5 lb.
Book of LSAT®
Practice Drills

Retail ISBN: 978-1-5062-4269-9

Course ISBN: 978-1-5062-5092-2

Layout Design: Joanna Graham
Production Editor: Chris Gage
Cover Design: Carly Schnur

TABLE OF CONTENTS

PART THREE: Getting the Most Out of Your Work

Letter to Students

Dear Student,

Thank you for picking up a copy of the *5 lb. Book of LSAT Practice Drills*. We hope this book provides you with exactly what you need as you prepare for the LSAT.

When we set out to write this book, it was because we believed there was something missing in the world of LSAT prep. There are plenty of tests and plenty of textbooks, but we wanted to give our students something different. One of the biggest challenges our students face when preparing for the LSAT is pinpointing areas of strength and weakness. Sure, they can say "I miss a lot of Assumption questions" but what does that really say about their skillset? This book is designed to help you figure out what skills you already have that are helping you get questions right and what skills you need to build to stop getting questions wrong. And once you've identified the skills you need to build, you can use this book to drill them until your weaknesses become your strengths.

We've also included supplementary materials to ensure that you get the most out of your practice, and more resources can be accessed online.

I'd like to thank all of the great writers and editors that contributed to this book, and in particular I'd like to thank Matt Shinners and Laura Damone for taking the idea for this book and making it into a reality.

We try to keep all of our books free from errors. But if you think we've goofed, please visit manhattanprep.com/lsat/errata.

And if you have any questions or comments in general, please email our Student Services team at lsat@mahnattanprep.com, or give us a shout at 212-721-7400 (or 800-576-4628 in the U.S. or Canada).

I look forward to hearing from you. Thanks again, and best of luck preparing for the LSAT!

Chris Ryan
Executive Director, Product Strategy
Manhattan Prep

How to Access Your Online Resources

If You Purchased a Physical Copy of This Book

1.   Go to: **www.manhattanprep.com/lsat/access**

2.   Follow the instructions on the screen.

You only need to register your product ONCE at the above URL. To use your online resources any time AFTER you have completed the registration process, log in to the following URL: **www.manhattanprep.com/lsat/studentcenter**

Please note that online access is nontransferable. This means that only NEW and UNREGISTERED copies of the book will grant you online access. Previously used books will NOT provide any online resources.

If You Purchased a Digital Version of This Book

1.   Create an account with Manhattan Prep at this website: **www.manhattanprep.com/lsat/register**

2.   Email a copy of your purchase receipt to **lsat@manhattanprep.com** to activate your resources. Please be sure to use the same email address to create an account that you used to purchase the book.

5 lb.
Book of LSAT®
Practice Drills

How to Use This Book

This book is designed to be a supplement to your LSAT preparation. If you're preparing for this exam, you've probably seen a whole lot of LSAT questions, and that's great—there's no substitute for that. But if you've been fed a steady diet of test, after question, after section, after test, there is definitely room for some healthy supplementation.

The drills in this book test what we like to call "microskills." When an expert takes this test, their brain is doing one hundred (and eighty!) things at once, and most of them intuitively. That's skill at the macro level. What we've done here is taken that expert process and broken it down from the macro level to the micro level. Instead of testing all of your skills at once, as a PrepTest would, we're testing skills in isolation so you can master them one at a time.

We believe that this mastery will come through the thoughtful execution of a systematic process. If you get into a drill and realize that you don't have much of a process, we suggest that you pause, consult the answers to the first few drill items, consider our explanations, and then resume the drill, attempting to put into practice what you've learned. Of course, you want to give yourself some time to find your footing in a tough drill before running to the answers, but avoid slogging through the drill just to get to the end; that all-too-common practice doesn't help anyone master anything.

The first section of this book, LSAT Foundations, is designed to build the most basic skills that are the foundation of a strong LSAT performance. There is one chapter devoted to each section of the exam. The drills in these chapters are appropriate for someone at any stage of their LSAT preparation. Whether you are very new to this test or already deep into your preparation, the LSAT Foundations chapter is an excellent starting point.

The next section of the book, LSAT Core Skills, is designed to cover all of the microskills that make up an expert performance. It is broken down first by the sections of the test, then further by the guiding principles of our 4-Step Process for each section. (Don't worry—we'll introduce you to those, and to our lexicon generally, in the next few pages of the book.) In the case of Logical Reasoning, the chapters are broken down further to examine each of the four "families" of Logical Reasoning questions. In the case of Logic Games, the chapters are broken down further to examine each of the three major game types.

If you'd like to use this book to target areas of strength or weakness that you've already identified, by all means do so—let the Table of Contents be your guide! But if you do use the book in this way, we suggest that, at least occasionally, you go exploring outside the areas you plan to target. You may find that the area of weakness you seek to improve upon is not as tied to a question or game type as you think, and that it is instead a function of a different sort of deficiency. Show us a student who struggles with Flaw questions, and we'll show you a student who cannot yet navigate abstract language. Show us a student who struggles with Strengthen questions, and we'll show you a student who cannot yet foresee potential objections to an argument.

The final section of this book, Getting the Most Out of Your Work, is composed of three appendices designed to help you maximize the impact of your study. The first, the Cheat Sheets, is part quiz and part textbook. Quiz yourself to see how much you really know about each question and game type, then check out our answer key where we break down the must-knows. The second appendix, the Recycling Bins, is a place to record the LSAT questions that typify a question type, game type, passage type, or strategy. By reviewing and redoing them regularly, you will make your process more consistent and more efficient, which translates to more effective. The last appendix, Planning and Review, is everything you need to effectively plan your study and thoroughly review your work. If you will be completing PrepTests and test sections as you work through this book, we recommend using the appendices early and often. There's no time like the present, and the more you use these resources, the bigger the dividends they'll pay.

Well, that about sums it up. As they say, there's nothing left to do but the work!

Sincerely,

The LSAT Team at Manhattan Prep

An Introduction to Our Lexicon and Approach

Logical Reasoning Lexicon

LR – This is how we'll usually refer to the Logical Reasoning section.

The Stem (aka The Question Stem) – This is the part that poses the actual question in LR, and is found beneath the argument or information that the question is about. It often begins *Which of the following…*

Stimulus – This is the information given, about which the question is asked. It will take the form of either an argument or a set of facts.

Premises – The evidence on which an argument is based.

Conclusion – The claim that the argument is trying to prove.

Argument Core – An argument's conclusion(s) and supporting premises, stripped of all background information, opposing points, and irrelevant information.

Assumption – The missing piece of an invalid argument (aka the gap between the premises and conclusion). It's what we can infer that the author believes, but hasn't established explicitly.

Prephrase – To predict what the correct answer will say (a specific prephrase) or do (a general prephrase).

Principle – A principle is a conditional rule that applies in a variety of circumstances.

Sufficient condition – In conditional logic, the "if" part of a conditional statement (aka the trigger). The sufficient condition is enough, by itself, to guarantee the necessary condition.

Necessary condition – In conditional logic, the "then" part of a conditional statement. The necessary condition necessarily happens if the trigger, or sufficient condition, occurs.

Contrapositive – In conditional logic, an inference you can reach by simultaneously reversing and negating a conditional statement. For example, if everyone in Manhattan is in New York, anyone *not* in New York *cannot* be in Manhattan.

Valid – In argumentation, when the premises, *if they were true*, would guarantee the truth of the conclusion. Whether the premises *are actually* true is inconsequential.

The 4-Step Process for Logical Reasoning

For every Logical Reasoning question, we go through a systematic four-step process. This is also the organizing principle of the LR chapters in the LSAT Core Skills section of this text. The process is as follows:

1. ID Your Task

    (Read the stem, ID the question type, and consider what you should be reading for in the stimulus.)

2. Work the Stimulus

    (Read the stimulus in a way that is dictated by your task. Break down arguments into their core components and, where appropriate, articulate the gap in their reasoning.)

3. Anticipate an Answer

    (Prephrase to the best of your ability. Some question types lend themselves to specific prephrases, others to general prephrases. Learn which are which, and prephrase accordingly—and yes, you guessed it, there's a drill for that!)

4. Answer Choice Analysis

    (Eliminate wrong answers for concrete reasons and select an answer with no fatal flaws, in accordance with your task.)

Question Families and Their Question Types

Each question type has its own unique profile, but there are a lot of commonalities between question types that often go unacknowledged. We believe these commonalities help lessen the intellectual distance between questions of different types, which is important in LR, given that you have to switch between question types twenty five times per section—essentially every minute! To that end, we like to think of the question types as belonging to one of four families, which we have outlined below.

Describe Family – These questions ask you to describe an argument, but they don't ask you to manipulate it.

> ID the Conclusion – These questions ask you to find the argument's main conclusion.
>
> Determine the Function – These questions task you with identifying the role played by a specific statement, identified in the stem.
>
> ID the (Dis)agreement – These questions present you with a dialogue between two speakers, and your task is generally to find the answer choice over which they'd disagree. Occasionally, though, the task is to find the answer choice over which they *would* agree, hence the funky parenthetical in the name.
>
> Procedure – *The author's argument proceeds by . . .* – Based on common argument structures, the answers will describe the author's method of argumentation.

Assumption Family – These questions ask you to address the gap in an argument's reasoning.

> Sufficient Assumption – *Which one of the following, if true, allows the author's conclusion to be properly drawn?* – The correct answer will completely bridge the gap between the premises and conclusion, making the argument valid.
>
> Necessary Assumption – *Which one of the following is an assumption on which the argument depends?* – The correct answer will be something that needs to be true and without which the argument would fall apart.
>
> ID the Flaw – *The argument is most vulnerable to which of the following criticisms?* – Sometimes abstract, sometimes specific, the correct answer will describe the gap in the argument. These questions pull from a list of Common Flaws (which will be outlined in the following pages and drilled into your brain by the time you finish this book!).

Strengthen – The correct answer will make the conclusion more likely to follow from the premises. These questions tend to feature arguments about cause and effect or about comparing entities to one another.

Weaken – The correct answer will make the conclusion less likely to follow from the premises. These questions also tend to feature arguments about cause and effect and comparisons.

Evaluate – *Which one of the following would be most useful in analyzing the argument above?* – The correct answer will point out the piece of information that would be helpful in figuring out if the author's conclusion is valid.

Principle Support – The correct answer will be a conditional principle that, if applied to the situation described in the premises of the argument, will help justify the judgment in the conclusion of the argument.

Inference Family – These questions don't give you arguments. Instead, they ask you to use facts provided in the stimulus to make a determination about the answer choices.

Must Be True – Often featuring conditional logic, Must Be True questions ask you to find an answer that you can be 100% certain of based on the givens in the stimulus.

Must Be False – This rare question type will have a correct answer that is directly contradicted by the stimulus.

Most Strongly Supported – Similar in most ways to a Must Be True question, these Inference questions leave open the possibility that there's a *small* chance the correct answer isn't true. These tend not to feature conditional logic, since conditional logic is all about guarantees.

Principle Example – These questions present you with a conditional principle (or two!) in the stimulus and ask you to find an answer choice that is an example of the principle(s) being applied.

Explain a Result – These questions present you with a surprising situation and ask you to choose an answer choice that explains why that surprising thing happened.

Matching Family – These questions sometimes rival Reading Comprehension passages in length! They ask you to find arguments that align in certain ways.

Match the Reasoning – *Which one of the following most closely parallels the pattern of reasoning in the argument above?* – The correct answer will mirror all relevant logical features of the given argument. Essentially, everything matches except the topic and the order of components.

Match the Flaw – *Which of the following flawed patterns of reasoning is most similar to the flawed pattern of reasoning above?* – These are essentially six ID the Flaw questions stacked on top of each other, with the correct answer being the one that would have the same answer as the stimulus.

Common Flaws

Most arguments on the LSAT are *invalid*—the truth of the conclusion is not guaranteed by the truth of the premises. Here is a list of the most common ways for invalid LSAT arguments to be built and the lexicon we'll use in this book to refer to them.

Ad Hominem – An argument that attacks the author or questions the author's motives instead of addressing the content of the opposing point.

Appeal to Emotion – An argument that relies on an emotional response rather than a logical one.

Appeal to Inappropriate Authority – An argument that relies on an expert whose expertise is not shown to apply to the situation at hand.

Causation Flaw – An argument that mistakenly concludes that one thing caused, causes, or is caused by another. The most common iteration is when a correlation between two things (e.g., when two things tend to happen together or in sequence) is taken to imply a causal relationship between the two things.

Circular Reasoning – An argument that presents a conclusion that is the same as one of its premises. This flaw is rarely exhibited by an argument but routinely shows up as an incorrect answer. (*The argument presupposes what it sets out to establish.*)

Comparison Flaw – An argument that relies on a comparison between two things that aren't shown to be comparable across all relevant metrics.

Equivocation – An argument that uses a single word in two different senses but acts as though the word has been used consistently throughout. This is not to be confused with a Term Shift, which is when an argument mistakenly equates two terms that are distinct.

False Choice – An argument that treats a list of options as if it's a complete list without establishing that it is.

Illegal Negation – An argument that uses a conditional statement (If you're in Manhattan, you're in New York.) as though one can simply negate each side of the conditional statement (If you're not in Manhattan, you're not in New York.).

Illegal Reversal – An argument that uses a conditional statement (If you're in Manhattan, you're in New York.) as though one can simply reverse the order of the conditional statement (If you're in New York, you're in Manhattan.).

Opinion vs. Fact – An argument that bases a claim about what is true on evidence about what someone *thinks* to be true.

Part vs. Whole – An argument that ascribes the features of each part of something to the whole entity, or the features of a whole entity to *each of its component parts*. This is not to be confused with a Sampling Flaw, which takes its evidence from a *small sample* of a whole, rather than *each part* of a whole.

Percent vs. Amount – An argument that jumps between absolute numbers and percents. This is math-y, which can be intimidating, but rest assured that you just need to know you that can't jump between these two types of figures. You won't ever have to crunch numbers in LR.

Possible vs. Certain – An argument that concludes that something is certain using evidence that merely shows the thing to be possible.

Sampling Flaw – An argument that draws a conclusion about a group from a sample that is either too small or not representative. A survey or study is usually referenced in an argument that exhibits this flaw.

Self-Contradiction – An argument with a conclusion that is directly contradicted by one of the premises. Like Circular Reasoning, this flaw is rarely exhibited by an argument but routinely shows up as an incorrect answer.

Straw Man – A man made of straw is easier to knock down than a man made of ... well ... man. This is the conceit from which this flaw gets its name, and the flaw occurs when the arguer takes his opponent's argument and misrepresents it, thereby making it easier to refute.

Term Shift – An argument that treats two terms as being equivalent when they are not (e.g., earnings vs. profit), or that treats one term as though it necessarily implies another when actually it does not.

Unproven vs. Untrue – An argument that treats the failure to prove a hypothesis as proof that the hypothesis is false. Just because no one has proven aliens don't exist doesn't mean they do, and just because no one has proven aliens do exist doesn't mean they don't.

Reading Comprehension Lexicon

RC – This is how we'll usually refer to the Reading Comprehension section.

The Scale – Most RC passages feature a debate. The Scale is a way to visually represent this, allowing you to track that debate.

Passage Map – A breakdown of the role each piece of the passage plays. Your map can be made either while reading or immediately after. Each time there's a paragraph break or a shift in content/viewpoint, jotting down a few notes in the margin can help you create your own table of contents to use when you go back to the passage to answer the questions.

The 4-Step Process for Reading Comprehension

For every RC passage, we go through another systematic four-step process. This is also the organizing principle of the RC chapter in the LSAT Core Skills section of this text. The process is as follows:

1. Read the Passage

    (Read and notate important information, possibly creating your passage map. Consider whether the passage has a central debate, where the author stands, and whether the passage is exhibiting a familiar format.)

2. Pause and Rehash

    (Between each paragraph, take a moment to collect your thoughts and consider where the author just went and where you think the author will go next. After your initial read, create your passage map, if you haven't already, and consider which side of the central debate your author falls on.)

3. ID the Question/Strategy

    (Consider the task of the first question and the strategies you should implement.)

4. Analyze the Answers

    (Eliminate wrong answers for concrete reasons and select an answer with no fatal flaws, in accordance with your task.)

RC Passage Types

Every RC passage deals with a unique subject, but the forms RC passages tend to take are less diverse than you might think. While these categories are neither exhaustive nor exclusive, we believe they are a helpful way to think about the passages, the way the test-writers have constructed them, and the features that are likely to be important.

The Old vs. the New – These passages discuss a catalyst for change and how the change is panning out.

A Traditional View Is Refuted – These passages are a riff on the Old vs. New dichotomy, wherein the old way is argued against.

A Debate Is Presented – These are passages in which the author takes no side.

A Debate Is Presented, and the Author Takes a Side – The name says it all.

The Author Reconciles Two Sides of a Debate – Another self-explanatory one.

A Thesis Is Illustrated with an Example(s) – These are often legal or scientific in nature.

An Artist Is Critiqued or Defended from Criticism – Defense from criticism will often take the form of a reconceptualization of the artist's work.

The Importance of Something Is Explored – The "something" can be a phenomenon, legal, social, or scientific, or a person, typically an artist or scientist.

A Problem Is Presented, with Solutions – These passages tend to be legal in nature. Sometimes the author will advocate for a particular solution, and other times the author will remain neutral.

RC Question Types

The questions generally take one of five forms, though the first three are the most well-represented:

1. Identification – A specific and explicitly mentioned detail must be identified.

2. Inference – The information in the passage is used to support an answer that isn't explicitly stated (but boy is it close!).

3. Synthesis – A "big picture" question that's asking about the overall debate, a viewpoint, or the structure of the argument.

4. Strengthen/Weaken – Questions that ask you to identify a detail that would impact one of the arguments in the passage.

5. Analogy/Application – Questions that call out some feature of the passage and ask you to choose either an answer that is analogous or an answer to which a called-out principle applies.

RC Answer Choice Analysis

For RC, we work wrong-to-right, eliminating answers before choosing one. Answer choices are, generally, wrong for one of the following reasons:

1. Contradicted – The answer is explicitly contradicted by the passage.

2. Unsupported – The answer may bring up similar concepts to the passage, but the actual answer doesn't have full support.

3. Out of Scope – The answer choice involves elements that aren't in the passage.

4. Narrow Scope – The answer choice involves elements from the passage, but it doesn't fully address the question (e.g., an answer about the first paragraph in a question about the passage as a whole).

5. Degree – The language in the answer choice is more extreme than the language in the passage.

Logic Games Lexicon

LG – This is how we'll usually refer to the Logic Games section.

The Scenario – This is the part of the game that lists the entities and describes the basic situation.

The Constraints – Aka the Rules.

The Elements – The things, usually letters but occasionally numbers, that you are tasked with putting in order or putting in groups.

Inferences – Something that must be true of the game but hasn't been explicitly stated by the rules. There are basic inferences (if H must be before J, then H can't be last and J can't be first), and more in-depth inferences (these generally come from combining two rules that talk about the same element, slot, or group).

Clouds – When we know an element has to be in one of a few adjacent slots, or a group of elements has to fill a series of slots but we don't know in what order, we represent that by floating the element(s) above the slots and circling them.

Strays – Elements that don't have any rules associated with them.

Frames – A series of diagrams that represents all possibilities for a game. Certain games are limited in a way that allows you to create multiple diagrams that cover every way the game can work out.

When considering whether to build frames, there are two questions:

1. Is there something in the game that can play out in only 2 or 3 ways?

2. In each of these possibilities, will there be inferences?

Numerical Distributions – A special type of inference that is derived from information about maximums, minimums, and the relationship between the sizes of groups or the frequency that elements can show up.

The 4-Step Process for Logic Games

As for LR and RC, there is a systematic process that you can use to approach every game.

1. Picture the Game

    (Visualize the real-world scenario the game describes.)

2. Notate the Rules and Make Inferences

    (Inferences are often spotted while you're notating the rules, which is why we list the two tasks as a single step.)

3. The Big Pause

    (Rushing into the questions is a mistake almost everyone has been guilty of. Step 3 is in place to combat that universal tendency and force you to pause and assess a few critical dimensions of the game. This will improve both accuracy and efficiency on the questions.)

    A. Are there any Stays?

    B. Are there any opportunities to Frame?

    C. What elements, rules, or relationships are likely to drive the game?

4. Attack the Questions

    (In accordance with the question type and task.)

Game Types

There are three basic tasks that a game might ask you to perform on the exam, and each has its own basic diagram.

1. Put things in Order

When the LSAT tasks you with putting things in order, your basic diagram is going to be a Number Line.

Common rules associated with Ordering games:

1. Relative Ordering – *S is delivered earlier than U.* If all of the rules are Relative Ordering rules, they should be linked into a single diagram we call the Tree.

2. Chunks – *S must be delivered immediately before U.*

3. Reversible chunks – *S and U must be delivered consecutively.*

4. Anti-chunks – *S and U cannot be delivered consecutively.*

5. Open chunks – *S must be delivered two hours before U.*

6. Options – *Either S or U is delivered fifth; or S is delivered either first or last.* These can be represented using fraction notation (for the former, S/U in slot 5; for the latter, S/ in the first slot and /S in the last slot).

7. Exclusions – *S cannot be delivered third.*

8. Assignments – *S is delivered second.*

2. Split things between two Groups

When the LSAT asks us to split things between two groups, it is almost always between a group of selected elements and the remaining unselected elements. For that reason, we call these In/Out games. The criteria for an In/Out game are as follows: there are exactly two groups, and all rules are conditional. Where these criteria are met, we use the Logic Chain to represent the relationship between the elements.

In the Logic Chain, the elements are listed in an In column and an Out column. Arrow diagrams represent conditional rules, which would normally be written out individually, in a manner that makes taking their contrapositives and connecting them much easier. These connections are the foundation of this game type, so being able to visualize them quickly and as a unified whole can lower the difficulty of the game.

3. Split things between more than two Groups

When the LSAT has you splitting things between more than two groups, we use a Grouping Board composed of slots and boxes above each of the groups, into which the elements are placed.

Common rules associated with Grouping games:

1. Chunks – *H and G must be assigned to the same department.*

2. Anti-chunks – *H and G cannot be assigned to the same department.*

3. Conditionals – *If H is assigned to Litigation, then G must be assigned to Copyright.*

4. Exclusions – *H cannot be assigned to Copyright.*

5. Assignments – *H must be assigned to Litigation.*

6. Distributions – *Twice as many lawyers are assigned to Copyright as Litigation.*

Twists

These are the things that complicate the basic tasks of ordering, splitting between two groups, and splitting between more than two groups. Twists include:

Relative Ordering – When all rules in an Ordering game are Relative Ordering rules. We build a special diagram called a Tree that connects them all.

Mismatches – When the number of elements doesn't equal the number of slots. We can either have too many elements, or not enough.

Repeating Elements – When elements that you're placing into your slots can show up more than once.

Defined Subgroups – When the elements are split up into defined categories by the scenario or rules.

Undefined Subgroups – When the elements are going to be split up into categories but the rules/scenario don't define up front which elements are in which subgroups.

3D – Games with Subgroups often require that you represent the subgroup characteristics separately from the elements themselves. (Think: *the third pitcher is right-handed.*) Where this is the case, a second row should be created atop your Number Line or Grouping Board, and we call these diagrams 3D.

Open – Basic Grouping games are "closed," meaning we're told how many elements will be assigned to each group. Open games don't tell us how many elements will be assigned. (Yes, this makes them harder!)

Special Positions – When one element is given a designation that the others don't have. For example, if one member of the board is the chairperson or one chef is the head chef.

Hybrid – Most games ask you to complete one of the primary tasks. Hybrid games ask you to complete more than one. Most often, you'll be tasked with putting elements into groups and putting the groups in order.

Final Notes

This crash-course in our lexicon and approach might seem like a lot of information, and if you've already been preparing for the LSAT using different approaches and systems of categorization, reconciling or replacing the approaches might seem daunting. While it's true that this sort of thing is a pain, we think you'll find it more intuitive than it might seem to be at the outset. As you complete our drills and read our explanations, the process should happen organically. And when it doesn't, these pages can be referenced as a guide.

And now, on to our main event: the drills!

LSAT Foundations

CHAPTER 1

Logical Reasoning, Meet the Stimulus

In This Chapter, We Will Cover:

- Argument Structure

- Premise and Conclusion Types

- Conditional Logic

- Causal Reasoning

- Debating an Argument

1

Meet the Stimulus

First thing's first: If you want to get to the correct answer on an LR problem, you've got to understand the stimulus! Stimuli can be either arguments or sets of facts, and stimuli that are arguments can be either valid or invalid. Some LR stimuli have a single premise and single conclusion while others have more complex structures with multiple premises, multiple conclusions, background information, and opposing points. That can be a lot to untangle! LR stimuli can also exhibit a variety of reasoning structures. Two of those reasoning structures, Conditional Logic and Causal Reasoning, are so central to the LSAT that it pays to focus on them early and often.

In this section, you will learn to:

ID Argument Structure

- Use Structural Indicators
- Break down arguments
- Get rid of extraneous information

Recognize Premise and Conclusion Types

- Distinguish premises from conclusions
- Recognize Causal, Conditional, and Comparative statements

Navigate Conditional Logic

- Diagram basic conditional statements
- Find the contrapositive of basic conditional statements

Navigate Causal Reasoning

- Recognize causal arguments
- Distinguish between correlation and causation

Debate Arguments

- Accept the truth of the premises while contesting the conclusion

Drill 1: Structural Indicators

Instructions: Arguments are the heart of the Logical Reasoning section. Every time you see one, you need to quickly and accurately break it down into its component parts, and Structural Indicators are there to help! Structural Indicators are words and phrases that clue you in to the way an argument is built and the role that each piece plays. Every structural indicator can be categorized as introducing a premise (P), a conclusion (C), or a shift (S). For the rest of this book, we'll refer to shift indicators as "pivot indicators," but for this drill, we're sticking with "shift" because we already used "P" for "premise."

For each of the following Structural Indicators, note on the preceding line the category that best describes the indicator: P, C, or S.

P	1. Owing to		S	18. Although		S	35. But
C	2. Shows that		S	19. Even though		S	36. Despite
S	3. Admittedly		C	20. So		C	37. Hence
C	4. Consequently		P	21. Since		P	38. In that
P	5. For example		C	22. Thus		S	39. On the other hand
P	6. Due to		S	23. While		C	40. Obviously
S	7. In contrast		S	24. However		S	41. Even so
S	8. Nevertheless		C	25. That is why		P	42. This is seen from
C	9. Clearly		C	26. For this reason		P	43. For the reason that
C	10. Must be that		P	27. It is clear from		C	44. It is clear
C	11. It follows that		C	28. Accordingly		C	45. This proves that
P	12. For		S	29. Still		S	46. Conversely
C	13. As a result		P	30. As indicated		P	47. Studies suggest
P	14. Because		S	31. Yet		S	48. Instead
S	15. In spite of		S	32. Whereas		C	49. And so
P	16. From the fact that		C	33. Conclude that		S	50. Surprisingly
C	17. Therefore		P	34. After all			

Answers

P	1.	Owing to	S	18.	Although	S	35.	But
C	2.	Shows that	S	19.	Even though	S	36.	Despite
S	3.	Admittedly	C	20.	So	C	37.	Hence
C	4.	Consequently	P	21.	Since	P	38.	In that
P	5.	For example	C	22.	Thus	S	39.	On the other hand
P	6.	Due to	S	23.	While	C	40.	Obviously
S	7.	In contrast	S	24.	However	S	41.	Even so
S	8.	Nevertheless	C	25.	That is why	P	42.	This is seen from
C	9.	Clearly	C	26.	For this reason	P	43.	For the reason that
C	10.	Must be that	P	27.	It is clear from	C	44.	It is clear
C	11.	It follows that	C	28.	Accordingly	C	45.	This proves that
P	12.	For	S	29.	Still	S	46.	Conversely
C	13.	As a result	P	30.	As indicated	P	47.	Studies suggest
P	14.	Because	S	31.	Yet	S	48.	Instead
S	15.	In spite of	S	32.	Whereas	C	49.	And so
P	16.	From the fact that	C	33.	Conclude that	S	50.	Surprisingly
C	17.	Therefore	P	34.	After all			

Drill 2: Premise or Conclusion?

Instructions: While it's not always possible to tell whether a statement is a premise or a conclusion without the context of the rest of the argument, there are trends you should familiarize yourself with that can help you make that determination. Data, statistics, correlations, and simple statements of fact are more likely to be premises, while predictions, recommendations, mandates, judgments, evaluations, and explanations are more likely to be conclusions. For each of the following, indicate whether it's more likely to be a premise (P) or conclusion (C).

_P_ 1. Water with high lead content is found more frequently near heavy industrial sites.

_C_ 2. Houses with lead paint ought to be inspected by an official to determine if they are safe to live in.

_C_ 3. Providing patients with access to a therapy dog would be a distraction to medical professionals working in the hospital.

_P_ 4. The city has never elected a mayor to serve a second consecutive term before.

_P_ 5. The American Cancer Society names alcohol consumption as a risk factor for cancer growth.

_C_ 6. The jump in participants is likely a result of increased advertising.

_P_ 7. Astronomers have discovered that hotter stars appear blue in color, while colder stars appear red.

_C_ 8. All people considering buying a house should first meet with a financial advisor.

_C_ 9. The philosopher's recommendation is impractical.

_C_ 10. Labor unions ought to ensure that all employees have paid parental leave.

_P_ 11. A recent study reported that nearly one third of the Great Barrier Reef has died.

_C_ 12. Regular aerobic exercise will likely decrease the risk of developing cardiovascular disease.

_P_ 13. Researchers have found that this chemical is produced in greater quantities during pregnancy.

_P_ 14. The manufacturer has recently altered the design of the car to include a greater number of airbags.

_C_ 15. Colleges that require community service hours prior to graduation are better at preparing students than those that do not require service hours.

_P_ 16. Some of the students were expelled for participating in the protest, and some others were suspended.

_C_ 17. Customers purchasing a drying machine must be informed about the potentially-faulty lint trap.

_C_ 18. The animals' strange behavior is probably a result of the deforestation occurring in their habitat.

_P_ 19. Research results show that racial discrimination and bias have lifelong health impacts on minority groups in the United States.

_C_ 20. Hotels that have stopped washing all linens and towels daily are making a choice that benefits the environment.

_P_ 21. The average American adult spends more than ten hours each day in front of a screen.

_P_ 22. Yeast is a commonly-used model organism for scientists studying molecular genetics.

_C_ 23. High school classes should start later in the day.

_C_ 24. The new flowers are likely a result of efforts to increase the bee population in this county.

_P_ 25. State legislators voted to increase the salary of all public employees by three percent.

_P_ 26. A recent study found that Sudden Infant Death Syndrome, or SIDS, is more likely to occur in infants born to mothers who smoked cigarettes during pregnancy.

_P_ 27. Turkey has the highest rate of coffee consumption in the world.

_C_ 28. The psychologists' claim is not adequately supported.

_P_ 29. The park has experienced increased levels of vandalism recently.

_C_ 30. All public employees should be required to sign an ethics agreement.

_C_ 31. Teaching Shakespeare each year from middle school onward will increase the average SAT scores of students in this school district.

_P_ 32. Geckos are capable of regrowing a tail that has been cut off.

_C_ 33. Future correspondence should be more clearly postmarked so as to avoid confusion.

_C_ 34. A nation that invests in renewable energy is making a rational choice that will benefit its economy.

_P_ 35. Heart attack symptoms experienced by women are different than those experienced by men.

_P_ 36. Healthy farm animals are often given antibiotics preventatively.

_C_ 37. The price of produce in Medville likely increased as a result of last summer's drought.

_P_ 38. Some biologists have recently been studying the migration pattern of turtles in Ohio.

_C_ 39. Zoo animals must be protected from exposure to the litter that visitors produce.

_C_ 40. A four-day school week for young children would result in a higher quality of learning.

_C_ 41. The policy analyst's recommendation is unrealistic.

_P_ 42. Large aerospace firms hire attorneys who have international legal experience.

_P_ 43. The budget was amended three times before being passed.

_C_ 44. Lowering the tax rate would result in less spending on roads and bridges.

_P_ 45. Carpal tunnel syndrome is most commonly diagnosed in those who spend several hours each day typing.

_P_ 46. According to findings from recent research, debris accumulating in space will make launching new satellites increasingly difficult in coming decades.

_C_ 47. Failing to invest in a retirement fund will result in financial difficulties for many aging adults.

_P_ 48. Solar energy is more commonly used in regions closer to the equator.

_C_ 49. Mr. B's restaurant must close in light of its failing health inspection grade.

_C_ 50. Fast food companies should not air television ads aimed at children.

Answers

Note: Any italicized word or phrase is one that can help you make your determination. Items that have no italicized words are just simple facts. We've also included the type of statement to help you start to think categorically about these things!

P   1. Water with high lead content *is found more frequently near* heavy industrial sites. *(Statistic/Correlation)*

C   2. Houses with lead paint *ought to* be inspected by an official to determine if they are safe to live in. *(Recommendation)*

C   3. Providing patients with access to a therapy dog *would be* a distraction to medical professionals working in the hospital. *(Prediction)*

P   4. The city has never elected a mayor to serve a second consecutive term before. *(Fact)*

P   5. *The American Cancer Society names* alcohol consumption as a risk factor for cancer growth. *(Data)*

C   6. The jump in participants *is likely a result of* increased advertising. *(Explanation)*

P   7. *Astronomers have discovered* that hotter stars appear blue in color, while colder stars appear red. *(Data)*

C   8. All people considering buying a house *should* first meet with a financial advisor. *(Recommendation)*

C   9. The *philosopher's recommendation is impractical. (Judgment)*

C   10. Labor unions *ought to* ensure that all employees have paid parental leave. *(Recommendation)*

P   11. A *recent study reported* that nearly one third of the Great Barrier Reef has died. *(Data)*

C   12. Regular aerobic exercise *will likely decrease* the risk of developing cardiovascular disease. *(Prediction)*

P   13. *Researchers have found* that this chemical is produced in greater quantities during pregnancy. *(Data)*

P   14. The manufacturer has recently altered the design of the car to include a greater number of airbags. *(Fact)*

C   15. Colleges that require community service hours prior to graduation *are better at preparing* students than those that do not require service hours. *(Evaluation)*

P   16. Some of the students were expelled for participating in the protest, and some others were suspended. *(Fact)*

C   17. Customers purchasing a drying machine *must be informed* about the potentially-faulty lint trap. *(Mandate)*

C   18. The animals' strange behavior *is probably a result of* the deforestation occurring in their habitat. *(Explanation)*

P   19. *Research results show that* racial discrimination and bias have lifelong health impacts on minority groups in the United States. *(Data)*

C   20. Hotels that have stopped washing all linens and towels daily *are making a choice that benefits the environment. (Evaluation)*

P   21. *The average American adult spends* more than ten hours each day in front of a screen. *(Statistic)*

P   22. Yeast is a commonly-used model organism for scientists studying molecular genetics. *(Fact)*

C   23. High school classes *should* start later in the day. *(Recommendation)*

C   24. The new flowers are *likely a result of* efforts to increase the bee population in this county. *(Explanation)*

P   25. State legislators voted to increase the salary of all public employees by three percent. *(Fact)*

P   26. *A recent study found* that Sudden Infant Death Syndrome, or SIDS, is more likely to occur in infants born to mothers who smoked cigarettes during pregnancy. *(Data)*

P   27. Turkey has *the highest rate* of coffee consumption in the world. *(Statistic)*

1

C   28. *The psychologists' claim* is not adequately supported. *(Judgment)*

P   29. The park has *experienced increased levels of* vandalism recently. *(Statistic)*

C   30. All public employees *should* be required to sign an ethics agreement. *(Recommendation)*

C   31. Teaching Shakespeare each year from middle school onward *will increase* the average SAT scores of students in this school district. *(Prediction)*

P   32. Geckos are capable of regrowing a tail that has been cut off. *(Fact)*

C   33. Future correspondence *should be* more clearly postmarked so as to avoid confusion. *(Recommendation)*

C   34. A nation that invests in renewable energy *is making a rational choice* that will benefit its economy. *(Judgment)*

P   35. Heart attack symptoms experienced by women are different than those experienced by men. *(Fact)*

P   36. Healthy farm animals are often given antibiotics preventatively. *(Fact)*

C   37. The price of produce in Medville *likely increased as a result of* last summer's drought. *(Explanation)*

P   38. Some biologists have recently been studying the migration pattern of turtles in Ohio. *(Fact)*

C   39. Zoo animals *must be protected* from exposure to the litter that visitors produce. *(Mandate)*

C   40. A four-day school week for young children *would result in* a higher quality of learning. *(Prediction)*

C   41. The policy analyst's recommendation *is unrealistic. (Judgment)*

P   42. Large aerospace firms hire attorneys who have international legal experience. *(Fact)*

P   43. The budget was amended three times before being passed. *(Fact)*

C   44. Lowering the tax rate *would result in* less spending on roads and bridges. *(Prediction)*

P   45. Carpal tunnel syndrome *is most commonly diagnosed* in those who spend several hours each day typing. *(Statistic/Correlation)*

P   46. *According to findings from recent research*, debris accumulating in space will make launching new satellites increasingly difficult in coming decades. *(Data)*

C   47. Failing to invest in a retirement fund *will result in* financial difficulties for many aging adults. *(Prediction)*

P   48. Solar energy *is more commonly used in* regions closer to the equator. *(Statistic/ Correlation)*

C   49. Mr. B's restaurant *must close* in light of its failing health inspection grade. *(Mandate)*

C   50. Fast food companies *should not* air television ads aimed at children. *(Recommendation)*

Drill 3: Pivot Premise, Pivot Conclusion

Instructions: Each of the following arguments contains a pivot indicator: a word or phrase that indicates that the author is changing directions within the argument. Pivot indicators typically pivot away from an opposing point or piece of counter evidence, marking a transition into the core of the argument. But which part of the Argument Core—premise or conclusion—is the author transitioning into? Use this drill to practice making that critical determination.

For each of the following arguments, decide whether the pivot indicator in **bold** is introducing the argument's conclusion or one of the argument's premises, and fill in a C or P accordingly in the preceding space.

_C_ 1. Ice cream is generally regarded as the most popular summer dessert. **However**, people should be careful how much ice cream they eat in one sitting, since eating too much too fast can cause a headache.

_C_ 2. The Kihansi Spray Toad is thought to be extinct in the wild today. Its population fell sharply in the two years following the damming of the waterfalls overlooking its habitat for a nearby hydropower plant, and the damming has been cited as the cause of the toad's extinction. **However**, this can't be the case, as the toad populations around other hydropower plants in the region have remained stable.

_P_ 3. Before the advent of online dating, individuals living in geographically-isolated communities were often severely limited in their dating options, while today they can connect with literally millions of prospective dates. **On the other hand**, this increased access has reduced the period of time spent evaluating a new connection and so has had a detrimental effect on dating as a whole.

_P_ 4. The commercial success of Thomas Nast's depiction of Santa Claus has anchored the character firmly in American culture for more than a century. Recently, **though**, new interpretations of the Krampus from German folklore have proven to be quite marketable. Therefore, the Krampus is likely to become a fixture in American culture over the coming century.

_C_ 5. A common conceit among pet owners is that the bond they share with their animals constitutes "love" just as much as what is deemed to be "love"

between two people. **But** this is impossible, since what is or is not felt by the animal remains a mystery.

_P_ 6. In the aftermath of a scandal, public figures can regain the public's trust in large measure by promoting their reformed behavior whenever possible. **Yet** there will always be those who remain skeptical that those changes are sincere or permanent. Thus, any reformation of one's image can never be completely successful.

_P_ 7. Our team's doctors claimed that if we attempted to ski without goggles we would suffer from snow blindness within a few hours. **Despite** their warnings, we have competed in several events without any incidents of snow blindness, so the doctors' warnings were without grounds.

_P_ 8. All of the promotions for the new 24-hour Health Clinic have stressed that it is a viable alternative to the downtown hospital for any minor ailment. This is doubtful, **however**, since often a patient is unaware of the severity of his or her condition until diagnosis.

_C_ 9. Most parents would love to have their child attend an expensive pre-kindergarten program, provided they could afford it. **Paradoxically**, this may not serve the child's best interests, as those earliest years are the ones in which continual interaction with the child's parents is most important.

_C_ 10. It has become the prevalent attitude lately that a low-sodium diet would benefit anyone who adopts it. Most athletes lose a substantial amount of sodium playing their sport, **though**, and such a diet may therefore be dangerous for some people in the long term.

_____ 11. To the untrained eye, the skill that professional jugglers display seems to be entirely muscle memory. **However**, this mischaracterizes the skill. Most jugglers use mathematics both to plan and execute their routines.

_____ 12. The French conception of separation of powers in government is in many ways akin to that in the United States, **but** with at least one important distinction: the French President is rarely subject to the same legislative oversight as the American one. This means that there are multiple ways of implementing the separation of powers successfully.

_____ 13. Husani boasts that he can solve the puzzle cube that appears in our textbook, **although** he is unwilling to explain what his solution might be. It is highly doubtful, then, that he can back up his claim.

_____ 14. *Return by This Route* has been hailed by some critics as the first drama to successfully integrate truffle hunting with a coming-of-age story. In the original director's cut of the film, **however**, the elements of truffle hunting are entirely absent. Thus, such praise is at odds with the filmmaker's true intentions.

_____ 15. Our GPS recommends that we stay on the state highway for the last leg of our journey, **but** this is a suggestion we should not heed, as there is a strong possibility that the GPS has not been updated with the latest information about construction along the highway.

_____ 16. A common portion of the pre-takeoff safety demonstration given by airlines assures passengers that in the unlikely event of a water landing, their seat cushions serve as floatation devices, and thus there is little risk of drowning. **On the other hand**, this kind of floatation device is only useful if the passenger is not overly disoriented or stunned by the landing and so does not represent a realistic safety measure.

_____ 17. Television viewership has been in a steady decline over the last decade, and many experts predict the death of the medium in the near future. **Yet** this must be balanced against the tendencies of an aging population, who represent a large segment of the population and will be less inclined to stop watching television altogether. The reports of TV's imminent demise, therefore, are greatly exaggerated.

_____ 18. The restaurant aggregator app on my phone ranks Mama Lucinda's above all other restaurants in our area. **Nevertheless**, I believe we should find somewhere else to eat, since the company that produces this app owns a financial stake in Mama Lucinda's.

_____ 19. Residents of Los Helena are seeing a large spike in the premiums they pay for volcano insurance, which insurance companies have justified by claiming that the region is due for another eruption. **Despite** these claims, none of the seismic patterns that usually precede an eruption have been recorded. So the insurance companies are not justified in raising the premiums.

_____ 20. Doctors caution against the overuse of antibiotics for treatment, especially in cases of viral infection, because it may lead to antibiotic-resistant strains of bacteria. **Conversely**, some studies show that many bacterial strains mimic the symptoms of a viral infection. Thus, it is difficult to ascertain when an antibiotic is being used needlessly.

_____ 21. The amount of dynamite used to carve Mount Rushmore has left fissures in the granite that some experts warn may leave the mountain susceptible to future collapse. No other mountains carved in this way have yet collapsed, **however**, so this warning is unfounded.

_____ 22. Recording music in the studio setting is a painstaking process that, to some minds, robs the music of its spontaneity and energy. And **yet,** many of the most exciting musical moments ever recorded were inspired by the quiet focus of the studio. Hence, studio recording should be regarded as something that gives energy as often as it takes energy.

_____ 23. Activist: In their efforts to increase the shelf life of their products, many cosmetics corporations have taken to adding preservatives to their formulas, claiming their motivation is to benefit consumers by giving them longer-lasting products. The majority of these preservatives have known allergenic effects, **though**, leading to our claim that the real motivation is profits.

_____ 24. Mikio says that he ought to be the one to handle the navigation for our kayaking trip, due to his extensive experience in the area's rivers. **Despite this**, I would nominate Georgette as navigator, since she worked at the hydroelectric dam that has very recently begun to affect the current patterns in those rivers.

_____ 25. Many scientists advocate for breaking apart an asteroid on a collision course with Earth. I, **however**, recommend the long-view "tugboat" option to gently deflect the asteroid fully intact, thereby avoiding a collision without incurring dangerous complications.

Answers

1

___C___ 1. Structural indicator word "since" introduces a premise, so when it comes in the middle of a sentence, we know that what comes before it is a conclusion.

___C___ 2. The final clause of the last sentence is a fact introduced by "as," which makes it a premise. The pivot is away from the opposing point to the conclusion that is a judgment on that point.

___P___ 3. "On the other hand" implies a counterbalance of evidence, meaning what follows is a contrasting premise.

___P___ 4. Pivot word introduces a fact (premise) that supports the prediction (conclusion) in the last sentence.

___C___ 5. Again, "since" introduces a premise, so when it comes in the middle of a sentence, we know that what comes before it is a conclusion.

___P___ 6. Pivot word introduces a statement that supports the last sentence (premise).

___P___ 7. Pivot word refers first to the opposing point, then pivots to the premise offered in support of the final claim, introduced by conclusion indicator "so."

___P___ 8. "However" pivots directly into a "since" statement, which is always a premise.

___C___ 9. The final clause introduces a premise with "as," which means that the pivot indicator precedes the conclusion.

___C___ 10. "Though" pivots to a "therefore" statement, which is a conclusion.

___C___ 11. Pivot word pivots to a judgment (conclusion) on the opposing point that precedes it.

___P___ 12. "This means that" introduces a conclusion in the last line, while the colon indicates a premise that precedes it.

___P___ 13. "Then" offset by commas indicates that the last sentence is a conclusion that builds from the prior sentence, which makes the statement introduced by "although" a premise.

___P___ 14. Pivot word introduces contrasting evidence from which the conclusion in the last line is drawn.

___C___ 15. "As" in the final line introduces a premise offered in support of the conclusion that comes before, which is introduced by the pivot indicator.

___P___ 16. "And so" in the final line introduces a conclusion supported by the premise that comes before it, which is introduced by the pivot indicator.

___P___ 17. "Therefore" in the final line introduces a conclusion supported by the premise that comes before it, which is introduced by the pivot indicator.

___C___ 18. "Since" in the middle of a sentence indicates that what comes before it is a conclusion supported by the premise that follows it.

___P___ 19. Pivot word refers first to the opposing point, then pivots to data (premise) offered in support of the judgment (conclusion) introduced by conclusion indicator "so."

___P___ 20. Pivot word introduces data (premise) offered in support of the judgment (conclusion) in the next line, introduced by "thus."

___C___ 21. Pivot word bisects a sentence in which the first part is a fact (premise) offered in support of the judgment on the opposing point (conclusion) in the second part.

___P___ 22. "Hence" in the final line tells us that the preceding line with the pivot word is a premise.

___C___ 23. "Leading to" introduces a conclusion. Pivot word pivots away from a fact, which is offered in support of that conclusion.

___C___ 24. Pivot word introduces a referent ("this") that refers to the opposing point, but then states an opinion (conclusion) that is supported by a fact (premise) introduced by "since."

___C___ 25. Pivot word introduces a recommendation (conclusion).

Drill 4: Insert Borrowed Language Here

Instructions: Some of the trickiest conclusions on the LSAT are those that refer to an aforementioned idea in an abbreviated way (e.g., "But *this view* is shortsighted."). These conclusions are challenging because, in order to fully understand them, you have to replace that abbreviated language with the complete idea it refers to. Borrowing language from elsewhere in the text and inserting it into your conclusion is the best way to go about this (e.g., "But *the view that camels will one day roam the plains of Iowa* is shortsighted."). Incorrect answers, particularly for ID the Conclusion and Determine the Function questions, will often hinge on a misunderstanding of what language, exactly, you should borrow. Use this drill to practice making that important determination.

Each of the following arguments has a conclusion that references another piece of the argument. Select the answer choice that best describes the text that you should borrow and insert.

1. The University Health Care System at Gladwell University is available to full-time students only. Some part-time students have petitioned the Dean to expand access to the University Health Care System to part-time students, but their entreaty is doomed to fail. The Gladwell University Board of Trustees would have to approve any such expansion, and the Board will not take any action that will increase expenditures without generating income to offset those increases.

    The phrase "their entreaty" in the conclusion refers to

    (A) the petition to the Dean to give part-time students all the privileges of full-time students.
    (B) the petition to the Board of Trustees to expand access to the University Health Care System.
    ⬤ the petition to the Dean to expand access to the University Health Care System.
    (D) the petition to the Board of Trustees to allow actions that would increase expenditures without generating income to offset those increases.

2. After observing the ability of microbes to survive in the harsh environment of space, scientists have suggested that life on Earth could have originated on Mars. Martian meteorites are routinely blasted from the surface of Mars by asteroid collisions, and microbes can cling to meteorites even as they leave their planetary atmosphere. However, there remain many reasons to doubt this hypothesis.

    The phrase "this hypothesis" in the conclusion refers to the possibility that

    (A) microbes can survive in the harsh environment of space.
    (B) meteorites are routinely blasted from the surface of Mars.
    ⬤ life on Earth originated on Mars.
    (D) microbes can cling to meteorites even as they leave their planetary atmosphere.

3. Despite contemporary evidence to the contrary, many people continue to believe, as the ancients sometimes did, that the earth is a hollow sphere. However, this theory can be rejected on the basis of seismic evidence alone. The speed of seismic waves produced by earthquakes is affected by the earth's internal composition. If the earth were hollow, seismic waves would travel much faster than is actually observed.

    The phrase "this theory" in the conclusion refers to the supposition that

    ⬤ the earth is a hollow sphere.
    (B) seismic evidence proves that the earth is not hollow.
    (C) seismic waves would be faster if the earth were hollow.
    (D) the earth has a solid inner composition.

1

4. While parking, Regina accidentally struck a car owned by Todd, causing minor damage to Todd's car. Regina offered to pay Todd directly for the cost of his repairs in order to avoid reporting the incident to her insurance company. Todd is considering accepting her offer because he thinks it would be more convenient than filing an insurance claim. However, Todd should reject her offer because his insurance policy requires him to file a claim for any damage, even if it is relatively minor.

    The phrase "her offer" in the conclusion refers to Regina's offer to

    (A) file an insurance claim on Todd's behalf.
    (B) pay Todd directly for the repairs to his car.
    (C) cooperate with Todd's insurance company if he files a claim.
    (D) reimburse Todd for the increase in his insurance premiums.

5. Doctors have developed a new treatment that they believe will delay the onset of Alzheimer's disease in patients who are diagnosed before the age of 70. The new protocol is similar to the previous one in that they both require patients to receive regular B12 injections, but the new protocol increases the dosage while reducing the frequency of the injections. This new protocol is likely to succeed because patients will be more likely to adhere to the schedule for injections if they do not have to be administered as frequently.

    The term "protocol" in the conclusion refers to

    (A) the process by which doctors developed a new treatment for Alzheimer's disease.
    (B) a new treatment for Alzheimer's disease that increases the dosage and frequency of B12 injections.
    (C) a new treatment for Alzheimer's disease that decreases the dosage and increases the frequency of B12 injections.
    (D) a new treatment for Alzheimer's disease that increases the dosage but decreases the frequency of B12 injections.

6. Our community pool requires swimmers under the age of 13 to be accompanied by an adult. While most young swimmers need adult supervision, the pool should not apply its policy to Tara, even though she is only 12 years old, because Tara is a competitive swimmer training for the Olympics.

    The phrase "its policy" in the conclusion refers to

    (A) the pool's policy requiring swimmers under the age of 13 to be accompanied by an adult.
    (B) the pool's policy that swimmers training for the Olympics must be accompanied by an adult.
    (C) the author's policy that Tara should be exempt from the pool's requirement that she be accompanied by an adult.
    (D) the author's policy that swimmers training for the Olympics should be exempt from the pool's requirement that swimmers under the age of 13 be accompanied by an adult.

7. A law student planning to work in public interest should take out student loans instead of paying for tuition from her own savings. This suggestion is sound advice because a public interest lawyer will be eligible for loan repayment assistance and loan forgiveness programs, in effect rendering her legal education retroactively cost-free.

    The phrase "this suggestion" in the conclusion refers to the recommendation that

    (A) all law students should take out student loans.
    (B) only law students planning to work in public interest should take out student loans.
    (C) a law student planning to work in public interest should take out student loans.
    (D) a lawyer working in public interest should be eligible for loan repayment and forgiveness programs.

8. Although the law requires asking for proof of age only when a person making an alcohol purchase appears to be younger than 30 years old, the Diamond Bar asks any customer who orders an alcoholic beverage for proof of age. This rule is sensible, as the penalties for violating the law are steep, and determining whether a person appears to be younger than 30 years old is a subjective judgment that can be difficult to make with reasonable certainty.

    The phrase "this rule" in the conclusion refers to

    (A) the law requiring proof of age for anyone making an alcohol purchase.

    (B) the law requiring proof of age for anyone who appears to be younger than 30 years old making an alcohol purchase.

    (C) the Diamond Bar's policy of asking for proof of age only when the customer appears to be younger than 30 years old.

    (D) the Diamond Bar's policy of asking for proof of age from any customer who orders an alcoholic beverage.

9. The Smith County Board of Elections has proposed that the county switch from using increasingly obsolete punch-card ballots to using modern touch-screen voting machines. Although the Board of Elections is correct that touch-screen machines produce more accurate results because voters are more likely to make mistakes when using a punch-card ballot, its proposal will almost certainly fail. A recent survey shows that more than two thirds of the voters in Smith County have serious concerns about the security and reliability of touch-screen voting machines.

    The phrase "its proposal" in the conclusion refers to the board's recommendation that Smith County

    (A) replace punch-card ballots with touch-screen voting machines in order to decrease the costs associated with administering an election.

    (B) use touch-screen voting machines rather than optical-scan ballots.

    (C) replace punch-card ballots with touch-screen voting machines in order to improve the overall accuracy of election results.

    (D) conduct a public awareness campaign to reassure voters that touch-screen voting machines are secure and reliable.

10. Many people have argued that the Electoral College should be abolished, but this position is misguided. While it is true that the winner of the Electoral College will not always be the candidate who receives the highest number of popular votes, a candidate cannot win the Electoral College without amassing a multi-regional coalition of voter support, thus ensuring that the candidate who wins the presidency will be representative of the nation as a whole.

    The term "position" in the conclusion refers to the assertion that

    (A) the Electoral College should be abolished.

    (B) the winner of the Electoral College will not necessarily receive the highest number of popular votes.

    (C) the winner of the Electoral College will be representative of the nation as a whole.

    (D) the Electoral College should not be abolished.

1

11. Many people believe that the flu shot can infect them with the flu virus, leading them to decline the flu vaccine each year. However, their belief is mistaken. Of the two versions of the flu shot that are currently administered, one contains only inactivated flu virus, and the other contains no flu virus at all, making it impossible to contract the flu virus from the flu shot.

     The phrase "their belief" in the conclusion refers to the belief that

     (A) everyone should decline the flu shot.
     (B) it is reasonable for a person to decline the flu shot.
     (C) the flu shot can infect a person with the flu virus.
     (D) it is impossible to contract the flu virus from the flu shot.

12. Some scientists contend that life may exist on other planets beyond our solar system. Although this possibility is intriguing, we should not commit resources to exploring the idea. It would take nearly 100 years to reach even the closest solar system to our own, and our planet faces a greater scientific challenge over the next century in working to halt global warming and reverse its effects.

     The term "idea" in the conclusion refers to the supposition that

     (A) we should investigate the possibility that life exists on other planets.
     (B) our planet faces a great challenge in working to reverse the effects of global warming.
     (C) we should not spend money to explore the possibility of life on other planets.
     (D) life may exist on other planets outside our own solar system.

13. Historically, the Patuxent Library has been closed on Sundays during the summer months. Recently, some residents have petitioned the library to remain open on Sundays throughout the year, but their attempt to change the library's policy will almost certainly be thwarted. The library's budget has already been finalized for the next two fiscal years, and the city council is unlikely to call a special session to consider any budgetary changes.

     The phrase "their attempt" in the conclusion refers to

     (A) the city council's attempt to call a special session to consider making a change to the library's budget.
     (B) the residents' attempt to keep the library open on Sundays during the summer.
     (C) the library's attempt to remain closed on Sundays during the summer.
     (D) the author's attempt to convince the reader that the residents' proposal will be thwarted.

14. Margaret has filed a petition to contest her late brother's will, arguing that the will is invalid because her brother was no longer of sound mind when he signed it. The court is likely to reject her claim, however, since her brother was still working as a professor when he signed the will, and there is no indication that he was unable to perform the complex functions of his job at that time.

     The term "claim" in the conclusion refers to the assertion that

     (A) a will is not valid unless the person who signs it is of sound mind.
     (B) a person must be of sound mind in order to execute a valid will.
     (C) the court is likely to reject Margaret's argument that her brother's will is invalid.
     (D) Margaret's brother's will is invalid because he was not of sound mind when he signed it.

15. Recently, Stratford Corporation asked its employees to offer ideas for reducing or eliminating unnecessary costs. Abizer, an employee at Stratford, has suggested that the company cancel its contract with a local janitorial service and redistribute the janitorial work to existing employees. While it is true that the company would save money if it no longer had to pay an outside contractor to perform janitorial work, Stratford should not adopt this recommendation because it would require employees to devote valuable work time to tasks that do not actively make the company any money.

The term "recommendation" in the conclusion refers to the suggestion that

(A) Stratford should cancel its contract for janitorial services.
(B) Stratford should reject Abizer's proposed cost-saving measure.
(C) Stratford should try to reduce or eliminate unnecessary expenses.
(D) Stratford should not ask its employees to perform janitorial work.

16. Manager: We recently learned that traffic coming into our store has decreased more than 50% over the past year. Lyle Baker, an outside consultant we hired to help us improve our business strategy, thinks that fewer customers are shopping with us because our largest competitor has started accepting coupons, whereas we do not accept coupons. However, this hypothesis is surely mistaken, since our prices are lower than our largest competitor's even after any coupon discount is applied.

The phrase "this hypothesis" refers to the supposition that

(A) customers have stopped shopping in the manager's store because the store's largest competitor is now accepting coupons.
(B) customers will always shop at the store that offers the lowest price.
(C) customer traffic coming into the manager's store has decreased by more than 50% over the past year.
(D) customers sometimes fail to consider a store's coupon policy when deciding whether or not to shop there.

17. In order to detain a suspected shoplifter, a store employee must directly observe the suspect taking unpaid merchandise out of the store. However, this requirement is unlikely to be met in any instance of shoplifting that takes place at Bee Happy Candle Store, since a large hanging sign at the front of the store makes it impossible to see the front door from the vantage point of the cash registers.

The phrase "this requirement" in the conclusion refers to the need for

(A) a store employee to detain a suspected shoplifter.
(B) a store employee to see a person leave the store with unpaid merchandise before detaining that person as a suspected shoplifter.
(C) Bee Happy Candle Store to take additional steps to prevent shoplifting.
(D) Bee Happy Candle Store to train its employees more thoroughly on how to approach a suspected shoplifter.

18. Student: Professor Jenkins asked us not to cite sources from the Internet in our term papers this semester. But in his most recent book on the cultural effects of social media, Professor Jenkins cites numerous sources from the Internet to support his claims. Thus, his request is hypocritical.

The phrase "his request" in the conclusion refers to

(A) Professor Jenkins's request that students cite numerous sources in their papers.
(B) Professor Jenkins's request that students read his book.
(C) Professor Jenkins's request that students not use any social media.
(D) Professor Jenkins's request that students not cite Internet sources in their papers.

1

19. A world-renowned French chef is seeking to open a new restaurant in Westerville. The restaurant will feature molecular cuisine, an innovative cooking style that emphasizes the scientific aspects of food and often utilizes dramatic or whimsical plate presentations. While some diners may find menu items like edible paper intriguing, such a restaurant is not likely to be well-received in Westerville, where most restaurant patrons have preferred more traditional dining options in the past.

The phrase "such a restaurant" in the conclusion refers to a restaurant that is characterized by

- (A) traditional French cuisine prepared by a world-famous chef.
- (B) innovative cooking techniques and dramatic presentations of food.
- (C) classic menu items prepared using modern cooking techniques.
- (D) modern French cuisine with dramatic plate presentations.

20. Automotive technology experts have predicted that in a few decades the majority of cars on the road will be self-driven, or will at least have the capacity to be autonomous. We should be skeptical of this possibility, however, because most drivers feel uneasy about surrendering their control to an automated car, making it unlikely that the technology will become very popular.

The phrase "this possibility" in the conclusion refers to the possibility that

- (A) drivers will feel uneasy about using autonomous cars.
- (B) self-driving cars will not become very popular.
- (C) the majority of cars on the road will be self-driven within the next few decades.
- (D) autonomous cars are not as safe as traditional driver-operated vehicles.

21. A group of high school students has developed a mentoring program that pairs students at their high school with underprivileged elementary and middle school students who are at risk of becoming high school dropouts. In order to receive funding for their program, the students must seek approval from the local school board. The school board should adopt their plan because the area has a high unemployment rate, and increasing the number of high school graduates will surely help improve that problem.

The phrase "their plan" in the conclusion refers to

- (A) the high school students' mentoring program.
- (B) the school board's approval of the students' mentoring program.
- (C) the elementary and middle school students' interest in the mentoring program.
- (D) the local government's plan to improve the unemployment situation in the area.

22. A group of local businesses has asked the city to build a park on an unimproved lot in the downtown area. The businesses contend that the lot has become an unofficial dump, and that the accumulating trash has attracted rats and other unwanted pests, deterring customers from shopping in the surrounding area. The city would build the proposed park if the businesses could demonstrate that the unimproved lot has had a detrimental economic impact, but in fact their petition will be denied because all of the businesses involved have actually seen their profits increase in the past year.

The phrase "their petition" in the conclusion refers to the request for

- (A) the city to turn the unimproved lot into an official dump.
- (B) the city to build a park on the unimproved lot.
- (C) the businesses to demonstrate that the lot has negatively affected their profits.
- (D) the businesses to show that building a park would improve the situation.

23. Aurora claims that the new baking competition show will fail to attract an audience because most viewers have tired of reality competition programming. While it is true that viewer fatigue has occurred with other types of programming, her assertion is inaccurate. Seven of the ten most highly rated shows last week were reality shows with a competition format.

The phrase "her assertion" in the conclusion refers to Aurora's claim that

(A) a majority of the most-watched shows on television have a reality competition format.

(B) the new baking competition show will not be popular among television viewers.

(C) viewers will not be interested in any new reality competition show.

(D) most people will probably watch the first episode of the new baking competition show but will quickly lose interest.

24. Job placement rates for graduates of Smith County Community College have been low in recent years, and an employment expert thinks that this is unlikely to change in the near future because Smith County has been experiencing an economic downturn that is expected to continue for several years. His prediction is probably wrong, however, because the community college recently opened a nursing school, and nurses are in high demand in Smith County.

The phrase "his prediction" refers to the expert's claim that

(A) job placement rates for graduates of the community college will definitely worsen in the next few years.

(B) job placement rates for graduates of the community college will probably not improve in the next few years.

(C) job placement rates for graduates of the community college will probably improve in the next few years.

(D) it is impossible to predict whether job placement rates for graduates of the community college will change in the next few years.

25. According to an article published in a well-known medical journal, cancer researchers have recently demonstrated the success of a new early detection screening tool for pancreatic cancer. Although a screening tool does not directly treat or cure cancer, the prospect is promising news for cancer patients, who tend to have a better prognosis the earlier a diagnosis is made.

The term "prospect" as used in the conclusion refers to the possibility that

(A) the new screening tool for pancreatic cancer may lead to an earlier detection of some pancreatic cancers.

(B) the new screening tool for pancreatic cancer will definitely save lives.

(C) additional research will confirm the efficacy of the new screening tool for pancreatic cancer.

(D) the researchers cited in the journal article were mistaken about the efficacy of the new screening tool.

26. Resident: During the last election, our local council member assured voters that she would not allow the city council to raise our taxes. But the councilwoman is one of eight council members, and raising taxes requires only a simple majority of council members to vote in favor of a proposed tax increase. Thus, it is impossible for the councilwoman to keep her promise.

The phrase "her promise" in the conclusion refers to

(A) the resident's promise to vote for the councilwoman because she is opposed to tax increases.

(B) the resident's promise to vote out the councilwoman for allowing the city council to raise taxes.

(C) the councilwoman's promise not to vote for a tax increase.

(D) the councilwoman's promise to prevent the city council from raising taxes.

1

27. Lawyer: Our legal system adheres to the at-will employment doctrine, meaning that an employee can be fired without notice for nearly any reason. Some people have argued that we should abandon the at-will doctrine in favor of a rule that requires an employer to provide a one-year notice period when terminating an employee, as many other countries have done. Proponents of this change argue that it would reduce our unemployment rate by giving people more time to find work while they are still employed, but this proposition is mistaken, as countries that have adopted the new rule actually have higher rates of employment due to the inherent lack of flexibility in their workforce.

The phrase "this proposition" in the conclusion refers to the claim that

(A) the lawyer's country should adopt a one-year notice period requirement.

(B) countries that require a one-year notice period have higher rates of unemployment.

(C) if the lawyer's country were to adopt a one-year notice period requirement, unemployment rates in the lawyer's country would decrease.

(D) the lawyer's country should abandon the at-will employment doctrine.

Answers

1. The University Health Care System at Gladwell University is available to full-time students only. Some part-time students have petitioned the Dean to expand access to the University Health Care System to part-time students, but their entreaty is doomed to fail. The Gladwell University Board of Trustees would have to approve any such expansion, and the Board will not take any action that will increase expenditures without generating income to offset those increases.

    The phrase "their entreaty" in the conclusion refers to

    (A) the petition to the Dean to give part-time students all the privileges of full-time students.

    (B) the petition to the Board of Trustees to expand access to the University Health Care System.

    ● **the petition to the Dean to expand access to the University Health Care System.**

    (D) the petition to the Board of Trustees to allow actions that would increase expenditures without generating income to offset those increases.

"Their entreaty" refers to the petition described in the first half of the sentence: "part-time students have petitioned the Dean to expand access to the University Health Care System to part-time students." Answer choice (A) is too broad. The part-time students are only asking for health care, as far as we know—not all the privileges of full-time students. Answer choices (B) and (D) inaccurately claim that the petition was directed at the Board of Trustees, rather than the Dean. Answer choice (D) describes something the Board would have to do in order for the student petition to be successful, but it doesn't describe the petition itself.

2. After observing the ability of microbes to survive in the harsh environment of space, scientists have suggested that life on Earth could have originated on Mars. Martian meteorites are routinely blasted from the surface of Mars by asteroid collisions, and microbes can cling to meteorites even as they leave their planetary atmosphere. However, there remain many reasons to doubt this hypothesis.

    The phrase "this hypothesis" in the conclusion refers to the possibility that

    (A) microbes can survive in the harsh environment of space.

    (B) meteorites are routinely blasted from the surface of Mars.

    ● **life on Earth originated on Mars.**

    (D) microbes can cling to meteorites even as they leave their planetary atmosphere.

In the first sentence, the idea of life on Earth originating on Mars is described as something that "scientists have suggested." In other words, that's the scientists' hypothesis. The other statements about microbes surviving in space, meteorites being blasted from the surface of Mars, and microbes clinging to meteorites, are presented as uncontested facts. These facts support the hypothesis, but are not part of the hypothesis.

1

3. Despite contemporary evidence to the contrary, many people continue to believe, as the ancients sometimes did, that the earth is a hollow sphere. However, this theory can be rejected on the basis of seismic evidence alone. The speed of seismic waves produced by earthquakes is affected by the earth's internal composition. If the earth were hollow, seismic waves would travel much faster than is actually observed.

    The phrase "this theory" in the conclusion refers to the supposition that

    ● **the earth is a hollow sphere.**
    Ⓑ seismic evidence proves that the earth is not hollow.
    Ⓒ seismic waves would be faster if the earth were hollow.
    Ⓓ the earth has a solid inner composition.

In the first sentence, the author states that many people "believe" the earth is a hollow sphere. This belief is the theory that the author rejects in the second sentence. The wrong answer choices represent the author's own position, or evidence that supports it, rather than the theory that the author rejects.

4. While parking, Regina accidentally struck a car owned by Todd, causing minor damage to Todd's car. Regina offered to pay Todd directly for the cost of his repairs in order to avoid reporting the incident to her insurance company. Todd is considering accepting her offer because he thinks it would be more convenient than filing an insurance claim. However, Todd should reject her offer because his insurance policy requires him to file a claim for any damage, even if it is relatively minor.

    The phrase "her offer" in the conclusion refers to Regina's offer to

    Ⓐ file an insurance claim on Todd's behalf.
    ● **pay Todd directly for the repairs to his car.**
    Ⓒ cooperate with Todd's insurance company if he files a claim.
    Ⓓ reimburse Todd for the increase in his insurance premiums.

The author is advising Todd to reject Regina's offer, which, according to the author's second sentence, was to pay Todd directly for the cost of his repairs without filing an insurance claim.

5. Doctors have developed a new treatment that they believe will delay the onset of Alzheimer's disease in patients who are diagnosed before the age of 70. The new protocol is similar to the previous one in that they both require patients to receive regular B12 injections, but the new protocol increases the dosage while reducing the frequency of the injections. This new protocol is likely to succeed because patients will be more likely to adhere to the schedule for injections if they do not have to be administered as frequently.

    The term "protocol" in the conclusion refers to

    Ⓐ the process by which doctors developed a new treatment for Alzheimer's disease.
    Ⓑ a new treatment for Alzheimer's disease that increases the dosage and frequency of B12 injections.
    Ⓒ a new treatment for Alzheimer's disease that decreases the dosage and increases the frequency of B12 injections.
    ● **a new treatment for Alzheimer's disease that increases the dosage but decreases the frequency of B12 injections.**

In the second sentence, the author states that the new protocol increases the dosage of the B12 injections while reducing their frequency. Answer choice (A) incorrectly references the process by which the treatment is developed, rather than the treatment itself, while answer choices (B) and (C) misstate the characteristics of the new protocol.

6.   Our community pool requires swimmers under the age of 13 to be accompanied by an adult. While most young swimmers need adult supervision, the pool should not apply its policy to Tara, even though she is only 12 years old, because Tara is a competitive swimmer training for the Olympics.

The phrase "its policy" in the conclusion refers to

⬤   **the pool's policy requiring swimmers under the age of 13 to be accompanied by an adult.**
Ⓑ   the pool's policy that swimmers training for the Olympics must be accompanied by an adult.
Ⓒ   the author's policy that Tara should be exempt from the pool's requirement that she be accompanied by an adult.
Ⓓ   the author's policy that swimmers training for the Olympics should be exempt from the pool's requirement that swimmers under the age of 13 be accompanied by an adult.

In the second sentence, the author states that "the pool" should not apply its policy to Tara, so the author is referring to the pool's policy rather than his own. As indicated by the first sentence, the pool's policy is to require swimmers under 13 to be accompanied by an adult, making (A) the correct answer choice.

7.   A law student planning to work in public interest should take out student loans instead of paying for tuition from her own savings. This suggestion is sound advice because a public interest lawyer will be eligible for loan repayment assistance and loan forgiveness programs, in effect rendering her legal education retroactively cost-free.

The phrase "this suggestion" in the conclusion refers to the recommendation that

Ⓐ   all law students should take out student loans.
Ⓑ   only law students planning to work in public interest should take out student loans.
⬤   **a law student planning to work in public interest should take out student loans.**
Ⓓ   a lawyer working in public interest should be eligible for loan repayment and forgiveness programs.

In the conclusion, the author endorses the advice given in the first sentence: namely, that a law student planning to work in public interest should take out student loans, making (C) the correct answer. Because this advice is directed toward students planning on a career in public interest, answer choice (A) is too broad. In addition, there could be other reasons why a law student might want to borrow money for school, so answer choice (B) is too narrow in its claim that "only" students intending to go into public interest work should take out student loans. Answer choice (D) is a reason to take the author's advice, but is not the advice itself.

8.   Although the law requires asking for proof of age only when a person making an alcohol purchase appears to be younger than 30 years old, the Diamond Bar asks any customer who orders an alcoholic beverage for proof of age. This rule is sensible, as the penalties for violating the law are steep, and determining whether a person appears to be younger than 30 years old is a subjective judgment that can be difficult to make with reasonable certainty.

The phrase "this rule" in the conclusion refers to

Ⓐ   the law requiring proof of age for anyone making an alcohol purchase.
Ⓑ   the law requiring proof of age for anyone who appears to be younger than 30 years old making an alcohol purchase.
Ⓒ   the Diamond Bar's policy of asking for proof of age only when the customer appears to be younger than 30 years old.
⬤   **the Diamond Bar's policy of asking for proof of age from any customer who orders an alcoholic beverage.**

The author is judging the Diamond Bar's rule to be sensible. We know this because the evidence provided in the second sentence explains why the Diamond Bar's policy make sense, not why the law itself is logical. Since the first sentence states that the Diamond Bar's policy is to ask any customer for proof of age, answer choice (D) is correct.

1

9. The Smith County Board of Elections has proposed that the county switch from using increasingly obsolete punch-card ballots to using modern touch-screen voting machines. Although the Board of Elections is correct that touch-screen machines produce more accurate results because voters are more likely to make mistakes when using a punch-card ballot, its proposal will almost certainly fail. A recent survey shows that more than two thirds of the voters in Smith County have serious concerns about the security and reliability of touch-screen voting machines.

The phrase "its proposal" in the conclusion refers to the board's recommendation that Smith County

(A) replace punch-card ballots with touch-screen voting machines in order to decrease the costs associated with administering an election.

(B) use touch-screen voting machines rather than optical-scan ballots.

● **replace punch-card ballots with touch-screen voting machines in order to improve the overall accuracy of election results.**

(D) conduct a public awareness campaign to reassure voters that touch-screen voting machines are secure and reliable.

The author states that the Board of Elections wants to replace punch-card ballots with touch-screen voting machines because touch-screen machines are more reliably accurate, making (C) the correct answer. Answer choices (A) and (B) are incorrect because they misconstrue some of the details of the proposal, and while the Board of Elections might want to conduct a campaign like the one suggested in answer choice (D), such a measure was not addressed in the argument.

10. Many people have argued that the Electoral College should be abolished, but this position is misguided. While it is true that the winner of the Electoral College will not always be the candidate who receives the highest number of popular votes, a candidate cannot win the Electoral College without amassing a multi-regional coalition of voter support, thus ensuring that the candidate who wins the presidency will be representative of the nation as a whole.

The term "position" in the conclusion refers to the assertion that

● **the Electoral College should be abolished.**

(B) the winner of the Electoral College will not necessarily receive the highest number of popular votes.

(C) the winner of the Electoral College will be representative of the nation as a whole.

(D) the Electoral College should not be abolished.

The author is arguing against the claim referred to earlier in the first sentence: namely, that the Electoral College should be abolished. Thus, (A) is the correct answer. Answer choice (B) supports that position, but it is not the position itself, while answer choices (C) and (D) refer to elements of the author's argument, not the position the author is arguing against.

11. Many people believe that the flu shot can infect them with the flu virus, leading them to decline the flu vaccine each year. However, their belief is mistaken. Of the two versions of the flu shot that are currently administered, one contains only inactivated flu virus, and the other contains no flu virus at all, making it impossible to contract the flu virus from the flu shot.

The phrase "their belief" in the conclusion refers to the belief that

Ⓐ everyone should decline the flu shot.

Ⓑ it is reasonable for a person to decline the flu shot.

● **the flu shot can infect a person with the flu virus.**

Ⓓ it is impossible to contract the flu virus from the flu shot.

The author is criticizing the belief mentioned in the first sentence: namely, that the flu shot can infect a person with the flu virus. We know this is the belief the author refers to in the conclusion because the author's evidence in the third sentence—that the flu shot contains either inactivated flu virus or no flu virus at all—is designed to rebut the belief that the flu shot can cause the flu.

12. Some scientists contend that life may exist on other planets beyond our solar system. Although this possibility is intriguing, we should not commit resources to exploring the idea. It would take nearly 100 years to reach even the closest solar system to our own, and our planet faces a greater scientific challenge over the next century in working to halt global warming and reverse its effects.

The term "idea" in the conclusion refers to the supposition that

Ⓐ we should investigate the possibility that life exists on other planets.

Ⓑ our planet faces a great challenge in working to reverse the effects of global warming.

Ⓒ we should not spend money to explore the possibility of life on other planets.

● **life may exist on other planets outside our own solar system.**

In the conclusion, the author states that we should not fund "this idea," which is a reference to the idea mentioned in the previous sentence: the belief held by some scientists that life may exist outside our solar system.

13. Historically, the Patuxent Library has been closed on Sundays during the summer months. Recently, some residents have petitioned the library to remain open on Sundays throughout the year, but their attempt to change the library's policy will almost certainly be thwarted. The library's budget has already been finalized for the next two fiscal years, and the city council is unlikely to call a special session to consider any budgetary changes.

The phrase "their attempt" in the conclusion refers to

Ⓐ the city council's attempt to call a special session to consider making a change to the library's budget.

● **the residents' attempt to keep the library open on Sundays during the summer.**

Ⓒ the library's attempt to remain closed on Sundays during the summer.

Ⓓ the author's attempt to convince the reader that the residents' proposal will be thwarted.

The attempt that the author is referring to is the residents' petition to keep the library open on Sundays during the summer months. We know this because the residents are the people mentioned in the argument who are actively trying to accomplish a particular goal.

14. Margaret has filed a petition to contest her late brother's will, arguing that the will is invalid because her brother was no longer of sound mind when he signed it. The court is likely to reject her claim, however, since her brother was still working as a professor when he signed the will, and there is no indication that he was unable to perform the complex functions of his job at that time.

The term "claim" in the conclusion refers to the assertion that

(A) a will is not valid unless the person who signs it is of sound mind.

(B) a person must be of sound mind in order to execute a valid will.

(C) the court is likely to reject Margaret's argument that her brother's will is invalid.

● **Margaret's brother's will is invalid because he was not of sound mind when he signed it.**

The author says that "her" claim will be rejected, so he must be referring to Margaret's claim that her brother's will is invalid. Since Margaret's claim is specific to her brother's will, we would not select answer choices (A) or (B), which are generalizations that support Margaret's claim, but are not the claim itself.

15. Recently, Stratford Corporation asked its employees to offer ideas for reducing or eliminating unnecessary costs. Abizer, an employee at Stratford, has suggested that the company cancel its contract with a local janitorial service and redistribute the janitorial work to existing employees. While it is true that the company would save money if it no longer had to pay an outside contractor to perform janitorial work, Stratford should not adopt this recommendation because it would require employees to devote valuable work time to tasks that do not actively make the company any money.

The term "recommendation" in the conclusion refers to the suggestion that

● **Stratford should cancel its contract for janitorial services.**

(B) Stratford should reject Abizer's proposed cost-saving measure.

(C) Stratford should try to reduce or eliminate unnecessary expenses.

(D) Stratford should not ask its employees to perform janitorial work.

The author is arguing against Abizer's recommendation, which was to cancel the contract with the janitorial service and redistribute the janitorial work to the company's employees. Answer choices (B) and (D) represent the author's own position, not the recommendation that the author is referring to in the conclusion.

16. Manager: We recently learned that traffic coming into our store has decreased more than 50% over the past year. Lyle Baker, an outside consultant we hired to help us improve our business strategy, thinks that fewer customers are shopping with us because our largest competitor has started accepting coupons, whereas we do not accept coupons. However, this hypothesis is surely mistaken, since our prices are lower than our largest competitor's even after any coupon discount is applied.

The phrase "this hypothesis" refers to the supposition that

● **customers have stopped shopping in the manager's store because the store's largest competitor is now accepting coupons.**

(B) customers will always shop at the store that offers the lowest price.

(C) customer traffic coming into the manager's store has decreased by more than 50% over the past year.

(D) customers sometimes fail to consider a store's coupon policy when deciding whether or not to shop there.

The manager's conclusion is referring to the explanation offered by the consultant, which was that customers are flocking to the competitor because the competitor now accepts coupons. Answer choices (B) and (D) are consistent with the manager's point of view, but not with the "hypothesis" that the manager references in the conclusion, while answer choice (C) is simply a background fact.

17. In order to detain a suspected shoplifter, a store employee must directly observe the suspect taking unpaid merchandise out of the store. However, this requirement is unlikely to be met in any instance of shoplifting that takes place at Bee Happy Candle Store, since a large hanging sign at the front of the store makes it impossible to see the front door from the vantage point of the cash registers.

The phrase "this requirement" in the conclusion refers to the need for

(A) a store employee to detain a suspected shoplifter.

● **a store employee to see a person leave the store with unpaid merchandise before detaining that person as a suspected shoplifter.**

(C) Bee Happy Candle Store to take additional steps to prevent shoplifting.

(D) Bee Happy Candle Store to train its employees more thoroughly on how to approach a suspected shoplifter.

The conclusion is referring to the legal requirement that an employee actually see a person leave the store with unpaid merchandise before detaining that person as a suspected shoplifter.

18. Student: Professor Jenkins asked us not to cite sources from the Internet in our term papers this semester. But in his most recent book on the cultural effects of social media, Professor Jenkins cites numerous sources from the Internet to support his claims. Thus, his request is hypocritical.

The phrase "his request" in the conclusion refers to

(A) Professor Jenkins's request that students cite numerous sources in their papers.

(B) Professor Jenkins's request that students read his book.

(C) Professor Jenkins's request that students not use any social media.

● **Professor Jenkins's request that students not cite Internet sources in their papers.**

Professor Jenkins's request was that students refrain from citing sources from the Internet in their term papers. The professor did not ask students to cite a specific number of resources (A) or refrain from using any social media at all (C).

19. A world-renowned French chef is seeking to open a new restaurant in Westerville. The restaurant will feature molecular cuisine, an innovative cooking style that emphasizes the scientific aspects of food and often utilizes dramatic or whimsical plate presentations. While some diners may find menu items like edible paper intriguing, such a restaurant is not likely to be well-received in Westerville, where most restaurant patrons have preferred more traditional dining options in the past.

The phrase "such a restaurant" in the conclusion refers to a restaurant that is characterized by

(A) traditional French cuisine prepared by a world-famous chef.

● **innovative cooking techniques and dramatic presentations of food.**

(C) classic menu items prepared using modern cooking techniques.

(D) modern French cuisine with dramatic plate presentations.

The conclusion refers to restaurants that feature molecular cuisine, which the author earlier described as characterized by a focus on the scientific aspects of food, innovative cooking techniques, and whimsical or dramatic plate presentations. While the chef-owner of the new restaurant is French, there is no indication that the food will be, making choices (A) and (D) incorrect. Similarly, answer choice (C) refers to classic menu items, but that was not a stated feature of molecular cuisine.

1

20. Automotive technology experts have predicted that in a few decades the majority of cars on the road will be self-driven, or will at least have the capacity to be autonomous. We should be skeptical of this possibility, however, because most drivers feel uneasy about surrendering their control to an automated car, making it unlikely that the technology will become very popular.

The phrase "this possibility" in the conclusion refers to the possibility that

(A) drivers will feel uneasy about using autonomous cars.

(B) self-driving cars will not become very popular.

● **the majority of cars on the road will be self-driven within the next few decades.**

(D) autonomous cars are not as safe as traditional driver-operated vehicles.

The conclusion refers to the possibility introduced earlier in the argument: namely, that self-driving cars will dominate the roads within the next few decades. The other answer choices contain statements that are consistent with the author's point of view, not possibilities that the author warns us to be "skeptical" of.

21. A group of high school students has developed a mentoring program that pairs students at their high school with underprivileged elementary and middle school students who are at risk of becoming high school dropouts. In order to receive funding for their program, the students must seek approval from the local school board. The school board should adopt their plan because the area has a high unemployment rate, and increasing the number of high school graduates will surely help improve that problem.

The phrase "their plan" in the conclusion refers to

● **the high school students' mentoring program.**

(B) the school board's approval of the students' mentoring program.

(C) the elementary and middle school students' interest in the mentoring program.

(D) the local government's plan to improve the unemployment situation in the area.

The author is recommending that the school board adopt the students' mentoring plan, which is the only plan referenced in the argument. None of the groups mentioned in the other answer choices have formulated a "plan" to do anything.

22. A group of local businesses has asked the city to build a park on an unimproved lot in the downtown area. The businesses contend that the lot has become an unofficial dump, and that the accumulating trash has attracted rats and other unwanted pests, deterring customers from shopping in the surrounding area. The city would build the proposed park if the businesses could demonstrate that the unimproved lot has had a detrimental economic impact, but in fact their petition will be denied because all of the businesses involved have actually seen their profits increase in the past year.

The phrase "their petition" in the conclusion refers to the request for

(A) the city to turn the unimproved lot into an official dump.

● **the city to build a park on the unimproved lot.**

(C) the businesses to demonstrate that the lot has negatively affected their profits.

(D) the businesses to show that building a park would improve the situation.

The author is referring to the business owners' petition to build a park on the unimproved lot. Answer choice (A) misstates the goal of the petition, and answer choices (C) and (D) refer to potential requests that were not actually mentioned in the argument.

23. Aurora claims that the new baking competition show will fail to attract an audience because most viewers have tired of reality competition programming. While it is true that viewer fatigue has occurred with other types of programming, her assertion is inaccurate. Seven of the ten most highly rated shows last week were reality shows with a competition format.

    The phrase "her assertion" in the conclusion refers to Aurora's claim that

    (A) a majority of the most-watched shows on television have a reality competition format.

    ● the new baking competition show will not be popular among television viewers.

    (C) viewers will not be interested in any new reality competition show.

    (D) most people will probably watch the first episode of the new baking competition show but will quickly lose interest.

Aurora's claim, according to the first sentence of the argument, is that the new show will not attract an audience. Answer choice (C) is too extreme, because we can't know that Aurora would say the same thing about any new reality competition show.

24. Job placement rates for graduates of Smith County Community College have been low in recent years, and an employment expert thinks that this is unlikely to change in the near future because Smith County has been experiencing an economic downturn that is expected to continue for several years. His prediction is probably wrong, however, because the community college recently opened a nursing school, and nurses are in high demand in Smith County.

    The phrase "his prediction" refers to the expert's claim that

    (A) job placement rates for graduates of the community college will definitely worsen in the next few years.

    ● job placement rates for graduates of the community college will probably not improve in the next few years.

    (C) job placement rates for graduates of the community college will probably improve in the next few years.

    (D) it is impossible to predict whether job placement rates for graduates of the community college will change in the next few years.

In the first sentence, the expert is cited as claiming that the low job placement rates are unlikely to change in the near future, meaning that the rates will probably not improve. Answer choice (A) is too extreme because the expert does not claim that the rates will worsen, just that they will not improve. Answer choices (C) and (D) are incompatible with the expert's position.

25. According to an article published in a well-known medical journal, cancer researchers have recently demonstrated the success of a new early detection screening tool for pancreatic cancer. Although a screening tool does not directly treat or cure cancer, the prospect is promising news for cancer patients, who tend to have a better prognosis the earlier a diagnosis is made.

    The term "prospect" as used in the conclusion refers to the possibility that

    ● the new screening tool for pancreatic cancer may lead to an earlier detection of some pancreatic cancers.

    (B) the new screening tool for pancreatic cancer will definitely save lives.

    (C) additional research will confirm the efficacy of the new screening tool for pancreatic cancer.

    (D) the researchers cited in the journal article were mistaken about the efficacy of the new screening tool.

The author believes that the new screening tool is promising because it may lead to successful early detection for some patients. Answer choices (B) and (C) are too extreme for the author's position, which is tentatively hopeful, while (D) is the opposite of the author's position.

1

26. Resident: During the last election, our local council member assured voters that she would not allow the city council to raise our taxes. But the councilwoman is one of eight council members, and raising taxes requires only a simple majority of council members to vote in favor of a proposed tax increase. Thus, it is impossible for the councilwoman to keep her promise.

The phrase "her promise" in the conclusion refers to

(A) the resident's promise to vote for the councilwoman because she is opposed to tax increases.

(B) the resident's promise to vote out the councilwoman for allowing the city council to raise taxes.

(C) the councilwoman's promise not to vote for a tax increase.

● **the councilwoman's promise to prevent the city council from raising taxes.**

According to the first sentence, the councilwoman promised that she would not allow the city council to raise taxes. This is different from promising that she herself would not vote for a tax increase, making (C) incorrect. (A) and (B) are incorrect because the resident is the author of the argument and would refer to her own promise as "my" promise, not "her" promise.

27. Lawyer: Our legal system adheres to the at-will employment doctrine, meaning that an employee can be fired without notice for nearly any reason. Some people have argued that we should abandon the at-will doctrine in favor of a rule that requires an employer to provide a one-year notice period when terminating an employee, as many other countries have done. Proponents of this change argue that it would reduce our unemployment rate by giving people more time to find work while they are still employed, but this proposition is mistaken, as countries that have adopted the new rule actually have higher rates of employment due to the inherent lack of flexibility in their workforce.

The phrase "this proposition" in the conclusion refers to the claim that

(A) the lawyer's country should adopt a one-year notice period requirement.

(B) countries that require a one-year notice period have higher rates of unemployment.

● **if the lawyer's country were to adopt a one-year notice period requirement, unemployment rates in the lawyer's country would decrease.**

(D) the lawyer's country should abandon the at-will employment doctrine.

The proposition the author is referring to in the conclusion is the one made earlier in the same sentence; namely, that unemployment rates would decrease if the author's country were to adopt a one-year notice period. We know this because the evidence offered in the next part of the sentence is intended to show that this claim is not true. Answer choices (A) and (D) are tempting, but the author is arguing against the reasoning for the recommendation, not against the recommendation itself.

Drill 5: What's Your Function? Round 1

Instructions: Breaking down an argument into its core components is step one for almost any Logical Reasoning question. To do this, you need to determine the role of each statement in the argument. There are two key questions here: 1) Is this part of the author's argument, or is it part of an opposing argument? 2) If this statement is part of the author's argument, is it the conclusion, support for the conclusion, or background?

Each of the following sets of items is an argument broken up into pieces. Some sentences within the argument are also broken into pieces because single sentences can have multiple clauses that each have a different function. For each numbered piece, note whether it's Background info (BG), an Opposing Point (OP), Counter Evidence that would support an opposing point (even if that point has not been explicitly articulated) (CE), a Premise of the argument (P), an Intermediate Conclusion of the argument (IC), or the argument's Main Conclusion (MC). Note that you will generally need to read the whole argument before making your determination, and that it's generally easiest to start by trying to identify the main conclusion and figure the rest out from there.

Argument 1

___P___ 1. The archaeological record shows that only the Alzonian clan had the ability to create the uniform and tightly-fitting bricks that were used in the construction of the Grand Temple.

___MC___ 2. Therefore, the Grand Temple was certainly built by the Alzonian clan.

Argument 2

___MC___ 3. My karate instructor is remarkably good at his job.

___P___ 4. After all, everyone who has studied at his school for at least two years is a competent martial artist.

___P___ 5. Furthermore, almost none of these students had any experience before attending classes there.

Argument 3

___CE___ 6. The giant greyback is a very aggressive species of lizard that nests in mountain caves and fissures.

___P___ 7. Since these lizards are nocturnal and sleep from dawn to dusk, however,

___MC___ 8. individuals traversing the mountains during daytime hours will not be attacked by them.

Argument 4

_____ 9. The faculty of Benjamin Harrison High School are debating the merits of a referendum that would ban students from carrying mobile phones on the school grounds.

_____ 10. The principle argues that the new rule would benefit both students and staff,

_____ 11. but she is certainly mistaken.

_____ 12. Forbidding mobile phones on campus will unfairly punish the students who are only using them for legitimate purposes.

Argument 5

_____ 13. Decreasing the temperature in the factory by 20 degrees Celsius would save a small amount of money on heating costs

_____ 14. but dramatically damage the morale and productivity of the workers.

_____ 15. Thus, the temperature change would hurt the factory's finances overall,

_____ 16. so the factory's owners would be foolish to endorse such a change.

1

Argument 6

_____ 17. I believe that Swirsky will be selected as the next conductor of the Springview Philharmonic orchestra.

_____ 18. After all, she has far more experience than the other candidates and is a virtuoso musician in her own right;

_____ 19. accordingly, she would be the best choice to improve the orchestra's international reputation.

Argument 7

_____ 20. In her editorial in yesterday's edition of the Weekly Tribune, Dr. Anderson argued that no one under the age of six should be permitted to play unattended near the Harden Pharmaceutical plant.

_____ 21. However, we can safely ignore her advice.

_____ 22. She cited a recent study which found that the runoff from the plant contains several compounds that may severely retard the physical development of young children,

_____ 23. but one of the principal researchers in that study is employed by a competitor of Harden Pharmaceutical.

Argument 8

_____ 24. The Q&B Diner has the best pancakes in the county.

_____ 25. If you doubt it, go and taste them yourself.

_____ 26. The batter has the perfect level of sweetness,

_____ 27. and the cooks only add the freshest fruit and nuts into the mix.

Argument 9

_____ 28. The board of directors of the Orner Corporation erred when it rejected the merger proposal from PolusTech.

_____ 29. In its statement, the board claimed that the terms of the proposal dramatically overstated PolusTech's value and that the merger would have constituted a disservice to Orner's stakeholders.

_____ 30. The board's position, however, was based on antiquated financial models that cannot properly value a cutting-edge business such as PolusTech.

Argument 10

_____ 31. Our offices are located on the 97th floor of the Chakrabarti Building.

_____ 32. In the event of a fire or similar emergency, it would take a great deal of time for our staff to descend to the ground floor via the stairs,

_____ 33. and their safety would presumably be at risk while doing so.

_____ 34. But the potential to be trapped or injured in a malfunctioning elevator is far riskier.

_____ 35. Since the stairs will always be the best exit route,

_____ 36. the company safety guide should explicitly instruct our staff to use them in the case of an emergency.

Argument 11

_____ 37. Stefan is the manager of the Willow Center, a day care facility.

_____ 38. Recently, he has come to believe that providing a greater number of toys never reduces the conflict between the children in the play area;

_____ 39. instead, the children continue to fight for the right to play with whichever toys are the most desirable.

_____ 40. He is probably correct:

_____ 41. recent psychological research suggests that all humans quickly adapt to improved material circumstances and continue to seek advantages over their peers.

Argument 12

_____ 42. It is common knowledge that carbon dioxide is the most abundant greenhouse gas generated by humans, accounting for over 80% of emissions.

_____ 43. This has led some pundits to argue that we should disregard the effects of other greenhouse gases.

_____ 44. Climate scientists, however, warn that the heat-trapping effect of a methane molecule may be up to 100 times greater than that of a carbon dioxide molecule.

_____ 45. So although methane emissions are already relatively low, industrialized nations should invest in initiatives to reduce them further.

Argument 13

_____ 46. Fugu, a dish originating in Japan and Korea, is considered a delicacy by many diners.

_____ 47. Although the species of pufferfish from which it is prepared is indeed poisonous to humans,

_____ 48. the danger posed by eating fugu has been greatly exaggerated throughout history.

_____ 49. One noteworthy example of its cultural prominence is the law that forbids its consumption by the Emperor of Japan; fugu is the only food item subject to such an edict.

_____ 50. Despite this aura of menace,

_____ 51. deaths due to fugu poisoning are extremely rare

_____ 52. since techniques to safely prepare the flesh of the pufferfish have been well-known for centuries.

Argument 14

_____ 53. The noted scholar Helen Isaacs was mistaken to assert that the Elkind manuscript could not have been produced by Sir Alan Pole.

_____ 54. In her letters, Isaacs argued that the text is written in a hand markedly different from Pole's own.

_____ 55. In the present day, however, a number of leading document experts disagree.

_____ 56. According to them, the differences highlighted by Isaacs are incidental and by no means conclusively exclude Pole as a potential author of the manuscript.

Argument 15

_____ 57. Recently, the sale of several fraudulent Old Master paintings for eight-digit sums has dealt a serious blow to the reputation of the high-end art market.

_____ 58. Prominent dealers admit that careful forgeries, ubiquitous and almost impossible to detect, have flooded galleries and auction houses in the past decade.

_____ 59. It is unlikely that many more pieces will be sold at such prices;

_____ 60. the pall of uncertainty ensures that wealthy collectors will only purchase those rare artworks that have impeccable provenance.

Answers

1

Argument 1

__P__ 1. The archaeological record shows that only the Alzonian clan had the ability to create the uniform and tightly-fitting bricks that were used in the construction of the Grand Temple.

__MC__ 2. Therefore, the Grand Temple was certainly built by the Alzonian clan.

Argument 2

__MC__ 3. My karate instructor is remarkably good at his job.

__P__ 4. After all, everyone who has studied at his school for at least two years is a competent martial artist.

__P__ 5. Furthermore, almost none of these students had any experience before attending classes there.

Argument 3

__CE__ 6. The giant greyback is a very aggressive species of lizard that nests in mountain caves and fissures.

__P__ 7. Since these lizards are nocturnal and sleep from dawn to dusk, however,

__MC__ 8. individuals traversing the mountains during daytime hours will not be attacked by them.

Argument 4

__BG__ 9. The faculty of Benjamin Harrison High School are debating the merits of a referendum that would ban students from carrying mobile phones on the school grounds.

__OP__ 10. The principal argues that the new rule would benefit both students and staff,

__MC__ 11. but she is certainly mistaken.

__P__ 12. Forbidding mobile phones on campus will unfairly punish the students who are only using them for legitimate purposes.

Argument 5

__CE__ 13. Decreasing the temperature in the factory by twenty degrees Celsius would save a small amount of money on heating costs

__P__ 14. but dramatically damage the morale and productivity of the workers.

__IC__ 15. Thus, the temperature change would hurt the factory's finances overall,

__MC__ 16. so the factory's owners would be foolish to endorse such a change.

Argument 6

__MC__ 17. I believe that Swirsky will be selected as the next conductor of the Springview Philharmonic orchestra.

__P__ 18. After all, she has far more experience than the other candidates and is a virtuoso musician in her own right;

__IC__ 19. accordingly, she would be the best choice to improve the orchestra's international reputation.

Argument 7

__OP__ 20. In her editorial in yesterday's edition of the Weekly Tribune, Dr. Anderson argued that no one under the age of six should be permitted to play unattended near the Harden Pharmaceutical plant.

__MC__ 21. However, we can safely ignore her advice.

__CE__ 22. She cited a recent study which found that the runoff from the plant contains several compounds that may severely retard the physical development of young children,

__P__ 23. but one of the principal researchers in that study is employed by a competitor of Harden Pharmaceutical.

Argument 8

_MC_ 24. The Q&B Diner has the best pancakes in the county.

_BG_ 25. If you doubt it, go and taste them yourself.

_P_ 26. The batter has the perfect level of sweetness,

_P_ 27. and the cooks only add the freshest fruit and nuts into the mix.

Argument 9

_MC_ 28. The board of directors of the Orner Corporation erred when it rejected the merger proposal from PolusTech.

_OP_ 29. In its statement, the board claimed that the terms of the proposal dramatically overstated PolusTech's value and that the merger would have constituted a disservice to Orner's stakeholders.

_P_ 30. The board's position, however, was based on antiquated financial models that cannot properly value a cutting-edge business such as PolusTech.

Argument 10

_BG_ 31. Our offices are located on the ninety-seventh floor of the Chakrabarti Building.

_CE_ 32. In the event of a fire or similar emergency, it would take a great deal of time for our staff to descend to the ground floor via the stairs,

_CE_ 33. and their safety would presumably be at risk while doing so.

_P_ 34. But the potential to be trapped or injured in a malfunctioning elevator is far riskier.

_P_ 35. Since the stairs will always be the best exit route,

_MC_ 36. the company safety guide should explicitly instruct our staff to use them in the case of an emergency.

Argument 11

_BG_ 37. Stefan is the manager of the Willow Center, a day care facility.

_P_ 38. Recently, he has come to believe that providing a greater number of toys never reduces the conflict between the children in the play area;

_P_ 39. instead, the children continue to fight for the right to play with whichever toys are the most desirable.

_MC_ 40. He is probably correct:

_P_ 41. recent psychological research suggests that all humans quickly adapt to improved material circumstances and continue to seek advantages over their peers.

Argument 12

_BG_ 42. It is common knowledge that carbon dioxide is the most abundant greenhouse gas generated by humans, accounting for over 80% of emissions.

_OP_ 43. This has led some pundits to argue that we should disregard the effects of other greenhouse gases.

_P_ 44. Climate scientists, however, warn that the heat-trapping effect of a methane molecule may be up to one hundred times greater than that of a carbon dioxide molecule.

_MC_ 45. So although methane emissions are already relatively low, industrialized nations should invest in initiatives to reduce them further.

Argument 13

_BG_ 46. Fugu, a dish originating in Japan and Korea, is considered a delicacy by many diners.

_CE_ 47. Although the species of pufferfish from which it is prepared is indeed poisonous to humans,

_MC_ 48. the danger posed by eating fugu has been greatly exaggerated throughout history.

1

__P__ 49. One noteworthy example of its cultural prominence is the law that forbids its consumption by the Emperor of Japan; fugu is the only food item subject to such an edict.

__CE__ 50. Despite this aura of menace,

__P__ 51. deaths due to fugu poisoning are extremely rare

__P__ 52. since techniques to safely prepare the flesh of the pufferfish have been well-known for centuries.

Argument 14

__MC__ 53. The noted scholar Helen Isaacs was mistaken to assert that the Elkind manuscript could not have been produced by Sir Alan Pole.

__CE__ 54. In her letters, Isaacs argued that the text is written in a hand markedly different from Pole's own.

__P__ 55. In the present day, however, a number of leading document experts disagree.

__P__ 56. According to them, the differences highlighted by Isaacs are incidental and by no means conclusively exclude Pole as a potential author of the manuscript.

Argument 15

__BG__ 57. Recently, the sale of several fraudulent Old Master paintings for eight-digit sums has dealt a serious blow to the reputation of the high-end art market.

__CE__ 58. Prominent dealers admit that careful forgeries, ubiquitous and almost impossible to detect, have flooded galleries and auction houses in the past decade.

__MC__ 59. It is unlikely that many more pieces will be sold at such prices;

__P__ 60. the pall of uncertainty ensures that wealthy collectors will only purchase those rare artworks that have impeccable provenance.

Drill 6: Conclusion Types

Instructions: While conclusions can feel as if they come in all different shapes and sizes, most of them fall into one of a small set of categories, each of which has its own strategic considerations. Some of the most common categories, along with their strategies, are:

Conditional – A sure sign you should be diagramming that question.

Qualified – When the author states the conclusion is true only under certain conditions. You should make sure those conditions are met, or pick an answer that does so.

Comparison – Be sure the author has established the criteria by which things will be judged and be sure to consider relevant similarities and differences.

Recommendation – Look for words such as *should* or *ought*. Check to see if the author established the criteria for making the recommendation. If not, the answer is likely to. Also, consider possible alternatives to the recommended course of action.

Causal – This type of conclusion is one of the most common on the LSAT, and, depending on the question type, there are a lot of more nuanced strategies that we will cover later in the book. For now, the basic strategy is to consider alternative causes to the one proposed in the causal conclusion.

Explanation – These questions usually have answers related to alternative explanations.

Prediction – The criteria for the prediction and alternative predictions are central to these questions.

Mandate – The author decrees that something must be true or needs to happen. Mandates should always make you consider alternatives to the mandate.

Judgment on Opposing Point – When you see this, be sure to rephrase the author's opinion as what she actually believes: *Those who say aliens exist are wrong* should be rephrased as *Aliens don't exist*.

Note that these categories can and will overlap. Explanations are often Causal in nature, explaining why two things are associated by claiming that one thing causes the other. Recommendations are also Causal, since if you make a recommendation, it is typically for a course of action in pursuit of a certain effect. Qualified conclusions are a subset of Conditional conclusions because they only hold under certain conditions. Mandates are often conditional as well, because they establish something that must be (a guarantee) or needs to be (a necessity).

For each of the following conclusions, fill in the subsequent blank with the category you think provides the best description. (Bonus points if you rephrase the Judgment on Opposing Point conclusions when possible.)

1. These unexpected survey results suggest that there has been a general decline in overall literacy in this country over the past 40 years.

   ___*Explanation*___

2. The plan will likely achieve different results from those intended by management.

   ___*Prediction*___

3. If reduction of unemployment is the priority, consumers have to be willing to pay higher prices for manufactured goods.

   ___*Qualified*___

4. Computer models are less reliable than historical trend analysis for predicting market behavior.

   ___*Comparison*___

5. It was the launch of the first Soviet satellite in 1957 that triggered the boom in popular science fiction in the 1960s.

   _____

6. The physical evidence shows that those who believed the witness's testimony were being misled.

   _____

7. So, economic factors cannot be an overriding consideration in life-or-death decisions.

   _____

8. The advantageous choice, therefore, is to lease the new car.

   _____

1

9. So, countries can take actions to curtail the use of fossil fuels only after ensuring that such actions will not cripple the economy.

_____

10. Increasing the tax on cigarettes will contribute to a reduction in the number of deaths from smoking-related diseases in the future.

_____

11. No member of this board has held a political office or been a lobbyist for a political cause.

_____

12. It is clear that the only reason for the mayor's unexpected victory was the scandal that haunted her opponent in the final month of the campaign.

_____

13. Dr. Smythe's conclusion that bonobos mate for life is therefore false.

_____

14. She must have gotten to the office late because of the change to daylight saving time.

_____

15. This bacteria can be deadly, but only in very young children and in adults with certain preexisting conditions.

_____

16. Although the sociologist attributes anxiety to societal pressures, that clearly cannot be the explanation in this case.

_____

17. When deciding which college to attend, a student should consider a school's culture as much as its academic factors.

_____

18. So, a proper daily dose of vitamin D_3 is as essential as calcium for maintaining strong bones.

_____

19. This makes it highly probable that Earth will experience a collision with a large asteroid within the next 100 million years.

_____

20. It was Germany's resumption of submarine attacks on passenger and merchant ships in 1917 that led to Wilson's decision to enter the United States into World War I.

_____

21. The standard American diet must be improved by replacing highly processed foods with whole grains and fresh or frozen vegetables as often as possible.

_____

22. Any truly complete jazz record collection is sure to include a copy of Dave Brubeck's finest album, _Take Five_.

_____

23. I can only conclude that someone in her family must have talked Emily into such an unwise investment decision.

_____

24. In drafting the new motorcycle law, the goal of enhancing public safety is more important than the concern for preserving individual freedom.

_____

25. Janie will need to refresh her knowledge of trigonometry if she hopes to do well in her introductory celestial mechanics class.

_____

Answers follow on the next page.

Answers

Note: The description we feel best captures the structure of the conclusion is listed first. If there is a secondary structure, we have listed it parenthetically.

1. These unexpected survey *results suggest* that there has been a general decline in overall literacy in this country over the past 40 years.

   Explanation

2. The plan *will likely* achieve different results from those intended by management.

   Prediction

3. *If reduction of unemployment is the priority,* consumers have to be willing to pay higher prices for manufactured goods.

   Qualified

4. Computer models *are less reliable than* historical trend analysis for predicting market behavior.

   Comparison

5. It was the launch of the first Soviet satellite in 1957 that *triggered* the boom in popular science fiction in the 1960s.

   Causal

6. The physical evidence shows that *those who believed the witness's testimony were being misled.*

   Judgment on Opposing Point (Rephrase: The witness gave misleading testimony.)

7. So, economic factors *cannot be* an overriding consideration in life-or-death decisions.

   Mandate (Conditional)

8. The a*dvantageous choice*, therefore, *is to* lease the new car.

   Recommendation

9. So, countries can take actions to curtail the use of fossil fuels *only after* ensuring that such actions will not cripple the economy.

   Qualified (Conditional)

10. Increasing the tax on cigarettes *will contribute to* a reduction in the number of deaths from smoking-related diseases in the future.

    Prediction

11. *No* member of this board has held a political office or been a lobbyist for a political cause.

    Conditional

12. It is clear that *the only reason for* the mayor's unexpected victory was the scandal that haunted her opponent in the final month of the campaign.

    Explanation (Causal)

13. *Dr. Smythe's conclusion* that bonobos mate for life *is therefore false.*

    Judgment on Opposing Point (Rephrase: Bonobos don't mate for life.)

14. She *must have* gotten to the office late *because of* the change to daylight saving time.

    Explanation (Causal)

15. This bacteria can be deadly, *but only* in very young children and in adults with certain preexisting conditions.

    Qualified

16. Although the sociologist attributes anxiety to societal pressures, *that clearly cannot be the explanation in this case.*

    Judgment on Opposing Point (Rephrase: Societal pressures don't explain this case of anxiety.)

17. When deciding which college to attend, a student *should* consider a school's culture as much as its academic factors.

    Recommendation

18. So, a proper daily dose of vitamin D_3 *is as essential as* calcium for maintaining strong bones.

    Comparison

19. This makes it *highly probable* that Earth will experience a collision with a large asteroid within the next 100 million years.

    Prediction

20. It was Germany's resumption of submarine attacks on passenger and merchant ships in 1917 *that led to* Wilson's decision to enter the United States into World War I.

    Causal

21. The standard American diet *must be* improved *by* replacing highly processed foods with whole grains and fresh or frozen vegetables as often as possible.

    Mandate (Causal)

22. *Any* truly complete jazz record collection *must* include a copy of Dave Brubeck's album, *Take Five*.

    Mandate (Conditional)

23. *I can only conclude that* someone in her family *must have* talked Emily into such an unwise investment decision.

    Explanation

24. In drafting the new motorcycle law, the goal of enhancing public safety *is more important than* the concern for preserving individual freedom.

    Comparison

25. Janie *will need to* refresh her knowledge of trigonometry *if she hopes to do well* in her introductory celestial mechanics class.

    Qualified (Conditional/Mandate)

Drill 7: The Three C's

1

Instructions: Each LSAT argument is unique in subject matter, which can make it easy to lose sight of how standardized LSAT arguments actually are. In fact, there are three categories of reasoning that LSAT arguments overwhelmingly fall into: **C**onditional, **C**omparative, and **C**ausal. We call these categories the Three C's.

When a question uses one of these types of reasoning, there are strategies you can deploy, but this drill isn't about that—we'll get to that later in the book. This drill is all about step one: recognizing which type of reasoning an argument uses.

For each of the following arguments, circle any words that are indicative of one of the Three C's. Then, select which type of reasoning the argument features by putting the argument's number into the appropriate field of the chart below.

Causal	Conditional	Comparative	Other
2,4,8,11,15 17	3, 6,10, 13, 18	1,5,7,12, 14, ,20	9,16,1

1. For the home hobbyist deciding which programming languages to learn, Python is preferable to C++. Although C++ is used in 95% of industrial computer systems, Python is easier for a beginner to use and can be acquired for free.

2. Although many believe certain foods contribute to the formation of kidney stones, the condition that is present in every case is an insufficient amount of water. Without enough water, the kidneys cannot dilute uric acid, and the uric acid then forms the accretions that become kidney stones.

3. A ripening banana does not develop its full flavor if it is kept cold in a refrigerator. So, to ensure the most flavorful bananas, refrigerate them only if they are already fully ripe.

4. Last year, the school instituted a system for students to evaluate the teaching effectiveness of their professors. Since the system was implemented, there has been a dramatic rise in student grades. Although it was hoped that the evaluation system would improve teaching, it is more likely that it has instead resulted in grade inflation by professors hoping to get good evaluations.

5. Contrary to some parents' belief, a large dog makes a good pet choice for families with small children. Unlike small breeds, which can be high-strung and skittish, the larger breeds tend to be calm and have even dispositions.

6. When a health plan allows the patient choices, it is worth paying somewhat higher premiums. So paying a little more for this PPO plan is worthwhile, because it allows the patient to choose any doctor in the plan.

7. The three common types of pillows to choose from are latex, memory foam, and feather. Because latex has more body and retains its shape well, it is generally a better choice for people who sleep on their sides.

8. More than any other single event, the extreme overbuilding of the nation's railroad system brought on the so-called "Panic of 1873." Clear evidence of this lies in the numerous failures immediately before the crash of banks that were heavily invested in the railroads.

9. Freedom of speech and expression are the foundation of the democratic form of government. We must therefore resist any governmental attempt to control information on the Internet.

10. Financial advisor: Saving enough money is essential for retirement, but savings alone is not enough. Wise investing is also necessary. Those, therefore, who only save but do not invest are unlikely to be financially prepared for retirement.

11. Editorial: Historically, whenever a country's debt has risen above 90% of its gross domestic product, slow economic growth is seen, and the country experiences economic recession. Congressional refusal to take action to reduce the national debt will plunge this country into a recession before the decade is out.

12. Because electronic tablet screens are backlit and emit blue light, they cause a reader greater eye fatigue than e-ink, the display used by e-readers. Although the technology in tablet screens is improving, e-readers will continue to be the more popular choice for book readers.

13. Jeweler: If a gemstone is common and readily available, it should not be considered an investment. Diamonds, contrary to popular belief, are very common and readily available. So unless you have a really special one-of-a-kind stone that is worth millions, a diamond should not be considered an investment.

14. Every school child is taught that Mount Everest is the highest mountain in the world. Scientifically, however, the highest mountain is Mount Chimborazo, a stratovolcano in Ecuador. Because Mount Chimborazo is closer to the equator, the oblate shape of the earth puts its peak farther from the earth's center than the peak of Everest.

15. Counselor: Excessive use of social media is compounding the growing problem of social anxiety among teenagers and young adults today. Comparing pictures posted on social media with one's own life creates feelings of self-consciousness, and those with social anxiety also report chronic feelings of self-consciousness.

16. Ethicist: Respect for others is the most important value that parents can teach their children. All of the other important values—honesty, kindness, fairness, and generosity—come naturally out of respect for the other person.

17. Patient: Years of prescription remedies for arthritis had little if any effect on my pain, but I finally experienced some relief when I switched to using an over-the-counter glucosamine supplement. In my opinion, glucosamine is surprisingly effective for reducing osteoarthritis discomfort.

18. Every citizen should be ready to respond to a jury summons and willingly serve as a juror when called. Fair and equal justice is an essential part of democracy, and without citizen participation, the court system would be unable to serve its vital function of providing justice for all.

19. The so-called Little Ice Age that occurred between the sixteenth and nineteenth centuries was not a true ice age. Areas around the globe experienced levels of cooling that varied greatly and occurred at different times.

20. Contrary to what is commonly believed, Einstein's theories did not replace Newton's physical laws. Everything that Einstein's equations describe is fully compatible with Newtonian law. The difference is that Einstein's equations explain phenomena that Newton's could not, so Einstein's theories are more complete.

Answers

1

Causal	Conditional	Comparative	Other
2, 4, 8, 11, 15, 17	3, 6, 10, 13, 18	1, 5, 7, 12, 14, 20	9, 16, 19

Causal:

2. Although many believe certain foods contribute to the formation of kidney stones, the condition that is present in every case is an insufficient amount of water. Without enough water, the kidneys cannot dilute uric acid, and the uric acid then forms the accretions that become kidney stones. *(Correlation: present in every case; causation: contribute, forms)*

4. Last year, the school instituted a system for students to evaluate the teaching effectiveness of their professors. Since the system was implemented, there has been a dramatic rise in student grades. Although it was hoped that the evaluation system would improve teaching, it is more likely that it has instead resulted in grade inflation by professors hoping to get good evaluations. *(Correlation: since the system was implemented; causation: resulted in)*

8. More than any other single event, the extreme overbuilding of the nation's railroad system brought on the so-called "Panic of 1873." Clear evidence of this lies in the numerous failures immediately before the crash of banks that were heavily invested in the railroads. *(Correlation: immediately before; causation: brought on)*

11. Editorial: Historically, whenever a country's debt has risen above 90% of its gross domestic product, slow economic growth is seen and the country experiences economic recession. Congressional refusal to take action to reduce the national debt will plunge this country into a recession before the decade is out. *(Correlation: whenever, is seen; causation: will plunge)*

15. Counselor: Excessive use of social media is compounding the growing problem of social anxiety among teenagers and young adults today. Comparing pictures posted on social media with one's own life creates feelings of self-consciousness, and those with social anxiety also report chronic feelings of self-consciousness. *(Correlation: also; causation: compounding, creates)*

17. Patient: Years of using prescription remedies for arthritis had little if any effect on my pain, but I finally experienced some relief when I switched to using an over-the-counter glucosamine supplement. In my opinion, glucosamine is surprisingly effective for reducing osteoarthritis discomfort. *(Correlation: when I switched; causation: effect, reducing)*

Conditional:

3. A ripening banana does not develop its full flavor if it is kept cold in a refrigerator. So, to ensure the most flavorful bananas, refrigerate them only if they are already fully ripe.

6. When a health plan allows the patient choices, it is worth paying somewhat higher premiums. So paying a little more for this PPO plan is worthwhile because it allows the patient to choose any doctor in the plan.

10. Financial advisor: Saving enough money is essential for retirement, but savings alone is not enough. Wise investing is also necessary. Those, therefore, who only save but do not invest are unlikely to be financially prepared for retirement.

13. Jeweler: If a gemstone is common and readily available, it should not be considered an investment. Diamonds, contrary to popular belief, are very common and readily available. So unless you have a really special one-of-a-kind stone that is worth millions, a diamond should not be considered an investment.

18. Every citizen should be ready to respond to a jury summons and willingly serve as a juror when called. Fair and equal justice is an essential part of democracy, and without citizen participation the court system would be unable to serve its vital function of providing justice for all.

Comparative:

1. For the home hobbyist deciding which programming languages to learn, Python is preferable to C⁺⁺. Although C⁺⁺ is used in 95% of industrial computer systems, Python is easier for a beginner to use and can be acquired for free.

5. Contrary to some parents' belief, a large dog makes a good pet choice for families with small children. Unlike small breeds, which can be high-strung and skittish, the larger breeds tend to be calm and have even dispositions.

7. The three common types of pillows to choose from are latex, memory foam, and feather. Because latex has more body and retains its shape well, it is generally a better choice for people who sleep on their sides.

12. Because electronic tablet screens are backlit and emit blue light, they cause a reader greater eye fatigue than e-ink, the display used by e-readers. Although the technology in tablet screens is improving, e-readers will continue to be the more popular choice for book readers.

14. Every school child is taught that Mount Everest is the highest mountain in the world. Scientifically, however, the highest mountain is Mount Chimborazo, a stratovolcano in Ecuador. Because Mount Chimborazo is closer to the equator, the oblate shape of the earth puts its peak farther from the earth's center than the peak of Everest.

20. Contrary to what is commonly believed, Einstein's theories did not replace Newton's physical laws. Everything that Einstein's equations describe is fully compatible with Newtonian law. The difference is that Einstein's equations explain phenomena that Newton's could not, so Einstein's theories are more complete.

Other:

9. Freedom of speech and expression are the foundation of the democratic form of government. We must therefore resist any governmental attempt to control information on the Internet. *(Mandate)*

16. Ethicist: Respect for others is the most important value that parents can teach their children. All of the other important values—honesty, kindness, fairness, and generosity—come naturally out of respect for the other person. *(Evaluation)*

19. The so-called Little Ice Age that occurred between the sixteenth and nineteenth centuries was not a true ice age. Areas around the globe experienced levels of cooling that varied greatly and occurred at different times. *(Evaluation)*

1

Drill 8: Diagramming 101, Round 1

Instructions: One of the most important skills you can build for the LR section is the ability to quickly and accurately diagram and contrapose conditional statements. Conditional logic is tested more often on this exam than just about anything else, and we hope that by the time you hit the test, you'll be able to diagram with your eyes closed (well…maybe not literally, but you get the idea). This drill is the first step toward that level of mastery, and there will be many more to come.

If this one feels like a breeze, feel free to skip over the subsequent "101" iterations of the drill and move right into the "201" or "301" versions. Or, if you want to add a level of difficulty to the subsequent rounds of "101," record your time on this first round and try to beat your time by at least a minute on each round that follows.

1. The carnival will happen only if we get the permit.

   C → P

   ~P → ~C

2. Whenever it rains, the snails and grasshoppers come out.

   If R → S and G

   If ~G or ~S → ~R

3. I never leave home without it.

   Have It → Leave

   Leave → Have It

4. Katrina must be the star of the show or the director.

   If K → S or D

   If ~D and ~S → ~K

5. Jerry is always accompanied by Tim.

   If J → T

   If ~T → ~J

6. The kingdom will be destroyed unless we stop the evil wizard.

   Not Stop Wiz → Kingdom destroyed

   No Kingdom dest. → Stop W

7. Basketball players cannot be slow.

   If B → Not slow

   Slow → ~B

8. If Mark and Johnny are together, then Denny is there too.

   If M and J → D

   If ~D → ~M or ~J

9. Balloons never rise above three feet unless they are filled with helium.

   Not H → Not Rise 3+

   Rise 3+ → H

10. Getting the promotion requires that you work weekends.

    If P → WW

    If ~WW → ~P

11. Either Tony or Angela is in charge of the house.

    If ~T → A

    If ~A → T

12. Terrence cannot be the best skier ever.

    If T → Not BS

    If BS → ~T

13. No computer can express real emotions.

    If C → NOT ERE

    If ERE → ~C

14. If you are lazy and inattentive, you will make a big mistake.

    If L and I → make mistake

    If No mistake → ~L or ~I

15. All hotdogs are made from wholesome ingredients.

If HD → WI
If ~WI → ~HD

16. Only the best employees can be managers or comanagers.

If BE → M or C
If ~M and ~C → ~BE

17. A healthy ecosystem depends on a wide variety of organisms.

HE → VO
~VO → ~HE

18. All cougars are fast.

If C → F
~F → ~C

19. Jim never goes to the meeting without Pam.

If J → P
If ~P → ~J

20. The store does not open until Erin arrives.

EA → O
O → EA

21. If you have confidence and integrity, it will guarantee your success.

If C and I → success
success → C or I

22. None of the flamingos are actually pink.

F → ~P
P → ~F

23. All veterinarians wear insoles.

V → I
~I → ~V

24. The volcano will erupt if there's an earthquake.

EQ → Erupt
~Erupt → ~EQ

25. Horns are all made of keratin.

If H → K
~K → ~H

26. Recycling will bring about world peace.

If R → WP.
~WP → ~R

27. Every bossa nova song is a masterpiece.

If BN → MP
~MP → ~BN

28. A baby has to be burped after every meal.

After Meal → BB
~BB → ~AM

29. Humans cannot be perfectly objective in their interactions with others.

If H → ~PO
PO → ~H

30. Either giraffes will take over the world or bonobos will.

If ~G → B take over
If ~B → G take over

31. Any interpretative dance must also be an expressive art form.

ID → EAF

~~EAF~~ → ~~ID~~

32. Using a coupon precludes earning points on your credit card purchases.

C → ~~R~~

P → ~~C~~

33. My garage sale will happen unless Bill buys it all beforehand.

~~BB~~ → GS

~~GS~~ → BB

34. Each job offer I received included a full benefits package as part of it.

JO → FBP

~~FBP~~ → ~~JO~~

35. When Gloria goes to the movies she is never late.

G → not late

late → ~~G~~

36. Without laws, there must be chaos.

~~L~~ → C

~~C~~ → L

37. When the lights come on, Charlie the ghost goes away.

L → ~~G~~

G → ~~L~~

38. No matchmakers are single.

If MM → ~~S~~

S → ~~MM~~

39. There will be no dessert except for those who finished their salads.

D → FS

~~FS~~ → ~~D~~

40. I get into a car accident whenever I try to eat a burrito while driving.

If eat bud → CA

~~CA~~ → NOT eat bud

Answers

1. The carnival will happen only if we get the permit.

   $C \rightarrow P$; $\sim P \rightarrow \sim C$

2. Whenever it rains, the snails and grasshoppers come out.

   $R \rightarrow G$ and S ; $\sim G$ or $\sim S \rightarrow \sim R$

3. I never leave home without it.

   $\sim HI \rightarrow \sim LH$; $LH \rightarrow HI$

4. Katrina must be the star of the show or the director.

   $K \rightarrow S$ or D ; $\sim S$ and $\sim D \rightarrow \sim K$

5. Jerry is always accompanied by Tim.

   $J \rightarrow T$; $\sim T \rightarrow \sim J$

6. The kingdom will be destroyed unless we stop the evil wizard.

   $\sim SW \rightarrow KD$; $\sim KD \rightarrow SW$

7. Basketball players cannot be slow.

   $BP \rightarrow \sim S$; $S \rightarrow \sim BP$

8. If Mark and Johnny are together, then Denny is there too.

   M and $J \rightarrow D$; $\sim D \rightarrow \sim M$ or $\sim J$

9. Balloons never rise above three feet unless they are filled with helium.

   $\sim H \rightarrow \sim BR3+$; $BR3+ \rightarrow H$

10. Getting the promotion requires that you work weekends.

    $P \rightarrow WW$; $\sim WW \rightarrow \sim P$

11. Either Tony or Angela is in charge of the house.

    $\sim TC \rightarrow AC$; $\sim AC \rightarrow TC$

12. Terrence cannot be the best skier ever.

    $T \rightarrow \sim BS$; $BS \rightarrow \sim T$

13. No computer can express real emotions.

    $C \to \sim RE \; ; RE \to \sim C$

14. If you are lazy and inattentive, you will make a big mistake.

    L and $I \to BM \; ; \sim BM \to \sim L$ or $\sim I$

15. All hotdogs are made from wholesome ingredients.

    $HD \to WI \; ; \sim WI \to \sim HD$

16. Only the best employees can be managers or comanagers.

    M or $CM \to BE \; ; \sim BE \to \sim M$ and $\sim CM$

17. A healthy ecosystem depends on a wide variety of organisms.

    $HE \to WV \; ; \sim WV \to \sim HE$

18. All cougars are fast.

    $C \to F \; ; \sim F \to \sim C$

19. Jim never goes to the meeting without Pam.

    $\sim P \to \sim J \; ; J \to P$

20. The store does not open until Erin arrives.

    $\sim EA \to \sim SO \; ; SO \to EA$

21. If you have confidence and integrity, it will guarantee your success.

    C and $I \to S \; ; \sim S \to \sim C$ or $\sim I$

22. None of the flamingos are actually pink.

    $F \to \sim P \; ; P \to \sim F$

23. All veterinarians wear insoles.

    $V \to I \; ; \sim I \to \sim V$

24. The volcano will erupt if there's an earthquake.

    $EQ \to VE \; ; \sim VE \to \sim EQ$

25. Horns are all made of keratin.

    $H \rightarrow K$; $\sim K \rightarrow \sim H$

26. Recycling will bring about world peace.

    $R \rightarrow WP$; $\sim WP \rightarrow \sim R$

27. Every bossa nova song is a masterpiece.

    $B \rightarrow M$; $\sim M \rightarrow \sim B$

28. A baby has to be burped after every meal.

    $AM \rightarrow BB$; $\sim BB \rightarrow \sim AM$

29. Humans cannot be perfectly objective in their interactions with others.

    $H \rightarrow \sim PO$; $PO \rightarrow \sim H$

30. Either giraffes will take over the world or bonobos will.

    $\sim GTOW \rightarrow BTOW$; $\sim BTOW \rightarrow GTOW$

31. Any interpretative dance must also be an expressive art form.

    $ID \rightarrow EA$; $\sim EA \rightarrow \sim ID$

32. Using a coupon precludes earning points on your credit card purchases.

    $CO \rightarrow \sim P$; $P \rightarrow \sim CO$

33. My garage sale will happen unless Bill buys it all beforehand.

    $\sim BB \rightarrow GS$; $\sim GS \rightarrow BB$

34. Each job offer I received included a full benefits package as part of it.

    $JO \rightarrow FB$; $\sim FB \rightarrow \sim JO$

35. When Gloria goes to the movies she is never late.

    $GM \rightarrow \sim L$; $L \rightarrow \sim GM$

36. Without laws, there must be chaos.

    $\sim L \rightarrow C$; $\sim C \rightarrow L$

37. When the lights come on, Charlie the ghost goes away.

    LO → CA ; ~CA → ~LO

39. There will be no dessert except for those who finished their salads.

    D → FS ; ~FS → ~D

38. No matchmakers are single.

    ´MM → ~S ; S → ~MM

40. I get into a car accident whenever I try to eat a burrito while driving.

    BWD → CA ; ~CA → ~BWD

Drill 9: Correlation vs. Causation

Instructions: The difference between correlation and causation is one of the fundamental concepts that the LSAT tests. Can you tell the difference? Use this drill to find out! Each of the following statements expresses either a corollary relationship or a causal one. Consider each statement and place its number into the appropriate field of the chart below.

Correlation	Causation
4, 5, 6, 9, 10, 11, 12, 13, 15, 17, 19 20, 22, 24, 26, 27	1, 2, 3, 7, 8, 14, 16, 18, 21 23, 25, 28, 29, 30

1. The icy road conditions led to twice as many accidents as occur on a typical Monday commute.

2. I ordered two entrees at the restaurant because I had just run a marathon.

3. Breaking in a new pair of skates makes even professional ice skaters more likely to fall.

4. Wearing glasses is linked to being more intelligent.

5. Books that are fewer than 200 pages sell more copies than longer books.

6. Left-handed tennis players scored more points in the championship than right-handed players.

7. Aquatic birds evolved to have larger wingspans, which allow them to fly longer distances.

8. Drinking a glass of water before eating triggers a fuller feeling after the meal.

9. Scientists measured 100 subjects and found that people who wear mittens have a higher body temperature than people who wear fingerless gloves.

10. Practicing yoga at least twice a week has been linked to lower blood pressure.

11. Cities that have a higher density of murals have been found to have stronger economies.

12. Everyone who qualified for the varsity basketball team had helped with the bake sale.

13. Whenever I add salt to the pasta water, it boils faster than when I don't add salt.

14. Distant fireworks can provoke a strong fear response in farm animals.

15. Every time that I order soup at the restaurant, I order breadsticks as well.

16. Assigning students detention more than once a year drove them to skip school more frequently.

17. Students who tried chewing gum while they studied got higher scores on the subsequent exam.

18. The company bought ergonomic chairs for all employees, which resulted in fewer absences.

19. The store's profits have increased 10% since the store updated its ordering system.

1

20. After the number of factories on the north shore of the lake doubled, the amount of pollution in the lake doubled as well.

21. When the condo board switched its meeting to Saturday, it sparked a rise in attendance.

22. The realty company found that apartments with hardwood floors were more likely to be rented.

23. Installing more traffic lights in downtown areas created greater traffic congestion.

24. Studies have shown that red cars are involved in the greatest number of highway accidents.

25. Correlation vs. causation drills lead to higher scores on the LSAT.

26. Parties with bounce houses have been rated as more enjoyable than parties without them.

27. Stores with neon signs attract more customers after 8pm than stores without neon signs.

28. A study found that adding fruit to water induced people to drink twice as much water in a day.

29. Being separated too early from their mother leads to aggression in dogs.

30. The tourism board's commercial prompted travelers to book more trips to the beach.

Answers follow on the next page.

Answers

1

Correlation	Causation
4, 5, 6, 9, 10, 11, 12, 13, 15, 17, 19, 20, 22, 24, 26, 27	1, 2, 3, 7, 8, 14, 16, 18, 21, 23, 25, 28, 29, 30

A note about #17, #19, and #20: Be careful not to confuse statements of time and sequence (one thing happens before or after another) for statements of causality (one thing causes or is caused by another). A causal statement implies a particular time and sequence—A caused B implies that A came before B—but a statement about time and sequence doesn't imply anything about causality. Just because A came before B doesn't mean A caused B.

A note about #13 and #15: These are both conditional statements, but they are not expressing a causal relationship. For #13, perhaps the cook only adds salt when the water is in a particular pot that happens to conduct heat better. For #15, perhaps soup and breadsticks are part of a package meal-deal.

1. The icy road conditions led to twice as many accidents as occur on a typical Monday commute.
2. I ordered two entrees at the restaurant because I had just run a marathon.
3. Breaking in a new pair of skates makes even professional ice skaters more likely to fall.
4. Wearing glasses is linked to being more intelligent.
5. Books that are fewer than 200 pages sell more copies than longer books.
6. Left-handed tennis players scored more points in the championship than right-handed players.
7. Aquatic birds evolved to have larger wingspans, which allow them to fly longer distances.
8. Drinking a glass of water before eating triggers a fuller feeling after the meal.
9. Scientists measured 100 subjects and found that people who wear mittens have a higher body temperature than people who wear fingerless gloves.
10. Practicing yoga at least twice a week has been linked to lower blood pressure.
11. Cities that have a higher density of murals have been found to have stronger economies.
12. Everyone who qualified for the varsity basketball team had helped with the bake sale.
13. Whenever I add salt to the pasta water, it boils faster than when I don't add salt.
14. Distant fireworks can provoke a strong fear response in farm animals.
15. Every time that I order soup at the restaurant, I order breadsticks as well.
16. Assigning students detention more than once a year drove them to skip school more frequently.
17. Students who tried chewing gum while they studied got higher scores on the subsequent exam.
18. The company bought ergonomic chairs for all employees, which resulted in fewer absences.
19. The store's profits have increased 10% since the store updated its ordering system.
20. After the number of factories on the north shore of the lake doubled, the amount of pollution in the lake doubled as well.
21. When the condo board switched its meeting to Saturday, it sparked a rise in attendance.
22. The realty company found that apartments with hardwood floors were more likely to be rented.
23. Installing more traffic lights in downtown areas created greater traffic congestion.
24. Studies have shown that red cars are involved in the greatest number of highway accidents.
25. Correlation vs. causation drills lead to higher scores on the LSAT.
26. Parties with bounce houses have been rated as more enjoyable than parties without them.
27. Stores with neon signs attract more customers after 8pm than stores without neon signs.
28. A study found that adding fruit to water induced people to drink twice as much water in a day.
29. Being separated too early from their mother leads to aggression in dogs.
30. The tourism board's commercial prompted travelers to book more trips to the beach.

Drill 10: Quantifiers: What Do They Mean?

Instructions: Quantifiers are some of the most important words on the LSAT. They can allow you to make quick eliminations, and they can break an otherwise good-looking answer choice. But using quantifiers to your advantage necessitates knowing exactly what each quantifier implies.

Use this drill to test your mettle. Circle the quantifier in each of the following statements. Then, place the statement's number into the most appropriate field of the chart below.

All/Always None/Never	Some are Sometimes	Some aren't Not always	Most Probably	Most aren't Probably not
2, 6, 10, 11	1, 3, 8, 12, 14, 15,	9, 18	4, 5, 13, 17	7, 16

1. Somebody from our committee needs to attend Friday's meeting.

2. Everyone who attended Keisha's party also attended Ray's party.

3. Some apples are red.

4. Most of the students in Professor Gabriel's class are sophomores.

5. Miguel usually spends his weekends practicing his archery.

6. No one on the basketball team skipped yesterday's practice.

7. Less than a majority of the country's citizens voted for the new prime minister.

8. A great many pianists find Chopin's music particularly difficult to play.

9. Not all doctors are surgeons.

10. In December of 1970, every snowfall in Peoria exceeded five inches.

11. Each of Judge Watkins's clerks attended Allerston Law School.

12. Kazuko often plays tennis on Fridays.

13. A great majority of the world's forests are currently threatened by logging and pollution.

14. In a recent survey, many fans of jazz music listed Ella Fitzgerald as their favorite jazz singer.

15. Our newest company policy will dramatically affect some of our employees.

16. In last year's election, the incumbent was unable to earn even half of the votes.

17. Jamila will probably attend the Doctor When convention this weekend.

18. Not everyone in our department has a master's degree.

5 lb.

All/Always None/Never	Some are Sometimes	Some aren't Not always	Most Probably	Most aren't Probably not
19, 20, 24, 25, 27, 37, 39,	26, 29, 32, 33, 34, 36	21, 41	22, 23, 31,	28, 30, 35, 38, 40

1

19. None of the movies playing at the cinema on Gerard Street are comedies.

20. Nobody who loves Donne's poetry dislikes that of Marvell.

21. Not everyone at the party convention is a party member.

22. Almost all of the restaurants on Blake Street serve french fries.

23. It is likely that if you walk into the household of an American, it will have a television.

24. To be successful, every engineer needs a basic understanding of theoretical mathematics.

25. Not a single television courtroom drama accurately represents the realities of the legal profession.

26. A significant proportion of the nation's offices could save money by using Compton brand printers.

27. None of the nation's wetlands are unaffected by increasing urbanization.

28. The director's latest film was unable to earn the praise of even half of the critics.

29. Queen regularly beats Raggs at tennis.

30. Few children regularly brush their teeth.

31. Since enrolling at Cinnabar College, Vakim has taken mostly courses in the Psychology department.

32. At least some runners prefer tracks with hard surfaces to tracks with soft ones.

33. Despite recent legislation requiring antilock brakes on all new cars, not every car in the state is equipped with antilock brakes.

34. There are so many beautiful paintings on display at the art museum.

35. Almost no new businesses have relocated to Mission City in the past five years.

36. Zack frequently ends up in trouble of his own making.

37. No zoo in Chesterton has ever housed more than one panda.

38. Only a very small number of English professors specialize in contemporary literature.

39. Any activity that involves movement at over 15 miles per hour is dangerous.

40. Fewer than 50% of the readers of *New Event Magazine* report that they read the horoscope page.

41. Tori often isn't in class during school hours.

All/Always None/Never	Some are Sometimes	Some aren't Not always	Most Probably	Most aren't Probably not
45	43, 44, 46, 47	42	48, 49	50

1

42. Despite recent droughts, not all regions of our country have seen a decrease in crop yields.

43. At least one of the members of the jury believes the defendant is not guilty.

44. At least some cases of back pain are not caused by injury to the spine.

45. There is currently no conclusive evidence of life on Jupiter's moon Europa.

46. Some chess players prefer playing with wooden pieces rather than plastic ones.

47. A great many prehistoric wooden tools have been found in South American peat bogs.

48. Most local historians underestimate the role of Mayor Juarez in shaping the design of our town square.

49. Interviews conducted in 2015 suggest that a majority of commercial airlines either already offer wireless Internet access on their flights or plan to within five years.

50. Of the players on our volleyball team, fewer than half played while in high school.

Answers

All/Always None/Never	Some are Sometimes	Some aren't Not always	Most Probably	Most aren't Probably not
2, 6, 10, 11, 19, 20, 24, 25, 27, 37, 39, 45	1, 3, 8, 12, 14, 15, 26, 29, 32, 33, 34, 36, 43, 44, 46, 47	9, 18, 21, 41, 42	4, 5, 13, 17, 22, 23, 31, 48, 49	7, 16, 28, 30, 35, 38, 40, 50

1. *Somebody* from our committee needs to attend Friday's meeting.
2. *Everyone* who attended Keisha's party also attended Ray's party.
3. *Some* apples are red.
4. *Most* of the students in Professor Gabriel's class are sophomores.
5. Miguel *usually* spends his weekends practicing his archery.
6. *No one* on the basketball team skipped yesterday's practice.
7. *Less than a majority* of the country's citizens voted for the new prime minister.
8. *A great many* pianists find Chopin's music particularly difficult to play.
9. *Not all* doctors are surgeons.
10. In December of 1970, *every* snowfall in Peoria exceeded five inches.
11. *Each* of Judge Watkins's clerks attended Allerston Law School.
12. Kazuko *often* plays tennis on Fridays.
13. A *great majority* of the world's forests are currently threatened by logging and pollution.
14. In a recent survey, *many* fans of jazz music listed Ella Fitzgerald as their favorite jazz singer.
15. Our newest company policy will dramatically affect *some* of our employees.
16. In last year's election, the incumbent was *unable* to earn *even half* of the votes.
17. Jamila will *probably* attend the Doctor When convention this weekend.
18. *Not everyone* in our department has a master's degree.
19. *None* of the movies playing at the cinema on Gerard Street are comedies.
20. *Nobody* who loves Donne's poetry dislikes that of Marvell.
21. *Not everyone* at the party convention is a party member.
22. *Almost all* of the restaurants on Blake Street serve french fries.
23. It is *likely* that if you walk into the household of an American, it will have a television.
24. To be successful, *every* engineer needs a basic understanding of theoretical mathematics.
25. *Not a single* television courtroom drama accurately represents the realities of the legal profession.
26. *A significant proportion* of the nation's offices could save money by using Compton brand printers.
27. *None* of the nation's wetlands are unaffected by increasing urbanization.
28. The director's latest film was *unable* to earn the praise of *even half* of the critics.
29. Queen *regularly* beats Raggs at tennis.
30. *Few* children regularly brush their teeth.
31. Since enrolling at Cinnabar College, Vakim has taken *mostly* courses in the Psychology department.
32. *At least some* runners prefer tracks with hard surfaces to tracks with soft ones.
33. Despite recent legislation requiring antilock brakes on all new cars, *not every* car in the state is equipped with antilock brakes.
34. There are *so many* beautiful paintings on display at the art museum.
35. *Almost no* new businesses have relocated to Mission City in the past five years.
36. Zack *frequently* ends up in trouble of his own making.
37. *No* zoo in Chesterton has ever housed more than one panda.
38. *Only a very small number* of English professors specialize in contemporary literature.
39. *Any* activity that involves movement at over 15 miles per hour is dangerous.
40. *Fewer than 50%* of the readers of *New Event Magazine* report that they read the horoscope page.
41. Tori *often* isn't in class during school hours.
42. Despite recent droughts, *not all* regions of our country have seen a decrease in crop yields.

43. *At least one* of the members of the jury believes the defendant is not guilty.
44. *At least some* cases of back pain are not caused by injury to the spine.
45. There is currently *no* conclusive evidence of life on Jupiter's moon Europa.
46. *Some* chess players prefer playing with wooden pieces rather than plastic ones.
47. *A great many* prehistoric wooden tools have been found in South American peat bogs.
48. *Most* local historians underestimate the role of Mayor Juarez in shaping the design of our town square.
49. Interviews conducted in 2015 suggest that a *majority* of commercial airlines either already offer wireless Internet access on their flights or plan to within five years.
50. Of the players on our volleyball team, *fewer than half* played while in high school.

1

Drill 11: Diagramming 101, Round 2

Instructions: Diagram and contrapose each of the following conditional statements in the space provided, again! If you feel that you're ready for a more challenging diagramming drill, feel free to skip ahead to the "Diagramming 201" versions in Chapter 4.

1. None of the best flautists are entomologists.

2. Rachel will keep talking until Joey arrives.

3. Stephanie will go to the concert only if Makeba does.

4. Finding true wisdom and being deeply happy are mutually incompatible.

5. If we don't get new tires and a replacement blinker, then we will crash the car or get a ticket.

6. Only chihuahuas can fit in my doggy backpack.

7. You will never see Marcy and Rich at the same party.

8. If you tell someone your wish, it will not come true.

9. Emily is always bored while she is at work.

10. All early Romans used to use porcupine quills as toothpicks.

11. Snakes never attack without warning.

12. If a child is allergic to cockroaches, that child is allergic to dogs.

13. Our hearts always beat faster in the morning.

14. Abigail will only work with Lindsey or Taylor.

15. Patricia thinks of her sister whenever the telephone rings.

23. If Jean does not file her taxes on time, she has to request an extension.

16. Walter and Jack always sleep through lunch.

24. Kevin's toast will burn unless he watches it.

17. Monica cannot exercise without her headphones.

25. All golfers and all tennis players practice daily.

G and T → Practice daily

practice daily → G or T

18. None of the attendees brought a business card with them.

26. People always get in car accidents when they drive while using their cell phones.

19. Unless it snows tomorrow, I'm going fishing.

27. Lashawn wears his raincoat whenever he walks to work.

20. Whenever I bring my lunch to work, someone orders pizza for the office.

28. At least one dinosaur fossil will be discovered under each mountain.

21. Every building in Detroit has a steel frame.

29. Nobody in this waiting room is actually sick.

22. If you get the job, you will have to install the company e-mail app.

30. Rhinos never charge vehicles that are larger than a Jeep.

1

31. Unless everyone stops preordering the game, it will be terrible.

32. Leaving the stadium early is the only way to beat the traffic.

33. Everyone at this party is famous and brilliant.

34. Stefan visited every college he was accepted to.

35. Dawn is always on time unless she wakes up late.

36. Only when the music stops will I stop dancing.

37. None of my friends drive a Porsche.

38. Tim buys ice cream each time he goes to the grocery store.

39. The grass is always greener on the other side of the fence.

40. My cat will meow at me until I feed him wet food.

Answers

1. None of the best flautists are entomologists.

   BF → ~E ; E → ~BF

2. Rachel will keep talking until Joey arrives.

   ~JA → RT ; ~RT → JA

3. Stephanie will go to the concert only if Makeba does.

   S → M ; ~M → ~S

4. Finding true wisdom and being deeply happy are mutually incompatible.

   TW → ~DH ; DH → ~TW

5. If we don't get new tires and a replacement blinker, then we will crash the car or get a ticket.

   ~NT or ~RB → C or T ; ~C and ~T → NT and RB

6. Only chihuahuas can fit in my doggy backpack.

   DB → C ; ~C → ~DB

7. You will never see Marcy and Rich at the same party.

   M → ~R ; R → ~M

8. If you tell someone your wish, it will not come true.

   TW → ~CT ; CT → ~TW

9. Emily is always bored while she is at work.

   W → B ; ~B → ~W

10. All early Romans used to use porcupine quills as toothpicks.

    ER → PQT ; ~PQT → ~ER

11. Snakes never attack without warning.

    SA → W ; ~W → ~SA

12. If a child is allergic to cockroaches, that child is allergic to dogs.

    ACR → AD ; ~AD → ~ACR

1

13. Our hearts always beat faster in the morning.

    M → HBF ; ~HBF → ~M

14. Abigail will only work with Lindsey or Taylor.

    AWW → L or T ; ~L and ~T → ~AWW

15. Patricia thinks of her sister whenever the telephone rings.

    TR → S ; ~S → ~TR

16. Walter and Jack always sleep through lunch.

    L → WS and JS ; ~WS or ~JS → ~L

17. Monica cannot exercise without her headphones.

    ~H → ~ME ; ME → H

18. None of the attendees brought a business card with them.

    A → ~BC ; BC → ~A

19. Unless it snows tomorrow, I'm going fishing.

    ~S → F ; ~F → S

20. Whenever I bring my lunch to work, someone orders pizza for the office.

    BL → P ; ~P → ~BL

21. Every building in Detroit has a steel frame.

    D → SF ; ~SF → ~D

22. If you get the job, you will have to install the company e-mail app.

    J → A ; ~A → ~J

23. If Jean does not file her taxes on time, she has to request an extension.

    ~FTOT → RE ; ~RE → FTOT

24. Kevin's toast will burn unless he watches it.

    ~W → B ; ~B → W

25. All golfers and all tennis players practice daily.

    G or TP → PD ; ~PD → ~G and ~TP

31. Unless everyone stops preordering the game, it will be terrible.

    ~SPO → T ; ~T → SPO

26. People always get in car accidents when they drive while using their cell phones.

    DCP → A ; ~A → ~DCP

32. Leaving the stadium early is the only way to beat the traffic.

    BT → LE ; ~LE → ~BT

27. Lashawn wears his raincoat whenever he walks to work.

    WW → RC ; ~RC → ~WW

33. Everyone at this party is famous and brilliant.

    P → F and B ; ~F or ~B → ~P

28. At least one dinosaur fossil will be discovered under each mountain.

    M → DF ; ~DF → ~M

34. Stefan visited every college he was accepted to.

    A → V ; ~V → ~A

29. Nobody in this waiting room is actually sick.

    WR → ~AS ; AS → ~WR

35. Dawn is always on time unless she wakes up late.

    ~WL → OT ; ~OT → WL

30. Rhinos never charge vehicles that are larger than a Jeep.

    RC → ~LJ ; LJ → ~RC

36. Only when the music stops will I stop dancing.

    SD → MS ; ~MS → ~SD

1

37. None of my friends drive a Porsche.

   F → ~P ; P → ~F

38. Tim buys ice cream each time he goes to the grocery store.

   GS → IC ; ~IC → ~GS

39. The grass is always greener on the other side of the fence.

   OS → GG ; ~GG → ~OS

40. My cat will meow at me until I feed him wet food.

   ~WF → M ; ~M → WF

Drill 12: Strip the Fat

Instructions: Wouldn't it be great if LSAT arguments told you only what you needed to know? Unfortunately, that's not how it works. Can you tell the relevant from the extraneous? Use this drill to find out!

For each of the arguments below, cross off any information that you believe is not part of the argument's core, such as background information and most opposing points. But, be careful: if an argument's conclusion is a judgment on the opposing point, that point is part of the core and should be left alone.

1. The emissions created by conventional vehicles—i.e., vehicles that burn gasoline and diesel fuel—are creating severe environmental problems that could have serious economic consequences in the near future. All countries must act immediately to replace the use of gasoline and diesel with alternative fuels that create fewer harmful emissions.

2. A large national magazine recently came under new ownership. The new owners shifted the focus of the magazine from family-friendly articles to stories about celebrity scandals and sensational crimes in an attempt to profit from a broader readership. In response to the changes to more prurient content, several of the magazine's major advertisers immediately withdrew their advertising. These advertisers were clearly choosing their moral standards over profits.

3. Many people are convinced that they have relieved their cold symptoms through the self-prescribed use of antibiotic drugs. However, antibiotics kill bacteria, not viruses, and the common cold is caused by a virus. So, no matter what someone's experience leads them to believe, you cannot relieve cold symptoms with antibiotics.

4. Pharmaceutical spokesperson: An industry-wide study demonstrated that the drugs that are most effective in treating serious illnesses can also cause potentially severe side effects. Homeopathic remedies, on the other hand, have no side effects, which is why some seriously ill patients turn to them instead of conventional therapies. These patients are making a dangerous choice, as this study has proven that side effects are a necessary risk of effective treatment.

5. Excess consumption of sugar is linked to several health problems, such as obesity, diabetes, and tooth decay. These health problems impose costs on individuals and society. It has been proposed that a tax be placed on sugar in order to discourage consumption and raise revenue to fund improved health care. However, a tax on sugar is unreasonable because it imposes the greatest financial burden on consumers with the lowest incomes.

6. For a scientific theory to be considered valid, scientists insist that the theory be capable of being tested and proven false. Cosmologists who study string theory have recently hypothesized about the possible existence of a multiverse, in which our universe is one of an infinite number of universes. Yet, by definition a theory about the existence of a multiverse cannot be tested from within our own universe. It follows, then, that a multiverse theory cannot be considered scientifically valid.

7. Analysts who see computer models as a potentially valuable tool for predicting market behavior are overly optimistic. No computer, even the most powerful and sophisticated supercomputer, is capable of processing the huge amounts of data necessary to create even very short-term forecasts of financial market trends.

8. Increasing numbers of homes and businesses throughout the United States are installing solar panels to meet most, if not all, of their electricity needs. Most homeowners and business owners install panels to reduce electricity bills and save money. However, this growing trend in the use of solar panels, if it continues, will result in an additional benefit of significantly reducing the use of fossil fuels in this country.

1

9. Current scientific consensus holds that the moon formed from red-hot debris left over after a Mars-sized object collided with Earth around four and a half billion years ago. Some astronomers are challenging this hypothesis using computer models simulating how the moon could have been captured by Earth's gravity instead. But discarding a well-established hypothesis simply because another explanation is possible goes too far. Astronomers need more physical evidence to support their computer models before they will be worthy of serious consideration.

10. Experts agree that the incidence of allergic rhinitis, or hay fever, is increasing in the United States. One explanation for this points to increased concentrations of airborne pollutants. An alternative explanation, the so-called hygiene hypothesis, focuses on increased levels of cleanliness and sanitation, speculating that an increasingly clean living environment gives our bodies fewer opportunities to build immunities. While experts typically hold one view or the other, there is no reason to believe that these explanations are not both correct.

11. It is a central tenet of free-market capitalism that self-interest is the driving motive for production and exchange. Narrow self-interest, however, is also the reason for theft, dishonesty, and other unethical and detrimental behaviors. Self-interest becomes less of a problem when we view economies as social contracts in which doing good for others helps oneself, too. So, teaching young children to replace narrow self-interest with a social contract view will lead them to do what is ethically right and socially beneficial as adults.

12. Home cooks learn that they should never cut lettuce with a knife because cutting causes the edges of the lettuce to turn unsightly brown. But this rule originated in restaurants, where salads are often prepared in advance and sit for hours in a cooler before being served. Most home cooks, on the other hand, serve the salads shortly after preparation, and the lettuce does not sit long enough to turn color. So, a no-knife rule is pointless in home cooking.

13. A management consulting group recently conducted a study of the effects of workplace stress on employee performance. The group examined complaints from a representative sample of workers in several of its major client corporations. This study found that a significant majority of worker complaints at all levels within the organization were about boredom rather than stress. Clearly, concern about workplace stress is greatly exaggerated.

14. Moon-landing conspiracy theories have existed since the first moon landing. Conspiracists claim either that the landings did not happen, or that they did happen but not in the way that has been told. However, even if one ignores the wealth of physical evidence supporting the authenticity of the moon landings, no rational thinker can truly believe that the NASA moon-landings were a hoax. To believe this one would have to believe that hundreds of thousands of people—astronauts, scientists, engineers, technicians, skilled workers, and administrators—have all kept the secret for almost a half century.

15. The Olympic Games frequently add new sports to attract new participants and spectators. In recent years, many of the new sports events feature so-called "extreme" sports, the inclusion of which is intended to draw young viewers to watch the games. Nevertheless, one sport that is long overdue for inclusion is karate. Karate is the most popular of the martial arts, consistently enjoying more popularity than either judo or taekwondo, both of which have been included in the Olympic Games.

16. Many psychologists have recently advocated for inclusion of "Internet addiction disorder" in the psychiatric diagnostic literature. These psychologists claim that the number of patients exhibiting this condition is growing exponentially and will soon present a serious mental health problem in society. Most psychiatrists, however, hold to a rigorous definition of what constitutes a psychiatric disorder, and they point out that so-called Internet addiction does not fit any definable category of disorder. The psychiatrists'

position is valid. Internet addiction disorder should not be included in the diagnostic literature until much more study has been done to define what it is.

17. When the current mayor came into office, the unemployment rate in the city was at 10%, despite the previous mayor's increased expenditures on job training and job placement programs. However, this administration has already experienced a drop in the unemployment rate of almost 3% in its first year. It's clear that current administration is doing a much better job of tackling the urgent problem of unemployment in the city.

18. Our mathematics education system is inequitable. Students are taught math in ways that alienate many students, causing them to graduate with poor math skills and a general distaste for mathematics. Mathematics education at all levels must be radically redesigned if we wish to improve the mathematical knowledge and skills of future generations.

19. A central tenet of supply-side economic theory is that minimal regulation and lower business tax rates will increase the government's overall revenue because the cuts will stimulate increased economic activity and result in more actual tax dollars collected. However, studies have consistently shown that cuts in business tax rates over the past several decades led to very little growth, and the government has seldom recouped revenue losses. This failure to produce the predicted revenue increases has proven supply-side economic theory to be fundamentally flawed.

20. No matter how much we might speculate, we will never know the identity of the infamous Victorian-era murderer known as Jack the Ripper. Many professional and amateur sleuths have proposed a variety of suspects— from doctors to lawyers to noblemen, and even a prince—based on bits of circumstantial evidence and a lot of imagination. But the fact remains that there exists no solid forensic evidence to establish with any certainty who the true killer was.

Answers

1. **No redactions.**

2. ~~A large national magazine recently came under new ownership. The new owners shifted the focus of the magazine from family-friendly articles to stories about celebrity scandals and sensational crimes in an attempt to profit from a broader readership.~~ In response to the changes to more prurient content, several of the magazine's major advertisers immediately withdrew their advertising. These advertisers were clearly choosing their moral standards over profits.

   Redaction: Background.

3. ~~Many people are convinced that they have relieved their cold symptoms through the self-prescribed use of antibiotic drugs.~~ However, antibiotics kill bacteria, not viruses, and the common cold is caused by a virus. So, no matter what someone's experience leads them to believe, you cannot relieve cold symptoms with antibiotics.

   Redaction: Opposing point.

4. **No redactions.**

5. ~~Excess consumption of sugar is linked to several health problems, such as obesity, diabetes, and tooth decay. These health problems impose costs on individuals and society. It has been proposed that a tax be placed on sugar in order to discourage consumption and raise revenue to fund improved health care.~~ However, a tax on sugar is unreasonable because it imposes the greatest financial burden on consumers with the lowest incomes.

   Redaction: Background and Opposing point.

6. For a scientific theory to be considered valid, scientists insist that the theory be capable of being tested and proven false. ~~Cosmologists who study string theory have recently hypothesized about the possible existence of a multiverse, in which our universe is one of an infinite number of universes.~~ Yet, by definition a theory about the existence of a multiverse cannot be tested from within our own universe. It follows, then, that a multiverse theory cannot be considered scientifically valid.

   Redaction: Background.

7. **No redactions.**

8. Increasing numbers of homes and businesses throughout the United States are installing solar panels to meet most, if not all, of their electricity needs. ~~Most homeowners and business owners install panels to reduce electricity bills and save money.~~ However, this growing trend in the use of solar panels, if it continues, will result in an additional benefit of significantly reducing the use of fossil fuels in this country.

   Redaction: Background.

9. ~~Current scientific consensus holds that the moon formed from red-hot debris left over after a Mars-sized object collided with Earth around four and a half billion years ago.~~ Some astronomers are challenging this hypothesis using computer models simulating how the moon could have been captured by Earth's gravity instead. But discarding a well-established hypothesis simply because another explanation is possible goes too far. Astronomers need more physical evidence to support their computer models before they will be worthy of serious consideration.

   Redaction: Background. The conclusion is a judgment on the opposing point, so the opposing point isn't extraneous.

10. **No redactions.**

11. ~~It is a central tenet of free-market capitalism that self-interest is the driving motive for production and exchange.~~ Narrow self-interest, however, is also the reason for theft, dishonesty, and other unethical and detrimental behaviors. Self-interest becomes less of a problem when we view economies as social contracts in which doing good for others helps oneself, too. So, teaching young children to replace narrow self-interest with a social contract view will lead them to do what is ethically right and socially beneficial as adults.

    Redaction: Background.

12. Home cooks learn that they should never cut lettuce with a knife because cutting causes the edges of the lettuce to turn unsightly brown. But this rule originated in restaurants, where salads are often prepared in advance and sit for hours in a cooler before being served. Most home cooks, on the other hand, serve the salads shortly after preparation, and the lettuce does not sit long enough to turn color. So, a no-knife rule is pointless in home cooking.

    No redactions. The conclusion is a judgment on the opposing point, so the opposing point isn't extraneous.

13. ~~A management consulting group recently conducted a study of the effects of workplace stress on employee performance.~~ The group examined complaints from a representative sample of workers in several of its major client corporations. This study found that a significant majority of worker complaints at all levels within the organization were about boredom rather than stress. Clearly, concern about workplace stress is greatly exaggerated.

    Redaction: Background.

14. ~~Moon-landing conspiracy theories have existed since the first moon landing. Conspiracists claim either that the landings did not happen or that they did happen but not in the way that has been told. Even if one ignores the wealth of physical evidence supporting the authenticity of the moon landings,~~ no rational thinker can truly believe that the NASA moon-landings were a hoax. To believe this one would have to believe that hundreds of thousands of people—astronauts, scientists, engineers, technicians, skilled workers, and administrators—have all kept the secret for almost a half century.

    Redaction: Opposing point.

15. ~~The Olympic Games frequently add new sports to attract new participants and spectators. In recent years, many of the new sports events feature so-called "extreme" sports, the inclusion of which is intended to draw young viewers to watch the games.~~ Nevertheless, one sport that is long overdue for inclusion is karate. Karate is the most popular of the martial arts, consistently enjoying more popularity than either judo or taekwondo, both of which have been included in the Olympic Games.

    Redaction: Background.

16. ~~Many psychologists have recently advocated for inclusion of "Internet addiction disorder" in the psychiatric diagnostic literature. These psychologists claim that the number of patients exhibiting this condition is growing exponentially and will soon present a serious mental health problem in society.~~ Most psychiatrists, however, hold to a rigorous definition of what constitutes a psychiatric disorder, and they point out that so-called Internet addiction does not fit any definable category of disorder. The psychiatrists' position is valid. Internet addiction disorder should not be included in the diagnostic literature until much more study has been done to define what it is.

    Redaction: Opposing point.

17. **No redactions.**

18. ~~Our mathematics education system is inequitable.~~ Students are taught math in ways that alienate many students, causing them to graduate with poor math skills and a general distaste for mathematics. Mathematics education at all levels must be radically redesigned if we wish to improve the mathematics knowledge and skills of future generations.

    Redaction: Background.

19. **No redactions.** The conclusion is a judgment on the opposing point, so the opposing point isn't extraneous.

20. No matter how much we might speculate, we will never know the identity of the infamous Victorian-era murderer known as Jack the Ripper. ~~Many professional and amateur sleuths have proposed a variety of suspects—from doctors to lawyers to noblemen, and even a prince—based on bits of circumstantial evidence and a lot of imagination.~~ But the fact remains that there exists no solid forensic evidence to establish with any certainty who the true killer was.

    Redaction: Background.

Drill 13: Mind the Gap

Instructions: The first step in any Logical Reasoning problem is to break down the stimulus, which in most cases will be an argument. The second step for most problems is to assess the argument in the stimulus and consider whether there is a gap in the reasoning. Gaps are most easily spotted when the premise of the argument and the conclusion of the argument deal with slightly different concepts. Use this drill to practice recognizing these sometimes subtle conceptual shifts.

For each of the following arguments, highlight the new concept introduced in the conclusion and the concept from the premise that the new concept doesn't quite link up with.

1. I have made a firm commitment to avoid consuming more than 2,500 calories per day. Therefore, I can guarantee that I will lose a significant amount of weight.

2. In the future, I will only purchase hardcover books for my personal library. By doing so, I will ensure that none of my new books have durability issues.

3. The laws of this municipality require that one be at least 18 years of age in order to rent an automobile, because it is vital that anyone driving a rented vehicle be able to make responsible decisions.

4. There is no way to avoid a catastrophic increase in the greenhouse gases that cause global warming because the human-created sources of these gases continue to grow.

5. My high-speed Internet service should have been working very smoothly yesterday. After all, there was no inclement weather such as lightning or strong winds.

6. This alloy is resistant to corrosion and has desirable mechanical properties. Therefore, it will be ideal for the applications that AvTech has in mind.

7. It is extremely unlikely that anyone who attempts to reach the South Pole on foot will survive if they depart without companions. So, since Aarne departed alone, her search for the South Pole will almost certainly lead to a tragic death.

8. The only way for a newly established state to avoid conflicts with its neighbors is to enter into trade relationships with them. So, since it is impossible to enter into a trade relationship unless the two parties have significant cultural overlap, a new state is bound to conflict with neighbors with which it has no languages in common.

9. Putting a small table in the corner of a large room will completely eliminate it as a usable surface. So to ensure that they have some utility, tables should be placed either against the middle of a wall or "floating" in the middle of the room.

10. Cape buffalo cannot outrun any predator that is smaller than them. Thus, if cape buffalo are ambushed by a pack of lions, which are much smaller in size, the buffalo will be helpless.

11. There are only two lieutenant's positions open in this department. So of the eight sergeants in this department who are seeking promotion to lieutenant, most won't achieve their goal.

12. The best wine comes from grapes grown in calcium-rich soil, and that level of calcium is only found in the soil of the Bordeaux region. Therefore, aspiring winemakers must grow their grapes in the Bordeaux region if they want to produce wine worthy of consumption.

13. All excellent carpenters were trained by a true master. Therefore, the carpenters who live in this village must not be excellent, because there hasn't been a true master here for over a century.

14. We cannot survive without fresh water, and our current supply has run out. We can't replenish it at the nearest known islands since they are all at least ten miles away from this one: too distant for us to reach alive, given the shark-infested waters. Since fresh water can only be found on islands, we have to find fresh water on this island if we want to survive.

15. The Barksdale breed of horses is always uniformly black in color, while the Clarkhorn and Euler breeds both have patches of white, black, and brown. These are the only three common breeds of horses located in this region. The horse on that distant hill doesn't have patches of different colors, so it is definitely a Barksdale horse.

16. Beeswax candles melt more slowly than any other sort of candle. Therefore, putting beeswax candles in the library will ensure a night's worth of light to read by.

17. If you want to find a valuable example of Navajo weaving, look for a rug with simple patterns and colors. Those designs are characteristic of the oldest and rarest Navajo rugs, while younger and more common examples are brighter and contain more complex shapes.

18. A black hole, as its name suggests, is a very dense collapsed star that emits no light. Because of this, it follows that black holes are undetectable to astronomers.

19. "Maple syrup" is a term protected under Canadian law: any product labeled as such should be composed of at least 99% material from the maple tree. But a recent study found that the majority of products labeled as maple syrup worldwide do not satisfy this condition. Therefore, most products sold as maple syrup worldwide are marketed illegally.

20. Rozen was the most successful managing editor in the history of Tech News. After all, profits increased 300% under her guidance, and the goal of any business, even a news publication, is to maximize profits.

21. One must be able to tolerate great heat without flinching in order to practice the craft of glassblowing. Therefore, you can't take it up as a profession if you have sensitive skin.

22. Professional basketball players have a considerably greater average height than the population generally. It is therefore unsurprising that they are prone to heart problems later in life.

23. The elbow has the highest concentrations of nerve endings on the human arm. It would be wise, then, for anyone with a low pain threshold seeking an arm tattoo to avoid designs that involve the elbow.

24. When a piece of jewelry fails to meet its reserve price at auction and remains unsold, those in the industry consider the piece's eventual sale price to be irrevocably diminished. They even go so far as to refer to them as "dead pieces." Thus, those who want to procure jewelry below market value can do so by seeking out and purchasing these "dead pieces."

25. The model Fx50 ceramics oven cannot also fire enamel. The art studio should therefore purchase the model Fx500, which can.

26. The accountant's records indicated that the company's cash reserves were approximately $100,000 less than they had been fewer than twenty-four hours ago. Since those records have been audited extensively and are certainly correct, and since only an employee of the company could access these cash reserves, someone has been embezzling money from the company.

27. A tent with a sloping roof is much less likely to collapse than a tent with a flat roof. Thus, for safety reasons, this campsite should mandate that only tents with sloping roofs will be used here.

28. In tennis, a tall player has the intrinsic advantages of being able to strike the ball with greater speed and at an angle that is challenging for the opponent. Therefore, a tall tennis player will always defeat a shorter one.

29. Coffee shops that serve as workspaces are clearly a function of universal access to wireless Internet connections. Before such access, coffee shops were primarily frequented by people engaging socially.

30. The breed of dog most maligned in the media is certainly the pitbull terrier. News reports of dog-fighting rings give the mistaken impression that this is a breed that poses a danger to humans, but the data does not support that theory. Far more canine attacks occur by members of other breeds than by pitbull terriers.

Answers

1. I have made a firm commitment to avoid consuming more than 2500 calories per day. Therefore, I can guarantee that I will lose a significant amount of weight.

The conclusion mentions losing weight, but the premise only mentions the calories consumed, so the argument assumes that consuming fewer than 2500 calories per day will guarantee significant weight loss.

2. In the future, I will only purchase hardcover books for my personal library. By doing so, I will ensure that none of my new books have durability issues.

The conclusion is about durability issues, but the premise only mentions hardcover books. The argument therefore assumes that hardcover books don't have durability issues.

3. The laws of this municipality require that one be at least 18 years of age in order to rent an automobile, because it is vital that anyone driving a rented vehicle be able to make responsible decisions.

The conclusion is about being 18 or older, but the premise is only about responsible decision making. The argument assumes that being 18 or older is necessary in order to be capable of responsible decision-making.

4. There is no way to avoid a catastrophic increase in the greenhouse gases that cause global warming because the human-created sources of these gases continue to grow.

The conclusion is about greenhouse gases in general, but the premise only mentions one specific source of these gases. The argument assumes that there is no way that decreasing other sources could avoid a net increase of greenhouse gases.

5. My high-speed Internet service should have been working very smoothly yesterday. After all, there was no inclement weather such as lightning or strong winds.

The conclusion says that the service should have been working, but the premise only mentions a lack of bad weather, so the argument assumes that bad weather is the only reason the service might not work smoothly.

6. This alloy is resistant to corrosion and has desirable mechanical properties. Therefore, it will be ideal for the applications that AvTech has in mind.

The conclusion mentions that the alloy is ideal for AvTech, but the premise only refers to several of the alloy's good qualities, so the argument assumes that these qualities make it perfect for AvTech's needs.

7. It is extremely unlikely that anyone who attempts to reach the South Pole on foot will survive if they depart without companions. So, since Aarne departed alone, her search for the South Pole will almost certainly lead to a tragic death.

The conclusion mentions searching for the South Pole, but the premise mentions searching for the South Pole on foot specifically. The argument assumes that Aarne searched on foot and not by other means.

8. The only way for a newly established state to avoid conflicts with its neighbors is to enter into trade relationships with them. So, since it is impossible to enter into a trade relationship unless the two parties have significant cultural overlap, a new state is bound to conflict with neighbors with which it has no languages in common.

The conclusion introduces the concept of lacking languages in common, but the premise is about having significant cultural overlap. The argument assumes that nations lacking languages in common can't have significant cultural overlap.

9. Putting a small table in the corner of a large room will completely eliminate it as a usable surface. So to ensure that they have some utility, tables should be placed either against the middle of a wall or "floating" in the middle of the room.

The conclusion concerns tables in general, but the premise only concerns small tables. The argument assumes that the claim in the premise applies to all tables.

10. Cape buffalo cannot outrun any predator that is smaller than them. Thus, if cape buffalo are ambushed by a pack of lions, which are much smaller in size, the buffalo will be helpless.

The argument concludes that the buffalo will be helpless in the face of a smaller predator, but the premise only states that they cannot outrun a smaller predator. The argument assumes that the buffalo cannot ensure their own safety without doing so.

11. There are only two lieutenant's positions open in this department. So of the eight sergeants in this department who are seeking promotion to lieutenant, most won't achieve their goal.

The argument concludes that most of the sergeants won't be promoted at all, but the premise only mentions positions open in this particular department, so the argument assumes that there are no lieutenant positions available elsewhere that sergeants in this department are eligible for.

12. The best wine comes from grapes grown in calcium-rich soil, and that level of calcium is only found in the soil of the Bordeaux region. Therefore, aspiring winemakers must grow their grapes in the Bordeaux region if they want to produce wine worthy of consumption.

The conclusion concerns wine that is worthy of consumption, but the premise only mentions the best wine. The argument assumes that only the best wine is worthy of consumption.

13. All excellent carpenters were trained by a true master. Therefore, the carpenters who live in this village must not be excellent, because there hasn't been a true master here for over a century.

The conclusion is about being trained by a true master, while the premise mentions a true master being in this village specifically. The argument assumes that carpenters in the village could only have been trained in this village.

14. We cannot survive without fresh water, and our current supply has run out. We can't replenish it at the nearest known islands since they are all at least ten miles away from this one: too distant for us to reach alive given the shark-infested waters. Since fresh water can only be found on islands, we have to find fresh water on this island if we want to survive.

The conclusion claims that we must find the life-saving fresh water on this island, but the premise only states that we can't get the water at the other nearest known islands. The argument assumes that there are no other currently-unknown islands where fresh water could be obtained.

15. The Barksdale breed of horses is always uniformly black in color, while the Clarkhorn and Euler breeds both have patches of white, black, and brown. These are the only three common breeds of horses located in this region. The horse on that distant hill doesn't have patches of different colors, so it is definitely a Barksdale horse.

The conclusion of the argument is about one particular horse, but the premise is about common breeds. The argument assumes that the horse couldn't be a member of an uncommon solid-colored breed.

16. Beeswax candles melt more slowly than any other sort of candle. Therefore, putting beeswax candles in the library will ensure a night's worth of light to read by.

The conclusion claims that there will be a night's worth of light with beeswax candles, but the premise only states that they are the slowest-melting type of candle. The argument assumes that being the slowest-melting means that they will last for a full night.

17. If you want to find a valuable example of Navajo weaving, look for a rug with simple patterns and colors. Those designs are characteristic of the oldest and rarest Navajo rugs, while younger and more common examples are brighter and contain more complex shapes.

The conclusion is concerned with value, but the premise only mentions age and rarity. The argument assumes that the oldest and rarest Navajo rugs are also the most valuable.

18. A black hole, as its name suggests, is a very dense collapsed star that emits no light. Because of this, it follows that black holes are undetectable to astronomers.

The premise states that a black hole emits no light, but the argument concludes that it is undetectable, which assumes that astronomers can only detect objects that emit light.

19. "Maple syrup" is a term protected under Canadian law: any product labeled as such should be composed of at least 99% material from the maple tree. But a recent study found that the majority of products labeled as maple syrup worldwide do not satisfy this condition. Therefore, most products sold as maple syrup worldwide are marketed illegally.

The conclusion refers to products sold worldwide, but the premise only refers to violations of Canadian law. The argument assumes that similar laws apply worldwide.

20. Rozen was the most successful managing editor in the history of Tech News. After all, profits increased 300% under her guidance, and the goal of any business, even a news publication, is to maximize profits.

The premise states that profits increased 300% under Rozen, but the conclusion states that she was the most successful editor. The argument assumes that no other editor increased profits by an even greater amount.

21. One must be able to tolerate great heat without flinching in order to practice the craft of glassblowing. Therefore, you can't take it up as a profession if you have sensitive skin.

The conclusion mentions sensitive skin, but the premise only refers to the ability to tolerate great heat. The argument assumes that someone with sensitive skin cannot tolerate great heat without flinching.

22. Professional basketball players have a considerably greater average height than the population generally. It is therefore unsurprising that they are prone to heart problems later in life.

The conclusion is about heart problems, whereas the premise is only about height. The argument therefore assumes that greater height predisposes one to heart problems later in life.

23. The elbow has the highest concentrations of nerve endings on the human arm. It would be wise, then, for anyone with a low pain threshold who is seeking an arm tattoo to avoid designs that involve the elbow.

The conclusion is about pain, but the premise is only about nerve endings. That means the argument assumes that a higher concentration of nerve endings in an area makes for a more painful tattoo.

24. When a piece of jewelry fails to meet its reserve price at auction and remains unsold, those in the industry consider the piece's eventual sale price to be irrevocably diminished. They even go so far as to refer to them as "dead pieces." Thus, those who want to procure jewelry below market value can do so by seeking out and purchasing these "dead pieces."

The conclusion deals with market value, whereas the premises only deal with sale price. This argument assumes that the reserve price was market value.

25. The model Fx50 ceramics oven cannot also fire enamel. The art studio should therefore purchase the model Fx500, which can.

The conclusion makes a recommendation of what the studio should purchase. The premises only give us facts about two models. The argument assumes that the enamel-firing feature is the overriding criterion for the studio's purchase.

26. The accountant's records indicated that the company's cash reserves were approximately $100,000 less than they had been fewer than twenty-four hours ago. Since those records have been audited extensively and are certainly correct, and since only an employee of the company could access these cash reserves, someone has been embezzling money from the company.

The conclusion states that money was embezzled, but the premise only states that funds have been removed from the cash reserves. The argument assumes that funds were not removed for a legitimate purpose.

27. A tent with a sloping roof is much less likely to collapse than a tent with a flat roof. Thus, for safety reasons, this campsite should mandate that only tents with sloping roofs will be used here.

The premise states that sloping roofs make a tent less likely to collapse, but the conclusion states that tents with such roofs should be adopted for safety reasons. So, the argument assumes both that roof collapse is a safety issue, and that people would not use tents with sloping roofs in the absence of a mandate.

28. In tennis, a tall player has the intrinsic advantages of being able to strike the ball with greater speed and at an angle that is challenging for the opponent. Therefore, a tall tennis player will always defeat a shorter one.

The conclusion mentions that a taller player will always win, but the premise only mentions that a taller player has intrinsic advantages. The argument assumes that these advantages are sufficient to guarantee victory.

29. Coffee shops that serve as workspaces are clearly a function of universal access to wireless Internet connections. Before such access, coffee shops were primarily frequented by people engaging socially.

The conclusion is about the use of coffee shops, whereas the premise is about their primary use. This argument therefore assumes that coffee shops were not secondarily frequented by people working in the era before wireless Internet.

30. The breed of dog most maligned in the media is certainly the pitbull terrier. News reports of dog-fighting rings give the mistaken impression that this is a breed that poses a danger to humans, but the data does not support that theory. Far more canine attacks occur by members of other breeds than by pitbull terriers.

The conclusion is about an absolute contention: pitbulls don't pose a danger to humans. The premise, on the other hand, presents only relative data: more attacks occur by other breeds than by pitbulls. The argument therefore assumes that if a breed does not account for the majority of attacks, that breed poses no risk to humans.

Drill 14: Objection, Your Honor!

Instructions: In the first drills of this section, you practiced breaking arguments down into their core components. In the last drill, you practiced breaking arguments down and spotting gaps in reasoning. For this drill, you're going to take it one step further: not only are you going to break arguments down and spot the gap in reasoning, you're also going to articulate the gaps by pointing out an assumption the author is making or a possible objection the author has failed to consider.

For each of the following arguments, take what we call The Debater's Stance: I accept (the premise), but that does not prove (the conclusion) because (objection/assumption). Fill in the first two blanks with your abbreviated version of the premise and conclusion, then choose an answer choice to fill the third blank from the three options that follow.

1. Scout: Since arriving in Spain, I have watched hundreds of professional basketball games. After observing that the Spanish players average about six and a half feet in height, I have concluded that the height of the typical Spanish citizen is around six and a half feet as well.

    I accept that _____

    _____,

    but that does not prove_____

    _____

    because_____

    _____.

    (A) The scout has not watched a sufficient number of games to exactly determine the average height of professional basketball players.

    (B) There is no reason to believe that the scout has received enough medical training to evaluate the overall health of professional athletes relative to individuals in other professions.

    (C) The scout fails to consider that in any nation, unusually tall individuals are more likely to become professional basketball players than are people of average height.

2. Benjamin: Suzanne is extremely charismatic, has great plans to improve campus facilities, and shows empathy for her classmates. Since these are all the qualities that voters would want their student body president to have, Suzanne will certainly win the upcoming election.

    I accept that _____

    _____,

    but that does not prove_____

    _____

    because_____

    _____.

    (A) Benjamin assumes that Suzanne is interested in pursuing politics as a career after graduation.

    (B) Benjamin fails to establish that Suzanne is the only candidate with all of the qualities he mentioned.

    (C) Benjamin ignores the extensive time commitment associated with the position of student body president.

3. Every circuit board with a flickering light must be replaced. After all, any circuit board that cannot be repaired must be replaced, and a flickering light on a circuit board indicates that it is not functioning properly.

    I accept that _____

    _____,

    but that does not prove _____

    _____

    because_____

    _____.

    (A) The argument assumes that circuit boards that cannot be repaired must not be functioning properly.

    (B) The argument assumes that a circuit board that is not functioning properly cannot be repaired.

    (C) The argument ignores the possibility that an electronic device may still function properly even if one of its circuit boards is not functioning properly.

4. Paleontologist: Every modern bird is a dinosaur. Therefore, the discovery of the species *capito barzoni* has increased the number of dinosaur species known to science.

    I accept that _____

    _____,

    but that does not prove _____

    _____

    because_____

    _____.

    (A) The paleontologist assumes that *capito barzoni* is a species of modern bird.

    (B) The paleontologist ignores the possibility that some dinosaurs were not modern birds.

    (C) The paleontologist ignores the fact that most dinosaur species are extinct.

5. The Bermuda Triangle has a reputation for supernatural mishaps, and a large number of vessels have vanished in it over the years. Therefore, the disappearances are clearly the result of supernatural events.

    I accept that _____

    _____,

    but that does not prove _____

    _____

    because_____

    _____.

    (A) The argument assumes that the Bermuda Triangle is the only region of the ocean with such an ominous reputation.

    (B) The argument makes the unwarranted assumption that every vessel entering the Bermuda Triangle has disappeared.

    (C) The argument neglects to consider that the supernatural reputation of the Bermuda Triangle may be the result of the disappearances rather than the cause of them.

1

6.   Analyst: In an effort to motivate the patrons of a local golf club to keep the ball on dry ground, a new rule was established that significantly increased the penalty for shots that land in the water. Since this rules change, data recorded by players at the club indicate a 78% decrease in the number of shots that land in the water per round of golf played. The new rule has evidently accomplished its goal.

I accept that _____

_____,

but that does not prove_____

_____

because_____

_____.

(A)   The analyst fails to demonstrate that the overall scores of golfers at the club have improved since the new rule was instituted.

(B)   The analyst assumes that the players have accurately reported how many of their shots land in the water.

(C)   The analyst did not consider whether or not similar rules instituted at other golf clubs have had a similar effect.

7.   Two hours of safety training under the guidance of a certified professional are required before one can participate in a paintball match at Stealthy Acres. Mark has completed the training, so he can compete in the match that will be held at Stealthy Acres as part of his future brother-in-law's bachelor party.

I accept that _____

_____,

but that does not prove_____

_____

because_____

_____.

(A)   The argument confuses a necessary condition for competing in a paintball match with a sufficient condition for competing in such a match.

(B)   The argument assumes that Mark is interested in attending his future brother-in-law's bachelor party.

(C)   The argument assumes that two hours of safety training guarantees that paintball players will conduct themselves safely during a match.

8. Patient: A nutritionist has advised me to dramatically reduce my consumption of refined sugars and fats, arguing that they are unhealthy for anyone. However, it would be perfectly healthy for me to ignore his advice, because he has been consuming sugary and fatty foods every time I have encountered him in private settings.

I accept that _____

_____,

but that does not prove_____

_____

because_____

_____.

(A) The patient assumes that the nutritionist's failure to follow his own advice indicates that the advice is inaccurate.

(B) The patient fails to consider that significant exercise may be needed to offset the negative health effects of consuming refined sugars and fats.

(C) The patient ignores the possibility that the nutritionist did not expect to have his own dietary habits revealed.

9. Principal: The students in your homeroom cannot join the rest of the class on today's field trip. I just reviewed the paperwork in the front office, and none of them have brought in a consent form signed by a legal guardian.

I accept that _____

_____,

but that does not prove_____

_____

because_____

_____.

(A) The principal assumes that some students have legal guardians who are not their parents.

(B) The principal ignores the fact that a signed consent form will not prevent the school from being held legally responsible if students are injured during a class trip.

(C) The principal's argument assumes that a signed consent form is required to attend the field trip.

1

10. Salesperson: The purchase of a flood insurance policy is guaranteed to save you money in the long run. After all, the policy covers all flood-related costs for only $1,000 per year, while any flood would cause at least $5,000 in damage to your home.

I accept that _____

_____,

but that does not prove_____

_____

because_____

_____.

(A) The policy that the salesperson is offering may not cover damages caused by other natural disasters.

(B) The salesperson provides no statistics to validate the claim that repairing flood damage would cost at least $5,000.

(C) The salesperson fails to recognize the possibility that floods may be very uncommon events where the customer's home is located.

11. The prominent musician Harriet Schroder has become an advocate for panspermia: a scientific hypothesis that meteorites containing simple organisms landed on Earth and led to the development of simple life on this planet. Schroder is deeply respected, so her support indicates that the theory of panspermia is probably correct.

I accept that _____

_____,

but that does not prove_____

_____

because_____

_____.

(A) Schroder has not personally written criticism of every possible alternative to the panspermia hypothesis.

(B) There is no reason to believe that Schroder is qualified to evaluate the merits of a scientific theory.

(C) Schroder has assumed, but not demonstrated, that advanced life exists on other planets.

12. Engineer: Our research staff have designed a new anti-pest machine, and they claim that it will deter all pests such as rats and cockroaches from remaining inside any home in which the machine is installed. However, I have personally tested each component that they propose to use in this machine, and none of them individually deter pests from staying nearby. Therefore, the researchers' claims are mistaken.

I accept that _____

_____,

but that does not prove_____

_____

because_____

_____.

(A) The engineer has not properly evaluated the anti-pest machine's effect on pets and other non-pest animals.

(B) The engineer does not understand the means by which the anti-pest machine is supposedly able to deter animals such as rats and cockroaches.

(C) The engineer assumes that if each part of an object lacks a certain characteristic, then the object as a whole must also lack that characteristic.

13. Comedian: I have performed at eight festivals across the country over the past month. Each time I arrived at the location of the next festival, I asked one random person on the street to identify his or her favorite genre of literature. Since the majority of these people responded that their favorite genre is science fiction, science fiction must be the most popular literary genre in the country.

I accept that _____

_____,

but that does not prove_____

_____

because_____

_____.

(A) Comedians are not qualified to collect data about people's literary preferences.

(B) The comedian assumed that many people in this country read literature regularly.

(C) The comedian did not poll enough people to draw a clear conclusion about the country's favorite literary genre.

1

14. Runner: Reducing one's body fat percentage is a factor in achieving better results in long races, and starvation will decrease anyone's percentage of body fat. So refusing to eat will improve my results in long races.

I accept that _____

_____,

but that does not prove_____

_____

because_____

_____.

(A) The runner overlooks the possibility that starvation may have unintended negative effects on performance in races.

(B) The runner assumes that the best preparation for long races is also the best preparation for shorter races.

(C) The definition of "results" changes illicitly in the course of the runner's argument.

15. Focusing our televised news coverage on sports and human interest stories would guarantee high ratings for the station. Therefore, devoting the majority of our airtime to other topics, such as history or technology, will ensure that the station receives poor ratings.

I accept that _____

_____,

but that does not prove_____

_____

because_____

_____.

(A) The argument assumes that there is only one set of programming choices that would achieve high ratings for the news station.

(B) The argument fails to consider that some sports and human interest stories will draw higher ratings than others.

(C) The argument assumes that most viewers are too unsophisticated to appreciate stories about history or technology.

16. Parent: I argue that it is safe to let my children wander outside alone at night, although my superstitious spouse believes that they may be attacked by werewolves. But since it is indisputably impossible that werewolves could exist, my original position is correct.

I accept that _____

_____,

but that does not prove_____

_____

because_____

_____.

(A) The parent maintains that werewolves do not exist simply because her or she has never seen one.

(B) The parent assumes that a claim is true simply because an argument against that claim has been refuted.

(C) The parent disregards the possibility that the spouse has greater concern for the children's safety than he or she does.

17. Art dealer: A painting from the 16th century is definitely more valuable than a 20th-century painting, and any 9th-century sculpture is worth more than a 16th-century sculpture. So this 9th-century sculpture is worth more than this 20th-century painting.

   I accept that _____

   _____,

   but that does not prove_____

   _____

   because_____

   _____.

   Ⓐ The art dealer assumes that a 16th-century sculpture must be worth as much as or more than a 16th-century painting.

   Ⓑ The art dealer fails to recognize that it is impossible to definitively determine whether one piece of art is more valuable than another.

   Ⓒ The art dealer assumes that any sculpture is more valuable than any painting.

18. Meteorologist: The last five blizzards in this state occurred immediately after a day of unseasonably warm weather. Therefore, I conclude that these blizzards were triggered by high temperatures.

   I accept that _____

   _____,

   but that does not prove_____

   _____

   because_____

   _____.

   Ⓐ The meteorologist doesn't consider the possibility that recent weather trends will not necessarily continue in the future.

   Ⓑ The meteorologist assumes that if one event preceded another, then the first event must have caused the second one.

   Ⓒ The meteorologist neglects to consider that blizzards only occur when the temperature is quite low.

19. Biology professor: A recently conducted national survey indicates that only 25% of adults have heard of the famous primatologist Jane Goodall. However, the survey must be flawed, because I've polled dozens of my own friends and they are all very familiar with Goodall and her scientific accomplishments.

   I accept that _____

   _____,

   but that does not prove_____

   _____

   because_____

   _____.

   Ⓐ The biology professor assumes that those who conducted the national poll are ignorant of all statistical principles.

   Ⓑ The biology professor neglects to consider that his or her friends may not be knowledgable about many other scientists aside from Jane Goodall.

   Ⓒ The biology professor ignores the possibility that his or her friends may be more likely than the average adult to be aware of other famous scientists.

20. Coach: If you practice extensively, you will be at peak performance for the upcoming chess match, and it is impossible that you will lose the match if you are at peak performance. Therefore, practice is all you need to guarantee victory.

I accept that _____

_____,

but that does not prove_____

_____

because_____

_____.

(A) The coach assumes that anyone can reach peak chess performance simply through practice.

(B) The coach fails to consider that it is very difficult to practice chess extensively without neglecting other necessary components of a victory in the upcoming match.

(C) The coach ignores the possibility that the chess match could be drawn or tied.

21. Astrologer: The exceptional value of astrology to the romantic is clearly demonstrated by the fact that nearly all of my clients have told me that my counsel on romantic relationships has served them well.

I accept that _____

_____,

but that does not prove_____

_____

because_____

_____.

(A) Astrology is not based on accepted scientific principles.

(B) The astrologer is assuming that his clients aren't afraid to give honest feedback.

(C) Many of the astrologer's clients were already happily married before they became his clients.

Answers

1. Scout: Since arriving in Spain, I have watched hundreds of professional basketball games. After observing that the Spanish players average about six and a half feet in height, I have concluded that the height of the typical Spanish citizen is around six and a half feet as well.

    I accept that <u>Spanish players average about six and a half feet in height</u>, but that does not prove <u>that the height of the typical Spanish citizen is around six and a half feet</u> because <u>the scout fails to consider that in any nation, unusually tall individuals are more likely to become professional basketball players than are people of average height</u>.

    (A) The scout has not watched a sufficient number of games to exactly determine the average height of professional basketball players.

    (B) There is no reason to believe that the scout has received enough medical training to evaluate the overall health of professional athletes relative to individuals in other professions.

    ⬤ **The scout fails to consider that in any nation, unusually tall individuals are more likely to become professional basketball players than are people of average height.**

(A) This choice would be appealing if there were a recognizable sampling error in the argument. But it addresses the sample size used to establish the premise of the argument (the average height of the players) rather than the conclusion of the argument (the average height of citizens). Since we accept the premise as true, this answer can't be correct.

(B) "Overall health" is outside the scope of this argument.

(C) Correct. The scout cites the height of a sample of Spanish people in order to draw a conclusion about the height of Spanish people in general. However, the scout has chosen a fundamentally unrepresentative sample, since professional basketball players are unusually tall compared to the general population. Always investigate both the size and representativeness of any sample cited by an LSAT argument!

2. Benjamin: Suzanne is extremely charismatic, has great plans to improve campus facilities, and shows empathy for her classmates. Since these are all the qualities that voters would want their student body president to have, Suzanne will certainly win the upcoming election.

    I accept that <u>these are all the qualities that voters would want their student body president to have</u>, but that does not prove <u>Suzanne will certainly win the upcoming election</u> because <u>Benjamin fails to establish that Suzanne is the only candidate with all of the qualities he mentioned</u>.

    (A) Benjamin assumes that Suzanne is interested in pursuing politics as a career after graduation.

    ⬤ **Benjamin fails to establish that Suzanne is the only candidate with all of the qualities he mentioned.**

    (C) Benjamin ignores the extensive time commitment associated with the position of student body president.

(A) Whether Suzanne will enter politics as a career is outside the scope of this argument.

(B) Correct. While Benjamin's argument shows that Suzanne is a well-qualified candidate, he fails to consider that other candidates may be equally well-qualified, in which case his conclusion that Suzanne will win the election is far from certain.

(C) The demands associated with the student presidency are irrelevant to Benjamin's argument, which focuses on who will win the election.

3. Every circuit board with a flickering light must be replaced. After all, any circuit board that cannot be repaired must be replaced, and a flickering light on a circuit board indicates that it is not functioning properly.

    I accept that <u>any circuit board that cannot be repaired must be replaced, and a flickering light on a circuit board indicates that it is not functioning properly</u>, but that does not prove <u>every circuit board with a flickering light must</u>

1

be replaced because the argument assumes that a circuit board that is not functioning properly cannot be repaired.

- (A) The argument assumes that circuit boards that cannot be repaired must not be functioning properly.
- ● **The argument assumes that a circuit board that is not functioning properly cannot be repaired.**
- (C) The argument ignores the possibility that an electronic device may still function properly even if one of its circuit boards is not functioning properly.

(A) This is the converse of the correct answer. The argument assumes that when a board isn't functioning properly, it cannot be repaired. We don't need to assume the reversal of this statement: that when a board cannot be repaired, it isn't functioning properly.

(B) Correct. In order to conclude that a board needs to be replaced, we need to establish that it cannot be repaired. But our premises only establish that a board with a flickering light isn't functioning properly. Thus, to reach the conclusion, we have to establish that a board that isn't functioning properly cannot be repaired.

(C) Devices that use circuit boards are outside the scope of the argument.

4. Paleontologist: Every modern bird is a dinosaur. Therefore, the discovery of the species *capito barzoni* has increased the number of dinosaur species known to science.

I accept that every modern bird is a dinosaur, but that does not prove the discovery of the species *capito barzoni* has increased the number of dinosaur species known to science because the paleontologist assumes that *capito barzoni* is a species of modern bird.

- ● **The paleontologist assumes that *capito barzoni* is a species of modern bird.**
- (B) The paleontologist ignores the possibility that some dinosaurs were not modern birds.
- (C) The paleontologist ignores the fact that most dinosaur species are extinct.

(A) Correct. If we assume that the new species is a modern bird, then it is also a dinosaur, which confirms the conclusion that another dinosaur species has been found. Otherwise, there is no reason to believe that the conclusion is true.

(B) The possibility that not every dinosaur is a modern bird is outside the scope of the paleontologist's argument, which concerns those dinosaurs that *are* modern birds.

(C) The number of dinosaur species that are extinct or living is outside the scope of the paleontologist's argument.

5. The Bermuda Triangle has a reputation for supernatural mishaps, and a large number of vessels have vanished in it over the years. Therefore, the disappearances are clearly the result of supernatural events.

I accept that the Bermuda Triangle has a reputation for supernatural mishaps, and a large number of vessels have vanished in it over the years, but that does not prove the disappearances are clearly the result of supernatural events because the argument neglects to consider that the supernatural reputation of the Bermuda Triangle may be the result of the disappearances rather than the cause of them.

- (A) The argument assumes that the Bermuda Triangle is the only region of the ocean with such an ominous reputation.
- (B) The argument makes the unwarranted assumption that every vessel entering the Bermuda Triangle has disappeared.
- ● **The argument neglects to consider that the supernatural reputation of the Bermuda Triangle may be the result of the disappearances rather than the cause of them.**

(A) The possible existence of other areas with supernatural reputations is irrelevant to this argument.

(B) The argument does not assume that all of the vessels in the Triangle have disappeared, only that many of them have.

(C) Correct. The argument states two facts about the Triangle and concludes that one of them must have caused the other, but the reverse causal relationship is equally plausible. Whenever an LSAT argument has a conclusion about one thing causing another, always ask yourself if the opposite could be true.

6.   Analyst: In an effort to motivate the patrons of a local golf club to keep the ball on dry ground, a new rule was established that significantly increased the penalty for shots that land in the water. Since this rules change, data recorded by players at the club indicate a 78% decrease in the number of shots that land in the water per round of golf played. The new rule has evidently accomplished its goal.

I accept that since this rules change, data recorded by players at the club indicate a 78% decrease in the number of shots that land in the water per round of golf played, but that does not prove the new rule has evidently accomplished its goal because the analyst assumes that the players have accurately reported how many of their shots land in the water.

- (A) The analyst fails to demonstrate that the overall scores of golfers at the club have improved since the new rule was instituted.
- ⬤ **The analyst assumes that the players have accurately reported how many of their shots land in the water.**
- (C) The analyst did not consider whether or not similar rules instituted at other golf clubs have had a similar effect.

(A) The goal of the new rule was specifically to minimize shots landing in the water, so overall golf scores are beyond the scope of the argument.

(B) Correct. The data in the analyst's premise are reported by the players themselves, and self-reported results are always suspect. Under the new rule, players at the club have more motivation to avoid reporting balls that fall in the water.

(C) This would be an attractive choice if the analyst had cited other golf clubs in the premise or argued that the results observed at this particular golf club were "typical." Since the analyst did not, events at other golf clubs are irrelevant to the argument.

7.   Two hours of safety training under the guidance of a certified professional are required before one can participate in a paintball match at Stealthy Acres. Mark has completed the training, so he can compete in the match that will be held at Stealthy Acres as part of his future brother-in-law's bachelor party.

I accept that Mark has completed the training, but that does not prove he can compete in the match that will be held at Stealthy Acres as part of his future brother-in-law's bachelor party because the argument confuses a necessary condition for competing in a paintball match with a sufficient condition for competing in such a match.

- ⬤ **The argument confuses a necessary condition for competing in a paintball match with a sufficient condition for competing in such a match.**
- (B) The argument assumes that Mark is interested in attending his future brother-in-law's bachelor party.
- (C) The argument assumes that two hours of safety training guarantees that paintball players will conduct themselves safely during a match.

(A) Correct. The premise states that Mark has completed safety training, which is necessary to participate in a match. But the conclusion is that completion of training is sufficient to play in a match. In confusing these two points, the argument overlooks the possibility of additional requirements beyond the training.

(B) Since the argument only concludes that Mark *can* attend the paintball match, whether or not he is interested in doing so is irrelevant.

(C) This is not assumed, since actual safe conduct during a match is beyond the scope of the argument.

1

8. Patient: A nutritionist has advised me to dramatically reduce my consumption of refined sugars and fats, arguing that they are unhealthy for anyone. However, it would be perfectly healthy for me to ignore his advice, because he has been consuming sugary and fatty foods every time I have encountered him in private settings.

I accept that <u>he has been consuming sugary and fatty foods every time I have encountered him in private settings</u>, but that does not prove <u>it would be perfectly healthy for me to ignore his advice</u> because <u>the patient assumes that the nutritionist's failure to follow his own advice indicates that the advice is inaccurate</u>.

⬤ **The patient assumes that the nutritionist's failure to follow his own advice indicates that the advice is inaccurate.**

Ⓑ The patient fails to consider that significant exercise may be needed to offset the negative health effects of consuming refined sugars and fats.

Ⓒ The patient ignores the possibility that the nutritionist did not expect to have his own dietary habits revealed.

(A) Correct. The patient concludes that the nutritionist is wrong about the health effects of certain foods based only on the nutritionist's consumption of those foods. Hypocrisy, however, does not necessarily imply inaccuracy. LSAT arguments that accuse the opposition of hypocrisy are virtually all flawed in this regard.

(B) The patient's argument concerns whether or not certain foods have a negative effect on one's health, so the activities necessary to offset this effect are beyond the scope of the argument.

(C) The patient's argument concludes that the nutritionist's advice about certain eating habits is inaccurate, so the nutritionist's belief about the privacy of his own eating habits is not relevant.

9. Principal: The students in your homeroom cannot join the rest of the class on today's field trip. I just reviewed the paperwork in the front office, and none of them have brought in a consent form signed by a legal guardian.

I accept that <u>none of them have brought in a consent form signed by a legal guardian</u>, but that does not prove <u>the students in your homeroom cannot join the rest of the class on today's field trip</u> because <u>the principal's argument assumes that a signed consent form is required to attend the field trip</u>.

Ⓐ The principal assumes that some students have legal guardians who are not their parents.

Ⓑ The principal ignores the fact that a signed consent form will not prevent the school from being held legally responsible if students are injured during a class trip.

⬤ **The principal's argument assumes that a signed consent form is required to attend the field trip.**

(A) The principal does not assume this. The consent form needs to be signed by a legal guardian, but the identity of that guardian is beyond the scope of the argument.

(B) The degree to which the school is legally responsible for the students on the field trip is beyond the scope of the principal's argument, which only concerns whether or not the students are allowed to go on the trip.

(C) Correct. The argument presents the lack of consent forms as the sole reason that the students cannot go on the trip, so it assumes that the consent form is necessary for attendance.

10. Salesperson: The purchase of a flood insurance policy is guaranteed to save you money in the long run. After all, the policy covers all flood-related costs for only $1,000 per year, while any flood would cause at least $5,000 in damage to your home.

I accept that <u>the policy covers all flood-related costs for only $1,000 per year, while any flood would cause at least $5,000 in damage to your home</u>, but that does not prove <u>the purchase</u>

of a flood insurance policy is guaranteed to save you money in the long run because the salesperson fails to recognize the possibility that floods may be very uncommon events where the customer's home is located.

(A) The policy that the salesperson is offering may not cover damages caused by other natural disasters.

(B) The salesperson provides no statistics to validate the claim that repairing flood damage would cost at least $5,000.

● **The salesperson fails to recognize the possibility that floods may be very uncommon events where the customer's home is located.**

(A) The salesperson's argument only concerns floods, so other natural disasters are irrelevant.

(B) Such statistics would only validate the premise of the argument, which we already accept as true. They would not justify the conclusion that the policy will save you money.

(C) Correct. If floods are very infrequent, then the cost of maintaining flood insurance until a flood occurs may be greater than the amount of money that is saved on the damage from that flood. In this case, purchasing the policy would not lead to overall savings for the customer.

11. The prominent musician Harriet Schroder has become an advocate for panspermia: a scientific hypothesis that meteorites containing simple organisms landed on Earth and led to the development of simple life on this planet. Schroder is deeply respected, so her support indicates that the theory of panspermia is probably correct.

I accept that <u>Schroder is deeply respected</u>, but that does not prove <u>her support indicates that the theory of panspermia is probably correct</u> because <u>there is no reason to believe that Schroder is qualified to evaluate the merits of a scientific theory</u>.

(A) Schroder has not personally written criticism of every possible alternative to the panspermia hypothesis.

● **There is no reason to believe that Schroder is qualified to evaluate the merits of a scientific theory.**

(C) Schroder has assumed, but not demonstrated, that advanced life exists on other planets.

(A) To support a hypothesis, is not necessary to write about every possible alternative to that hypothesis. And even if Schroder had done so, her support would still be suspect because her reputation is musical, rather than scientific, in nature.

(B) Correct. This argument appeals to an inappropriate authority, since Schroder's status as a respected musician does not qualify her to determine the accuracy of the panspermia hypothesis. Whenever an LSAT argument relies on an expert opinion, be sure to investigate whether what's at issue is actually within that person's realm of expertise. In many cases, it will not be.

(C) Advanced life is irrelevant to the argument, as the panspermia hypothesis is only about simple life.

12. Engineer: Our research staff have designed a new anti-pest machine, and they claim that it will deter all pests such as rats and cockroaches from remaining inside any home in which the machine is installed. However, I have personally tested each component that they propose to use in this machine, and none of them individually deter pests from staying nearby. Therefore, the researchers' claims are mistaken.

I accept that <u>I have personally tested each component that they propose to use in this machine, and none of them individually deter pests from staying nearby</u>, but that does not prove <u>the researchers' claims are mistaken</u> because <u>the engineer assumes that if each part of an object lacks a certain characteristic, then the object as a whole must also lack that characteristic</u>.

(A) The engineer has not properly evaluated the anti-pest machine's effect on pets and other non-pest animals.

(B) The engineer does not understand the means by which the anti-pest machine is supposedly able to deter animals such as rats and cockroaches.

1

⬤ **The engineer assumes that if each part of an object lacks a certain characteristic, then the object as a whole must also lack that characteristic.**

(A) The engineer and the researchers only made claims about pest animals, so the machine's effect on other animals is outside the scope of the argument.

(B) The engineer's argument concerns whether the machine works, so how it works is irrelevant.

(C) Correct. The engineer assumes that the completed machine cannot be greater than the sum of its parts, overlooking the possibility that the components must work together in order to deter pests. Whenever an LSAT argument takes evidence about each component of a thing and draws its conclusion about the thing as a whole, or vica versa, the logic is suspect and will likely be the crux of the question.

13. Comedian: I have performed at eight festivals across the country over the past month. Each time I arrived at the location of the next festival, I asked one random person on the street to identify his or her favorite genre of literature. Since the majority of these people responded that their favorite genre is science fiction, science fiction must be the most popular literary genre in the country.

   I accept that <u>the majority of these people responded that their favorite genre is science fiction</u>, but that does not prove <u>science fiction must be the most popular literary genre in the country</u> because <u>the comedian did not poll enough people to draw a clear conclusion about the country's favorite literary genre</u>.

   (A) Comedians are not qualified to collect data about people's literary preferences.

   (B) The comedian assumed that many people in this country read literature regularly.

   ⬤ **The comedian did not poll enough people to draw a clear conclusion about the country's favorite literary genre.**

(A) This criticism attacks the premise of the argument, not its conclusion. Since we must accept the premise that that the majority of polled individuals preferred science fiction, the comedian's qualifications are not relevant.

(B) Such an assumption is beyond the scope of the comedian's argument, as a person doesn't need to read literature regularly to have an opinion of which genre is best.

(C) Correct. Eight individuals is a very small sample, so the comedian's conclusion is not statistically sound. Whenever an LSAT argument relies on a sample, be sure to consider whether the sample is large enough and representative enough to draw the conclusion. Often it will not be, and this will be the crux of the question.

14. Runner: Reducing one's body fat percentage is a factor in achieving better results in long races, and starvation will decrease anyone's percentage of body fat. So refusing to eat will improve my results in long races.

   I accept that <u>reducing one's body fat percentage is a factor in achieving better results in long races, and starvation will decrease anyone's percentage of body fat</u>, but that does not prove <u>refusing to eat will improve my results in long races</u> because <u>the runner overlooks the possibility that starvation may have unintended negative effects on performance in races</u>.

   ⬤ **The runner overlooks the possibility that starvation may have unintended negative effects on performance in races.**

   (B) The runner assumes that the best preparation for long races is also the best preparation for shorter races.

   (C) The definition of "results" changes illicitly in the course of the runner's argument.

(A) Correct. While lower body fat generally improves one's results, denying oneself food may be a particularly poor way to achieve it. For example, it is very plausible that starvation would rob a runner of the energy needed to complete a long race. Whenever an LSAT argument concludes that because something is good in one respect, it is good in all respects, be suspicious! Try to consider possible objections that the argument overlooked.

(B) The runner's argument only concerns long races, so short races are beyond its scope.

(C) The meaning of "results" does not change; in both the premise and the conclusion, it is a general way of referring to the quality of the runner's performance in a race.

15. Focusing our televised news coverage on sports and human interest stories would guarantee high ratings for the station. Therefore, devoting the majority of our airtime to other topics, such as history or technology, will ensure that the station receives poor ratings.

I accept that <u>focusing our televised news coverage on sports and human interest stories would guarantee high ratings for the station</u>, but that does not prove <u>devoting the majority of our airtime to other topics, such as history or technology, will ensure that the station receives poor ratings</u> because <u>the argument assumes that there is only one set of programming choices that would achieve high ratings for the news station</u>.

⬤ **The argument assumes that there is only one set of programming choices that would achieve high ratings for the news station.**

Ⓑ The argument fails to consider that some sports and human interest stories will draw higher ratings than others.

Ⓒ The argument assumes that most viewers are too unsophisticated to appreciate stories about history or technology.

(A) Correct. The argument's premise establishes that a focus on sports and human interest will get high ratings, but the conclusion presumes that no other focus could receive high ratings as well.

(B) The different ratings achieved by particular sports and human interest stories are beyond the scope of the argument.

(C) The reasons that viewers might choose not to watch stories about history or technology are also beyond the scope of the argument.

16. Parent: I argue that it is safe to let my children wander outside alone at night, although my superstitious spouse believes that they may be attacked by werewolves. But since it is indisputably impossible that werewolves could exist, my original position is correct.

I accept that <u>it is indisputably impossible that werewolves could exist</u>, but that does not prove <u>it is safe to let my children wander outside alone at night</u> because <u>the parent assumes that a claim is true simply because an argument against that claim has been refuted</u>.

Ⓐ The parent maintains that werewolves do not exist simply because her or she has never seen one.

⬤ **The parent assumes that a claim is true simply because an argument against that claim has been refuted.**

Ⓒ The parent disregards the possibility that the spouse has greater concern for the children's safety than he or she does.

(A) The parent's argument is not based on personal experience, but rather on the inherent impossibility of the existence of werewolves.

(B) Correct. The argument's premise does not rule out other good reasons to keep your children from wandering outside at night.

(C) The argument concerns whether or not the children are safe, so each person's degree of concern for the children's safety is irrelevant.

17. Art dealer: A painting from the 16th century is definitely more valuable than a 20th-century painting, and any 9th-century sculpture is worth more than a 16th-century sculpture. So this 9th-century sculpture is worth more than this 20th-century painting.

I accept that <u>a painting from the 16th century is definitely more valuable than a 20th-century painting, and any 9th-century sculpture is worth more than a 16th-century sculpture</u>, but that does not prove <u>this 9th-century sculpture is worth more than this 20th-century painting</u>

because <u>the art dealer assumes that a 16th-century sculpture must be worth as much as or more than a 16th-century painting</u>.

● **The art dealer assumes that a 16th-century sculpture must be worth as much as or more than a 16th-century painting.**

Ⓑ The art dealer fails to recognize that it is impossible to definitively determine whether one piece of art is more valuable than another.

Ⓒ The art dealer assumes that any sculpture is more valuable than any painting.

(A) Correct. To establish that something is more valuable than a 20th-century painting, it must be worth as much as or more than a 16th-century painting. But all the argument states about 9th-century sculpture is that it is worth more than a 16th-century sculpture. So the art critic must have assumed that a 16th-century sculpture is worth as much as or more than a 16th-century painting.

(B) The premises of the argument, which we must accept as true, make it clear that one piece of art can in fact be definitively more valuable than another.

(C) The argument does not make this broad of an assumption, since its conclusion is about the relative value of sculptures and paintings from particular centuries.

18. Meteorologist: The last five blizzards in this state occurred immediately after a day of unseasonably warm weather. Therefore, I conclude that these blizzards were triggered by high temperatures.

I accept that <u>the last five blizzards in this state occurred immediately after a day of unseasonably warm weather</u>, but that does not prove <u>that these blizzards were triggered by high temperatures</u> because <u>the meteorologist assumes that if one event preceded another, then the first event must have caused the second one</u>.

Ⓐ The meteorologist doesn't consider the possibility that recent weather trends will not necessarily continue in the future.

● **The meteorologist assumes that if one event preceded another, then the first event must have caused the second one.**

Ⓒ The meteorologist neglects to consider that blizzards only occur when the temperature is quite low.

(A) Future weather is beyond the scope of the meteorologist's argument, which does not predict anything.

(B) Correct. The argument assumes a causal relationship between the high temperatures and the blizzards that followed, without demonstrating a clear connection. Whenever an LSAT argument uses the order of events to justify a claim that the first event caused the second, be suspicious. Order doesn't prove causality, and this is likely to be the crux of the question.

(C) This consideration is irrelevant to the argument, as it does not necessarily mean that the blizzards couldn't have been caused by a prior day of high temperature.

19. Biology professor: A recently conducted national survey indicates that only 25% of adults have heard of the famous primatologist Jane Goodall. However, the survey must be flawed, because I've polled dozens of my own friends and they are all very familiar with Goodall and her scientific accomplishments.

I accept that <u>I've polled dozens of my own friends and they are all very familiar with Goodall and her scientific accomplishments</u>, but that does not prove <u>the survey must be flawed</u> because <u>the biology professor ignores the possibility that his or her friends may be more likely than the average adult to be aware of other famous scientists</u>.

Ⓐ The biology professor assumes that those who conducted the national poll are ignorant of all statistical principles.

Ⓑ The biology professor neglects to consider that his or her friends may not be knowledgable about many other scientists aside from Jane Goodall.

● **The biology professor ignores the possibility that his or her friends may be more likely than the average adult to be aware of other famous scientists.**

(A) The professor's conclusion is not based upon the ignorance of those who conducted the national poll, but rather on the fact that a personal poll yielded different results.

(B) The friends' knowledge of other scientists is beyond the scope of the professor's argument.

(C) Correct. Most people may be less familiar with Goodall than are the friends of a highly educated person who works in a related field. Since this argument relies on a sample, you need to consider both the sample's size and its representativeness.

20. Coach: If you practice extensively, you will be at peak performance for the upcoming chess match, and it is impossible that you will lose the match if you are at peak performance. Therefore, practice is all you need to guarantee victory.

I accept that <u>if you practice extensively, you will be at peak performance for the upcoming chess match, and it is impossible that you will lose the match if you are at peak performance</u>, but that does not prove <u>practice is all you need to guarantee victory</u> because <u>the coach ignores the possibility that the chess match could be drawn or tied</u>.

(A) The coach assumes that anyone can reach peak chess performance simply through practice.

(B) The coach fails to consider that it is very difficult to practice chess extensively without neglecting other necessary components of a victory in the upcoming match.

● **The coach ignores the possibility that the chess match could be drawn or tied.**

(A) The coach does not assume that this is true of anyone, merely claiming as a premise that it is true for the subject of the argument.

(B) The compromises that extensive practice requires are beyond the scope of the coach's argument, which only concerns the results of extensive practice.

(C) Correct. The coach's argument equates "not losing the match" with "winning the match," but this is only true if a tie/draw is impossible.

21. Astrologer: The exceptional value of astrology to the romantic is clearly demonstrated by the fact that nearly all of my clients have told me that my counsel on romantic relationships has served them well.

I accept that <u>nearly all of the astrologer's clients have told him that his counsel on romantic relationships has served them well</u>, but that does not prove <u>the exceptional value of astrology to the romantic</u> because <u>the astrologer is assuming that his clients aren't afraid to give honest feedback</u>.

(A) Astrology is not based on accepted scientific principles.

● **The astrologer is assuming that his clients aren't afraid to give honest feedback.**

(C) Many of the astrologer's clients were already happily married before they became his clients.

(A) Astrology may not be based on accepted scientific principles, but that's not an objection to the link between the premise and the conclusion of this particular argument.

(B) Correct. Whenever an argument's premise is self-reported data, there's always a risk that people aren't self-reporting accurately. This astrologer is taking for granted that the reports are accurate, so he's assuming his clients aren't afraid to give honest feedback.

(C) This claim isn't an objection; it doesn't provide us any reason to believe that astrology might not be of exceptional value to the romantic.

Drill 15: Diagramming 101, Round 3

Instructions: Diagram and contrapose each of the following conditional statements in the space provided, again! And remember, if you feel that you're ready for a more challenging diagramming drill, feel free to skip ahead to the "Diagramming 201" versions in Chapter 4.

1. Anyone who can't make eye contact when telling you something is lying.

2. Charlie will not do his homework until he gets his fruit roll-up.

3. Ronald will not attend the bar mitzvah if Donald goes.

4. It's impossible to be rich and unhappy at the same time.

5. If Raul drives quickly and the airport is empty, he will make his flight.

6. Only if we hire Katie will we be able to fix the Web site.

7. Either Eloise or Barbara will win the weightlifting competition.

8. Neither Harrison nor Billy will find the treasure.

9. If I cook breakfast, I make the only thing I know: pancakes.

10. The dryer will continue to run until the clothes are completely dry.

11. The team will lose if David doesn't play in the second half.

12. If you do not know how to use a protractor, you cannot make the blueprints.

13. Except for Saturdays, I always wear a red shirt.

14. Whenever Kayla says something mean, she's only joking.

15. Penny doesn't cook anything except gourmet meals.

16. If we get up early tomorrow, we will go to the MOMA or the LACMA, or both.

17. The only way to get an A in the class is to go to class and do the homework.

18. If, and only if, I get a new computer will I program that fun app.

19. If Vera and Wallace both buy a new car, I will have to buy one as well.

20. Only those who pass the medical evaluation can enter the race.

21. If Deshawn buys the sofa, then he will not buy the table.

22. Only reptiles are iguanas.

23. You can't go to the movies until you finish your homework.

24. Jessica will go to a baseball game if Liam goes, too.

25. Whenever Arden oversleeps, he misses the first train to work.

26. Dragan and Petar cannot both have the leftover pizza.

27. All of the Paralympic athletes at the opening ceremonies are excited and well-trained.

28. Each volunteer will work for exactly one shift.

29. The violets will bloom again only if there is bright light.

30. Either Alejandro or David will be the lead dancer.

1

31. Any teachers with a PhD will be asked to teach next year.

32. All romance novels include a kiss.

33. The book club has not chosen any mystery novels.

34. Only during the six weeks before April 15th do accountants work too much.

35. If Brooke adds strawberries to the smoothie, she will add raspberries, too.

36. The bridge will last 100 years if it is built properly.

37. Cynthia will win the election if Travis serves as her campaign manager.

38. Any elected official will be a public figure.

39. Only if it rains will Diego go to the movies.

40. A contract is legally binding only when it includes an offer and an acceptance.

Answers

1. Anyone who can't make eye contact when telling you something is lying.

    ~MEC → L ; ~L → MEC

2. Charlie will not do his homework until he gets his fruit roll-up.

    ~FR → ~HW ; HW → FR

3. Ronald will not attend the bar mitzvah if Donald goes.

    D → ~R ; R → ~D

4. It's impossible to be rich and unhappy at the same time.

    R → ~U ; U → ~R

5. If Raul drives quickly and the airport is empty, he will make his flight.

    DQ and AE → MF ; ~MF → ~DQ or ~AE

6. Only if we hire Katie will we be able to fix the Web site.

    FW → HK ; ~HK → ~FW

7. Either Eloise or Barbara will win the weightlifting competition.

    ~ E → B ; ~ B → E

8. Neither Harrison nor Billy will find the treasure.

    H or B → ~FT ; FT → ~H and ~B

9. If I cook breakfast, I make the only thing I know: pancakes.

    CB → P ; ~P → ~CB

10. The dryer will continue to run until the clothes are completely dry.

    ~CCD → DR ; ~DR → CCD

11. The team will lose if David doesn't play in the second half.

    ~DSH → L ; ~L → DSH

12. If you do not know how to use a protractor, you cannot make the blueprints.

    ~KP → ~MBP ; MBP → KP

1

13. Except for Saturdays, I always wear a red shirt.

    ~S → WRS ; ~WRS → S

19. If Vera and Wallace both buy a new car, I will have to buy one as well.

    VNC and WNC → INC ; ~INC → ~VNC or ~WNC

14. Whenever Kayla says something mean, she's only joking.

    M → J ; ~J → ~M

20. Only those who pass the medical evaluation can enter the race.

    ER → ME ; ~ME → ~ER

15. Penny doesn't cook anything except gourmet meals.

    ~GM → ~PC ; PC → GM

21. If Deshawn buys the sofa, then he will not buy the table.

    S → ~T ; T → ~S

16. If we get up early tomorrow, we will go to the MOMA or the LACMA, or both.

    GUET → M or L ; ~M and ~L → ~GUET

22. Only reptiles are iguanas.

    I → R ; ~R → ~I

17. The only way to get an A in the class is to go to class and do the homework.

    A → C and HW ; ~C or ~HW → ~A

23. You can't go to the movies until you finish your homework.

    M → H ; ~H → ~M

18. If, and only if, I get a new computer will I program that fun app.

    NC ←→ FA ; ~FA ←→ ~NC

24. Jessica will go to a baseball game if Liam goes, too.

    L → J ; ~J → ~L

25. Whenever Arden oversleeps, he misses the first train to work.

    $OS \rightarrow MT$; $\sim MT \rightarrow \sim OS$

26. Dragan and Petar cannot both have the leftover pizza.

    $D \rightarrow \sim P$; $P \rightarrow \sim D$

Note that for *cannot be both* statements, it doesn't matter which entity you choose to be the sufficient condition. Just pick one to be the sufficient, and negate the other to form the necessary.

27. All of the Paralympic athletes at the opening ceremonies are excited and well-trained.

    $PA \rightarrow E$ and WT ; $\sim E$ or $\sim WT \rightarrow \sim PA$

28. Each volunteer will work for exactly one shift.

    $V \rightarrow 1$; $\sim 1 \rightarrow \sim V$

29. The violets will bloom again only if there is bright light.

    $VB \rightarrow BL$; $\sim BL \rightarrow \sim VB$

30. Either Alejandro or David will be the lead dancer.

    $\sim A \rightarrow D$; $\sim D \rightarrow A$

Note that for *either/or* statements, it doesn't matter which entity you choose to be the sufficient condition. Just pick one to be the sufficient and negate it. The other, not negated, forms the necessary.

31. Any teachers with a PhD will be asked to teach next year.

    $PhD \rightarrow AT$; $\sim AT \rightarrow \sim PhD$

32. All romance novels include a kiss.

    $RN \rightarrow K$; $\sim K \rightarrow \sim RN$

33. The book club has not chosen any mystery novels.

    $BC \rightarrow \sim MN$; $MN \rightarrow \sim BC$

34. Only during the six weeks before April 15th do accountants work too much.

    $AWTM \rightarrow 6wk$ before $4/15$; $\sim 6wk$ before $4/15 \rightarrow \sim AWTM$

1

35. If Brooke adds strawberries to the smoothie, she will add raspberries, too.

    S → R ; ~R → ~S

36. The bridge will last 100 years if it is built properly.

    BP → 100 ; ~100 → ~BP

37. Cynthia will win the election if Travis serves as her campaign manager.

    TCM → CW ; ~CW → ~TCM

38. Any elected official will be a public figure.

    EO → PF ; ~PF → ~EO

39. Only if it rains will Diego go to the movies.

    M → R ; ~R → ~M

40. A contract is legally binding only when it includes an offer and an acceptance.

    LB → O and A ; ~O or ~A → ~LB

CHAPTER 2

Logic Games, Meet the Setup

In This Chapter, We Will Cover:

- Game Type

- Rule Representation

- Basic Inferences

- The Big Pause

Meet the Setup

A strong setup is the foundation of a strong Logic Games section. This chapter will cover the basics: representing the information you're given in a way that is clear, concise, and complete.

In this section, you will learn to:

2

Approach Common Game Types

- Distinguish between games of different tasks
- Create complete setups for common game types

Represent Rules

- Use notation that is clear and consistent
- Use shorthand when necessary

Make Basic Inferences

- Determine whether elements in a game can, cannot, or must repeat
- Use single rules to generate multiple inferences

Take The Big Pause

- Identify the least restricted elements of a game
- Predict the elements that are likely to drive the game

Drill 16: Game Type

Instructions: The first step in any logic game is to determine your task. For the vast majority of logic games, that task will be to order elements (O), to group them (G), or to do both (B). For each of the logic game scenarios below, fill in the letter that best describes the task of the game.

_O_   1.   A local bookstore is organizing speakers on five topics—Fantasy, Horror, Mystery, Romance, and Science Fiction—Monday through Friday. Each topic will be discussed once, and one topic will be discussed each day, in accordance with the following conditions:

_G_   2.   Seven trapeze artists—Isherwood, Laughlin, Monroe, Plath, Solo, Wittig, and Zahn—will join two circuses. Four of the artists will join a circus in Boston, and three of the artists will join a circus in Charleston. No artist will be permitted to join more than one circus, and each artist must join one of the two circuses, according to the following restrictions:

_G_   3.   A wedding planner is designing bouquets for three members of a wedding. She will select flowers from among the following six types—lily, orchid, peony, rose, snapdragon, and tulip—in accordance with the following conditions:

_G_   4.   A grocer has seven new flavors of ice cream pints—Mint Chip, Neapolitan, Orange Sherbet, Raspberry, Strawberry, Triple Chocolate, and Vanilla Bean—to arrange on three shelves. Each flavor will go on exactly one shelf, and every shelf will have one or more flavors, with the following restrictions:

_O_   5.   A high school senior is planning a road trip to visit his top five choices for college—Ardvard, Bailer, Conch State, Edmondson, and Ferrier—during a week off from school. The order in which he visits the schools must meet the following conditions:

_B_   6.   The HR department is scheduling interviews on Tuesday for five applicants—Farouk, Garcia, Han, Ibaka, and Jagger. Each applicant will meet with exactly one of three HR specialists—Tonks, Viney, and Woo. Each specialist will interview at least one of the applicants, in either a morning or afternoon session, in accordance with the following conditions:

_G_   7.   Eight club members—Altinoglu, Brady, Chang, Dov, Embiid, Federoff, Ghosh, and Halabi—are competing in their annual golf championship. The players will be split into two teams of exactly four players. The assignment of players to foursomes is subject to the following constraints:

_O_   8.   This week, The Coffee House will feature coffees from five regions: Ethiopia, Guatemala, Hawaii, Java, and Kenya. One coffee will be featured each day, from Monday through Friday, in accordance with the following conditions:

_O_   9.   Vitaly must visit exactly six places today—the barber, the chiropractor, the deli, the farmer's market, the gym, and the hospital. He will visit each place exactly once and no two places are visited at the same time. The order of his visits is determined by the following constraints:

_B_   10.   A tutor is creating a three-day lesson plan for his student. There will be exactly eight math questions: three probability questions, two quadratics questions, two ratio questions, and one standard deviation question. Low difficulty questions will be done before medium difficulty questions and high difficulty questions will be done last. The questions will be scheduled in accordance with the following constraints:

2

11. A fire commissioner must inspect the firehouses in exactly seven towns—Peoria, Rockford, Salem, Tempe, Vallejo, Waymarsh, and Youngstown. Each town will be inspected exactly once and no two towns will be inspected at the same time. The order of the inspections has the following constraints:

12. A landscaper is designing two rock gardens, one for the South garden and one for the North. Each garden will have two or more of the following rock types—limestone, marble, norite, pumice, obsidian, quartzite, and shale. The composition of the gardens must conform to the following constraints:

13. Over the next six years, Fallon plans to run in exactly six major marathons: Athens, Boston, Great Wall, New York, Rome, and Tokyo. She will run exactly one marathon per year according to the following constraints:

14. A genealogist is tracing the ancestry of seven members of a family—Gene, Harriet, Irma, John, Kathleen, Laura, and Matthew—to determine the parentage of each. Each family member is either the parent or the child of at least one other family member, subject to the following conditions:

15. A talent agency will schedule auditions for six voice-over actors—Linton, Ming, Nazir, Oren, Petra, and Rina. Exactly one audition will be held each hour from 1pm to 6pm. Each actor will audition exactly once, in accordance with the following constraints:

16. Students at a culinary school are given a project to prepare exactly three meals—breakfast, lunch, and dinner. Each meal must contain at least two of the following five flavors—bitter, pungent, salty, sour, and sweet—subject to the following constraints:

17. Seven differently colored cars—red, orange, yellow, green, blue, indigo, and violet—are driving to Central City, each on exactly one of three single-lane roads—Central Avenue, Daily Drive, and Easy Street. Each road will be taken by at least one car, subject to the following conditions:

18. Nine contestants—Faith, Gopal, Henry, Ian, Jamaica, Kaat, Liam, Myani, and Nanda—will compete in exactly one of three challenges—relay race, sack race, three-legged race. Each challenge will be completed by exactly three players. The assignment of players to challenges must meet the following conditions:

19. A community center is hosting a seminar every night this week. Exactly one of the following five seminars—Fire Safety, Gymnastics, Health Awareness, Kickboxing, and Lighting Design—will be featured each night, from Monday through Friday. The schedule for the seminars will meet the following conditions:

20. Rodeo Night at Horseshoe Park will include the following five events: barrel racing, calf roping, flag racing, goat wrangling, and hog tying. Exactly one event per hour will be scheduled starting at 6pm, according to the following conditions:

Answers follow on the next page.

Answers

1.	O	6.	B	11.	O	16.	B
2.	G	7.	G	12.	G	17.	G
3.	G	8.	O	13.	O	18.	G
4.	G	9.	O	14.	O	19.	O
5.	O	10.	B	15.	O	20.	O

2

Drill 17: Repeat Customers

Instructions: Once you're determined the basic task of a game, the next step is to make your roster of elements. In the most straightforward games, each element will have one corresponding slot, but in more complicated games, the elements and slots might not have a one-to-one relationship. Contained within the scenario of every logic game are hidden rules that dictate whether all the elements must be used and the extent to which any can repeat. Practice spotting these hidden rules with this drill!

For each of the following scenarios, determine the description that most accurately characterizes the game, and fill the item number into the appropriate field of the chart below. Follow these instructions for both parts of this drill.

Possible Unused Elements	Definite Unused Elements	Elements Used Exactly Once	Elements Could Repeat	Elements Must Repeat

1.	All Sports Network will play a different evening program at 6:00pm, 6:30pm, 7:00pm, 7:30pm, and 8:00pm. Each program must have a host, and the available hosts are Newman, Ogilvie, and Phan, each of whom must host at least one program.

2.	A city manager is overseeing the design of a new city flag. The flag will be composed of at least four vertical stripes and one star. The flag must contain the colors lemon yellow, magenta, navy blue, orange, and purple, each of which represents an aspect of the city's history.

3.	A chef is choosing the vegetables for the daily soup special. He will choose from the vegetables that are available in the walk-in, which are broccoli, cabbage, daikon, eggplant, fennel, and garlic. The soup must contain at least four vegetables.

4.	The principal of a school is choosing three students for a leadership committee. The principal will choose from among the students who scored the highest on a recent exam: Belinda, Cathy, Dale, Edward, Fernando, and Gail.

5.	The editor of Lifestyle Magazine must assign a writer to each of five features for this week's edition: a celebrity feature, a dress feature, an exercise feature, a food feature, and a games feature. Each feature has exactly one writer. Three writers are available to write the features—O'Connell, Packwood, and Quinn—each of whom writes at most two features.

6.	There are six houses on a certain block, numbered one through six. The houses are occupied by the Jones family, the Kaur family, the Lawrence family, the Mann family, the Nunez family, and the O'Neill family.

7.	The manager of an art gallery is scheduling employees to staff two shifts, am and pm, on both Monday and Tuesday. Each shift must be staffed by at least one employee. The employees are Tao, Uma, Valerie, Wilson, and Xavier, each of whom can work at most one shift.

8.	The professor of a biology course must choose at least three students to join her on a field trip. She will choose from among the six students who have expressed interest in attending—Raquel, Suki, Taylor, Ursula, Valentino, and Walter.

2

9. The executive chef at Le Petit Chablis is selecting the day's specials. The specials will include a salad, two main courses, and a dessert. The possible salads are the salade niçoise and the tomato salad; the possible main courses are the beef bourguignon, the Cajun gumbo, and the duck à l'orange; and the possible desserts are macarons and the Norman tarte.

10. A city manager is overseeing the design of a new city flag. The flag will be composed of exactly four vertical stripes and one star, each of which is a different color. The flag will contain only the colors lemon yellow, magenta, navy blue, orange, and purple, each of which represents an aspect of the city's history.

11. A high school has six sections of English I, scheduled at 9:00am, 10:00am, 11:00am, 12:00pm, 1:00pm, and 2:00pm. The English teachers who can teach the classes are Ferreira, Gibson, and Hamm. Each teacher will teach exactly two sections of English I.

12. Lauren is choosing two outfits to wear on her first two days at a new job. Each outfit will contain at least two colors. Her wardrobe contains only blue, carmine, dandelion, and ecru items. Together, her outfits will contain at least one of each color in her wardrobe.

13. A college professor is scheduling the classes he will teach in the Fall Semester and the Spring Semester. He needs to teach at least one section each of Algebra I, Algebra II, Calculus I, and Calculus II.

14. A teacher is putting students into pairs for an upcoming project. He plans to make three pairs from the students Jack, Katrina, Lulu, Monira, Ning, and Patrice. No student will be in more than one pair.

15. A city manager is overseeing the design of a new city flag. The flag will be composed of exactly three vertical stripes and a star, each of which is a different color. The flag can contain only the colors lemon yellow, magenta, navy blue, orange, and purple, each of which represents an aspect of the city's history.

Answers

Possible Unused Elements	Definite Unused Elements	Elements Used Exactly Once	Elements Could Repeat	Elements Must Repeat
3, 7, 8	4, 9, 15	6, 10, 14	2, 12, 13	1, 5, 11

1. "Each of whom must host at least one program" means all the hosts are used. There are five programs and three hosts, so at least one host must host more than one program. That means elements must repeat.

2. "Must contain the colors" means all the colors are used. "At least four vertical stripes and one star" means there is a minimum of five spaces for colors, but there could be more spaces. That means elements could repeat.

3. "At least four" tells us that it is possible that four, five, or six vegetables will be chosen. That means it is possible that some of the elements are unused.

4. "Choosing three students" means three elements will be used. There are six students to choose from, so three elements will definitely be unused.

5. "Each of whom writes at most two features" means each of the three writers has to write at least one feature, so all writers are used. Five features and three writers means at least one writer writes more than one feature. That means some elements must repeat.

6. There are six elements (the six houses), and six slots to put them in (numbers 1–6). That means each element is used exactly once.

7. There are four total shifts and five employees who can cover them. "Each of whom can work at most one shift" means each employee can be scheduled a maximum of one time, and "each shift must be staffed by at least one employee" means a minimum of four employees will be scheduled. The fifth employee could be scheduled on the same shift as one of the other four, but doesn't have to be. That means one of the elements may be unused.

8. "At least three" tells us that it is possible that three, four, five, or six students will be chosen. That means it is possible that some of the elements are unused.

2

9. "The specials will include a salad, two main courses, and a dessert" means that exactly one element from the salad category will be used, exactly two elements from the main course category will be used, and exactly one element from the dessert category will be used. The listing of the elements means that the salad category contains two elements, the main course category contains three elements, and the dessert category contains two elements. That means one element in each category will definitely be unused.

10. "Each of which is a different color" means the colors are not repeated. Then "exactly four vertical stripes and one star" means five total colors are used. Since there are five colors to choose from, all elements must be used exactly once.

11. "Each teacher will teach exactly two sections" means each element is used exactly twice.

12. "Together, her outfits will contain at least one of each color in her wardrobe" means that all four colors in her wardrobe will be used at least once. "At least two colors" for each of the two outfits means that each color could be used more than once, so the elements could repeat.

13. "At least one section each" means all the elements will be used. There is no language about how many total classes the professor will teach, so he could teach one section or more than one section of any (or all!) of the four classes. That means elements could repeat.

14. "Three pairs" means six students will be in the pairs. There are six students to distribute, and "no student will be in more than one pair" means all six students will be used. That means all elements are used exactly once.

15. "Each of which is a different color" means the colors are not repeated. "Exactly three vertical stripes and a star" means four colors are used. Since there are five colors to choose from, one of the colors is definitely unused.

Drill 17: Repeat Customers Part 2

Possible Unused Elements	Definite Unused Elements	Elements Used Exactly Once	Elements Could Repeat	Elements Must Repeat

16. A city manager is overseeing the design of a new city flag. The flag will be composed of exactly six vertical stripes. The flag must contain the colors lemon yellow, magenta, navy blue, orange, and purple, each of which represents an aspect of the city's history.

17. An upcoming consignment sale has morning and afternoon shifts on Monday and Tuesday, and a morning shift on Wednesday. The volunteers—Vanessa, Will, Xavier, Yseult, and Zane—will each staff one shift.

18. The photography editor of Right Now! Magazine is arranging photos for this month's centerfold. The photos from which he is choosing are "Grass is Greener," "Here We Go," "Iota of Truth," "Joking Around," "Katya's Lament," and "Lion's Lair," none of which can appear more than once. There are three positions in the layout that must be occupied by photos: upper left, upper right, and lower left. Each position can hold up to two photos.

19. A shopkeeper is arranging items in a display that has a top shelf, a middle shelf, and a bottom shelf. Each shelf will contain at least two items. The items he plans to display are cotton swabs, rat traps, sunflowers, toothpaste, utensils, and vacuums, each of which will be displayed on at least one shelf.

20. The CEO of Orion Inc. plans to launch three new initiatives. Each initiative will have a lead project manager and an associate project manager. The available project managers are Irving, Jackson, and Khan, each of whom will be either the lead project manager or associate project manager on at least one initiative.

21. A city manager is overseeing the design of a new city flag. The flag will be composed of three or four vertical stripes and a star, each of which is a different color. The flag can contain only the colors lemon yellow, magenta, navy blue, orange, and purple, each of which represents an aspect of the city's history.

22. The DJ at a radio station releases a weekly list of her top-five favorite songs. The songs she is considering for this week's list are "Highways and Byways," "In it to Win it," "Just Keep Moving," "Kale Monster," "Laughter Laws," "Mother's Mementos," and "No Sleep for the Wicked."

23. The leader of a scout troop is packing four backpacks for an upcoming camping trip. Each pack can contain two or three different items. The items to pack are kites, lanterns, matches, and napkins, each of which must be contained in at least one pack.

24. A couple is choosing the flavors for their three-layer wedding cake. Each layer will be a different flavor. The bakery making the cake offers the flavors Red Velvet, Spiced Apple, Tropical, Ube, and Vanilla.

25. There are three apartments in a building, occupied by the Quaglios, the Robinsons, and the Shaws. There are six pets living in the building—a cat, a dog, a falcon, a gerbil, a hamster, and an iguana—with two pets living in each apartment.

26. The city council is proposing a special parks project. A committee of at least three council members will lead the proposal. The city council members are Molina, Nagai, Olivier, Pratt, Quaid, Rogers, and Sullivan.

27. For a class project, a teacher is assigning students to three organizational committees: the monetary committee, the nutrition committee, and the planning committee. Each committee must have at least one member. The students who will participate are Allie, Brad, Calista, Dieter, and Eleni, each of whom will serve on at least one committee.

28. The curator of a museum is arranging artifacts for a central exhibit. The exhibit will contain three artifacts, one on the left, one in the middle, and one on the right. The artifacts she will choose from are a stone carving, a text, a violin, and a weaving.

29. A teacher's aid is choosing classroom pets for her fourth-grade class. She plans to have at least one of each of the following pets: ladybugs, mice, newts, and opossum.

30. Friends Qin, Roberto, Selma, and Tauriq are forming a four-piece band. Each friend will play one instrument in the band, and no two friends will play the same instrument. The instruments will be a fiddle, a guitar, a hand drum, and an Irish flute.

Answers

Possible Unused Elements	Definite Unused Elements	Elements Used Exactly Once	Elements Could Repeat	Elements Must Repeat
18, 21, 26	22, 24, 28	17, 25, 30	19, 27, 29	16, 20, 23

16. "Must contain the colors" means all the colors are used. "Exactly six vertical stripes" means there are six spaces that must be filled with colors. Since there are five colors to choose from, that means one element must repeat.

17. "Will each staff one shift" means each volunteer will work exactly once. There are five volunteers and five shifts, so each element will be used exactly once.

18. "Three positions ... must be occupied by photos" and "none of which can appear more than once" means at least three photos will be used. "Each position can hold up to two photos" means that each position holds one or two photos. So it is possible that three, four, five, or six photos are used. That means one or more of the elements may be unused.

19. "Each of which will be displayed on at least one shelf" means all the items are used. "Each shelf will contain at least two items" means any given shelf could contain more than two items, so some elements could repeat.

20. "Each of whom will be ... on at least one initiative" means all three managers will be used at least once. Each of the three projects needs two leaders, so six total leadership roles must be filled. That means at least some elements must repeat.

21. "Each of which is a different color" means the colors are not repeated. "Three or four vertical stripes and a star" means four (three stripes plus the star) or five (four stripes plus the star) colors are used. Since there are five colors to choose from, it is possible that one of the colors is unused.

22. "Top-five favorite songs" means the list will contain exactly five songs. There are seven songs to choose from, so two elements will definitely be unused.

23. "Each of which must be contained in at least one pack" means all the elements will be used. There are 4 packs and each contains 2 or 3 different items, so between 8 and 12 total items will be contained in the packs. Since there are 4 items to choose from, some elements must repeat.

24. "Each layer will be a different flavor" means the flavors will not be repeated. Then "three-layer wedding cake" means three flavors will be used. There are five flavors to choose from, so two flavors will definitely be unused.

25. Three apartments and two pets per apartment means there are six pets total in the apartment building. There are six pets to choose from, so all elements are used exactly once.

26. "At least three" tells us that it is possible that three, four, five, six, or seven council members will be on the committee. That means it is possible that some of the elements are unused.

27. "Each of whom will serve on at least one committee" means all of the students will be used. "Each committee must have at least one member" means there is no limit (until we get the rules!) to the number of students who can serve on each committee. That means the students can serve on multiple committees, so elements could repeat.

28. "Will contain three artifacts" means that exactly three elements will be used. There are four elements to choose from, so one element will definitely be unused.

29. "At least one of each" means all elements will be used, but allows that there may be more than one of some (or all!) of the pets. That means elements could repeat.

30. "No two friends will play the same instrument" means at least as many instruments must be used as there are band members. Then "each friend will play one instrument" means exactly as many instruments as band members will be used. There are four friends in the band and four instruments, so each element will be used exactly once.

Drill 18: Rules Represent, Round 1

Instructions: Once you've determined your task and your roster, the next step in any logic game is to diagram the rules, and that's what this drill is all about. Diagram each of the following rules in the space provided. There are rules in this drill from all different game types and twists, so be prepared to think about what kind of game a given rule is likely to appear in as you figure out the ideal diagram. You also might need to sketch out a mini game diagram, such as a Number Line or Grouping Board, in which to place some rules.

1. The felt must be purchased at some time before the denim is purchased.

   F — D

2. Queenstown must be built either immediately before or immediately after Newville.

3. Xavier must be booked during week 5.

4. Janet must perform during week 2 or week 6.

   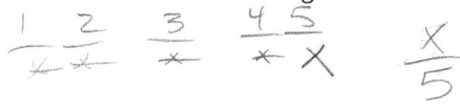

5. Paprika is acquired either first or seventh.

6. The driver delivers the cog at some time after delivering the drill.

   D — C

7. The engineer designs the fluxor at some time before designing the energizer.

   F — e

8. The shopper buys exactly one product between buying the lava lamp and buying the octopus statue, whether or not the lava lamp is bought before the octopus statue.

9. Neither instructor is assigned a room next to a professor's room.

10. Wanda is not assigned to a room next to Vicky's room unless Rachel is also assigned a room next to Vicky's room.

11. The two days on which a given workshop is in session are consecutive.

    W W

12. Frieda arrives later than Helga, and earlier than Ivan.

    H — F — I

13. Lot A has more cars than Lot B.

    L > B

14. Quentin must perform at least two days later than Priscilla.

15. Harvey and George must be separated by exactly three days.

H/G _ _ _ H/G

16. The oranges will be delivered two days before the lemons.

O _ L

17. There is exactly one space between Ralph and Mercutio.

R _ M   or
M _ R

18. Abby and Bart will perform together exactly once.

AB = 1

19. *Carpeteers* will air the week before any week that *Huffaluffs* airs.

C _ H

20. Foot treatments are always immediately preceded by dermabrasion treatments.

F ⟹ DF

21. On each of the five days, at least one, but no more than two, of the workshops are in session.

1 2 3 4 5

22. Martha is either after Louis or before Pretsie, but not both. (no ties)

L > M   or   M < L
P   P

23. Any Monet must have a Picasso hung immediately after it.

M ⟹ MP

24. Elderberries are harvested before huckleberries.

E — H

25. If Charles performs fifth, he also performs first.

$\frac{C}{5}$ ⟹ $\frac{C}{1}$

$\cancel{C \atop 1}$ ⟹ $\cancel{C \atop 5}$

26. Khan and Touré appear together at least once.

KT = 1+

27. If she selects geology, she can select neither historiography nor fine arts.

G ⟹ H̶F̶

HF ⟹ G̶

28. She cannot select the pumpkin unless she selects the zucchini.

P ⟹ z

z̶ ⟹ P̶

29. Jakarta will always be the destination after Nepal.

N ⟹ NJ

30. If he redoes the kitchen, he must also redo the living room.

K ⟹ L

L̶ ⟹ K̶

31. If both Goethe and Shakespeare are reviewed, Whitman is also reviewed.

    G and S → W

    ~W → ~G or ~S

32. There must be at least two seats in between Romy and Michele.

    R/m _ _ _ R/m

33. Dwight must present either immediately after or immediately before Jim.

    DJ or JD

34. If Soto is a wallaby, Garamond is a ferret.

    Sw → Gf

    ~Gf → ~Sw

35. Michael will only perform in week 1 or week 6.

    M _ _ _ _ M

    If M → M₁ or M₆

36. If Steve is on the team, neither Ralph nor Takahashi will be on the team.

    S → ~R and ~T

    T or R → ~S

37. If either the robot or the ducky is given, they must both be given and boxed together.

    R or D → [R / D]

38. Marco and Paulo cannot both be chosen.

    M → ~P

    P → ~M

39. If either the jeans or the blouse is selected, the other must also be selected.

    [JB] B → J

40. Frank is selected.

    [In]
    [F]

Answers

Note: Some of these include partial diagrams. If yours are a bit more fleshed out, that's fine. There are also times where more than one way to represent a rule would be correct. We've often included different representations for these rules, but just as often provided only our preferred representation.

1. The felt must be purchased at some time before the denim is purchased.

    F — D

2. Queenstown must be built either immediately before or immediately after Newville.

    or

3. Xavier must be booked during week 5.

    $\dfrac{X}{5}$

4. Janet must perform during week 2 or week 6.

5. Paprika is acquired either first or seventh.

    ᴾ⁄ ___ ___ ___ ___ ___ ⁄ᴾ
    1   2   3   4   5   6   7

6. The driver delivers the cog at some time after delivering the drill.

    D — C

7. The engineer designs the fluxor at some time before designing the energizer.

    F - E

8. The shopper buys exactly one product between buying the lava lamp and buying the octopus statue, whether or not the lava lamp is bought before the octopus statue.

    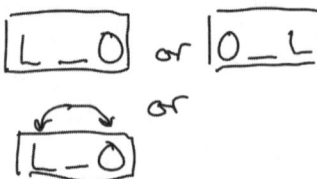

    or

9. Neither instructor is assigned a room next to a professor's room.

    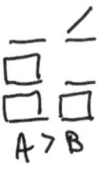

    Note: In #2 and #8 we showed you two ways of representing these types of rules, which we call reversible chunks. One way is to draw the chunk in one order and add a set of arrows on top denoting that the elements could switch places. The other way is to draw out two chunks, each representing one of the two possible orders. Moving forward, we'll mostly be showing one way or the other, not both. But, if you have a preference for the one we don't show, go ahead and use it. Our feelings won't be hurt.

10. Wanda is not assigned to a room next to Vicky's room unless Rachel is also assigned a room next to Vicky's room.

    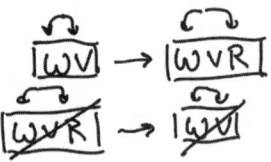

11. The two days on which a given workshop is in session are consecutive.

    WW

12. Frieda arrives later than Helga, and earlier than Ivan.

    H — F — I

13. Lot A has more cars than Lot B.

    A > B

14. Quentin must perform at least two days later than Priscilla.

    P — ___ — Q

15. Harvey and George must be separated by exactly three days.

16. The oranges will be delivered two days before the lemons.

17. There is exactly one space between Ralph and Mercutio.

18. Abby and Bart will perform together exactly once.

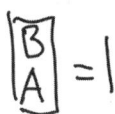

19. *Carpeteers* will air the week before any week that *Huffaluffs* airs.

H → [CH]

Note: We can't simply represent this with a CH chunk, because it's possible to have C without H following. Also, a chunk would imply that both C and H air. It's possible that neither airs, or that just C airs. All we know is that if H airs, C must precede it.

20. Foot treatments are always immediately preceded by dermabrasion treatments.

21. On each of the five days, at least one, but no more than two, of the workshops are in session.

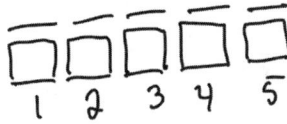

22. Martha is either after Louis or before Pretsie, but not both. (no ties)

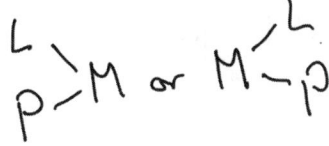

23. Any Monet must have a Picasso hung immediately after it.

M → [MP]

24. Elderberries are harvested before huckleberries.

E – H

25. If Charles performs fifth, he also performs first.

$\frac{C}{5} → \frac{C}{1}$

$\frac{\cancel{C}}{\cancel{1}} → \frac{\cancel{C}}{\cancel{5}}$

26. Khan and Toure appear together at least once.

$\begin{bmatrix} T \\ K \end{bmatrix}$ = 1+

27. If she selects geology, she can select neither historiography nor fine arts.

G → $\cancel{H}$ + $\cancel{F}$

H or F → $\cancel{G}$

28. She cannot select the pumpkin unless she selects the zucchini.

$\cancel{Z}$ → $\cancel{P}$

P → Z

29. Jakarta will always be the destination after Nepal.

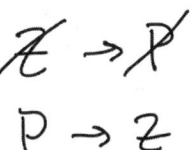

30. If he redoes the kitchen, he must also redo the living room.

K → L

$\cancel{L}$ → $\cancel{K}$

31. If both Goethe and Shakespeare are reviewed, Whitman is also reviewed.

G & S → W

$\cancel{W}$ → $\cancel{G}$ or $\cancel{S}$

32. There must be at least two seats in between Romy and Michele.

R – ___ ___ – M

33. Dwight must present either immediately after or immediately before Jim.

34. If Soto is a wallaby, Garamond is a ferret.

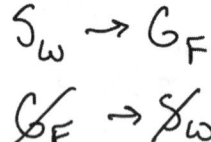

35. Michael will only perform in week 1 or week 6.

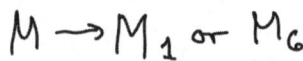

36. If Steve is on the team, neither Ralph nor Takahashi will be on the team.

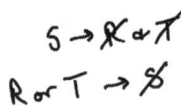

37. If either the robot or the ducky is given, they must both be given and boxed together.

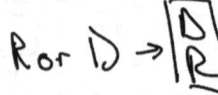

38. Marco and Paulo cannot both be chosen.

$M \rightarrow \not{P}$

$P \rightarrow \not{M}$

39. If either the jeans or the blouse is selected, the other must also be selected.

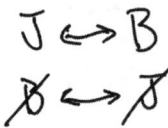

40. Frank is selected.

$$\frac{In \quad | \quad Out}{F \quad | \quad}$$

Drill 19: Basic Inferences

Instructions: Once you've got the rules in place, it's time to look for inferences. In logic games, there are some inferences that can be derived from a single rule and others that can only be derived by combining multiple rules. We call the former basic inferences and the latter advanced inferences. Basic inferences are repeatable, in that every time you have a certain type of rule, you can make certain types of basic inferences.

For this drill, we have provided five game scenarios. Each scenario is accompanied by a series of rules. Each rule is accompanied by a series of potential inferences. Your job is to determine if the basic inference listed can (Y) or cannot (N) be derived from the stated rule. Note that the rules are to be taken individually. Don't combine them in order to assess your potential inferences because we're not looking for advanced inferences; that's a drill for another day!

Scenario 1 – Relative Ordering:

Six fishing boats—F, H, I, Q, R, and S—arrive in the harbor during one afternoon. The boats arrive one at a time.

H arrives before S.

___N___ 1. H cannot be first.

___Y___ 2. H cannot be last.

___Y___ 3. S cannot be first.

___N___ 4. S cannot be last.

Q arrives after F.

___Y___ 5. Q cannot be first.

___N___ 6. Q cannot be last.

___N___ 7. F cannot be first.

___Y___ 8. F cannot be last.

R must arrive either before H or before I, but not both.

R H or R I but not RHI

___Y___ 9. R cannot be first.

___Y___ 10. R cannot be last.

___N___ 11. H cannot be first.

___N___ 12. H cannot be last.

___N___ 13. I cannot be first.

___N___ 14. I cannot be last.

___Y___ 15. Either H or I must arrive before R.

___Y___ 16. Either H or I must arrive after R.

F must arrive after Q or before S, but not both.

Q-F or F-S not both

___N___ 17. F cannot be first.

___N___ 18. F cannot be second.

___N___ 19. F cannot be fifth.

___N___ 20. F cannot be last.

___N___ 21. Q cannot be first.

___N___ 22. Q cannot be second.

___N___ 23. Q cannot be fifth.

___Y___ 24. Q cannot be last.

Q F S (crossed out)

___Y___ 25. S cannot be first at the same time that Q is last.

___Y___ 26. Q cannot be first at the same time that S is last.

___N___ 27. Either Q or S must arrive before F.

___N___ 28. Either Q or S must arrive after F.

I must arrive after H or after R, but not both.

H-I or R-H not both

___Y___ 29. I cannot be first.

___Y___ 30. I cannot be last.

___N___ 31. H cannot be first.

___N___ 32. H cannot be last.

___N___ 33. R cannot be first.

___N___ 34. R cannot be last.

___Y___ 35. Either H or R must arrive before I.

___Y___ 36. Either H or R must arrive after I.

G O
1 2 3 4 5 6 7

Scenario 2 – Basic Ordering:

A car dealership has seven spaces in its showroom, numbered 1 to 7 from left to right, in which to display cars. The showroom has seven cars in seven different colors: gold, indigo, jade, olive, purple, ruby, and silver. Each car occupies exactly one space.

1 2 3 4 5 6 7

The purple car is in the space immediately to the left of the indigo car.

PI

_N_ 37. The purple car cannot be first.

_X_ 38. The purple car cannot be last.

_Y_ 39. The purple car cannot be in a slot immediately to the left of a filled-in slot.

_N_ 40. The purple car cannot be in a slot immediately to the right of a filled-in slot.

_Y_ 41. The indigo car cannot be first.

_N_ 42. The indigo car cannot be last.

_N_ 43. The indigo car cannot be in a slot immediately to the left of a filled-in slot.

_Y_ 44. The indigo car cannot be in a slot immediately to the right of a filled-in slot.

The olive car and jade car are in adjacent spaces.

_N_ 45. The jade car cannot be first.

_N_ 46. The jade car cannot be last.

_N_ 47. The olive car cannot be first.

_N_ 48. The olive car cannot be last.

OJ or
JO

The ruby car is exactly three spaces to the left of the silver car.

_N_ 49. The silver car cannot be in spaces 1, 2, 3, or 4.

_Y_ 50. The silver car cannot be in spaces 1, 2, or 3.

_N_ 51. The silver car cannot be in spaces 5, 6, or 7.

_N_ 52. The ruby car cannot be in spaces 1, 2, or 3.

_Y_ 53. The ruby car cannot be in spaces 5, 6, or 7.

_N_ 54. The ruby car cannot be in spaces 4, 5, 6, or 7.

If the olive car is in space 3, then the gold car must be to its left.

_N_ 55. If the olive car is not in space 3, the gold car must be to its right.

_N_ 56. If the gold car is to the left of the olive car, then the olive car is in space 3.

_Y_ 57. If the gold car is to the right of the olive car, then the olive car is not in space 3.

Scenario 3 – In/Out Grouping:

A photographer is choosing photos for an exhibition. She will display photos from at least three of the following seven nations: Oman, Poland, Russia, Switzerland, Tanzania, Uruguay, and Venezuela.

At least 3   O P R S T Z ✓

If the photographer displays photographs from Poland, then she also displays photographs from Oman.

P → O

_N_ 58. Either photographs from Poland or Oman are displayed.

_N_ 59. Either photographs from Poland or Oman are not displayed.

_N_ 60. Either photographs from both Poland and Oman are displayed, or photographs from neither Poland nor Oman are displayed.

If the photographer displays photographs from Venezuela, then she does not display photographs from Uruguay.

V → U
U → V

_N_ 61. Either photographs from Venezuela or Uruguay are displayed.

_Y_ 62. Either photographs from Venezuela or Uruguay are not displayed.

If the photographer does not display photographs from Switzerland, then she does display photographs from Tanzania.

_Y_ 63. Either photographs from Switzerland or Tanzania are displayed.

_N_ 64. Either photographs from Switzerland or Tanzania are not displayed.

The photographer will display photographs from either Oman or Russia, but not both.

_Y_ 65. Either photographs from Oman or Russia are displayed.

_Y_ 66. Either photographs from Oman or Russia are not displayed.

1 2 3 4 5 6 7

R _ _ S

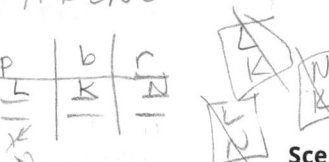

Scenario 4 – Basic Grouping:

On a children's game show, six competitors—F, H, K, L, N, and O—are split evenly between three teams—the Purple Monkeys, the Blue Snakes, and the Red Iguanas. Each competitor will be on exactly one team.

F and K must be on the same team.

_____ Y 67. No one else can be on the same team as F and K.

_____ Y 68. Once F and K are placed, there are only two available teams for the remaining competitors to be placed on.

H and O cannot be on the same team.

_____ N 69. K is on the same team as either H or O.

_____ N 70. K is on the same team as either F or L.

_____ N 71. K is on the same team as either H, O, or N.

L and K cannot be on the same team; L and N cannot be on the same team; N and K cannot be on the same team.

_____ N 72. Two of F, H, and O have to be on the same team.

_____ N 73. F is either with L or N.

_____ Y 74. F is either with L, N, or K.

_____ Y 75. F, H, and O each have to be on a different team.

If F is not on the Red Iguanas, then H is on the Blue Snakes.

_____ N 76. If F is on the Red Iguanas, then H is not on the Blue Snakes.

_____ N 77. If H is on the Blue Snakes, then F is not on the Red Iguanas.

_____ Y 78. If H is not on the Blue Snakes, then F is on the Red Iguanas.

_____ Y 79. Either F is on the Red Iguanas, or H is on the Blue Snakes.

_____ Y 80. If F is on the Blue Snakes, then so is H.

_____ N 81. If H is on the Red Iguanas, then F is not.

_____ Y 82. If H is on the Red Iguanas, then so is F.

_____ Y 83. If H is on the Purple Monkeys, then F is on the Red Iguanas.

Scenario 5 – Open Grouping:

A charitable organization has teams that pick up donations in three cities: F, G, and H. Each city is covered by one team that must consist of at least two but no more than four volunteers. On one particular day, the organization has eight volunteers: Peter, Quan, Roopsi, Sam, Tyrone, Veronica, Wanda, and Xavier. Each volunteer will be assigned to at least one team.

Sam and Tyrone are assigned to the same city at least once.

_____ N 84. No one else is assigned to the city to which Sam and Tyrone are assigned.

_____ N 85. At least one other person is assigned to the city to which Sam and Tyrone are assigned.

_____ Y 86. At most two other people are assigned to the city to which Sam and Tyrone are assigned.

Peter and Roopsi are never assigned to the same city.

_____ 87. Peter must be assigned to the same city as Quan at least once.

_____ 88. Roopsi must be assigned to the same city as Quan at least once.

City F has fewer volunteers assigned to it than City G.

_____ 89. F has a maximum of three volunteers assigned to it.

_____ 90. F has a minimum of three volunteers assigned to it.

_____ 91. G has a maximum of three volunteers assigned to it.

_____ 92. G has a minimum of three volunteers assigned to it.

_____ 93. F and G have no volunteers in common.

_____ 94. F and G must have at least one volunteer in common.

_____ 95. G must have at least one volunteer in common with each other city.

2

City H has exactly one more volunteer assigned to it than City G.

_____ 96. H has a maximum of three volunteers assigned to it.

_____ 97. H has a minimum of three volunteers assigned to it.

_____ 98. G has a maximum of three volunteers assigned to it.

_____ 99. G has a minimum of three volunteers assigned to it.

_____ 100. H has either two or three volunteers assigned to it.

_____ 101. H has either three or four volunteers assigned to it.

_____ 102. G has either two or three volunteers assigned to it.

_____ 103. G has either three or four volunteers assigned to it.

_____ 104. Either three volunteers are assigned to H and two to G, or four to H and three to G.

Any volunteer assigned to City F cannot be assigned to City H.

_____ 105. F cannot have four volunteers assigned to it.

_____ 106. F has exactly two volunteers assigned to it.

_____ 107. H cannot have four volunteers assigned to it.

_____ 108. If both F and H have exactly four volunteers assigned, then at least two volunteers are assigned to more than one city.

Veronica is assigned to twice as many cities as Wanda.

_____ 109. Either Veronica and Wanda are not assigned to any cities, or Veronica is assigned to exactly one city and Wanda is assigned to exactly two.

_____ 110. Either Veronica and Wanda are not assigned to any cities, or Wanda is assigned to exactly one city and Veronica is assigned to exactly two.

_____ 111. Veronica is assigned to exactly one city and Wanda is assigned to exactly two.

_____ 112. Wanda is assigned to exactly one city and Veronica is assigned to exactly two.

Answers follow on the next page.

Answers

1.	N	29.	Y	57.	Y	85.	N
2.	Y	30.	Y	58.	N	86.	Y
3.	Y	31.	N	59.	N	87.	N
4.	N	32.	N	60.	N	88.	N
5.	Y	33.	N	61.	N	89.	Y
6.	N	34.	N	62.	Y	90.	N
7.	N	35.	Y	63.	Y	91.	N
8.	Y	36.	Y	64.	N	92.	Y
9.	Y	37.	N	65.	Y	93.	N
10.	Y	38.	Y	66.	Y	94.	N
11.	N	39.	Y	67.	Y	95.	N
12.	N	40.	N	68.	Y	96.	N
13.	N	41.	Y	69.	N	97.	Y
14.	N	42.	N	70.	N	98.	Y
15.	Y	43.	N	71.	N	99.	N
16.	Y	44.	Y	72.	N	100.	N
17.	N	45.	N	73.	N	101.	Y
18.	N	46.	N	74.	Y	102.	Y
19.	N	47.	N	75.	Y	103.	N
20.	N	48.	N	76.	N	104.	Y
21.	N	49.	N	77.	N	105.	N
22.	N	50.	Y	78.	Y	106.	N
23.	N	51.	N	79.	Y	107.	N
24.	N	52.	N	80.	Y	108.	Y
25.	Y	53.	Y	81.	N	109.	N
26.	Y	54.	N	82.	Y	110.	N
27.	N	55.	N	83.	Y	111.	N
28.	N	56.	N	84.	N	112.	Y

2

Drill 20: Strays and Other Important Elements, Round 1

Instructions: Before diving into the questions of a game, you should always take time to identify the game's key elements. "Strays" are elements that don't show up in the rules. "Twins" are pairs of elements that are equivalent in all ways. "Game Drivers" are elements that, alone or in a relationship, seem likely to drive the play of the game. Game Drivers tend to be more restricted, and usually appear in multiple rules.

For each of the following, identify the key elements and list them on the provided lines. If you don't see a type of element in a game, write in *None*.

[handwritten: oldest   T—W—R   youngest   S _ Q   P   V↗Vₓ   W V]

Set 1

Game Roster: P, Q, R, S, T, V, W, X

    W is older than R, but younger than T.

    There is exactly one person born between S and Q.

    P is either the oldest or the youngest.

    V is younger than S, but is not the youngest.

    W and V were not born in consecutive years.

_X_   1.   Strays?

___   2.   Twins?

SVW 3.   Game Drivers?

Set 2

Game Roster: B, C, D, H, J, K, M, N, P

    K is selected only if both N and C are selected.

    P is not selected unless B is selected.

    M cannot be selected if B is selected.

    J is selected if, but only if, C is not.

    H is selected only if D is selected.

_____   4.   Strays?

_____   5.   Twins?

_____   6.   Game Drivers?

Set 3

Game Roster: R, O, Y, G, B, I, V, W

    All colors must appear in exactly one quilt.

    The first quilt has more colors than the second or third quilt.

    Red and Orange are not used in the same quilt.

    Indigo is in the same quilt as Yellow.

    White is used with at least two other colors.

    A quilt can have at most two of Green, Blue, and Violet.

_____   7.   Strays?

_____   8.   Twins?

_____   9.   Game Drivers?

Set 4

Game Roster: D, K, L, M, P, S, V

    She will not dust after she vacuums.

    She will paint before she does laundry or dusts.

    She will study immediately before or immediately after watching a movie.

_____   10.   Strays?

_____   11.   Twins?

_____   12.   Game Drivers?

2

Set 5

Game Roster: boys: H, L, M, P, R, S; girls: I, J, K, N, O, Q

    M will not be paired with P or any of the girls.

    H and R will each be paired with a girl.

    If I is paired with Q, then N is paired with O.

    If I is paired with S, then J is paired with O.

_____ 13. Strays?

_____ 14. Twins?

_____ 15. Game Drivers?

Set 6

Game Roster: A, B, H, K, M, S, Z

    If they go hiking, they will not go kayaking.

    The music lesson cannot be consecutive to a visit to the art gallery.

    They will not go shopping on either the first or the last day of her five-day visit.

    If they have a music lesson, it will be earlier in her visit than bowling.

_____ 16. Strays?

_____ 17. Twins?

_____ 18. Game Drivers?

Set 7

Game Roster: A, B, C, D, E, F, H, I, J, K (letters)

Bins: local, national, global

    Each letter is used exactly once.

    Each bin contains at least one letter.

    E and F are not in the same bin.

    The local bin contains more letters than the global bin.

    B and D are not in the same bin.

    There are exactly two other letters in the bin with H.

    If K is in the local bin, then C is in the national bin.

_____ 19. Strays?

_____ 20. Twins?

_____ 21. Game Drivers?

Set 8

Game Roster: M, N, P, Q, R, S, T, V (gold/blue teams)

    Whichever team she is on, Q is always last.

    If M is on the gold team, N is on the blue team.

    R is always earlier in the relay than P or V.

    S and T are never on the same team.

_____ 22. Strays?

_____ 23. Twins?

_____ 24. Game Drivers?

Set 9

Game Roster: A, C, F, G, L, P, S, T

    L is added before A.

    P is added after G, but before C.

    F is not added fourth.

    T and C are added consecutively.

_____ 25. Strays?

_____ 26. Twins?

_____ 27. Game Drivers?

Set 10

Game Roster: C, E, F, L, O, P, W

    He reads O at some point after reading L.

    P is neither first nor last.

    He reads W before F, but after E.

    E and P are not consecutive.

_____ 28. Strays?

_____ 29. Twins?

_____ 30. Game Drivers?

Set 11

Game Roster: A, B, C, P, S, T, W, Z

    She will plant no more than six types of plants.

    If she plants C, she will not plant S.

    She will not plant A unless she plants Z.

    She will plant W if she does not plant T.

    If she does not plant B, she will plant P.

_____ 31. Strays?

_____ 32. Twins?

_____ 33. Game Drivers?

Set 12

Game Roster: H, I, J, K, L, M, N, O

> There are four chocolate and four vanilla cupcakes.
>
> Hannah and Laura have different flavors.
>
> Jamal has chocolate if Osha has chocolate.
>
> Marcos has the same flavor as Katia.

_____ 34. Strays?

_____ 35. Twins?

_____ 36. Game Drivers?

Set 13

Game Roster: A, B, C, D, L, N, P, S (autumn/spring)

> He never visits any city more than once.
> If he visits N in autumn, he will visit S in spring.
>
> He will visit A and B the same season.
>
> If he does not visit C in autumn, he will visit D in autumn.
>
> He will not visit A and P in the same season.

_____ 37. Strays?

_____ 38. Twins?

_____ 39. Game Drivers?

Set 14

Game Roster: P, Q, R, S, T, U, V

> S is closer to the corner than V.
>
> There is exactly one house between P and U.
>
> Q is closer to the corner than either R or T.
>
> U does not live on the corner.

_____ 40. Strays?

_____ 41. Twins?

_____ 42. Game Drivers?

Set 15

Game Roster: D, H, I, L, S, T (front/back)

> Five flowers will be planted.
>
> If S is planted, it will be planted beside I.
>
> I and T are never planted beside one another.
>
> L are never first in the row.
>
> If H is planted, it will be before T.
>
> D must be planted beside H or T.

_____ 43. Strays?

_____ 44. Twins?

_____ 45. Game Drivers?

Answers

Set 1

X	1.	Strays?
	2.	Twins?
W, V, S	3.	Game Drivers?

Set 2

	4.	Strays?
	5.	Twins?
B, C	6.	Game Drivers?

Set 3

	7.	Strays?
R/O, I/Y	8.	Twins?
quilt 1, #'s	9.	Game Drivers?

This game is driven by numeric restrictions. The eight colors must all be used exactly once, and quilt 1 must have more colors than the other two. This severely limits the possible ways the colors can be arranged.

Set 4

K	10.	Strays?
	11.	Twins?
D	12.	Game Drivers?

Set 5

L, K	13.	Strays?
H/R	14.	Twins?
M	15.	Game Drivers?

Set 6

Z	16.	Strays?
K/H	17.	Twins?
M, unused elements	18.	Game Drivers?

The rule set of this game tells us that not all the elements are used. Whenever there are unused elements, who gets used and who doesn't tends to drive the game.

Set 7

A, I, J	19.	Strays?
E/F, B/D	20.	Twins?
H, #'s	21.	Game Drivers?

We have ten letters that must be sorted into three bins. Knowing that H is with exactly two others limits the possible numeric breakdowns to three options: 3-6-1, 3-5-2, and 3-4-3. In the final distribution, we can also infer that the local bin has 4 letters, since it has to have more than the global bin.

Set 8

	22.	Strays?
P/V, S/T	23.	Twins?
R	24.	Game Drivers?

Set 9

	25.	Strays?
L/G	26.	Twins?
C	27.	Game Drivers?

Set 10

C	28.	Strays?
	29.	Twins?
E	30.	Game Drivers?

Set 11

	31.	Strays?
T/B P/W	32.	Twins?
#'s	33.	Game Drivers?

There is no overlap in the rules here. What will drive the game are the maxima/minima.

Set 12

I, N	34.	Strays?
H/L	35.	Twins?
O	36.	Game Drivers?

Set 13

__L__	37.	Strays?
_____	38.	Twins?
__A__	39.	Game Drivers?

Set 14

_____	40.	Strays?
__R/T__	41.	Twins?
__U__	42.	Game Drivers?

Set 15

_____	43.	Strays?
_____	44.	Twins?
__T__	45.	Game Drivers?

2

2

Drill 21: Rules Represent, Round 2

Instructions: You can't master the games section without mastering the rules, so diagram each rule in the space provided, again! There are rules in this drill from all different game types and twists, so be prepared to think about what kind of game a given rule is likely to appear in as you figure out the ideal diagram. You also might need to sketch out a mini game diagram, such as a Number Line or Grouping Board, in which to place some rules. Or, if you're ready for more of a challenge, check out Drill 132 - Rude Rules.

1. If Marishka is hired, and Tina is interviewed, then Oliver is hired.

$$M_h \text{ and } T_i \rightarrow O_h$$
$$\cancel{O_h} \rightarrow \cancel{M_h} \text{ or } \cancel{T_i}$$

2. The borscht is served after the tempura.

$$T - B$$

3. Natalia did not receive the lowest score.

$$\cancel{N_L}$$

4. Baseball was ranked lower than football but higher than hockey and higher than soccer.

$$F - B \overset{H}{\underset{S}{<}}$$

5. Velma will not be scheduled next to Ingrid unless Emily is also scheduled next to Velma.

$$\boxed{VI} \rightarrow \boxed{EVI} \text{ or } \boxed{IVE}$$
$$\cancel{\boxed{EVI} \text{ or } \boxed{IVE}} \rightarrow \cancel{\boxed{VI}}$$

6. *Kook-off* airs earlier in the evening than both *Freekshow* and *Loozers*.

$$K < \overset{L}{\underset{F}{}}$$

7. Romeo has to arrive later than Mercutio, but earlier than Tybalt.

$$M - R - T$$

8. If Stefan placed lower than Paul, Mike placed lower than Stefan.

$$\boxed{P-S} \rightarrow \boxed{S-M}$$
$$\cancel{\boxed{S-M}} \rightarrow \cancel{\boxed{P-S}}$$

9. At least three of the dishes include cumin.

$$\frac{3+}{C}$$

10. The London office has more employees than the Madrid office.

$$L > M$$

11. If Genevieve purchases a TV, then Felicia must purchase a microwave.

$$\boxed{G_+} \rightarrow \boxed{F_m}$$
$$\cancel{\boxed{F_m}} \rightarrow \cancel{\boxed{G_+}}$$

12. There are no more than three rappers.

$$R = Max\ 3$$

13. The fruit is not sliced.

$$F\cancel{s}$$

14. Leeloo and Korbin will travel together exactly twice.

$$\boxed{\begin{matrix} L \\ K \end{matrix}} = 2$$

15. Any racer who places first at either the relay or the marathon must place no higher than third at the long jump.

$$R1 \text{ or } M1 \rightarrow \cancel{L_1}, L_2$$
$$L_1, L_2 \rightarrow \boxed{\cancel{R1}} \text{ and } \boxed{\cancel{M1}}$$

16. If a sandwich has lettuce, it must also have tomato.

$$L \rightarrow T$$
$$\cancel{T} \rightarrow \cancel{L}$$

17. The red thread will be used at most two times.

$$Red = 2 \text{ max}$$

18. The Magritte was auctioned for more than the Picasso but for less than the Klimt or the Dali.

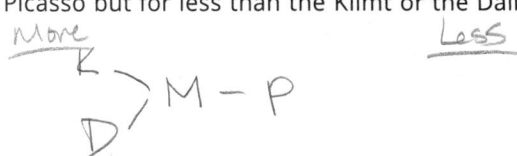

19. The moviehouse will play *Deathsickle* directly after any showing of *Murdercat*.

$$M \rightarrow MD$$

20. If Candice performs heart surgery, and Amandeep performs a transplant, then Amandeep also performs a skin graft.

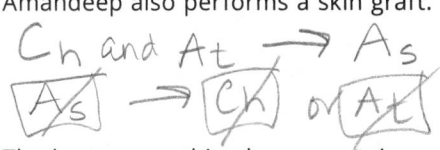

21. The berry smoothie always contains strawberries.

22. Albert will present third.

23. The love letter is delivered before the bill, which is delivered before the postcard, which is delivered after the newsletter.

24. There are at least two other performers in between Simran and Jeet.

$$S - \_ \_ - J \text{ or}$$
$$J - \_ \_ - S$$

25. Matt appeared after both Skip and Bryan.

$$\begin{array}{c} S \\ B \end{array} > M$$

26. If neither Hannah nor Clara is convicted of a crime, then Duke will be.

27. Belem will not go to the concert unless Irene goes.

28. Marcus plays his ballad before any of his rock songs.

29. If she visits Greece, she must not visit Haiti.

$$G \rightarrow \cancel{H}$$
$$H \rightarrow \cancel{G}$$

30. The publisher will sell *The Linguini Code* at some time after *Plaguenomics*.

$$P - L$$

2

31. Whenever a cake is baked, a pie is baked immediately before it.

$$C \Rightarrow PC$$

32. If Leo turned in his work later than Donnie, Ralph turned in his work earlier than Donnie.

$$D-L \Rightarrow R-D$$

$$\cancel{R-D} \Rightarrow \cancel{D-L}$$

33. The food critic will eat at Heartwise before Pizza Shack.

$$H-P$$

34. If Kristin does not take the fourth slot, she will not be included at all.

$$\cancel{K}_4 \Rightarrow \cancel{K}$$

$$K \Rightarrow \frac{K}{4}$$

35. Ellen is number one or number two in the rankings.

$$\frac{E}{1 \text{ or } 2}$$

36. The toy box has fewer items than the shopping cart.

$$S > T$$

37. Elizabeth and Henry will never be scheduled on the same day.

38. If Bruce drives a Lambo, Gary drives a Porchetta.

$$B\ell \Rightarrow G_p$$

$$\cancel{G_R} \Rightarrow \cancel{B\ell}$$

39. Logan is either before Scott or after Raven, but not both. (no ties)

$$L-S \quad \text{or} \quad R\diagup L$$
$$\diagdown R \qquad S$$

40. There will be exactly two sessions on both Monday and Wednesday.

$$\underline{M} \qquad \underline{W}$$
$$= \qquad =$$

Answers

Note: Some of these include partial diagrams. If yours are a bit more fleshed out, that's fine. There are also times when it would be correct to represent a rule more than one way. We've sometimes included different representations for these rules but more often provided only diagrams of our preferred representation.

1. If Marishka is hired, and Tina is interviewed, then Oliver is hired.

$$M_H + T_I \rightarrow O_H$$
$$\cancel{O}_H \rightarrow \cancel{M}_H \text{ or } \cancel{T}_I$$

2. The borscht is served after the tempura.

$$T - B$$

3. Natalia did not receive the lowest score.

$$\overset{last}{\cancel{N}}$$

4. Baseball was ranked lower than football but higher than hockey and higher than soccer.

$$F - B \overset{H}{\underset{S}{<}}$$

5. Velma will not be scheduled next to Ingrid unless Emily is also scheduled next to Velma.

6. *Kook-off* airs earlier in the evening than both *Freekshow* and *Loozers*.

$$K \overset{F}{\underset{L}{<}}$$

7. Romeo has to arrive later than Mercutio, but earlier than Tybalt.

$$M - R - T$$

8. If Stefan placed lower than Paul, Mike placed lower than Stefan.

$$P - S \rightarrow S - M$$
$$\cancel{S-M} \rightarrow \cancel{P-S}$$

9. At least three of the dishes include cumin.

$$C = 3+$$
or
$$\square$$
$$\square$$
$$\square$$
$$C$$

10. The London office has more employees than the Madrid office.

$$L > M$$
$$\overset{\diagup}{\underset{L \quad M}{\square}}$$

11. If Genevieve purchases a TV, then Felicia must purchase a microwave.

$$G_{TV} \rightarrow F_M$$
$$\cancel{F}_M \rightarrow \cancel{G}_{TV}$$

12. There are no more than three rappers.

$$R = max. 3$$
$$\overset{\leq}{\underset{R}{=}}$$

13. The fruit is not sliced.

Sl	Unsl
	(fruit)

14. Leeloo and Korbin will travel together exactly twice.

$$\boxed{\begin{matrix}K\\L\end{matrix}} = 2$$

15. Any racer who places first at either the relay or the marathon must place no higher than third at the long jump.

$$R_1 \text{ or } M_1 \rightarrow \cancel{L}_1 + \cancel{L}_2$$
$$L_1 \text{ or } L_2 \rightarrow \cancel{R}_1 + \cancel{M}_1$$

16. If a sandwich has lettuce, it must also have tomato.

$$L \rightarrow T$$
$$\cancel{T} \rightarrow \cancel{L}$$

2

17. The red thread will be used at most two times.

$$R = 2\ max$$

$$\frac{\leq}{\overline{R}}$$

18. The Magritte was auctioned for more than the Picasso but for less than the Klimt or the Dali.

$$K \searrow M - P$$
$$D \nearrow$$

19. The moviehouse will play *Deathsickle* directly after any showing of *Murdercat*.

$$M \rightarrow \boxed{MD}$$

20. If Candice performs heart surgery, and Amandeep performs a transplant, then Amandeep also performs a skin graft.

$$\frac{H}{C} \text{ or } \frac{T}{A} \rightarrow \frac{S}{\frac{T}{A}}$$

$$\frac{S}{A} \rightarrow \frac{T}{A} \text{ or } \frac{H}{C}$$

21. The berry smoothie always contains strawberries.

$$\frac{S}{B}$$

22. Albert will present third.

$$\frac{A}{3}$$

23. The love letter is delivered before the bill, which is delivered before the postcard, which is delivered after the newsletter.

$$L - B - P$$
$$N \nearrow$$

24. There are at least two other performers in between Simran and Jeet.

$$S - \_\_\_ - J$$

Note: Remember, for reversible chunks and chains you can always write out both ordered options if you prefer that to a single diagram where arrows indicate that the elements can switch places.

25. Matt appeared after both Skip and Bryan.

$$S \searrow M$$
$$B \nearrow$$

26. If neither Hannah nor Clara is convicted of a crime, then Duke will be.

$$\cancel{H} \text{ or } \cancel{C} \rightarrow D$$
$$\cancel{D} \rightarrow H \text{ or } C$$

27. Belem will not go to the concert unless Irene goes.

$$\cancel{I} \rightarrow \cancel{B}$$
$$B \rightarrow I$$

28. Marcus plays his ballad before any of his rock songs.

$$B = 1$$
$$\boxed{\frac{B}{M}} - \boxed{\frac{R}{M}}_{all}$$

29. If she visits Greece, she must not visit Haiti.

$$G \rightarrow \cancel{H}$$
$$H \rightarrow \cancel{G}$$

30. The publisher will sell *The Linguini Code* at some time after *Plaguenomics*.

$$P - L$$

31. Whenever a cake is baked, a pie is baked immediately before it.

$$C \rightarrow \boxed{PC}$$

32. If Leo turned in his work later than Donnie, Ralph turned in his work earlier than Donnie.

$$D - L \rightarrow R - D$$
$$\cancel{R-D} \rightarrow D\cancel{-L}$$

33. The food critic will eat at Heartwise before Pizza Shack.

$$H - P$$

34. If Kristin does not take the fourth slot, she will not be included at all.

$$\cancel{K_4} \rightarrow \cancel{K}$$
$$K \rightarrow K_4$$

35. Ellen is number one or number two in the rankings.

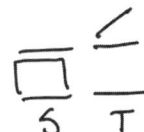

36. The toy box has fewer items than the shopping cart.

S > T

37. Elizabeth and Henry will never be scheduled on the same day.

38. If Bruce drives a Lambo, Gary drives a Porchetta.

$B_L \rightarrow G_P$

$\cancel{G_P} \rightarrow \cancel{B_L}$

39. Logan is either before Scott or after Raven, but not both. (no ties)

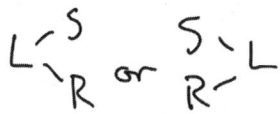

40. There will be exactly two sessions on both Monday and Wednesday.

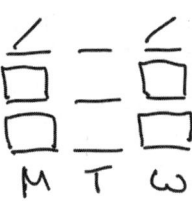

M   T   W

Drill 22: Quickfire Setups, Round 1

Instructions: To end this chapter on meeting the setup, we want you to pull it all together and set up the following games. Give yourself 2.5 minutes to diagram each scenario and rules, along with any inferences you can find. If you're really brave, try to knock these out in 2 minutes!

2

1. Seven actors—Jones, Klein, Larson, Morales, Nanette, O'Meara, and Parvik—are auditioning for a role in a new movie. There are seven time slots available. Each actor will audition in a single time slot, and no two auditions are scheduled for the same time slot. The scheduling of the auditions will meet the following constraints:

    Klein auditions sometime after Quan.
    Morales auditions before both Klein and O'Meara.
    Jones auditions before Larson and after Klein.
    Larson auditions after Parvik.

2. Five candidates for student president—Gupta, Han, Isaacs, Jabari, and Lopez—are scheduled to give campaign speeches. One candidate will speak each day, from Monday through Friday, with the following restrictions:

    Han speaks on the day immediately after the day on which Lopez speaks.
    Isaacs speaks on Thursday.
    Lopez speaks sometime before Gupta speaks.

3. A biology professor must assign four students—Abboud, Barnes, Chou, and Diya—to one or more of three projects—Metabolism, Obesity, and Sleep. Each project will have at least one student assigned, according to the following conditions:

Barnes and Diya are not assigned to Sleep.
Chou is assigned to Obesity.
If Barnes is assigned to Obesity, then Abboud is assigned to Sleep.
Sleep cannot have fewer students assigned to it than Metabolism.

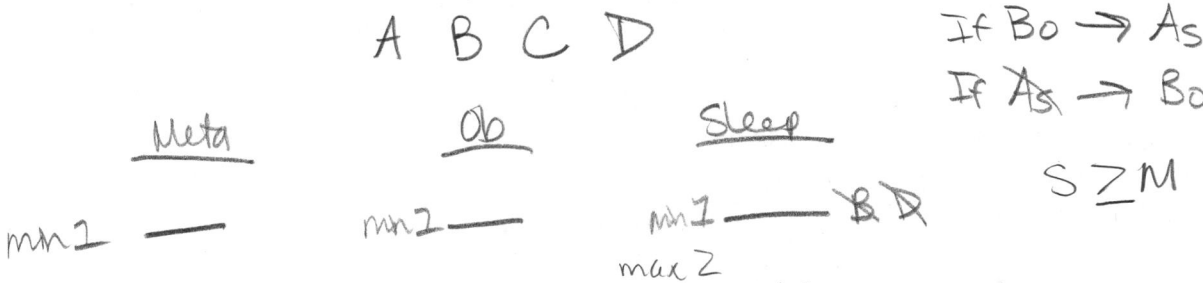

4. Each of six cruise-ship passengers—Kim, Long, Mendoza, Okafor, Pinto, and Shigeru—signs up for exactly one of two activities: bingo or a cooking class. Each activity will be attended by at least one passenger. The following conditions apply:

If Long attends bingo, then Okafor attends the cooking class.
Pinto and Shigeru attend different activities.
Kim and Okafor attend the same activity.
If Kim attends the cooking class, then Pinto attends bingo.

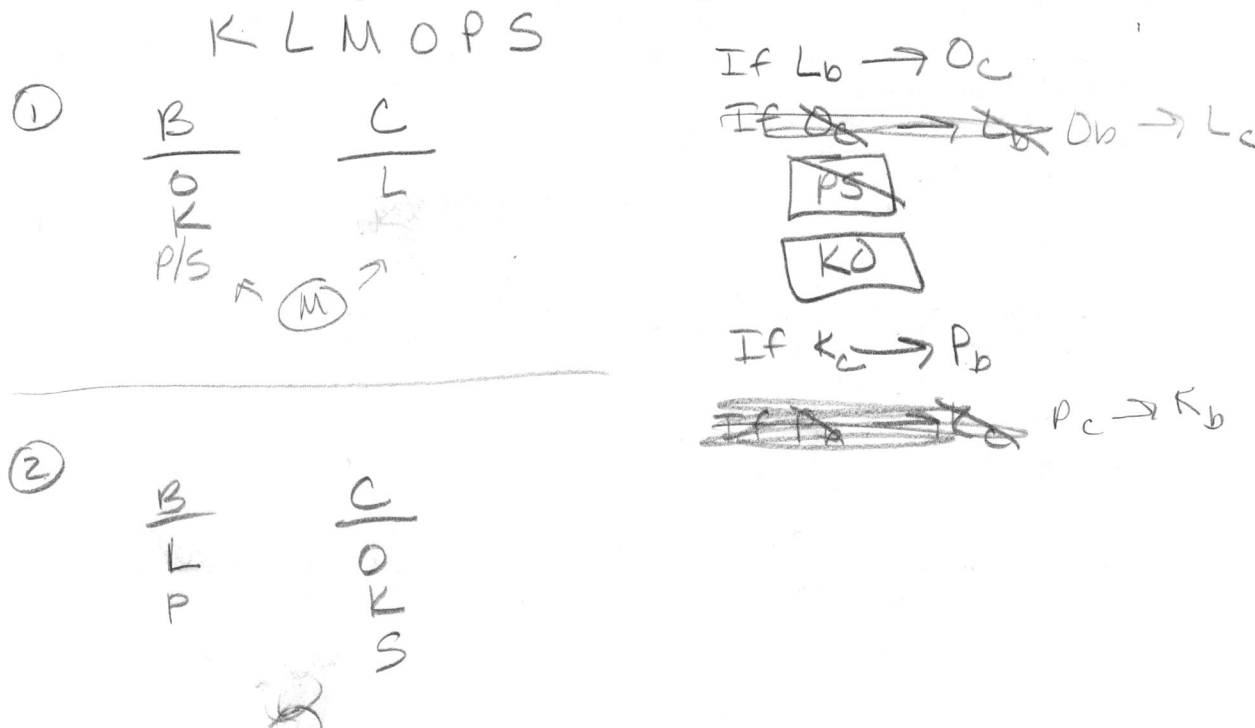

Answers

Your diagrams may differ from ours somewhat, and that's OK! Just make sure that your diagram communicates the same information as ours, and consider whether doing it our way next time would make the game easier, faster, neater, etc.

1. Seven actors—Jones, Klein, Larson, Morales, Nanette, O'Meara, and Parvik—are auditioning for a role in a new movie. There are seven time slots available. Each actor will audition in a single time slot, and no two auditions are scheduled for the same time slot. The scheduling of the auditions will meet the following constraints:

    Klein auditions sometime after Quan.
    Morales auditions before both Klein and O'Meara.
    Jones auditions before Larson and after Klein.
    Larson auditions after Parvik.

2. Five candidates for student president—Gupta, Han, Isaacs, Jabari, and Lopez—are scheduled to give campaign speeches. One candidate will speak each day, from Monday through Friday, with the following restrictions:

    Han speaks on the day immediately after the day on which Lopez speaks.
    Isaacs speaks on Thursday.
    Lopez speaks sometime before Gupta speaks.

Because I speaks on Thursday, there are only two places that the LH chunk can be placed: Monday/Tuesday or Tuesday/Wednesday. This split is the starting point for the two frames.

3. A biology professor must assign four students—Abboud, Barnes, Chou, and Diya—to one or more of three projects—Metabolism, Obesity, and Sleep. Each project will have at least one student assigned, according to the following conditions:

   Barnes and Diya are not assigned to Sleep.
   Chou is assigned to Obesity.
   If Barnes is assigned to Obesity, then Abboud is assigned to Sleep.
   Sleep cannot have fewer students assigned to it than Metabolism.

   The last rule of this Open Grouping game establishes that group M cannot have more members than group S. Because the first rule prevents two of the four elements from being placed in group S, the maximum number of elements that can be placed in group M is also two.

4. Each of six cruise-ship passengers—Kim, Long, Mendoza, Okafor, Pinto, and Shigeru—signs up for exactly one of two activities: bingo or a cooking class. Each activity will be attended by at least one passenger. The following conditions apply:

   If Long attends bingo, then Okafor attends the cooking class.
   Pinto and Shigeru attend different activities.
   Kim and Okafor attend the same activity.
   If Kim attends the cooking class, then Pinto attends bingo.

   Although this game doesn't have an In group and an Out group, it still meets the criteria for using the Logic Chain: There are exactly two groups and all of the rules are conditional. Rule three establishes an OK chunk, and the placement of that chunk is the starting point for the two frames.

CHAPTER 3

Reading Comprehension, Meet the Passage

In This Chapter, We Will Cover:

- What to Read For

- Small Words with Big Impacts

- The Scale

- Common Structures

Meet the Passage

If you don't understand what you read, you can't answer questions about it. This holds true for the big-picture considerations of The Scale and passage structure all the way down to the minutiae of vocabulary. This chapter of the book will cover the whole gamut.

In this section, you will learn to:

Read for What the Questions Test

- Summarize succinctly
- Separate the relevant from the extraneous

Understand LSAT Vocab

- Navigate reference words
- Define vocabulary words that appear on the test

Use The Scale

- Articulate the two sides of a debate
- Determine which side of the debate a given statement aligns with

Recognize Common Passage Structures

- Predict the direction of a paragraph
- Outline a passage from its opening line

Drill 23: What's Important? Round 1

Instructions: Have you ever looked at an RC passage you just read and realized that you underlined most of a paragraph but can't remember why? If so, you're not alone. Many of us are not selective enough about what we deem noteworthy on RC. Use this drill to practice making the tough determination of what's really important. Mark up each of the following paragraphs as you would an RC passage.

1. Throughout the twentieth century, Picasso and Matisse have been touted as the quintessential artistic rivalry. In *Matisse and Picasso*, Yve-Alain Bois follows Hubert Damisch in proposing that the interaction between Picasso and Matisse should be seen as a dynamic game rather than a static conflict of artistic polarities. Bois employs the metaphor of chess, arguing that the game represents the artists' exchange as "a competitive rivalry and a complex temporality" that can be viewed both as a linear process and a simultaneous structure.

2. What, then, would be a better tool to use in the high school classroom than textbooks or timelines for creating an effective learning environment that could reflect the dynamic nature of historical study? Out of all the various alternatives, the most promising is film. Movies can be a window into history for even the most resistant naysayer of historical study. Film is a rich medium for depicting history, with various genres—everything from documentaries to dramas—that not only present facts, but dramatize the human relationships behind those facts.

3. But trends following the Civil War produced a drastic shift away from the adventurous optimism of the pre-war era and toward a more subdued appreciation for the details of American life. In this new social context, the paintings now seemed too decadent, too gaudy, for the new philosophy taking root in the country following the horrors of war. As one commentator in 1866 put it, Bierstadt's work "may impose upon the senses, but does not affect the heart." In a sense, then, that same American pride upon which Bierstadt had capitalized to advance his success was now, in its fickleness, the source of his downfall.

4. Indeed, the final evidence that one can, in fact, have "half a mind" came in the 1960s, from the famous studies by Roger Sperry in which he discovered the functional specialization of the cerebral hemispheres and for which he was awarded the Nobel Prize in 1981. Working with people with epilepsy who had been treated via the cutting of the corpus callosum, or division between the two hemispheres, Sperry was able to observe "odd behavior" in these patients—each half of the brain could gain new information, but one hemisphere was entirely unaware of what the other had learned or experienced.

3

5. Boal has documented various successful instances of so-called "invisible theater" in which non-performers actively listen, participate in public-spirited discussion, and even take unplanned public-minded action in response to the dialogue and events set up by invisible theater performers. Because onlookers think they are witnessing real life events, intervention is common. For this reason, invisible theater is able to instigate political conversation within an everyday context, creating, according to its adherents, public forums out of thin air.

6. Mark di Suvero's *Iroquois* is composed of several industrial-sized I-beams. The materials are so heavy and large that the artist used cranes and other construction tools to manipulate and connect the beams, all of which have been painted a bright red-orange. The result is an intruding work of almost architectural dimensions that one can immediately sense is terribly heavy and somewhat precarious, yet stable and balanced. As one contemplates *Iroquois*, walking in and around its structure, backing away to see it from a distance, the linear forms become considerably more complex than one might presume. The tangled steel was obviously constructed with great care, yet each piece seems to threaten the viewer with its weight and size, jutting out away from the central nexus, daring the entire form to topple over. At the same time, the piece seems to exude stability, balance, even serenity. *Iroquois* resonates with an energy born not of the physical quality of the sculpture, which is quite passive and stable, but rather of the gestural quality of the forms.

7. More recent probes have investigated whether there was once liquid water on Mars. Some scientists believe that the presence of certain geological landforms definitively resolves this question. Others posit that wind erosion or carbon dioxide oceans may be responsible for these formations. Mars rovers *Opportunity* and *Spirit*, which landed on Mars in 2004, have both discovered geological evidence of past water activity. These findings substantially bolster claims that there was once life on Mars.

8. After 22 years of observations in Shark Bay, Australia, behavioral biologist Janet Mann and her colleagues have discovered that certain bottlenose dolphins, known as spongers, form social networks, showing the first hints of culture among nonhuman animals. Spongers are dolphins that wear marine basket sponges on their beaks as hunting tools, using them to root around on deep sandy bottoms and find fish concealed below the sand. Sponging is a complex hunting technique passed on from mother to offspring. A sponger must know where the sponges grow, how to pick the right sponge, how to remove the sponge intact from the ocean floor, and how and where to properly hunt.

9. The ensuing stability and peace brought a commercial prosperity that lasted nearly two hundred years. However, as psychologists and social historians have observed, humans inevitably fail to anticipate unintended consequences. In the Tokugawa period, the fixed social hierarchy placed the samurai on top; they and the government were essentially supported by levies on the peasantry, as the other two classes were demographically and economically inconsequential. However, prosperity brought riches to the commercial classes and their numbers burgeoned. Eventually, their economic power dwarfed that of their supposed superiors, the samurai.

10. Homer's *The Odyssey* is an epic poem that put a popular oral myth into writing for the first time. *The Histories* is an attempt by its author Herodotus to provide an unbiased account of historical conflicts in the Hellenistic world. These two works share two important motifs: the interference of the gods in the events of the mortal world and the concept of a predetermined and unavoidable destiny. One might assume that these two themes are one and the same—a predetermined fate set forth by the gods. However, Homer's and Herodotus's gods are presented as acting in a political fashion—each one acting within certain boundaries to accomplish his or her own agenda. As such, the wills of the gods do not coincide to allow for the formulation of a cohesive "master plan." Instead of destiny created by the gods, Homer and Herodotus present fate as something beyond the gods—a driving force under which the actions of gods and mortals lead to the realization of destiny. In *The Odyssey* and *The Histories*, the idea of gods with limited power leads to a conception of fate wherein the gods act not as the creators of destiny, but as agents of its fulfillment.

3

Answers

Note: How we notate is subjective, but what we notate shouldn't be. We've included here the important material that you should have noted, but we leave it up to you to come up with a notation system. We find that bracketing is superior to underlining for multiple lines of text, and that labeling anything you bracket or underline with shorthand is a good way to help you relocate relevant information to answer questions later.

1. The conflict between Picasso and Matisse should have been noted, as well as Bois and Damisch's assessment of it ("a dynamic game"). Also, you should have tagged the chess metaphor. It's almost guaranteed to have a question asked about it.

2. This paragraph introduces a question/answer (or problem/solution) passage. You should have noted the question (How should history be taught?) and the answer (film).

3. This paragraph deals with a transition. The societal shift should have been noted, and the effect this had on Bierstadt's career (and the criticism of his work) should have been connected to it.

4. Don't worry about the science/specifics here. Note the conclusion (the halves of the brain can act independently) and the topic of the study (people with epilepsy). Reread to answer any detail questions.

5. "Because X…" and "For this reason…" should tell you that the causality is important. You should note that invisible theater, presumably defined elsewhere, causes political conversation.

6. Keep it simple. Note that this paragraph is a description of the sculpture. The last sentence—the author's assessment of its importance—should have been underlined.

7. The debate should have been noted here, as well as the shift the author makes to her opinion in the last sentence (life vs. liquid water).

8. The author uses "discovered," showing that he agrees with the discovery. You also should have also noted the definition of sponger (when the passage defines a term, the term is important), and the evidence for the conclusion (the last sentence, which is implicit support).

9. That second sentence should have been noted as the conclusion, with the rest of the paragraph serving as an example of it.

10. This paragraph brings up similarities between *The Odyssey* and *The Histories*, so you should have tagged it as such. This discussion builds to the conclusion in the last line, which would be the most important takeaway from the paragraph.

Drill 24: What Are You Talking About?

Instructions: RC passages are full of words and phrases that refer to earlier concepts. To understand the passage, you have to understand exactly what these words refer to. For each of the following selections, choose the answer choice that best describes the earlier concept being referenced.

1. Many studies have shown that cable locks are an ineffective deterrent against professional bike thieves. However, they are still used frequently and provide bicycle owners with a false sense of security.

    What does the word "they" in the second sentence refer to?

    (A) Studies of cable locks
    (B) Cable locks
    (C) Professional bike thieves

2. A new office policy increased the number of vacation days that can be carried over to the following year. Since the policy change, employees have taken, on average, 20% less time off from work per month. This is likely due to employees planning to take longer or more frequent vacations in the near future.

    What does the word "This" in sentence three refer to?

    (A) The introduction of the new vacation policy
    (B) Employees taking less time off
    (C) Employees going on vacation

3. The scene features a waitress working her first day at a restaurant and a powerful businessman who was recently fired from his job. By the end of the scene, the audience has developed greater sympathy for the latter character.

    What does the word "latter" in the second sentence refer to?

    (A) The waitress
    (B) The restaurant
    (C) The businessman

4. Of the nearly 200 works by Shakespeare in the collection, there are only 38 plays. Of these, only 10 are devoted to actual historical figures.

    What does the word "these" in sentence two refer to?

    (A) All of the works in the collection
    (B) The 200 works by Shakespeare
    (C) The 38 plays by Shakespeare

5. Some cuckoos will lay their eggs in the nests of other birds, who will then act as hosts and become responsible for feeding and raising the cuckoo chicks when they hatch. This behavior is a form of parasitism and can be particularly harmful to the host.

    What does the phrase "This behavior" in the second sentence refer to?

    (A) Cuckoos laying eggs in other birds' nests
    (B) Birds feeding cuckoo chicks
    (C) Cuckoo chicks hatching

6. Unlike the gods in Greek mythology, the gods in Norse mythology were not immortal—the Norse god Baldr was killed by a spear thrown by his own brother, and even Odin eventually dies after being attacked by the wolf Fenrir. This constitutes one of the key differences between Greek and Norse mythology.

    What does the word "This" in the last sentence refer to?

    (A) Baldr being killed by a spear
    (B) Odin being attacked by Fenrir
    (C) Norse gods not being immortal

7. Some parents have argued that teachers should not permit the use of cell phones as an educational tool (e.g., as a calculator) and that, despite students' complaints, cell phones should be turned off, and not just on silent mode, for the duration of the school day. Their arguments have served as a basis for broader discussions about the increased role of technology in the education system.

    Who does the word "Their" in the second sentence refer to?

    (A) Parents
    (B) Teachers
    (C) Students

8. Urban runoff consists of waste, oil, and other debris that can be washed away from homes and contaminate local rivers and lakes. To combat the effects of urban runoff, the city has proposed that any home being built or renovated must install a drainage system. Opponents have expressed concerns. Such action, they argue, could have a detrimental effect on the soil causing it to shift or even collapse.

    What does the phrase "Such action" in the last sentence refer back to?

    (A) Waste, oil, and debris being washed away from homes
    (B) Expressing concerns about the city proposal
    (C) Installing drainage systems in homes being built or renovated

9. Because they don't have eardrums, many snakes rely on sensory nerves in the skin called mechanoreceptors for hearing. Sound waves stimulate the mechanoreceptors, which then send messages to the inner ear. And snakes are not alone. Many fish use this same method.

    What does the word "this" in the last line refer back to?

    (A) Sending messages to the inner ear
    (B) Using mechanoreceptors in the skin to hear
    (C) Stimulating mechanoreceptors with sound waves

10. Eustress, like distress, is brought about by stressors—events or conditions that bring about stress. However, unlike the negative stressors that bring about distress, the stressors associated with eustress can provide numerous benefits such as greater focus, increased motivation, and improved performance in daily activities. These stressors can arise from situations both personal (e.g., getting married) and work-related (e.g., getting a promotion).

    What does the word "These" in the last sentence refer to?

    (A) Eustress and distress

    (B) Conditions that bring about distress

    (C) Events or conditions associated with eustress

11. A committee was formed consisting of several actors, directors, and producers who were frustrated by the increased restrictions studios were placing on film production. This group drafted a manifesto designed to encourage, rather than stifle, creativity.

    What does the word "this" in the last sentence refer to?

    (A) Actors

    (B) Directors

    (C) The committee

12. Many critics believe that the novelist's view of society as chaotic and devoid of redemption is unnecessarily pessimistic. This belief is supported by observing the multitude of charitable actions carried out by prominent members of society.

    What does the word "This" in the second sentence refer to?

    (A) The idea that society is chaotic and devoid of redemption

    (B) The idea that the novelist's view is pessimistic

    (C) The critic's idea that the novelist's works are unnecessary

13. Scientists researching macular degeneration are facing several setbacks. For one thing, funding is a major issue. Not only are fewer grants being offered, but most grants are being offered for shorter periods of time. In addition, information has become increasingly difficult and costly to access and disseminate. While these are understandably sources of great concern, there are still several reasons to be optimistic.

    What does the word "these" in the final sentence refer to?

    (A) The setbacks facing scientists researching macular degeneration

    (B) The grants being offered

    (C) Scientists accessing and disseminating information

14. Organizational experts offer a three-step method to reduce the amount of clutter in a room. First, determine the primary functions of the room. Then, remove any items from the room that do not serve those functions. Finally, decide whether any removed items can be used elsewhere in the home or should be given or thrown away. This approach can be utilized in any room and repeated throughout the year.

    What does the word "This" in the final sentence refer to?

    (A) The method offered by experts
    (B) The decision to keep certain items and to throw others away
    (C) The decision to reduce clutter in a room

15. Many people purchase products advertised on infomercials, particularly ones that offer seemingly ingenious solutions to everyday problems. However, many of them fail to see the promised results, leading to feelings of disappointment and frustration.

    What does the word "them" in the second sentence refer to?

    (A) The people who buy products advertised on infomercials
    (B) The products advertised on infomercials
    (C) The infomercials

16. The Phoenicians are rightfully praised for developing many techniques and inventions in the fields of science, technology, mathematics, and writing. However, despite so many undeniable accomplishments, they cannot be credited with having invented the alphabet.

    What does the word "they" in the last sentence refer to?

    (A) The Phoenicians
    (B) The accomplishments of the Phoenicians
    (C) The fields of science, technology, mathematics, and writing

17. Using the new tilling technique, the farmers produced greater yields of corn that were better able to withstand dry conditions, even in soil that historically produced very little corn. Other farmers have since experienced similar results with wheat and soybean crops.

    What does the word "similar" in the last sentence refer to?

    (A) Using the new tilling technique
    (B) Producing dry conditions
    (C) Producing greater crop yields in dry conditions

18. Sociologists have offered many theories to explain why juveniles are committing an increasing number of crimes. They are often based on understanding interactions that occur both in home and at school.

    What does the word "They" in the second sentence refer to?

    (A) Sociologists
    (B) Juveniles
    (C) The sociologists' theories

19. Berkeley's theory of idealism rejects the commonly held belief that all physical objects are composed of matter. Instead, it asserts that everything is composed of ideas and can only be perceived in one's mind.

    What does the word "it" in the second sentence refer back to?

    (A) Berkeley's theory of idealism
    (B) The belief that all physical objects are composed of matter
    (C) The matter that composes all physical objects

20. After new managers were hired, the store introduced a new policy. The new policy removes restrictions on the number of sale items that an individual may purchase. This has angered many customers who worry that popular products will be harder to obtain because other customers will purchase more than they need.

    What does the word "This" at the beginning of the last sentence refer back to?

    (A) The hiring of new managers
    (B) The new policy introduced by the store
    (C) Restrictions on the number of sale items an individual may purchase

3

Answers

1.	B	6.	C	11.	C	16.	A
2.	B	7.	A	12.	B	17.	C
3.	C	8.	C	13.	A	18.	C
4.	C	9.	B	14.	A	19.	A
5.	A	10.	C	15.	A	20.	B

3

Drill 25: Function Junction, Round 1

Instructions: "RC" passages have a LOT of words, and in order to get through all those words efficiently, you need to ensure that you can pick up the meaning of the big-picture words that indicate structure and tone. These subtle yet important words are often overlooked by students too focused on the details of a passage.

In each of the following selections, a portion has been highlighted. In the space provided, write a brief description of the function of the highlighted text, and/or what it conveys about the direction the selection is likely to take.

1. While new census data reveals that unemployment numbers are more dire than was previously suspected, it is not clear that the forecast for American entrepreneurship is equally alarming.

2. An epic dramatization of the internal consequences of the quest for power, Macbeth is thus considered one of Shakespeare's best works.

3. For example, as women's participation in the workforce has increased, there has been a corresponding increase in jobs in the childcare industry.

4. Surprisingly, Kyle did not rebut Johanna's assertion.

5. Although best known for her poetry, Emily Dickinson was also a consummate baker.

6. The winds are forecasted to exceed 58 miles per hour; therefore, the National Weather Service will issue a Severe Thunderstorm Warning.

7. *Fun in the Sun* was an audience favorite, but *Yonder Horizon* ultimately won the award.

8. Though they were once thought to increase cholesterol, eggs are now recommended by many dieticians as part of a healthy diet.

9. Some have claimed that the rise of automation will actually lead to a decline in manufacturing sector employment.

10. In an American wedding ceremony, a bride is traditionally escorted down the aisle by her father.

11. The depiction of light was especially important in the Impressionists' paintings.

12. It is Tuesday, so Tina will do her shopping.

13. He further asserted that the commissioner's recommendation would be detrimental to the residents of the eastern part of the city.

14. Pluto is no longer classified as a planet, despite the protests of many amateur astronomers.

15. The majority of the council voted in favor of the proposal; however, the dissenting minority wrote a strongly contrary editorial opposing it.

16. Thomas usually agrees with Lina.

_____

17. A samurai's primary role was to function as a warrior for a lord, who would be a member of the middle or upper class.

_____

18. The kidneys also play a crucial role in blood pressure regulation, by producing a hormone involved in the constriction of the blood vessels.

_____

19. Unfortunately, Reina decided to accept the job offer from Westcorp rather than the one from Ionics, Inc.

_____

20. We should move forward with the plan, even if the CEO objects.

_____

21. The Bobcats will win the title because of the strength of their passing game.

_____

22. Though it is often celebrated as an early example of the use of magical realism, Hesse's _Steppenwolf_ is equally important for its use of epiphany as a tool of character development.

_____

23. Installing outdoor dining will increase sales from foot traffic; furthermore, the general manager has always wanted to design an outdoor dining space.

_____

24. This policy has been in place since the company filed articles of incorporation.

_____

25. Theoretically, we could route power from auxiliary systems to boost the strength of the shielding.

_____

26. I suggest that Dizzy Gillespie was actually heavily influenced by Roy Eldridge.

_____

27. The committee has not yet decided whether to schedule a public hearing on the matter.

_____

28. Red brick is the best choice for the new facade because the style will match the other homes in the neighborhood; moreover, it is a cost-effective option.

_____

29. To illustrate her claim about modernist philosophers, Dr. Katana used the example of Hume's _A Treatise on Human Nature_.

_____

30. Firstly, the initiative is popular with stockholders, secondly, it has been highly rated by employees, and finally, it will raise revenue.

_____

Answers follow on the next page.

Answers

Note: Your answers may be slightly different than ours, but they should convey similar ideas.

1. Introduce a fact from which to pivot to a contrasting/surprising fact

2. Introduce a conclusion that follows from previously stated evidence

3. Give an example of a previously stated claim

4. Describe the author's attitude about an event

5. Introduce a fact from which to pivot to a contrasting/surprising fact

6. Introduce a conclusion that follows from previously stated evidence

7. Introduce a contrasting fact

8. Introduce a fact from which to pivot to a contrasting/surprising fact

9. Introduce an opinion with which the author may or may not agree

10. Describe the context of an event

11. Indicate ranking/importance

12. Introduce a conclusion that follows from previously stated evidence

13. Continue to introduce evidence/premises

14. Introduce a contrasting view/fact

15. Introduce a contrasting view/fact

16. Indicate an expected/typical outcome

17. Indicate ranking/importance

18. Indicate ranking/importance

19. Indicate negative attitude by the author

20. Indicate a contrary opinion

21. Introduce evidence

22. Introduce a fact from which to pivot to a contrasting/surprising fact

23. Continue to introduce evidence/premises

24. Indicate timing/sequence of events (a different use of *since* than the usual premise indicator)

25. Qualify the nature of an assertion

26. Offer an opinion

27. Indicate that a decision is not final

28. Build on the previous statement/conclusion

29. Introduce a supporting example

30. Offer a final assertion/conclusion

Drill 26: Vocab Lab #1 – Definition Match

Instructions: The LSAT doesn't test your vocabulary as explicitly as some standardized tests do, but let's face it: sometimes the LSAT uses words that many of us aren't that comfortable with…yet. Enter the Vocab Lab series! We've mined the LSAT for 300 of the trickiest words it has ever used. Do you know what they mean? Use this series of drills to find out!

For your first lab, 45 LSAT words below are grouped in 3 sets of 15 words apiece. Within each set, match the words to their definitions.

Set A

1. Abide - E
2. Abrasive - G
3. Aptitude - L
4. Avant-garde - C
5. Cognitive - A
6. Cohesive - O
7. Collude - J
8. Deride - m
9. Derive - D
10. Dissuade - N
11. Evaluative - F
12. Inductive - K
13. Inquisitive - H
14. Intuitive - B
15. Oppressive - I

a. having to do with the process of knowledge/perception
b. instinctive; perceived by quick insight
c. ahead of its time; innovative; on the forefront
d. acquire from a specific source
e. follow; conform; tolerate
f. based on assessing something to determine its value
g. rough; causing irritation or annoyance
h. curious; having a desire to know more or investigate
i. burdensome; harsh; cruel
j. conspire; cooperate for illegal or fraudulent purposes
k. characterized by the use of particular ideas or instances to form general principles
l. an inherent ability to do something
m. mock; scoff at; laugh at contemptuously
n. prevent or deter from taking a course of action
o. united; connected; causing the forming of a whole

Set B

16. Anecdotal - M
17. Apparent - L
18. Chastise - F
19. Connoisseur - B
20. Curtail - A
21. Disdain - I
22. Emit - N
23. Flourishing - E
24. Incite - C
25. Merit - D
26. Proprietary - K
27. Refrain - G
28. Sedentary - O
29. Superimpose - J
30. Teeming - H

a. make less, cut down, or put a restraint on
b. expert who is able to pass critical judgment on the fine arts or matters of taste
c. instigate, stir up, or promote the growth of
d. excellence or worthiness
e. growing quickly and prosperously
f. intensely scold or condemn
g. hold back, especially from something bad or unhealthy
h. swarming; full of things; abundantly filled
i. having contempt toward someone, or a feeling that they're undeserving of interest or respect
j. set or lay something over something else
k. related to ownership of exclusive rights to something
l. obvious; clearly understood
m. based on reports made through observation or personal accounts rather than data
n. send, give forth, or issue
o. seated most of the time

Set C

31. Abstraction – E
32. Determinant – m

33. Diffuse – C
34. Envisage – O
35. Expend – N

36. Heed – K
37. Implicit – F
38. Indelible – B
39. Intermittent – G
40. Manifest – J
41. Perplexing – L
42. Receptivity – H
43. Sentimental – I
44. Susceptible – D
45. Vehement – A

a. exhibiting forceful, intense feeling or energy
b. incapable of being forgotten, removed, or erased (as in a pen mark)
c. spread out over a large area
d. capable of being influenced by something
e. the act of considering ideas or concepts that are not attached to any one event
f. understood without being plainly expressed
g. existing in intervals
h. the state of being open and responsive
i. overly emotional, or romantic in an extravagant way
j. readily perceived by the eye or mind
k. take notice of
l. utterly baffling
m. an element that influences the nature or result of something
n. pay out or use up
o. conceive of as a future possibility

Answers

Set A

1. e

Abide = follow; conform; tolerate. If a document doesn't *abide* by certain standards, you might not *abide* the situation.

2. g

Abrasive = rough; causing irritation or annoyance. Think sandpaper, which can literally *abrade*, or scrape, your skin.

3. l

Aptitude = an inherent ability to do something. Fun fact: "SAT" used to be an acronym for Scholastic *Aptitude* Test because the Harvard president who championed the test's wide adoption insisted that the SAT only measured inherent ability. Now that this insistence is a thing of the past, SAT is no longer an acronym.

4. c

Avant-garde = ahead of its time; innovative; on the forefront. From the French for "advance guard" (*avant* = before).

5. a

Cognitive = having to do with the process of knowledge/perception. Overly simplified, *cognition* is thinking, rather than feeling.

6. o

Cohesive = united; connected; causing the forming of a whole. You want your teams to be *cohesive*, to "stick together" as the Latin root of *cohere* means.

7. j

Collude = conspire; cooperate for illegal or fraudulent purposes. The noun form *collusion* has found its way into recent news, although it does not refer to a specific crime.

8. m

Deride = mock; scoff at; laugh at contemptuously. It's no fun to be *derided*, to be the subject of *derision* or *derisive* laughter. Find better people to be around.

9. d

Derive = acquire from a specific source. You can say that an idea *derives* from some inspiration, or that you derived that idea from that inspiration. In logic or math, a formal *derivation* is a step-by-step proof of a result.

10. n

Dissuade = prevent or deter from taking a course of action. *Persuade* and *dissuade* are antonyms. As a lawyer, you will likely be in the business of both *persuasion* and *dissuasion*.

11. f

Evaluative = based on assessing something to determine its value. An *evaluative* framework is one by which you'd *evaluate* something.

12. k

Inductive = characterized by the use of particular ideas or instances to form general principles. That is, you *induce* the general principles from the specific examples. In contrast, *deductive* logic *deduces* specific examples from general principles.

13. h

Inquisitive = curious; having a desire to know more or investigate. Being *inquisitive* is generally thought to be good; simply *inquiring* is neutral; and running an *inquisition* is bad.

14. b

Intuitive = instinctive; perceived by quick insight. When you want to dress up your wild guess, call it *intuitive*, or based on *intuition*.

15. i

Oppressive = burdensome; harsh; cruel. Whether physical, emotional, or political, *oppression* is always a negative thing, with the connotation of downward, stifling *pressure*.

3

Set B

16. m

Anecdotal = based on reports made through observation or personal accounts rather than data. *Anecdotal* evidence can be very useful, but is seldom deemed to be scientifically conclusive.

17. l

Apparent = obvious; clearly understood. From the same root as *appear*. As in the case of the verb, sometimes *apparent* is used to indicate the surface level of something, in contrast with a deeper reality.

18. f

Chastise = intensely scold or condemn. No one likes to be *chastised*, a word that carries with it the hint of being reprimanded by a teacher or another authority figure.

19. b

Connoisseur = expert who is able to pass critical judgment on the fine arts or matters of taste. From a Latin root (via French) meaning "to know." A *connoisseur* knows certain kinds of things.

20. a

Curtail = make less, cut down, or put a restraint on. *Curtail* shares a root with *curt*, in the sense of "short." The verb is now not used in a physical sense, but it was once used to describe the literal shortening of horses' tails.

21. i

Disdain = having contempt toward someone, or a feeling that they're undeserving of interest or respect (as a noun). *Disdain* can also be a verb.

22. n

Emit = send, give forth, or issue. From the Latin *e-* (= out) + *mittere* (= send). *Emission* is the noun form, either the act of *emitting* something or that something itself.

23. e

Flourishing = growing quickly and prosperously. From the same root, ultimately, as *flower*.

24. c

Incite = instigate, stir up, or promote the growth of. Usually what you're *inciting* is something negative, like trouble.

25. d

Merit = excellence or worthiness. To have *merit* (or to be *meritorious*) is to be worthy of praise. From a Latin root meaning "earn, deserve."

26. k

Proprietary = related to ownership of exclusive rights to something. *Proprietary* is related to *property*, unsurprisingly.

27. g

Refrain = hold back, especially from something bad or unhealthy. A horse's bridle in Latin is *frenum*. The ancestor of *refrain* conveyed the image of a horse being held in check by its headgear.

28. o

Sedentary = seated most of the time. Physically inactive. A possible pitfall of being a lawyer may be that you could slip into a *sedentary* lifestyle. Avoid this trap, for instance by using a standing desk.

29. j

Superimpose = set or lay something over something else. The prefix *super-* means "over, above, on top of."

30. h

Teeming = swarming; full of things; abundantly filled (yes, with things). These things are usually moving, such as bugs or people.

Set C

31. e

Abstraction = the act of considering ideas or concepts that are not attached to any one event. *Abstractions* are great, but to avoid getting lost in the clouds, anchor your *abstractions* in concrete examples.

32. m

Determinant = an element that influences the nature or result of something. That is, a *determinant determines* the course of events.

33. c

Diffuse = spread out over a large area. The adjective form (e.g., this effect is *diffuse*) is pronounced "diff-yooss." In contrast, the verb form (e.g., the aroma will *diffuse* throughout the room) is pronounced "diff-yooz," with a *z*- sound at the end. Don't confuse *diffuse* with *defuse*.

34. o

Envisage = conceive of as a future possibility. *Envisage* can also simply mean "regard or view" something in some way. *Envisage* and *envision* are very close in meaning.

35. n

Expend = pay out or use up. You can *expend* things other than money, but the noun forms *expense* and *expenditure* are frequently used in financial contexts.

36. k

Heed = take notice of. As a noun, *heed* can also mean "attention, notice." It's a rather formal word, so when you tell people to take *heed*, they will.

37. f

Implicit = understood without being plainly expressed. An *implicit* message is *implied*, not *explicitly* written or spoken.

38. b

Indelible = incapable of being forgotten, removed, or erased (as in a pen mark). *Indelible* is much more common than its nearly obsolete opposite *delible*.

39. g

Intermittent = existing in intervals; happening occasionally or irregularly. In environmental science, an *intermittent* stream comes and goes with the seasons, sometimes drying up completely.

40. j

Manifest = readily perceived by the eye or mind. *Manifest* may also be a verb (= become or make evident) and even a noun (= a list of the cargo or passengers on a vehicle).

41. l

Perplexing = utterly baffling; bewildering. Some LSAT questions are *perplexing* at first. With practice, you can become *unperplexed* (although that's not really a word).

42. h

Receptivity = the state of being open and responsive. That is, if your *receptivity* is high and you are being *receptive*, you are ready to *receive* whatever's coming.

43. i

Sentimental = overly emotional, or romantic in an extravagant way. *Sentiment* is a neutral word that means "feeling, emotion," but *sentimental* is decidedly not neutral.

44. d

Susceptible = capable of being influenced by something; impressionable; unresistant. Some adjectives in *-ible* or *-able* are easy to decode, because the verb from which they're built exists in English. For instance, *acceptable* = able to be accepted. But *susceptible* doesn't mean "able to be *suscepted*," because there's no such verb. That's just the way it is.

45. a

Vehement = exhibiting forceful, intense feeling or energy, even to the point of being antagonistic or otherwise negative. *Vehement* may come from the same root as *vehicle*, namely *veh-* = carry. According to this etymology, *vehement* originally meant "really carried away."

Drill 27: Whose Side Are You On?

Instructions: We've all heard the old adage that there are two sides to every story. For the most part, RC passages are no exception. Identifying the central debate is a critical part of your initial read, and when you get to the questions, you'll have to decide for some answers what side of the debate they align with. Use this drill to practice that skill!

For each of the following debates, consider the two diverging opinions articulated, then categorize the ten accompanying statements as aligning with viewpoint A (A), viewpoint B (B), or neither (N).

Set A

(A) Some music historians view punk rock as a premeditated rejection of the materialism of the pop music of the time and a rebellion against the histrionics that had overwhelmed the spare and forthright character of rock music. (B) On the other hand, some believe that punk, like its various predecessors and descendants, was just another natural and unconscious evolution of the art form called rock and roll.

N 1. Some art forms feature periods of vigorous activity followed by periods of slower development.

B 2. Punk rock musicians who eventually transitioned to playing New Wave rock music were not necessarily reacting against the aims of punk music.

A 3. Negative reactions to musicians altering one style of music can spur others to develop a new musical style of their own.

A 4. Punk rock was not as much a natural progression to a new musical style as it was a reaction against an established musical style.

N 5. Some musical genres are developed in response to the cultural and social conditions of the time.

B 6. Some musicians unintentionally created new styles of rock and roll music.

A 7. Punk rock was designed to be spare and forthright.

N 8. Punk rock music was not intended to appeal to listeners of pop music.

N 9. Not all art forms change solely in response to prior works.

N 10. Punk rock did not share any musical components with the pop music of its time.

Set B

(A) To help increase productivity, many corporate executives recommend rewarding employees with incentives such as extra vacation time, office parties, or sizeable bonuses. (B) However, some psychologists argue that offering such rewards can actually run counter to the executives' goal by creating undue and debilitating pressure on employees.

A 11. Financial rewards can have a positive effect in motivating people to boost their own performance.

B 12. The pressure involved in trying to earn a bonus can lead some workers to perform worse than they would have without such an incentive.

N 13. Increasing productivity is not a realistic goal for many corporate executives.

A 14. Employees can be motivated by both monetary and non-monetary incentives.

N 15. Increasing employee productivity is the most important goal when running a company.

B 16. It would not be unexpected for productivity to drop when employees are given the opportunity to earn more money.

N 17. Office parties can serve as a distraction and could actually decrease employee productivity in the long run.

B 18. Actions that can be perceived as having a positive impact on people can instead lead to undesirable circumstances.

N 19. A system in which employees are penalized for poor performance would be an ineffective way to increase productivity.

A 20. The results gained from providing employees with bonuses can compensate for the expense of providing those bonuses.

Set C

(A) Based on what fractured historical data was available at the time, 19th-century paleontologists and archaeologists nearly unanimously held that, before the arrival of Europeans, the Americas were sparsely populated by indigenous peoples. (B) Despite having access to data that is no less fragmented, modern researchers argue that the American indigenous population before European contact was substantially larger than previously reported, with some estimates at over 100 million people.

B 21. Paleontologists and archaeologists in the 19th century did not have access to the most accurate data for estimating the indigenous population of the Americas.

A 22. Despite the lack of consistent data, there is little reason to believe that the Americas had a dense population of indigenous people before the arrival of the Europeans.

N 23. When Europeans arrived in the Americas, they were unlikely to have observed a substantial population of indigenous peoples.

N 24. One does not need more complete data to produce a vastly different estimate of the same statistic.

B 25. Extensive cross-referencing of the existing data has led to substantial gains in scholars' ability to interpret documents to make inferences about population.

B 26. The diseases brought over to the Americas by the Europeans had a more devastating effect on the indigenous population than was previously estimated.

A 27. Modern nations with populations over 100 million people are far more heavily populated than all of the Americas were before the arrival of the Europeans.

B 28. The methods used in the 19th century for estimating indigenous populations in the Americas were not accurate.

N 29. The data available for indigenous populations is not complete enough to produce a reasonable estimate of birth rates prior to the arrival of Europeans.

A 30. Recent analysis suggests that early agricultural practices among indigenous peoples in the Americas would have been insufficient to support a total population exceeding 50 million people.

Set D

(A) Proponents of a strict constructionist interpretation of the Constitution decry judicial activists' nullification of the original intent of the document in favor of a justice's preferred interpretation, (B) but, in actuality, strict constructionism and judicial activism are both merely instances of justices' interpretations as shaped by preference and the circumstances of their times.

B 31. When interpreting a document, even those who adhere to the document's original intent are exhibiting a conscious preference.

A 32. The idea of the Constitution as a living document that can be molded to fit contemporary circumstances is unacceptable.

A 33. The original rules and regulations as laid out in the Constitution are infallible.

B 34. Strict constructionism and judicial activism involve similar interpretations of the Constitution.

B 35. Interpretations that follow the tenets of strict constructionism constitute an indication of one's preference.

N 36. Strict constructionism entails nullifying the original intent of a document.

3

N 37. It is acceptable for judicial activists to favor a preferred interpretation over one that follows the original intent of the Constitution.

B 38. The circumstances surrounding an interpretation can influence justices to adhere to a document's original intent.

N 39. Some of the most significant judicial rulings have been influenced by the major social and cultural circumstances of the time.

A 40. A justice's preferred interpretation of a document is acceptable only if such an interpretation is consistent with the original intent of the document.

3

Answers

Set A

__N__ 1. Both views focus on the motivation behind punk rock, not the speed at which it developed.

__B__ 2. Viewpoint B argues that evolution was unconscious for punk rock musicians and their descendants.

__A__ 3. As Viewpoint A claims, punk rock developed partially as a reaction against people adding histrionics to rock music.

__A__ 4. Viewpoint A asserts that punk rock was a reaction against the materialistic nature of pop music.

__N__ 5. Neither view addresses cultural and social conditions; they are all about the music.

__B__ 6. Viewpoint B claims that punk rock, like other styles, evolved unconsciously, i.e., without intent.

__A__ 7. Viewpoint A claims that punk rock rebelled against those who added histrionics to what had once been spare and forthright. Such rebellion would logically entail eliminating the histrionics and going back to the original style. The word "designed" implies that this was an intentional change, rather than an unconscious evolution.

__N__ 8. While punk rock is said to reject the nature of pop music, that says nothing about appealing to listeners. It's possible that punk rockers were trying to get pop music listeners to switch and join them in rejecting materialism.

__N__ 9. This might seem to reject Viewpoint A, but in saying "not solely," it doesn't take a stand on whether responding to prior works is one possible way that art forms change. In any case, merely rejecting Viewpoint A wouldn't constitute support for Viewpoint B, which describes a "natural and unconscious evolution."

__N__ 10. Punk rock rejected the materialist nature of pop music, the two still could have shared certain musical components.

Set B

__A__ 11. This is, in essence, the main idea behind the recommendation of bonuses in Viewpoint A.

__B__ 12. Viewpoint B claims that bonuses can create "undue and debilitating pressure."

__N__ 13. Viewpoint B claims that bonuses won't help with the goal. However, that doesn't mean the goal is unrealistic. There may be other methods that actually would help achieve that goal.

__A__ 14. Viewpoint A describes both monetary and non-monetary rewards, and this suggests that both may work.

__N__ 15. This is the only goal mentioned, and neither viewpoint evaluates its importance. They simply differ on whether incentives can help to achieve it.

__B__ 16. If we cut through the double negative, this says that we might expect productivity to decrease in response to bonuses, and that is exactly what Viewpoint B argues.

__N__ 17. This runs counter to one element of Viewpoint A, but it doesn't support Viewpoint B, which warns that incentives can create pressure, not that they are distracting. Note that Viewpoint B does not state whether incentives should actually be used. Maybe parties are great even if they make workers less productive!

__B__ 18. This is the principle behind Viewpoint B. Bonuses are perceived by executives as beneficial, but Viewpoint B claims that they can lead to undesirable circumstances: decreased productivity.

__N__ 19. Both viewpoints address positive, rather than negative, reinforcement, so we don't know what either would have to say about this.

__A__ 20. For this to be true, bonuses would have to produce gains for the company, which is what Viewpoint A proposes.

Set C

B 21. This provides a reason to favor the more recent estimates. Even if the available data is still fragmented, it may be more accurate.

A 22. This supports the description of a sparse population in Viewpoint A.

N 23. This might seem to support Viewpoint A, but evidence that a large population was unlikely to be seen isn't evidence that a large population didn't exist.

N 24. This is something that we can infer by comparing the two viewpoints, but it doesn't align with either on its own.

B 25. If this is true, then scholars today may be able to make better estimates even without any improvement in the completeness of the data.

B 26. If more people died than was previously thought, this suggests that the pre-European population may have been higher than early estimates indicated.

A 27. This is a roundabout way of saying that the estimates in B are too high, and that means that the earlier, lower estimates may be correct.

B 28. If this is true, then perhaps the estimates were too low despite similarly fragmented data. Note that it's also possible that the estimates were too high, which would not support B, but this gives us reason to agree that a revision of the earlier estimates is in order.

N 29. This would only be a problem if the estimates of population size relied on birth rates, and even then it would be a problem for both viewpoints rather than a support for either one.

A 30. Although this mentions recent work, it actually suggests that some of the current estimates may be too high. We don't know what the 19th-century estimates were—perhaps 50 million is still closer to the new estimates than the old—but this still supports pushing the estimates down rather than up.

Set D

B 31. Strict constructionism involves adhering to the Constitution's original intent, and Viewpoint B suggests that such interpretation is shaped by preference.

A 32. The idea of a living, changing document is just the kind of preferred interpretation concept that Viewpoint A decries.

A 33. This supports the idea in Viewpoint A that we should stick with the Constitution's original intent. Although this statement seems more extreme and specific than Viewpoint A, extremes are not generally a problem when we're providing support.

B 34. Again, this is more than we need, but it supports Viewpoint B by indicating that both views involve interpretation.

B 35. This is the heart of Viewpoint B on strict constructionism.

N 36. This is the opposite of how Viewpoint A describes constructionism. However, it also doesn't fit Viewpoint B, which doesn't take a stance on how successful strict constructionists are in following the original intent.

N 37. This is the opposite of Viewpoint A, which decries such favoritism. However, Viewpoint B never addresses whether this is acceptable. Viewpoint B only suggests that following the Constitution's original intent is itself a preferred interpretation.

B 38. Viewpoint B argues that adhering to a document's original intent, i.e., strict constructionism, is indeed influenced by circumstances of the time. Note that while this choice supports Viewpoint B, it doesn't necessarily go against Viewpoint A, which never addresses how or why justices choose to be constructionists.

__N__ 39. This only tells us that justices may be influenced by outside factors in their decisions, but it doesn't address whether this is true of strict constructionists or only of judicial activists. For that reason, it could be consistent with both viewpoints.

__A__ 40. Viewpoint A does not say preference is wrong. Viewpoint A only decries favoring preference over original intent. If the preference and the original intent are one and the same, then Viewpoint A would have no qualms.

3

Drill 28: Sum It Up, Round 1

Instructions: Most students try to retain too much information while working through an RC passage, or they take notes that are almost as long as the paragraph they're summarizing! For each of the following paragraphs, sum it up as succinctly as possible. Try to capture the paragraph in fewer than ten words.

1. The debate continues over the regulation of the process of hydraulic fracturing, which is used to extract oil and natural gas from previously unavailable reserves. Environmentalists and public health advocates strongly support stricter regulation and oversight of the industry, citing concerns about potentially severe impacts on the environment and public health. Industry advocates, on the other hand, minimize concerns.

2. While some critics continue to refuse to acknowledge the literary merit of genre fiction, others have begun to see past such outdated distinctions. For example, the Nobel Prize for Literature was recently awarded to Kazuo Ishiguro, an author who has blended elements of science fiction and fantasy into what would have been considered more traditional literary fiction.

3. A supernova is a stellar explosion so luminous that it can briefly outshine an entire galaxy. While the explosion itself takes less than fifteen seconds, supernovae take weeks or months to fade from view. During that time, a supernova can emit an amount of energy equivalent to the amount of energy the sun is expected to radiate over its entire lifespan. Supernovae generate enough heat to create heavy elements, such as mercury, gold, and silver.

4. From assemblages of found objects to bizarre video installations and digital interactive experiments, much of contemporary art has been criticized as cold, unapproachable, impersonal, and emotionless. One link between the immediately appealing, expressive paintings that are often the most popular museum attractions and the constructivist school of art pioneered in the early twentieth century is the notion of gesture as an expressive tool.

5. *Homo economicus*, or economic human, denotes the idea of human beings as rational, narrowly self-interested agents who, given total information about opportunities and possible constraints, seek to obtain the highest possible well-being for themselves at the least possible cost. In the late 19th century, a host of economists built mathematical models based on the conception of real humans as *Homo economicus*.

6. While new census data reveals that unemployment numbers are more dire than previously suspected, the forecast for American entrepreneurship may not be as alarming. Recent data show that new companies are being founded at higher rates than before the recession, despite the contraction in hiring at existing companies. One reason for the increase in new companies is that college graduates, unable to find traditional jobs, are instead opting to start their own businesses.

7. One critique of the use of historical film in the classroom cites the often rampant inaccuracies and biases found in such films. However, some historians believe that these flaws are part of the reason why film is a useful teaching tool. Not only does film allow students to see history come to life, but it can also foster deep critical thinking skills if instructors lead critical discussions after film viewings.

8. The Parthenon has long been regarded as one of the great architectural and artistic products of the High Classical Period. Yet scholars have struggled to reach a consensus interpretation for the meaning of the Parthenon frieze. The study of this particular sculptural element of the Parthenon, a continuous band of sculpture that ran around the top of the building's temple chamber, has proven quite difficult.

9. In traditional theater forms, the roles of performer and audience are completely separate, so that performance space is divided into an actor sphere and a spectator sphere. Pursuant to this model, even when performers move out into the audience or when there is scripted audience interaction, spectators do not become performers.

10. Modern thinkers take for granted an idea that would have perplexed philosophers from Aristotle through Descartes. Recent scholars posit that the mind is physically located in the brain and that our intellect, personality, and selfhood are attributable to physical processes in the brain and can therefore be altered by brain injuries.

Answers

Note: Your summaries will probably be different than ours, but make sure that they convey the same information. Also, our summaries aren't always grammatically correct—these are essentially shorthand, so don't confine yourself to thinking in full sentences!

1. Fracking debate; industry wrong?
(The author stating the industry minimizes concerns suggests she disagrees with that view.)

2. Some critics now OK genre fiction.

3. Supernovae: brief but bright and really hot.

4. Contemporary art sometimes cold. Gesture → appealing.

5. 19th-century economists: math models of economic human.

6. Despite unemployment, many new companies.

7. Benefits to teaching history w/ film?
(The author seems to be on the yay side, since he gives more explanation for that side.)

8. Why Parthenon frieze?

9. Traditional theater: actor/audience separate.

10. Modern thinkers: mind is brain → brain injuries are mind injuries.

Drill 29: Vocab Lab #2 – Match the Verbs

Instructions: The LSAT verbs in the first set below all end in *-ate* or *-ify*. In the second set, the verbs all end in *-ate* or *-duce*. Within each set, match the words to their definitions.

Set A

1. Allocate –H
2. Deteriorate –O
3. Disseminate –K
4. Emulate – F
5. Exemplify –L
6. Fabricate –N
7. Mollify –J
8. Necessitate – B
9. Proliferate –I
10. Rectify –m
11. Relegate – E
12. Repudiate –A
13. Simulate – C
14. Transliterate –D
15. Typify –G

a. reject, cast off; deny that something has authority
b. require as a result of; be grounds for
c. imitate how something looks or acts
d. represent using the corresponding letters of another alphabet or language
e. downgrade; lower the rank or position of
f. copy in an attempt to equal or be better than
g. be an ideal or representative example of
h. portion out for specific purpose
i. increase or spread rapidly or excessively
j. calm or soothe (an angry person); lessen or soften
k. scatter, spread about, broadcast
l. illustrate, demonstrate by example
m. correct, amend, make right
n. make up, construct (often something false)
o. continuously worsen; go downhill

Set B

16. Adduce – B
17. Deduce –H
18. Deviate – F
19. Dissipate – E
20. Eradicate –I
21. Expropriate –J
22. Induce – A
23. Instantiate – D
24. Mandate – C
25. Subordinate –G

a. persuade or influence into action; give rise to
b. give reason or proof to support a theory
c. instruct or command someone to act a certain way (as a verb); an official order or command (as a noun)
d. represent by an occurrence or use of a concrete example
e. steadily disappear or cause to steadily disappear; disperse
f. drift from established or standard course
g. put in such a position (as a verb); in a lower position (as an adjective)
h. draw a conclusion based on logic or reasoning
i. obliterate, remove or destroy completely
j. seize property from, dispossess (especially for public use)

Answers

Set A

1. h

Allocate = portion out for specific purpose. *Allocate* and *allot* seem to have different origins, but they basically mean the same thing.

2. o

Deteriorate = continuously worsen; go downhill. If the weather *deteriorates* on the mountain, don't go skiing.

3. k

Disseminate = scatter; spread about; broadcast. The object of *disseminate* is usually not physical but informational. You *disseminate* a story, a message, etc. From the Latin for "scatter seeds."

4. f

Emulate = copy in an attempt to equal or be better than. *Emulate* shares a really ancient root with *imitate* and *image*. They all come from the Proto-Indo-European word for "copy."

5. l

Exemplify = illustrate; demonstrate by example. *Exemplify* is basically "*example-fy*," but with a fancier set of vowels. The *-ify* or *-fy* suffix means "make." (By the way, *exemplify* and *typify* are close enough in meaning that if you chose (g), that's fine too.)

6. n

Fabricate = make up; construct (often something false). *Fabricate* can be used simply to mean "make" or "create" in a physical sense, without negative judgment. The particular meaning of the word depends on what's being *fabricated*. *Fabricated* sandals are fine; *fabricated* stories are not.

7. j

Mollify = calm or soothe (an angry person); lessen or soften (hurt feelings, etc.). In Latin, the ancestor verb meant "make soft" in a physical sense, but in English the meaning of *mollify* is always more abstract.

8. b

Necessitate = require as a result of; be grounds for. This word shares an obvious root with *necessary* and *necessity.*

9. i

Proliferate = increase or spread rapidly or excessively. The verb was backformed from *proliferation*. If asked, most people would be against nuclear *proliferation*, i.e., the spread of nuclear weapons.

10. m

Rectify = correct, amend; make right. The Latin root *rect-* (= right) has many English descendants, such as *correct* and *rectangle*.

11. e

Relegate = downgrade; lower the rank or position of. Some multitiered sports leagues practice *relegation*, which is the downgrading of poorly performing teams to the next tier down.

12. a

Repudiate = reject; cast off; deny that something has authority. Contrast *repudiate* with *renounce*, a similar word with a key distinction. If you *renounce* chocolate, that means you're giving it up (and you used to eat it). But if you *repudiate* chocolate, you're rejecting it forcefully. It's unknown whether you used to eat the stuff.

13. c

Simulate = imitate how something looks or acts. A computer *simulation* is a program that performs such an imitation.

14. d

Transliterate = represent using the corresponding letters of another alphabet or language. This is not the same thing as *translation*. If you *transliterate* the Russian word нет into the Latin alphabet, you get *nyet*, which you can pronounce if you don't read the Cyrillic alphabet. *Translated*, the word means "no."

15. g

Typify = be an ideal or representative example of. If this painting *typifies* Rembrandt's approach, then the painting is *typical* of his approach and represents the approach well. (By the way, *exemplify* and *typify* are close enough in meaning that if you chose (l), that's fine too.)

Set B

16. b

Adduce = give reason or proof to support a theory. A document may *adduce* a certain piece of evidence to argue a particular position.

17. h

Deduce = draw a conclusion based on logic or reasoning. You will do a lot of *deducing* as you prepare for the LSAT, as you proceed through law school, as you practice law, and (one hopes) as you live your life.

18. f

Deviate = drift from an established or standard course. Sometimes, there is no value judgment in the words *deviate* or *deviation*; at other times, there is a negative judgment. And *deviant* is always pejorative.

19. e

Dissipate = steadily disappear or cause to steadily disappear; disperse. The context is sometimes that of money, so *dissipate* can mean "spend foolishly" or "live a spendthrift, drunken life."

20. i

Eradicate = obliterate; remove or destroy completely. From Latin *e-* (= out) + *radix* (= root). When you *eradicate* something, you're not just trimming back the leaves. You're pulling it out by the roots.

21. j

Expropriate = seize property from; dispossess (especially for public use). The Latin prefix *ex-* (= out) indicates that the *property* is being taken out or away from someone.

22. a

Induce = persuade or influence into action; give rise to. You can also use *induce* to mean "infer a general principle from specific examples," but this primary meaning of *induce* (persuade or cause) may interfere. Use the terms *inductive logic* or *induction* if you want to draw a contrast with *deductive logic* or *deduction*.

23. d

Instantiate = represent by an occurrence or use of a concrete example. That is, a concrete thing *instantiates* an abstract principle or pattern.

24. c

Mandate = instruct or command someone to act a certain way (as a verb); an official order or command (as a noun). Probably from *man-* (hand) + *dare* (= give), so *mandate* meant "give into someone's hand" or "give by hand." What was given was an order.

25. g

Subordinate = put in such a position (as a verb); in a lower position (as an adjective). The Latin prefix *sub-* (= under, below) tells you most of what you need to know here.

Drill 30: Where Are You Going with This? Round 1

Instructions: The first sentence in a paragraph can tell you a lot, and the better you know this test, the more true that becomes. This test is standardized, and trends in argument structure should help you make accurate predictions about the direction a paragraph is likely to take. Use this drill to practice that skill by writing out the direction you think a paragraph will take after each of the introductory sentences below.

1. For years, many scientists believed that the best explanation for changes in monarch butterfly migration patterns was gradual temperature changes caused by climate change.

2. Surprisingly, the legalization of marijuana in California was followed by an increase in the volume of black-market marijuana, grown without compliance with the new licensing regulations.

3. Overlaying a graph of the Federal Reserve's benchmark interest rate for the last 50 years upon a graph of inflation for the same period highlights corresponding trends in the two economic indicators.

4. Opponents of the death penalty have routinely relied on moral arguments that have failed to persuade a majority of the voting public.

5. One example of the dominance of GeoMap, Inc. in the geographic information system (GIS) market is that its mapping software is used exclusively in the top five most prestigious university Geography departments in North America.

6. The Darwinian view of evolution long ago triumphed over the Lamarckian view.

7. For those born into lower socioeconomic strata, upward mobility depends not only upon access to educational opportunity, but also on some mechanism that functions as a surrogate for the continuous support systems available to those born into higher socioeconomic classes.

8. It was long thought that mean sea level was at the same elevation all over the world; after all, the oceans are all connected.

9. The recent rise in sea levels in conjunction with subsidence of the ground in areas of large-scale groundwater pumping has resulted in routine tidal flooding of densely populated coastal areas throughout South Florida, even in the absence of storms.

10. The two data formats in geographic information systems are raster and vector.

11. The novels of Milan Kundera, a Czech émigré, explore the emotional lives of people that escaped Socialist Czechoslovakia after the Soviet invasion and later tried to return to their old lives in a newly capitalistic state.

12. Island biogeographers examining the historical record have noted that the arrival of humans on previously uninhabited islands typically preceded, by about two decades, a 30% decline in the species diversity of resident songbirds.

13. The physical and biological environment in Abalone Bay, where new oil drilling has been proposed, is similar in most respects to that in Farland Sound, where oil drilling has been ongoing for three decades.

14. While the financial benefit of a college degree has continued to increase in recent decades, over the same period, the college graduation rate of students from lower income houses has remained stagnant, despite increased college enrollment in that demographic.

15. Bob Dylan's lyrics, long-described as poetry by his devoted fan base, were held at a distance by the literary community, who cited, among other criticisms, the necessity of the accompanying music to fully realize the art pieces that Dylan had created.

16. Starting in the 14th century in Italy, the Renaissance is classically viewed as a rebirth of art and culture, as well as humanistic philosophy, following the "dark" Middle Ages.

17. A group of state legislators have proposed raising the speed limit on approximately a dozen segments of the state highway system, asserting that their goal is the reduction of traffic accidents.

18. Some people claim that happiness is ultimately dependent upon managing one's own expectations rather than exceeding them.

19. Many claim that Internet-based video streaming giants—financed in large part by tech money—are ushering in a new golden age for movies and television, while others bemoan the final nail in the coffin for the shared cultural experience of the hit broadcast television show that was watched across all regions and socioeconomic groups and discussed the next day at the water cooler at work.

20. In a broad survey of college statistics courses, those in which the students were expected to complete homework collaboratively had higher course completion rates than those in which students were expected to complete their homework independently.

3

21. Warmer temperatures are melting peat bogs in the northern latitudes, the melting of which, in turn, releases substantial quantities of carbon dioxide into the atmosphere.

22. Many of the rules and common practices of English grammar are different, or even opposite, in Great Britain and America.

23. Academic analysis of the work of the Anarchist philosophers of the late 19th century is typically marred by association with the violence carried out by those ostensibly acting in the cause of Anarchist beliefs.

24. In a recent medical study, one group of participants was given a high salt diet, a second group was given a diet with salt levels typical of an American diet, and a third was given a reduced salt diet.

25. It should be noted that for a twenty year period across major league sports, if the top defensive team and the top offensive team in any particular year met in the championship, the top defensive team won almost twice as often.

26. Integrated pest management (IPM), while not eschewing the use of chemical pesticides as in organic farming, has transformed traditional agriculture to the benefit of farmers, consumers, and the environment.

27. Teaching children to play chess at a young age greatly increases the likelihood of success in high school mathematics classes.

28. Most species of large marine mammals have gone through a genetic bottleneck within the last two centuries as population levels were reduced dramatically through hunting for meat and skins.

29. Leonardo da Vinci is best known among the general population for his paintings, sculptures, and other works of art.

30. Some ecologists believe that small isolated nature preserves provide little value in the long term for the conservation of large-bodied mammalian species.

Answers

Note: Your answers will differ from ours. That's OK! Consider where you landed and where we landed, and if they differ substantially, ask yourself, "Which of these sounds more like the LSAT?" Maybe both do, in which case, great! But if only one does, consider how you might align your thinking with ours the next time.

1. The LSAT often uses a past/present dichotomy to structure its passages. When long-held beliefs are presented early on, the rest of the passage will likely describe new evidence that challenges the old way of thinking, a competing theory that has been introduced, or a problem that has been discovered with the old idea. In this case, the author will likely introduce a new explanation for the observed phenomenon.

2. If an LSAT author describes an unexplained observed phenomenon, especially an unexpected one, the point of the argument will be to provide an explanation for it.

3. As with number 2, it can be expected that the author will provide an explanation for the observation presented in this sentence.

4. The rest of the paragraph will likely take issue with opponents of the death penalty. The author could present an argument in favor of the death penalty (either on moral or other grounds) or could suggest an alternative strategy for opposing the death penalty. The latter is more likely here, as the focus is on the effectiveness of the opponents' arguments, not the death penalty itself.

5. From such a strong assertion supported by an example, the author will either provide additional examples and/or elaborate on the significance of GeoMap's market dominance. But, it's not impossible that the author could be setting up a pivot from current market dominance to a new era of market diversity.

6. This author will definitely expound on the two different views in this debate. Since the triumph of the Darwinian view is acknowledged, this line is likely to introduce a new discovery that lends some credence to an aspect of the Lamarckian view, or reconciles the two views in some way.

7. After articulating a principle, the author can be expected to expand on it and then either apply it or justify it. In this case, expect some description or examples of the "mechanism" that the author identifies as a requirement.

8. This is a traditional belief along with the reason for it. The author likely will explain how the traditional belief is wrong despite that evidence.

9. The author is describing a problem, which signals the Problems and Solutions structure. The passage will likely discuss further implications of this problem and possible solutions to it.

10. This non-opinionated factual statement regarding the existence of two types of systems is likely to preface a compare/contrast structure. Note if the author indicates a preference or remains neutral.

11. An LSAT passage will often laud the work of a writer, artist, or some other notable figure. In some cases, the passage will rebut a criticism of the person's work, but this purely descriptive opening line lays the groundwork for a passage that is not a defense from criticism.

12. Description of an observed phenomenon will typically lead to an explanation of the cause. Since the mechanism for the causal connection between the correlated trends is not obvious, the author will likely describe *how* one phenomenon caused the other.

13. This compare/contrast scenario will likely lead to a conclusion regarding the proposed drilling based on the ongoing drilling in an area identified as similar.

14. This observation will likely lead to an explanation for the puzzling phenomenon and/or a proposed solution for this problematic situation.

15. When an artist is criticized, expect that the author will defend that artist from criticism.

16. When a classical view is presented, expect that the author will offer something in contrast with that view. In this case, a re-envisioning of the Middle Ages seems likely, as the quotations around "dark" suggest that the author may take issue with this characterization.

17. When a proposal is mentioned, expect a consideration of pros and cons, though be aware that authors often neglect to balance the two, focusing instead on a preferred outcome. Due to the counter-intuitive nature of proposal, expect some explanation of this paradox, and take note of the author's position.

18. On the LSAT, the phrase "some people claim" is typically a prelude to a rebuttal.

19. Expect elaboration of both sides of the debate, though not necessarily evenly, and note the author's ultimate position on the two views, if it is articulated. Note that in this example, the author could hold both views.

20. When statistics are presented, expect the passage to explore causal explanations of the statistic.

21. When a problem is presented, expect that potential solutions will be explored. Resultant problems are often part of the passage, too.

22. Expect examples of this phenomenon and then its reasons and/or its implications.

23. Expect a reassessment or a defense from criticism structure.

24. Expect results of the study and an exploration of the causes of these results.

25. Expect an explanation of the trend and its implications.

26. Expect the author to compare/contrast IPM and organic farming, explain how IPM has transformed agriculture, and/or expand on the benefits of IPM. In a passage about the benefits of something, it is also common that the author raises a potential downside.

27. Expect an explanation of this statistic, and possibly its implications.

28. Expect a discussion of the implications for the future from these past events and/or a discussion of a possible solution(s) for the problem.

29. Expect a transition to other aspects of da Vinci's life and work.

30. Expect a rebuttal of this belief.

Drill 31: Outline a Passage

Instructions: In the last drill, we asked you to practice predicting the direction of a single paragraph based on its introductory sentence. In this drill, we're asking you to take that one step further and predict the direction of an entire passage.

For each of the following introductory sentences, construct an outline for a passage (aka a passage map). Your answers will invariably differ from those you see listed in the explanations and that's OK! Use this drill to practice thinking about structure, and use our explanations to start recognizing common structural patterns.

1. Contrary to popular belief, most people find it easier to understand quantum physics than traditional, Newtonian physics.

2. Despite arguments to the contrary, universities should actually spend more money on athletics programs.

3. Those who consider Charlie Chaplin to be merely a slapstick comedian fail to appreciate the life of one of history's greatest champions in the struggle against fascistic militarism.

4. Without intending to be, Thomas Jefferson, through his devotion to science, the advancement of knowledge, and good government, is arguably responsible for the discovery that mean sea level is not at a consistent elevation around the globe—a discovery that spurred further advancements in the fields of surveying and cartography.

5. The most significant point of contention regarding Abraham Lincoln is whether he was first and foremost an idealist committed to the freeing of the enslaved or a pragmatist committed to preserving the Union.

6. What preceded the Big Bang that formed the universe is, for now, beyond the scope of human comprehension, but three intriguing ideas are at the fore of current thinking.

7. The most important educational reform would be a shift from rote exposition of information to the development of critical thinking skills.

8. The realization that a virus fatal to livestock and other ungulates was at the core of the enduring mystery regarding the uniform age structure of the great stands of acacia trees in Africa epitomizes the interdisciplinary sleuthing required to solve such ecological puzzles.

3

9. The primary questions regarding Universal Basic Income proposals are how long until automation in the workplace throughout all sectors of the economy makes it an absolute necessity, and how much societal upheaval must ensue before it becomes politically palatable.

10. Unlike nihilism, to which it is often compared, anarchism would not inevitably lead to a breakdown of civil society, even if it were to become the predominant ideology of humanity.

11. Though it receives relatively little attention and is primarily viewed as an aesthetic issue, the massive tonnage of plastics discharged into the oceans is probably the greatest threat, including climate change, to the survival of marine mammals, most of which were only recently on the brink of extinction due to intensive harvesting for oil and fur.

12. Though it is currently in vogue to proclaim Nikola Tesla the true genius in the early study of electricity and Thomas Edison a usurper of that genius, there are valid reasons why Edison initially was viewed as the superior inventor and still should be considered as such.

13. The Rorschach Test, once lauded and then roundly criticized, is enjoying a minor resurgence with some psychologists, but one that is sure to be short-lived.

14. There is no simple answer as to whether it is better to buy or rent in the vast majority of regional housing markets throughout the United States in the current economic climate.

15. As human society and technology continue to evolve at an exponentially increasing rate, Strict Constructionism as a philosophy for guiding application of the Constitution to modern legal disputes grows increasingly impractical.

16. While there are a multitude of beliefs as to the ostensible purpose of Daylight Saving Time, the only thing about Daylight Saving Time that can be known for certain is that it is time to get rid of this antiquated practice.

17. Paradoxically, global "warming," properly known as climate change, could usher in an era of extreme cold weather to northern Europe because it appears to be shutting down the Gulf Stream—an ocean current that continually funnels warm water from the Caribbean toward England resulting in much warmer average temperatures in northern Europe than would be expected based on its latitude alone.

18. How is it that the United States Treasury continues to mint new pennies each year?

19. The federal judiciary's extremely broad reading of the Constitution's Commerce Clause has had a profound role in shaping American life well beyond matters of pure commerce.

20. The most likely explanation for the persistence of high rates of homelessness in a country with vast wealth and highly advanced technological capabilities is either an inherent defect in the political system or a complete failure of human spirit.

Answers

Note: Your outlines will differ from ours. That's okay! Use our examples to get familiar with common structures, not worrying whether you got this "right."

1.
Paragraph 1—Introduction to Newtonian vs. quantum physics

Paragraph 2—Description of popular belief toward quantum physics

Paragraph 3—Explanation of why it's not actually difficult to understand

Paragraph 4—Information about how most people understand it when explained to them

2.
Paragraph 1—Outline of current spending programs at universities

Paragraph 2—Arguments that schools are spending too much

Paragraph 3—Arguments that schools are spending an appropriate amount

Paragraph 4—The author's argument that schools should spend more for various reasons

3.
Paragraph 1—Background biographical information on Chaplin

Paragraph 2—Author's characterization of the views of those dismissing Chaplin

Paragraph 3—Author's refutation of views of critics of Chaplin

Paragraph 4—Author extolling the virtues of Chaplin

4.
Paragraph 1—A brief focus on Jefferson's devotion to science, etc.

(The discovery and its implications are the likely focus of this passage, not Jefferson)

Paragraph 2—Discussion of the prior state of knowledge regarding global mean sea levels

Paragraph 3—What Jefferson did that led to advancement of knowledge on mean sea levels

Paragraph 4—The advancements in surveying and cartography spurred by this discovery

5.
Paragraph 1—Background on Lincoln

Paragraph 2—Lincoln as idealist

Paragraph 3—Lincoln as pragmatist

Paragraph 4—Author view (neutral, favoring one view, or arguing a combination of both)

6.
Paragraph 1—Information regarding the formation of the universe and Idea 1

Paragraph 2—Idea 2

Paragraph 3—Idea 3

Paragraph 4—Author's view on ideas

3

7.

Paragraph 1—Inadequacies of current approach

Paragraph 2—Benefits of proposed shift

Paragraph 3—Potential counter argument and rebuttal

Paragraph 4—How to accomplish the proposed shift; potential obstacles and how to overcome them

(*Author directly making a claim/recommendation/ judgment right off the bat is often comforting but this statement leaves a lot open as to how the author will structure the supporting evidence; even more than for the other examples, it is to be expected that your proposed structure might look very different than this one.*)

8.

Paragraph 1—Background on the observation regarding uniform age of acacias in Africa

Paragraph 2—Some history on dead ends in trying to solve the mystery

Paragraph 3—How the virus is responsible

Paragraph 4—How the virus connection was discovered, and likely an author plug for more such interdisciplinary investigations

9.

Paragraph 1—Define Universal Basic Income

Paragraph 2—Explain how automation in the workplace will make it a necessity

Paragraph 3—Discuss why it is politically unpalatable

Paragraph 4—Discuss the societal upheaval the author anticipates and likely some recommendations for how to minimize it and facilitate the implementation of a Universal Basic Income

10.

Paragraph 1—Definitions and history of nihilistic and anarchistic ideologies

Paragraph 2—Compare and contrast the two ideologies, particularly as they relate to the potential to result in breakdown of civil society

Paragraph 3—Explain why nihilism as a dominant ideology would inevitably result in the breakdown of civil society

Paragraph 4—Explain why anarchism would not

11.

Paragraph 1—History of marine mammal harvesting and current population status

Paragraph 2—Survey of various current threats to marine mammals

Paragraph 3—Details regarding discharge of plastics into the ocean

Paragraph 4—How plastics impact marine mammals, why greatest threat, and proposed solutions, if any

12.

Paragraph 1—Background on the work of Edison and Tesla

Paragraph 2—Explanation for Edison getting early credit

Paragraph 3—View of those now asserting that Tesla deserves more credit

Paragraph 4—Author's argument that Edison is the superior inventor

13.

Paragraph 1—Description of the Rorschach Test and reasons it was once widely used

Paragraph 2—Views of critics

Paragraph 3—Explanation of its resurgent use

Paragraph 4—Author's argument for why resurgence will be short-lived

14.
Paragraph 1—Compare/contrast pros and cons of buying and renting

Paragraph 2—Analysis and examples of how such comparison might vary in different housing markets

Paragraph 3—Description of how current economic climate makes the calculus different than in the past

Paragraph 4—Compare/contrast claims of others as to whether it is better to buy or rent

15.
Paragraph 1—Define Strict Constructionism

Paragraph 2—Explain how changes in society and technology affect the practicality of relying on it

Paragraph 3—Examples of modern legal issues that illustrate the challenges of applying Strict Constructionism

Paragraph 4—Identification of a potentially valid factor for continuing to apply Strict Constructionism, rebuttal, and summary of argument for abandoning Strict Constructionism

16.
Paragraph 1—Discussion of beliefs about Daylight Savings Time

Paragraph 2—Rebuttal of various potential benefits of it

Paragraph 3—Claims regarding costs or harms of it

Paragraph 4—Balancing of pros and cons, with conclusion to get rid of it

17.
Paragraph 1—Description of the Gulf Stream and how it moderates weather in northern Europe

Paragraph 2—Discussion of evidence that Gulf Stream is shutting down

Paragraph 3—Implications for weather in northern Europe

Paragraph 4—Prediction of effects of changing weather pattern on people and environment in northern Europe

18.
Paragraph 1—Reasons pennies are not necessary/important/useful

Paragraph 2—Historical reasons for minting pennies

Paragraph 3—Why those reasons are outdated

Paragraph 4—More reasons we shouldn't keep minting pennies

(*Occasionally, a Reading Comprehension passage author will express the main idea as a question that the rest of passage is designed to answer*).

19.
Paragraph 1—Introductory information on the Commerce Clause

Paragraph 2—Explanation of how judicial interpretation has been broader than it might have been

Paragraph 3—Reasons for the broad interpretation

Paragraph 4—Examples of impact of broad interpretation

20.
Paragraph 1—Description of the current levels of homelessness and comparisons to the past

Paragraph 2—Other proposed explanations and their rebuttals

Paragraph 3—Explanation of the type of defect in the political system the author's believes could be responsible

Paragraph 4—Explanation of what the author means by a complete failure of human spirit and how it could be responsible; potentially author judgment regarding which of the two is more likely or more significant

Drill 32: Vocab Lab #3 – Match the Nouns

Instructions: The LSAT nouns in the first set below all end in *-ion*, indicating an action or a result. In the second set, they all end in *-ity*, indicating a quality.

In each set, match the words to their definitions.

Set A

1. Allegation -m
2. Coalition - G
3. Contention - B
4. Evasion - I
5. Fragmentation - A
6. Nullification - F
7. Overestimation - K
8. Pretension - E
9. Prevarication - C
10. Procession - H
11. Protrusion - N
12. Reiteration - D
13. Rendition - J
14. Retention - O
15. Supposition - L

a. the process of being broken into smaller pieces
b. an assertion
c. a lie; a deviation from the truth
d. the act of restating or repeating something for emphasis or clarity
e. a claim or an attempt to establish a claim, often doubtfully
f. the process of eliminating any legal or binding force
g. an alliance or union joining together for action
h. a group moving forward in an orderly way, likely for a ceremony of some sort
i. avoidance; the act of dodging something
j. the performance of a dramatic role or musical piece
k. the act of judging or approximating something too highly
l. hypothesis, conjecture, a belief formed without certainty
m. a claim for which proof has not yet been provided
n. something that sticks out
o. the act of keeping possession or use of something

Set B

16. Acuity - B
17. Affinity - D
18. Ambiguity - G
19. Animosity - E
20. Civility - F
21. Commonality - C
22. Domesticity - O
23. Fallibility - H
24. Feasibility - J
25. Multiplicity - K
26. Plasticity - L
27. Precocity - m
28. Propensity - A
29. Veracity - I
30. Virtuosity - N

a. tendency to act a certain way
b. keenness in perception or hearing
c. a shared feature or characteristic
d. a natural liking or feeling of kinship toward someone or something
e. hostility
f. polite or courteous behavior
g. lack of clarity, openness to interpretation in more than one way
h. inclination to make mistakes
i. habitual adherence to truth; accuracy
j. capability of being carried out or easily done
k. a large number; a big variety
l. ability to be easily shaped or molded
m. mental development that is achieved abnormally early
n. great skill, aptitude, or mastery within the fine arts
o. life at home and/or with family

Answers follow on the next page.

Answers

Set A

1. m

Allegation = a claim for which proof has not yet been provided. A good word to bring to law school. The *leg-* core came from the same root as *litigation*, but semantic twists occurred along the way to arrive at the current meaning.

2. g

Coalition = an alliance or union joining together for action. There is always a temporary sense about the term *coalition*; right after the action in question, the components of the *coalition* will likely disband.

3. b

Contention = an assertion. *Contention* has a variety of meanings, but on the LSAT it is most commonly used to express an assertion made as part of an argument. However, it can also mean an area of disagreement between parties, e.g., a *point of contention*.

4. i

Evasion = avoidance; the act of dodging something. Infamous gangster Al Capone was eventually caught for the nontrivial crime of tax *evasion*.

5. a

Fragmentation = the process of being broken into smaller pieces, i.e., *fragments*. Since *fragment* can also be a verb, it makes sense that you can make this action noun out of it.

6. f

Nullification = the process of eliminating any legal or binding force. According to the theory of *jury nullification*, juries are said to be able to vote a defendant not guilty of a crime as an act of protest against the classification of the crime or the severity of the punishment, essentially *nullifying* the law.

7. k

Overestimation = the act of judging or approximating something too highly. *Estimate* = assess, judge, value, and the prefix *over-* does what it says on the package: you go over, or overshoot.

8. e

Pretension = a claim or an attempt to establish one, often doubtfully. *Pretension* can also mean "aspiration that falls short" or "*pretentiousness*, being stuck up."

9. c

Prevarication = a lie; a deviation from the truth. Ultimately from a Latin word meaning "walk crookedly, in a bowlegged fashion."

10. h

Procession = a group moving forward in an orderly way, likely for a ceremony of some sort. The phrase *in procession* means "in an orderly sequence," whether the objects in question are actually people in a ceremony or not.

11. n

Protrusion = something that sticks out. *Protrusion* can also indicate the act itself of *protruding* something, or of something *protruding* on its own.

12. d

Reiteration = the act of restating or repeating something for emphasis or clarity. Telling someone that you'd like to repeat a point may come across as condescending or aggressive. But if you tell that person that you'd like to *reiterate* a point, the medicine will go down more smoothly.

13. j

Rendition = the performance of a dramatic role or musical piece. Just as the underlying verb *render* has a variety of meanings, so too does *rendition*, which can also mean "a surrender of something" or "a translation."

14. o

Retention = the act of keeping possession or use of something. That is, *retention* is the action noun derived from the verb *retain*.

15. l

Supposition = hypothesis; conjecture; a belief formed without certainty. *Supposition* is the act or result of *supposing*.

Set B

16. b

Acuity = keenness in perception or hearing. *Acuity* is the quality of being *acute*.

17. d

Affinity = a natural liking or feeling of kinship toward someone or something. Interestingly, the underlying Latin adjective didn't make it into English, so there's no modern adjective that corresponds etymologically to the idea of having an *affinity* for something.

18. g

Ambiguity = lack of clarity; openness to interpretation in more than one way; the state of being *ambiguous*. The root *ambi-* means "both" in Latin.

19. e

Animosity = hostility. Unlike *hostility*, however, which can be parsed as "the state of being hostile," the word *animosity* doesn't break down into "the state of being … *animous*." However, one can feel *animus* (no "o") toward something, which is the same thing as *animosity*.

20. f

Civility = polite or courteous behavior; the state of being *civil* (not in the legal sense, but in the nice and *civilized* sense).

21. c

Commonality = a shared feature or characteristic; something that is in *common*. Communities may have many or few *commonalities*.

22. o

Domesticity = life at home and/or with family, or the quality of being domestic. From Latin *domus* (= house), which gave rise to *domicile, dominion,* and a host of other words.

23. h

Fallibility = inclination to make mistakes; the quality of being *fallible*. Speaking formally *ex cathedra* (= from the chair), the Pope is believed by Catholics to be *infallible,* a belief first defined formally in 1870.

24. j

Feasibility = capability of being carried out or easily done, the quality of being *feasible*.

25. k

Multiplicity = a large number; a big variety. This noun is derived from the adjective *multiple*, but the noun goes bigger. Compare "I have *multiple* friends" (= more than one) with "I have a *multiplicity* of friends" (= now you're bragging and probably wrong).

26. l

Plasticity = ability to be easily shaped or molded. The noun form *plasticity* has not deviated as much from its original meaning as the underlying adjective *plastic* has, which originally only meant "moldable." Since the successful launch of *plastic*, moldable materials a century ago, the word *plastic* became a noun, and the adjective form added the sense of "synthetic, artificial, glossy like *plastic*."

27. m

Precocity = mental development that is achieved abnormally early; the quality of being *precocious*, which may be both a blessing and a curse.

28. a

Propensity = tendency to act a certain way; a disposition toward or in favor of something. As with *affinity* and *animosity*, no adjective form of *propensity* survived into modern English. So if you have an affinity for chocolate, then you might have a *propensity* to eat it, as well as an animosity toward people who might take it away from you.

29. i

Veracity = habitual adherence to truth; accuracy. *Veracity* can also mean "a truth" itself. The adjective form is *veracious*, not be confused with voracious, which is more applicable to the propensity to each chocolate than to the strict adherence to truth.

30. n

Virtuosity = great skill, aptitude, or mastery within the fine arts. In other words, *virtuosity* is the quality of being a *virtuoso* (= master of an art), from Italian.

Drill 33: Vocab Lab #4 – Match the Adjectives

Instructions: The LSAT adjectives in the first set below all end in *-al* or *-le*. In the second set, they all end in *-ic* or *-ive*. In each set, match the words to their definitions.

Set A

1. Aboriginal – G
2. Archetypal – L
3. Canonical – E
4. Dialectical – M
5. Fundamental – C
6. Hierarchical – A
7. Inviolable – I
8. Irreducible – O
9. Nominal – F
10. Pedagogical – H
11. Peripheral – N
12. Proportional – D

13. Trivial – K
14. Unfathomable – J
15. Viable – B

a. arranged by rank
b. capable of functioning successfully
c. essential to structure or function
d. corresponding in size or degree
e. conforming to accepted rule or orthodox procedures
f. existing in name form only
g. first of its kind to inhabit a land or region
h. having to do with teaching or instruction
i. incapable of being broken, dishonored, or breached
j. incomprehensible; incapable of being fully understood
k. insignificant, unimportant, of little value
l. original type in which all those of the same type are modeled after; representative of a certain type of person or thing
m. related to discussion and reasoning via dialogue
n. relating to the edge or boundary, e.g., of the field of vision
o. unable to diminish or to put in simpler form

Set B

16. Aesthetic – K
17. Archaic – F
18. Conducive – H
19. Corrosive – C
20. Counterintuitive – O
21. Erratic – B
22. Idiosyncratic – D
23. Idyllic – I
24. Imperative – E
25. Irrespective – L
26. Lucrative – A
27. Pragmatic – G
28. Prohibitive – N
29. Putative – J
30. Successive – M

a. profitable
b. inconsistent, wandering, having no fixed course
c. causing to wear away, destructive
d. peculiar, distinctive, individualistic
e. crucial, critical, vital
f. very old, out of date
g. dealing with actual facts and reality
h. promoting or assisting; helping make something possible
i. pleasant in a natural, simple way
j. generally regarded as such
k. concerning the appreciation of beauty or good taste
l. regardless of, without considering
m. consecutive, following after
n. forbidding, preventing
o. contrary to what instinct or common sense would lead one to expect

3

Answers follow on the next page.

Answers

Set A

1. g

Aboriginal = first of its kind to inhabit a land or region. If you are specifically referring to the *Aboriginal* peoples of Australia, then you should capitalize the adjective.

2. l

Archetypal = original type which all those of the same type are modeled after; representative of a certain type of person or thing. In the psychological theories of Carl Jung, an *archetype* is a powerful subconscious pattern inherited by all individuals in a group. However, you can generally use *archetype* and *archetypal* more broadly without fear of misinterpretation.

3. e

Canonical = conforming to accepted rule or orthodox procedures. The original meaning was "according to canon," the law of the Catholic Church. But just as *canon* can now mean "an accepted body of principles" in many other contexts, so too has the meaning of *canonical* broadened.

4. m

Dialectical = related to discussion and reasoning via dialogue, i.e., via a dialectic. There are various more technical definitions, which you can avoid unless you're deep in a philosophical powwow.

5. c

Fundamental = essential to structure or function. The word is also commonly used as a plural noun: *the fundamentals* = the basic foundations of a field.

6. a

Hierarchical = arranged by rank. The words *hierarchy* and *hierarchical* come from the Greek roots *hier-* (= sacred, holy) and *arkh-* (= rule, govern).

7. i

Inviolable = incapable of being broken, dishonored, or breached. Something *inviolable* cannot (or should not) be *violated*.

8. o

Irreducible = unable to diminish or to put in simpler form. That is, *irreducible* = unable to be *reduced*.

9. f

Nominal = existing in name form only, in contrast to an underlying reality. Alternatively, something *nominal* may be real but small and insignificant.

10. h

Pedagogical = having to do with teaching or instruction. In ancient Greece, a *pedagogue* was someone who led children to school. *Ped-* (= child) + *agogos* (= leader).

11. n

Peripheral = relating to the edge or boundary, e.g., of the field of vision. *Peripheral* and its noun form *periphery* come from Greek roots *peri-* (= around) and *pher-* (= carry).

12. d

Proportional = corresponding in size or degree. Two things that are *proportional* are in *proportion*: they have a sensible correspondence according to an important measure.

13. k

Trivial = insignificant; unimportant; of little value. The original Latin word *trivium* meant "crossroads, where three roads meet": *tri-* (= three) + *via* (= road, way), and thus *trivialis* meant "of the streets, common." The word *trivium* also came to be applied to the first three classical liberal arts: grammar, rhetoric, and logic.

14. j

Unfathomable = incomprehensible; incapable of being fully understood. In Old English, *faethm* meant "the width of the outstretched arms." So you can't *fathom*, or get your arms around, something *unfathomable*.

15. b

Viable = capable of functioning successfully. From French *vie* = life. Something *viable* is able to live.

Set B

16. k

Aesthetic = concerning the appreciation of beauty or good taste. *Aesthetic* is one of the very few words beginning with *ae-* that survive in common modern usage.

17. f

Archaic = very old; out of date. *Archaic* and *archaeology* both come from the same Greek root *arkhe-* (= beginning).

18. h

Conducive = promoting or assisting; helping make something possible. The rarer verb form *conduce* means "lead to a result," usually a good one.

19. c

Corrosive = causing to wear away; destructive; tending to *corrode*. Think saltwater on exposed iron, rusting it away.

20. o

Counterintuitive = contrary to what instinct or common sense would lead one to expect. That is, it's *counter* to, or against, *intuition*.

21. b

Erratic = inconsistent; wandering; having no fixed course. The Latin verb *errare* meant either "wander" or "make a mistake." *Erratic* and *errant* both stayed closer to the "wander" side, while *err, error,* etc. wandered over to the "mistake" side.

22. d

Idiosyncratic = peculiar; distinctive; individualistic. Just remember the *idio-* prefix, which means "one's own, personal, private." The original meaning of *idiot* was "private person," which morphed into "uneducated person" and worse.

23. i

Idyllic = pleasant in a natural, simple way. Alfred Lord Tennyson wrote a long cycle of narrative poems about King Arthur, titled *Idylls of the King*.

24. e

Imperative = crucial; critical, vital. From the same Latin root *imperare* (= command) as *emperor* and *empire*.

25. l

Irrespective = regardless of; without considering. Avoid saying or writing *irregardless*, a confusion of *regardless* and *irrespective*, unless in jest.

26. a

Lucrative = profitable. In Latin, *lucrum* meant "profit, gain." Its modern descendant, *lucre*, is mostly used tongue in cheek, as in *filthy lucre*.

27. g

Pragmatic = dealing with actual facts and reality. *Pragmatism* is the principle of taking such practical approaches. *Pragmatic* and *practical* are near-synonyms, but they took different routes from ancient Greek to modern English.

28. n

Prohibitive = forbidding; preventing. If a sports car has a *prohibitive* cost, you are in essence *prohibited* from buying it.

29. j

Putative = generally regarded as such; supposed; presumed; assumed; ostensible. *Putative* is an even fancier word than these synonyms, but *prima facie* (= on the face) takes the whole fancy cake.

30. m

Successive = consecutive; following after or next. This word draws on what was originally the primary meaning of *succeed*, that is, "follow after."

3

UNIT TWO

LSAT Core Skills

CHAPTER 4

Logical Reasoning, The 4-Step Process

In This Chapter, We Will Cover:

- Step 1 – ID Your Task

- Step 2 – Work the Stimulus

- Step 3 – Anticipate an Answer

- Step 4 – Answer Choice Analysis

Step 1 – ID Your Task

Before you tackle the stimulus of an LR question, we recommend that you first read the question stem. That way, you know the task of the question and can tailor your approach to the stimulus accordingly. For some types of questions, you'll need to break down an argument. For others, you'll need to break down *and* debate an argument. For others still, there's no argument at all! Knowing your task from the outset will give you confidence approaching the stimulus and can help ensure that you don't do any extraneous work. That's why ID'ing Your Task is Step 1 of our 4-Step Process for Logical Reasoning.

In this section, you will learn to:

Match Question Types to Question Stems

Match Principle Questions to Their Primary Tasks

Use the Question Task to Guide Answer Analysis

4

Drill 34: Stem the Tide, Round 1

Instructions: The first step in any LR question is to read the question stem and identify the question type. It might feel counterintuitive to read the stem before the stimulus that precedes it, but there is good reason to do so. The stem communicates the task of the question, and that should impact how you read the stimulus. The stem will tell you whether you should be looking for a conclusion or whether the stimulus is just going to be a set of facts. If you *are* looking at an argument, the stem will tell you whether you need to assess its validity or not. Knowing what you need to do is the foundation of an effective process, and doing only what you need to do is the foundation of an efficient process, so mastering the art of question type identification can pay big dividends in the realms of both accuracy and speed. This drill is the first step toward that level of mastery, and there will be more to come, because this is a skill that is worth a lot of practice!

For this drill, we tell you the question stem and you tell us the question type! The 18 major question types are as follows: ID the Conclusion, Determine the Function, Procedure, ID the (Dis)agreement, Sufficient Assumption, Necessary Assumption, ID the Flaw, Strengthen, Weaken, Evaluate, Principle Support, Must Be True, Must Be False, Most Strongly Supported, Principle Example, Match the Reasoning, Match the Flaw, Explain a Result.

1. Which of the following is an assumption on which the argument depends?

   _____

2. Which of the following most accurately expresses the conclusion of the argument?

   _____

3. The essayist's argument proceeds by

   _____

4. Marita and Hassan's statements provide the most support for concluding that they disagree over which one of the following?

   _____

5. Which one of the following, if true, most weakens the argument?

   _____

6. Which one of the following is an assumption the argument requires?

   _____

7. Which of the following judgments conforms most closely to the principles cited above?

   _____

8. Which one of the following is an assumption on which the argument depends?

   _____

9. Which of the following principles, if valid, most helps to justify the reasoning above?

   _____

10. Which one of the following statements is most supported by the information above?

    _____

11. Which one of the following most accurately describes the role played in the argument by the claim that increasing global carbon dioxide emissions are correlated with increasing average global temperatures?

    _____

12. Which of the following arguments is most similar in its pattern of reasoning to the argument above?

    _____

13. If the statements above are true, which one of the following must also be true?

    _____

14. Which one of the following, if true, most helps to resolve the apparent paradox described above?

_____

15. The flawed pattern of reasoning exhibited by which one of the following is most similar to that exhibited by the argument above?

_____

16. Which one of the following most accurately expresses a flaw in the reasoning of the ethnologist's argument?

_____

17. Which of the following, if true, most strengthens the argument?

_____

18. Which one of the following most accurately describes the technique of reasoning employed by the critic?

_____

19. Which one of the following, if true, most strongly supports the reasoning in the argument above?

_____

20. The information above, if true, most strongly supports which one of the following?

_____

21. The argument is most vulnerable to criticism on the grounds that the argument

_____

22. Which one of the following identifies a reasoning error in the argument?

_____

23. Which one of the following, if true, most strengthens the argument?

_____

24. The reasoning in the argument is most vulnerable to criticism because the argument

_____

25. Which one of the following can be properly inferred from the company president's statements?

_____

Answers follow on the next page.

Answers

1. Necessary Assumption
2. ID the Conclusion
3. Procedure
4. ID the (Dis)agreement
5. Weaken
6. Necessary Assumption
7. Principle Example
8. Necessary Assumption
9. Principle Support
10. Most Strongly Supported
11. Determine the Function
12. Match the Reasoning
13. Must Be True

14. Explain a Result
15. Match the Flaw
16. ID the Flaw
17. Strengthen
18. Procedure
19. Strengthen
20. Most Strongly Supported
21. ID the Flaw
22. ID the Flaw
23. Strengthen
24. ID the Flaw
25. Must Be True

4

Drill 35: Standing on Principle

Instructions: The word "principle" gets thrown around a lot in LR question stems. So much, in fact, that you might think it's a type of question. But actually, "principle" is more a flavor than a question type. A principle question that asks you to support the argument is just a different flavor of Strengthen question. A principle question that asks you to exemplify a principle is a just a different flavor of Most Strongly Supported question—one that asks which argument must be valid if the principle given is true. There can be principle Matching questions, principle Assumption questions, and even principle Weaken questions. For this drill, consider each of the following principle question stems and categorize it by the broader question type to which it belongs.

1. The principle underlying the argument above is most similar to the principle underlying which one of the following?

   _____

2. Which one of the following principles, if valid, would most help to justify Carina's decision?

   _____

3. Which one of the following generalizations does the situation described above most clearly illustrate?

   _____

4. The principles cited by the ethicist most help to justify the reasoning in which one of the following?

   _____

5. Which one of the following propositions is best illustrated by the statements above?

   _____

6. The principle stated above, if valid, most helps to justify the reasoning in which one of the following arguments?

   _____

7. The engineer's argument can most reasonably be interpreted as invoking which one of the following principles?

   _____

8. Which one of the following principles, if valid, most helps to justify the politician's criticism?

   _____

9. Each of the following is supported by the principle above EXCEPT:

   _____

10. Which one of the following conforms most closely to the principle illustrated above?

    _____

11. Which one of the following principles, if valid, most helps to justify the reasoning above?

    _____

12. Each of the following conforms to the principle illustrated above EXCEPT:

    _____

13. The situation described above conforms most closely to which one of the following generalizations?

    _____

14. The argument requires assuming which one of the following principles?

    _____

15. Which one of the following is a principle that, if valid, most helps to justify the restaurant critic's reasoning?

    _____

16. The claims made above are incompatible with which one of the following generalizations?

    _____

17. Which of the following best illustrates the principle underlying the reasoning above?

_____

18. Which one of the following most accurately expresses the principle underlying the reasoning above?

_____

19. Which one of the following principles, if valid, most helps to justify the business owner's argument?

_____

20. Which one of the following judgments conforms to the principle illustrated above?

_____

4

Answers follow on the next page.

Answers

1.	Match the Reasoning	11.	Strengthen
2.	Strengthen	12.	Match the Reasoning (EXCEPT)
3.	Most Strongly Supported	13.	Most Strongly Supported
4.	Most Strongly Supported	14.	Necessary Assumption
5.	Strengthen	15.	Strengthen
6.	Most Strongly Supported	16.	Must Be False
7.	Strengthen	17.	Match the Reasoning
8.	Strengthen	18.	Strengthen
9.	Most Strongly Supported (EXCEPT)	19.	Strengthen
10.	Match the Reasoning	20.	Match the Reasoning

4

Drill 36: Talking to Yourself, Select the Question Edition

Instructions: We all know that the key to efficiency is to do only what you need to do and nothing that you don't. What is often overlooked, though, is how much this can improve your accuracy. A laser-like focus on only the task at hand can make otherwise tricky eliminations a breeze. This drill is about honing that focus and canceling out the noise.

Ten question stems will be provided. For each, a series of questions follows. These are questions that test takers might ask themselves as they evaluate an answer choice. Mark Y for the ones that focus on the right things and N for the the ones that don't.

Which of the following, if true, allows the conclusion to be properly drawn?

_____ 1. Does the argument need this to be true in order to work?

_____ 2. Does this answer address the new concept in the conclusion?

_____ 3. Does this seem true, based on the argument?

_____ 4. If this isn't true, does the argument fall apart?

_____ 5. Is this the reverse of what I'm looking for?

_____ 6. Does this make the argument airtight?

_____ 7. If this is true, does it make the argument better?

_____ 8. Is this the contrapositive of my prephrase?

Which of the following is an assumption on which the argument depends?

_____ 9. Does the argument need this to be true in order to work?

_____ 10. Does this answer seem too weakly worded?

_____ 11. Is this just about the evidence or does it relate to the conclusion?

_____ 12. If this isn't true, does the argument fall apart?

_____ 13. Is this a reversal or negation of the author's thinking?

_____ 14. Does this make the argument airtight?

_____ 15. If this is true, does it make the argument better?

_____ 16. Does this answer seem too strongly worded?

Which of the following, if true, most helps to resolve the apparent discrepancy?

_____ 17. Does this address a gap between the evidence and the conclusion?

_____ 18. Is this explanation bulletproof?

_____ 19. Does this answer actually exacerbate the discrepancy?

_____ 20. Does this answer provide a new distinction?

_____ 21. Is this answer too strong or too weird of an idea?

_____ 22. Does this answer provide a potential way to explain the surprise?

_____ 23. Is this answer only talking about the background condition?

_____ 24. Is this answer something I can basically prove using only the provided text?

Which of the following best expresses the main conclusion of the argument?

_____ 25. Was this idea ever mentioned in the argument?

_____ 26. Is there a flaw with drawing this conclusion from that evidence?

_____ 27. Do I just like this answer because it's the last claim of the paragraph?

_____ 28. Given all the author said, would she probably believe this claim too?

_____ 29. Is it possible that this is an intermediate conclusion?

_____ 30. Did the author give me any supporting reason why I should believe this claim?

_____ 31. What is the author assuming in drawing this conclusion?

_____ 32. Is this answer choice equivalent in meaning to the author's explicit conclusion?

Which one of the following is most supported by the statements above?

_____ 33. If this idea were true, would it make the argument more plausible?

_____ 34. To support this idea, would I need to combine multiple facts?

_____ 35. Does this answer tie the whole stimulus together?

_____ 36. Is any word in this answer stronger than what was said in the paragraph?

_____ 37. If I were to negate this idea, would the paragraph fall apart?

_____ 38. Is this the most provable answer I can find?

_____ 39. Is this the most interesting inference I can derive from these facts?

_____ 40. Is this testing one of the famous flaws?

Which one of the following contains the most similar reasoning to the argument above?

_____ 41. Does this argument have the same number of premises as the original argument?

_____ 42. What assumptions are being made by this argument?

_____ 43. Should I look at the conclusion before I bother reading the rest of this answer choice?

_____ 44. Is this answer presenting its ingredients in the same order as the original argument?

_____ 45. Do I like this only because it has a similar topic to the original?

_____ 46. Does this answer reuse any specific words from the original argument?

_____ 47. This answer definitely works. Can I pick it and move on?

_____ 48. Is this valid logic or flawed logic?

Which one of the following, if true, most undermines the argument?

_____ 49. Does this answer have much punching power or is it weakly worded?

_____ 50. With this answer, can I successfully refute the author's conclusion?

_____ 51. Does this answer neutralize or outweigh the value of the author's evidence?

_____ 52. Should I disqualify this answer since I would need to add common sense to make it work?

_____ 53. Is this answer an illegal reversal of what I wanted?

_____ 54. Does this answer contradict one of the premises?

_____ 55. Is this answer unlikely to be true in the real world?

_____ 56. If I were the lawyer arguing *against* the author's conclusion, would this be a smart thing to say?

Which one of the following principles, if valid, does most to justify the argument?

_____ 57. If this answer weren't true, would the argument fall apart?

_____ 58. Is this answer an illegal reversal or negation of the argument core?

_____ 59. Is this answer stronger or broader than it should be?

_____ 60. Does this answer choice guarantee the truth of the conclusion?

_____ 61. Can I match half of this answer to the evidence and half to the conclusion?

_____ 62. Does this answer deal with the new term or concept in the conclusion?

_____ 63. Can I think of counterexamples to this rule?

_____ 64. Does this answer tie together everything in the stimulus?

The reasoning in the argument is most vulnerable to criticism on the grounds that it

_____ 65. Does this answer accurately describe the argument core?

_____ 66. Would this answer strengthen the argument, if true?

_____ 67. Is this describing a famous flaw?

_____ 68. If I were the lawyer arguing *against* the author's conclusion, would this be a smart thing to say?

_____ 69. Does this answer choice relate to an intermediate conclusion?

_____ 70. Would this answer choice weaken the argument, if true?

_____ 71. Is this the reverse of what actually happened?

_____ 72. Can I eliminate this answer because this word is too strong?

Their dialogue provides the most support for the claim that Person 1 and Person 2 disagree over whether

_____ 73. Does this answer accurately describe the argument core?

_____ 74. Does this answer effectively capture the flaw in each person's reasoning?

_____ 75. Can I eliminate this answer, since I don't know what Person 1 would say about this?

_____ 76. Would this answer be an effective rebuttal for Person 1?

_____ 77. Can I infer whether Person 2 would agree or disagree with this?

_____ 78. Can I find a spot in each person's statements where this idea is addressed?

_____ 79. If I negated this idea, would it hurt either person's argument?

_____ 80. Is this so strongly worded that neither person would agree to it?

4

Answers

Which of the following, if true, allows the conclusion to be properly drawn?

__N__ 1. Does the argument need this to be true in order to work?

__Y__ 2. **Does this answer address the new concept in the conclusion?**

__N__ 3. Does this seem true, based on the argument?

__Y__ 4. **If this isn't true, does the argument fall apart?**

__Y__ 5. **Is this the reverse of what I'm looking for?**

__Y__ 6. **Does this make the argument airtight?**

__N__ 7. If this is true, does it make the argument better?

__Y__ 8. **Is this the contrapositive of my prephrase?**

This is a Sufficient Assumption stem, so you need an answer that makes the argument airtight (6). That means that if there is a new concept in the argument's conclusion, the correct answer has to address it (2). Sufficient Assumption questions are often conditional, so you need to be on the lookout for wrong answer choices that reverse your prephrase (5) and correct answers that contrapose it (8). 1 and 4 are questions you would ask yourself for a Necessary Assumption question, but they won't make or break a Sufficient Assumption answer; a yes wouldn't make you select it, and a no wouldn't make you eliminate it. 7 is what you would ask yourself for a Strengthen question, but asking it about a Sufficient Assumption answer choice doesn't get you very far. 3 is one of the biggest distractions on the LSAT. When your question stem has the phrase "if true" in it, whether the answer seems *likely* to be true is totally irrelevant.

Which of the following is an assumption on which the argument depends?

__Y__ 9. **Does the argument need this to be true in order to work?**

__N__ 10. Does this answer seem too weakly worded?

__Y__ 11. **Is this just about the evidence or does it relate to the conclusion?**

__Y__ 12. **If this isn't true, does the argument fall apart?**

__Y__ 13. **Is this a reversal or negation of the author's thinking?**

__N__ 14. Does this make the argument airtight?

__N__ 15. If this is true, does it make the argument better?

__Y__ 16. **Does this answer seem too strongly worded?**

This is a Necessary Assumption stem, so we're looking for an idea that is embedded in or required by the author's logic (9). Some trap answers only address the evidence (Premise Boosters), whereas we are examining the move from evidence to conclusion (11). We can judge or confirm an answer by submitting it to the Negation Test: "If this idea *weren't true*, would that badly weaken the argument?" (12). Trap answers that are written in conditional form are often just reversals or negations of the author's thinking (13). Other trap answers overstate what the author is assuming by using overly harsh or specific wording (16). We don't have to worry about an answer being too weak (10); if someone is assuming "Bob has at least $40," then they are also assuming "Bob has at least $1." We don't need the answer to guarantee the conclusion (14) as we do with Sufficient Assumption, and we don't want to ask ourselves "if true, does this support the argument?" as we do with Strengthen (16).

Which of the following, if true, most helps to resolve the apparent discrepancy?

__N__ 17. Does this address a gap between the evidence and the conclusion?

__N__ 18. Is this explanation bulletproof?

__Y__ 19. **Does this answer actually exacerbate the discrepancy?**

__Y__ 20. **Does this answer provide a new distinction?**

__N__ 21. Is this answer too strong or too weird of an idea?

__Y__ 22. **Does this answer provide a potential way to explain the surprise?**

__Y__ 23. **Is this answer only talking about the background condition?**

__N__ 24. Is this answer something I can basically prove using only the provided text?

This is an Explain/Resolve question stem. We're not reading an argument (17); we're reading a series of facts that lead to a surprise, and then we're looking for a potential way to account for that surprise (22).

4

The story line that the correct answer hints at doesn't need to be a lock, as 18 suggests; the correct answer just does *the most* to explain the surprise. Correct answers almost always introduce some new distinction (20) (something that has changed or something that is different), whereas answers that just talk about the background (23) aren't helping us to better understand the surprise. Many trap answers *intensify* the paradox (19), making the result more surprising, not less. Since the question stem contains "if true," we never have to worry about an answer being too strong or too exotic a possibility (21), and we need new ideas to explain the surprise, not something we can infer from the facts (24).

Which of the following best expresses the main conclusion of the argument?

_Y_	25.	**Was this idea ever mentioned in the argument?**
_N_	26.	Is there a flaw with drawing this conclusion from that evidence?
_Y_	27.	**Do I just like this answer because it's the last claim of the paragraph?**
_N_	28.	Given all the author said, would she probably believe this claim too?
_Y_	29.	**Is it possible that this is an intermediate conclusion?**
_Y_	30.	**Did the author give me any supporting reason why I should believe this claim?**
_N_	31.	What is the author assuming in drawing this conclusion?
_Y_	32.	**Is this answer choice equivalent in meaning to the author's explicit conclusion?**

This is an ID the Conclusion stem. Our task is to find the conclusion, which for this question type is usually located *earlier* than the supporting evidence. Test writers almost never put the conclusion in the last sentence, but they know people are often attracted to that last claim simply because it is last (27). Other times, an idea toward the end *is* a conclusion, but it's an intermediate conclusion (29). The conclusion is an actual claim that the author made (25 and 32) and supported (30), not a speculation about what *else* the author might say (28). We only need to identify the conclusion, not judge the argument for flaws (26) or assumptions (31).

Which one of the following is most supported by the statements above?

_N_	33.	If this idea were true, would it make the argument more plausible?
_Y_	34.	**To support this idea, would I need to combine multiple facts?**
_N_	35.	Does this answer tie the whole stimulus together?
_Y_	36.	**Is any word in this answer stronger than what was said in the paragraph?**
_N_	37.	If I were to negate this idea, would the paragraph fall apart?
_Y_	38.	**Is this the most provable answer I can find?**
_N_	39.	Is this the most interesting inference I can derive from these facts?
_N_	40.	Is this testing one of the famous flaws?

This is an Inference (Most Strongly Supported) stem. That means there's a 99.9% chance that we are reading facts, not arguments, as 33 and 40 are suggesting. The correct answer will almost always be supported by synthesizing two or more facts from the paragraph (34). It does not need to connect all the facts (35), even though in many cases it will. It also doesn't need to be a particularly interesting inference (39). We're just looking for the most provable answer we can find (38), so strong language is a big red flag (36). After all, it's much easier to prove a weakly worded claim than a strongly worded one. Although negating the correct answer probably *would* feel like it went against the paragraph in some way (37), we only use the Negation Test on Necessary Assumption questions.

Which one of the following contains the most similar reasoning to the argument above?

_Y_	41.	**Does this argument have the same number of premises as the original argument?**
_N_	42.	What assumptions are being made by this argument?
_Y_	43.	**Should I look at the conclusion before I bother reading the rest of this answer choice?**
_N_	44.	Is this answer presenting its ingredients in the same order as the original argument?
_Y_	45.	**Do I like this only because it has a similar topic to the original?**

4

___N___ 46. Does this answer reuse any specific words from the original argument?

___Y___ 47. **This answer definitely works. Can I pick it and move on?**

___Y___ 48. **Is this valid logic or flawed logic?**

This is a Match the Reasoning stem. Our job is to read the original argument and extract from it an abstract logical "recipe." The correct answer will follow that recipe. It will almost always have the same number of premises as the original argument (41). It will also have a conclusion that is of a similar type and degree as the original argument's conclusion, so starting there is an efficient way to eliminate answer choices (43). We don't care in what order we receive these ingredients (44) because only the logical structure needs to match, not the linguistic structure. If the original argument was valid logic, then the correct answer will be as well. If the original was flawed, the correct answer will be also (48). But we don't otherwise have to evaluate the argument for assumptions (42). We need similar logic, not a similar topic or similar words (46), though many trap answers try to lure us in that way (45). If you find an answer that works, take stock of your timing and your level of certainty. If you're short on time and reasonably certain, especially if you have a matching diagram or matching flaw to rely on, you can probably take it and move on (47).

Which one of the following, if true, most undermines the argument?

___Y___ 49. **Does this answer have much punching power or is it weakly worded?**

___N___ 50. With this answer, can I successfully refute the author's conclusion?

___Y___ 51. **Does this answer neutralize or outweigh the value of the author's evidence?**

___N___ 52. Should I disqualify this answer since I would need to add common sense to make it work?

___N___ 53. Is this answer an illegal reversal of what I wanted?

___N___ 54. Does this answer contradict one of the premises?

___N___ 55. Is this answer unlikely to be true in the real world?

___Y___ 56. **If I were the lawyer arguing against the author's conclusion, would this be a smart thing to say?**

This is a Weaken stem. We are looking for an answer that sounds like a potential rebuttal (56), and it usually works by making the author's evidence seem less relevant or less persuasive than the author believed, or by introducing a totally new consideration that might outweigh the author's evidence (51). It would almost never contradict any premise (54), and it does not need to definitively prove the author's conclusion is wrong; it only needs to introduce some doubt (50). We almost never have to worry about conditional logic with Weaken questions (53), and we don't need to analyze whether an answer is too strong or too weird because the stem says "if true" (55). We will often have to supply a little bit of common sense to explain to ourselves why a correct answer is relevant to the conversation (52). We should be wary of weak words and phrases such as "some," "many," and "not all" because these words indicate "at least one/at least a handful," which might not be powerful enough to do any damage to the argument (49).

Which one of the following principles, if valid, does most to justify the argument?

___N___ 57. If this answer weren't true, would the argument fall apart?

___Y___ 58. **Is this answer an illegal reversal or negation of the argument core?**

___N___ 59. Is this answer stronger or broader than it should be?

___N___ 60. Does this answer choice guarantee the truth of the conclusion?

___Y___ 61. **Can I match half of this answer to the evidence and half to the conclusion?**

___Y___ 62. **Does this answer deal with the new term or concept in the conclusion?**

___N___ 63. Can I think of counterexamples to this rule?

___N___ 64. Does this answer tie together everything in the stimulus?

This is a Principle Support stem. Principle Support questions often feel like Sufficient Assumptions, in that for both question types the answer is usually a Bridge Assumption connecting the premise to the conclusion (61) and for both question types any new term or concept in the conclusion will need to be in the correct answer (62). Unlike Sufficient Assumption, however, Principle Support is a task that does not actually require that our answer guarantee the conclusion (60) or that it tie together everything in the paragraph (64) even though it usually does. The answers are offered to us as "if true/if valid," so we don't have worry about whether the answer is necessary (57) or whether it has exceptions in the real world (63). We just evaluate whether we could apply the rule provided in the answer choice to the argument we just read, in order to better draw the conclusion, which makes strength and breadth good characteristics, not bad ones (59). Principles are by definition conditional statements, so we need to be wary of Illegal Reversals and Negations (58) and be receptive to seeing our predicted answer in contrapositive form.

The reasoning in the argument is most vulnerable to criticism on the grounds that it

Y 65. **Does this answer accurately describe the argument core?**

N 66. Would this answer strengthen the argument, if true?

Y 67. **Is this describing a famous flaw?**

Y 68. **If I were the lawyer arguing** against **the author's conclusion, would this be a smart thing to say?**

N 69. Does this answer choice relate to an intermediate conclusion?

Y 70. **Would this answer choice weaken the argument, if true?**

Y 71. **Is this the reverse of what actually happened?**

Y 72. **Can I eliminate this answer because this word is too strong?**

This is a Flaw stem. Our correct answer will be something opposing counsel could say after listening to the author's argument and then saying "Objection!" (68), so you wouldn't want the answer to *strengthen* the author's case (66). About 50% of Flaw questions exhibit one of the famous flaws (67). A flaw can take place between a premise and an intermediate conclusion or an intermediate conclusion and the main one (69), so an answer dealing with the intermediate conclusion isn't grounds for dismissal. Wrong answers often accuse the argument of doing something it didn't, so we need to make sure that what's said in an answer matches the Argument Core (65) while

making sure it describe things backward (71) (e.g., "Parts to Whole" instead of "Whole to Parts"). Lots of answers call out an assumption the author supposedly made, and we can eliminate these if any word in the answer is stronger than what the author needed to assume (72). Many other answers raise a potential objection, but if the objection wouldn't actually weaken the argument (70), it's not a good enough objection to constitute a flaw.

Their dialogue provides the most support for the claim that Person 1 and Person 2 disagree that

N 73. Does this answer accurately describe the argument core?

N 74. Does this answer effectively capture the flaw in each person's reasoning?

Y 75. **Can I eliminate this answer, since I don't know what Person 1 would say about this?**

N 76. Would this answer be an effective rebuttal for Person 1?

Y 77. **Can I infer whether Person 2 would agree or disagree with this?**

Y 78. **Can I find a spot in each person's statements where this idea is addressed?**

N 79. If I negated this idea, would it hurt either person's argument?

Y 80. **Is this so strongly worded that neither person would agree to it?**

This is an ID the (Dis)agreement stem. The two people may or may not make actual arguments (73), and we do not need to judge the merits of their reasoning (74) or look for necessary assumptions (79). We're simply looking for some overlapping issue (78) on which the people offer contrasting claims. The correct answer will be something one person would agree about and the other person would not (77). If we don't know how one of the people would feel about an answer choice, we can eliminate it (75). If the answer is so strong that neither person would agree to it (80) or so weak that neither person would fight it, then we can eliminate it. The answer is just *describing* the source of disagreement, not introducing some new idea that changes the conversation (76).

Drill 37: Stem the Tide, Round 2

Instructions: We tell you the stem, you tell us the type, again! The 18 major question types are as follows: ID the Conclusion, Determine the Function, Procedure, ID the (Dis)agreement, Sufficient Assumption, Necessary Assumption, ID the Flaw, Strengthen, Weaken, Evaluate, Principle Support, Must Be True, Must Be False, Most Strongly Supported, Principle Example, Match the Reasoning, Match the Flaw, Explain a Result.

1. The conclusion of the argument can be properly inferred if which one of the following is assumed?

   _____

2. The situation described above best illustrates which one of the following generalizations?

   _____

3. Each of the following, if true, supports the botanist's argument EXCEPT:

   _____

4. Which one of the following is an assumption required by the surveyor's argument?

   _____

5. Which one of the following, if true, justifies the application of the principle above?

   _____

6. On the basis of their statements, Karina and Brown are committed to disagreeing over the truth of which one of the following statements?

   _____

7. Which one of the following most logically completes the argument?

   _____

8. Which one of the following, if true, most strongly supports the argument above?

   _____

9. The argument's conclusion follows logically if which one of the following is assumed?

   _____

10. The history teacher's statements provide the most support for which one of the following?

    _____

11. The reasoning is most vulnerable to criticism on the grounds that it

    _____

12. The statements above, if true, most strongly support which one of the following?

    _____

13. Which one of the following, if true, most helps to resolve the apparent discrepancy in the information above?

    _____

14. Which one of the following principles, if valid, most helps to justify the reasoning above?

    _____

15. Which one of the following most accurately expresses the conclusion drawn in the consumer advocate's argument?

    _____

16. Which one of the following exhibits flawed reasoning most similar to that exhibited by the argument above?

    _____

17. The reasoning in the argument is flawed in that the argument

    _____

18. Each of the following, if true, weakens the argument EXCEPT:

    _____

19. Which one of the following arguments is most closely parallel in its reasoning to the reasoning in the argument above?

_____

20. Which of the following allows the conclusion of the argument to be properly drawn?

_____

21. The conclusion of the argument logically follows if

_____

22. The conclusion of the argument logically follows only if

_____

23. Which one of the following most accurately expresses the conclusion drawn in the argument?

_____

24. Which one of the following, if true, most strengthens the expert's reasoning?

_____

25. Each of the following, if true, undermines the conclusion of the argument EXCEPT:

_____

4

Answers

1. Sufficient Assumption
2. Principle Support
3. Strengthen (EXCEPT)
4. Necessary Assumption
5. Principle Support
6. ID the (Dis)agreement
7. Most Strongly Supported
8. Strengthen
9. Sufficient Assumption
10. Most Strongly Supported
11. ID the Flaw
12. Most Strongly Supported
13. Explain a Result

14. Principle Support
15. ID the Conclusion
16. Match the Flaw
17. ID the Flaw
18. Weaken (EXCEPT)
19. Match the Reasoning
20. Sufficient Assumption
21. Sufficient Assumption
22. Necessary Assumption
23. ID the Conclusion
24. Strengthen
25. Weaken (EXCEPT)

Drill 38: Vocab Lab #5 – Pick the Definition, Round 1

Instructions: Multiple choice! This batch of LSAT words darts around the alphabet a couple of times. For each word, choose the answer closest in meaning.

1. Acclaim
    - (A) praise
    - (B) demand
    - (C) blame

2. Barter
    - (A) exchange
    - (B) give away
    - (C) persuade

3. Compel
    - (A) support
    - (B) tempt
    - (C) force

4. Deplete
    - (A) hoard
    - (B) use up
    - (C) exclude

5. Frivolous
    - (A) serene
    - (B) ignorant
    - (C) senseless

6. Impetus
    - (A) falling object
    - (B) driving force
    - (C) ulterior motive

7. Norm
    - (A) aberration
    - (B) exception
    - (C) standard

8. Recoup
    - (A) resist
    - (B) renew
    - (C) regain

9. Superfluous
    - (A) excessive
    - (B) steep
    - (C) grandiose

10. Vacuous
    - (A) aware
    - (B) mindless
    - (C) vague

11. Amorphous
    - (A) cowardly
    - (B) shapeless
    - (C) tenacious

12. Contemporaneous
    - (A) occurring at the same time
    - (B) occurring at distinct times
    - (C) occurring throughout history

13. Contiguous
    - (A) endless
    - (B) distant
    - (C) adjoining

14. Erroneous
    - (A) erratic or irregular
    - (B) wrong or false
    - (C) cheap or lousy

4

15. Impervious
    - (A) reprehensible
    - (B) susceptible
    - (C) impenetrable

16. Ingenious
    - (A) inventive
    - (B) inept
    - (C) innate

17. Innocuous
    - (A) damaging
    - (B) harmless
    - (C) foolish

18. Multitudinous
    - (A) confined
    - (B) abundant
    - (C) rebellious

19. Ominous
    - (A) auspicious
    - (B) enigmatic
    - (C) threatening

20. Overzealous
    - (A) too confident
    - (B) too eager
    - (C) too forbearing

21. Rigorous
    - (A) dangerous
    - (B) meticulous
    - (C) tenuous

22. Ruinous
    - (A) destructive
    - (B) trivial
    - (C) revolting

23. Treacherous
    - (A) forthright
    - (B) noxious
    - (C) untrustworthy

24. Vicarious
    - (A) callous
    - (B) secondary
    - (C) causative

25. Voracious
    - (A) insatiable
    - (B) bounteous
    - (C) abstemious

4

Answers follow on the next page.

Answers

1. A

Acclaim = praise, excitedly approve, applaud. *Acclaim* can also be a noun. The Latin root *clamare* means "shout, cry out," which in the word *acclaim* becomes a shout of joy or praise.

2. A

Barter = exchange, trade in goods or services for other goods or services. In its modern definition, *barter* indicates an exchange that lacks money.

3. C

Compel = force, urge a course of action. If you find an activity particularly *compelling*, you might even become a bit *compulsive* about it.

4. B

Deplete = use up, completely or almost completely. *Ego depletion* is a term from social psychology, indicating the exhaustion of mental resources, leading one to make worse decisions.

5. C

Frivolous = senseless, lacking seriousness, excessively carefree. *Frivolous* and *frivolity* came before the verb *frivol*, which is what linguists call a "backformation."

6. B

Impetus = driving force, momentum, impulse. The word is neutral, but it originally meant "attack" or "violence" in Latin.

7. C

Norm = a standard, principle, or average. From the same root as *normal*, as would be *normal* for you to suppose.

8. C

Recoup = regain, make up for. As in, after an injury, or a long night out, it is necessary to rest and *recuperate*.

9. A

Superfluous = excessive, not needed, more than enough. The prefix *super-* means "over," and the root *flu-* means "flow." So the word corresponds well to its Latin components: "overflowing."

10. B

Vacuous = mindless, empty, lack of thought or intelligence. The Latin root of *vacuous* is *vac-*, meaning "empty." *Vac-* shows up in *vacant, vacuity,* and *vacuum.*

11. B

Amorphous = shapeless, without structure. The Greek roots tell the tale. *Morph-* means "form, shape," and, in this case, the prefix *a-* means "without, not."

12. A

Contemporaneous = occurring at the same time (appropriate for describing people or events that are active in the same time period). The Latin root *temp-*, meaning "time," shows up in many English words.

13. C

Contiguous = adjoining, touching, sharing a border. For instance, the *contiguous* United States does not include Hawaii or Alaska, since touching through water or another country doesn't count.

14. B

Erroneous = wrong, false, mistaken. To *err* is human; to be *erroneous* is, also.

15. C

Impervious = impenetrable, not able to be harmed or emotionally disturbed, as in "impervious to criticism." The positive form *pervious* is today very rare, perhaps by taboo confusion with *perversion* and related words. It's fine to call a vapor seal in your crawl space impervious, but don't say to the installer that you don't want the seal to be too pervious.

16. A

Ingenious = inventive, brilliant, clever. It's important to realize that *genius* and *ingenious* are nearly synonyms, not antonyms, as many erroneously believe. Both come from the same root *gen-*, meaning "give birth, create."

17. B

Innocuous = harmless, inoffensive. Both *innocuous* and its cousin *innocent* only really survive with the prefix *in-*, meaning "not." Technically, yes, *nocuous* and *nocent* still skulk around in dictionaries, but no one will know what you mean if you use them.

18. B

Multitudinous = abundant, numerous, existing in great number. *Multitudinous* is the adjective corresponding to *multitude*, famously included in Walt Whitman's lines from *Song of Myself*: "Do I contradict myself? Very well then I contradict myself. (I am large, I contain multitudes.)"

19. C

Ominous = threatening, giving the feeling that something bad is about to happen. *Ominous* comes from *omen*, which was borrowed into English from Latin to mean "a sign of things to come." Omens aren't always bad, but ominous things are.

20. B

Overzealous = too eager in the pursuit of something. *Zealous* and *zeal* by themselves aren't necessarily negative, but they do get right up to the line of acceptable enthusiasm and partisanship. Then *over* flings the word deep past the line into the darkness.

21. B

Rigorous = meticulous, extremely thorough. *Rigor* (outside of *rigor mortis*) and *rigorous* are typically used in a positive sense, but *rigid* is not. Call your friend's organized study plan *rigorous*; don't call your friend *rigid*.

22. A

Ruinous = destructive, harmful, devastating. Just like it says on the box, something *ruinous* causes *ruin*.

23. C

Treacherous = untrustworthy or unfaithful, not dependable, dangerous or deceptive. *Treachery* is betrayal.

24. B

Vicarious = secondary, experienced through imagined participation in another's experience. A *vicarious* thrill is what you get when you see your friend jump into a ravine with a bungee cord tied to his or her legs.

25. A

Voracious = insatiable, having a really big appetite, having an extremely eager approach. The Latin root *vor-*, meaning "devour," is at the core of *devour* itself, as well as *voracity*, and the various *-vorous* words, such as *carnivorous*.

4

Drill 39: Stem the Tide, Round 3

Instructions: We tell you the stem, you tell us the type, again! The 18 major question types are as follows: ID the Conclusion, Determine the Function, Procedure, ID the (Dis)agreement, Sufficient Assumption, Necessary Assumption, ID the Flaw, Strengthen, Weaken, Evaluate, Principle Support, Must Be True, Must Be False, Most Strongly Supported, Principle Example, Match the Reasoning, Match the Flaw, Explain a Result.

1. Each of the following, if true, undermines the conclusion of the argument EXCEPT:

   _____

2. The argument is most vulnerable to criticism on the grounds that it

   _____

3. The dialogue provides the most support for the claim that Naoki and Patek disagree over whether

   _____

4. Which one of the following exhibits flawed reasoning most similar to the flawed reasoning exhibited by the argument above?

   _____

5. Which one of the following, if true, would most strengthen the argument?

   _____

6. Which one of the following, if true, most weakens the architect's argument?

   _____

7. The reasoning in the argument is flawed in that it

   _____

8. The conclusion of the argument can be properly drawn if which one of the following is assumed?

   _____

9. Which one of the following, if true, most helps to explain the findings above?

   _____

10. If the statements above are true, which one of the following must also be true?

    _____

11. Which one of the following, if true, provides the most support for the researchers' hypothesis?

    _____

12. The pattern of reasoning in the argument above is most similar to that in which one of the following arguments?

    _____

13. The argument depends on assuming which one of the following?

    _____

14. Which one of the following is an assumption required by the argument?

    _____

15. Which one of the following most accurately expresses the conclusion of the argument as a whole?

    _____

16. Which one of the following arguments most closely conforms to the principle underlying the reasoning in the analyst's argument?

    _____

17. The reasoning is most vulnerable to the criticism that it takes for granted that

    _____

18. The statement that democracy requires an objective and rigorous media figures in the argument in which one of the following ways?

    _____

19. Which one of the following situations most closely corresponds to the principles of justice described above?

_____

20. The argument is most vulnerable to criticism on the grounds that it overlooks the possibility that

_____

21. Which one of the following principles, if valid, most helps to justify the argumentation?

_____

22. Ito and Harris disagree over whether

_____

23. Which one of the following is an assumption on which the argument depends?

_____

24. Which one of the following, if true, most calls into question the editor's reasoning?

_____

25. The argument is most vulnerable to criticism because it fails to consider that

_____

Answers

1. Weaken (EXCEPT)

2. ID the Flaw

3. ID the (Dis)agreement

4. Match the Flaw

5. Strengthen

6. Weaken

7. ID the Flaw

8. Sufficient Assumption

9. Explain a Result

10. Must Be True

11. Strengthen

12. Match the Reasoning

13. Necessary Assumption

14. Necessary Assumption

15. ID the Conclusion

16. Match the Principle

17. Necessary Assumption *(If you thought this was an ID the Flaw question, you're partially right. But because it ends with "takes for granted that," you're looking for an answer that's a necessary assumption.)*

18. Determine the Function

19. Principle Example

20. Weaken *(If you thought this was an ID the Flaw question, again, you're partially right. But because it ends with "overlooks the possibility that," you're looking for an answer that is a possibility that, if true, would weaken the argument.)*

21. Principle Support

22. ID the (Dis)agreement

23. Necessary Assumption

24. Weaken

25. Weaken *(If you thought this was an ID the Flaw question, yet again, you're partially right. But because it ends with "fails to consider," you're looking for an answer that is a consideration that, if true, would weaken the argument.)*

Drill 40: Vocab Lab #6 – How Much?

Instructions: Quantity is expressed in a lot of different ways on the LSAT. See if you can recognize the most subtle with this Vocab Lab!

Choose the answer closest in meaning.

1. Bereft

    Ⓐ deprived
    Ⓑ abundant
    Ⓒ measured

2. Chronic

    Ⓐ recurring
    Ⓑ scarce
    Ⓒ well-timed

3. Deficit

    Ⓐ charge
    Ⓑ lack
    Ⓒ budget

4. Devoid

    Ⓐ limited
    Ⓑ average
    Ⓒ empty

5. Myriad

    Ⓐ priceless
    Ⓑ countless
    Ⓒ worthless

6. Profusion

    Ⓐ insufficient quantity
    Ⓑ thorough mixture
    Ⓒ extravagant amount

7. Quorum

    Ⓐ minimum number of words in a formal declaration
    Ⓑ minimum amount of energy or other physical quantity
    Ⓒ minimum number of members needed for a meeting

8. Scant

    Ⓐ excessively much
    Ⓑ barely enough
    Ⓒ completely barren

9. Substantial

    Ⓐ brisk
    Ⓑ ample
    Ⓒ base

10. Subpopulation

    Ⓐ reduction in a group of people
    Ⓑ subset of a group of people
    Ⓒ people in underwater vehicles

4

Answers

1.   A

Bereft = deprived. It can imply a sense of loss or abandonment. *Bereave* = deprive someone of a loved one.

2.   A

Chronic = recurring, persistent, long-standing. *Chronos* = time, in Greek.

3.   B

Deficit = lack, gap. A budget *deficit* is a gap between revenue (money coming in) and expenses (money going out) over a period of time.

4.   C

Devoid = empty, vacant, completely lacking. Like the *void* itself.

5.   B

Myriad = countless (as an adjective), huge in number, or (as a noun) a huge number. From the Greek word for "ten thousand."

6.   C

Profusion = extravagant amount, a great (maybe even excessive) quantity. *Profuse* = abundant, prolific.

7.   C

Quorum = minimum number of members needed for a meeting. When you have a *quorum*, the meeting can be official. From the Latin word "of whom," used in a longer phrase to appoint justices of the peace.

8.   B

Scant = barely enough. A *scant* increase in your wages provides a minimal, almost negligible uptick in your bank account.

9.   B

Substantial = ample. Something *substantial* has real *substance*, weight, or heft to it.

10. B

Subpopulation = subset of a group of people. *Sub-* is a prefix meaning under, as in *submarine*.

Step 2 – Work the Stimulus

The work you do in the stimulus sets the tone for the whole question. That's why it's Step 2 in our 4-Step Process for Logical Reasoning. In Chapter 1, you got to meet the stimulus and get familiar with the core issues of argument type and argument structure. This section of the book will help you refine those skills and add some important new ones to your arsenal.

In this section, you will learn to:

Master Argument Breakdown

Manage Complicated Conditional Statements

Recognize Subtle Implied Causality

Identify the Most Common Flawed Methods of Reasoning

4

Drill 41: What's Your Function? Round 2

Instructions: Breaking down arguments into their core components is still step one for almost any Logical Reasoning question, so here is another round of practice!

Each of the following sets of items is an argument broken up into pieces. Some sentences within the argument are also broken into pieces because single sentences can have multiple clauses that each have a different function. For each numbered piece, note whether it's Background info (BG), an Opposing Point (OP), Counter Evidence that would support an opposing point (even if that point has not been explicitly articulated) (CE), a Premise of the argument (P), an Intermediate Conclusion of the argument (IC), or the argument's Main Conclusion (MC). Note that you will generally need to read the whole argument before making your determination, and that it's generally easiest to start by trying to identify the main conclusion and figure the rest out from there.

4

Set A

_____ 1. The Atlantic halibut is one of the largest members of the flounder family.

_____ 2. When born, a halibut larva has one eye on each side of its body.

_____ 3. Subsequently, it will undergo a metamorphosis in which the eye on the left side migrates to the right side, where it remains for the rest of the fish's life.

_____ 4. At the same time, the right side of the halibut's body darkens and the left side lightens in color.

_____ 5. These adaptations indicate that the species is ideally suited for the ecological niche it occupies,

_____ 6. because each one makes the halibut a more effective hunter or protects it from predators.

Set B

_____ 7. The Capestrano film industry will inevitably suffer if current regulations are not made stricter.

_____ 8. At present, there is no mechanism in place to prevent conflicts of interest;

_____ 9. it is a simple matter for studios to secure government funding for projects and then use the money to pay contractors with close personal and financial ties to the studio heads themselves.

_____ 10. Taxpayers are already growing disgusted with this corruption,

_____ 11. and the withdrawal of public funds would make it extremely difficult for any of the local studios to continue operations.

Set C

_____ 12. A major ad campaign for Hark Toothpaste has launched recently,

_____ 13. but it will not have a major effect on sales.

_____ 14. The ads heavily emphasize Hark's ability to protect gums and tooth enamel,

_____ 15. but market research indicates that the overwhelming majority of customers choose a toothpaste based on its flavor and how fresh-feeling it leaves the mouth.

_____ 16. Therefore, this campaign won't connect with customers.

Set D

_____ 17. Emily always wakes up early in the morning unless she went to a concert the previous night.

_____ 18. On any morning that she wakes up early she goes for a run,

_____ 19. and she needs to take a long shower immediately after running.

_____ 20. So, she definitely took a long shower on Tuesday

_____ 21. because she didn't attend a concert on Monday.

Set E

_____ 22. Dr. Meadows argues vigorously that Marcus should refrain from chewing smokeless tobacco.

_____ 23. According to Dr. Meadows, medical research has categorically demonstrated that no other form of tobacco is more addictive or has a greater carcinogenic effect.

_____ 24. He also regularly points out the efficacy of new treatments that can minimize the effects of withdrawal.

_____ 25. Marcus is correct to continue his habit, however,

_____ 26. since he has been told by a nurse that Dr. Meadows secretly chews smokeless tobacco as well.

Set F

_____ 27. Savvy consumers will book their flights with Yearling Airlines rather than Apso Airlines.

_____ 28. The Isley Guide notes that Yearling charges significantly higher fares than Apso

_____ 29. and accordingly recommends that frugal flyers patronize the latter.

_____ 30. However, the editors of the guide overlook the fact that Yearling includes in its fares many services, such as the option to carry a small bag into the cabin, that are essential for air travel.

_____ 31. Apso charges additional fees for these services,

_____ 32. and thus the overall cost of flying with Apso is greater than the cost of flying with Yearling.

Set G

_____ 33. Madeleine, who owns a poultry farm, has noticed a connection between the colors of a chicken's feathers and the colors of the eggs it lays.

_____ 34. At her farm, chickens with black feathers almost always produce brown eggs,

_____ 35. while chickens with brown, white, or yellow feathers lay white eggs an overwhelming majority of the time.

_____ 36. This has led her to conclude that most of the eggs laid by any chicken without black feathers will also be white.

_____ 37. She is correct to believe this,

_____ 38. since her prior observations involved many thousands of chickens.

Set H

_____ 39. Yoshida and Klein are both professional badminton players in the Q League.

_____ 40. In the course of a season, each individual in the league plays five one-on-one matches against every other league member.

_____ 41. Yoshida has defeated Klein in their only match so far this season.

_____ 42. However, it is likely that Klein will win most or all of the remaining matches between the two.

_____ 43. Over the past few years, Klein's total record in the league has been much better than Yoshida's.

Set I

_____ 44. In order to graduate at the end of the academic year, Jordan must take an upper-level psychology course this semester.

_____ 45. Another unavoidable requirement is a seminar on classical Sanskrit literature, which meets every Tuesday and Thursday afternoon.

_____ 46. While many upper-level psychology courses are offered this semester at Jordan's university,

_____ 47. all of them except Personality Disorders have a lab component that meets for the entirety of either Tuesday or Thursday afternoon.

_____ 48. Since regularly failing to attend any course will prevent a student from receiving credit for that course,

_____ 49. Jordan must take Personality Disorders if she wishes to graduate this year.

4

Set J

_____ 50. The Marygate Library does not use a common method, such as the Dewey Decimal or Library of Congress systems, to organize its books.

_____ 51. Instead, the librarians at Marygate have devised a unique schematic representation of knowledge.

_____ 52. The concepts most fundamental to civilization are located at the center of the building,

_____ 53. while the more sophisticated fields of thought that are derived from them branch away, creating a "family tree" of all human endeavors.

_____ 54. So, if you would like to locate a book corresponding to the culinary arts, find the shelves devoted to hunting and agriculture and move toward the perimeter of the room.

Set K

_____ 55. The top priority of the newly-founded Bear City Fire Department is to protect human life,

_____ 56. with the secondary goal of minimizing financial losses from damaged property.

_____ 57. The best way to accomplish both of these goals is for the department to begin work as soon as possible after a fire is reported,

_____ 58. but Bear City can afford only one station from which to dispatch fire crews.

_____ 59. The northern half of the city is more heavily populated and affluent than the southern half

_____ 60. and fires that take place there will have an enormous economic impact.

_____ 61. Nonetheless, it would be better to construct the fire station in the southern half of the city,

_____ 62. where there are many wooden buildings and even small fires pose an immediate danger to the residents.

Answers

Set A

BG 1. The Atlantic halibut is one of the largest members of the flounder family.

BG 2. When born, a halibut larva has one eye on each side of its body.

P 3. Subsequently, it will undergo a metamorphosis in which the eye on the left side migrates to the right side, where it remains for the rest of the fish's life.

P 4. At the same time, the right side of the halibut's body darkens and the left side lightens in color.

MC 5. These adaptations indicate that the species is ideally suited for the ecological niche it occupies,

P 6. because each one makes the halibut a more effective hunter or protects it from predators.

Set B

MC 7. The Capestrano film industry will inevitably suffer if current regulations are not made stricter.

P 8. At present, there is no mechanism in place to prevent conflicts of interest;

P 9. it is a simple matter for studios to secure government funding for projects and then use the money to pay contractors with close personal and financial ties to the studio heads themselves.

P 10. Taxpayers are already growing disgusted with this corruption,

P 11. and the withdrawal of public funds would make it extremely difficult for any of the local studios to continue operations.

Set C

BG 12. A major ad campaign for Hark Toothpaste has launched recently,

MC 13. but it will not have a major effect on sales.

P 14. The ads heavily emphasize Hark's ability to protect gums and tooth enamel,

P 15. but market research indicates that the overwhelming majority of customers choose a toothpaste based on its flavor and how fresh-feeling it leaves the mouth.

IC 16. Therefore, this campaign won't connect with customers.

Set D

P 17. Emily always wakes up early in the morning unless she went to a concert the previous night.

P 18. On any morning that she wakes up early she goes for a run,

P 19. and she needs to take a long shower immediately after running.

MC 20. So, she definitely took a long shower on Tuesday

P 21. because she didn't attend a concert on Monday.

Set E

OP 22. Dr. Meadows argues vigorously that Marcus should refrain from chewing smokeless tobacco.

CE 23. According to Dr. Meadows, medical research has categorically demonstrated that no other form of tobacco is more addictive or has a greater carcinogenic effect.

CE 24. He also regularly points out the efficacy of new treatments that can minimize the effects of withdrawal.

MC 25. Marcus is correct to continue his habit, however,

P 26. since he has been told by a nurse that Dr. Meadows secretly chews smokeless tobacco as well.

Set F

MC   27. Savvy consumers will book their flights with Yearling Airlines rather than Apso Airlines.

CE   28. The Isley Guide notes that Yearling charges significantly higher fares than Apso

OP   29. and accordingly recommends that frugal flyers patronize the latter.

P   30. However, the editors of the guide overlook the fact that Yearling includes in its fares many services, such as the option to carry a small bag into the cabin, that are essential for air travel.

P   31. Apso charges additional fees for these services,

IC   32. and thus the overall cost of flying with Apso is greater than the cost of flying with Yearling.

Set G

P   33. Madeleine, who owns a poultry farm, has noticed a connection between the colors of a chicken's feathers and the colors of the eggs it lays.

P   34. At her farm, chickens with black feathers almost always produce brown eggs,

P   35. while chickens with brown, white, or yellow feathers lay white eggs an overwhelming majority of the time.

P   36. This has led her to conclude that most of the eggs laid by any chicken without black feathers will also be white.

MC   37. She is correct to believe this,

P   38. since her prior observations involved many thousands of chickens.

Set H

BG   39. Yoshida and Klein are both professional badminton players in the Q League.

BG   40. In the course of a season, each individual in the league plays five one-on-one matches against every other league member.

CE   41. Yoshida has defeated Klein in their only match so far this season.

MC   42. However, it is likely that Klein will win most or all of the remaining matches between the two.

P   43. Over the past few years, Klein's total record in the league has been much better than Yoshida's.

Set I

P   44. In order to graduate at the end of the academic year, Jordan must take an upper-level psychology course this semester.

P   45. Another unavoidable requirement is a seminar on classical Sanskrit literature, which meets every Tuesday and Thursday afternoon.

BG   46. While many upper-level psychology courses are offered this semester at Jordan's university,

P   47. all of them except Personality Disorders have a lab component that meets for the entirety of either Tuesday or Thursday afternoon.

P   48. Since regularly failing to attend any course will prevent a student from receiving credit for that course,

MC   49. Jordan must take Personality Disorders if she wishes to graduate this year.

Set J

BG   50. The Marygate Library does not use a common method, such as the Dewey Decimal or Library of Congress systems, to organize its books.

BG   51. Instead, the librarians at Marygate have devised a unique schematic representation of knowledge.

P   52. The concepts most fundamental to civilization are located at the center of the building,

P   53. while the more sophisticated fields of thought that are derived from them branch away, creating a "family tree" of all human endeavors.

MC   54. So, if you would like to locate a book corresponding to the culinary arts, find the shelves devoted to hunting and agriculture and move toward the perimeter of the room.

4

Set K

P   55. The top priority of the newly-founded Bear City Fire Department is to protect human life,

P   56. with the secondary goal of minimizing financial losses from damaged property.

BG 57. The best way to accomplish both of these goals is for the department to begin work as soon as possible after a fire is reported,

P   58. but Bear City can afford only one station from which to dispatch fire crews.

CE 59. The northern half of the city is more heavily populated and affluent than the southern half

CE 60. and fires that take place there will have an enormous economic impact.

MC 61. Nonetheless, it would be better to construct the fire station in the southern half of the city,

P   62. where there are many wooden buildings and even small fires pose an immediate danger to the residents.

Drill 42: Diagramming 201, Round 1

Instructions: Pop quiz: How do you diagram "Diagramming 101 is a prerequisite for Diagramming 201"?
Answer: D201 → D101

This is where the diagramming gets trickier. Try your hand at diagramming and contraposing these more complicated conditionals, but if you start to feel lost, don't be afraid to go back and review the basics with a round of Diagramming 101. For an added twist, some of these statements might not even be conditional, in which case you should note that.

1. Josh can't go to the party on Friday unless he passes his history midterm.

2. Ethan will paint his room, but only if Ingrid helps him.

3. Every comet has a nucleus of icy rock and a tail formed by jets of gas.

4. Unless the politician changes her stance on this issue, her constituents will not reelect her.

5. It's a prerequisite for this class that you supply either your own camera or tripod.

6. Even if I try my best, I cannot beat Rodney in the competition.

7. Among the cars on this lot, none has a GPS system included as standard.

8. Until the city changes the speed limit for this road, it will remain both noisy and unsafe.

9. All good friendships are based either on shared interests or mutual respect.

10. Her parents will have a fit if she dyes her hair that color.

11. The dentist can neither diagnose nor treat your condition without an X-ray.

12. The VR will be immersive if, but only if, it is both fluid and vivid.

13. Only mammals are pachyderms.

14. In order to brush his teeth, Steve must use the upstairs bathroom.

15. Things made of sugar and spice are neither naughty nor nice.

16. Pablo finished the season with the league's highest batting average, so he's ensured to be nominated either for rookie of the year or MVP.

17. Our dog just goes crazy whenever a nature documentary comes on TV.

18. The researchers will be vindicated and the critics will be silenced, but only if our team can show that the data is statistically significant.

19. Unless it snows or there's an impending asteroid collision, there will be school tomorrow.

20. To work on a Formula 1 race car is every mechanic's dream.

21. Not only does most of the best animation come out of Korea, but that animation is usually more efficiently produced.

22. No helicopters fly over that park except when there's an emergency.

23. A winning smile is all it takes to have a chance to be crowned homecoming queen.

24. Maintaining a healthy weight is a prerequisite for anyone who wants sustainably low blood pressure and cholesterol.

25. Until this tree is downed, our neighborhood is going to remain a haven for squirrels and chipmunks.

Answers

1. Josh can't go to the party on Friday unless he passes his history midterm.

   PF → PM ; ~PM → ~PF

2. Ethan will paint his room, but only if Ingrid helps him.

   EP → IP ; ~IP → ~EP

3. Every comet has a nucleus of icy rock and a tail formed by jets of gas.

   C → NIR and TJG ; ~NIR or ~TJG → ~C

4. Unless the politician changes her stance on this issue, her constituents will not reelect her.

   R → CS ; ~CS → ~R

5. It's a prerequisite for this class that you supply either your own camera or tripod.

   C → OC or OT ; ~OC and ~OT → ~C

6. Even if I try my best, I cannot beat Rodney in the competition.

   Not a conditional statement.

7. Among the cars on this lot, none has a GPS system included as standard.

   CL → ~GPS ; GPS → ~CL

8. Until the city changes the speed limit for this road, it will remain both noisy and unsafe.

   ~CSL → N and ~S ; ~N or S → CSL

   (Note: It's preferable to use "-S" to represent "not safe" than to use "U" to represent "unsafe," because when you negate "unsafe," you get a double negative.)

9. All good friendships are based either on shared interests or mutual respect.

   GF → SI or MR ; ~SI and ~MR → ~GF

10. Her parents will have a fit if she dyes her hair that color.

    D → PHF ; ~PHF → ~D

11. The dentist can neither diagnose nor treat your condition without an X-ray.

    D or T → X ; ~X → ~D and ~T

16. Pablo finished the season with the league's highest batting average, so he's ensured to be nominated either for rookie of the year or MVP.

    This is an argument, not a conditional statement. It *assumes* a conditional relationship (if highest batting average, then rookie of the year or MVP nomination) but it doesn't *state* it.

12. The VR will be immersive if, but only if, it is both fluid and vivid.

    I ↔ F and V ; ~F or ~V ↔ ~I

17. Our dog just goes crazy whenever a nature documentary comes on TV.

    ND → DC ; ~DC → ~ND

13. Only mammals are pachyderms.

    P → M ; ~M → ~P

18. The researchers will be vindicated and the critics will be silenced, but only if our team can show that the data is statistically significant.

    RV and CS → DSS ; ~DSS → ~RV or ~CS

14. In order to brush his teeth, Steve must use the upstairs bathroom.

    BT → UB ; ~UB → ~BT

19. Unless it snows or there's an impending asteroid collision, there will be school tomorrow.

    ~Sch → Sn or IAC ; ~Sn and ~IAC → Sch

15. Things made of sugar and spice are neither naughty nor nice.

    Su and Spi → ~Nau and ~Ni ; Nau or Ni → ~Su or ~Spi

20. To work on a Formula 1 race car is every mechanic's dream.

    M → F1D ; ~F1D → ~M

4

21. Not only does most of the best animation come out of Korea, but that animation is usually more efficiently produced.

    Not a conditional statement.

22. No helicopters fly over that park except when there's an emergency.

    H → E ; ~E → ~H

23. A winning smile is all it takes to have a chance to be crowned homecoming queen.

    WS → CHQ ; ~CHQ → ~WS

    (Note: This doesn't say that a winning smile is sufficient to be elected. It only says that it's sufficient to give one the chance to be.)

24. Maintaining a healthy weight is a prerequisite for anyone who wants sustainably low blood pressure and cholesterol.

    LBP and LC → MHW ;
    ~MHW → ~LBP or ~LC

25. Until this tree is downed, our neighborhood is going to remain a haven for squirrels and chipmunks.

    ~TD → HS and HC ; ~HS or ~HC → TD

Drill 43: What's That Indicate?

Instructions: Indicator words come in different flavors. Some tell us about the way an argument is built by introducing premises, conclusions, and opposing points. We call these Structural Indicators. Other indicators clue us in to the fact that the argument is using conditional reasoning. We call these Conditional Indicators. For each of the following words or phrases, determine whether it is a Structural Indicator (S), a Conditional Indicator (C), or neither (N).

_____ 1. Until	_____ 18. And	_____ 35. Even if
_____ 2. Without	_____ 19. Each	_____ 36. Except
_____ 3. However	_____ 20. But	_____ 37. The only
_____ 4. Thus	_____ 21. Moreover	_____ 38. Prerequisite
_____ 5. Most	_____ 22. Unless	_____ 39. Many
_____ 6. Whenever	_____ 23. Because	_____ 40. Requires
_____ 7. Any	_____ 24. Since	_____ 41. Nevertheless
_____ 8. Therefore	_____ 25. For example	_____ 42. For
_____ 9. After all	_____ 26. Never	_____ 43. Guarantees
_____ 10. Hence	_____ 27. Always	_____ 44. Once
_____ 11. No	_____ 28. Also	_____ 45. Necessitates
_____ 12. Some	_____ 29. Additionally	_____ 46. As a result
_____ 13. Unlike	_____ 30. Often	_____ 47. Despite
_____ 14. Although	_____ 31. If	_____ 48. Furthermore
_____ 15. Only	_____ 32. It follows that	_____ 49. So
_____ 16. None	_____ 33. Only if	_____ 50. Must
_____ 17. Every	_____ 34. Consequently	

4

Answers

C 1. Until
C 2. Without
S 3. However
S 4. Thus
N 5. Most
C 6. Whenever
C 7. Any
S 8. Therefore
S 9. After all
S 10. Hence
C 11. No
N 12. Some
S 13. Unlike
S 14. Although
C 15. Only
C 16. None
C 17. Every

N 18. And
C 19. Each
S 20. But
S 21. Moreover
C 22. Unless
S 23. Because
S 24. Since
S 25. For example
C 26. Never
C 27. Always
S 28. Also
S 29. Additionally
N 30. Often
C 31. If
S 32. It follows that
C 33. Only if
S 34. Consequently

C 35. Even if
N 36. Except
C 37. The only
C 38. Prerequisite
N 39. Many
C 40. Requires
S 41. Nevertheless
S 42. For
C 43. Guarantees
N 44. Once
C 45. Necessitates
S 46. As a result
S 47. Despite
S 48. Furthermore
S 49. So
C 50. Must

Drill 44: Famous Flaws, Round 1

Instructions: Famous flaws appear all over the LSAT, and being able to recognize them quickly is a must if you're looking for a top score. This drill is the first step toward that level of mastery, and there will be more to come.

For each of the following abbreviated arguments, select the famous flaw that is exhibited. Since there is some overlap between the different flaws, you might prephrase an answer that doesn't appear. That's fine! Figure out which answer is correct, and then spend time thinking about why it's correct and how you could have prephrased both answers (assuming, of course, that you were also correct with your initial prephrase).

1. Based on a recent survey of college seniors, it can be concluded that the average American spends at least two hours each day reading and writing.

   (A) Ad Hominem
   (B) Circular Reasoning
   (C) Sampling Flaw

2. For decades, no one has been able to identify the disc-shaped object in the picture as anything that we know of on Earth, so it clearly cannot be of earthly origin.

   (A) Circular Reasoning
   (B) Unproven vs. Untrue
   (C) Sampling Flaw

3. Senator Jones has consistently voted for any bill that lowers taxes, so she can be counted on to support the tax reduction bill being proposed in this session.

   (A) Unproven vs. Untrue
   (B) Circular Reasoning
   (C) Unwarranted Prediction

4. Smokers suffer from depression at a significantly higher rate than nonsmokers. This shows that depression can be one more negative side effect of smoking.

   (A) Causation Flaw
   (B) Percent vs. Amount
   (C) Equivocation

5. The superintendent has proposed a reduction in the amount of money allocated in the school's budget for the music department. We should seek to hire a new superintendent, because the idea of eliminating music from our schools is unthinkable.

   (A) Appeal to Inappropriate Authority
   (B) Opinion vs. Fact
   (C) Straw Man

6. I didn't see a taxi arrive, so she must have taken the bus to get here.

   (A) Circular Reasoning
   (B) False Choice
   (C) Term Shift

7. Without a library card, you can't check out any books. Since she didn't check out books needed for her research paper, she must not have a library card.

   (A) Illegal Reversal
   (B) Self-Contradiction
   (C) False Choice

8. The defense attorney called the sentencing unfair, claiming that the penalty for his client was considerably harsher than was warranted by the crime. However, the sentencing was perfectly fair. Both the attorney's client and the other defendant got the same sentence for the same crime.

   (A) Ad Hominem
   (B) Equivocation
   (C) Comparison Flaw

9. A good quarterback has to be the best passer on the team. After all, if he didn't throw the ball better than all the other players, he wouldn't be a good quarterback.

   (A) Comparison Flaw
   (B) Unproven vs. Untrue
   (C) Circular Reasoning

10. Jesse had a fender bender shortly after she received a C on her term paper. It must have been stress over her grade that led to the accident.

    (A) Unproven vs. Untrue
    (B) Causation Flaw
    (C) Appeal to Emotion

11. My favorite actor just starred in a new action drama. The comedy he was in last year was very enjoyable, so this new movie is certainly going to be enjoyable as well.

    (A) Comparison Flaw
    (B) Relative vs. Absolute
    (C) Sampling Flaw

12. This song from the artist's newly-released album is far below the quality of his usual work. Clearly, he did not put as much effort into this album as he put into his prior albums.

    (A) Sampling Flaw
    (B) Part vs. Whole
    (C) Equivocation

13. In recent years, increasing numbers of students have been choosing to take Mandarin for their foreign language requirement. It would seem, then, that more students are choosing Mandarin over the European languages traditionally chosen in the past.

    (A) Sampling Flaw
    (B) Comparison Flaw
    (C) Percent vs. Amount

14. People should always be free to speak out without restraint against their government. Restraint on free speech can only be tolerated when the speech would undermine the authority of agencies to perform their legitimate functions.

    (A) Self-Contradiction
    (B) Opinion vs. Fact
    (C) Circular Reasoning

15. The recent successful launch of a privately built rocket demonstrated that commercial space travel is possible. Tourists will be traveling to the moon before this century is out!

    (A) Unproven vs. Untrue
    (B) Causation Flaw
    (C) Possible vs. Certain

16. That author's new book on business ethics isn't worth reading. Everyone knows that he was caught plagiarizing at the university when he was an undergraduate there.

    (A) Circular Reasoning
    (B) Ad Hominem
    (C) Appeal to Inappropriate Authority

17. International crises have always been accompanied by a downturn in the stock market. So, it is no surprise that the recent stock market slump happened shortly after the diplomatic incident.

    (A) Term Shift
    (B) Causation Flaw
    (C) Part vs. Whole

18. The popularity of Afghan hounds as pets cannot be due to their intelligence because they are not particularly smart dogs. So, people must like them for their good looks and silky coats.

    (A) Comparison Flaw
    (B) Unproven vs. Untrue
    (C) False Choice

19. The district attorney should have asked for a stiffer penalty for the offense. After all, how would you feel if your son or daughter had been the victim of this terrible crime?

    (A) Circular Reasoning
    (B) Appeal to Emotion
    (C) Opinion vs. Fact

20. If he had taken his usual route, he would be stuck in that big traffic jam on the freeway and arrive at the office late. Fortunately, he took a different route this morning, so he will make it to work on time.

    (A) Circular Reasoning
    (B) Causation Flaw
    (C) Illegal Negation

21. Statistics show that the number of near collisions of aircraft has increased around the country's largest airports. Efforts taken to reduce the likelihood of such incidents have clearly not been effective.

    (A) Percent vs. Amount
    (B) Unproven vs. Untrue
    (C) Opinion vs. Fact

22. Time is merely an illusion of the mind. None of Einstein's equations require that time exists, and physicists have been unable to establish mathematically that it does.

    (A) Appeal to Inappropriate Authority
    (B) Unproven vs. Untrue
    (C) Equivocation

23. The local café began giving out discount coupons. Since then, it has seen a noticeable increase in customers coming in for its lunchtime buffet. Clearly, the coupons have helped the café to attract customers.

    (A) Sampling Flaw
    (B) Percent vs. Amount
    (C) Causation Flaw

24. People on the East Coast read more foreign affairs magazines than people read on the West Coast. Clearly, people on the East Coast are better informed about world events.

    (A) Straw Man
    (B) Term Shift
    (C) Causation Flaw

25. My history teacher, who has written an authoritative and respected textbook on medieval England, concludes that the legislation was constitutional. So, the court's decision to strike it down was obviously politically motivated.

    (A) Ad Hominem
    (B) Appeal to Inappropriate Authority
    (C) Circular Reasoning

4

Answers

1.	C	8.	B	15.	C	22.	B
2.	B	9.	C	16.	B	23.	C
3.	C	10.	B	17.	A	24.	B
4.	A	11.	A	18.	C	25.	B
5.	C	12.	B	19.	B		
6.	B	13.	C	20.	C		
7.	A	14.	A	21.	A		

4

Drill 45: Conditional Fill-in-the-Blank, Round 1

Instructions: Taking the LSAT at the highest level requires that you know your formal logic backward and forward. This drill pulls from the backward side of things by presenting you with a diagram and *most* of the statement that would generate it, but *without* its conditional indicator words. Your task is to look at the diagram and reverse-engineer the statement, filling in the blank(s) with the conditional indicator word(s) that will make the diagram accurate.

1. The competitors _must_ be older than 18 or licensed.

    Competitor → 18+ or Licensed

2. _None_ of the plates were yellow.

    Plate → ~Yellow

3. She will buy the knives _if_ they are made in Germany.

    German → Buy knives

4. _Each_ radio DJ wears velour.

    Radio DJ → Velour

5. _Everyone_ at the gala was wearing a hat.

    Gala → Hat

6. The tree will be uprooted _only if_ the storm comes tomorrow.

    Uprooted → Storm tomorrow

7. Lawyers _cannot_ be engineers.

    Lawyer → ~Engineer

8. If Ron or Leslie goes, then Andy _does not_ go.

    Ron or Leslie → ~Andy

9. _Only if_ she wins two thirds of the votes will she be elected.

    Elected → Two-thirds votes

10. _Only_ professionals are allowed.

    Allowed → Professional

11. You _cannot_ be an artist if you like finger painting.

    Like FP → ~Artist

12. Daphne _never_ goes where Fred goes.

    Daphne → ~Fred

13. The bill _____ pass _____ Senator Lucius sponsors it.

    Lucius sponsors → Bill passes

14. _____ you are wearing pants and a jacket, you _____ be allowed into the restaurant.

    Pants and Jacket → Allowed in

15. _____ of the coats are made of wool.

    Coat → Wool

16. Everyone likes frozen yogurt _____ they like ice cream.

    ~Like IC → Like FY

17. A successful businessperson _____ to have connections.

    Successful → Connections

18. _____ moviegoer had a good time.

    Moviegoer → ~Good time

19. The Fooltown Footballers _____ play their games without a mascot.

    FF game → ~Mascot

20. It's not a real party _____ Barry is there.

    Barry → ~Real party

21. _____ at the funeral was crying.

    At funeral → ~Crying

4

22. Marcie was _____ one who got a ride home.

    Ride home → Marcie

23. _____ athletes have dentures.

    Athlete → ~Dentures

24. The check will clear _____ it is cashed today.

    Check clears → Cashed today

25. _____ nuclear reactors contain protoplasm.

    Nuclear reactor → ~Protoplasm

Answers follow on the next page.

Answers

Note: We've included a few options for some of these, but if you have a different answer than ours, it still could be correct. Make sure that if your answer is different, it serves the same function as the answer we've provided.

1. The competitors **must** be older than 18 or licensed.

    Competitor → 18+ or Licensed

2. **None** of the plates were yellow.

    Plate → ~Yellow

3. She will buy the knives **if** they are made in Germany.

    German → Buy knives

4. **Every/Each** radio DJ wears velour.

    Radio DJ → Velour

5. **Everybody/Everyone** at the gala was wearing a hat.

    Gala → Hat

6. The tree will be uprooted **only if** the storm comes tomorrow.

    Uprooted → Storm tomorrow

7. Lawyers **cannot** be engineers.

    Lawyer → ~Engineer

8. If Ron or Leslie goes, then Andy **cannot/must not** go.

    Ron or Leslie → ~Andy

9. **Only if** she wins two thirds of the votes will she be elected.

    Elected → Two-thirds votes

10. **Only** professionals are allowed.

    Allowed → Professional

11. You **cannot** be an artist if you like finger painting.

    Like FP → ~Artist

12. Daphne **never** goes where Fred goes.

    Daphne → ~Fred

13. The bill **will** pass if Senator Lucius sponsors it.

    Lucius sponsors → Bill passes

14. **If** you are wearing pants and a jacket, you **will** be allowed into the restaurant.

    Pants and Jacket → Allowed in

15. **All** of the coats are made of wool.

    Coat → Wool

16. Everyone likes frozen yogurt **unless** they like ice cream.

    ~Like IC → Like FY

17. A successful businessperson **needs** to have connections.

    Successful → Connections

18. **No** moviegoer had a good time.

    Moviegoer → ~Good time

19. The Fooltown Footballers **always** play their games without a mascot.

    FF game → ~Mascot

20. It's not a real party **if** Barry is there.

    Barry → ~Real party

21. **Nobody/No one** at the funeral was crying.

    At funeral → ~Crying

22. Marcie was **the only** one who got a ride home.

    Ride home → Marcie

23. **No** athletes have dentures.

    Athlete → ~Dentures

24. The check will clear **only if** it is cashed today.

    Check clears → Cashed today

25. **No** nuclear reactors contain protoplasm.

    Nuclear reactor → ~Protoplasm

Drill 46: 6 Degrees of Separation

Instructions: Degree is a critical dimension of RC passages, LR stimuli, and answer choices in both sections. Authors and arguers have a degree of opinion. Conditional, causal, and quantified statements all exhibit a degree. So do predictions, evaluations, and recommendations. Practice homing in on this important feature by highlighting any words you see that indicate degree in the statements that follow.

1. Dog breeders have failed to preserve genetic variety due to years of inbreeding.

2. It is seldom the case that short-term and long-term interests perfectly align.

3. The opportunity to appoint a new justice to the Supreme Court is a rare one for American presidents.

4. The efficacy of border checkpoints in preventing the movement of contraband across borders has been questioned by many in the security community.

5. In desert climates where vegetation is scarce, herbivorous animals are at a disadvantage relative to their omnivorous and carnivorous counterparts.

6. The flea market is closed during inclement weather, but the temperate climate ensures that such closures are infrequent.

7. Workers should be compensated not only for their work, but also for the risks they take in dangerous working conditions.

8. Although skydiving accidents are relatively rare, they typically result in fatalities.

9. For firms that insure real estate along shorelines, sea level rise is of particular concern.

10. Psychiatrists often struggle to convince ill patients that medications must be taken regularly in order to be effective.

11. Transportation options for those in wheelchairs have historically been limited to public paratransit or hired drivers, but the advent of driverless vehicles may soon change that.

12. Public notaries must periodically renew their certification.

13. It is therefore unlikely that the patent will be granted.

14. A new study sheds light upon a long-overlooked segment of the porcupine population.

15. A definitive connection has yet to be established.

16. Competition has driven down prices at nearby tailors, compromising profitability.

17. The entire hospital staff was given a pay raise after the recent vote by the board of directors.

18. A recent outbreak of bovine conjunctivitis coincided with a successful mad cow vaccination campaign.

19. Sharply declining birth rates in the area have virtually eliminated the local practice of midwifery.

20. The Vatican's team of archivists regularly monitors the manuscript archive for signs of decomposition.

21. All new buildings on the campus will be fully equipped with solar panels.

22. Caregivers at Sunshine Daycare are always put through a background check before being offered employment.

23. Reservoir water is continually tested to ensure that it is safe for consumption.

24. The ability to fly for free on standby is a benefit usually included in the compensation package of flight attendants.

4

25. Many ancient tombs were raided before archaeologists discovered them, limiting the possible extent of archeological discovery.

26. Pediatricians never recommend allowing infants or young children to drink soda.

27. Even dormant volcanoes may sporadically erupt.

28. Although she does write about indigenous Polynesian tribes, the researcher's motives in traveling to the tropical islands may not have been purely academic.

29. Sales of coffee grinders have declined as a result of the surging popularity of pre-ground coffee.

30. These new findings cast doubt on theories long held to be true by most astronomers.

31. Military barracks are devoid of entertainment or leisure items such as television sets, books, games, and music.

32. For many modern couples, having fewer children means being able to save more money for the rising cost of higher education.

33. Significant gains cannot be made without sacrifices from all members of the team.

34. The economist's prediction rests on a misinterpretation of the data.

35. It is therefore undeniable that human activity is contributing to the warming of Earth's atmosphere.

36. Anticorruption laws merit careful reevaluation after recent scandals exposed illegal activity in the state's capital.

37. There is general agreement in the scientific community about the issue, but public opinion is divided nonetheless.

38. Drug trials depend on sugar-based placebos.

39. The National Basketball Association has been roundly criticized by those in the collegiate sports industry for allowing the drafting of players directly out of high school.

40. Jury members in high-profile cases are generally prohibited from watching or reading news sources for the duration of the trial.

41. Some glaciers in the Arctic Circle are projected to melt considerably more over the next decade than they did over the previous one.

42. Pedro Almodóvar's storied directorial career began on a low-budget, self-produced film that quickly garnered him a cult following in Spain.

43. The museum lacks engaging material for children.

44. Former manufacturing districts in cities across the country have been experiencing a revitalization as the so-called creative class has become an increasingly dominant force of urban economic growth.

45. The evidence in the case was insufficient to prove the guilt of the accused.

46. Camphor oil can alleviate a cough when applied to the patient's chest.

47. Paradoxically, the opera owes its success to its outstanding orchestral compositions.

48. The small section of the Berlin Wall that remains standing will probably remain standing indefinitely as a memorial to those who perished in the East German liberation struggle.

49. Despite being fraternal twins, the boys have virtually identical faces.

50. Even the most skilled scientists regularly conduct experiments that produce little to no viable data.

Answers

1. Dog breeders have failed to preserve genetic variety due to years of inbreeding.

2. It is seldom the case that short-term and long-term interests perfectly align.

3. The opportunity to appoint a new justice to the Supreme Court is a rare one for American presidents.

4. The efficacy of border checkpoints in preventing the movement of contraband across borders has been questioned by many in the security community.

5. In desert climates where vegetation is scarce, herbivorous animals are at a disadvantage relative to their omnivorous and carnivorous counterparts.

6. The flea market is closed during inclement weather, but the temperate climate ensures that such closures are infrequent.

7. Workers should be compensated not only for their work, but also for the risks they take in dangerous working conditions.

8. Although skydiving accidents are relatively rare, they typically result in fatalities.

9. For firms that insure real estate along shorelines, sea level rise is of particular concern.

10. Psychiatrists often struggle to convince ill patients that medications must be taken regularly in order to be effective.

11. Transportation options for those in wheelchairs have historically been limited to public paratransit or hired drivers, but the advent of driverless vehicles may soon change that.

12. Public notaries must periodically renew their certification.

13. It is therefore unlikely that the patent will be granted.

14. A new study sheds light upon a long-overlooked segment of the porcupine population.

15. A definitive connection has yet to be established.

16. Competition has driven down prices at nearby tailors, compromising profitability.

17. The entire hospital staff was given a pay raise after the recent vote by the board of directors.

18. A recent outbreak of bovine conjunctivitis coincided with a successful mad cow vaccination campaign.

19. Sharply declining birth rates in the area have virtually eliminated the local practice of midwifery.

20. The Vatican's team of archivists regularly monitors the manuscript archive for signs of decomposition.

21. All new buildings on the campus will be fully equipped with solar panels.

22. Caregivers at Sunshine Daycare are always put through a background check before being offered employment.

23. Reservoir water is continually tested to ensure that it is safe for consumption.

24. The ability to fly for free on standby is a benefit usually included in the compensation package of flight attendants.

4

25. Many ancient tombs were raided before archaeologists discovered them, limiting the possible extent of archeological discovery.

26. Pediatricians never recommend allowing infants or young children to drink soda.

27. Even dormant volcanoes may sporadically erupt.

28. Although she does write about indigenous Polynesian tribes, the researcher's motives in traveling to the tropical islands may not have been purely academic.

29. Sales of coffee grinders have declined as a result of the surging popularity of pre-ground coffee.

30. These new findings cast doubt on theories long held to be true by most astronomers.

31. Military barracks are devoid of entertainment or leisure items such as television sets, books, games, and music.

32. For many modern couples, having fewer children means being able to save more money for the rising cost of higher education.

33. Significant gains cannot be made without sacrifices from all members of the team.

34. The economist's prediction rests on a misinterpretation of the data.

35. It is therefore undeniable that human activity is contributing to the warming of Earth's atmosphere.

36. Anti-corruption laws merit careful reevaluation after recent scandals exposed illegal activity in the state's capital.

37. There is general agreement in the scientific community about the issue, but public opinion is divided nonetheless.

38. Drug trials depend on sugar-based placebos.

39. The National Basketball Association has been roundly criticized by those in the collegiate sports industry for allowing the drafting of players directly out of high school.

40. Jury members in high-profile cases are generally prohibited from watching or reading news sources for the duration of the trial.

41. Some glaciers in the Arctic Circle are projected to melt considerably more over the next decade than they did over the previous one.

42. Pedro Almodóvar's storied directorial career began on a low-budget, self-produced film that quickly garnered him a cult following in Spain.

43. The museum lacks engaging material for children.

44. Former manufacturing districts in cities across the country have been experiencing a revitalization as the so-called creative class has become an increasingly dominant force of urban economic growth.

45. The evidence in the case was insufficient to prove the guilt of the accused.

46. Camphor oil can alleviate a cough when applied to the patient's chest.

47. Paradoxically, the opera owes its success to its outstanding orchestral compositions.

48. The small section of the Berlin Wall that remains standing will probably remain standing indefinitely as a memorial to those who perished in the East German liberation struggle.

49. Despite being fraternal twins, the boys have virtually identical faces.

50. Even the most skilled scientists regularly conduct experiments that produce little to no viable data.

Drill 47: To Chain or Not to Chain?

Instructions: Chaining conditional statements to one another on test day tends to feel harder than it does in practice because when you look at statements on the test, you're not guaranteed that they can even chain together. Practice making that call with this drill.

A conditional statement will be given, followed by a series of statements. Indicate for each statement whether it can be chained to the conditional statement (Y) or not (N).

It will probably be helpful to diagram the given conditional statement and its contrapositive on different lines, like so:

Everyone who likes apples likes berries.

A → B

~B → ~A

A statement can chain to the left side of the statement if it has A or ~B as its necessary condition. A statement can chain to the right side of the statement if it has B or ~A as its sufficient condition. When your original statement is diagrammed in this way, it's easy to diagram the answer choices and quickly assess whether they, or their contrapositives, can chain.

Items:

If Kenneth visits Istanbul, he will not visit Athens.

_____ 1. Penelope never visits Istanbul.

_____ 2. Whenever Kenneth takes the train, he visits Istanbul.

_____ 3. Unless Kenneth goes to Athens, he will visit Rome.

_____ 4. Kenneth visits Athens only when he visits Rome as well.

_____ 5. If Kenneth does not visit Istanbul, Penelope visits Istanbul.

Anyone who listens to world music will enjoy the festival.

_____ 6. All those who listen to world music would enjoy jazz.

_____ 7. All those who enjoy the festival will return the following year.

_____ 8. Anyone who doesn't listen to world music is missing out.

_____ 9. If you didn't enjoy the festival, you weren't paying attention.

_____ 10. No one at the party listens to world music.

Michael will order pizza unless he orders wings.

_____ 11. Jackson will order fried rice unless Michael orders pizza for dinner.

_____ 12. If Michael orders wings, Jackson orders fried rice.

_____ 13. If Michael orders a cheesesteak, he will not order pizza.

_____ 14. Unless Michael orders pizza, he will not order breadsticks.

_____ 15. Michael orders soup only if he orders wings.

Whenever she goes to Georgia, Gladys takes the train.

_____ 16. When Gladys is driving her car, she wears her glasses.

_____ 17. When Gladys takes the train, she doesn't wear her glasses.

_____ 18. If Gladys goes to Kentucky, she doesn't take the train.

_____ 19. When Gladys doesn't go to Georgia, she goes to Kentucky.

_____ 20. When Gladys is ill, she doesn't go to Georgia.

There will be no cake for those who do not eat their peas.

_____ 21. If Roger eats his salad, he will not eat his peas.

_____ 22. If David eats his salad, then he will have cake.

_____ 23. Unless Richard eats his peas, he will not eat ice cream.

_____ 24. Unless Nick eats cake, he will not eat his roast beef.

_____ 25. Whenever Syd eats his peas, he is allowed to eat cake.

If Clarence joins the band, then Steve joins the band.

_____ 26. If Bruce joins the band, then Steve joins the band.

_____ 27. Unless Patti joins the band, Steve will join the band.

_____ 28. Whenever Max joins the band, Clarence will join the band.

_____ 29. Garry will not join the band unless Clarence joins the band.

_____ 30. Bruce joins the band only if Clarence does not join the band.

The flowers will grow only if they are watered.

_____ 31. If it does not rain, Bill will water the flowers.

_____ 32. If Bill watered the flowers, it did not rain.

_____ 33. The flowers will not grow unless they are fertilized.

_____ 34. The flowers will grow only if they are fertilized.

_____ 35. If Bill is not home, the flowers will not be watered.

No partners at the firm are taking a vacation.

_____ 36. Everyone on team A is a partner at the firm.

_____ 37. No one on team B is taking a vacation.

_____ 38. No one on team C is a partner at the firm.

_____ 39. No partner at the firm will attend the gala.

_____ 40. Everyone on team D is on vacation.

Martha will not make pancakes unless she makes bacon.

_____ 41. If Martha has no milk, she will not make pancakes.

_____ 42. Whenever Martha has syrup she makes pancakes.

_____ 43. Martha always has coffee with her pancakes.

_____ 44. Martha never has pancakes with her coffee.

_____ 45. Martha never makes bacon without eggs.

Unless it rains, the kids play baseball.

_____ 46. When playing baseball, the kids chew gum.

_____ 47. When it is overcast, it will rain.

_____ 48. If it is not raining, the sun is shining.

_____ 49. The kids play baseball only if their parents allow it.

_____ 50. The kids will play video games only if it rains.

4

Answers

If Kenneth visits Istanbul, he will not visit Athens:

$$KI \rightarrow \sim KA$$
$$KA \rightarrow \sim KI$$

__N__ 1. Penelope never visits Istanbul (P → ~I)

__Y__ 2. **Whenever Kenneth takes the train, he visits Istanbul. (KT → KI → ~KA)**

__Y__ 3. **Unless Kenneth goes to Athens, he will visit Rome. (~KR → KA → ~KI)**

__N__ 4. Kenneth visits Athens only when he visits Rome as well. (KA → KR)

__Y__ 5. **If Kenneth does not visit Istanbul, Penelope visits Istanbul. (KA → ~KI → PI)**

Anyone who listens to world music will enjoy the festival:

$$LWM \rightarrow EF$$
$$\sim EF \rightarrow \sim LWM$$

__N__ 6. All those who listen to world music would enjoy jazz. (LWM → EJ)

__Y__ 7. **All those who enjoy the festival will return the following year. (LWM → EF → R)**

__Y__ 8. **Anyone who doesn't listen to world music is missing out. (~EF → ~LWM → MO)**

__N__ 9. If you didn't enjoy the festival, you weren't paying attention. (~EF → ~PA)

__N__ 10. No one at the party listens to world music. (P → ~LWM)

Michael will order pizza unless he orders wings:

$$\sim MP \rightarrow MW$$
$$\sim MW \rightarrow MP$$

__N__ 11. Jackson will order fried rice unless Michael orders pizza for dinner. (~JFR → MP)

__Y__ 12. **If Michael orders wings, Jackson orders fried rice. (~MP → MW → JFR)**

__Y__ 13. **If Michael orders a cheesesteak, he will not order pizza. (MC → ~MP → MW)**

__N__ 14. Unless Michael orders pizza, he will not order breadsticks. (MB → MP)

__N__ 15. Michael orders soup only if he orders wings. (MS → MW)

Whenever she goes to Georgia, Gladys takes the train:

$$GG \rightarrow TT$$
$$\sim TT \rightarrow \sim GG$$

__N__ 16. When Gladys is driving her car, she wears her glasses. (GD → WG)

__Y__ 17. **When Gladys takes the train, she doesn't wear her glasses. (GG → TT → ~WG)**

__Y__ 18. **If Gladys goes to Kentucky, she doesn't take the train. (GK → ~TT → ~GG)**

__Y__ 19. **When Gladys doesn't go to Georgia she goes to Kentucky. (~TT → ~GG → GK)**

__N__ 20. When Gladys is ill, she doesn't go to Georgia. (GI → ~GG)

There will be no cake for those who do not eat their peas:

$$\sim EP \rightarrow \sim C$$
$$C \rightarrow EP$$

__Y__ 21. **If Roger eats his salad, he will not eat his peas. (RS → ~EP → ~C)**

__Y__ 22. **If David eats his salad, then he will have cake. (DS → C → EP)**

__N__ 23. Unless Richard eats his peas, he will not eat ice cream. (IC → REP)

__Y__ 24. **Unless Nick eats cake, he will not eat his roast beef. (ERB → C → EP)**

__N__ 25. Whenever Syd eats his peas, he is allowed to eat cake. (SEP → AC)

4

If Clarence joins the band, then Steve joins the band:

> C → S
> ~S → ~C

__N__ 26. If Bruce joins the band, then Steve joins the band. (B → S)

__N__ 27. Unless Patti joins the band, Steve will join the band. (~S → P)

__Y__ **28. Whenever Max joins the band, Clarence will join the band. (M → C → S)**

__Y__ **29. Garry will not join the band unless Clarence joins the band. (G → C → S)**

__N__ 30. Bruce joins the band only if Clarence does not join the band. (B → ~C)

The flowers will grow only if they are watered:

> FG → W
> ~W → ~FG

__N__ 31. If it does not rain, Bill will water the flowers. (~R → W)

__Y__ **32. If Bill watered the flowers, it did not rain. (FG → W → ~R)**

__N__ 33. The flowers will not grow unless they are fertilized. (FG → F)

__N__ 34. The flowers will grow only if they are fertilized. (FG → F)

__Y__ **35. If Bill is not home, the flowers will not be watered. (~BH → ~W → ~FG)**

No partners at the firm are taking a vacation:

> P → ~V
> V → ~P

__Y__ **36. Everyone on team A is a partner at the firm. (A → P → ~V)**

__N__ 37. No one on team B is taking a vacation. (B → ~V)

__N__ 38. No one on team C is a partner at the firm. (C → ~P)

__N__ 39. No partner at the firm will attend the gala. (P → ~G)

__Y__ **40. Everyone on team D is on vacation. (D → V → ~P)**

Martha will not make pancakes unless she makes bacon:

> P → B
> ~B → ~P

__N__ 41. If Martha has no milk, she will not make pancakes. (~M → ~P)

__Y__ **42. Whenever Martha has syrup she makes pancakes. (S → P → B)**

__N__ 43. Martha always has coffee with her pancakes. (P → C)

__N__ 44. Martha never has pancakes with her coffee. (C → ~ P)

__Y__ **45. Martha never makes bacon without eggs. (P → B → E)**

Unless it rains, the kids play baseball:

> ~KB → R
> ~R → KB

__Y__ **46. When playing baseball, the kids chew gum. (~R → KB → CG)**

__N__ 47. When it is overcast, it will rain. (O → R)

__N__ 48. If it is not raining, the sun is shining. (~R → S)

__Y__ **49. The kids play baseball only if their parents allow it. (~R → KB → PA)**

__N__ 50. The kids will play video games only if it rains. (KVG → R)

Drill 48: Implied Causality

Instructions: Noticing an argument that commits a Causation Flaw is an important step to tackle any question that deals with that concept. That can get tricky when the test writers *imply* causality in an argument instead of explicitly stating it. For each of the following conclusions, fill in the blanks with the cause and effect implied. It's possible that there is no causality implied, in which case you should write NA.

1. If you want to lower your cholesterol, you should eat more whole grains.

    _____ causes _____.

2. People who regularly take a vitamin C supplement have better health.

    _____ causes _____.

3. Sleeping more than eight hours a night can add years to your life.

    _____ causes _____.

4. I left twenty minutes late, and then I ran out of gasoline on the way to work.

    _____ causes _____.

5. If you want to prevent tooth decay, you should floss after every meal.

    _____ causes _____.

6. The dog ate only grain-free food and lived indoors.

    _____ causes _____.

7. If you are planning to graduate in June, you should order a yearbook by March 1.

    _____ causes _____.

8. Turning off your phone two hours before bed will help you fall asleep faster.

    _____ causes _____.

9. Simply forgetting to put on gloves before you go outside can lead to frostbite in Antarctica.

    _____ causes _____.

10. Dragons who fly are more likely to die of accidental causes.

    _____ causes _____.

11. Studies show those who break a bone before age 10 are more likely to develop arthritis by age 45.

    _____ causes _____.

12. If you want to be on time, you should leave ten minutes earlier than you think.

    _____ causes _____.

13. Couples who go on dates together once a week are more likely to stay married.

    _____ causes _____.

14. If you drive too slowly in the fast lane, you are more likely to get rear-ended.

    _____ causes _____.

15. If you want to lose weight quickly, you should fast two days a week.

    _____ causes _____.

16. If you want to win the beauty pageant, you should hire a coach.

    _____ causes _____.

17. One way to increase your earnings is to take a second job.

    _____ causes _____.

18. Your car won't start in the morning if you forget to turn off the lights the night before.

    _____ causes _____.

19. If you want to learn to play the piano, you need to set aside time to practice every day.

    _____ causes _____.

20. Students are ignorant because they don't do enough homework.

    _____ causes _____.

Answers

1. <u>Eating more whole grains</u> causes <u>lower cholesterol.</u>

2. <u>Taking a vitamin C supplement</u> causes <u>better health.</u>

3. <u>Sleeping more than eight hours a night</u> causes <u>longer life.</u>

4. NA

5. <u>Flossing after every meal</u> causes <u>less tooth decay.</u>

6. NA

7. NA

8. <u>Turning off your phone two hours before bed</u> causes <u>sleep to come faster.</u>

9. <u>Forgetting to put on gloves before going outside in Antarctica</u> causes <u>frostbite.</u>

10. <u>Flying</u> causes <u>accidental death.</u>

11. <u>Breaking a bone before age 10</u> causes <u>arthritis to develop by age 45.</u>

12. <u>Leaving ten minutes earlier than you think</u> causes <u>increased likelihood of timely arrivals.</u>

13. <u>Going on a date together once a week</u> causes <u>staying married.</u>

14. <u>Driving too slowly in the fast lane</u> causes <u>greater chance of being rear-ended.</u>

15. <u>Fasting two days a week</u> causes <u>quick weight loss.</u>

16. <u>Hiring a coach</u> causes <u>beauty pageant success.</u>

17. <u>Taking a second job</u> causes <u>increased earnings.</u>

18. <u>Forgetting to turn off car lights</u> causes <u>car to not start in morning.</u>

19. NA

20. <u>Not doing enough homework</u> causes <u>student ignorance.</u>

Drill 49: Paraphrase the Haze

Instructions: One of the most important skills on the LSAT is the ability to paraphrase complicated statements without changing their meaning. Without this skill, it is extremely difficult to get through the LR and RC sections in the time allotted. Use this drill to practice that skill!

For each of the following statements or arguments, pick the answer that is the most complete and accurate paraphrase.

1. Some complex organisms, such as humans and octopodes, use their appendages to manipulate found objects to accomplish work that they wouldn't be able to do unaided.

    (A) Complex organisms all use tools to accomplish goals.
    (B) Some animals use tools to achieve certain goals.
    (C) Humans and octopodes are among the few animals that use their hands to do work.

2. Economists and historians with extensive expertise on the subject have not reached a consensus on the effects that government economic policies might have had in exacerbating or ameliorating the Great Depression.

    (A) Experts do not agree about how government policies affected the Great Depression.
    (B) Neither economists nor historians know what caused the Great Depression.
    (C) Economists and historians have different theories about the cause of the Great Depression.

3. To maintain their status as athletic participants, student athletes are required not only to fulfill the obligations of team participation, but also to ensure that their academic performance remains at the required level for graduation.

    (A) Students athletes must keep grades up or risk losing their ability to participate on the team.
    (B) Student athletes must meet team obligations and academic obligations in order to graduate.
    (C) Student athletes have heavier obligations than students who do not participate in athletics.

4. It is often necessary, even in an open society, to restrict the free flow of certain categories of information, such as information about advanced military or commercial technology, in order to safeguard the economic and national security interests of the country.

    (A) A country must always act to protect its economic and security interests.
    (B) Advanced technology that affects a country's military and commerce must always be protected.
    (C) Some kinds of information may need to be restricted to protect national interests.

5. A special ad hoc committee convened to investigate allegations of police misconduct made public its findings, concluding that the allegations are unsubstantiated by the known facts surrounding the incident in question.

    (A) A committee found that allegations of police misconduct are false.
    (B) A special committee concluded it did not know all the facts supporting alleged police misconduct.
    (C) An investigating committee concluded that the facts do not support allegations of police misconduct.

6. Those nations that are, and will continue to be, considered the most economically successful are those that ensure the education of as many of their citizens as possible in skills necessary to develop, operate, and support the most state-of-the-art technologies.

   (A) Economically successful countries educate their citizens in the newest technology skills.

   (B) Universal education in science and technology is essential for a successful economy.

   (C) State-of-the-art technology is necessary for a nation's economic success.

7. Although leadership is thought to be a skill attained through education and adherence to specific management principles, the skills needed for effective leadership are more often acquired through the circumstances of a person's life experience rather than from any particular form of formal education.

   (A) Education is not necessary to become a good leader.

   (B) Leadership skills can be taught through informal rather than formal education.

   (C) Effective leaders learn leadership skills through experience.

4

8. Commercial art is created for no higher purpose than to appeal to those who finance its production, and thus it is incapable of expressing the individual artistic vision and conscience of the artist.

   (A) Art created for profit fails to express artistic vision and conscience.

   (B) Art created to please the buyer cannot express the mind of its artist.

   (C) Art should have a higher purpose of expressing the vision and conscience of the artist.

9. The theory that an asteroid collision caused the global extinction event affecting the dinosaurs was made more plausible with the discovery of a unique chemical in a layer of dust deposited worldwide at the time of the mass extinction.

   (A) An asteroid collision caused the extinction of the dinosaurs.

   (B) The asteroid theory of the dinosaur extinction is now more plausible than other theories.

   (C) Chemical evidence has been discovered that strengthens the asteroid theory of the dinosaur extinction.

10. Because the primary function of multinational corporations is to maximize profit, management decisions that appear to support social reform do so merely as an incidental consequence of a strategy to increase profit.

    (A) Decisions that increase corporate profits often benefit society as a whole.

    (B) Corporate decisions that seem to support social causes are really intended to increase profit.

    (C) Making profit does not prevent a corporation from also supporting social reform.

11. The most common objection to the moral theory called utilitarianism lies in the practical impossibility of accurately predicting the benefits that will result from our actions in order to determine the morality of those actions.

    (A) A potential problem with utilitarianism as a moral theory is that we cannot predict the results of actions.

    (B) Utilitarianism is a failed moral theory because predicting its benefits is impossible.

    (C) Judging the morality of actions is practically impossible.

12. As a result of the inherent difficulty in determining when a species has reached extinction, it is not uncommon for ecologists and biologists to encounter a situation in which a species that was presumed extinct abruptly reappears after a period of apparent absence.

    (A) Scientists can never be completely sure that a species is really extinct.

    (B) Extinct species can sometimes come back from extinction.

    (C) Because it's hard to know when a species is extinct, they can sometimes reappear.

13. Attributing the cause of World War I to the assassination of an archduke trivializes the complex history of European treaties, alliances, and military buildups that made the conflict inevitable.

    (A) It is too simple to say that the assassination caused World War I.

    (B) Assassinations don't make conflict inevitable.

    (C) The assassination of an archduke didn't cause World War I.

14. Educating the public about the neurochemical causes of problems ranging from serious mental illness to less serious but disturbing behaviors can help to promote more compassion for those who are afflicted with a condition beyond their control.

    (A) Mental health education gives afflicted people more compassion.

    (B) More compassion is needed for those afflicted with mental illness.

    (C) Teaching people about the causes of mental problems helps people to feel empathy toward those afflicted with such problems.

15. Although the resemblance between the genome and physiology of great apes and those of humans is close, some scientists hold that the resemblance ends at the use of language as a primary means of expression and communication.

    (A) Great apes and humans are genetically similar but cannot communicate with each other.

    (B) The similarity between great apes and humans does not include language.

    (C) Great apes and humans, being similar, communicate primarily through the use of language.

16. Historians have recently come to the realization, through the increasingly common use of DNA analysis of archaeological remains, that the fearsome Viking warriors of history were not exclusively male.

    (A) DNA evidence shows some Viking warriors were women.

    (B) Historians realized they can use DNA to study the gender of Vikings.

    (C) Analyzing DNA is the most common way of studying male and female Viking remains.

17. Hummingbirds, tiny birds of the family Trochilidae, possess an astounding fourteen or fifteen neck vertebrae, depending on the particular species, whereas most mammals, even those that are many times larger, possess only seven vertebrae in the neck.

    (A) Hummingbirds have the most vertebrae of any animal.

    (B) Hummingbirds have more bones in their necks than most mammals have.

    (C) Small species of animals often have more bones than larger species.

18. Social democrats, unlike free market capitalists, typically regard government intervention in the economy as a desirable means of constraining markets and engaging in redistributive efforts for the benefit of the lower classes in order to establish a more equitable society.

    (A) Social democratic economic intervention is more desirable than free market capitalism.
    (B) Social democrats believe that the only way to make society fair is for the government to intervene in the economy.
    (C) Social democrats believe government intervention in the economy can make society more fair.

19. Despite strong views and convincing theories held by modern cosmologists, it remains an open question whether the universe came into being in one instant of time 13.8 billion years ago or is merely one manifestation of an infinite chain of universes that have always been.

    (A) Cosmologists' strong and convincing views about the beginning of the universe have all been called into question.
    (B) Scientists don't know if the universe had a beginning or has always existed.
    (C) Scientists should question even strong and convincing views on the universe's beginnings.

4

20. Serious allergic reactions to foods typically develop early in an individual's childhood. Yet, there exist many documented cases in which an adult suddenly manifests life-threatening reactions to a particular food, such as shellfish or nuts, that had never been known to trigger an immune response previously.

    (A) Adults can develop food allergies that they didn't have before.
    (B) An adult who is not allergic to a food can still have serious reactions to it.
    (C) All food allergies are serious, in children and in adults.

21. So-called progressive rock albums of the 1970s differed from other popular albums of that time in that they consisted of complex collections of songs that were created to be experienced as a unified whole within the context of one sitting rather than individually as distinct works.

    (A) Creators of progressive rock albums created works that were distinctly different from what had ever been done before.
    (B) Progressive rock albums were created in a single sitting rather than in separate sittings, as albums were before.
    (C) Unlike other albums, progressive rock albums were intended to be a single work rather than a collection of individual songs.

22. What is clear is that there are many sufficient conditions that lead to armed conflict between nations, even if only a few apply to any given conflict, but there are very few necessary conditions for conflict to arise.

    (A) War always has many causes but leads to very few necessary outcomes.
    (B) Many things guarantee a war, but few things are needed to start one.
    (C) Many things are sufficient to make armed conflict necessary, but few apply in any one case.

23. In an attempt to explain why the prevalence of multiple sclerosis is lower in tropical and subtropical countries than in countries at higher latitudes, a recent study found a correlation between the disease and consumption of dairy products, which is significantly more common in northern populations.

    (A) People who eat more dairy products are more likely to get multiple sclerosis.

    (B) The higher rate of consumption of dairy products in northern countries accounts for their higher rate of multiple sclerosis.

    (C) Countries with higher rates of multiple sclerosis also have higher rates of dairy product consumption.

24. Despite recognition by leading baseball officials that the popularity of "America's national pastime" has been in steep decline for decades, baseball managers and commissioners have been doggedly resistant to introducing changes to the sport that might invigorate its existing fans as well as attract a new generation of fans.

    (A) Baseball officials don't want to change the game to try to make it more popular again.

    (B) Baseball's popularity has declined because of officials' resistance to changes in past decades.

    (C) Baseball could become as popular as it was in the past if officials would allow changes to the game.

25. Although the term "social media" evades an agreed-upon definition, social media, whether stand-alone or embedded into other applications, is generally recognized by a set of common characteristics, such as interactivity and user-generated content.

    (A) An application cannot be called "social media" unless it possesses interactivity and user-generated content.

    (B) "Social media" could be defined as stand-alone or embedded applications with interactivity and user-generated content.

    (C) Although "social media" has no common definition, various social media share some characteristics.

26. The twin reform policies of glasnost and perestroika, introduced as part of a larger program to promote prosperity in the USSR in the 1980s, loosened governmental controls over the Soviet people and made possible new social movements that eventually brought about the collapse of the Soviet republic.

    (A) Social reforms intended to promote prosperity led to the end of the USSR.

    (B) If the USSR had not loosened its control over the people, it would not have collapsed in the 1980s.

    (C) Reform policies that loosen governmental control lead eventually to the collapse of a totalitarian society.

27. Many fans of calypso music familiar with its more popular hits of the '50s and '60s are largely ignorant of the genre's origins as a populist means of promulgating news and articulating political protest against the corruption of authoritarian colonial governments in the Caribbean.

    (A) Many fans of calypso did not know about the political corruption that it originated to protest.

    (B) Many fans don't know that calypso music started out as a form of political protest.

    (C) Calypso music was more popular as a populist music form than as a means of political protest.

28. The most recent mortgage crisis was believed by some to have been the inevitable result of federal policies that nullified state consumer protection laws; the subsequent lack of oversight created incentives for lending institutions to engage in higher levels of risky lending.

    (A) When federal regulations nullify state laws, the inevitable result is a lack of oversight.

    (B) Many believe that the recent mortgage crisis was the result of conflicting federal and state regulations regarding risky lending.

    (C) Some think that federal policies removing state oversight of lenders created the recent mortgage crisis.

29. Just as the human taste for sweetness evolved as a means of promoting the consumption of foods with high caloric content and the loathing for bitter tastes evolved to ensure avoidance of toxins, the craving for umami has evolved as a means of ensuring that humans seek and consume essential amino acids needed for survival.

    (A) Humans could not survive without a taste for sweetness, bitterness, and umami.

    (B) Like other tastes, umami evolved to promote human survival.

    (C) The most essential tastes that humans have evolved are sweet, bitter, and umami.

30. Although technology has been developed to accelerate and manage Earth's hydrologic cycle (the natural recycling of the finite supply of water), diverse natural or man-made factors, such as drought, population growth, or contamination, often create conditions in which a water supply does not meet the community's needs.

    (A) Even with water recycling technology, communities can often experience water shortages.

    (B) Hydrologic technology will never be able to prevent natural and man-made water shortages.

    (C) Technologies developed to manage water cycles created by droughts, population growth, or contamination often fail to meet communities' needs.

31. Lessons learned from examination of the regulatory and operational failures that led to the tragic sinking of the RMS Titanic bore fruit with the passing of new wireless communications regulations by nations around the world, implementing procedures that, had they existed at the time of the tragedy, would have saved many more passengers.

    (A) The lack of regulatory and operational wireless communications led to the sinking of the Titanic.

    (B) Many lives were unnecessarily lost because the crew of the RMS Titanic failed to learn new communications regulations.

    (C) Learning from the causes of the Titanic tragedy, countries passed new life-saving regulations for wireless communications.

32. Unlike a will, which becomes effective only when entered into probate after an individual's death, a living trust bypasses the costly and time-consuming process of probate and enables the trust's instructions to be carried out not only at the time of death, but also in the event of the individual's physical or mental incapacity.

    (A) A will only goes into effect when a person dies, while a trust only goes into effect when the person becomes disabled.

    (B) A trust, unlike a will, avoids probate and can be implemented before a person dies.

    (C) The difference between a will and a trust is a difference in the process of probate at death or incapacity.

33. Two separate referendums seeking to decide if the territory of Gibraltar, granted by treaty to Great Britain in 1713, should be ceded back to Spain culminated in an overwhelming affirmation by the resident population to retain its status as a British overseas territory.

    (A) The territory of Gibraltar should be returned to Spain if residents overwhelmingly agree.

    (B) The people of Gibraltar voted twice to remain a British territory and not return to Spain.

    (C) Gibraltar will permanently retain its status as a British overseas territory.

34. Tinnitus, a subjective experience of continual noise in one or both ears, usually in people over fifty years old, can arise as the result of damage inflicted by excessive or cumulative noise exposure, head and neck injuries, or ear infections, but is generally not indicative of a serious underlying physical condition needing treatment.

    (A) Tinnitus can be caused by physical damage but is never a serious medical condition in people over fifty.

    (B) Tinnitus can be caused by physical damage but can be cured with treatment of the underlying condition.

    (C) Tinnitus can be caused by physical damage but is usually not a serious medical problem.

35. To explain observations indicating that the universe is expanding at an accelerating rate, physical cosmologists hypothesize the cause to be a gravitational effect of an unknown form of energy, termed dark energy, that, although so far undetected, is believed to permeate all of space.

    (A) Scientists hypothesize that dark energy is causing the expansion of the universe to speed up.

    (B) Dark matter is hypothesized to cause the expansion of the universe even though it is undetectable.

    (C) Cosmologists hypothesize that the observed gravitational acceleration of the universe is the cause of dark energy.

36. Libertarians, whether their political inclinations tend to the left or the right, are characterized by a deep skepticism toward governmental authority but diverge on the scope of their opposition to existing political systems, presenting a range of perspectives on the legitimate role of government.

    (A) Any libertarian who is skeptical of government authority opposes existing political systems and the legitimacy of government.

    (B) Some libertarians are deeply skeptical of government, while others believe it has a legitimate role.

    (C) Libertarians are skeptical of government but differ in their views of its proper role.

37. The label cryptozoology refers to a pseudoscientific discipline that purports to study animals and plants, termed cryptids, whose presumed existence is based on anecdotal evidence derived from the indigenous folklore of a region and considered insufficient by mainstream science.

    (A) Cryptozoology is the study of folklore animals and plants whose existence is not supported by standard scientific evidence.

    (B) Cryptozoology is a discipline that proves the existence of cryptids, unusual animals that mainstream science rejects.

    (C) Cryptozoology is a pseudoscience because mainstream science does not support its evidence for the existence of cryptids.

4

38. For legal disputes in which the parties disagree on the applicable law, a common law court examines prior relevant decisions of related courts, synthesizes the principles set forth in the past cases as applicable to the current facts, and renders a decision consistent with those precedential principles.

    (A) Legal disputes over past decisions must be decided in a way consistent with relevant common law principles.

    (B) Common law courts use relevant decisions of past courts to reach a decision in a current case.

    (C) A common law court cannot ignore the decisions of past courts when deciding a legal dispute.

39. Whereas a corporate bondholder, as a creditor of the corporation, profits through the receipt of interest on the amount of the bond, a shareholder, as a part-owner of the corporation, receives a portion of the company's profits in the form of dividends.

    (A) Corporate bondholders can only profit from interest, while shareholders can only profit from dividends.

    (B) A corporation's bondholder profits from an interest in a company instead of from receiving dividends.

    (C) A bondholder earns interest on the bond, while a shareholder gets a share of the company's profits.

4

40. The hazards of asbestos to human health arise mainly from the microscopic nature of its strong and durable fibers, which are so minute that they easily become airborne and are inhaled, lodging in the respiratory system where they result in severe irritation and damage to tissues.

    (A) The microscopic nature of asbestos makes it hazardous only when inhaled.

    (B) Asbestos becomes airborne and causes severe damage to the microscopic fibers in lung tissues.

    (C) Asbestos is dangerous because the fibers are very small and tough, causing tissue damage when inhaled.

41. The English name of the Hoopoe, a colorful bird of Afro-Eurasia notable for its distinctive crown of feathers, was conferred as an onomatopoeic imitation of the call that the bird emits in the wild, as was its Latin name, *upupa*.

    (A) The Hoopoe is known for its onomatopoeic call in the wild.

    (B) Both the English and Latin names of the Hoopoe imitate its cry.

    (C) The Hoopoe has both an English and a Latin name that make note of its distinctive feathers.

42. Sometimes labeled "failed stars," brown dwarfs are relatively cool stellar objects that possess too little mass to become ordinary stars because they are incapable of sustaining nuclear fusion in their cores the way main sequence stars such as our Sun are able to do.

    (A) Brown dwarfs are too small to support the nuclear fusion found in ordinary stars.

    (B) Brown dwarfs could only be successful stars if they had as much mass as our Sun.

    (C) Brown dwarfs will be failed stars until they gain enough mass to sustain nuclear fusion.

43. While "Khan" is known to be a traditional title meaning "leader" or "ruler," historians remain uncertain as to the origin and meaning of "Genghis," the name conferred by a meeting of the kurultai tribal council on a man previously known as Temujin when he was proclaimed leader of the Mongols.

    (A) Mongol leaders were all given the title "Khan," but only Temujin was given the unknown name of "Genghis."

    (B) Nobody knows the origin of the name "Genghis" or why it was given to a man named Temujin.

    (C) Historians know "Khan" means leader but don't know the meaning of the name "Genghis" given to the Mongol ruler.

44. The sport of curling, which originated in Scotland, got its intriguing name from the tendency of the heavy curling stones to deviate from a straight path due to tiny water droplets that form on the surface of the ice, for which players compensate by sweeping the ice ahead of the sliding stone.

    (A) Curling stones cause water droplets to form on the surface of ice, which players sweep smooth to keep the path from deviating.

    (B) The name "curling" comes from the curved path of the stone caused by drops of water on the ice.

    (C) The Scottish sport of curling was named for the heavy stone hurled in a curved path on the ice, which players sweep in an effort to keep the stone straight.

45. Young border collies have been found to be capable of mastering a new command in under 5 seconds and following the command accurately at least 95% of the time, making this exceptionally intelligent breed a consistently popular choice as a reliable working dog and an easily-trainable animal companion.

    (A) Border collies are exceptionally intelligent working dogs that can be trained in under 5 seconds to obey 95% of the time.

    (B) Border collies make good working dogs and pets because of their ability to learn and follow commands.

    (C) Young border collies make the best working dogs and pets because of their exceptional intelligence.

46. While a dearth of empirical evidence relating to the origins of human language has led some scholars to regard the entire topic as unsuitable for serious study, some linguists have built academic careers around a variety of theories based on either cultural or genetic causal factors.

    (A) Some people think language origins can never be studied, but others study various theories about the causes of language.

    (B) A lack of evidence has caused some linguists to abandon academic careers focused on the cultural and genetic theories of language.

    (C) Some scholars are unaware of cultural and genetic evidence for the origins of language that others have built careers around.

47. Cryptocurrency mining consumes large quantities of energy to generate even small amounts of currency, so those who engage in large-scale mining of cryptocurrencies often operate in locales such as Iceland in order to avail themselves of abundant natural energy sources and cool climates.

    (A) Cryptocurrency miners consume more energy than can be provided in places such as the United States.

    (B) Mining cryptocurrency in Iceland is made easier by that country's good climate and natural resources.

    (C) Cryptocurrency miners often locate in places where natural resources help to meet their energy needs.

48. The potential for inadvertent errors in the continuity of characters, plot, and scene during filmmaking is a special concern, requiring close monitoring of the filming process by a script supervisor to try to avoid the expense of rectifying discontinuities discovered after the completion of shooting.

 (A) Discontinuity errors do not occur when a script supervisor monitors the filming process.

 (B) Film production requires a script supervisor to monitor filming and fix costly continuity errors after shooting.

 (C) Filmmakers use script supervisors to watch for and avoid costly continuity errors during the filming process.

49. Whereas humans and almost all of their domesticated animals manifest a sexual dimorphism in which the average male of the species is larger than the average female, a significant majority of animal species on Earth exhibit the opposite dimorphism, with females often possessing a marked size advantage.

 (A) The females of most animal species have a significant advantage over human females and domesticated animals because of their greater size.

 (B) In most animal species other than humans and their domesticated animals, the females are larger than the males.

 (C) Sexual dimorphism is a problem in all species, but especially in nonhuman and non-domesticated species.

50. Explanations for an observed correlation between sugar consumption and depression commonly assume that sugar in the bloodstream triggers various chemical processes resulting in depression, but there are some who note that the opposite might be the case: i.e., that people self-medicate with sweet foods when depressed.

 (A) Most assume that sugar triggers depression, but it's possible that depression triggers sugar consumption.

 (B) Eating sugar triggers depression, which in turn causes people to eat more sugar.

 (C) Consumption of sugar is correlated with mental health problems, but nobody is sure how.

4

Answers

Note: The portions of text that are crossed out are the parts that make an answer choice incorrect.

1. Some complex organisms, such as humans and octopodes, use their appendages to manipulate found objects to accomplish work that they wouldn't be able to do unaided.

    (A) Complex organisms all use tools to accomplish goals.

    ● **Some animals use tools to achieve certain goals.**

    (C) Humans and octopodes are among ~~the few~~ animals that use their ~~hands~~ to do work.

2. Economists and historians with extensive expertise on the subject have not reached a consensus on the effects that government economic policies might have had in exacerbating or ameliorating the Great Depression.

    ● **Experts do not agree about how government policies affected the Great Depression.**

    (B) Neither economists nor historians ~~know what~~ ~~caused~~ the Great Depression.

    (C) Economists and historians have different theories ~~about the cause of~~ the Great Depression.

3. To maintain their status as athletic participants, student athletes are required not only to fulfill the obligations of team participation, but also to ensure that their academic performance remains at the required level for graduation.

    ● **Students athletes must keep grades up or risk losing their ability to participate on the team.**

    (B) Student athletes must meet team obligations and academic obligations ~~in order to graduate~~.

    (C) Student athletes have ~~heavier~~ obligations ~~than students who do not participate~~ in athletics.

4. It is often necessary, even in an open society, to restrict the free flow of certain categories of information, such as information about advanced military or commercial technology, in order to safeguard the economic and national security interests of the country.

    (A) A country ~~must always act~~ to protect its economic and security interests.

    (B) Advanced technology that affects a country's military and commerce ~~must always be protected~~.

    ● **Some kinds of information may need to be restricted to protect national interests.**

5. A special ad hoc committee convened to investigate allegations of police misconduct made public its findings concluding that the allegations are unsubstantiated by the known facts surrounding the incident in question.

    (A) A committee found that allegations of police misconduct ~~are false~~.

    (B) A special committee concluded it ~~did not know all the facts~~ supporting alleged police misconduct.

    ● **An investigating committee concluded that the facts do not support allegations of police misconduct.**

6. Those nations that are, and will continue to be, considered the most economically successful are those that ensure the education of as many of their citizens as possible in skills necessary to develop, operate, and support the most state-of-the-art technologies.

    ● **Economically successful countries educate their citizens in the newest technology skills.**

    (B) ~~Universal~~ education in science and technology is ~~essential for a~~ successful economy.

    (C) ~~State-of-the-art technology is necessary~~ for a nation's economic success.

4

7. Although leadership is thought to be a skill attained through education and adherence to specific management principles, the skills needed for effective leadership are more often acquired through the circumstances of a person's life experience rather than from any particular form of formal education.

   (A) Education is ~~not necessary~~ to become a good leader.

   (B) Leadership skills ~~can be taught through informal rather than~~ formal education.

   ● **Effective leaders learn leadership skills through experience.**

8. Commercial art is created for no higher purpose than to appeal to those who finance its production, and thus it is incapable of expressing the individual artistic vision and conscience of the artist.

   (A) Art ~~created for profit~~ fails to express artistic vision and conscience.

   ● **Art created to please the buyer cannot express the mind of its artist.**

   (C) Art ~~should have~~ a higher purpose of expressing the vision and conscience of the artist.

9. The theory that an asteroid collision caused the global extinction event affecting the dinosaurs was made more plausible with the discovery of a unique chemical in a layer of dust deposited worldwide at the time of the mass extinction.

   (A) An asteroid collision ~~caused~~ the extinction of the dinosaurs.

   (B) The asteroid theory of the dinosaur extinction is now more plausible ~~than other theories~~.

   ● **Chemical evidence has been discovered that strengthens the asteroid theory of the dinosaur extinction.**

10. Because the primary function of multinational corporations is to maximize profit, management decisions that appear to support social reform do so merely as an incidental consequence of a strategy to increase profit.

    (A) Decisions that increase corporate profits ~~often benefit society~~ as a whole.

    ● **Corporate decisions that seem to support social causes are really intended to increase profit.**

    (C) Making profit does ~~not prevent~~ a corporation from also supporting social reform.

11. The most common objection to the moral theory called utilitarianism lies in the practical impossibility of accurately predicting the benefits that will result from our actions in order to determine the morality of those actions.

    ● **A potential problem with utilitarianism as a moral theory is that we cannot predict the results of actions.**

    (B) Utilitarianism ~~is a failed moral theory~~ because predicting its benefits is impossible.

    (C) ~~Judging the morality~~ of actions is practically impossible.

12. As a result of the inherent difficulty in determining when a species has reached extinction, it is not uncommon for ecologists and biologists to encounter a situation in which a species that was presumed extinct abruptly reappears after a period of apparent absence.

    (A) Scientists ~~can never be completely sure~~ that a species is really extinct.

    (B) Extinct species can sometimes ~~come back from extinction~~.

    ● **Because it's hard to know when a species is extinct, they can sometimes reappear.**

13. Attributing the cause of World War I to the assassination of an archduke trivializes the complex history of European treaties, alliances, and military buildups that made the conflict inevitable.

    ⬤ **It is too simple to say that the assassination caused World War I.**

    Ⓑ Assassinations ~~don't make conflict inevitable~~.

    Ⓒ The assassination of an archduke ~~didn't cause World War I~~.

14. Educating the public about the neurochemical causes of problems ranging from serious mental illness to less serious but disturbing behaviors can help to promote more compassion for those who are afflicted with a condition beyond their control.

    Ⓐ Mental health education ~~gives afflicted people more compassion~~.

    Ⓑ ~~More compassion is needed~~ for those afflicted with mental illness.

    ⬤ **Teaching people about the causes of mental problems helps people to feel empathy toward those afflicted with such problems.**

15. Although the resemblance between the genome and physiology of great apes and those of humans is close, some scientists hold that the resemblance ends at the use of language as a primary means of expression and communication.

    Ⓐ Great apes and humans are genetically similar, but ~~cannot communicate with each other~~.

    ⬤ **The similarity between great apes and humans does not include language.**

    Ⓒ Great apes and humans, being similar, ~~communicate primarily through~~ the use of language.

16. Historians have recently come to the realization, through the increasingly common use of DNA analysis of archaeological remains, that the fearsome Viking warriors of history were not exclusively male.

    ⬤ **DNA evidence shows some Viking warriors were women.**

    Ⓑ Historians ~~realized they can use~~ DNA to study the gender of Vikings.

    Ⓒ Analyzing DNA ~~is the most common~~ way of studying male and female Viking remains.

17. Hummingbirds, tiny birds of the family Trochilidae, possess an astounding fourteen or fifteen neck vertebrae, depending on the particular species, whereas most mammals, even those that are many times larger, possess only seven vertebrae in the neck.

    Ⓐ Hummingbirds have ~~the most vertebrae of any animal~~.

    ⬤ **Hummingbirds have more bones in their necks than most mammals have.**

    Ⓒ ~~Small species of animals~~ often have more bones than larger species.

18. Social democrats, unlike free market capitalists, typically regard government intervention in the economy as a desirable means of constraining markets and engaging in redistributive efforts for the benefit of the lower classes in order to establish a more equitable society.

    Ⓐ Social democratic economic intervention is ~~more desirable than free market capitalism~~.

    Ⓑ Social democrats believe that ~~the only way~~ to make society fair is for the government to intervene in the economy.

    ⬤ **Social democrats believe government intervention in the economy can make society more fair.**

19. Despite strong views and convincing theories held by modern cosmologists, it remains an open question whether the universe came into being in one instant of time 13.8 billion years ago or is merely one manifestation of an infinite chain of universes that have always been.

(A) Cosmologists' strong and convincing views about the beginning of the universe ~~have all been called into question~~.

● **Scientists don't know if the universe had a beginning or has always existed.**

(C) Scientists ~~should question~~ even strong and convincing views on the universe's beginnings.

20. Serious allergic reactions to foods typically develop early in an individual's childhood. Yet, there exist many documented cases in which an adult suddenly manifests life-threatening reactions to a particular food, such as shellfish or nuts, that had never been known to trigger an immune response previously.

● **Adults can develop food allergies that they didn't have before.**

(B) An ~~adult who is not allergic~~ to a food can still have serious reactions to it.

(C) All food allergies ~~are serious~~, in children and in adults.

4

21. So-called progressive rock albums of the 1970s differed from other popular albums of that time in that they consisted of complex collections of songs that were created to be experienced as a unified whole within the context of one sitting rather than individually as distinct works.

(A) Creators of progressive rock albums created works that were distinctly different ~~from what had ever been done before~~.

(B) Progressive rock albums ~~were created in a single sitting~~ rather than in separate sittings, as albums were before.

● **Unlike other albums, progressive rock albums were intended to be a single work rather than a collection of individual songs.**

22. What is clear is that there are many sufficient conditions that lead to armed conflict between nations, even if only a few apply to any given conflict, but there are very few necessary conditions for conflict to arise.

(A) War always has many causes but ~~leads to~~ very few ~~necessary outcomes~~.

● **Many things guarantee a war, but few things are needed to start one.**

(C) Many things are sufficient ~~to make armed conflict necessary~~, but few apply in any one case.

23. In an attempt to explain why the prevalence of multiple sclerosis is lower in tropical and subtropical countries than in countries at higher latitudes, a recent study found a correlation between the disease and consumption of dairy products, which is significantly more common in northern populations.

(A) People who eat more dairy products ~~are more likely~~ to get multiple sclerosis.

(B) The higher rate of consumption of dairy products in northern countries ~~accounts~~ for their higher rate of multiple sclerosis.

● **Countries with higher rates of multiple sclerosis also have higher rates of dairy product consumption.**

24. Despite recognition by leading baseball officials that the popularity of "America's national pastime" has been in steep decline for decades, baseball managers and commissioners have been doggedly resistant to introducing changes to the sport that might invigorate its existing fans as well as attract a new generation of fans.

    ● **Baseball officials don't want to change the game to try to make it more popular again.**

    Ⓑ Baseball's popularity has declined ~~because of~~ officials' resistance to changes in past decades.

    Ⓒ Baseball ~~could become as popular~~ as it was in the past if officials would allow changes to the game.

25. Although the term "social media" evades an agreed-upon definition, social media, whether stand-alone or embedded into other applications, is generally recognized by a set of common characteristics, such as interactivity and user-generated content.

    Ⓐ An application ~~cannot be called~~ "social media" ~~unless~~ it possesses interactivity and user-generated content.

    Ⓑ "Social media" ~~could be defined as~~ stand-alone or embedded applications with interactivity and user-generated content.

    ● **Although "social media" has no common definition, various social media share some characteristics.**

26. The twin reform policies of glasnost and perestroika, introduced as part of a larger program to promote prosperity in the USSR in the 1980s, loosened governmental controls over the Soviet people and made possible new social movements that eventually brought about the collapse of the Soviet republic.

    ● **Social reforms intended to promote prosperity led to the end of the USSR.**

    Ⓑ If the USSR had not loosened its control over the people, ~~it would not have collapsed~~ in the 1980s.

    Ⓒ ~~Reform policies~~ that loosen governmental control ~~lead eventually to the collapse of a totalitarian society~~.

27. Many fans of calypso music familiar with its more popular hits of the '50s and '60s are largely ignorant of the genre's origins as a populist means of promulgating news and articulating political protest against the corruption of authoritarian colonial governments in the Caribbean.

    Ⓐ Many fans of calypso did not ~~know about the political corruption~~ that it originated to protest.

    ● **Many fans don't know that calypso music started out as a form of political protest.**

    Ⓒ Calypso music was ~~more popular~~ as a populist music form than as a means of political protest.

28. The most recent mortgage crisis was believed by some to have been the inevitable result of federal policies that nullified state consumer protection laws; the subsequent lack of oversight created incentives for lending institutions to engage in higher levels of risky lending.

    Ⓐ When federal regulations nullify state laws, ~~the inevitable result is a lack of oversight~~.

    Ⓑ Many believe that the recent mortgage crisis was the result of conflicting federal and state regulations regarding risky lending.

    ● **Some think that federal policies removing state oversight of lenders created the recent mortgage crisis.**

29. Just as the human taste for sweetness evolved as a means of promoting the consumption of foods with high caloric content and the loathing for bitter tastes evolved to ensure avoidance of toxins, the craving for umami has evolved as a means of ensuring that humans seek and consume essential amino acids needed for survival.

   Ⓐ Humans ~~could not survive without~~ a taste for sweetness, bitterness, and umami.

   ⬤ **Like other tastes, umami evolved to promote human survival.**

   Ⓒ The ~~most essential tastes~~ that humans have evolved are sweet, bitter, and umami.

30. Although technology has been developed to accelerate and manage Earth's hydrologic cycle (the natural recycling of the finite supply of water), diverse natural or man-made factors, such as drought, population growth, or contamination, often create conditions in which a water supply does not meet the community's needs.

   ⬤ **Even with water recycling technology, communities can often experience water shortages.**

   Ⓑ Hydrologic technology ~~will never be able to prevent~~ natural and man-made water shortages.

   Ⓒ ~~Technologies~~ developed to manage water cycles created by droughts, population growth, or contamination ~~often fail to meet communities' needs~~.

31. Lessons learned from examination of the regulatory and operational failures that led to the tragic sinking of the RMS Titanic bore fruit with the passing of new wireless communications regulations by nations around the world, implementing procedures that, had they existed at the time of the tragedy, would have saved many more passengers.

   Ⓐ The lack of regulatory and operational wireless communications ~~led to~~ the sinking of the Titanic.

   Ⓑ Many lives were unnecessarily lost because the crew of the RMS Titanic ~~failed to learn~~ new communications regulations.

   ⬤ **Learning from the causes of the Titanic tragedy, countries passed new life-saving regulations for wireless communications.**

32. Unlike a will, which becomes effective only when entered into probate after an individual's death, a living trust bypasses the costly and time-consuming process of probate and enables the trust's instructions to be carried out not only at the time of death, but also in the event of the individual's physical or mental incapacity.

   Ⓐ A will only goes into effect when a person dies, while a ~~trust only goes into effect~~ when the person becomes disabled.

   ⬤ **A trust, unlike a will, avoids probate and can be implemented before a person dies.**

   Ⓒ The difference between a will and a trust is ~~a difference in the process of probate~~ at death or incapacity.

33. Two separate referendums seeking to decide if the territory of Gibraltar, granted by treaty to Great Britain in 1713, should be ceded back to Spain culminated in an overwhelming affirmation by the resident population to retain its status as a British overseas territory.

   Ⓐ The territory of Gibraltar ~~should be~~ returned to Spain if residents overwhelmingly agree.

   ⬤ **The people of Gibraltar voted twice to remain a British territory and not return to Spain.**

   Ⓒ Gibraltar ~~will permanently retain its status~~ as a British overseas territory.

34. Tinnitus, a subjective experience of continual noise in one or both ears, usually in people over fifty years old, can arise as the result of damage inflicted by excessive or cumulative noise exposure, head and neck injuries, or ear infections, but is generally not indicative of a serious underlying physical condition needing treatment.

    (A) Tinnitus can be caused by physical damage but ~~is never~~ a serious medical condition in people over fifty.

    (B) Tinnitus can be caused by physical damage but ~~can be cured~~ with treatment of the underlying condition.

    ● **Tinnitus can be caused by physical damage but is usually not a serious medical problem.**

35. To explain observations indicating that the universe is expanding at an accelerating rate, physical cosmologists hypothesize the cause to be a gravitational effect of an unknown form of energy, termed dark energy, that, although so far undetected, is believed to permeate all of space.

    ● **Scientists hypothesize that dark energy is causing the expansion of the universe to speed up.**

    (B) Dark matter is hypothesized ~~to cause the expansion~~ of the universe even though it is undetectable.

    (C) Cosmologists hypothesize that the observed gravitational acceleration of the universe ~~is the cause of dark energy~~.

36. Libertarians, whether their political inclinations tend to the left or the right, are characterized by a deep skepticism toward governmental authority but diverge on the scope of their opposition to existing political systems, presenting a range of perspectives on the legitimate role of government.

    (A) ~~Any libertarian who~~ is skeptical of government authority ~~opposes~~ existing political systems and the legitimacy of government.

    (B) Some libertarians are deeply skeptical of government, while ~~others believe it has a legitimate role~~.

    ● **Libertarians are skeptical of government but differ in their views of its proper role.**

37. The label cryptozoology refers to a pseudoscientific discipline that purports to study animals and plants, termed cryptids, whose presumed existence is based on anecdotal evidence derived from the indigenous folklore of a region and considered insufficient by mainstream science.

    ● **Cryptozoology is the study of folklore animals and plants whose existence is not supported by standard scientific evidence.**

    (B) Cryptozoology is a discipline that ~~proves~~ the existence of cryptids, unusual animals that mainstream science ~~rejects~~.

    (C) Cryptozoology is a pseudoscience ~~because~~ mainstream science does not support its evidence for the existence of cryptids.

38. For legal disputes in which the parties disagree on the applicable law, a common law court examines prior relevant decisions of related courts, synthesizes the principles set forth in the past cases as applicable to the current facts, and renders a decision consistent with those precedential principles.

    (A) Legal disputes over past decisions ~~must be decided~~ in a way consistent with relevant common law principles.

    ● **Common law courts use relevant decisions of past courts to reach a decision in a current case.**

    (C) A common law court ~~cannot ignore~~ the decisions of past courts when deciding a legal dispute.

39. Whereas a corporate bondholder, as a creditor of the corporation, profits through the receipt of interest on the amount of the bond, a shareholder, as a part-owner of the corporation, receives a portion of the company's profits in the form of dividends.

    (A) Corporate bondholders ~~can only profit from~~ interest, while shareholders can only profit from dividends.

    (B) A corporation's bondholder ~~profits from an interest in a company~~ instead of from receiving dividends.

    ● **A bondholder earns interest on the bond, while a shareholder gets a share of the company's profits.**

40. The hazards of asbestos to human health arise mainly from the microscopic nature of its strong and durable fibers, which are so minute that they easily become airborne and are inhaled, lodging in the respiratory system where they result in severe irritation and damage to tissues.

    (A) The microscopic nature of asbestos makes it hazardous ~~only when~~ inhaled.

    (B) Asbestos becomes airborne and causes severe damage to ~~the microscopic fibers in lung tissues~~.

    ● **Asbestos is dangerous because the fibers are very small and tough, causing tissue damage when inhaled.**

41. The English name of the Hoopoe, a colorful bird of Afro-Eurasia notable for its distinctive crown of feathers, was conferred as an onomatopoeic imitation of the call that the bird emits in the wild, as was its Latin name, *upupa*.

    (A) The Hoopoe is known for its ~~onomatopoeic call~~ in the wild.

    ● **Both the English and Latin names of the Hoopoe imitate its cry.**

    (C) The Hoopoe has both an English and a Latin name ~~that make note of its distinctive feathers~~.

42. Sometimes labeled "failed stars," brown dwarfs are relatively cool stellar objects that possess too little mass to become ordinary stars because they are incapable of sustaining nuclear fusion in their cores the way main sequence stars such as our Sun are able to do.

    ● **Brown dwarfs are too small to support the nuclear fusion found in ordinary stars.**

    (B) Brown dwarfs ~~could only be successful stars if~~ they had as much mass as our Sun.

    (C) Brown dwarfs ~~will be failed stars until~~ they gain enough mass to sustain nuclear fusion.

43. While "Khan" is known to be a traditional title meaning "leader" or "ruler," historians remain uncertain as to the origin and meaning of "Genghis," the name conferred by a meeting of the kurultai tribal council on a man previously known as Temujin when he was proclaimed leader of the Mongols.

    (A) Mongol leaders ~~were all given~~ the title "Khan," ~~but only~~ Temujin was given the unknown name of "Genghis."

    (B) Nobody knows the origin of the name "Genghis" ~~or why it was given to~~ a man named Temujin.

    ● **Historians know "Khan" means leader but don't know the meaning of the name "Genghis" given to the Mongol ruler.**

44. The sport of curling, which originated in Scotland, got its intriguing name from the tendency of the heavy curling stones to deviate from a straight path due to tiny water droplets that form on the surface of the ice, for which players compensate by sweeping the ice ahead of the sliding stone.

    Ⓐ Curling stones ~~cause~~ water droplets to form on the surface of ice, which players sweep smooth to keep the path from deviating.

    ⬤ **The name "curling" comes from the curved path of the stone caused by drops of water on the ice.**

    Ⓒ The Scottish sport of curling was ~~named for the heavy stone~~ hurled in a curved path on the ice, which players sweep in an effort to keep the stone straight.

45. Young border collies have been found to be capable of mastering a new command in under 5 seconds and following the command accurately at least 95% of the time, making this exceptionally intelligent breed a consistently popular choice as a reliable working dog and an easily-trainable animal companion.

    Ⓐ Border collies are exceptionally intelligent working dogs that can be trained in under 5 seconds ~~to obey~~ 95% of the time.

    ⬤ **Border collies make good working dogs and pets because of their ability to learn and follow commands.**

    Ⓒ Young border collies make ~~the best~~ working dogs and pets because of their exceptional intelligence.

46. While a dearth of empirical evidence relating to the origins of human language has led some scholars to regard the entire topic as unsuitable for serious study, some linguists have built academic careers around a variety of theories based on either cultural or genetic causal factors.

    ⬤ **Some people think language origins can never be studied, but others make careers studying various theories about the causes of language.**

    Ⓑ A lack of evidence has caused some linguists to ~~abandon academic careers~~ focused on the cultural and genetic theories of language.

    Ⓒ Some scholars are ~~unaware of~~ cultural and genetic evidence for the origins of language that others have built careers around.

47. Cryptocurrency mining consumes large quantities of energy to generate even small amounts of currency, so those who engage in large-scale mining of cryptocurrencies often operate in locales such as Iceland in order to avail themselves of abundant natural energy sources and cool climates.

    Ⓐ Cryptocurrency miners consume ~~more~~ energy ~~than can be provided~~ in places such as the United States.

    Ⓑ Mining cryptocurrency in Iceland ~~is made easier by that country's good climate and natural resources~~.

    ⬤ **Cryptocurrency miners often locate in places where natural resources help to meet their energy needs.**

48. The potential for inadvertent errors in the continuity of characters, plot, and scene during filmmaking is a special concern, requiring close monitoring of the filming process by a script supervisor to try to avoid the expense of rectifying discontinuities discovered after the completion of shooting.

    Ⓐ Discontinuity errors ~~do not occur~~ when a script supervisor monitors the filming process.

    Ⓑ Film production requires a script supervisor to monitor filming ~~and fix~~ costly continuity errors after shooting.

    ⬤ **Filmmakers use script supervisors to watch for and avoid costly continuity errors during the filming process.**

49. Whereas humans and almost all of their domesticated animals manifest a sexual dimorphism in which the average male of the species is larger than the average female, a significant majority of animal species on Earth exhibit the opposite dimorphism, with females often possessing a marked size advantage.

   (A) The females of most animal species ~~have a significant advantage over human females~~ and domesticated animals because of their greater size.

   ● **In most animal species other than humans and their domesticated animals, the females are larger than the males.**

   (C) Sexual dimorphism ~~is a problem~~ in all species, but especially in nonhuman and non-domesticated species.

50. Explanations for an observed correlation between sugar consumption and depression commonly assume that sugar in the bloodstream triggers various chemical processes resulting in depression, but there are some who note that the opposite might be the case: i.e., that people self-medicate with sweet foods when depressed.

   ● **Most assume that sugar triggers depression, but it's possible that depression triggers sugar consumption.**

   (B) Eating sugar triggers depression, ~~which in turn causes~~ people to eat more sugar.

   (C) Consumption of sugar is correlated with ~~mental health problems~~, but ~~nobody is sure how~~.

4

Drill 50: Famous Flaws, Round 2

Instructions: For each of the following abbreviated arguments, select which famous flaw is being committed. Since there is some overlap between the different flaws, you might prephrase an answer that doesn't appear. That's fine! Figure out which answer is correct, and then spend time thinking about why it's correct and how you could have prephrased both answers (assuming, of course, that you were correct with your initial prephrase).

1. The local newspaper conducted a poll of its readers. An overwhelming majority responded that they prefer to read their news in print rather than online. Clearly, newspapers are still the preferred way to get news.

   (A) Percent vs. Amount
   (B) Comparison Flaw
   (C) Sampling Flaw

2. The junior varsity team has won its last eight consecutive games—more consecutive wins than any junior varsity team has ever had. It is therefore unlikely that they will win a ninth game in a row.

   (A) Unwarranted Prediction
   (B) Illegal Reversal
   (C) Causation Flaw

3. Ninety percent of Americans are convinced that intelligent extraterrestrial beings exist and can be communicated with. NASA should, therefore, make every effort to establish communication with these beings.

   (A) Sampling Flaw
   (B) Percent vs. Amount
   (C) Opinion vs. Fact

4. Katelyn should have no problem deciding which college she will attend. She certainly had no problem deciding which friend's New Year's Eve party to attend this year.

   (A) False Choice
   (B) Comparison Flaw
   (C) Relative vs. Absolute

5. A recent study found that older people who regularly practiced yoga for longer than six months had less joint pain than those who tried yoga and quit. This is good evidence that regularly practicing yoga decreases joint pain.

   (A) Causation Flaw
   (B) Comparison Flaw
   (C) Relative vs. Absolute

6. Nobody who has a criminal record can own a gun in this county. But George has never had a criminal record of any kind, so he can own one.

   (A) Appeal to Emotion
   (B) Illegal Negation
   (C) Circular Reasoning

7. Marianne says she joined the debate club to learn to argue better. But I disagree with her intentions. In my opinion, the world needs less arguing and more cooperation.

   (A) Appeal to Emotion
   (B) Opinion vs. Fact
   (C) Equivocation

8. Astrology can reveal things about a person's personality. Why else would so many people continue to practice it and believe its predictions for so many centuries?

   (A) Appeal to Inappropriate Authority
   (B) Opinion vs. Fact
   (C) Unproven vs. Untrue

4

9. If a person becomes chilled, it can become easier for the body's defenses to be overwhelmed when exposed to a virus. So, she obviously caught her cold when she went out in the snow without her coat.

   (A) Possible vs. Certain
   (B) Unproven vs. Untrue
   (C) Unwarranted Prediction

10. Preparing for retirement requires putting money into savings regularly. After all, no one would go without eating for weeks or months at a time. Just as your body needs regular meals, your savings need regular infusions of cash.

    (A) Appeal to Emotion
    (B) Illegal Reversal
    (C) Comparison Flaw

11. The brain is made up entirely of organic molecules, and organic molecules have no consciousness. So, it cannot be true that the brain possesses consciousness.

    (A) Causation Flaw
    (B) Part vs. Whole
    (C) Relative vs. Absolute

12. Paying bills is a necessary part of life. After all, the bills have to be paid.

    (A) Circular Reasoning
    (B) Opinion vs. Fact
    (C) Self-Contradiction

13. All of the polls show that consumers are feeling confident about the state of the economy. The economist's claim that the economy is booming must therefore be correct!

    (A) Appeal to Emotion
    (B) Possible vs. Certain
    (C) Opinion vs. Fact

14. Buying stock in this new computer startup company is going to be a good investment. My barber, whose wife is a programmer for a big company downtown, says it is sure to be profitable.

    (A) Term Shift
    (B) Opinion vs. Fact
    (C) Appeal to Inappropriate Authority

15. Brazil nuts are an outstanding source of selenium. This makes brazil nuts an excellent addition to a healthy diet.

    (A) Term Shift
    (B) Relative vs. Absolute
    (C) Causation Flaw

16. The accusation that council member Brown misused public funds is nothing more than a lie by her opponents. The ethics committee's month-long investigation uncovered no facts to support any of the allegations made against her.

    (A) Appeal to Inappropriate Authority
    (B) Unproven vs. Untrue
    (C) Equivocation

17. Animal lovers were polled by the magazine *Puppy People* to determine American pet preferences. The poll showed that Americans prefer owning dogs over cats by a wide margin.

    (A) Percent vs. Amount
    (B) Sampling Flaw
    (C) Appeal to Emotion

18. It's clear that ignorance of the law cannot be used as an excuse. Because this local ordinance is so little known, though, the officer should not have given her that ticket.

    (A) Self-Contradiction
    (B) Term Shift
    (C) Appeal to Emotion

4

19. My aunt is familiar with the characters in Harry Potter, though she has never read the books. She must have watched the movies.

    (A) Unproven vs. Untrue
    (B) Opinion vs. Fact
    (C) False Choice

20. The theory of evolution is unbelievable. It is absurd to think that pond scum somehow became the human race!

    (A) Straw Man
    (B) Causation Flaw
    (C) Appeal to Emotion

21. The Democratic candidate has no chance of winning the congressional seat this year. In every election for the past 20 years, the majority in this district has voted for the Republican candidate.

    (A) Sampling Flaw
    (B) Causation Flaw
    (C) Unwarranted Prediction

22. The health columnist for the local paper received undeserved praise for his series on the dangers of drug and alcohol use. His recent incident of public drunkenness has called his judgment and sincerity into serious question.

    (A) Ad Hominem
    (B) Straw Man
    (C) Opinion vs. Fact

23. Vegetarianism is not just a healthy choice; it's the most ethical lifestyle. We all should want to put an end to the needless suffering and brutal slaughter of helpless animals.

    (A) Opinion vs. Fact
    (B) Appeal to Emotion
    (C) Relative vs. Absolute

24. Grilled chicken is healthier than fried chicken. To provide a healthy menu, the restaurant should stop serving fried chicken.

    (A) Term Shift
    (B) False Choice
    (C) Relative vs. Absolute

25. Philosophers who argue that free will is an illusion are correct. Nobody is free to lie, cheat, steal, or kill at will, for example.

    (A) Equivocation
    (B) Appeal to Emotion
    (C) Opinion vs. Fact

4

5 lb.

Answers

1.	C	8.	B	15.	A	22.	A
2.	A	9.	A	16.	B	23.	B
3.	C	10.	C	17.	B	24.	C
4.	B	11.	B	18.	A	25.	A
5.	A	12.	A	19.	C		
6.	B	13.	C	20.	A		
7.	C	14.	C	21.	C		

4

Drill 51: Classic Flaws Checklist

Instructions: The LSAT has a set of classic flaws that show up over and over again in Logical Reasoning stimuli. You know what we're talking about: Illegal Reversal and Illegal Negation, Causation Flaw, and Sampling Flaw, to name a few. But there are sometimes cases where the LSAT will present a valid argument that has many of the same features as these famous flaws. Can you tell the difference between a valid argument and a flawed one? For the argument types listed below, indicate whether each of the accompanying items is a criterion that needs to be met (Y) or not (N) in order to make a valid argument. (Note: The parentheses tell you which classic flaw is associated with that type of reasoning.)

An argument with a data sample as its evidence (Sampling Flaw):

_____ 1. A sample representative of the group about which the conclusion is drawn

_____ 2. A sample collected in a way that is impervious to bias

_____ 3. A sample that consists of at least ten percent of the overall population being studied

_____ 4. A large enough sample size

An argument that relies on the opinion of an expert (Appeal to Inappropriate Authority):

_____ 5. Evidence of expertise

_____ 6. Expertise in a field relevant to the argument

_____ 7. Proof that the expert is not alone in their thinking

_____ 8. A consensus among experts in the field

A causal argument (Causation Flaw):

_____ 9. Proof that no other possible causes for the observed effect exist

_____ 10. Evidence that no alternative explanation is equally likely

_____ 11. A timeline that places the alleged cause before the observed effect

_____ 12. A conclusion that is calibrated to the strength of the evidence

An argument that hinges on an analogy (Comparison Flaw):

_____ 13. One or more relevant similarities between the items being compared

_____ 14. A lack of relevant differences between the items being compared

_____ 15. A thorough examination of all differences between the items being compared

_____ 16. A conclusion that takes into account the strength of the comparison

A conclusion that proposes a single course of action (False Choice):

_____ 17. The consideration of more than two potential options

_____ 18. Evidence that the proposed course of action will have the desired effect

_____ 19. Evidence that alternative actions are less justified than the proposition

_____ 20. A lack of predictable unintended negative consequences that would logically stem from the proposition

An argument that makes a prediction (Unwarranted Prediction):

_____ 21. Evidence that the prediction is a widely held belief

_____ 22. Evidence that the predicted outcome is likely to occur

_____ 23. Evidence that the predicted outcome has occurred before under the same circumstances

_____ 24. A qualified conclusion that is calibrated to the strength of the evidence

An argument with premises based on opinion (Opinion vs. Fact):

_____ 25. An opinion that cannot be demonstrated to be false

_____ 26. An opinion that is relevant to the conclusion made by the argument

_____ 27. Evidence that the opinion is justified

_____ 28. Evidence that the opinion is shared by others

4

An argument that concludes something about an entity based on evidence about the entity's components (Part vs. Whole):

_____ 29. Evidence that the entity shares other characteristics with its components

_____ 30. Evidence that a characteristic is shared by a sufficient portion of the entity's components to be projected onto the entity as a whole

_____ 31. Evidence that the entity as a whole must share that characteristic with the entity's components

_____ 32. Evidence that the components of the entity are not dissimilar in any way

An argument that concludes a change in amount based on a change in percent (Percent vs. Amount):

_____ 33. A percentage greater than 50 percent

_____ 34. Evidence that there was not a change in the size of the whole that accounts for the change in percent

_____ 35. The raw numbers that make up the percent

_____ 36. Evidence that rules out alternative explanations for the change in percentage

An argument that concludes that a general principle applies to a specific case (Conditional Logic Flaw):

_____ 37. Evidence that the specific case fulfills the necessary condition of the principle

_____ 38. Evidence that the specific case fulfills the sufficient condition of the principle

_____ 39. A conclusion that the specific case fulfills the necessary condition of the principle

_____ 40. A conclusion that the specific case fulfills the sufficient condition of the principle

4

Answers

An argument with a data sample as its evidence (Sampling Flaw):

__Y__ 1. A sample representative of the group about which the conclusion is drawn

__Y__ 2. A sample collected in a way that is impervious to bias

__N__ 3. A sample that consists of at least ten percent of the overall population being studied

__Y__ 4. A large enough sample size

While a sample needs to be "large enough," sufficient size hasn't ever been quantified in terms of the percent of the whole.

An argument that relies on the opinion of an expert (Appeal to Inappropriate Authority):

__Y__ 5. Evidence of expertise

__Y__ 6. Expertise in a field relevant to the argument

__N__ 7. Proof that the expert is not alone in their thinking

__N__ 8. A consensus among experts in the field

As long as you're told the authority is an expert in a relevant field, you don't need to know if their expert opinion is shared by others.

A causal argument (Causation Flaw):

__N__ 9. Proof that no other possible causes for the observed effect exist

__Y__ 10. Evidence that no alternative explanation is equally likely

__Y__ 11. A timeline that places the alleged cause before the observed effect

__Y__ 12. A conclusion that is calibrated to the strength of the evidence

Most valid causal arguments don't conclude definitive causality because that's just so hard to prove. So, a total lack of other possible causes isn't a requirement.

An argument that hinges on an analogy (Comparison Flaw):

__Y__ 13. One or more relevant similarities between the items being compared

__Y__ 14. A lack of relevant differences between the items being compared

__N__ 15. A thorough examination of all differences between the items being compared

__Y__ 16. A conclusion that takes into account the strength of the comparison

For an analogy to work, the two things have to be similar in relevant respects. But they don't have to be similar in all respects, and the irrelevant differences don't need to be examined.

A conclusion that proposes a single course of action (False Choice):

__N__ 17. The consideration of more than two potential options

__Y__ 18. Evidence that the proposed course of action will have the desired effect

__Y__ 19. Evidence that alternative actions are less justified than the proposition

__Y__ 20. A lack of predictable unintended negative consequences that would logically stem from the proposition

Most valid arguments of this type have one premise that sets up two possible courses of action and another premise that rules out one of the possibilities. More than two possibilities don't need to be discussed, as long as the argument doesn't fail to consider a middle ground between two extremes.

An argument that makes a prediction (Unwarranted Prediction):

__N__ 21. Evidence that the prediction is a widely held belief

__Y__ 22. Evidence that the predicted outcome is likely to occur

__N__ 23. Evidence that the predicted outcome has occurred before under the same circumstances

__Y__ 24. A qualified conclusion that is calibrated to the strength of the evidence

A prediction doesn't need to be widely held to be valid, and while many of these arguments use evidence of previous outcomes to support the prediction, they don't necessarily have to; they could also be argued by ruling out alternative outcomes.

An argument with premises based on opinion (Opinion vs. Fact):

__Y__ 25. An opinion that cannot be demonstrated to be false

__Y__ 26. An opinion that is relevant to the conclusion made by the argument

__Y__ 27. Evidence that the opinion is justified

__N__ 28. Evidence that the opinion is shared by others

4

As long as the opinion is relevant, thoroughly evinced, and irrefutable, there's no need for it to be shared by others.

An argument that concludes something about an entity based on evidence about the entity's components (Part vs. Whole):

__N__ 29. Evidence that the entity shares other characteristics with its components

__Y__ 30. Evidence that a characteristic is shared by a sufficient portion of the entity's components to be projected onto the entity as a whole

__Y__ 31. Evidence that the entity as a whole must share that characteristic with the entity's components

__N__ 32. Evidence that the components of the entity are not dissimilar in any way

For an argument like this to work, the characteristic has to be such that an entity composed of parts with that characteristic must be a whole with that characteristic (e.g., a chair composed entirely of wooden parts must be entirely wooden). It does not have to share other characteristics with the component parts, nor do the component parts have to share any other characteristics with each other.

An argument that concludes a change in amount based on a change in percent (Percent vs. Amount):

__N__ 33. A percentage greater than 50 percent

__Y__ 34. Evidence that there was not a change in the size of the whole that accounts for the change in percent

__N__ 35. The raw numbers that make up the percent

__Y__ 36. Evidence that rules out alternative explanations for the change in percentage

If the percent of a population that does something increases, either the number of folks doing it increased or the total population surveyed shrank. In order to conclude that it's one of those, you need to rule out the other. The starting percentage and the exact numbers that make up the percent, however, are unnecessary.

An argument that concludes that a general principle applies to a specific case (Conditional Logic Flaw):

__N__ 37. Evidence that the specific case fulfills the necessary condition of the principle

__Y__ 38. Evidence that the specific case fulfills the sufficient condition of the principle

__Y__ 39. A conclusion that the specific case fulfills the necessary condition of the principle

__N__ 40. A conclusion that the specific case fulfills the sufficient condition of the principle

To apply a principle to a specific case, the evidence of the argument must show that the case fulfills the principle's sufficient condition and the argument must conclude that the necessary condition of the principle is also fulfilled. An argument that does the opposite is an Illegal Reversal.

Drill 52: Predict the Flawed Conclusion

Instructions: Each of the following flawed arguments is missing its conclusion. Experts predict the direction each argument will take as they're reading, so use the premises to predict what flawed conclusion the author is about to draw.

1. Many fad diets eschew consumption of carbohydrates completely. Generally, however, people who have diets low in carbohydrates are heavier than those who consume plenty of carbohydrates. Therefore, _____.

2. Some string theorists claim that we live in a multiverse with infinite parallel universes. However, since they have never been able to provide any tangible proof of this claim, _____.

3. Almost all great professional quarterbacks were successful at the college level. Doug Oboey has had an absolutely stellar college career, so _____.

4. Technological products that consumers believe do not distinctly improve on previous models rarely become financial success stories. Despite the initial hype surrounding the newest NextGen smartphone, its specs are nearly identical to the specs of the previous generation. Therefore, _____.

5. Every component of SFG's new backpack, including the straps, pockets, and hip belt, is made from ultralight Domino Fiber. We can be sure, then, that _____.

6. Prism Motors plans to introduce its fully electric autonomous vehicle to market next year. Asimov Autos has enjoyed immense success with its fully electric and semi-autonomous Model 3, despite the fact that the Model 3 costs almost twice what Prism's car will cost. Therefore, _____.

7. Nutritionist: The results of a new study clearly show that sugar causes less harm than the top selling artificial sweetener. So, _____.

8. The global temperature has risen by an average of one tenth of one degree each of the last ten years. It would be catastrophic if it rises another degree, so _____.

9. Research has shown that people who floss are less than half as likely to develop cancer as those who do not. Clearly, _____.

10. Pundit: Income tax revenue from the top one percent is expected to fall sharply as a result of the new tax bill. When budget shortfalls occur, the government must cut social services to stay within the budget. Therefore, _____.

11. All of the candidates running for office are well qualified and have lots of experience. But only Representative Johnson has a record of success in the business world. For this reason, _____.

12. The incidence of wheat allergies in the United States has soared over the last twenty years. The rise began around the time that the United States approved a controversial new genetically modified super-wheat. Thus, _____.

13. Sequels of successful movies almost always make more money at the box office than the originals, despite the fact that they consistently receive worse reviews. It seems that if you want to make a successful movie, _____.

14. In countries where tipping is not the custom, restaurant workers tend to make more money than their counterparts in the United States, who rely largely on tips. Therefore, _____.

15. My teacher, who's working on a dissertation on the history of science, insists that the hypothesis about multiple universes is nonsense, so _____.

16. Carlisle types faster than his coworker, Gina. When he updates his resume, he should add that he _____.

17. All of the managers at that company have master's degrees. Jack is a technician in the company, not a manager, so _____.

18. It would seem that either the defendant lied to his lawyer or the lawyer lied to the court. Since his lawyer has an undisputed reputation for honesty, _____.

19. The longer food stays in contact with teeth, the greater the chance that a cavity will result. Since cotton candy dissolves in the mouth faster than french fries dissolve, _____.

4

20. The unemployment rate in the state has reduced from ten percent to eight percent in the past three years. It is clear that the current administration _____.

21. The city banned access to this stretch of riverbank because it is claimed that pedestrians are causing ecological damage to rare plants growing there. But it is very saddening to think that people will no longer be able to enjoy the sublime beauty of walking in that area, so the city _____.

22. If a person does not inform herself about important issues, she should abstain from criticizing the views of others on those issues. For this reason, Martha _____ _____.

23. Everyone in my filmmaking class is under thirty years old, and every one of them said they loved the new superhero movie. So, _____.

24. The median grade point average of applicants admitted to this law school has gone up by at least a tenth of a point every year for the past three years. No doubt this year _____.

25. Chuck started using positive affirmations every morning to increase success in his career. Two months later he got a promotion. That proves _____.

26. The cafeteria stopped serving macaroni and cheese. But mac and cheese is so yummy and satisfying that surely nobody dislikes it. The choice to discontinue _____.

27. Each and every component in this computer was manufactured overseas. So, the company cannot claim that _____.

28. Despite finding numerous exoplanets orbiting other stars, scientists have not found any evidence of another planet that is capable of supporting life as we know it. So, we can be sure that _____.

29. This graduate level course has two prerequisite courses that must be taken. Heidi has taken both of the prerequisites, so _____.

30. Scientists are cloning increasing varieties of mammals using technology that could also be used to clone humans. Human cloning, therefore, _____.

31. Studies show that people who use the over-the-counter medication ibuprofen report suffering more headaches than people who never use it. We can conclude from this that _____.

32. Virginia is looking for a pet that is very easy to care for. Cats are easier to care for than dogs, so Virginia _____.

33. Despite his devoted practice, Kurt has never been able to break his 225-point high score record in bowling. So, in the upcoming league, _____.

34. That artist has been highly praised by critics for the originality of her works. But her sketch used for this magazine cover is not particularly original, so in truth, _____ _____.

35. Any novel that deals with controversial topics makes a good book club choice. The novel Nick proposed for next month's book club discussion, however, doesn't deal with any controversial issues, so _____.

36. Far more people are injured in automobile accidents than in motorcycle accidents each year. Since the cost of insurance premiums is based on risk, automobile premiums _____.

37. I told my yoga instructor about my chronic heartburn, and she recommended apple cider vinegar as an effective remedy. I should _____.

38. People who join social clubs tend to possess more self-assurance than people who engage in solitary hobbies. So, a person who wants to develop more self-assurance _____.

39. Most people polled are convinced that voter fraud is an urgent problem that needs an immediate legislative solution. Therefore, Congress _____ _____.

40. Important historical documents should be preserved for future generations. That is why the president's personal journal _____.

41. All of the evidence that has been offered to show that Sir Francis Bacon wrote Shakespeare's plays is unconvincing, proving once and for all _____ _____.

42. Astronomers conducting a survey to determine the largest object in the Kuiper Belt now know that Pluto is larger than Eris. This finally establishes _____ _____.

43. Each article submitted for inclusion in this journal is very short. The journal itself _____.

44. Taxpayers will be willing to pay for a solution to the current water shortage problems. If the technology continues to improve, one solution could be desalination. So, _____.

45. A characteristic that all of the greatest artists share is a passionate nature. Genevieve is a passionate woman, so her artworks _____.

46. Many people drink orange juice as a means of getting vitamin C in the morning. Yet, a cup of broccoli has more vitamin C than a cup of orange juice. So, _____.

47. Marco has been training hard for the 2020 Olympics and has high hopes. But an Olympic medal has never been taken home by a San Marino athlete. So, because he's competing for San Marino, _____.

48. Sara has been using this salve daily for months now, and her skin is moist and smooth. The television infomercial had said that using it daily would keep skin from becoming dry and rough, so _____.

49. A small New York City newspaper polled its readers and 87% of respondents were opposed to the increase in farm subsidies being considered by Congress. This confirms that Americans _____.

50. Propositions that cannot be tested are not scientific. Therefore, the belief that life exists in other galaxies _____.

4

Answers

Note: Our conclusions may differ slightly from yours—that's OK! Just make sure that they represent the same famous flaw.

1. Many fad diets eschew consumption of carbohydrates completely. Generally, however, people who have diets low in carbohydrates are heavier than those who consume plenty of carbohydrates. Therefore, <u>these fad diets are counterproductive for those trying to lose weight</u>. *(Flaw: Causation Flaw)*

2. Some string theorists claim that we live in a multiverse with infinite parallel universes. However, since they have never been able to provide any tangible proof of this claim, <u>it must be the case that there is only a single universe</u>. *(Flaw: Unproven vs. Untrue)*

3. Almost all great professional quarterbacks were successful at the college level. Doug Oboey has had an absolutely stellar college career as a quarterback, so <u>he will almost certainly see success in the same position in the pros</u>. *(Flaw: Illegal Reversal)*

4. Technological products that consumers believe do not distinctly improve on previous models rarely become financial success stories. Despite the initial hype surrounding the newest NextGen smartphone, its specs are nearly identical to the specs of the previous generation. Therefore, <u>this phone is unlikely to be a financial success</u>. *(Flaw: Opinion vs. Fact. People may still believe the phone has innovations even if it does not.)*

5. Every component of SFG's new backpack, including the straps, pockets, and hip belt, is made from ultralight Domino Fiber. We can be sure, then, that <u>the backpack as a whole won't weigh you down while you're hiking!</u> *(Flaw: Part vs. Whole)*

6. Prism Motors plans to introduce its fully electric autonomous vehicle to market next year. Asimov Autos has enjoyed immense success with its fully electric and semi-autonomous Model 3, despite the fact that the Model 3 costs almost twice what <u>Prism's car will cost. Therefore, Prism Motors is sure to have a successful launch for its new car</u>. *(Flaw: Comparison Flaw)*

7. Nutritionist: The results of a new study clearly show that sugar causes less harm than the top-selling artificial sweetener. So, <u>anyone looking to eat a healthy diet should feel free to include sugar in all of their meals</u>. *(Flaw: Relative vs. Absolute. Even if it's less harmful, it could still be really harmful!)*

8. The global temperature has risen by an average of one tenth of one degree each of the last ten years. It would be catastrophic if it rises another degree, so <u>we're merely one decade away from the end of the world</u>. *(Flaw: Unwarranted Prediction. The trend over the past decade could reverse.)*

9. Research has shown that people who floss are less than half as likely to develop cancer as those who do not. Clearly, <u>people who wish to decrease their chances of developing cancer should work flossing into their daily routine</u>. *(Flaw: Causation Flaw)*

10. Pundit: Income tax revenue from the top one percent is expected to fall sharply as a result of the new tax bill. When budget shortfalls occur, the government must cut social services to stay within the budget. Therefore, <u>the new tax bill will lead to a reduction in social services</u>. *(Flaw: Term Shift/Sampling Flaw. A loss of income tax revenue from the top one percent doesn't necessarily mean there will be a budget shortfall.)*

11. All of the candidates running for office are well qualified and have lots of experience. But only Representative Johnson has a record of success in the business world. For this reason, <u>Representative Johnson is the best candidate for the job</u>. *(Flaw: Term Shift/Comparison Flaw)*

4

12. The incidence of wheat allergies in the United States has soared over the last twenty years. The rise began around the time that the United States approved a controversial new genetically modified super-wheat. Thus, <u>GM wheat is probably responsible for the increase in wheat allergies</u>. *(Flaw: Causation Flaw)*

13. Sequels of successful movies almost always make more money at the box office than the originals, despite the fact that they consistently receive worse reviews. It seems that if you want to make a successful movie, <u>you should not consider how it will be received</u>. *(Flaw: Sampling Flaw. Sequels aren't representative of movies in general.)*

14. In countries where tipping is not the custom, restaurant workers tend to make more money than their counterparts in the United States, who rely largely on tips. Therefore, <u>restaurant workers in the United States would make more money if we eliminated tipping</u>. *(Flaw: Causation Flaw. This conclusion implies that the lack of tipping is what causes the higher take-home pay, when in fact, it is likely that the opposite is true.)*

15. My history teacher, who's working on a dissertation on the history of science, insists that the hypothesis about multiple universes is nonsense, so <u>the hypothesis cannot be true</u>. *(Flaw: Appeal to Inappropriate Authority. A history teacher, even one who knows the history of science, is not necessarily an appropriate expert on cosmological theories.)*

16. Carlisle types faster than his coworker, Gina. When he updates his resume, he should add that he <u>is a fast typist</u>. *(Flaw: Relative vs. Absolute. He could still be a slow typist, even though he's faster than Gina.)*

17. All of the managers at that company have master's degrees. Jack is a technician in the company, not a manager, so <u>he doesn't have a master's degree</u>. *(Flaw: Illegal Negation)*

18. It would seem that either the defendant lied to his lawyer or the lawyer lied to the court. Since his lawyer has an undisputed reputation for honesty, <u>the defendant must have lied to him</u>. *(Flaw: False Choice. While it seems to be the case that one of the two lied, it isn't definitely the case that one of them did so.)*

19. The longer food stays in contact with teeth, the greater the chance that a cavity will result. Since cotton candy dissolves in the mouth faster than french fries dissolve, <u>cotton candy is less likely than french fries to cause cavities in teeth</u>. *(Flaw: Comparison Flaw. Cotton candy and french fries are different in other ways relevant to the development of cavities that haven't been considered here.)*

20. The unemployment rate in the state has reduced from ten percent to eight percent in the past three years. It is clear that the current administration <u>has reduced the number of unemployed workers.</u> *(Flaw: Percent vs. Amount. If the total population grew during that time, the percent could go down while the actual number of unemployed stayed the same or grew.)*

21. The city banned access to this stretch of riverbank because it is claimed that pedestrians are causing ecological damage to rare plants growing there. But it is very saddening to think that people will no longer be able to enjoy the sublime beauty of walking in that area, so the city <u>should not bar pedestrian access</u>. *(Flaw: Appeal to Emotion)*

22. If a person does not inform herself about important issues, she should abstain from criticizing the views of others on those issues. For this reason, Martha <u>should abstain from criticizing others' views on this very important issue</u>. *(Flaw: Conditional Logic Flaw. This is a misapplication of the principle, since we're given no evidence that this principle should apply to Martha.)*

23. Everyone in my filmmaking class is under thirty years old, and every one of them said they loved the new superhero movie. So, <u>any person under thirty must love the new superhero movie</u>. *(Flaw: Sampling Flaw. This is an unrepresentative sample.)*

24. The median grade point average of applicants admitted to this law school has gone up by at least a tenth of a point every year for the past three years. No doubt this year <u>the average GPA will continue to rise</u>. *(Flaw: Unwarranted Prediction)*

25. Chuck started using positive affirmations every morning to increase success in his career. Two months later he got a promotion. That proves <u>affirmations work</u>. *(Flaw: Causation Flaw)*

26. The cafeteria stopped serving macaroni and cheese. But mac and cheese is so yummy and satisfying that surely nobody dislikes it. The choice to discontinue <u>was a mistake</u>. *(Flaw: Opinion vs. Fact)*

27. Each and every component in this computer was manufactured overseas. So, the company cannot claim that <u>the computer was made in this country</u>. *(Flaw: Part vs. Whole)*

28. Despite finding numerous exoplanets orbiting other stars, scientists have not found any evidence of another planet that is capable of supporting life as we know it. So, we can be sure that <u>Earth is the only planet with life as we know it</u>. *(Flaw: Unproven vs. Untrue)*

29. This graduate-level course has two prerequisite courses that must be taken. Heidi has taken both of the prerequisites, so <u>she can sign up for this course</u>. *(Flaw: Illegal Reversal)*

30. Scientists are cloning increasing varieties of mammals using technology that could also be used to clone humans. Human cloning, therefore, <u>will be a reality very soon</u>. *(Flaw: Possible vs. Certain. Just because scientists have technology that can clone humans does not mean they will.)*

31. Studies show that people who use the over-the-counter medication ibuprofen report suffering more headaches than people who never use it. We can conclude from this that <u>ibuprofen causes headaches</u>. *(Flaw: Causation Flaw)*

32. Virginia is looking for a pet that is very easy to care for. Cats are easier to care for than dogs, so Virginia <u>should get a cat</u>. *(Flaw: Relative vs. Absolute. Although cats are easier to care for than dogs are, that does not necessarily mean that cats are very easy to care for.)*

33. Despite his devoted practice, Kurt has never been able to break his 225-point high-score record in bowling. So, in the upcoming league, <u>he won't break his high score</u>. *(Flaw: Unwarranted Prediction)*

34. That artist has been highly praised by critics for the originality of her works. But her sketch used for this magazine cover is not particularly original, so in truth, <u>she is not a particularly original artist</u>. *(Flaw: Sampling Flaw. One sketch used on a magazine cover is not a large enough sample.)*

35. Any novel that deals with controversial topics makes a good book club choice. The novel Nick proposed for next month's book club discussion, however, doesn't deal with any controversial issues, so <u>it won't be a good choice</u>. *(Flaw: Illegal Negation)*

36. Far more people are injured in automobile accidents than in motorcycle accidents each year. Since the cost of insurance premiums is based on risk, automobile premiums <u>should cost less than motorcycle premiums</u>. *(Flaw: Percent vs. Amount. Relative risk is determined by the percent of those injured, not the number of those injured. There are far fewer motorcyclists than people in automobiles, so the smaller number of motorcyclists in accidents doesn't mean riding a motorcycle is less risky than driving a car.)*

37. I told my yoga instructor about my chronic heartburn, and she recommended apple cider vinegar as an effective remedy. I should <u>get some apple cider vinegar</u>. *(Flaw: Appeal to Inappropriate Authority. Neither the question nor the recommendation are within her field of expertise.)*

38. People who join social clubs tend to possess more self-assurance than people who engage in solitary hobbies. So a person who wants to develop more self-assurance <u>should join a social club</u>. *(Flaw: Causation Flaw. It could be that more self-assured people are the ones who join social clubs, rather than vice versa.)*

39. Most people polled are convinced that voter fraud is an urgent problem that needs an immediate legislative solution. Therefore, Congress <u>needs to pass a law immediately to solve the problem</u>. *(Flaw: Opinion vs. Fact)*

40. Important historical documents should be preserved for future generations. That is why the president's personal journal <u>should be preserved for future generations</u>. *(Flaw: Conditional Logic Flaw. This is a misapplication of the principle. Unless we're told the president's personal journal is an important historical document, we can't conclude that it should be preserved.)*

41. All of the evidence offered to show that Sir Francis Bacon wrote Shakespeare's plays is unconvincing, proving once and for all <u>that Bacon did not write them</u>. *(Flaw: Unproven vs. Untrue.)*

42. Astronomers conducting a survey to determine the largest object in the Kuiper Belt now know that Pluto is larger than Eris. This finally establishes <u>that Pluto is the largest object in the Kuiper Belt</u>. *(Flaw: Relative vs. Absolute)*

43. Each article submitted for inclusion in this journal is very short. The journal itself <u>must be very short</u>. *(Flaw: Part vs. Whole)*

44. Taxpayers will be willing to pay for a solution to the current water shortage problems. If the technology continues to improve, one solution could be desalination. So, <u>taxpayers will be willing to pay for desalination</u>. *(Flaw: Possible vs. Certain)*

45. A characteristic that all of the greatest artists share is a passionate nature. Genevieve is a passionate woman, so her artworks <u>will be among the greatest</u>. *(Flaw: Illegal Reversal)*

46. Many people drink orange juice as a means of getting vitamin C in the morning. Yet, a cup of broccoli has more vitamin C than a cup of orange juice. So, <u>people should eat a cup of broccoli in the morning</u>. *(Flaw: Comparison Flaw)*

47. Marco has been training hard for the 2020 Olympics and has high hopes. But an Olympic medal has never been taken home by a San Marino athlete. So, because he's competing for San Marino, <u>Marco will not win a medal in 2020</u>. *(Flaw: Unwarranted Prediction)*

48. Sara has been using this salve daily for months now, and her skin is moist and smooth. The television infomercial had said that using it daily would keep skin from becoming dry and rough, so <u>the infomercial was accurate</u>. *(Flaw: Causation Flaw. This takes for granted that the salve caused the moist smooth condition of Sara's skin.)*

49. A small New York City newspaper polled its readers and 87% of respondents were opposed to the increase in farm subsidies being considered by Congress. This confirms that Americans <u>are largely opposed to increased farm subsidies</u>. *(Flaw: Sampling Flaw. Readers of a small New York City paper may have opinions about farm subsidies that are not representative of the country's opinion as a whole.)*

50. Propositions that cannot be tested are not scientific. Therefore, the belief that life exists in other galaxies <u>is not scientific</u>. *(Flaw: Conditional Logic Flaw. This is a misapplication of the principle. There's no evidence in this argument that we cannot test a belief about life in other galaxies, so we can't conclude that the belief is not scientific.)*

Drill 53: Diagramming 201, Round 2

Instructions: Diagram and contrapose these more complicated conditionals, but if you start to feel lost, don't be afraid to go back and review the basics with a round of Conditionals 101. For an added twist, some of these statements might not even be conditional, in which case you should note that.

1. A lifeguard has to be on duty in order for anyone to swim in the pool.

2. To be able to afford both a new phone and a new panini press, you need to supplement your income.

3. None of Husani's tasks can be completed if he wakes up late for work or if he forgets his lanyard.

4. Only those with a pure heart will avoid being eaten by the Minotaur.

5. Provided she can maintain her composure, Eloise is ensured a standing ovation.

6. We will enjoy a profitable quarter and boost our market presence if either our company's stock value rises or our competitor's product falters.

7. Whenever Simone gets the flu, she's sure to have gotten it from either her brother or from one of her coworkers.

8. It's not until the clouds part that the aurora borealis becomes visible.

9. Our neighbor will watch our cat if, but only if we promise to bring him back a souvenir from our trip.

10. There is no need to worry because all the snakes in this region are neither venomous nor aggressive.

11. Every side item is included in the sampler meal except for the jalapeño poppers.

12. Fujiko will refuse the promotion but only if it involves moving into a new department.

4

13. None of the cars for sale is both fuel efficient and a convertible.

14. Madagascar cannot protect its natural resources without regulating its logging industry.

15. Making Hans his favorite strudel will ensure that he remembers to invite you to his next party.

16. In order to properly greet the Bosnian ambassador or impress her staff, Randall will have to study Bosnia's history.

17. Not a single firework will be lit until the bonfire is extinguished.

18. If every specialist approves of it and at least one study supports its efficacy, the experimental drug will be released to the public.

19. The screen door will not close whenever the temperature drops suddenly.

20. Some brains can be fooled by an optical illusion, even if there is a history of previous exposure to the illusion.

21. The plastic used to make those toys is safe, except for when it's been exposed to direct sunlight for a prolonged period and had its coating rubbed off.

22. Either Curtis or Sandra will lead the evening shift if both Max and Vanessa fail to show up.

23. Only guests who have been issued credentials and who have checked their equipment with the front desk may photograph the art exhibit.

24. A sense of humor is a prerequisite for anyone wishing to learn to dance.

25. Jasmine will be admitted to the space program if, but only if, she passes the preliminary physical.

Answers

1. A lifeguard has to be on duty in order for anyone to swim in the pool.

   $S \rightarrow L$; $\sim L \rightarrow \sim S$

2. To be able to afford both a new phone and a new panini press, you need to supplement your income.

   NP and $PP \rightarrow SI$; $\sim SI \rightarrow \sim NP$ or $\sim PP$

3. None of Husani's tasks can be completed if he wakes up late for work or if he forgets his lanyard.

   WL or $FL \rightarrow \sim TC$; $TC \rightarrow \sim WL$ and $\sim FL$

4. Only those with a pure heart will avoid being eaten by the Minotaur.

   $\sim E \rightarrow PH$; $\sim PH \rightarrow E$

5. Provided she can maintain her composure, Eloise is ensured a standing ovation.

   $MC \rightarrow SO$; $\sim SO \rightarrow \sim MC$

6. We will enjoy a profitable quarter and boost our market presence if either our company's stock value rises or our competitor's product falters.

   SVR or $CPF \rightarrow PQ$ and BMP ; $\sim PQ$ or $\sim BMP \rightarrow \sim SRV$ and $\sim CPF$

7. Whenever Simone gets the flu, she's sure to have gotten it from either her brother or from one of her coworkers.

   $F \rightarrow B$ or C : $\sim B$ and $\sim C \rightarrow \sim F$

8. It's not until the clouds part that the aurora borealis becomes visible.

   $\sim CP \rightarrow \sim ABV$; $ABV \rightarrow CP$

9. Our neighbor will watch our cat if, but only if, we promise to bring him back a souvenir from our trip.

   $WC \longleftrightarrow S$; $\sim WC \longleftrightarrow \sim S$

10. There is no need to worry because all the snakes in this region are neither venomous nor aggressive.

    $SR \rightarrow \sim V$ and $\sim A$; V or $A \rightarrow \sim SR$

11. Every side item is included in the sampler meal except for the jalapeño poppers.

    SI and ~JP → SM ; ~SM → ~SI or JP

12. Fujiko will refuse the promotion but only if it involves moving into a new department.

    RP → MD ; ~MD → ~RP

13. None of the cars for sale is both fuel efficient and a convertible.

    CFS → ~FE or ~C ; FE and C → ~CFS

14. Madagascar cannot protect its natural resources without regulating its logging industry.

    P → R ; ~R → ~P

15. Making Hans his favorite strudel will ensure that he remembers to invite you to his next party.

    MS → I ; ~I → ~MS

16. In order to properly greet the Bosnian ambassador or impress her staff, Randall will have to study Bosnia's history.

    PG or IS → SH ; ~SH → ~PG and ~IS

17. Not a single firework will be lit until the bonfire is extinguished.

    ~BE → ~FL ; FL → BE

18. If every specialist approves of it and at least one study supports its efficacy, the experimental drug will be released to the public.

    ESA and 1SS → RP : ~RP → ~ESA or ~1SS

19. The screen door will not close whenever the temperature drops suddenly.

    TD → ~SDC ; SCD → ~TD

20. Some brains can be fooled by an optical illusion, even if there is a history of previous exposure to the illusion.

    Not a conditional statement.

21. The plastic used to make those toys is safe, except for when it's been exposed to direct sunlight for a prolonged period and had its coating rubbed off.

    ES and CRO → ~S ; S → ~ES or ~CRO

22. Either Curtis or Sandra will lead the evening shift if both Max and Vanessa fail to show up.

    ~M and ~V → C or S ; ~C and ~S → M or V

23. Only guests who have been issued credentials and who have checked their equipment with the front desk may photograph the art exhibit.

    PE → IC and CE ; ~IC or ~CE → ~PE

24. A sense of humor is a prerequisite for anyone wishing to learn to dance.

    LD → SH ; ~SH → ~LD

25. Jasmine will be admitted to the space program if, but only if, she passes the preliminary physical.

    A ←→ PPP ; ~A ←→ ~PPP

4

Drill 54: Vocab Lab #7 – Pick a Definition, Round 2

Instructions: Here's an array of LSAT adjectives. Some end in *-ed*; others end in *-able, -ible,* or even *-uble*. For each word, choose the answer closest in meaning.

1. Aggrieved
   - (A) tempered
   - (B) assuaged
   - (C) afflicted

2. Convoluted
   - (A) twisted
   - (B) discerned
   - (C) succinct

3. Disinclined
   - (A) heedless
   - (B) imbued
   - (C) unwilling

4. Dispersed
   - (A) paid out
   - (B) scattered
   - (C) condensed

5. Diversified
   - (A) varied
   - (B) confined
   - (C) retained

6. Emboldened
   - (A) instilled with condescension
   - (B) instilled with knowledge
   - (C) instilled with courage

7. Entrenched
   - (A) vacillating
   - (B) well-established
   - (C) cultivated

8. Fortified
   - (A) strengthened
   - (B) impermanent
   - (C) hardened

9. Muddled
   - (A) clarified
   - (B) disordered
   - (C) distinguished

10. Obscured
    - (A) concealed
    - (B) displayed
    - (C) perplexed

11. Predisposed
    - (A) assumed
    - (B) inclined
    - (C) resistant

12. Protracted
    - (A) lengthy
    - (B) intermittent
    - (C) repealed

13. Reputed
    - (A) factual
    - (B) refined
    - (C) believed

14. Uninflected
    - (A) unimposed
    - (B) monotonous
    - (C) flowing

15. Vested

   Ⓐ tractable
   Ⓑ guaranteed
   Ⓒ unspent

16. Amenable

   Ⓐ unwilling to cooperate
   Ⓑ willing to take suggestion
   Ⓒ able to be repaired

17. Discernible

   Ⓐ questionable
   Ⓑ detestable
   Ⓒ observable

18. Dispensable

   Ⓐ functional
   Ⓑ nonessential
   Ⓒ compulsory

19. Foreseeable

   Ⓐ able to be anticipated
   Ⓑ able to be managed
   Ⓒ able to be avoided

20. Impermissible

   Ⓐ improbable
   Ⓑ unendurable
   Ⓒ unallowable

21. Inexplicable

   Ⓐ uncontrollable
   Ⓑ undeniable
   Ⓒ unexplainable

22. Innumerable

   Ⓐ featureless
   Ⓑ countless
   Ⓒ worthless

23. Insoluble

   Ⓐ cannot be forgiven
   Ⓑ cannot be disputed
   Ⓒ cannot be solved

24. Ostensible

   Ⓐ professed
   Ⓑ implausible
   Ⓒ unsuitable

25. Permeable

   Ⓐ able to be argued
   Ⓑ able to be penetrated
   Ⓒ able to be believed

4

Answers

4

1. C

Aggrieved = afflicted, resentful, or distressed from experiencing unfair treatment. If you frequently feel *aggrieved* in your life, look for ways to turn your frowns upside down. See, it worked!

2. A

Convoluted = twisted; very complicated. The Latin root *vol-* means "roll, turn, twist," giving rise to such words besides *convoluted* as *evolution, revolve,* and *involve.*

3. C

Disinclined = unwilling; hesitant; unenthusiastic. This word is nice to deploy in conversation when you really don't want to do something: "I'm *disinclined* right now to wash these pans."

4. B

Dispersed = scattered over a broad area. As work-forces become more and more physically *dispersed,* good Internet connections and effective tools for collaboration have become all the more critical.

5. A

Diversified = varied; assorted; mixed. The only free lunch in financial investing is to have a *diversified* portfolio: don't put all your savings eggs in the basket of just one or two companies.

6. C

Emboldened = instilled with courage; given bravery to take action; encouraged. After you've said that you're disinclined to wash the pans, your roommate may feel *emboldened* to wash them (or to punch you).

7. B

Entrenched = securely established; ingrained; rooted. Visualize a big trench in the ground, and now envision something solidly stuck in that trench.

8. A

Fortified = defensible (due to walls offering protec-tion); strengthened; supported; reinforced. From the Latin roots *fort-* (= strong) + *-fy* (= make).

9. B

Muddled = disordered; in a confused or disorderly state. Physical mud does not have to be involved, but that's the original image underneath. When mixing cocktails, bartenders use *muddlers* to *muddle,* or mash, various ingredients, including herbs and spices (but certainly not mud!).

10. A

Obscured = concealed; darkened; cast over. Even in the densest of legal writings, one hopes that the point is rarely *obscured* by flights of fancy language…but alas, this hope may be in vain.

11. B

Predisposed = inclined or liable to do something. Interestingly, you can be either *predisposed* or just *disposed,* and either way, you're in the same state of readiness.

12. A

Protracted = lengthy; continuing for a long time or longer than usual. From a Latin term meaning "draw out." Your high school geometry class, which is where you probably last used a protractor, may have felt rather *protracted.*

13. C

Reputed = believed to be or act a certain way. The verb *repute* is almost never used without the *-ed* on the end ("This movie is *reputed* to be excellent."). The longer noun *reputation* is much more common in both speech and writing.

14. B

Uninflected = monotonous; without change in pitch or tone. *Inflections* give life and emotion to speech. Do not deliver an *uninflected* closing argument, when the time comes.

15. B

Vested = guaranteed; fixed; absolute; without contingency. Typically used as part of the phrase *vested interest,* which most often means "a personal stake" ("I have a *vested interest* in the success of this book."), but can also describe an individual who has a *vested interest* ("I cannot objectively review this book, as I am a *vested interest.*").

16. B

Amenable = willing to take suggestion; able to be influenced or controlled. "I am *amenable* to your suggestion" is nice to say to your friend. *Amenable* can also mean "suitable; appropriate."

17. C

Discernible = observable; perceptible; able to be seen or detected. That is, you can *discern* something *discernible*. If you are especially good at *discerning* things and understanding them, you have good *discernment*.

18. B

Dispensable = nonessential; can be done without; unneeded because there's more than enough. You can *dispense* with an item that's *dispensable*.

19. A

Foreseeable = able to be anticipated or predicted. In some sense, nothing is perfectly *foreseeable*, but there are important degrees of difference. The sun continuing to rise in the east and set in the west is pretty *foreseeable*.

20. C

Impermissible = unallowable; unacceptable; not legitimate or lawful; lacking permission. In contrast, something *permissible* is allowed.

21. C

Inexplicable = unexplainable; unaccountable. You cannot *explicate* the *inexplicable*.

22. B

Innumerable = countless; numberless; very many. Although many things in life can theoretically be counted with a number, it still makes sense to call the stars in the sky or the grains of sand on a beach *innumerable*.

23. C

Insoluble = cannot be solved; unsolvable or unanswerable. An *insoluble* problem cannot be solved; it simply must be worked around. In chemistry, an *insoluble* substance cannot be dissolved in whatever solution you're using.

24. A

Ostensible = professed; evident or pretended; outwardly appearing in a certain way. Don't confuse *ostensible*, which indicates surface characteristics in a relatively neutral way, with *ostentatious*, which passes a negative judgment on people as "showy, gaudy, seeking to attract envy."

25. B

Permeable = able to be penetrated. If the disposable diaper has a *permeable* barrier, then something unfortunate might *permeate* (= pass, spread) right through it.

4

Step 3 – Anticipate an Answer

The third step in our 4-Step Process for Logical Reasoning is often overlooked by students rushing to finish the section on time. We all know how hard it is to do 26 questions in 35 minutes, so we understand why students are hesitant any time we ask them to stop mid-question. But in fact, a moment spent pausing to anticipate an answer can save you lots of time on answer choice analysis. Students who consistently anticipate, or prephrase, a correct answer are more likely to move efficiently through the questions and less likely to get caught by trap answers.

In this section, you will learn to:

Recognize Scenarios for General Prephrases

Recognize Scenarios for Specific Prephrases

Prephrase Answers of Appropriate Strength for the Question Type

Prephrase for Questions about Percentages and Amounts

4

Drill 55: Strength Expectations

Instructions: While each question needs to be considered individually, there are some general rules for which question types are more likely to have strong answers, which are more likely to have weak answers, and which don't have an inherent preference. For each of the following question types, write in whether, as a general rule, you'd expect a strong answer (S), a weak answer (W), or whether there's no preference (NP). Again, these general rules won't always hold true, but they're a good place to start and they're great to fall back on when you're stuck!

_____ 1. ID the Conclusion

_____ 2. Determine the Function

_____ 3. Procedure

_____ 4. Sufficient Assumption

_____ 5. Necessary Assumption

_____ 6. ID the Flaw

_____ 7. Strengthen

_____ 8. Weaken

_____ 9. Evaluate

_____ 10. Principle Support

_____ 11. Must Be True

_____ 12. Must Be False

_____ 13. Most Strongly Supported

_____ 14. Principle Example

_____ 15. Match the Reasoning

_____ 16. Match the Flaw

_____ 17. Explain a Result

4

Answers

NP 1. ID the Conclusion

The answer should match the strength of the conclusion.

NP 2. Determine the Function

The answer should match the strength of the statement in the argument.

NP 3. Procedure

The answer should match the strength of the argument.

S 4. Sufficient Assumption

The answer needs to bridge the gap between evidence and the conclusion entirely, and that's typically done with a strong conditional statement.

W 5. Necessary Assumption

The answer has to be something that, if negated, totally destroys the argument. When you negate a weak answer, it becomes strong and is thus more likely to destroy an argument.

NP 6. ID the Flaw

The answer should match the strength of the flaw.

S 7. Strengthen

The answer should make the conclusion more likely to be valid, so it needs to be strong enough to have an impact.

S 8. Weaken

The answer should make the conclusion less likely to be valid, so it also needs to be strong enough to have an impact.

S 9. Evaluate

The answer should help you assess whether the argument is valid, so it needs to be strong enough to make or break the argument.

S 10. Principle Support

The answer will be a principle, usually stated as a conditional, which is strong.

NP 11. Must Be True

The answer must match the strength of the stimulus. If the stimulus is conditional, the correct answer is likely to be as well, meaning it could be strong. If the stimulus is not conditional, the correct answer is likely to be weak.

NP 12. Must Be False

The answer must be strong enough to contradict a claim in the stimulus or an inference you can make from the stimulus, but that isn't a high bar to set. If the stimulus claims "All dogs are good companions," one dog that's a bad companion is strong enough to contradict.

W 13. Most Strongly Supported

These stimuli aren't typically conditional, so unlike Must Be True questions, for these you won't usually be able to conclude a strong statement.

NP 14. Principle Example

The answer should match the strength of the principle expressed in the stimulus.

NP 15. Match the Reasoning

The answer should match the strength of the argument. Many wrong answer choices can be eliminated because they fail to do so!

NP 16. Match the Flaw

Same as Match the Reasoning—the answer should match the strength of the original argument.

S 17. Explain a Result

The answer should be strong enough to reconcile the seeming contradiction.

Drill 56: Famous Flaws, Round 3

Instructions: We've said it before: Famous flaws appear all over the LSAT, and being able to recognize them quickly is a must if you're looking for a top score.

For each of the following abbreviated arguments, select the famous flaw that is exhibited (again!). Remember, since there is some overlap between the different flaws, you might prephrase an answer that doesn't appear. That's fine! Figure out which answer is correct, and then spend time thinking about why it's correct and how you could have prephrased both answers (assuming, of course, that you were also correct with your initial prephrase).

1. If you want to live longer, eat more fish. The residents of the island of Okinawa eat a diet that consists primarily of fish, and they are also known to have the longest average lifespan of any population on earth.

   (A) False Choice
   (B) Causation
   (C) Opinion vs. Fact

2. If rice is left standing at room temperature, it can grow bacteria that have been known to create symptoms similar to food poisoning. That means my nausea came from the rice being left at room temperature by the restaurant last night.

   (A) Possible vs. Certain
   (B) Ad Hominem
   (C) Circular Reasoning

3. It is unreasonable to simply reject outright the claim that Bigfoot exists. After all, we accept that neutrinos exist without ever having actually seen one.

   (A) Equivocation
   (B) Comparison Flaw
   (C) Opinion vs. Fact

4. If ACMECorp management and the labor union reach an agreement to raise workers' wages by 10% over the next five years, ACMEcorp will spend $4 million more per year on wages. So, if ACMECorp management and the labor union reach an agreement to raise wages by 10%, ACMECorp will have to sell at least one of its overseas subsidiaries.

   (A) Percent vs. Amount
   (B) False Choice
   (C) Term Shift

5. All of the professors in the History Department have written books on the Medieval Period. Clearly, the History Department is a Medieval History Department.

   (A) Appeal to Inappropriate Authority
   (B) Part vs. Whole
   (C) Ad Hominem

6. Alicia has made it known that she would drop out of the contest for class president if George ran. Since George has just announced that he is running, he will be unopposed.

   (A) False Choice
   (B) Self-Contradiction
   (C) Circular Reasoning

7. Teenager: You should extend my curfew to 11pm instead of 10pm, because I should be able to stay out later.

   (A) Equivocation
   (B) Circular Reasoning
   (C) Appeal to Emotion

8. The number of personal watercraft accidents has risen steadily over the past two years. Riding a personal watercraft has apparently become more hazardous despite technological advances, which is of particular concern given the increasing popularity of the activity.

   (A) Causation
   (B) Self-Contradiction
   (C) Percent vs. Amount

4

9. Our Anarchist Club should have no rules, because the only rule for anarchists should be that there are no rules.

   Ⓐ Self-Contradiction
   Ⓑ Equivocation
   Ⓒ Illegal Reversal

10. That talented new teenage actor deserves to get the Best Actor award this year, but it's unlikely that he'll get it. There has only been one male actor under the age of 30 who ever won Best Actor, and that was over 15 years ago.

   Ⓐ Opinion vs. Fact
   Ⓑ Unwarranted Prediction
   Ⓒ Appeal to Emotion

11. My friends didn't like the wine I served last night, but this only shows how little they know about fine wines. This same wine was praised by the maître d' of Paree, one of the most expensive restaurants in New York City.

   Ⓐ Comparison Flaw
   Ⓑ Appeal to Inappropriate Authority
   Ⓒ Straw Man

12. Tsar Nicholas inspired great respect and loyalty in the people of Russia. This was evident in the strong loyalty shown by his bodyguards and servants.

   Ⓐ Sampling
   Ⓑ Relative vs. Absolute
   Ⓒ Appeal to Emotion

13. We put out poison traps last autumn to keep rodents off the property. We have seen no rodents on the property all winter, so the traps have served their purpose well.

   Ⓐ Equivocation
   Ⓑ Term Shift
   Ⓒ Causation

14. A realtor who fails to reveal a known problem is dishonest. That's why I know my realtor is honest: she told us about the minor drainage problem on the property.

   Ⓐ Opinion vs. Fact
   Ⓑ Illegal Negation
   Ⓒ Circular Reasoning

15. The newspaper's food critic wrote a mediocre review of that new downtown bistro. But his recommendation is suspect. He only became a food critic because he wasn't a successful restaurant manager, so he's envious of success.

   Ⓐ Ad Hominem
   Ⓑ Appeal to Emotion
   Ⓒ Comparison Flaw

16. If you're looking for a good book to read, try this author's first book, because her first is much better than her later books.

   Ⓐ Relative vs. Absolute
   Ⓑ Comparison Flaw
   Ⓒ Part vs. Whole

17. Chloe must have Professor Wright as her American Literature teacher. Everyone in Wright's class has to read Cather's *My Antonia*, and I saw Chloe in the student commons reading it today.

   Ⓐ Sampling
   Ⓑ Illegal Reversal
   Ⓒ Circular Reasoning

18. Accepting gifts from the client seems to be self-serving, but it is really self-defeating. Any unethical act is always, in the end, self-defeating.

   Ⓐ Self-Contradiction
   Ⓑ Relative vs. Absolute
   Ⓒ Term Shift

19. Scientists have been searching for elementary particles that must exist if string theory is accurate. But the most powerful particle collider ever built has failed to find these theoretical particles, so string theory is a failed theory.

    (A) Unwarranted Prediction
    (B) Causation
    (C) Unproven vs. Untrue

20. Any budget increase in the coming year should be allocated to programs other than sports. Almost 90% of students have expressed the belief that the university is spending an appropriate portion of its budget on sports programs.

    (A) Opinion vs. Fact
    (B) Comparison Flaw
    (C) Illegal Reversal

21. The leaders of both the House and the Senate have proposed amendments to the bill. But the Senate proposal has been shown to be flawed and possibly unconstitutional. So, Congress will have to adopt the House amendment.

    (A) Opinion vs. Fact
    (B) False Choice
    (C) Illegal Negation

22. Carla is wasting her money buying a raffle ticket. She was the person who won the prize in last year's raffle.

    (A) Term Shift
    (B) Illegal Reversal
    (C) Unwarranted Prediction

23. The U.S. Census has become far too expensive. The first census in 1790 cost only $44,000 to complete, while the most recent census cost a whopping $6.5 billion!

    (A) Opinion vs. Fact
    (B) Comparison Flaw
    (C) Causation

24. Apparently, fewer people today have an interest in American impressionism. Only about half of this year's museum visitors stopped to view the American impressionist collection, a smaller portion than five years ago.

    (A) Comparison Flaw
    (B) Percent vs. Amount
    (C) Relative vs. Absolute

25. If the post office raises the price of Forever Stamps by two cents, then they experience an increase in revenue. The post office has recently experienced an increase in revenue, so they must have raised the price of Forever Stamps by two cents.

    (A) Illegal Reversal
    (B) False Choice
    (C) Circular Reasoning

4

Answers

1. B	8. C	15. A	22. C
2. A	9. A	16. A	23. B
3. B	10. B	17. B	24. B
4. C	11. B	18. C	25. A
5. B	12. A	19. C	
6. A	13. C	20. A	
7. B	14. B	21. B	

Drill 57: Prephrase – Specific vs. General

Instructions: Anticipating an answer is an important step in any Logical Reasoning question. It's important to know when you can have specific prephrase—an idea of exactly what the correct answer is likely to say—or a general prephrase—an idea of what the correct answer is likely to do, but not necessarily how the answer will do it.

For each of the following, read the question type and/or short description of the stimulus and indicate whether you think it would be possible to have a specific prephrase (S) or if you'd need to keep it general (G).

_____ 1. A Must Be True question in which each statement is conditional

_____ 2. A Weaken question presenting a causal argument

_____ 3. A Sufficient Assumption question with a Term Shift from premise to conclusion

_____ 4. An ID the Flaw question in which the argument confuses sufficient and necessary terms

_____ 5. An Explain a Result question presenting an unexpected outcome of a study

_____ 6. A Strengthen question in which a recommendation is made

_____ 7. An ID the Conclusion question

_____ 8. A Strengthen question in which an explanation is offered

_____ 9. An ID the Flaw question with none of the Common Flaws

_____ 10. A Principle Support question in which a recommendation is made

_____ 11. A Most Strongly Supported question

_____ 12. A Determine the Function question

_____ 13. A Strengthen question in which the argument already seems solid

_____ 14. A Weaken question

_____ 15. An ID the Flaw question in which a characteristic of an entity was concluded to also be a characteristic of each of the entity's components

_____ 16. An ID the Flaw question that accuses someone of hypocrisy

_____ 17. An Explain a Result question presenting a surprising disparity

_____ 18. A Necessary Assumption question in which the argument already seems solid

_____ 19. A Procedure question

_____ 20. A Weaken question presenting a comparative argument

_____ 21. An ID the Flaw question that cites a study

_____ 22. A Strengthen question presenting a causal argument

_____ 23. A Must Be True question made up entirely of quantity statements

_____ 24. A Must Be False question that is conditional

_____ 25. A Necessary Assumption question with a clear Term Shift

_____ 26. An ID the Flaw question that makes a comparison

_____ 27. A Must Be True question in which statements are not conditional

_____ 28. A Sufficient Assumption question in which a recommendation is made

_____ 29. A Weaken question that presents a conclusion about proportion based on evidence about raw numbers

_____ 30. A Necessary Assumption question without a clear Term Shift

_____ 31. A Strengthen question that offers an explanation

_____ 32. A Weaken question that recommends a course of action

_____ 33. A Principle Example question with two principles

_____ 34. A Strengthen question presenting a comparative argument

_____ 35. A Necessary Assumption question with a weak conclusion

_____ 36. A Match the Reasoning question

_____ 37. An ID the Flaw question that presents a conclusion about raw numbers based on evidence about proportion

_____ 38. A Principle Support question in which an evaluation is made

4

_____ 39. A Necessary Assumption question with a strong conclusion

_____ 40. A Match the Flaw question with a common flaw

_____ 41. A Match the Flaw question without a common flaw

_____ 42. A Most Strongly Supported question in which the stimulus presents an argument

_____ 43. An ID the (Dis)agreement question

_____ 44. A Must Be False question in which the stimulus is not conditional

_____ 45. A Match the Principle question

_____ 46. An Evaluate the Argument question with a proportion in the conclusion

_____ 47. A Principle Example question with one principle

_____ 48. A Logically Completes question in which the blank follows the word "thus"

_____ 49. An ID the Agreement question

_____ 50. A Weaken question in which an explanation is offered

4

Answers

___S___ 1. A Must Be True question in which each statement is conditional

Diagram and make a specific prediction.

___G___ 2. A Weaken question presenting a causal argument

Expect one of the main causal weakeners: alternative cause, counterexample, attack the sequence, reverse the causality.

___S___ 3. A Sufficient Assumption question with a Term Shift from premise to conclusion

Bridge that gap!

___S___ 4. An ID the Flaw question in which the argument confuses sufficient and necessary terms

Look for an answer describing an Illegal Reversal or Illegal Negation.

___G___ 5. An Explain a Result question presenting an unexpected outcome of a study

Reconcile it with the expected outcome in some way.

___G___ 6. A Strengthen question in which a recommendation is made

Expect to rule out alternative recommendations, add evidence that the recommended course of action will have the desired result, or rule out unintended consequences.

___S___ 7. An ID the Conclusion question

ID the conclusion in the stimulus and look for a paraphrase.

___G___ 8. A Strengthen question in which an explanation is offered

Expect to rule out alternative explanations or add evidence supporting the proposed explanation.

___G___ 9. An ID the Flaw question with none of the Common Flaws

Expect the correct answer to call out an assumption the argument makes or an objection the argument overlooks.

___S___ 10. A Principle Support question in which a recommendation is made

The right answer will establish the premise as the criterion for the recommendation that's made.

___G___ 11. A Most Strongly Supported question

Succinctly delineate the individual statements in the stimulus and look for an answer that aligns with one statement or a combination of statements and doesn't overshoot.

___S___ 12. A Determine the Function question

Articulate what role the quoted piece of text serves before looking at those answers!

___G___ 13. A Strengthen question in which the argument already seems solid

Anticipate what overlooked possibility an opposing counsel might expose to weaken the argument, and then look for answer that counters that possibility.

___G___ 14. A Weaken question

ID the argument's reasoning structure (Causal, Comparative, Survey) and predict one of the common weakeners for that type of argument.

___S___ 15. An ID the Flaw question in which a characteristic of an entity was concluded to also be characteristic of each of the entity's components

Part vs. Whole flaw!

___S___ 16. An ID the Flaw question that accuses someone of hypocrisy

Ad Hominem flaw!

___G___ 17. An Explain a Result question presenting a surprising disparity

Expect to introduce a possible cause of the disparity.

___G___ 18. A Necessary Assumption question in which the argument already seems solid

Expect a Defender Assumption that defends against an objection you hadn't considered.

___S___ 19. A Procedure question

Articulate the structure before looking at the answers. Look for the common ones such as reduction to the absurd, application of a general principle to a specific case, arguing by analogy, supporting a general principle with a specific example, and Common Flaws.

___S___ 20. A Weaken question presenting a comparative argument

If the argument concludes two things are similar, the right answer will show them to be different. If the argument concludes two things are different, the right answer will show them to be similar.

___G___ 21. An ID the Flaw question that cites a study

Sometimes the studies are flawed (Sampling Flaw), other times they're mistakenly cited as proving something they don't (Unproven vs. Untrue), and still other times they're fine and it's the rest of the argument that's the problem.

___G___ 22. A Strengthen question presenting a causal argument

Expect the right answer to rule out alternate causes, demonstrate other instances of the causal relationship, establish the temporal sequence, or establish a control group.

___S___ 23. A Must Be True question made up entirely of quantity statements

Identify the extent to which the quantified groups overlap.

___S___ 24. A Must Be False question that is conditional

Show a sufficient condition with the wrong necessary condition, in either a statement that is given or a chain you can infer. Be wary of false contrapositives (Illegal Reversal and Illegal Negation)—though we are trained to recognize them as faulty logic, they represent ideas that could be true and thus do not constitute correct answers.

___G___ 25. A Necessary Assumption question with a clear Term Shift

Bridge that gap! But, remember, these questions still tend to be based on ideas the author has failed to consider and the answers won't read the same as Sufficient Assumption questions.

___G___ 26. An ID the Flaw question that makes a comparison

Expect an answer about what is assumed or an objection the argument has failed to consider.

___G___ 27. A Must Be True question in which statements are not conditional

Try to infer what you can by visualizing the connections between individual statements, then rely on process of elimination. Remember that the correct answer can align with any single statement or it can be a deduction reached by combining multiple statements.

___S___ 28. A Sufficient Assumption question in which a recommendation is made

The right answer will establish the premise as the criterion for the recommendation.

___S___ 29. A Weaken question that presents a conclusion about proportion based on evidence about raw numbers

Attack the Percent vs. Amount flaw by offering alternative explanations.

___G___ 30. A Necessary Assumption question without a clear Term Shift

Expect a Defender Assumption that rules out possible objections.

___G___ 31. A Strengthen question that offers an explanation

Expect the right answer to rule out an alternate explanation or demonstrate other relationships that could reasonably be explained by the conclusion.

___G___ 32. A Weaken question that recommends a course of action

Expect alternatives to be presented, unintended consequences to be raised, or the extent to which the action will achieve the desired effect to be questioned.

___G___ 33. A Principle Example question with two principles

Predict that at least one will be exemplified, but possibly both.

___S___ 34. A Strengthen question presenting a comparative argument

If it concludes two things are similar, rule out a difference. If it concludes two things are different, rule out a similarity.

___G___ 35. A Necessary Assumption question with a weak conclusion

Predict a weaker correct answer.

___S___ 36. A Match the Reasoning question that presents a conditional argument

Diagram it and hunt for an exact match.

___S___ 37. An ID the Flaw question that presents a conclusion about raw numbers based on evidence about proportion

Percent vs. Amount flaw!

___S___ 38. A Principle Support question in which an evaluation is made

All Principle Support questions will link the new concept in the conclusion back to a concept from the premise.

__G__ 39. A Necessary Assumption question with a strong conclusion

Predict that the correct answer might be stronger than you'd normally expect from a Necessary Assumption question, but otherwise this won't change your prephrase.

__G__ 40. A Match the Flaw question with a common flaw

Define the flaw, but you'll have no idea what the answer choice will look like specifically!

__G__ 41. A Match the Flaw question without a common flaw

If it doesn't have one (or you don't recognize the flaw), rely on other Mismatches just as you would in a Match the Reasoning question.

__S__ 42. A Most Strongly Supported question in which the stimulus presents an argument

These are extremely rare, almost non-existent, but when they occur, the correct answer is a necessary assumption that bridges the gap between the premise and conclusion of the argument presented.

__S__ 43. An ID the (Dis)agreement question

Know exactly what piece of the first speaker's argument the second speaker is responding to.

__G__ 44. A Must Be False question in which the stimulus is not conditional

Attempt to draw a valid conclusion by constructing a concise flow chart of the individual statements, then look for its negation in the answers.

__G__ 45. A Match the Principle question

Articulate the principle and look for an argument based on the same type of logic.

__S__ 46. An Evaluate the Argument question with a proportion in the conclusion

This is indicative of a Percent vs. Amount flaw, and the correct answer choice will establish the extent to which one led to the other.

__S__ 47. A Principle Example question with one principle

Diagram and contrapose it: the right answer will fulfill the sufficient and conclude the necessary of the original or the contrapositive.

__S__ 48. A Logically Completes question in which the blank follows the word "thus"

Draw a valid conclusion based on the evidence given and find it in the answers.

__S__ 49. An ID the Agreement question

Find the common ground before assessing the answer choices.

__G__ 50. A Weaken question in which an explanation is offered

Expect alternatives to the explanation or things that would get in the way of the explanation being appropriate.

4

Drill 58: Lies, Damn Lies, and Statistics

Instructions: In this drill, you'll be evaluating statements from Explanation stimuli that include math elements. Ugh, math! It rarely shows its face on the LSAT, but when it does, it can mean you're in for a tough question.

For the most part, math on the LSAT will deal with statistics. On Assumption Family questions, you'll need to know when you can and can't jump between statements about rates and statements about quantity. (If you're thinking Percent vs. Amount flaw right now, kudos!) For Explanation questions, you'll need to recognize which answer choices do and do not help to account for statistical changes. The common thread here is the idea that every statistic or statistical change can have multiple explanations, some of which involve a change in rate and others of which involve a change in quantity. Can you tell a good explanation from a bogus one? Use this drill to find out!

For each of the following sets, write an E on the line if what follows would help explain the situation in the stimulus, and write an N if the statement does not help explain the situation.

4

The number of traffic fatalities in Springfield decreased in 2017 from the previous year's total.

_____ 1.   The speed limits in Springfield were lowered in 2017.

_____ 2.   The winter of 2016 was an unusually stormy one that frequently created icy road conditions.

_____ 3.   Springfield had the highest rate of traffic fatalities of any city in the region in 2016.

_____ 4.   Due to poor economic conditions, many residents of Springfield moved elsewhere in 2017.

_____ 5.   Springfield's city council passed an ordinance that went into effect in 2017 that required two years, rather than one year, of driver education before new drivers can take the driving test.

The average global life span has increased by more than ten years in the last century.

_____ 6.   Family planning services that allow families to have fewer children have spread to countries with high infant mortality rates over the last 15 years.

_____ 7.   The global population has increased by more than 4 billion over the last 100 years.

_____ 8.   The prevalence of wars, which were one of the leading causes of death among young men in the 20th century, has decreased significantly in the last few decades.

_____ 9.   The average life span has increased by as much as 20 years in some cities over the last century.

_____ 10.   Improvements in medical care have significantly increased the lifespan of people who suffer a heart attack, one of the most common causes of death for older people.

More people have cancer now than at any other time in human history.

_____ 11.   Doctors have made marked improvements to cancer treatments that prolong the life of cancer patients over the last fifty years.

_____ 12.   The global population is currently the highest it has ever been.

_____ 13.   Researchers have discovered that many patients long thought to have been cured of cancer are, in fact, still suffering from the disease.

_____ 14.   Recent developments in treatment have significantly improved the quality of life of those suffering from cancer.

_____ 15.   Smoking cigarettes, which tends to cause cancer over a period of twenty or thirty years, was at its peak thirty years ago.

Springfield's rate of voter participation in the last mayoral election was the lowest in the last 40 years.

_____ 16. Normally there are only two viable candidates, but last year Councilwoman Garcia ran a successful third-party candidacy.

_____ 17. Springfield's population has shrunk significantly over the last 40 years.

_____ 18. Springfield has established two new universities over the last decade, and college students have the lowest rate of voter participation of any age demographic.

_____ 19. Election day has previously been held on a Sunday, but this last election it was held on a Tuesday, when many people have to work.

_____ 20. The rate of voter participation in Springfield had been steadily decreasing over the 40 years leading up to last year's election.

Fewer people watched the Super Bowl this year than in any other year in recent memory.

_____ 21. Many people have digital video recorders that allow them to watch recordings of games at a later time.

_____ 22. The matchup in this year's Super Bowl was the first one between two teams from small cities, neither of which has a large fan base.

_____ 23. The series premiere of a highly-touted new show coincided with the Super Bowl.

_____ 24. The commercials, which generally entice many people who aren't football fans to watch the Super Bowl, were available on a separate online stream for the first time this year.

_____ 25. This year, the human population was decimated by disease.

The amount of economic damage due to hurricanes was greater last year than ever before.

_____ 26. There was a record-breaking number of hurricanes last year.

_____ 27. The budget for hurricane relief was slashed last year in many cities.

_____ 28. Regulations intended to limit hurricane damage by requiring increased structural integrity of all new buildings will not go into effect until the coming year.

_____ 29. Some of the cities hit by the worst hurricanes last year were in regions that typically do not get hit by hurricanes, and the infrastructure was not built to handle the resulting flooding.

_____ 30. Even though meteorologists have improved their ability to track and project the path of incoming hurricanes, there is not much anyone can do to prevent damage in a severe storm.

The proportion of Americans responding "no religion" to a survey that asks about religious affiliation is at an all-time high.

_____ 31. It is becoming increasingly socially acceptable not to affiliate with any organized religion.

_____ 32. The survey has started calling cell phones instead of landlines, shifting the population of those surveyed from older and more religious people to younger people less likely to be religiously affiliated.

_____ 33. The survey reached more people last year than it had in previous years.

_____ 34. The survey reached fewer people last year than it had in previous years.

_____ 35. The company that conducts the survey is under new ownership as of last year.

The recidivism rate (the rate at which people released from prison return to prison) is much lower in Canada than it is in the United States.

_____ 36. The United States has a significantly higher incarceration rate than Canada.

_____ 37. Canada recently instituted programs aimed to intervene and help inmates deemed most likely to recidivate upon their release.

_____ 38. In the United States, but not in Canada, parolees can be sent back to prison for violations of their parole.

_____ 39. The population of the United States is ten times that of Canada.

_____ 40. The United States incarcerates a larger number of low-level drug offenders, who are some of the most likely people to recidivate.

The acceptance rate at Stevens Law School has dropped each of the last four years.

_____ 41. The number of applicants to Stevens Law School has increased each of the last four years, while the size of its incoming class has remained the same.

_____ 42. Stevens Law School lowered the size of its incoming class five years ago in an effort to increase its prestige.

_____ 43. The admissions team at Stevens Law School has been consistently improving its ability to predict which accepted students will eventually enroll.

_____ 44. The law schools with similar rankings to Stevens Law School have all decreased their acceptance rates each of the past four years.

_____ 45. The number of people applying to law school four years ago hit a twenty-year low.

The on-time percentage of the top airlines was significantly higher last year than it was the previous year.

_____ 46. As budget airlines have cropped up in recent years, top airlines have felt pressure to distinguish themselves from their competitors.

_____ 47. Many top airlines have begun to increase the published duration of their flights.

_____ 48. A volcanic eruption in Iceland two years ago delayed thousands of flights for days due to the resulting ash.

_____ 49. Web sites that report the on-time percentage of different airlines have become popular in the last few years.

_____ 50. Last year saw a record-breaking number of flights throughout the world.

4

Answers

1–5. The number of traffic fatalities in Springfield decreased in 2017 from the previous year's total.

  E   1.
  E   2.
  N   3.
  E   4.
  N   5.

To explain this statistic, we need something that will demonstrate a difference between 2016 and 2017 that could account for the reduction of traffic fatalities. This could take the form of safer driving conditions in 2017 (1), more dangerous driving conditions in 2016 (2), or a reduction of total driving from one year to the next (4). Statements 3 and 5 don't address a difference between the two years so they can't explain a statistical change. Statement 5, by the way, is easy to misinterpret. Does it imply that the annual variation could just be the standard, if it happened between both sets of years? In fact, it doesn't—statement 5 just gives another statistic without attributing it to any particular cause. Resist the urge to project your interpretation of the possible shared cause of both statistics onto an answer choice that doesn't state or imply that cause.

6–10. The average global life span has increased by more than ten years in the last century.

  E   6.
  N   7.
  E   8.
  N   9.
  E   10.

To explain this statistic, we need something that will explain why people across the world are living 10+ years longer today than they were a century ago. Because this statistic is about average lifespan, it could be explained by improvements in medical care that extend life (10) or by a significant reduction in early mortality (6 and 8). Statement 7 addresses the size of the population, not the average life span. Statement 9 only addresses the increase in lifespan in a subset of the global population, and it doesn't provide an explanation as to why.

11–15. More people have cancer now than at any other time in human history.

  E   11.
  E   12.
  N   13.
  N   14.
  E   15.

To explain this statistic, we need something that explains why the number of people living with cancer today is higher than it's ever been. Perhaps a leading cause of cancer has become more prevalent (15), or maybe people with cancer are living longer (11). Alternatively, this could result from the fact that there are more people alive today (12), since the statistic is about the absolute number, not the percentage, of people living with cancer today. Statement 13 only addresses a change in whether researchers *know* that patients have cancer, not whether the patients actually have cancer. Statement 14 addresses the quality of life, which will not impact the number of people living with cancer.

16–20. Springfield's rate of voter participation in the last mayoral election was the lowest in the last 40 years.

  N   16.
  N   17.
  E   18.
  E   19.
  N   20.

To explain this statistic, we need to demonstrate a difference between last year and the previous four decades that accounts for the reduction in the *rate* of Springfield's voter participation. We aren't necessarily looking for a drop in total voters, but for a drop in voters per capita. This could be due to Springfield's demographic shifts toward a population that's less likely to vote (18), or some factor that made it more difficult to vote last year (19). Statement 16 would, if anything, explain an increase in voter participation. Statement 17 explains a reduction in the total number of voters, but not the percentage of the population who voted. Statement 20 establishes a trend but fails to justify why that trend would continue.

4

21–25. Fewer people watched the Super Bowl this year than in any other year in recent memory.

   N   21.
   E   22.
   E   23.
   E   24.
   E   25.

To explain this statistic, we need to demonstrate a difference between last year's Super Bowl and the other Super Bowls in recent memory that explains why the telecast last year garnered fewer viewers. One explanation could be that the teams involved had fewer fans than the teams in previous years (22). There could also have been something competing for viewership (23). Alternatively, one of the main reasons many people typically watch the Super Bowl may no longer apply (24), or maybe there were just fewer people in the world to watch (25)! Remember, you can always explain a change in the number of a subset by a change in the number of the whole. Statement 21 explains why fewer people may watch the Super Bowl live, but it does not explain a reduction in total viewership.

26–30. The amount of economic damage due to hurricanes was greater last year than ever before.

   E   26.
   N   27.
   N   28.
   E   29.
   N   30.

To explain this statistic, we need to demonstrate a difference between last year and the previous years that accounts for the record amount of economic damage resulting from hurricanes. Perhaps there were simply more hurricanes than ever before (26), or the hurricanes did more damage, on average, because they hit areas less prepared to deal with hurricanes (29). Statement 27 explains why relief efforts were limited, not why the hurricanes did more damage in the first place. If neither regulations (28) nor meteorology (30) helped last year, that would justify why economic damage did not decrease last year, but it does not articulate a difference between last year and prior years that accounts for record-breaking damage.

31–35. The proportion of Americans responding "no religion" to a survey that asks about religious affiliation is at an all-time high.

   E   31.
   E   32.
   N   33.
   N   34.
   N   35.

To explain this statistic, we either need to demonstrate a difference between the survey last year vs. other years, or the people surveyed last year vs. other years. Perhaps more Americans are admitting their lack of religiosity as social pressure to affiliate religiously declines (31). Or, perhaps the survey reached a different population of respondents than it did in past years (32). Statements 33 and 34 indicate a change in the raw number of survey respondents, but those changes don't explain the change in proportion. Statement 35 indicates that ownership of the company conducting the survey changed but gives no indication that the survey itself changed.

36–40. The recidivism rate (the rate at which people released from prison return to prison) is much lower in Canada than it is in the United States.

   N   36.
   E   37.
   E   38.
   N   39.
   N   40.

To explain this statistic, we need to find a difference between the criminal justice systems in Canada and the United States that explains why prisoners recidivate at a higher rate in the United States than they do in Canada. It may be that Canada takes active measures to reduce recidivism (37) or that former inmates can be sent back to prison for lesser crimes in the United States (38). Statements 36 and 39 both address a difference in the size of the incarcerated populations in the United States and Canada, but a difference in size cannot explain a difference in the rate, because rate is proportional to size. Statement 40 addresses a difference in the composition of the prison population; however, it refers only to the number, rather than the proportion, of low-level drug offenders who are incarcerated in the United States, so, like statements 36 and 39, it cannot explain a difference in rate.

41–45. The acceptance rate at Stevens Law School has dropped each of the last four years.

__E__	41.
__N__	42.
__E__	43.
__N__	44.
__N__	45.

To explain this statistic, we need something that explains why the acceptance rate at Stevens Law School has dropped continuously over the past four years. Note that a one-time change four years ago would not account for a reduction in *each* of the last four years. The continuous reduction could be explained by an increase in the number of applicants without a comparable increase in class size over each of the last four years (41), or by some factor that has allowed the admissions committee to accept fewer students each year while maintaining the same number of students who decide to attend (43). Statements 42 and 45 explain a one-time reduction, but neither explains a trend that would continue for four years. Statement 44 describes a trend about other law schools that won't necessarily translate to Stevens Law School.

46–50. The on-time percentage of the top airlines was significantly higher last year than it was the previous year.

__E__	46.
__E__	47.
__E__	48.
__E__	49.
__N__	50.

To explain this statistic, we need something that changed from two years ago to last year that explains why a higher proportion of flights from top airlines are on time. Some external pressure, whether from low-cost competitors (46) or increased awareness of on-time performance (49), could push top airlines to improve their service. Or, the top airlines could also have maintained their level of service and simply extended the published duration of their flights, setting a lower bar so that more flights come in on time (47). Alternatively, if there was an external event that decreased average on-time percentage two years ago (48), then a return to normal last year could also explain the improvement in on-time performance. Statement 50 indicates a change in the total number of flights, which doesn't address the proportion of those flights that come in on time.

4

Drill 59: Vocab Lab #8 – Bad Words

Instructions: These are the bad boys of the LSAT world. Each word will have a negative connotation. Choose the answer closest in meaning.

1. Censure
   - (A) edit out unacceptable parts
   - (B) disapprove strongly and officially
   - (C) record distasteful details

2. Contemptuous
   - (A) insolvent
   - (B) disgusting
   - (C) scornful

3. Denounce
   - (A) accuse of being evil or wrong
   - (B) give up doing something evil
   - (C) join forces with someone evil

4. Lament
   - (A) limp feebly
   - (B) connive secretly
   - (C) mourn passionately

5. Malign
   - (A) speak ill of
   - (B) distort in shape
   - (C) indicate incorrectly

6. Objectionable
   - (A) impersonal
   - (B) offensive
   - (C) insignificant

7. Reprehensible
   - (A) suspicious
   - (B) disgraceful
   - (C) outraged

8. Sardonic
   - (A) mocking
   - (B) depressed
   - (C) selfish

9. Subversive
   - (A) dismissive
   - (B) acquisitive
   - (C) disruptive

10. Unconscionable
    - (A) inanimate
    - (B) indefensible
    - (C) inconceivable

Answers follow on the next page.

Answers

1.   B

Censure = disapprove strongly and officially. As a noun, it means strong, official disapproval. Not to be confused with *censor* = edit out unacceptable parts.

2.   C

Contemptuous = scornful; full of disrespect for something or someone. Related to, but not to be confused with, *contemptible* = worthy of *contempt* or disgust. If you are *contemptuous* of quinoa, then you feel that quinoa is *contemptible*.

3.   A

Denounce = accuse of being evil or wrong, generally publicly and loudly. The root of *denounce* and *announce* is the same: *nuntius* = messenger in Latin.

4.   C

Lament = mourn passionately. It is true that not all *laments* are poetic. Sometimes *laments* are just wailing and gnashing of teeth.

5.   A

Malign = speak ill of; slander. As an adjective, it means "evil, bad, *malignant*," the opposite of *benign*.

6.   B

Objectionable = offensive; off-putting. You *object* to, or raise an *objection* to, something *objectionable*.

7.   B

Reprehensible = disgraceful; dishonorable. The underlying verb *reprehend*, which means "reprimand, rebuke," has become rare in modern English.

8.   A

Sardonic = mocking, often with laughter; spiteful. The word seems to have an interesting origin. Long ago, some believed that a plant that grew on the island of Sardinia caused people to laugh *sardonically* and then die.

9.   C

Subversive = disruptive; trying to undermine some kind of established order. *Subvert* = turn upside down, from *sub* (under) + *vert* (turn).

10.   B

Unconscionable = indefensible; unreasonable. Connect this word, not to *consciousness*, but to *conscience*. An *unconscionable* action is one that disregards *conscience* or reason.

4

Step 4 – Answer Choice Analysis

The final step in our 4-Step Process for Logical Reasoning is Answer Choice Analysis. One of the most common mistakes students make when approaching the answer choices is focusing too much on looking for one that's right. Looking for the right answer is great if you have a solid prephrase, but if you don't have one, or if you don't see your prephrase in the answers on your first pass, we recommend focusing on the four incorrect answers instead. That's why we call our approach Working Wrong to Right. In most LR questions, there are at least a couple of answer choices that can be eliminated for concrete reasons on a first pass. Looking for what makes them definitively wrong is more efficient than considering whether they could be right, and for the answer choices that remain, it's generally easier to find fatal flaws than it is to find qualities that make one definitively correct.

In this section, you will learn to:

Spot Red Flags

Untangle Abstract Answer Choices

Work from Wrong to Right

Recognize the Most Common Traps

4

Drill 60: A Test of Strength

Instructions: Strength, also known as degree, can make or break an answer choice, and what is or is not an acceptable strength is largely determined by the interaction between the question type and the conclusion. For the following question type/conclusion breakdowns, determine for each answer choice fragment whether it's likely to be too strong (TS), too weak (TW), or an acceptable strength (AS).

A Necessary Assumption question with the conclusion: "Thus, captive-born guinea pigs are unlikely to ever experience success in the wild."

_____ 1. No guinea pigs...

_____ 2. Some captive-born guinea pigs...

_____ 3. Most captive-born guinea pigs...

_____ 4. Captive-born guinea pigs have been known to...

_____ 5. Most guinea pigs...

A Weaken question with the conclusion: "This study demonstrates that cooperative grooming is much rarer among male chimpanzees than among female chimpanzees."

_____ 6. The chimpanzee population observed for this study...

_____ 7. Some male chimpanzees...

_____ 8. Other chimpanzee populations...

_____ 9. ...among males is not infrequent.

_____ 10. ...among females has been observed.

A Strengthen question with the conclusion: "It is expected that the board president will be voted out of office in the next election."

_____ 11. Some of the voting members...

_____ 12. A majority of the voting members...

_____ 13. All of the voting members...

_____ 14. A majority of the members...

_____ 15. All of the members...

A Sufficient Assumption question with the conclusion: "The council should adopt the Parks Department's land-use proposal."

_____ 16. Some of the other departments' proposals...

_____ 17. Some of the Parks Department's proposals...

_____ 18. All land use proposals...

_____ 19. All of the Parks Department's proposals...

_____ 20. Some land use proposals...

A Necessary Assumption question with the conclusion: "The new bakery in town will probably be successful."

_____ 21. A majority of the town's residents...

_____ 22. Some visitors to the town...

_____ 23. All tourists...

_____ 24. Some of the town's residents...

_____ 25. A bakery in a nearby town...

A Weaken question with the conclusion: "The experimental results show that the new drug is effective at lowering blood pressure in men over 50."

_____ 26. Among the study participants...

_____ 27. In a study with a similar design...

_____ 28. A study of another new drug...

_____ 29. In previous studies of men...

_____ 30. In previous studies of men over 50...

A Flaw question with the conclusion: "...is the only possible reason Thompson's project did not win first prize."

_____ 31. Assumes that all of the projects...

_____ 32. ...the projects that were ranked higher than Thompson's...

_____ 33. ...Thompson's project...

_____ 34. Fails to consider that some projects that were ranked lower than Thompson's...

_____ 35. ...the scoring criteria for the projects...

A Strengthen question with the conclusion: "Therefore, the pottery shards found at Mexico's Chichen Itza archeological site are unlikely to have played a role in the religious practices of the indigenous Mayan population there."

_____ 36. The religious practices of indigenous Mexican civilizations...

_____ 37. Pottery was often...

_____ 38. Pottery was typically...

_____ 39. Pottery may...

_____ 40. Pottery was rarely...

4

A Flaw question with the conclusion: "Clearly, the recent change in the law caused the crime wave."

_____ 41. The first incident associated with the crime wave . . .

_____ 42. Fails to consider that some changes in the law . . .

_____ 43. Fails to consider that all crime waves . . .

_____ 44. Presumes that all crime waves . . .

_____ 45. Presupposes that the majority of crimes in the city . . .

A Necessary Assumption question with the conclusion: "Hence, the library books were probably lost rather than stolen."

_____ 46. Library books never . . .

_____ 47. Thieves typically . . .

_____ 48. It is unlikely that . . .

_____ 49. Library books frequently . . .

_____ 50. It is possible that . . .

Answers

1–5. A Necessary Assumption question with the conclusion: "Thus, captive-born guinea pigs are unlikely to ever experience success in the wild."

<u>TS</u> 1. No guinea pigs ...

<u>AS</u> 2. Some captive-born guinea pigs ...

<u>AS</u> 3. Most captive-born guinea pigs ...

<u>AS</u> 4. Captive born guinea pigs have been known to ...

<u>TS</u> 5. Most guinea pigs ...

In order to conclude something about captive-born guinea pigs, we don't need info about guinea pigs in general: these answers (1 and 5) are too strong. "Some" statements are the gold standard for Necessary Assumption answers, so 2 and 4 are an acceptable strength. Because our conclusion is so strong ("unlikely to ever"), a "most" statement could also be acceptable (3).

6–10. A Weaken question with the conclusion: "This study demonstrates that cooperative grooming is much rarer among male chimpanzees than among female chimpanzees."

<u>AS</u> 6. The chimpanzee population observed for this study ...

<u>TW</u> 7. Some male chimpanzees ...

<u>AS</u> 8. Other chimpanzee populations ...

<u>TW</u> 9. ... among males is not infrequent.

<u>TW</u> 10. ... among females has been observed.

To weaken a conclusion about comparative rarity, it won't suffice to simply have observed something in one of the two groups being compared. 7, 9, and 10 are thus too weak. On the other hand, answers that address both of the groups being compared by looking at the whole population (6 and 8) are acceptably strong.

11–15. A Strengthen question with the conclusion: "It is expected that the board president will be voted out of office in the next election."

<u>TW</u> 11. Some of the voting members ...

<u>AS</u> 12. A majority of the voting members ...

<u>AS</u> 13. All of the voting members ...

<u>TW</u> 14. A majority of the members ...

<u>AS</u> 15. All of the members ...

To strengthen a conclusion that is a prediction about an election, we need information about how a majority of voting members will vote (12 and 13). Thus, 11 is too weak. 14 is also too weak because what the majority of members think doesn't necessarily reflect what the majority of *voting* members think. 15, on the other hand, is acceptable because it addresses all members, which includes all voting members.

16–20. A Sufficient Assumption question with the conclusion: "The council should adopt the Parks Department's land-use proposal."

<u>TW</u> 16. Some of the other departments' proposals ...

<u>TW</u> 17. Some of the Parks Department's proposals ...

<u>AS</u> 18. All land use proposals ...

<u>AS</u> 19. All of the Parks Department's proposals ...

<u>TW</u> 20. Some land use proposals ...

A sufficient assumption for a conclusion that is a recommendation must specifically address the recommendation, or must apply broadly to everything in a category into which the recommendation falls (18 and 19). Anything less specific or less broadly applicable is too weak (16, 17, and 20).

21–25. A Necessary Assumption question with the conclusion: "The new bakery in town will probably be successful."

<u>TS</u> 21. A majority of the town's residents ...

<u>AS</u> 22. Some visitors to the town ...

<u>TS</u> 23. All tourists ...

<u>AS</u> 24. Some of the town's residents ...

<u>TW</u> 25. A bakery in a nearby town ...

The conclusion is a qualified, weak prediction about the success of a new business. A necessary assumption is that the business will have some customers (22 and 24). 21 and 23 discuss much bigger groups of potential customers and are likely to be too strong for this weak prediction. 25, on the other hand, introduces an irrelevant comparison, and is too weak even for this qualified prediction.

26–30. A Weaken question with the conclusion: "The experimental results show that the new drug is effective at lowering blood pressure in men over 50."

<u>AS</u> 26. Among the study participants ...

<u>AS</u> 27. In a study with a similar design ...

<u>TW</u> 28. A study of another new drug ...

<u>TW</u> 29. In previous studies of men ...

<u>AS</u> 30. In previous studies of men over 50 ...

To weaken a causal conclusion about an experiment, we can show that there was something specific about the experiment's participants that does not generalize (26). We could also compare the result across similar experiments (27) or experiments on similar populations (30). It does not suffice to compare the result to other experiments more broadly (28 and 29).

31–35. A Flaw question with the conclusion: "... is the only possible reason Thompson's project did not win first prize."

TS	31.	Assumes that all of the projects...
AS	32.	... the projects that were ranked higher than Thompson's...
AS	33.	... Thompson's project...
TW	34.	Fails to consider that some projects that were ranked lower than Thompson's...
AS	35.	... the scoring criteria for the projects...

The conclusion is a singular explanation, which suggests that the flaw may be that the argument overlooked alternative explanations (other reasons Thompson's project did not win). 34 is irrelevant, since information about projects ranked lower than Thompson's can't provide an alternative explanation of why Thompson's project did not win. 31 articulates an assumption too broad to be necessary, given that the conclusion is only about Thompson and not those he beat out. 32 and 33 specifically address the projects in question. Like 31, 35 applies broadly, but because 35 isn't necessarily articulating an assumption, its breadth is acceptable. An overlooked alternative explanation could be broad and still correct.

36–40. A Strengthen question with the conclusion: "Therefore, the pottery shards found at Mexico's Chichen Itza archeological site are unlikely to have played a role in the religious practices of the indigenous Mayan population there."

AS	36.	The religious practices of indigenous Mexican civilizations...
TW	37.	Pottery was often...
AS	38.	Pottery was typically...
TW	39.	Pottery may...
AS	40.	Pottery was rarely...

Because the conclusion is a negatively ("unlikely") qualified assertion of fact, correct answer choices could give evidence for more likely alternative uses of the pottery by the inhabitants of Chichen Itza

(38 and 40). 39 and 37 could give evidence of alternative uses, but they are too weak to make the alternatives more likely than use in religious practice. 36 applies more broadly than the argument, but that's OK because the Chichen Itza Mayans fall into the category "indigenous Mexican civilizations," and a strengthener just needs to apply; it doesn't have to be a perfect match.

41–45. A Flaw question with the conclusion: "Clearly, the recent change in the law caused the crime wave."

AS	41.	The first incident associated with the crime wave...
TW	42.	Fails to consider that some changes in the law...
AS	43.	Fails to consider that all crime waves...
TS	44.	Presumes that all crime waves...
TS	45.	Presupposes that the majority of crimes in the city...

The correct answer can address the specific topics of the argument (41), or it could suggest a broadly applicable objection that necessarily applies to the topics of the argument (43). An objection not broadly applicable enough to necessarily apply is too weak (42). On the other hand, an assumption that is too broad to be necessary is too strong (44 and 45).

46–50. A Necessary Assumption question with the conclusion: "Hence, the library books were probably lost rather than stolen."

TS	46.	Library books never...
TS	47.	Thieves typically...
AS	48.	It is unlikely that...
TS	49.	Library books frequently...
AS	50.	It is possible that...

The degree of this conclusion, as indicated by the word "probably," and its specificity to a set of particular books, means this argument will never require assumptions as strong or as broad as 46, 47, or 49. To conclude that something is probable may require the assumption that another thing is unlikely (48), but the lesser degree of mere possibility (50) is acceptable as well.

4

Drill 61: A Flag Has Been Thrown

Instructions: Without even seeing a stimulus, there is certain language that should give you pause as you evaluate an answer choice. Consider each of the following question stems, and highlight any red-flag language in the accompanying answer choices that would make you think the answer is unlikely to be correct. If an answer choice seems OK, just leave it alone.

The argument presupposes which of the following?

1. The only use of ceramic vessels was ceremonial.

2. All civilizations that existed at that time used ceramic vessels.

3. Ceramic vessels were used ceremonially by the civilizations that existed at the time.

4. Ceramic vessels were used ceremonially more frequently than they were used culinarily.

5. Ceramic vessels were not a currency of trade in the region.

Which of the following is an assumption that the argument depends on?

6. Wind energy is the best source of renewable power.

7. Wind and solar energy are the only renewable energy sources that can power a large city.

8. If the city relies on solar energy, it will be able to meet the energy needs of at least some of its citizens.

9. The energy efficiency of a city increases in direct proportion to its reliance on wind energy.

10. Wind energy is far more efficient than solar energy.

Which of the following is most strongly supported by the evidence above?

11. A bicycle is the ideal way for any employee to commute to work.

12. It is impossible for most employees to drive to work.

13. People who ride bicycles to work should never be penalized for arriving late.

14. Riding a bicycle to work is likely to have at least some health benefits.

15. People who ride bicycles to work are healthier than people who do not.

Which of the following criticisms is the argument most vulnerable to?

16. The argument presupposes that no one ever purchases paper copies of newspapers anymore.

17. The argument fails to consider that the only way for newspapers to make revenue is through digital sales.

18. The argument fails to consider that the highest quality newspapers sell both print and digital versions of their news.

19. The argument presupposes that newspapers depend at least in part on digital sales for revenue.

20. The argument assumes that digital advertising brings in revenue at a rate that is inversely proportional to the number of consumers purchasing paper copies.

Which of the following is most strongly supported by the statements above?

21. The flood was unquestionably due to the above average rainfall.

22. The flood was a direct result of a tidal wave.

23. No damage that resulted from the flood was covered by insurance.

24. Every insurance company offered to pay for damage from the flood.

25. The flooding was at least partially caused by an inadequate drainage system.

Which of the following, if true, allows the conclusion to be properly drawn?

26. Some bridges have been improperly inspected.

27. No bridges have been properly inspected.

28. All bridge inspectors have given proper inspections.

29. Most bridges have been improperly inspected.

30. Not all bridges have been properly inspected.

4

Answers

The argument presupposes which of the following?

1. The only use of ceramic vessels was ceremonial.

2. All civilizations that existed at that time used ceramic vessels.

3. Ceramic vessels were used ceremonially by the civilizations that existed at the time.

4. Ceramic vessels were used ceremonially more frequently than they were used culinarily.

5. Ceramic vessels were not a currency of trade in the region.

(While "not" might seem too strong, be careful: Defender Assumptions often rule out alternatives to the conclusion and that requires strong negative language.)

Which of the following is an assumption that the argument depends on?

6. Wind energy is the best source of renewable power.

7. Wind and solar energy are the only renewable energy sources that can power a large city.

8. If the city relies on solar energy, it will be able to meet the energy needs of at least some of its citizens.

9. The energy efficiency of a city increases in direct proportion to its reliance on wind energy.

10. Wind energy is far more efficient than solar energy.

Which of the following is most strongly supported by the evidence above?

11. A bicycle is the ideal way for any employee to commute to work.

12. It is impossible for most employees to drive to work.

13. People who ride bicycles to work should never be penalized for arriving late.

14. Riding a bicycle to work is likely to have at least some health benefits.

15. People who ride bicycles to work are healthier than people who do not.

Which of the following criticisms is the argument most vulnerable to?

16. The argument presupposes that no one ever purchases paper copies of newspapers anymore.

17. The argument fails to consider that the only way for newspapers to make revenue is through digital sales.

("The only" is strong, limiting language, and if this answer described an assumption, it would be a red flag. But, because this answer choice describes an objection, a strong degree isn't problematic.)

18. The argument fails to consider that the highest quality newspapers sell both print and digital versions of their news.

19. The argument presupposes that newspapers depend at least in part on digital sales for revenue.

20. The argument assumes that digital advertising brings in revenue at a rate that is inversely proportional to the number of consumers purchasing paper copies.

Which of the following is most strongly supported by the statements above?

21. The flood was unquestionably due to the above average rainfall.

22. The flood was a direct result of a tidal wave.

23. No damage that resulted from the flood was covered by insurance.

24. Every insurance company offered to pay for damage from the flood.

25. The flooding was at least partially caused by an inadequate drainage system.

Which of the following, if true, allows the conclusion to be properly drawn?

26. Some bridges have been improperly inspected.

(Weak language; Sufficient Assumption questions need answers that are strong enough to make an argument valid.)

27. No bridges have been properly inspected.

28. All bridge inspectors have given proper inspections.

29. Most bridges have been improperly inspected.

30. Not all bridges have been properly inspected.

Drill 62: Talking to Yourself, Supply the Type Edition

Instructions: Getting to the right answers is all about asking yourself the right questions. Questions that will make or break an answer for one type of question are completely irrelevant to others. Can you tell one from the other? Use this drill to find out!

For each of the following, identify which question types our hypothetical test taker could be working on from the question they are asking themselves while analyzing the answers. Note that many of these will have multiple right answers, so don't stop at one—try to find them all!

1. If this isn't true, does it make my argument fall apart?

2. Is this the contrapositive of my prephrase?

3. Does this rule out a possible alternative?

4. Did the argument actually say that?

5. Wait . . . is this the opposite of what I want?

6. Does this have to be true?

7. Would this help my argument?

8. What type of conclusion is that?

9. Is this something the author failed to consider?

10. Does this make the argument valid?

11. Is this too strong?

12. Is this too weak?

13. Is this the reversal of my prephrase?

14. Do both speakers talk about this?

15. Does something in the stimulus fulfill this sufficient condition?

16. Does this situation fulfill the sufficient condition presented in the stimulus?

17. Can I name the line of reasoning this describes?

18. Looks pretty good...should I diagram it to confirm?

19. Does this contradict a valid conclusion I could draw?

20. Does this argument conclude the necessary condition from the stimulus?

4

Answers

1. If this isn't true, does it make my argument fall apart?

    Necessary Assumption

2. Is this the contrapositive of my prephrase?

    Must Be True, Sufficient Assumption, Principle Support

3. Does this rule out a possible alternative?

    Strengthen, Necessary Assumption

4. Did the argument actually say that?

    ID the Conclusion, Procedure, Determine the Function, ID the Flaw, ID the (Dis)agreement

5. Wait ... is this the opposite of what I want?

    Strengthen, Weaken, Explain a Result, ID the (Dis)agreement

6. Does this have to be true?

    Must Be True, Necessary Assumption

7. Would this help my argument?

    Strengthen, Principle Support, Evaluate

8. What type of conclusion is that?

    Match the Reasoning, Match the Flaw

9. Is this something the author failed to consider?

    Flaw, Weaken, Necessary Assumption, Strengthen

10. Does this make the argument valid?

    Sufficient Assumption

11. Is this too strong?

    Necessary Assumption, Most Strongly Supported

12. Is this too weak?

    Strengthen, Weaken, Sufficient Assumption, Explain a Result, Principle Support

4

13. Is this the reversal of my prephrase?

    Must Be True, Sufficient Assumption, Principle Support

14. Do both speakers talk about this?

    ID the (Dis)agreement

15. Does something in the stimulus fulfill this sufficient condition?

    Sufficient Assumption, Principle Support

16. Does this situation fulfill the sufficient condition presented in the stimulus?

    Principle Example

17. Can I name the line of reasoning this describes?

    ID the Flaw, Procedure

18. Looks pretty good … should I diagram it to confirm?

    Match the Reasoning, Match the Flaw, Sufficient Assumption, Principle Example, Must Be True

19. Does this contradict a valid conclusion I could draw?

    Must Be False

20. Does this argument conclude the necessary condition from the stimulus?

    Principle Example

Drill 63: Abstract Answer Choices

Instructions: The abstract language in answer choices—especially Determine the Function and Procedure answer choices—can be difficult to understand. Use this drill to build familiarity with the most common abstract terms on the LSAT! For each abstract answer given, determine if the words that follow could replace the highlighted term without changing the meaning of the answer choice (Y) or not (N).

A phenomenon for which a causal explanation is offered.

_____ 1. Situation

_____ 2. Occurrence

_____ 3. Result

_____ 4. Premise

A claim used to support the argument.

_____ 5. Disclaimer

_____ 6. Assertion

_____ 7. Opinion

_____ 8. Question

The committee, however, posits that an increase in taxes would drive out low-income families.

_____ 9. Understands

_____ 10. Thinks

_____ 11. Knows

_____ 12. Believes

Which of the following does the author use to refute the statement that owning a cat is better than owning a dog?

_____ 13. Repudiate

_____ 14. Support

_____ 15. Contradict

_____ 16. Bolster

The teacher is unpopular because he teaches the class with the presupposition that students will already have some knowledge of biology.

_____ 17. Knowledge

_____ 18. Hope

_____ 19. Premise

_____ 20. Assumption

The analogy reduces this argument to the absurd.

_____ 21. Silly

_____ 22. Unusual

_____ 23. Unreasonable

_____ 24. Preposterous

Which of the following most helps to justify the reasoning used by the economist in her argument?

_____ 25. Interrogate

_____ 26. Prove

_____ 27. Weaken

_____ 28. Uphold

The politician referred to Alaska's oil reserves primarily in order to . . .

_____ 29. Only

_____ 30. Wholly

_____ 31. Partially

_____ 32. Mainly

It is used to refute an argument the economist deemed spurious.

_____ 33. Invalid

_____ 34. Genuine

_____ 35. Dubious

_____ 36. Legitimate

The argument relies on a term that is ambiguous.

_____ 37. Imprecise

_____ 38. Of more than one possible meaning

_____ 39. Unclear

_____ 40. Strange

4

Answers

A phenomenon for which a causal explanation is offered.

__Y__	1.	**Situation**
__Y__	2.	**Occurrence**
__Y__	3.	**Result**
__N__	4.	Premise

In the real world, we often think of a "phenomenon" as being something phenomenal. But in LSAT world, a phenomenon is just anything that has happened or is happening; it doesn't have to be anything exciting or unique.

A claim used to support the argument.

__N__	5.	Disclaimer
__Y__	6.	**Assertion**
__Y__	7.	**Opinion**
__N__	8.	Question

The committee, however, posits that an increase in taxes would drive out low-income families.

__N__	9.	Understands
__Y__	10.	**Thinks**
__N__	11.	Knows
__Y__	12.	**Believes**

Which of the following does the author use to refute the statement that owning a cat is better than owning a dog?

__Y__	13.	**Repudiate**
__N__	14.	Support
__Y__	15.	**Contradict**
__N__	16.	Bolster

The teacher is unpopular because he teaches the class with the presupposition that students will already have some knowledge of biology.

__N__	17.	Knowledge
__N__	18.	Hope
__N__	19.	Premise
__Y__	20.	**Assumption**

The analogy reduces this argument to the absurd.

__N__	21.	Silly
__N__	22.	Unusual
__Y__	23.	**Unreasonable**
__Y__	24.	**Preposterous**

In the real world, we tend to associate the word "absurd" with words like "wacky," "zany," and "ridiculous." But in LSAT world, an argument is "absurd" if its logic leads to a conclusion that is clearly false; it doesn't have to be weird, funny, or off the wall.

Which of the following most helps to justify the reasoning used by the economist in her argument?

__N__	25.	Interrogate
__Y__	26.	**Prove**
__N__	27.	Weaken
__Y__	28.	**Uphold**

The politician referred to Alaska's oil reserves primarily in order to . . .

__N__	29.	Only
__N__	30.	Wholly
__N__	31.	Partially
__Y__	32.	**Mainly**

It is used to refute an argument the economist deemed spurious.

__Y__	33.	**Invalid**
__N__	34.	Genuine
__N__	35.	Dubious
__N__	36.	Legitimate

When "spurious" refers to an argument, it means "illogical." When "spurious" refers to a claim, it means "false." Both usages exceed the degree of "dubious," which only means "doubtful."

The argument relies on a term that is ambiguous.

__N__	37.	Imprecise
__Y__	38.	**Of more than one possible meaning**
__Y__	39.	**Unclear**
__N__	40.	Strange

In the real world, "ambiguous" can mean "imprecise." But in LSAT world, a term is only "ambiguous" when it has multiple possible meanings and it is unclear which meaning is implied by the usage.

Drill 64: Counterexample Sample, Round 1

Instructions: Counterexamples often feature in answer choices. Sometimes, a correct answer choice points out a potential counterexample (Weaken, Flaw, and Must Be False questions). Other times, a correct answer rules out a potential counterexample (Strengthen and Necessary Assumption questions). Use this drill to practice recognizing these logical phenomena. For each of the following causal or conditional statements, indicate the answers that would serve as a counterexample (Y) and those what would not (N).

Inclement weather causes delays on the railroad and makes commuters late to work.

_____ 1. Commuters usually take an earlier train when they know construction is being performed on the railroad.

_____ 2. Last week, there was inclement weather on four days and trains were late on only one of those days.

_____ 3. There was no inclement weather yesterday and the railroad experienced severe delays.

_____ 4. Electrical problems cause longer delays in train service than does inclement weather.

_____ 5. Commuters who took the railroad last month arrived at work on time every day there was inclement weather.

The new restaurant is responsible for the increased business at the local shopping center.

_____ 6. Business at the shopping center had been increasing steadily for years prior to the restaurant opening.

_____ 7. Business decreased in another town's shopping center after a restaurant opened there.

_____ 8. Most shoppers at the shopping center do not eat at the new restaurant.

_____ 9. There were already five other restaurants in the shopping center before the new restaurant opened.

_____ 10. Many people complain that meals at the new restaurant are too expensive.

A mixture of cornstarch and water helps relieve the pain caused by sunburn.

_____ 11. Vanessa used aloe instead of cornstarch and experienced relief from her sunburn pain.

_____ 12. The pain from Thom's sunburn diminished greatly after using a mixture of cornstarch and water, but he still felt some pain.

_____ 13. Kelly applied a mixture of cornstarch and water to his sunburn and felt no relief.

_____ 14. The pain of Raul's sunburn got worse after he applied a mixture of cornstarch and water.

_____ 15. Carla continued to experience pain from her sunburn after refusing to try using cornstarch and water.

Anyone who purchases a VIP ticket is offered a backstage tour to meet the band.

_____ 16. Leah purchased a VIP ticket and was not offered a backstage tour.

_____ 17. Patrick is a primary donor to the concert arena and was offered a backstage tour despite not buying a VIP ticket

_____ 18. Elijah purchased a VIP ticket but had no intention of taking a backstage tour.

_____ 19. Felipe did not purchase a VIP ticket and was denied his request for a backstage tour.

_____ 20. Remy was not offered a backstage tour because she bought her VIP ticket the day of the concert.

It is difficult to become emotionally invested in novels with disreputable characters.

_____ 21. The characters in Anson's novel are not disreputable, yet it is difficult to become emotionally invested in her novel.

_____ 22. It is easy to become emotionally invested in Britten's novel despite it being filled with disreputable characters.

_____ 23. The characters in Chen's novel are emotionally complex, yet they are highly disreputable.

_____ 24. All of Duncan's novels feature disreputable characters, and it is easy to become emotionally invested in most of her novels.

4

4

_____ 25. Some of Eriksson's novels lack disreputable characters, yet it is difficult to become emotionally invested in any of his novels.

The steep drop in the mayor's approval ratings was due to the law passed last month that increased property taxes.

_____ 26. The mayor's approval ratings were at their highest immediately before the law was passed.

_____ 27. The mayor passed several laws last year and did not experience a drop in approval ratings after any of them passed.

_____ 28. Mayors in neighboring cities also passed laws recently and had no change in their approval ratings.

_____ 29. The mayor's approval ratings had been dropping considerably following a scandal that was first reported months before the new law passed.

_____ 30. The steep drop in the mayor's approval ratings parallels an earlier drop that occurred after the passage of a law that increased the local income tax.

Negative reviews from film critics are to blame for the reduced number of tickets sold for the action movie last weekend.

_____ 31. The most positively reviewed movie sold fewer tickets than the action movie.

_____ 32. The action movie sold more tickets than any other movie last weekend.

_____ 33. Reviews for the action movie were not published until after last weekend.

_____ 34. Other movies received even worse reviews than the action movie.

_____ 35. The number of tickets sold for the action movie next weekend are expected to be the same as the number sold last weekend.

The swimming pool is closed for at least half an hour whenever lightning is sighted.

_____ 36. No lightning was expected during the rain storm, yet the pool was closed.

_____ 37. Lightning was sighted in the distance but the pool remained open because the storm was moving away from the pool.

_____ 38. After lightning was first sighted, the pool remained open until lightning was sighted a second time, at which point the pool was closed for half an hour.

_____ 39. Despite the threat of lightning, the pool was not closed.

_____ 40. The pool was supposed to be open for another five hours but was closed for the day after lightning was sighted.

Jensen's restless sleep is entirely the result of eating desserts with too much sugar.

_____ 41. Marty slept well last night after eating a sugary dessert.

_____ 42. Marty slept restlessly last night, but hadn't had any dessert.

_____ 43. Jensen has had restless sleep for the past five days, during which time he did not have dessert.

_____ 44. Jensen slept well all last week, even after consuming too much sugar at dessert each night.

_____ 45. Jensen doesn't always finish the desserts he eats.

Vandalizing any part of the school property will result in being charged a steep fine.

_____ 46. Ariel did not vandalize any school property, but she was recently charged a steep fine.

_____ 47. Kris vandalized the school's gymnasium, but was required to perform community service in lieu of paying a fine.

_____ 48. Erik has been an exemplary student and was not charged a fine after he offered to clean up the school classroom he vandalized.

_____ 49. Leonard was one of seven students who vandalized the school auditorium, and the other six students received steeper fines.

_____ 50. Stella was caught vandalizing the public library yet was not given any fine.

Mad cow disease is only caused by the presence of ground meat and bone meal in cattle feed.

_____ 51. Ground meat and bone meal were present in the cattle feed of farmer Egbert's herd, but the herd did not develop mad cow disease.

_____ 52. Farmer Percival's cattle herd developed mad cow disease before the ground meat and bone were added to their feed.

_____ 53. After the ground meat and bone were added to the feed of the cattle at Pengrove Farms, the herd developed mad cow disease.

_____ 54. The herd at Diamond Ranch developed mad cow disease, and ground meat and bone have never been part of their feed.

_____ 55. Farmer Gautama's herd of cattle was never fed feed with ground meat and bone, and never developed mad cow disease.

An excess of sugar in the diet results in a proliferation of candida albicans in the lower gut.

_____ 56. Yorba's diet is high in excess sugar and he is experiencing a proliferation of candida albicans in his lower gut.

_____ 57. Fatima has a proliferation of candida albicans in her lower gut but has never had a diet containing excessive amounts of sugar.

_____ 58. Meyer has been steadily increasing the amount of sugar in his diet, but does not have a proliferation of candida albicans in his lower gut.

_____ 59. Graham does not have a proliferation of candida albicans in his lower gut but does have a diet that is high in excess sugar.

_____ 60. Pimma developed a proliferation of candida albicans in her lower gut before her diet increased in excess sugar.

4

Answers

Inclement weather causes delays on the railroad and makes commuters late to work.

__N__ 1. Commuters usually take an earlier train when they know construction is being performed on the railroad.

__Y__ 2. **Last week, there was inclement weather on four days and trains were late on only one of those days.**

__N__ 3. There was no inclement weather yesterday and the railroad experienced severe delays.

__N__ 4. Electrical problems cause longer delays in train service than does inclement weather.

__Y__ 5. **Commuters who took the railroad last month arrived at work on time every day there was inclement weather.**

This causal claim tells us that bad weather causes delays and tardiness, but not that bad weather is the only cause of delays and tardiness. So, showing an instance of delay without bad weather (3) is still consistent with the claim, not counter to it. We need something that shows bad weather without delays (2) or tardiness (5).

The new restaurant is responsible for the increased business at the local shopping center.

__Y__ 6. **Business at the shopping center had been increasing steadily for years prior to the restaurant opening.**

__N__ 7. Business decreased in another town's shopping center after a restaurant opened there.

__N__ 8. Most shoppers at the shopping center do not eat at the new restaurant.

__N__ 9. There were already five other restaurants in the shopping center before the new restaurant opened.

__N__ 10. Many people complain that meals at the new restaurant are too expensive.

Because this is a claim of one specific observable thing causing another specific observable thing, the only counterexample that wouldn't contradict the observable facts is that the effect predated the cause (6).

A mixture of cornstarch and water helps relieve the pain caused by sunburn.

__N__ 11. Vanessa used aloe instead of cornstarch and experienced relief from her sunburn pain.

__N__ 12. The pain from Thom's sunburn diminished greatly after using a mixture of cornstarch and water, but he still felt some pain.

__Y__ 13. **Kelly applied a mixture of cornstarch and water to his sunburn and felt no relief.**

__Y__ 14. **The pain of Raul's sunburn got worse after he applied a mixture of cornstarch and water.**

__N__ 15. Carla continued to experience pain from her sunburn after refusing to try using cornstarch and water.

This causal claim is that one thing helps to achieve another thing. An instance of the thing not helping (13) or making the situation worse (14) is a counterexample. An instance of the thing helping but not fully resolving the problem (12) is consistent with the claim, as is an instance of a different thing helping the situation (11).

Anyone who purchases a VIP ticket is offered a backstage tour to meet the band.

__Y__ 16. **Leah purchased a VIP ticket and was not offered a backstage tour.**

__N__ 17. Patrick is a primary donor to the concert arena and was offered a backstage tour despite not buying a VIP ticket

__N__ 18. Elijah purchased a VIP ticket but had no intention of taking a backstage tour.

__N__ 19. Felipe did not purchase a VIP ticket and was denied his request for a backstage tour.

__N__ 20. Remy was not offered a backstage tour because she bought her VIP ticket the day of the concert.

This claim is conditional, and there's only one way to form a counterexample for a conditional statement: show an instance of its sufficient condition without its necessary condition (16 and 20), thereby proving that that the sufficient doesn't always guarantee the necessary.

It is difficult to become emotionally invested in novels with disreputable characters.

__N__ 21. The characters in Anson's novel are not disreputable, yet it is difficult to become emotionally invested in her novel.

4

___Y___ 22. **It is easy to become emotionally invested in Britten's novel despite it being filled with disreputable characters.**

___N___ 23. The characters in Chen's novel are emotionally complex, yet they are highly disreputable.

___Y___ 24. **All of Duncan's novels feature disreputable characters, and it is easy to become emotionally invested in most of her novels.**

___N___ 25. Some of Eriksson's novels lack disreputable characters, yet it is difficult to become emotionally invested in any of his novels.

We're told that it's hard to get emotionally invested in novels with disreputable characters, and this implies that it's hard to get emotionally invested in ALL novels with disreputable characters. That makes this a conditional statement, so we need our counterexamples to show the sufficient condition without the necessary condition: instances of novels with disreputable characters that are not hard to get emotionally invested in (22 and 24).

The steep drop in the mayor's approval ratings was due to the law passed last month that increased property taxes.

___N___ 26. The mayor's approval ratings were at their highest immediately before the law was passed.

___N___ 27. The mayor passed several laws last year and did not experience a drop in approval ratings after any of them passed.

___N___ 28. Mayors in neighboring cities also passed laws recently and had no change in their approval ratings.

___Y___ 29. **The mayor's approval ratings had been dropping considerably following a scandal that was first reported months before the new law passed.**

___N___ 30. The steep drop in the mayor's approval ratings parallels an earlier drop that occurred after the passage of a law that increased the local income tax.

Because this is a causal claim about observed facts, we need a counterexample that will attack the order in which the facts were observed (29).

Negative reviews from film critics are to blame for the reduced number of tickets sold for the action movie last weekend.

___N___ 31. The most positively reviewed movie sold fewer tickets than the action movie.

___N___ 32. The action movie sold more tickets than any other movie last weekend.

___Y___ 33. **Reviews for the action movie were not published until after last weekend.**

___N___ 34. Other movies received even worse reviews than the action movie.

___N___ 35. The number of tickets sold for the action movie next weekend are expected to be the same as the number sold last weekend.

Because this is a causal claim about observed facts, we need a counterexample that will attack the order in which they were observed (33).

The swimming pool is closed for at least half an hour whenever lightning is sighted.

___N___ 36. No lightning was expected during the rain storm, yet the pool was closed.

___Y___ 37. **Lightning was sighted in the distance but the pool remained open because the storm was moving away from the pool.**

___Y___ 38. **After lightning was first sighted, the pool remained open until lightning was sighted a second time, at which point the pool was closed for half an hour.**

___N___ 39. Despite the threat of lightning, the pool was not closed.

___N___ 40. The pool was supposed to be open for another five hours but was closed for the day after lightning was sighted.

"Whenever" indicates a conditional claim, so we need to show an instance of the sufficient condition— observed lighting—without the necessary condition— pool closure (37 and 38).

Jensen's restless sleep is entirely the result of eating desserts with too much sugar.

___N___ 41. Marty slept well last night after eating a sugary dessert.

___N___ 42. Marty slept restlessly last night, but hadn't had any dessert.

4

__Y__ 43. **Jensen has had restless sleep for the past five days, during which time he did not have dessert.**

__N__ 44. Jensen slept well all last week, even after consuming too much sugar at dessert each night.

__N__ 45. Jensen doesn't always finish the desserts he eats.

When you're told that A is entirely the result of B, that's akin to saying A is only caused by B, so showing A without B (effect without cause—43) is a counterexample. Since the original claim does not imply that B always causes A, showing B without A (cause without effect—44) is not a counterexample.

Vandalizing any part of the school property will result in being charged a steep fine.

__N__ 46. Ariel did not vandalize any school property, but she was recently charged a steep fine.

__Y__ 47. **Kris vandalized the school's gymnasium, but was required to perform community service in lieu of paying a fine.**

__Y__ 48. **Erik has been an exemplary student and was not charged a fine after he offered to clean up the school classroom he vandalized.**

__N__ 49. Leonard was one of seven students who vandalized the school auditorium, and the other six students received steeper fines.

__N__ 50. Stella was caught vandalizing the public library yet was not given any fine.

"Any ... will ... " indicates a conditional statement, so we need the sufficient condition without the necessary to form a counterexample (47 and 48).

Mad cow disease is only caused by the presence of ground meat and bone meal in cattle feed.

__N__ 51. Ground meat and bone meal were present in the cattle feed of farmer Egbert's herd, but the herd did not develop mad cow disease.

__Y__ 52. **Farmer Percival's cattle herd developed mad cow disease before the ground meat and bone were added to their feed.**

__N__ 53. After the ground meat and bone were added to the feed of the cattle at Pengrove Farms, the herd developed mad cow disease.

__Y__ 54. **The herd at Diamond Ranch developed mad cow disease, and ground meat and bone have never been part of their feed.**

__N__ 55. Farmer Gautama's herd of cattle was never fed feed with ground meat and bone, and never developed mad cow disease.

We're told one thing is only caused by another, which means that a counterexample needs the effect without the cause (54). Showing the effect before the cause (52) accomplishes the same thing. Showing the cause without the effect (51) does not.

An excess of sugar in the diet results in a proliferation of candida albicans in the lower gut.

__N__ 56. Yorba's diet is high in excess sugar and he is experiencing a proliferation of candida albicans in his lower gut.

__N__ 57. Fatima has a proliferation of candida albicans in her lower gut but has never had a diet containing excessive amounts of sugar.

__N__ 58. Meyer has been steadily increasing the amount of sugar in his diet, but does not have a proliferation of candida albicans in his lower gut.

__Y__ 59. **Graham does not have a proliferation of candida albicans in his lower gut but does have a diet that is high in excess sugar.**

__N__ 60. Pimma developed a proliferation of candida albicans in her lower gut before her diet increased in excess sugar.

We're told that one thing causes another, so we need to counter that with an example of the cause not leading to the effect (59). Examples of the effect without the cause (57), or the events happening in the opposite order (60) don't work, because we're never told that the effect has no other cause.

Drill 65: Screening Interview

Instructions: In Logical Reasoning, there are often three answers that can be quickly eliminated...if your process of elimination skills are on point. Are yours? Use this drill to find out!

In each of the following sets, a description of a question will be given. For each of the potential answers, determine if it's a quick elimination (X) or one that you'd keep for further consideration (OK).

Set A

A Sufficient Assumption question with a new concept in the conclusion: all basketball players.

_X_ 1. Most athletes practice for countless hours.

_OK_ 2. Exceptional cardiovascular health is a trait of all sports players.

_____ 3. Many athletes, and most basketball players, have above average lung capacity.

_____ 4. Almost all basketball players stretch daily.

_____ 5. Football players all train using free weights.

_____ 6. Except for some basketball players, all athletes can run a mile in under eight minutes.

_OK_ 7. Football players, like basketball players, can all squat at least their body weight.

_____ 8. Many athletes are ambidextrous.

_____ 9. Few basketball players lack hand-eye coordination.

_OK_ 10. Anyone who has played a sport has had to learn to lose with grace.

Set B

A Principle Support question with this premise: Estella has never intentionally harmed anyone.

_____ 11. If someone is always kind, then that person has good character.

_____ 12. Anyone who never harms others on purpose can be considered a kind person.

_____ 13. Some people who intentionally harm others are evil.

_____ 14. Avoiding intentional harm of others guarantees that one will never go to jail.

_____ 15. Maria sometimes harms others, but never on purpose.

_____ 16. If someone intentionally harms others, then that person has bad character.

_____ 17. Most people who never intentionally harm others are good people.

_____ 18. Only people who intentionally harm others have questionable character.

_____ 19. Many acts of harm are unintentional.

_____ 20. Despite Margo's intentions, she sometimes harms others.

Set C

A Determine the Function question in which you have determined that the quoted piece of the argument supports the final conclusion.

_____ 21. A premise that supports the claim that airplane travel is safe.

_____ 22. The argument's main conclusion that airplane travel is safe.

_____ 23. A counterclaim to the argument's main conclusion that airplane travel is safe.

_____ 24. An intermediate conclusion based on the premise that all airplanes are inspected regularly.

_____ 25. Background information to provide context for an argument about airplane safety.

_____ 26. An assumption made without any evidence to support it.

_____ 27. The final conclusion based on the premise that airplanes are inspected regularly.

_____ 28. A subsidiary conclusion that provides evidence for the claim that airplane travel is safe.

_____ 29. A premise to defend the conclusion that airplane travel is not safe.

_____ 30. Evidence to contradict the conclusion that airplane travel is safe.

4

Set D

A Must Be True question composed of two *most* statements about medical students.

_____ 31. Some medical students will never complete their studies.

_____ 32. All medical students who complete their studies take at least eight years.

_____ 33. No medical students ever complete their studies in less than eight years.

_____ 34. Some students who complete their studies in less than eight years are medical students.

_____ 35. Anyone who completed their studies in more than eight years could not have been a medical student.

_____ 36. Everyone who is a medical student completes their studies in less than eight years.

_____ 37. Some people who are medical students complete their studies in over eight years.

_____ 38. Only people who go to medical school take longer than eight years to complete their studies.

_____ 39. Most medical students take less than eight years to complete their studies.

_____ 40. None of the students who go to medical school will take less than eight years to complete their studies.

Set E

A Match the Reasoning question with an either/or statement in the conclusion.

_____ 41. The Lubitz family can either go to Disney World or Niagara Falls for their next vacation. Their daughter prefers Disney World. Therefore, if the Lubitz family values their daughter's opinion, the family will go to Disney World.

_____ 42. Steve was told that the surgery would not be covered by his insurance. Therefore, Steve either paid for the surgery himself, or he did not have the surgery.

_____ 43. If Austin writes a book, it will be about indigenous history. If he does not write a book, he will never become famous. Therefore, Austin will either write a book about indigenous history or he will not become famous.

_____ 44. Most people who live in Boston are accustomed to the cold. Most people who live in Boston also own a snow shovel. Therefore, Angie, who lives in Boston and is accustomed to the cold, owns a snow shovel.

_____ 45. Dave ran out of his favorite soda, Minty Dawn, in his mini fridge. He wants a soda, so he must either go to the store or drink a different type of soda.

_____ 46. Mustang convertibles are considered safe to drive with the top down unless there is a thunderstorm. Since a thunderstorm is coming, Linda should not drive her Mustang convertible with the top down.

_____ 47. Chaise lounges are available for purchase online or in the local home improvement store. Buying a chaise lounge online provides more alternatives, but buying it in the local home improvement store is less expensive. Therefore, Elle, who is buying a chaise lounge, may either have more alternatives or save money.

_____ 48. A rare jade vine was recently planted in Erin's garden. It will thrive as long as it has the right balance of shade to sunlight and adequate water. Erin waters the plant daily and keeps it on the porch, so the jade vine will thrive.

_____ 49. The black bear population in the Shenandoah National Park has grown in recent years. Park rangers hope to keep the bears separated from the visiting public. Therefore, the park rangers would be wise to build fences around known bear habitats.

_____ 50. Middle school students tend to have shorter attention spans than high school students. Since there is no major difference between middle and high school students besides age, this must be due to the younger age of middle school students.

Set F

A Strengthen question with the following Argument Core:

Premise: Backpacks are lighter and more portable than rolling suitcases.

Conclusion: Frequent travelers would benefit from using backpacks instead of suitcases.

_____ 51. The average backpack weighs five pounds less than a rolling suitcase.

_____ 52. Backpacks are not allowed on all commercial flights, but rolling suitcases are.

_____ 53. Backpacks are typically more colorful than rolling suitcases.

_____ 54. Frequent travelers generally benefit from using luggage that is as lightweight and portable as possible.

_____ 55. Most backpacks cannot hold as much as rolling suitcases can.

_____ 56. Duffel bags are superior to both backpacks and rolling suitcases.

_____ 57. Weight and portability are the only criteria that frequent travelers should use in determining which luggage to carry.

_____ 58. Backpacks can typically be carried more easily than rolling suitcases.

_____ 59. Rolling suitcases cause fewer back problems than backpacks.

_____ 60. For people who are not frequent travelers, rolling suitcases are preferable to backpacks.

Set G

A Necessary Assumption question with the following Argument Core:

Premise: Reusable water bottles prevent disposable plastic water bottle waste.

Conclusion: Providing free reusable water bottles to citizens of Town X would help the environment.

_____ 61. Providing reusable water bottles is the only way that this town can help the environment.

_____ 62. Disposable plastic water bottle waste is the worst environmental problem in Town X.

_____ 63. Waste of disposable plastic water bottles harms the environment in Town X.

_____ 64. Providing free, reusable water bottles would not cause significant environmental harm.

_____ 65. Providing reusable water bottles to all towns in the United States would help the environment.

_____ 66. Responsible citizens should never use disposable plastic water bottles.

_____ 67. The problem of plastic water bottle waste has not already been solved in Town X.

_____ 68. Everyone should drink from only reusable water bottles.

_____ 69. Town X has the most environmental problems of any town in the country.

_____ 70. Preventing unnecessary waste of plastic water bottles would help the environment.

Set H

An ID the Conclusion question with the following conclusion: They are using faulty reasoning.

_____ 71. It is unreasonable to say that technology will replace textbooks in schools within the next five years.

_____ 72. Fewer schools are using textbooks than ever before.

_____ 73. The argument that fewer schools are using textbooks than ever before relies on a logical fallacy.

_____ 74. Some experts believe that schools will never stop using textbooks.

_____ 75. Textbooks are less expensive than technology.

_____ 76. Technology and textbooks can be used together for effective learning.

_____ 77. People who believe that technology will not replace textbooks within the next five years are relying on problematic reasoning.

_____ 78. Technology will not replace textbooks within the next five years.

_____ 79. People who believe that textbooks are less expensive than technology are correct.

_____ 80. No school could ever function without textbooks.

Set I

An ID the Flaw question in which you are confident that the flaw is conflating causation and correlation.

_____ 81. The argument presupposes that a statement that applies to a certain part of a group applies to the whole group.

_____ 82. The argument confuses a condition that is necessary for an event to happen with a condition that is sufficient for that event to happen.

_____ 83. The argument fails to establish that because two events coincided, one event caused the other.

_____ 84. The argument equivocates with respect to the term "mad."

_____ 85. The argument assumes that because event A was followed by event B, event A must have caused event B.

_____ 86. The argument fails to consider that there may have been more than two alternatives.

_____ 87. The argument assumes that a small sample is representative of a larger population.

_____ 88. The argument fails to consider that a third variable may have caused both of the events.

_____ 89. The argument rests on a generalization.

_____ 90. The argument conflates the term "healthy" with the term "happy."

Set J

An ID the (Dis)agreement question with the following setup:

Speaker A: Sofia needs a new chair. Comfort is important to her. Recliners are the most comfortable chairs. Thus, Sofia should purchase a recliner.

Speaker B: Recliners break easily. Thus, Sofia should not purchase a recliner.

_____ 91. Sofia should purchase a new chair.

_____ 92. Comfort is not important to Sofia.

_____ 93. Sofia should purchase a recliner.

_____ 94. Recliners are not the most comfortable chairs.

_____ 95. Recliners do not break easily.

_____ 96. Recliners are more affordable than other types of chairs.

_____ 97. Sofia's last recliner broke too quickly, even though it was comfortable.

_____ 98. The best option for Sofia's next purchase is not a recliner.

_____ 99. Recliners are the most reliable type of chair.

_____ 100. Sofia cares more about the appearance of a chair than comfort.

Answers

Set A

The correct answer must include a concept equivalent to "all basketball players" or a concept that is sufficiently broad to apply to "all basketball players" (see 2, "all sports players," and 10, "anyone who has played a sport"). Any answer that doesn't is a quick elimination.

<u> X </u>   1.   Most athletes practice for countless hours.

<u>OK</u>   2.   Exceptional cardiovascular health is a trait of all sports players.

<u> X </u>   3.   Many athletes, and most basketball players, have above average lung capacity.

<u> X </u>   4.   Almost all basketball players stretch daily.

<u> X </u>   5.   Football players all train using free weights.

<u> X </u>   6.   Except for some basketball players, all athletes can run a mile in under eight minutes.

<u>OK</u>   7.   Football players, like basketball players, can all squat at least their body weight.

<u> X </u>   8.   Many athletes are ambidextrous.

<u> X </u>   9.   Few basketball players lack hand-eye coordination.

<u>OK</u>   10.   Anyone who has played a sport has had to learn to lose with grace.

Set B

A Principle Support correct answer will link the premise to the conclusion. Eliminate answers that aren't broad enough to definitely include Estella (see "Most people" in 17 and "Many acts" in 19). And any answer that doesn't go beyond the premise to include some kind of judgment based on it (19 and 20). Keep answers that negate the premise (16 says "intentionally harm" instead of "never intentionally harm") because it's possible for the correct answer to be the contrapositive of the premise-conclusion link.

<u> X </u>   11.   If someone is always kind, then that person has good character.

<u>OK</u>   12.   Anyone who never harms others on purpose can be considered a kind person.

<u> X </u>   13.   Some people who intentionally harm others are evil.

<u>OK</u>   14.   Avoiding intentional harm of others guarantees that one will never go to jail.

<u> X </u>   15.   Maria sometimes harms others, but never on purpose.

<u>OK</u>   16.   If someone intentionally harms others, then that person has bad character.

<u> X </u>   17.   Most people who never intentionally harm others are good people.

<u>OK</u>   18.   Only people who intentionally harm others have questionable character.

<u> X </u>   19.   Many acts of harm are unintentional.

<u> X </u>   20.   Despite Margo's intentions, she sometimes harms others.

Set C

The correct answer must categorize the quoted piece of the argument as something that supports the main conclusion (e.g., Premise, Intermediate Conclusion, or Subsidiary Conclusion). Eliminate an answer choice as soon as you see that it incorrectly categorizes the piece in question.

<u>OK</u>   21.   A premise that supports the claim that airplane travel is safe.

<u> X </u>   22.   The argument's main conclusion that airplane travel is safe.

<u> X </u>   23.   A counterclaim to the argument's main conclusion that airplane travel is safe.

<u>OK</u>   24.   An intermediate conclusion based on the premise that all airplanes are inspected regularly.

<u> X </u>   25.   Background information to provide context for an argument about airplane safety.

<u> X </u>   26.   An assumption made without any evidence to support it.

<u> X </u>   27.   The final conclusion based on the premise that airplanes are inspected regularly.

<u>OK</u>   28.   A subsidiary conclusion that provides evidence for the claim that airplane travel is safe.

<u>OK</u>   29.   A premise to defend the conclusion that airplane travel is not safe.

<u> X </u>   30.   Evidence to contradict the conclusion that airplane travel is safe.

4

4

Set D

Two *most* statements overlap to create a *some* statement under certain conditions, but never anything stronger. Eliminate any answer that uses stronger language than *some*!

OK 31. Some medical students will never complete their studies.

X 32. All medical students who complete their studies take at least eight years.

X 33. No medical students ever complete their studies in less than eight years.

OK 34. Some students who complete their studies in less than eight years are medical students.

X 35. Anyone who completed their studies in more than eight years could not have been a medical student.

X 36. Everyone who is a medical student completes their studies in less than eight years.

OK 37. Some people who are medical students complete their studies in over eight years.

X 38. Only people who go to medical school take longer than eight years to complete their studies.

X 39. Most medical students take less than eight years to complete their studies.

X 40. None of the students who go to medical school will take less than eight years to complete their studies.

Set E

The structure of the correct answer's conclusion must match that of the original conclusion.

X 41. The Lubitz family can either go to Disney World or Niagara Falls for their next vacation. Their daughter prefers Disney World. Therefore, if the Lubitz family values their daughter's opinion, the family will go to Disney World.

OK 42. Steve was told that the surgery would not be covered by his insurance. Therefore, Steve either paid for the surgery himself, or he did not have the surgery.

OK 43. If Austin writes a book, it will be about indigenous history. If he does not write a book, he will never become famous. Therefore, Austin will either write a book about indigenous history or he will not become famous.

X 44. Most people who live in Boston are accustomed to the cold. Most people who live in Boston also own a snow shovel. Therefore, Angie, who lives in Boston and is accustomed to the cold, owns a snow shovel.

OK 45. Dave ran out of his favorite soda in his mini fridge. He wants a soda, so he must either go to the store or drink a different type of soda.

X 46. Mustang convertibles are considered safe to drive with the top down unless there is a thunderstorm. Since a thunderstorm is coming, Linda should not drive her Mustang convertible with the top down.

OK 47. Chaise lounges are available for purchase online or in the local home improvement store. Buying a chaise lounge online provides more alternatives, but buying it in the local home improvement store is less expensive. Therefore, Elle, who is buying a chaise lounge, may either have more alternatives or save money.

X 48. A rare jade vine was recently planted in Erin's garden. It will thrive as long as it has the right balance of shade to sunlight and adequate water. Erin waters the plant daily and keeps it on the porch, so the jade vine will thrive.

X 49. The black bear population in the Shenandoah National Park has grown in recent years. Park rangers hope to keep the bears separated from the visiting public. Therefore, the park rangers would be wise to build fences around known bear habitats.

X 50. Middle school students tend to have shorter attention spans than high school students. Since there is no major difference between middle and high school students besides age, this must be due to the younger age of middle school students.

Set F

A correct answer should establish a connection between lightness/portability and benefits for frequent travelers. Common incorrect answers to eliminate include premise boosters (51 and 58), answers that weaken the argument (52, 55, and 59), and answers that introduce new information that doesn't affect the conclusion (53, 56, and 60).

X	51.	The average backpack weighs five pounds less than a rolling suitcase.
X	52.	Backpacks are not allowed on all commercial flights, but rolling suitcases are.
X	53.	Backpacks are typically more colorful than rolling suitcases.
OK	54.	Frequent travelers generally benefit from using luggage that is as lightweight and portable as possible.
X	55.	Most backpacks cannot hold as much as rolling suitcases can.
X	56.	Duffel bags are superior to both backpacks and rolling suitcases.
OK	57.	Weight and portability are the only criteria that frequent travelers should use in determining which luggage to carry.
X	58.	Backpacks can typically be carried more easily than rolling suitcases.
X	59.	Rolling suitcases cause fewer back problems than backpacks.
X	60.	For people who are not frequent travelers, rolling suitcases are preferable to backpacks.

Set G

If the premise and conclusion don't use strong language, it's unlikely that a very extreme statement will need to be true in order for the conclusion to hold. Be wary of answers with extreme modifiers (61, 65, and 68) and ranking indicators (62 and 69).

X	61.	Providing reusable water bottles is the only way that this town can help the environment.
X	62.	Disposable plastic water bottle waste is the worst environmental problem in Town X.

OK	63.	Waste of disposable plastic water bottles harms the environment in Town X.
OK	64.	Providing free, reusable water bottles would not cause significant environmental harm.
X	65.	Providing reusable water bottles to all towns in the United States would help the environment.
X	66.	Responsible citizens should never use disposable plastic water bottles.
OK	67.	The problem of plastic water bottle waste has not already been solved in Town X.
X	68.	Everyone should drink from only reusable water bottles.
X	69.	Town X has the most environmental problems of any town in the country.
OK	70.	Preventing unnecessary waste of plastic water bottles would help the environment.

Set H

The correct answer needs to include a judgment on an opposing point but be careful: the judgment is that the opposing point was reached using faulty logic, but not necessarily that the opposing point is factually incorrect (78).

OK	71.	It is unreasonable to say that technology will replace textbooks in schools within the next five years.
X	72.	Fewer schools are using textbooks than ever before.
OK	73.	The argument that fewer schools are using textbooks than ever before relies on a logical fallacy.
X	74.	Some experts believe that schools will never stop using textbooks.
X	75.	Textbooks are less expensive than technology.
X	76.	Technology and textbooks can be used together for effective learning.
OK	77.	People who believe that technology will not replace textbooks within the next five years are relying on problematic reasoning.
X	78.	Technology will not replace textbooks within the next five years.

__X__ 79. People who believe that textbooks are less expensive than technology are correct.

__X__ 80. No school could ever function without textbooks.

Set I

If you can identify the flaw, you're more than halfway home! Eliminate anything that clearly describes a different flaw. Keep answers that mention causality.

__X__ 81. The argument presupposes that a statement that applies to a certain part of a group applies to the whole group.

__X__ 82. The argument confuses a condition that is necessary for an event to happen with a condition that is sufficient for that event to happen.

__OK__ 83. The argument fails to establish that because two events coincided, one event caused the other.

__X__ 84. The argument equivocates with respect to the term "mad."

__OK__ 85. The argument assumes that because event A was followed by event B, event A must have caused event B.

__X__ 86. The argument fails to consider that there may have been more than two alternatives.

__X__ 87. The argument assumes that a small sample is representative of a larger population.

__OK__ 88. The argument fails to consider that a third variable may have caused both of the events.

__X__ 89. The argument rests on a generalization.

__X__ 90. The argument conflates the term "healthy" with the term "happy."

Set J

For an ID the (Dis)agreement question, wrong answers will typically be half scope (only one speaker discusses the idea) or out of scope (neither speaker discusses the idea). The only idea discussed by both speakers is whether Sofia should purchase a recliner. Eliminate any answer that doesn't address this.

__X__ 91. Sofia should purchase a new chair.

__X__ 92. Comfort is not important to Sofia.

__OK__ 93. Sofia should purchase a recliner.

__X__ 94. Recliners are not the most comfortable chairs.

__X__ 95. Recliners do not break easily.

__X__ 96. Recliners are more affordable than other types of chairs.

__X__ 97. Sofia's last recliner broke too quickly, even though it was comfortable.

__OK__ 98. The best option for Sofia's next purchase is not a recliner.

__X__ 99. Recliners are the most reliable type of chair.

__X__ 100. Sofia cares more about the appearance of a chair than comfort.

Drill 66: It's a Trap! LR Matching Edition

Instructions: The most adept test takers don't tend to get caught in the LSAT's standard traps precisely because they recognize them as such. Hone your trap-recognition skills by matching the trap answer on the right to the question type on the left in which you are most likely to find that trap.

Question Type	Trap Answer Type
1. ID the Conclusion	Premise Booster
2. Sufficient Assumption	Strengthener
3. Strengthen	Misquotes the Argument
4. Determine the Function	Illegal Reversal
5. Weaken	Last Thing You Read

Question Type	Trap Answer Type
6. Necessary Assumption	Only One Side References It
7. ID the Conclusion	Self-Contradiction
8. ID the (Dis)agreement	Strong Language
9. ID the Flaw	Illegal Negation
10. Principle Support	Intermediate Conclusion

Question Type	Trap Answer Type
11. Most Strongly Supported	Refers to Something That Did Not Occur
12. ID the Flaw	Therefore or Thus
13. Weaken	Strong Language
14. Match the Argument	Illegal Reversal
15. ID the Conclusion	Weak Language

Question Type	Trap Answer Type
16. Procedure	Refers to Something That Did Not Occur
17. Principle Example	Attacks the Premise
18. Explain a Result	Valid Argument
19. Match the Flaw	Supports the Expected
20. Weaken	Wrong Direction

Answers

1. **ID the Conclusion** questions almost never end with the conclusion, but that's where many test takers think it should be. That's why the **Last Thing You Read** trap is so effective.

2. **Sufficient Assumption** questions are often conditional and allow for prephrasing, so the **Illegal Reversal** of the prephrase is often a trap answer.

3. **Strengthen** questions are about strengthening the link between premise and conclusion, not about proving the premises to be true. **Premise Boosters** just support the premise, not the link.

4. **Determine the Function** answer choices often paraphrase the argument. When an answer refers to a claim the argument made, look out: it might be a **Misquotes the Argument** trap.

5. **Weaken** questions, somewhat counterintuitively, often have one answer that is a **Strengthener**.

6. **Necessary Assumption** questions require you to build a bridge from the premises to the conclusion with language that doesn't exceed what's required. A common trap in this question type is an answer that builds the right bridge with the right pieces and in the right direction, but with language that is **too strong (Strong Language)** to be necessary.

7. **ID the Conclusion** questions often have **Intermediate Conclusions** preceded by conclusion indicator words such as *thus* or *therefore*.

8. **ID the (Dis)agreement** questions ask you to pinpoint the point of contention between two speakers. Wrong answer choices often describe something that **Only One Side References**.

9. **ID the Flaw** questions exhibit a rotating cast of famous flaws: Illegal Reversal, Causation Flaw, Part vs. Whole, etc. One flaw that's almost never the right answer, though, is **Self-Contradiction**.

10. **Principle Support** questions tend to function like Sufficient Assumption questions, with lots of conditional logic ripe for an **Illegal Negation** trap.

11. **Most Strongly Supported** questions ask you to find an answer with really strong support in the stimulus, and the more **Strong Language** there is, the harder that thing is to support.

12. **ID the Flaw** answer choices usually describe real flaws, meaning that most wrong answer choices **Refer to Something That Did Not Occur** in the given argument.

13. **Weaken** questions ask you to undermine the link between the premises and the conclusion. An answer with **Weak Language** is unlikely to significantly damage that link because it isn't strong enough to have an impact.

14. **Match the Argument** questions are rife with conditional logic, and any time conditional logic is present, watch out for **Illegal Reversals**.

15. **ID the Conclusion** questions try to hide the main conclusion by using indicators such as **Therefore** or **Thus** before Intermediate Conclusions. Be careful though: this is a tendency but once or twice we've seen it go the other way.

16. **Procedure** questions tend to use abstract language. Fill in the abstractions with the details of the argument, because the trap answers will often **Refer to Something That Did Not Occur**.

17. **Principle Example** questions have answers that are often reminiscent of Illegal Reversals, tempting you with an example that goes in the **Wrong Direction** (from judgment to example, rather than from example to judgment).

18. **Explain a Result** questions ask you to reconcile a surprising result with an expected result; an incorrect answer often **Supports the Expected** result instead.

19. **Match the Flaw** questions ask you to select the answer that contains the same flaw as the initial argument. One surefire way to spot a wrong answer choice? When it's actually a **Valid Argument**!

20. **Weaken** questions ask you to attack the link between the premises and the conclusion, but you have to accept the premises as true. Tempting wrong answer choices on Weaken questions will **Attack the Premise** instead of the link.

Drill 67: Vocab Lab #9 – Pick the Definition, Round 3

Instructions: The words in the first half of this set all begin with the letter *a*. The rest of the words begin with the letter *c*. That pattern might make you think of air conditioning, alternating current, or the athlete who played in the most consecutive NBA games in history (A.C. Green, with 1,192 games). Try not to be biased against poor, lonely choice (B) when choosing the answer closest in meaning.

1. Abstain
   - (A) absorb
   - (B) refrain
   - (C) concede

2. Acute
   - (A) dull or blunt
   - (B) unhealthy or harmful
   - (C) sharp or intense

3. Adherent
   - (A) reneger
   - (B) competitor
   - (C) supporter

4. Antithetical
   - (A) opposite
   - (B) unrelated
   - (C) complacent

5. Apex
   - (A) dip
   - (B) nadir
   - (C) peak

6. Arbitrary
   - (A) having a direction
   - (B) having no basis
   - (C) having power

7. Ascertain
   - (A) misunderstand
   - (B) make certain
   - (C) make light of

8. Ascribe
   - (A) attribute
   - (B) discredit
   - (C) construe

9. Assert
   - (A) reveal hesitantly
   - (B) shout frantically
   - (C) state forcefully

10. Asymmetry
    - (A) insincerity
    - (B) artificiality
    - (C) imbalance

11. Circumspect
    - (A) brash
    - (B) cautious
    - (C) dubious

12. Circumvent
    - (A) verbalize
    - (B) bypass
    - (C) accede

13. Cogent
    - (A) ineffective
    - (B) baseless
    - (C) compelling

14. Compulsory
    - (A) mandatory
    - (B) remissible
    - (C) retaliatory

4

15. Concurrence
    - (A) circumstance
    - (B) accident
    - (C) agreement

16. Conform
    - (A) collide
    - (B) comply
    - (C) belie

17. Constitute
    - (A) admonish
    - (B) establish
    - (C) relinquish

18. Construe
    - (A) interpret
    - (B) devise
    - (C) confuse

19. Continuum
    - (A) an interrupted cycle
    - (B) an endless sequence
    - (C) a winding path

20. Converse
    - (A) a median
    - (B) an equivalent
    - (C) the reverse

4

Answers follow on the next page.

Answers

1. B

Abstain = refrain (from), especially something bad or unhealthy. If you are *abstaining* from something but find your willpower weakening, ask your friends to remind you of your commitment.

2. C

Acute = sharp or intense, usually marked by a sudden onset. The underlying Latin root *ac-* means "sharp."

3. C

Adherent = supporter; follower; devotee. *Adhere* means "hold fast to, stick by, support" things such as ideas, people, or political parties.

4. A

Antithetical = opposite; directly opposed. In formal rhetoric, *antithesis* is the linguistic act of placing two phrases that have opposite meanings next to each other for contrast, as in "love me or hate me."

5. C

Apex = peak; high point. The town of Apex, North Carolina, is on a physical *apex*, as is the larger town of High Point, North Carolina. In 2015, *Money* magazine named Apex the best place to live in the country.

6. B

Arbitrary = having no basis; capricious; unreasonable. Based entirely on one's discretion.

7. B

Ascertain = make certain; find out for sure; determine. Be sure to pronounce *ascertain* with the stress on the final syllable ("TANE"), not as "uh-CERT-in."

8. A

Ascribe = attribute; chalk up to. The Latin root *scrib-* (= write) is found within numerous English words.

9. C

Assert = state forcefully. The verb *assert*, the noun *assertion*, and the adjective *assertive* are all positive.

10. C

Asymmetry = imbalance. Lack of balanced proportions, equal parts, or aspects of something. Here, the *a-* prefix means "not," as in "not *symmetry*."

11. B

Circumspect = cautious; prudent; careful to consider the circumstances and consequences. *Circum-* (= around) + *spect* (= look), from Latin.

12. B

Circumvent = bypass or avoid, such as circumventing the rules. Again, *circum-* means "around," but the *vent* part means "go."

13. C

Cogent = compelling; powerfully persuasive. May all your briefs be brief and *cogent*.

14. A

Compulsory = mandatory; enforced by rule. *Compulsory* education until age 16 is credited with lifting the economy of the United States and the fortunes of its people.

15. C

Concurrence = agreement in point of view, or a simultaneous occurrence. From the same root *cur-* (= run) as *current* and many, many other words.

16. B

Conform = comply; act in line with standards that are socially acceptable. The latter definition is more common in everyday speech, while the former is more common on the LSAT. If, for example, you're asked which argument *conforms* to a given principle, you're looking for an argument that complies with, or goes along with, the conditional relationship the principle proposes.

17. B

Constitute = establish (as in by law); make up; form. If you don't know this word by now, you'll get it in spades in law school, both the verb and the noun forms.

4

18. A

Construe = interpret, make sense of. No matter how precise lawmakers are with their statutes, there are always unforeseen ambiguities. In such cases, the intent of the lawmakers will need to be *construed* by the courts, in the absence of further legislation.

19. B

Continuum = an endless sequence in which the elements close to each other do not differ greatly, but the starting and ending points do.

20. C

Converse = the reversal of something. In formal logic, the *converse* of a conditional statement is what we call, in our lexicon, an illegal reversal. The *converse* of "if a person is in Manhattan, the person is in New York" is "if a person is in New York, the person is in Manhattan." The first claim is a true story. The second claim is not.

Logical Reasoning, Skills by Family

In This Chapter, We Will Cover:

- The Describe Family

- The Assumption Family

- The Inference Family

- The Matching Family

The Describe Family

The Describe Family of questions consists of the question types ID the Conclusion, Determine the Function, Procedure, and ID the (Dis)agreement. These questions run the difficulty-level gamut, testing the most basic task of argument breakdown through the most high-level abstract task of argument description. Work toward mastering this range of skills with the drills in this section of the book. Within the section, the drills are organized by the steps in our 4-Step Process for Logical Reasoning, but because Step 1 (ID Your Task) is so straightforward in this family, we're going to skip Step 1 and move right into Step 2.

In this section, you will learn to:

Work the Stimulus

- Master Argument Breakdown
- ID the point at issue between two speakers

Anticipate an Answer

- Recognize common valid argument structures
- Name each piece of an argument

Analyze the Answers

- Navigate abstract answer choices

Drill 68: Find the Friction Point

Instructions: In ID the (Dis)agreement questions, the second speaker's conclusion often begins with a short rebuttal of something from the first speaker's argument. However, it's usually not explicit what, exactly, the second speaker objects to. Sometimes the second speaker contests one of the first speaker's premises. Other times, the second speaker accepts the premises but contests their application. Sometimes an objection is raised in the form of something the first speaker failed to consider, such as an alternative explanation or evidence to the contrary. Other times an assumption or common reasoning error is called out. The second speaker could even agree with the first speaker's conclusion, but not with how the first speaker reached it.

For each of the following exchanges, we're limiting the second speaker to a short rebuttal without much context. Identify what part of the first speaker's argument the second speaker takes issue with, and articulate it in the space provided.

1. Insurance Agent: Floods and tornadoes are two of the most catastrophic events that can affect your home. So, if you purchase our joint flood and tornado insurance policy, then your home will be fully insured against catastrophic events.

    Prospective Client: You're ignoring other possibilities.

    The IA lists two but not all possibilities, but concludes the home will be "fully insured" against c. events.

2. Researcher: I smoke at least three packs of cigarettes per day. However, smoking three or more packs of cigarettes every day is detrimental to health. Therefore, no one else should smoke three or more packs of cigarettes per day.

    Critic: How is anyone to believe such a hypocritical assertion?

    Ad Hominem

3. Automotive Executive: Since midsize sedans have been found to have a minimal impact on the environment, it is safe to conclude that our midsize sedans are environmentally friendly.

    Environmentalist: While historically, that has been true...

    It leaves out the qualities & aspects of the AE's sedan. It could be worse, could be better.

4. Prosecutor: Anyone would agree that breaking the law is wrong. In addition, anyone who does something wrong deserves to be punished. Jim broke the law by speeding, so he deserves to be sent to prison.

    Defense Attorney: You rest your argument on principles that are indeed accurate, and yet...

    Why does punished = prison?

5. Administrator: Students learn best when they are challenged with material that is at their level. When challenged with difficult material, they can become discouraged because they feel overwhelmed. However, when facing material that is too easy, students can quickly become disengaged. As a result, we should put students in different tracks based on their understanding so that they can have the best possible education.

Teacher: In theory, I agree. *The solution proposed doesn't fully address the premise — how does this guarantee the best possible education?*

6. Realtor: Families in the process of selling their homes often believe that location is the key factor in determining the value of a piece of real estate. However, a simple analysis of sale prices indicates that this is not the case; houses on a particular street, for example, will not consistently sell for dramatically more or less than the comparable houses on another street. To predict the likely selling price more realistically, one should instead determine which feature of the home itself is the most uniquely desirable.

Colleague: I disagree. While the sale prices do indeed indicate... *It doesn't adequately address how the location can impact and if houses on a different street offer a "better" or "worse" location. And why does this then mean features are a better factor?*

7. Judge: The plaintiff has sent a message explaining why she cannot be present at today's hearing and asks that it be delayed. If this were the first time, the court would be inclined to honor her request. However, she has repeatedly failed to appear for scheduled hearings pertaining to this case and, therefore, the plaintiff's suit is dismissed.

Plaintiff's attorney: That isn't a fair basis for this decision. *What is the reason why she can't be present? Is it legit?*

8. Director: Unfortunately, funding delays have forced the production schedule for the film project to be compressed into a shorter period than was originally planned. Union guidelines permit film crews to work up to ten hours per day, and I estimate that the remaining filming for this project will take only two hundred hours. So, we can finish filming, at least, twenty days from today.

Producer: Your arithmetic is accurate, but we have to be practical.

9. Veterinary student: This dog has exhibited a fever for the past two days, despite routine tests and treatments indicating negative results for a number of potential ailments. None of his organs are failing, he lacks any tumors or other abnormalities visible to the naked eye, and antibiotic drugs have had no effect, indicating that the infection is not bacterial. In light of this, his ailment must be viral.

   Veterinarian: Not necessarily...

10. Psychologist: When you become angry but cannot identify the object of your anger, it's very likely that you are subconsciously angry at yourself. Studies have consistently demonstrated that people generally overestimate their own competence and accept little responsibility for negative outcomes in their lives, even where there is strong evidence that they are directly responsible for these outcomes. This excessive self-esteem makes it difficult to be aware of self-directed anger.

    Patient: But some people...

11. Police captain: We should train our officers that refusal to comply with a request to exit one's vehicle should always be treated as an indication that a person may have committed a crime. Statistics in our department show that 46% of individuals who refuse to exit their vehicles when asked are ultimately arrested for crimes, evidence of which was present either on their persons or in the vehicles. This is a startlingly large percentage, especially given that fewer than 1% of routine traffic stops ever lead to arrests for more serious crimes.

    Superintendent: But what percentage of those who refuse to exit the vehicle during a routine traffic stop are ultimately arrested for a more serious crime?

12. Politician: The largest problem in my district is that the schools are routinely under-funded. My opponents may tell you that we need to raise taxes to provide these schools with the resources that they need, but my opponents are mistaken. We should initiate an investigation into wasteful spending to find these additional funds.

    Constituent: That will do nothing to increase the total allocated budget for the schools, which is insufficient with or without the wasteful spending you believe to exist.

13. Shepherd: The six sheep that are missing from the flock were probably taken by wolves. While there are many bears and wolves in this area, and both animals have been known to attack sheep, the area in which this flock grazes during the day is surrounded by a fence. The fence was unbroken this morning, and all of the sheep were present inside. There is now a hole in that fence that is large enough for wolves, but not bears, to have slipped through.

    Livestock farmer: But what if . . .

14. Biologist: Microscopic organisms have been discovered living around sulfur-producing vents on the deep ocean floor. This is an extreme environment consisting of very high pressure, almost no light, and a chemical cocktail fatal to most known forms of life. As a result, it has proven very difficult to study these organisms where they were found or to remove them alive to another location. However, the environment itself may provide a clue to their nature. Since this sort of environment was much more common in earlier stages of Earth's development, we posit that these organisms are remnants of the life forms that originally evolved billions of years ago.

    Director: The environment you describe, while more like those of yesteryear than those of today, has nonetheless undergone significant changes since the early stages of Earth's development, which have no doubt impacted the life therein.

15. Car Salesman: Our truck has the same fuel economy, interior, and lighting system as our competitor's truck. However, the price of our truck is significantly lower. So, compared with our competitor, our truck provides the same quality at a lower price.

    Customer: But the competitor's truck . . .

5

Answers follow on the next page.

Answers

1. The prospective client doesn't contest that floods and tornadoes are *two of the most* catastrophic events that could occur, but does contest the agent's implicit assumption that they are *the only* catastrophic events that can occur.

2. The critic is challenging the researcher's conclusion because the researcher doesn't abide by his own recommendation—an example of the common Ad Hominem flaw.

3. The environmentalist is contesting the automotive executives premise, suggesting that there is some new information that differs from the evidence that the automotive executive provided.

4. The attorney objects to the way the principles are being applied. We can validly conclude Jim should be punished, but we cannot conclude *how*.

5. The teacher agrees "in theory," which implies that there is a practical consideration that undermines a part of the administrator's argument, though it is not clear from this selection which part.

6. The colleague accepts the premise of the realtor's argument but disagrees with the conclusion that home prices can be more realistically predicted using the method described.

7. The defense attorney believes that the suit should not be dismissed merely because of the plaintiff's failure to appear. Be careful: the attorney does not necessarily maintain that there is *no valid reason* to dismiss the suit, just that *this particular reason* is insufficient.

8. The producer accepts the director's premises but believes that practical considerations will prevent photography from being completed in twenty days, nonetheless.

9. The veterinary student reaches the conclusion that the illness *must* be viral. When the veterinarian says not *necessarily*, we can infer that the objection is to the degree of the student's claim.

10. In raising the issue of what *some people* do, think, or feel, the patient is not disputing the studies the psychologist cites, but instead is arguing that you can't apply their findings universally.

11. The superintendent doesn't question the accuracy of the statistics but rather the captain's application of them. The data doesn't tell us whether refusing to exit the vehicle *at a routine traffic stop* is correlated with a higher than 1% likelihood of being arrested for a more serious crime, because the data only addresses police approaching people in their vehicles *in general*.

12. The constituent doesn't confirm or deny the politician's assumption that wasteful spending is indeed a problem. Instead, the constituent disputes that recovered funds could be sufficient to make up for the current budget shortfall.

13. "But what if" indicates that the farmer is going to raise an alternative possibility. Because the shepherd concludes that there is only one explanation, the farmer must have an alternative one.

14. The director accepts that this sort of environment was more common in the early stages of Earth's development but objects to the biologist's claim that this relative difference can be extended to the life-forms within that environment.

15. The salesman's argument hinges on similarities between the two trucks. The beginning of the customer's objection implies that a relevant difference is about to be raised.

5

Drill 69: What's Your Function? Round 3

Instructions: Breaking down arguments into their core components is still step one for almost any Logical Reasoning question, so here is another round of practice!

Each of the following sets of items is an argument broken up into pieces. Some sentences within the argument are also broken into pieces because single sentences can have multiple clauses that each have a different function. For each numbered piece, note whether it's Background info (BG), an Opposing Point (OP), Counter Evidence that would support an opposing point (even if that point has not been explicitly articulated) (CE), a Premise of the argument (P), an Intermediate Conclusion of the argument (IC), or the argument's Main Conclusion (MC). Note that you will generally need to read the whole argument before making your determination, and that it's generally easiest to start by trying to identify the main conclusion and figure the rest out from there.

Argument 1

_____ 1. The General Grant rose is far more striking than the Admiral Oakley rose.

_____ 2. While amateur flower enthusiasts are struck by an enormous bloom or a pleasant scent,

_____ 3. the true connoisseur is familiar with known varieties and can recognize when a flower contains an entirely novel pattern of colors.

_____ 4. The General Grant is smaller and less fragrant than the Admiral Oakley,

_____ 5. but the swirls of orange and blue on its petals are an unmatched achievement in horticulture.

Argument 2

_____ 6. To the naked eye, Sirius (located in the constellation Canis Major) is the brightest star in the night sky.

_____ 7. However, it merely seems the brightest to us because of its proximity to Earth.

_____ 8. Sirius is a white main-sequence star, which means that it is much less intrinsically luminous than any number of other stars, such as the blue supergiant Rigel.

_____ 9. Thus, humans who settle on a planet that is equidistant from both stars would find Rigel brighter to the naked eye than Sirius.

Argument 3

_____ 10. Currently, the top professional basketball players are comfortable playing both offense and defense on any part of the court.

_____ 11. Torry, however, argues that it is counterproductive for young players to diversify their skills in this way.

_____ 12. Like Torry, many coaches of youth teams teach a style of play that does not focus on diversifying skills and has not been successful at the professional level for decades.

_____ 13. This is inadvisable,

_____ 14. since it alienates players and limits team success.

_____ 15. Children and young adults who are developing basketball skills want to emulate the habits of the top contemporary players.

Argument 4

_____ 16. In its most recent issue, the magazine *Gardening Weekly* included a guide to growing tropical fruits and vegetables in cool climates.

_____ 17. To grow okra, it recommended using an enclosed, heated space to mimic the environment in which the plant naturally grows.

_____ 18. Nelson followed these instructions precisely and built a structure according to the magazine's specifications.

_____ 19. Within a season, this space produced a bountiful crop of high-quality okra.

_____ 20. Since *Gardening Weekly*'s advice led to excellent results for growing one tropical plant,

_____ 21. its suggestions for growing mangoes, another tropical plant, will probably also yield excellent results if followed.

Argument 5

_____ 22. The recent data breach at Helios Bank can only be explained by the participation of one of the bank's top officials.

_____ 23. While auditing the computer system used by Helios to prevent unauthorized access to its customers' online accounts, a security firm found that the breach was facilitated by the rollback of a vital update immediately beforehand.

_____ 24. The circumstances strongly suggest that those behind the breach were aware that the rollback would occur,

_____ 25. and only the chief executive officer and chief technical officer of Helios have the authority to order such a rollback.

Argument 6

_____ 26. The Department of Agricultural Sciences is developing a breeding population of longhorn cattle for a new study on the connection between bovine nutrition and fertility.

_____ 27. The successful execution of the study will require at least one hundred male and one hundred female longhorn,

_____ 28. and local laws forbid the acquisition of more than five longhorns of each gender per week.

_____ 29. Since the department currently possesses eighty-five female and fifty male longhorn,

_____ 30. the study cannot be successfully executed in less than ten weeks.

Argument 7

_____ 31. The city event planner has determined that the championship-winning hockey team's parade should follow a route that is two miles in length.

_____ 32. Based on the expected number of attendees, this will permit everyone to have a good view of the festivities.

_____ 33. In addition, such a length will require only a modest police presence and will not unduly disrupt rush-hour traffic in the city center.

Argument 8

_____ 34. Ordinances in our city limit the time of day that certain products, such as alcoholic beverages, can be advertised on television.

_____ 35. Mayor Jardin has argued in favor of loosening these restrictions.

_____ 36. She has stated in public forums and debates that the ordinances reduce the city's tax revenue,

_____ 37. and that allowing such ads to air at any time will help to fund the public schools and fire department.

_____ 38. This is not the case, however:

_____ 39. the city would derive only modest income from the previously forbidden ads.

_____ 40. Therefore, her proposal would have a negligible impact on either of these public institutions and is not in the city's best interest.

Argument 9

_____ 41. Monroe County has produced almost all of the great lacrosse players in the state over the past ten years.

_____ 42. The ten highest-ranked players in the county at the end of this calendar year will be eligible for a tournament to determine the members of next year's all-state team.

_____ 43. Andersen is currently ranked twelfth in Monroe County and will need to perform brilliantly in at least three matches in order to rise multiple positions in the rankings.

_____ 44. There are four matches remaining in this calendar year,

_____ 45. but one of them conflicts with a serious family obligation.

_____ 46. So, he probably will not qualify for the tournament

_____ 47. since it is unlikely that he will have an excellent performance in three consecutive matches that he plays.

Argument 10

_____ 48. The research department has proposed that health-promoting animal genes be inserted into the cereal grains that are our company's main products.

_____ 49. This course of action would cause significant damage to our international reputation.

_____ 50. It is true that our researchers have exhaustively tested samples of the genetically modified grains and found that they present no additional health risk compared to unmodified grains.

_____ 51. But since the public as a whole lacks the expertise to appreciate these test results,

_____ 52. the revelation that the company is selling genetically modified foods will lead to harsh criticism.

Argument 11

_____ 53. All technicians at Bhatt Industries receive annual evaluations, in the course of which their overall performance is given one of three ratings: "inadequate," "adequate," or "excellent."

_____ 54. A technician must demonstrate skill in both lab safety and electronics in order to receive an "excellent" rating,

_____ 55. and no technician that has been cited for mishandling radioactive material can be considered skilled in lab safety.

_____ 56. Thus, any technician that has been cited for mishandling radioactive materials will be rated as either "inadequate" or "adequate."

Answers

Argument 1

__MC__ 1. The General Grant rose is far more striking than the Admiral Oakley rose.

__OP__ 2. While amateur flower enthusiasts are struck by an enormous bloom or a pleasant scent,

__P__ 3. the true connoisseur is familiar with known varieties and can recognize when a flower contains an entirely novel pattern of colors.

__CE__ 4. The General Grant is smaller and less fragrant than the Admiral Oakley,

__P__ 5. but the swirls of orange and blue on its petals are an unmatched achievement in horticulture.

Argument 2

__OP__ 6. To the naked eye, Sirius (located in the constellation Canis Major) is the brightest star in the night sky.

__MC__ 7. However, it merely seems the brightest to us because of its proximity to Earth.

__P__ 8. Sirius is a white main-sequence star, which means that it is much less intrinsically luminous than any number of other stars, such as the blue supergiant Rigel.

__IC__ 9. Thus, humans who settle on a planet that is equidistant from both stars would find Rigel brighter to the naked eye than Sirius.

Argument 3

__BG__ 10. Currently, the top professional basketball players are comfortable playing both offense and defense on any part of the court.

__OP__ 11. Torry, however, argues that it is counterproductive for young players to diversify their skills in this way.

__OP__ 12. Like Torry, many coaches of youth teams teach a style of play that does not focus on diversifying skills and has not been successful at the professional level for decades.

__MC__ 13. This is inadvisable,

__P__ 14. since it alienates players and limits team success.

__P__ 15. Children and young adults who are developing basketball skills want to emulate the habits of the top contemporary players.

Argument 4

__BG__ 16. In its most recent issue, the magazine *Gardening Weekly* included a guide to growing tropical fruits and vegetables in cool climates.

__BG__ 17. To grow okra, it recommended using an enclosed, heated space to mimic the environment in which the plant naturally grows.

__BG__ 18. Nelson followed these instructions precisely and built a structure according to the magazine's specifications.

BG   19. Within a season, this space produced a bountiful crop of high-quality okra.

P   20. Since *Gardening Weekly*'s advice led to excellent results for growing one tropical plant,

MC   21. its suggestions for growing mangoes, another tropical plant, will probably also yield excellent results if followed.

Argument 5

MC   22. The recent data breach at Helios Bank can only be explained by the participation of one of the bank's top officials.

P   23. While auditing the computer system used by Helios to prevent unauthorized access to its customers' online accounts, a security firm found that the breach was facilitated by the rollback of a vital update immediately beforehand.

P   24. The circumstances strongly suggest that those behind the breach were aware that the rollback would occur,

P   25. and only the chief executive officer and chief technical officer of Helios have the authority to order such a rollback.

Argument 6

BG   26. The Department of Agricultural Sciences is developing a breeding population of longhorn cattle for a new study on the connection between bovine nutrition and fertility.

P   27. The successful execution of the study will require at least one hundred male and one hundred female longhorn,

P   28. and local laws forbid the acquisition of more than five longhorns of each gender per week.

P   29. Since the department currently possesses eighty-five female and fifty male longhorn,

MC   30. the study cannot be successfully executed in less than ten weeks.

Argument 7

MC   31. The city event planner has determined that the championship-winning hockey team's parade should follow a route that is two miles in length.

P   32. Based on the expected number of attendees, this will permit everyone to have a good view of the festivities.

P   33. In addition, such a length will require only a modest police presence and will not unduly disrupt rush-hour traffic in the city center.

Argument 8

BG   34. Ordinances in our city limit the time of day that certain products, such as alcoholic beverages, can be advertised on television.

OP   35. Mayor Jardin has argued in favor of loosening these restrictions.

CE   36. She has stated in public forums and debates that the ordinances reduce the city's tax revenue,

CE   37. and that allowing such ads to air at any time will help to fund the public schools and fire department.

IC   38. This is not the case, however:

P   39. the city would derive only modest income from the previously forbidden ads.

MC   40. Therefore, her proposal would have a negligible impact on either of these public institutions and is not in the city's best interest.

Argument 9

BG   41. Monroe County has produced almost all of the great lacrosse players in the state over the past ten years.

P   42. The ten highest-ranked players in the county at the end of this calendar year will be eligible for a tournament to determine the members of next year's all-state team.

P   43. Andersen is currently ranked twelfth in Monroe County and will need to perform brilliantly in at least three matches in order to rise multiple positions in the rankings.

5

CE   44. There are four matches remaining in this calendar year,

P   45. but one of them conflicts with a serious family obligation.

MC   46. So, he probably will not qualify for the tournament

P   47. since it is unlikely that he will have an excellent performance in three consecutive matches that he plays.

Argument 10

OP   48. The research department has proposed that health-promoting animal genes be inserted into the cereal grains that are our company's main products.

MC   49. This course of action would cause significant damage to our international reputation.

CE   50. It is true that our researchers have exhaustively tested samples of the genetically modified grains and found that they present no additional health risk compared to unmodified grains.

P   51. But since the public as a whole lacks the expertise to appreciate these test results,

IC   52. the revelation that the company is selling genetically modified foods will lead to harsh criticism.

Argument 11

P   53. All technicians at Bhatt Industries receive annual evaluations, in the course of which their overall performance is given one of three ratings: "inadequate," "adequate," or "excellent."

P   54. A technician must demonstrate skill in both lab safety and electronics in order to receive an "excellent" rating,

P   55. and no technician that has been cited for mishandling radioactive material can be considered skilled in lab safety.

MC   56. Thus, any technician that has been cited for mishandling radioactive materials will be rated as either "inadequate" or "adequate."

The Assumption Family

The Assumption Family of questions consists of the question types Necessary Assumption, Sufficient Assumption, ID the Flaw, Strengthen, Weaken, and Principle Support. That's a lot of question types, and together they make up more than 50% of the Logical Reasoning section and 25% of the LSAT as a whole! Work toward mastering this important family of questions with the drills in this section of the book. Within the section, the drills are organized by the steps in our 4-Step Process for Logical Reasoning, beginning with question stem identification and ending with answer choice analysis.

In this section, you will learn to:

ID Your Task

- Distinguish between Sufficient and Necessary Assumption Stems
- Distinguish between Strengthen and Most Strongly Supported Stems
- Use the task of the question to drive your approach to the answers

Work the Stimulus

- Break down arguments into their Argument Cores
- Master the most common flawed methods of reasoning

Anticipate an Answer

- Predict the likelihood of a Bridge Assumption vs. a Defender Assumption
- Prephrase answers for conditional questions
- Prephrase answers for causal questions
- Relate the question types within the Assumption Family

Analyze the Answers

- Negate statements
- Recognize answers that describe the most common flaws
- Distinguish between answers that describe assumptions vs. objections
- Assess the impact that answers have on comparative arguments

Drill 70: Determine the Function Abstract Answers

Instructions: It would be nice if the answers to Determine the Function questions used words like *premise* and *conclusion* to describe the statements in question. Unfortunately, that's all too rare. Practice determining what piece of the argument abstractly-written phrases are referring to with this drill.

For each of the following answer choice snippets, identify whether it's most likely referring to a premise (P), a conclusion (C), or whether it's totally uncertain (U).

_____ 1. The phenomenon observed...

_____ 2. A statement supported by...

_____ 3. Cited as an example...

_____ 4. Serves to cast doubt...

_____ 5. A subsidiary...

_____ 6. Represents...

_____ 7. Illustrates...

_____ 8. The only reason...

_____ 9. It both supports and is supported...

_____ 10. Supports an earlier statement...

_____ 11. Introduces a solution...

_____ 12. Presented to counter...

_____ 13. Generalization supported by...

_____ 14. A particular instance...

_____ 15. Claimed to follow from ...

_____ 16. Used to weaken the claim...

_____ 17. A hypothesis supported by...

_____ 18. A specific instance...

_____ 19. Used as an illustration...

_____ 20. What the argument is attempting to establish...

_____ 21. An assertion...

_____ 22. It is offered as one reason...

_____ 23. An insufficient reason...

_____ 24. Offered as an example...

_____ 25. Presents an objection...

_____ 26. The overall...

_____ 27. Offered as an explanation...

_____ 28. A general principle...

_____ 29. Used to suggest...

_____ 30. A statement that supports...

5

Answers follow on the next page.

Answers

P	1.	The phenomenon observed...
C	2.	A statement supported by...
P	3.	Cited as an example...
P	4.	Serves to cast doubt...
C	5.	A subsidiary...
U	6.	Represents...
P	7.	Illustrates...
P	8.	The only reason...
C	9.	It both supports and is supported...
P	10.	Supports an earlier statement...
C	11.	Introduces a solution...
P	12.	Presented to counter...
C	13.	Generalization supported by...
P	14.	A particular instance...
C	15.	Claimed to follow from...

P	16.	Used to weaken the claim...
C	17.	A hypothesis supported by...
U	18.	A specific instance...

(A specific instance can be used to support a general claim, or it can be a conclusion reached by the application of a general principle.)

P	19.	Used as an illustration...
C	20.	What the argument is attempting to establish...
C	21.	An assertion...
P	22.	It is offered as one reason...
P	23.	An insufficient reason...
P	24.	Offered as an example...
P	25.	Presents an objection...
C	26.	The overall...
C	27.	Offered as an explanation...
U	28.	A general principle...

(A general principle can be a premise applied to a specific case or a conclusion reached by inferring from specific cases or linking principles together.)

P	29.	Used to suggest...
P	30.	A statement that supports...

Drill 71: Procedure Abstract Answers

Instructions: Procedure questions tend to have very abstract answer choices. The best test takers are unfazed by this because they replace the abstract language in an answer choice with concrete language from the stimulus. Each of the following arguments is accompanied by a correct abstract Procedure answer choice. After each abstract description is a blank. Fill that blank with the specific idea or ideas from the argument that the abstract description is referring to.

1. Philosopher: It is never ethically justified to be untruthful, even as a means to an end. And every statement is either truthful or untruthful. Therefore, to live an ethical life, one must always tell the truth.

    Establishing two mutually exclusive possibilities (1._____ and 2._____) and arguing that since one (_____) cannot be reconciled with a certain condition (_____), the alternative (_____) necessarily results from that condition (_____).

2. Early human civilizations were located exclusively near large sources of fresh, potable water. There are signs that some human groups attempted to settle in other locations, but they all abandoned those locations quickly after constructing only a few initial buildings. Therefore, large sources of drinking water must have been necessary for early human civilizations to establish themselves fully.

    Concludes a requirement (_____) based on examining the results of both having (_____) and not having (_____) that requirement.

3. In a recent study, homing pigeons were fed varying diets before being released miles away from their home locations. After measuring the flight times home, the ornithologists in the study concluded that a diet including a high concentration of protein from insect sources leads to the fastest return flight times for messenger birds.

    Uses a study about a limited subset of a group (_____) in order to draw a conclusion about the group as a whole (_____).

4. The clans of Caledonia each developed their own currencies. However, each clan relied heavily on intra-clan trade to maintain their economies. Hence, these seemingly independent currencies were actually a part of a larger monetary system and thus should be considered the same.

    Additional context (_____) is added to a historical fact (_____) in order to reevaluate (_____) that fact and promote an alternative interpretation (_____).

5. Canoes and kayaks are the two most popular water vessels. Despite many differences, including paddle shape and sitting position, the physical requirements to pilot these vehicles are almost identical. Therefore, it should be expected that strong kayakers will also be strong canoers.

    Differences are raised (_____) and dismissed as relatively unimportant (_____) compared to similarities (_____) when reaching a conclusion about two distinct activities (1. _____ and 2. _____).

6. It is commonly believed that an asteroid impact was the cause of the last great extinction period. However, reanalysis of the age of the crater of the asteroid impact primarily believed to be at fault indicates that it struck near the beginning of the extinction period but did not fully precede it. Thus, it could not possibly be the cause of any of the extinctions associated with that period.

    A previously accepted cause (_____) of a phenomenon (_____) is determined not to have caused the phenomenon based on evidence (_____) that precludes it from being the only cause of the phenomenon.

7. In most major urban areas throughout the nation, increased law enforcement budgets, targeted community-based policing strategies, and advances in surveillance technologies have allegedly produced dramatic declines in violent crimes and grand theft. However, complaints to police regarding acts of vandalism and petty theft have increased at even greater rates in most of these cities. Therefore, it is likely that the declines in violent crimes and grand theft are part of a cyclical trend unrelated to law enforcement efforts.

    An asserted contradictory correlation (_____) is used to undermine a claim of causation (_____).

8. Sunnyvale Community College's recent "Year to Career" marketing strategy—in which the coursework from two-year certificate programs was condensed into one year—clearly has not been detrimental to the learning experience of students in its Civil Engineering Technology programs. Since the change, overall employment rates for certificate recipients are up by 12.5%, and highly technical CET jobs demand advanced skills.

    A judgment (_____) is rendered regarding an initiative (_____) based on a recent trend (_____) and an implication of that trend (_____).

9. Many of the most successful rock musicians have extensive formal musical training in their backgrounds. However, others are self-trained and most, whether formally trained or self-trained, prefer to give the impression that their talent comes naturally and that they only really apply themselves to partying and living the rock and roll lifestyle. As a result, it will become less and less common for the best rock music to be created by formally trained musicians.

    Two mutually exclusive traits (1._____ and 2._____) present in a category of individuals (_____) are described and one (_____) is identified as more preferred, either in fact or in reputation, in order to support a prediction (_____).

10. Ecologists consider a species to be a "keystone species" if its removal from an ecosystem precipitates a cascade of changes across trophic levels. The decimation of sea otters through harvesting for their fur over vast areas of the Pacific resulted in dramatic losses of kelp forests, since sea otters are the only species to feed on sea anemones. In the absence of the otters, sea anemone populations explode and quickly denude kelp forests. Clearly, the sea otter qualifies as a keystone species.

    A definition (_____) is presented and applied to an entity (_____) in order to support a classification (_____).

11. It is indisputable that the rise of social media has transformed our global society and has been a profound force for democratization and free exchange of information. This is evidenced by the strict censorship that totalitarian regimes have tried to impose on social media sites. However, the most significant measure of the impact of social media is at the level of the individual. The perpetual focus on the incessantly changing images on a screen as a substitute for real interaction has made the individual more isolated rather than more connected. Thus, social media is a net detriment to humanity.

    The overall value (_____) of a phenomenon (_____) to humanity is weighed over two different scales of analysis (1._____ and 2. _____), partially due to a balancing of the relative significance of the two different scales (_____).

12. In order to be a success in today's technology-driven workplace it is necessary that one be fluent in the computer sciences and well-grounded in mathematics. Eventually, this imperative will produce a renaissance in mathematics education down to the elementary school level. As a result, America's students will start showing improvement in all areas, including reading, critical thinking, and even the humanities.

    An assertion of a necessary condition regarding the present (_____) is used to support a specific related prediction (_____), which in turn provides support for a broader prediction (_____).

13. The recent discovery that a whale beached on the coast of Spain died because it had ingested over 60 pounds of plastic shocked that nation. Tragically, but unsurprisingly, millions of marine mammals die painful deaths in this manner. However, land mammals tend to have extremely sensitive taste buds that aid them in selecting healthful foods. The fact that multitudes of marine mammals die from ingesting plastic must indicate that, in their evolutionary adaptation to life in the sea, these creatures have lost the keen sense of taste of their terrestrial ancestors.

    An occurrence (_____) provides context for the discussion of a broader phenomenon of which the occurrence is a part (_____), which stands in contrast to a counter-phenomenon (_____) from which a causal conclusion (_____) is drawn.

14. The recent petition submitted to the State of California to split the state into three different states should be decided solely by the people of California. After all, it is wholly appropriate that matters relating only to internal matters of a state and not affecting citizens of other states should be decidedly solely by the citizens of that state.

    A recommendation on how to reach a determination (_____) regarding a proposal (_____) is supported by a principle (_____).

15. A resurgence of interest in Mark Twain has been driven not by any reexamination of his literary works, but by the "discovery" of his personal, typically cantankerous, musings on any and all matters of human nature, politics, and society, of which most people were previously unaware. So, unfortunately, this renewed interest is unlikely to restore his books to their rightful place in the literary education of our youth.

    The reason (_____) for a phenomenon (_____) is used to discount the likelihood of one potential effect (_____) of the phenomenon.

16. Many people believe that they can identify edible mushrooms and distinguish them from poisonous ones through the use of field guides. However, the authors and publishers of such guides advise that most people, without some specialized training in mycology, are unable to make such distinctions safely using such guides alone. Therefore, those that claim that they are capable of utilizing field guides to identify edible mushrooms are likely mistaken.

A claim (_____) is refuted based on the statement of an authoritative source (_____) that includes two qualifications (1. _____ and 2. _____) that might or might not apply to the claimants.

17. A truly great food experience depends not only on superb ingredients and a masterful chef, but also on diners capable of leaving behind their worldly concerns and immersing themselves in the culinary moment. Thus, while the greatest chefs will be found in the economic and cultural meccas of the world, such as New York and London, the greatest food experiences are savored in little villages in France, Italy, India, China, and other birthplaces of the world's great cuisines.

A relative judgment (_____) is claimed based on three requirements of an absolute standard (_____requires 1. _____, 2. _____, and 3. _____), despite relative counter-evidence (_____).

18. I must wholly agree with those who believe that a compelling premise in the hands of a skilled writer guarantees a good read. Similarly, it seems indisputable that what constitutes a good read depends on the taste of the reader. Since I cannot reconcile these beliefs, nor can I refute them, I must consider them to be mere platitudes rather than formal principles from which to make logical deductions.

Two statements classified as principles are presented (1. _____ and 2. _____), followed by an assertion of their contradictory nature, resulting in a reclassification of the two statements (_____).

19. Pursuing success in life is tantamount to searching for beauty in abstract art. The more one is personally invested in finding it, the less likely it is to be there. Thus, those who can truly appreciate abstract art are far more likely to judge their lives a success.

An analogy (_____) is claimed based on an asserted shared principle (_____) in order to support a relative judgment (_____).

20. Forests can contain more biomass per unit area than grasslands and thus can store more carbon at any one time. However, in native grasslands a far greater percentage of the biomass is stored underground in the root system than in a forest. Thus, a fire in a forest will release a greater proportion of the stored carbon back to the atmosphere than a grassland fire. So while restoring forests is a critical tool in combating climate change, it would be counterproductive to such efforts to try to convert well-established native grasslands into forests.

A comparison (_____) that supports one course of action (_____) is weighed against a comparison (_____) that supports maintaining the status quo.

Answers

1. Philosopher: It is never ethically justified to be untruthful, even as a means to an end. And every statement is either truthful or untruthful. Therefore, to live an ethical life, one must always tell the truth.

   Establishing two mutually exclusive possibilities (1. **being truthful** and 2. **being untruthful**) and arguing that since one (**being untruthful**) cannot be reconciled with a certain condition (**livingan ethical life**), the alternative (**being truthful**) necessarily results from that condition (**living an ethical life**).

2. Early human civilizations were located exclusively near large sources of fresh, potable water. There are signs that some human groups attempted to settle in other locations, but they all abandoned those locations quickly after constructing only a few initial buildings. Therefore, large sources of drinking water must have been necessary for early human civilizations to establish themselves fully.

   Concludes a requirement (**drinking water**) based on examining the results of both having (**early civilizations located near fresh water**) and not having (**other locations**) that requirement.

3. In a recent study, homing pigeons were fed varying diets before being released miles away from their home locations. After measuring the flight times home, the ornithologists in the study concluded that a diet including a high concentration of protein from insect sources leads to the fastest return flight times for messenger birds.

   Uses a study about a limited subset of a group (**homing pigeons**) in order to draw a conclusion about the group as a whole (**messenger birds**).

4. The clans of Caledonia each developed their own currencies. However, each clan relied heavily on intra-clan trade to maintain their economies. Hence, these seemingly independent currencies were actually a part of a larger monetary system and thus should be considered the same.

   Additional context (**intra-clan trade**) is added to a historical fact (**the clans' different currencies**) in order to reevaluate (**were actually**) that fact and promote an alternative interpretation (**should be considered the same currency**).

5. Canoes and kayaks are the two most popular water vessels. Despite many differences, including paddle shape and sitting position, the physical requirements to pilot these vehicles are almost identical. Therefore, it should be expected that strong kayakers will also be strong canoers.

   Differences are raised (**paddle shape/sitting position**) and dismissed as relatively unimportant (**despite**) compared to similarities (**physical requirements**) when reaching a conclusion about two distinct activities (1. **canoeing** and 2. **kayaking**).

6. It is commonly believed that an asteroid impact was the cause of the last great extinction period. However, reanalysis of the age of the crater of the asteroid impact primarily believed to be at fault indicates that it struck near the beginning of the extinction period but did not fully precede it. Thus, it could not possibly be the cause of any of the extinctions associated with that period.

   A previously accepted cause (**a particular asteroid impact**) of a phenomenon (**a period of extinctions**) is determined not to have caused the phenomenon based on evidence (**the start of the extinction period preceded the impact**) that precludes it from being the only cause of the phenomenon.

7. In most major urban areas throughout the nation, increased law enforcement budgets, targeted community-based policing strategies, and advances in surveillance technologies have allegedly produced dramatic declines in violent crimes and grand theft. However, complaints to police regarding acts of vandalism and petty theft have increased at even greater rates in most of these cities. Therefore, it is likely that the declines in violent crimes and grand theft are part of a cyclical trend unrelated to law enforcement efforts.

    An asserted contradictory correlation (<u>**a rise in complaints for vandalism and petty theft coinciding with declines in violent crimes and grand theft in conjunction with various policing initiatives**</u>) is used to undermine a claim of causation (<u>**that the policing initiatives are responsible for the declines in violent crimes and grand theft**</u>).

8. Sunnyvale Community College's recent "Year to Career" marketing strategy—in which the coursework from two-year certificate programs was condensed into one year—clearly has not been detrimental to the learning experience of students in its Civil Engineering Technology programs. Since the change, overall employment rates for certificate recipients are up by 12.5%, and highly technical CET jobs demand advanced skills.

    A judgment (<u>**not detrimental**</u>) is rendered regarding an initiative (<u>**"Year to Career" certificate programs**</u>) based on a recent trend (<u>**increase in employment rates for certificate recipients**</u>) and an implication of that trend (<u>**certificate recipients have advanced skills**</u>).

9. Many of the most successful rock musicians have extensive formal musical training in their backgrounds. However, others are self-trained and most, whether formally trained or self-trained, prefer to give the impression that their talent comes naturally and that they only really apply themselves to partying and living the rock and roll lifestyle. As a result, it will become less and less common for the best rock music to be created by formally trained musicians.

    Two mutually exclusive traits (1. <u>**formally trained**</u> and 2. <u>**self-taught**</u>) present in a category of individuals (<u>**successful rock musicians**</u>) are described and one (<u>**self-taught**</u>) is identified as more preferred, either in fact or in reputation, in order to support a prediction (<u>**less common for best rock music to be created by formally trained musicians**</u>).

10. Ecologists consider a species to be a "keystone species" if its removal from an ecosystem precipitates a cascade of changes across trophic levels. The decimation of sea otters through harvesting for their fur over vast areas of the Pacific resulted in dramatic losses of kelp forests, since sea otters are the only species to feed on sea anemones. In the absence of the otters, sea anemone populations explode and quickly denude kelp forests. Clearly, the sea otter qualifies as a keystone species.

    A definition (<u>**keystone species—removal causes changes across levels**</u>) is presented and applied to an entity (<u>**sea otter**</u>) in order to support a classification (<u>**sea otter is a keystone species**</u>).

11. It is indisputable that the rise of social media has transformed our global society and has been a profound force for democratization and free exchange of information. This is evidenced by the strict censorship that totalitarian regimes have tried to impose on social media sites. However, the most significant measure of the impact of social media is at the level of the individual. The perpetual focus on the incessantly changing images on a screen as a substitute for real interaction has made the individual more isolated rather than more connected. Thus, social media is a net detriment to humanity.

    The overall value (<u>**net detriment**</u>) of a phenomenon (<u>**the rise of social media**</u>) to humanity is weighed over two different scales of analysis (1. <u>**global society**</u> and 2. <u>**the individual**</u>), partially due to a balancing of the relative significance of the two different scales (<u>**individual as the most significant measure**</u>).

12. In order to be a success in today's technology-driven workplace it is necessary that one be fluent in the computer sciences and well-grounded in mathematics. Eventually, this imperative will produce a renaissance in mathematics education down to the elementary school level. As a result, America's students will start showing improvement in all areas, including reading, critical thinking, and even the humanities.

    An assertion of a necessary condition regarding the present (<u>aptitude in computer sciences and math</u>) is used to support a specific related prediction (<u>revitalization in mathematics education</u>), which in turn provides support for a broader prediction (<u>broad-based improvements in education across subject matters</u>).

13. The recent discovery that a whale beached on the coast of Spain died because it had ingested over 60 pounds of plastic shocked that nation. Tragically, but unsurprisingly, millions of marine mammals die painful deaths in this manner. However, land mammals tend to have extremely sensitive taste buds that aid them in selecting healthful foods. The fact that multitudes of marine mammals die from ingesting plastic must indicate that, in their evolutionary adaptation to life in the sea, these creatures have lost the keen sense of taste of their terrestrial ancestors.

    An occurrence (<u>death of a whale from ingesting plastic</u>) provides context for the discussion of a broader phenomenon of which the occurrence is a part (<u>death of marine mammals from ingesting plastic</u>), which stands in contrast to a counter-phenomenon (<u>land mammals less prone to ingest plastic because of their sensitive taste buds</u>) from which a causal conclusion (<u>marine mammals lost those sensitive taste buds as they evolved</u>) is drawn.

14. The recent petition submitted to the State of California to split the state into three different states should be decided solely by the people of California. After all, it is wholly appropriate that matters relating only to internal matters of a state and not affecting citizens of other states should be decidedly solely by the citizens of that state.

    A recommendation on how to reach a determination (<u>assessing the will of people of California only</u>) regarding a proposal (<u>to split California in three</u>) is supported by a principle (<u>internal matters not affecting citizens of other states should be decided solely by citizens of that state</u>).

15. A resurgence of interest in Mark Twain has been driven not by any reexamination of his literary works, but by the "discovery" of his personal, typically cantankerous, musings on any and all matters of human nature, politics, and society, of which most people were previously unaware. So, unfortunately, this renewed interest is unlikely to restore his books to their rightful place in the literary education of our youth.

    The reason (<u>new interest in Twain's musings on human nature, etc.</u>) for a phenomenon (<u>resurgence of interest in Twain</u>) is used to discount the likelihood of one potential effect (<u>Twain's books restored to their rightful place in literary education</u>) of the phenomenon.

16. Many people believe that they can identify edible mushrooms and distinguish them from poisonous ones through the use of field guides. However, the authors and publishers of such guides advise that most people, without some specialized training in mycology, are unable to make such distinctions safely using such guides alone. Therefore, those that claim that they are capable of utilizing field guides to identify edible mushrooms are likely mistaken.

    A claim (<u>ability to identify edible mushrooms</u>) is refuted based on the statement of an authoritative source (<u>mycology field guides</u>) that includes two qualifications (1. <u>no specialized training in mycology</u> and 2. <u>relying solely on field guides</u>) that might or might not apply to the claimants.

17. A truly great food experience depends not only on superb ingredients and a masterful chef, but also on diners capable of leaving behind their worldly concerns and immersing themselves in the culinary moment. Thus, while the greatest chefs will be found in the economic and cultural meccas of the world, such as New York and London, the greatest food experiences are savored in little villages in France, Italy, India, China, and other birthplaces of the world's great cuisines.

    A relative judgment (**greatest food experiences in little villages**) is claimed based on three requirements of an absolute standard (**great food experience requires** 1. **superb ingredients**, 2. **masterful chef**, and 3. **diner "in the culinary moment"**), despite relative counter-evidence (**greatest chefs in New York and London, etc.**).

18. I must wholly agree with those who believe that a compelling premise in the hands of a skilled writer guarantees a good read. Similarly, it seems indisputable that what constitutes a good read depends on the taste of the reader. Since I cannot reconcile these beliefs, nor can I refute them, I must consider them to be mere platitudes rather than formal principles from which to make logical deductions.

    Two statements classified as principles are presented (1. **compelling premise** + **skilled writer** → **"good read"** and 2. **"good read"** → **taste of reader**), followed by an assertion of their contradictory nature, resulting in a reclassification of the two statements (**as mere platitudes rather than formal principles**).

19. Pursuing success in life is tantamount to searching for beauty in abstract art. The more one is personally invested in finding it, the less likely it is to be there. Thus, those who can truly appreciate abstract art are far more likely to judge their lives a success.

    An analogy (**pursuing success in life compared to searching for beauty in abstract art**) is claimed based on an asserted shared principle (**more invested in finding it** → **less likely it is to be there**) in order to support a relative judgment (**appreciate abstract art** → **more likely to judge life a success**).

20. Forests can contain more biomass per unit area than grasslands and thus can store more carbon at any one time. However, in native grasslands a far greater percentage of the biomass is stored underground in the root system than in a forest. Thus, a fire in a forest will release a greater proportion of the stored carbon back to the atmosphere than a grassland fire. So while restoring forests is a critical tool in combating climate change, it would be counterproductive to such efforts to try to convert well-established native grasslands into forests.

    A comparison (**total stored carbon in forests vs. grasslands**) that supports one course of action (**converting native grasslands to forests to fight climate change**) is weighed against a comparison (**carbon stored below ground in forests vs. grasslands**) that supports maintaining the status quo.

Drill 72: Police Procedural – The Usual Suspects

Instructions: Just as ID the Flaw questions test your knowledge of common *flawed* ways of reasoning, Procedure questions often test your knowledge of common *valid* ways of reasoning. These include:

- **Reduction to the Absurd** – Disputing someone's argument by using their logic to reach a clearly false conclusion.
- **Application of a Principle** – Applying a general rule to a specific case.
- **Arguing by Analogy** – Supporting an argument by means of a similar argument that is assumed to be valid.
- **Ruling Out Alternatives** – Reaching a conclusion by ruling out the other options.

For each of the following arguments, determine which common procedure is employed and fill the item numbers into the appropriate field in the chart.

Reduction to the Absurd	Application of a Principle	Arguing by Analogy	Ruling Out Alternatives

1. Tamara will only eat pizza, sushi, or tacos for lunch. She ate pizza this morning and refuses to eat the same meal twice in one day. There's no place to get tacos close enough for her to eat and get back in time for a meeting she must make. Therefore, she'll get sushi.

2. Discrete math is a complicated, abstract subject. Therefore, it takes several years to master the subject, since any complicated, abstract topic requires several years to master.

3. The *San Dimas Times* recently praised Representative Smith for promoting a bill that provided assistance to local homeless shelters. Thus, they should also praise Representative Patel for her promotion of a bill supporting free medical clinics, since both clinics and shelters assist those who have the greatest need.

4. Parent: You refuse to make your bed because you'll just need to make it again later. However, by similar logic, you shouldn't breathe because you'll just have to breathe again later. Since you'd clearly agree that you should keep breathing, make your bed!

5. We've already tried all other feasible methods for reducing our budget deficit, which is required by our state constitution, so we must enact this cost-cutting bill.

6. *Romeo and Juliet* is considered to be Shakespeare's greatest tragedy. The two closest contenders are *Hamlet* and *Macbeth*, but neither of these has achieved the same degree of both literary stature and popular appeal.

7. When choosing the restaurant's daily special, the chef can opt for a meat dish or a vegetarian dish. On Fridays the special is always vegetarian, so, since today is Friday, the special will not feature meat.

8. A corollary of the law of supply and demand is that as demand increases for an item that is limited in supply, the price of that item will also increase. So, it is not surprising that the price of the highly sought-after, limited edition Tiny Trina dolls reached record levels during the holiday season.

9. The Green candidate's plan to invest all local tax revenue in building and maintaining a new mixed-use outdoor space in town is too extreme. After all, no one would agree, no matter how much they value the outdoors, that all of our federal tax dollars should be used to build and maintain national parks.

10. A recent study corroborated the conjecture that the grass-eating behavior of domesticated dogs can likely be tied back to their evolution from wolves, which eat grass to help pass bacteria and other organisms through the digestive system. The researchers also considered the possibilities that domesticated dogs eat grass for specific nutritional reasons or simply because they like the taste, but found these explanations unlikely.

11. Citizen: Mayor Teddington should resign over his involvement in the embezzlement scandal. After all, 15 years ago when former Mayor Covey was involved in a tax scandal that was similar in scope and impact, he resigned.

12. Researchers have concluded that pottery fragments found at ancient Aztec archaeological sites can nearly always be tied to domestic practices. Therefore, the recent cache of pottery shards found at the Aztec site of Tenochtitlan was almost certainly from pottery used domestically rather than ceremonially.

13. Stanley is likely to be elected city council president, given that the two other candidates running for the position are both implicated in the recent corruption scandal.

14. To understand why the new boutique dress shop in the downtown shopping district will be successful, we need only look at the success of the handmade guitar store that occupies the unit next door.

15. The plan to reduce truancy by lengthening the suspension penalty will be effective. The school district increased the severity of the punishment for academic integrity violations, and such violations decreased by 20%.

16. Some people advocate for the lifting of all restrictions on speech. But free speech, however valuable, cannot go completely unchecked. That would be akin to nullifying all traffic laws and giving people free reign behind the wheel.

17. Increased funding for genetics research can be attributed not only to its development as a rigorous scientific discipline, but also to its rise as a pop culture phenomenon, as indicated by the similar case of neuroscience research 20 years ago as it entered the popular consciousness.

18. As technology advances in any given sector, traditional business practices decline. Therefore, as Internet shopping engines become more sophisticated, more brick and mortar stores will close.

19. Doctor: The patient should have surgery to remove the tumors. We have already tried the other two available treatments, medication and irradiation, and they have not been effective.

20. The social stigma associated with being a quitter is illogical. According to the law of diminishing returns, there is a reasonable endpoint to every action beyond which the investment in the action no longer produces a return worth the energy expended on the endeavor.

Answers follow on the next page.

Answers

Reduction to the Absurd	Application of a Principle	Arguing by Analogy	Ruling Out Alternatives
4, 9, 16, 20	2, 7, 8, 12, 18	3, 11, 14, 15, 17	1, 5, 6, 10, 13, 19

Reduction to the Absurd

4. Parent: You refuse to make your bed because you'll just need to make it again later. However, by similar logic, you shouldn't breathe because you'll just have to breathe again later. Since you'd clearly agree that you should keep breathing, make your bed!
9. The Green candidate's plan to invest all local tax revenue in building and maintaining a new mixed-use outdoor space in town is too extreme. After all, no one would agree, no matter how much they value the outdoors, that all of our federal tax dollars should be used to build and maintain national parks.
16. Some people advocate for the lifting of all restrictions on speech. But free speech, however valuable, cannot go completely unchecked. That would be akin to nullifying all traffic laws and giving people free reign behind the wheel.
20. The social stigma associated with being a quitter is illogical. According to the law of diminishing returns, there is a reasonable endpoint to every action beyond which the investment in the action no longer produces a return worth the energy expended on the endeavor.

Application of a General Principle

2. Discrete math is a complicated, abstract subject. Therefore, it takes several years to master the subject, since any complicated, abstract topic requires several years to master.
7. When choosing the restaurant's daily special, the chef can opt for a meat dish or a vegetarian dish. On Fridays the special is always vegetarian, so, since today is Friday, the special will not feature meat.
8. A corollary of the law of supply and demand is that as demand increases for an item that is limited in supply, the price of that item will also increase. So, it is not surprising that the price of the highly sought-after, limited edition Tiny Trina dolls reached record levels during the holiday season.
12. Researchers have concluded that pottery fragments found at ancient Aztec archaeological sites can nearly always be tied to domestic practices. Therefore, the recent cache of pottery shards found at the Aztec site of Tenochtitlan was almost certainly from pottery used domestically rather than ceremonially.
18. As technology advances in any given sector, traditional business practices decline. Therefore, as Internet shopping engines become more sophisticated, more brick and mortar stores will close.

Arguing by Analogy

3. The *San Dimas Times* recently praised Representative Smith for promoting a bill that provided assistance to local homeless shelters. Thus, they should also praise Representative Patel for her promotion of a bill supporting free medical clinics, since both clinics and shelters assist those who have the greatest need.
11. Citizen: Mayor Teddington should resign over his involvement in the embezzlement scandal. After all, 15 years ago when former Mayor Covey was involved in a tax scandal that was similar in scope and impact, he resigned.
14. To understand why the new boutique dress shop in the downtown shopping district will be successful, we need only look at the success of the handmade guitar store that occupies the unit next door.

15. The plan to reduce truancy by lengthening the suspension penalty will be effective. The school district increased the severity of the punishment for academic integrity violations, and such violations decreased by 20%.

17. Increased funding for genetics research can be attributed not only to its development as a rigorous scientific discipline, but also to its rise as a pop culture phenomenon, as indicated by the similar case of neuroscience research 20 years ago as it entered the popular consciousness.

Ruling Out Alternatives

1. Tamara will only eat pizza, sushi, or tacos for lunch. She ate pizza this morning and refuses to eat the same meal twice in one day. There's no place to get tacos close enough for her to eat and get back in time for a meeting she must make. Therefore, she'll get sushi.

5. We've already tried all other feasible methods for reducing our budget deficit, which is required by our state constitution, so we must enact this cost-cutting bill.

6. *Romeo and Juliet* is considered to be Shakespeare's greatest tragedy. The two closest contenders are *Hamlet* and *Macbeth*, but neither of these has achieved the same degree of both literary stature and popular appeal.

10. A recent study corroborated the conjecture that the grass-eating behavior of domesticated dogs can likely be tied back to their evolution from wolves, which eat grass to help pass bacteria and other organisms through the digestive system. The researchers also considered the possibilities that domesticated dogs eat grass for specific nutritional reasons or simply because they like the taste, but found these explanations unlikely.

13. Stanley is likely to be elected city council president, given that the two other candidates running for the position are both implicated in the recent corruption scandal.

19. Doctor: The patient should have surgery to remove the tumors. We have already tried the other two available treatments, medication and irradiation, and they have not been effective.

A Note on 7: This argument presents two alternatives—a meat dish and a vegetarian dish—and concludes that it will be one, rather than the other. This may have looked to you like a Ruling Out Alternatives argument. However, the argument doesn't make its case for one option by ruling out the other. Instead, it makes its case by offering a general principle—the special is always vegetarian on Friday—and applying it to a specific case—today.

Drill 73: Vocab Lab #10 – Legal Lexicon

Instructions: These are words you can expect to see in law school and beyond! Choose the answer closest in meaning.

1. Compensatory
   - (A) intended to punish
   - (B) extreme in amount
   - (C) offsetting to an injury

2. Contingency
   - (A) positive expectation
   - (B) required condition
   - (C) possible future event

3. Corroborate
   - (A) entirely disprove
   - (B) partially weaken support for
   - (C) provide more evidence for

4. Culpable
   - (A) admissible as evidence
   - (B) worthy of blame
   - (C) able to be challenged

5. Extenuating
   - (A) mitigating
   - (B) aggravating
   - (C) abbreviating

6. Extralegal
   - (A) extremely lawful
   - (B) not regulated by law
   - (C) covered by several laws

7. Fallacious
   - (A) logically convincing
   - (B) logically incorrect
   - (C) logically unimportant

8. Illegitimate
   - (A) unlawful
   - (B) statutory
   - (C) unverified

9. Inconclusive
   - (A) lacking a definite result
   - (B) summarizing prior work
   - (C) demonstrating a point

10. Indubitable
    - (A) problematic
    - (B) unquestionable
    - (C) convertible

11. Plausible
    - (A) debatable
    - (B) believable
    - (C) suggestible

12. Preponderance
    - (A) neutral authority
    - (B) natural inflexibility
    - (C) numerical superiority

13. Presuppose
    - (A) perceive
    - (B) assume
    - (C) depict

14. Stipulate
    - (A) testify as a witness
    - (B) justify as a circumstance
    - (C) specify as a demand

15. Transgressor
    - (A) scribe
    - (B) lawbreaker
    - (C) judge

5

Answers follow on the next page.

Answers

1. C

Compensatory = offsetting to an injury; making *recompense* or *compensating* for that injury. *Compensatory* damages that may be awarded are different from *punitive* damages, which are intended to punish.

2. C

Contingency = possible future event. It can also refer to a provision made for such an event: *contingency plan. Contingent* = dependent (on). If your lawyer charges you a *contingency* fee, you only pay in the *contingency*, or event, that you win your case.

3. C

Corroborate = provide more evidence for; support; strengthen. *Corroborate* can even mean confirm or authenticate; that is, *corroborating* evidence can prove a case beyond a reasonable doubt.

4. B

Culpable = worthy of blame; guilty; at fault. *Culpa* = fault; blame in Latin, as in *mea culpa* = my bad.

5. A

Extenuating = mitigating; excusing; making more forgivable. Almost always followed by *circumstances*. When you cite "*extenuating* circumstances," you're making an excuse.

6. B

Extralegal = not regulated by law. Note: *Extralegal* isn't the same as *illegal* = against the law. Rather, something *extralegal* is just outside of the scope of the law. Also, *extralegal* doesn't mean "super *legal*," whatever that might be.

7. B

Fallacious = logically incorrect. You will find much that is *fallacious* in LSAT Logical Reasoning arguments, as well as in the world at large.

8. A

Illegitimate = unlawful; illegal; improper. The word was first created in the 1500s to mean "born out of wedlock," a narrower sense that predates the broader meaning. The phrase *illegitimi non carborundum* ("Don't let the bastards grind you down.") is *illegitimate* Latin.

9. A

Inconclusive = lacking a definite result. *In* (not) + *conclusive* (definite or final, as in "conclusion"). May none of your trials be *inconclusive*, and may none of your juries be hung.

10. B

Indubitable = unquestionable; without a *doubt*. The *-dubit-* part means "*doubt*" in Latin. The final word sung in the Schoolhouse Rock tune "Lolly Lolly Lolly Get Your Adverbs" is "*Indubitably*."

11. B

Plausible = believable; credible; possible. Something *plausible* seems to be true or worthy of acceptance. The Latin root *plaus-* is related to "*applaud*," so the word originally meant "worthy of *applause*."

12. C

Preponderance = numerical superiority; majority; greater importance or weight. From the same Latin root *pond-* (weight) as *ponderous* (heavy, clumsy) and *pound* (unit of weight). You want a *preponderance* of evidence on your side of the case.

13. B

Presuppose = assume; presume; require as a condition. Useful for pointing out unjustified assumptions in someone else's thinking: "Your line of reasoning *presupposes* the existence of truly impartial justice."

14. C

Stipulate = specify as a demand. Well-written contracts *stipulate* clearly the terms of the deal on both sides.

15. B

Transgressor = lawbreaker; criminal; someone who violates rules or codes. *Trans-* (across) + *-gress* (walk, go, as in *progress* and *regress*).

5

5 lb.

Chapter 5: **Logical Reasoning, Skills by Family**

Drill 74: Family Feud: Assumption vs. Inference, Round 1

Instructions: Strengthen questions, a bulwark of the Assumption Family, have stems very similar to Most Strongly Supported stems, a mainstay of the Inference Family. Needless to say, the two question types have very different approaches and criteria for correct answers, so it's important to be able to distinguish them from one another at the outset.

For each of the following stems, indicate whether it's a Strengthen question (S) or an Inference question (I). Note that there will be repetition among these stems because this is a rapid-fire drill to practice making quick determinations. Set your timer for ninety seconds and have at it!

_____ 1. Which one of the following, if true, most strongly supports the argument above?

_____ 2. Which one of the following is most strongly supported by the information above?

_____ 3. The statements above, if true, most strongly support which one of the following?

_____ 4. Which one of the following, if true, most strongly supports the ethicist's conclusion?

_____ 5. Which one of the following does the information above most strongly support?

_____ 6. Which one of the following, if true, most strongly supports the reasoning above?

_____ 7. The commentator's statements, if true, most strongly support which of the following?

_____ 8. Which one of the following, if assumed, most strongly supports the reasoning above?

_____ 9. Which one of the following is most strongly supported by the information above?

_____ 10. Sophia's statements, if true, most strongly support which one of the following?

_____ 11. Which one of the following, if true, adds the most support for the argument's conclusion?

_____ 12. Which one of the following, if true, most strongly supports the ecologist's conclusion?

_____ 13. The mayor's statements, if true, provide the most support for which one of the following?

_____ 14. Which one of the following principles, if valid, most strongly supports the reasoning above?

_____ 15. Which one of the following, if true, provides the most support for the argument in the letter to the editor?

_____ 16. The conclusion of the commissioner's argument is most strongly supported if which one of the following is assumed?

_____ 17. The lecturer's statements, if true, most strongly support which one of the following statements?

_____ 18. Which one of the following, if true, adds the most support to the historian's reasoning?

_____ 19. Which one of the following is most strongly supported by the information above?

_____ 20. Which one of the following, if true, most strongly supports the philosopher's line of reasoning?

Answers

S	1.	Which one of the following, if true, most strongly supports the argument above?
I	2.	Which one of the following is most strongly supported by the information above?
I	3.	The statements above, if true, most strongly support which one of the following?
S	4.	Which one of the following, if true, most strongly supports the ethicist's conclusion?
I	5.	Which one of the following does the information above most strongly support?
S	6.	Which one of the following, if true, most strongly supports the reasoning above?
I	7.	The commentator's statements, if true, most strongly support which of the following?
S	8.	Which one of the following, if assumed, most strongly supports the reasoning above?
I	9.	Which one of the following is most strongly supported by the information above?
I	10.	Sophia's statements, if true, most strongly support which one of the following?
S	11.	Which one of the following, if true, adds the most support for the argument's conclusion?
S	12.	Which one of the following, if true, most strongly supports the ecologist's conclusion?
I	13.	The mayor's statements, if true, provide the most support for which one of the following?
S	14.	Which one of the following principles, if valid, most strongly supports the reasoning above?
S	15.	Which one of the following, if true, provides the most support for the argument in the letter to the editor?
S	16.	The conclusion of the commissioner's argument is most strongly supported if which one of the following is assumed?
I	17.	The lecturer's statements, if true, most strongly support which one of the following statements?
S	18.	Which one of the following, if true, adds the most support to the historian's reasoning?
I	19.	Which one of the following is most strongly supported by the information above?
S	20.	Which one of the following, if true, most strongly supports the philosopher's line of reasoning?

5

Drill 75: Sufficient vs. Necessary Assumption Stem

Instructions: Sufficient and Necessary Assumption questions are often lumped together, but their tasks are different and so are their criteria for correct answer choices. That means it's crucial to determine what type of Assumption question you are looking at before tackling the question. Use this drill to master that skill! Indicate whether each of the following stems is a Necessary stem (N) or a Sufficient one (S).

_____ 1. Which of the following, if assumed, allows the conclusion to be properly drawn?

_____ 2. Which of the following is an assumption on which the argument depends?

_____ 3. The conclusion of the argument follows logically if which one of the following is assumed?

_____ 4. The argument depends on assuming which one of the following?

_____ 5. Which one of the following is an assumption required by the argument?

_____ 6. The argument's conclusion can be properly inferred if which one of the following is true?

_____ 7. Which one of the following, if true, allows the conclusion to be properly drawn?

_____ 8. The argument makes which one of the following assumptions?

_____ 9. The economist's conclusion follows logically if which of the following is assumed?

_____ 10. The argument presupposes...

_____ 11. Which one of the following is an assumption made by the argument?

_____ 12. The conclusion above follows logically if which one of the following is assumed?

_____ 13. The conclusion of the argument follows logically only if which one of the following is assumed?

_____ 14. The ecologist's argument is valid only if...

_____ 15. The climatologist's argument is valid if...

_____ 16. The governor's reasoning is questionable because it takes for granted that...

_____ 17. The professor's conclusion is properly drawn if which one of the following is true?

_____ 18. The argument is flawed because it presumes...

_____ 19. Which of the following justifies the application of the principle above?

_____ 20. The speechwriter's conclusion is not valid unless which of the following is assumed?

5

Answers

___S___ 1. Which of the following, *if* assumed, allows the conclusion to be *properly drawn*?

___N___ 2. Which of the following is an assumption on which the argument *depends*?

___S___ 3. The conclusion of the argument *follows logically if* which one of the following is assumed?

___N___ 4. The argument *depends* on assuming which one of the following?

___N___ 5. Which one of the following is an assumption *required* by the argument?

___S___ 6. The argument's conclusion can be *properly inferred if* which one of the following is true?

___S___ 7. Which one of the following, *if true*, allows the conclusion to be *properly drawn*?

___N___ 8. The argument makes which one of the following assumptions?

If a stem just asks for an assumption without any additional language, it is a Necessary Assumption question, though the correct answer will also often be Sufficient.

___S___ 9. The economist's conclusion *follows logically if* which of the following is assumed?

___N___ 10. The argument presupposes...

A presupposition is the same thing as an assumption, similar to #8.

___N___ 11. Which one of the following is an *assumption made* by the argument?

___S___ 12. The conclusion above *follows logically if* which one of the following is assumed?

___N___ 13. The conclusion of the argument *follows logically only if* which one of the following is assumed?

This very rare question stem sounds like a Sufficient Assumption question, but the "only if" instead of the usual "if" makes it a Necessary Assumption question.

___N___ 14. The ecologist's argument is valid *only if*...

Only if introduces something necessary.

___S___ 15. The climatologist's argument is valid *if*...

___N___ 16. The governor's reasoning is questionable because it takes for granted that...

Takes for granted" is the same as saying "it assumes," and if the reasoning is bad because of an assumption, that assumption must be necessary.

___S___ 17. The professor's conclusion is *properly drawn if* which one of the following is true?

___N___ 18. The argument is flawed because it *presumes*...

___S___ 19. Which of the following *justifies* the application of the principle above?

This is a rare one, but if you're asked to justify the application of the principle, you're being asked to provide information that is sufficient to ensure that the principle is correctly applied. We categorize this as a Sufficient Assumption question with a Principle Twist.

___N___ 20. The speechwriter's conclusion is *not valid unless* which of the following is assumed?

Another rare one, but if the conclusion isn't valid unless an assumption is made, that assumption must be necessary in order for the argument to work.

5

Drill 76: Which Stem Doesn't Belong?

Instructions: The question stem tells you a lot of information about the stimulus. Will there be an argument? If so, do you have to evaluate it? What strategies are you likely to use, and which flaws are likely to be involved? When you're in the Assumption Family of questions you'll be looking to break down the argument into its core components, spot the gap in reasoning, and articulate the assumption(s). That's a lot of work, so before you do it, you'd better be sure you're actually looking at an Assumption Family question! For each of the following, indicate whether it is (Y) or is not (N) a question stem from the Assumption Family. Bonus points if you identify the question type!

_____ 1. Which one of the following is most supported by the information above?

_____ 2. Which one of the following, if true, most supports the conclusion of the architect?

_____ 3. Which one of the following most accurately states the conclusion of the argument as a whole?

_____ 4. If the statements above are true, which one of the following must also be true?

_____ 5. Which one of the following, if true, constitutes the logically strongest counter to the scientist's argument?

_____ 6. The flawed reasoning in which one of the following most closely parallels the flawed reasoning in the argument above?

_____ 7. Which of the following, if assumed, enables the conclusion to be properly drawn?

_____ 8. The claim that pioneering space travel will probably improve aeronautical flight plays which of the following roles in the argument?

_____ 9. If all of the statements above are true, which of the following must be true?

_____ 10. The principles stated by the lawyer most strongly support which one of the following judgments?

_____ 11. Which of the following statements, if true, most strongly strengthens the argument?

_____ 12. Which one of the following principles most helps to justify the reasoning in the argument?

_____ 13. The reasoning in which one of the following is most similar to the reasoning above?

_____ 14. Which one of the following, if true, most helps to explain the phenomenon described above?

_____ 15. Which one of the following is an assumption on which the argument depends?

_____ 16. The professor's argument proceeds by . . .

_____ 17. The argument above is valid if . . .

_____ 18. Which of the following is required for the author to infer that outward displacement is a valid theory?

_____ 19. The dialogue provides the most support for the claim that Newton and Isaac disagree over whether . . .

_____ 20. Which one of the following principles, if valid, most helps to justify the argument?

_____ 21. Each of the following, if true, would call into question the author's conclusion EXCEPT: . . .

_____ 22. Which one of the following, if true, most helps to resolve the apparent conflict between Jason's and Amanda's statements?

_____ 23. Which one of the following propositions is best illustrated by the statements above?

_____ 24. The critic's argument is most vulnerable to criticism on which of the following grounds?

_____ 25. The principles cited by the ethicist most help to justify the reasoning in which one of the following?

_____ 26. If the scientist's statements are true, which one of the following must be false?

_____ 27. The reasoning in the argument is most vulnerable to criticism on the grounds that the argument . . .

_____ 28. The conclusion drawn above follows logically if which one of the following is assumed?

_____ 29. The argument proceeds by . . .

_____ 30. Which one of the following is an assumption on which the argument depends?

_____ 31. Which of the following best describes an error in reasoning on the part of the economist?

_____ 32. Which one of the following most accurately describes a flaw in the physician's argument?

_____ 33. Which one of the following arguments exhibits a pattern of questionable reasoning most similar to that exhibited by the argument above?

_____ 34. The reasoning above is questionable because the argument . . .

_____ 35. The professor's statements, if true, most strongly support which one of the following statements?

_____ 36. Which one of the following, if true, most contributes to a resolution of the apparent discrepancy mentioned above?

_____ 37. If the statements above are true, which one of the following must be true?

_____ 38. Which one of the following, if true, adds the most support to the challenge from the critics?

_____ 39. The argument requires the assumption that . . .

_____ 40. Which one of the following most logically completes the argument?

_____ 41. Of the following claims, which one can most justifiably be rejected on the basis of the statements above?

_____ 42. Dean and Jerry disagree with each other about which one of the following?

_____ 43. Which one of the following, if true, provides the most support for the meteorologist's argument?

_____ 44. The flawed pattern of reasoning exhibited by the argument above most closely parallels that exhibited by which one of the following?

_____ 45. The salesperson's inference is most strongly supported if which of the following is assumed?

_____ 46. Which of the following, if true, most helps to justify the environmentalist's position?

_____ 47. Which one of the following best illustrates the principle that the passage illustrates?

_____ 48. The answer to which one of the following questions would most help in evaluating the argument above?

_____ 49. The conclusion of the politician's argument follows logically if which one of the following is assumed?

_____ 50. Which one of the following generalizations does the situation described above most clearly illustrate?

5

Answers

___N___ 1. Which one of the following is most supported by the information above? **(Most Strongly Supported)**

___Y___ 2. Which one of the following, if true, most supports the conclusion of the architect? **(Strengthen)**

___N___ 3. Which one of the following most accurately states the conclusion of the argument as a whole? **(ID the Conclusion)**

___N___ 4. If the statements above are true, which one of the following must also be true? **(Must Be True)**

___Y___ 5. Which one of the following, if true, constitutes the logically strongest counter to the scientist's argument? **(Weaken)**

___N___ 6. The flawed reasoning in which one of the following most closely parallels the flawed reasoning in the argument above? **(Match the Flaw)**

___Y___ 7. Which of the following, if assumed, enables the conclusion to be properly drawn? **(Sufficient Assumption)**

___N___ 8. The claim that pioneering space travel will probably improve aeronautical flight plays which of the following roles in the argument? **(Determine the Function)**

___N___ 9. If all of the statements above are true, which of the following must be true? **(Must Be True)**

___N___ 10. The principles stated by the lawyer most strongly support which one of the following judgments? **(Principle Example)**

___Y___ 11. Which of the following statements, if true, most strongly strengthens the argument? **(Strengthen)**

___Y___ 12. Which one of the following principles most helps to justify the reasoning in the argument? **(Principle Support)**

___N___ 13. The reasoning in which one of the following is most similar to the reasoning above? **(Match the Reasoning)**

___N___ 14. Which one of the following, if true, most helps to explain the phenomenon described above? **(Explain a Result)**

___Y___ 15. Which one of the following is an assumption on which the argument depends? **(Necessary Assumption)**

___N___ 16. The professor's argument proceeds by . . . **(Procedure)**

___Y___ 17. The argument above is valid if . . . **(Sufficient Assumption)**

___Y___ 18. Which of the following is required for the author to infer that outward displacement is a valid theory? **(Necessary Assumption)**

___N___ 19. The dialogue provides the most support for the claim that Newton and Isaac disagree over whether . . . **(ID the (Dis)agreement)**

___Y___ 20. Which one of the following principles, if valid, most helps to justify the argument? **(Principle Support)**

___Y___ 21. Each of the following, if true, would call into question the author's conclusion EXCEPT: . . . **(Weaken: Except)**

___N___ 22. Which one of the following, if true, most helps to resolve the apparent conflict between Jason's and Amanda's statements? **(ID the (Dis)agreement)**

___N___ 23. Which one of the following propositions is best illustrated by the statements above? **(Principle Example)**

___Y___ 24. The critic's argument is most vulnerable to criticism on which of the following grounds? **(Weaken)**

___N___ 25. The principles cited by the ethicist most help to justify the reasoning in which one of the following? **(Principle Example)**

___N___ 26. If the scientist's statements are true, which one of the following must be false? **(Must Be False)**

___Y___ 27. The reasoning in the argument is most vulnerable to criticism on the grounds that the argument . . . **(ID the Flaw)**

5

___Y___ 28. The conclusion drawn above follows logically if which one of the following is assumed? **(Sufficient Assumption)**

___N___ 29. The argument proceeds by . . . **(Procedure)**

___Y___ 30. Which one of the following is an assumption on which the argument depends? **(Necessary Assumption)**

___Y___ 31. Which of the following best describes an error in reasoning on the part of the economist? **(ID the Flaw)**

___Y___ 32. Which one of the following most accurately describes a flaw in the physician's argument? **(ID the Flaw)**

___N___ 33. Which one of the following arguments exhibits a pattern of questionable reasoning most similar to that exhibited by the argument above? **(Match the Flaw)**

___Y___ 34. The reasoning above is questionable because the argument . . . **(ID the Flaw)**

___N___ 35. The professor's statements, if true, most strongly support which one of the following statements? **(Most Strongly Supported)**

___N___ 36. Which one of the following, if true, most contributes to a resolution of the apparent discrepancy mentioned above? **(Explain a Result)**

___N___ 37. If the statements above are true, which one of the following must be true? **(Must Be True)**

___Y___ 38. Which one of the following, if true, adds the most support to the challenge from the critics? **(Strengthen)**

___Y___ 39. The argument requires the assumption that . . . **(Necessary Assumption)**

___N___ 40. Which one of the following most logically completes the argument? **(Most Strongly Supported)**

___N___ 41. Of the following claims, which one can most justifiably be rejected on the basis of the statements above? **(Must Be False)**

___N___ 42. Dean and Jerry disagree with each other about which one of the following? **(ID the (Dis)agreement)**

___Y___ 43. Which one of the following, if true, provides the most support for the meteorologist's argument? **(Strengthen)**

___N___ 44. The flawed pattern of reasoning exhibited by the argument above most closely parallels that exhibited by which one of the following? **(Match the Flaw)**

___Y___ 45. The salesperson's inference is most strongly supported if which of the following is assumed? **(Sufficient Assumption)**

___Y___ 46. Which of the following, if true, most helps to justify the environmentalist's position? **(Strengthen)**

___N___ 47. Which one of the following best illustrates the principle that the passage illustrates? **(Match the Principle)**

___N___ 48. The answer to which one of the following questions would most help in evaluating the argument above? **(Evaluate)**

___Y___ 49. The conclusion of the politician's argument follows logically if which one of the following is assumed? **(Sufficient Assumption)**

___N___ 50. Which one of the following generalizations does the situation described above most clearly illustrate? **(Principle Example)**

Drill 77: Talking to Yourself, Assumption Family Edition

Instructions: We've said it before: the key to efficiency is to do only what you need to do and nothing that you don't. A laser-like focus on only the task at hand can make otherwise tricky eliminations a breeze. This drill is about honing that focus and canceling out the noise.

For this edition of the Talking To Yourself series, a question stem from each of the Assumption Family question types will be provided, followed by a series of questions. These are questions that test takers might ask themselves as they evaluate an answer choice. Mark Y for the ones that focus on the right things. Mark N for the ones that don't.

Which of the following, if true, provides the most support for the ethicist's argument?

_____ 1. Does this eliminate a possible objection to the argument?

_____ 2. Does this answer introduce new information?

_____ 3. Is the language in this answer strong enough to impact the argument?

_____ 4. Does this make the argument airtight?

_____ 5. Does this answer shrink the gap between the premise and the conclusion?

_____ 6. If this isn't true, does the argument fall apart?

Which of the following allows the conclusion to be properly drawn?

_____ 7. Does the argument need this to be true?

_____ 8. Does the argument prove this to be true?

_____ 9. Does this prove the argument's conclusion to be true?

_____ 10. Can the argument work if this isn't true?

_____ 11. Does this mention the new term from the argument's conclusion?

_____ 12. Is this the reverse of my prephrase?

The professor's argument is most vulnerable to criticism because it

_____ 13. Does each abstract noun in the answer refer to a tangible noun in the argument?

_____ 14. Does this disprove the professor's conclusion?

_____ 15. Does this match my prephrase?

_____ 16. Is this the only flaw in the argument?

_____ 17. How would the professor respond to this charge?

_____ 18. Does this undermine one of the pieces of evidence the professor used to construct her argument?

Which of the following, if true, does most to undermine the economist's argument?

_____ 19. Does this strengthen the argument?

_____ 20. Did the economist imply this?

_____ 21. Is this an alternative to the economist's conclusion?

_____ 22. Does this make the economist's premises less relevant?

_____ 23. Does this seem likely to be true?

_____ 24. Is this too strong?

Which of the following assumptions is required for the politician's argument?

_____ 25. If this weren't true, would it seriously damage the politician's argument?

_____ 26. If this were true, would it guarantee the politician's conclusion?

_____ 27. Does this bring in a new concept?

_____ 28. Is this a response to a possible objection?

_____ 29. Is the language too strong to be necessary?

_____ 30. Does this support the author's conclusion?

Which of the following principles offers the most support for the argument above?

_____ 31. Does this establish the criteria for the judgment in the conclusion?

_____ 32. Does this make the argument valid?

_____ 33. Does the argument imply that this is true?

_____ 34. Do the premises fulfill this sufficient condition?

_____ 35. Does this seem like a reasonable claim?

_____ 36. Is this necessary condition the judgment the argument makes?

Answers

Which of the following, if true, provides the most support for the ethicist's argument?

__Y__ **1. Does this eliminate a possible objection to the argument?**

This is one of the most common ways of strengthening an argument.

__N__ 2. Does this answer introduce new information?

Answers on Strengthen/Weaken questions will always bring in new information, but you don't need to be on the lookout for it.

__Y__ **3. Is the language in this answer strong enough to impact the argument?**

Sometimes the only difference between a right and wrong answer on a Strengthen/Weaken question is that the right answer has stronger language.

__N__ 4. Does this make the argument airtight?

Nope—that's a Sufficient Assumption. While this would certainly strengthen the argument, the right answer doesn't have to have this quality, so it's not the right question to ask here.

__Y__ **5. Does this answer shrink the gap between the premise and the conclusion?**

That's exactly what the right answer ought to do!

__N__ 6. If this isn't true, does the argument fall apart?

Nope—that's a Necessary Assumption. While this would definitely strengthen, the right answer doesn't have to have this quality, so it's not the right question to ask here.

Which of the following allows the conclusion to be properly drawn?

__N__ 7. Does the argument need this to be true?

"Allows the conclusion to be properly drawn" indicates that this is a Sufficient Assumption question. Needing to be true is a criterion for Necessary Assumption questions.

__N__ 8. Does the argument prove this to be true?

We're not looking for an answer that's a properly drawn conclusion—that would be a Must Be True question.

__Y__ **9. Does this prove the argument's conclusion to be true?**

That's the task of Sufficient Assumption questions—make that argument valid!

__N__ 10. Can the argument work if this isn't true?

Nope—that's Necessary Assumption talk.

__Y__ **11. Does this mention the new term from the argument's conclusion?**

Most Sufficient Assumption questions have a new term in the conclusion, and whenever they do, that term, or its equivalent, has to feature in the correct answer. Anything that doesn't address that new concept can be eliminated.

__Y__ **12. Is this the reverse of my prephrase?**

Sufficient Assumption questions are often conditional, and when they are, you should always be on the lookout for incorrect answers that illegally reverse or negate your prephrase, and correct answers that contrapose it.

The professor's argument is most vulnerable to criticism because it . . .

__Y__ **13. Does each abstract noun in the answer refer to a tangible noun in the argument?**

It's easy to get lost in the abstract language of an ID the Flaw answer choice. To combat this, try to replace the abstract language in the answer with the specific language from the stimulus you think it's referencing.

__N__ 14. Does this disprove the professor's conclusion?

Even if the answer you're evaluating begins "Fails to consider," it only needs to introduce something that makes the conclusion less likely to follow from the premises; it doesn't need to prove the conclusion false.

__Y__ **15. Does this match my prephrase?**

ID the Flaw questions are some of the most predictable on the LSAT; you should definitely be prephrasing here. If the argument contains one of the named flaws, you should be able to effectively prephrase the answer.

__N__ 16. Is this the only flaw in the argument?

Not relevant—there's normally only one glaring flaw, but there can sometimes be more than one.

__N__ 17. How would the professor respond to this charge?

Not what you need to discern—if it's the flaw, it's the flaw, regardless of how the author might respond.

__N__ 18. Does this undermine one of the pieces of evidence the professor used to construct her argument?

While correct answers may attack the usefulness or the completeness of the evidence, they will not attack the truth or the accuracy of the evidence!

Which of the following, if true, does the most to undermine the economist's argument?

___Y___ **19. Does this strengthen the argument?**

Somewhat counterintuitively, many Weaken questions will contain a wrong answer that strengthens the argument. Be on the lookout for this trap and keep your eye on the task at hand!

___N___ 20. Did the economist imply this?

Not what we're concerned with. Though many bad arguments will suggest potential objections, they certainly don't have to be suggested in order to be correct answers for Weaken questions.

___Y___ **21. Is this an alternative to the economist's conclusion?**

Alternatives are classic weakeners, especially if the conclusion is an explanation, a claim of causation, or a recommendation.

___Y___ **22. Does this make the economist's premises less relevant?**

While we can't attack the accuracy of a premise to weaken an argument, we can definitely attack its relevance. This is particularly common in questions where the argument rests on a single premise.

___N___ 23. Does this seem likely to be true?

The stem says explicitly that we should evaluate the answers as though they were—"Which of the following, if true..."

___N___ 24. Is this too strong?

A weakener can never be too strong! You do, however, have to look out for answers that are too weak. "Some" statements and the like tend not to be impactful enough to weaken.

Which of the following assumptions is required for the politician's argument?

___Y___ **25. If this weren't true, would it seriously damage the politician's argument?**

This is a Necessary Assumption question, so this is exactly what you're looking for. Since the right answer is necessary, if it's not true, the argument falls apart.

___N___ 26. If this were true, would it guarantee the politician's conclusion?

Nope—that's Sufficient Assumption territory.

___N___ 27. Does this bring in a new concept?

Correct answers on Necessary Assumption questions may or may not bring in a new piece of information, depending on whether they're Bridge or Defender assumptions.

___Y___ **28. Is this a response to a possible objection?**

This is what a Defender Assumption looks like: it defends the argument against a potential objection. These can be harder to recognize than Bridge Assumptions, so definitely ask this question!

___Y___ **29. Is the language too strong to be necessary?**

Many Necessary Assumption incorrect answers contain the right content but have language that makes them too strong to be absolutely necessary.

___N___ 30. Does this support the author's conclusion?

Necessary Assumptions support the conclusion, whether by building a bridge from premise to conclusion or eliminating a possible objection, but answering this question in the positive won't allow you to pick the answer because the answer may be a strengthener that isn't necessary.

Which of the following principles offers the most support for the argument above?

___Y___ **31. Does this establish the criteria for the judgment in the conclusion?**

That's what Principle Support questions are all about—the arguments conclude judgments but the criteria for those judgments hasn't been established by the premises. Your job is to find a principle that establishes criteria that make the judgment appropriate.

___N___ 32. Does this make the argument valid?

Often the correct answer will, but answering this question in the negative doesn't allow you to eliminate an answer, because it isn't actually a requirement.

___N___ 33. Does the argument imply that this is true?

As in other Strengthen questions, we're trying to evaluate the impact each answer would have if it were true. We're not trying to evaluate whether it is likely to be true.

___Y___ **34. Do the premises fulfill this sufficient condition?**

In order for a principle to support an argument, it has to apply, and principles only apply in situations that fulfill their sufficient conditions. If the principle is about mammals and the argument is about birds, you've got a problem.

__N__ 35. Does this seem like a reasonable claim?

Principles are often sweeping claims that, in the real world, would definitely have exceptions. That's OK! You're just worried about whether the answer helps connect the concept in the premise to the judgment in the conclusion.

__Y__ **36. Is this necessary condition the judgment the argument makes?**

A principle supports an argument by establishing that if the premises are true, they basically guarantee the judgment in the conclusion. The thing that's guaranteed is always the necessary condition, so the judgment has to be in the necessary position in order for the principle to do its job. Beware of answers that move in the opposite direction—they're traps!

Drill 78: Quick Core Breakdown

Instructions: Whenever you see a dense argument on the LSAT, you need to quickly assess what information is critical and what information is extraneous. Enter the argument core! In our lexicon, we use the phrase "argument core" to refer to an argument's premise(s) and conclusion(s). Background info is not included. Opposing points are only included insofar as they provide information to clarify conclusions that are a judgment on an opposing point. Breaking an argument down into its core components and getting rid of all the excess is hard to do quickly and accurately. Hone both speed and accuracy with this drill by setting your timer to ten minutes... or seven if you're really brave!

Some experts argue that, since most lawyers rarely enter courtrooms, trial advocacy training should not be a priority for law schools. But that opinion is nonsense. Even if they never actually litigate, lawyers have permission to appear in court on behalf of clients once they are admitted to the bar. To give them this ability without the training to properly use it would be a disservice to their clients and the public interest.

1. **Premise(s):**

2. **Intermediate Conclusion (if one exists):**

3. **Main Conclusion:**

Publishers would greatly increase their sales by marketing original versions of fairy tales to adults. Modern versions of fairy tales have often been marketed to children. However, many of these tales have been greatly altered from their original form in order to be seen as appropriate for young readers. As a result, adult interest in fairy tales has declined.

4. **Premise(s):**

5. **Intermediate Conclusion (if one exists):**

6. **Main Conclusion:**

An eruption of the Yellowstone caldera, one of the largest in the world, would likely have global consequences. Scientists have determined that it is fairly consistent since it erupts approximately every 600,000 years. Since it has been over 640,000 years since its last eruption, it is apparent that something has changed geologically. So, it is at least possible that there will not be another eruption for tens of thousands of years.

7. **Premise(s):**

8. **Intermediate Conclusion (if one exists):**

9. **Main Conclusion:**

Drastic measures are required to address the cost of living in major coastal cities, such as San Francisco and Seattle. Teachers, artists, nurses, and civil servants are getting priced out of our urban communities. If a city becomes unaffordable for the people who underpin civic society, the city will lose its identity.

10. **Premise(s):**

11. **Intermediate Conclusion (if one exists):**

12. **Main Conclusion:**

Many homeowners concerned about drought have replaced their lawns with patios and other artificial surfaces. But, the more impervious the cover—such as concrete and paving—in a watershed, the faster rainwater funnels into streams and is rushed out to sea rather than soaking into the ground and recharging aquifers. Thus, those who wish to help save water should instead add compost to their soil and replant with drought-tolerant vegetation in order to recharge groundwater.

13. **Premise(s):**

14. **Intermediate Conclusion (if one exists):**

15. **Main Conclusion:**

A sense of having control over one's own life, from big-picture control such as being able to choose one's career to the ability to make mundane, everyday choices, is at the root of attaining a sense of satisfaction. Many psychologists propose myriad other factors that can influence one's sense of satisfaction, such as wealth, family, support network, or love, but only a feeling of personal autonomy is consistently correlated with "high life satisfaction" in psychological studies.

16. **Premise(s):**

17. **Intermediate Conclusion (if one exists):**

18. **Main Conclusion:**

5

Stimulus spending by the federal government is traditionally viewed as the most effective way of ending a long-term economic recession or depression. A vast array of domestic spending programs preceded the emergence of the U.S. economy from the Great Depression in the years leading up to World War II. Thus, it is clear that stimulus spending on domestic programs was responsible for lifting the U.S. economy out of the Great Depression.

19. **Premise(s):**

20. **Intermediate Conclusion (if one exists):**

21. **Main Conclusion:**

Skiing is an optimal form of exercise. After all, a skier must utilize every major muscle group in the course of a few minutes on the slope. Skiing, which has been a popular form of recreation for centuries, should thus be incorporated into many more people's exercise regimens, rather than merely viewed as a vacation activity.

22. **Premise(s):**

23. **Intermediate Conclusion (if one exists):**

24. **Main Conclusion:**

Some people advocate in favor of mind-altering drugs on the grounds that they have been used for centuries by indigenous cultures around the world. But that basis is irrelevant to our modern society, in which the routine traumas of life in the complex, harsh world we have created impedes efforts to incorporate indigenous practices into modern life.

25. **Premise(s):**

26. **Intermediate Conclusion (if one exists):**

27. **Main Conclusion:**

Light Detection and Ranging (LiDAR) technology uses pulsed lasers from planes or satellites to construct incredibly detailed mapping of topography, landforms, vegetation, and even long-buried ancient structures. Since LiDAR has more varied capabilities than standard photography-based remote sensing systems, it is highly likely that remote sensing photography will become obsolete, even for uses for which remote sensing photography is completely adequate.

28. **Premise(s):**

29. **Intermediate Conclusion (if one exists):**

30. **Main Conclusion:**

The decline in enrollment among recent high school graduates at junior colleges will result in reduced recruitment of new faculty at such institutions. As a result, the junior college system, which has played a major role in broadening access to higher education in many segments of American society, will be less able to adapt its course offerings to changes in the employment marketplace. Thus, older workers looking to develop new skills in order to change career direction are the most likely to suffer from the decline in prestige of junior colleges among recent high school graduates.

31. **Premise(s):**

32. **Intermediate Conclusion (if one exists):**

33. **Main Conclusion:**

Japan has the most homogenous population of any major industrialized society and low rates of immigration. Because automation of manufacturing and other tactics that improve economic productivity will reduce the need for human labor in Japan, as it will throughout the world, Japan must allow increased immigration in order to regain its past stature as an economic powerhouse.

34. **Premise(s):**

35. **Intermediate Conclusion (if one exists):**

36. **Main Conclusion:**

It is often claimed that large campaign donations are a corrupting influence on the workings of our government. Such claims should not be taken seriously, since those making such claims typically could not afford to make such large campaign donations and are not in agreement with how government is run. It is a simple matter of human nature that people who are unable to get their way will routinely seek to demonize those who aren't.

37. **Premise(s):**

38. **Intermediate Conclusion (if one exists):**

39. **Main Conclusion:**

If a goal seems out of reach, but an intermediary goal is readily achievable, then it is always worthwhile to make reasonable efforts to achieve the intermediary goal, whether it has its own intrinsic worth or is only a step toward the ultimate goal. However, if the intermediary goal is itself unlikely to be achieved, then it is rarely worth making any substantial efforts toward achieving it, unless it by itself has some significant intrinsic value. As a result, those who fail to focus on balancing the intrinsic value of their goals with the difficulty of achieving them will seldom prioritize their efforts properly.

40. **Premise(s):**

41. **Intermediate Conclusion (if one exists):**

42. **Main Conclusion:**

No matter how much people think they want love at first sight, the most fulfilling relationships are often between those who were brought together by circumstances and who forged a lasting bond through overcoming some sort of adversity together. The most reasonable explanation for this disparity between ambition and reality is that feelings partners have for each other are primarily shaped by how they enrich each other's lives, and this cannot be known until the partners are already in some sort of social relationship.

43. **Premise(s):**

44. **Intermediate Conclusion (if one exists):**

45. **Main Conclusion:**

Answers

Some experts argue that, since most lawyers rarely enter courtrooms, trial advocacy training should not be a priority for law schools. But that opinion is nonsense. Even if they never actually litigate, lawyers have permission to appear in court on behalf of clients once they are admitted to the bar. To give them this ability without the training to properly use it would be a disservice to their clients and the public interest.

1. **Premise(s):**

   All lawyers can advocate in court.

2. **Intermediate Conclusion (if one exists):**

   It would be a disservice to their clients and the public interest not to train them to advocate in court.

3. **Main Conclusion:**

   Trial advocacy training should be a priority for law schools.

Publishers would greatly increase their sales by marketing original versions of fairy tales to adults. Modern versions of fairy tales have often been marketed to children. However, many of these tales have been greatly altered from their original form in order to be seen as appropriate for young readers. As a result, adult interest in fairy tales has declined.

4. **Premise(s):**

   Fairy tales are marketed to kids.
   +
   Fairy tales were watered down to make them kid-friendly.

5. **Intermediate Conclusion (if one exists):**

   Adult interest in fairy tales declined.

6. **Main Conclusion:**

   Publishers could increase sales of fairy tales by marketing original versions to adults.

An eruption of the Yellowstone caldera, one of the largest in the world, would likely have global consequences. Scientists have determined that it is fairly consistent since it erupts approximately every 600,000 years. Since it has been over 640,000 years since its last eruption, it is apparent that something has changed geologically. So, it is at least possible that there will not be another eruption for tens of thousands of years.

7. **Premise(s):**

   Volcano erupts about every 600,000 years.
   +
   Last eruption over 640,000 years ago.

8. **Intermediate Conclusion (if one exists):**

   Geological conditions changed.

9. **Main Conclusion:**

   Next eruption may not be for tens of thousands of years.

Drastic measures are required to address the cost of living in major coastal cities, such as San Francisco and Seattle. Teachers, artists, nurses, and civil servants are getting priced out of our urban communities. If a city becomes unaffordable for the people who underpin civic society, the city will lose its identity.

10. **Premise(s):**

    If those who underpin civic society cannot afford to live in a city, that city will lose its identity.
    +
    Teachers, artists, nurses, and civil servants are getting priced out.

11. **Intermediate Conclusion (if one exists):**

    None

12. **Main Conclusion:**

    Major coastal cities need to take drastic measures to address unaffordability.

Many homeowners concerned about drought have replaced their lawns with patios and other artificial surfaces. But, the more impervious the cover—such as concrete and paving—in a watershed, the faster rainwater funnels into streams and is rushed out to sea rather than soaking into the ground and recharging aquifers. Thus, those who wish to help save water should instead add compost to their soil and replant with drought-tolerant vegetation in order to recharge groundwater.

13. **Premise(s):**

    Increased impervious cover (e.g., concrete) leads to increased stormwater runoff and decreased aquifer recharge.

14. **Intermediate Conclusion (if one exists):**

    None

15. **Main Conclusion:**

    Concerned homeowners should compost and plant drought-tolerant vegetation (instead of constructing patios, etc.) in order to recharge groundwater.

A sense of having control over one's own life, from big-picture control such as being able to choose one's career to the ability to make mundane, everyday choices, is at the root of attaining a sense of satisfaction. Many psychologists propose myriad other factors that can influence one's sense of satisfaction, such as wealth, family, support network, or love, but only a feeling of personal autonomy is consistently correlated with "high life satisfaction" in psychological studies.

16. **Premise(s):**

    "Feeling of personal autonomy" is uniquely and consistently correlated with "high life satisfaction."

17. **Intermediate Conclusion (if one exists):**

    None

18. **Main Conclusion:**

    Control over one's life leads to satisfaction with one's life.

Stimulus spending by the federal government is traditionally viewed as the most effective way of ending a long-term economic recession or depression. A vast array of domestic spending programs preceded the emergence of the U.S. economy from the Great Depression in the years leading up to World War II. Thus, it is clear that stimulus spending on domestic programs was responsible for lifting the U.S. economy out of the Great Depression.

19. **Premise(s):**

    Lots of domestic spending occurred before the U.S. emerged from the Great Depression (chronological correlation).

20. **Intermediate Conclusion (if one exists):**

    None

21. **Main Conclusion:**

    Domestic stimulus spending caused the emergence of the U.S. from the Great Depression.

Skiing is an optimal form of exercise. After all, a skier must utilize every major muscle group in the course of a few minutes on the slope. Skiing, which has been a popular form of recreation for centuries, should thus be incorporated into many more people's exercise regimens, rather than merely viewed as a vacation activity.

22. **Premise(s):**

    Skiing uses all the muscles all the time.

23. **Intermediate Conclusion (if one exists):**

    Skiing is optimal exercise.

24. **Main Conclusion:**

    People should ski for exercise, not just for vacation.

Some people advocate in favor of mind-altering drugs on the grounds that they have been used for centuries by indigenous cultures around the world. But that basis is irrelevant to our modern society, in which the routine traumas of life in the complex, harsh world we have created impedes efforts to incorporate indigenous practices into modern life.

25. **Premise(s):**

    Modern traumas make it hard to incorporate indigenous practices into modern life.

26. **Intermediate Conclusion (if one exists):**

    None

27. **Main Conclusion:**

    The use of mind-altering drugs by indigenous cultures is not relevant to their use in modern society.

Light Detection and Ranging (LiDAR) technology uses pulsed lasers from planes or satellites to construct incredibly detailed mapping of topography, landforms, vegetation, and even long-buried ancient structures. Since LiDAR has more varied capabilities than standard photography-based remote sensing systems, it is highly likely that remote sensing photography will become obsolete, even for uses for which remote sensing photography is completely adequate.

28. **Premise(s):**

    LiDAR can do more than photo-based remote sensing systems can.

29. **Intermediate Conclusion (if one exists):**

    None

30. **Main Conclusion:**

    Remote sensing photography will become obsolete.

The decline in enrollment among recent high school graduates at junior colleges will result in reduced recruitment of new faculty at such institutions. As a result, the junior college system, which has played a major role in broadening access to higher education in many segments of American society, will be less able to adapt its course offerings to changes in the employment marketplace. Thus, older workers looking to develop new skills in order to change career direction are the most likely to suffer from the decline in prestige of junior colleges among recent high school graduates.

31. **Premise(s):**

    Fewer recent high school grads going to junior college will lead to reduced faculty recruitment.

32. **Intermediate Conclusion (if one exists):**

    Junior colleges will be less able to adapt course offerings to the job market.

33. **Main Conclusion:**

    Older career changers are the most likely to suffer from the declining prestige of junior colleges among recent high school grads.

Japan has the most homogenous population of any major industrialized society and low rates of immigration. Because automation of manufacturing and other tactics that improve economic productivity will reduce the need for human labor in Japan, as it will throughout the world, Japan must allow increased immigration in order to regain its past stature as an economic powerhouse.

34. **Premise(s):**

    Japan has a highly homogenous society and low rates of immigration.

35. **Intermediate Conclusion (if one exists):**

    None

36. **Main Conclusion:**

    Increased immigration is required for Japan to regain its economic stature.

It is often claimed that large campaign donations are a corrupting influence on the workings of our government. Such claims should not be taken seriously, since those making such claims typically could not afford to make such large campaign donations and are not in agreement with how government is run. It is a simple matter of human nature that people who are unable to get their way will routinely seek to demonize those who aren't.

37. **Premise(s):**

People who oppose big campaign donations can't make them.
+
It is human nature to demonize those who can do what you can't.

38. **Intermediate Conclusion (if one exists):**

None

39. **Main Conclusion:**

Don't take seriously the claims of those arguing against large campaign donations.

If a goal seems out of reach, but an intermediary goal is readily achievable, then it is always worthwhile to make reasonable efforts to achieve the intermediary goal, whether it has its own intrinsic worth or is only a step toward the ultimate goal. However, if the intermediary goal is itself unlikely to be achieved, then it is rarely worth making any substantial efforts toward achieving it, unless it by itself has some significant intrinsic value. As a result, those who fail to focus on balancing the intrinsic value of their goals with the difficulty of achieving them will seldom prioritize their efforts properly.

40. **Premise(s):**

If the ultimate goal is out of reach but the intermediary goal isn't, it's worth it is worth it to pursue the intermediary one.
+
If the intermediary goal is out of reach, it is not worth it to pursue unless it has value apart from the ultimate goal.

41. **Intermediate Conclusion (if one exists):**

None

42. **Main Conclusion:**

If you don't balance the value of your goals with how hard they are to achieve, you'll seldom prioritize your efforts properly.

No matter how much people think they want love at first sight, the most fulfilling relationships are often between those who were brought together by circumstances and who forged a lasting bond through overcoming some sort of adversity together. The most reasonable explanation for this disparity between ambition and reality is that feelings partners have for each other are primarily shaped by how they enrich each other's lives, and this cannot be known until the partners are already in some sort of social relationship.

43. **Premise(s):**

Feelings partners have for each other are primarily shaped by how they enrich each other's lives.
+
This cannot be known until the partners are already in some sort of social relationship.
+
The best relationships are often those in which the people overcame adversity together.

44. **Intermediate Conclusion (if one exists):**

None

45. **Main Conclusion:**

Love at first sight rarely results in lasting relationships because the feelings partners have can't be established until they are in a social relationship.

Drill 79: Famous Flaws Match-Up

Instructions: Match each argument on the left with the flaw the argument exhibits.

Set A

1. Jane can't eat bread, so she'll have to eat rice instead.

2. Troy said he would go shopping on Wednesday if Vanessa would also go. Troy went shopping on Wednesday, so Vanessa must have gone shopping also.

3. Our accountant insisted that using a professional tax preparer was the best choice, but since she clearly just wants our business, we'll do our taxes ourselves.

4. The attitude of the team is that fast but incremental change is more valuable than sweeping reforms that take more time to achieve. As a team member, Aditya surely prefers the incremental approach as well.

5. Poetry professor: My mentor argues that William Carlos Williams's "*This is Just to Say*" offers his best example of the Imagist style, so it's not worth considering any of his other poems as better examples.

6. Physicist: Many of my colleagues argue for the existence of the graviton as an elementary particle involved in the force of gravity. But its existence has never been verified in an experiment, so it clearly does not exist.

7. The high school newspaper gave the opera an unfavorable review. Since the review was clearly written by someone with great linguistic skill, one should trust her opinion on the matter.

8. Individuals with a higher percentage of meat in their diets tend to be less responsive to antibiotics. There must be something in the meat—perhaps high levels of livestock antibiotics—that reduces the effectiveness in antibiotics in humans.

9. The last two times I washed my car, it rained the next day. I plan to wash my car today, so it will probably rain tomorrow, ruining my wash job.

10. Columnist: Commissioner Steven's claim that the referendum is in the public interest is misleading. We can see from the fact that the turnout in the election where it was on the ballot was under 20% that the public is not interested in the referendum.

A. Equivocation

B. Opinion vs. Fact

C. False Choice

D. Unproven vs. Untrue

E. Causation Flaw

F. Illegal Reversal

G. Unwarranted Prediction

H. Appeal to Inappropriate Authority

I. Part vs. Whole

J. Ad Hominem

Set B

1. All mathematicians are expert logicians. Van is not a mathematician, so she must not be an expert in logic either.

2. The lungs of marathon runners can be shown to use oxygen more efficiently than those of individuals who have never run a marathon. This respiratory efficiency must predispose an individual to run a marathon.

3. Councilman Silva's insistence that an indoor smoking ban would improve health outcomes in our community lacks credibility. After all, he is a smoker himself.

4. The assertions made in this book are clearly evidence-based. After all, the book's truth is guaranteed in its first chapter.

5. Politician: From my conversations with folks who attend my campaign rallies, it's clear that my platform has broad support.

6. Connie prefers almond butter over peanut butter, so it must be that almond butter is the superior nut butter.

7. The candidate for district commissioner's claims that she has high support among residents over age 65 is false; she has consistently failed to provide evidence to support that assertion.

8. The candidate for district commissioner asserted that a greater proportion of residents over age 65 supported her initiatives than young residents under 25. Her facts are clearly wrong, however; our surveys show that for every resident over 65 who supports her plans, two residents under 25 do.

9. All of Dr. Oliveira's patients should follow his dietary recommendations. After all, he is the county's most highly-ranked podiatrist.

10. A second term for the incumbent mayor is all but guaranteed. When surveyed, a representative sample of likely voters responded "Yes" to the question "Will you vote to reelect Mayor Cooper?"

A. Appeal to Inappropriate Authority

B. Possible vs. Certain

C. Illegal Negation

D. Unproven vs. Untrue

E. Circular Reasoning

F. Sampling Flaw

G. Ad Hominem

H. Causation Flaw

I. Opinion vs. Fact

J. Percent vs. Amount

Set C

1. Electric blankets are safe as long as they have an automatic shut-off mechanism. SleepWell Co. recently issued a recall notice for its top-selling electric blanket as it was reported to have caused several fires. It must not have an automatic shut-off mechanism.

2. The city council voted to adopt the recent rule change, so Councilman Robinson must be eager to celebrate a unanimous victory.

3. At story time, Mrs. Reed's first grade class always votes for *The Big White Dog* over *Tatiana's Tongue Twisters*. Clearly, *The Big White Dog* is their favorite book.

4. Dolphins and sharks are aerodynamically very similar, which is often raised as an example of parallel evolution. Additionally, dolphins breathe through a blowhole, so sharks likely breathe through blowholes as well.

5. The discovery of textile fragments at an archaeological site classifies the site as domestic. The archaeological site described in the recent paper was classified as domestic, so textile fragments must have been discovered there.

6. Professor Sato's claim that having grown up in poverty makes a person more likely to have contact with the criminal justice system is suspect, since she has never experienced poverty herself.

7. General: Bringing the war to an end requires the eventual removal of all ground troops. But pulling 50,000 soldiers out now will send the country into chaos. We must therefore remain militarily engaged in the nation for the foreseeable future.

8. Sarah is not voting for Edwards, so she must be voting for Adams.

9. More than half of subjects in the treatment group found relief. We can now say conclusively that this medicine is curative.

10. Cicadas are known for their distinctive, high-pitched singing. Some scientists have advanced the theory that a plausible explanation for the singing is that it serves as a mating call. Since we now know that this is the reason for the cicada's call, more research should be done in this field of study in light of this new fact.

A. Illegal Reversal

B. False Choice

C. Term Shift

D. Illegal Negation

E. Straw Man

F. Ad Hominem

G. Possible vs. Certain

H. Relative vs. Absolute

I. Comparison Flaw

J. Part vs. Whole

Answers

Note: Nobody wants to look at a bunch of messy lines so, instead of connecting the arguments to the flaws that way, we've opted to list the correct flaw directly across from the argument that exhibits it.

Set A

1. Jane can't eat bread, so she'll have to eat rice instead.

2. Troy said he would go shopping on Wednesday if Vanessa would also go. Troy went shopping on Wednesday, so Vanessa must have gone shopping also.

3. Our accountant insisted that using a professional tax preparer was the best choice, but since she clearly just wants our business, we'll do our taxes ourselves.

4. The attitude of the team is that fast but incremental change is more valuable than sweeping reforms that take more time to achieve. As a team member, Aditya surely prefers the incremental approach as well.

5. Poetry professor: My mentor argues that William Carlos Williams's "*This is Just to Say*" offers his best example of the Imagist style, so it's not worth considering any of his other poems as better examples.

6. Physicist: Many of my colleagues argue for the existence of the graviton as an elementary particle involved in the force of gravity. But its existence has never been verified in an experiment, so it clearly does not exist.

7. The high school newspaper gave the opera an unfavorable review. Since the review was clearly written by someone with great linguistic skill, one should trust her opinion on the matter.

8. Individuals with a higher percentage of meat in their diets tend to be less responsive to antibiotics. There must be something in the meat—perhaps high levels of livestock antibiotics—that reduces the effectiveness in antibiotics in humans.

9. The last two times I washed my car, it rained the next day. I plan to wash my car today, so it will probably rain tomorrow, ruining my wash job.

10. Columnist: Commissioner Steven's claim that the referendum is in the public interest is misleading. We can see from the fact that the turnout in the election where it was on the ballot was under 20% that the public is not interested in the referendum.

A. **False Choice**

B. **Illegal Reversal**

C. **Ad Hominem**

D. **Part vs. Whole**

E. **Opinion vs. Fact**

F. **Unproven vs. Untrue**

G. **Appeal to Inappropriate Authority**

H. **Causation Flaw**

I. **Unwarranted Prediction**

J. **Equivocation**

Set B

1. All mathematicians are expert logicians. Van is not a mathematician, so she must not be an expert in logic either.

2. The lungs of marathon runners can be shown to use oxygen more efficiently than those of individuals who have never run a marathon. This respiratory efficiency must predispose an individual to run a marathon.

3. Councilman Silva's insistence that an indoor smoking ban would improve health outcomes in our community lacks credibility. After all, he is a smoker himself.

4. The assertions made in this book are clearly evidence-based. After all, the book's truth is guaranteed in its first chapter.

5. Politician: From my conversations with folks who attend my campaign rallies, it's clear that my platform has broad support.

6. Connie prefers almond butter over peanut butter, so it must be that almond butter is the superior nut butter.

7. The candidate for district commissioner's claims that she has high support among residents over age 65 is false; she has consistently failed to provide evidence to support that assertion.

8. The candidate for district commissioner asserted that a greater proportion of residents over age 65 supported her initiatives than young residents under 25. Her facts are clearly wrong, however; our surveys show that for every resident over 65 who supports her plans, two residents under 25 do.

9. All of Dr. Oliveira's patients should follow his dietary recommendations. After all, he is the county's most highly-ranked podiatrist.

10. A second term for the incumbent mayor is all but guaranteed. When surveyed, a representative sample of likely voters responded "Yes" to the question "Will you vote to reelect Mayor Cooper?"

A. **Illegal Negation**

B. **Causation Flaw**

C. **Ad Hominem**

D. **Circular Reasoning**

E. **Sampling Flaw**

F. **Opinion vs. Fact**

G. **Unproven vs. Untrue**

H. **Percent vs. Amount**

I. **Appeal to Inappropriate Authority**

J. **Possible vs. Certain**

Set C

1. Electric blankets are safe as long as they have an automatic shut-off mechanism. SleepWell Co. recently issued a recall notice for its top-selling electric blanket as it was reported to have caused several fires. It must not have an automatic shut-off mechanism.

2. The city council voted to adopt the recent rule change, so Councilman Robinson must be eager to celebrate a unanimous victory.

3. At story time, Mrs. Reed's first grade class always votes for *The Big White Dog* over *Tatiana's Tongue Twisters*. Clearly, *The Big White Dog* is their favorite book.

4. Dolphins and sharks are aerodynamically very similar, which is often raised as an example of parallel evolution. Additionally, dolphins breathe through a blowhole, so sharks likely breathe through blowholes as well.

5. The discovery of textile fragments at an archaeological site classifies the site as domestic. The archaeological site described in the recent paper was classified as domestic, so textile fragments must have been discovered there.

6. Professor Sato's claim that having grown up in poverty makes a person more likely to have contact with the criminal justice system is suspect, since she has never experienced poverty herself.

7. General: Bringing the war to an end requires the eventual removal of all ground troops. But pulling 50,000 soldiers out now will send the country into chaos. We must therefore remain militarily engaged in the nation for the foreseeable future.

8. Sarah is not voting for Edwards, so she must be voting for Adams.

9. More than half of subjects in the treatment group found relief. We can now say conclusively that this medicine is curative.

10. Cicadas are known for their distinctive, high-pitched singing. Some scientists have advanced the theory that a plausible explanation for the singing is that it serves as a mating call. Since we now know that this is the reason for the cicada's call, more research should be done in this field of study in light of this new fact.

A. **Illegal Negation**

B. **Part vs. Whole**

C. **Relative vs. Absolute**

D. **Comparison Flaw**

E. **Illegal Reversal**

F. **Ad Hominem**

G. **Straw Man**

H. **False Choice**

I. **Term Shift**

J. **Possible vs. Certain**

5

Drill 80: Famous Flaws, Round 4

Instructions: We've said it before: Famous flaws appear all over the LSAT, and being able to recognize them quickly is a must if you're looking for a top score.

For each of the following abbreviated arguments, select the famous flaw that is exhibited (again!). Remember, since there is some overlap between the different flaws, you might prephrase an answer that doesn't appear. That's fine! Figure out which answer is correct, and then spend time thinking about why it's correct and how you could have prephrased both answers (assuming, of course, that you were also correct with your initial prephrase).

1. It was simply wrong of my writing professor to tell me to be more discriminating in my choice of words. I was taught never to discriminate in word or deed.

    A Self-Contradiction
    B Equivocation
    C Opinion vs. Fact

2. A Jackson is the best car in its class. After making the movie *The Jackson Kid*, the lead actor switched to driving a Jackson and swears he would never drive anything else.

    A Comparison Flaw
    B Relative vs. Absolute
    C Appeal to Inappropriate Authority

3. Corporations hire managers who are motivated by financial success. Therefore, corporations are unlikely to hire an applicant with a liberal arts major for a management position.

    A Unwarranted Prediction
    B False Choice
    C Term Shift

4. The club president has repeatedly criticized members for speaking rudely to other members. She should step down from her position, because the club cannot have a president who wants to abolish the First Amendment and take away our freedom of speech.

    A Ad Hominem
    B Straw Man
    C Opinion vs. Fact

5. Throughout history, population growth has been accompanied by a growth in material prosperity. Therefore, we should continue to promote population growth as a means of stimulating increased prosperity.

    A Causation
    B Illegal Reversal
    C Circular Reasoning

6. Some scientists speculate that intelligent machines could develop beyond our control and end up destroying mankind. Now is the time to take action to save future generations.

    A Appeal to Inappropriate Authority
    B Equivocation
    C Appeal to Emotion

7. One very popular romance novelist has written and published over 160 books which have sold over 800 million copies. Yet three of my best friends have each read one of her books, and all said they didn't enjoy them. I don't know why so many people keep buying her books if they are not enjoyable.

    A Percent vs. Amount
    B Sampling
    C Appeal to Emotion

8. The pinstripe-wearing team has the best players in Major League Baseball this year. They are, therefore, the best team in Major League Baseball this year.

    A Term Shift
    B Unwarranted Prediction
    C Part vs. Whole

9. Getting into Brody Law School requires a high GPA and a good LSAT score. Rachel wasn't accepted to Brody, so either her GPA was too low or she didn't do well on the LSAT.

    (A) False Choice
    (B) Illegal Negation
    (C) Circular Reasoning

10. Congressman Jones's effort to override restrictions imposed by the current environmental regulations must be opposed. The congressman apparently does not care about the future health of our children and grandchildren, or else he would not oppose these restrictions.

    (A) Relative vs. Absolute
    (B) Term Shift
    (C) Appeal to Emotion

11. The independent candidate would conduct himself with honesty and integrity if elected. In his career, he has been the target of the fewest investigations of all the candidates running.

    (A) Relative vs. Absolute
    (B) Unproven vs. Untrue
    (C) Sampling

12. Astronomers theorize that dark matter could either be elusive particles called axions or a property of space itself. But the latter explanation is flawed because it is based on a discarded assumption about gravity. So, efforts must focus on detecting the axions that make up dark matter.

    (A) False Choice
    (B) Opinion vs. Fact
    (C) Circular Reasoning

13. A law can restrict the rights of citizens only if it serves a compelling societal interest. Although this legislation will restrict some forms of public speech, all parties agree that it serves a compelling social interest. Therefore, it should be enacted.

    (A) Opinion vs. Fact
    (B) Circular Reasoning
    (C) Illegal Reversal

14. More people are killed each year by shark attacks than by terrorist acts, and we don't have an anti-shark unit. Clearly, allocating more money in the budget for an anti-terrorism unit is an overreaction.

    (A) False Choice
    (B) Comparison Flaw
    (C) Term Shift

15. The company should not have withdrawn its ads in response to the public criticism. Business decisions should not be made in response to political correctness.

    (A) Term Shift
    (B) Comparison Flaw
    (C) Illegal Negation

16. Benjamin Franklin has been accused of being an atheist, but this position is patently untrue. Reading his autobiography, his writings, and his public speeches, one finds nothing that could be taken as evidence that he did not believe in God.

    (A) Opinion vs. Fact
    (B) Possible vs. Certain
    (C) Unproven vs. Untrue

17. New York City residents were stopped outside the Museum of Modern Art and asked if the city was spending enough on public art projects, and a large majority answered "no." The city government should respond to its citizens by allocating more money to public arts.

    (A) Possible vs. Certain
    (B) Sampling
    (C) Percent vs. Amount

5

18. If you are unable to get a flu shot, a good alternative is to consume large amounts of vitamin C every day. My whole family has been taking large doses of vitamin C this winter, and not one of us has contracted the flu.

    (A) Sampling
    (B) Unwarranted Prediction
    (C) Causation

19. Lewis Carroll's stories make no sense to me, so they are illogical, and are therefore unsuitable reading for children.

    (A) Self-Contradiction
    (B) Opinion vs. Fact
    (C) Equivocation

20. Scarlet said she left her government job because she wanted to retire, but that was clearly not the reason. Not two weeks after her retirement ceremony, she was opening her own flower shop and working longer hours than ever.

    (A) Equivocation
    (B) Self-Contradiction
    (C) Circular Reasoning

21. The cloning of mammals, such as cattle and sheep, is already being done. Human cloning uses the same technology and methods, and is therefore soon to become a reality.

    (A) Ad Hominem
    (B) Term Shift
    (C) Possible vs. Certain

22. The film left much to be desired. It is therefore unlikely that any of the actors will be nominated for awards for their performances.

    (A) Self-Contradiction
    (B) Part vs. Whole
    (C) Circular Reasoning

23. The philosopher Hume was clearly a pessimist. This is obvious from his view that humans are basically selfish.

    (A) Term Shift
    (B) Self-Contradiction
    (C) Illegal Negation

24. The councilman argues that lifting zoning restrictions in this neighborhood will boost the local economy, but his concern isn't the economy. His family is heavily invested in real estate, and they will benefit from lifting the restrictions.

    (A) Relative vs. Absolute
    (B) Straw Man
    (C) Ad Hominem

25. The downtown mall has been a great success since its opening. Sara's new boutique in the mall must surely be very successful.

    (A) Sampling
    (B) Part vs. Whole
    (C) Possible vs. Certain

5

Answers follow on the next page.

Answers

1.	B	8.	C	15.	A	22.	B
2.	C	9.	B	16.	C	23.	A
3.	C	10.	C	17.	B	24.	C
4.	B	11.	A	18.	C	25.	B
5.	A	12.	A	19.	B		
6.	C	13.	C	20.	A		
7.	B	14.	B	21.	C		

Drill 81: Enough Is Enough!

Instructions: Sufficient Assumption questions take prephrasing to the next level. More than any other question type in the Assumption Family, Sufficient Assumption questions allow you to anticipate the correct answer. That is, as long as you can identify the gap that needs to be bridged and come up with an assumption that is enough to bridge it. By now, you should be pretty well-practiced at spotting the gap in reasoning. This drill is all about anticipating the Bridge Assumption. For each of the following arguments, prephrase an assumption that is enough to make the argument valid. (Hint: If the conclusion of the argument deals with a concept the premises don't address, bridge the gap by connecting the concepts in the premise to the new one in the conclusion.)

1. Biking to work burns more calories than walking to work. Therefore, biking to work is healthier than walking to work.

2. Julia will become successful. After all, everyone who is highly educated becomes financially independent. And no financially independent people fail to become successful.

3. Marie won the tennis game against Ally by focusing on her opponent's weaknesses. Thus, the best strategy for any tennis player who wants to beat Ally at tennis is to focus on Ally's weaknesses.

4. Computer simulations all point to the space station crashing into the Arctic somewhere. Therefore, anyone who lives in South America shouldn't worry about being hit by falling debris when the space station crashes to Earth next week.

5. In a recent study, more people lowered their blood pressure through exercise than through diet. Therefore, for most people with the goal of lowering their blood pressure, it is better to focus on exercise than diet.

6. All amoebas reproduce without a genetic contribution from an external entity. This has been definitively proven by our observations of amoebic mitosis: reproduction by means of the division of the nucleus of a single entity into two genetically identical entities.

5

7. I need to get to work in 30 minutes, and there's a forty-minute backup on the bridge due to an accident. If I'm going to get to work on time, I'll have to take the tunnel.

8. I've increased my iron supplement to 30 mg per day, so I know I am getting enough iron in my diet to be healthy.

9. Unless Jakarta is able to dramatically reduce its pumping of groundwater, the combination of ground-level subsidence and sea-level rise will result in the submergence of the vast majority of the city within ten years. Thus, in approximately a decade, most of Jakarta will be underwater.

10. Professor: Anybody who attends my class every day and does all assignments will at least pass the class. So, no matter how you feel about mathematics, if you make a reasonable effort at passing my class, you will do so.

11. A genetic mutation that occurred within the last 25 years has resulted in a new species of crayfish in which the females reproduce solely by producing clones of themselves. Thus, any remaining males play no role in the survival of the species.

12. Pediatrician: The latest data shows that defects in child car seats that cost $300 or less have been responsible for only 25 more injuries than were caused by defects in child car seats that cost more than $300. Thus, spending more than $300 on a car seat does not provide significant extra protection against the likelihood of sustaining an injury attributed to a car seat defect.

13. Visitors to South Dakota for last week's motorcycle rally indicated by a large majority that improving the condition of the highways is the best way to lure more tourism to the state. Thus, it is true, as I have long argued, that most visitors to our state believe that fixing the roads is the best way to increase tourism.

14. In order to be emotionally fluent, one must be capable of empathy. Enrique has a strong understanding of human nature, thus he is surely capable of empathy.

15. If it is at all possible to secure a grant for building a facility for preschool education in this neighborhood, Claudia will do it. If the grant is secured, then construction will begin before the end of this year and finish in six months. So, in less than eighteen months, we will have our new preschool education facility.

16. The Southtown Snapping Turtles lead their division by ten games. This late in the season, that guarantees that the Turtles will win the division.

17. The newly discovered species of an ancient marine mammal should be classified as a pinniped, since traditional taxonomic principles dictates such a classification.

18. A bacterial infection is the most likely cause of the unusual and disparate symptoms in this patient, since a bacterial infection is the only single potential cause of all of these symptoms.

19. Extraordinarily, DNA analysis has identified the closest living relatives of the mummified remains of a human released from the melting ice of a glacier thousands of years after his death. The scientists examining the remains should desist, and the remains should be sent to his descendants for burial, since that is their wish.

20. I forgot to apply for a passport 180 days in advance of my planned international flight, so I won't be able to take that flight.

21. I got a 180 on the LSAT! I'll be able to go to any law school!

22. Police Officer: The bad guys were ready for us, as if they knew we were coming. There must be a leak inside our department.

23. A population of macaques in northern Japan started using hot spring pools constructed by a hotel for its guests. It was thought that they wanted to warm up in cold weather, but it has recently been discovered that bathing in the pools lowers stress hormones. Thus, the macaques must be bathing in the pools in order to de-stress.

24. One cannot tango well unless one possesses an impeccable sense of timing. So, Harry is almost certain to not tango well, since he lacks rhythm.

25. So far in this game nearly every time his pitcher was behind in the count, the catcher called for a fastball. Once again, the pitcher has fallen behind in the count, so it is highly likely that the catcher will signal for a fastball.

Answers

1. Biking to work burns more calories than walking to work. Therefore, biking to work is healthier than walking to work.

    If something burns more calories, then it is healthier. *(Corrects the Term Shift)*

2. Julia will become successful. After all, everyone who is highly educated becomes financially independent. And no financially independent people fail to become successful.

    Julia is (or will be) highly educated. *(Shows that the principle applies)*

3. Marie won the tennis game against Ally by focusing on her opponent's weaknesses. Thus, the best strategy for any tennis player who wants to beat Ally at tennis is to focus on Ally's weaknesses.

    If a strategy works against a given opponent, then it is always the best strategy for beating that opponent. *(Corrects the overgeneralization)*

4. Computer simulations all point to the space station crashing into the Arctic somewhere. Therefore, anyone who lives in South America shouldn't worry about being hit by falling debris when the space station crashes to Earth next week.

    The computer simulations are correct. *(Shows that the principle applies)*

5. In a recent study, more people lowered their blood pressure through exercise than through diet. Therefore, for most people with the goal of lowering their blood pressure, it is better to focus on exercise than diet.

    The people in the study are a representative sample. *(Corrects the Sampling Flaw)*

6. All amoebas reproduce without a genetic contribution from an external entity. This has been definitively proven by our observations of amoebic mitosis: reproduction by means of the division of the nucleus of a single entity into two genetically identical entities.

    All amoebas reproduce using mitosis. *(Corrects the Sampling Flaw—shows the sample to be representative)*

7. I need to get to work in 30 minutes, and there's a forty-minute backup on the bridge due to an accident. If I'm going to get to work on time, I'll have to take the tunnel.

    Taking the bridge or the tunnel are the only commuting options that could be used to commute to work in 30 minutes. *(Corrects the False Choice—establishes a binary)*

8. I've increased my iron supplement to 30 mg per day, so I know I am getting enough iron in my diet to be healthy.

    No individual requires more than 30 mg per day of iron in order to be healthy. *(Corrects the Term Shift)*

9. Unless Jakarta is able to dramatically reduce its pumping of groundwater, the combination of ground-level subsidence and sea-level rise will result in the submergence of the vast majority of the city within ten years. Thus, in approximately a decade, most of Jakarta will be underwater.

    It will not be possible for Jakarta to dramatically reduce its pumping of groundwater. *(Shows that the principle applies)*

10. Professor: Anybody who attends my class every day and does all assignments will at least pass the class. So, no matter how you feel about mathematics, if you make a reasonable effort at passing my class, you will do so.

    Any reasonable effort to pass the class must include attending class every day and doing all assignments. (Corrects the Term Shift)

11. A genetic mutation that occurred within the last 25 years has resulted in a new species of crayfish in which the females reproduce solely by producing clones of themselves. Thus, any remaining males play no role in the survival of the species.

    If males don't help the females reproduce, then they can play no role in the survival of the species. (Corrects the Term Shift)

12. Pediatrician: The latest data shows that defects in child car seats that cost $300 or less have been responsible for only 25 more injuries than were caused by defects in child car seats that cost more than $300. Thus, spending more than $300 on a car seat does not provide significant extra protection against the likelihood of sustaining an injury attributed to a car seat defect.

    25 injuries is a very small percentage of total overall injuries attributed to car seat defects. (Corrects the Percent vs. Amount Flaw—25 may be a small number, but if it is a large percentage of injuries, the pricier seats may actually provide significant protection.)

13. Visitors to South Dakota for last week's motorcycle rally indicated by a large majority that improving the condition of the highways is the best way to lure more tourism to the state. Thus, it is true, as I have long argued, that most visitors to our state believe that fixing the roads is the best way to increase tourism.

    The motorcyclists surveyed are representative of visitors to the state generally. (Corrects the Sampling Flaw)

14. In order to be emotionally fluent, one must be capable of empathy. Enrique has a strong understanding of human nature, thus he is surely capable of empathy.

    Anybody who possesses a strong understanding of human nature is emotionally fluent. (Corrects the Term Shift)

15. If it is at all possible to secure a grant for building a facility for preschool education in this neighborhood, Claudia will do it. If the grant is secured, then construction will begin before the end of this year and finish in six months. So, in less than eighteen months, we will have our new preschool education facility.

    It is possible to secure a grant. (Shows that the principle applies)

16. The Southtown Snapping Turtles lead their division by ten games. This late in the season, that guarantees that the Turtles will win the division.

    A ten-game lead is insurmountable this late in the season. (Corrects the Term Shift)

17. The newly discovered species of an ancient marine mammal should be classified as a pinniped, since traditional taxonomic principles dictates such a classification.

    Traditional taxonomic principles supersede any other potential taxonomic principles in the classification of ancient marine mammals. (Establishes criteria for the recommendation)

18. A bacterial infection is the most likely cause of the unusual and disparate symptoms in this patient, since a bacterial infection is the only single potential cause of all of these symptoms.

    It is most likely that all of the patient's symptoms had a single cause. (Corrects the Term Shift)

19. Extraordinarily, DNA analysis has identified the closest living relatives of the mummified remains of a human released from the melting ice of a glacier thousands of years after his death. The scientists examining the remains should desist, and the remains should be sent to his descendants for burial, since that is their wish.

    The only consideration as to what should be done with the remains is the wishes of the descendants. *(Establishes criteria for the recommendation)*

20. I forgot to apply for a passport 180 days in advance of my planned international flight, so I won't be able to take that flight.

    Applying for a passport 180 days in advance of an international flight is a requirement. *(Corrects the Term Shift)*

21. I got a 180 on the LSAT! I'll be able to go to any law school!

    A 180 on the LSAT is sufficient by itself to guarantee anybody admission to any law school. *(Corrects the Term Shift—not actually the case, of course!)*

22. Police Officer: The bad guys were ready for us, as if they knew we were coming. There must be a leak inside our department.

    A leak within the department is the only way that the bad guys could have been ready for the police. *(Corrects the False Choice)*

23. A population of macaques in northern Japan started using hot spring pools constructed by a hotel for its guests. It was thought that they wanted to warm up in cold weather, but it has recently been discovered that bathing in the pools lowers stress hormones. Thus, the macaques must be bathing in the pools in order to de-stress.

    If an action has a particular effect, then the action must have been undertaken in pursuit of that effect. *(Corrects the Causation Flaw)*

24. One cannot tango well unless one possesses an impeccable sense of timing. So, Harry is almost certain to not tango well, since he lacks rhythm.

    If one lacks rhythm, one doesn't possess an impeccable sense of timing. *(Corrects the Term Shift)*

25. So far in this game nearly every time his pitcher was behind in the count, the catcher called for a fastball. Once again, the pitcher has fallen behind in the count, so it is highly likely that the catcher will signal for a fastball.

    When a pitcher is behind in the count, the catcher will call for a pitch that is likely to be called a strike. *(Corrects the Term Shift)*

5

Drill 82: Bridge or Defend?

Instructions: Arguments in the Assumption Family can rest on either Bridge Assumptions, which link a concept in the premise to a concept in the conclusion, or Defender Assumptions, which defend against possible objections to the argument. For each of the following statements, determine whether the correct answer is more likely to bridge the gap between two concepts (B) or defend the argument against a possible objection (D).

_____ 1. People who own cats are more likely to be introverted. Therefore, most cat owners lack social skills.

_____ 2. Those who work from home spend an average of six work hours per workday. Those who work at an office spend an average of eight work hours per workday. The distractions in the home environment must therefore account for the difference.

_____ 3. Those who own a tablet device spend, on average, two more hours per day in front of a screen than those who don't own a tablet. Clearly, owning a tablet makes one more likely to spend the day in front of a screen.

_____ 4. Research shows that books with mass-market appeal are more likely to be made into movies than books without mass-market appeal. Movies made from books, therefore, are predisposed to doing well at the box office.

_____ 5. Vegetarians consume, on average, fewer dietary fats than meat eaters. This explains the lower incidence of obesity in vegetarians.

_____ 6. Introverts require sufficient alone time in order to recharge their energy. Therefore, to be happy, introverted people must have sufficient alone time.

_____ 7. Libraries are public resources that benefit people of all ages and demographics. Therefore, governments should prioritize libraries in their annual budgets.

_____ 8. Kell left his wallet at home. Therefore, he will ask his friend to pay for dinner.

_____ 9. Mia's plant died this morning. It is obvious that she must not have watered it adequately.

_____ 10. Cutting coupons from the weekly newspaper can help families save money. Therefore, cutting coupons is the only way families can save money.

_____ 11. The newest diesel vehicles are fuel efficient. Therefore, purchasing one of the newest diesel vehicles is an act of conservation.

_____ 12. Jana received a high grade on her recent project. Therefore, Jana impressed her teacher.

_____ 13. Being in a room painted the color blue is known to calm people when they are feeling stressed. Thus, anyone who wishes to have a peaceful life would benefit from painting his or her bedroom blue.

_____ 14. In order to be happy, one must be healthy. Good health requires eating fruits and vegetables. Therefore, those with good lives are those who eat fruits and vegetables.

_____ 15. People who have highly demanding jobs often check their e-mail more than ten times per day. Marquel checks his e-mail more than ten times per day. Therefore, he must have a highly demanding job.

_____ 16. A recent study showed that individuals who purchase a home next to the ocean tend to be happier than those who do not. Therefore, living next to the ocean must inevitably lead to happiness.

_____ 17. Bob has read more books than anyone else in his sixth grade class. Therefore, Bob is the smartest person in his sixth-grade class.

_____ 18. Despite years of efforts by conservationists, many species of whales are still endangered. Therefore, the efforts of conservationists must not be helping whales at all.

_____ 19. Mark has the most creative costume. Therefore, his chances of winning the costume contest are high.

_____ 20. This phone is the least expensive one on the market. Consequently, it must be the worst phone on the market.

5

Answers follow on the next page.

Answers

There's a bit of a trick to this drill: arguments with Term Shifts and arguments that make recommendations are those most likely to have a Bridge Assumption as their correct answer. Arguments that make predictions, offer explanations, or conclude limitations are those most likely to have Defender Assumptions that rule out alternatives as their correct answers.

B	1.	Term Shift	D	8.	Prediction	D	15.	Explanation
D	2.	Explanation	D	9.	Explanation	D	16.	Explanation
D	3.	Explanation	D	10.	Limitation	B	17.	Term Shift
B	4.	Term Shift	B	11.	Term Shift	D	18.	Limitation
D	5.	Explanation	B	12.	Term Shift	D	19.	Prediction
B	6.	Term Shift	B	13.	Term Shift	B	20.	Term Shift
B	7.	Recommendation	B	14.	Term Shift			

Drill 83: Causal 2-Pronged Prephrase

Instructions: One of the most frequently tested concepts in the Assumption Family is the relationship between correlation and causation. This relationship can take a variety of forms, but the most common is a conclusion that explains a correlation expressed in the premises by claiming that one of the correlated things causes the other.

For each of the following arguments, practice recognizing that common form by filling in the blanks of the accompanying sentence. Bonus points if you highlight the keywords that denote correlation and causation. (Note: Some of the arguments mark not feature a correlation or a causal statement, in which case you should mark NA in the relevant field.)

1. Last week, Manny focused more on sleep than on studying and saw his score improve on the LSAT. Therefore, the focus on sleep must have resulted in his improvement.

    The author explains the correlation between _____ and _____ by

    claiming that _____ causes _____.

2. This year was warmer than usual and also saw an increase in the production of yellow roses at Peacock's Nursery. The warmer temperatures must be good for yellow-rose production.

    The author explains the correlation between _____ and _____ by

    claiming that _____ causes _____.

3. Whenever the hot tubs at Hot Tub Paradise are discounted, the hot tubs at Hot Tub Fairer-Price are discounted even more. The managers at Hot Tub Fairer-Price must be attempting to beat the sale prices of their competitor.

    The author explains the correlation between _____ and _____ by

    claiming that _____ causes _____.

4. Patients with a medical history of narcolepsy have been found to have significantly higher blood iron levels than patients with no history of narcolepsy. Thus, in order to curb the narcolepsy epidemic, we must require narcolepsy patients to donate blood and platelets, thereby lowering their blood iron levels.

    The author explains the correlation between _____ and _____ by

    claiming that _____ causes _____.

5. Those who consume primarily organ meats and leafy greens are more likely to have diabetes than those who consume a typical diet that is full of sugar and simple carbohydrates. Thus, contrary to popular belief, those who wish to avoid diabetes do not need to avoid overconsumption of sugar and simple carbohydrates after all, and should instead avoid organ meats and greens.

    The author explains the correlation between _____ and _____ by

    claiming that _____ causes _____.

6. When the Kansas City Kangaroos play on my birthday, they always win. So, they should always schedule a game on my birthday because they are guaranteed to win if they do.

    The author explains the correlation between _____ and _____ by

    claiming that _____ causes _____.

7. Forested areas that are replete with oak trees tend to have higher oxygen levels than forested areas that are thick with maples and elms but nearly devoid of oaks. Oaks must therefore produce more oxygen than maple and elm trees.

   The author explains the correlation between _____ and _____ by claiming that _____ causes _____.

8. Impoverished areas tend to have more graffiti than affluent areas. It follows that those areas are impoverished precisely because their denizens are defacing public property with graffiti rather than working or looking for work.

   The author explains the correlation between _____ and _____ by claiming that _____ causes _____.

9. Cherise and her boyfriend tend to fight whenever there is a full moon. So, the full moon must be affecting their moods, making them irritable and hot tempered.

   The author explains the correlation between _____ and _____ by claiming that _____ causes _____.

10. Lakes that have a lot of blue algae never have lots of catfish, but they do tend to be more acidic than other bodies of water. Since catfish need less-acidic environments in order to breed, blue algae must increase the acidity of any surrounding body of water.

    The author explains the correlation between _____ and _____ by claiming that _____ causes _____.

11. Both Mercury and Venus are extremely warm planets, and both have extremely slow rotational periods compared to Earth and Mars. Both Earth and Mars complete a full rotation approximately once every day. In contrast, Mercury rotates once about every 60 days, and Venus rotates once every 243 days. Hence, a slower rotation time must be the reason why these planets are so much hotter than Earth and Mars.

    The author explains the correlation between _____ and _____ by claiming that _____ causes _____.

12. *Ankylosaurus* was a dinosaur with armor plating and a large club tail. Paleontologists have found *Ankylosaurus* fossils near the fossils of Cretaceous plants whose leaves would have been at a height too tall for *Ankylosaurus* to reach, but whose trunks could have been easily crushed by the tail of an *Ankylosaurus*. The scientists concluded that *Ankylosauruses* must have evolved their tail to knock down these trees in order to obtain nutrients from their leaves.

    The author explains the correlation between _____ and _____ by claiming that _____ causes _____.

13. Yelise is the most tired on Wednesday afternoons. She eats spaghetti for lunch on Wednesdays, so she blames the spaghetti for her Wednesday-afternoon fatigue.

    The author explains the correlation between _____ and _____ by claiming that _____ causes _____.

14. The highest-paid actors in television are the stars of *The Comic Shop*, which is the highest-rated comedy on television. So, to improve their ratings, the lowest-rated show on television, *Doctors with Personal Issues*, should pay its actors more.

    The author explains the correlation between _____ and _____ by claiming that _____ causes _____.

15. Every time my grocery bill is really high, I've had to get pickles that week. Clearly, pickles are among the most expensive things I buy at the grocery store.

    The author explains the correlation between _____ and _____ by claiming that _____ causes _____.

16. The best soccer players in the world wear Nitro cleats. So, aspiring soccer players should buy Nitro cleats because those cleats must improve touch and passing abilities; otherwise, great soccer players wouldn't wear them.

    The author explains the correlation between _____ and _____ by claiming that _____ causes _____.

17. The board game *Dark Cavern* is remarkably intricate, and it was the highest-rated board game of last year. Dustin and Rick are designing their own board game. If they want to get a high rating and sell a lot of copies, they should make their game equally intricate.

    The author explains the correlation between _____ and _____ by claiming that _____ causes _____.

18. William Shakespeare is the most famous author in the English-speaking world, and he used lyrical, elevated language, often creating brand-new words. So, if she wants her own novel to be famous, Tegara should use lyrical, elevated language and invent some new words.

    The author explains the correlation between _____ and _____ by claiming that _____ causes _____.

19. The five most-recent films to win Best-Picture awards were all over two hours long. So, if any production team hopes for its film to be considered for Best Picture next year, the team should make sure not to edit the movie to have a runtime of less than two hours.

    The author explains the correlation between _____ and _____ by claiming that _____ causes _____.

20. Bowlers that use pink bowling balls have a higher-scoring average than bowlers that use any other color ball. Everyone on Reva's bowling team has a pink bowling ball, so they'll surely beat Jose's team, which has a few players that roll green balls.

    The author explains the correlation between _____ and _____ by claiming that _____ causes _____.

21. A Mediterranean diet, which is often consumed with red wine, has been associated with a decreased risk of heart disease. Anyone at risk of heart disease, then, should increase the amount of red wine she drinks on a daily basis.

    The author explains the correlation between _____ and _____ by claiming that _____ causes _____.

22. People who play chess tend to be more intelligent than people who do not. Clearly, playing chess increases intelligence.

    The author explains the correlation between _____ and _____ by claiming that _____ causes _____.

23. Last year saw a steep rise in the number of parkour athletes that use Sporting Plaza to practice parkour. Sporting Plaza saw a steep decline in the number of shoppers last year as well. It follows that many shoppers left because of the presence of the parkour athletes in Sporting Plaza.

    The author explains the correlation between _____ and _____ by claiming that _____ causes _____.

24. Five months ago, they added a carpool lane to the Taft Freeway. Since then, travel times have decreased significantly for people that use the Taft Freeway. Clearly, the carpool lane is responsible for this decrease in travel time.

    The author explains the correlation between _____ and _____ by claiming that _____ causes _____.

25. Jesper's house is full of scented candles, and Jesper's house is never dirty. People with dirty houses should therefore buy scented candles because the smell of scented candles clearly increases a person's propensity to clean.

    The author explains the correlation between _____ and _____ by claiming that _____ causes _____.

Answers

1. Last week, Manny focused more on sleep than on studying and saw his score improve on the LSAT. Therefore, the focus on sleep must have resulted in his improvement.

   The author explains the correlation between **more sleep** and **higher score** by claiming that **more sleep** causes **score improvement**.

2. This year was warmer than usual and also saw an increase in the production of yellow roses at Peacock's Nursery. The warmer temperatures must be good for yellow-rose production.

   The author explains the correlation between **warm temperatures** and **yellow rose production** by claiming that **warmer temperatures** cause **increased rose production**.

3. Whenever the hot tubs at Hot Tub Paradise are discounted, the hot tubs at Hot Tub Fairer-Price are discounted even more. The managers at Hot Tub Fairer-Price must be attempting to beat the sale prices of their competitor.

   The author explains the correlation between **HT Paradise discounts** and **HT Fairer-Price discounts** by claiming that **HT Paradise discounts** cause **HT Fairer-Price discounts**.

4. Patients with a medical history of narcolepsy have been found to have significantly higher blood iron levels than patients with no history of narcolepsy. Thus, in order to curb the narcolepsy epidemic, we must require narcolepsy patients to donate blood and platelets, thereby lowering their blood iron levels.

   The author explains the correlation between **higher blood iron** and **narcolepsy** by claiming that **higher blood iron** causes **narcolepsy**.

The causality here isn't quite explicit, but when we're told that a requirement should be instituted in order to curb an epidemic, it is implied that the requirement will address the cause of the epidemic.

5. Those who consume primarily organ meats and leafy greens are more likely to have diabetes than those who consume a typical diet that is full of sugar and simple carbohydrates. Thus, contrary to popular belief, those who wish to avoid diabetes do not need to avoid overconsumption of sugar and simple carbohydrates after all, and should instead avoid organ meats and greens.

   The author explains the correlation between **leafy greens/organ meat diet** and **diabetes** by claiming that **this diet** causes **diabetes**.

This is another case of implied causality. Here, the conclusion is a recommendation to avoid a diet in order to avoid a disease. It is implied, then, that the diet causes the disease. (Henceforth, instances of this will simply be tagged as "Implied Causality.")

6. When the Kansas City Kangaroos play on my birthday, they always win. So, they should always schedule a game on my birthday because they are guaranteed to win if they do.

   The author explains the correlation between **the Kangaroos playing on his birthday** and **the Kangaroos winning** by claiming that **playing on his birthday** causes **the Kangaroo victory.**

7. Forested areas that are replete with oak trees tend to have higher oxygen levels than forested areas that are thick with maples and elms but nearly devoid of oaks. Oaks must therefore produce more oxygen than maple and elm trees.

   The author explains the correlation between **higher oxygen levels** and **larger populations of oak trees** by claiming that **oak trees** cause **higher oxygen levels**.

8. Impoverished areas tend to have more graffiti than affluent areas. It follows that those areas are impoverished precisely because their denizens are defacing public property with graffiti rather than working or looking for work.

    The author explains the correlation between **poverty** and **graffiti** by claiming that **graffiti** causes **poverty.**

9. Cherise and her boyfriend tend to fight whenever there is a full moon. So, the full moon must be affecting their moods, making them irritable and hot-tempered.

    The author explains the correlation between **Cherise's fighting with her boyfriend** and **the full moon** by claiming that **the full moon** causes **the fights between Cherise and her boyfriend.**

10. Lakes that have a lot of blue algae never have lots of catfish, but they do tend to be more acidic than other bodies of water. Since catfish need less-acidic environments in order to breed, blue algae must increase the acidity of any surrounding body of water.

    The author explains the correlation between **blue algae** and **lack of catfish** by claiming that **blue algae** causes **an increase in acidity** (which in turn guarantees **a lack of catfish**).

11. Both Mercury and Venus are extremely warm planets, and both have extremely slow rotational periods compared to Earth and Mars. Both Earth and Mars complete a full rotation approximately once every day. In contrast, Mercury rotates once about every 60 days, and Venus rotates once every 243 days. Hence, a slower rotation time must be the reason why these planets are so much hotter than Earth and Mars.

    The author explains the correlation between **rotation time** and **temperature** by claiming that **slow rotation time** causes **warmer temperatures.**

12. *Ankylosaurus* was a dinosaur with armor plating and a large club tail. Paleontologists have found *Ankylosaurus* fossils near the fossils of Cretaceous plants whose leaves would have been at a height too tall for *Ankylosaurus* to reach, but whose trunks could have been easily crushed by the tail of an *Ankylosaurus*. The scientists concluded that *Ankylosauruses* must have evolved their tail to knock down these trees in order to obtain nutrients from their leaves.

    The author explains the correlation between ***Ankylosaurus* fossils** and **plant fossils** by claiming that **the plants** caused **the evolution of *Ankylosaurus's* club tail**.

13. Yelise is the most tired on Wednesday afternoons. She eats spaghetti for lunch on Wednesdays, so she blames the spaghetti for her Wednesday-afternoon fatigue.

    The author explains the correlation between **fatigue** and **spaghetti** by claiming that **spaghetti** causes **fatigue**.

14. The highest-paid actors in television are the stars of *The Comic Shop*, which is the highest-rated comedy on television. So, to improve their ratings, the lowest-rated show on television, *Doctors with Personal Issues,* should pay its actors more.

    The author explains the correlation between **highly-paid actors** and **high ratings** by claiming that **highly-paid actors** cause **great ratings**. *(Implied Causality)*

15. Every time my grocery bill is really high, I've had to get pickles that week. Clearly, pickles are among the most expensive things I buy at the grocery store.

    The author explains the correlation between **high grocery bills** and **pickles** by claiming that **buying pickles** causes **high grocery bills**. *(Implied Causality)*

16. The best soccer players in the world wear Nitro cleats. So, aspiring soccer players should buy Nitro cleats because those cleats must improve touch and passing abilities; otherwise, great soccer players wouldn't wear them.

   The author explains the correlation between **wearing Nitro cleats** and **being a great soccer player** by claiming that **Nitro cleats** cause **greatness in soccer players.**

17. The board game *Dark Cavern* is remarkably intricate, and it was the highest-rated board game of last year. Dustin and Rick are designing their own board game. If they want to get a high rating and sell a lot of copies, they should make their game equally intricate.

   The author explains the correlation between **intricacy** and **high ratings** by claiming that **intricacy** causes **high ratings**. *(Implied Causality)*

18. William Shakespeare is the most famous author in the English-speaking world, and he used lyrical, elevated language, often creating brand-new words. So, if she wants her own novel to be famous, Tegara should use lyrical, elevated language and invent some new words.

   The author explains the correlation between **famous literature** and **lyrical, elevated language and new words** by claiming that **lyrical, elevated language and newly coined words** cause **a work/author to become famous**. *(Implied Causality)*

19. The five most-recent films to win Best-Picture awards were all over two hours long. So, if any production team hopes for its film to be considered for Best Picture next year, the team should make sure not to edit the movie to have a runtime of less than two hours.

   The author explains the correlation between **winning a Best-Picture award** and **having a runtime well over two hours** by claiming that **long runtimes** cause **films to be award-winning**. *(Implied Causality)*

20. Bowlers that use pink bowling balls have a higher-scoring average than bowlers that use any other color ball. Everyone on Reva's bowling team has a pink bowling ball, so they'll surely beat Jose's team, which has a few players that roll green balls.

   The author explains the correlation between **high-scoring average** and **using pink bowling balls** by claiming that **a pink bowling ball** causes **higher scores**.

21. A Mediterranean diet, which is often consumed with red wine, has been associated with a decreased risk of heart disease. Anyone at risk of heart disease, then, should increase the amount of red wine she drinks on a daily basis.

   The author explains the correlation between **consuming red wine** and **a decreased risk of heart disease** by claiming that **red wine** causes **a lowered risk of heart disease**.

22. People who play chess tend to be more intelligent than people who do not. Clearly, playing chess increases intelligence.

   The author explains the correlation between **playing chess** and **being more intelligent** by claiming that **playing chess** causes **increased intelligence**.

23. Last year saw a steep rise in the number of parkour athletes that use Sporting Plaza to practice parkour. Sporting Plaza saw a steep decline in the number of shoppers last year as well. It follows that many shoppers left because of the presence of the parkour athletes in Sporting Plaza.

   The author explains the correlation between **increased parkour** and **decreased shoppers** by claiming that **parkour athletes** caused **the decrease in shoppers**.

24. <mark>Five months ago,</mark> they added a carpool lane to the Taft Freeway. <mark>Since then,</mark> travel times have decreased significantly for people that use the Taft Freeway. Clearly, the carpool lane is <mark>responsible for</mark> this decrease in travel time.

The author explains the correlation between **decreased travel times** and **adding a carpool lane** by claiming that **the carpool lane** caused **the drop in travel times**.

25. Jesper's house <mark>is full of</mark> scented candles, <mark>and</mark> Jesper's house <mark>is never</mark> dirty. People with dirty houses should therefore buy scented candles because the smell of scented candles <mark>clearly increases</mark> a person's propensity to clean.

The author explains the correlation between **scented candles** and **cleanliness** by claiming that **the smell of scented candles** causes **a desire to clean**.

Drill 84: Causal Fill-In, Round 1

Instructions: Strengthen and Weaken questions frequently feature a Causation Flaw. When they do, there are some common formats from which correct answer choices tend to be drawn. For each of the following causal relationships, fill in a potential answer that follows each of the given formats. Note: For some relationships, there may be some formats that cannot be logically produced or that have no logical impact.

Regular exercise results in improved memory.

1. Weaken—ID an Alternative Cause: _____

2. Weaken—Cause Without Effect: _____

3. Weaken—Effect Without Cause: _____

4. Weaken—Reverse Causality: _____

5. Strengthen—Eliminate an Alternative Cause: _____

6. Strengthen—Same Cause, Same Effect: _____

7. Strengthen—No Cause, No Effect: _____

Playing a musical instrument improves one's ability to solve math problems.

8. Weaken—ID an Alternative Cause: _____

9. Weaken—Cause Without Effect: _____

10. Weaken—Effect Without Cause: _____

11. Weaken—Reverse Causality: _____

12. Strengthen—Eliminate an Alternative Cause: _____

13. Strengthen—Same Cause, Same Effect: _____

14. Strengthen—No Cause, No Effect: _____

Income-tax cuts cause saving rates to rise.

15. Weaken—ID an Alternative Cause: _____

16. Weaken—Cause Without Effect: _____

17. Weaken—Effect Without Cause: _____

18. Weaken—Reverse Causality: _____

19. Strengthen—Eliminate an Alternative Cause: _____

20. Strengthen—Same Cause, Same Effect: _____

21. Strengthen—No Cause, No Effect: _____

When Westmont County shut down a lane of traffic on Highway 105, the average time needed to travel from Pittsville to Rowan during the morning rush hour decreased. The county should thus keep a lane permanently closed to mitigate the long morning commute times.

22. Weaken—ID an Alternative Cause: _____

23. Weaken—Cause Without Effect: _____

24. Weaken—Effect Without Cause: _____

25. Weaken—Reverse Causality: _____

26. Strengthen—Eliminate an Alternative Cause: _____

27. Strengthen—Same Cause, Same Effect: _____

28. Strengthen—No Cause, No Effect: _____

The president of country X must have sparked the civil war when he convinced the country's parliament to allow him to serve for life instead of one ten-year term.

29. Weaken—ID an Alternative Cause: _____

30. Weaken—Cause Without Effect: _____

31. Weaken—Effect Without Cause: _____

32. Weaken—Reverse Causality: _____

33. Strengthen—Eliminate an Alternative Cause: _____

34. Strengthen—Same Cause, Same Effect: _____

35. Strengthen—No Cause, No Effect: _____

The wastewater from the fertilizer factory on the Mennel River is probably responsible for this year's harmful algae blooms near the river's mouth, 50 miles downriver.

36. Weaken—ID an Alternative Cause: _____

37. Weaken—Cause Without Effect: _____

38. Weaken—Effect Without Cause: _____

39. Weaken—Reverse Causality: _____

40. Strengthen—Eliminate an Alternative Cause: _____

41. Strengthen—Same Cause, Same Effect: _____

42. Strengthen—No Cause, No Effect: _____

It is the carbon dioxide produced by yeast that causes dough to rise.

43. Weaken—ID an Alternative Cause: _____

44. Weaken—Cause Without Effect: _____

45. Weaken—Effect Without Cause: _____

46. Weaken—Reverse Causality: _____

47. Strengthen—Eliminate an Alternative Cause: _____

48. Strengthen—Same Cause, Same Effect: _____

49. Strengthen—No Cause, No Effect: _____

Increasing the driving age from 16 to 20 is the best way to decrease the number of deaths in automobile crashes.

50. Weaken—ID an Alternative Cause: _____

51. Weaken—Cause Without Effect: _____

52. Weaken—Effect Without Cause: _____

53. Weaken—Reverse Causality: _____

54. Strengthen—Eliminate an Alternative Cause: _____

55. Strengthen—Same Cause, Same Effect: _____

56. Strengthen—No Cause, No Effect: _____

The crashed computer program lacks an error routine to safely handle division by zero. To prevent crashes, such error routines should therefore be standard in all computer programs released by our company.

57. Weaken—ID an Alternative Cause: _____

58. Weaken—Cause Without Effect: _____

59. Weaken—Effect Without Cause: _____

60. Weaken—Reverse Causality: _____

61. Strengthen—Eliminate an Alternative Cause: _____

62. Strengthen—Same Cause, Same Effect: _____

63. Strengthen—No Cause, No Effect: _____

The general manager of the baseball team announced that the number-one pitcher would not be re-signed because the team couldn't afford his salary demands for next season.

64. Weaken—ID an Alternative Cause: _____

65. Weaken—Cause Without Effect: _____

66. Weaken—Effect Without Cause: _____

67. Weaken—Reverse Causality: _____

68. Strengthen—Eliminate an Alternative Cause: _____

69. Strengthen—Same Cause, Same Effect: _____

70. Strengthen—No Cause, No Effect: _____

Answers

Note: Your answers may differ, especially when identifying alternative causes. That's OK! Just make sure that your answers serve the same function as ours.

Regular exercise results in improved memory.

1. Weaken—ID an Alternative Cause: <u>Those who regularly exercise also often eat foods high in so-called "brain nutrients."</u>

2. Weaken—Cause Without Effect: <u>Those who train for marathons tend to show severe recall problems throughout the training process.</u>

3. Weaken—Effect Without Cause: <u>Those who regularly win memory competitions state that they don't have time to exercise because of all the brain training they engage in.</u>

4. Weaken—Reverse Causality: <u>People with better memories tend to be able to incorporate healthier habits in their routines more easily.</u>

5. Strengthen—Eliminate an Alternative Cause: <u>Those who regularly exercise don't regularly use brain-training puzzles to improve their recall.</u>

6. Strengthen—Same Cause, Same Effect: <u>In a new study, those who exercised the most had the best memories.</u>

7. Strengthen—No Cause, No Effect: <u>People who hardly exercise also demonstrate a lower level of recall on simple memory tasks.</u>

Playing a musical instrument improves one's ability to solve math problems.

8. Weaken—ID an Alternative Cause: <u>Individuals who take up a musical instrument typically already possess the abstract reasoning skills required to solve math problems.</u>

9. Weaken—Cause Without Effect: <u>High school students who play a musical instrument have lower math scores on standardized tests than those who do not.</u>

10. Weaken—Effect Without Cause: <u>The people who win math competitions overwhelmingly do not play musical instruments.</u>

11. Weaken—Reverse Causality: <u>Improving one's ability to solve math problems makes it easier to read music and play an instrument.</u>

12. Strengthen—Eliminate an Alternative Cause: <u>People who learn to play a musical instrument do not simultaneously take courses to become better at mathematics.</u>

13. Strengthen—Same Cause, Same Effect: <u>A scientific study showed that, after learning to play a musical instrument, participants solved math problems 10% faster than before learning to play.</u>

14. Strengthen—No Cause, No Effect: <u>People who do not play a musical instrument tend to perform poorly on measures of mathematical ability.</u>

Income-tax cuts cause saving rates to rise.

15. Weaken—ID an Alternative Cause: <u>In the last 50 years, all income-tax cuts have occurred in years in which average gross income has risen.</u>

16. Weaken—Cause Without Effect: <u>The last time income taxes were reduced, the saving rate actually fell.</u>

17. Weaken—Effect Without Cause: <u>Saving rates at Bank of Blovarica tend to increase only when taxes are raised and customers feel the need for extra savings.</u>

18. Weaken—Reverse Causality: <u>The government wants to encourage saving, and thus cuts taxes when it sees an increase in saving rates.</u>

19. Strengthen—Eliminate an Alternative Cause: <u>Income-tax cuts never occur during time periods in which average gross income is rising.</u>

20. Strengthen—Same Cause, Same Effect: <u>When income taxes were cut ten years ago, saving rates doubled within a year.</u>

21. Strengthen—No Cause, No Effect: <u>In the absence of tax cuts, people have shown no desire to increase their saving rates.</u>

When Westmont County shut down a lane of traffic on Highway 105, the average time needed to travel from Pittsville to Rowan during the morning rush hour decreased. The county should thus keep a lane permanently closed to mitigate the long morning commute times.

22. Weaken—ID an Alternative Cause: <u>Because a factory in Rowan shut down, the number of cars traveling from Pittsville to Rowan each day decreased.</u>

23. Weaken—Cause Without Effect: <u>Shutting down a lane of traffic typically causes commute times to increase.</u>

24. Weaken—Effect Without Cause: <u>The average time needed to travel from Pittsville continued to decrease after the lane had been reopened.</u>

25. Weaken—Reverse Causality: <u>The lane of traffic was closed in response to the decreased number of commuters and the concomitant lower commute times.</u>

26. Strengthen—Eliminate an Alternative Cause: <u>Westmont County did not increase the speed limit on the remaining lanes.</u>

27. Strengthen—Same Cause, Same Effect: <u>When Westmont County shut down a lane of traffic between two other cities, travel time decreased.</u>

28. Strengthen—No Cause, No Effect: <u>When the county restored the traffic lane, the average commute time returned to normal.</u>

The president of country X must have sparked the civil war when he convinced the country's parliament to allow him to serve for life instead of one ten-year term.

29. Weaken—ID an Alternative Cause: <u>The change in term limit coincided with a severe drought that left 20% of the population homeless.</u>

30. Weaken—Cause Without Effect: <u>No country in the last century that has allowed a leader to serve for life has seen a civil war as a result.</u>

31. Weaken—Effect Without Cause: <u>The civil war began a month before the increase in term length was announced.</u>

32. Weaken—Reverse Causality: <u>The president, warning of the imminent threat of civil war, convinced the parliament to lengthen his term.</u>

33. Strengthen—Eliminate an Alternative Cause: <u>There were no major changes to country X's economy that could spark civil unrest.</u>

34. Strengthen—Same Cause, Same Effect: <u>When the president of neighboring country Y lengthened his term in the same way, a civil war resulted.</u>

35. Strengthen—No Cause, No Effect: <u>Civil wars in that part of the world have occurred only after presidents have sought to serve for life.</u>

The wastewater from the fertilizer factory on the Mennel River is probably responsible for this year's harmful algae blooms near the river's mouth, 50 miles downriver.

36. Weaken—ID an Alternative Cause: <u>Another factory closer to the mouth produces five times as much pollution.</u>

37. Weaken—Cause Without Effect: <u>The amount of pollution from the fertilizer factory has remained the same for decades, but this is the first year with algae blooms.</u>

38. Weaken—Effect Without Cause: <u>The species of algae that causes these blooms is known to cause blooms in unpolluted water.</u>

39. Weaken—Reverse Causality: <u>As a response to the algae blooms, the fertilizer factory released the wastewater in the hopes that it would poison the algae.</u>

40. Strengthen—Eliminate an Alternative Cause: <u>There are no other factories whose wastewater reaches the river's mouth.</u>

41. Strengthen—Same Cause, Same Effect: <u>Other rivers containing the same chemicals found in the wastewater have seen algae blooms.</u>

42. Strengthen—No Cause, No Effect: <u>These algae blooms are not seen where there is no wastewater from fertilizer factories.</u>

It is the carbon dioxide produced by yeast that causes dough to rise.

43. Weaken—ID an Alternative Cause: <u>Baker's yeast also releases nitrogen gas, which is known to cause dough to rise.</u>

44. Weaken—Cause Without Effect: <u>Some types of unleavened bread, in which the dough never rises, are made with baker's yeast.</u>

45. Weaken—Effect Without Cause: <u>Some bread rises due to fermentation, rather than yeast.</u>

46. Weaken—Reverse Causality: <u>Some doughs start rising spontaneously, drawing in yeasts from the environment that produce carbon dioxide.</u>

47. Strengthen—Eliminate an Alternative Cause: <u>No other compound produced by yeast is produced in large-enough amounts to account for the size increase observed when bread rises.</u>

48. Strengthen—Same Cause, Same Effect: <u>The amount by which dough rises is directly proportional to the amount of carbon dioxide produced by the yeast.</u>

49. Strengthen—No Cause, No Effect: <u>When strains of yeast that don't produce carbon dioxide are used, dough never rises.</u>

Increasing the driving age from 16 to 20 is the best way to decrease the number of deaths in automobile crashes.

50. Weaken—ID an Alternative Cause: <u>Drunk driving by adults over 21 causes far more traffic fatalities than occur when drivers aged 16-20 are behind the wheel.</u>

51. Weaken—Cause Without Effect: <u>Places where the driving age is 20-years old already have approximately the same rate of traffic fatalities as places where the age is 16.</u>

52. Weaken—Effect Without Cause: <u>The rate of traffic fatalities in one country decreased, while the number of drivers aged 16-19 increased.</u>

53. Weaken—Reverse Causality: <u>A decrease in the rate of traffic fatalities prompted legislators to seek an increase in the driving age.</u> *(Yeah, we know this one doesn't make a lot of sense. The takeaway? The type of causal claim should impact your causal prephrasing!)*

54. Strengthen—Eliminate an Alternative Cause: <u>One state found that banning cell phone use prevented 100 deaths, but drivers aged 16-19 were responsible for 500 deaths.</u>

55. Strengthen—Same Cause, Same Effect: <u>A review of safety measures has found that raising the driving age leads to a larger decrease in the number of deaths than any other measure.</u>

56. Strengthen—No Cause, No Effect: <u>Countries that have not raised the minimum driving age have not seen a decrease in the number of deaths from car crashes.</u>

The crashed computer program lacks an error routine to safely handle division by zero. To prevent crashes, such error routines should therefore be standard in all computer programs released by our company.

57. Weaken—ID an Alternative Cause: <u>The attempt to divide by zero itself, and not the lack of an error routine, causes a program to crash.</u>

58. Weaken—Cause Without Effect: <u>Many programs lack error routines for division by zero, but never crash.</u>

59. Weaken—Effect Without Cause: <u>Many programs that have error routines for division by zero crash for other reasons.</u>

60. Weaken—Reverse Causality: <u>The crashing of a program can cause changes in the program's code that could delete some error routines.</u>

61. Strengthen—Eliminate an Alternative Cause: <u>There is no other way of coding in the operating system that regulates division by zero.</u>

62. Strengthen—Same Cause, Same Effect: <u>Removing the routine to handle division by zero from programs known to function properly causes them to start crashing.</u>

63. Strengthen—No Cause, No Effect: <u>Adding an error routine to programs known to crash because of division by zero errors causes them to stop crashing.</u>

The general manager of the baseball team announced that the number-one pitcher would not be re-signed. The team must not have been able to afford his salary demands for next season.

64. Weaken—ID an Alternative Cause: <u>Although he was the best pitcher on the team, he was not a very good pitcher.</u>

65. Weaken—Cause Without Effect: <u>An inability to meet a salary request can be mitigated by trading other players on the team.</u>

66. Weaken—Effect Without Cause: <u>Teams often release certain players because they are not the best use of their funds, even though they can technically afford to pay them.</u>

67. Weaken—Reverse Causality: <u>The team decided not to re-sign the pitcher, who then demanded a high salary in response.</u> *(As with item 53, this doesn't seem particularly realistic!)*

68. Strengthen—Eliminate an Alternative Cause: <u>The pitcher's performance did not decline compared to previous years.</u>

69. Strengthen—Same Cause, Same Effect: <u>The team did not re-sign their last number one pitcher, who also demanded a salary that it could not afford.</u>

70. Strengthen—No Cause, No Effect: <u>The team has a history of re-signing players who make salary demands that it can afford.</u>

Drill 85: Famous Flaws, Short Answer Edition, Round 1

Instructions: By now, you should be familiar enough with the famous flaws that you can name them without looking at a list of options. For each of the following abbreviated arguments, record which famous flaw is being committed. Since there is some overlap between flaws, there may be instances in which more than one flaw feels appropriate. That's fine! You can list more than one in these cases.

1. I've increased my GPA each of the last four semesters, so I know I'll achieve a 3.9 GPA next semester.

   _____

2. Certain frog populations decimated by the fungus Bd have rebounded slightly in areas in which the average temperature has increased to the point that it is no longer suitable for the Bd fungus to thrive. Since the Earth is going to keep getting hotter, these frog populations should start growing even faster soon.

   _____

3. My recent purchase of many shares of stock in Exciting Co. was driven by a leaked version of their earnings report, showing they outperformed estimates. However, that leaked report has since been revealed to be a fake, so the real version will almost certainly show a negative forecast and cause my shares to lose value.

   _____

4. While my congressional representative has made many reasonable speeches extolling the new infrastructure bill, her donors are going to benefit from the increase in government spending, so I don't believe the infrastructure bill is good for the average citizen.

   _____

5. Renaldo composes intricately crafted paintings in which the juxtaposition of each element tells a wondrous short story, rather than just presenting a single scene as most paintings do. Seeing a series of his paintings hung across a gallery wall must be like spending an afternoon with a beloved novel as one painting seamlessly flows into the next.

   _____

6. Strawberries grow well in my side yard. However, if I were to plant my entire side yard with strawberries, I would need to cover that area of the yard in mesh netting in order to protect them from birds, which I'm unwilling to do. Therefore, I will have to grow another plant in my side yard this year.

   _____

7. In a scientific study, one group of students was told that they would do well on an exam, and another group of students was admonished to try harder. The average score of the group told to try harder was significantly lower, so intensity of effort during a test does not positively influence performance on tests.

   _____

8. Every time I go to Madrid, I have the most amazing time! If you want to have real fun, it is the only place to go.

   _____

9. Scientists had believed that isolated vernal pools inaccessible to humans would not be contaminated with a certain strain of fungal disease because it was thought to most commonly be transported on the boots of hikers. However, after establishing similar pools in a testing environment, the fungus was discovered at these pools within a few weeks. Since the fungus appears to spread more easily than initially thought, the scientists concluded that the inaccessible vernal pools are likely already contaminated.

   _____

10. Resort Owner: In 2000, 22% of tourist dollars spent at Hawaiian resorts were spent on the island of Oahu. Every year since that percentage has climbed, hitting 37% this year. However, in 2000 net revenue for our Oahu resort was $1.1 million, and in recent years we have averaged under $1 million per year. The only explanation is that our competitors on Oahu are getting a higher share of the tourist dollars spent on Oahu than back in 2000.

_____

11. So far this year, every time our team wears their "throwback" uniforms, they have won. If they wear those throwback uniforms this Sunday, they're certain to beat the other team.

_____

12. If the low-pressure system over Greenland remains in place through the week, then the jet stream will undoubtedly usher in a series of powerful storms across Northern Europe. Luckily, meteorologists are nearly certain that system will dissipate, so the region should have clear weather.

_____

13. Residential rooftop solar energy users in Arizona and Florida report yearly savings of over $2,000, on their utility bills. So, homeowners all across the country can do the right thing for the environment and save lots of money at the same time.

_____

14. The recent economic recovery has lasted well over five years, and the economy always fluctuates over time. However, unemployment is at a record low, interest rates are at historic lows, and the stock market has hit a record high. This combination is unprecedented in the last 100 years. Thus, there is no reason to believe that such conditions cannot persist for another five years.

_____

15. Football, a notoriously violent sport, has recently seen a decline in viewership, while basketball, which has penalties for almost all physical contact, is seeing unprecedented high levels of viewership. It's clear that the desire to watch a less violent sport is driving the shift in viewer preferences.

_____

16. Georgia needs to drop a package off at the post office today before it closes. Since the post office closes at 5pm, Georgia will be sure to arrive at the post office before that time.

_____

17. The Debson is the instrument of choice for all the best-selling country artists. That particular guitar must create a great sound that results in hit songs.

_____

18. Mayor: Restoring community morale in the wake of last year's natural disasters is my highest priority. Therefore, I will focus my efforts on passing this bill that reduces property taxes.

_____

19. Anybody who seeks true enlightenment is destined to fall short of that goal. Thus, those who routinely fall short of their goals should take heart, as that is a sure path to true enlightenment.

_____

20. Whenever Tom and Bob train for marathons together, they both individually run faster times than when they train independently. Thus, Bob must be a great motivator.

_____

21. The exquisite weight balance of the SureShot2000 helps any golfer maintain a proper stance through the drive and follow-through. As a result, any golfer using the SureShot2000 is far more likely to strike the ball at the optimal angle.

_____

22. Darveston makes far superior touring motorcycles than Satsumi. So, even though Satsumi is known for its off-road dirt bikes, Darveston's announced entry into the dirt-bike market will likely overtake Satsumi's as top sellers.

_____

23. A fully functional democracy is dependent upon a voting populace informed on the important issues of the day. Therefore, it is vital to the health of our democracy that funding for K–12 education be dramatically increased.

_____

24. My neighbor claims that the color scheme I used to paint the exterior of my house violates the restrictions imposed by our homeowners' association. However, his bland taste in home decor means that no one should take any of his criticisms seriously.

_____

25. Harmony takes all her friends for granted. After all, she doesn't have a single friend that she doesn't take for granted.

_____

Answers

1. I've increased my GPA each of the last four semesters, so I know I'll achieve a 3.9 GPA next semester.

   Relative vs. Absolute

2. Certain frog populations decimated by the fungus Bd have rebounded slightly in areas in which the average temperature has increased to the point that it is no longer suitable for the Bd fungus to thrive. Since the Earth is going to keep getting hotter, these frog populations should start growing even faster soon.

   Unwarranted Prediction

3. My recent purchase of many shares of stock in Exciting Co. was driven by a leaked version of their earnings report, showing they outperformed estimates. However, that leaked report has since been revealed to be a fake, so the real version will almost certainly show a negative forecast and cause my shares to lose value.

   Unproven vs. Untrue

4. While my congressional representative has made many reasonable speeches extolling the new infrastructure bill, her donors are going to benefit from the increase in government spending, so I don't believe the infrastructure bill is good for the average citizen.

   Ad Hominem

5. Renaldo composes intricately crafted paintings in which the juxtaposition of each element tells a wondrous short story, rather than just presenting a single scene as most paintings do. Seeing a series of his paintings hung across a gallery wall must be like spending an afternoon with a beloved novel as one painting seamlessly flows into the next.

   Part vs. Whole

6. Strawberries grow well in my side yard. However, if I were to plant my entire side yard with strawberries, I would need to cover that area of the yard in mesh netting in order to protect them from birds, which I'm unwilling to do. Therefore, I will have to grow another plant in my side yard this year.

   False Choice

7. In a scientific study, one group of students was told that they would do well on an exam, and another group of students was admonished to try harder. The average score of the group told to try harder was significantly lower, so intensity of effort during a test does not positively influence performance on tests.

   Term Shift

8. Every time I go to Madrid, I have the most amazing time! If you want to have real fun, it is the only place to go.

   Illegal Reversal

9. Scientists had believed that isolated vernal pools inaccessible to humans would not be contaminated with a certain strain of fungal disease because it was thought to most commonly be transported on the boots of hikers. However, after establishing similar pools in a testing environment, the fungus was discovered at these pools within a few weeks. Since the fungus appears to spread more easily than initially thought, the scientists concluded that the inaccessible vernal pools are likely already contaminated.

   Sampling Flaw

10. Resort Owner: In 2000, 22% of tourist dollars spent at Hawaiian resorts were spent on the island of Oahu. Every year since that percentage has climbed, hitting 37% this year. However, in 2000 net revenue for our Oahu resort was $1.1 million, and in recent years we have averaged under $1 million per year. The only explanation is that our competitors on Oahu are getting a higher share of the tourist dollars spent on Oahu than back in 2000.

Percent vs. Amount

11. So far this year, every time our team wears their "throwback" uniforms, they have won. If they wear those throwback uniforms this Sunday, they're certain to beat the other team.

Unwarranted Prediction

12. If the low-pressure system over Greenland remains in place through the week, then the jet stream will undoubtedly usher in a series of powerful storms across Northern Europe. Luckily, meteorologists are nearly certain that system will dissipate, so the region should have clear weather.

Illegal Negation

13. Residential rooftop solar energy users in Arizona and Florida report yearly savings of over $2,000, on their utility bills. So, homeowners all across the country can do the right thing for the environment and save lots of money at the same time.

Comparison Flaw

14. The recent economic recovery has lasted well over five years, and the economy always fluctuates over time. However, unemployment is at a record low, interest rates are at historic lows, and the stock market has hit a record high. This combination is unprecedented in the last 100 years. Thus, there is no reason to believe that such conditions cannot persist for another five years.

Self-Contradiction

15. Football, a notoriously violent sport, has recently seen a decline in viewership, while basketball, which has penalties for almost all physical contact, is seeing unprecedented high levels of viewership. It's clear that the desire to watch a less violent sport is driving the shift in viewer preferences.

Causation Flaw

16. Georgia needs to drop a package off at the post office today before it closes. Since the post office closes at 5pm, Georgia will be sure to arrive at the post office before that time.

Opinion vs. Fact

17. The Debson is the instrument of choice for all the best-selling country artists. That particular guitar must create a great sound that results in hit songs.

Causation Flaw

18. Mayor: Restoring community morale in the wake of last year's natural disasters is my highest priority. Therefore, I will focus my efforts on passing this bill that reduces property taxes.

Term Shift

19. Anybody who seeks true enlightenment is destined to fall short of that goal. Thus, those who routinely fall short of their goals should take heart, as that is a sure path to true enlightenment.

Illegal Reversal

20. Whenever Tom and Bob train for marathons together, they both individually run faster times than when they train independently. Thus, Bob must be a great motivator.

False Choice

21. The exquisite weight balance of the SureShot2000 helps any golfer maintain a proper stance through the drive and follow-through. As a result, any golfer using the SureShot2000 is far more likely to strike the ball at the optimal angle.

Term Shift

22. Darveston makes far superior touring motorcycles than Satsumi. So, even though Satsumi is known for its off-road dirt bikes, Darveston's announced entry into the dirt-bike market will likely overtake Satsumi's as top sellers.

    Comparison Flaw

23. A fully functional democracy is dependent upon a voting populace informed on the important issues of the day. Therefore, it is vital to the health of our democracy that funding for K–12 education be dramatically increased.

    Term Shift

24. My neighbor claims that the color scheme I used to paint the exterior of my house violates the restrictions imposed by our homeowners' association. However, his bland taste in home decor means that no one should take any of his criticisms seriously.

    Ad Hominem

25. Harmony takes all her friends for granted. After all, she doesn't have a single friend that she doesn't take for granted.

    Circular Reasoning

Drill 86: Assumption Family Portrait

Instructions: All the questions in the Assumption Family have something in common: the correct answer deals with the gap in the argument—aka the assumption. For each of the following arguments, write out the assumption, then prephrase an answer for each question type in the Assumption Family. Don't worry if there's overlap between your answers—that's why we call it the Assumption *Family*. The tasks therein are a lot more similar than they may at first appear.

Argument 1

The school board's proposed 5% reduction in the after-school care budget has been widely criticized by members of the parent-teacher association. But what these critics fail to understand is the resiliency of the after-school care program. Only two years ago, the program withstood a 7% budget reduction, and it continues to offer quality care at no cost to qualifying families. Thus, the critics are mistaken when they claim the program might fold under the new budget.

The argument assumes:

1. Sufficient Assumption: _____

2. Necessary Assumption: _____

3. ID the Flaw Objection: _____

4. Strengthen: _____

5. Weaken: _____

6. Principle Support: _____

Argument 2

The recent immigration of just three Arctic foxes into Sweden from a healthy population of the species in Norway has reduced inbreeding by over 40% in the Swedish population, which biologists assumed would go extinct. Thus, those three Norwegian foxes paying a visit to their Swedish neighbors have saved that imperiled population.

The argument assumes:

7. Sufficient Assumption: _____

8. Necessary Assumption: _____

9. ID the Flaw Objection: _____

10. Strengthen: _____

11. Weaken: _____

12. Principle Support: _____

Argument 3

Modern dishwashing machines, on average, use 0.5 liters less water to wash a load of dishes compared to a person washing that same load of dishes by hand, if the person is being highly conscientious about water use. The differential rises to 2 liters for more typical hand-washing of dishes, during which most people leave the faucet running throughout the process. Clearly, in the face of our current severe drought conditions, Westerly Water District should move forward immediately with plans to offer $200 rebates to any low- and middle-income households that install a dishwasher, as the District was recently granted the authority to do.

The argument assumes:

13. Sufficient Assumption: _____

14. Necessary Assumption: _____

15. ID the Flaw Objection: _____

16. Strengthen: _____

17. Weaken: _____

18. Principle Support: _____

Argument 4

On the 3rd, 7th, 12th, 19th, and 30th of last month, dramatic solar flare activity was recorded by scientists at the National Aeronautics and Space Administration. On each of those days, the Federal Aviation Administration received multiple reports of communication failures between planes and air traffic controllers. Since the solar flares are predicted to continue into this month, travelers should anticipate the possibility of communication failures on their flights.

The argument assumes:

19. Sufficient Assumption: _____

20. Necessary Assumption: _____

21. ID the Flaw Objection: _____

22. Strengthen: _____

23. Weaken: _____

24. Principle Support: _____

Argument 5

Many legal theorists claim that the context of an action supersedes the substance of the action. Such a principle is impractical in our legal system, for the context of an action is far more subjective than the substance of an action.

The argument assumes:

25. Sufficient Assumption: _____

26. Necessary Assumption: _____

27. ID the Flaw Objection: _____

28. Strengthen: _____

29. Weaken: _____

30. Principle Support: _____

Argument 6

Commuter: To determine the most efficient way to get to work, I conducted an experiment. On one Friday I took the train, on another I took the tunnel, on another I took the bus, and on the last I took the bridge. The Friday I took the tunnel was the quickest of my Friday commutes; therefore, I should take the tunnel every day if I want to have the quickest commute to work.

The argument assumes:

31. Sufficient Assumption: _____

32. Necessary Assumption: _____

33. ID the Flaw Objection: _____

34. Strengthen: _____

35. Weaken: _____

36. Principle Support: _____

Argument 7

The Canada lynx, *Felix canadensis*, is wholly dependent upon one prey—the snowshoe hare—for its survival. Graphs of lynx and hare populations show cyclical ups and downs that mirror each other, but there is a time lag. As hare populations increase, lynx populations will subsequently increase in response to more available food. But the large numbers of lynx will soon drive down the hare population, which presages lynx die-offs from lack of food. Relieved of predation pressure, the nearly-depleted hare population rebounds, and the cycle starts anew. Thus, only the lynx's own hunting prowess can bring about this magnificent feline's demise, if it were ever successful in catching every last hare.

The argument assumes:

37. Sufficient Assumption: _____

38. Necessary Assumption: _____

39. ID the Flaw Objection: _____

40. Strengthen: _____

41. Weaken: _____

42. Principle Support: _____

Argument 8

The new web drama Isle of the Conquerors is a harbinger of the future of entertainment. Its weekly episodes will immediately provide the content for downloaded updates to a companion video game. Since the video game is certain to be popular with young viewers, they will be drawn to watch new episodes each week, rather than waiting to binge-watch at the end of the season, as most young viewers now prefer. As a result, the cross-generational cultural experience of a hit television show will be reborn.

The argument assumes:

43. Sufficient Assumption: _____

44. Necessary Assumption: _____

45. ID the Flaw Objection: _____

46. Strengthen: _____

47. Weaken: _____

48. Principle Support: _____

Argument 9

Toy company executive: Typically, the greater the complexity of a board game, the less suitable that game will be for entertainment at a party. So, complex board games based on hit sci-fi series are unlikely to sell well.

The argument assumes:

49. Sufficient Assumption: _____

50. Necessary Assumption: _____

51. ID the Flaw Objection: _____

52. Strengthen: _____

53. Weaken: _____

54. Principle Support: _____

Argument 10

Transparency in the decision-making process increases public confidence in the fairness of administrative agency adjudications and regulations. New procedures dictate that agencies in this county publish on the Internet responses to all public comments on proposed agency decisions. As a result, it can be expected that future decisions of the zoning board, which is subject to the new procedural rules, will be more popular with the public.

The argument assumes:

55. Sufficient Assumption: _____

56. Necessary Assumption: _____

57. ID the Flaw Objection: _____

58. Strengthen: _____

59. Weaken: _____

60. Principle Support: _____

Answers

Note: Your answers will be different than ours—that's OK! Check to see if they perform the same function, and if they don't, try to rethink your answers to come up with ones that do.

The argument assumes: Since the program was able to withstand a similar reduction in the past, it will be able to withstand this reduction.

1. Sufficient Assumption: Any program that can withstand a 7% budget reduction can withstand a subsequent 5% reduction.

2. Necessary Assumption: The after-school care program's previous 7% budget reduction did not leave the program without the ability to withstand a further reduction in its budget down the road.

3. ID the Flaw Objection: The cumulative effects of the budget reductions may be more than the program can withstand.

4. Strengthen: The after-school care program's budget as of three years ago far exceeded the spending of the program.

5. Weaken: An in-depth study of the program's budget after the 5% reduction showed that there was only another 1 to 2% that could possibly be cut from the budget without risking the entire program.

6. Principle Support: Programs that have found a way to cope with previous budget reductions will always find ways to deal with single-digit future reductions.

The argument assumes: Reduced inbreeding will save the population.

7. Sufficient Assumption: Inbreeding is the only threat to the population, and a 40% reduction eliminates it.

8. Necessary Assumption: A reduction in inbreeding improves the chance of survival of the population.

9. ID the Flaw Objection: There may be other threats to the survival of the species.

10. Strengthen: The Swedish Arctic fox's population is no longer imperiled by hunting. *(This answer strengthens by eliminating a potential objection.)*

11. Weaken: The Swedish Arctic fox population is threatened by the warming of its habitat.

12. Principle Support: The elimination of inbreeding guarantees the conservation of a species.

The argument assumes: The conditions described warrant proceeding with the recommendation (to offer the rebates for dishwashers).

13. Sufficient Assumption: Westerly Water District should do anything within its authority to save water.

14. Necessary Assumption: The District has enough money to fund the rebate plan. *(Any proposal or recommendation necessarily assumes that it is feasible to carry out.)*

15. ID the Flaw Objection: $200 might be an insufficient incentive.

16. Strengthen: Dishwashers in Westerly can be purchased for under $200.

17. Weaken: The Easterly Water District recently was forced to raise its dishwasher rebate to $300 in order to increase participation in its rebate program.

18. Principle Support: It is the obligation of a water district to do everything it can to reduce water use when facing a severe drought.

The argument assumes: The communication failures are caused by solar flare activity.

19. Sufficient Assumption: Solar flares are the only possible cause of the observed communication failures.

20. Necessary Assumption: It is possible that solar flares interfere with the communication between airplanes and air traffic controllers.

21. ID the Flaw Objection: Multiple reports of communication failures between planes and air traffic controllers are received daily, regardless of solar flare activity.

22. Strengthen: Communication failures between planes and air traffic controllers are uncommon in the absence of solar flares.

23. Weaken: The communication equipment in airplanes is designed to prevent environmental effects such as solar flares from interfering with the planes' ability to communicate with air traffic controllers.

24. Principle Support: Any failure in the normal functioning of an airplane is likely due to solar flares.

The argument assumes: Reliance on something more subjective is impractical in the legal system.

25. Sufficient Assumption: In order for a criterion to be practical in the legal system, it must be the least subjective of the available criteria.

26. Necessary Assumption: The subjectivity of a criterion is relevant to its practicality in the legal system.

27. ID the Flaw Objection: Just because one criterion is more subjective than another doesn't mean it is too subjective to be practical. *(This points out the Relative vs. Absolute flaw: confusing something relative—"more subjective"—for something absolute—"too subjective.")*

28. Strengthen: The functioning of the legal system across many levels depends upon adherence to objective standards.

29. Weaken: Equity and fairness, both of which are highly subjective, are at the foundation of our legal system.

30. Principle Support: The more subjective a criterion is, the less practical it is.

The argument assumes: The commute times for the different methods of transportation on those four Fridays are representative of the average commute times for each method of transportation in general.

31. Sufficient Assumption: The typical commute time for each method of transportation on all days of the week was accurately measured by the experiment on the four Fridays.

32. Necessary Assumption: Traffic and travel times were not very different on the four Fridays of the experiment than they are on Fridays in general.

33. ID the Flaw Objection: Fridays might not be representative of other days. *(Sampling Flaw)*

34. Strengthen: Mass transit use in the region is relatively consistent on all weekdays.

35. Weaken: A large employer in the region has its employees on a four-day workweek, Monday to Thursday.

36. Principle Support: One should always determine the most efficient way to achieve a task based on your most recent experience completing that task.

The argument assumes: Nothing else besides loss of its snowshoe hare prey could cause the extinction of the lynx.

37. Sufficient Assumption: Nothing else could cause the extinction of the Canada lynx besides loss of food supply.

38. Necessary Assumption: The Canada lynx is not at risk of extinction from loss of habitat.

39. ID the Flaw Objection: Other factors could result in the extinction of the lynx.

40. Strengthen: The Canada lynx population is not being threatened by poaching.

41. Weaken: The habitat of the Canada lynx is being threatened by logging.

42. Principle Support: A predator's total dependence on a single prey species makes extinction of that prey the only threat to the predator's existence.

The argument assumes: The show will be popular with other generations as well.

43. Sufficient Assumption: Any show that is popular with young viewers is guaranteed to be popular across generations.

44. Necessary Assumption: It is possible for a current television show to be a hit across generations.

45. ID the Flaw Objection: The show might not be a hit with other generations.

46. Strengthen: Older television viewers have increasingly migrated from broadcast television to web-streaming services, but many have maintained the habit of watching one episode of a show per week.

5

47. Weaken: Older generations in recent years have taken to binge-watching even more than younger viewers, as streaming services provide access to classic shows.

48. Principle Support: Other generations typically adopt the habits of the younger generation in matters of viewing habits.

The argument assumes: In order to sell well, board games must be suitable for entertainment at parties.

49. Sufficient Assumption: Only games suitable for entertainment at parties are capable of selling well.

50. Necessary Assumption: There is a threshold of complexity beyond which a game will not sell well.

51. ID the Flaw Objection: A game doesn't have to be suitable for party entertainment to sell well.

52. Strengthen: With the increasing popularity of electronic games with children, the board game market has shifted to adults seeking entertainment for large gatherings.

53. Weaken: As their overall popularity has decreased in recent decades, underlying trends in the board-game market have become increasingly short-lived.

54. Principle Support: Sales of entertainment items tend to be proportional to their suitability for large gatherings.

The argument assumes: Public confidence in fairness will translate into popularity.

55. Sufficient Assumption: Perceived fairness in zoning decisions inexorably increases public approval.

56. Necessary Assumption: The perception of fairness is a factor in determining the popularity of decisions.

57. ID the Flaw Objection: A process perceived as fair could nonetheless result in decisions that the public doesn't like.

58. Strengthen: Decisions of the zoning board do not directly affect the vast majority of the public. *(This eliminates a potential objection— that how decisions affect people will override how fair they feel the decisions to have been.)*

59. Weaken: The zoning board is charged with making decisions that, however fairly they are made, will negatively impact the majority of the public.

60. Principle Support: Perceptions regarding the decision-making process of governmental bodies tend to outweigh other factors in public judgments of those bodies' actions.

Drill 87: Negation Nation

Instructions: Necessary Assumption answer choices have a tried-and-true method of evaluation: the negation technique. The correct answer, when negated, will destroy the argument. The incorrect answers, when negated, will not. That is, as long as you negate everything properly! Improper negations—those that go too far in the opposite direction or that fail to actually contradict the original statement—will throw a wrench in the process and could lead you to pick an incorrect answer. To ensure that doesn't happen, use this drill to hone your statement negation skills.

To negate a statement with a quantifier word (e.g., all, none, some, most), change the quantifier to the bare minimum that will make the original untrue. That means, for example, that "all" should become "not all" rather than "none." If there is no quantifier to negate, negate the sentence's main verb. If the statement is conditional, negate it by stating that the sufficient condition might not guarantee the necessary condition.

Negate each of the following statements in the space provided.

1. The sales team is unlikely to meet its quota by the end of this month, regardless of the new incentives being offered.

2. The decrease in price is not due to the use of lower quality materials.

3. At least some of the advertisements in the magazine are for nutritional supplements.

4. Students who want to attend the ceremony must submit a request for tickets.

5. Sharks are more likely to attack a solitary individual than a group of swimmers.

6. The recycling machine will not accept the bottle if the label is removed.

7. Over the last twenty years, the theater group has performed every operetta by Gilbert and Sullivan.

8. The author's longest novels have too many characters.

9. A faster processor is not the primary reason people purchase new computers.

10. Watermelon, which is only available during the summer, is the store's most popular flavor of sherbet.

11. Most of the city's apartment buildings have an elevator.

12. The art museum will have to close unless it can increase attendance.

13. Each of the animals at the ecology center was found injured in the wild.

14. The esteemed scientist, who is well-known for giving lengthy speeches, is not a good choice for tonight's lecture.

15. There will be some patients who experience severe side effects from the new medication.

16. The plates on the top shelf are the most expensive.

17. The tournament is always won by a professional player.

18. A cactus grown indoors is no more likely to thrive than a cactus grown outdoors.

19. It's very difficult to cut one's sugar intake in half.

20. The bank will charge a fee when you use a debit card from another bank.

21. There is no reason for history students to purchase the new version of the textbook.

22. Dendrochronology, a scientific method that analyzes tree rings, is useful for dating ancient wooden artifacts.

23. Customers usually purchase items that are not on their shopping lists.

24. Baroque composers, unlike romantic composers, did not include written cadenzas in their works.

25. Anyone attending the conference is eligible for a discounted rate at the hotel.

26. High cholesterol levels do not increase the risk of coronary heart disease.

27. Due to budgetary pressure, the executive cannot hire a new assistant.

28. Luggage without wheels must be carried through the entrance.

29. The time spent maintaining the machine is not significantly greater than the time saved by using it.

30. Some of the coins in the collection are not in mint condition.

31. In addition to being aesthetically appealing, a blue shade of paint can have a calming effect on people.

32. Each customer orders at least one appetizer and at least one dessert.

33. There are no devices that are more effective at reducing coughing.

34. The belief that people have free will is inconsistent with the philosopher's writings.

35. There is no convincing evidence that sauropods swam.

36. The taller an office building is, the greater the number of offices there are in the building.

37. None of the movies being shown at the multiplex this weekend are horror movies.

38. The vegetables at the farm stand, as well as the fruit sold there, are sold by weight, not quantity.

39. Baking a moist cake requires neither milk nor eggs.

40. The decrease in ticket sales was greater this year than in any of the previous five years.

5

Answers

Note: Your answers may differ slightly from ours. That's OK, as long as they serve the same function.

1. The sales team is unlikely to meet its quota by the end of this month, regardless of the new incentives being offered.

   The sales team will likely meet its quota by the end of this month.

The dependent clause about incentives is irrelevant (as suggested by the word "regardless") and need not be negated.

2. The decrease in price is not due to the use of lower quality materials.

   The decrease in price is due to the use of lower quality materials.

It's tempting to negate easily negated words such as "decrease" and "lower quality." However, focus on the main verb ("is due to"). The price did decrease, and that can't be negated. What can be negated is whether or not lower quality materials were the cause of that decrease.

3. At least some of the advertisements in the magazine are for nutritional supplements.

   None of the advertisements in the magazine are for nutritional supplements.

When a statement has a quantifier (e.g., "some"), negate the quantifier. Don't negate "some are" to "some aren't."

4. Students who want to attend the ceremony must submit a request for tickets.

   Students who want to attend the ceremony do not have to submit a request for tickets.

The word "must" indicates an absolute necessity. That is negated by suggesting the supposed requirement is not, in fact, necessary.

5. Sharks are more likely to attack a solitary individual than a group of swimmers.

   Sharks are not more likely to attack a solitary individual than a group of swimmers.

If something is said to be "more likely," negate that by saying it's *not* more likely. Don't say it's absolutely less likely. It may be equally likely, just not more.

6. The recycling machine will not accept the bottle if the label is removed.

   The recycling machine may accept the bottle, even if the label is removed.

When a statement provides a condition that would produce a certain result, do not negate the condition itself. Negate the result that would follow from that condition.

7. Over the last twenty years, the theater group has performed every operetta by Gilbert and Sullivan.

   The theater group has not performed every operetta by Gilbert and Sullivan over the last twenty years OR There is at least one operetta by Gilbert and Sullivan that the theater group has not performed over the last twenty years.

"Every" is a quantifier that indicates totality. You can simply negate the quantifier (*not every*) or establish an exceptional case (*there is one that was not*).

8. The author's longest novels have too many characters.

   The author's longest novels do not have too many characters.

The statement is only about the longest novels, so don't negate "longest" to "shortest." Instead, negate the main verb, "have," to "do not have." And don't negate too much. If there are not too many characters, that doesn't mean there are too few. There may be just the right number.

9. A faster processor is not the primary reason people purchase new computers.

   A faster processor is the primary reason people purchase new computers.

Look to negate the main verb of a sentence (e.g., "is not") instead of adjectives (e.g., "faster").

10. Watermelon, which is only available during the summer, is the store's most popular flavor of sherbet.

    Watermelon is not the store's most popular flavor of sherbet.

The statement "which is only available during the summer" is a dependent clause—it cannot stand alone as a sentence. Don't negate that part. Stick to the main, independent clause: "Watermelon is the store's most popular flavor of sherbet."

11. Most of the city's apartment buildings have an elevator.

    At least half of the city's apartment buildings do not have an elevator OR No more than half of the city's apartment buildings have an elevator.

The word "most" means more than half. To negate a statement with "most," you can negate the quantity to 50% or less (*No more than half…*), or you can show that at least 50% do not have the stated quality (*At least half … do not have an elevator*). Unlike with other quantitative words such as "some" or "all," you could also just negate the quality (*Most … do not have an elevator*). This technically omits the possibility of exactly half-and-half, which would also negate the statement. However, for the negation technique, it should be sufficient to indicate whether the answer choice is necessary or not.

12. The art museum will have to close unless it can increase attendance.

    The art museum might not have to close even if it can't increase attendance OR The art museum does not have to increase attendance to stay open.

This statement claims that increased attendance is necessary to keep the art museum open. When a condition is claimed as necessary to produce a result, negate that by showing the condition is not, in fact, necessary (*The museum does not have to increase attendance*).

13. Each of the animals at the ecology center was found injured in the wild.

    Not every animal at the ecology center was found injured in the wild OR At least one of the animals at the ecology center was not found injured in the wild.

The word "each" is an absolute quantifier. To negate such a claim, negate the quantifier (*Not each was injured*) or find at least one exceptional case (*At least one was not injured*).

14. The esteemed scientist, who is well-known for giving lengthy speeches, is not a good choice for tonight's lecture.

    The esteemed scientist is a good choice for tonight's lecture.

Stick to the primary, independent clause. The dependent clause, "who is well-known for giving lengthy speeches," is not necessary to the statement and need not be negated.

15. There will be some patients who experience severe side effects from the new medication.

    No patients will experience severe side effects from the new medication.

The word "some" is a quantifier representing any possible number. The only possible negation is for there to be "no" result that fits the given criterion.

16. The plates on the top shelf are the most expensive.

    The plates on the top shelf are not the most expensive.

Don't negate too much. If they're not the most expensive, they don't have to be the least.

17. The tournament is always won by a professional player.

    The tournament is not always won by a professional player OR At least one non-professional has won the tournament.

Always is an absolute quantifier, allowing for no exceptions. So, negate it by taking away the absolute (*The winner is not always a pro*) or declaring a possible exception (*At least one non-professional has won*).

18. A cactus grown indoors is no more likely to thrive than a cactus grown outdoors.

    A cactus grown indoors is more likely to thrive than a cactus grown outdoors.

The statement is about whether one event is more likely than another, so that's what needs to be negated.

19. It's very difficult to cut one's sugar intake in half.

    It's not very difficult to cut one's sugar intake in half.

Avoid the temptation to negate "difficult" to "easy." "Easy" is the polar opposite, not the bare minimum required to make the original untrue.

20. The bank will charge a fee when you use a debit card from another bank.

    The bank might not charge a fee when you use a debit card from another bank.

The word "when" indicates a conditional statement. Negate by showing that the sufficient condition might not lead to the necessary result.

21. There is no reason for history students to purchase the new version of the textbook.

    There is at least one reason why history students should purchase the new version of the textbook.

If it's claimed that no reason exists whatsoever to do something, then even one reason is enough to negate that belief.

22. Dendrochronology, a scientific method that analyzes tree rings, is useful for dating ancient wooden artifacts.

    Dendrochronology is not useful for dating ancient wooden artifacts.

The phrase "a scientific method that analyzes tree rings" defines the scientific term dendrochronology and should not be negated. Instead, negate whether that method is useful.

23. Customers usually purchase items that are not on their shopping lists.

    Customers do not usually purchase items that are not on their shopping lists OR *Customers usually purchase only items that are on their shopping lists.*

When something is said to be "usually" true, negate that by saying it's not usually the case (*Customers don't usually deviate from their list*) or by saying the alternative is actually more common (*Customers usually stick to their list*).

24. Baroque composers, unlike romantic composers, did not include written cadenzas in their works.

    Baroque composers did include written cadenzas in their works.

The main verb in this statement is "did not include." "Unlike romantic composers" is a dependent clause that can be left out of the negation.

25. Anyone attending the conference is eligible for a discounted rate at the hotel.

    Not everyone attending the conference is eligible for a discounted rate at the hotel OR *At least one conference attendee is not eligible for a discounted rate at the hotel.*

The word "anyone" is an absolute quantifier. Negate that by negating the qualifier (*Not anyone ...*) or by declaring an exception (*At least one person is not ...*).

26. High cholesterol levels do not increase the risk of coronary heart disease.

    High cholesterol levels do increase the risk of coronary heart disease.

Do not negate "high" to "low." High cholesterol levels is the subject. Negate the verb "do not increase" to "do increase."

27. Due to budgetary pressure, the executive cannot hire a new assistant.

    The executive can hire a new assistant.

The phrase about budgetary pressure is presented as reasoning to support the primary claim and should not be negated. Instead, negate the main point.

5

28. Luggage without wheels must be carried through the entrance.

    Luggage without wheels does not have to be carried through the entrance.

When a "must" is negated, it does not get negated to "must not." It gets negated to "does not have to" or "could not."

29. The time spent maintaining the machine is not significantly greater than the time saved by using it.

    The time spent maintaining the machine is significantly greater than the time saved by using it.

When the phrase "is not" is used, that's usually the part that should be negated, regardless of the wordiness that surrounds it.

30. Some of the coins in the collection are not in mint condition.

    All of the coins in the collection are in mint condition.

"Some" is a quantifier that indicates any number of items, and is typically negated to "none." In this case, that leads to a double negative (*None* of the coins are *not* in mint condition), which can be more clearly expressed in positive language (*All* of the coins *are* in mint condition).

31. In addition to being aesthetically appealing, a blue shade of paint can have a calming effect on people.

    A blue shade of paint can not have a calming effect on people.

The phrase about being aesthetically appealing is a modifying phrase and should not be negated.

32. Each customer orders at least one appetizer and at least one dessert.

    At least one customer does not order both an appetizer and a dessert OR At least one customer orders no appetizer, no dessert, or neither.

"Each" is an absolute quantifier, so even one exception will negate the statement. And when negating a statement with "and," the negation is not necessarily "neither." If even one thing is rejected (*no appetizer* or *no dessert*), then the statement is negated.

33. There are no devices that are more effective at reducing coughing.

    There is at least one device that is more effective at reducing coughing.

The word "no" is very strong and suggests no exceptions. A single exception negates it.

34. The belief that people have free will is inconsistent with the philosopher's writings.

    The belief that people have free will is not inconsistent (i.e., is consistent) with the philosopher's writings.

Do not negate the belief. The claim is about whether that belief is consistent with the writings.

35. There is no convincing evidence that sauropods swam.

    There is convincing evidence that sauropods swam.

Don't negate whether these dinosaurs swam. Just negate whether or not there's convincing evidence.

36. The taller an office building is, the greater the number of offices there are in the building.

    A taller office building does not necessarily have more offices than a shorter office building.

When a direct relationship is presented, negate it by showing that the relationship does not have to be direct. Do not just say the inverse is true (*The taller an office building is, the fewer number of offices there are*). That would be the polar opposite, not the logical negation.

37. None of the movies being shown at the multiplex this weekend are horror movies.

    At least one of the movies being shown at the multiplex this weekend is a horror movie.

A single counterexample negates "none." Don't go to the extreme and suggest *all* movies that weekend are horror movies.

38. The vegetables at the farm stand, as well as the fruit sold there, are sold by weight, not quantity.

    The vegetables and the fruit at the farm stand are sold by quantity, not weight.

When one thing is selected over another (i.e., weight over quantity), the negation will usually favor the reverse situation (i.e., quantity over weight).

5

39. Baking a moist cake requires neither milk nor eggs.

   Baking a moist cake requires either milk or eggs.

The phrase "neither … nor" is negated by changing it to "either … or."

40. The decrease in ticket sales was greater this year than in any of the previous five years.

   The decrease in ticket sales was not greater this year than any of the previous five years. OR *At least one of the previous five years saw ticket sales decrease as much or more than they did this year.*

Do not negate "decrease." That happened and cannot be negated. The claim is that this year's decrease was the greatest, so the negation should show that it wasn't the greatest or that at least one other year's decrease was equal to or greater than this year.

Drill 88: Flaws – Answer Choice Lead-Ins

Instructions: ID the Flaw answer choices that don't directly describe a common flaw tend to follow one of two patterns: they point out an assumption, or they point out an objection. In order to evaluate the answer choice's content, you need to know which of the two patterns it's following, and that requires careful attention to language. Use this drill to master the tricky phrasing patterns of ID the Flaw answer choices.

For each of the following answer choices, first write in whether it's phrased as an assumption (A) or an objection (O), and then *flip* that answer by rewriting it to be phrased in the opposite way.

_____ 1. The argument fails to consider that some predators use smell as their primary sense while hunting.

_____ 2. The argument takes for granted that the popularity of a concerto is evidence of its musical quality.

_____ 3. The argument presumes, without providing justification, that the methods used by the scientist are the only methods capable of producing accurate results.

_____ 4. The argument fails to take into account the possibility that at least some of the environmental cleanup efforts were performed by the same crew.

_____ 5. The argument overlooks the possibility that many readers disagree with Jordan's criticisms of Cole's novel.

_____ 6. The argument takes for granted that the method used by the pollsters for gathering data was reliable.

_____ 7. The argument fails to consider the possibility that salamanders and humans share a common ancestor.

_____ 8. The argument ignores the possibility that the gymnasium will be built in spite of opposition from the general public.

_____ 9. The argument fails to justify its presumption that profits from the company's hardware division were higher than profits from its software division.

_____ 10. The argument presumes, without providing justification, that the new radio program has at least some educational value.

_____ 11. The argument fails to consider that the total number of students at the university who follow its tennis team may be greater than the total number of students at the university who follow its rugby team.

_____ 12. The argument takes for granted that the ordinance is unpopular with the majority of citizens just because it is unpopular with a majority of city council members.

_____ 13. The argument overlooks the possibility that seismologists can estimate the magnitude of an earthquake without using a seismograph.

_____ 14. The argument presumes without warrant that people never feel comfortable approaching a police officer.

_____ 15. The argument presumes, without providing justification, that the government is at least partially responsible for the success in rehabilitating the valley's ecosystem.

_____ 16. The argument fails to take into account that some technicians may have successfully created computers capable of processing sensory images

_____ 17. The argument takes for granted that the effectiveness of a command is always directly proportional to the number of times the command is issued.

_____ 18. The argument ignores the possibility that a city-state can be neither thriving nor in decline.

_____ 19. The argument assumes that people who do not eat veal do so because they dislike the flavor of veal.

_____ 20. The argument fails to justify its presumption that a majority of voters in Malden will vote for a candidate who favors developing the city center.

_____ 21. The argument presumes without warrant that a novel must address social injustices to be considered socially relevant.

_____ 22. The argument ignores the possibility that the company closed the warehouse for reasons other than safety concerns.

_____ 23. The argument fails to establish that at least some patients will stay in the hospital long enough for an ulcer to develop.

_____ 24. The argument fails to take into account the possibility that the birds in the sanctuary are not natural predators of the short-horned grasshopper.

_____ 25. The argument provides no justification for the presumption that history students prefer newspaper stories covering serious political issues.

_____ 26. The argument assumes that the penalty imposed on the company will motivate the company to alter its unethical practices.

_____ 27. The argument ignores the possibility that the modern humans whose DNA partially resembles the DNA of _Australopithecus_ may have inherited the similar DNA from ancestors other than _Australopithecus_.

_____ 28. The argument does not consider that actions intended to cause harm are not necessarily morally reprehensible.

_____ 29. The argument fails to address the possibility that criticism can be intended not to hurt, but to help, the recipient of the criticism.

_____ 30. The argument fails to justify its presupposition that fresh fruits and vegetables are more nutritious than frozen fruits and vegetables.

_____ 31. The argument presumes that what is true of the country's population as a whole is also true of each citizen of the country.

_____ 32. The argument presumes, without providing justification, that at least some substances in cheese are capable of causing increases in blood pressure when consumed in typical quantities.

_____ 33. The argument fails to consider that the majority of teachers have master's degrees.

_____ 34. The argument fails to establish that the students at the university lack the initiative necessary to solve socioeconomic problems.

_____ 35. The argument fails to take into account the possibility that people are more likely to notice other cars on the road that are the same make and model as their own.

_____ 36. The argument presumes, without providing justification, that hares are capable of moving faster than their predators.

_____ 37. The argument provides no justification for its presumption that the parrots' squawking was a response to the threatening behavior of their handlers.

_____ 38. The argument does not consider the possibility that the instructors who indicated that they had very positive attitudes toward their students' work were misrepresenting their true feelings about their students' work.

_____ 39. The argument overlooks the possibility that none of the residents owned any pets even before the landlord's prohibition was enacted.

_____ 40. The argument fails to establish that imitating the behavior of other people promotes harmony with other people.

5

Answers

___O___ 1. The argument fails to consider that some predators use smell as their primary sense while hunting.

The argument assumes that no predators use smell as their primary sense while hunting.

___A___ 2. The argument takes for granted that the popularity of a concerto is evidence of its musical quality.

The argument fails to consider that a concerto can be popular without being of high musical quality.

___A___ 3. The argument presumes, without providing justification, that the methods used by the scientist are the only methods capable of producing accurate results.

The argument fails to consider that methods other than the scientist's might also produce accurate results.

___O___ 4. The argument fails to take into account the possibility that at least some of the environmental cleanup projects were completed by the same crew.

The argument assumes that each of the environmental cleanup projects was completed by a different crew.

___O___ 5. The argument overlooks the possibility that many readers disagree with Jordan's criticisms of Cole's novel.

The argument assumes that few readers disagree with Jordan's criticisms of Cole's novel.

___A___ 6. The argument takes for granted that the method used by the pollsters for gathering data was reliable.

The argument overlooks the possibility that the method used by the pollsters for gathering data was not reliable.

___O___ 7. The argument fails to consider the possibility that salamanders and humans share a common ancestor.

The argument assumes that salamanders and humans do not share a common ancestor.

___O___ 8. The argument ignores the possibility that the gymnasium will be built in spite of opposition from the general public.

The argument assumes that the gymnasium will not be built if the general public opposes it.

___A___ 9. The argument fails to justify its presumption that profits from the company's hardware division were higher than profits from its software division.

The argument overlooks the possibility that profits from the company's hardware division were equal to or lower than profits from its software division.

___A___ 10. The argument presumes, without providing justification, that the new radio program has at least some educational value.

The argument fails to consider the possibility that the new radio program has no educational value.

___O___ 11. The argument fails to consider that the total number of students at the university who follow its tennis team may be greater than the total number of students at the university who follow its rugby team.

The argument assumes that the total number of students at the university who follow its tennis team is equal to or less than the total number of students at the university who follow its rugby team.

5

___A___ 12. The argument takes for granted that the ordinance is unpopular with the majority of citizens just because it is unpopular with a majority of city council members.

The argument overlooks the possibility that the ordinance is popular with a majority of citizens even though it is unpopular with a majority of city council members.

___O___ 13. The argument overlooks the possibility that seismologists can estimate the magnitude of an earthquake without using a seismograph.

The argument assumes that seismologists can estimate the magnitude of an earthquake only by using a seismograph.

___A___ 14. The argument presumes without warrant that people never feel comfortable approaching a police officer.

The argument fails to consider that people may sometimes feel comfortable approaching a police officer.

___A___ 15. The argument presumes, without providing justification, that the government is at least partially responsible for the success in rehabilitating the valley's ecosystem.

The argument overlooks the possibility that the success in rehabilitating the valley's ecosystem has been achieved without any help from the government.

___O___ 16. The argument fails to take into account that some technicians may have successfully created computers capable of processing sensory images.

The argument assumes that no technicians have ever successfully created computers capable of processing sensory images.

___A___ 17. The argument takes for granted that the effectiveness of a command is always directly proportional to the number of times the command is issued.

The argument overlooks the possibility that the effectiveness of a command may be inversely proportional, or even unrelated, to the number of times the command is issued.

___O___ 18. The argument ignores the possibility that a city-state can be neither thriving nor in decline.

The argument assumes that a city-state must either be thriving or in decline.

___A___ 19. The argument assumes that people who do not eat veal do so because they dislike the flavor of veal.

The argument overlooks the possibility that people who do not eat veal do so for reasons other than flavor (e.g., ethical reasons).

___A___ 20. The argument fails to justify its presumption that a majority of voters in Malden will vote for a candidate who favors developing the city center.

The argument fails to consider the possibility that a majority of voters in Malden will not vote for a candidate who favors developing the city center.

___A___ 21. The argument presumes without warrant that a novel must address social injustices to be considered socially relevant.

The argument overlooks the possibility that a novel that does not address social injustices can nevertheless be considered socially relevant.

___O___ 22. The argument ignores the possibility that the company closed the warehouse for reasons other than safety concerns.

The argument assumes that the company only closed the warehouse because of safety concerns.

5

__A__ 23. The argument fails to establish that at least some patients will stay in the hospital long enough for an ulcer to develop.

The argument overlooks the possibility that no patients will stay in the hospital long enough for an ulcer to develop.

__O__ 24. The argument fails to take into account the possibility that the birds in the sanctuary are not natural predators of the short-horned grasshopper.

The argument takes for granted that the birds in the sanctuary are natural predators of the short-horned grasshopper.

__A__ 25. The argument provides no justification for the presumption that history students prefer newspaper stories covering serious political issues.

The argument fails to consider that history students may prefer newspaper stories that do not address serious political issues.

__A__ 26. The argument assumes that the penalty imposed on the company will motivate the company to alter its unethical practices.

The argument fails to consider that the company will continue its unethical practices in spite of the penalty imposed upon it.

__O__ 27. The argument ignores the possibility that the modern humans whose DNA partially resembles the DNA of *Australopithecus* may have inherited the similar DNA from ancestors other than *Australopithecus*.

The argument assumes that the modern humans whose DNA partially resembles the DNA of Australopithecus inherited the similar DNA from Australopithecus.

__O__ 28. The argument does not consider that actions intended to cause harm are not necessarily morally reprehensible.

The argument assumes that actions intended to cause harm are necessarily morally reprehensible.

__O__ 29. The argument fails to address the possibility that criticism can be intended not to hurt, but to help, the recipient of the criticism.

The argument assumes that all criticism is intended to hurt the recipient of the criticism.

__A__ 30. The argument fails to justify its presupposition that fresh fruits and vegetables are more nutritious than frozen fruits and vegetables.

The argument overlooks the possibility that frozen fruits and vegetables are as nutritious as fresh fruits and vegetables.

__A__ 31. The argument presumes that what is true of the country's population as a whole is also true of each citizen of the country.

The argument fails to consider that what is true of the country's population as a whole may not be true of each citizen of the country.

__A__ 32. The argument presumes, without providing justification, that at least some substances in cheese are capable of causing increases in blood pressure when consumed in typical quantities.

The argument overlooks the possibility that no substances in cheese are capable of causing increases in blood pressure when consumed in typical quantities.

__O__ 33. The argument fails to consider that the majority of teachers have master's degrees.

The argument assumes that no more than half of teachers have master's degrees.

__A__ 34. The argument fails to establish that the students at the university lack the initiative necessary to solve socioeconomic problems.

The argument fails to consider that students at the university have the initiative necessary to solve socioeconomic problems.

___O___ 35. The argument fails to take into account the possibility that people are more likely to notice other cars on the road that are the same make and model as their own.

The argument assumes that people are not more likely to notice other cars on the road that are the same make and model as their own.

___A___ 36. The argument presumes, without providing justification, that hares are capable of moving faster than their predators.

The argument overlooks the possibility that hares are incapable of moving faster than their predators.

___A___ 37. The argument provides no justification for its presumption that the parrots' squawking was a response to the threatening behavior of their handlers.

The argument fails to consider that the parrots' squawking was caused by something other than the threatening behavior of their handlers.

___O___ 38. The argument does not consider the possibility that the instructors who indicated that they had very positive attitudes toward their students' work were misrepresenting their true feelings about their students' work.

The argument assumes that the instructors who indicated that they had very positive attitudes toward their students' work were representing their true feelings about their students' work.

___O___ 39. The argument overlooks the possibility that none of the residents owned any pets even before the landlord's prohibition was enacted.

The argument assumes that at least some of the residents owned pets before the landlord's prohibition was enacted.

___A___ 40. The argument fails to establish that imitating the behavior of other people promotes harmony with other people.

The argument fails to consider that imitating the behavior of other people may not promote harmony with other people.

Drill 89: What Flaw Is This? Abstract Edition

Instructions: ID the Flaw questions are notorious for the abstract language of their answer choices. Not to worry: the ways that famous flaws are described in these answers is remarkably consistent from test to test. With practice, you can learn to recognize the famous flaws almost instantaneously and quickly eliminate those you know the stimulus didn't exhibit.

For this drill, match each flaw to the answer choice that describes it.

Set A

1. The argument presupposes what it sets out to establish.

2. The author assumes that a guaranteed means of achieving a result is the only means of achieving that result.

3. The argument predicts that a certain outcome will occur on the basis that a similar outcome occurred on a previous occasion.

4. The author concludes from a mere association between two phenomena that those phenomena are causally related.

5. The argument fails to recognize that expertise in one area of medicine does not imply expertise in all areas of medicine.

6. The conclusion relies on one of two outcomes being possible when in fact many outcomes are possible.

7. The argument rejects a conclusion on the grounds that it was offered by someone who is biased.

8. The physicist argues that the mathematician's conjecture is false on the basis that the mathematician has not offered adequate evidence to justify that conjecture.

9. The reasoning takes for granted that because an outcome would be disappointing to a certain group, the outcome is undesirable.

10. The argument presumes without justification that because two phenomena are alike in one respect, they are also alike in another respect.

A. Ad Hominem

B. False Choice

C. Illegal Reversal

D. Appeal to Inappropriate Authority

E. Circular Reasoning

F. Comparison Flaw

G. Unproven vs. Untrue

H. Causation Flaw

I. Unwarranted Prediction

J. Appeal to Emotion

Set B

11. The author fails to consider that a property shared by each part of something may not be shared by the thing itself.

12. The argument assumes, without providing justification, that the company's actions are in line with the dictates of its policies.

13. The argument confuses a claim about a group's proportional makeup for a claim about a group's numeric makeup.

14. The conclusion about the population as a whole relies on a sample that is unlikely to be representative of that population.

15. The argument presumes that an event which guarantees an outcome must take place in order for that outcome to occur.

16. The author argues against a position that is not equivalent to the one put forth by his opponent.

17. The argument offers a conclusion that is in direct opposition to one of its central premises.

18. The author concludes that an assertion is true on the basis that someone believes it to be true.

19. The argument trades on an ambiguity in the term "great."

20. The conclusion mistakes a set of circumstances that could bring about a certain result for a set of circumstances that will bring about that result.

A. Sampling Flaw

B. Illegal Negation

C. Term Shift

D. Opinion vs. Fact

E. Equivocation

F. Possible vs. Certain

G. Percent vs. Amount

H. Self-Contradiction

I. Part vs. Whole

J. Straw Man

5

Set C

21. The argument treats a necessary factor as though it were sufficient.

22. The conclusion takes for granted that a characteristic of a whole can be attributed to any individual member of the set.

23. The argument relies on a premise which is incompatible with its conclusion.

24. The argument improperly assumes that because a phenomenon occurred less frequently than expected during a given period, it will occur less frequently than expected in the future.

25. The argument assumes, without providing justification, that an increase in sales corresponded with a commensurate increase in profitability.

26. The scientist improperly claims that an experiment is of great importance while establishing only that is more important than a similar experiment.

27. The conclusion is merely a restatement of the premise.

28. The author questions the validity of an argument because its conclusion serves the interests of the person making it.

29. An explanation is given on the basis of data when there is reason to believe that the data was unduly influenced by its method of collection.

30. The argument takes for granted that the phenomena are similar in all ways, after establishing that they are similar in one way.

A. Term Shift

B. Self-Contradiction

C. Ad Hominem

D. Relative vs. Absolute

E. Sampling Flaw

F. Circular Reasoning

G. Part vs. Whole

H. Illegal Reversal

I. Comparison Flaw

J. Unwarranted Prediction

Set D

31. The argument treats two extremes as though there is no middle ground between them.

32. The argument takes for granted that lack of evidence for a phenomenon is sufficient to conclude that the phenomenon did not occur.

33. The conclusion relies on questionable expertise.

34. The conclusion relies on a set of circumstances being sufficient to bring about a certain result, while the premises indicate that those circumstances are only necessary to bring about that result.

35. The conclusion improperly assumes that because one event preceded another, the first event caused the second.

36. The conclusion states as factual what the premises establish as merely the scholar's viewpoint.

37. The argument presumes, without providing adequate evidence, that the occurrence of an event in the past ensures its occurrence in the future.

38. The argument takes for granted that an attribute of a group must likewise be an attribute of each member of a group individually.

39. The argument presumes what it sets out to prove.

40. The argument rests on a single explanation for a phenomenon that could have multiple explanations.

A. Opinion vs. Fact

B. Circular Reasoning

C. Causation Flaw

D. Part vs. Whole

E. Unwarranted Prediction

F. Possible vs. Certain

G. False Choice

H. Unproven vs. Untrue

I. Appeal to Inappropriate Authority

J. Illegal Reversal

5

Set E

41. The conclusion fails to consider that both incidents may have had a mutual, alternative possible cause.

42. The reasoning is based on an appeal to the views of someone with questionable authority in the matter.

43. The conclusion widens the scope of a key concept beyond the narrow application that is established by the evidence.

44. The author assumes that an outcome that will always occur in the presence of a certain factor cannot occur in the absence of that factor.

45. The argument makes an overgeneralization from a data set that is insufficient to support the breadth of the claim.

46. The argument allows the meaning of a key term to shift throughout the argument.

47. The argument presumes that if a certain outcome may occur, then it will occur.

48. The premises exclude only one alternative to the explanation given in the conclusion, when in fact many alternatives are possible.

49. The conclusion overlooks the possibility that an explanation for a phenomenon may be true, despite not being adequately justified.

50. The argument fails to justify the claim that an explanation is reasonable, offering evidence only that the explanation is more reasonable than a competing explanation.

A. Illegal Negation

B. Equivocation

C. Relative vs. Absolute

D. Sampling Flaw

E. False Choice

F. Possible vs. Certain

G. Unproven vs. Untrue

H. Appeal to Inappropriate Authority

I. Causation Flaw

J. Term Shift

Answer Key

Note: Nobody wants to look at a bunch of messy lines so, instead of connecting the answer choices to the flaws that way, we've opted to list the correct flaw directly across from the answer choice that describes it.

Set A

1. The argument presupposes what it sets out to establish.

2. The author assumes that a guaranteed means of achieving a result is the only means of achieving that result.

3. The argument predicts that a certain outcome will occur on the basis that a similar outcome occurred on a previous occasion.

4. The author concludes from a mere association between two phenomena that those phenomena are causally related.

5. The argument fails to recognize that expertise in one area of medicine does not imply expertise in all areas of medicine.

6. The conclusion relies on one of two outcomes being possible when in fact many outcomes are possible.

7. The argument rejects a conclusion on the grounds that it was offered by someone who is biased.

8. The physicist argues that the mathematician's conjecture is false on the basis that the mathematician has not offered adequate evidence to justify that conjecture.

9. The reasoning takes for granted that because an outcome would be disappointing to a certain group, the outcome is undesirable.

10. The argument presumes without justification that because two phenomena are alike in one respect, they are also alike in another respect.

E. **Circular Reasoning**

C. **Illegal Reversal**

I. **Unwarranted Prediction**

H. **Causation Flaw**

D. **Appeal to Inappropriate Authority**

B. **False Choice**

A. **Ad Hominem**

G. **Unproven vs. Untrue**

J. **Appeal to Emotion**

F. **Comparison Flaw**

5

Set B

11. The author fails to consider that a property shared by each part of something may not be shared by the thing itself.

12. The argument assumes, without providing justification, that the company's actions are in line with the dictates of its policies.

13. The argument confuses a claim about a group's proportional makeup for a claim about a group's numeric makeup.

14. The conclusion about the population as a whole relies on a sample that is unlikely to be representative of that population.

15. The argument presumes that an event which guarantees an outcome must take place in order for that outcome to occur.

16. The author argues against a position that is not equivalent to the one put forth by his opponent.

17. The argument offers a conclusion that is in direct opposition to one of its central premises.

18. The author concludes that an assertion is true on the basis that someone believes it to be true.

19. The argument trades on an ambiguity in the term "great."

20. The conclusion mistakes a set of circumstances that could bring about a certain result for a set of circumstances that will bring about that result.

I. **Part vs. Whole**

C. **Term Shift**

G. **Percent vs. Amount**

A. **Sampling Flaw**

B. **Illegal Negation**

J. **Straw Man**

H. **Self-Contradiction**

D. **Opinion vs. Fact**

E. **Equivocation**

F. **Possible vs. Certain**

Set C

21. The argument treats a necessary factor as though it were sufficient.

22. The conclusion takes for granted that a characteristic of a whole can be attributed to any individual member of the set.

23. The argument relies on a premise which is incompatible with its conclusion.

24. The argument improperly assumes that because a phenomenon occurred less frequently than expected during a given period, it will occur less frequently than expected in the future.

25. The argument assumes, without providing justification, that an increase in sales corresponded with a commensurate increase in profitability.

26. The scientist improperly claims that an experiment is of great importance while establishing only that is more important than a similar experiment.

27. The conclusion is merely a restatement of the premise.

28. The author questions the validity of an argument because its conclusion serves the interests of the person making it.

29. An explanation is given on the basis of data when there is reason to believe that the data was unduly influenced by its method of collection.

30. The argument takes for granted that the phenomena are similar in all ways, after establishing that they are similar in one way.

H. **Illegal Reversal**

G. **Part vs. Whole**

B. **Self-Contradiction**

J. **Unwarranted Prediction**

A. **Term Shift**

D. **Relative vs. Absolute**

F. **Circular Reasoning**

C. **Ad Hominem**

E. **Sampling Flaw**

I. **Comparison Flaw**

Set D

31. The argument treats two extremes as though there is no middle ground between them.

32. The argument takes for granted that lack of evidence for a phenomenon is sufficient to conclude that the phenomenon did not occur.

33. The conclusion relies on questionable expertise.

34. The conclusion relies on a set of circumstances being sufficient to bring about a certain result, while the premises indicate that those circumstances are only necessary to bring about that result.

35. The conclusion improperly assumes that because one event preceded another, the first event caused the second.

36. The conclusion states as factual what the premises establish as merely the scholar's viewpoint.

37. The argument presumes, without providing adequate evidence, that the occurrence of an event in the past ensures its occurrence in the future.

38. The argument takes for granted that an attribute of a group must likewise be an attribute of each member of a group individually.

39. The argument presumes what it sets out to prove.

40. The argument rests on a single explanation for a phenomenon that could have multiple explanations.

G. **False Choice**

H. **Unproven vs. Untrue**

I. **Appeal to Inappropriate Authority**

J. **Illegal Reversal**

C. **Causation Flaw**

A. **Opinion vs. Fact**

E. **Unwarranted Prediction**

D. **Part vs. Whole**

B. **Circular Reasoning**

F. **Possible vs. Certain**

Set E

41. The conclusion fails to consider that both incidents may have had a mutual, alternative possible cause.

42. The reasoning is based on an appeal to the views of someone with questionable authority in the matter.

43. The conclusion widens the scope of a key concept beyond the narrow application that is established by the evidence.

44. The author assumes that an outcome that will always occur in the presence of a certain factor cannot occur in the absence of that factor.

45. The argument makes an overgeneralization from a data set that is insufficient to support the breadth of the claim.

46. The argument allows the meaning of a key term to shift throughout the argument.

47. The argument presumes that if a certain outcome may occur, then it will occur.

48. The premises exclude only one alternative to the explanation given in the conclusion, when in fact many alternatives are possible.

49. The conclusion overlooks the possibility that an explanation for a phenomenon may be true, despite not being adequately justified.

50. The argument fails to justify the claim that an explanation is reasonable, offering evidence only that the explanation is more reasonable than a competing explanation.

I. **Causation Flaw**

H. **Appeal to Inappropriate Authority**

J. **Term Shift**

A. **Illegal Negation**

D. **Sampling Flaw**

B. **Equivocation**

F. **Possible vs. Certain**

E. **False Choice**

G. **Unproven vs. Untrue**

C. **Relative vs. Absolute**

5

Drill 90: What Flaw Is This? Topical Edition

Instructions: ID the Flaw questions frequently couch descriptions of famous flaws in topical language from the stimulus. For this drill, write in the famous flaw that serves as the basis for each answer choice.

1. The argument assumes that the inability of each team member to afford the entrance fee to the tournament means the team cannot afford that fee. _____

2. The argument ignores the possibility that algae blooms could occur in the absence of excess agricultural runoff. _____

3. The incumbent points out the hypocrisy of the challenger in taking large campaign donations without addressing the merits of the challenger's proposal to ban such donations. _____

4. The philosophy student purports to support the conclusion that humans are mortal solely with the equivalent premise that whatever is immortal cannot be human. _____

5. The defense attorney neglects to consider the possibility that the failure of the witness to accurately describe the gun used by the defendant does not preclude the possibility that the witness is capable of identifying the perpetrator of the crime. _____

6. Maude presumes the stock will go down in value simply because the stock analyst who advised her that it would go up in value admitted that he doesn't actually research his stock picks. _____

7. The argument overlooks the possibility that Brett's success over the past decade in games played in snow will not prevent Tom's team from prevailing tomorrow. _____

8. The company only surveyed those customers who had favorably reviewed their products in determining how to increase overall customer satisfaction. _____

9. The representative fails to distinguish the two possible interpretations of the term in concluding that there is insufficient "public interest" in the project to warrant supporting it. _____

10. The argument concludes that the decline in quarterly sales was a consequence of the new marketing strategy due to the release of the latter preceding the former by a matter of a few weeks. _____

11. The fact that there is occasionally a spring freeze in late April in this region leads the new farmer to believe that it is never possible to plant lettuces and other freeze-sensitive greens any earlier than early May. _____

12. The argument purports to claim that snowboarding is safer than traditional skiing based on comparing the data on injuries incurred in each sport without considering the relative level of participation in each sport. _____

13. The argument fails to recognize that even substantial improvements in the healthiness of the diets of the captive animals at the facility might not qualify the diets for classification as healthy pursuant to the regulations. _____

14. The advocate, in detailing the impressive qualifications of the expert in microbiology, fails to establish the relevance of that expertise to the question of how best to raise public awareness of measures for preventing the spread of the disease. _____

15. The chemical company spokesperson implicitly acknowledges that there will, by mass, soon be more plastic in the oceans than fish before explicitly concluding that it is not plausible that there could ever be more plastic in the ocean than fish. _____

16. The claims adjuster fails to consider that the insurance company's process for selecting claims to use as a basis for determining rates for all policyholders could influence the results. _____

17. The year-over-year decline in the number of right whale deaths is not necessarily an indication of a declining mortality rate. _____

18. The argument fails to consider that above-average summer temperatures may be the cause of the increased insect activity in the orchard as well as the increased damage to apples from diseases without any increase in insect-transmitted diseases. _____

19. The absence of ritual burial markers does not preclude the possibility that the inhabitants of the village believed in an afterlife, even though the presence of such markers would clearly be indicative of such beliefs. _____

20. The argument implicitly equates sound fiscal policy with maintaining prime interests below three percent. _____

21. In his claim, Faraday treats the recorded beliefs of the village leaders as indicative of the actual circumstances surrounding the apparent clan feud that purportedly led to abandonment of the village. _____

22. The acknowledged bias of the arbiter should not affect a reasoned analysis of the validity of the arbiter's reasoning in reaching a decision in favor of the defendant. _____

23. The logic of Ricardo's ostensible rebuttal of Faulray does not actually address Faulray's claim that the proposed changes to the zoning code will be impractical. _____

24. The author fails to consider that low levels of iron and low levels of magnesium are not the only possible side effects of the prescribed medication. _____

25. The committee's projections regarding the national debt do not factor in recently enacted changes in national tax policy. _____

26. While the assessment of the reading level of the middle school's students is greatly improved, that does not necessarily imply that it meets state standards for grades seven through eight. _____

27. Falwell's claim that nonhuman primates cannot be extended certain rights belonging to humans is supported only by various reiterations of the premise that such rights are reserved to humans. _____

28. The argument fails to take into account that even though fossil fuels make up a smaller percentage of the county's energy consumption, the gross tonnage of fossil fuels combusted annually in the county has continued to grow each year. _____

29. Even though the prosecutor did not claim that nobody but the defendant had a motive to kill the victim, the defense counsel's argument focuses solely on rebutting such a claim. _____

30. Johnson ignores the possibility that while cyanide poisoning would be sufficient to cause such symptoms, such symptoms could also occur in the absence of cyanide poisoning. _____

31. The author overlooks the possibility that limiting the study group to those with preexisting heart conditions potentially precludes applying the result of the study to the entire population. _____

32. The argument trades on the ambiguity of the term "professional." _____

33. The author assumes without warrant that the data collected was of sufficient breadth. _____

34. The author fails to consider that ruling out job candidate Haines is not in itself sufficient to guarantee the hiring of candidate Sherman, as other candidates may exist. _____

35. The disqualification of the existing evidence against Monroe does not necessary imply his innocence, even if a guilty verdict cannot be supported. _____

36. Neither proponents of increased access to drug treatment facilities nor proponents of increased indictments for narcotics trafficking appeared to consider that the two proposals were not mutually exclusive. _____

37. The argument treats a probable interest rate hike as though it were inevitable. _____

38. The author fails to consider the possibility that interest rates do not necessarily have to increase or decrease—they could remain unchanged. _____

39. The author ignores the possibility that while loss of a job can result in depression, it is as likely that having depression could result in the sufferer's losing his or her employment. _____

40. The author assumes that putting together five exceptional musicians will produce an exceptional band. _____

41. The forecast presumes that there will not be any volatility in the price of oil. _____

42. That Daniel routinely beats Nguyen in chess does not necessarily dictate a similar result in a game such as poker, which is not limited to pure strategic ability and skill. _____

43. The author treats the fact that the indictment preceded the precipitous decline in stock prices to imply that the indictment led to the sharp decline. _____

44. Evidence of a genetic predisposition to the condition does not preclude a potential role of diet and other lifestyle factors in assessing the likelihood of its occurrence. _____

45. The argument makes a claim regarding the fairness of the judge's decision without directly offering any premises regarding what constitutes fairness in this context. _____

46. The argument assumes that a problematic study cannot nonetheless arrive at a factually accurate conclusion. _____

47. The author neglects the possibility that although the presence of rain guarantees the presence of clouds, the presence of clouds does not guarantee that it is raining. _____

48. The conclusion that the experimental treatment is effective in reducing blood pressure depends on the absence of confounding variables in the study and the control group. _____

49. The selection of participants utilized a process that was unlikely to ensure representativeness of the entire student body. _____

50. The corporate executive's dismissal of the claims of the protesters as well-meaning and motivated by a desire to help others failed to address the protesters' argument that the company's treatment of its workers violated international agreements. _____

Answers

1. The argument assumes that the inability of each team member to afford the entrance fee to the tournament means the team cannot afford that fee. **Part vs. Whole**

2. The argument ignores the possibility that algae blooms could occur in the absence of excess agricultural runoff. **Illegal Negation**

3. The incumbent points out the hypocrisy of the challenger in taking large campaign donations without addressing the merits of the challenger's proposal to ban such donations. **Ad Hominem**

4. The philosophy student purports to support the conclusion that humans are mortal solely with the equivalent premise that whatever is immortal cannot be human. **Circular Reasoning**

5. The defense attorney neglects to consider the possibility that the failure of the witness to accurately describe the gun used by the defendant does not preclude the possibility that the witness is capable of identifying the perpetrator of the crime. **Term Shift**

6. Maude presumes the stock will go down in value simply because the stock analyst who advised her that it would go up in value admitted that he doesn't actually research his stock picks. **Unproven vs. Untrue**

7. The argument overlooks the possibility that Brett's success over the past decade in games played in snow will not prevent Tom's team from prevailing tomorrow. **Unwarranted Prediction**

8. The company only surveyed those customers who had favorably reviewed their products in determining how to increase overall customer satisfaction. **Sampling Flaw**

9. The representative fails to distinguish the two possible interpretations of the term in concluding that there is insufficient "public interest" in the project to warrant supporting it. **Equivocation**

10. The argument concludes that the decline in quarterly sales was a consequence of the new marketing strategy due to the release of the latter preceding the former by a matter of a few weeks. **Causation Flaw**

11. The fact that there is occasionally a spring freeze in late April in this region leads the new farmer to believe that it is never possible to plant lettuces and other freeze-sensitive greens any earlier than early May. **Possible vs. Certain**

12. The argument purports to claim that snowboarding is safer than traditional skiing based on comparing the data on injuries incurred in each sport without considering the relative level of participation in each sport. **Percent vs. Amount**

13. The argument fails to recognize that even substantial improvements in the healthiness of the diets of the captive animals at the facility might not qualify the diets for classification as healthy pursuant to the regulations. **Relative vs. Absolute**

14. The advocate, in detailing the impressive qualifications of the expert in microbiology, fails to establish the relevance of that expertise to the question of how best to raise public awareness of measures for preventing the spread of the disease. **Appeal to Inappropriate Authority**

15. The chemical company spokesperson implicitly acknowledges that there will, by mass, soon be more plastic in the oceans than fish before explicitly concluding that it is not plausible that there could ever be more plastic in the ocean than fish. **Self-Contradiction**

16. The claims adjuster fails to consider that the insurance company's process for selecting claims to use as a basis for determining rates for all policyholders could influence the results. **Sampling Flaw**

17. The year-over-year decline in the number of right whale deaths is not necessarily an indication of a declining mortality rate. **Percent vs. Amount or Term Shift**

18. The argument fails to consider that above-average summer temperatures may be the cause of the increased insect activity in the orchard as well as the increased damage to apples from diseases without any increase in insect-transmitted diseases. **Causation Flaw**

19. The absence of ritual burial markers does not preclude the possibility that the inhabitants of the village believed in an afterlife, even though the presence of such markers would clearly be indicative of such beliefs. **Illegal Negation**

20. The argument implicitly equates sound fiscal policy with maintaining prime interests below three percent. **Term Shift**

21. In his claim, Faraday treats the recorded beliefs of the village leaders as indicative of the actual circumstances surrounding the apparent clan feud that purportedly led to abandonment of the village. **Opinion vs. Fact**

22. The acknowledged bias of the arbiter should not affect a reasoned analysis of the validity of the arbiter's reasoning in reaching a decision in favor of the defendant. **Ad Hominem**

23. The logic of Ricardo's ostensible rebuttal of Faulray does not actually address Faulray's claim that the proposed changes to the zoning code will be impractical. **Straw Man**

24. The author fails to consider that low levels of iron and low levels of magnesium are not the only possible side effects of the prescribed medication. **False Choice**

25. The committee's projections regarding the national debt do not factor in recently enacted changes in national tax policy. **Unwarranted Prediction**

26. While the assessment of the reading level of the middle school's students is greatly improved, that does not necessarily imply that it meets state standards for grades seven through eight. **Relative vs. Absolute**

27. Falwell's claim that nonhuman primates cannot be extended certain rights belonging to humans is supported only by various reiterations of the premise that such rights are reserved to humans. **Circular Reasoning**

28. The argument fails to take into account that even though fossil fuels make up a smaller percentage of the county's energy consumption, the gross tonnage of fossil fuels combusted annually in the county has continued to grow each year. **Number vs. Percent**

29. Even though the prosecutor did not claim that nobody but the defendant had a motive to kill the victim, the defense counsel's argument focuses solely on rebutting such a claim. **Straw Man**

30. Johnson ignores the possibility that while cyanide poisoning would be sufficient to cause such symptoms, such symptoms could also occur in the absence of cyanide poisoning. **Illegal Negation**

31. The author overlooks the possibility that limiting the study group to those with preexisting heart conditions potentially precludes applying the result of the study to the entire population. **Sampling Flaw**

32. The argument trades on the ambiguity of the term "professional." **Equivocation**

33. The author assumes without warrant that the data collected was of sufficient breadth. **Sampling Flaw**

34. The author fails to consider that ruling out job candidate Haines is not in itself sufficient to guarantee the hiring of candidate Sherman, as other candidates may exist. **False Choice**

35. The disqualification of the existing evidence against Monroe does not necessary imply his innocence, even if a guilty verdict cannot be supported. **Unproven vs. Untrue**

36. Neither proponents of increased access to drug treatment facilities nor proponents of increased indictments for narcotics trafficking appeared to consider that the two proposals were not mutually exclusive. **False Choice**

37. The argument treats a probable interest rate hike as though it were inevitable. **Possible vs. Certain**

38. The author fails to consider the possibility that interest rates do not necessarily have to increase or decrease—they could remain unchanged. **False Choice**

39. The author ignores the possibility that while loss of a job can result in depression, it is as likely that having depression could result in the sufferer's losing his or her employment. **Causation Flaw**

40. The author assumes that putting together five exceptional musicians will produce an exceptional band. **Part vs. Whole**

41. The forecast presumes that there will not be any volatility in the price of oil. **Unwarranted Prediction**

42. That Daniel routinely beats Nguyen in chess does not necessarily dictate a similar result in a game such as poker, which is not limited to pure strategic ability and skill. **Comparison Flaw**

43. The author treats the fact that the indictment preceded the precipitous decline in stock prices to imply that the indictment led to the sharp decline. **Causation Flaw**

44. Evidence of a genetic predisposition to the condition does not preclude a potential role of diet and other lifestyle factors in assessing the likelihood of its occurrence. **False Choice**

45. The argument makes a claim regarding the fairness of the judge's decision without directly offering any premises regarding what constitutes fairness in this context. **Term Shift**

46. The argument assumes that a problematic study cannot nonetheless arrive at a factually accurate conclusion. **Unproven vs. Untrue**

47. The author neglects the possibility that although the presence of rain guarantees the presence of clouds, the presence of clouds does not guarantee that it is raining. **Illegal Reversal**

5

48. The conclusion that the experimental treatment is effective in reducing blood pressure depends on the absence of confounding variables in the study and the control group. <u>**Causation Flaw**</u>

49. The selection of participants utilized a process that was unlikely to ensure representativeness of the entire student body. <u>**Sampling Flaw**</u>

50. The corporate executive's dismissal of the claims of the protesters as well-meaning and motivated by a desire to help others failed to address the protesters' argument that the company's treatment of its workers violated international agreements. <u>**Ad Hominem**</u>

Drill 91: Compare for Impact

Instructions: When the LSAT asks you to strengthen or weaken a comparative argument, the correct answer will usually deal with relevant similarities or differences between the entities being compared. For each of the following arguments, determine whether each item strengthens (S), weakens (W), or does nothing (DN). Bonus points for determining whether answers that impact the argument do so by pointing out a relevant similarity or a relevant difference!

Set A

Video game players often spend long periods of time staring at a computer, phone, or television screen. Their eyes follow repetitive patterns and are constantly refocusing, leading to a form of eye strain known as computer vision syndrome. Symptoms of this syndrome include headaches, blurred vision, and sensitivity to bright light. Thus, although studies have shown that juggling and playing video games are two equally effective ways to improve hand-eye coordination, juggling is the safer method of the two.

_____ 1. A juggler's eyes tend to follow repetitive patterns and must continually refocus as she looks at the objects being juggled.

_____ 2. The edges of objects on computers screens are not as sharply defined as real-life objects, causing our eyes to continually refocus as we look at any object on a screen.

_____ 3. On average, learning how to juggle requires fewer hours of practice than learning to play a video game.

_____ 4. Professional jugglers and competitive video game players often find it easy to learn sleight-of-hand magic tricks, which also require good hand-eye coordination.

Set B

Many Americans are fans of baseball. When asked what about the sport appeals to them, the most commonly cited features are the deliberate pace, sudden moments of excitement, and long-standing rivalries that have developed over the sport's decades-long history. Thus, these Americans would enjoy cricket if they gave it a chance.

_____ 5. Cricket teams tend to last for an average of five years before breaking up.

_____ 6. The pace of cricket prevents sudden moments of excitement.

_____ 7. The pace of cricket is determined by the umpires, who are wildly inconsistent.

_____ 8. Cricket has a yearly tournament similar to baseball's World Series championship.

Set C

The mayor's plan to reduce city traffic congestion is to construct a comprehensive trolley system that would provide convenient access to and from all areas of the city between downtown and the city limits. The mayor claims that constructing and operating such a trolley system would cost less than reengineering the streets to add traffic lanes and would reduce the amount of car traffic in the city.

_____ 9. For most commuters, riding the trolley daily will cost more per month than driving their cars.

_____ 10. The majority of city drivers commute to and from offices and homes within the city limits.

_____ 11. Most city traffic consists of incoming truck shipments from remote locations outside the city.

_____ 12. The new trolley rails will supplant some of the lanes that currently carry traffic in the city.

Set D

Advertisements for dietary supplements claim that one supplement tablet per day offers a full 100% of the recommended daily allowance of several essential vitamins. However, many doctors argue that taking supplements is an unnecessary expense because a balanced diet that includes a variety of meats, fruits, and grains provides all of the essential vitamins a body needs. Therefore, supplements should not be recommended by physicians.

_____ 13. Meat, fruit, and grains also contain other nutrients that aid the body's absorption of all essential vitamins, whereas supplements do not.

_____ 14. Most busy people today are not able to prepare a balanced menu of meats, fruit, and grains every day.

_____ 15. When a person consumes more vitamins than are needed, most of the extra vitamins are flushed from the body unabsorbed.

_____ 16. Most processed foods are fortified with many of the essential vitamins that were lost during processing.

Set E

Employees who spend long hours typing on a computer keyboard often develop tension headaches. A study examined treatments believed by many to relieve these headaches, including acupuncture and massage, and concluded that acupuncture, unlike massage, has no effectiveness as a headache treatment because its needles have no direct physiological impact on the sufferer's body.

_____ 17. The severity of headaches can be lessened by feelings of well-being achieved when the sufferer believes that a treatment is effective.

_____ 18. The number of people seeking acupuncture treatment for headaches and other symptoms of stress and tension has increased dramatically over the past decade.

_____ 19. Headaches from computer use are caused by eyestrain, a purely physiological condition in minute eye muscles treatable exclusively through the physical manipulation of the head and neck.

_____ 20. Advances in the technology of computer monitors are greatly reducing the incidence of computer-induced headaches.

Set F

The number of people attending concerts at the arena in Ableville is far greater than the number of people attending concerts at the arena in Zetaville. This clearly shows that the residents of Ableville are considerably more interested in seeing live music than the residents of Zetaville.

_____ 21. The arena in Ableville seats almost twice as many people as the arena in Zetaville.

_____ 22. Zetaville has many more local music clubs than Ableville, and Zetaville residents prefer the setting of a smaller club over that of a larger arena.

_____ 23. Almost all of the musicians who perform in the Ableville arena also perform in the Zetaville arena.

_____ 24. Concert tickets for the Ableville arena can be purchased online as well as at the arena itself, while concert tickets for the Zetaville arena can only be purchased online.

5

Set G

To promote a more active lifestyle for students, a local high school has offered extra credit to those who attend an optional physical education program held outside of normal school hours. Until this year, the program was held in the morning before school began. This past year, the program was held in the afternoon, immediately after school. The percent of students taking part in the program this year was more than double that in any prior year. It's clearly better to hold the program after school than to hold it before school.

_____ 25. Most students who attend the program for the first time this past year already had active lifestyles.

_____ 26. This past year, the activities in the program were changed to better reflect the interests of the school's students.

_____ 27. The school provides additional busing in the morning and in the afternoon for all students participating in extracurricular activities.

_____ 28. Students who were most in need of a more active lifestyle were unavailable for the afternoon program but would have been available in the morning.

Set H

Power plants fueled by natural gas and by oil emit pollutants into the air. However, plants burning coal, as they are presently engineered, emit far greater quantities of more noxious air pollutants and are implicated in the creation of acid rain that can fall many hundreds of miles from the plants themselves. Therefore, in order to reduce air pollution, coal-fired power plants should be closed and replaced with gas- and oil-fueled plants.

_____ 29. As supplies of oil and gas decline, demand for these fuels will increase and prices will go up.

_____ 30. Gas-fueled power plants are more cost efficient than coal-fueled power plants.

_____ 31. Engineers have developed a model to reduce emissions from plants fueled by oil and gas to almost undetectable levels.

_____ 32. Coal-fueled plants can easily be redesigned to eliminate most emissions into the atmosphere.

Set I

Classes in public speaking have been proven to raise self-confidence, and self-confidence is very important to the performance of many employees, especially sales representatives. So, for sales representatives who suffer from low self-confidence, taking a public speaking class could help improve job performance better than reading the frequently recommended books on developing self-confidence.

_____ 33. It is easier for people to develop self-confidence when they learn in an environment with other people.

_____ 34. Many jobs do not require a high level of self-confidence.

_____ 35. Books on developing self-confidence can contain information about other work-related skills that public speaking classes would not address.

_____ 36. Research has shown that people have raised their self-confidence by reading the frequently recommended books on developing self-confidence.

Set J

A recently developed drug that is valuable in the treatment of cancer currently can only be made from the endangered mayapple plant or the more readily available camellia plant. The drug is far easier to make from the mayapple plant, but it takes such large quantities of the mayapple to make one pound of the drug that this method of production will decimate the existing mayapple population. The manufacturer should therefore switch over all its production to the camellia-derived version of the drug.

_____ 37. The camellia-derived version of the drug is no more effective than the mayapple-derived version of the drug.

_____ 38. The camellia population will not be endangered by the production of the drug.

_____ 39. Raw camellia is a known poison, whereas raw mayapple is not.

_____ 40. The quantities of plant matter needed to produce the camellia-derived version of the drug are even greater than those needed to produce the mayapple-derived version of the drug.

Answers

Set A

Video game players often spend long periods of time staring at a computer, phone, or television screen. Their eyes follow repetitive patterns and are constantly refocusing, leading to a form of eye strain known as computer vision syndrome. Symptoms of this syndrome include headaches, blurred vision, and sensitivity to bright light. Thus, although studies have shown that juggling and playing video games are two equally effective ways to improve hand-eye coordination, juggling is the safer method of the two.

__W__ 1. A juggler's eyes tend to follow repetitive patterns and must continually refocus as he or she looks at the objects being juggled.

(In an argument that concludes a difference, relevant similarities will serve as weakeners.)

__S__ 2. The edges of objects on computers screens are not as sharply defined as real-life objects, causing our eyes to continually refocus as we look at any object on a screen.

(In an argument that concludes a difference, relevant differences will serve as strengtheners.)

__DN__ 3. On average, learning how to juggle requires fewer hours of practice than learning to play a video game.

(Time spent practicing/learning isn't necessarily relevant to overall eye strain, though overall time spent on the activities in order to see improvement in hand-eye coordination would be.)

__DN__ 4. Professional jugglers and competitive video game players often find it easy to learn sleight-of-hand magic tricks, which also require good hand-eye coordination.

(While this supports the contention that both juggling and gaming predict good hand-eye coordination, it doesn't support the actual conclusion, which is that juggling is safer than gaming.)

Set B

Many Americans are fans of baseball. When asked what about the sport appeals to them, the most commonly cited features are the deliberate pace, sudden moments of excitement, and long-standing rivalries that have developed over the sport's decades-long history. Thus, these Americans would enjoy cricket if they gave it a chance.

__W__ 5. Cricket teams tend to last for an average of five years before breaking up.

(This provides a relevant difference because it would prevent the rivalries from being long-standing.)

__W__ 6. The pace of cricket prevents sudden moments of excitement.

(Relevant difference.)

__W__ 7. The pace of cricket is determined by the umpires, who are wildly inconsistent.

(Relevant difference.)

__DN__ 8. Cricket has a yearly tournament similar to baseball's World Series championship.

(Since the championship wasn't mentioned as an appeal, this isn't a relevant similarity.)

Set C

The mayor's plan to reduce city traffic congestion is to construct a comprehensive trolley system that would provide convenient access to and from all areas of the city between downtown and the city limits. The mayor claims that constructing and operating such a trolley system would cost less than reengineering the streets to add traffic lanes and would reduce the amount of car traffic in the city.

__DN__ 9. For most commuters, riding the trolley daily will cost more per month than driving their cars.

(The relative costs to the commuters is irrelevant to the conclusion, which compares the costs of construction.)

__S__ 10. The majority of city drivers commute to and from offices and homes within the city limits.

(Relevant similarity.)

__W__ 11. Most city traffic consists of incoming truck shipments from remote locations outside the city.

(Relevant difference.)

__DN__ 12. The new trolley rails will supplant some of the lanes that currently carry traffic in the city.

(While this may seem at first that it would weaken the argument by showing that the trolley would take up an existing traffic route rather than creating a new one, the quantifier "some" only implies that this will happen in at least one circumstance, so we can't infer that the impact will be widespread enough to matter.)

Set D

Advertisements for dietary supplements claim that one supplement tablet per day offers a full 100% of the recommended daily allowance of several essential vitamins. However, many doctors argue that taking supplements is an unnecessary expense because a balanced diet that includes a variety of meats, fruits, and grains provides all of the essential vitamins a body needs. Therefore, supplements should not be recommended by physicians.

__S__ 13. Meat, fruit, and grains also contain other nutrients that aid the body's absorption of all essential vitamins, whereas supplements do not.

(Relevant difference.)

__W__ 14. Most busy people today are not able to prepare a balanced menu of meats, fruit, and grains every day.

(Relevant difference.)

__DN__ 15. When a person consumes more vitamins than are needed, most of the extra vitamins are flushed from the body unabsorbed.

(Irrelevant—makes no distinction between how the vitamins are ingested.)

__DN__ 16. Most processed foods are fortified with many of the essential vitamins that were lost during processing. *(Irrelevant—deals with neither supplements nor a balanced diet.)*

Set E

Employees who spend long hours typing on a computer keyboard often develop tension headaches. A study examined treatments believed by many to relieve these headaches, including acupuncture and massage, and concluded that acupuncture, unlike massage, has no effectiveness as a headache treatment because its needles have no direct physiological impact on the sufferer's body.

__W__ 17. The severity of headaches can be lessened by feelings of well-being achieved when the sufferer believes that a treatment is effective.

(Makes the difference in the stimulus less relevant.)

__DN__ 18. The number of people seeking acupuncture treatment for headaches and other symptoms of stress and tension has increased dramatically over the past decade.

(Irrelevant.)

__S__ 19. Headaches from computer use are caused by eyestrain, a purely physiological condition in minute eye muscles treatable exclusively through the physical manipulation of the head and neck.

(Makes the difference in the stimulus more relevant.)

__DN__ 20. Advances in the technology of computer monitors are greatly reducing the incidence of computer-induced headaches.

(Irrelevant.)

Set F

The number of people attending concerts at the arena in Ableville is far greater than the number of people attending concerts at the arena in Zetaville. This clearly shows that the residents of Ableville are considerably more interested in seeing live music than the residents of Zetaville.

__W__ 21. The arena in Ableville seats almost twice as many people as the arena in Zetaville.

(Relevant difference.)

__W__ 22. Zetaville has many more local music clubs than Ableville, and Zetaville residents prefer the setting of a smaller club over that of a larger arena.

(Relevant difference.)

__S__ 23. Almost all of the musicians who perform in the Ableville arena also perform in the Zetaville arena.

(Relevant similarity.)

__DN__ 24. Concert tickets for the Ableville arena can be purchased online as well as at the arena itself, while concert tickets for the Zetaville arena can only be purchased online.

(Irrelevant.)

5

Set G

To promote a more active lifestyle for students, a local high school has offered extra credit to those who attend an optional physical education program held outside of normal school hours. Until this year, the program was held in the morning before school began. This past year, the program was held in the afternoon, immediately after school. The percent of students taking part in the program this year was more than double that in any prior year. It's clearly better to hold the program after school than to hold it before school.

__DN__ 25. Most students who attend the program for the first time this past year already had active lifestyles.

(Irrelevant—they could still have even more active lifestyles, which may be beneficial.)

__W__ 26. This past year, the activities in the program were changed to better reflect the interests of the school's students.

(Relevant difference.)

__S__ 27. The school provides additional busing in the morning and in the afternoon for all students participating in extracurricular activities.

(Relevant similarity.)

__DN__ 28. Students who were most in need of a more active lifestyle were unavailable for the afternoon program but would have been available in the morning.

(Irrelevant—a program can still be worthwhile even if those most in need are not served by it, so long as enough of those in need still are. Consider, for example, if the three kids who need it most couldn't participate in the afternoon, but 100 kids who needed it were available in the afternoon but not in the morning.)

Set H

Power plants fueled by natural gas and by oil emit pollutants into the air. However, plants burning coal, as they are presently engineered, emit far greater quantities of more noxious air pollutants and are implicated in the creation of acid rain that can fall many hundreds of miles from the plants themselves. Therefore, in order to reduce air pollution, coal-fired power plants should be closed and replaced with gas- and oil-fueled plants.

__DN__ 29. As supplies of oil and gas decline, demand for these fuels will increase and prices will go up.

(Irrelevant—the recommendation is qualified solely on environmental considerations, so financial ones have no impact.)

__DN__ 30. Gas-fueled power plants are more cost efficient than coal-fueled power plants.

(Irrelevant, for the same reason as #29.)

__S__ 31. Engineers have developed a model to reduce emissions from plants fueled by oil and gas to almost undetectable levels.

(Relevant difference.)

__W__ 32. Coal-fueled plants can easily be redesigned to eliminate most emissions into the atmosphere.

(Makes a difference in the stimulus less relevant.)

Set I

Classes in public speaking have been proven to raise self-confidence, and self-confidence is very important to the performance of many employees, especially sales representatives. So, for sales representatives who suffer from low self-confidence, taking a public speaking class could help improve job performance better than reading the frequently recommended books on developing self-confidence.

_S_   33. It is easier for people to develop self-confidence when they learn in an environment with other people.

(Relevant difference.)

_DN_   34. Many jobs do not require a high level of self-confidence.

(Irrelevant.)

_DN_   35. Books on developing self-confidence can contain information about other work-related skills that public speaking classes would not address.

(Irrelevant—it's not clear what these "other work-related skills" are, nor whether they would be beneficial to sales representatives.)

_W_   36. Research has shown that people have raised their self-confidence by reading the frequently recommended books on developing self-confidence.

(Relevant similarity.)

Set J

A recently-developed drug that is valuable in the treatment of cancer currently can only be made from the endangered mayapple plant or the more readily-available camellia plant. The drug is far easier to make from the mayapple plant, but it takes such large quantities of the mayapple to make one pound of the drug that this method of production will decimate the existing mayapple population. The manufacturer should therefore switch over all its production to the camellia-derived version of the drug.

_DN_   37. The camellia-derived version of the drug is no more effective than the mayapple-derived version of the drug.

(A difference in efficacy would be relevant if it were established, but this claim doesn't actually do that—it just says that one is not more effective than the other, so they could still be equally effective.)

_S_   38. The camellia population will not be endangered by the production of the drug.

(Relevant difference.)

_DN_   39. Raw camellia is a known poison, whereas raw mayapple is not.

(Irrelevant—this is a difference between the plants in their raw states that has no bearing on their population strength or drug production qualities.)

_DN_   40. The quantities of plant matter needed to produce the camellia-derived version of the drug are even greater than those needed to produce the mayapple-derived version of the drug.

(Irrelevant—even if it takes more camellia to make the drug, camellia may be so readily available that it doesn't matter.)

5

Drill 92: Principled Objections

Instructions: Principle Support questions describe a situation with a judgment made in the conclusion, often a recommendation in the form of a *should* statement. Your job is to find the answer choice, in the form of a principle, that justifies that conclusion. The correct answer will almost always take this general form: *If (criteria from the premises), then (judgment from conclusion).* For each of the following sets, a judgment and criteria will be provided. Determine for each item whether it shows that the criteria justify the judgment and fill in yes (Y) or no (N) accordingly.

Thus, Megan, who clearly treated Bishop poorly, should be held accountable for her own blameworthy actions.

_____ 1. Anyone who treats another person poorly is a blameworthy person.

_____ 2. Someone who is treated poorly by others should impart judgment upon those people for their actions.

_____ 3. All people should be held accountable for all of their actions.

_____ 4. People who treat others poorly should be held accountable for their own blameworthy actions.

_____ 5. Accountability requires someone to be blameworthy for performing a given action.

Dan, therefore, ought to be immediately fired from his position for his theft.

_____ 6. Anyone who steals from the company should be immediately fired.

_____ 7. Immediate firing requires probable cause.

_____ 8. No one should be immediately fired unless their transgression involves theft.

_____ 9. Stealing from the company should always be punished.

_____ 10. A person should be immediately fired if and only if they steal.

So the council should adopt the infrastructure plan, given its clear benefits.

_____ 11. All potential impacts of adopting a plan should be considered before its adoption.

_____ 12. Any plan having demonstrable beneficial impact should be adopted.

_____ 13. No plan that will not improve infrastructure should be adopted.

_____ 14. Plans that may improve infrastructure should always be adopted.

_____ 15. Plans that will improve infrastructure should always be considered carefully.

Therefore, cardiologists should prescribe the recently approved medication to patients with a hypertension diagnosis.

_____ 16. Doctors should always prescribe the newest available medications to treat their patients' conditions.

_____ 17. Medications which pass regulatory approval should be prescribed.

_____ 18. Only medications which pass regulatory approval should be prescribed.

_____ 19. Cardiologists are responsible for providing their patients with the best available care.

_____ 20. Any medication which has shown promise in research studies should be prescribed.

Employees should never send their passwords by e-mail because doing so endangers company security.

_____ 21. Employees should avoid any action which could endanger company security.

_____ 22. Any action which could endanger company security should be discussed with an employee's supervisor.

_____ 23. Employees are required to follow all company rules.

_____ 24. An employee should engage in any action that protects company security.

_____ 25. Sending passwords by e-mail exposes a company to risk.

In light of past successes, the sales manager at Chairs! Chairs! Chairs! ought to institute another 10% discount on new merchandise.

_____ 26. Any discount on new merchandise would increase revenue at Chairs! Chairs! Chairs!.

_____ 27. Instituting any discount at Chairs! Chairs! Chairs! requires the approval of the general manager.

_____ 28. Promotions which could increase sales should be implemented.

_____ 29. If a promotion has been successful in the past, it should be tried again.

_____ 30. A promotion should be implemented only if it may draw new customers to a business.

Thus, retaining contextual data alongside specimens will ease the job of future researchers and is therefore a paleontology best practice.

_____ 31. If a policy will make it easier for future researchers to continue their work, it can be considered a best practice.

_____ 32. Paleontologists should retain contextual data only if doing so allows for better record keeping.

_____ 33. Retaining contextual data is advisable for paleontologists if and only if it is reasonably easy to do so.

_____ 34. In order for a policy to be considered a best practice, the policy must have benefits.

_____ 35. Paleontologists should practice any policy that makes current or future research easier.

Therefore, it is advisable that parents limit their children to one hour per day of screen time with non-educational content, per the pediatrician's recommendation.

_____ 36. If a pediatrician recommends a policy, parents should adopt it.

_____ 37. Parents should engage in any action which improves their children's education.

_____ 38. A parent should allow a child more than an hour per day of screen time only if the content is educational.

_____ 39. If parents limit their children to one hour per day of screen time with non-educational content, pediatricians should recommend the practice.

_____ 40. It is incumbent upon parents to teach their children discipline.

So, the judge should rule in favor of the defendant, given the questionability of the witness's character.

_____ 41. If a judge believes the character of a witness to be questionable, he should rule in favor of the defendant.

_____ 42. If a judge rules in favor of a defendant, he must believe that the witness to the crime is questionable.

_____ 43. If a judge believes that a defendant is not wholly responsible, he should send the case to arbitration.

_____ 44. The law requires judges to take all available information under consideration.

_____ 45. A judge should not rule in favor of a defendant unless he believes that all witnesses have unquestionable characters.

The park rangers should therefore conduct a controlled burn in the portion of the forest affected by Dutch elm disease.

_____ 46. A controlled burn should be conducted to combat any tree disease.

_____ 47. A controlled burn should only be conducted to combat Dutch elm disease.

_____ 48. An outbreak of Dutch elm disease requires responsive management.

_____ 49. The park rangers are responsible for maintaining the health of the forest.

_____ 50. A controlled burn should be conducted if, but only if, there is an outbreak of Dutch elm disease.

5

Answers

Note: We've crossed out the offending text in the ones that don't justify the judgment.

Thus, Megan, who clearly treated Bishop poorly, should be held accountable for her own blameworthy actions.

__N__ 1. Anyone who treats another person poorly is ~~a blameworthy person~~.

(Wrong judgment—we need to conclude she should be held accountable, not that she should be considered blameworthy.)

__N__ 2. Someone who is treated poorly by others should ~~impart judgment upon those people for their actions~~.

(Wrong judgment—we need to conclude that someone is accountable for their own actions, not passing judgment on the actions of others.)

__Y__ 3. **All people should be held accountable for all of their actions.**

(This is broader than necessary, but if Megan is responsible for all of her actions, that includes the blameworthy ones.)

__Y__ 4. **People who treat others poorly should be held accountable for their own blameworthy actions.**

__N__ 5. Accountability requires someone to be blameworthy for performing a given action.

(In order to conclude that Megan should be held accountable, we need accountability to be the necessary condition. In this principle, it's the sufficient. Henceforth, we'll call this a Reversal.)

Dan, therefore, ought to be immediately fired from his position for his theft.

__Y__ 6. **Anyone who steals from the company should be immediately fired.**

__N__ 7. Immediate firing ~~requires probable cause~~.

(Reversal.)

__N__ 8. ~~No one should be immediately fired~~ unless their transgression involves theft.

(This principle could only help us conclude that someone should not be fired since it presents theft as a necessary condition for firing rather than a sufficient one. Henceforth, we'll call this a Negation.)

__N__ 9. Stealing from the company should always be ~~punished~~.

(Wrong judgment—while firing is a punishment, it's not the only one, so this answer doesn't justify the specific punishment of firing.)

__Y__ 10. **A person should be immediately fired if and only if they steal.**

("If and only if" indicates biconditionality, meaning that the recommendation to fire someone is both a sufficient and a necessary condition. Being sufficient doesn't help us here, but since it's necessary, too, it meets the criterion we're testing for.)

So the council should adopt the infrastructure plan, given its clear benefits.

__N__ 11. All potential impacts of adopting a plan should ~~be considered before its adoption~~.

(Wrong judgment—we need to conclude that a thing should be adopted, not that things should be considered.)

__Y__ 12. **Any plan having demonstrable beneficial impact should be adopted.**

(Broader than what is necessary, but that's OK for Principle Support questions!)

__N__ 13. ~~No plan~~ that will not improve infrastructure ~~should be adopted~~.

(Negation.)

__Y__ 14. **Plans that may improve infrastructure should always be adopted.**

__N__ 15. Plans that will improve infrastructure should always ~~be considered carefully~~.

(Wrong judgment—what we need is adoption!)

Therefore, cardiologists should prescribe the recently approved medication to patients with a hypertension diagnosis.

__N__ 16. Doctors should always prescribe the ~~newest available~~ medications to treat their patients' conditions.

(Wrong criteria—we don't know if our medicine is the newest available.)

__Y__ 17. **Medications which pass regulatory approval should be prescribed.**

(Broad, but OK!)

__N__ 18. ~~Only~~ medications which pass regulatory approval ~~should be prescribed~~.

(Reversal.)

__N__ 19. Cardiologists ~~are responsible for providing~~ their patients with the ~~best available care~~.

(Wrong judgment—we need a prescription, not the "best available care.")

__N__ 20. Any medication which has shown promise in ~~research studies~~ should be prescribed.

(Wrong criteria—there's no evidence of any research study results.)

Employees should never send their passwords by e-mail because doing so endangers company security.

__Y__ 21. **Employees should avoid any action which could endanger company security.**

__N__ 22. Any action which could endanger company security should ~~be discussed with an employee's supervisor~~.

(Wrong judgment.)

__N__ 23. Employees are required to follow ~~all company rules~~.

(Wrong criteria—we don't know if it's against the rules to send passwords by e-mail, only that it's being recommended against.)

__N__ 24. An employee ~~should engage~~ in any action that protects company security.

(Negation—the recommendation is about avoiding an action rather than engaging in an action.)

__N__ 25. Sending passwords by e-mail ~~exposes a company to risk~~.

(This isn't even a principle; it's just a statement of fact.)

In light of past successes, the sales manager at Chairs! Chairs! Chairs! ought to institute another 10% discount on new merchandise.

__N__ 26. Any discount on new merchandise ~~would~~ increase revenue at Chairs! Chairs! Chairs!.

(We need a principle about what should happen, not what would happen.)

__N__ 27. Instituting any discount at Chairs! Chairs! Chairs! ~~requires the approval of the general manager~~.

(Reversal, signaled by "requires.")

__Y__ 28. **Promotions which could increase sales should be implemented.**

__Y__ 29. **If a promotion has been successful in the past, it should be tried again.**

__N__ 30. A promotion should be implemented ~~only if~~ it may draw new customers to a business.

(Reversal, signaled by "only if.")

Thus, retaining contextual data alongside specimens will ease the job of future researchers and is therefore a paleontology best practice.

__Y__ 31. **If a policy will make it easier for future researchers to continue their work, it can be considered a best practice.**

__N__ 32. Paleontologists should retain contextual data ~~only if~~ doing so allows for better record keeping.

(Reversal, signaled by "only if.")

__N__ 33. Retaining contextual data is advisable for paleontologists if and only if it is ~~reasonably easy to do so~~.

(Wrong criteria—we don't know whether it's easy to do so, but we still need to conclude that it's a best practice.)

__N__ 34. In order for a policy to be considered a best practice, the policy ~~must have~~ benefits.

(Reversal, signaled by "must.")

__Y__ 35. **Paleontologists should practice any policy that makes current or future research easier.**

Therefore, it is advisable that parents limit their children to one hour per day of screen time with non-educational content, per the pediatrician's recommendation.

__Y__ 36. **If a pediatrician recommends a policy, parents should adopt it.**

__N__ 37. Parents should engage in any action which ~~improves their children's education~~.

(Wrong criteria—we don't know whether this practice will improve education.)

___Y___ 38. **A parent should allow a child more than an hour per day of screen time only if the content is educational.**

(The contrapositive of this principle allows us to conclude that non-educational screen time should be limited to one hour.)

___N___ 39. If parents limit their children to one hour per day of screen time with non-educational content, ~~pediatricians should recommend the practice~~.

(Reversal.)

___N___ 40. It is incumbent upon parents to ~~teach their children discipline~~.

(Wrong criteria—will this teach discipline? We don't know!)

So the judge should rule in favor of the defendant, given the questionability of the witness's character.

___Y___ 41. **If a judge believes the character of a witness to be questionable, he should rule in favor of the defendant.**

___N___ 42. ~~If a judge rules in favor~~ of a defendant, ~~he must believe~~ that the witness to the crime is questionable.

(Reversal.)

___N___ 43. If a judge believes that a defendant is ~~not wholly responsible~~, he should ~~send the case to arbitration~~.

(Wrong criteria and wrong judgment.)

___N___ 44. The law requires judges to take ~~all available information~~ under consideration.

(Wrong judgment.)

___Y___ 45. **A judge should not rule in favor of a defendant unless he believes that all witnesses have unquestionable characters.**

The park rangers should therefore conduct a controlled burn in the portion of the forest affected by Dutch elm disease.

___Y___ 46. **A controlled burn should be conducted to combat any tree disease.**

(Broad, but OK!)

___N___ 47. A controlled burn should ~~only~~ be conducted to combat Dutch elm disease.

(Reversal, signaled by "only.")

___N___ 48. An outbreak of Dutch elm disease requires ~~responsive management~~.

(Wrong judgment.)

___N___ 49. The park rangers are responsible for ~~maintaining the health of the forest~~.

(Wrong judgment.)

___Y___ 50. **A controlled burn should be conducted if, but only if, there is an outbreak of Dutch elm disease.**

("If, but only if" signals a biconditional; the "if" clause provides sufficient support for the recommendation.)

Drill 93: Vocab Lab #11 – Confused and Confusing

Instructions: Some of these LSAT words are commonly confused with each other (or with other words). The rest have something about them that's just plain confusing. Choose the answer closest in meaning.

1. Abate
   - (A) compensate
   - (B) provoke
   - (C) diminish

2. Allegorical
   - (A) having a hidden meaning
   - (B) expressing an unambiguous meaning
   - (C) stating a possibly doubtful meaning

3. Allusion
   - (A) image
   - (B) myth
   - (C) hint

4. Analogous
   - (A) comparable
   - (B) incongruous
   - (C) sensitive

5. Anomalous
   - (A) akin
   - (B) aloof
   - (C) abnormal

6. Comprise
   - (A) shake up
   - (B) agree on
   - (C) consist of

7. Elicit
   - (A) call forth (e.g., a reaction)
   - (B) enact (e.g., a crime)
   - (C) allow (e.g., a lapse)

8. Equivocate
   - (A) express different meanings using the same term
   - (B) compare two different ideas
   - (C) measure proportionally

9. Illicit
   - (A) imperceptible
   - (B) impermissible
   - (C) impenetrable

10. Indigenous
    - (A) destitute
    - (B) native
    - (C) incensed

11. Qualified
    - (A) thrilled
    - (B) expected
    - (C) limited

12. Supplant
    - (A) install
    - (B) provide
    - (C) replace

13. Tenacious
    - (A) persistent
    - (B) insubstantial
    - (C) impassioned

14. Tenuous
    - (A) dogged
    - (B) flimsy
    - (C) plentiful

15. Vindicate
    - (A) clear of blame
    - (B) take vengeance upon
    - (C) capitulate in the face of

Answers

1. C

Abate = diminish; lessen in force. *Abatement* = reduction; alleviation, e.g., of a property tax. *Abate* isn't necessarily that confusing, but its cousin *bate* has chiefly survived in the phrase "with *bated* breath" = with restrained or held-in breath (due to suspense). "Baited breath," on the other hand, implies that your breath smells like you've been eating fishing bait, so be careful with your spelling.

2. A

Allegorical = having a hidden meaning. It does not have anything to do with *alleged* = so-called; supposed.

3. C

Allusion = hint; indirect reference. A text may *allude* to something by subtly referring to it, without making a direct citation. Don't confuse *allusion* with *illusion* = false image.

4. A

Analogous = comparable; similar. When you make an *analogy*, you're comparing X to Y in order to explain X (through its similarity to Y). Don't mix up *analogous* and *anomalous*, which are practically antonyms.

5. C

Anomalous = abnormal; deviant; out of the ordinary. An *anomaly* is something unique or unusual.

6. C

Comprise = consist of; include. If you don't want to annoy certain professors, use *comprise* only in this way: "The whole *comprises* (consists of) three parts." Avoid "Three parts *comprise* the whole" or "The whole is *comprised* of three parts," as tempting (and even justifiable) as these uses are.

7. A

Elicit = call forth (a reaction); evoke; bring out. The *e-* is a form of *ex-* (out in Latin). Don't confuse *elicit* with *illicit* (illegal; unlawful).

8. A

Equivocate = express different meanings using the same term. On the LSAT, this refers to a logical fallacy in which the author uses the same word or phrase in two different senses within an argument. (For example: "Residents shouldn't be concerned about the new plant being built; I have several plants in my yard, and they make my home look beautiful." The meaning of "plant" changes from an industrial facility to a living organism.) This logical definition is based on the roots *equi-* (same) and *voc-* (voice, sound). It's worth noting that, in common usage, *equivocate* has evolved to mean "express ambiguously, often with an intent to deceive or conceal."

9. B

Illicit = impermissible; unlawful. The grounds could be legal or ethical. The *il-* is a form of *in-* (not). The opposite of *illicit* is *licit* (legal; permissible). Don't confuse *illicit* with *elicit*, which sounds nearly the same.

10. B

Indigenous = native (to a place). Don't confuse *indigenous* with *indigent* (destitute; impoverished) or with *indignant* (incensed; angry).

11. C

Qualified = limited; restricted in some way. You often encounter *qualified* in the positive "skilled" sense: "she is highly *qualified* for the position." But you should be ready with the less common (and negative) meaning as well: "She gave only *qualified* approval to the plan." Likewise, *unqualified* can mean "unskilled; unsuitable," or it can mean "unrestricted; unlimited."

12. C

Supplant = replace; supersede. Often, *supplant* is used when one idea becomes outdated and is replaced by a new, better idea. For instance, a new scientific theory may *supplant* an older one if the new theory is better supported by experiments and observations.

13. A

Tenacious = persistent; steadfast; holding onto
something. The Latin root *ten-* within *tenacity*
literally means "hold." However, a related Latin root,
also *ten-*, means "thin." Don't confuse *tenacious* with
tenuous.

14. B

Tenuous = flimsy; unsubstantiated; weak; vague. The
underlying Latin root *ten-* comes from the same
distant Proto-Indo-European root as the English
word *thin* and has the same meaning.

15. A

Vindicate = clear of blame; justify; defend; substanti-
ate. Don't confuse the positive word *vindicate* with
the negative word *vindictive* (= vengeful; unforgiv-
ing). These words have the same Latin roots, and in
fact, once upon a time, *vindicate* primarily meant
"avenge; get revenge for." Nowadays, however, that
meaning is very much secondary, if not obsolete.
(And it certainly never meant "take vengeance *upon*,"
but rather "take vengeance *on behalf of.*")

The Inference Family

The Inference Family of questions consists of the question types Must Be True, Must Be False, Most Strongly Supported, Principle Example, and Explain a Result. As the family name suggests, what these questions have in common is that they ask you to take what's said in the stimulus and infer from that information something that is definitely true, probably true, or definitely false, depending on the question type. Within this section, the drills are organized by the steps in our 4-Step Process for Logical Reasoning, beginning with question stem identification and ending with answer choice analysis.

In this section, you will learn to:

ID Your Task

- Use the task to ask the right questions about the answers
- Distinguish between Most Strongly Supported and Strengthen Stems (again!)

Work the Stimulus

- Chain conditional statements for Must Be True and Must Be False questions
- Zero in on the paradox for Explain a Result questions

Anticipate an Answer

- Predict what can and cannot be concluded
- Combine quantified statements

Analyze the Answers

- Contradict conditional statements
- Apply general principles to specific cases

Drill 94: Talking to Yourself, Inference Family Edition

Instructions: We've said it before: the key to efficiency is to do only what you need to do and nothing that you don't. This drill is about honing that focus and canceling out the noise.

Question stems will be provided. For each, a series of questions follows. These are questions that test takers might ask themselves as they evaluate an answer choice. Mark Y for the ones that focus on the right things. Mark N for the ones that don't.

Which of the following is most strongly supported by the statements above?

_____ 1. Is it possible for this to be false?

_____ 2. Does this answer bring in new information?

_____ 3. Does this support the argument's conclusion?

_____ 4. Is the wording in the answer too strong to be justified?

_____ 5. Is this the contrapositive of my prephrase?

_____ 6. Does this connect all the different ideas in the stimulus?

Which of the following can be properly inferred on the basis of the geneticist's claims?

_____ 7. Is it possible for this to be false?

_____ 8. Does this answer bring in new information?

_____ 9. Does this support the argument's conclusion?

_____ 10. Is the wording in the answer too strong to be justified?

_____ 11. Is this the contrapositive of my prephrase?

_____ 12. Does this connect all the different ideas in the stimulus?

Which one of the following most logically completes the argument above?

_____ 13. Is it possible for this to be false?

_____ 14. Does this answer bring in new information?

_____ 15. Does this support the argument's conclusion?

_____ 16. Is the wording in the answer too strong to be justified?

_____ 17. Is this the contrapositive of my prephrase?

_____ 18. Does this connect all the different ideas in the stimulus?

Which of the following, if true, would best reconcile the astronomer's seemingly contradictory observations?

_____ 19. Is this likely to be true?

_____ 20. If I'd known this was true before reading the stimulus, would the observation still have seemed contradictory?

_____ 21. Does this match my prephrase?

_____ 22. Does this make the observations seem more contradictory?

_____ 23. Is this specific or comprehensive enough to affect the given situation?

_____ 24. Does this explain not only why the surprising thing happened, but also why the surprising thing happened in spite of the obstacle presented, or instead of the thing we would have expected to happen?

Which one of the following examples best illustrates the principle described in the argument?

_____ 25. Does the example in the answer trigger the sufficient condition of the principle?

_____ 26. If there are two principles in the stimulus, does this example illustrate both of them?

_____ 27. Does this example conclude the principle's necessary condition?

_____ 28. Does this follow the same order as the given principle?

_____ 29. Is this an example of the contrapositive of the principle?

_____ 30. Does this example conclude the principle's sufficient condition?

5

If the statements above are true, then each of the following statements could be true EXCEPT:

_____ 31. Does this contradict information in the stimulus?

_____ 32. Does this contradict a conclusion that could validly be drawn from the information in the stimulus?

_____ 33. Does this seem likely to be false in the real world?

_____ 34. If the stimulus is conditional, does this show a statement's sufficient condition without its necessary condition?

_____ 35. If this were true, would it weaken the argument in the stimulus?

_____ 36. Given the information in the stimulus, is this answer possibly true?

5

Answers

Which of the following is most strongly supported by the statements above?

__N__ 1. Is it possible for this to be false?

This is a criterion for Must Be True questions but not for Most Strongly Supported. If you feel like an answer does have to be true, by all means select it, but answering this in the negative doesn't mean the answer is wrong.

__Y__ 2. Does this answer bring in new information?

Inferences have to deal with the information presented. The one caveat is that an answer might introduce an entity that fulfills a condition set forth in the stimulus, but that's not the same thing as bringing in a totally new concept.

__N__ 3. Does this support the argument's conclusion?

Nope—the language of the stem is similar in Most Strongly Supported and Strengthen questions, so be sure you know what you're looking at before you start thinking about the answer choices.

__Y__ 4. Is the wording in the answer too strong to be justified?

So many incorrect answers on Most Strongly Supported questions are wrong because they exceed the degree of the stimulus. Strong language is the primary red flag for this question type.

__N__ 5. Is this the contrapositive of my prephrase?

Most Strongly Supported questions don't tend to be conditional, and they are typically hard to prephrase.

__N__ 6. Does this connect all the different ideas in the stimulus?

The correct answer might do this, but it doesn't have to.

Which of the following can be properly inferred on the basis of the geneticist's claims?

__Y__ 7. Is it possible for this to be false?

This is exactly what you want to ask for a Must Be True question. If it can't be false, it has to be true!

__Y__ 8. Does this answer bring in new information?

It can't bring in any new concepts, but it might introduce a new entity that fulfills a condition from the stimulus.

__N__ 9. Does this support the argument's conclusion?

99.9% of Inference Family questions don't deal with arguments, so there's no conclusion to support.

__Y__ 10. Is the wording in the answer too strong to be justified?

Even if you're looking at a Must Be True question with a conditional structure, you still need the strength of the answer to be calibrated to the strength of the stimulus. Strong language isn't a red flag, exactly, but you always need to be sure it doesn't exceed the strength of the claims in the stimulus.

__Y__ 11. Is this the contrapositive of my prephrase?

Must Be True questions that are heavy in conditional logic should be fairly predictable—whenever you prephrase a conditional answer, always be on the lookout for its contrapositive.

__N__ 12. Does this connect all the different ideas in the stimulus?

The correct answer needs to tell a true story, but it doesn't need to tell the whole story.

Which one of the following most logically completes the argument above?

__N__ 13. Is it possible for this to be false?

The right answer is most likely a valid conclusion, but there might be a little wiggle room, so treat these fill-in-the-blank Inference questions as Most Strongly Supported rather than Must Be True.

__Y__ 14. Does this answer bring in new information?

It shouldn't!

__Y__ 15. Does this support the argument's conclusion?

The correct answer will usually be the argument's conclusion, not support it. But, if you are presented with a stimulus that already includes a conclusion, the blank will probably be filled with a premise that supports the conclusion given.

__Y__ 16. Is the wording in the answer too strong to be justified?

This is always a concern with an Inference Family question.

__N__ 17. Is this the contrapositive of my prephrase?

These questions tend not to be conditional.

___Y___ 18. **Does this connect all the different ideas in the stimulus?**

Unlike the other Inference Family questions, fill-in-the-blank ones almost always have a conclusion that ties the whole stimulus together because you're looking for the logical completion of the argument, not just something that is true, or likely true, based on what you've been given.

Which of the following, if true, would best reconcile the astronomer's seemingly contradictory observations?

___N___ 19. Is this likely to be true?

When the stem includes the phrase "if true," treat every answer as though it were and don't worry about whether that seems realistic or not.

___Y___ 20. **If I'd known this was true before reading the stimulus, would the observation still have seemed contradictory?**

This is exactly what you want to ask. The right answer should make you say, "Ooooh, now those two things make sense together."

___N___ 21. Does this match my prephrase?

Explain a Result questions don't lend themselves well to specific prephrasing. You want to be clear on why the initial situation is unexpected, but don't expect to predict the exact way the LSAT will choose to reconcile the situation.

___Y___ 22. **Does this make the observations seem more contradictory?**

Many wrong answer choices on Explain a Result questions actually do the opposite of what you're looking for, so asking this question can help you ID those bad answers.

___Y___ 23. **Is this specific or comprehensive enough to affect the given situation?**

If the observation is about male squid, the correct answer must deal with that subset of squid or deal broadly enough with squid (or sea creatures) in general that it definitely applies to the subset you've been given. But be careful: sometimes broad answers are not comprehensive enough to apply to the subset in question. "All squid . . ." would work, whereas "Squid generally . . ." would not.

___Y___ 24. **Does this explain not only why the surprising thing happened, but also why the surprising thing happened in spite of the obstacle presented, or instead of the thing we would have expected to happen?**

Some of the most tempting Explain a Result incorrect answers will give a good reason that the surprising thing happened, but without reconciling it with the obstacle presented or the result we would have expected. These answers might seem right, but they only tell half the story.

Which one of the following examples best illustrates the principle described in the argument?

___Y___ 25. **Does the example in the answer trigger the sufficient condition of the principle?**

This is one of the two criteria for a correct answer choice!

___N___ 26. If there are two principles in the stimulus, does this example illustrate both of them?

Many Principle Example questions present you with two principles, but the correct answer will not necessarily illustrate both.

___Y___ 27. **Does this example conclude the principle's necessary condition?**

This is the other criteria for a correct answer choice!

___N___ 28. Does this follow the same order as the given principle?

Order is insignificant; a correct answer might open with the conclusion and end with the premise.

___Y___ 29. **Is this an example of the contrapositive of the principle?**

It's not as common as the alternative, but it has been known to happen, so you should always both diagram and contrapose the principle(s) given and compare each answer to both versions.

___Y___ 30. **Does this example conclude the principle's sufficient condition?**

Many, many incorrect answers will mistakenly conclude the principle's sufficient condition. A quick and easy screening technique is to check the conclusion of each answer and eliminate all those that aren't the necessary condition of the principle or the principle's contrapositive.

If the statements above are true, then each of the following statements could be true EXCEPT:

___Y___ 31. **Does this contradict information in the stimulus?**

If it does, then it must be false, which is exactly what we're looking for.

__Y__   32. **Does this contradict a conclusion that could validly be drawn from the information in the stimulus?**

Conditional Must Be False questions can be especially tricky because they often require that you deduce what must be true, and then find an answer that contradicts it.

__N__   33. Does this seem likely to be false in the real world?

You're only concerned with whether it contradicts the stimulus.

__Y__   34. **If the stimulus is conditional, does this show a statement's sufficient condition without its necessary condition?**

That's how you contradict a conditional statement!

__N__   35. If this were true, would it weaken the argument in the stimulus?

Like other Inference Family questions, Must Be False questions don't have arguments in the stimulus.

__Y__   36. **Given the information in the stimulus, is this answer possibly true?**

Worth asking, because if an answer choice is possibly true, it's wrong!

5

Drill 95: Family Feud: Assumption vs. Inference, Round 2

Instructions: You already know that Most Strongly Supported question stems have very similar language to Strengthen question stems. The two question types, however, have very different approaches and criteria for correct answers. For each of the following stems, write in whether it's a Strengthen question (S) or an Inference question (I). Note: There will be repetition among these stems. That's because this is a rapid-fire drill to practice making quick determinations. Since you've done this drill once before, set your timer for only 45 seconds—or 30 seconds, if you're feeling bold!

_____ 1. Which one of the following, if true, adds the most support for the conclusion of the argument?

_____ 2. The information above, if true, most strongly supports which one of the following?

_____ 3. Which one of the following is most strongly supported by the statements above?

_____ 4. Which one of the following principles, if valid, most strongly supports the reasoning above?

_____ 5. The photographer's statements, if true, provide the most support for which one of the following?

_____ 6. The argument's conclusion is most strongly supported if which one of the following is assumed?

_____ 7. The sociologist's statements, if true, most strongly support which one of the following?

_____ 8. Which one of the following, if true, most strongly supports the climatologist's reasoning?

_____ 9. The facts cited above most strongly support which one of the following?

_____ 10. Which one of the following, if assumed, most strongly supports the reasoning above?

5

Answers follow on the next page.

Answers

  __S__   1. Which one of the following, if true, adds the most support for the conclusion of the argument?

  __I__   2. The information above, if true, most strongly supports which one of the following?

  __I__   3. Which one of the following is most strongly supported by the statements above?

  __S__   4. Which one of the following principles, if valid, most strongly supports the reasoning above?

  __I__   5. The photographer's statements, if true, provide the most support for which one of the following?

  __S__   6. The argument's conclusion is most strongly supported if which one of the following is assumed?

  __I__   7. The sociologist's statements, if true, most strongly support which one of the following?

  __S__   8. Which one of the following, if true, most strongly supports the climatologist's reasoning?

  __I__   9. The facts cited above most strongly support which one of the following?

  __S__   10. Which one of the following, if assumed, most strongly supports the reasoning above?

Drill 96: Chain Chain Chain, Round 1

Instructions: Combining conditional statements is a skill that is tested throughout the exam, but it is particularly important for Inference Family questions. In this drill, groups of conditional statements will be given. Think of each one as a stimulus in a conditional Inference Family Question. Use the space provided to diagram the statements, chain them together, and take the contrapositive of the chains, just as you would if you were prephrasing correct answer choices from these stimuli.

1. All video games require hand-eye coordination. Anything requiring hand-eye coordination should be considered a sport, and schools should offer scholarships for anything that's considered a sport.

2. If Genevieve attends the party, Jamal will as well. And Martese won't attend any party that Rochelle attends. However, Genevieve will attend any party that Martese does not attend.

3. All bicycling promotes cardiovascular health, which, in turn, always promotes a longer life span.

4. According to Professor Simmons, any machine equipped with a processor qualifies as a computer. No computers can operate without electricity, and electricity requires both generation and storage.

5. All the members of Club Moon are doctors. No one can become a doctor without first attending medical school. And all medical schools require a bachelor's degree.

6. The only shellfish Ruth eats is lobster. No lobsters are mammals. Mammals are the only organisms that grow hair.

7. Shauri will be marked tardy unless she arrives at school on time, and she will only arrive at school on time if she catches the bus. She only catches the bus when she wakes up before 6:00am, and for Shauri to wake up before 6:00am, she will have to set an alarm.

8. To be eligible to vote in Ravania, one must be both a citizen and over the age of 18. Everyone in the Ravania Populist Party is an eligible voter, and all members of the Basni family are members of the Ravania Populist Party.

9. At the Conservancy Botanic Gardens, all daffodils are planted outside, and everything planted outside is watered by sprinklers and not by hand.

10. Lincoln will serve on the committee only if Gavan does not. Gavan will serve on the committee unless Yusuf serves. Yusuf will never serve on a committee on which Howin serves.

11. At Brandt College, Professor Marquis is the only professor who teaches Postmodern Literature, and she refuses to teach on any day except Tuesday. Majoring in English at Brandt College requires taking Postmodern Literature.

12. Each of the songs on Montgomery's new album is a punk rock song. No punk rock song features more than four chords, but all punk rock songs feature electric guitar.

13. None of the houses on Mavis Street have rooftop solar panels, nor do any of them have satellite dishes. Every member of the neighborhood's Anti-litter Committee lives in a house on Mavis Street.

14. Parking in Lot J at City College requires either a valid parking permit or a $5.00 daily fee, and Lot J is the only parking lot at the college with a station for recharging electric car batteries. To receive the college's Electric Car Tuition Credit, one must recharge one's electric car's battery at the college at least once per week.

15. Otavia will enroll in an athletic club only if it has a swimming pool. The only athletic club in Brighton with a swimming pool is Workout Central. No one can enter Workout Central without a membership, but a membership with Workout Central guarantees access to the club's climbing wall.

16. None of Wallens's shorter compositions features the flute, and Devona will never agree to perform a composition that doesn't feature the flute. If our concert next month is to be a success, it is essential that Devona perform on every piece we play.

17. Unless our organization procures additional funding, we will not be able to advertise our summer charity event. Without advertising, our summer charity event will have few attendees.

18. If Jiang decides to buy a pet, he will definitely buy a reptile. All reptiles are cold-blooded, and cold-blooded animals require sunlight for warmth.

19. Each member of the Committee on International Relations is bilingual. Every association member who is not on the Energy Committee is on the Committee on International Relations. Fumiko, an association member, has never and will never serve on the Energy Committee.

20. Williams is never selected if Jodh is selected. Gardner is selected unless Jodh is selected. If Hollyn is not selected, then neither is Gardner.

21. The Clean Curb waste removal company requires all customers to sort their recycling into three categories: glass, paper, and plastic. The only recycling service in Milletton is Clean Curb, and Hermia, a resident of Milletton, insists on always patronizing a recycling service.

22. Invasive species always threaten both indigenous flora and indigenous fauna. The red palm mite is an invasive species, and the only arthropods on Palm Frond Island are red palm mites.

23. Jeremy will subscribe to *Cyclists Monthly* unless he subscribes to *Trail Cyclist.* If he subscribes to *Trail Cyclist*, he will learn about new bicycling trails in the Spiny Mountains, in which case he will purchase higher quality mountain-biking tires than he currently owns.

24. Without a faster processor, Iyesha's computer will not be able to run *Castle Quest*, a new video game. The only processor currently on the market that is faster than Iyesha's current processor is the Accucomp SX-9.

25. Jevette, a local musician, always includes in her live performances "Step Out," one of the first songs she ever wrote. Each performance of "Step Out" features sudden rhythm changes, and sudden rhythm changes are never easy to perform.

5

Answers

Note: Your shorthand may differ from ours, but the concepts should be related in the correct direction. We're also going to get more succinct with our abbreviations as we go, which is an important, time-saving skill to develop.

1. All video games require hand-eye coordination. Anything requiring hand-eye coordination should be considered a sport, and schools should offer scholarships for anything that's considered a sport.

   Video Game → HE Coord → Sport → Scholarships
   ~Scholarships → ~Sport → ~HE Coord → ~Video Game

2. If Genevieve attends the party, Jamal will as well. And Martese won't attend any party that Rochelle attends. However, Genevieve will attend any party that Martese does not attend.

   Roch → ~Mar → Gen → Jam
   ~Jam → ~Gen → Mar → ~Roch

3. All bicycling promotes cardiovascular health, which, in turn, always promotes a longer life span.

   Bic → Card H → Longer LS
   ~Longer LS → ~Card H → ~Bic

4. According to Professor Simmons, any machine equipped with a processor qualifies as a computer. No computers can operate without electricity, and electricity requires both generation and storage.

   Mach w/ proc → Comp → Elec → Gen + Stor
   ~Stor OR ~Gen → ~Elec → ~Comp → ~Mach w/ proc

5. All the members of Club Moon are doctors. No one can become a doctor without first attending medical school. And all medical schools require a bachelor's degree.

   Memb CM → Doc → Med Sch → Bach Deg
   ~Bach Deg → ~Med Sch → ~Doc → ~Memb CM

6. The only shellfish Ruth eats is lobster. No lobsters are mammals. Mammals are the only organisms that grow hair.

   Ruth eat shell → Lobs → ~Mamm → ~Hair
   Hair → Mamm → ~Lobs → ~Ruth eat shell

7. Shauri will be marked tardy unless she arrives at school on time, and she will only arrive at school on time if she catches the bus. She only catches the bus when she wakes up before 6:00am, and for Shauri to wake up before 6:00am, she will have to set an alarm.

   ~Tardy → On time → Bus → Wake before 6 → Alarm
   ~Alarm → ~Wake before 6 → ~Bus → ~On time → Tardy

8. To be eligible to vote in Ravania, one must be both a citizen and over the age of 18. Everyone in the Ravania Populist Party is an eligible voter, and all members of the Basni family are members of the Ravania Populist Party.

   Basni → RPP → Vote Rav → Cit AND Over 18
   ~Cit OR ~Over 18 → ~Vote Rav → ~RPP → ~Basni

9. At the Conservancy Botanic Gardens, all daffodils are planted outside, and everything planted outside is watered by sprinklers and not by hand.

   CBG Daff → Planted Out → Sprink AND ~By hand
   By hand OR ~Sprink → ~Planted Out → ~CBG Daff

10. Lincoln will serve on the committee only if Gavan does not. Gavan will serve on the committee unless Yusuf serves. Yusuf will never serve on a committee on which Howin serves.

    Linc → ~Gav → Yus → ~How
    How → ~Yus → Gav → ~Linc

11. At Brandt College, Professor Marquis is the only professor who teaches Postmodern Literature, and she refuses to teach on any day except Tuesday. Majoring in English at Brandt College requires taking Postmodern Literature.

    Eng Maj at Brandt → Post Lit → Marq teach → Tues
    ~Tues → ~Marq teach → ~Post Lit → ~Eng Maj at Brandt

12. Each of the songs on Montgomery's new album is a punk rock song. No punk rock song features more than four chords, but all punk rock songs feature electric guitar.

    Song on M's new alb → Punk Rock → ~more than four chords + electric guitar
    More than four chords OR ~electric guitar → ~Punk Rock → ~Song on M's new alb

13. None of the houses on Mavis Street have rooftop solar panels, nor do any of them have satellite dishes. Every member of the neighborhood's Anti-litter Committee lives in a house on Mavis Street.

    Memb of ALC → Mav Str → ~RSP AND ~Sat Dish
    Sat Dish OR RSP → ~Mav Str → ~Memb of ALC

14. Parking in Lot J at City College requires either a valid parking permit or a $5.00 daily fee, and Lot J is the only parking lot at the college with a station for recharging electric car batteries. To receive the college's Electric Car Tuition Credit, one must recharge one's electric car's battery at the college at least once per week.

    Elec Car Tuit Cred → Rech Batt at Coll → Lot J → Val Perm OR Daily Fee
    ~Val Perm + ~Daily Fee → ~Lot J → ~Rech Batt at Coll → ~Elec Car Tuit Cred

15. Otavia will enroll in an athletic club only if it has a swimming pool. The only athletic club in Brighton with a swimming pool is Workout Central. No one can enter Workout Central without a membership, but a membership with Workout Central guarantees access to the club's climbing wall.

    Ot Enroll → Pool → Work Cent → Memb → Acc to Climbing Wall
    ~Acc to Climbing Wall → ~Memb → ~Work Cent → ~Pool → ~Ot Enroll

16. None of Wallens's shorter compositions features the flute, and Devona will never agree to perform a composition that doesn't feature the flute. If our concert next month is to be a success, it is essential that Devona perform on every piece we play.

    W's Shorter Comps → ~Feature Flute → ~Dev Perf → ~Succ at Conc
    Succ at Conc → Dev Perf → Feature Flute → ~W's Shorter Comps

17. Unless our organization procures additional funding, we will not be able to advertise our summer charity event. Without advertising, our summer charity event will have few attendees.

    ~Addl Fund → ~Adv Event → Few Attend
    ~Few Attend → Adv Event → Addl Fund

18. If Jiang decides to buy a pet, he will definitely buy a reptile. All reptiles are cold-blooded, and cold-blooded animals require sunlight for warmth.

    J pet → Rept → Cold Blood → Sun for Warm
    ~Sun for Warm → ~Cold Blood → ~Rept → ~J pet

19. Each member of the Committee on International Relations is bilingual. Every association member who is not on the Energy Committee is on the Committee on International Relations. Fumiko, an association member, has never and will never serve on the Energy Committee.

    Fum → ~En Comm → Int Rel Comm → Biling
    ~Biling → ~Int Rel Comm → En Comm → ~Fum

20. Williams is never selected if Jodh is selected. Gardner is selected unless Jodh is selected. If Hollyn is not selected, then neither is Gardner.

    ~H → ~G → J → ~W
    W → ~J → G → H

21. The Clean Curb waste removal company requires all customers to sort their recycling into three categories: glass, paper, and plastic. The only recycling service in Milletton is Clean Curb, and Hermia, a resident of Milletton, insists on always patronizing a recycling service.

    Herm → Recyc in Mill → CC → Sort
    ~Sort → ~CC → ~Recyc in Mill → ~Herm

22. Invasive species always threaten both indigenous flora and indigenous fauna. The red palm mite is an invasive species, and the only arthropods on Palm Frond Island are red palm mites.

    Arth on PFI → RPM → Inv → Threat Ind Flor AND Threat Ind Faun
    ~Threat Ind Flor OR ~Threat Ind Faun → ~Inv → ~RPM → ~Arth on PFI

23. Jeremy will subscribe to *Cyclists Monthly* unless he subscribes to *Trail Cyclist*. If he subscribes to *Trail Cyclist*, he will learn about new bicycling trails in the Spiny Mountains, in which case he will purchase higher quality mountain-biking tires than he currently owns.

    ~Purch better tires → ~Learn new SM trails → ~Subscr TC → Subscr CM
    ~Subscr CM → Subscr TC → Learn new SM trails → Purch better tires

24. Without a faster processor, Iyesha's computer will not be able to run *Castle Quest*, a new video game. The only processor currently on the market that is faster than Iyesha's current processor is the Accucomp SX-9.

    ~SX-9 → ~Faster Proc → ~CQ
    CQ → Faster Proc → SX-9

25. Jevette, a local musician, always includes in her live performances "Step Out," one of the first songs she ever wrote. Each performance of "Step Out" features sudden rhythm changes, and sudden rhythm changes are never easy to perform.

    Jev Live Perf → SO → Sudd Rhy Change → ~Easy
    Easy → ~Sudd Rhy Change → ~SO → ~Jev Live Perf

Drill 97: Expect the Unexpected

Instructions: Explain a Result questions are about the relationship between what we *think* would happen and what *actually* happened. And in these questions, what *actually* happened is puzzling because it happened in spite of some fact that would make us think it wouldn't.

Practice breaking this type of stimulus into its core components by filling in the blanks in the following sentence: *How come _____ in spite of _____, because I would have expected _____.*

1. Five years ago, the local university spent millions of dollars improving its campus and facilities. This year, both the university's enrollment and its overall ranking declined for the third year in a row.

   How come _____

   in spite of _____,

   because I would have expected _____.

2. Playing a musical instrument is known to correlate with strong academic achievement. When Jamie began playing a musical instrument, her grades declined.

   How come _____

   in spite of _____,

   because I would have expected _____.

3. In country Z, regulations that protect the environment are popular with voters. In this year's presidential election, no candidate in country Z supported regulations to protect the environment.

   How come _____

   in spite of _____,

   because I would have expected _____.

4. Literary critics typically define a classic as any work that is still widely read after fifty years from the date it was published. In Julia's classic literature course, three of the assigned works were published within the last forty years.

   How come _____

   in spite of _____,

   because I would have expected _____.

5. A powerful hurricane recently struck country X, knocking down trees with life-threatening wind gusts, flooding buildings, and wiping out the electricity grid. Such damage usually correlates with a high number of casualties. However, no injuries or deaths were reported after the hurricane.

   How come _____

   in spite of _____,

   because I would have expected _____.

6. Museum curators typically choose to spend their annual budgets on a variety of exhibits and collections projects in order to attract a wide array of visitors and donors. A small museum recently invested over 75 percent of its annual budget into the restoration and display of a single artifact. Since then, the museum has seen record-breaking attendance and donations.

    How come _____

    in spite of _____,

    because I would have expected _____.

7. People who wear glasses require an annual vision screening, which is 100% covered by all vision insurance plans. Linda recently had an annual vision screening and had to pay a significant portion of the cost.

    How come _____

    in spite of _____,

    because I would have expected _____.

8. Sports reporters widely described football team A as the underdog in the championship game, with almost no chance of winning. Dave, a fan of football team A, was shocked and disappointed when his team lost the championship game.

    How come _____

    in spite of _____,

    because I would have expected _____.

9. Expert advisers to the city's charter schools recommended that each school spend at least one month preparing its students for the end-of-year test. School A spent only two weeks preparing, and its students outperformed students at every other charter school in the district.

    How come _____

    in spite of _____,

    because I would have expected _____.

10. In the past, late spring frosts have caused cherry blossom trees to produce fewer blooms than average in those years. This year, there was a frost in late May. The cherry blossom trees produced an average number of blooms compared to years past.

    How come _____

    in spite of _____,

    because I would have expected _____.

11. Emily was the most highly qualified candidate for an engineering job, with the greatest number of years of experience in the field. Another candidate with fewer qualifications and less experience was given the engineering job.

    How come _____

    in spite of _____,

    because I would have expected _____.

12. Studies have shown that spending significant amounts of time in front of electronic screens late at night diminishes one's ability to fall asleep quickly. Angie spent half an hour video chatting with her sister on the phone after 11pm one night, but she was still able to fall asleep directly afterward.

    How come _____

    in spite of _____,

    because I would have expected _____.

13. A particular American bird species is listed as endangered. Citizen scientists in Florida, however, report seeing the bird very frequently.

    How come _____

    in spite of _____,

    because I would have expected _____.

14. It is widely known that yoga is an effective method for combating stress. However, a recent study showed that only 20 percent of people who feel highly stressed practice yoga.

    How come _____

    in spite of _____,

    because I would have expected _____.

15. Jerome purchased child safety plugs for his electrical outlets to protect his children from the risk of electrical shock. Jerome's children are now far past the age when they were at risk of accidentally shocking themselves with an outlet, but he has not stopped using the child safety plugs.

    How come _____

    in spite of _____,

    because I would have expected _____.

16. The local pottery painting studio recently invested heavily in an advertising campaign to attract families with young children. They offered Wednesday night family classes, discounts for children, and kid-friendly "unbreakable" pottery. The studio has not seen any increase in the number of young children brought in to paint pottery.

    How come _____

    in spite of _____,

    because I would have expected _____.

17. In an effort to combat seasonal affective disorder, in which individuals experience depressed moods due to the change of seasons, Maria recently installed natural lighting in her home. Access to natural lighting has been proven to enhance the mood of individuals with seasonal affective disorder. Maria has not seen any mood improvement since installing the lighting.

    How come _____

    in spite of _____,

    because I would have expected _____.

18. George was the fastest person in his high school, had the best cross-country coach in the county, and trained daily. However, George did not win the county's annual marathon.

    How come _____

    in spite of _____,

    because I would have expected _____.

19. Three years ago, the state transportation department invested a record-setting sum of money in a series of three-year projects to upgrade the state's roads and highways. A survey conducted this year showed that citizens of the state have never been more displeased with the roads and highways in the state.

    How come _____

    in spite of _____,

    because I would have expected _____.

20. A local town recently reduced its taxes and regulations in an effort to attract more businesses. Since then, more businesses have left the town than have come to it.

    How come _____

    in spite of _____,

    because I would have expected _____.

Answers

1. Five years ago, the local university spent millions of dollars improving its campus and facilities. This year, both the university's enrollment and its overall ranking declined for the third year in a row.

    How come <u>enrollment and ranking declined again</u>
    in spite of <u>the millions spent improving the campus</u>,
    because I would have expected <u>enrollment and ranking to increase</u>.

2. Playing a musical instrument is known to correlate with strong academic achievement. When Jamie began playing a musical instrument, her grades declined.

    How come <u>Jamie's grades declined when she started playing a musical instrument</u>
    in spite of <u>the correlation between playing an instrument and strong academic achievement</u>,
    because I would have expected <u>Jamie's grades to improve</u>.

3. In country Z, regulations that protect the environment are popular with voters. In this year's presidential election, no candidate in country Z supported regulations to protect the environment.

    How come <u>no candidate in country Z supported regulations to protect the environment</u>
    in spite of <u>the popularity of such regulations with voters</u>,
    because I would have expected <u>candidates to support what's popular with voters</u>.

4. Literary critics typically define a classic as any work that is still widely read after fifty years from the date it was published. In Julia's classic literature course, three of the assigned works were published within the last forty years.

    How come <u>Julia's classic lit course is using works published in the last forty years</u>
    in spite of <u>the fact that literary critics' definition of classics says they must have been published at least fifty years ago</u>,
    because I would have expected <u>a classic literature class to use works that meet the literary critics' definition of a classic</u>.

5. A powerful hurricane recently struck country X, knocking down trees with life-threatening wind gusts, flooding buildings, and wiping out the electricity grid. Such damage usually correlates with a high number of casualties. However, no injuries or deaths were reported after the hurricane.

    How come <u>no casualties were reported after the hurricane</u>
    in spite of <u>damage that would typically correlate with a high number of casualties</u>,
    because I would have expected <u>a high number of casualties after a damaging hurricane</u>.

6. Museum curators typically choose to spend their annual budgets on a variety of exhibits and collections projects in order to attract a wide array of visitors and donors. A small museum recently invested over 75 percent of its annual budget into the restoration and display of a single artifact. Since then, the museum has seen record-breaking attendance and donations.

    How come <u>the museum has seen record-breaking attendance and donations</u>
    in spite of <u>choosing to spend so much of its budget on a single artifact</u>,
    because I would have expected <u>the museum to attract fewer donors and visitors</u>.

7. People who wear glasses require an annual vision screening, which is 100% covered by all vision insurance plans. Linda recently had an annual vision screening and had to pay a significant portion of the cost.

    How come Linda had to pay a significant portion of the cost of her vision screening
    in spite of the fact that vision screenings are 100% covered by all vision insurance plans,
    because I would have expected Linda's screening to be 100% covered by a vision insurance plan.

8. Sports reporters widely described football team A as the underdogs in the championship game, with almost no chance of winning. Dave, a fan of football team A, was shocked and disappointed when his team lost the championship game.

    How come Dave was shocked and disappointed when his team lost the game
    in spite of wide reporting that the team was likely to lose,
    because I would have expected Dave to be unsurprised that his team lost.

9. Expert advisers to the city's charter schools recommended that each school spend at least one month preparing its students for the end-of-year test. School A spent only two weeks preparing, and its students outperformed students at every other charter school in the district.

    How come school A outperformed other charter schools,
    in spite of spending less time preparing for the end-of-year test than recommended,
    because I would have expected school A to perform worse.

10. In the past, late spring frosts have caused cherry blossom trees to produce fewer blooms than average in those years. This year, there was a frost in late May. The cherry blossom trees produced an average number of blooms compared to years past.

    How come the cherry blossoms produced an average number of blooms
    in spite of the frost in late May,
    because I would have expected a lower number of blooms than average.

11. Emily was the most highly qualified candidate for an engineering job, with the greatest number of years of experience in the field. Another candidate with fewer qualifications and less experience was given the engineering job.

    How come Emily was not given the engineering job
    in spite of her being the most highly qualified and experienced candidate,
    because I would have expected the most highly qualified and experienced candidate to get the job.

12. Studies have shown that spending significant amounts of time in front of electronic screens late at night diminishes one's ability to fall asleep quickly. Angie spent half an hour video chatting with her sister on the phone after 11pm one night, but she was still able to fall asleep directly afterward.

    How come Angie was able to fall asleep quickly
    in spite of spending a significant amount of time on an electronic screen late at night,
    because I would have expected her ability to fall asleep to have been diminished.

13. A particular American bird species is listed as endangered. Citizen scientists in Florida, however, report seeing the bird very frequently.

     How come <u>the bird is frequently sighted in Florida</u>
     in spite of <u>its endangered status</u>,
     because I would have expected <u>sightings of the bird to be rare</u>.

14. It is widely known that yoga is an effective method for combating stress. However, a recent study showed that only 20 percent of people who feel highly stressed practice yoga.

     How come <u>only a small percentage of highly stressed people practice yoga</u>
     in spite of <u>widespread knowledge that yoga is an effective way to combat stress</u>,
     because I would have expected <u>that if people knew that a technique is an effective way to combat their stress, they would use that technique</u>.

15. Jerome purchased child safety plugs for his electrical outlets to protect his children from the risk of electrical shock. Jerome's children are now far past the age when they were at risk of accidentally shocking themselves with an outlet, but he has not stopped using the child safety plugs.

     How come <u>Jerome has not stopped using the child safety plugs</u>
     in spite of <u>the fact that his children are now old enough to be safe around electrical outlets</u>,
     because I would have expected <u>Jerome to stop using the plugs when there was no longer a risk to his children</u>.

16. The local pottery painting studio recently invested heavily in an advertising campaign to attract families with young children. They offered Wednesday night family classes, discounts for children, and kid-friendly "unbreakable" pottery. The studio has not seen any increase in the number of young children brought in to paint pottery.

     How come <u>the pottery studio has not seen an increase in children visiting the studio</u>
     in spite of <u>recent advertising efforts targeted toward kids</u>,
     because I would have expected <u>the advertising efforts to attract more families with children into the studio</u>.

17. In an effort to combat seasonal affective disorder, in which individuals experience depressed moods due to the change of seasons, Maria recently installed natural lighting in her home. Access to natural lighting has been proven to enhance the mood of individuals with seasonal affective disorder. Maria has not seen any mood improvement since installing the lighting.

     How come <u>Maria has not seen any improvement in her mood</u>
     in spite of <u>installing natural lighting</u>,
     because I would have expected <u>the natural lighting to help combat seasonal affective disorder</u>.

18. George was the fastest person in his high school, had the best cross-country coach in the county, and trained daily. However, George did not win the county's annual marathon.

     How come <u>George did not win the county's annual marathon</u>
     in spite of <u>being the fastest person in his school, training daily, and having the best cross-country coach</u>,
     because I would have expected <u>George to win</u>.

19. Three years ago, the state transportation department invested a record-setting sum of money in a series of three-year projects to upgrade the state's roads and highways. A survey conducted this year showed that citizens of the state have never been more displeased with the roads and highways in the state.

   How come <u>citizens of the state are so displeased with the roads and highways</u>
   in spite of <u>the recent investments in upgrading the state's roads and highways</u>,
   because I would have expected <u>the citizens to be more satisfied after projects to upgrade the roads</u>.

20. A local town recently reduced its taxes and regulations in an effort to attract more businesses. Since then, more businesses have left the town than have come to it.

   How come <u>more businesses have left the town than come to it</u>
   in spite of <u>reduced taxes and regulations</u>,
   because I would have expected <u>more growth in business</u>.

Drill 98: Principle Example, Quick Elimination Edition

Instructions: Principle Example questions ask you to find situations that demonstrate a given principle in action. That means the situation in the correct answer has to be one in which the principle can be applied. Principles can only be applied in situations that fulfill their sufficient conditions, and when they are applied, their necessary condition is concluded. If an answer choice concludes something that is not the principle's necessary condition or has as its premise something that is not the principle's sufficient condition, it should be a quick elimination.

Because so many Principle Example questions provide you with not one but two principles, that is the format this drill will take. For each of the following pairs of principles, decide for each accompanying item if an answer containing the feature described could be correct (Y) or not (N). Two things to keep in mind: (1) you're not deciding whether the statement could be true, but only whether it could correctly serve as an example of the principle in question, and (2) a correct answer might fulfill a sufficient condition of a principle's contrapositive and conclude that contrapositive's necessary condition.

Set A

Doesn't take recipient's tastes into account → Gift not thoughtful

Something recipient wants AND Costs gift-giver time → Gift thoughtful

_____ 1. Conclusion: The gift was thoughtful.

_____ 2. Conclusion: The gift was not thoughtful.

_____ 3. Conclusion: The gift does take the recipient's tastes into account.

_____ 4. Premise: The recipient didn't want the gift.

Set B

Steam locomotive → Powered by pressure-driven piston AND Labor-intensive operation

Powered by internal combustion → ~Steam locomotive

_____ 5. Premise: Labor-intensive to operate

_____ 6. Premise: Powered by internal combustion

_____ 7. Conclusion: Powered by a pressure-driven piston

_____ 8. Conclusion: Steam locomotive

Set C

Majority of council members oppose the measure → Bad for local community

Good for local community → Improves roads AND Lowers commute times

_____ 9. Conclusion: The measure is bad for the local community.

_____ 10. Conclusion: The measure would result in lengthier commute times.

_____ 11. Premise: Most council members support the measure.

_____ 12. Conclusion: Most community members oppose the measure.

Set D

Mutation decreases risk of predation OR Increases attractiveness of phenotypic traits → Evolutionary advantage

Mutation weakens the genetic pool → Evolutionary disadvantage

_____ 13. Premise: A mutation increases attractiveness of phenotypic traits.

_____ 14. Conclusion: A mutation results in an evolutionary disadvantage.

_____ 15. Premise: A mutation does not weaken the host's genetic pool.

_____ 16. Conclusion: A mutation creates neither advantage nor disadvantage (no effect).

Set E

Clinical study identifies only minor side effects →
FDA should approve new drug therapy

Clinical study identifies major side effects → FDA
should not approve new drug therapy

_____ 17. Premise: Clinical study results are
inconclusive.

_____ 18. Conclusion: FDA will not approve the
new drug therapy.

_____ 19. Conclusion: FDA should approve the
new drug therapy.

_____ 20. Premise: Clinical study finds that the
new drug therapy's benefits outweigh
its risks.

Set F

"Marginal" OR "Poor" rating in crash safety test →
Likely to result in serious injury

"Good" rating in crash safety test → Likely to be
purchased by families with children

_____ 21. Premise: "Poor" rating in crash safety
test

_____ 22. Premise: "Acceptable" rating in crash
safety test

_____ 23. Conclusion: Likely to be most popular
among consumers with children

_____ 24. Conclusion: Unlikely to cause serious
injury

Set G

Best art → Elicits strong emotion OR Highly
memorable

Bad art → Uninteresting

_____ 25. Premise: Good art

_____ 26. Premise: Best art

_____ 27. Premise: Highly memorable

_____ 28. Conclusion: Not interesting

Set H

Reason to believe it will help and no reason to
believe it will harm → Act justifiable

Act questionable → Reason to believe that the
harm might outweigh the help

_____ 29. Premise: No reason to believe an act
will harm

_____ 30. Premise: No reason to believe an act
will help

_____ 31. Conclusion: Act questionable

_____ 32. Conclusion: Act justifiable

Set I

Competing courses of action each benefit some
and hurt others → Moral quandary

Course of action the morally right choice → No
choice that would benefit more and hurt fewer

_____ 33. Premise: Not a moral quandary

_____ 34. Premise: Not the morally right choice

_____ 35. Conclusion: Not the morally right
choice

_____ 36. Conclusion: Not a moral quandary

Set J

Performed for the benefit of no one but oneself →
Selfish action

Egomaniacal → Performed with complete disregard
for how others will be impacted

_____ 37. Premise: Egomaniacal

_____ 38. Premise: Selfish action

_____ 39. Conclusion: Not egomaniacal

_____ 40. Conclusion: Not selfish

Answers

Set A

Doesn't take recipient's tastes into account → Gift not thoughtful;

Gift thoughtful → Takes recipient's tastes into account

Something recipient wants AND Costs gift-giver time → Gift thoughtful;

~Gift thoughtful → ~Something recipient wants OR ~Costs gift giver time

__Y__ 1. **Conclusion: The gift was thoughtful.**

(Because this conclusion matches a necessary condition in one of our principles, this conclusion could be properly drawn if the sufficient condition were supplied.)

__Y__ 2. **Conclusion: The gift was not thoughtful.**

(This also matches a necessary condition in one of our principles, so this conclusion could also be properly drawn by supplying the sufficient condition.)

__Y__ 3. **Conclusion: The gift does take the recipient's tastes into account.**

(This statement is the necessary condition of the principle's contrapositive, so it can be properly concluded by supplying the contrapositive's sufficient condition.)

__N__ 4. Premise: The recipient didn't want the gift.

(This is one of the necessary conditions of the principle's contrapositive, so it can't serve as a premise.)

Set B

Steam locomotive → Powered by pressure-driven piston AND Labor-intensive operation;

~Powered by pressure-driven piston OR ~Labor-intensive operation → ~Steam locomotive

Powered by internal combustion → ~Steam locomotive;

Steam locomotive → ~Powered by internal combustion

__N__ 5. Premise: Labor-intensive to operate

(This term only appears as a necessary condition, so it can't serve as a premise.)

__Y__ 6. **Premise: Powered by internal combustion**

(This term is the sufficient condition of the second principle, so it could serve as a premise.)

__Y__ 7. **Conclusion: Powered by a pressure-driven piston**

(This is the necessary condition of our first principle, so it can serve as a conclusion.)

__N__ 8. Conclusion: Steam locomotive

(The necessary condition of either the principle or its contrapositive could serve as a conclusion. This statement is the sufficient condition of the first principle as well as the sufficient condition of the second principle's contrapositive, neither of which can serve as a conclusion.)

Set C

Majority of council members oppose the measure → Bad for local community;

~Bad for local community → ~Majority of council members oppose the measure

Good for local community → Improves roads AND Lowers commute times;

~Improves roads OR ~Lowers commute times → ~Good for local community

__Y__ 9. **Conclusion: The measure is bad for the local community.**

(Being bad for the local community is a necessary condition in our first principle, so this works.)

__N__ 10. Conclusion: The measure would result in lengthier commute times.

("Lengthier commute times" is similar to the sufficient condition of the second principle's contrapositive, so it could not serve as a conclusion.)

__N__ 11. Premise: Most council members support the measure.

(If most council members support the measure, that's similar to the necessary condition of the first principle's contrapositive. Thus, it can't be a premise. And if you look carefully, it actually can't be a conclusion either. While we could apply the contrapositive to conclude that most council members do not oppose the measure, that's not the same as saying most of them support it—perhaps most are neutral.)

__N__ 12. Conclusion: Most community members oppose the measure.

(Careful! The principle discusses whether *council* members oppose the measure and makes no mention of *community* members at all.)

Set D

Mutation decreases risk of predation OR Increases attractiveness of phenotypic traits → Evolutionary advantage;

~Evolutionary advantage → ~Mutation decreases risk of predation AND ~Increases attractiveness of phenotypic traits

Mutation weakens the genetic pool → Evolutionary disadvantage;

~Evolutionary disadvantage → ~Mutation weakens the genetic pool

___Y___ 13. Premise: A mutation increases attractiveness of phenotypic traits.

(This is one of two sufficient conditions in the first principle. Since we have an "OR" connecting the two sufficient conditions, either one alone will lead to the necessary condition.)

___Y___ 14. Conclusion: A mutation results in an evolutionary disadvantage.

(An "evolutionary disadvantage" is the necessary condition of our second principle.)

___N___ 15. Premise: A mutation does not weaken the host's genetic pool.

(This is the necessary condition of the second principle's contrapositive, meaning it could serve as the conclusion, but not as the premise.)

___N___ 16. Conclusion: A mutation creates neither advantage nor disadvantage (no effect).

(This statement fulfills the sufficient condition of the first principle's contrapositive, meaning it could serve as the premise, but not as the conclusion.)

Set E

Clinical study identifies only minor side effects → FDA should approve new drug therapy;

~FDA should approve new drug therapy → ~Clinical study identifies only minor side effects

Clinical study identifies major side effects → FDA should not approve new drug therapy;

FDA should approve new drug therapy → ~Clinical study identifies major side effects

___N___ 17. Premise: Clinical study results are inconclusive.

(This scenario satisfies neither of the sufficient conditions of the principles, so it cannot serve as a premise.)

___N___ 18. Conclusion: FDA will not approve the new drug therapy.

(While this conclusion resembles the necessary condition in the second principle, it is not a match. The principle provides only a recommendation, while this conclusion states that something will be done. The principle can allow us to conclude what *should* be done, but does not tell us what *will* be done.)

___Y___ 19. Conclusion: FDA should approve the new drug therapy.

(This conclusion matches the necessary condition in the first principle.)

___N___ 20. Premise: Clinical study finds that the new drug therapy's benefits outweigh its risks.

(The sufficient conditions of the principles mention "minor" side effects and "major" side effects, respectively. Neither is concerned with risks overall or with the ratio of benefit to risk. This premise does not provide enough information to determine whether the side effects, if any, are "minor" or "major" and so it does not supply a sufficient condition for either principle.)

Set F

"Marginal" OR "Poor" rating in crash safety test → Likely to result in serious injury;

~Likely to result in serious injury → ~"Marginal" AND ~"Poor" rating in crash safety test

"Good" rating in crash safety test → Likely to be purchased by families with children;

~Likely to be purchased by families with children → ~"Good" rating in crash safety test

___Y___ 21. Premise: "Poor" rating in crash safety test

(The first principle provides two sufficient conditions, and this is one of them.)

___N___ 22. Premise: "Acceptable" rating in crash safety test

(Neither principle discusses an "Acceptable" rating in a crash safety test.)

___N___ 23. Conclusion: Likely to be most popular among consumers with children

("Likely to be purchased" is not necessarily the same as "likely to be popular," and even if we were to equate these two things, we definitely can't conclude the relative aspect of the claim: that it is likely to be *most* popular with that group.)

___N___ 24. Conclusion: Unlikely to cause serious injury

(This is the sufficient condition of the contrapositive of the first principle, so it could serve as a premise but not a conclusion.)

Set G

Best art → Elicits strong emotion OR Highly memorable;

~Elicits strong emotion AND ~Highly memorable → ~Best art

Bad art → Uninteresting;

~Uninteresting → ~Bad art

___N___ 25. Premise: Good art

(Neither principle refers to "good art," so the principles cannot be applied.)

___Y___ **26. Premise: Best art**

(Because this premise matches a sufficient condition in one of our principles, it leads us to conclude the corresponding necessary condition.)

___N___ 27. Premise: Highly memorable

(This premise matches a necessary condition of the first principle, so it does not lead us to conclude anything.)

___Y___ **28. Conclusion: Not interesting**

("Uninteresting" and "not interesting" are synonyms, so this conclusion is a match for the necessary condition in our second principle.)

Set H

Reason to believe it will help AND no reason to believe it will harm → Act justifiable;

~Act justifiable → ~Reason to believe it will help OR reason to believe it will harm

Act questionable → Reason to believe that the harm might outweigh the help;

~Reason to believe that the harm might outweigh the help → ~Act questionable

___Y___ **29. Premise: No reason to believe an act will harm**

(This is one of the first principle's two sufficient conditions. Note that because they are linked with "and" rather than "or," the other condition would have to be fulfilled as well.)

___N___ 30. Premise: No reason to believe an act will help

(This negates one of the first principle's sufficient conditions.)

___N___ 31. Conclusion: Act questionable

(This is the second principle's sufficient condition. Be careful: lots of Principle Example questions will present you with two judgments—one in the sufficient position and the other in the necessary position. You can't conclude a judgment if it's in a sufficient position. You can only conclude its negation through the application of the principle's contrapositive.)

___Y___ **32. Conclusion: Act justifiable**

(This is the necessary condition of the first principle.)

Set I

Competing courses of action each benefit some and hurt others → Moral quandary;

~Moral quandary → ~Competing courses of action each benefit some and hurt others

Course of action the morally right choice → No choice that would benefit more and hurt fewer;

~No choice that would benefit more and hurt fewer → ~Course of action the morally right choice

___Y___ **33. Premise: Not a moral quandary**

(This would be our premise if we want to apply the contrapositive of the first principle.)

___N___ 34. Premise: Not the morally right choice

(This is the negation of the second principle's sufficient condition, so it could serve as the conclusion but not the premise.)

___Y___ **35. Conclusion: Not the morally right choice**

(This would be our conclusion if we want to apply the contrapositive of the second principle.)

___N___ 36. Conclusion: Not a moral quandary

(We can't conclude the negation of a principle's necessary condition—this could only serve as a premise.)

Set J

Performed for the benefit of no one but oneself →
Selfish action;

*~Selfish action → ~Performed for the benefit of no
one but oneself*

Egomaniacal → Performed with complete disregard
for how others will be impacted;

*~Performed with complete disregard for how others
will be impacted → ~Egomaniacal*

___Y___ 37. **Premise: Egomaniacal**

(This is the second principle's sufficient condition.)

___N___ 38. Premise: Selfish action

(This appears only as a necessary condition.)

___Y___ 39. **Conclusion: Not egomaniacal**

(This would be our conclusion if we apply the second
principle's contrapositive.)

___N___ 40. Conclusion: Not selfish

(We can't conclude the negation of a principle's
necessary condition—this could only serve as a
premise.)

Drill 99: Quanti-YAY or Quanti-NAY? Round 1

Instructions:

Some of the trickiest Inference Family questions test whether or not you can combine quantified statements. Consider the following pairs of quantified statements. Can they be combined? Use the provided space to either write in the inference or write in that you can't make one.

Some guidelines: The *only* way to combine a pair of quantified statements that doesn't include an "All" or a "None" statement is to combine two "Most" statements that have the same first condition. When you do so, you can infer a "Some" statement that links the two second conditions. An example of this would be:

> Most students study hard, and most students improve their score; therefore, some people who study hard improve their score.

To combine a "Most" or "Some" statement with an "All" or "None" statement (aka a conditional statement), the conditional statement's *sufficient* condition *has* to be the shared term. Examples of this would be:

> All students want to improve, and most students try to improve; therefore, some people who want to improve try to do so.

> All students try their best, and some students achieve their best, so some people who try their best achieve their best.

> Most students practice regularly, and everyone who practices regularly will be prepared; therefore, most students will be prepared.

Notice that in the first two combinations, we could only infer a "Some" statement. This will be true in *all* cases *except* those that follow the format of the last case. If you can build a chain that starts with a "Most" statement and links to a conditional statement like so—Most A's are B's and all B's are C's"—then you can infer that "Most A's are C's."

Use these guidelines when tackling the items below!

1. All cats are nimble, and most nimble things are flexible.

2. The plant recycles many types of plastic, and many clothes hangers are made of plastic.

3. All dogs are loyal, and some dogs are dirty.

4. Most drivers own cars, and most people who own cars can change a tire.

5. All Olympic athletes are in good shape, and all Olympic athletes travel a lot.

6. Most of the hotels in the area have an indoor pool, and most of the hotels in the area offer a free continental breakfast.

7. Some animals that live in the forest have been spotted along the hiking trail, and the forest is home to some foxes.

8. Most ice cream is delicious, and most ice cream is served freezing cold.

9. Most basketball players are tall, and some basketball players are point guards.

10. A piece of luggage must fit in the overhead compartment to be accepted as a carry-on. Some rolling luggage is accepted as a carry-on.

11. Suspects who post bail will not be repaid unless they appear in court when ordered to do so. Most suspects who post bail appear in court when ordered to do so.

12. Any video game with intense violence is given a "mature" rating. Not all video games involving military combat are given a "mature" rating.

13. Most tea drinkers drink tea in the morning, and some tea drinkers only drink decaffeinated tea.

14. Most coffee drinkers enjoy caffeine, and most coffee drinkers enjoy the smell of coffee.

15. Most of the donations for the school event were made by local businesses, and most local businesses are owned by people who graduated from that school.

16. Everyone who plays video games enjoys Hill Droplets soda, and most people who play video games have good hand-eye coordination.

17. Anyone with an open laceration is admitted to the intensive care unit. Most serious flu cases are admitted to the intensive care unit.

18. Most poker games do not use the jokers from a deck of cards, and many card games described in the book use jokers.

19. At least four tickets are required to ride any of the roller coasters at the carnival. Exactly three tickets are required for the most popular attraction at the carnival.

20. All of the wrenches in the tool kit are made of chrome vanadium steel. Some of the wrenches in the tool kit are adjustable.

21. Many New Yorkers enjoy pizza, and a significant number of New Yorkers are lactose intolerant.

22. Most sommeliers have an impeccable palate, and no one with an impeccable palate would eat at S.C.'s Roast Joint.

23. Many craters on Earth are formed by meteorite impacts, and many craters on Earth contain lakes.

24. All of the paintings in the museum's third-floor gallery are oil paintings. All of the paintings by Degas are in the second-floor gallery.

25. Most children at the fair jump in the bounce house. Children are not allowed in the bounce house without socks.

26. Most books are released first in hardcover, and most books are by first-time authors.

27. Some smokers have quit smoking using hypnosis therapy, and some smokers have quit smoking after 20 years of trying to quit.

28. All of the questions on the math test require algebra, and some of the questions on the math test involve geometry.

29. Most swimming pools use chlorine to control the growth of algae, and most swimming pools are used more heavily in the summer.

30. All music majors understand music theory, and most people who understand music theory are good at math.

31. All of the electronic toys in the house are battery-powered, and most battery-powered items in the house use AA batteries.

5

32. All streaming TV services feature exclusive content, and most of these services cost around $15 per month.

33. Most hyenas are carnivorous, and aardwolves are a species of hyena.

34. Some twins are born on different days, and some twins have different blood types.

35. All professional skiers have their own equipment and don't need to rent skis. Most skiers staying at the resort for the competition had to rent skis.

5

Answers follow on the next page.

Answers

Note: Remember that "Some" statements are reversible, so if you presented yours in a different order than ours, no big deal!

1. No inference.

2. No inference.

3. Some loyal things are dirty.

4. No inference.

5. Some people who are in good shape travel a lot.

6. Some hotels in the area with an indoor pool offer a free continental breakfast.

7. No inference.

8. Some delicious things are served freezing cold.

9. No inference.

10. Some rolling luggage fits in the overhead compartment.

11. No inference.

12. Some video games involving military combat do not contain intense violence.

13. No inference.

14. Some who love caffeine also love the smell of coffee.

15. No inference.

16. Some people who enjoy Hill Droplets soda have good hand-eye coordination.

17. No inference.

18. No inference.

19. The most popular attraction is not a roller coaster.

20. Some adjustable wrenches in the tool kit are made from chrome vanadium steel.

21. No inference.

22. Most sommeliers would never eat at S.C.'s Roast Joint.

23. No inference.

24. Some of the museum's oil paintings are not by Degas.

25. Most children at the fair have socks.

26. Some books in hardcover are by first-time authors.

27. No inference.

28. Some algebra questions require geometry.

29. Some things that use chlorine to control the growth of algae are used more heavily in the summer.

30. No inference.

31. No inference.

32. Some services with exclusive content cost around $15 per month.

33. No inference.

34. No inference.

35. Most skiers staying at the resort are not professional skiers.

Drill 100: False, I Say!

Instructions: Must Be False questions almost always have a conditional structure, so it pays to be able to recognize (and predict!) when a statement contradicts a conditional. Practice recognition with this drill by filling in a Y beside every item that contradicts the conditional provided and an N beside every item that does not.

Anyone who orders two entrees is eligible for a free dessert.

_____ 1. Steve ordered two entrees but, because they were the cheapest on the menu, isn't eligible for a free dessert.

_____ 2. Free desserts are only given to people who order two entrees.

_____ 3. Amy only ordered a single entree, so she's not eligible for a free dessert.

_____ 4. Aloysius was correctly told that he was ineligible for a free dessert, despite having ordered two entrees.

_____ 5. If Constance gets a free dessert, then she must have ordered two entrees.

If you learn the concepts and practice on questions, your LSAT score will improve.

_____ 6. Alanna practiced on many questions, but she never learned the concepts, and her LSAT score didn't improve.

_____ 7. Barton's LSAT score didn't improve after learning the concepts and practicing them on questions.

_____ 8. Claudia practiced on LSAT questions, so her score will improve.

_____ 9. David's LSAT score improved despite not practicing any questions.

_____ 10. Enid neither learned the concepts nor practiced on any questions, yet her score improved.

If you go to the beach, you must bring an umbrella and sunscreen.

_____ 11. Deanna went to the beach with only an umbrella and a blanket.

_____ 12. Carlos has an umbrella and sunscreen and is at the beach.

_____ 13. Robin does not have an umbrella and is not at the beach.

_____ 14. Maryam is not at the beach and does not have an umbrella and sunscreen.

_____ 15. Anusha does not have sunscreen, but she is at the beach.

Any item on the third shelf must cost more than any item on a lower-numbered shelf.

_____ 16. Item A is on the third shelf, so it must be the most expensive item.

_____ 17. Item B costs more than an item on the first shelf, so it must be on the third shelf.

_____ 18. Item D is on the first shelf and has the same cost as item E, which is on the third shelf.

_____ 19. Item F is not on the third shelf, so it does not cost more than the items on the first two shelves.

_____ 20. Item J on the third shelf costs less than item K on the second shelf.

In order to naturally control cucumber beetle populations, either tomatoes or peppers, but not both, must be planted in any garden that is planted with cucumbers.

_____ 21. Phillip planted tomatoes, so he will plant cucumbers but not peppers.

_____ 22. Gavin planted only rosemary, zucchini, and cucumbers in his garden, but controlled cucumber beetles naturally.

_____ 23. Peppers, eggplant, cucumbers, and tomatoes are planted in Elena's garden.

_____ 24. Jacquelyn's garden contains tomatoes, mint, cucumbers, and peppers and keeps cucumber beetles under control naturally.

_____ 25. Marcus planted peppers and tomatoes in his garden, so he cannot plant cucumbers.

This semester, students must take biology if they take neither chemistry nor psychology.

_____ 26. Pamela took biology, so she will not take chemistry or psychology.

_____ 27. Gina took both biology and chemistry this semester.

_____ 28. Zohal did not take biology, so she must take chemistry or psychology.

_____ 29. Sumit took chemistry and psychology this semester, so he will not take biology.

_____ 30. Riley did not take biology, chemistry, or psychology this semester.

Anyone who does not adopt a cat will adopt a dog.

_____ 31. Matthew adopts only a bird and a hamster.

_____ 32. Filippa adopts a dog, so she will not adopt a cat.

_____ 33. Reagan adopts only a bird and a dog.

_____ 34. Dustin does not adopt a cat, so he will adopt a dog.

_____ 35. Giuseppe adopts both a cat and a dog.

No one can enter the party without wearing a costume and having an invitation.

_____ 36. Eva did not enter the party, but was wearing a costume and had an invitation.

_____ 37. Angelo is wearing a costume and has an invitation, so he can enter the party.

_____ 38. Stella entered the party wearing a costume but without an invitation.

_____ 39. James is not wearing a costume, but does have an invitation, so he can enter the party.

_____ 40. Mariah, who does not have an invitation, cannot enter the party.

No person will purchase a couch unless that person also purchases a lamp and a table.

_____ 41. Alberto did not purchase a couch, so he cannot purchase a lamp and a table.

_____ 42. Jacinda did not purchase a lamp, but she did purchase a couch and a table.

_____ 43. Neha purchased only a lamp and a table.

_____ 44. Brodie purchased a lamp and a table, so he will purchase a couch.

_____ 45. Donald purchased a couch and a lamp, but nothing else.

Answers

Anyone who orders two entrees is eligible for a free dessert.

2E's → EFD

~EFD → ~2E's

__Y__ 1. **Steve ordered two entrees but, because they were the cheapest on the menu, isn't eligible for a free dessert.**

(Showing an instance in which the sufficient condition happens but the necessary condition doesn't is the most common way conditional contradictions play out!)

__N__ 2. Free desserts are only given to people who order two entrees.

(Illegal Reversals aren't contradictions.)

__N__ 3. Amy only ordered a single entree, so she's not eligible for a free dessert.

(Illegal Negations aren't contradictions.)

__Y__ 4. **Aloysius was correctly told that he was ineligible for a free dessert, despite having ordered two entrees.**

(Sufficient without the necessary = must be false!)

__N__ 5. If Constance gets a free dessert, then she must have ordered two entrees.

(Illegal Reversals aren't contradictions.)

If you learn the concepts and practice on questions, your LSAT score will improve.

LC and PQ → LSI

~LSI → ~LC or ~PQ

__N__ 6. Alanna practiced on many questions, but she never learned the concepts, and her LSAT score didn't improve.

__Y__ 7. **Barton's LSAT score didn't improve after learning the concepts and practicing them on questions.**

(Sufficient without the necessary = must be false!)

__N__ 8. Claudia practiced on LSAT questions and her score will improve.

__N__ 9. David's LSAT score improved despite not practicing any questions.

(Showing the necessary condition without the sufficient condition doesn't contradict: only showing the sufficient without the necessary does!)

__N__ 10. Enid neither learned the concepts nor practiced on any questions, yet her score improved.

(Illegal Negations aren't contradictions.)

If you go to the beach, you must bring an umbrella and sunscreen.

B → U and S

~U or ~S → ~B

__Y__ 11. **Deanna went to the beach with only an umbrella and a blanket.**

(Sufficient without the necessary = must be false!)

__N__ 12. Carlos has an umbrella and sunscreen and is at the beach.

__N__ 13. Robin does not have an umbrella and is not at the beach.

(This must be true.)

__N__ 14. Maryam is not at the beach and does not have an umbrella and sunscreen.

__Y__ 15. **Anusha does not have sunscreen, but she is at the beach.**

(Sufficient without the necessary = must be false!)

Any item on the third shelf must cost more than any item on a lower-numbered shelf.

3 → > 1 and 2

~ > 1 or 2 → ~3

__N__ 16. Item A is on the third shelf, so it must be the most expensive item.

__N__ 17. Item B costs more than an item on the first shelf, so it must be on the third shelf.

(Illegal Reversals aren't contradictions.)

__Y__ 18. **Item D is on the first shelf and has the same cost as item E, which is on the third shelf.**

(Items on the third shelf are more expensive than any item on the first shelf, so this must be false.)

__N__ 19. Item F is not on the third shelf, so it does not cost more than the items on the first two shelves.

(Illegal Negations aren't contradictions).

__Y__ 20. **Item J on the third shelf costs less than item K on the second shelf.**

(Sufficient without the necessary = must be false!)

In order to naturally control cucumber beetle populations, either tomatoes or peppers, but not both, must be planted in any garden that is planted with cucumbers.

C → T or P (not both)

~T and ~P → ~C

T and P → ~C

(Note: when "either X or Y but not both" is the necessary condition, think of it as a compound condition to be contraposed. On one line, negate the condition that requires one or the other by showing neither. On a separate line, negate the condition that prohibits both by showing both.)

N 21. Phillip planted tomatoes, so he will plant cucumbers but not peppers.

(This isn't a straight Illegal Reversal, but it still starts by fulfilling a necessary condition, and contradictions can only show the sufficient without the necessary.)

Y **22. Gavin planted only rosemary, zucchini, and cucumbers in his garden, but controlled cucumber beetles naturally.**

(You can't control the beetles naturally without tomatoes or peppers.)

N 23. Peppers, eggplant, cucumbers, and tomatoes are planted in Elena's garden.

(This could be true, but she won't be controlling cucumber beetles naturally.)

Y **24. Jacquelyn's garden contains tomatoes, mint, cucumbers, and peppers and keeps cucumber beetles under control naturally.**

(You can't control the beetles naturally with both tomatoes and peppers.)

N 25. Marcus planted peppers and tomatoes in his garden, so he cannot plant cucumbers.

(This must be true, if he wants to control cucumber beetle populations naturally.)

This semester, students must take biology if they take neither chemistry nor psychology.

~C and ~P → B

~B → C or P

N 26. Pamela took biology, so she will not take chemistry or psychology.

(Illegal Reversals are not contradictions.)

N 27. Gina took both biology and chemistry this semester.

(Necessary without the sufficient isn't a contradiction.)

N 28. Zohal did not take biology, so she must take chemistry or psychology.

(This must be true.)

N 29. Sumit took chemistry and psychology this semester, so he will not take biology.

(Illegal Negations are not contradictions.)

Y **30. Riley did not take biology, chemistry, or psychology this semester.**

(At least one of the classes must be taken this semester, so this must be false.)

Anyone who does not adopt a cat will adopt a dog.

~C → D

~D → C

Y **31. Matthew adopts only a bird and a hamster.**

(At least a cat or a dog must be adopted, so this must be false.)

N 32. Filippa adopts a dog, so she will not adopt a cat.

(Illegal Reversals are not contradictions.)

N 33. Reagan adopts only a bird and a dog.

(This could be true.)

N 34. Dustin does not adopt a cat, so he will adopt a dog.

(This must be true.)

N 35. Giuseppe adopts both a cat and a dog.

(Nothing prevents someone from adopting both a cat and a dog. What's prohibited is adopting neither.)

No one can enter the party without wearing a costume and having an invitation.

E → C and I

~C or ~I → ~E

N 36. Eva did not enter the party, but was wearing a costume and had an invitation.

(Necessary without the sufficient isn't a contradiction.)

N 37. Angelo is wearing a costume and has an invitation, so he can enter the party.

(Illegal Reversals are not contradictions.)

___Y___ 38. **Stella entered the party wearing a costume but without an invitation.**

(You need an invitation to enter the party, so this must be false.)

___Y___ 39. **James is not wearing a costume, but does have an invitation, so he can enter the party.**

(You need a costume to enter the party, so this must be false, too.)

___N___ 40. Mariah, who does not have an invitation, cannot enter the party.

(This must be true.)

No person will purchase a couch unless that person also purchases a lamp and a table.

$C \rightarrow L$ and T

$\sim L$ or $\sim T \rightarrow \sim C$

___N___ 41. Alberto did not purchase a couch, so he cannot purchase a lamp and a table.

(Illegal Negations are not contradictions.)

___Y___ 42. **Jacinda did not purchase a lamp, but she did purchase a couch and a table.**

(A couch without a coffee table is the sufficient without the necessary, so this must be false!)

___N___ 43. Neha purchased only a lamp and a table.

(The necessary without the sufficient isn't a contradiction.)

___N___ 44. Brodie purchased a lamp and a table, so he will purchase a couch.

(Illegal Reversals are not contradictions.)

___Y___ 45. **Donald purchased a couch and a lamp but nothing else.**

(A couch without a table is the sufficient without the necessary, so this must be false!)

5

Drill 101: Principle Example, Full Monty Edition

Instructions: Principle Example questions typically give you two principles that deal with similar subjects but can't be chained together. Your job is to determine whether the answer choices exemplify one or both of the principles. The easiest way to do that is to diagram both principles and their contrapositives. The correct answer will have a premise that fulfills the sufficient condition of one of your diagrams and a conclusion that fulfills its necessary condition. Most incorrect answer choices will conclude something that isn't one of the necessary conditions. The rest will conclude a necessary condition but without fulfilling the appropriate sufficient condition.

For this drill, diagram out each principle and its contrapositive in the space provided. Then, use your diagrams to determine whether each item exemplifies a principle, and fill in a Y for those that do and an N for those that don't.

Set A

A person can be considered informed about an event if that person witnessed the event directly. However, only those who studied the event extensively can be considered experts on the event.

Set B

An act is altruistic when it deliberately puts the interest of another above one's own interest. An act is selfish when it is performed without considering the interests of others.

_____ 1. Jeff was directly involved in the fender bender as a passenger, but he was asleep, so he can't be considered informed about the event.

_____ 2. Anna is knowledgeable about the crime, but she learned about it secondhand from her boss, so she's not actually informed.

_____ 3. Tara witnessed the eclipse from an observatory and is therefore informed about the event.

_____ 4. Rob, a college freshman and witness to the crime, is not considered an expert on the crime. This must be because he hasn't studied the crime extensively enough.

_____ 5. Jessica conducted extensive interviews of all of the witnesses to the bank heist and can therefore be considered an expert on the event.

_____ 6. Chris took the last piece of cake because he knew nobody wanted it. So taking the last piece of cake was not selfish.

_____ 7. Katy decided to postpone her vacation to help her sister with her new baby. Even though she would be able to take her vacation at another time, her decision was altruistic.

_____ 8. Carrie spent her lunch money on her favorite author's new book. After reading it, she shared it with her husband, who also liked that author, so her sharing was an altruistic gesture.

_____ 9. After thinking about it, Mike decided that it was more important to go to his office party rather than agree to a last-minute dinner with his girlfriend. His decision to go to the party despite her wishes was selfish.

_____ 10. Rebecca brought home a rescued cat from the animal shelter. However, she did not consider how this would affect her roommate, who is allergic to cats. Rebecca's adoption of the cat was selfish.

Set C

If one can carry on a simple conversation in a foreign language, one can be considered proficient in the language. Fluency, however, requires both ease and accuracy in using the language.

_____ 11. Ginger is able to converse in Japanese easily and with very few errors. She can be considered a fluent speaker of Japanese.

_____ 12. Thomas can speak Swedish easily, but he frequently chooses the wrong words. Hence, he is not yet fluent in Swedish.

_____ 13. Ana can be considered proficient in Canadian French. While in Quebec, she is capable of talking to shopkeepers and asking locals for directions in that language.

_____ 14. Jon is not considered proficient in Russian because even though he tries to converse in Russian with visitors, he cannot make his ideas understood most of the time.

_____ 15. Josephine prefers not to speak with her family in Italian and is therefore not fluent in that language.

Set D

A person has no responsibility to help a stranger unless something the person did caused the stranger to need help. However, when a dependency relationship exists—such as parent/child or caregiver/patient—then there is a legal duty to help.

_____ 16. Although Winston's bike missed hitting the elderly man, the near miss caused the man to fall. So, Winston had a responsibility to stop and help the injured man.

_____ 17. Felicia lives down the street from Ed, but they have never been introduced. Nevertheless, Felicia had a responsibility to get help when she witnessed Ed slipping on the ice in front of his house.

_____ 18. Nate is a volunteer home-visiting nurse assigned by Social Services to visit Mr. Jackson twice a week. Nate had a duty to call for help when Mr. Jackson said he was having pains in his chest.

_____ 19. Rick's cousin visits him once a year. This year his cousin forgot to bring his medication. Because he is family, Rick has a duty to help his cousin to obtain the medicine he needs.

_____ 20. Melissa observed a fellow shopper stumble on the escalator, and her quick assistance prevented a serious injury to the shopper. Her act was very kind, but she had no responsibility to help.

Set E

It is right to share controversial articles on the Internet only if you have verified the article's authenticity. If you cannot confirm the accuracy of the information, cite the source of the article for others to check.

_____ 21. Juanita verified that this controversial article about a local politician is authentic, so she was right to share it.

_____ 22. Pete cited the source of this controversial article he shared, so he must not have been able to confirm the accuracy of the information in it.

_____ 23. This contentious article about the health care debate was shared by both Francis and Tom. So, it must be true that they each verified the authenticity of the article.

_____ 24. Ralph confirmed the accuracy of this article's information on global warming, so it was not necessary for him to cite the source of the article.

_____ 25. Carrie tried but was unable to confirm the accuracy of the information on this tax reform article, so she should cite her source if she wishes to share the article.

5

Set F

A belief is rational if it conforms to the rules of logic and is consistent with the known facts. To be reasonable, however, a belief needs to be something that an average person might believe to be true.

_____ 26. There's no chance that an average person would believe Carla's explanation for her own behavior. Thus, it would be unreasonable for Carla to believe her own explanation.

_____ 27. Lynn's professor called her views on universal health care irrational. If that's true, Lynn's beliefs must either be illogical or inconsistent with the available facts.

_____ 28. Hannah's political views on the current immigration issue are illogical when examined closely, so her position can be judged irrational.

_____ 29. Numerous polls have consistently shown that the majority of Americans believe in the existence of ghosts and spirits, so this belief is a reasonable one.

_____ 30. The speaker's position in favor of the proposal seems to fit all the facts and makes perfect logical sense. So, agree with it or not, his support appears to be rational.

Set G

A person who has good health and material comfort can always feel contentment in life. But one can't be truly happy without the feeling that one's life has a purpose.

_____ 31. Reading to the elderly makes Roberto feel his life has a purpose. That sense of purpose makes Roberto a truly happy person.

_____ 32. Despite her current financial difficulties, Sylvia's health is good and she is comfortable in her ability to supply her modest needs. So, overall, Sylvia is content with her life.

_____ 33. Marlon must feel that he lacks a purpose in his life because he has been seeing a psychologist for many years to treat chronic depression and unhappiness.

_____ 34. Agnes has chronic and serious health problems, which make it unlikely that she can feel content with her life.

_____ 35. Since losing his job, Zack has lost all feeling of purpose in his life. He cannot be truly happy right now.

Set H

For an individual to be considered ethical, that individual must act honestly and fairly. But regardless of whether an individual is ethical, those who act according to their values possess integrity.

_____ 36. Louise has a reputation for always being honest and acting fairly in all of her transactions with clients. This shows her to be an ethical person.

_____ 37. Martha's lie on her job applications proves her to be an unethical person.

_____ 38. The arbitrator was deemed to be unethical when it was demonstrated that he had shown favoritism toward the plaintiff in the dispute.

_____ 39. Joe values generosity. Because he is a person of integrity, he can be counted on to treat his friends with generosity.

_____ 40. Sonya was recognized by her professional organization for her ethical practices. Colleagues can know, therefore, that she will always be honest and fair in her professional conduct.

Set I

To effectively correct a child's behavior, one must avoid being critical. Additionally, setting clear guidelines for acceptable behavior will prevent the child from experiencing anxiety over the behavior.

_____ 41. Nathaniel succeeded in getting his toddler to stop hitting others. He must have been able to correct the child without being critical of him.

_____ 42. Cecilia's daughter exhibits anxious behavior when asked to share her toys. Cecilia clearly failed to give her clear guidelines about how to share.

_____ 43. Turner told the kindergarten student to stop being rowdy, but he did not make it clear to the boy what behavior he expected. This lack of guidance will surely create anxiety in the youngster.

_____ 44. The assistant principal counseled the disobedient student about proper behavior, maintaining a positive, non-critical tone. This will ensure that the student will correct his behavior in the future.

_____ 45. Beth's intervention in her son's misbehavior did not change his actions at all. She clearly took a critical tone when lecturing him.

Set J

Customer service cannot be considered adequate unless the product it provides meets the customer's expectations. A customer who returns for another purchase in the future or recommends the product to another can be considered a satisfied customer.

_____ 46. Marco wrote an online customer review stating that the new restaurant's customer service was inadequate, so the meal must not have been as good as he expected it would be.

_____ 47. Sara was very satisfied with the computer she purchased at a local electronics retailer. When the time comes to upgrade to a new computer, she will undoubtedly go back to that retailer.

_____ 48. Reggie was dissatisfied with his experience at the car dealership where he got his new SUV. Although he did not speak badly of the dealership, we can be sure that he will not go back, nor will he recommend that dealership to his friends.

_____ 49. The weed whacker that Melissa purchased did not operate as easily as she had expected. The garden shop that sold it to her must not have provided her with adequate customer service.

_____ 50. The furniture store at the mall must provide quite adequate customer service since the mattress that Bethany purchased there was as comfortable and durable as she expected it would be.

5

Answers

The highlighted portions of the items marked "N" are the portions that make the item incorrect. Just as on real Principle Example questions, these items are incorrect either because they conclude something that isn't one of the necessary conditions or because they fail to fulfill the sufficient condition of the necessary condition they conclude.

Set A

Witness Directly → Informed;
~Informed → ~Witness Directly

Expert → Studied Extensively;
~Studied Extensively → ~Expert

N 1. Jeff was directly involved in the fender bender as a passenger, but he was asleep, so he can't be considered informed about the event.

N 2. Anna is knowledgeable about the crime, but she learned about it second hand from her boss, so she's not actually informed.

Y 3. **Tara witnessed the eclipse from an observatory and is therefore informed about the event.**

N 4. Rob, a college freshman and witness to the crime, is not considered an expert on the crime. This must be because he hasn't studied the crime extensively enough.

N 5. Jessica conducted extensive interviews of all of the witnesses to the bank heist and can therefore be considered an expert on the event.

Set B

Other deliberately above self → Altruistic;
~Altruistic → ~Other deliberately above self

~Consider others → Selfish;
~Selfish → Consider others

N 6. Chris took the last piece of cake because he knew nobody wanted it. So taking the last piece of cake was not selfish.

Y 7. **Katy decided to postpone her vacation to help her sister with her new baby. Even though she would be able to take her vacation at another time, her decision was altruistic.**

N 8. Carrie spent her lunch money on her favorite author's new book. After reading it, she shared it with her husband, who also liked that author, so her sharing was an altruistic gesture.

N 9. After thinking about it, Mike decided that it was more important to go to his office party rather than agree to a last-minute dinner with his girlfriend. His decision to go to the party despite her wishes was selfish.

Y 10. **Rebecca brought home a rescued cat from the animal shelter. However, she did not consider how this would affect her roommate, who is allergic to cats. Rebecca's adoption of the cat was selfish.**

Set C

Simple conversation → Proficient;
~Proficient → ~Simple conversation

Fluent → Ease and Accuracy;
~Ease or ~Accuracy → ~Fluent

N 11. Ginger is able to converse in Japanese easily and with very few errors. She can be considered a fluent speaker of Japanese.

Y 12. **Thomas can speak Swedish easily, but he frequently chooses the wrong words. Hence, he is not yet fluent in Swedish.**

Y 13. **Ana can be considered proficient in Canadian French. While in Quebec, she is capable of talking to shopkeepers and asking locals for directions in that language.**

N 14. Jon is not considered proficient in Russian because even though he tries to converse in Russian with visitors, he cannot make his ideas understood most of the time.

N   15. Josephine prefers not to speak with her family in Italian and is therefore not fluent in that language.

(Josephine's preference when speaking with her family does not necessarily indicate a lack of ease or accuracy with Italian.)

Set D

Responsibility to stranger → Caused need;
~Caused need → ~Responsibility to stranger

Dependent relationship → Legal duty;
~Legal duty → ~Dependent relationship

N   16. Although Winston's bike missed hitting the elderly man, the near miss caused the man to fall. So, Winston had a responsibility to stop and help the injured man.

N   17. Felicia lives down the street from Ed, but they have never been introduced. Nevertheless, Felicia had a responsibility to get help when she witnessed Ed slipping on the ice in front of his house.

Y   **18. Nate is a volunteer home-visiting nurse assigned by Social Services to visit Mr. Jackson twice a week. Nate had a duty to call for help when Mr. Jackson said he was having pains in his chest.**

N   19. Rick's cousin visits him once a year. This year his cousin forgot to bring his medication. Because he is family, Rick has a duty to help his cousin to obtain the medicine he needs.

Y   **20. Melissa observed a fellow shopper stumble on the escalator, and her quick assistance prevented a serious injury to the shopper. Her act was very kind, but she had no responsibility to help.**

Set E

Right to share article → Verify authenticity;
~Verify authenticity → ~Right to share article

~Confirm accuracy → Cite source;
~Cite source → Confirm accuracy

N   21. Juanita verified that this controversial article about a local politician is authentic, so she was right to share it.

N   22. Pete cited the source of this controversial article he shared, so he must not have been able to confirm the accuracy of the information in it.

N   23. This contentious article about the health care debate was shared by both Francis and Tom. So, it must be true that they each verified the authenticity of the article.

(The first principle's sufficient condition concerns whether or not it is right to share a controversial article, not whether or not the article was, in fact, shared.)

N   24. Ralph confirmed the accuracy of this article's information on global warming, so it was not necessary for him to cite the source of the article.

Y   **25. Carrie tried but was unable to confirm the accuracy of the information on this tax reform article, so she should cite her source if she wishes to share the article.**

Set F

Logical and Consistent → Rational;
~Rational → ~Logical or ~Consistent

Reasonable → Average person might believe;
~Average person might believe → ~Reasonable

Y   **26. There's no chance that an average person would believe Carla's explanation for her own behavior. Thus, it would be unreasonable for Carla to believe her own explanation.**

Y   **27. Lynn's professor called her views on universal health care irrational. If that's true, Lynn's beliefs must either be illogical or inconsistent with the available facts.**

N   28. Hannah's political views on the current immigration issue are illogical when examined closely, so her position can be judged irrational.

N   29. Numerous polls have consistently shown that the majority of Americans believe in the existence of ghosts and spirits, so this belief is a reasonable one.

Y   **30. The speaker's position in favor of the proposal seems to fit all the facts and makes perfect logical sense. So, agree with it or not, his support appears to be rational.**

Set G

Health and Comfort → Contentment;
~Contentment → ~Health or ~Comfort

True happiness → Feeling of purpose;
~Feeling of purpose → ~True happiness

N   31. Reading to the elderly makes Roberto feel his life has a purpose. That sense of purpose makes Roberto a truly happy person.

Y   32. **Despite her current financial difficulties, Sylvia's health is good and she is comfortable in her ability to supply her modest needs. So, overall, Sylvia is content with her life.**

N   33. Marlon must feel that he lacks a purpose in his life because he has been seeing a psychologist for many years to treat chronic depression and unhappiness.

N   34. Agnes has chronic and serious health problems, which make it unlikely that she can feel content with her life.

Y   35. **Since losing his job, Zack has lost all feeling of purpose in his life. He cannot be truly happy right now.**

Set H

Ethical → Honest and Fair;
~Honest or ~Fair → ~Ethical

Act according to values → Has integrity;
~Has integrity → ~Act according to values

N   36. Louise has a reputation for always being honest and acting fairly in all of her transactions with clients. This shows her to be an ethical person.

Y   37. **Martha's lie on her job applications proves her to be an unethical person.**

Y   38. **The arbitrator was deemed to be unethical when it was demonstrated that he had shown favoritism toward the plaintiff in the dispute.**

N   39. Joe values generosity. Because he is a person of integrity, he can be counted on to treat his friends with generosity.

Y   40. **Sonya was recognized by her professional organization for her ethical practices. Colleagues can know, therefore, that she will always be honest and fair in her professional conduct.**

(Even though it is the practices, not the person, that are deemed ethical in this case, it is the person that is recognized for such practices, which implies that she has been considered to be personally ethical as well.)

Set I

Effectively correct → ~Critical;
Critical → ~Effectively correct

Clear guidelines → ~Anxiety;
Anxiety → ~Clear guidelines

Y   41. **Nathaniel succeeded in getting his toddler to stop hitting others. He must have been able to correct the child without being critical of him.**

Y   42. **Cecilia's daughter exhibits anxious behavior when asked to share her toys. Cecilia clearly failed to give her clear guidelines about how to share.**

N   43. Turner told the kindergarten student to stop being rowdy, but he did not make it clear to the boy what behavior he expected. This lack of guidance will surely create anxiety in the youngster.

N   44. The assistant principal counseled the disobedient student about proper behavior, maintaining a positive, non-critical tone. This will ensure that the student will correct his behavior in the future.

N   45. Beth's intervention in her son's misbehavior did not change his actions at all. She clearly took a critical tone when lecturing him.

Set J

Adequate service → Product as expected;
~Product as expected → ~Adequate service

Returns or Recommends → Satisfied;
~Satisfied → ~Return and ~Recommend

N 46. Marco wrote an online customer review stating that the new restaurant's customer service was inadequate, so the meal must not have been as good as he expected it would be.

N 47. Sara was very satisfied with the computer she purchased at a local electronics retailer. When the time comes to upgrade to a new computer, she will undoubtedly go back to that retailer.

Y 48. **Reggie was dissatisfied with his experience at the car dealership where he got his new SUV. Although he did not speak badly of the dealership, we can be sure that he will not go back, nor will he recommend that dealership to his friends.**

Y 49. **The weed whacker that Melissa purchased did not operate as easily as she had expected. The garden shop that sold it to her must not have provided her with adequate customer service.**

(While this seems a bit counterintuitive if we're thinking about the real world, it does apply the principle, and that's all that matters!)

N 50. The furniture store at the mall must provide quite adequate customer service, since the mattress that Bethany purchased there was as comfortable and durable as she expected it would be.

Drill 102: Vocab Lab #12 – Adverb Ad Lib

Instructions: Adverbs on the LSAT are always there for a reason, telling you the how, how much, when, where, or why of some event. Even more crucially, they can reveal the author's opinion or stance, as in this very sentence with "even more crucially." Choose the answer closest in meaning to each of the adverbs below.

1. Appreciably
    - (A) considerably
    - (B) inconsequentially
    - (C) conditionally

2. Astonishingly
    - (A) in a very surprising fashion
    - (B) in a very disgraceful fashion
    - (C) in a very indifferent fashion

3. Diametrically
    - (A) in a vicious cycle
    - (B) in direct opposition
    - (C) in complete alignment

4. Effusively
    - (A) involving a physical breakdown
    - (B) in a calm, tranquil manner
    - (C) expressed with strong emotion

5. Egregiously
    - (A) understandably
    - (B) outrageously
    - (C) incorrectly

6. Empirically
    - (A) within a particular domain
    - (B) according to observation
    - (C) by means of force

7. Facilely
    - (A) in a laborious way
    - (B) in a deceptive way
    - (C) in an oversimplified way

8. Indistinguishably
    - (A) in an undignified manner
    - (B) in a manner that cannot be described
    - (C) in exactly the same manner

9. Invariably
    - (A) irregularly
    - (B) without exception
    - (C) in an elevated fashion

10. Inventively
    - (A) ingeniously
    - (B) derivatively
    - (C) predictably

11. Inversely
    - (A) as a consequence
    - (B) from right to left
    - (C) in the opposite way

12. Presumably
    - (A) hopefully
    - (B) certainly
    - (C) supposedly

13. Presumptuously
    - (A) wordlessly
    - (B) arrogantly
    - (C) guilelessly

14. Sequentially
    - (A) in logical order
    - (B) in descending fashion
    - (C) in alternation

15. Tacitly
    - (A) in an unspoken manner
    - (B) in an aggrieved fashion
    - (C) in an explicit way

Answers

1.   A

Appreciably = considerably; in a manner that is enough to be perceived. If the stock market has declined *appreciably*, then one can *appreciate*, or notice, how much the stock market has declined.

2.   A

Astonishingly = in a very surprising fashion. The surprise is often that of the author. When you encounter *astonishingly*, the author is typically revealing his or her own *astonishment* at whatever is described in the rest of the sentence.

3.   B

Diametrically = in direct opposition; opposite; utterly or completely (opposed). Picture two enemies at opposite ends of a *diameter*, facing each other across a circle. They are *diametrically* opposed, without even a hint of alignment.

4.   C

Effusively = expressed with strong emotion; enthusiastically. To be *effusive* is to gush with emotion or enthusiasm.

5.   B

Egregiously = outrageously; shockingly; in an outstandingly terrible way. *Egregiously* frequently expresses the author's perspective on just how awful something is, just how beyond the bounds of normalcy that thing has gone.

6.   B

Empirically = according to observation; in an observed or experienced manner. *Empirical* evidence is factual data gathered by observation from the world.

7.   C

Facilely = in an oversimplified way; superficially. *Facilely* is often used to describe verbal communication that is too fast or easy, especially arguments that skip over important nuances.

8.   C

Indistinguishably = in exactly the same manner; in a way that cannot be *distinguished* (recognized as different or *distinct*).

9.   B

Invariably = without exception; always; on every occasion. In other words, there is absolutely no *variability* in whatever is happening. *Invariably* is quite an extreme word; don't miss it sneaking by.

10. A

Inventively = ingeniously; imaginatively; in an original, creative fashion. In contrast, something done *derivatively* may be new, but it is an unoriginal *derivation* of something else.

11. C

Inversely = in the opposite way; backward; in reverse or in a contrary way somehow. If two phenomena are *inversely* related, then when one goes up, the other goes down. This is also known as negative correlation.

12. C

Presumably = supposedly; apparently; "one can *presume* that…" An author using *presumably* is stating his or her belief that the statement is likely to be true without expressing absolute certainty.

13. B

Presumptuously = arrogantly; shamelessly; too boldly or confidently. *Presumptuously* is derived from the same underlying verb, *presume,* as in *presumably*, but the two adverbs have very different meanings. In *presumptuously*, someone *presumes* too much.

14. A

Sequentially = in logical order; one thing naturally following another in time or space or according to some other governing principle.

15. A

Tacitly = in an unspoken manner; in an implied or implicit fashion. If you *tacitly* agree with someone to cease hostilities, then your agreement is never spoken or expressed in words.

The Matching Family

The Matching Family of questions consists of the question types Match the Reasoning and Match the Flaw. Though limited in their representation, this family accounts for some of the longest, hardest questions in LR. This family forces you to synthesize a lot of different skills, and each question consists of a whopping six arguments. Still, with the right approach, these questions are entirely manageable. Within this section, the drills are organized by the steps in our 4-Step Process for Logical Reasoning, but because Step 1 (ID Your Task) is so straightforward in this family, we're going to begin with Step 2.

In this section, you will learn to:

Work the Stimulus

- Diagram conditional arguments

Anticipate an Answer

- Identify elements likely to be mismatched

Analyze the Answers

- Spot mismatches in answer choices
- Determine when to stop diagramming a conditional answer choice

5

Drill 103: Diagram the Argument

Instructions: Diagramming conditional arguments is a skill that many Matching Family questions hinge on. Sometimes, you'll have to diagram as many as six arguments to answer the question correctly, so it pays to be able to diagram both quickly and accurately!

Many conditional Matching Family questions ask you to distinguish arguments composed entirely of conditional statements from arguments containing entities that fulfill some of those conditions. To illustrate the difference, consider these two arguments:

1. All poodles are dogs, and every dog has its day. Therefore, all poodles will have their day.
2. All poodles are dogs, and every dog has its day. Ralph is a poodle. Therefore, Ralph will have his day.

Argument 1 is entirely composed of conditional statements, including the conclusion:

$$P \rightarrow D \rightarrow HD$$
_____
$$P \rightarrow HD$$

Argument 2, on the other hand, introduces Ralph, who fulfills one condition from the premises (being a poodle). The conclusion is that he fulfills another condition from the premises (having his day).

$$P \rightarrow D \rightarrow HD$$
$$P$$
_____
$$HD$$

For this drill, a series of conditional arguments will be given. Use the space provided to diagram them in accordance with the examples above.

1. Anything requiring hand-eye coordination should be considered a sport, and universities should offer scholarships for anything that's considered a sport. Video games require hand-eye coordination. Universities should therefore offer video game scholarships.

2. Every Friday, Cassius goes to the movies, and he always has popcorn at the movies. Whenever Cassius has popcorn, he also has a soda. Cassius did not have any soda yesterday, so it wasn't Friday.

3. Amelia never goes to a party without Zach. Megan will not go to the party if Sarah doesn't go, and Zach will not go if Megan doesn't go. Sarah will not attend the party, so Amelia will not attend the party either.

4. Anyone who wants to attend Amazon Law School this fall must take the LSAT. Taking the LSAT requires registering before the deadline and uploading a passport photo. Olga forgot to upload her passport photo, so she won't be going to Amazon Law School this fall.

5

5. Stephan got a C on his midterm project, so he cannot go on his class field trip. Students are not permitted to go on the field trip unless they get a guardian's permission and pass physics. Students will not pass physics if they don't get at least a B on the midterm project.

6. Clearly, Martin is never late for work on Tuesday or Friday. Martin uses the HOV lane whenever he's not alone in a car, and he's never late for work when he uses the HOV lane. Martin carpools with his neighbor every Tuesday and Friday.

7. DeShawn will not go to regionals unless he wins his local tournament. Winning the local tournament requires practice and skill. DeShawn is going to regionals, so he must have practiced.

8. Every Saturday, a farmer supplements his chicken feed, and the only supplement he uses is fishmeal. Fishmeal makes his coop smell terrible, so, every Saturday, the farmer's coop must smell terrible.

9. Jyoti cannot vote to provide funding for the girls' soccer team. Jyoti is a freshman, and freshmen cannot serve on the Student Council. Students not on the Student Council are prohibited from voting on funding issues.

10. Nylah cannot take both AP U.S. History and AP World History. If she doesn't take AP World History, then she will take AP Japanese and AP Chemistry, but she won't take AP Japanese unless she takes AP Music. Nylah decided to take AP U.S. History, so she will be taking AP Music also.

11. We need new drugs to eliminate superbugs such as CRE that have become resistant to known drugs. New drugs require FDA approval, but FDA approval depends on funding for research. Funding for drug research was not available this year, so CRE will not be eradicated this year.

12. Chantel read all of the books that Manolo read this month. However, Chantel did not read any of the books that Gopal read this month. Hence, Gopal did not read any of the books that Manolo read this month.

13. Tonya can't go to the festival until she receives her ticket, but the tour promoter will not send tickets until they get a payment. Tonya can't pay for the ticket unless she gets a bonus. She got a bonus, so she must be going to the festival.

14. Hiro will get the promotion only if Sonia does not. Sonia will get the promotion unless Emir leaves the company. Emir will not leave if Aria is hired. Aria was hired, so Hiro will not get the promotion.

5

15. The bill would pass if, and only if, Senator Appel voted for it. Senators cannot vote if they are not present in the chamber. Senator Appel would not be present to vote if she were too ill to travel. The bill passed, so Senator Appel was not too ill to travel.

16. If Chang is eating in the cafeteria today, it can't be Friday. Chang never eats in the cafeteria unless Alvarez does, and Alvarez never eats in the cafeteria on Friday.

17. Tino is at a party where no one is both a Philly fan and a Washington fan. Everyone at the party is a Philly fan except the New York fans, and New York fans cannot be Boston fans. Tino is a Washington fan, so he cannot be a Boston fan.

18. The Aoki family will visit either Milan or Naples, and if they go to Naples they will also stop in Pompeii. They can't go to Florence if they see Pompeii, but if they skip Florence, they will get to see Rome. Thus, if they fail to visit Milan, the family will surely visit Rome.

19. Every dinosaur is classified as either a saurischian or an ornithischian but not both. Velociraptors were theropods, and all theropods were saurischians. All armored dinosaurs were ornithischians, so velociraptors did not have armor.

20. At the local grocery store, Ross and Mendez never work together. If White is working, so is Mendez. If Ross is not working, then Kim is working, but Bolt cannot work with Kim. White is working today, so Bolt is not.

Answers

1. H → S → U$
    V → H
    _____
    V → U$

2. F → M → P → S
    ~S
    _____
    ~F

3. ~Z → ~A
    ~S → ~M → ~Z
    ~S
    _____
    ~A

4. A → L → R and P
    ~P
    _____
    ~A

5. FT → GP and PP
    ~B → ~PP
    ~B
    _____
    ~FT

6. M + 1 → HOV → ~L
    T or F → M+1
    _____
    T or F → ~L

    Note: The stimulus says "every Tuesday and Friday," but we have used "or" in our diagram. That's because, if something happens every Tuesday and every Friday, either day is sufficient, by itself, to trigger the conditional.

7. R → WL → P and S
    R
    _____
    P

8. Sa → SC → F → ST
    _____
    Sa → ST

5

9. $J \to F \to {\sim}S \to {\sim}V$

   _____

   $J \to {\sim}V$

10. $U \to {\sim}W$
    ${\sim}W \to J$ and C
    $J \to M$
    U

    _____

    M

Note: Because this one contains trickier conditional language, we've diagrammed each statement separately, as we would on test day. When chained, the diagram would appear like so: $U \to {\sim}W \to J \to M$

11. $EC \to ND \to FA \to \$$
    ${\sim}\$$

    _____

    ${\sim}EC$

12. $M \to C$
    $G \to {\sim}C$

    _____

    $M \to {\sim}G$

Note: If you diagrammed the second premise as we have, you will need to contrapose it to make the chain. The second premise and the conclusion both use the indicator word "any," which introduces the sufficient condition. It is equally valid, however, to diagram a statement that says "A didn't do anything B did" as $A \to {\sim}B$.

13. $F \to T \to P$
    $P \to B$
    B

    _____

    F

Note: This is an invalid argument. Can you spot the flaw? That's right—Illegal Reversal.

14. $HP \to {\sim}SP \to EL$
    $AH \to {\sim}EL$
    AH

    _____

    ${\sim}HP$

Note: This argument fulfills the sufficient condition of the second premise, which then triggers the contrapositive of the initial chain.

15. $AV \to BP$; $BP \to AV$
    $AV \to P$
    $TI \to {\sim}P$
    BP

    _____

    ${\sim}TI$

Note: The first statement is biconditional, so we need two diagrams. Double arrows, while great for LG, are unwieldy in LR. If we contrapose the third premise, we get $P \to {\sim}TI$, which allows us to make this chain: $BP \to AV \to P \to {\sim}TI$.

16. CC → AC → ~F

    _____

    CC → ~F

    Note: "A is never B" statements can be diagrammed A → ~B or B → ~A. If you diagrammed the second premise F → ~AC, that's OK. Just contrapose to make your chain.

17. W → ~P; P → ~W

    ~P → N; N → ~P

    N → ~B

    W

    _____

    ~B

    Note: This one is full of tricky conditionals that need two diagrams: "no one is both" means if you are one, you're not the other. "Everyone's an A except the B's" is biconditional - if you're not an A, you're a B, and if you're a B, you're not an A. These can chain up like so: W → ~P → N → ~B.

18. ~M → N; ~N → M

    N → P

    P → ~F → R

    _____

    ~M → R

    Note: "Either A or B" statements tell us if you don't have one, you have the other. As that can be translated two ways, it is advisable to write out both translations until it is clear which one can be chained. In this case, we can chain the ~M → N version to the rest of the premises, giving us: ~M → N → P → ~F → R.

19. O → ~S; S → ~O

    ~O → S; ~S → O

    V → T

    T → S

    A → O

    _____

    V → ~A

    Note: "Either/or but not both: statements are biconditional, meaning we need multiple diagrams. Start by diagramming out each relationship the biconditional represents and its contrapositive. Then see which chain to the other premises. In this case, it's V → T → S → ~O → ~A.

20. R → ~M; M → ~R

    W → M

    ~R → K → ~B

    W

    _____

    ~B

    Note: "Never both" statements mean that if you have one, then you cannot have the other, so it's advisable to jot down both translations until it's clear which one can be chained to the other premises, just as we've done for "either/or" statements and biconditionals. In this case, the M → ~R translation provides the link that allows us to chain the other premises: W → M → ~R → K → ~B.

5

Drill 104: Plan Your Hunt

Instructions: Matching Family questions are primarily driven by process of elimination. You look in the answer choices for things that don't match the stimulus. But you can make that process a lot more efficient by identifying elements in the stimulus that wrong answers are likely to botch. Anything unique in an argument's structure can fall into this category, but a few that occur frequently are chained conditional statements, contrapositive reasoning, famous flaws, recommendations, evaluations, qualified conclusions, compound premises, compound conclusions, and either/or statements.

Practice identifying these elements by highlighting them in the stimuli below.

1. Recently completed research demonstrates that, in hypertensive patients, coenzyme Q10 has the potential to significantly reduce blood pressure without significant side effects. Thus, unless the supplement is contraindicated with a patient's current medications, it would be a wise addition to the treatment regimen of anyone battling high blood pressure.

2. If we leave for the basketball game after 5pm, we will be in rush-hour traffic on Interstate 40. Driving anywhere on Interstate 40 always takes twice as long during rush hour. Jules cannot leave for the basketball game until after 5pm. Therefore, Jules should find his own ride to the game instead of riding with us.

3. Sam will either miss work this evening or turn his history paper in late. After all, he needs to spend at least three hours this evening finishing his paper, but he needs to be at work in 30 minutes.

4. Tigers and wolves are both considered carnivores. However, while a tiger's diet must include nutrients found only in meat, wolves can survive on plant matter for a relatively long period of time. Thus, it is a mistake to use the term "carnivore" to mean "an animal that only eats meat."

5. We will go to the seafood restaurant if we aren't going to the concert tonight. If we can't get tickets this afternoon, we can't go to the concert. So, we must be going to the seafood restaurant, since there aren't any more tickets available.

6. Either Wilson or Santos must be in the building when we test the fire alarm. Wilson is afraid of the noise the fire alarm makes, but Santos slipped on a banana peel and will be in the hospital all week. Thus, the only way we can test the fire alarm this week is for Wilson to overcome his fear.

7. Companies that manufacture electronic goods often announce upgraded versions of their products at major electronics shows. Many people purchase these new products because they find the new features exciting. However, retailers will often deeply discount the previous year's models once the new models have been announced, even though the previous models' features still serve most users' needs. Thus, the best option is to buy a previous year's model when it goes on sale just after a major electronics show.

8. Persistence allows a person to continue working toward a difficult goal in the face of dispiriting hardships, which inevitably arise when working toward such a goal. Discipline allows a person to make consistent progress toward a goal. Thus, anyone who wishes to achieve a difficult goal should strive to develop persistence and discipline.

9. The Cleveland Caterpillars hockey team is the highest scoring team in the Southwestern Hockey League this year. All of the people on my bowling team are also on the Cleveland Caterpillars hockey team. Therefore, the people on my bowling team are the highest scoring players in the Southwestern Hockey League this year.

5

10. All mustelids are carnivorans. Although they are similar to mustelids in some ways, lemurs are not carnivorans. Therefore, lemurs are not mustelids.

11. Any sailboat that sets a new nautical mile speed record in the future will employ hydrofoils, since a boat that does not employ hydrofoils will have its speed limited severely by drag, and a boat cannot have its speed limited severely by drag if it is to set a new nautical mile speed record.

12. Most hotels in Florida are located near fast-food restaurants, since the majority of hotels in Florida seek to attract families, and most hotels that seek to attract families are located near fast-food restaurants.

13. Jones must be at the dock by 8:30am if he wishes to take the ferry to Hall Island. His car needs to be repaired, however, and the only shop that is authorized to repair it is the dealership. Thus, if Jones wishes to take the ferry to Hall Island, he cannot take the car to the dealership himself, since he cannot take his car to the dealership before 9:30am.

14. Leah will not eat any dessert made using a recipe from her mother's cookbook, since all of the dessert recipes in her mother's cookbook require eggs. Vegan desserts are never made with eggs, and Leah only eats vegan desserts.

15. It will take two hours to drive to the beach tomorrow. The foosball tournament tomorrow morning only lasts for three hours. Thus, since we don't have to do anything else tomorrow, we can compete in the foosball tournament and still drive to the beach.

16. MacArthur must either stay on Earth, which is about to be destroyed, or board a spaceship full of potentially hostile alien creatures. MacArthur clearly should board the spaceship, since his friend Clifford, who has experience travelling through space in the company of potentially hostile creatures, is recommending that they do so.

17. All new employees must either attend Tuesday's orientation or complete the optional online training on Wednesday afternoon. As a result, all new employees in the IT department will have to complete the online training unless Davis comes to the office on Tuesday, since Davis is the only person who can conduct the orientation.

18. All players on the Cincinnati Coyotes basketball team are from Canada. Thus, only players who once played for the Brooklyn Bonobos are members of the Cincinnati Coyotes, since everyone who has ever played for the Brooklyn Bonobos is from Canada.

19. No dog that belongs to the hotel clerk will bite. The dog in the hotel lobby bit the inspector. Thus, it is not the hotel clerk's dog.

20. Raúl and Michael both need new backpacks. They can save money by buying backpacks online instead of buying them at Jack's Backpack Shack. However, Jack's Backpack Shack is having a 50% off sale. So, Raúl and Michael will buy their backpacks at Jack's Backpack Shack.

21. Everyone who went on the camping trip hiked to the waterfall, and everyone who hiked to the waterfall was in the group photo. Therefore, everyone who was in the group photo went on the camping trip.

22. A fantasy story that features elves as characters will inevitably describe powerful magic. Thus, any fantasy story that features elves as characters is a great fantasy story, since all fantasy stories that describe powerful magic are great stories.

23. When looking for a watchdog, few people would consider the Lhasa Apso to be a good choice. Small dogs known for their long, dense coat, Lhasa Apsos seem better suited to the life of a lapdog than to the life of a guard dog. However, these dogs were originally bred by Tibetan Buddhist monks to help guard temples from intruders. Known for their keen hearing and alertness, and for being suspicious of strangers, Lhasa Apsos make excellent sentinels who will alert homeowners to any attempted intrusion.

24. No one who is overly confident in her abilities will succeed for a sustained period of time, and sustained success is a requirement for one to achieve true proficiency. Therefore, no one who is swayed by insincere praise will achieve true proficiency, since being swayed by insincere praise guarantees that one will become overconfident in her abilities.

25. Most procyonids are cute, but some procyonids chew on furniture and attack their owners. People should avoid buying pets that might harm them or their belongings. Therefore, people should avoid keeping procyonids as pets.

26. If Joe was aware that Rachael and Richard had a child, he would have asked Morton about the child. Since Joe did not ask Morton about this, we can be sure he did not know that Richard and Rachael had a child.

27. Unless a restaurant's oysters are local, Sergei will not eat them raw. Sam's Shuck and Shake Shack serves local oysters, so Sergei will eat raw oysters there.

28. Anyone who is studying for the LSAT ought not to drink several cups of coffee every afternoon. After all, drinking several cups of coffee late in the afternoon will make many people sleep poorly or not at all. People who are preparing for the LSAT need to get sufficient sleep.

29. Jeanette cannot grow grass in her front yard, since grass cannot grow without abundant sunlight, and the giant oak trees in Jeanette's front yard allow very little sunlight to reach the ground.

30. In order to gain the trust of someone who is speaking, a listener must be genuinely interested in what the speaker is saying. This is evident from the following facts: if a person is genuinely interested in what another person is saying, then the speaker will believe that the listener is sympathetic, and a listener will gain a speaker's trust if the speaker believes that the listener is sympathetic.

31. When looking for a vacation destination, most parents with young children prefer a location featuring attractions that they will enjoy and activities that will entertain their children. For this reason, parents with young children should consider Charleston, South Carolina when choosing a vacation destination. The beaches will keep their children entertained, and adults will enjoy the city's many shops, restaurants, and historical sites.

32. Managed hunts are often used to control populations of herd animals like deer. These animals can become a nuisance to humans when their numbers grow too large. Overpopulation can cause the animals themselves to suffer from malnutrition and disease as their numbers grow too large to be supported by available food resources. However, this overpopulation often occurs because the herd animals' natural predators, such as cougars and wolves, have themselves been hunted to extinction. Thus, protecting these natural predators is a more effective solution to the problem than managed hunts.

33. It is not worth eating at a restaurant unless one enjoys the main course. Thus, we cannot eat any nachos before dinner if eating at the restaurant this evening is to be worthwhile. Every time we eat nachos before dinner, we eat too many, and eating too many nachos guarantees that we will be too full to enjoy the main course.

34. The company only needs one person for the open sales position but has the option of hiring more than one person. As a result, it is likely that it will hire both Siobhan and Reed. Siobhan has more sales experience than any other applicant, but Reed was the top salesperson for three years in a row at the last company where he worked.

35. Any recipe from Chef Jane's cookbook that includes hot peppers as an ingredient will be featured in her cooking show even though they are not the most popular recipes. So, her macaroni and cheese recipe will not be featured in the show, since it does not include hot peppers.

36. Neither Wilson nor Yang knows how to drive a boat, and if you don't know how to drive a boat, you cannot drive the boat. The only other people on the boat are Ortega and her brother, but Ortega's brother is too young to drive the boat. Therefore, Ortega will drive.

37. No one will want to rent a house in this part of town if the walls in every room are covered in old, peeling wallpaper. So, the new owner will need to remove the wallpaper and install new carpet before putting this house up for rent, since the walls in every room are covered in old, peeling wallpaper and the carpet is so badly stained that it has to be replaced.

38. Most people who enjoy eating pie also enjoy eating ice cream, and some people who drink coffee also enjoy eating ice cream, so some people who enjoy eating pie also drink coffee.

39. Fans of *The Flaming Hedgehogs*, a famous punk-rock tuba quartet, post more about the band on social media immediately after the band gives a live performance than at any other time. However, the band receives more coverage from mainstream journalists when it releases a new album. Therefore, instead of spending time redesigning its website, the band should either go on tour or record a new album.

40. The azaleas at the library flower only during the spring. Photos of the library inevitably look drab unless the azaleas are flowering. Because of this, any photos of the library used in the new brochure must be ones that were taken in the spring, since the brochure cannot include any drab photos of the library.

Answers

1. Recently completed research demonstrates that, in hypertensive patients, coenzyme Q10 has the potential to significantly reduce blood pressure without significant side effects. Thus, unless the supplement is contraindicated with a patient's current medications, it would be a wise addition to the treatment regimen of anyone battling high blood pressure.

Thus, unless – qualified conclusion. The conclusion of this argument is that the supplement would be a wise addition to the treatment regimen of anyone battling high blood pressure … anyone, that is, except those whose current medications contraindicate it. When there are exceptions to the conclusion, it's a qualified conclusion.

would be a wise addition – evaluation.

2. If we leave for the basketball game after 5pm, we will be in rush-hour traffic on Interstate 40. Driving anywhere on Interstate 40 always takes twice as long during rush hour. Jules cannot leave for the basketball game until after 5pm. Therefore, Jules should find his own ride to the game instead of riding with us.

If, always, cannot – chained conditional statements. Each of these words by itself indicates that a sentence contains conditional logic. When we see several, there is likely to be a chain of conditional statements that we can link, so we should diagram the stimulus to confirm.

should – recommendation in the conclusion.

3. Sam will either miss work this evening or turn his history paper in late. After all, he needs to spend at least three hours this evening finishing his paper, but he needs to be at work in 30 minutes.

either … or – either/or statement in conclusion. The correct answer must also have an either/or structure in the conclusion.

Famous flaw alert: False Choice! The premises do not prove that the two options presented in the conclusion are the only ones possible. Maybe Sam can finish the paper after work.

4. Tigers and wolves are both considered carnivores. However, while a tiger's diet must include nutrients found only in meat, wolves can survive on plant matter for a relatively long period of time. Thus, it is a mistake to use the term "carnivore" to mean "an animal that only eats meat."

and – compound premise.

while … can – contrast. This premise establishes that two things are different in some way. A correct answer must include the same kind of premise. Any answer that doesn't is immediately suspect.

it is a mistake – evaluation.

5. We will go to the seafood restaurant if we aren't going to the concert tonight. If we can't get tickets this afternoon, we can't go to the concert. So, we must be going to the seafood restaurant, since there aren't any more tickets available.

If, if, must – chained conditional statements. Multiple conditionals means you can probably chain.

6. Either Wilson or Santos must be in the building when we test the fire alarm. Wilson is afraid of the noise the fire alarm makes, but Santos slipped on a banana peel and will be in the hospital all week. Thus, the only way we can test the fire alarm this week is for Wilson to overcome his fear.

Either … or – either/or statement in premise.

the only – conditional.

7. Companies that manufacture electronic goods often announce upgraded versions of their products at major electronics shows. Many people purchase these new products because they find the new features exciting. However, retailers will often deeply discount the previous year's models once the new models have been announced even though the previous models' features still serve most users' needs. Thus, the best option is to buy a previous year's model when it goes on sale just after a major electronics show.

best – evaluation. Expect wrong answers to have a different type of conclusion.

often, Many, often – weak quantifiers. Expect wrong answers to exceed this degree.

8. Persistence allows a person to continue working toward a difficult goal in the face of dispiriting hardships, which inevitably arise when working toward such a goal. Discipline allows a person to make consistent progress toward a goal. Thus, anyone who wishes to achieve a difficult goal should strive to develop persistence and discipline.

should – recommendation.

Thus … and – compound conclusion.

9. The Cleveland Caterpillars hockey team is the highest scoring team in the Southwestern Hockey League this year. All of the people on my bowling team are also on the Cleveland Caterpillars hockey team. Therefore, the people on my bowling team are the highest scoring players in the Southwestern Hockey League this year.

All … are – conditional logic.

highest scoring team … highest scoring players –
Famous Flaw alert: Part vs. Whole! We don't know that what is true of the team as a whole is true of the individual players.

10. All mustelids are carnivorans. Although they are similar to mustelids in some ways, lemurs are not carnivorans. Therefore, lemurs are not mustelids.

All – conditional logic.

not carnivorans … not mustelids – contrapositive reasoning. One premise contains a conditional statement. Another premise negates the necessary condition of the conditional statement, and the conclusion negates the sufficient condition of the conditional statement.

11. Any sailboat that sets a new nautical mile speed record in the future will employ hydrofoils, since a boat that does not employ hydrofoils will have its speed limited severely by drag, and a boat cannot have its speed limited severely by drag if it is to set a new nautical mile speed record.

Any, will, if – chained conditional statements. Multiple conditionals mean you should diagram the stimulus to see if they chain.

12. Most hotels in Florida are located near fast-food restaurants, since the majority of hotels in Florida seek to attract families, and most hotels that seek to attract families are located near fast-food restaurants.

Most, the majority, most – quantified logic.
Flaw alert: We're told that most hotels seek to attract families and that most are located near fast-food restaurants, but that doesn't mean most are both. It could be that 51% have each quality, and there is only a 1% overlap.

13. Jones must be at the dock by 8:30am if he wishes to take the ferry to Hall Island. His car needs to be repaired, however, and the only shop that is authorized to repair it is the dealership. Thus, if Jones wishes to take the ferry to Hall Island, he cannot take the car to the dealership himself, since he cannot take his car to the dealership before 9:30am.

Thus, if – qualified conclusion.

if; the only – conditional logic.

14. Leah will not eat any dessert made using a recipe from her mother's cookbook, since all of the dessert recipes in her mother's cookbook require eggs. Vegan desserts are never made with eggs, and Leah only eats vegan desserts.

will not eat, all … require, are never, only –
conditional logic, contrapositive reasoning.

15. It will take two hours to drive to the beach tomorrow. The foosball tournament tomorrow morning only lasts for three hours. Thus, since we don't have to do anything else tomorrow, we can compete in the foosball tournament and still drive to the beach.

Thus … and – compound conclusion.

16. MacArthur must either stay on Earth, which is about to be destroyed, or board a spaceship full of potentially hostile alien creatures. MacArthur clearly should board the spaceship, since his friend Clifford, who has experience travelling through space in the company of potentially hostile creatures, is recommending that they do so.

Either … or – either/or statement in premise.

clearly should – recommendation in the conclusion.

17. All new employees must either attend Tuesday's orientation or complete the optional online training on Wednesday afternoon. As a result, all new employees in the IT department will have to complete the online training unless Davis comes to the office on Tuesday, since Davis is the only person who can conduct the orientation.

All ... must, the only – conditional logic.

Either ... or – either/or structure in premise.

As a result ... unless – qualified conclusion.

18. All players on the Cincinnati Coyotes basketball team are from Canada. Thus, only players who once played for the Brooklyn Bonobos are members of the Cincinnati Coyotes, since everyone who has ever played for the Brooklyn Bonobos is from Canada.

All ... are; only ... are; everyone ... is – conditional logic.

Famous Flaw alert: Conditional Flaw! The premises cannot be linked together to draw this conclusion, since both have "from Canada" as their necessary condition. To reach this conclusion, the second premise would need to be reversed and state, "all basketball players from Canada have played for the Brooklyn Bonobos."

19. No dog that belongs to the hotel clerk will bite. The dog in the hotel lobby bit the inspector. Thus, it is not the hotel clerk's dog.

No ... will – conditional logic.

bit ... not the hotel clerk's dog – contrapositive reasoning.

20. Raúl and Michael both need new backpacks. They can save money by buying backpacks online instead of buying them at Jack's Backpack Shack. However, Jack's Backpack Shack is having a 50% off sale. So, Raúl and Michael will buy their backpacks at Jack's Backpack Shack.

and – compound premise

can ... However – one option is possible, but there is reason to choose another. Expect the correct answer to have this same structure, and incorrect answers to botch it.

So ... and – compound conclusion.

21. Everyone who went on the camping trip hiked to the waterfall, and everyone who hiked to the waterfall was in the group photo. Therefore, everyone who was in the group photo went on the camping trip.

Everyone – conditional logic.

Famous Flaw alert: Conditional Flaw! The conclusion is an illegal reversal of what you could actually conclude: everyone who went on the camping trip was in the group photo.

22. A fantasy story that features elves as characters will inevitably describe powerful magic. Thus, any fantasy story that features elves as characters is a great fantasy story, since all fantasy stories that describe powerful magic are great stories.

inevitably, any, all – conditional logic; chained conditional statements.

23. When looking for a watchdog, few people would consider the Lhasa Apso to be a good choice. Small dogs known for their long, dense coat, Lhasa Apsos seem better suited to the life of a lapdog than to the life of a guard dog. However, these dogs were originally bred by Tibetan Buddhist monks to help guard temples from intruders. Known for their keen hearing and alertness, and for being suspicious of strangers, Lhasa Apsos make excellent sentinels who will alert homeowners to any attempted intrusion.

few people would consider ... to be a good choice... However... excellent – the premises in the argument present a view that is refuted by the conclusion. Wrong answers will botch this structure.

excellent – evaluation.

24. No one who is overly confident in their abilities will succeed for a sustained period of time, and sustained success is a requirement for one to achieve true proficiency. Therefore, no one who is swayed by insincere praise will achieve true proficiency, since being swayed by insincere praise guarantees that one will become overconfident in her abilities.

No one who ... will, requirement, guarantees – conditional logic, chained conditional statements.

25. Most procyonids are cute, but some procyonids chew on furniture and attack their owners. People should avoid buying pets that might harm them or their belongings. Therefore, people should avoid keeping procyonids as pets.

and, or – compounds.

should – recommendation in the conclusion.

26. If Joe was aware that Rachael and Richard had a child, he would have asked Morton about the child. Since Joe did not ask Morton about this, we can be sure he did not know that Richard and Rachael had a child.

If – conditional logic.

did not ask ... did not know – contrapositive reasoning.

27. Unless a restaurant's oysters are local, Sergei will not eat them raw. Sam's Shuck and Shake Shack serves local oysters, so Sergei will eat raw oysters there.

Unless – conditional logic.

so Sergei will eat raw oysters – Famous Flaw alert: Conditional Flaw! The first premise is a conditional statement: if the restaurant does not serve local oysters, then Sergei will not eat them raw. The conclusion is based on an Illegal Negation of that statement.

28. Anyone who is studying for the LSAT ought not to drink several cups of coffee every afternoon. After all, drinking several cups of coffee late in the afternoon will make many people sleep poorly or not at all. People who are preparing for the LSAT need to get sufficient sleep.

ought not to – recommendation in the conclusion.

Anyone – conditional conclusion.

or – compound premise.

29. Jeanette cannot grow grass in her front yard, since grass cannot grow without abundant sunlight, and the giant oak trees in Jeanette's front yard allow very little sunlight to reach the ground.

cannot – conditional logic.

cannot grow grass ... very little sunlight – contrapositive reasoning.

30. In order to gain the trust of someone who is speaking, a listener must be genuinely interested in what the speaker is saying. This is evident from the following facts: if a person is genuinely interested in what another person is saying, then the speaker will believe that the listener is sympathetic, and a listener will gain a speaker's trust if the speaker believes that the listener is sympathetic.

must, if, then, will, if – conditional logic.

Famous Flaw alert: Conditional Flaw. The conclusion is based on an invalid reversal of the conditional statements in the premises.

31. When looking for a vacation destination, most parents with young children prefer a location featuring attractions that they will enjoy and activities that will entertain their children. For this reason, parents with young children should consider Charleston, South Carolina when choosing a vacation destination. The beaches will keep their children entertained, and adults will enjoy the city's many shops, restaurants, and historical sites.

and – compound premise.

For this reason ... should – recommendation in the conclusion.

32. Managed hunts are often used to control populations of herd animals like deer. These animals can become a nuisance to humans when their numbers grow too large. Overpopulation can cause the animals themselves to suffer from malnutrition and disease as their numbers grow too large to be supported by available food resources. However, this overpopulation often occurs because the herd animals' natural predators, such as cougars and wolves, have themselves been hunted to extinction. Thus, protecting these natural predators is a more effective solution to the problem than managed hunts.

more effective – evaluation. This is also relative information, which is ripe for mismatching.

33. It is not worth eating at a restaurant unless one enjoys the main course. Thus, we cannot eat any nachos before dinner if eating at the restaurant this evening is to be worthwhile. Every time we eat nachos before dinner, we eat too many, and eating too many nachos guarantees that we will be too full to enjoy the main course.

Thus ... if – qualified conclusion.

Unless, if, Every time, guarantees – conditional logic, chained conditional statements.

34. The company only needs one person for the open sales position but has the option of hiring more than one person. As a result, it is likely that it will hire both Siobhan and Reed. Siobhan has more sales experience than any other applicant, but Reed was the top salesperson for three years in a row at the last company where he worked.

it is likely – prediction.

As a result ... and – compound conclusion.

35. Any recipe from Chef Jane's cookbook that includes hot peppers as an ingredient will be featured in her cooking show even though they are not the most popular recipes. So, her macaroni and cheese recipe will not be featured in the show, since it does not include hot peppers.

Any ... will – conditional logic

So ... will not be ... since it does not include – Famous Flaw alert: Conditional Flaw! The conclusion is based on an invalid negation of the conditional statement in the first premise.

36. Neither Wilson nor Yang knows how to drive a boat, and if you don't know how to drive a boat, you cannot drive the boat. The only other people on the boat are Ortega and her brother, but Ortega's brother is too young to drive the boat. Therefore, Ortega will drive.

Neither ... nor – neither/nor statement in premise.

and – compound premise.

Therefore ... will drive. – Famous Flaw alert: False Choice! We don't know that anyone on the boat is qualified to drive it.

37. No one will want to rent a house in this part of town if the walls in every room are covered in old, peeling wallpaper. So, the new owner will need to remove the wallpaper and install new carpet before putting this house up for rent, since the walls in every room are covered in old, peeling wallpaper and the carpet is so badly stained that it has to be replaced.

if – conditional logic.

So ... and – compound conclusion.

since ... and – compound premise.

38. Most people who enjoy eating pie also enjoy eating ice cream, and some people who drink coffee also enjoy eating ice cream, so some people who enjoy eating pie also drink coffee.

Most, some – quantified logic.

Famous Flaw alert: Even if the statements in the premises are true, there isn't a guaranteed overlap between those who eat pie and those who drink coffee.

39. Fans of *The Flaming Hedgehogs*, a famous punk-rock tuba quartet, post more about the band on social media immediately after the band gives a live performance than at any other time. However, the band receives more coverage from mainstream journalists when it releases a new album. Therefore, instead of spending time redesigning its website, the band should either go on tour or record a new album.

Therefore, instead of ... should – recommendation.

either ... or – either/or statement in conclusion.

40. The azaleas at the library flower only during the spring. Photos of the library inevitably look drab unless the azaleas are flowering. Because of this, any photos of the library used in the new brochure must be ones that were taken in the spring, since the brochure cannot include any drab photos of the library.

only, inevitably ... unless, must, cannot – conditional logic; contrapositive reasoning.

Drill 105: Mismatch Attack!

Instructions: Matching Family questions can take a lot of time. However, noticing small mismatches between statements can often lead to a quick elimination. For each of the following sets, determine whether the statements in the choices match the logical structure of the given statement. Write Y if it does and N if it does not. On the test, some of these mismatches will be fatal. Others will be "yellow flags"—a reason to doubt the answer but not, in and of itself, a reason to scrap it. Multiple "yellow flags," however, can definitely be grounds for dismissal! Note: There may be more than one match in each set.

Set A

The majority of students will improve, given sufficient practice.

_____ 1. Most arguments on the LSAT are invalid.

_____ 2. Most arguments on the LSAT can be proven to be invalid with the right logical tools.

_____ 3. Most arguments on the LSAT will be proven to be invalid if someone capable sets out to do so.

_____ 4. A majority of the arguments on the LSAT are valid.

_____ 5. A minority of the arguments on the LSAT are invalid.

Set B

Fermented vegetables are unlikely to spoil in a cool cellar.

_____ 6. Most prepared foods don't spoil in the refrigerator.

_____ 7. Bread is likely to rise better in the oven, where temperatures are warmer than on the counter.

_____ 8. Kombucha will probably not ferment in temperatures under 60 degrees Fahrenheit.

_____ 9. Generally speaking, leaving the key in the ignition overnight doesn't drain the battery.

_____ 10. Leaving the key in the ignition overnight tends not to drain the battery.

Set C

Making the best jewelry requires patience and skill.

_____ 11. Good clothes are always made of good fabric.

_____ 12. You can't have the best garden without sun and fresh wind protection.

_____ 13. Since these pears are the best I've ever tasted, they must have been picked right before ripening and grown in fecund soil.

_____ 14. Writing the best LSAT essay requires stamina and circumspection.

_____ 15. The best apples come from regions with cold temperatures or nitrogenated soil.

Set D

Shade-grown coffee is superior in taste and better for the environment than plantation-grown coffee.

_____ 16. Analog recordings are considered by some to have a more authentic sound, but even analog fans acknowledge the superior versatility of digital recording.

_____ 17. Reducing caffeine intake results in both physical and psychological benefits.

_____ 18. Forests managed for roadless, low-intensity timber harvesting can be superior in aesthetic value, as well as wildlife habitat suitability, compared to unmanaged forests.

_____ 19. A high-fat, suet-based bird feed will typically attract more birds and a greater diversity of birds than a simple bird seed mix.

_____ 20. Manual transmissions, when compared to automatic transmissions, provide improved engine control and greater fuel efficiency.

Set E

It is likely that drought conditions will persist.

_____ 21. General P's scabies infestation will undoubtedly continue through August.

_____ 22. Rob will probably succumb to the injuries he sustained in the marsupial attack.

_____ 23. Ecological conditions tend to change very slowly.

_____ 24. The falling anvil will probably land on Christina.

_____ 25. The department has probably crumbled since the professors' departure.

Set F

The possibility of a major earthquake in the region increased dramatically after the sizable shift in the tectonic plates last week, which was measured by seismologists.

_____ 26. There will almost certainly be substantial wildfires this summer due to the likelihood of drought predicted by meteorologists.

_____ 27. According to biologists, the red-tailed coot will probably go extinct since the hurricane wiped out its nesting ground.

_____ 28. Aviation experts have indicated that most airlines have increased their safety inspections, so the risk of a plane crash should be substantially lower.

_____ 29. The possibility of a recession has sharply increased since major investors started to pull out of the stock market in favor of safer investments.

_____ 30. Cardiologists agree that the risk of a heart attack is positively correlated with a sedentary lifestyle.

Set G

Routinely attempting challenging crossword puzzles is a good way to improve critical thinking skills.

_____ 31. The more adept one is at reading maps, the less likely one is to get lost.

_____ 32. Practicing yoga consistently will benefit overall muscle conditioning.

_____ 33. Occasional practice riding a bicycle might be sufficient to improve riding proficiency in safe conditions.

_____ 34. Investing in the stock market at a young age is the best way to guarantee a comfortable retirement.

_____ 35. Few people can excel on graduate school admissions tests without substantial preparation.

Set H

People will often neglect going to the dentist until a serious problem has developed.

_____ 36. Many car repairs could have been undertaken sooner.

_____ 37. Frequently, procrastination gets the better of people.

_____ 38. It is not unusual for a student to wait to seek tutoring for months after falling behind in a class.

_____ 39. There is some likelihood that a patient will not tell an attending physician about a source of pain unless it becomes unbearable.

_____ 40. It is probable that a Labrador will persist in play or exercise long after exhaustion, dehydration, or severe pain has set in.

Set I

Either a Merlot or a Riesling will pair well with this menu.

_____ 41. Maple and mahogany woods complement each other well when paired in a piece of furniture.

_____ 42. Either the apples or the peaches at the farmers market will be good for making pies.

_____ 43. The song will sound great with either a violin or mandolin accompaniment.

_____ 44. You can only get beer or wine at my favorite bar.

_____ 45. Most foods pair well with subtle wines.

Set J

It is healthiest to follow national guidelines for fat intake.

_____ 46. Sticking to the speed limit is safest.

_____ 47. The slower you drive, the more gas you will save.

_____ 48. The wealthiest in society have the greatest influence.

_____ 49. You would be healthier if you cut back on salt in your diet.

_____ 50. People tend to eat too much sugar.

Set K

Without a major star, this type of action-adventure movie usually flops.

_____ 51. If it lacks a snappy hook, a dance-pop song like this will probably not catch on.

_____ 52. A fine French restaurant must have a master chef and an evolving menu to stay in business for more than a few years.

_____ 53. Unless the team picks up an ace reliever, it will not make the playoffs.

_____ 54. The ideal investment portfolio is well diversified.

_____ 55. Only a silicone sealant can diminish the tendency of this sort of roof to leak.

Set L

American companies make excellent watches, but they are not as good as Swiss-made watches.

_____ 56. Sonoma wines are arguably better than Napa wines, but Sonoma wines are not as well-known.

_____ 57. Persian rugs are the best in the world, but Indian rugs are also sold around the world.

_____ 58. California oranges are better for eating, but Florida oranges are the best for juicing.

_____ 59. Though not as high in quality as German performance automobiles, Japanese models are impressive.

_____ 60. African and South American coffee varieties are both excellent, but the African varieties might be better.

5

Answers

Note: We've highlighted the parts of the given statements that need to be matched and the offending portions of the mismatched statements that follow.

Set A

The majority of students will improve, given sufficient practice.

  N   1.   Most arguments on the LSAT are invalid.

"Are" is about what's happening now, whereas "will" predicts happenings in the future. We'll call this a Temporal Mismatch. It is a yellow flag, but not necessarily a fatal flaw. However, this statement also lacks a qualifying phrase to match "given sufficient practice," so it can be safely dismissed.

  N   2.   Most arguments on the LSAT can be proven to be invalid with the right logical tools.

"Can be" doesn't match the strength of "will." We'll call this a Strength Mismatch.

  Y   **3.**   **Most arguments on the LSAT will be proven to be invalid if someone capable sets out to do so.**

  N   4.   A majority of the arguments on the LSAT are valid.

Temporal Mismatch.

  N   5.   A minority of the arguments on the LSAT are invalid.

"Minority" is a yellow flag, but since the existence of a majority does imply the existence of a minority, this isn't quite fatal until we get to "are," which is a Temporal Mismatch. Two yellow flag mismatches create pretty safe grounds for dismissal.

Set B

Fermented vegetables are unlikely to spoil in a cool cellar.

  N   6.   Most prepared foods don't spoil in the refrigerator.

This states a tendency rather than a prediction. This is a fatal flaw, and one the LSAT loves to test!

  N   7.   Bread is likely to rise better in the oven, where temperatures are warmer than on the counter.

"Is likely" is positive whereas "are unlikely" is negative. We'll call this yellow flag mismatch a Negative vs. Positive Mismatch. "Better" and "warmer than" are comparative, whereas the original statement is not, so they constitute a Type Mismatch.

  Y   **8.**   **Kombucha will probably not ferment in temperatures under 60 degrees Fahrenheit.**

  N   9.   Generally speaking, leaving the key in the ignition overnight doesn't drain the battery.

Tendency vs. Prediction Mismatch.

  N   10. Leaving the key in the ignition overnight tends not to drain the battery.

Tendency vs. Prediction Mismatch.

Set C

Making the best jewelry requires patience and skill.

  N   11. Good clothes are always made of good fabric.

Strength Mismatch, and not a compound.

  Y   **12.** **You can't have the best garden without sun and fresh wind protection.**

  N   13. Since these pears are the best I've ever tasted, they must have been picked right before ripening and grown in fecund soil.

Type Mismatch – this is an argument, whereas the initial statement was not.

  Y   **14.** **Writing the best LSAT essay requires stamina and circumspection.**

  N   15. The best apples come from regions with cold temperatures or nitrogenated soil.

Compound statements need to have a matching conjunction.

Set D

Shade-grown coffee is superior in taste and better for the environment than plantation-grown coffee.

___N___ 16. Analog recordings are considered by some to have a more authentic sound, but even analog fans acknowledge the superior versatility of digital recording.

Strength Mismatch, and no pivot words in the original.

___N___ 17. Reducing caffeine intake results in both physical and psychological benefits.

Type Mismatch – not comparative.

___N___ 18. Forests managed for roadless, low-intensity timber harvesting can be superior in aesthetic value, as well as wildlife habitat suitability, compared to unmanaged forests.

Strength Mismatch.

___N___ 19. A high-fat, suet-based bird feed will typically attract more birds and a greater diversity of birds than a simple bird seed mix.

Strength Mismatch.

___Y___ **20. Manual transmissions, when compared to automatic transmissions, provide improved engine control and greater fuel efficiency.**

Set E

It is likely that drought conditions will persist.

___N___ 21. General P's scabies infestation will undoubtedly continue through August.

Strength Mismatch.

___Y___ **22. Rob will probably succumb to the injuries he sustained in the marsupial attack.**

___N___ 23. Ecological conditions tend to change very slowly.

Tendency vs. Prediction Mismatch.

___Y___ **24. The falling anvil will probably land on Christina.**

___N___ 25. The department has probably crumbled since the professors' departure.

Temporal Mismatch.

Set F

The possibility of a major earthquake in the region increased dramatically after the sizable shift in the tectonic plates last week, which was measured by seismologists.

___N___ 26. There will almost certainly be substantial wildfires this summer due to the likelihood of drought predicted by meteorologists.

Strength Mismatch.

___N___ 27. According to biologists, the red-tailed coot will probably go extinct since the hurricane wiped out its nesting ground.

Strength Mismatch.

___N___ 28. Aviation experts have indicated that most airlines have increased their safety inspections, so the risk of a plane crash should be substantially lower.

"Most" can be considered a Quantifier Mismatch or a Strength Mismatch. "Lower" is a Negative vs. Positive yellow flag. "Should be" is a Strength Mismatch, as it suggests the risk may or may not have actually changed, while the possibility changed for certain in the original statement.

___Y___ **29. The possibility of a recession has sharply increased since major investors started to pull out of the stock market in favor of safer investments.**

___N___ 30. Cardiologists agree that the risk of a heart attack is positively correlated with a sedentary lifestyle.

Type Mismatch.

Set G

Routinely attempting challenging crossword puzzles is a good way to improve critical thinking skills.

___N___ 31. The more adept one is at reading maps, the less likely one is to get lost.

Type Mismatch – this is a statement of correlation whereas the original statement is causal.

___Y___ **32. Practicing yoga consistently will benefit overall muscle conditioning.**

___N___ 33. Occasional practice riding a bicycle might be sufficient to improve riding proficiency in safe conditions.

Strength Mismatch.

__N__   34. Investing in the stock market at a young age is the best way to guarantee a comfortable retirement.

We could consider this a Strength Mismatch or a Type Mismatch, since this is comparative whereas the original statement is not.

__N__   35. Few people can excel on graduate school admissions tests without substantial preparation.

"Few" is a Quantifier Mismatch and "without" indicates a conditional statement, meaning we also have a Type Mismatch.

Set H

People will often neglect going to the dentist until a serious problem has developed.

__N__   36. Many car repairs could have been undertaken sooner.

Doesn't match the "until" clause of the original.

__N__   37. Frequently, procrastination gets the better of people.

Doesn't match the "until" clause of the original.

__Y__   **38. It is not unusual for a student to wait to seek tutoring for months after falling behind in a class.**

__N__   39. There is some likelihood that a patient will not tell an attending physician about a source of pain unless it becomes unbearable.

Tendency vs. Prediction Mismatch – the original is a tendency, not predictive.

__N__   40. It is probable that a Labrador will persist in play or exercise long after exhaustion, dehydration, or severe pain has set in.

Tendency vs. Prediction Mismatch – the original is a tendency, not predictive.

Set I

Either a Merlot or a Riesling will pair well with this menu.

__N__   41. Maple and mahogany woods complement each other well when paired in a piece of furniture.

The conjunction doesn't match; the two things should complement a third thing, not one another.

__Y__   **42. Either the apples or the peaches at the farmers market will be good for making pies.**

__Y__   **43. The song will sound great with either a violin or mandolin accompaniment.**

__N__   44. You can only get beer or wine at my favorite bar.

Strength Mismatch.

__N__   45. Most foods pair well with subtle wines.

Quantifier Mismatch.

Set J

It is healthiest to follow national guidelines for fat intake.

__Y__   **46. Sticking to the speed limit is safest.**

__N__   47. The slower you drive, the more gas you will save.

Type Mismatch – sets up a direct proportion. Temporal Mismatch—what will happen vs. what is healthiest.

__N__   48. The wealthiest in society have the greatest influence.

Type Mismatch – shows a correlation.

__N__   49. You would be healthier if you cut back on salt in your diet.

Type Mismatch – conditional. Strength Mismatch – healthier vs. healthiest.

__N__   50. People tend to eat too much sugar.

Type Mismatch – tendency.

Set K

Without a major star, this type of action-adventure movie usually flops.

__N__   51. If it lacks a snappy hook, a dance-pop song like this will probably not catch on.

Tendency vs. Prediction Mismatch.

__N__   52. A fine French restaurant must have a master chef and an evolving menu to stay in business for more than a few years.

The original argument is not a compound, and there is a Strength Mismatch because of the absence of "usually."

__N__   53. Unless the team picks up an ace reliever, it will not make the playoffs.

Strength Mismatch.

___N___   54. The ideal investment portfolio is well diversified.

Type Mismatch – comparative instead of conditional.

___Y___   **55. Only a silicone sealant can diminish the tendency of this sort of roof to leak.**

Set L

American companies make excellent watches, but they are not as good as Swiss-made watches.

___N___   56. Sonoma wines are arguably better than Napa wines, but Sonoma wines are not as well-known.

"Arguably" is a Strength Mismatch. This also adds a second consideration while the original does not.

___N___   57. Persian rugs are the best in the world, but Indian rugs are also sold around the world.

Strength Mismatch.

___N___   58. California oranges are better for eating, but Florida oranges are the best for juicing.

This adds a second consideration while the original does not.

___Y___   **59. Though not as high in quality as German performance automobiles, Japanese models are impressive.**

___N___   60. African and South American coffee varieties are both excellent, but the African varieties might be better.

Strength Mismatch.

5

Drill 106: Know When to Fold 'Em, Round 1

Instructions: When a Matching Family question has a conditional stimulus, your first move should always be to diagram it. This is something that a lot of students resist because they feel like they won't have time to diagram the stimulus and all five answer choices, and they may be right. Luckily for them (and you!), diagramming the stimulus can ensure you *don't* have to slog through diagramming a bunch of answers because it will allow you to clearly see how answer choices diverge from the original. Once you see such a divergence, stop reading. You're done there. Move on.

Eliminating an answer choice this way can be a hard thing to do on test day, so practice it with this drill. We've done the first step for you—we've diagrammed your stimulus. Each diagram will form a set with five accompanying arguments for you to evaluate. Highlight the part where the non-matching answers go awry.

Set A

~B or ~A → ~C
D → C
~D → ~C
_____
~B → ~D

1. If Anna and Maria both attend the party, Julio will not. If Julio does not attend the party, Jerome also will not attend the party. Ann will not attend the party, so Jerome will not attend the party.

2. If either the coach or the team captain does not show up to the game, the game will not be played. As long as it is a Monday night, the game will be played. If it is not Monday night, the game is not played. The coach did not show up to the game, so it is not Monday night.

3. If it either rains or hails, school will be canceled. School was not canceled, so it must not have rained or hailed.

4. Many people who play soccer also play basketball. Anyone who plays basketball is athletic. So, some people who play soccer are athletic.

5. There are no history books that cover every possible perspective on history. Any history book that claims to do so is misleading its readers. This history book claims to cover every possible perspective on history; therefore, it is misleading its readers.

Set B

A
B → C
A → B
_____
C

6. If Ally's computer breaks within the next month, she will purchase a new one. If she purchases a new computer, she will have to spend over $200 from her savings. Ally's computer will break within the next month. Therefore, Ally will have to spend over $200 from her savings.

7. Today is a fall day. When the leaves have not changed colors, it cannot be a fall day unless there are only evergreen trees or no trees at all. The leaves have not changed colors, and there are no evergreen trees in this location, so there must be no trees at all.

8. Irma uses only gel pens to write. This pen is not gel. Therefore, Irma will not use it to write.

9. Some home repairs can be done without professional assistance and some cannot. Marge is able to do her home repair without professional assistance. Therefore, Marge will do her home repair without professional assistance.

10. David will do any math problem required by his job. He will not do any math problems that are not required by his job. Therefore, if David is doing a math problem, it must be for his job.

Set C

X → Y and Z

~Z

_____

~X

11. Imported wine is generally perceived to be more of a luxury good than domestically produced wine. Keisha would like to impress the guests coming to her next party. They appreciate the finer things in life. Therefore, Keisha would be wise to provide imported wine at her next party.

12. Whenever Marianne listens to music before work, she arrives at work in a good mood. Marianne did not arrive to work in a good mood this morning. Thus, she must not have listened to music before work.

13. Alicia reads the newspaper only on Sundays and only when the news contains a story that relates personally to her life. It is Sunday, and the news contains a story relevant to Alicia's life today. Hence, Alicia might read the newspaper today.

14. A high-quality raincoat always provides protection and makes its wearer look stylish. Hunter's raincoat does not make him look stylish. Thus, it is not a high-quality raincoat.

15. If Megan adopts an animal, it will be either a dog or a cat. The animal shelter currently does not have any cats available for adoption. Consequently, if Megan adopts an animal, it will be a dog.

Set D

A → B

A → C

D → ~C

_____

D → ~A

16. All notebooks sold at this store contain wide-ruled paper. Also, all notebooks sold at this store contain at least 100 sheets of paper. Notebooks sold online always contain fewer than 100 sheets of paper. Therefore, notebooks sold online are not sold at this store.

17. Home fires are sometimes caused by candles. In addition, home fires are often caused by fireplaces. Therefore, if someone wants to prevent a home fire, she would be wise to avoid candles and fireplaces.

18. If Emily goes running today, she will get exercise. And if she goes running today, Emily will be late for work. Emily does not want to be late for work, so she will not go running today.

19. Pedro has a pet hedgehog. Every time he needs to buy food for it, he must go to the exotic pet supply store. The exotic pet supply store is over 35 miles from Pedro's home. Thus, every time Pedro needs food for his hedgehog, he must drive over 35 miles.

20. Alyssa will move to New York if her friends move there. She will also move to New York if she gets a job offer there. Alyssa's friends moved to New York, and she got a job offer there. It follows that Alyssa will move to New York.

5

Set E

A or B → C

Not C

_____

Not A and Not B

21. If Julia is accepted into a top-tier graduate school, then she will attend. If she attends a top-tier graduate school, then she will have to move out of state. Therefore, if Julia does not have to move out of state for graduate school, then she was not accepted into a top-tier graduate school.

22. Most zebras in zoos are animals that were injured in the wild and are being rehabilitated. Most penguins in zoos were born in captivity. The local zoo contains both zebras and penguins. Therefore, the zoo must contain at least some animals that were born in captivity.

23. Any time that Austin purchases a new car or a new home, he must take out a loan to help pay for it. Austin did not take out a loan this year. Therefore, Austin neither purchased a new car nor a new home this year.

24. Everyone who works in software development either studied computer science in school or learned computer science outside of school. Radha did not study computer science in school, so she must have learned it outside of school.

25. If Sarah goes to law school or business school, she will make her parents happy. Sarah will go to law school. Therefore, she will make her parents happy.

Set F

X → Y and Z

Z → Q

_____

X → Q

26. Any time that a person moves, they must file a change of address form and obtain a new driver's license. If someone obtains a new driver's license, they will get a new photo taken. Therefore, anyone who files a change of address form will get a new photo taken.

27. Some restaurants that regularly feature specials allow their servers to try the specials in advance. This allows the servers to make recommendations and accurately describe the specials. Therefore, allowing servers to try specials in advance is advisable.

28. Every child loves both ice cream and balloons. Therefore, in order to have a successful children's birthday party, one should provide both ice cream and balloons.

29. If Dave orders a cheeseburger, he will order it with both ketchup and mustard. Anytime Dave orders something with mustard, he requests spicy mustard. Thus, if Dave orders a cheeseburger, he will request spicy mustard.

30. In many grocery stores, plastic bags are more popular than paper bags. As a result, the local grocery store carries more plastic bags than paper bags. Customers who prefer paper bags are more likely than customers who prefer plastic bags to be disappointed in the check-out line.

Set G

~A → ~B

A → C

B

_____

C

Set H

A → B

C → B

B → D

_____

C → D

31. Anyone who does not recycle does not care about the environment. Furthermore, everyone who recycles is a conscientious person. Amelia cares about the environment. Therefore, Amelia is a conscientious person.

32. All exotic pets are illegal in country X. Monkeys are exotic pets. Therefore, monkeys are illegal in this country.

33. Luke does not like to travel to foreign countries where he does not speak the primary language. Luke's friends recently invited him to travel to a country where he does not speak the primary language. Luke will most likely turn down his friends' invitation.

34. Everyone who came to class without a pen also came to class without a pencil. All students who brought a pen to class also brought paper. Melinda came to class without a pen; therefore, she also came to class without paper.

35. Customers at this restaurant may choose either chocolate or vanilla milkshakes. The restaurant's chocolate milkshakes are known to be the best in town, so most customers will choose the chocolate milkshake.

36. All bird cages are on sale at the home goods store. Nothing that is on sale at the home goods store is discounted by more than 20% from its original price. Therefore, no bird cage at the home goods store is discounted by more than 20% from its original price.

37. All lizards are reptiles. All alligators are reptiles. Any alligator in the United States lives in Florida. Thus, there are at least some reptiles in Florida.

38. Most monarch butterflies migrate south in the winter. Some of the butterflies that migrate south stop to feed from milkweed in Texas. Therefore, Texas is the best place to see a monarch butterfly in the winter.

39. Every light bulb in Angela's house is an energy-saving light bulb. Also, all the light bulbs at Angela's workplace are energy-saving light bulbs. Energy-saving light bulbs are always more expensive than standard light bulbs. It is clear that the light bulbs at Angela's workplace must be more expensive than standard light bulbs.

40. The spring flowers will probably not bloom in April this year. After all, it has been unusually cold, and the spring flowers typically bloom late when it has been colder than average.

5

Answers

Set A

~B or ~A → ~C
D → C
~D → ~C
_____
~B → ~D

1. If Anna and Maria both attend the party

(We get an "and" condition instead of an "or" and a positive instead of a negative right out of the gate!)

2. If either the coach or the team captain does not show up to the game, the game will not be played. As long as it is a Monday night, the game will be played. If it is not Monday night, the game is not played. The coach did not show up to the game, so it is not Monday night.

(A match!)

3. If it either rains or hails, school will be canceled. School was not canceled,

(All positives instead of negatives in the first conditional is a yellow flag, but we can throw this out when we get a statement of fact —there were none of those in the original.)

4. Many people who play soccer also play basketball.

("Many" means this is not a conditional statement.)

5. There are no history books that cover every possible perspective on history. Any history book that claims to do so is misleading its readers.

(It is tempting to rule this out when we don't see an "or," but remember that "or" in the sufficient condition means the condition can split into two statements with the same necessary condition. Keep reading to make sure that's not what's going to happen here. But when we get all new terms in the second sentence, we know it's not a match.)

Set B

A
B → C
A → B
_____
C

6. If Ally's computer breaks within the next month, she will purchase a new one. (A → B) If she purchases a new computer, she will have to spend over $200 from her savings. (B → C) Ally's computer will break within the next month. (A) Therefore, Ally will have to spend over $200 from her savings. (C)

(A match! Remember that only the logical pattern matters, not the order. This has all the parts, just in a different order.)

7. Today is a fall day. When the leaves have not changed colors, it cannot be a fall day unless there are only evergreen trees or no trees at all.

(Too complex! Nothing in our original diagram matches this.)

8. Irma uses only gel pens to write. This pen is not gel.

(A negative statement of fact paired with all positive conditional terms = mismatch!)

9. Some home repairs can be done without professional assistance and some cannot.

("Some" is not conditional language.)

10. David will do any math problem required by his job. He will not do any math problems that are not required by his job.

(The second sentence is the negation of the first; there is nothing like that in the original.)

Set C

$X \rightarrow Y$ and Z

$\sim Z$

$\sim X$

11. Imported wine is generally perceived to be more of a luxury good than domestically produced wine.

(A comparison with no conditional logic = mismatch.)

12. Whenever Marianne listens to music before work, she arrives to work in a good mood. Marianne did not arrive at work in a good mood this morning.

(The absence of "and" in the first line is suspect, but remember that "and" in the necessary condition means the compound conditional can be presented as two separate statements. That means we have to keep reading past the first sentence to see if the second sentence diagrams that way. But no, the second sentence negates the outcome of the first, and that doesn't match our original.)

13. Alicia reads the newspaper only on Sundays and only when the news contains a story that relates personally to her life. It is Sunday, and the news contains a story relevant to Alicia's life today.

(We're looking for a negation of one outcome from the prior conditional, and instead we get a positive statement of both outcomes.)

14. A high-quality raincoat always provides protection and makes its wearer look stylish. Hunter's raincoat does not make him look stylish. Thus, it is not a high-quality raincoat.

(A match!)

15. If Megan adopts an animal, it will be either a dog or a cat.

("Or" instead of "and.")

Set D

$A \rightarrow B$

$A \rightarrow C$

$D \rightarrow \sim C$

$D \rightarrow \sim A$

16. All notebooks sold at this store contain wide-ruled paper. Also, all notebooks sold at this store contain at least 100 sheets of paper. Notebooks sold online always contain fewer than 100 sheets of paper. Therefore, notebooks sold online are not sold at this store.

(A match!)

17. Home fires are sometimes caused by candles.

("Sometimes" is not conditional logic.)

18. If Emily goes running today, she will get exercise. And if she goes running today, Emily will be late for work. Emily does not want to be late for work, so she will not go running today.

(The last sentence is not a conditional—it gives us a statement of fact and a prediction for the future.)

19. Pedro has a pet hedgehog. Every time he needs to buy food for it, he must go to the exotic pet supply store. The exotic pet supply store is over 35 miles from Pedro's home.

(There are no statements of fact in the original argument, so the first sentence here is a red flag. The fatal flaw, though, comes in the third sentence, which sets up an $A \rightarrow B \rightarrow C$ transitive chain with the second. In the argument we're trying to match, two conditional premises share the same sufficient condition, and a third needs to be contraposed in order to link up with the second.)

20. Alyssa will move to New York if her friends move there. She will also move to New York if she gets a job offer there.

(The first two lines need to share the same sufficient condition, not the same necessary condition.)

Set E

A or B → C

Not C
_____

Not A and Not B

21. If Julia is accepted into a top-tier graduate school, she will attend. If she attends a top-tier graduate school, she will have to move out of state. Therefore . . .

As soon as we know that the first two sentences are premises, eliminate. Neither one contains an "or."

22. Most zebras in zoos are animals that were injured in the wild and are being rehabilitated.

23. Any time that Austin purchases a new car or a new home, he must take out a loan to help pay for it. Austin did not take out a loan this year. Therefore, Austin neither purchased a new car nor a new home this year.

(A match!)

24. Everyone who works in software development either studied computer science in school or learned computer science outside of school.

The "or" makes this tempting, but it diagrams as A → B or C. In our original, the "or" was in the sufficient condition. Eliminate!

25. If Sarah goes to law school or business school, she will make her parents happy. Sarah will go to law school.

The first premise matches A or B → C, but the second premise is A, and we need not C. Eliminate!

Set F

X → Y and Z

Z → Q
_____

X → Q

26. Any time that a person moves, they must file a change of address form and obtain a new driver's license. If someone obtains a new driver's license, they will get a new photo taken. Therefore, anyone who files a change of address form will get a new photo taken.

A match until the conclusion, which diagrams as Y → Q.

27. Some restaurants that regularly feature specials allow their servers to try the specials in advance.

28. Every child loves both ice cream and balloons. Therefore, in order to have a successful children's birthday party, one should provide both ice cream and balloons.

The conclusion introduces a new element as the sufficient condition, and has a compound necessary condition: Q → Y and Z. Eliminate!

29. If Dave orders a cheeseburger, he will order it with both ketchup and mustard. Anytime Dave orders something with mustard, he requests spicy mustard. Thus, if Dave orders a cheeseburger, he will request spicy mustard.

(A match!)

30. In many grocery stores, plastic bags are more popular than paper bags.

Set G

~A → ~B

A → C

B

_____

C

31. Anyone who does not recycle does not care about the environment. Furthermore, everyone who recycles is a conscientious person. Amelia cares about the environment. Therefore, Amelia is a conscientious person.

(A match!)

32. All exotic pets are illegal in country X. Monkeys are an exotic pet. Therefore . . .

The premises here could be diagrammed as A → C and B → A (~A → ~B), which is a match, but there are only two premises. We're missing the third "B" premise in the original.

33. Luke does not like to travel to foreign countries where he does not speak the primary language. Luke's friends recently invited him to travel to a country where he does not speak the primary language.

The first premise doesn't look like conditional logic, but could possibly be diagrammed as ~Speak Primary Language → ~Like to Travel, a match for ~A → ~B. The second premise, however, brings in a new idea (Luke's friends inviting him) that doesn't have a match in the original argument. You could possibly stretch this into Country Invited to Visit → ~Speak Primary Language, but this still isn't a match.

34. Everyone who came to class without a pen also came to class without a pencil. All students who brought a pen to class also brought paper. Melinda came to class without a pen.

A match until we hit this statement, which would be ~A. We're looking for a B at this point.

35. Customers at this restaurant may choose either chocolate or vanilla milkshakes.

Set H

A → B

C → B

B → D

_____

C → D

36. All bird cages are on sale at the home goods store. Nothing that is on sale at the home goods store is discounted by more than 20% from its original price.

The first premise matches A → B, but the second premise is B → ~C. Eliminate!

37. All lizards are reptiles. All alligators are reptiles. Any alligator in the United States lives in Florida.

The first two premises match, but the third premise needs reptiles in the sufficient condition, not "alligator in the United States." Eliminate!

38. Most monarch butterflies migrate south in the winter.

39. Every light bulb in Angela's house is an energy-saving light bulb. Also, all the light bulbs at Angela's workplace are energy-saving light bulbs. Energy-saving light bulbs are always more expensive than standard light bulbs. It is clear that the light bulbs at Angela's workplace must be more expensive than standard light bulbs.

(A match!)

40. The spring flowers will probably not bloom in April this year.

5

Drill 107: Conclusion Considerations

Instructions: When a Match the Reasoning question has a conditional structure, one quick and easy way to make eliminations is to compare the conclusion of each answer choice against the conclusion of the stimulus. A stimulus with a conditional conclusion needs a match with a conditional conclusion. On the other hand, a stimulus that applies conditional statements to a specific case needs a match that isn't a conditional statement.

For each of the following conditional arguments, determine whether the argument's conclusion is a conditional statement (Y) or not (N).

_____ 1. The best pizza is found at Italian restaurants, and Italian restaurants never serve frozen pizza. Therefore, if the pizza is frozen, it must not be the best pizza.

_____ 2. Weather forecasters use equipment and models that are most accurate when the prediction is close to the weather event predicted. So, predictions for tomorrow's weather should be the most accurate predictions these equipment and models can make.

_____ 3. When people go to a grocery store hungry, they will be tempted by what they see and buy more items than they need. So, if people go grocery shopping when full, they will only buy what they need.

_____ 4. Impatiens don't grow well when planted in direct sunlight, and the impatiens in Lily's garden are doing very well. Therefore, Lily must have planted them in at least partial shade.

_____ 5. Learning to play a musical instrument well requires extensive practice, and extensive practice will be abhorrent to all but the most dedicated students. Only the most dedicated students, therefore, will ever learn to play their instruments well.

_____ 6. In order to play varsity sports, students must maintain at least a 2.5 GPA. Dante has a 3.0 GPA, so he will be able to play varsity sports.

_____ 7. LED bulbs last significantly longer than incandescent bulbs and also use less energy. Thus, if Dave replaces all of his incandescent bulbs with LED bulbs, he will save money.

_____ 8. The freezing and thawing of pavement during the winter creates stress and causes potholes, and potholes require paving. Pavers are therefore likely to be very busy this spring.

_____ 9. Major coastal storms can cause significant flooding and damage to beachfront properties. Properties at risk of such damage are more difficult to insure. The beach house, therefore, will be difficult to insure.

_____ 10. Maintaining a long-distance romantic relationship has always presented challenges, but as platforms for interactive long-distance communications have improved, so has the ability to remain closely connected. Therefore, if such platforms continue to improve indefinitely, long-distance relationships, which require these close connections, will continue to improve as well.

_____ 11. Parents who fly with their children must be exceptionally patient, and patient adults are incapable of raising impatient children. Therefore, all the children one sees on an airline flight must be patient children.

_____ 12. When airline flights are full, they now require that larger carry-on bags be gate-checked because there is not enough room in the overhead compartments to accommodate them. Thus, because this flight is full, it is likely that passengers with larger carry-on bags will have to gate-check them.

_____ 13. People who frequently change time zones experience frequent disruptions in their sleep patterns. Therefore, since all flight attendants frequently change time zones, they must experience frequent sleep disruptions.

_____ 14. Avid sports fans wear the emblem of their team on their clothing when attending a game. Thus, all people at a game wearing team shirts must be avid sports fans.

_____ 15. Excellent baking requires mathematical precision, since quantities need to be measured precisely and directions followed exactly. All elite musicians possess mathematical precision, so it is clear that all elite musicians must be excellent bakers.

_____ 16. Children today have grown up with technology, which makes them more comfortable with electronic devices than older generations, even those devices with which they are unfamiliar. This comfort allows children to navigate unfamiliar devices more successfully than those who are uncomfortable with an unfamiliar device. Children, therefore, are more likely than their parents to be able to navigate unfamiliar devices successfully.

_____ 17. Louie is a six-year-old boy, and all six-year-old boys like gross humor. From this we can conclude that Louie likes gross humor.

_____ 18. All softball players wear cleats on the field, and anyone wearing cleats increases their chances of injuring another person in a collision. Therefore, all softball players increase their chances of injuring another person in a collision when they take the field.

_____ 19. If it's Tuesday and Tim has no appointments in the afternoon, then his car will get waxed. Since it's Tuesday and all of Tim's afternoon appointments were canceled, Tim's car was waxed today.

_____ 20. Voting is both a right and a responsibility, and responsibilities should not be handed to the irresponsible. It is therefore imperative that the young people of our country learn to be responsible if they are to be granted the right to vote.

_____ 21. Kathy always rolls her eyes when Alan looks at his phone during a conversation. Therefore, because Alan will surely look at his phone while they converse over dinner this evening, we can be assured that Kathy will be rolling her eyes at dinner tonight.

_____ 22. Headaches are a classic sign of caffeine withdrawal. Maura, who used to drink three cups of coffee a day, has decided to stop drinking caffeine. Therefore, she will start having headaches.

_____ 23. People who do not get all the nutrients they need from their diets take supplements. Gina's diet is lacking in essential nutrients, so she should start taking a dietary supplement.

_____ 24. Cameras take better pictures than do cell phones. Hobby photographers should always attempt to take the best pictures possible. Hobby photographers should therefore take pictures on their cameras rather than their cell phones whenever possible.

_____ 25. People who are conscientious pay attention to details and meet deadlines. Giovanni does not meet deadlines, so he is clearly not conscientious.

5

Answers

___Y___ 1. **Therefore, if the pizza is frozen, it must not be the best pizza.**

___N___ 2. So, predictions for tomorrow's weather should be the most accurate predictions these equipment and models can make.

___Y___ 3. **So, if people go grocery shopping when full, they will only buy what they need.**

___N___ 4. Therefore, Lily must have planted them in at least partial shade.

   (Note: The stimulus maps as follows: if direct sunlight → impatiens ~ do well; impatiens do well → ~ direct sunlight. However, since the conclusion contains only the necessary condition (~direct sunlight), it is not by itself a conditional statement.)

___Y___ 5. **Only the most dedicated students, therefore, will ever learn to play their instruments well.**

___N___ 6. So, he will be able to play varsity sports. *(See explanation for Q. 4)*

___Y___ 7. **Thus, if Dave replaces all of his incandescent bulbs with LED bulbs, he will save money.**

___N___ 8. Pavers are therefore likely to be very busy this spring.

___N___ 9. The beach house, therefore, will be difficult to insure.

___Y___ 10. **Therefore, if such platforms continue to improve indefinitely, long-distance relationships will continue to improve as well.**

___Y___ 11. **Therefore, all the children one sees on an airline flight must be patient children.**

___N___ 12. Thus, it is likely that passengers with larger carry-on bags will have to gate-check them.

___N___ 13. Therefore, flight attendants must experience frequent sleep disruptions. *(See explanation for Q. 4)*

___Y___ 14. **Thus, all people at a game wearing team shirts must be avid sports fans.**

___Y___ 15. **So, it is clear that all elite musicians must be excellent bakers.**

___N___ 16. Children, therefore, are more likely than their parents to be able to navigate unfamiliar devices successfully.

___N___ 17. From this we can conclude that Louie likes gross humor. *(See explanation for Q. 4)*

___Y___ 18. **Therefore, all softball players increase their chances of injuring another person in a collision when they take the field.**

___N___ 19. Therefore, Tim's car was waxed today. *(See explanation for Q. 4)*

___Y___ 20. **It is therefore imperative that the young people of our country learn to be responsible if they are to be granted the right to vote.**

___N___ 21. Therefore, we can be assured that Kathy will be rolling her eyes at dinner tonight. *(See explanation for Q. 4)*

___N___ 22. Therefore, she will start having headaches.

___N___ 23. So, she should start taking a dietary supplement.

___N___ 24. Hobby photographers should therefore take pictures on their cameras rather than their cell phones whenever possible.

___N___ 25. So, he is clearly not conscientious. *(See explanation for Q. 4)*

Drill 108: Vocab Lab #13 – Root of All Evil

Instructions: Knowing Latin and Greek roots can help a great deal with English vocabulary. It can also help you guess at the meanings of unknown words when you encounter them.

Match the LSAT words below to the meanings of their core Latin or Greek roots.

1.	Adjoining	a.	different + kind
2.	Commensurate	b.	forward + kind
3.	Disanalogous	c.	holy + make
4.	Disconfirming	d.	inward + look
5.	Heterogeneity	e.	reverse + establish
6.	Introspective	f.	reverse + proportional
7.	Misdescribe	g.	straight + belief
8.	Orthodox	h.	to + connect
9.	Progenitor	i.	together + measure
10.	Sanctify	j.	wrong + represent

Answers

1. h

Adjoining = to *(ad)* + connect *(join)* = next to; in direct contact with.

2. i

Commensurate = together *(com)* + measure *(mensur)* = proportional; proportionate; equal in measure.

3. f

Disanalogous = reverse *(dis)* + proportional *(analogous)* = not comparable; unrelated.

4. e

Disconfirming = reverse *(dis)* + establish *(confirm)* = proving something invalid.

5. a

Heterogeneity = different *(hetero)* + kind *(gen)* = diversity; being made of many different parts.

6. d

Introspective = inward *(intro)* + look *(spect)* = inward-looking; self-examining.

7. j

Misdescribe = wrong *(mis)* + represent *(describe)* = describe incorrectly or misleadingly.

8. g

Orthodox = straight *(ortho)* + belief *(dox)* = in agreement with an established tradition.

9. b

Progenitor = forward *(pro)* + kind *(gen)* = ancestor; forebear.

10. c

Sanctify = holy *(sanct)* + make *(ify)* = declare or make holy.

CHAPTER 6

Logic Games, The 4-Step Process

In This Chapter, We Will Cover:

- Step 1 – Picture the Game

- Step 2 – Notate the Rules and Make Inferences

- Step 3 – The Big Pause

- Step 4 – Attack the Questions

Logic Games, The 4-Step Process

In order to approach logic games effectively, you have to approach logic games consistently. That's why we've created the 4-Step process for Logic Games. The first step is always to picture the game in your mind's eye. This will help the game feel less abstract and orient you to the task of the game. The next step is to represent the game on paper. In Chapter 2, you practiced the basic skills for this step of the process. This chapter will help you take those skills to the next level. The third step in our 4-Step Process is The Big Pause. Before diving into the questions of the game, you should always take a moment to identify the elements that are likely to drive the game, the elements that are likely to get lost in the shuffle, and opportunities to use high-level techniques such as Framing and Numerical Distributions. The fourth step is where all that hard work finally comes to fruition as you attack the questions and rake in the points.

In this section, you will learn to:

Picture the Game

- Recognize twists on common game types

Notate the Rules and Make Inferences

- Navigate hard-to-diagram rules
- Deal with complex conditional statements
- Spot binary and biconditional relationships
- Combine rules to make inferences

Take The Big Pause

- Catch your mistakes
- Master identifying the most and least restricted elements in a game

Attack the Questions

- Mow down Orientation questions
- Characterize correct and incorrect answers on questions about truth
- Test drive answers
- Use previous work
- Use frames

6

Step 1–Picture the Game

Drill 109: Twist and Shout

Instructions: Some logic games are boilerplate examples of their game type, but many, if not most, contain some sort of twist. Lots of these twists show up over and over again, so it pays to know how to recognize them. For this drill, you'll see a list of twists in the left column. In the right column is language that describes the twist or language pulled from a game that has the twist. Match each twist to its identifying language.

Twists	Rule/Description
1. Open Grouping *j*	a. A game where none of the rules deal with the numbered slots.
2. Mismatch: Repeating Elements *e*	b. "Each student will attend at least one class, and each class will have at least one student."
3. Relative Ordering *a*	
4. Hybrid *c*	c. "Larry and Omar must attend the same seminar, and it must be given after the seminar Pierre attends."
5. In/Out *d*	d. "The zookeeper will select at least five and no more than seven animals for her display."
	e. "The four-person cast will perform all seven of the play's parts."

Twists	Rule/Description
6. Interchangeable Groups	f. "The duets are performed Friday through Sunday."
7. Special Positions	g. Something gets passed from one element to another element.
8. Mismatch: Open Slots	h. "One member of each team is the captain."
9. Process	i. Each element must be used exactly once, but there are more slots than elements.
10. Hybrid	j. A grouping game in which the individual groups have no rules.

Twists	Rule/Description
11. Relative Ordering	k. "The top five out of seven runners will make the final heat."
12. Open Grouping	l. "If Alice is selected, then exactly one of the men will also be selected."
13. Mismatch: Out Group	m. "Frank will go before Gabe or after Hannah, but not both."
14. 3D Ordering	n. "Victor will sell more items than any of the other merchants."
15. In/Out Grouping with Subgroups	o. "Zach is the third pitcher and is left-handed."

Twists		Rule/Description
16.	Mismatch: Elements Double Up	p.	"David sits across the table from Rachel."
17.	3D Grouping	q.	"Exactly five of the eight foods will be used in the meal."
18.	Circular Ordering	r.	"All eight patients schedule an appointment during the five-day work week."
19.	Undefined Subgroups	s.	"The Craftsman house is either red or green and is not located at the beach."
20.	Closed In/Out Grouping	t.	"Four of the students are sophomores, and three of the students are freshmen."

Twists		Rule/Description
21.	Mismatch: Repeating Elements	u.	"Proposal one gets twice as many votes as proposal two."
22.	Open Grouping	v.	"Teddy, Ursula, and Velma are junior partners. Javier, Khaled, and Louise are senior partners."
23.	Defined Subgroups	w.	"Either five or six of the students make the team."
24.	3D Grouping	x.	"One of the four shows is performed on every day of the week."
25.	Open In/Out Grouping	y.	Teams of two finish first, second, and third in a relay race.

Answers

Note: Nobody wants to look at a bunch of messy lines so, instead of connecting the twists to their rule/description that way, we've opted to list the correct rule/description directly across from its associated twist in this answer key.

Twists		Rule/Description	
1.	Open Grouping	b.	"Each student will attend at least one class, and each class will have at least one student."
2.	Mismatch: Repeating Elements	e.	"The four-person cast will perform all seven of the play's parts."
3.	Relative Ordering	a.	A game where none of the rules deal with the numbered slots.
4.	Hybrid	c.	"Larry and Omar must attend the same seminar, and it must be given after the seminar Pierre attends."
5.	In/Out	d.	"The zookeeper will select at least five and no more than seven animals for her display."

Twists		Rule/Description	
6.	Interchangeable Groups	j.	A grouping game in which the individual groups have no rules.
7.	Special Positions	h.	"One member of each team is the captain."
8.	Mismatch: Open Slots	i.	Each element must be used exactly once, but there are more slots than elements.
9.	Process	g.	Something gets passed from one element to another element.
10.	Hybrid	f.	"The duets are performed Friday through Sunday."

Twists		Rule/Description	
11.	Relative Ordering	m.	"Frank will go before Gabe or after Hannah, but not both."
12.	Open Grouping	n.	"Victor will sell more items than any of the other merchants."
13.	Mismatch: Out Group	k.	"The top five out of seven runners will make the final heat."
14.	3D Ordering	o.	"Zach is the third pitcher and is left-handed."
15.	In/Out Grouping with Subgroups	l.	"If Alice is selected, then exactly one of the men will also be selected."

Twists		Rule/Description
16. Mismatch: Elements Double Up	r.	"All eight patients schedule an appointment during the five-day work week."
17. 3D Grouping	s.	"The Craftsman house is either red or green and is not located at the beach."
18. Circular Ordering	p.	"David sits across the table from Rachel."
19. Undefined Subgroups	t.	"Four of the students are sophomores, and three of the students are freshmen."
20. Closed In/Out Grouping	q.	"Exactly five of the eight foods will be used in the meal."

Twists		Rule/Description
21. Mismatch: Repeating Elements	x.	"One of the four shows is performed on every day of the week."
22. Open Grouping	u.	"Proposal one gets twice as many votes as proposal two."
23. Defined Subgroups	v.	"Teddy, Ursula, and Velma are junior partners. Javier, Khaled, and Louise are senior partners."
24. Hybrid	y.	Teams of two finish first, second, and third in a relay race.
25. Open In/Out Grouping	w.	"Either five or six of the students make the team."

Drill 110: Do the Twist, Mixed Edition

Instructions: For each of these tricky games, identify the game type and twist. Bonus points for any strategic considerations you can fill in! No need to diagram the full games. For now, just practice spotting the game type, twist, and strategic considerations. Be on the lookout for the chance to use advanced strategies such as Framing and Numerical Distribution and for high-level inferences such as those that stem from Limited Group Space and Interchangeable Groups!

1. An accounting firm is assigning nine employees to audit three companies: Amtech, Baxter, and Cypher. Each employee will audit exactly one company. Feld, Garcia, Han, Inoglu, and Jones are senior consultants; Kuhl, Lee, Mejia, and Okafor are junior consultants. Each company is assigned a team of exactly three auditors, and each team must have a senior consultant and a junior consultant. The employee assignments are made according to the following constraints:

   Inoglu and Feld audit the same company.
   Jones and Okafor audit the same company.
   Kuhl and Mejia audit different companies.
   Han and Garcia audit different companies.

2. Seven dogs—Fido, Goldie, Hercules, Jumper, Kittens, Luna, and Meatball—are competing in the Westville Dog Show. The dogs finish the competition according to the following rules:

   Fido finishes before Goldie.
   Either Hercules finishes before Jumper or Hercules finishes before Kittens, but not both.
   Luna finishes before Meatball if, and only if, Goldie also finishes before Meatball.
   Kittens finishes before Meatball.

3. Nine friends—Frank, Gavin, Huang, Ilene, Juan, Kevin, Laura, Molly, and Nancy—are voting on whether to go out for Italian or Mexican food. Each time they vote, a supermajority of exactly six of the friends will vote for one or the other type of food. They vote according to the following rules:

   Juan and Kevin always vote together.
   Huang and Juan never vote together.
   Ilene and Laura never vote together.
   If Molly votes for Italian, so does Nancy.
   If Nancy votes for Italian, so does Laura.

4. Seven players—Paul, Quinn, Rei, Shira, Ty, Valerie, and Walter—are vying for five starting spots on a basketball team: point guard, shooting guard, small forward, power forward, and center. They are selected according to the following rules:

   If Paul makes the team, then Walter also makes the team.
   Valerie starts at one of the two guard spots.
   Rei and Shira cannot be the two starting forwards.
   Ty and Quinn cannot both make the team.

5. A realtor is showing an apartment to seven prospective buyers—F, G, H, K, L, M, and N—through the week. She normally works Monday through Friday, but this week she will take one vacation day. She shows the apartment according to the following rules:

    She shows the apartment to more people on Monday than on any other day of the week.
    F and G see the apartment on different days.
    H and K see the apartment on different days.
    L sees the apartment before M.
    M sees the apartment before N.

6. Pizza Palace is revealing three brand new specialty pizzas. There are three vegetable toppings; artichoke, broccoli, and cauliflower; three fruit toppings; lemon, mango, and orange; and three meat toppings; quail, swordfish, and tuna. Each topping will be used exactly once, except for mango which is used twice. The combinations will be decided according to the following rules:

    Each pizza has at least two but at most four toppings.
    No two meat toppings can be on one pizza.
    Quail does not go with any fruit.
    Broccoli does not go with mango.
    Tuna goes with lemon.

7. A genealogist is charting the lineage of six male family members—P, Q, R, S, V, and W. The genealogist knows the following information:

    Everyone fits on one connected family tree.
    P and Q are brothers.
    No one had more than two sons.
    W is V's father.
    S is one generation older than Q.
    Either S or V is R's father.

8. An agent is booking six performances—L, M, N, O, R, and P—at three venues—A, B, and C. Each venue has one opening act followed by one headlining act. One venue's shows will be on Thursday, another venue's shows will be on Friday, and the third venue's shows will be on Saturday. The acts are booked according to the following rules:

    L is a headlining act at venue A.
    M is an opening act at venue C.
    N and O do not perform on the same day.
    R performs at some time before P.
    Venue A's shows are before venue C's shows.

9. An airline is scheduling one flight each to France, Germany, Holland, Iceland, Japan, and Kuwait. The flights are scheduled according to the following restrictions:

   Each flight departs on the hour, and only one flight can depart at a time.
   The first flight departs at 1:00pm, and the last flight departs at 9:00pm on the same day.
   The flight to Germany departs at least two hours after the flight to France.
   The flight to Holland departs at 5:00pm or 6:00pm.
   The flight to Kuwait departs the hour after the flight to Japan.
   Hours in which no flight departs are not consecutive.
   No flight takes off at 3:00pm.

10. A designer is creating a circular merry-go-round for a children's playground that has six seats, and she is painting a picture of an animal on each seat. The animals are a snail, a tiger, a unicorn, a walrus, a yak, and a zebra. She paints them in accordance with the following rules:

    The snail and tiger are next to each other.
    The unicorn and walrus are not next to each other.
    The walrus and the zebra are directly across from each other.

Answers

1. Basic Grouping, Subgroups, Interchangeable Groups (Fill In Elements.)

2. Relative Ordering, Either/Or Rule (Consider Frames.)

3. Closed In/Out Grouping (Look for Limited Group Space Inferences and consider Frames.)

4. Basic Grouping, Mismatch: Too Many Elements (Make an Out group and look for Limited Group Space Inferences.)

5. Hybrid, Open Grouping (Consider Numerical Distributions.)

6. Open Grouping, Interchangeable Groups (Fill In Elements.)

7. Process, Either/Or Rule, Transposition (Consider Frames.)

8. Hybrid, 3D Grouping, Undefined Group Order (Consider Framing Group Order.)

9. Ordering, Mismatch: Too Many Slots (Consider Framing Open Slots.)

10. Circular Ordering (Diagram Circle.)

6

Step 2–Notate the Rules and Make Inferences

Drill 111: Rules Represent, Round 3

Instructions: We've said it before and we'll say it again: you can't master the games section without mastering the rules, so diagram each Logic Games rule in the space provided, again! There are rules in this drill from all different game types and twists, so be prepared to think about what kind of game a given rule is likely to appear in as you figure out the ideal diagram. You also might need to sketch out a mini game diagram, such as a Number Line or Grouping Board, in which to place some rules.

1. Chad picks at least one but no more than three of the movies.

2. Neither of the guitars will be displayed next to the harp.

3. The second band will not be a rock band.

4. The magician will never perform two card tricks in a row.

5. Pamela must precede Dominic.

6. The derby will air at least three days before the golf tournament.

7. Flight 63 arrives before Flight 20 but after Flight 50.

8. Gretchen will not eat the entrée unless she also eats the appetizer.

9. Any portrait will be appraised for more than any still life.

10. If he visits Vietnam, he must visit Cambodia or Japan as well.

11. Bob's fruit stand has more items than Prakesh's.

12. If Cristal works on Project A, both Rubi and Emeril will be on Project B.

6

13. The pizza and the sushi are dropped off simultaneously.

14. The talk show must always immediately precede or be immediately preceded by the promotional show.

15. There is at least one singer performing between after Selena and before Marsha.

16. The blue paint cans are two aisles away from the red paint cans.

17. The video game was rated lower than the board game.

18. Ahoova will not be seated next to Yoav if Shira is seated next to Yoav.

19. Andy will never be the only person on Team B.

20. The advertiser runs exactly one show between the news show and the sports show.

21. Stevie finishes the quiz after Maureen.

22. No men sit next to each other.

23. If Susan goes to Germany, then she will not visit Belgium.

24. Myers and Olafson present exactly one award together.

25. Penelope will perform if, and only if, Kate does as well.

26. Squirrels and chipmunks are always found together.

27. If Nathan takes the tennis racket and Sabila takes the golf clubs, then Marlis will not play any sports today.

34. R is finished at least two days before M.

28. Sinnott's presentation takes place exactly two days after Howell's.

35. All extra terrestrials have a personal computer.

29. The piece by Schubert is performed after the piece by Adams if the piece by Dvořák is performed before the piece by Adams.

36. Zora will run the marathon unless Reshmi does.

30. Robin and Gemma have offices immediately adjacent to one another.

37. The third dessert is chocolate and contains flour.

31. The singer and the guitarist do not arrive onstage before the flute player.

38. Each of the three boats has room for up to three passengers.

32. Astrid begins the race at least four lanes to the left of Evelyn.

39. Ken sits exactly two spaces before Morgan.

33. Only wheat crackers can be served with cheddar.

40. Eliza will pack either purple boots or red sandals.

Answers

Note: Some of these include partial diagrams. If yours are a bit more fleshed out, that's fine. There are also times when more than one way to represent a rule would be correct. We've sometimes included different representations for these rules but just as often included only diagrams of our preferred representation.

1. Chad picks at least one but no more than three of the movies.

2. Neither of the guitars will be displayed next to the harp.

3. The second band will not be a rock band.

4. The magician will never perform two card tricks in a row.

5. Pamela must precede Dominic.

   $$P - D$$

6. The derby will air at least three days before the golf tournament.

   $$D - \_\_\_ - G$$

7. Flight 63 arrives before Flight 20 but after Flight 50.

   $$50 - 63 - 20$$

8. Gretchen will not eat the entrée unless she also eats the appetizer.

9. Any portrait will be appraised for more than any still life.

   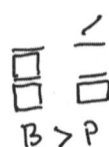

10. If he visits Vietnam, he must visit Cambodia or Japan as well.

    $$V \rightarrow C \text{ or } J$$

    $$\cancel{C} + \cancel{J} \rightarrow \cancel{V}$$

11. Bob's fruit stand has more items than Prakesh's.

    $$B > P$$

12. If Cristal works on Project A, both Rubi and Emeril will be on Project B.

    $$C_A \rightarrow R_B \,\&\, E_B$$

    $$\cancel{R}_B \text{ or } \cancel{E}_B \rightarrow \cancel{C}_A$$

13. The pizza and the sushi are dropped off simultaneously.

14. The talk show must always immediately precede or be immediately preceded by the promotional show.

15. There is at least one singer performing between after Selena and before Marsha.

    $$S \sim \_\_ - M$$

16. The blue paint cans are two aisles away from the red paint cans.

17. The video game was rated lower than the board game.

    $$B - V$$

18. Ahoova will not be seated next to Yoav if Shira is seated next to Yoav.

19. Andy will never be the only person on Team B.

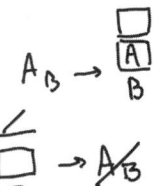

20. The advertiser runs exactly one show between the news show and the sports show.

21. Stevie finishes the quiz after Maureen.

M ~ S

22. No men sit next to each other.

23. If Susan goes to Germany, then she will not visit Belgium.

S_G → S̸_B

S_B → S̸_G

24. Myers and Olafson present exactly one award together.

25. Penelope will perform if, and only if, Kate does as well.

P ↔ K

K̸ ↔ P̸

26. Squirrels and chipmunks are always found together.

S ↔ C

C̸ ↔ S̸

27. If Nathan takes the tennis racket and Sabila takes the golf clubs, then Marlis will not play any sports today.

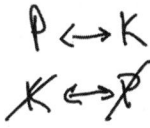

28. Sinnott's presentation takes place exactly two days after Howell's.

29. The piece by Schubert is performed after the piece by Adams if the piece by Dvořák is performed before the piece by Adams.

D–A → A–S

A̸/S → D̸/A

30. Robin and Gemma have offices immediately adjacent to one another.

31. The singer and the guitarist do not arrive onstage before the flute player.

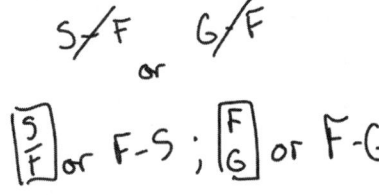

32. Astrid begins the race at least four lanes to the left of Evelyn.

A – _ _ _ _ – E

33. Only wheat crackers can be served with cheddar.

C → ⬚C or W̶C

34. R is finished at least two days before M.

R – ⬚ – M

35. All extra terrestrials have a personal computer.

ET → PC

P̸C → E̸T

36. Zora will run the marathon unless Reshmi does.

$$\cancel{R} \rightarrow Z$$
$$\cancel{Z} \rightarrow R$$

37. The third dessert is chocolate and contains flour.

$$\frac{\frac{F}{C}}{3}$$

38. Each of the three boats has room for up to three passengers.

— — —
— — —
$\overline{B_1} \ \overline{B_2} \ \overline{B_3}$

39. Ken sits exactly two spaces before Morgan.

$$\boxed{K \ \_ \ M}$$

40. Eliza will pack either purple boots or red sandals.

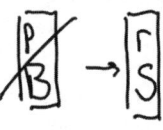

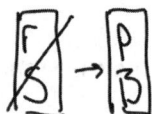

6

Drill 112: Reverse Engineer the Rule, Round 1

Instructions: Knowing how to diagram a rule is one thing. Remembering how to interpret a rule that you've diagrammed is another. Practice that second skill by decoding the rule diagrams you've been given and reverse engineering the text of the rule. Fill in the text version of each rule in the space provided.

1.

2.

3. J – K – L

4. J → J – L

5.

6. C ↛ D

7. K̸ → K̸

8. M̸ → N

9. F –[___] ~T

10. A → [B / A]

11. P → [P S]

12. L → [K / L]

    M → [K / M]

13.
$$\boxed{\begin{matrix} Z \\ W \end{matrix}}$$

17. R ⋵ S → T

14.
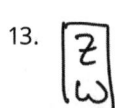
$$\boxed{T \; V}$$

18. J - _ _ - K

15.
$$\boxed{\begin{matrix} b \\ \underline{} \end{matrix}} \rightarrow \boxed{\begin{matrix} \_ \; b \\ C \_ \end{matrix}}$$

19.
$$\boxed{\begin{matrix} S \\ R \end{matrix}}$$

6

16. G → K̸
    H → K̸

20.
T
J ⟍ S

Answers follow on the next page.

Answers

Note: While you may have phrased the rules differently than we have, make sure that they're conveying the same information. Minor changes can make a big difference in LG rules!

1.

   S and M cannot be in the same group.

2.

   C is exactly three spaces before D.

3. J — K — L

   K is after J but before L.

4. J → J–L

   If J is included, J must be before L.

5.

   R and S cannot be next to each other.

6. C → D

   If C is included, D is included.

7. ̷L → ̷K

   If L is not included, K is not included.

8. ̷M → N

   If M is not included, N is included.

9. F – |__ __| ~ T

   There must be at least two consecutive slots after F and before T.

10. A → B / A

    If A is included, A and B will be in the same group.

11. P → PS

    If P is included, it will be directly before S.

12. L → K / L

    M → K / M

    If L or M is included in a group, K will also be included in that group.

13. Z / W

    W and Z will be in the same group.

14.  | T V |

    T and V are next to each other.

15.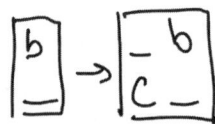

    C will be directly before any entity that is colored blue.

16. G → ̷K

    H → ̷K

    If G or H is included, K will not be included.

17. R & S → T

    If R and S are included, T will be included.

18. J – __ __ – K

    J is at least two spaces before K.

19. S / R

    R and S will be in the same group.

20. T ↘ S / J ↗

    T and J will both come before S.

Drill 113: Binaries and Biconditionals

Instructions: Binaries are rules that split your game into exactly two scenarios. Biconditionals are a specific type of binary—one that's given using conditional language that establishes that each condition is both necessary in order for the other to occur and sufficient to guarantee that the other will occur.

Sometimes, it can be hard to tell when a rule creates a binary situation or when a conditional is really a biconditional. There are certain turns of phrase that indicate binaries and biconditionals across game types and these are relatively easy to spot. But there are other times when the nature of the game is what makes a rule binary. Use this drill to practice spotting binaries and biconditionals of both varieties!

Each of the following game descriptions is accompanied by two rules. Indicate whether each rule does (Y) or doesn't (N) create a binary or biconditional.

This is an In/Out game in which you are selecting toppings for a sundae.

_____ 1. If a cherry is on the sundae, then caramel cannot be.

_____ 2. Sprinkles will be included if, but only if, raspberries are as well.

This is a Grouping game in which you are assigning people to boats A or B.

_____ 3. If Peter is in boat B, then Wendy is as well.

_____ 4. Either Jack or Rose is in boat A, but not both.

This is an Ordering game in which you are scheduling visits to six exhibits at the zoo.

_____ 5. Either the lions or the tigers are visited first.

_____ 6. The bears must be visited in the second half of the schedule.

This is an Ordering game in which you are scheduling four cities on a European tour.

_____ 7. London must be visited immediately before Amsterdam.

_____ 8. Paris must be visited in the second half of the schedule.

This is a Grouping game in which seven colors of yarn are available to be used in two sweaters.

_____ 9. If blue yarn is used in a sweater, pink yarn is not.

_____ 10. The green yarn and purple yarn must be used in the same sweater.

This is an In/Out game in which a conference attendee is choosing six of seven seminars.

_____ 11. If Sensitivity Training is attended, then Resume Building cannot be.

_____ 12. Either Interview Skills or Handshakes 101 must be attended.

This is a Grouping game in which five ice cream flavors are available to be used in three cones.

_____ 13. Ken's cone has butterscotch if, and only if, it has salted caramel.

_____ 14. Chocolate and mint must be on the same cone.

This is a Hybrid game in which you are parking six cars in adjacent lots 1, 2, and 3.

_____ 15. The red car and the yellow car must be in the same lot.

_____ 16. The green car must be in the lot immediately to the left of the white car's lot.

This is an In/Out game in which you are choosing five of eight available classes.

_____ 17. Math and physics cannot both be taken.

_____ 18. She must take either French or ethics but cannot take both.

This is an In/Out game in which you are selecting fish for a koi pond.

_____ 19. Clown fish are in the pond if, and only if, blue tang are as well.

_____ 20. If the pond includes flounder, it cannot include eel.

This is a Grouping game in which you are dividing players into a blue team and a gray team.

_____ 21. Ashley and Melanie cannot both be on the gray team.

_____ 22. Rhett and Scarlett must be on different teams.

This is an Ordering game in which you are ranking the greatness of landmarks.

_____ 23. Either the pyramids are ranked higher than the Nile or Machu Picchu is, but not both.

_____ 24. There are at least two landmarks ranked lower than the Grand Canyon.

This is a Grouping game in which you are distributing school supplies to students.

_____ 25. Student X gets pencils if, and only if, she also gets erasers.

_____ 26. Any student who gets a binder does not get a ruler.

This is an In/Out game in which you are choosing four out of five dentists.

_____ 27. If Dr. T is chosen, then Dr. S is not.

_____ 28. If either Dr. O or Dr. W is chosen, so is Dr. L.

This is a Grouping game in which six colors are available to be used in three paintings.

_____ 29. Any painting that includes yellow also includes blue.

_____ 30. Either two paintings have green or none do.

This is an Ordering game in which you assign rooms to the top, middle, or bottom floor.

_____ 31. The library must be on the floor directly above the kitchen's floor.

_____ 32. The bedroom is the only room on its floor.

This is an In/Out game in which you are placing people on the naughty list or the nice list.

_____ 33. Tom is naughty if, but only if, Jenny is nice.

_____ 34. If Lucy is naughty, then Ethel is nice.

This is a Grouping game in which you are choosing toppings for two pizzas.

_____ 35. Any pizza with pepperoni cannot have sausage.

_____ 36. Both olives and anchovies must be on a pizza, but not together.

This is an Ordering game in which you are scheduling a workout.

_____ 37. Cardio must be done either first or last.

_____ 38. If lunges are third, then weightlifting must be second.

This a Grouping game in which you are dividing six people into teams—Rock, Paper, and Scissors—with no "empty" teams.

_____ 39. If Beth is on team Paper, then Gina is on team Paper.

_____ 40. Neither Elliot nor Alec can be on team Rock, nor can they be together on a team.

6

Answers

Note: In cases where the language of the rule indicates biconditionality across all game types, that language appears in bold and no further explanation is given. "If, and only if," "if, but only if," and "either/or ... but not both" are the most common examples of this.

This is an In/Out game in which you are selecting toppings for a sundae.

   N   1. If a cherry is on the sundae, then caramel cannot be.

   Y   2. Sprinkles will be included **if, but only if,** raspberries are as well.

This is a Grouping game in which you are assigning people to boats A or B.

   N   3. If Peter is in boat B, then Wendy is as well.

   Y   4. **Either** Jack **or** Rose is in boat A, **but not both**.

This is an Ordering game in which you are scheduling visits to six exhibits at the zoo.

   Y   5. **Either** the lions **or** the tigers are visited first.

   N   6. The bears must be visited in the second half of the schedule.

This is an Ordering game in which you are scheduling four cities on a European tour.

   N   7. London must be visited immediately before Amsterdam.

   Y   8. Paris must be visited in the second half of the schedule.

Since there are only four slots, "the second half" gives only two options—third or fourth.

This is a Grouping game in which seven colors of yarn are available to be used in two sweaters.

   N   9. If blue yarn is used in a sweater, pink yarn is not.

   Y   10. The green yarn and purple yarn must be used in the same sweater.

10 is a chunk rule, and chunks are inherently biconditional—where one goes, so goes the other, and vica versa. 9 is a conditional rule that creates an anti-chunk. This would be biconditional if we knew each color of yarn was selected, but the language of the scenario doesn't guarantee that, saying only that the seven colors of yarn are "available."

This is an In/Out game in which a conference attendee is choosing six of seven seminars.

   Y   11. If Sensitivity Training is attended, then Resume Building cannot be.

   N   12. Either Interview Skills or Handshakes 101 must be attended.

In this tricky one, 11 is biconditional only because of the numeric restrictions on the Out group. Normally, a rule such as this would only establish that ST and RB can't both be in, but since there is only one slot in the Out group, it's not possible that ST and RB are out together. Thus one must be in and the other out—a biconditional.

This is a Grouping game in which five ice cream flavors are available to be used in three cones.

   Y   13. Ken's cone has butterscotch **if, and only if,** it has salted caramel.

   N   14. Chocolate and mint must be on the same cone.

This is a Hybrid game in which you are parking six cars in adjacent lots 1, 2, and 3.

   N   15. The red car and the yellow car must be in the same lot.

   Y   16. The green car must be in the lot immediately to the left of the white car's lot.

Since this game has only three lots, 16 establishes two mutually exclusive options, one of which must take place. The GW chunk is in either 1 and 2 or 2 and 3, which makes this rule binary!

This is an In/Out game in which you are choosing five of eight available classes.

   N   17. Math and physics cannot both be taken.

   Y   18. She must take **either** French **or** ethics **but cannot take both**.

This is an In/Out game in which you are selecting fish for a koi pond.

__Y__ 19. Clown fish are in the pond **if, and only if,** blue tang are as well.

__N__ 20. If the pond includes flounder, it cannot include eel.

This is a Grouping game in which you are dividing players into a blue team and a gray team.

__N__ 21. Ashley and Melanie cannot both be on the gray team.

__Y__ 22. Rhett and Scarlett must be on different teams.

Because there are only two teams, the anti-chunk rule in 22 creates a binary situation.

This is an Ordering game in which you are ranking the greatness of landmarks.

__Y__ 23. The pyramids are ranked higher than either the Nile or Machu Picchu, but not both.

__N__ 24. There are at least two landmarks ranked lower than the Grand Canyon.

This is a Grouping game in which you are distributing school supplies to students.

__Y__ 25. Student X gets pencils **if, and only if,** she also gets erasers.

__N__ 26. Any student who gets a binder does not get a ruler.

This is an In/Out game in which you are choosing four out of five dentists.

__Y__ 27. If Dr. T is chosen, then Dr. S is not.

__N__ 28. If either Dr. O or Dr. W is chosen, so is Dr. L.

Since there is only one slot in the Out group, 27, which establishes that at least one of S and T must be out, also establishes that at least one of them must be in, making binary!

This is a Grouping game in which six colors are available to be used in three paintings.

__N__ 29. Any painting that includes yellow also includes blue.

__Y__ 30. Either two paintings have green or none do.

30 sets up mutually exclusive possibilities, at least one of which must be true, which makes 30 biconditional. Be careful with 29—if it established a definite chunk, it would be biconditional, too. But 29 only establishes a chunk when yellow is included. The absence of yellow doesn't guarantee the absence of blue, so this one isn't biconditional.

This is an Ordering game in which you assign rooms to the top, middle, or bottom floor.

__Y__ 31. The library must be on the floor directly above the kitchen's floor.

__N__ 32. The bedroom is the only room on its floor.

Because there are only three floors, 31 can only pan out two different ways, making it binary.

This is an In/Out game in which you are placing people on the naughty list or the nice list.

__Y__ 33. Tom is naughty **if, but only if,** Jenny is nice.

__N__ 34. If Lucy is naughty, then Ethel is nice.

This is a Grouping game in which you are choosing toppings for two pizzas.

__N__ 35. Any pizza with pepperoni cannot have sausage.

__Y__ 36. Both olives and anchovies must be on a pizza, but not together.

36 establishes an anti-chunk which, because there are only two groups, is binary.

This is an Ordering game in which you are scheduling a workout.

__Y__ 37. Cardio must be done either first or last.

__N__ 38. If lunges are third, then weightlifting must be second.

37 establishes mutually exclusive options, one of which must happen. That makes it binary. Historically, however, "one element with two possible slots" rules lead to good Frames much less often than "one slot with two possible elements" rules.

This a Grouping game in which you are dividing six people into teams—Rock, Paper, and Scissors—with no "empty" teams.

__N__ 39. If Beth is on team Paper, then Gina is on team Paper.

__Y__ 40. Neither Elliot nor Alec can be on team Rock, nor can they be together on a team.

Elliot and Alec form an anti-chunk, and because they cannot occupy Rock, they must be spread across the other two, making item 40 binary.

6

Drill 114: Diagramming 301, Round 1

Instructions: This is where the rubber meets the road! These conditionals are the hardest of the hard. Try your hand at diagramming and contraposing them, but if you feel lost, don't be afraid to return to a round of Diagramming 201 or even Diagramming 101 for a refresher course.

1. She will not take biology unless she takes German or history.

2. The exhibit cannot have both tarantulas and black widows.

3. The tapestry will contain gold or maroon thread unless it contains brown thread.

4. The tapestry will not have both brown and olive threads.

5. The tapestry will contain maroon or purple thread if it does not contain navy.

6. The tapestry has silver thread if, and only if, it does not have gold thread.

7. The bouquet cannot contain both roses and lilies.

8. A bouquet will contain carnations if, and only if, it does not contain roses.

9. Papyrus must be used unless quartz is used.

10. Glass is used if, but only if, metal is used.

11. If the project does not contain ceramic, it will contain glass or bamboo.

12. She will go to the art gallery unless she goes to the baseball game or the zoo.

13. She goes to the movie if, and only if, she does not go to the play.

14. If she goes to the beach and the museum, she won't go to the zoo.

15. She will not visit both the museum and the art gallery.

16. They will visit the tiger exhibit unless they visit the bear and penguin exhibits.

17. If they visit the zoo, they will visit the bear exhibit or the turtle enclosure, but not both.

18. They will visit the crocodiles if they see the otters and the hippopotamuses.

19. The bouquet cannot contain both roses and carnations.

20. A bouquet will not contain tulips unless it contains fern or ivy.

21. The menu will not include pasta unless chicken is included and the mushroom dish is not included.

22. Consommé is served if, but only if, salad is not served.

23. Ice cream will be on the menu unless both pie and cake are.

24. He will not visit both Dallas and Houston.

25. If the trip includes Burkina Faso, it will include either Mali or Ghana, but not both.

26. She will not attend C's concert unless she also attends W's and X's.

27. She will see band L if, but only if, she does not see band X.

28. She will attend T's concert unless she attends S's.

29. She will not see both M and W in concert.

30. Whenever pasta is on the menu, either tiramisu or crème brûlée is also on the menu.

Answers

1. She will not take biology unless she takes German or history.

   B → G or H ; ~G and ~H → ~B

2. The exhibit cannot have both tarantulas and black widows.

   T → ~B ; B → ~T

3. The tapestry will contain gold or maroon thread unless it contains brown thread.

   ~B → G or M ; ~G and ~M → B

4. The tapestry will not have both brown and olive threads.

   B → ~O ; O → ~B

5. The tapestry will contain maroon or purple thread if it does not contain navy.

   ~N → M or P ; ~M and ~P → N

6. The tapestry has silver thread if, and only if, it does not have gold thread.

   S ↔ ~G ; G ↔ ~S

7. The bouquet cannot contain both roses and lilies.

   R → ~L ; L → ~R

8. A bouquet will contain carnations if, and only if, it does not contain roses.

   C ↔ ~R ; R ↔ ~C

9. Papyrus must be used unless quartz is used.

   ~P → Q ; ~Q →P

10. Glass is used if, but only if, metal is used.

    G ↔ M ; ~M ↔ ~G

11. If the project does not contain ceramic, it will contain glass or bamboo.

    ~C → G or B ; ~G and ~B → C

12. She will go to the art gallery unless she goes to the baseball game or the zoo.

    ~A → B or Z ; ~B and ~Z → A

13. She goes to the movie if, and only if, she does not go to the play.

    M ↔ ~P ; P ↔ ~M

14. If she goes to the beach and the museum, she won't go to the zoo.

    B and M → ~Z ; Z → ~B or ~M

15. She will not visit both the museum and the art gallery.

    M → ~A ; A → ~M

16. They will visit the tiger exhibit unless they visit the bear and penguin exhibits.

    ~T → B and P ; ~B or ~P → T

17. If they visit the zoo, they will visit the bear exhibit or the turtle enclosure, but not both.

    Z → B or T (not both) ; ~B and ~T → ~Z ;
    B and T → ~Z

18. They will visit the crocodiles if they see the otters and the hippopotamuses.

    O and H → C ; ~C → ~O or ~H

19. The bouquet cannot contain both roses and carnations.

    C → ~R ; R → ~C

20. A bouquet will not contain tulips unless it contains fern or ivy.

    T → F or I ; ~F and ~I → ~T

21. The menu will not include pasta unless chicken is included and the mushroom dish is not included.

    P → C and ~M ; M or ~C → ~P

22. Consommé is served if, but only if, salad is not served.

    C ↔ ~S ; S ↔ ~C

23. Ice cream will be on the menu unless both pie and cake are.

    ~I → P and C ; ~P or ~C → I

24. He will not visit both Dallas and Houston.

    D → ~H ; H → ~D

6

25. If the trip includes Burkina Faso, it will include either Mali or Ghana, but not both.

    B → M or G (not both) ; M and G → ~B ; ~M and ~G → ~B

26. She will not attend C's concert unless she also attends W's and X's.

    C → W and X ; ~W or ~ X → ~C

27. She will see band L if, but only if, she does not see band X.

    L ↔ ~X ; X ↔ ~L

28. She will attend T's concert unless she attends S's.

    ~T → S ; ~S → T

29. She will not see both M and W in concert.

    M → ~W ; W → ~M

30. Whenever pasta is on the menu, either tiramisu or crème brûlée is also on the menu.

    P → T or C ; ~T and ~C → ~P

6

Drill 115: Rude Rules, Mixed Edition

Instructions: By now, you should be well-versed in diagramming the most straightforward rules. But how about the rude rules? Use this drill to find out how you fare when the rules get ugly! Diagram each of the following tricky rules in the space provided. Some might include information that doesn't diagram neatly. Where this is the case, use a shorthand you understand. If a rule is conditional or biconditional, contrapose it.

1. The smoothie cannot contain both turmeric and blueberries.

2. The parasol is sold neither before both the hat and the wrap nor after both of them. (no ties)

3. S is either more expensive than both L and H or less expensive than both L and H.

4. Q finished the race before T or after Y, but not both. (no ties)

5. G is delivered either before H or before I, but not both. (no ties)

6. Q is included if and only if Y is included.

7. G is second if H is third. H is third if G is second.

8. Either J is included, or M is included, but not both.

9. T is on duty twice as often as S is on duty.

10. U arrives before W if T arrives before S; otherwise, U arrives after W. (no ties)

11. There are exactly three auditions between J and N.

12. K displays her artwork two days after I.

13. Neither G nor K ranks higher than L.

14. If S is not second, Q is third.

6

15. Either Y or T finishes the race before U.

16. Exactly two gymnasts scored higher than T but lower than V.

17. Q finished the tournament three ranks lower than G.

18. Either X or Y receives its delivery before Z.

19. G is seventh if, and only if, H is second.

20. If F is included, so is J. If J is included, so is F.

21. H is neither first nor third.

22. L is before I if, and only if, I is before H.

23. G runs immediately before any race in which K runs.

24. S is scheduled either before T or after U, but not both. (no ties)

25. V is selected for the team if, and only if, W is not.

26. F is neither second nor immediately after S.

27. A classic novel is always placed on the shelf immediately before any nonfiction work.

28. Either W or Y is delivered immediately before Z.

29. R is either more expensive than S or less expensive than T, but not both. (no ties)

30. Whenever an assembly line is assigned to paint cars green, the assembly line immediately before it is assigned to paint cars red.

31. S finished the race either immediately before T or immediately after R, but not both. (no ties)

32. J is not selected unless K is selected, and K is not selected unless J is selected.

33. Exactly three cookies were ranked higher than the snickerdoodles but lower than the oatmeal raisin.

34. If S is included, then R is included. If R is included, then S is included.

35. Neither I nor M is the fourth- or fifth-ranked tennis player.

36. Pierre is scheduled exactly three days before Quinn.

37. Exactly two restaurants were ranked higher than T but lower than V.

38. A long lecture is always scheduled immediately before any short lecture.

39. Neither T nor V can be shown before Y.

40. If X is not included on the blue team, Y is included on the blue team.

41. K is either more expensive than J or less expensive than L, but not both.

42. K is either more expensive than J or more expensive than L, but not both. (no ties)

43. H is cast in the play if, and only if, J is also cast in the play.

44. If X is not delivered second, X is delivered after S.

6

45. Either T is red and second, or T is blue and third.

46. S appears immediately ahead of R if, and only if, R appears third.

47. There are exactly two events held after the rodeo but before the shindig.

48. J is second only if R is third. If R is third, then J is second.

49. A hot dish is always served immediately after any cold dish.

50. Either Q is hired, or P is hired, but not both.

6

Answers

Note: Your notations might differ slightly from ours, but make sure that they convey the same information. Small changes can make a big difference, so be sure that any differences aren't meaningful.

1. The smoothie cannot contain both turmeric and blueberries.

   $T \rightarrow \not{B}$

   $B \rightarrow \not{T}$

2. The parasol is sold neither before both the hat and the wrap nor after both of them. (no ties)

   H - P - W or W - P - H

3. S is either more expensive than both L and H or less expensive than both L and H.

   $S\overset{L}{\underset{H}{\diagdown}}$ or $\overset{L}{\underset{H}{\diagup}}S$

4. Q finished the race before T or after Y, but not both. (no ties)

   $Q\overset{T}{\underset{Y}{\diagdown}}$ or $\overset{T}{\underset{Y}{\diagup}}Q$

5. G is delivered either before H or before I, but not both. (no ties)

   H - G - I or I - G - H

6. Q is included if and only if Y is included.

   $Q \leftrightarrow Y$

   $\not{Y} \leftrightarrow \not{Q}$

7. G is second if H is third. H is third if G is second.

   $G_2 \leftrightarrow H_3$

   $\not{H_3} \leftrightarrow \not{G_2}$

8. Either J is included, or M is included, but not both.

   $J \leftrightarrow \not{M}$

   $M \leftrightarrow \not{J}$

9. T is on duty twice as often as S is on duty.

   $T = 2 \times S$

   Note: Since there are usually sharp limits on the total number of elements, a rule of this type will usually create just a few numeric possibilities, such as TT S or TTTT SS. With such limited possibilities, we may also be able to frame out the number arrangements for other elements and go into the questions with a pretty strong sense of what can happen in the game.

10. U arrives before W if T arrives before S; otherwise, U arrives after W. (no ties)

    T - S $\leftrightarrow$ U - W

    W - U $\leftrightarrow$ S - T

11. There are exactly three auditions between J and N.

12. K displays her artwork two days after I.

13. Neither G nor K ranks higher than L.

    $\not{G} \cdot L$ $\left|\begin{array}{l}\boxed{\begin{array}{c}G\\L\end{array}} \text{ or } L - G \\ \boxed{\begin{array}{c}K\\L\end{array}} \text{ or } L - K\end{array}\right.$

    $\not{K} \cdot L$

14. If S is not second, Q is third.

    $\not{S_2} \rightarrow Q_3$

    $\not{Q_3} \rightarrow S_2$

15. Either Y or T finishes the race before U.

    $Y\!/\!T - U$

16. Exactly two gymnasts scored higher than T but lower than V.

17. Q finished the tournament three ranks lower than G.

18. Either X or Y receives its delivery before Z.

19. G is seventh if, and only if, H is second.

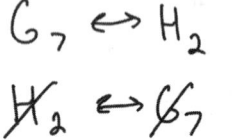

20. If F is included, so is J. If J is included, so is F.

21. H is neither first nor third.

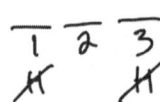

22. L is before I if, and only if, I is before H.

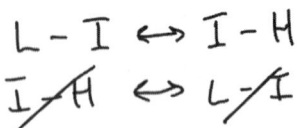

23. G runs immediately before any race in which K runs.

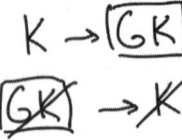

24. S is scheduled either before T or after U, but not both. (no ties)

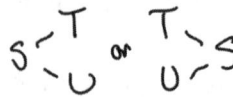

25. V is selected for the team if, and only if, W is not.

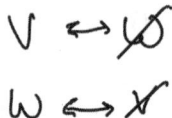

26. F is neither second nor immediately after S.

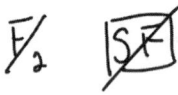

27. A classic novel is always placed on the shelf immediately before any nonfiction work.

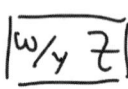

28. Either W or Y is delivered immediately before Z.

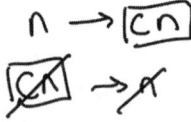

29. R is either more expensive than S or less expensive than T, but not both. (no ties)

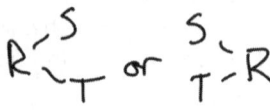

30. Whenever an assembly line is assigned to paint cars green, the assembly line immediately before it is assigned to paint cars red.

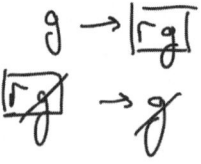

31. S finished the race either immediately before T or immediately after R, but not both. (no ties)

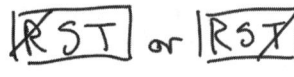

32. J is not selected unless K is selected, and K is not selected unless J is selected.

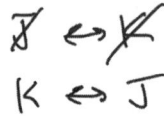

33. Exactly three cookies were ranked higher than the snickerdoodles but lower than the oatmeal raisin.

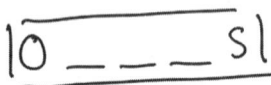

34. If S is included, then R is included. If R is included, then S is included.

S ⟷ R
R̸ ⟷ S̸

35. Neither I nor M is the fourth- or fifth-ranked tennis player.

36. Pierre is scheduled exactly three days before Quinn.

37. Exactly two restaurants were ranked higher than T but lower than V.

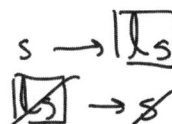

38. A long lecture is always scheduled immediately before any short lecture.

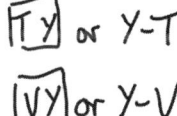

39. Neither T nor V can be shown before Y.

$$\boxed{TY} \text{ or } Y\text{-}T$$
$$\boxed{VY} \text{ or } Y\text{-}V$$

40. If X is not included on the blue team, Y is included on the blue team.

$$\cancel{X_B} \rightarrow Y_B$$
$$\cancel{Y_B} \rightarrow X_B$$

41. K is either more expensive than J or less expensive than L, but not both. (no ties)

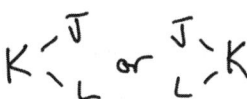

42. K is either more expensive than J or more expensive than L, but not both. (no ties)

$$J\text{-}K\text{-}L$$
$$\text{or}$$
$$L\text{-}K\text{-}J$$

43. H is cast in the play if, and only if, J is also cast in the play.

$$H \leftrightarrow J$$
$$\cancel{J} \leftrightarrow \cancel{H}$$

44. If X is not delivered second, X is delivered after S.

$$\cancel{X_2} \rightarrow S\text{-}X$$
$$S\cancel{X} \rightarrow X_2$$

45. Either T is red and second, or T is blue and third.

$$\frac{r}{\frac{T}{2}} \text{ or } \frac{b}{\frac{T}{3}}$$

46. S appears immediately ahead of R if, and only if, R appears third.

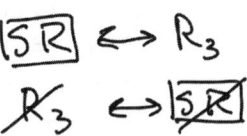

47. There are exactly two events held after the rodeo but before the shindig.

48. J is second only if R is third. If R is third, then J is second.

$$J_2 \leftrightarrow R_3$$
$$\cancel{R_3} \leftrightarrow \cancel{J_2}$$

49. A hot dish is always served immediately after any cold dish.

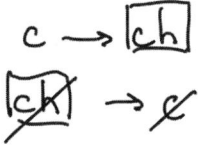

50. Either Q is hired, or P is hired, but not both.

$$Q \leftrightarrow \cancel{P}$$
$$P \leftrightarrow \cancel{Q}$$

Drill 116: Conditional Fill-in-the-Blank, Round 2

Instructions: Taking the LSAT at the highest level requires that you know your formal logic backward and forward. This drill pulls from the backward side of things by presenting you with a diagram and *most* of the statement that would generate it but *without* its conditional indicator word(s). Your task is to look at the diagram and reverse-engineer the statement, filling in the blank(s) with the conditional indicator word(s) that will make the diagram accurate.

1. You will make the team _____ you abandon your friends.

    Abandon friends → Make team

2. _____ of the motorcycle helmets will be on sale.

    Motorcycle helmet → ~On sale

3. I never go to work _____ I feel happy.

    At work → Happy

4. _____ of the cats are fat.

    Cat → Fat

5. There is room for the cars to park _____ they come before 3:00pm.

    Before 3 → Room

6. _____ of the invites have a signature.

    Invite → ~Signature

7. _____ stamp collectors invest in gold.

    Invest in gold → Stamp collector

8. We'll go to the concert _____ DJ Formuhl Lojik performs.

    Concert → DJ FL

9. DJ Formuhl Lojik will perform at the concert _____ the stadium sells out.

    Sell out → DJ FL

10. The stadium will sell out of tickets _____ DJ Formuhl Lojik doesn't perform.

    DJ FL → Sell out

11. _____ Becky goes, _____ Jay will go.

    Becky → Jay

12. Jay _____ go _____ Kenny.

    Jay → Kenny

13. Ida _____ go _____ Kenny goes.

    Ida → Kenny

14. _____ it is a national holiday, I will wear my suit.

    ~Suit → Nat'l holiday

15. It is easy to find a babysitter _____ I am going out.

    Going out → Babysitter

16. _____ of the guitarists are Spanish.

    Guitarist → Spanish

17. You _____ take physics or calculus _____ you are student body president.

    President → Physics or Calculus

18. You _____ take physics or calculus _____ you are student body president.

    Physics or Calculus → President

19. If I drive my SUV, I _____ go to the post office.

    SUV → ~Post office

20. I will go to the post office _____ Carmen comes along.

    Post office → Carmen

21. _____ she is hungry, Carmen will not come with me.

    Carmen comes → Hungry

22. There will _____ be lightning during a hurricane.

    Hurricane → Lightning

23. Erik will _____ put himself before his family.

    Erik → Self before family

24. If the stew has fish and clams, it _____ be delicious.

    Fish and Clams → ~Delicious

25. Hayden always has his uniform on _____ he is at a party.

    Party → Uniform

Answers

Note: We've included a few options for some of these, but if you have a different answer than ours, it still could be correct. Make sure that if your answer is different, it serves the same function as the answer we've provided.

1. You will make the team **if** you abandon your friends.

   Abandon friends → Make team

2. **None** of the motorcycle helmets will be on sale.

   Motorcycle helmet → ~On sale

3. I never go to work **unless** I feel happy.

   At work → Happy

4. **All** of the cats are fat.

   Cat → Fat

5. There is room for the cars to park **if** they come before 3:00pm.

   Before 3 → Room

6. **None** of the invites have a signature.

   Invite → ~Signature

7. **Only** stamp collectors invest in gold.

   Invest in gold → Stamp collector

8. We'll go to the concert **only if** DJ Formuhl Lojik performs.

   Concert → DJ FL

9. DJ Formuhl Lojik will perform at the concert **if** the stadium sells out.

   Sell out → DJ FL

10. The stadium will sell out of tickets **unless** DJ Formuhl Lojik doesn't perform.

    DJ FL → Sell out

11. **If** Becky goes, **then** Jay will go.

    Becky → Jay

12. Jay **cannot** go **without** Kenny.

    Jay → Kenny

13. Ida **cannot** go **unless** Kenny goes.

    Ida → Kenny

14. **Unless** it is a national holiday, I will wear my suit.

    ~Suit → Nat'l holiday

15. It is easy to find a babysitter **if/when** I am going out.

    Going out → Babysitter

16. **All** of the guitarists are Spanish.

    Guitarist → Spanish

17. You **must** take physics or calculus **if** you are student body president.

    President → Physics or Calculus

18. You **cannot** take physics or calculus **unless** you are student body president.

    Physics or Calculus → President

19. If I drive my SUV, I **cannot** go to the post office.

    SUV → ~Post office

20. I will go to the post office **only if** Carmen comes along.

    Post office → Carmen

21. **Unless** she is hungry, Carmen will not come with me.

    Carmen comes → Hungry

22. There will **always** be lightning during a hurricane.

    Hurricane → Lightning

23. Erik will **always** put himself before his family.

    Erik → Self before family

24. If the stew has fish and clams, it **cannot** be delicious.

    Fish and Clams → ~Delicious

25. Hayden always has his uniform on **if** he is at a party.

    Party → Uniform

Drill 117: Inferences

Instructions: In Drill 19, we looked at basic inferences—the ones that can be made from a single rule. Now, it's time to tackle the more advanced inferences that are derived from rules working in combination. For this drill, a scenario and two rules are given. Draw a diagram that includes the rules and any inferences, both basic and advanced, that can be derived.

1. Seven movies—H, I, J, K, L, M, and N—will be screened on seven days. One movie will be screened per day, and all seven movies must be screened at least once.

   H is screened at some time before K.
   I is screened at some time after J and at some time after K.

   HIJKLMN = at least once

   1 2 3 4 5 6 7   H~K~
   K̶ I̶ I̶   H̶ H̶   J~I
   I̶   J̶   H~K
                    K̶

2. Francine, Gerry, Harold, and Irene are eating dinner at a restaurant. Each person will order one entrée and one dessert. The entrées are A, B, C, D, and E, and the desserts are W, X, Y, and Z.

   Gerry and Harold order the same dessert.
   If Harold orders W, then Francine orders X.

   E = ABCDE
   d = wxyz

   F | G | H
   _   _   _   ABCDE (E)   G and H = (same d)
   _   _   _   wxyz (d)
                              If Hw → Fx → Gw
                              If Fx → Hw → Gw

3. Eight skaters—four men: L, N, O, and P; and four women: S, T, U, and V—are skating as pairs in a figure skating competition. The competition consists of four routines, each performed one at a time, with exactly one woman and one man performing in each routine.

L does not compete in the first or third routine.
S skates with L.

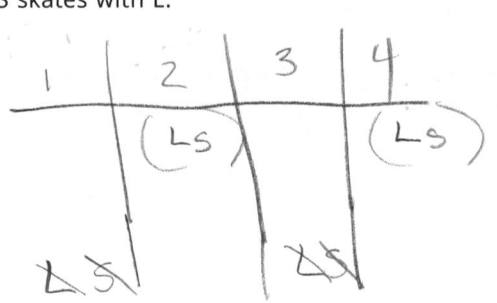

4. Professor Stanton is selecting five of seven books—L, M, N, O, P, Q, and R—to be required reading for her history class this semester.

If L is selected, N is not selected.
If O is selected, P is selected.

LMNOPQR

In
① L _ _ _ _ _ _

② N _ _ _ _ _ _

Out
N _ _ _ _ _
L

If L ⇒ N̸
If N ⇒ L̸

If O ⇒ P
If R ⇒ O̸

Because of

P, must be in

6

5. Seven cars—S, T, U, V, W, X, and Y—will be loaded onto a tractor trailer truck for delivery.

   T will be loaded either first or last.
   If S is loaded third, W will be loaded last.

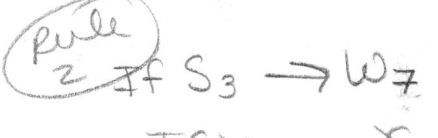

STUVWXY

T̄ ‾2̄ ‾3̄ ‾4̄ ‾5̄ ‾6̄ 7̄
1 2 3 4 5 6
  T̶ T̶ T̶ T̶ T̶

① T ‾ S ‾ ‾ ‾ 7
   1 2 3 4 5 6 7

② ‾ ‾ ‾ ‾ ‾ ‾ T
   1 2 3 4 5 6

6. A piano teacher has six students—F, G, H, I, J, and L—scheduled for the afternoon, each starting on a different hour from 1pm to 7pm.

   F's lesson is either immediately before or immediately after G's lesson.
   I's lesson is exactly three hours before J's lesson.

FGHIJL

‾ ‾ ‾ ‾ ‾ ‾ ‾
1 2 3 4 5 6 7
   I̶ I̶ I̶

① I ‾ ‾ J ‾ ‾

② ‾ I ‾ ‾ J ‾

③ ‾ ‾ I ‾ ‾ J

7. Three farm stands—F, G, and H—each sell exactly two of the following four types of fruit: apricots, strawberries, blueberries, and peaches.

   H does not sell any fruit that G sells.
   If H sells strawberries, then F sells blueberries.

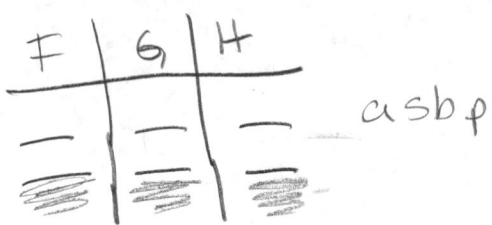

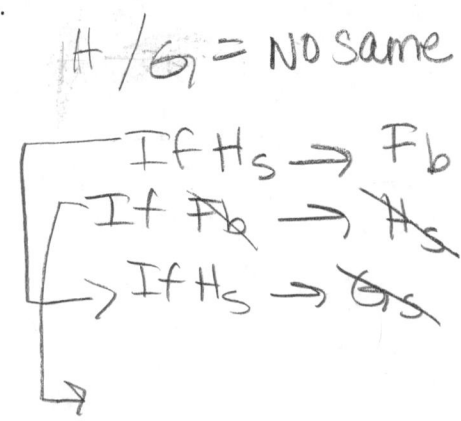

8. A tax services group invoices by location. There are seven invoices—A, B, C, D, E, F, and G—and three locations—the United Kingdom, the European Union, and the United States.

   There is at least one invoice for every location.
   Twice as many invoices originate in the European Union as the United States.

9. Eight students—D, E, F, G, H, I, J, and K—are singing in a choir. They will stand on the stage in order from left to right. Each student wears either a red or green shirt.

   The students in positions 1 and 3 are wearing green shirts.
   Any student wearing a green shirt must have a student in a red shirt immediately to the right.

   D E F G H I J K

   $\overline{\quad}_1 \; \overline{\quad}_2 \; \overline{\quad}_3 \; \overline{\quad}_4 \; \overline{\quad}_5 \; \overline{\quad}_6 \; \overline{\quad}_7 \; \overline{\quad}_8$

   $\frac{G}{1} \; \frac{R}{2} \; \frac{G}{3} \; \frac{R}{4} \; \frac{\quad}{5} \; \frac{\quad}{6} \; \frac{\quad}{7} \; \frac{R}{8}$

   R or G

G
R

10. Seven new employees—N, O, P, Q, R, S, and T—will be trained by four managers—F, G, H, and I. Each manager will train at least one new employee, and each new employee will only be trained by one manager.

    G will train more employees than H.
    The manager who trains P will not train anyone else.

F	G	H	I
—	—	—	—
	R		

    N O P Q R S T   ⑦

    G > H

P only

11. Blue, green, magenta, pink, red, yellow, and white streamers will be put up for a party.

Blue will be put up before magenta and white.
White will be put up before yellow, and yellow will be put up before magenta.

B G m P R Y W

$$B < \frac{m}{W}$$

W – Y – M

B – W – Y – m

12. A tourist is going on a restaurant tour. During the tour, she will visit six restaurants in this order—D, E, F, G, H, and I. At each restaurant she will get to taste either an appetizer, an entrée, or a dessert from the menu. Whatever type of menu item she chooses at a restaurant, she will choose a different type of menu item at the next restaurant.

At restaurant H, she chooses a dessert.
She chooses the same type of menu item at restaurant E and restaurant G.

D E F G H I

EG = same

13. A committee for county affairs will be selected from among residents of Bedminster—D, E, and F—residents of Springfield—L, M, and N—and residents of Townsend—U, V, W, and X.

   F cannot be selected unless W is selected.
   F and D cannot both be selected.

   Bed   Spring   Toon
   D E F   L m N   U V W X

   F → W
   W → F

   F̶D̶

   In | Out
        | F/D

14. Six fishing boats—F, H, I, Q, R, and S—arrive in a harbor one afternoon.

   The boats arrive one at a time.
   H arrives immediately before S.
   Q arrives third.

   F H I Q R S

   ___ ___ Q ___ ___ ___   HS
    1   2   3   4   5   6

   ① H S Q ___ ___ ___

   ② ___ ___ Q H S ___

   ③ ___ ___ Q ___ H S

15. Six supermarket items—F, G, H, I, J, and K—will be in one of three shopping carts numbered 1, 2, and 3. Each item will be in a cart, and each cart will have at least one item.

    H is in a higher numbered cart than F.
    H is in the same cart as either J or K, but not both.

F G H I J K

1	2	3
—	—	—
—	—	—

H̶ (under 1)   F̶ (under 3)

H higher # → F

If H → J or K

If J and K → H̶

16. Guests are being selected to give a toast at a party. The guests will be selected from the following group: F, G, H, I, J, K, and L.

    If H gives a toast, then J does not give a toast.
    If J does not give a toast, then K must give a toast.

F G H I J K L

①
In	out
H	J
K	

If H → J̶
If J̶ → H̶
If J̶ → K
If K̶ → J

6

Answers

Note: At the top of every logic game diagram you should list your roster of elements, but for the purpose of this drill, we have omitted this standard to conserve space on the page.

1. Seven movies—H, I, J, K, L, M, and N—will be screened on seven days. One movie will be screened per day, and all seven movies must be screened at least once.

   H is screened at some time before K.
   I is screened at some time after J and at some time after K.

   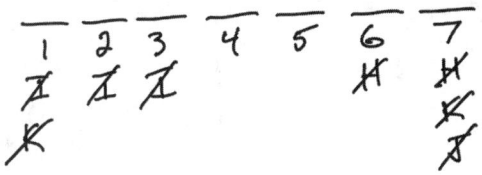

   The two relative ordering rules share an element and can therefore be combined into a tree. From this, we can infer exclusions for each element in the tree.

2. Francine, Gerry, Harold, and Irene are eating dinner at a restaurant. Each person will order one entrée and one dessert. The entrées are A, B, C, D, and E, and the desserts are W, X, Y, and Z.

   Gerry and Harold order the same dessert.
   If Harold orders W, then Francine orders X.

   $$D \_\_\_\_\_ \quad WXYZ - \text{at least } 1 \text{ out}$$
   $$E \_\_\_\_\_ \quad ABCDE - \text{at least } 1 \text{ out}$$

   $$H_O \leftrightarrow G_O$$
   $$\cancel{H_O} \leftrightarrow \cancel{G_O}$$

   $$H_W \rightarrow F_X$$
   $$\cancel{F_X} \rightarrow \cancel{H_W}$$

   $$G_W \rightarrow F_X$$
   $$\cancel{F_X} \rightarrow \cancel{G_W}$$

   "Gerry and Harold order the same dessert" tells us that all four desserts cannot be selected: at least one must be out. The fact that there are five entrees and only four diners tells us that all five entrees cannot be selected: at least one must be out. Since Harold and Gerry order the same dessert, Gerry ordering W will also guarantee that Francine orders X.

6

3. Eight skaters—four men: L, N, O, and P; and four women: S, T, U, and V—are skating as pairs in a figure skating competition. The competition consists of four routines, each performed one at a time, with exactly one woman and one man performing in each routine.

   L does not compete in the first or third routine.
   S skates with L.

   W _ _ _ _ STUV
   M _ _ _ _ LNOP
       1 2 3 4
        L̸   L̸
        S̸   S̸   [S / L]

   The men and women will be paired for each routine, and the first rule tells us that the four routines will be in order. Since L cannot compete first or third and L and S must compete together, L and S will compete either second or fourth, giving us a frameable split. If the other rules of the game are impacted, this would make for a great framing opportunity!

4. Professor Stanton is selecting five of seven books—L, M, N, O, P, Q, and R—to be required reading for her history class this semester.

   If L is selected, N is not selected.
   If O is selected, P is selected.

   L M N O P Q R

   L → N̸
   N → L̸

   O → P
   P̸ → O̸

In	Out
P	L/N
—	—
—	
~	
—	

   The first rule tells us that if L is selected, then N will not be selected. The contrapositive of this rule tells us that if N is selected, then L is not selected. This means that L and N will never be selected together; therefore, at least one of them must be out. The second rule doesn't chain to the first, but the contrapositive of the second rule combined with the L/N Placeholder inference allows us to infer that P must always be in. There are only two spots in the out group, one of which is filled by the L/N placeholder. That leaves only one out slot remaining. If P were to be out, it would need to bring O out with it, which would exceded the limited number of slots in the outgroup: a classic Limited Group Space inference! P, therefore, must always be in.

5. Seven cars—S, T, U, V, W, X, and Y—will be loaded onto a tractor trailer truck for delivery.

    T will be loaded either first or last.
    If S is loaded third, W will be loaded last.

    The first rule tells us that if S is loaded third, then W must be loaded seventh. Since T must be loaded first or last, we know that if W is loaded seventh, then T will be loaded first. Thus, S loaded third guarantees T loaded first, and when T is not loaded first, S is not loaded third.

6. A piano teacher has six students—F, G, H, I, J, and L—scheduled for the afternoon, each starting on a different hour from 1pm to 7pm.

    F's lesson is either immediately before or immediately after G's lesson.
    I's lesson is exactly three hours before J's lesson.

    The first rule tells us that F and G are a reversible chunk. The second rule tells us that I and J are also a chunk, with exactly two slots between them: an open chunk. Although there are not outright inferences here, this chunk has only three placement options (1/4, 2/5, and 3/6) and will influence where the FG chunk can be placed. A three-way split that will constrain other elements indicates a great framing opportunity!

7. Three farm stands—F, G, and H—each sell exactly two of the following four types of fruit: apricots, strawberries, blueberries, and peaches.

    H does not sell any fruit that G sells.
    If H sells strawberries, then F sells blueberries.

    H and G can never sell the same fruit, and there are only four fruits total. That tells us that whichever fruits are not sold by H are sold by G and vica versa. When combined with the second rule, we can infer that when F doesn't sell blueberries, G must, and the contrapositive.

8. A tax services group invoices by location. There are seven invoices—A, B, C, D, E, F, and G—and three locations—the United Kingdom, the European Union, and the United States.

    There is at least one invoice for every location. Twice as many invoices originate in the European Union as the United States.

    Since the European Union must have twice as many invoices as the United States, and every location must have at least one invoice, there are only two ways this game can break down numerically: US1-EU2-UK4 or US2-EU4-UK1. These two numeric breakdowns will likely interact with other rules to produce inferences that would make this split worth framing!

9. Eight students—D, E, F, G, H, I, J, and K—are singing in a choir. They will stand on the stage in order from left to right. Each student wears either a red or green shirt.

The students in positions 1 and 3 are wearing green shirts.
Any student wearing a green shirt must have a student in a red shirt immediately to the right.

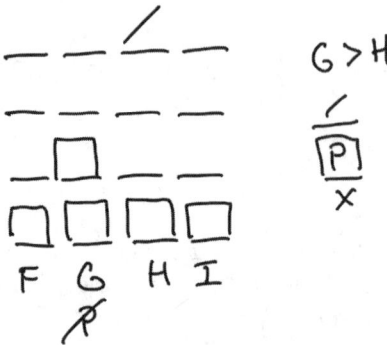

Since the students in positions 1 and 3 are wearing green shirts, and students in green shirts must have a student in a red shirt immediately to the right, we know that students in positions 2 and 4 must be wearing red shirts. We also know that the student in position 8 must be wearing a red shirt, because there can be no student in a red shirt immediately to his or her right.

10. Seven new employees—N, O, P, Q, R, S, and T—will be trained by four managers—F, G, H, and I. Each manager will train at least one new employee, and each new employee will only be trained by one manager.

G will train more employees than H.
The manager who trains P will not train anyone else.

P will not be trained with anyone else. Since G must train more employees than H and H must train at least one employee, G must train at least two employees, so G cannot train P. We can also use numerical distribution to determine the possible breakdown of seven elements over four groups, and make additional inferences. In the 1-1-1-4 distribution, G must have 4 and H must have 1. In the 1-1-2-3 distribution, G must have 2 or 3 and H must have 1 or 2. In the 1-2-2-2 distribution, G must have 2 and H must have 1, which also guarantees that P is trained by H.

6

11. Blue, green, magenta, pink, red, yellow, and white streamers will be put up for a party.

    Blue will be put up before magenta and white. White will be put up before yellow, and yellow will be put up before magenta.

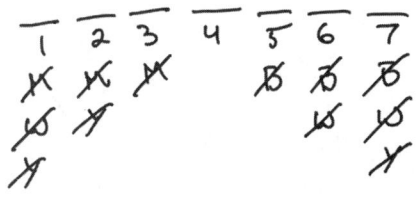

    The two relative ordering rules share elements, and can therefore be combined into a tree. From this, we can infer exclusions for each element in the tree.

12. A tourist is going on a restaurant tour. During the tour, she will visit six restaurants in this order—D, E, F, G, H, and I. At each restaurant she will get to taste either an appetizer, an entrée, or a dessert from the menu. Whatever type of menu item she chooses at a restaurant, she will choose a different type of menu item at the next restaurant.

    At restaurant H, she chooses a dessert. She chooses the same type of menu item at restaurant E and restaurant G.

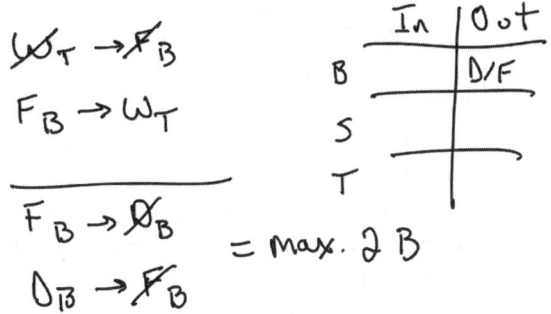

    Since the tourist chooses a dessert at restaurant H, and she must not try the same dish at restaurants in consecutive order, she must choose an appetizer or an entrée at restaurant I and an appetizer or an entrée at restaurant G. She must also select an appetizer or an entrée at restaurant E, since she must select the same kind of menu item at restaurants E and G.

13. A committee for county affairs will be selected from among residents of Bedminster—D, E, and F—residents of Springfield—L, M, and N—and residents of Townsend—U, V, W, and X.

    F cannot be selected unless W is selected.
    F and D cannot both be selected.

This In/Out game has the Subcategories of Elements twist, so we want to use subscripts to indicate the subcategories in our Rule Chart, and subdivide our T chart and our Logic Chain. Since the rest of the game is undefined, we've omitted the Logic Chain and opted to use the Rule Chart instead. The second rule tells us that F and D will never be on the committee together. This leads to the Placeholder inference that at least one must be out. Since F and D are both from Bedminster, we also can infer that there will never be more than two residents from Bedminster on the committee.

6

14. Six fishing boats—F, H, I, Q, R, and S—arrive in a harbor one afternoon.

    The boats arrive one at a time.
    H arrives immediately before S.
    Q arrives third.

    H and S form a chunk, so the first in the chunk can't go in position 6 and the last in the chunk can't go in position 1. Because the chunk can't overlap with Q in position 3, H can't be in position 2, and S can't be in position 4.

15. Six supermarket items—F, G, H, I, J, and K—will be in one of three shopping carts numbered 1, 2, and 3. Each item will be in a cart, and each cart will have at least one item.

    H is in a higher numbered cart than F.
    H is in the same cart as either J or K, but not both.

    Since H is in a higher numbered cart than F, H cannot go in cart 1 and F cannot go in cart 3. Since H must be in a cart with either J or K, but not both, there must be an HJ or HK chunk in cart 2 or cart 3. We can use numerical distribution to breakdown the options for the number of elements per cart to 1-1-4, 1-2-3, and 2-2-2. In the 1-1-4 distribution, the group with 4 would have to have the H chunk, meaning that group 1 can never have 4 elements.

16. Guests are being selected to give a toast at a party. The guests will be selected from the following group: F, G, H, I, J, K, and L.

    If H gives a toast, then J does not give a toast.
    If J does not give a toast, then K must give a toast.

    The first rule tells us that if H is selected to give a toast, then J will not be selected to give a toast. The contrapositive tells us that if J is selected, then H will not be selected. This means that H and J will never both be selected, leading to the Placeholder inference that at least one must be out. The second rule tells us that If J is not selected, then K must be selected. The contrapositive tells us that if K is not selected, then J must be selected. This leads to the Placeholder inference that at least one of them must be in.

Drill 118: Quickfire Setups, Round 2

Instructions: Here we go again! Give yourself ten minutes to set up the following games. Proceed all the way through The Big Pause.

1. Five building inspectors—Perea, Quam, Ricci, Singh, and Tanaka—will be assigned to complete the inspection of six floors in a new office building. Each inspector will inspect at least one floor, and each floor will be inspected by exactly one inspector. The floors will be assigned in accordance with the following constraints:

    No two consecutive floors will be inspected by the same inspector.
    Perea inspects the first floor or the top floor, but no other floor.
    Tanaka and Quam inspect adjacent floors.
    Singh inspects the fifth floor.
    Ricci inspects one of the first three floors.

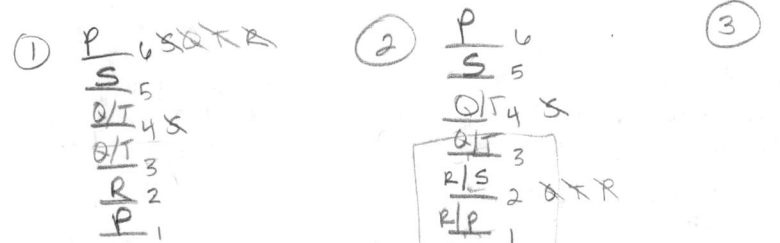

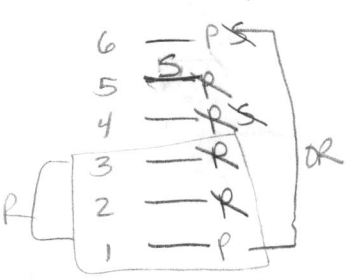

2. The cafeteria is planning its lunch menu for the next six days, Monday through Saturday. Exactly one of six entrées will be served each day—mac and cheese, nachos, pizza, quesadillas, ramen, and sandwiches. There will also be one of two desserts served each day—brownies or gelato. The menus will meet the following constraints:

    Gelato will be offered with the pizza.
    Nachos will be offered exactly two days after the ramen.
    Mac and cheese will be offered on Wednesday.
    The quesadillas and sandwiches will not be offered on consecutive days.
    Brownies will never be offered on consecutive days.

3. A track coach must assign eight students—Pedro, Qadim, Raj, Sven, Thu, Victor, Will, and Zain—to compete in one of two relay events—the 4×100 meter and the 4×400 meter. Each relay has four legs, in order, from one to four. The coach will also designate which leg each student will run, with the following constraints:

    Raj and Zain do not run in the same relay.
    Thu runs the 4×400 relay.
    Pedro runs a lower numbered leg than Sven.
    Will runs the third leg of his relay.

4. There are exactly four remaining seats available on a flight to Honolulu. The following six passengers have unconfirmed seat reservations—Garcia, Holt, Ikeda, Jepson, King, and Mahdi. The available seats will be assigned to exactly four of the waiting passengers with the following constraints:

    Either Holt gets a seat or King gets a seat, but not both.
    If Garcia does not get a seat, then Mahdi does.
    If Ikeda gets a seat, then Jepson also gets a seat.

Answers

1. Five building inspectors—Perea, Quam, Ricci, Singh, and Tanaka—will be assigned to complete the inspection of six floors in a new office building. Each inspector will inspect at least one floor, and each floor will be inspected by exactly one inspector. The floors will be assigned in accordance with the following constraints:

No two consecutive floors will be inspected by the same inspector.
Perea inspects the first floor or the top floor, but no other floor.
Tanaka and Quam inspect adjacent floors.
Singh inspects the fifth floor.
Ricci inspects one of the first three floors.

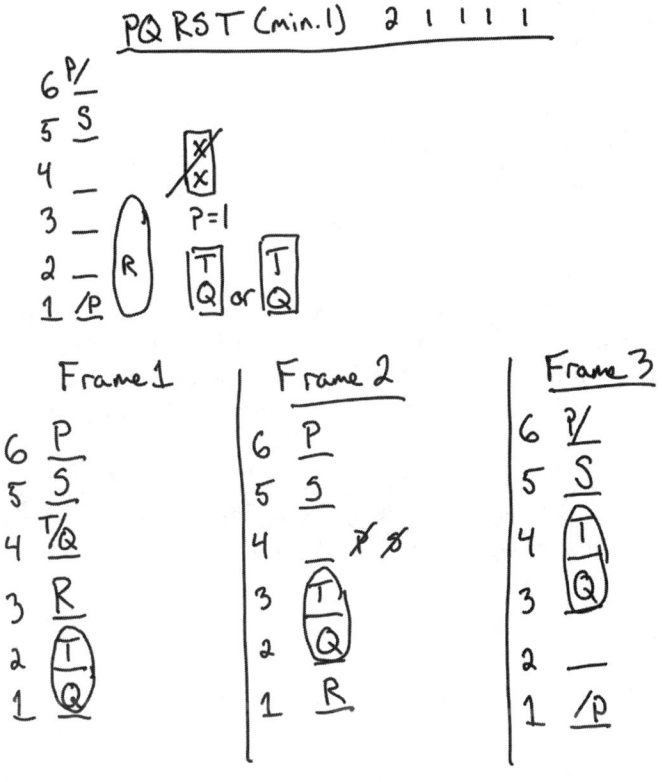

The ordering scenario in this game is inherently vertical, so our Number Line should be arranged vertically with floor 6 at the top and floor 1 at the bottom. Because S inspects floor 5, there are only three placement options for the TQ chunk. Because those options intersect with the rules about Ricci on floors 1 through 3 and Perea on 1 or 6, the placement of the chunk represents a good framing opportunity.

2. The cafeteria is planning its lunch menu for the next six days, Monday through Saturday. Exactly one of six entrées will be served each day—mac and cheese, nachos, pizza, quesadillas, ramen, and sandwiches. There will also be one of two desserts served each day—brownies or gelato. The menus will meet the following constraints:

Gelato will be offered with the pizza.
Nachos will be offered exactly two days after the ramen.
Mac and cheese will be offered on Wednesday.
The quesadillas and sandwiches will not be offered on consecutive days.
Brownies will never be offered on consecutive days.

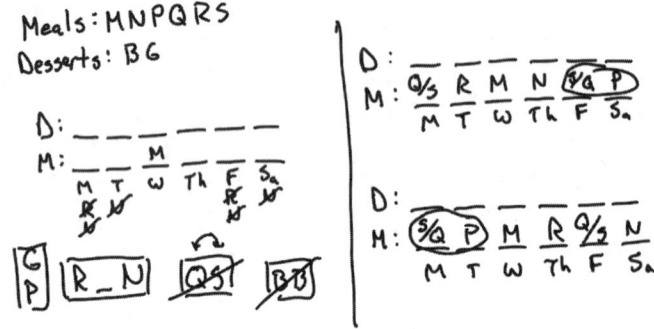

This 3D game is pretty sparse on the top row, but the bottom row frames out nicely. The RN open chunk either has to be placed on Tuesday/Thursday or on Thursday/Saturday. Each placement creates a frame with two adjacent blank slots, and a third blank slot elsewhere. Because Q and S cannot be adjacent, one of them must occupy the solo slot, leaving the other one, with P, in the adjacent slots.

3. A track coach must assign eight students—Pedro, Qadim, Raj, Sven, Thu, Victor, Will, and Zain—to compete in one of two relay events—the 4×100 meter and the 4×400 meter. Each relay has four legs, in order, from one to four. The coach will also designate which leg each student will run, with the following constraints:

Raj and Zain do not run in the same relay.
Thu runs the 4×400 relay.
Pedro runs a lower numbered leg than Sven.
Will runs the third leg of his relay.

PQ RST VW Z

W

100 ___ ___ ___ ___   (R)
400 ___ ___ ___ ___   (Z) T
     1   2   3   4

P−S

This Hybrid game can be organized in two tiers. There are no major inferences beyond the exclusions for P and S. Be sure to keep your eye on twin floaters Q and V.

4. There are exactly four remaining seats available on a flight to Honolulu. The following six passengers have unconfirmed seat reservations—Garcia, Holt, Ikeda, Jepson, King, and Mahdi. The available seats will be assigned to exactly four of the waiting passengers with the following constraints:

Either Holt gets a seat or King gets a seat, but not both.
If Garcia does not get a seat, then Mahdi does.
If Ikeda gets a seat, then Jepson also gets a seat.

This In/Out game doesn't have rules that share elements, but the Logic Chain is still your best bet because there aren't unsplittable rules. The HK biconditional fills one of the two spots in the Out group. That doesn't leave enough room for J to be out and bring I with it, which leads to the Limited Group Space inference that J must, therefore, be in.

Step 3–The Big Pause

Drill 119: Find the Mistake

Instructions: We all want to be able to notate the rules correctly, but it's also important to be able to spot mistakes in your own work because, let's face it, they happen. Catching a mistake might happen right after notating a tricky rule, during The Big Pause as you look for inferences, or even while working through an early question (after eliminating all five answer choices!).

For each of the following rules, we've included a notation. Your job is to state whether the rule is represented correctly (Y) or not (N). If the rule would only be correctly notated in certain game types, list that as an N (yes, we're making this hard!). Bonus points if you fix the mistakes.

_____ 1. J is visited three days after I is visited.

_____ 2. If Inga arrives before Jessica, then Inga arrives at least three hours before Jessica.

$$I - J \rightarrow \boxed{I \_ \_ \_ \_ J}$$

_____ 3. Either G is delivered before H or after I, but not both.

$$G \overset{H}{\underset{I}{<}} \quad or \quad \overset{H}{\underset{I}{>}} G$$

_____ 4. Every deciduous tree is planted immediately before a coniferous tree.

_____ 5. The schnauzer is not adopted on a day before the whippet.

$$W - S$$

_____ 6. Hannibal cannot attend fewer of the events than Godfrey.

$$H > G$$

_____ 7. F and H cannot both be selected.

$$F \rightarrow \cancel{H}$$
$$H \rightarrow \cancel{F}$$

_____ 8. There are at least three paintings hanging on the wall between the Matisse and the Picasso.

$$M - \_ \_ \_ \_ - P$$

_____ 9. Charlotte competes in every event that Dave competes in.

$$C \rightarrow D$$
$$\cancel{D} \rightarrow \cancel{C}$$

_____ 10. Either J or L is selected for the team.

$$\cancel{J} \rightarrow L$$
$$\cancel{L} \rightarrow J$$

_____ 11. Green and magenta appear together in exactly one of the quilts.

_____ 12. Isabel attends exactly twice as many of the events as Leanne.

$$2 \times I = L$$

_____ 13. If G is delivered before H, then it is delivered after I.

$$G - H \rightarrow I - G - H$$

_____ 14. R is assigned to the night shift on the same night that Q is assigned to his first night shift.

_____ 15. Either Q or R is selected, but not both.

$$Q \rightarrow \cancel{R}$$
$$R \rightarrow \cancel{Q}$$

_____ 16. Exactly two events precede the Gala and are preceded by the Hootenanny.

$$|\underline{H \_ \_ \_ G}|$$

_____ 17. G is less expensive than I or more expensive than K, but not both.

$$G \overset{I}{\underset{K}{<}} \quad or \quad \overset{I}{\underset{K}{>}} G$$

_____ 18. G is less expensive than I or less expensive than K, but not both.

K-I-G or G-I-K

_____ 19. Every hot dish has a cold dish served immediately before it.

$$h \rightarrow \boxed{ch}$$

_____ 20. K is delivered after H.

$$K - H$$

_____ 21. J and L have exactly one presentation in between their presentations.

$$|\overline{J \_ L}|$$

_____ 22. J's presentation is exactly two presentations after L's presentation.

$$|\overline{L \_ \_ \_ J}|$$

_____ 23. G or F is at the party unless H and K are.

$$\cancel{H} \ or \ \cancel{K} \rightarrow G \ or \ F$$

_____ 24. Either S and U are both selected for the committee or neither are selected for the committee.

$$S \longleftrightarrow U$$
$$\cancel{S} \longleftrightarrow \cancel{U}$$

_____ 25. Each visit to a thrift shop is immediately followed by a visit to a fabric shop.

$$\boxed{F \ T}$$

6

Answers

___N___ 1. J is visited three days after I is visited.

$$\boxed{I \_\_\_ J}$$

___N___ 2. If Inga arrives before Jessica, then Inga arrives at least three hours before Jessica.

$$I-J \rightarrow I-\_\_-J$$

___Y___ 3. Either G is delivered before H or after I, but not both.

___N___ 4. Every deciduous tree is planted immediately before a coniferous tree.

$$d \rightarrow \boxed{dc}$$

___N___ 5. The schnauzer is not adopted on a day before the whippet.

$$\boxed{\begin{array}{c}S\\W\end{array}} \text{ or } W-S$$

___N___ 6. Hannibal cannot attend fewer of the events than Godfrey.

$$H > G$$
$$\text{or}$$
$$H = G$$

___Y___ 7. F and H cannot both be selected.

___N___ 8. There are at least three paintings hanging on the wall between the Matisse and the Picasso.

$$M-\_\_\_-P$$

___N___ 9. Charlotte competes in every event that Dave competes in.

$$D \rightarrow C$$
$$\cancel{C} \rightarrow \cancel{D}$$

___Y___ 10. Either J or L is selected for the team.

___N___ 11. Green and Magenta appear together in exactly one of the quilts.

 $= 1$

___N___ 12. Isabel attends exactly twice as many of the events as Leanne.

$$I = 2 \times L$$

___Y___ 13. If G is delivered before H, then it is delivered after I.

___N___ 14. R is assigned to the night shift on the same night that Q is assigned to his first night shift.

$$\boxed{\begin{array}{c}R\\Q_1\end{array}}$$

___N___ 15. Either Q or R is selected, but not both.

$$Q \leftrightarrow \cancel{R}$$
$$R \leftrightarrow \cancel{Q}$$

___Y___ 16. Exactly two events precede the Gala and are preceded by the Hootenanny.

___Y___ 17. G is less expensive than I or more expensive than K, but not both.

___Y___ 18. G is less expensive than I or less expensive than K, but not both.

___Y___ 19. Every hot dish has a cold dish served immediately before it.

___N___ 20. K is delivered after H.

$$H - K$$

___N___ 21. J and L have exactly one presentation in between their presentations.

$$\boxed{J \_ L}$$

N 22. J's presentation is exactly two presentations after L's presentation.

Y 23. G or F is at the party unless H and K are.

Y 24. S and U are either both selected for the committee or are both not selected for the committee.

N 25. Each visit to a thrift shop is immediately followed by a visit to a fabric shop.

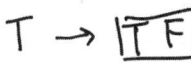

6

Drill 120: Strays and Other Important Elements, Round 2

Instructions: Before diving into the questions of a game, you should always take time to identify the game's key elements. "Strays" are elements that don't show up in the rules. "Twins" are pairs of elements that are equivalent in all ways. "Game Drivers" are elements that, alone or in a relationship, seem likely to drive the play of the game. Game Drivers tend to be more restricted, and usually appear in multiple rules.

For each of the following, identify the key elements and list them on the provided lines. If you don't see a type of element in a game, write in *None*.

Set 1

Game A: F L N O R V Z

F is placed before V and O.

R is placed after V, but before Z.

N and L are placed after R.

_____ 1. Strays?

_____ 2. Twins?

_____ 3. Game Drivers?

Set 2

Game B: J K M Q W Y

J will play fourth.

Q will play exactly two spots before W.

Y will play after M.

K will play either immediately before or immediately after Q.

_____ 4. Strays?

_____ 5. Twins?

_____ 6. Game Drivers?

Set 3

Game C: B Q R S T Y

At least four entities must precede Y.

Exactly two spaces separate S and Q.

T runs before Y but after R.

_____ 7. Strays?

_____ 8. Twins?

_____ 9. Game Drivers?

Set 4

Game D: C F H J M S

H immediately follows S.

C arrives some time after S.

Either J or F goes last.

_____ 10. Strays?

_____ 11. Twins?

_____ 12. Game Drivers?

Set 5

Game E: E L O P V X

V comes either before O or before P, but not both.

Both X and L come before V.

_____ 13. Strays?

_____ 14. Twins?

_____ 15. Game Drivers?

Set 6

Game F: G Q S U W Z

If U is not first, it is last.

Z is third.

W is after Z, but before Q.

_____ 16. Strays?

_____ 17. Twins?

_____ 18. Game Drivers?

Set 7

Game G: C J K N V X

K and J are the two farthest from the door, but not necessarily in that order.

X and C are closer to the door than N.

X is farther away from the door than V.

_____ 19. Strays?

_____ 20. Twins?

_____ 21. Game Drivers?

Set 8

Game H: B D I M N R Y

M is either immediately before B or immediately before Y.

Y is before R and after D.

N is fourth.

_____ 22. Strays?

_____ 23. Twins?

_____ 24. Game Drivers?

Set 9

Game I: F J K O S U

F performs before J.

J performs before S and K.

At most one performer performs before U.

_____ 25. Strays?

_____ 26. Twins?

_____ 27. Game Drivers?

Set 10

Game J: A G R S T Y

A and Y cannot appear next to each other.

G and S appear directly next to each other, but not necessarily in that order.

There is exactly one space between R and G.

_____ 28. Strays?

_____ 29. Twins?

_____ 30. Game Drivers?

Set 11

Game K: B E O V X Z

V does not come immediately before or after E.

E does not come immediately before or after X.

X does not come immediately before or after V.

Z comes before both O and B.

_____ 31. Strays?

_____ 32. Twins?

_____ 33. Game Drivers?

Set 12

Game L: G H J N Q U Y

Y dances immediately before Q.

Two dancers go between N and G.

Q dances before J and U.

_____ 34. Strays?

_____ 35. Twins?

_____ 36. Game Drivers?

6

Answers

Set 1

__None__ 1. Strays?
__N & L__ 2. Twins?
__R, V__ 3. Game Drivers?

Set 2

__None__ 4. Strays?
__None__ 5. Twins?
__Q__ 6. Game Drivers?

Set 3

__B__ 7. Strays?
__S & Q__ 8. Twins?
__Y__ 9. Game Drivers?

Set 4

__M__ 10. Strays?
__J & F__ 11. Twins?
__S__ 12. Game Drivers?

Set 5

__E__ 13. Strays?
__X & L; O & P__ 14. Twins?
__V__ 15. Game Drivers?

Set 6

__S, G__ 16. Strays?
__S & G__ 17. Twins?
__Z__ 18. Game Drivers?

Set 7

__None__ 19. Strays?
__K & J__ 20. Twins?
__X, N__ 21. Game Drivers?

Set 8

__I__ 22. Strays?
__None__ 23. Twins?
__Y__ 24. Game Drivers?

Set 9

__O__ 25. Strays?
__S & K__ 26. Twins?
__J__ 27. Game Drivers?

Set 10

__T__ 28. Strays?
__None__ 29. Twins?
__G__ 30. Game Drivers?

Set 11

__None__ 31. Strays?
__O & B; V & E & X (triplets!)__ 32. Twins?
__Z, V, E, X__ 33. Game Drivers?

Set 12

__H__ 34. Strays?
__N & G; J & U__ 35. Twins?
__Q__ 36. Game Drivers?

Drill 121: We Need More Space!

Instructions: For this drill, you'll be given a series of diagrams in which all the rules of the game have been represented and inferences have been made. The questions that follow each represent a condition that could be given in a conditional question. Your job is to determine whether each new condition leads to any inferences from or about the space in the groups. An example of an inference *about* the space in the groups would be an inference that determines that group X has a maximum of three members. An example of an inference *from* the space in the groups but not necessarily *about* it would be an inference that P can't go in the out group because it would have to bring Q with it and the rules tell us there isn't room for both. Mark (Y) if the condition would lead to a group space inference. Mark (N) if the condition would not.

Towns: FGHI
Tourists: STUVWX

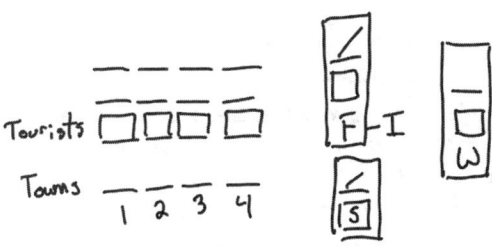

_____ 1. V visits with W.

_____ 2. I is the second town visited.

_____ 3. I is the fourth town visited.

_____ 4. W visits a town with two other tourists.

_____ 5. S visits the third town visited.

JKLMOPQR

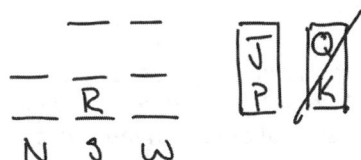

_____ 11. L is included in group N.

_____ 12. If J is in a group, then so is M.

_____ 13. If M is included in a group, then O is not.

_____ 14. O is included in group W.

_____ 15. P is included in group S.

HIJKL (up to 2x)

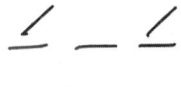

S   T > V

_____ 6. Exactly two workers work on exactly two projects.

_____ 7. S has assigned to it exactly twice as many workers as V.

_____ 8. J works on V.

_____ 9. K and L work together on exactly one project.

_____ 10. V has exactly three workers assigned to it.

STUVWXYZ

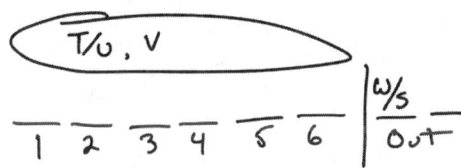

_____ 16. X is included in the rankings.

_____ 17. If Z is ranked, then Y is not.

_____ 18. If U is ranked, then so is X.

_____ 19. If W is not ranked, then Z is.

_____ 20. W is ranked third.

Answers

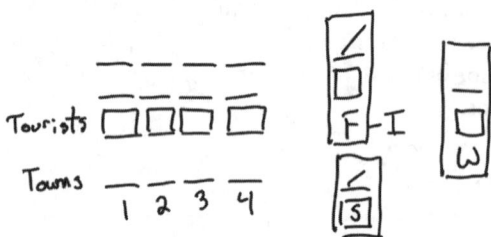

Towns: F G H I
Tourists: S T U V W X

Tourists ☐☐☐☐
Towns ‾1‾ ‾2‾ ‾3‾ ‾4‾

[diagram: F–I column, S box]

HIJKL (up to 2x)

/ _ /

[diagram: S, T > V columns]

S   T > V

N   1.   V visits with W.

While we now know which tourist must travel with W, another tourist still could travel with these two, so we can't make inferences from or about group sizes.

Y   2.   **I is the second town visited.**

If I is second, then F is first, and we can infer that the first town visited only has one tourist and that tourist can't be W.

N   3.   I is the fourth town visited.

I being visited fourth leaves open several options for F, and thus we can't make any inferences from or about group size.

Y   4.   **W visits a town with two other tourists.**

Since the W group is now three, and each town is visited by at least one tourist, we can infer that all the other groups are only visited by a single tourist, as long as we know that the tourists each visit only one town.

Y   5.   **S visits the third town visited.**

We can infer the third town is visited by only a single tourist, but if you didn't view that as an inference big enough to put Y down, that's fine.

Y   6.   **Exactly two workers work on exactly two projects.**

With this information, we know two workers work twice and three work once, meaning that we have at most seven slots filled, and those are already determined in our diagram.

Y   7.   **S has assigned to it exactly twice as many workers as V.**

With this information, we can determine that S is assigned four workers, V is assigned two, and T is assigned either three or four.

N   8.   J works on V.

There are no rules about V, so it'll take up one of the needs-to-be-filled slots without inferences.

N   9.   K and L work together on exactly one project.

Be careful here! K and L could each work on two projects as long as the second isn't together. No inferences because there's not enough information to make distributions.

Y   10.   **V has exactly three workers assigned to it.**

If V has exactly three slots filled in, then T must have at least four. With S's minimum of two, this accounts for nine of our ten possible slots, meaning that S could have a maximum of 3 workers.

J K L M O P Q R

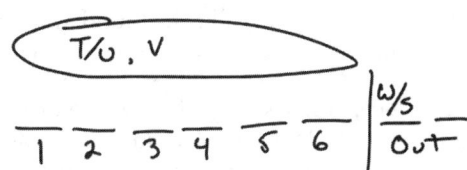

$$\overline{}\ \overline{}\ \overline{}$$

N S W

J T U V W X Y Z

T/U, V

1 2 3 4 5 6 | W/S — Out

__Y__ **11. L is included in group N.**

There's no longer room in N for the PJ chunk.

__Y__ **12. If J is in a group, then so is M.**

The PJ chunk becomes the PJM chunk and must be assigned to W. This creates an Anti-chunk Standoff with Q and K: one of them must be in N and the other must be in S.

__N__ 13. If M is included in a group, then O is not.

Even with M and O split up, there's still room to shuffle things around and get the PJ chunk into any group. There will be some forced overlap from members of the two anti-chunks, but not overlap that we can predict well enough to document.

__N__ 14. O is included in group W.

Since O is the first element in W, there's still room for the PJ chunk.

__Y__ **15. P is included in group S.**

We can infer that the PJ chunk is in S, which fills that group. That means that the anti-chunk must be split between groups N and W: another Anti-Chunk Standoff!

__N__ 16. X is included in the rankings.

There is plenty of space for X and other elements, so no inferences here.

__Y__ **17. If Z is ranked, then Y is not.**

Either Z or Y is out, filling up the out group and forcing the rest of the elements to be ranked.

__Y__ **18. If U is ranked, then so is X.**

The contrapositive is ~X→~U. Since there's only one open slot in the out group, X must be ranked, because otherwise, X, U, and W/S would all have to go out.

__N__ 19. If W is not ranked, then Z is.

This rule forces either W or Z to be ranked, but there's more than enough room for that to happen without filling up the ranked group, so there's no group space inference here.

__N__ 20. W is ranked third.

We can infer that S is out, but there are no group space inferences.

Drill 122: Quickfire Setups, Round 3

Instructions: A strong setup is (still!) the foundation of a strong performance on the Logic Games section, so here's another round of practice! Set your timer for 10 minutes and proceed through The Big Pause.

1. A baseball manager is creating the batting order for today's game. The nine players starting today are Figueroa, Galvan, Hideki, Ives, Jackson, Kidd, Midori, Novak, and Olivier. Each player bats left-handed or right-handed, but not both. The lineup will meet the following conditions:

   There are more right-handed hitters than left-handed hitters.
   Kidd bats before Hideki and Novak.
   Hideki and Novak, both right-handed, bat before Ives, who is also right-handed.
   If Galvan doesn't bat first, he bats last.
   If Jackson doesn't bat last, he bats first.
   No two right-handed hitters bat consecutively.

6

2. At Company K, there are three rounds of interviews that must be passed in order to get hired. If an applicant passes the first round—the audition—then they are invited to a technical interview. If they pass the technical interview, then they will be interviewed by a manager. Five applicants—Ferro, Gao, Hurtado, Inouye, and Joyce—are scheduled for an audition, and at least one of them will ultimately be interviewed by the manager. The interviews proceed according to the following conditions:

   Ferro and Inouye do not both pass the audition.
   Joyce and Hurtado do not both pass the audition.
   Not all applicants who are invited to the technical interview pass the technical interview.
   Gao passes the audition.
   If Inouye passes the audition, then Joyce is interviewed by the manager.

3. Seven foreign correspondents—Santos, Tung, Uranga, Volz, Wren, Yoshi, and Zarakolu—each decide to go see exactly one of three movies—*Dead People*, *The Meaning of Life*, and *The Point*. Which movie the correspondents see is determined by the following constraints:

   Tung and Yoshi see the same movie.
   Uranga and Wren see the same movie.
   More correspondents see *The Point* than see *Dead People*.
   Exactly two correspondents see *The Meaning of Life*.
   Tung and Uranga see different movies.
   Volz and Zarakolu see different movies.
   Santos sees *Dead People*.
   Volz doesn't see *The Point*.

4. Seven musicians—Lorraine, Marcos, Nandi, Paul, Quan, Rafiki, and Teresa—are on call to fill in for absent musicians at the Bridgetown Classical Music Festival. There are five absent musicians, each of whom is scheduled to perform a solo piece, a chamber music piece, or an orchestral piece. There is at least one absent musician scheduled to perform each type of piece, subject to the following constraints:

   All solo pieces are scheduled to be performed before any chamber music, and all chamber music is scheduled to be performed before any orchestral pieces.
   Teresa will fill in for an absent musician.
   Paul will fill in for the second absent soloist.
   If Quan fills in for an absent musician, then so does Marcos.
   If Lorraine fills in for an absent musician, then so does Rafiki.
   If either Marcos or Rafiki fills in for an absent musician, that musician was scheduled to perform chamber music.

Answers

1. A baseball manager is creating the batting order for today's game. The nine players starting today are Figueroa, Galvan, Hideki, Ives, Jackson, Kidd, Midori, Novak, and Olivier. Each player bats left-handed or right-handed, but not both. The lineup will meet the following conditions:

   There are more right-handed hitters than left-handed hitters.
   Kidd bats before Hideki and Novak.
   Hideki and Novak, both right-handed, bat before Ives, who is also right-handed.
   If Galvan doesn't bat first, he bats last.
   If Jackson doesn't bat last, he bats first.
   No two right-handed hitters bat consecutively.

This tricky 3D Ordering game is full of subtle inferences. The fact that there must be more righties than lefties, combined with the prohibition on consecutive righties, establishes the order of the top row. Since you can't have two R's in a row and you can't have more R's than L's, it follows that you can't have two L's in a row. Because there are nine slots, the only way to alternate R's and L's and ensure more R's than L's is to begin and end with R's. Rules 4 and 5 combine to establish a G/J dual option in the first and last slots. Both batters either bat first or last, so it follows that one bats first and the other last. Because we know the first and last slots are righties, that leaves only three remaining righty slots for H, N, and I, and since I must bat after H and N, I must bat seventh in the lineup and H and N must bat third and fifth (though we don't know in which order). This establishes that K must bat second, because slot 2 is the only open slot that precedes both H and N.

6

2.   At Company K, there are three rounds of interviews that must be passed in order to get hired. If an applicant passes the first round—the audition—then they are invited to a technical interview. If they pass the technical interview, then they will be interviewed by a manager. Five applicants—Ferro, Gao, Hurtado, Inouye, and Joyce—are scheduled for an audition, and at least one of them will ultimately be interviewed by the manager. The interviews proceed according to the following conditions:

Ferro and Inouye do not both pass the audition.
Joyce and Hurtado do not both pass the audition.
Not all applicants who are invited to the technical interview pass the technical interview.
Gao passes the audition.
If Inouye passes the audition, then Joyce is interviewed by the manager.

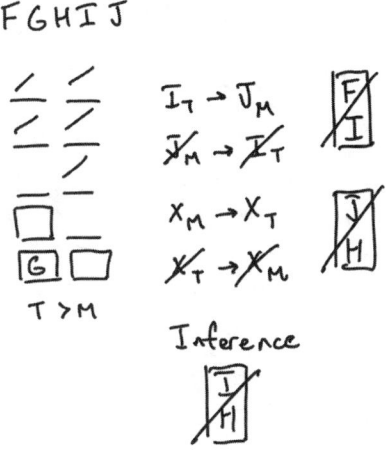

This Open Grouping game could be represented with three groups, but since every applicant auditions, the composition of the audition group is already determined. For that reason, we've left it out, but if you find it helpful as a reference point there's no harm in including it. The third rule establishes that more applicants are in the technical interview group than the manager interview group (henceforth the T group and the M group). This is what leads to the inference that we need at least two applicants in the T group. The first two rules combine to establish a maximum of three applicants in the T group, which leads to the inference that there is a maximum of two applicants in the M group. The final inference comes from the combination of the second and fifth rules with an easily overlooked rule from the scenario: everyone in group M is also in group T. If I in the T group means J is in the M group, and everyone in M is also in T, I in T means J in T. If J is in T, H is not, so I and H can never be in T together. Since they cannot be in T together, it follows that they also cannot be in M together. Hence, the IH anti-chunk.

6

3.   Seven foreign correspondents—Santos, Tung, Uranga, Volz, Wren, Yoshi, and Zarakolu—each decide to go see exactly one of three movies—*Dead People*, *The Meaning of Life*, and *The Point*. Which movie the correspondents see is determined by the following constraints:

Tung and Yoshi see the same movie.
Uranga and Wren see the same movie.
More correspondents see *The Point* than see *Dead People*.
Exactly two correspondents see *The Meaning of Life*.
Tung and Uranga see different movies.
Volz and Zarakolu see different movies.
Santos sees *Dead People*.
Volz doesn't see *The Point*.

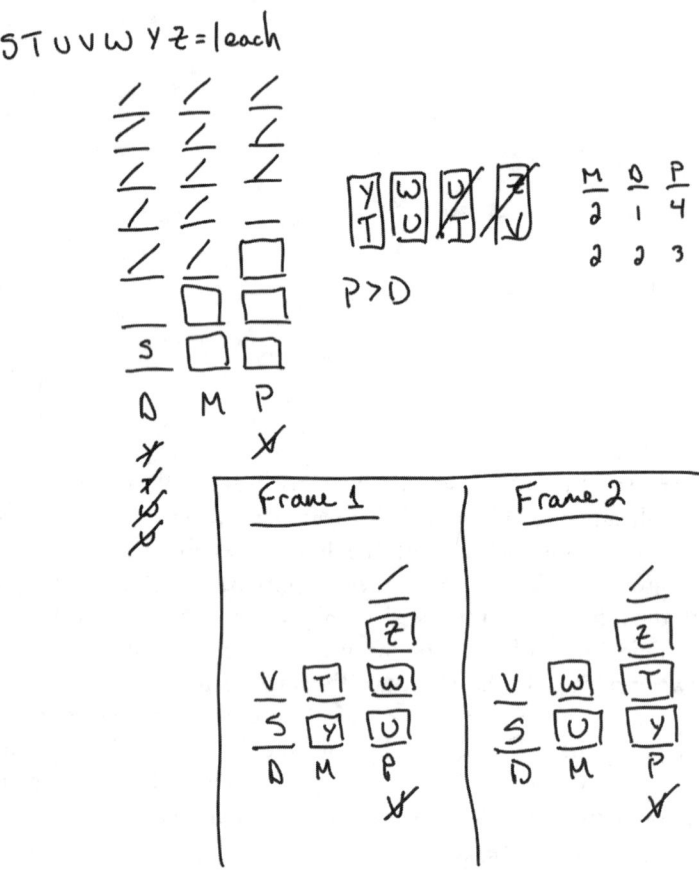

This is another Open Grouping game, this time with three groups: D, M, and P. Group M has exactly two members and group P has to have more members than group D. That leaves two numerical distributions for D, M, and P, respectively: 2-2-3 and 1-2-4. The first two rules establish two chunks and the fifth rule establishes that the chunks have to go in different groups. Because of the numeric restrictions on group D, and because group D already contains S, we can infer that the chunks have to go in groups M and P. Which chunk goes where forms the basis for the two frames. Once the chunks and S are placed, only V and Z remain. Because they cannot go in the same group, and because group M is already filled, V and Z must be split over groups D and P. The last rule tells us that V cannot be in group P, so in both frames, V is in group D and Z is in group P. Our frames thereby invalidate the 1-2-4 distribution.

6

4. Seven musicians—Lorraine, Marcos, Nandi, Paul, Quan, Rafiki, and Teresa—are on call to fill in for absent musicians at the Bridgetown Classical Music Festival. There are five absent musicians, each of whom is scheduled to perform a solo piece, a chamber music piece, or an orchestral piece. There is at least one absent musician scheduled to perform each type of piece, subject to the following constraints:

All solo pieces are scheduled to be performed before any chamber music, and all chamber music is scheduled to be performed before any orchestral pieces.
Teresa will fill in for an absent musician.
Paul will fill in for the second absent soloist.
If Quan fills in for an absent musician, then so does Marcos.
If Lorraine fills in for an absent musician, then so does Rafiki.
If either Marcos or Rafiki fills in for an absent musician, that musician was scheduled to perform chamber music.

This Mismatch 3D Ordering game with an out group opens up with a rule that establishes that all S's come before any C's, and that all C's come before any O's. When that is combined with the rule from the scenario that there is at least one musician performing each type of music, we can infer that the first piece must be an S and the last piece must be an O. We can also infer that the second piece could only be an S or a C and that the fourth piece could only be a C or an O. The third rule tells us that P fills in for the second absent soloist, and since the first absent soloist is the musician who fills slot one, we know P fills slot two. That means that slot three could only be an S or a C. The fact that M and R can only play chamber music prohibits them from going in slots one or five. Finally, the combination of the fourth and fifth rules leads to a Limited Group Space inference. Like most Limited Group Space inferences, this one is found by looking at the contrapositives of conditional rules. The fourth rule's contrapositive tells us that if M is out, so is Q. The fifth rule's contrapositive tells us that if R is out, then so is L. Each of these out group pairs could happen individually, but there isn't enough space in the out group for them to happen at the same time. Therefore, it can never be the case that both M and R are out, leading to our inference that at least one of them must perform.

6

Step 4–Attack the Questions

Drill 123: Target Practice

Instructions: If you're going to attack the questions, you have to know your target: is the correct answer something that could be true, could be false, must be true, or must be false?

For each of the following question stems or descriptions, decide if the target for the correct answer is Could Be True (CBT), Could Be False (CBF), Must Be True (MBT), or Must Be False (MBF).

_____ 1. The four incorrect answers all could be true.

_____ 2. Each of the following must be true EXCEPT:

_____ 3. The incorrect answers must be false.

_____ 4. Each of the following could be true EXCEPT:

_____ 5. The four incorrect answers all must be true.

_____ 6. The incorrect answers could be false.

_____ 7. Each of the following could be false EXCEPT:

_____ 8. Each of the following could be true EXCEPT:

_____ 9. The incorrect answers must be true.

_____ 10. Each of the following could be true EXCEPT:

_____ 11. Which of the following cannot be true?

_____ 12. The four incorrect answers all could be false.

_____ 13. The four incorrect answers are not necessarily true.

_____ 14. Each of the following must be false EXCEPT:

_____ 15. The four incorrect answers must be false.

Answers follow on the next page.

6

Answers

MBF   1.   The four incorrect answers all could be true.

CBF   2.   Each of the following must be true EXCEPT:

CBT   3.   The incorrect answers must be false.

MBF   4.   Each of the following could be true EXCEPT:

CBF   5.   The four incorrect answers all must be true.

MBT   6.   The incorrect answers could be false.

MBT   7.   Each of the following could be false EXCEPT:

MBF   8.   Each of the following could be true EXCEPT:

CBF   9.   The incorrect answers must be true.

MBF   10.   Each of the following could be true EXCEPT:

MBF   11.   Which of the following cannot be true?

MBT   12.   The four incorrect answers all could be false.

MBT   13.   The four incorrect answers are not necessarily true.

CBT   14.   Each of the following must be false EXCEPT:

CBT   15.   The four incorrect answers must be false.

6

Drill 124: Orientation Domination

Instructions: Orientation questions—those initial ones that ask for an acceptable list of elements—should be fast, free points. To ensure you get these points quickly and easily, take the first rule of the game and check each answer choice against it. Cross off any answer that breaks that rule, rinse, and repeat.

In most cases, a rule will eliminate only one answer, but this isn't always the case, especially when there are fewer than four rules. It's also advisable to consider using the rules out of order. If, for example, the first rule is a complex conditional and the rest are chunks and exclusions, it's probably better to do the easy rules first so you're only checking a couple of answers against the harder rule.

For each of the following sets, we've provided the type of game, rules, and some lists of elements. Follow the process outlined above and fill in the slot beside each answer with the rule number(s) that it violates. Note that some answers will be eliminated by more than one rule, some sets will have all the answers eliminated, and others will have multiple answers that are not eliminated. This is NOT a four wrong/one right scenario! We're not going to make it easy for you.

Game 1—An In/Out Grouping Game

1. K is selected only if N and C are both also selected.
2. P is not selected unless B is selected.
3. M is not selected if B is.
4. J is selected if, but only if, C is not selected.
5. H is selected unless D is selected.

_____ A) H, J, M, N, P

_____ B) C, D, J, M, N

_____ C) B, D, J, M, P

_____ D) B, C, H, K, P

_____ E) B, C, K, N, P

Game 2—An Ordering Game (ordered from oldest to youngest)

1. Y is older than M but younger than L.
2. There is exactly one person born between E and D.
3. K is either the oldest or the youngest.
4. M is younger than S but is not the youngest.
5. D and S were not born in consecutive years.

_____ A) L, Y, S, K, E, M, D

_____ B) S, E, L, D, Y, M, K

_____ C) Y, S, E, L, D, M, K

_____ D) K, L, Y, E, S, M, D

_____ E) K, L, S, Y, D, M, E

Game 3—An Open Grouping Game

1. The first quilt has more colors than the second or third quilt.
2. Red and orange are not used in the same quilt.
3. Indigo is in the same quilt as yellow.
4. White is used with at least two other colors.
5. A quilt can have at most two of the following colors: green, blue, and violet.

_____ A) 1: red, yellow, green, white

2: orange, blue

3: indigo, violet

_____ B) 1: yellow, green, indigo, blue

2: white, red, orange

3: violet

_____ C) 1: white, green, blue, violet

2: red, yellow, indigo

3: orange

_____ D) 1: yellow, indigo, violet

2: red, blue

3: orange, green, white

_____ E) 1: orange, yellow, indigo, violet

2: red, green

3: white, blue

Game 4—An Open Grouping Game

1. Bonnie visits more cities than Lise.
2. No one visits both Osaka and Sendai.
3. Anyone visiting Hiroshima will visit only one other city.
4. Anyone who doesn't visit Tokyo will visit Kyoto.
5. Exactly one person visits Yokohama.

_____ A) Bonnie: Hiroshima, Osaka, Yokohama

Lise: Kyoto, Yokohama

Anna: Sendai, Tokyo

_____ B) Bonnie: Tokyo, Yokohama

Lise: Kyoto

Anna: Kyoto, Osaka, Sendai, Tokyo

_____ C) Bonnie: Kyoto, Osaka, Yokohama

Lise: Osaka, Tokyo, Sendai

Anna: Hiroshima, Kyoto

_____ D) Bonnie: Kyoto, Osaka, Tokyo

Lise: Hiroshima, Osaka

Anna: Sendai, Tokyo

_____ E) Bonnie: Kyoto, Osaka, Tokyo, Yokohama

Lise: Kyoto, Hiroshima

Anna: Sendai, Tokyo

Game 5—A Mismatch Ordering Game

1. If they go hiking, they will not go kayaking.
2. The music lesson cannot be consecutive to a visit to the art gallery.
3. They will not go shopping on either the first or the last day of her five-day visit.
4. If they have a music lesson, they will also go bowling, and the music lesson will be earlier in her visit than bowling.
   (Zoo is a stray)

_____ A) hiking, bowling, shopping, music lesson, zoo

_____ B) music lesson, hiking, shopping, bowling, kayaking

_____ C) shopping, hiking, art gallery, music lesson, kayaking

_____ D) music lesson, art gallery, bowling, shopping, zoo

_____ E) shopping, art gallery, kayaking, zoo, bowling

Game 6—A 3D Ordering Game

1. He will never read three fiction or three nonfiction works in a row.
2. _Law_ and _Crime_ are not the same genre.
3. The fourth of the seven books is fiction.
4. He reads _Order_ at some point after reading _Law_.
5. He reads a fiction book immediately before and immediately after reading _Punishment_.
6. He reads _Wind_ before _Fire_ but after _Earth_.

_____ A) _Law, Punishment, Earth, Fire, Crime, Wind, Order_

_____ B) _Law, Punishment, Order, Earth, Crime, Wind, Fire_

_____ C) _Punishment, Earth, Law, Wind, Order, Fire, Crime_

_____ D) _Earth, Wind, Order, Punishment, Fire, Law, Crime_

_____ E) _Crime, Law, Wind, Earth, Order, Punishment, Fire_

Game 7—A 3D Grouping Game

1. There are exactly four chocolate and four vanilla cupcakes.
2. Exactly two of each flavor have sprinkles.
3. Henry and Leah have different flavors.
4. Jen has chocolate if Oscar has chocolate.
5. Nina does not have sprinkles.
6. Kylie and Meghan do not have identical cupcakes.
7. Ira has the same flavor as Nina.

_____ A) chocolate: Henry, Ira (sprinkles), Jen, Oscar (sprinkles)

vanilla: Kylie (sprinkles), Leah (sprinkles), Meghan, Nina

_____ B) chocolate: Kylie (sprinkles), Leah, Meghan, Oscar (sprinkles)

vanilla: Henry (sprinkles), Ira (sprinkles), Jen, Nina

_____ C) chocolate: Ira (sprinkles), Jen (sprinkles), Leah, Nina

vanilla: Henry, Kylie (sprinkles), Meghan (sprinkles), Oscar

_____ D) chocolate: Ira (sprinkles), Jen, Kylie (sprinkles), Nina

vanilla: Henry (sprinkles), Leah, Meghan, Oscar (sprinkles)

_____ E) chocolate: Henry, Ira, Kylie (sprinkles), Nina (sprinkles)

vanilla: Jen (sprinkles), Leah, Meghan, Oscar (sprinkles)

6

Game 8—A Hybrid Game

1. Q runs the last leg of the relay team she is on.
2. If M is on the gold team, N is on the blue team.
3. R runs an earlier leg in the relay than both P and V.
4. S and T are not on the same team.

_____ A) gold: T, R, M, P

blue: N, S, V, Q

_____ B) gold: M, S, R, V

blue: N, T, Q, P

_____ C) gold: S, M, N, Q

blue: T, R, P, V

_____ D) gold: M, S, R, V

blue: N, T, P, Q

_____ E) gold: R, S, T, Q

blue: M, N, V, P

Game 9—A Mismatch Grouping Game

1. He will not plant both cabbage and sprouts.
2. If asparagus is planted in the left garden, zucchini is planted in the right garden.
3. He will plant both tomatoes and watermelon, but in separate gardens.
4. If he does not plant beans, he will plant peas.

_____ A) left: asparagus, beans, cabbage

right: peas, watermelon, zucchini

_____ B) left: asparagus, beans, tomatoes, zucchini

right: cabbage, peas, watermelon

_____ C) left: cabbage, watermelon, zucchini

right: asparagus, sprouts, tomatoes

_____ D) left: tomatoes, zucchini

right: beans, peas, watermelon

_____ E) left: beans, watermelon

right: asparagus, peas, sprouts, tomatoes

Game 10—A 3D Grouping Game

1. Exactly two of the four beverages ordered will be the small size.
2. She will never order both grape soda and berry tea.
3. If she orders water, she will order a large water.
4. If she orders cola, she will order a medium cola.
5. If she orders orange soda, she will not order lemon-lime soda.
6. If both orange soda and grape soda are ordered, the orange soda will be a larger size than the grape soda.

_____ A) berry tea, cola, grape soda, lemon-lime soda

_____ B) berry tea, cola, orange soda, water

_____ C) cola, grape soda, lemon-lime soda, water

_____ D) berry tea, cola, lemon-lime soda, orange soda

_____ E) cola, grape soda, orange soda, water

6

Answers

Game 1

A. 2
B. 4
C. 3
D. 1
E. 5

Game 2

A. 3
B. Not eliminated
C. 1
D. 2
E. Not eliminated

Game 3

A. 3
B. 2
C. 5
D. 1
E. 4

Game 4

A. 3, 4, 5
B. 2
C. 1, 2
D. 4, 5
E. Not eliminated

Game 5

A. 4
B. 1
C. 1, 2, 3, 4
D. 2
E. 3

Game 6

A. 6
B. Not eliminated
C. 5
D. 4
E. 6

Game 7

A. 7
B. 4
C. 6
D. 3
E. 5

Game 8

A. Not eliminated
B. 1
C. 2
D. 3
E. 4

Game 9

A. 3
B. 2
C. 1, 4
D. Not eliminated
E. Not eliminated

Game 10

A. 2
B. Not eliminated
C. Not eliminated
D. 5
E. 6, 1, 3, 4—great job if you caught this one!

6

Drill 125: Haven't I Seen You Before? Round 1

Instructions: Over the course of a logic game, you put pencil to paper … a lot! This drill is about getting the most out of all that hard work that you're already doing.

Whenever you've drawn out a valid hypothetical scenario, even one that's incomplete, you can often get more out of it than the answer to a single question, or the elimination of a single wrong answer choice. Valid hypotheticals from your prior work can assist you on subsequent questions, but only if you know how to use them properly.

Consider this scenario: you've got a hypothetical that shows P, R, and T, all in the same group. A subsequent question asks you what could be true. How might the hypothetical help? Well, if P, R, and T, or any pair of those three, occupying the same group is one of the answers, you know that answer is correct, because the hypothetical demonstrates that this could be true.

Next, consider a subsequent question that asks you what *must* be true. How does the hypothetical help now— would P, R, and T in the same group still be a correct answer? No, because the hypothetical only shows that this is *possible*, not that it is *necessary*. That doesn't mean, however, that the hypothetical is useless. What if an answer said P and T had to be in different groups? The hypothetical demonstrates that this *doesn't* have to be true, allowing you to eliminate the answer.

Similar rules hold for Could Be False and Must Be False questions. On Could Be False questions, you can pick any answer choice that *is false* in a valid hypothetical. On Must Be False questions, you can eliminate any answer that *is not false* in a valid hypothetical.

For each of the following sets below, use the prior work provided to assess each potential answer choice. Determine whether each answer is demonstrated to be correct (C), demonstrated to be incorrect (I), or cannot be assessed using the prior work (?).

Note: More than one answer, or no answer, might be demonstrated to be correct.

Diagram 1

Which of the following could be true?

_____ 1. S appears before H.

_____ 2. I and U appear consecutively.

_____ 3. U appears immediately after G.

_____ 4. T appears immediately before H.

Which of the following must be true?

_____ 5. U appears at some point before V.

_____ 6. G and H appear consecutively.

_____ 7. S appears before I.

_____ 8. T appears before I.

Which of the following must be false?

_____ 9. T and G appear consecutively.

_____ 10. I appears after S but before T.

_____ 11. V and U do not appear consecutively.

_____ 12. G appears at some point before V.

Which of the following could be false?

_____ 13. G appears at some point before V.

_____ 14. H and G do not appear consecutively.

_____ 15. S and T appear consecutively.

_____ 16. I appears before G.

Diagram 2

$$\frac{\quad}{N}\overset{R}{\underset{1}{S}}\overset{\overset{L}{M}}{\underset{2}{S}}\overset{}{\underset{3}{T}} \qquad \overset{}{\underset{1}{S}}\overset{R}{\underset{2}{N}}\overset{\overset{T}{L}}{\underset{3}{M}} \qquad \overset{}{\underset{1}{S}}\overset{T}{\underset{2}{R}}\overset{\overset{L}{M}}{\underset{3}{N}}$$

Which of the following must be true?

_____ 17. M and L are placed in the same room.

_____ 18. S and N cannot be placed in the same room.

_____ 19. If T is placed in the third room, then N is placed in the first room.

_____ 20. If N is placed in the first room, then T is placed in the third room.

Which of the following must be false?

_____ 21. S and N are placed in the same room.

_____ 22. N is in the first room and T is in the second room.

_____ 23. N is in the first room and T is in the third room.

_____ 24. M is placed in the first room.

Which of the following could be true?

_____ 25. T and N are both placed in the second room.

_____ 26. L and T are placed in different rooms.

_____ 27. R is placed in a higher numbered room than N.

_____ 28. S and N are placed in the same room.

Which of the following could be false?

_____ 29. L is not placed in a higher numbered room than T.

_____ 30. M and L are not placed in different rooms.

_____ 31. N isn't placed in room 3.

_____ 32. S and R are placed in consecutively-numbered rooms.

Diagram 3

Which of the following could be true?

_____ 33. One engineer is assigned to all three projects.

_____ 34. G and F are not assigned to a project together.

_____ 35. H is assigned to a project with I but without J.

_____ 36. F is assigned to only one project.

Which of the following must be false?

_____ 37. S and V are assigned the same number of engineers.

_____ 38. S and U are assigned the same number of engineers.

_____ 39. H is assigned to a project with neither I nor J.

_____ 40. F is assigned to only one project.

Which of the following must be true?

_____ 41. F is assigned to exactly two projects.

_____ 42. V is assigned more engineers than any other project.

_____ 43. S is assigned more engineers than any other project.

_____ 44. S is assigned more engineers than U.

Which of the following could be false?

_____ 45. H is assigned to a project with either I or J.

_____ 46. F is assigned to exactly two projects.

_____ 47. V is assigned more engineers than both other projects combined.

_____ 48. H is assigned to more projects than F.

6

Diagram 4

$$\frac{Z}{1} \quad \frac{V}{2} \quad \frac{W}{3} \quad \frac{T}{4} \quad \frac{\boxed{U \quad S}}{5 \quad 6}$$

$$\frac{T}{1} \quad \frac{U}{2} \quad \frac{W}{3} \quad \frac{V}{4} \quad \frac{Z}{5} \quad \frac{S}{6}$$

Which of the following must be true?

_____ 49. If V is fourth, Z is fifth.

_____ 50. If V is ranked higher than Z, then S is last.

_____ 51. T is ranked higher than S.

_____ 52. T is ranked third.

Which of the following must be false?

_____ 53. T is ranked fifth.

_____ 54. V is ranked fourth and Z is ranked second.

_____ 55. V and Z are not ranked consecutively.

_____ 56. U is ranked consecutively with T.

Which of the following could be true?

_____ 57. Z and T have at least two other athletes ranked between them.

_____ 58. W and T have at most one other athlete ranked between them.

_____ 59. Z is ranked second.

_____ 60. V is ranked fourth and Z is ranked last.

Which of the following could be false?

_____ 61. W is ranked fourth.

_____ 62. S is ranked last.

_____ 63. V and W are ranked consecutively.

_____ 64. Z is not ranked last.

6

Answers

There's a bit of a trick to this drill. Because of the rules outlined in the introduction, on *Must Be* questions (both true and false), you can only prove answers to be incorrect answer choices, so you should only have I's and ?'s as answers for those questions. On *Could Be* questions (both true and false), you can only prove answers to be correct answer choices, so you should only have C's and ?'s as answers for those.

Diagram 1	Diagram 2	Diagram 3	Diagram 4
1. C	17. ?	33. C	49. ?
2. C	18. ?	34. C	50. ?
3. ?	19. I	35. C	51. ?
4. ?	20. ?	36. ?	52. I
5. I	21. ?	37. ?	53. ?
6. I	22. ?	38. ?	54. ?
7. ?	23. I	39. ?	55. ?
8. ?	24. ?	40. ?	56. I
9. I	25. ?	41. ?	57. C
10. ?	26. C	42. I	58. C
11. I	27. C	43. I	59. ?
12. I	28. ?	44. I	60. ?
13. ?	29. C	45. ?	61. C
14. C	30. ?	46. ?	62. C
15. ?	31. C	47. C	63. ?
16. C	32. C	48. C	64. ?

6

Drill 126: Testing, Testing, 1, 2, 3

Instructions: Testing answer choices is a reality of the Logic Games section. It's great when you can get to the correct answer through your elegant prework, but sometimes you just have to get in the trenches and test. Many students go to great lengths to avoid testing answers because they think it's too time-consuming and they end up creating a mountain of inconclusive prework or making guesses instead. But the fact is, if you commit to testing answer choices without a lot of foot-dragging, and if you know how to test efficiently, you'll have plenty of time to execute this strategy as often as you need to. Use this drill to build that efficiency!

For each of the question stem and answer choice pairs below, select the best method for testing out the answer choice.

1. Question: If Ronald is interviewed third, which of the following could be false?

    Answer: Susan is interviewed before Taren.

    A. Place R third and S somewhere before T.
    B. Place R third and S somewhere after T.

2. Question: Which of the following must be true?

    Answer: Kalil will bat fourth.

    A. Place K in any spot other than fourth.
    B. Place K in the fourth spot.

3. Question: If Sydney is in the Spanish class, which of the following could be true?

    Answer: Helena is in the French class.

    A. Place S in Spanish and H in French.
    B. Place both S and H in Spanish.

4. Question: If Liza is last, which of the following must be false?

    Answer: Taryn is fifth.

    A. Place L last and T in fifth.
    B. Place L last and T anywhere except fifth.

5. Question: Each of the following must be true EXCEPT:

    Answer: The second wall is red.

    A. Place R in the second slot.
    B. Place R in any slot other than the second slot.

6. Question: Each of the following could be true EXCEPT:

    Answer: Virginia is assigned to the asbestos project.

    A. Assign V to any project except asbestos.
    B. Assign V to asbestos.

7. Question: If Rina does not ski, each of the following could be false EXCEPT:

    Answer: Tom is in the skiing group.

    A. Place R in a group other than the skiing group, and T in the skiing group.
    B. Place R in a group other than the skiing group, and T in a group other than the skiing group.

8. Question: Each of the following must be false EXCEPT:

    Answer: Mary reads first.

    A. Place M first.
    B. Place M anywhere other than first.

9. Question: Which of the following could be a complete and accurate list of students in room 1?

    Answer: Juan, Lenore, and Neti.

    A. Place Juan, Lenore, and Neti in room 1 together in a single hypothetical.
    B. Place Juan, Lenore, and Neti in room 1, each in their own hypothetical.

10. Question: Which of the following is a complete and accurate list of flowers that could be planted in Bobbi's garden?

    Answer: Daffodils, gardenias, hibiscus

    A. Place daffodils, gardenias, and hibiscus in Bobbi's garden together in a single hypothetical.
    B. Place daffodils, gardenias, and hibiscus in Bobbi's garden, each in their own hypothetical.

Answers

1. Question: If Ronald is interviewed third, which of the following could be false?

    Answer: Susan is interviewed before Taren.

    A. Place R third and S somewhere before T.
    B. Place R third and S somewhere after T.

To test if something could be false, create a hypothetical where it is false. If it works, that's your answer.

2. Question: Which of the following must be true?

    Answer: Kalil will bat fourth.

    A. Place K in any spot other than fourth.
    B. Place K in the fourth spot.

To test if something must be true, try making it false. If it could be false, it doesn't have to be true—eliminate!

3. Question: If Sydney is in the Spanish class, which of the following could be true?

    Answer: Helena is in the French class.

    A. Place S in Spanish and H in French.
    B. Place both S and H in Spanish.

To test if something could be true, just try it out. If it works, that's your answer!

4. Question: If Liza is last, which of the following must be false?

    Answer: Taryn is fifth.

    A. Place L last and T in fifth.
    B. Place L last and T anywhere except fifth.

To test if something must be false, try making it true. If it works, it doesn't have to be false—eliminate!

5. Question: Each of the following must be true EXCEPT:

    Answer: The second wall is red.

    A. Place R in the second slot.
    B. Place R in any slot other than the second slot.

The correct answer to a Must Be True Except question is an answer choice that could be false, so treat it like a Could Be False question and try to create a hypothetical in which the answer choice isn't true. If you can, that's your answer.

6. Question: Each of the following could be true EXCEPT:

    Answer: Virginia is assigned to the asbestos project.

    A. Assign V to any project except asbestos.
    B. Assign V to asbestos.

The correct answer to a Could Be True Except question is an answer choice that must be false, so treat it like a Must Be False question and try to create a hypothetical in which the answer choice is true. If you can't, that's your answer.

7. Question: If Rina does not ski, each of the following could be false EXCEPT:

    Answer: Tom is in the skiing group.

    A. Place R in a group other than the skiing group, and T in the skiing group.
    B. Place R in a group other than the skiing group, and T in a group other than the skiing group.

The correct answer to a Could Be False Except question is an answer choice that must be true, so treat it like a Must Be True question and test whether the answer choice could be false. If it can, eliminate. If it can't, that's your answer!

8. Question: Each of the following must be false EXCEPT:

    Answer: Mary reads first.

    A. Place M first.
    B. Place M anywhere other than first.

The correct answer to a Must Be False Except question is an answer choice that could be true, so treat it like a Could Be True question and try it out. If it works, that's your answer.

9. Question: Which of the following could be a complete and accurate list of students in room 1?

    Answer: Juan, Lenore, and Neti.

    A. Place Juan, Lenore, and Neti in room 1 together in a single hypothetical.
    B. Place Juan, Lenore, and Neti in room 1, each in their own hypothetical.

The placement of the word "could" before the words "complete and accurate" tells us that we're looking for a list that could all happen together at the same time.

10. Question: Which of the following is a complete and accurate list of flowers that could be planted in Bobbi's garden?

    Answer: Daffodils, gardenias, hibiscus

    A. Place daffodils, gardenias, and hibiscus in Bobbi's garden together in a single hypothetical.
    B. Place daffodils, gardenias, and hibiscus in Bobbi's garden, each in their own hypothetical.

The placement of the word "could" after the words "complete and accurate" tells us that we're looking for a list that includes every flower that could be planted in Bobbi's garden in any hypothetical but not necessarily in the same hypothetical.

6

Drill 127: Frames. What Are They Good For?
Absolutely Everything!

Instructions: When a facet of a game can pan out in only two or three different ways, and at least one of the ways leads to a domino effect of element placement, you should draw out a separate master diagram for each way the game can pan out. We call this "framing."

This drill is about the final step in a framing game: using the frames to assess the answer choices.

We've provided several sets of frames below. For each item associated with the frames, determine whether it Must Be True (MBT), Must Be False (MBF), or Could Be Either True or False (CB).

Diagram 1

F₁   (G H)   I   J   F   K

F₂   F   J   I   K   (G H)

1   2   3   4   5   6

_____ 1.   J ranks higher than K.

_____ 2.   G ranks higher than H.

_____ 3.   H ranks higher than K.

_____ 4.   Exactly one chef ranks higher than G but lower than I.

_____ 5.   F ranks last.

Diagram 2

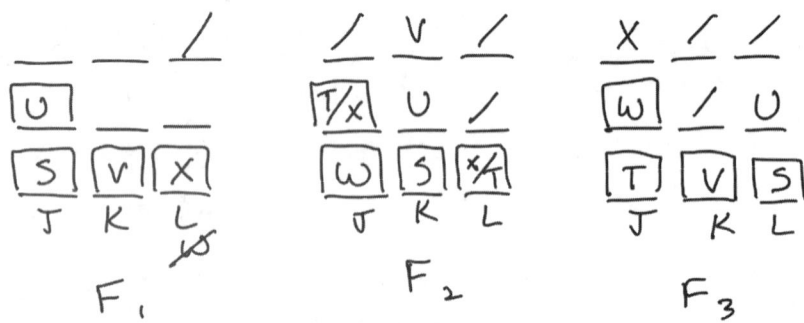

_____ 6.   Two projects have the same number of managers assigned to them.

_____ 7.   W and X are not assigned to the same project.

_____ 8.   S and X are both assigned to J.

_____ 9.   W and T are assigned to the same project.

_____ 10. U is assigned to a project with more engineers than any other project.

Diagram 3

_____ 11. J ranks consecutively with G.

_____ 12. J and H do not rank consecutively.

_____ 13. K ranks first or last.

_____ 14. G ranks higher than I.

_____ 15. L is either unranked or ranks higher than I.

Diagram 4

_____ 16. T is performed immediately after S and immediately before U.

_____ 17. Neither Z nor W is performed last.

_____ 18. Neither P nor Q is performed first.

_____ 19. Q is performed fourth.

_____ 20. Z is performed fifth.

Diagram 5

_____ 21. L and J play in the same game.

_____ 22. H and K play in the same game.

_____ 23. L plays in the game with the most participants.

_____ 24. G plays in the same game as L.

_____ 25. I and M do not play in the same game as each other.

Answers

Diagram 1	Diagram 2	Diagram 3	Diagram 4	Diagram 5
1. MBT	6. CB	11. CB	16. CB	21. CB
2. CB	7. CB	12. CB	17. CB	22. CB
3. CB	8. MBF	13. MBF	18. CB	23. MBT
4. CB	9. CB	14. MBF	19. CB	24. MBF
5. MBF	10. CB	15. MBT	20. CB	25. CB

6

Drill 128: Getting Down to Specifics

Instructions: Conditional questions in the Logic Games section provide you with a new rule. This will generally require you to draw a new diagram that incorporates the new rule and make some new inferences. For this drill, we've provided four master diagrams, each of which is accompanied by five new rules. In the space provided, draw a new diagram for each of the new rules. If you think breaking the new diagram into frames would be helpful, do it!

Set A

FGHISTUV

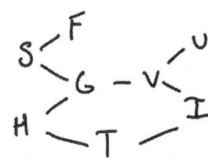

1. H is third.

2. V is fifth.

3. G and T are consecutive.

4. S is second, and F is last.

5. T is fifth.

Set B

FGHI STU

H/_____ _____ _____ M/_____ _____ _____ _____
     1   2   3   4   5   6   7

U – |S _ _ F|

G ⟨ I
   ⟨ T

6. S is fourth.

7. F is fifth.

8. H is fourth, and U is second.

9. G is in the highest-numbered slot possible.

10. H and U are separated by as many slots as possible.

6

Set C

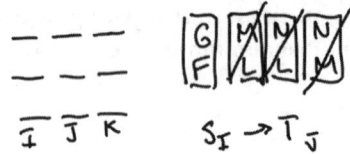

11. S is assigned to I.

12. T is assigned to I.

13. F is assigned to J.

14. M is assigned to J, and N is assigned to I.

15. H and V cannot be assigned to the same group.

Set D

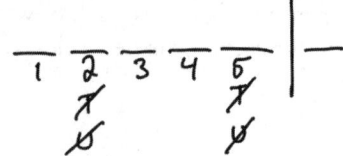

$R \rightarrow R_3$

$Q \rightarrow Q_5$

$P + S \rightarrow \boxed{PS}$

16. R and Q are both selected.

17. U and T cannot both be selected.

18. U is third.

19. T is fifth.

20. T and U are selected consecutively.

6

Answers follow on the next page.

Answers

Set A

1. H is third.

    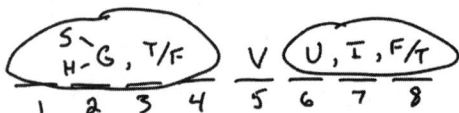

    $$\frac{S}{1} \ \frac{F}{2} \ \frac{H}{3} \ \frac{}{4} \ \frac{}{5} \ \frac{}{6} \ \frac{}{7} \ \frac{}{8}$$
    G – V ⌐U / ⌐I T – I

2. V is fifth.

    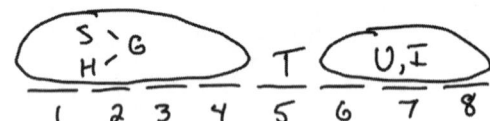

3. G and T are consecutive.

    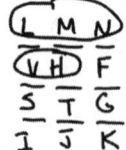

4. S is second, and F is last.

    $$\frac{H}{1} \ \frac{S}{2} \ \frac{}{3} \ \frac{T}{4} \ \frac{}{5} \ \frac{}{6} \ \frac{}{7} \ \frac{F}{8}$$
    G – V ⌐U / ⌐I T – I

5. T is fifth.

    $$\frac{}{1} \ \frac{}{2} \ \frac{}{3} \ \frac{}{4} \ \frac{T}{5} \ \frac{}{6} \ \frac{}{7} \ \frac{}{8}$$
    S G / H G   U, I

Set B

6. S is fourth.

    $$\frac{H}{1} \ \frac{UG}{2 \ 3} \ \frac{S}{4} \ \frac{I \ T}{5 \ 6} \ \frac{F}{7}$$

7. F is fifth.

    $$\frac{U}{1} \ \frac{S}{2} \ \frac{G}{3} \ \frac{H}{4} \ \frac{F}{5} \ \frac{I \ T}{6 \ 7}$$

8. H is fourth, and U is second.

    $$\frac{G}{1} \ \frac{U}{2} \ \frac{S}{3} \ \frac{H}{4} \ \frac{I/T}{5} \ \frac{F}{6} \ \frac{T/I}{7}$$

9. G is in the highest-numbered slot possible.

    $$\frac{H}{1} \ \frac{U}{2} \ \frac{S}{3} \ \frac{G}{4} \ \frac{I/T}{5} \ \frac{F}{6} \ \frac{T/I}{7}$$

10. H and U are separated by as many slots as possible.

    $$\frac{U}{} \ \frac{G}{} \ \frac{S}{} \ \frac{H}{} \ \frac{I/T}{} \ \frac{F}{} \ \frac{T/I}{}$$
    $$\frac{U}{1} \ \frac{S}{2} \ \frac{G}{3} \ \frac{H}{4} \ \frac{F}{5} \ \frac{I \ T}{6 \ 7}$$

Set C

11. S is assigned to I.

    $$\frac{L \ M \ N}{}$$
    $$\frac{V H}{} \ \frac{F}{}$$
    $$\frac{S}{I} \ \frac{T}{J} \ \frac{G}{K}$$

12. T is assigned to I.

    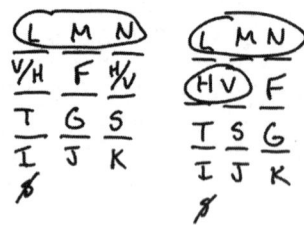

    $$\frac{L \ M \ N}{}$$
    $$\frac{V/H}{} \ \frac{F}{} \ \frac{H/V}{}$$
    $$\frac{T}{I} \ \frac{G}{J} \ \frac{S}{K}$$
    8

    $$\frac{L \ M \ N}{}$$
    $$\frac{H V}{} \ \frac{F}{}$$
    $$\frac{T}{I} \ \frac{S}{J} \ \frac{G}{K}$$
    8

13. F is assigned to J.

    $$\frac{L \ M \ N}{}$$
    $$\frac{G}{}$$
    $$\frac{F}{} \ \frac{S}{}$$
    $$\frac{}{I} \ \frac{}{J} \ \frac{}{K}$$

14. M is assigned to J, and N is assigned to I.

    $$\frac{N}{I} \ \frac{M}{J} \ \frac{L}{K}$$

6

15. H and V cannot be assigned to the same group.

Set D

16. R and Q are both selected.

In   Out   In | Out
                           | H/J
H ⟶ H
J ⤬ J   J/K |
K ⟵ K

17. U and T cannot both be selected.

$$\frac{P}{1} \quad \frac{S}{2} \quad \frac{R}{3} \quad \frac{T/U}{4} \quad \frac{Q}{5} \Big| \frac{U/T}{}$$

18. U is third.

$$\frac{P}{1} \quad \frac{S}{2} \quad \frac{U}{3} \quad \frac{T}{4} \quad \frac{Q}{5} \Big| R$$

19. T is fifth.

$$\frac{P}{1} \quad \frac{S}{2} \quad \frac{R}{3} \quad \frac{U}{4} \quad \frac{T}{5} \Big| Q$$

20. T and U are selected consecutively.

$$\frac{P}{1} \quad \frac{S}{2} \quad \frac{\boxed{T \; U}}{3 \quad 4} \quad \frac{Q}{5} \Big| R$$

Drill 129: One at a Time, or All at Once?

Instructions: Complete and Accurate List questions are among the most confusing on the LSAT. What are they even asking for? Well, some ask you to list everything that could fulfill a criterion in independent hypotheticals. Others ask you to generate a list of things that could all happen in a single hypothetical. Figuring out what the question is asking is often the hardest part of the question, and you can bank on seeing a wrong answer choice that would answer the opposite question. A general rule is that if the word "could" comes before the word "list," the question is asking for a list of elements that could appear in a "snapshot" of a single hypothetical. If the word "list" comes before the word "could," or you see the phrase "any one of which/whom," the question is asking for a wide-angle view of all possibilities.

For each of the following question stems, identify whether it's asking for a list from a single hypothetical (1) or a list covering all possible hypotheticals (All).

_____ 1. Which one of the following is a complete and accurate list of the athletes, any of whom could compete in all three tournaments?

_____ 2. Which of the following could be a complete and accurate list of the songs chosen for the concert?

_____ 3. If the blanket is dyed yellow, which of the following could be an accurate list of the items dyed green?

_____ 4. Which of the following is a complete and accurate list of the rangers, each of whom could patrol the park on Tuesday?

_____ 5. Which of the following could be a complete and accurate list of the rangers who patrol the park on Tuesday?

_____ 6. If the copier is the third machine repaired, which of the following is a complete and accurate list of the machines that could be repaired first?

_____ 7. Which of the following could be a complete and accurate list of materials used in the art projects?

_____ 8. Which of the following is a complete and accurate list of the students who could speak first in one of the debates?

_____ 9. Which of the following lists all of the toys that could be donated to charity X?

_____ 10. Which of the following could be a complete and accurate list of the projects that are NOT assigned to Martinez?

_____ 11. If car V is ranked fourth, which of the following could be a complete and accurate list of the cars ranked first through third, in order?

_____ 12. If car V is ranked fourth, which of the following is a complete and accurate list of cars that could be ranked first through third?

_____ 13. Which of the following is a complete and accurate list of the games, any of which can be played on day two?

_____ 14. If Leanne is a contestant on the first episode, then the complete list of contestants on the second episode could be:

_____ 15. If Leanne is a contestant on the first episode, then the complete list of contestants who could be on the second episode is:

Answers follow on the next page.

Answers

__All__ 1. Which one of the following is a complete and accurate list of the athletes, any of whom could compete in all three tournaments?

__1__ 2. Which of the following could be a complete and accurate list of the songs chosen for the concert?

__1__ 3. If the blanket is dyed yellow, which of the following could be an accurate list of the items dyed green?

__All__ 4. Which of the following is a complete and accurate list of the rangers, each of whom could patrol the park on Tuesday?

__1__ 5. Which of the following could be a complete and accurate list of the rangers who patrol the park on Tuesday?

__All__ 6. If the copier is the third machine repaired, which of the following is a complete and accurate list of the machines that could be repaired first?

__1__ 7. Which of the following could be a complete and accurate list of materials used in the art projects?

__All__ 8. Which of the following is a complete and accurate list of the students who could speak first in one of the debates?

__All__ 9. Which of the following lists all of the toys that could be donated to charity X?

__1__ 10. Which of the following could be a complete and accurate list of the projects that are NOT assigned to Martinez?

__1__ 11. If car V is ranked fourth, which of the following could be a complete and accurate list of the cars ranked first through third, in order?

__All__ 12. If car V is ranked fourth, which of the following is a complete and accurate list of cars that could be ranked first through third?

__All__ 13. Which of the following is a complete and accurate list of the games, any of which can be played on day two?

__1__ 14. If Leanne is a contestant on the first episode, then the complete list of contestants on the second episode could be:

__All__ 15. If Leanne is a contestant on the first episode, then the complete list of contestants that could be on the second episode is:

6

Drill 130: Haven't I Seen You Before? Round 2

Instructions: You already know that over the course of a logic game, you put pencil to paper ... a lot! This drill is (still!) about getting the most out of all that hard work that you're already doing.

For each of the following sets below, use the prior work provided to assess each potential answer choice. Determine whether each answer is demonstrated to be correct (C), demonstrated to be incorrect (I), or cannot be assessed using the prior work (?).

Note: More than one answer, or no answer, might be demonstrated to be correct.

Diagram 1

Which of the following could be true?

_____ 1.   J is selected and K is not.

_____ 2.   M is selected and G is not.

_____ 3.   Both M and G are selected.

_____ 4.   Neither M nor G is selected.

Which of the following must be true?

_____ 5.   If J is selected, so is K.

_____ 6.   Either M and N are both selected, or neither is selected.

_____ 7.   I is selected but N is not.

_____ 8.   Both I and L are not selected.

Which of the following must be false?

_____ 9.   Neither N nor I is selected.

_____ 10. Both I and L are selected.

_____ 11. K and N are both selected.

_____ 12. Only two songs are selected.

Which of the following could be false?

_____ 13. Exactly three songs are selected.

_____ 14. M is selected and N is not.

_____ 15. N is selected and M is not.

_____ 16. J is selected and G is not.

Diagram 2

Which of the following must be true?

_____ 17. Blue and yellow presents are opened in alternating order.

_____ 18. S and U are opened consecutively.

_____ 19. P is a yellow present.

_____ 20. P is opened before at least two other presents.

Which of the following must be false?

_____ 21. Q is one of the first three presents opened.

_____ 22. Q is opened immediately before P.

_____ 23. The last present opened is yellow.

_____ 24. The third present opened is blue.

Which of the following could be true?

_____ 25. Two blue presents are opened in a row.

_____ 26. Two yellow presents are opened in a row.

_____ 27. R is opened before T.

_____ 28. The first present opened is yellow.

Which of the following could be false?

_____ 29. The last present opened is blue.

_____ 30. The first and last presents opened are the same color.

_____ 31. R is the third present opened.

_____ 32. P and Q are not opened consecutively.

Diagram 3

$$\frac{}{}$$

K
F J I
L G H
M T ω

J
K F I
L H G
M T ω

Which of the following could be true?

_____ 33. K and L are assigned to consecutive days.

_____ 34. G and I are assigned to the same day.

_____ 35. I is assigned to a day preceding F.

_____ 36. J is assigned to the day immediately before K.

Which of the following must be false?

_____ 37. K is assigned to the day immediately following J.

_____ 38. K and I are assigned to different days.

_____ 39. H and G are assigned to the same day.

_____ 40. H and L are assigned to the same day.

Which of the following must be true?

_____ 41. I is assigned to Wednesday.

_____ 42. H, G, and L are all assigned to different days.

_____ 43. I is assigned later in the week than H.

_____ 44. J is not assigned to the day immediately before K.

Which of the following could be false?

_____ 45. F is assigned to an earlier day than I.

_____ 46. J and K are assigned to the same day.

_____ 47. H and G are assigned to different days.

_____ 48. L and G are assigned to different days.

Diagram 4

K G I J F | H L
1 2 3 4 5

H L I (J K) | G F
1 2 3 4 5

Which of the following must be true?

_____ 49. If G is selected for the team, G races second.

_____ 50. If F is selected for the team, so is J.

_____ 51. K is selected for the team.

_____ 52. If H is selected for the team, then so is I.

Which of the following must be false?

_____ 53. If both I and J are selected, I runs in an earlier race than J.

_____ 54. I is selected while H is not.

_____ 55. H is selected while I is not.

_____ 56. G is selected and runs in the third race.

Which of the following could be true?

_____ 57. K and I run in consecutive races.

_____ 58. Neither G nor H is selected to run in a race.

_____ 59. F and I run in consecutive races.

_____ 60. K runs in the first race and I runs in an earlier race than H.

Which of the following could be false?

_____ 61. K and J are both selected to run in races.

_____ 62. K is selected to run in a race while J is not.

_____ 63. I and J run in consecutive races.

_____ 64. K isn't selected to run in a race.

Answers follow on the next page.

6

Answers

Remember the trick to this drill? For *Must Be* questions (either True or False), you can only eliminate answers, not select them (because there are other hypotheticals that haven't been provided), so you should only have I's and ?'s as answers for those questions. For *Could Be* questions (either True or False), you can only select answer choices, not eliminate them, for the same reason, so you should only have C's and ?'s as answers for those.

Diagram 1	Diagram 2	Diagram 3	Diagram 4
1. ?	17. I	33. C	49. ?
2. ?	18. ?	34. C	50. ?
3. C	19. ?	35. ?	51. ?
4. C	20. ?	36. ?	52. ?
5. ?	21. I	37. ?	53. I
6. ?	22. I	38. I	54. I
7. I	23. ?	39. ?	55. ?
8. I	24. I	40. ?	56. ?
9. ?	25. C	41. ?	57. C
10. ?	26. ?	42. ?	58. ?
11. ?	27. C	43. I	59. ?
12. ?	28. ?	44. ?	60. ?
13. ?	29. ?	45. ?	61. ?
14. C	30. ?	46. C	62. C
15. C	31. C	47. ?	63. C
16. C	32. C	48. ?	64. C

6

CHAPTER 7

Logic Games, Skills by Family

In This Chapter, We Will Cover:

- Ordering Games

- In/Out Games

- Grouping and Hybrid Games

- Unusual Games

Ordering Games

Roughly 50% of the logic games on modern LSATs have had ordering as their primary task. But this family of games is as varied as any family can be. Some ordering games ask you to relate the elements to a Number Line. Others ask you to relate elements only to one another. Still others give you multiple sets of elements to relate, or a set of elements that doesn't correspond numerically to the number of available slots. Ordering games are typically arranged horizontally, but sometimes you need a vertical Number Line, or even a circular one! Get to know this important family of games in this chapter of the book. Within this section of the book, the drills are organized according to our 4-Step Process for Logic Games.

In this section, you will learn to:

Picture the Game

- Recognize the most common Ordering Family twists

Notate the Rules and Make Inferences

- Diagram tricky ordering rules
- Use Numerical Distributions in Mismatch Ordering Games

Take The Big Pause

- Spot framing opportunities

Attack the Questions

- Tackle Minimum/Maximum questions

7

Drill 131: Do the Twist, Ordering Edition

Instructions: For each of these tricky games, identify the game type and twist. Bonus points for any strategic considerations you can fill in! No need to diagram the full games. For now, just practice spotting the game type, twist, and strategic considerations. Be on the lookout for the chance to use advanced strategies such as Framing and Numerical Distribution and for high-level inferences such as those that stem from Limited Group Space!

1. A movie critic is ranking seven films—F, G, H, J, K, L, and M—from best to worst. They are ranked according to the following rules:

   F is ranked ahead of G and H.

   Either J or K is ranked lower than L, but not both.

   L is ranked ahead of M.

2. Seven high school students—P, Q, R, S, T, V, and W—are participating in a math competition. Some of the students are freshmen, some are sophomores, and one is a junior. They finish according to the following rules:

   Neither P nor Q is a junior.

   R finishes ahead of S.

   T finishes no worse than third place.

   The last place finisher is not a sophomore.

   The junior finishes ahead of all sophomores.

3. King Arthur has called a meeting of some of his knights—Gawain, Lancelot, Kay, Percivale, and Tristan—at the round table. They are seated according to the following rules:

   King Arthur sits next to Lancelot.

   Lancelot sits directly across from Gawain.

   Kay and Percivale do not sit next to each other.

4. Alex has job interviews scheduled with seven different companies—F, G, H, J, K, L, and M—from Monday through Thursday. He schedules the interviews according to the following rules:

   At least one interview is scheduled for every day from Monday through Thursday.

   F is scheduled for the day before G.

   H is scheduled before J, who is scheduled before K.

   L is scheduled exactly two days before M.

5. A network is deciding which four out of six ads—P, Q, R, S, T, and V—it is going to run, and in what order, during a commercial break. The network will choose the ads according to the following rules:

   If P is selected, then it is the first ad shown.

   If Q is selected, then it is the first ad shown.

   If R is selected, then S is directly after it.

   T cannot be the third ad shown.

6. Betty is test driving eight cars: three convertibles—F, G, and H—three hatchbacks—J, K, and L—and two sedans—M and N. Afterward, she lists them in order of how much she enjoyed driving each car, in accordance with the following rules:

   F is her favorite convertible.

   None of the hatchbacks are ranked directly next to another hatchback.

   One of the sedans is the lowest ranked car.

7. A contractor is setting her schedule for the week. She has five projects—P, Q, R, S, and T—to complete from Monday through Sunday. She works on one project per day, except for her two days off. She chooses her schedule according to the following rules:

    She works on exactly two projects in between her off days.
    She works on either P or Q on Monday.
    She works on both R and S before T.
    If Q is before S, then S is on Saturday.

8. A newspaper editor is paring down the articles to be published in the first seven pages of next week's paper. Currently, F, G, H, J, K, and L are all set to be included. However, one or two articles must be cut to make space. The articles are selected according to the following rules:

    F is one of two articles that takes up two pages, and every other article takes up exactly one page.
    If G is selected, it will be on page 1.
    H is selected.
    If K is not selected, then neither is L.

9. Eight residents—Quintana, Reuben, Stella, Tara, Vince, Willy, Xavier, and Zach—all live in a high-rise apartment building, each on a separate floor. Their apartments are arranged according to the following constraints:

    Reuben lives on a higher floor than Willy.
    Tara lives two floors below Xavier.
    Willy lives at least two floors above Zach.
    Vince and Quintana live on consecutive floors.

10. A food truck menu consists of three items—a sandwich, a burger, and a wrap. Eight customers visit the food truck and order one item each, according to the following conditions:

    The first order is not a sandwich.
    The third customer places the same order as the fifth customer.
    More customers order wraps than order burgers.
    A sandwich is ordered before the first burger is ordered.

Answers follow on the next page.

Answers

1. Relative Ordering, Either/Or Rule (Consider framing)

2. 3D Ordering (Draw a 3D Number Line)

3. Circular Ordering (Draw a circle diagram)

4. Basic Ordering, Mismatch: Too Many Elements (Double up slots, consider Numerical Distributions)

5. Basic Ordering, Mismatch: Too Many Elements (Out group, look for Limited Group Space inferences)

6. Basic Ordering, Subgroups (Draw a 3D Number Line or use subscripts)

7. Basic Ordering, Mismatch: Too Few Elements (Empty slots, consider framing options for empty slots)

8. Basic Ordering, Mismatch: Too Few Elements (Out group, look for Limited Group Space inferences)

9. Basic Ordering, Vertical (Draw a vertical Number Line)

10. Basic Ordering, Mismatch: Too Few Elements (Elements must repeat, consider Numerical Distributions)

Drill 132: Rude Rules, Ordering Edition

Instructions: The bad boys of the LG section are back! Diagram each of the following tough ordering rules in the space provided. Some might include information that doesn't diagram neatly. When this is the case, use a shorthand you understand. If a rule is conditional or biconditional, contrapose it.

1. Neither the tempeh nor the bisque is sampled before the waffle.

2. J ranks higher than H or higher than K, but not both. (no ties)

3. P is delivered either immediately before R or immediately after T, but not both.

4. Q is inspected either after T or after U, but not both. (no ties)

5. H arrives to the party before G or after I, but not both. (no ties)

6. Project L is completed before Project M or before Project O, but not both. (no ties)

7. T is lower in cost than U or higher in cost than S, but not both. (no ties)

8. V is more expensive than W or less expensive than Z, but not both. (no ties)

9. There are exactly three movies that are shown before X but after Y.

10. *Zombies: The Musical* is shown after *Yellow Dog Returns* or before *Ugh, More Zombies*, but not both. (no ties)

11. T is scheduled before S or before U, but not both. (no ties)

12. H appears in the magazine before I or before M, but not both. (no ties)

13. L is inspected later in the week than Q or earlier in the week than R, but not both. (no ties)

14. G is older than M or younger than O, but not both. (no ties)

15. If T is delivered before Y, then Z is delivered after Q.

16. N gets out of the car after P or after R, but not both. (no ties)

17. If X is delivered first, then V is delivered after R.

18. If J is delivered second, then G is delivered third; otherwise, G is delivered after J.

19. S is not delivered on a day after V is delivered.

20. Exactly three courses are served after the quail eggs but before the tart.

21. Exactly three cars finish the race between V and P.

22. R places higher than S or lower than V, but not both. (no ties)

23. Q does not arrive on any day before T arrives.

24. G is delivered after I or after L, but not both. (no ties)

25. If Mary is third, then Lionel precedes Niles by exactly two slots.

26. Z arrives either before T or before V, but not both. (no ties)

27. Q finished the tournament ranked exactly two spots higher than P.

28. U is more expensive than T or less expensive than V, but not both. (no ties)

7

29. U is less expensive than V or more expensive than T, but not both. (no ties)

30. Ilan is ranked third unless Pavel ranks higher than Shanna.

31. Neither the Donatello nor the Michelangelo can be auctioned before the Raphael.

32. Genevieve and Lance perform in slots separated by at least two other performers.

33. R arrives either before S or before T, but not both. (no ties)

34. If K is delivered third, then J is delivered before both K and L.

35. There are three days between when Marcy drives and when Quinlan drives.

36. Every math lesson is immediately preceded by a violin lesson.

37. Neither the kayak nor the canoe is more expensive to rent than the yacht.

38. The shanty is sung immediately after neither the dirge nor the aria.

39. *Heights Scare Me* is scheduled to be aired before *The Vultures* or after *Crazy Person*, but not both. (no ties)

40. W is either immediately before X or immediately after Y, but not both.

41. Unless Yuki is fourth, Zola is fifth.

42. Exactly two bands will perform before Killer Vegan Food and after Pandapocalypse.

43. Unless P is delivered before Q, Q is delivered immediately before T.

44. If orange is the first color in the friendship bracelet, then red is the third color; otherwise, red isn't one of the first three colors used.

45. G ranks at least two spots higher than H.

46. Sally takes out the trash exactly three days after Terence does.

47. If *Oily* is scheduled before *The Queen and You*, then *East Side Tale* is scheduled after *Pomade*; otherwise, *East Side Tale* is scheduled second.

48. If Q is placed fourth, then either Q is placed earlier than X or later than Y, but not both. (no ties)

49. If Chinchilla Rat performs before Spinal Spigot, then Spinal Spigot performs second; otherwise, both of those bands perform after Untamed Stallyns.

50. W is earlier in the schedule than Z or later in the schedule than Y, but not both. (no ties)

Answers

1. Neither the tempeh nor the bisque is sampled before the waffle.

   ┌─┐
   │T│ or W — T
   │W│
   └─┘

   ┌─┐
   │B│ or W — B
   │W│
   └─┘

2. J ranks higher than H or higher than K, but not both. (no ties)

   H – J – K   or   K – J – H

3. P is delivered either immediately before R or immediately after T, but not both.

   ┌──────┐   ┌──────┐
   │T̶ P R │ or   │ T P̶ R̶ │
   └──────┘   └──────┘

4. Q is inspected either after T or after U, but not both. (no ties)

   T – Q – U   or   U – Q – T

5. H arrives to the party before G or after I, but not both. (no ties)

   H⟨ᴳ or ᴳ⟩H
    ᴵ   ᴵ

6. Project L is completed before Project M or before Project O, but not both. (no ties)

   M – L – O   or   O – L – M

7. T is lower in cost than U or higher in cost than S, but not both. (no ties)

   T⟨ᵁ or ᵁ⟩T
    ₛ   ₛ

8. V is more expensive than W or less expensive than Z, but not both. (no ties)

   V⟨ᵂ or ᵂ⟩V
    ᶻ   ᶻ

9. There are exactly three movies that are shown before X but after Y.

   ┌──────────┐
   │Y ___ X│
   └──────────┘

10. *Zombies: The Musical* is shown after *Yellow Dog Returns* or before *Ugh, More Zombies*, but not both. (no ties)

    Z⟨ʸ or ʸ⟩Z
     ᵁ   ᵁ

11. T is scheduled before S or before U, but not both. (no ties)

    S – T – U   or   U – T – S

12. H appears in the magazine before I or before M, but not both. (no ties)

    I – H – M   or   M – H – I

13. L is inspected later in the week than Q or earlier in the week than R, but not both. (no ties)

    L⟨ᵠ or ᵠ⟩L
     ᴿ   ᴿ

14. G is older than M or younger than O, but not both. (no ties)

    G⟨ᴹ or ᴹ⟩G
     ᴼ   ᴼ

15. If T is delivered before Y, then Z is delivered after Q.

    T – Y → Q – Z

    Q̶ ̶Z̶ → T̶ ̶Y̶

16. N gets out of the car after P or after R, but not both. (no ties)

$$P - N - R \quad \text{or} \quad R - N - P$$

17. If X is delivered first, then V is delivered after R.

$$X_1 \rightarrow R - V$$
$$\cancel{R\!-\!V} \rightarrow \cancel{X_1}$$

18. If J is delivered second, then G is delivered third; otherwise, G is delivered after J.

$$J_2 \rightarrow G_3$$
$$\cancel{G_3} \rightarrow \cancel{J_2}$$
$$\cancel{J_2} \rightarrow J - G$$
$$J\cancel{/}G \rightarrow J_2$$

Note: If you noticed that these conditionals chain together, great! When faced with a single rule that creates multiple conditionals, it's wise to diagram them singly first and then see if they chain up. There's more than one way to connect these, depending on whether you start or end with a contrapositive. You may not want to notate them all, because that can get long and messy, but it's good to pause and notice that there are chains so you can refer to them on questions as necessary.

19. S is not delivered on a day after V is delivered.

$$\boxed{\begin{array}{c} V \\ S \end{array}} \quad \text{or} \quad S - V$$

20. Exactly three courses are served after the quail eggs but before the tart.

$$\boxed{Q\, \_\,\_\,\_\,\_\, T}$$

21. Exactly three cars finish the race between V and P.

$$\boxed{V\,\_\,\_\,\_\, P} \quad \text{or} \quad \boxed{P\,\_\,\_\,\_\, V}$$

22. R places higher than S or lower than V, but not both. (no ties)

$$R \overset{S}{\underset{V}{<}} \quad \text{or} \quad \overset{S}{\underset{V}{>}} R$$

23. Q does not arrive on any day before T arrives.

$$\boxed{\begin{array}{c} T \\ Q \end{array}} \quad \text{or} \quad T - Q$$

24. G is delivered after I or after L, but not both. (no ties)

$$I - G - L \quad \text{or} \quad L - G - I$$

25. If Mary is third, then Lionel precedes Niles by exactly two slots.

$$M_3 \rightarrow \boxed{L\,\_\, N}$$
$$\boxed{L\,\cancel{\_}\, N} \rightarrow \cancel{M_3}$$

26. Z arrives either before T or before V, but not both. (no ties)

$$T - Z - V \quad \text{or} \quad V - Z - T$$

27. Q finished the tournament ranked exactly two spots higher than P.

$$\boxed{Q\,\_\, P}$$

28. U is more expensive than T or less expensive than V, but not both. (no ties)

$$U \overset{T}{\underset{V}{<}} \quad \text{or} \quad \overset{T}{\underset{V}{>}} U$$

29. U is less expensive than V or more expensive than T, but not both. (no ties)

$$U \overset{T}{\underset{V}{<}} \quad or \quad T \overset{}{\underset{V}{>}} U$$

30. Ilan is ranked third unless Pavel ranks higher than Shanna.

$$\boxed{\begin{array}{c}P\\S\end{array}} \; or \; S\text{-}P \to I_3$$

$$\cancel{I_3} \to P\text{-}S$$

31. Neither the Donatello nor the Michelangelo can be auctioned before the Raphael.

$$\boxed{\begin{array}{c}D\\R\end{array}} \; or \; R\text{-}D$$

$$\boxed{\begin{array}{c}M\\R\end{array}} \; or \; R\text{-}M$$

32. Genevieve and Lance perform in slots separated by at least two other performers.

$$G - \_\_\_ - L \quad or \quad L - \_\_\_ - G$$

33. R arrives either before S or before T, but not both. (no ties)

$$S - R - T \quad or \quad T - R - S$$

34. If K is delivered third, then J is delivered before both K and L.

$$K_3 \to J \overset{K}{\underset{L}{<}}$$

$$\cancel{J/K} \; or \; \cancel{J/L} \to \cancel{K_3}$$

35. There are three days between when Marcy drives and when Quinlan drives.

$$\boxed{M \_\_\_ Q} \; or \; \boxed{Q \_\_\_ M}$$

36. Every math lesson is immediately preceded by a violin lesson.

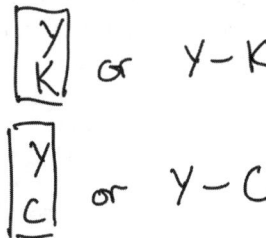

$$M \to \boxed{VM}$$

$$\cancel{\boxed{VM}} \to \cancel{M}$$

37. Neither the kayak nor the canoe is more expensive to rent than the yacht.

$$\boxed{\begin{array}{c}Y\\K\end{array}} \; or \; Y\text{-}K$$

$$\boxed{\begin{array}{c}Y\\C\end{array}} \; or \; Y\text{-}C$$

38. The shanty is sung immediately after neither the dirge nor the aria.

$$\cancel{\boxed{DS}}$$

$$\cancel{\boxed{AS}}$$

39. *Heights Scare Me* is scheduled to be aired before *The Vultures* or after *Crazy Person*, but not both. (no ties)

$$H \overset{V}{\underset{C}{<}} \quad or \quad C \overset{V}{\underset{}{>}} H$$

40. W is either immediately before X or immediately after Y, but not both.

$$\cancel{\boxed{Y}} \boxed{WX} \; or \; \boxed{YW} \cancel{\boxed{X}}$$

41. Unless Yuki is fourth, Zola is fifth.

$$\cancel{Y_4} \to Z_5$$

$$\cancel{Z_5} \to Y_4$$

42. Exactly two bands will perform before Killer Vegan Food and after Pandapocalypse.

$$\boxed{P \_\_\_ K}$$

43. Unless P is delivered before Q, Q is delivered immediately before T.

$$P\text{-}Q \rightarrow \boxed{QT}$$

$$\boxed{\cancel{QT}} \rightarrow P\text{-}Q$$

44. If orange is the first color in the friendship bracelet, then red is the third color; otherwise, red isn't one of the first three colors used.

$$O_1 \rightarrow R_3$$

$$\cancel{X}_3 \rightarrow \cancel{O}_1$$

$$\cancel{O}_1 \rightarrow \cancel{R}_{1\text{-}3}$$

$$R_{1\text{-}3} \rightarrow O_1$$

Note: As in 18, these can be chained together. In this case, that leads to the inference that R cannot ever be in position 1 because any time R is in positions 1-3, O must be in position 1. It also leads to the inference that R cannot ever be in position 2, because that would guarantee O in position 1 which puts R in position 3.

45. G ranks at least two spots higher than H.

$$G - \boxed{\text{\_}} - H$$

46. Sally takes out the trash exactly three days after Terence does.

$$\boxed{T \text{\_ \_ \_} S}$$

47. If *Oily* is scheduled before *The Queen and You*, then *East Side Tale* is scheduled after *Pomade*; otherwise, *East Side Tale* is scheduled second.

$$O\text{-}Q \rightarrow P\text{-}E$$

$$P\cancel{E} \rightarrow O\cancel{Q}$$

$$O\cancel{Q} \rightarrow E_2$$

$$\cancel{E}_2 \rightarrow O\text{-}Q$$

Note: As in 18, these can be chained together.

48. If Q is placed fourth, then either Q is placed earlier than X or later than Y, but not both. (no ties)

$$Q_4 \rightarrow Q{<}^{X}_{Y} \quad \text{or} \quad {}^{X}_{Y}{>}Q$$

$$\begin{matrix} X - Q - Y \\ \text{or} \\ Y - Q - X \end{matrix} \rightarrow \cancel{Q}_4$$

49. If Chinchilla Rat performs before Spinal Spigot, then Spinal Spigot performs second; otherwise, both of those bands perform after Untamed Stallyns.

$$C - S \rightarrow S_2$$

$$\cancel{S}_2 \rightarrow C\cancel{S}$$

$$C\cancel{S} \rightarrow U{<}^{C}_{S}$$

$$U\cancel{C} \text{ or } U\cancel{S} \rightarrow C - S$$

Note: As in 18, these can be chained together.

50. W is earlier in the schedule than Z or later in the schedule than Y, but not both. (no ties)

$$W{<}^{Z}_{Y} \quad \text{or} \quad {}^{Z}_{Y}{>}W$$

Drill 133: Should I Frame or Should I Go? Ordering Edition

Instructions: Building frames is an invaluable strategy for Logic Games. When building frames, you identify a rule that splits the game into two or three possibilities, and then you draw out each of those possibilities as its own diagram.

While a single rule by itself can't tell you that building frames will be a solid strategy for attacking a given game, the decision starts with certain rules that tend to lead to good frames. For each of the following, determine whether you would (Y) or would not (N) consider building frames around that rule, depending, of course, on the information from the other rules.

_____ 1. Either H is ranked higher than L, or lower than K, but not both.

_____ 2. P is first or seventh.

_____ 3. If Regina is the first candidate to be interviewed, Quaid is the last.

_____ 4. M is immediately before or after K.

_____ 5. S will be placed sixth.

_____ 6. Teresa will perform her solo exactly two hours after Isaac.

_____ 7. There are exactly two spots between F and M.

_____ 8. Morgan will bat first or last.

_____ 9. Laila and Ingrid will both read before Raul.

_____ 10. V is later than K, or W is later than K, but not both.

_____ 11. N will not be third.

_____ 12. If J is eighth, O is second.

_____ 13. G is before L.

_____ 14. Forrest and Ulani will both juggle after Nina.

_____ 15. The recital must end with a solo by either Patricia or Renaud.

_____ 16. If Q is last, Y will be first.

_____ 17. There is exactly one painting between the Kandinsky and the Picasso.

_____ 18. I is placed exactly two spots after V.

_____ 19. W is not fourth.

_____ 20. O or H must be second.

_____ 21. M is after L and U.

_____ 22. F is later than K, but before G.

_____ 23. Gabriella will be placed either immediately before or after Polly.

_____ 24. Ollala will not be last.

_____ 25. J is first only if Q is not second.

_____ 26. H is before I and T.

_____ 27. U will be at least one spot after V.

_____ 28. Justine must be seated sixth.

_____ 29. Etta and Rachel must be placed on either side of Veronica.

_____ 30. Either R is immediately after S, or R is immediately after T.

_____ 31. P is third.

_____ 32. L is third if K is second.

_____ 33. M and R must be after J.

_____ 34. Hillary is exactly three spaces after Fei.

_____ 35. Kayle is immediately before or after Rebecca.

_____ 36. J is always first.

_____ 37. If F is not first, then I is first.

_____ 38. L and U must be exactly two spots apart.

_____ 39. K and P are both later than Y.

_____ 40. Henrietta and Daniella cannot be placed after, or at the same time as, Sayid.

_____ 41. Muneeza will play before Joey.

_____ 42. U is exactly one spot before O.

_____ 43. N is exactly two spots after X.

_____ 44. Jean will read last.

_____ 45. The red team and the green team will play after the white team.

_____ 46. If Morales bats sixth, Garrison will bat seventh.

_____ 47. M is fourth only if T is eighth.

_____ 48. V must be exactly three spaces before W.

_____ 49. Either Paul or Nathaniel must sing immediately before Zara.

_____ 50. Owen will not dance seventh.

_____ 51. X and Y are before Z.

_____ 52. K is not seventh.

_____ 53. F and J are exactly two spots apart.

_____ 54. If H is first, then O is second.

_____ 55. Only M or L is last.

_____ 56. K cannot be fourth.

_____ 57. I is immediately before or after P.

_____ 58. T is immediately after N.

_____ 59. O is exactly two spots before F.

_____ 60. Q is fourth.

_____ 61. There are exactly two performances between Linda and Paulson.

_____ 62. M is after U and R.

_____ 63. Either G or R is second.

_____ 64. Neither H nor P is third.

_____ 65. Either J is after R, or J is after V, but not both.

_____ 66. If K is not last, then X is last.

_____ 67. I and S are after R.

_____ 68. Q and W are next to each other.

_____ 69. Z is not last.

_____ 70. H is after O.

Answers

__Y__   1.   **Either H is ranked higher than L, or lower than K, but not both.**

Relative Ordering games don't often frame, but when they do, they frame around Either/Or rules. Diagram each option, then build each into its own tree.

__Y__   2.   **P is first or seventh.**

P1 vs. P7 is a split. If it leads to other definite placements, it's a frameable split.

__N__   3.   If Regina is the first candidate to be interviewed, Quaid is the last.

This doesn't create a split. We know what happens when R is in 1, but we don't know what happens when it isn't. That's why conditional rules are almost never frameable.

__N__   4.   M is immediately before or after K.

On its own, this isn't enough to create a frameable split, since presumably MK or KM could be placed anywhere. However, if there's another reversible chunk that has either K or M, the overlap might be worth trying out.

__N__   5.   S will be placed sixth.

If a rule only provides one piece of information, it doesn't create a split.

__N__   6.   Teresa will perform her solo exactly two hours after Isaac.

No split here. We know T is two spots after I but that's all.

__Y__   7.   **There are exactly two spots between F and M.**

Either it's F _ _ M or M _ _ F. Depending on the rest of your rules and how restricted this chunk is, it could be an opportunity to make frames. Unlike "immediately before or after rules," open chunks like this take up a lot of space, which often restricts their possible placements enough to frame.

__Y__   8.   **Morgan will bat first or last.**

Clear split. If having M first or last influences the placement of other elements, frame away!

__N__   9.   Laila and Ingrid will both read before Raul.

No split here, just L and I before R.

__Y__   10. **Either V is later than K, or W is later than K, but not both.**

Either/or, but not both? Great place to start making frames.

__N__   11. N will not be third.

Not enough information to create a split.

__N__   12. If J is eighth, O is second.

Remember, conditional rules are often poor framing options. The contrapositive allows a lot of different possibilities.

__N__   13. G is before L.

No split, just one piece of information.

__N__   14. Forrest and Ulani will both juggle after Nina.

No split. Whatever happens, F and U are after N.

__Y__   15. **The recital must end with a solo by either Patricia or Renaud.**

Clear split, since only P or R can be last. Whether you make frames depends on whether P and R are in other rules.

__N__   16. If Q is last, Y will be first.

Almost never for conditionals. If Q is not last, we have no idea where Y is.

__N__   17. There is exactly one painting between the Kandinsky and the Picasso.

This creates a three-slot reversible chunk: either K_P or P_K. Unless P and K are central to a bunch of other rules, this is unlikely to create a two- or three-way split.

__N__   18. I is placed exactly two spots after V.

This creates a three-slot chunk, which is probably not big enough to create framing opportunities on its own. But if there are other ordering rules dealing with those elements that further restrict the chunk's placement, then it would be worth exploring.

__N__   19. W is not fourth.

Nope, just a single piece of information.

__Y__   20. **O or H must be second.**

One spot, only two possibilities? Clear split.

__N__   21. M is after L and U.

No split. You get the idea. We'll stop harping on it now.

__N__   22. F is later than K, but before G.

__N__   23. Gabriella will be placed either immediately before or after Polly.

"Immediately before or after" rules tend not to create frames.

__N__   24. Ollala will not be last.

__N__   25. J is first only if Q is not second.

Watch out with conditionals! No split here, since J could be lots of places other than first. OK…we'll stop harping on that, too.

__N__   26. H is before I and T.

N   27. U will be at least one spot after V.

U is definitely going to be after V—the only thing we don't know is exactly how many spots. There are likely too many possibilities for a frameable split.

N   28. Justine must be seated sixth.

Y   **29. Etta and Rachel must be placed on either side of Veronica.**

This is EVR or RVE, and if any of those elements are restricted in their placement and/or overlap in other rules, you probably have some good framing opportunities.

N   30. Either R is immediately after S, or R is immediately after T.

It's worth noting the either/or, but how useful it is will depend on how restricted these elements are. Since this just creates two options for a chunk, SR or TR, it will only be frameable if the placement of the chunks is severely limited.

N   31. P is third.

N   32. L is third if K is second.

N   33. M and R must be after J.

Y   **34. Hillary is exactly three spaces after Fei.**

Since this is a four-slot open chunk, it's going to take up a lot of room on a Number Line. This means it is likely limited enough to frame.

N   35. Kayle is immediately before or after Rebecca.

Immediately before or after.

N   36. J is always first.

Y   **37. If F is not first, then I is first.**

This is a rare exception to the general rule about conditionals and frames, because it creates an either/ or situation. The rule is if no F in spot 1, then I in spot 1—and the contrapositive is if no I in spot 1, then F in spot 1. So either F or I must fill spot 1.

Y   **38. L and U must be exactly two spots apart.**

Big reversible open chunk!

N   39. K and P are both later than Y.

N   40. Henrietta and Daniella cannot be placed after, or at the same time as, Sayid.

If H and D are not after or at the same time, they're both before. No split.

N   41. Muneeza will play before Joey.

N   42. U is exactly one spot before O.

N   43. N is exactly two spots after X.

N   44. Jean will read last.

N   45. The red team and the green team will play after the white team.

N   46. If Morales bats sixth, Garrison will bat seventh.

N   47. M is fourth only if T is eighth.

Y   **48. V must be exactly three spaces before W.**

Big open chunk!

N   49. Either Paul or Nathaniel must sing immediately before Zara.

This might be a useful split, but only if the placement of any of these elements is restricted by other rules.

N   50. Owen will not dance seventh.

N   51. X and Y are before Z.

N   52. K is not seventh.

Y   **53. F and J are exactly two spots apart.**

Big reversible open chunk!

N   54. If H is first, then O is second.

Y   **55. Only M or L is last.**

One spot—two possibilities.

N   56. K cannot be fourth.

N   57. I is immediately before or after P.

Immediately before or after.

N   58. T is immediately after N.

N   59. O is exactly two spots before F.

N   60. Q is fourth.

Y   **61. There are exactly two performances between Linda and Paulson.**

Big open chunk!

N   62. M is after U and R.

Y   **63. Either G or R is second.**

One spot—two possibilities.

N   64. Neither H nor P is third.

Y   **65. Either J is after R, or J is after V, but not both.**

Either/or, but not both!

Y   **66. If K is not last, then X is last.**

Another exception to the rule about conditionals and frames, again because it creates an either/or situation: either K not last and X is, or (the contrapositive) X is not last and K is.

N   67. I and S are after R.

N   68. Q and W are next to each other.

Doesn't create a split: just a small chunk.

N   69. Z is not last.

N   70. H is after O.

 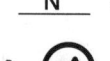

Drill 134: Numerical Distribution, Mismatch Edition

Instructions: When the number of slots in an ordering game isn't the same as the number of elements, you're looking at a Mismatch twist. These twists can play out four different ways, but this drill is just about the games with too many slots in which all slots must be filled, meaning elements will have to repeat. When you have repeating elements, you can use Numerical Distributions to figure out how often elements will need to repeat to fill the slots.

To execute this strategy, consider the elements to be digits that you need to add together to equal the number of slots. So, for example, if you had six elements and nine slots, you need to add six digits together to reach nine. If you have some concrete information, such as a relationship between elements (e.g., P has to go twice as often as R) or a maximum number of times any element can repeat (e.g., no dancer performs more than three solos), that's the logical starting place for any distribution. If you're given a relationship, think about all the ways it can pan out (it's usually just 2!), then distribute the rest of the numbers accordingly. If you're given a maximum, start by assigning the maximum to as many elements as you can without violating the minimum requirement (usually 1), and go from there.

In the absence of a relationship or a maximum, start by making each digit 1, then dump the remaining number of slots onto the last element:

$$1 + 1 + 1 + 1 + 1 + 4 = 9$$

Then, take one away from the element with the most and give it to the next element in line:

$$1 + 1 + 1 + 1 + 2 + 3 = 9$$

Continue in this way until the numbers are as close to even as you can get them:

$$1 + 1 + 1 + 2 + 2 + 2 = 9$$

That means you have three possible distributions of the elements:

One element goes four times and the rest go once (4-1-1-1-1-1).

One element goes three times, another goes twice, and the rest go once (3-2-1-1-1-1).

Three elements go twice and three elements go once (2-2-2-1-1-1).

One last thing: once you figure out the general distributions, you can sometimes make bonus inferences. Consider, for instance, in the game above, if your six elements were P, Q, R, S, T, and V, and you had a rule that said V has to be used more times than R. What can you infer? Well, V can't ever be used only once. That means in the first distribution, you can infer that V is the element that goes four times; in the second, V either goes thrice or twice; and in the third, V goes twice and R goes once.

Now, it's your turn! Map out the distributions and look for any bonus inferences.

1. Chapters from each of five books on five subjects—learning science, mindfulness, nepotism, oligarchy, and patriarchy—are to be assigned over the course of an eight-week class. Each week will cover a chapter from exactly one of the five books, and no book will be assigned in more than three weeks. The following conditions apply:

    A chapter from the book on mindfulness must be assigned in any week preceding a week in which a chapter from nepotism or patriarchy is assigned.

2. Quinn, Ryan, Shani, and Ty are each going to present at a conference. The conference runs from Monday through Friday, and there is one presentation each morning and one presentation each afternoon. The presenters are scheduled according to the following rules:

    Quinn presents exactly one time more than Ryan.

    No one presents more than Quinn.

    Ty presents on any day that Shani presents.

3. A circus is scheduling six performances, choosing from the following acts: partner acrobatics, Russian bar, silk, trapeze, and unicycle. The performances are scheduled according to the following rules:

    The same act opens and closes the show.

    No act is scheduled to perform twice in a row.

    If silk is scheduled, then trapeze is not.

4. John, Kai, and Lola each purchase tickets to a show. The seats are in a row, with seats labeled 101 through 109. The tickets are purchased according to the following rules:

    Each person purchases at least two tickets.

    No one purchases three tickets in a row.

5. Four horse owners—Frank, Gary, Helen, and Ian—are entering their horses into a derby. The horses are assigned to the eight lanes in accordance with the following rules:

    Each owner enters at least one horse into the derby.

    Frank enters more horses than Ian.

    Only Ian can enter horses in consecutive lanes.

7

Answers and explanations follow on the next page.

Answers

Note: The Bonus Inferences only apply to the distribution they share a line with.

1. The Books Game

3-2-1-1-1	Bonus Inferences: M can't be a 1 and N and P can't be the 3.
2-2-2-1-1	Bonus Inferences: N and P must be 1's and M must be a 2.

This game tells us the maximum number of times an element can repeat: three. We should begin our distribution there because it's the most concrete information we have. If one book goes three times and every other book goes one time, we're still one short. That means we have to have two repeaters: one who goes three times and one who goes twice: 3-2-1-1-1. Because M has to precede all N's and all P's, it must go at least twice, so it can't be a 1. And if N or P went three times, M would have to as well. This isn't possible, so neither N nor P can be the three-peat. The other distribution is 2-2-2-1-1. In this arrangement, M can only go two times, which means that it precedes N once and P once and that's it. That means N and P each go only once in this distribution.

2. The Conference Game

4-3-2-1	Bonus Inferences: Q goes 4 times, R goes 3 times, T goes twice, and S goes once.
3-3-2-2	Bonus Inferences: Q and T go 3 times, and R and S go twice.

This game has ten slots (five days, two presentations per day) and four elements. The first two rules combine to give us a piece of numerical info that should be our jumping-off point because it is so limiting: Quinn has the most repeats and Ryan has one less. Start by gaming out those options. 6 and 5 won't work, because that's more slots that we have. 5 and 4 won't work because that only leaves one more slot and there are two more elements that need to go. 4 and 3 would work; that would leave three more slots for the two other elements. So, 4-3-2-1 is our first distribution. 3 and 2 would also work. That would leave five slots for the other two elements, so 3-3-2-2 is our second distribution. 2 and 1 would not work, because that would leave seven slots to distribute over the other two elements, meaning they would both have more slots than Q, which isn't

allowed. Now, for bonus inferences: in the 4-3-2-1 distribution, Q and R are 4 and 3, respectively. That leaves S and T. Since T goes every time S goes, S can't go more frequently than T, meaning that T must go twice and S once. In the 3-3-2-2 distribution, Q goes three times and R goes twice. And again, since S can't go more often than T, T must go three times and S must go twice.

3. The Circus Game

3-1-1-1	Bonus Inferences: partner acrobatics, Russian bar, and unicycle all perform.
2-2-1-1	Bonus Inferences: partner acrobatics, Russian bar, and unicycle all perform.
3-2-1	
2-2-2	

Five elements and six slots is a pretty classic mismatch, and it usually pans out with one repeater. But the third rule tells us that S and T can't both go, so at least one of them must be excluded. That means we actually have a maximum of four elements to distribute over the six slots. The easiest way to start this distribution is to let everyone go once, then dump the remaining two slots onto one element: 1-1-1-3. Then, take one away from the element with the most and give it to the next element in line: 1-1-2-2. If we kept on that way, we would end up with the same numbers in a different order, so we're done with that set.

Now it's time to see what happens if we only have three elements. If we follow the same process, letting everyone go once and then dumping the remaining slots on one element, we get 1-1-4. But there's no way for an element to go four times without going twice in a row, so that one's out. Then we take one from the most and give it to the next element in line: 3-2-1. Once more, and we get 2-2-2. The numbers are even, so we're done with that set.

What if only two elements go? We already know that we can't have anyone go four times, so that leaves 3-3. But if we alternated two elements three times each, the first and last act wouldn't be the same, so that's impossible, too.

As far as bonus inferences go, it's pretty slim pickings. Because we can't have both S and T, any distribution that uses four elements must exclude one of those two, meaning that all the other elements—P, R, and U—must go.

4. The Tickets Game

5-2-2

4-3-2

3-3-3

Everyone purchases at least two tickets, so start with that. If we give the minimum to everyone, then dump the rest onto one element, we get 2-2-5. Then we take one from the person with the most and give it to the person with the least until the numbers are as even as they're going to get, giving us 4-3-2 and 3-3-3. No bonus inferences for this one.

5. The Derby Game

4-2-1-1	Bonus Inferences: Frank – 4 or 2, Ian – 2 or 1
3-3-1-1	Bonus Inferences: Frank – 3, Ian – 1
3-2-2-1	Bonus Inferences: Frank – 3 or 2, Ian – 2 or 1

We have four elements that each have to go at least once. If we give each the minimum, then dump the rest onto one element, we get 1-1-1-5. But if one element went five times, it would have to go consecutively at least once. Only I is allowed to do that, but F has to go more often than I. That means this one doesn't work. Next we try 4-2-1-1. This doesn't require an element to go twice in a row, and there are two different ways F can be more than I, so it looks good. If we take one away from the element with the most and give it to the next one, we get 3-3-1-1, which also looks good, then 3-2-2-1, which works as well. 2-2-2-2 is out, since F has to go more than I. Bonus inferences: In the 4-2-1-1, F has to be 4 or 2 and I has to be 1 or 2. Similarly, in the 3-2-2-1, F has to be 3 or 2 and I has to be 2 or 1. In the 3-3-1-1, F has to be 3 and I has to be 1.

7

Drill 135: Got a Min, Max?

Instructions: Minimum and Maximum questions can be found across virtually all game types but they're most prevalent in Relative Ordering games. Check out the completed Relative Ordering Tree diagrams below and answer each of the Minimum or Maximum questions in the space provided. Assume that the diagrams include all of the elements for each game.

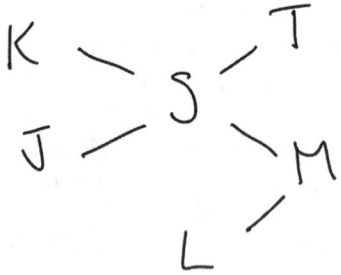

_____ 1. What is the minimum number of elements that must follow S?

_____ 2. What is the maximum number of elements between K and L?

_____ 3. What is the minimum number of elements between T and J?

_____ 4. What is the maximum number of elements between T and J?

_____ 5. What is the minimum number of elements that must precede L?

_____ 6. What is the minimum number of elements that must follow K?

_____ 7. What is the maximum number of elements that could follow K?

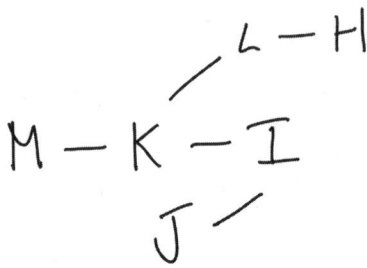

_____ 8. What is the minimum number of elements that must follow J?

_____ 9. What is the minimum number of elements that must follow M?

_____ 10. What is the minimum number of elements between J and H?

_____ 11. What is the maximum number of elements between K and H?

_____ 12. What is the minimum number of elements between M and J?

_____ 13. What is the maximum number of elements between M and J?

_____ 14. What is the maximum number of elements that could follow I?

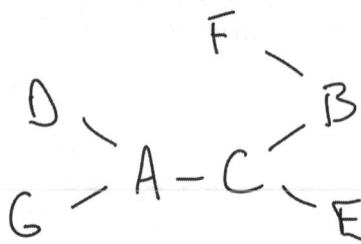

_____ 15. What is the minimum number of elements that must follow A?

_____ 16. What is the maximum number of elements that could follow A?

_____ 17. What is the minimum number of elements between D and E?

_____ 18. What is the maximum number of elements between A and B?

_____ 19. What is the minimum number of elements between D and F?

_____ 20. What is the maximum number of elements between F and E?

_____ 21. What is the minimum number of elements between G and E?

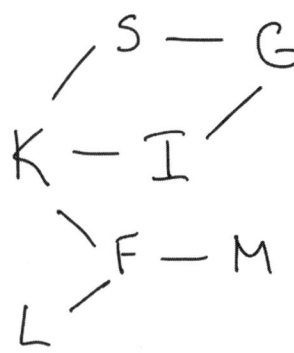

_____ 22. What is the minimum number of elements that follow Q?

_____ 23. What is the minimum number of elements that follow R?

_____ 24. What is the maximum number of elements that follow N?

_____ 25. What is the minimum number of elements that precede P?

_____ 26. What is the maximum number of elements between R and S?

_____ 27. What is the minimum number of elements between T and O?

_____ 28. What is the maximum number of elements between T and O?

_____ 29. What is the minimum number of elements that precede M?

_____ 30. What is the minimum number of elements that follow K?

_____ 31. What is the minimum number of elements between F and G?

_____ 32. What is the maximum number of elements between M and S?

_____ 33. What is the minimum number of elements between L and G?

_____ 34. What is the maximum number of elements between K and M?

_____ 35. What is the maximum number of elements that could follow I?

7

Answers

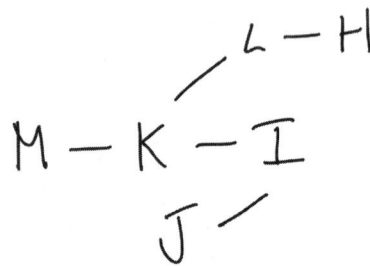

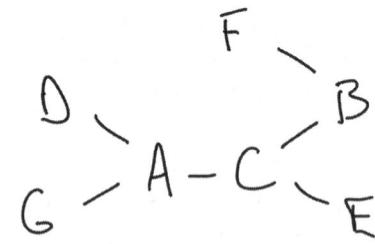

_2_ 1. T and M must follow. L could, but doesn't have to.

_3_ 2. To get these two as far apart as possible, we'd make K first and L second to last.

_1_ 3. S must come between them.

_4_ 4. Getting these two as far apart as possible means making J first and T last.

_0_ 5. Even though L appears toward the right in our diagram, there's no element connected before it, meaning it could go first.

_3_ 6. S must follow K, and M and T both must follow S.

_5_ 7. K could be first, since no element is connected before it. All five other elements could follow K.

_1_ 8. I must follow J, but no elements must follow I.

_4_ 9. K must follow M, I and L must follow K, and H must follow L.

_0_ 10. If I is last, J and H can be right next to each other.

_3_ 11. Getting K and H as far apart as possible means placing K second and H last.

_0_ 12. M and J can be as early as we like, so we can make one first and the other second.

_3_ 13. Getting M and J as far apart as possible means placing M first and J second to last.

_2_ 14. L and H are the only elements that do not have to precede I.

_3_ 15. C must follow A, and B and E must follow C.

_4_ 16. Putting A as early as possible means A is third, leaving four elements to follow A.

_2_ 17. E is connected to D through A and C.

_3_ 18. Getting A and B as far apart as possible means putting A third and B last.

_0_ 19. Nothing has to precede F or D, so they could be first and second, in either order.

_5_ 20. Getting F and E as far apart as possible means putting F first and E last.

_2_ 21. G is connected to E through A and C.

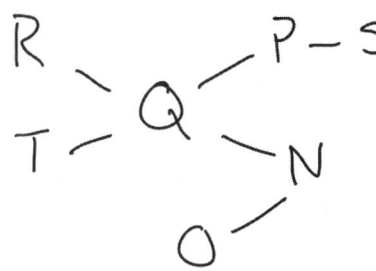

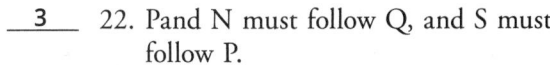

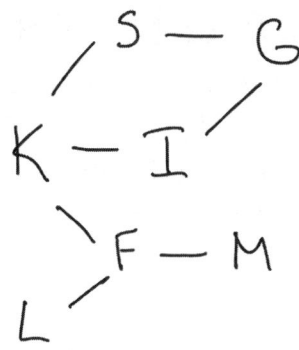

___3___ 22. P and N must follow Q, and S must follow P.

___4___ 23. Q must follow R, P and N must follow Q, and S must follow P.

___2___ 24. P and S are the only elements that do not have to precede N.

___3___ 25. Q must precede P, and R and T must precede Q.

___5___ 26. Getting R and S as far apart as possible means putting R first and S last.

___0___ 27. Nothing has to precede T or O, so they could be first and second, in either order.

___4___ 28. Getting T and O as far apart as possible means putting T first and O second to last.

___3___ 29. F comes before M, and K and L come before F.

___5___ 30. S, I, and F follow K, M follows F, and G follows S and I.

___0___ 31. F only has to be followed by M, so it can go late in the order, immediately preceding or following G.

___4___ 32. Getting M and S as far apart as possible means putting S second and M last.

___0___ 33. L and G could be fourth and fifth, in either order.

___5___ 34. Getting K and M as far apart as possible means putting K first and M last.

___5___ 35. Only K must come before I, so I could be second.

7

Drill 136: Diagramming 301, Round 2

Instructions: Need more practice with the hardest conditional rules? You've come to the right place! Diagram and contrapose each of the following complex conditional rules in the space provided.

1. Steak will be on the menu if the mushroom or chicken dish is included.

2. The menu will never include both pie and tarts.

3. A tapestry will not have gold or silver thread without purple.

4. Any tapestry that contains navy and gold will also contain white.

5. The tapestry cannot contain both maroon and purple thread.

6. The romance film will not be shown without the noir film being shown.

7. The film festival will never show both the silent and the noir films.

8. The film festival will show either the art film or the foreign film.

9. They will not visit the reptile house unless they also visit the elephants and the tigers.

10. They will visit the tiger enclosure if, and only if, they also visit the lion exhibit.

11. They will not see lions unless they also see giraffes and rhinoceroses.

12. They won't visit both the penguin exhibit and the elephant enclosure.

13. He will buy a wallet unless he buys shoes or a belt.

14. She will buy a scarf if she buys a wallet or purse.

15. He will never buy both a cardigan and a jacket.

16. He will buy a tie if, and only if, he buys a shirt as well.

17. Exactly one painting will be selected from the "Picasso and Dali" exhibit.

18. The Rembrandt and the Picasso will not both be displayed unless the Gleizes is displayed.

19. He will not buy a shirt and tie unless he buys a jacket.

20. He will not purchase both a belt and suspenders.

21. If Reese or Tiana are in the group, then Jeremy is not.

22. Kate is in the group unless Lexie and Mary are.

23. Jason will not be in the group unless Kori or Roy is with him.

24. She will buy socks or pantyhose if she buys loafers.

25. She will not go to both the pool and the beach this weekend.

26. She will visit the farm if, but only if, she does not go to the mall.

27. A playlist containing an instrumental piece will also include either a pop or country song.

28. The playlist will not contain both a country song and a golden oldie.

29. She will not go rock climbing unless she goes to the beach or the museum.

30. If the Whistler painting is displayed, either the Vermeer or Caravaggio painting will be as well.

Answers

1. Steak will be on the menu if the mushroom or chicken dish is included.

   M or C → S ; ~S → ~M and ~C

2. The menu will never include both pie and tarts.

   P → ~T ; T → ~P

3. A tapestry will not have gold or silver thread without purple.

   G or S → P ; ~P → ~G and ~S

4. Any tapestry that contains navy and gold will also contain white.

   N and G → W ; ~W → ~N or ~G

5. The tapestry cannot contain both maroon and purple thread.

   M → ~W ; P → ~M

6. The romance film will not be shown without the noir film being shown.

   R → N ; ~N → ~R

7. The film festival will never show both the silent and the noir films.

   S → ~N ; N → ~S

8. The film festival will show either the art film or the foreign film.

   ~A → F ; ~F → A

9. They will not visit the reptile house unless they also visit the elephants and the tigers.

   R → E and T ; ~E or ~T → ~R

10. They will visit the tiger enclosure if, and only if, they also visit the lion exhibit.

    T ↔ L ; ~L ↔ ~T

11. They will not see lions unless they also see giraffes and rhinoceroses.

    L → G and R ; ~G or ~R → ~L

12. They won't visit both the penguin exhibit and the elephant enclosure.

    P → ~E ; E → ~P

13. He will buy a wallet unless he buys shoes or a belt.

    ~W → S or B ; ~S and ~B → W

14. She will buy a scarf if she buys a wallet or purse.

    W or P → S ; ~S → ~W and ~P

7

15. He will never buy both a cardigan and a jacket.

    C → ~J ; J → ~C

16. He will buy a tie if, and only if, he buys a shirt as well.

    T ↔ S ; ~S ↔ ~T

17. Exactly one painting will be selected from the "Picasso and Dali" exhibit.

    D ↔ ~P ; P ↔ ~D

18. The Rembrandt and the Picasso will not both be displayed unless the Gleizes is displayed.

    R and P → G ; ~G → ~R or ~P

19. He will not buy a shirt and tie unless he buys a jacket.

    S and T → J ; ~J → ~S or ~T

20. He will not purchase both a belt and suspenders.

    B → ~S ; S → ~B

21. If Reese or Tiana are in the group, then Jeremy is not.

    R or T → ~J ; J → ~R and ~T

22. Kate is in the group unless Lexie and Mary are.

    ~K → L and M ; ~L or ~M → K

23. Jason will not be in the group unless Kori or Roy is with him.

    J → K or R ; ~K and ~R → ~J

24. She will buy socks or pantyhose if she buys loafers.

    L → S or P ; ~S and ~P → ~L

25. She will not go to both the pool and the beach this weekend.

    P → ~B ; B → ~P

26. She will visit the farm if, but only if, she does not go to the mall.

    F ↔ ~M ; M ↔ ~F

27. A playlist containing an instrumental piece will also include either a pop or country song.

    I → P or C ; ~P and ~C → ~I

28. The playlist will not contain both a country song and a golden oldie.

    C → ~G ; G → ~C

29. She will not go rock climbing unless she goes to the beach or the museum.

    R → B or M ; ~B and ~M → ~R

30. If the Whistler painting is displayed, either the Vermeer or Caravaggio painting will be as well.

    W → V or C ; ~V and ~C → ~W

In/Out Games

While In/Out games make up only a small percentage of the games on modern LSATs, anyone who has attempted one knows they are tough enough to merit their own section of the book! We characterize a game as being an In/Out game if it meets two criteria: 1) there are exactly 2 groups, and 2) all, or almost all, of the rules are conditional. Notice that one common criteria for In/Out games is conspicuously absent: The game doesn't actually have to be about an In group vs. an Out group. We find that the techniques we use to tackle In/Out games are every bit as effective for games in which you're tasked with splitting entities into two groups, regardless of whether those two groups are In vs. Out or Team 1 vs. Team 2.

In this section, you will learn to:

Split Compound Conditional Rules

Generate Placeholder Inferences

Navigate Questions about Element Pairs

7

Drill 137: Split Ends

Instructions: Complex conditionals—conditional statements that include *and* or *or*—are frequently used to increase the difficulty of a Logic Game, especially In/Out games. Some of them can be split into two individual conditionals; others can't. When you can split them, you should, because then they can be built into the unified conditional diagram we call the Logic Chain. For each of the following conditional statements, fill in Y if you can split it into two simple conditionals and N if you can't.

_____ 1. Jack will go to the party only if Mary and Louise also go.

_____ 2. If either Kate or Aisha is selected, then Vernon is not.

_____ 3. Annika will be fired if Charlene and Sefu are fired.

_____ 4. Anyone who is trained as both a teacher and a physicist is qualified to teach Physics 100.

_____ 5. The car will not turn on unless the battery is charged and the brake pedal is depressed.

_____ 6. If Hernandez wins the election, he will appoint either Merton or Santos as his vice president.

_____ 7. Neither Zack nor Louise is qualified to perform the operation.

_____ 8. All applicants must provide a recommendation letter from either a former employer or a former colleague.

_____ 9. Only surgeons and internists attended the conference.

_____ 10. Quentin performs third only if Sharon or Verner performs fourth.

_____ 11. No reporter that is assigned both a sports story and a lifestyle story will be assigned an international story.

_____ 12. Grecia's painting cannot be displayed if either Ray's or Hassan's painting is displayed.

_____ 13. Harris and May coach volleyball whenever Olga coaches swimming.

_____ 14. As long as Sheila works on Thursday or Friday, she will make enough money to pay her rent for October.

_____ 15. No one from Denver and no one from Dallas served on the committee.

_____ 16. Each of the apprentices will train in blacksmithing or woodworking.

_____ 17. Every concert featuring both Una and Jane on guitar will feature Stephany on piano.

_____ 18. Madeleine will not get in the canoe without a life jacket and a paddle.

_____ 19. Anyone who eats a kebab or a pita for lunch will not eat a taco.

_____ 20. A mixture of chemicals X and Z must never be mixed with chemical W.

_____ 21. Membership in Club Zeta requires both an annual fee and attendance at monthly meetings.

_____ 22. When pelicans are present in the bird sanctuary, neither spoonbills nor egrets are.

_____ 23. Matsuba will attend the meeting if Lihua or Kalu attend.

_____ 24. The animal shelter has greyhounds only when it also has schnauzers or huskies.

_____ 25. All archaeologists and all paleontologists are interested in ancient history.

_____ 26. Santiago always plays chess when both Lulu and Xavier play checkers.

_____ 27. As long as the houseplant receives sunlight and water, it will thrive.

_____ 28. The only types of trees in Groveland Forest are cedars and pines.

_____ 29. Javier does not go to the movies without buying both popcorn and candy.

_____ 30. Every large civilization requires both irrigation and agriculture.

_____ 31. Unless either Jenkins or Powell demands it, the chairperson will not appoint Pankaj as treasurer.

_____ 32. Raleigh cannot be selected if both Shae and Rhonda are selected.

_____ 33. Cookbook J cannot be published unless cookbook Q or cookbook R is published.

_____ 34. Hakeem always complains whenever Shoshanna is late or Zelda is absent.

_____ 35. No one who has both a master's degree and a doctorate is undereducated.

_____ 36. Only animals that are both docile and easy to care for make good pets for children.

_____ 37. Unless both Penhurst and Raynes vote against the bill, it will pass.

_____ 38. Each member of Club Savannah is either a doctor or a lawyer.

_____ 39. Neither Kevin nor Phillips will be selected unless Grant is selected.

_____ 40. The only person both available and qualified for the position is Jermain.

_____ 41. If Kieron or Sefina leads the finance subcommittee, Loto will lead the infrastructure subcommittee.

_____ 42. Any song that features both the guitar and the keyboard will feature the xylophone.

_____ 43. Ziegfeld will speak in the Garnet room whenever Yancey speaks in either the Primrose Room or the Garnet Room.

_____ 44. The Jacksons will remodel their kitchen only if they remodel neither their bathroom nor their bedroom.

_____ 45. Either roses or peonies must be included in any bouquet that includes tulips.

_____ 46. Unless the display includes oil paintings, it will include either watercolors or pastels.

_____ 47. The weaver will not use red thread unless she also uses purple thread and white thread.

_____ 48. Mayburn will train as a journalist if Watkins or Mikal trains as a photographer.

_____ 49. Both the GraphicX corporation and the FinanceAce corporation require a background check for all new employees.

_____ 50. The landscaper never plants walnuts in a park where she plants both oaks and plums.

Answers follow on the next page.

Answers

1.	Y	14.	Y	27.	N	40.	N
2.	Y	15.	Y	28.	N	41.	Y
3.	N	16.	N	29.	Y	42.	N
4.	N	17.	N	30.	Y	43.	Y
5.	Y	18.	Y	31.	N	44.	Y
6.	N	19.	Y	32.	N	45.	N
7.	Y	20.	N	33.	N	46.	N
8.	N	21.	Y	34.	Y	47.	Y
9.	N	22.	Y	35.	N	48.	Y
10.	N	23.	Y	36.	Y	49.	Y
11.	N	24.	N	37.	Y	50.	N
12.	Y	25.	Y	38.	N		
13.	Y	26.	N	39.	Y		

7

Drill 138: Hold My Place

Instructions: The first step for tackling an In/Out game is to create the Logic Chain diagram. Because the Logic Chain gives you so much information, it's tempting to stop there. But there are often inferences to be found about pairs of elements, at least one of which must be in, at least one of which must be out, or both. We call these Placeholder Inferences, and we represent them by creating a space in the appropriate column(s) of a T-chart and putting an Either/Or option in the chart to hold that place.

For example, if we're told that Fred and Garret cannot both be out, we'd draw a T-chart, put a slot in the In column, and put F/G in the slot. If they can't both be out, at least one of them has to be in. If, instead, we were told that Fred and Garret can't both be in, we'd put the Placeholder in the Out column. If we had a biconditional where one had to go in and the other had to go out, we'd put a Placeholder in both columns.

For each of the following rules, determine if it creates a Placeholder in the In group (In), a Placeholder in the Out group (Out), both (B), or neither (N).

_____ 1. If Paul is selected, Quinn is not selected.

_____ 2. If Melika is not cast in the production, then neither is Nguyen.

_____ 3. If Thayer is not presenting at the conference, then Sofia is.

_____ 4. Belinda and Camille cannot both attend the seminar.

_____ 5. Salim goes on the field trip if, but only if, Tasha does not.

_____ 6. If the armchair is sold, then the bureau, the desk, and the furnace are not.

_____ 7. Johannes and Mireya cannot both be excluded.

_____ 8. If Jennifer laughs, then Toshi laughs and Bjorn stays quiet.

_____ 9. Pickles and jelly beans are eaten at different meals.

_____ 10. If meditation is offered, then so is yoga.

_____ 11. Kaira will work at the event, provided that Maiko does not.

_____ 12. If Peter is admitted, then all of the drama majors are admitted.

_____ 13. If the bassist is offstage, then the guitar player or the saxophonist must be offstage.

_____ 14. If astrology or phrenology is taught, then logic is not.

_____ 15. At least one of each type of dessert is sampled.

_____ 16. Matchbooks are displayed when sheet music is not, and only then.

_____ 17. The game console is on whenever the television is on and at no other time.

_____ 18. Cashew milk is not available unless soy milk is available.

_____ 19. If at least one rayon garment is used, then no linen garment is used.

_____ 20. If no goats are petted, then at least two pigs are.

7

Answers

__Out__ 1. If Paul is selected, Quinn is not selected.

If P is in, Q is out, and if Q is in, P is out. That means they can't both be in, so at least one is out. Any rule that crosses from in to out will produce a Placeholder in the Out column.

__N__ 2. If Melika is not cast in the production, then neither is Nguyen.

If M is out, so is N. If N is in, so is M. That means they could both be out or in together. A rule that doesn't cross columns (from in to out or vice versa) won't create a Placeholder.

__In__ 3. If Thayer is not presenting at the conference, then Sofia is.

If T is out, S is in. If S is out, T is in. That means they can't both be out, so at least one is in. Any rule that crosses from out to in will produce a Placeholder in the In column.

__Out__ 4. Belinda and Camille cannot both attend the seminar.

They can't both be in, so at least one must be out.

__B__ 5. Salim goes on the field trip if, and only if, Tasha does not.

"If, but only if" creates a biconditional: T being out is both necessary and sufficient for S to be in. That means S and T can never be in or out together, so one must be in and the other out. Any biconditional that crosses columns will put a Placeholder on both sides.

__Out__ 6. If the armchair is sold, then the bureau, the desk, and the furnace are not.

If A is in, then B, D, and F are out. If any of B, D, or F are in, then A is out. That leaves at least one out.

__In__ 7. Johannes and Mireya cannot both be excluded.

They can't both be out, so at least one must be in.

__Out__ 8. If Jennifer laughs, then Toshi laughs and Bjorn stays quiet.

This may be a bit hard to interpret, but we can split the conditional (as we would when making a Logic Chain) to get a clearer view:

$J \rightarrow T$ $J \rightarrow \sim B$

$\sim T \rightarrow \sim J$ $B \rightarrow \sim J$

Now we can see that the first conditional doesn't create a Placeholder, but the second one does: J/B in the Out group. Remember, if a conditional has "or" in the sufficient condition or "and" in the necessary condition, you can (and should!) split it.

__B__ 9. Pickles and jelly beans are eaten at different meals.

Pickles must be in one column and jelly beans in the other. Like #5, this is a biconditional linking an in and an out.

__N__ 10. If meditation is offered, then so is yoga.

This rule doesn't cross from one column to another, so it doesn't create a Placeholder.

__In__ 11. Kaira will work at the event, provided that Maiko does not.

If Maiko does not work, Kaira will. If Kaira doesn't work, Maiko will.

__N__ 12. If Peter is admitted, then all of the drama majors are admitted.

This rule doesn't cross from one column to another, so it doesn't create a Placeholder.

__N__ 13. If the bassist is offstage, then the guitar player or the saxophonist must be offstage.

This rule doesn't cross from one column to another, so it doesn't create a Placeholder.

__Out__ 14. If astrology or phrenology is taught, then logic is not.

Because "or" is in the sufficient, this can be split:

$A \rightarrow \sim L$ $P \rightarrow \sim L$

$L \rightarrow \sim A$ $L \rightarrow \sim P$

The elements can't all be in together: at least L or both P and A must be out. This gives us a Placeholder in the Out group: L/PA.

__In__ 15. At least one of each type of dessert is sampled.

This will create a Placeholder in the In column for each category of dessert identified in the game.

__B__ 16. Matchbooks are displayed when sheet music is not, and only then.

Any time sheet music is off display, matchbooks are on. When sheet music is on display, matchbooks are off. Either way, one of the two is on display and the other is off.

__N__ 17. The game console is on whenever the television is on and at no other time.

This is a biconditional but it doesn't cross columns. The two machines are on together or off together, so we don't have a Placeholder.

7

___N___ 18. Cashew milk is not available unless soy milk is available.

If C is in, then S is in. If S is out, then C is out. This rule doesn't cross from one column to another, so it doesn't create a Placeholder.

__Out__ 19. If at least one rayon garment is used, then no linen garment is used.

If any rayon is in, all the linen is out. If any linen is in, all the rayon is out.

___In___ 20. If no goats are petted, then at least two pigs are.

If the goats are left out, then two or more pigs are in. If one or zero pigs are petted, then at least one goat is. Either way, someone gets petted.

Drill 139: Element Pairs

Instructions: Some of the most challenging questions in In/Out games ask you to name a pair of elements, at least one of which must be in or out. Your Placeholder Inferences are gold for these tricky questions.

For each of the following games, draw out the Logic Chain and the T-chart for Placeholders on a piece of scratch paper. Then, for each pair of elements listed below, determine whether at least one of the two must be out (Out), at least one of the two must be in (In), both (B), or neither (N).

A circus must select at least four clowns from among a group of seven—Marny, Nifty, Oscar, Porky, Rascal, Sunny, and Vinny—to perform in a traveling show. The selection of clowns must conform to the following conditions:

If Rascal is selected, then Sunny is not.

If Nifty is not selected, then Oscar must be selected.

Oscar cannot be selected unless Rascal is selected.

Porky cannot be selected unless Sunny is selected.

If Marny is selected, then Nifty cannot be selected.

If Vinny is not selected, then neither is Nifty.

_____ 1. O and N
_____ 2. R and S
_____ 3. M and N
_____ 4. V and R
_____ 5. O and M
_____ 6. S and M
_____ 7. R and P
_____ 8. O and V
_____ 9. N and R
_____ 10. O and P

A coach is deciding which five out of eight players—F, G, H, J, K, L, M, and N—will make the starting lineup. The starters are chosen according to the following rules:

F and G do not both start.

If J starts, then so does K.

Either K or L, but not both, start.

N starts unless M starts.

_____ 11. L and K
_____ 12. F and G
_____ 13. F and H
_____ 14. J and H
_____ 15. M and N
_____ 16. J and G
_____ 17. N and K
_____ 18. L and J
_____ 19. M and K
_____ 20. G and K

Answers follow on the next page.

7

Answers

In 1. The second rule establishes that O and N can't both be out, so at least one of them must be in.

Out 2. The first rule establishes that R and S can't both be in, so at least one of them must be out.

Out 3. The fifth rule establishes that M and N can't both be in, so at least one of them must be out.

In 4. This is where things start to get tricky. The second rule tells us that either O or N must be in. The third rule tells us that if O is in, so is R. The fifth rule tells us that if N is in, so is V. So, if either O or N must be in, either R or V must be in as well.

N 5. The second and fifth rules combine to establish that O and M are either both in or both out, but that isn't what we're looking for.

Out 6. Another tricky one, combining the first, second, third, and fifth rules. The first establishes that either S or R is out. And because R out leads to O out, which leads to N in, which leads to M out, we could replace the R in "either S or R is out" with M and infer that either S or M is out, too.

Out 7. The first rule and the fourth rule combine to establish that R and P can't both be in.

In 8. The second rule and the sixth rule combine to establish that O and V can't both be out.

In 9. The second rule and the third rule combine to establish that N and R can't both be out.

Out 10. The first, third, and fourth rules combine to establish that O and P can't both be in. If they were, they would force R and S to be in together, which violates the first rule.

B 11. "Either/or, but not both" is a chain-crossing biconditional; this type of rule always has a Placeholder for one in, one out.

Out 12. "F and G do not both start" is another way of saying that if F starts, G does not start. The crossing conditional always has a Placeholder Inference on the side it's pointing toward.

N 13. H is a floater, but because this is a closed game (exactly three out), it could still pop up in some Placeholder Inferences. In this case, though, FHL could be out, and FH could also both be in.

In 14. Here's where H has a Placeholder Inference even though it's a floater: since F/G accounts for one spot in the Out group and L/K accounts for the other spot, there's only one spot left for an element not in those two pairs. Thus, if J is out, H must be in and vice versa.

In 15. The unless language can be tricky—diagram it as "if not." If M does not start, then N starts. This chain-crossing conditional always has a Placeholder Inference on the side it's pointing toward.

N 16. No Inference here; any combination of J and G is possible.

In 17. K being out fills the Out group, forcing N to be in, and if they can't be out at the same time, at least one must be in.

Out 18. L forces K out, which in turn forces J out. Thus, if L is in, J is out. The contrapositive dictates that if J is in, L is out. Thus, one of L and J must always be out.

In 19. Like in 17, K being out fills the Out group, forcing M to be in, and if they can't be out at the same time, at least one must be in.

N 20. This time, even though K fills up the Out group, there's no Placeholder Inference because G is already part of another Placeholder in the Out group.

7

Grouping and Hybrid Games

Grouping and Hybrid games come in a lot of different flavors, and some of them are among the trickiest on the test. At their most basic, grouping games give us groups of predetermined sizes and ask us to figure out who goes where. Things start to get more complicated when group size isn't predetermined, and if you have to both group *and* order the elements, watch out! Within the chapter, the drills are organized according to our 4-Step Process for Logic Games.

In this section, you will learn to:

Recognize the Most Common Grouping Twists

Choose the Best Base for Grouping Boards

Use Numerical Distributions in Open Grouping Games

Spot Framing Opportunities in Grouping and Hybrid Games

Drill 140: Do the Twist, Grouping and Hybrid Edition

Instructions: For each of these tricky games, identify the game type and twist. Bonus points for any strategic considerations you can fill in! No need to diagram the full games. For now, just practice spotting the game type, twist, and strategic considerations. Be on the lookout for the chance to use advanced strategies such as Framing and Numerical Distribution, and for high-level inferences such as those that stem from Limited Group Space and Interchangeable Groups!

1. Seven friends—Pete, Quinn, Ryu, Sasi, Tamir, Ursula, and Vinny—are taking a canoe trip. Each canoe can hold either one or two people. They arrange themselves according to the following rules:

    Pete and Quinn canoe with a friend, but not each other.

    The only person Tamir is willing to have in his canoe is Ursula.

    Vinny travels with either Quinn or Ryu.

2. Three children—Flo, Gil, and Hannah—are choosing among a number of ice cream toppings—Orbeos, Peppermint Paddies, Reeze's, sprinkles, and Twinx. They will each choose exactly three toppings in accordance with the following rules:

    No one chooses the same exact toppings as anyone else.

    Gil does not choose Peppermint Paddies.

    If someone chooses Orbeos, he or she also choose Reeze's.

    Only one person chooses Twinx.

    Reeze's cannot be chosen by all three children.

3. Eight students—Julio, Kareem, Lexie, Mikhail, Natasha, Owen, Penelope, and Quinn—are each taking at least one language course. The school offers courses in Dutch, English, French, and German, and each language course is taken by at least one student. The students enroll in the courses according to the following rules:

    More students take Dutch than any other language.

    Fewer students take German than any other language.

    Julio and Lexie do not take any of the same languages.

    Owen and Penelope do not take any of the same languages.

4. A group of eight hikers—Faruq, Greg, Heidi, Juan, Kendra, Lori, Miguel, and Nakitomi—come to a break in the trail, and they can't decide which route to take. Some of the hikers decide to take the western route, and others decide to take the eastern route, in accordance with the following rules:

    If Faruq and Greg take the western route, then so does Heidi.

    If Juan takes the eastern route, then either Kendra or Lori takes the western route.

    If Lori and Miguel take the eastern route, then Nakitomi takes the western route.

5. Six figure skaters—P, Q, R, S, T, and V—are going to be paired up and assigned to perform to a specific piece of music—F, G, or H—before competing against each other. Each team will be ranked first, second, or third based on its performance. Teams will be assigned, and rankings given, in accordance with the following rules:

   P and Q are not on the same team.

   V and R are on the same team.

   R's team finishes ahead of S's team.

   If V is assigned to G, then V's team will win.

   If Q and T are on the same team, then they will win.

6. Ten employees—F, G, H, J, K, L, M, N, O, and P—are traveling to work either by ride share, subway, taxi, or walking. They travel according to the following rules:

   F and G travel together, but not by subway.

   H walks.

   J and K each travel with exactly one other person.

   L and M take the same method of transportation.

   N either takes a ride share or a taxi.

   O and P do not travel together.

   More people take a ride share than a taxi.

7. A group of nine high schoolers are running for the six open seats on the student council. There are three freshmen—A, B, and C—three sophomores—F, G, and H—and three juniors—R, S, and T. They are selected according to the following rules:

   At least one junior is selected.

   If A is not selected, then B is selected.

   If C is selected, then so is F.

   Either F or G is selected, but not both.

   H is selected if, and only if, R is not selected.

   If S is selected, then so is T.

8. Eight players—P, Q, R, S, T, V, W, and X—are going to be broken up into three different teams, each of which has a team leader. The teams are made according to the following rules:

   No team consists only of the team leader.

   P and Q are not on the same team.

   If R and S are on the same team, then X is the leader of that team.

   T is on a team with exactly one other person.

   V and W are on the same team, but neither of them is the leader.

7

9. Six friends—Felix, George, Howie, Junior, Kathy, and Laura—go out for sushi. They order from a specials menu consisting of rainbow, shrimp, and tuna sushi, in accordance with the following rules:

   Each person orders at least one type of sushi.

   Felix and George order the same types of sushi.

   Howie orders fewer types of sushi than Junior.

   Kristin does not order tuna.

   Junior and Kathy order no types of sushi in common.

   Howie and Kathy order exactly one type of sushi in common.

10. Eight classmates—F, G, H, J, K, L, M, and N—are each assigned to one of three groups—P, Q, and R—for a group project and challenged to see which group can finish first. Each group has at least two people and no more than three. The groups, and the order in which each finishes, are determined in accordance with the following rules:

    The group with the fewest number of students cannot finish first.

    F finishes ahead of G.

    H and J are in the same group.

    K and L are in different groups.

    G is in group P.

    F is not in group Q.

    M and N are in different groups, and neither of them is with G.

Answers follow on the next page.

Answers

1. Open Grouping, Interchangeable Groups (Fill-In Elements), Undefined Number of Groups (Consider Numerical Distributions)

2. Basic Grouping, Repeating Elements

3. Open Grouping, Repeating Elements

4. Open In/Out Grouping, Unsplittable Rules (Rule Chart instead of Logic Chain)

5. Hybrid, Undefined Group Order (Consider Framing), Chunks and Anti-chunk (look for Anti-Chunk Standoff)

6. Open Grouping, Non-Repeating Elements (Consider Numerical Distributions)

7. Closed In/Out Grouping, Subgroups (Subdivided Logic Chain, Numerical Distributions, Placeholder Inferences, Limited Group Space Inferences)

8. Open Grouping, Special Positions, Non-Repeating Elements (Consider Numerical Distributions)

9. Open Grouping, Repeating Elements

10. Hybrid, Undefined Group Order (Consider Framing), Chunks and Anti-chunks—look for Anti-Chunk Standoff

Drill 141: Rude Rules, Grouping and Hybrid Edition

Instructions: The rude rules are back, and this time, they're in groups! Diagram each of the nasty rules in the space provided. Some might include information that doesn't diagram neatly. When this is the case, use a shorthand you understand. If a rule is conditional or biconditional, contrapose it.

1. Neither the cockroaches nor the butterflies can be displayed before the ants.

2. Dina's article can be featured only if it is next to Carla's and next to Andy's.

3. Tony is scheduled earlier than Uli only if Uli is scheduled fourth.

4. The spread must contain a fashion feature or a dance feature, but not both.

5. The bouquet contains nasturtiums if, but only if, it doesn't contain mums.

6. If Tomas is a residential assistant, he is assigned to Baker Hall or Delphin Hall.

7. Zerotti has more toys than Van.

8. If Yuki makes the cast, Tyler is not a novice performer.

9. The exhibit judged by Graham on the first day must be judged by Ibott on the third or fourth day.

10. The tart will be served before the pie or after the spice cake, but not both. (no ties)

11. Either Kevin manages the parks project and Jalen does not manage the occupational project, or Kevin does not manage the parks project and Jalen manages the occupational project.

12. Leena has an appointment on Monday, Wednesday, or Friday.

13. If the cake does not have a berry layer, then it will have a chocolate layer.

14. The author of the baseball journal does not write any other journals.

15. If a pack does not contain matches, then it contains napkins or a lantern, but not both.

16. Unless Adrian works before Defne, Cristian works before Defne.

17. The logo has at least two blue stars.

18. The fiddle piece comes before the guitar piece, or the guitar piece comes before the hand drum piece or the Irish flute piece, but not both.

19. Unless Stefan works the crafts counter, Quinn works the fudge counter.

20. Joanie won't go to the party unless Lim doesn't go to the party.

21. Either both a cappuccino and a macchiato are ordered, or neither is ordered.

22. The terrier doesn't compete in any portion until the Chihuahua competes in the agility portion.

23. If Dacia and Freja both have works in the show, their works are different media.

24. If Sonia plays the cello, Valencia does not play the guitar.

25. Any show that is on the schedule more than once must not be repeated in consecutive time slots.

26. All of the first tier reviews are posted before any of the second tier reviews.

27. The flag contains either fewer than three or more than five blue stripes.

28. Only group leaders can hold the High Esteem rating.

29. The coffee demonstration happens after either Sven or Val does the beer demonstration.

30. McKenna doesn't speak at the workshop unless she is the third speaker.

31. Rabine and Tate both teach linear algebra if either one of them does.

32. Neither the Radcliffe lecture nor the Pope lecture happens on Wednesday.

33. If Susanna's exhibition takes place earlier than Tuesday, Qing's exhibition takes place on Tuesday.

34. The executive who manages the financial oversight project manages at least one other project.

35. Engels plans the unit on *Twelfth Night* only if he does not plan the unit on *The Winter's Tale*.

36. The visit to Abbotsford takes place prior to the visits to Fernie and Delta, or else after both.

37. At least one of the first four artist's pieces will be a pastel.

38. Anyone who brings chips also brings banana pudding.

39. Neither Easton nor Graves is seeded higher than third.

40. The poster on Descartes will be displayed before the poster on Hobbes only if the poster on Descartes is displayed before the poster on Berkeley.

Answers

1. Neither the cockroaches nor the butterflies can be displayed before the ants.

$$\boxed{\begin{array}{c}C\\A\end{array}} \text{ or } A\text{-}C$$

$$\boxed{\begin{array}{c}B\\A\end{array}} \text{ or } A\text{-}B$$

2. Dina's article can be featured only if it is next to Carla's and next to Andy's.

$$D \to \boxed{CDA} \text{ or } \boxed{ADC}$$

3. Tony is scheduled earlier than Uli only if Uli is scheduled fourth.

$$T\text{-}U \to U_4$$

$$\cancel{U_4} \to \boxed{\begin{array}{c}T\\U\end{array}} \text{ or } U\text{-}T$$

4. The spread must contain a fashion feature or a dance feature, but not both.

$$F \leftrightarrow \cancel{D}$$

$$D \leftrightarrow \cancel{F}$$

5. The bouquet contains nasturtiums if, but only if, it doesn't contain mums.

$$N \leftrightarrow \cancel{M}$$

$$M \leftrightarrow \cancel{N}$$

6. If Tomas is a residential assistant, he is assigned to Baker Hall or Delphin Hall.

$$\boxed{\begin{array}{c}r\\T\end{array}} \to \begin{array}{c}r\\T\\B/D\end{array}$$

$$\cancel{\begin{array}{c}r\\T\\B/D\end{array}} \to \boxed{\cancel{\begin{array}{c}r\\T\end{array}}}$$

7. Zerotti has more toys than Van.

$$Z > V \qquad \overline{\square} \begin{array}{c}<\\ \_\end{array}$$
$$\qquad\qquad Z \quad V$$

8. If Yuki makes the cast, Tyler is not a novice performer.

$$Y \to \cancel{T}_N$$

$$T_N \to \cancel{Y}$$

9. The exhibit judged by Graham on the first day must be judged by Ibott on the third or fourth day.

$$G_1 \to I_3 \text{ or } I_4$$

$$\cancel{I}_3 \cdot \cancel{I}_4 \to \cancel{G}_1$$

10. The tart will be served before the pie or after the spice cake, but not both. (no ties)

$$T \begin{array}{c}^{-P}\\ _{-S}\end{array} \text{ or } \begin{array}{c}^{P}\\ _{S}\end{array} \cdot T$$

11. Either Kevin manages the parks project and Jalen does not manage the occupational project, or Kevin does not manage the parks project and Jalen manages the occupational project.

$$K_P \leftrightarrow \cancel{J}_O$$

$$J_O \leftrightarrow \cancel{K}_P$$

12. Leena has an appointment on Monday, Wednesday, or Friday.

$$L_M \text{ or } L_W \text{ or } L_F$$

13. If the cake does not have a berry layer, then it will have a chocolate layer.

$$\cancel{B} \to C \quad (B \text{ or } C)$$
$$\cancel{C} \to B$$

14. The author of the baseball journal does not write any other journals.

$$\boxed{\begin{array}{c}<\\ \_\\B\end{array}}$$

15. If a pack does not contain matches, then it contains napkins or a lantern, but not both.

$$\cancel{M} \rightarrow (N \& \cancel{L}) \text{ or } (\cancel{N} \& L)$$

$$(\cancel{N} \& \cancel{L}) \text{ or } (N \& L) \rightarrow M$$

16. Unless Adrian works before Defne, Cristian works before Defne.

$$A\cancel{D} \rightarrow C-D$$

$$C\cancel{D} \rightarrow A-D$$

or

$$A/_C - D$$

17. The logo has at least two blue stars.

$$B = 2+$$

18. The fiddle piece comes before the guitar piece, or the guitar piece comes before the hand drum piece or the Irish flute piece, but not both.

$$F-G \leftrightarrow G \cancel{/}^{H}/_I$$

$$G - {}^{H}/_I \leftrightarrow F/_G$$

19. Unless Stefan works the crafts counter, Quinn works the fudge counter.

$$\cancel{S}_C \rightarrow Q_F$$

$$\cancel{Q}_F \rightarrow S_C$$

20. Joanie won't go to the party unless Lim doesn't go to the party.

$$L \rightarrow \cancel{J}$$

$$J \rightarrow \cancel{L}$$

21. Either both a cappuccino and a macchiato are ordered, or neither is ordered.

$$C \leftrightarrow M$$

$$\cancel{M} \leftrightarrow \cancel{C}$$

22. The terrier doesn't compete in any portion until the Chihuahua competes in the agility portion.

$$\boxed{{}^a_C} - \text{all } T$$

23. If Dacia and Freja both have works in the show, their works are different media.

$$D \& F \rightarrow \boxed{\cancel{\substack{D\\F}}}$$

24. If Sonia plays the cello, Valencia does not play the guitar.

$$S_C \rightarrow \cancel{V}_G$$

$$V_G \rightarrow \cancel{S}_C$$

25. Any show that is on the schedule more than once must not be repeated in consecutive time slots.

$$\cancel{\boxed{SS}}$$

26. All of the first tier reviews are posted before any of the second tier reviews.

$$1 - 2$$

27. The flag contains either fewer than three or more than five blue stripes.

$$B = 2^- \text{ or } 6+$$

28. Only group leaders can hold the High Esteem rating.

$$HE \rightarrow GL$$

$$\cancel{GL} \rightarrow \cancel{HE}$$

29. The coffee demonstration happens after either Sven or Val does the beer demonstration.

$$^S/_V{}_B - {}^?_C$$

30. McKenna doesn't speak at the workshop unless she is the third speaker.

$$\cancel{M}_3 \to \cancel{M}$$

$$M \to M_3$$

31. Rabine and Tate both teach linear algebra if either one of them does.

$$R_{LA} \leftrightarrow T_{LA}$$

$$\cancel{T}_{LA} \leftrightarrow \cancel{R}_{LA}$$

32. Neither the Radcliffe lecture nor the Pope lecture happens on Wednesday.

$$\overset{\overline{w}}{\underset{\cancel{P}}{\cancel{R}}}$$

33. If Susanna's exhibition takes place earlier than Tuesday, Qing's exhibition takes place on Tuesday.

$$S - \overline{}_{T} \to \frac{Q}{T}$$

$$\frac{\cancel{Q}}{T} \to \frac{S}{T} \text{ or } \overline{}^{-S}_{T}$$

34. The executive who manages the financial oversight project manages at least one other project.

$$\overset{\square}{\underset{\overline{?}}{F}}$$

35. Engels plans the unit on *Twelfth Night* only if he does not plan the unit on *The Winter's Tale*.

$$T_E \to \cancel{W}_E$$

$$W_E \to \cancel{T}_E$$

36. The visit to Abbotsford takes place prior to the visits to Fernie and Delta, or else after both.

$$A \overset{F}{\underset{D}{\diagdown}} \text{ or } \overset{F}{\underset{D}{\diagup}} A$$

37. At least one of the first four artist's pieces will be a pastel.

$$\overline{}_1 \ \overline{}_2 \ \overline{}_3 \ \overline{}_4$$

38. Anyone who brings chips also brings banana pudding.

$$C \to B$$

$$\cancel{B} \to \cancel{C}$$

39. Neither Easton nor Graves is seeded higher than third.

$$\overset{\overline{}_1}{\underset{\cancel{G}}{\cancel{E}}} \ \overset{\overline{}_2}{\underset{\cancel{G}}{\cancel{E}}}$$

40. The poster on Descartes will be displayed before the poster on Hobbes only if the poster on Descartes is displayed before the poster on Berkeley.

$$D-H \to D-B$$

$$\cancel{D-B} \to \cancel{D-H}$$

7

Drill 142: Base Desires

Instructions: The first step in standard grouping game is to choose which set of entities should form the base of your diagram. When you picture the game in your mind, clues about the most appropriate base can be found in the real-world scenario the game describes. If one set of entities is immobile, for example, and the other mobile, in many cases the immobile entities will be the base and the mobile entities will be the elements. (As an example—in the real world, buildings are immobile because they have foundations, but architects are mobile because they have legs.)

We can also find clues about the most appropriate base in the language of the scenario. In Open Grouping games, for example, in which the number of members each group has is unknown, the phrase "at least one" tends to follow the base and introduce the elements. In a game that tells us "each prey species has at least one predator," we should choose the prey species to be the base and the predators to be the elements. This is a more concrete indicator of the most appropriate base than the mobility consideration, so if the scenario language and mobility consideration point in conflicting directions, rely on the language of the scenario first and foremost.

There are times when "at least one" language is inconclusive, as in this example: "each prey species has at least one predator, and each predator preys upon at least one prey species." When "at least one" is used to introduce both sets of entities, we must turn to the constraints to help us. In these cases, the constraints will favor one set of entities as the base by presenting us with more concrete numerical information about that set. "The foxes prey on more species than the hounds" gives us good cause to make the predators the base, for example, because we know that the number of slots in group F must exceed the number in group H.

For each of the following game scenarios, circle the set of entities that you would use as the base of the diagram. In some cases, a few rules have been added to help you make the call.

1. To celebrate National Fish Day on August 27, the local pet store will display three aquariums in its store window. Each aquarium will have at least one of the following seven types of fish: angelfish, blowfish, clownfish, dartfish, eel, flatfish, and goatfish. Each type of fish will appear in at least one of the aquariums. The following conditions apply:

   (A) Fish
   (B) Aquariums

2. A manager at Spendco is doing her staffing for the following week. Each day, there are three work shifts to be covered: morning, afternoon, and night. She must assign at least one of the following employees to each shift: Brad, Carlos, Dev, Emily, Fiona, Gina, and Hadi. The staffing has the following constraints:

   (A) Employees
   (B) Shifts

3. The curator at the Metropolitan Art Center has received a donation of masterpieces featuring one work by each of the following artists: Matisse, Picasso, Rembrandt, Titian, and van Gogh. The curator will display each new work of art in one of three exhibit rooms—East, West, or North—in accordance with the following guidelines:

   (A) Exhibit Rooms
   (B) Artists

4. A travel blogger will be posting video blogs about six cities over the course of the next three months. The blogger will visit the following cities: Montreal, New York, Paris, Rome, Sydney, and Tokyo. Each city will be featured during one of the months, and each month at least one city will be featured. The blog postings will meet the following requirements:

   (A) Cities
   (B) Months

7

5. Six cousins need transportation to a family wedding. There are two cars available: a four-seat coupe and a five-seat sedan. Only three of the cousins can drive: Justin, Kiara, and Madison; Isaiah, Laila, and Nathan will be passengers. The following constraints apply:

   (A) Cars

   (B) Cousins

6. Today's Health Screening Fair offers three types of screening by health care professionals: a blood test, an EKG, and a vision screening. There are five visitors waiting to be screened: Jones, Kim, Morris, Nguyen, and Perez. Each visitor will be screened for at least one of the tests. Each type of screening will be performed at least once. The screening sessions will be conducted in accordance with the following conditions:

   More visitors get the blood test than the EKG. Morris and Perez do not get the same screening.

   (A) Visitors

   (B) Screenings

7. Two food critics, Beard and Child, will review one or more of exactly five new restaurants: Lord of the Fries, Mustard's Last Stand, Pita Pan, Thaitanic, and Sufficient Grounds Cafe. Each restaurant will be reviewed by exactly one critic according to the following constraints:

   (A) Critics

   (B) Restaurants

8. Bob is going to paint three rooms of his house—the den, the family room, and the living room. Exactly five paint colors will be used—Flagstone, Heavy Cream, Lotus Flower, Morning Sun, and Ocean Storm. Each room will use between one and three of the colors, according to the following constraints:

   (A) Rooms

   (B) Colors

9. Ronit has to staff five LSAT classes—L101, L201, L301, L401, and L501. Each class will be taught by exactly one of three instructors: Ed, Ken, or Tom. The following constraints apply:

   (A) Instructors

   (B) Classes

10. Ashton has three types of bread left—rye, pumpernickel, and sourdough—to make one sandwich for each of his three children. There are five fillers available: ham, jarlsberg, liverwurst, muenster, and prosciutto. Each type of bread will be used for a sandwich, and each sandwich will contain two or more fillers. The sandwiches will be made subject to the following conditions:

    (A) Breads

    (B) Fillers

11. ABC Corp has hired six new interns: Jennifer, Kyle, Liam, Megan, Nicholas, and Preston. Each intern will be assigned to exactly one of three departments: Finance, Human Resources, or IT. Every department will be assigned at least one intern. The following constraints apply:

    (A) Departments

    (B) Interns

12. Three friends—Abdul, Bella, and Charlie—are each ordering an ice cream cone. They can select up to three of the following six flavors—mango, Neapolitan, pistachio, raspberry, strawberry, and vanilla—for each cone. Each flavor will be selected at least once. The following conditions apply:

    (A) Flavors

    (B) Friends

7

13. There are five customers at the bank waiting to see exactly one of three tellers: Garcia, Han, and Johnson. Two customers are men—Alvarez and Bianco; the other three are women—Connors, Diaz, and El Moussa. Each teller will serve at least one customer, subject to the following constraints:

    (A) Customers
    (B) Tellers
    (C) Gender

14. Three art students—Ben, Carrie, and Diego—are working on seven books—J, K, L, M, N, O, and P. Each book cover will be worked on by at least one student. The following constraints apply:

    (A) Art students
    (B) Books

15. The local farmers' market has three colors of baskets for sale: auburn, beach sand, and charcoal. Each basket will have at least one of three fruits—mango, nectarine, and plum—and at least one of three vegetables—radicchio, squash, and tomatillo. The baskets will be filled in accordance with the following conditions:

    (A) Baskets
    (B) Fruits
    (C) Vegetables

16. Five census takers—Chou, Daniels, Farukh, Gupta, and Harris—will canvass two towns—Riverdale and Smallville. Each town will be canvassed by one or more census takers, but no census taker will canvass both towns. The canvassing will meet the following conditions:

    (A) Census Takers
    (B) Towns

17. The makers of a popular brand of popcorn will conduct a blind taste test. Five taste testers—Jasmine, Keith, Lara, Martin, and Nalla—will choose their favorite popcorn from among three different brands—X, Y, and Z. The test results must meet the following conditions:

    (A) Popcorn brands
    (B) Taste testers

18. Global News Network must assign foreign correspondents to Uzbekistan, Vietnam, and Zimbabwe. The candidates are Jabari, Kholova, Luc, Mupanda, and Ngu. At least one correspondent will be assigned to each country and no correspondent will be assigned to more than one country. The assignments must meet the following constraints:

    (A) Correspondents
    (B) Countries

19. Jury alternates are being selected for a grand theft trial and a family court trial. The jury pool consists of Ferro, Gupta, Han, Inez, and James. Each trial will be assigned at least one juror and no juror will be assigned to more than one trial. The assignment of jurors to trial will have the following constraints:

    (A) Jurors
    (B) Trials

20. Four students—Allen, Bazinga, Chukwa, and Duval—are competing for two positions on their school's basketball team—point guard and shooting guard. Each position will be filled by one or more students. Each student will be selected for exactly one of the positions, in accordance with the following conditions:

    (A) Students
    (B) Positions

Answers

1. B. Aquariums

"At least one" language is inconclusive because it introduces both sets of entities, so we fall back on the fact that aquariums are immobile, whereas fish are mobile.

2. B. Shifts

Shifts are immobile, whereas the employees are mobile. "At least one" introduces the employees. The shifts also come in order, which will be important if this turns out to be a Hybrid game. Whenever a game has entities that come in a specific order, use them as the base in case order becomes important.

3. A. Exhibit Rooms

Rooms are immobile, whereas artwork is mobile.

4. B. Months

Months come in order, so they should be the base.

5. A. Cars

If the cousins were the base, it wouldn't be a grouping game anymore because each "group" would only have one member. It would also be hard to keep track of the special position (the driver) if the cars were not the base.

6. B. Screenings

"At least" language is inconclusive because it introduces both sets of entities, and neither set is immobile or limited to one appearance. That means we need to turn to the rules to look for information. Rule 1 is numerical and points to the screenings to be the base. Rule 2 can be an anti-chunk if the screenings are the base.

7. A. Critics

"One or more" functions like "at least one," making the restaurants the elements and the critics the base.

8. A. Rooms

The rooms are immobile, and the numerical constraint that each has one, two, or three colors makes it the best choice for a base.

9. A. Instructors

Like game 5, this game has one set of entities that goes exactly once (the classes) and another that must go more than once (the instructors). In these cases, the entities that go exactly once need to be the elements, otherwise each group would be a group of one.

10. A. Breads

"Two or more" functions like "at least one" and introduces the elements, making the bread the base.

11. A. Departments

"At least one intern" tells us the interns are the elements and the departments are the base.

12. B. Friends

"Up to three of the following six flavors" is numerical information about group size pointing to the flavors as the elements and the cones as the base.

13. B. Tellers

When given three sets of entities, consider how they relate to one another. Here, the customers have a gender, so it makes sense to let the customers be the main element so we can have a 3D setup with the gender in the "characteristic row" above the main elements. The tellers should therefore be the base. This is confirmed by the fact that the tellers each serve "at least one" customer, but each customer is served by exactly one teller.

14. B. Books

"At least one student" tells us that the students are the elements, since a book could be worked on by multiple students. Students often get too hung up on the number of groups in games like this and try to make the smaller set the base. But many Open Grouping games with repeating elements will have a large number of groups and a small number of elements. This actually makes your Open Grouping Board easier because you won't have to use numerical distribution to figure out how many rows you need—you just make one for each element in every group!

15.   A. Baskets

The question of fruits vs. vegetables is a subdivision of the elements, meaning the baskets must be the base. Use a 3D Grouping Board with the produce name as the main element and the produce type as the characteristic.

16.   B. Towns

"One or more" functions like "at least one" and introduces the elements, making the towns the base. The towns are also immobile, whereas the census takers are not.

17.   A. Popcorn brands

The testers will each choose only one brand as best, so if they were the base, each group would be a group of one, which is usually a sign you've chosen the wrong base.

18.   B. Countries

"At least one" introduces the correspondents, making the countries the base. The countries are also immobile, whereas the correspondents are not.

19.   B. Trials

"At least one" introduces the jurors, making the trials the base.

20.   B. Positions

"One or more" functions like "at least one" and introduces the students, who should be the elements, making the positions the base.

Drill 143: Should I Frame or Should I Go?
Grouping/Hybrid Edition

Instructions: Building frames is (still!) an invaluable strategy for Logic Games. Remember, when building frames, you identify a rule that splits the game into two or three possibilities and then you draw out each one.

While a single rule by itself can't tell you that building frames will be a solid strategy for attacking a given game, the decision starts with certain rules that tend to lead to good frames. For each of the following, determine whether you would (Y) or would not (N) consider building frames around that rule, depending on what the other rules stated.

_____ 1. Twice as many students sign up for biology as sign up for chemistry.

_____ 2. L and R must be in the same group.

_____ 3. Group 1 must have more members than group 2.

_____ 4. V will not be in group 2.

_____ 5. Henry and Sarah cannot both be on the Red Team.

_____ 6. If Dahlia is with group 1, then Xavier is with group 3.

_____ 7. M and T cannot be in the same group.

_____ 8. Group 1 and group 3 have no members in common.

_____ 9. Either F or U must be in a group alone.

_____ 10. Benita must be on the NYC tour.

_____ 11. The second mural cannot contain flowers.

_____ 12. Either all of the orangutans are selected, or all of the gorillas are selected, but not both.

_____ 13. Both Fido and Spot must be walked on the same day.

_____ 14. Jill and Kyle cannot both be at the Westhaven site.

_____ 15. If K is not in group 2, I will be in group 4.

_____ 16. Half as many animals will be sent to the Oakland Zoo as will be sent to the San Diego Zoo.

_____ 17. O and P must be in group 1.

_____ 18. Zalena will be in the acting class only if Yoshi is not.

_____ 19. If N is in group 1, it must be the only element in that group.

_____ 20. G must be in group 2 or group 3.

_____ 21. U and W cannot be in the same group.

_____ 22. Neither Omar nor Tanya will be in the group that visits Buenos Aires.

_____ 23. The baritone group will have two or three members.

_____ 24. If J is with group 2, then P is with group 3.

_____ 25. Q and V must be in the same group.

7

Answers follow on the next page.

Answers

____Y____ 1. **Twice as many students sign up for biology as sign up for chemistry.**

There's unlikely to be more than two ways this can pan out, so it's a split!

____Y____ 2. **L and R must be in the same group.**

For Grouping games, chunks and anti-chunks are the big drivers of frames. In games with only a few groups, you can sometimes frame by placing the chunk in each group and seeing what happens.

____N____ 3. Group 1 must have more members than group 2.

Without more information—for example, restricted elements for each group—it's hard to make a clear split, especially since we don't know how many more group 1 will have.

____N____ 4. V will not be in group 2.

No split here—all we know is one place where V is not going.

____N____ 5. Henry and Sarah cannot both be on the Red Team.

Anti-chunks can be good framing indicators, but this isn't quite an anti-chunk. All we know is that H and S can't both be on the Red Team.

____N____ 6. If Dahlia is with group 1, then Xavier is with group 3.

Conditionals rarely make good frames. What if D is in another group? Then we don't know where X is.

____Y____ 7. **M and T cannot be in the same group.**

Anti-chunks can be good framing indicators, especially if the elements involved are otherwise restricted or if there are additional chunks or anti-chunks in the game.

____Y____ 8. **Group 1 and group 3 have no members in common.**

Knowing these two groups have no members in common doesn't create a split, since we don't which elements, or how many, will end up in each group.

____N____ 9. Either F or U must be the chairperson.

This either/or creates a clear split.

____N____ 10. Benita must be on the NYC tour.

____N____ 11. The second mural cannot contain flowers.

____Y____ 12. **Either all of the orangutans are selected, or all of the gorillas are selected, but not both.**

This either/or creates a clear split and two ways you can play the game depending on whether it's all the Os or all the Gs.

____Y____ 13. **Both Fido and Spot must be walked on the same day.**

Chunk!

____N____ 14. Jill and Kyle cannot both be at the Westhaven site.

Careful: this isn't an anti-chunk. We just know they can't both be at Westhaven.

____N____ 15. If K is not in group 2, I will be in group 4.

____Y____ 16. **Half as many animals will be sent to Oakland Zoo as will be sent to San Diego Zoo.**

There are typically only one or two ways this will pan out.

____N____ 17. O and P must be in group 1.

This is a chunk, but it doesn't create a split since we know they're in group 1. This may end up limiting the game enough to frame around another rule, but it is not a framing opportunity in and of itself.

____N____ 18. Zalena will be in the acting class only if Yoshi is not.

____N____ 19. If N is in group 1, it must be the only element in that group.

____Y____ 20. **G must be in group 2 or group 3.**

Two placement options!

____Y____ 21. **U and W cannot be in the same group.**

Anti-chunk!

____N____ 22. Neither Omar nor Tanya will be in the group that visits Buenos Aires.

____Y____ 23. **The baritone group will have two or three members.**

This creates a split in the numerical distribution of the elements.

____N____ 24. If J is with group 2, then P is with group 3.

____Y____ 25. **Q and V must be in the same group.**

Chunk!

Drill 144: Numerical Distribution, Grouping Edition

Instructions: Numerical Distributions feature frequently in Grouping games. Sometimes they'll be used to figure out how many times a given repeating element can be used. Other times they'll be used in Open Grouping games to figure out the limitations on group size. For each of the following scenarios and abbreviated rule sets, use the space provided to derive the Numerical Distributions.

1. At a recent ice cream convention, Danielle, Ilan, Judy, Kristin, Matt, Nicole, Pavel, and Sean were selected to sample bold new flavors and vote on their favorite. The flavors tested were chili chocolate, southern strawberry, and violet vanilla. Each ice cream enthusiast got a single vote.

    Twice as many enthusiasts selected chili chocolate as violet vanilla.

2. Five technicians—Gilius, Henrietta, Jaxer, Katelyn, and Leona—are each assigned to at least one of three different projects. Each project will have three technicians assigned to it.

    Jaxer works on exactly two of the projects.

3. Four athletes—Louise, Jared, Rich, and Suzie—are on a team competing at a track meet. The team will send two members to each of four events—high jump, long jump, mile run, and sprint.

    No team member will compete in all four events.

4. Five fifth graders—Leroy, Manna, Nanette, Ophelia, and Peyton—are each assigned to take care of at least one of the following class pets—a chinchilla, a ferret, and a rabbit. Each pet needs to have at least one student assigned to it, but no more than three.

    Manna is assigned to take care of two of the pets.
    More students must be assigned to take care of the rabbit than any other animal.

Answers

Note: For some of these Numerical Distributions, concrete information about a particular element or elements was the jumping-off point. In these cases, the elements are listed in a given order, and the distributions beneath reflect that order. If a single element was the jumping-off point but the other elements are interchangeable, the order will be presented as "**concrete element**-everybody else" and the distributions beneath will list the numbers for the concrete element first and in bold.

1. **Chocolate-Strawberry-Vanilla (Distributions represent number of votes)**

   2-5-1
   4-2-2

   In order for chocolate to receive twice as many votes as vanilla, either vanilla must receive one vote and chocolate two, or vanilla must receive two votes and chocolate four.

2. **(Distributions represent how many projects technicians are on)**

   Jaxer-everybody else

   2-3-2-1-1
   2-2-2-2-1

   Because Jaxer works on exactly two projects, the remaining four technicians must fill the seven remaining openings.

3. **(Distributions represent how many events athletes compete in)**

   3-3-2-0
   3-3-1-1
   3-2-2-1
   2-2-2-2

   Although we know that the team itself competes, it isn't specified that each team *member* must compete. It's possible for one team member not to compete in any event without violating the other numeric requirement: the maximum of three events per athlete.

4. **(Distributions represent number of students per pet)**

   Rabbit-everybody else

   ~~**2**-1-1~~ *(not enough slots based on the student rules)*
   3-2-1
   3-2-2

   (Distributions represent number of pets per student)

   Manna-everybody else

   2-2-1-1-1
   2-1-1-1-1

   This tricky game has two sets of distributions: one for the number of students per pet and another for the number of pets per student. Since the Rabbit has more students assigned to it than any other pet, it must have the maximum of three. If the Rabbit had two and the other pets only one, there wouldn't be enough slots to accommodate Manna's two assignments. Once we have the two distributions for students per pet, we know that there are either six or seven total assignments. Manna gets two of these, and the rest are distributed over the other four children.

Drill 145: Diagramming 301, Round 3

Instructions: Here's another round of practice with the hardest of the hard! Diagram and contrapose each of the following complex conditional rules in the space provided.

1. The Gleizes painting will be displayed if, and only if, the Ernst painting is displayed.

2. The Seurat painting will be displayed whenever the Dali and Monet paintings both are.

3. The Rembrandt and the Monet paintings will not both be displayed.

4. The Monet painting will be displayed unless the Ernst painting is displayed.

5. If she sees D in concert, she will also see L and M.

6. She will not see both band T and band S.

7. If she sees C or K in concert, she will also see R.

8. Either Mei or Suki, but not both, will lead the expedition.

9. Sam and Ami will try out unless Hiro tries out.

10. Ken will not try out without Lee.

11. Keiko will try out if, but only if, Hiro tries out.

12. If Theo visits the Adirondacks, he will read a science fiction or a mystery novel, but not both.

13. Any family that purchases a bird will purchase neither a cat nor a snake.

14. The class will choose a lizard or a toad, but not both.

15. Anna will try out only if Sam and Hiro do as well.

16. Mia and Anna will not both try out.

17. They will buy a seahorse if, but only if, they also buy a frog.

18. If they buy a snake, they will either not buy a fish or not buy a hamster.

19. He will read the crime novel if, but only if, he doesn't read the mystery.

20. He will not read the crime novel if he reads the how-to or the biography.

21. He will read the crime novel unless he reads the mystery or the biography.

22. He will not read both the biography and the how-to.

23. He will not read the how-to or the biography unless he reads the cookbook.

24. He will read the fantasy and mystery novels only if he also reads the poetry collection.

25. She will take calculus and physics only if she does not take English.

26. She will take the literature class if, and only if, she takes calculus.

27. The class will have a hamster as a pet unless it has a mouse or a fish.

28. They will not purchase both a kitten and a hamster.

29. She will select a potion for her character if, but only if, she does not select an amulet.

30. If she purchases a robot, she will also purchase a computer or a tablet, but not both.

Answers

1. The Gleizes painting will be displayed if, and only if, the Ernst painting is displayed.

   G ↔ E ; ~E ↔ ~G

2. The Seurat painting will be displayed whenever the Dali and Monet paintings both are.

   D and M → S ; ~S → ~D or ~M

3. The Rembrandt and the Monet paintings will not both be displayed.

   R → ~M ; M → ~R

4. The Monet painting will be displayed unless the Ernst painting is displayed.

   ~M → E ; ~E → M

5. If she sees D in concert, she will also see L and M.

   D → L and M ; ~L or ~M → ~D

6. She will not see both band T and band S.

   T → ~S ; S → ~T

7. If she sees C or K in concert, she will also see R.

   C or K → R ; ~R → ~C and ~K

8. Either Mei or Suki, but not both, will lead the expedition.

   M ↔ ~S ; S ↔ ~M

9. Sam and Ami will try out unless Hiro tries out.

   ~H → S and A ; ~S or ~A → H

10. Ken will not try out without Lee.

    K → L ; ~L → ~K

11. Keiko will try out if, but only if, Hiro tries out.

    H ↔ K ; ~K ↔ ~H

12. If Theo visits the Adirondacks, he will read a science fiction or a mystery novel, but not both.

    A → S or M (not both) ; ~S and ~M → ~A ; S and M → ~A

13. Any family that purchases a bird will purchase neither a cat nor a snake.

    B → ~C and ~S ; C or S → ~B

14. The class will choose a lizard or a toad, but not both.

    L ↔ ~T ; ~L ↔ T

15. Anna will try out only if Sam and Hiro do as well.

    A → S and H ; ~S or ~H → ~A

16. Mia and Anna will not both try out.

    M → ~A ; A → ~M

17. They will buy a seahorse if, but only if, they also buy a frog.

    S ↔ F ; ~F ↔ ~S

18. If they buy a snake, they will either not buy a fish or not buy a hamster.

    S → ~F or ~H ; F and H → ~S

19. He will read the crime novel if, but only if, he doesn't read the mystery.

    C ↔ ~M ; M ↔ ~C

20. He will not read the crime novel if he reads the how-to or the biography.

    H or B → ~C ; C → ~H and ~B

21. He will read the crime novel unless he reads the mystery or the biography.

    ~C → M or B ; ~M and ~B → C

22. He will not read both the biography and the how-to.

    B → ~H ; H → ~B

23. He will not read the how-to or the biography unless he reads the cookbook.

    H or B → C ; ~C → ~H and ~B

24. He will read the fantasy and mystery novels only if he also reads the poetry collection.

    F and M → P ; ~P → ~F or ~M

25. She will take calculus and physics only if she does not take English.

    C and P → ~E ; E → ~C or ~P

26. She will take the literature class if, and only if, she takes calculus.

    C ↔ L ; ~L ↔ ~C

27. The class will have a hamster as a pet unless it has a mouse or a fish.

    ~M and ~F → H ; ~H → M or F

28. They will not purchase both a kitten and a hamster.

    K → ~H ; H → ~K

29. She will select a potion for her character if, but only if, she does not select an amulet.

    P ↔ ~A ; A ↔ ~P

30. If she purchases a robot, she will also purchase a computer or a tablet, but not both.

    R → C or T (not both) ; ~C and
    ~T → ~R ; C and T → ~R

7

Unusual Games

In the LSAT Games section, abnormal is the new normal. Increasingly, we're seeing games that seem to defy the standards that we've all come to expect. The key word, however, is *seem*. As intimidating as these weird games can feel, we've actually found that most of them bend to the same approaches as your more standard games, *if* you know how to make them fit the mold. That's why there's only one drill in this section, and it's all about cracking a non-standard game with a standard approach.

In this section, you will learn to:

Spot the Standard Game Type an Unusual Game Is Riffing On

Use a Standard Approach for a Nonstandard Game

Drill 146: Neutralize the Threat

Instructions: In the LG section, nonstandard is the new standard. You should go into test day expecting to see a game with an unfamiliar structure or an unexpected twist. This is one of the hardest things to prep for because there's only so much LSAT material out there that has these increasingly common curveballs. Not to worry— this drill has you covered.

Each of the following games will have an unusual feature. But, like all unusual games, each of them can also be approached using one of our standard base diagrams. Your task is to practice your test day approach, which should be to pause, set the oddball feature aside, and identify which base diagram is most appropriate.

1. A gardener is planting lilies in a row in front of the town square. There will be nine lilies total, available in five colors: orange, purple, red, white, and yellow. The lilies must be planted according to the following specifications:

   A single white lily must be planted after any two lilies that are not white.

   The fifth lily must be orange.

   Two white lilies cannot be planted next to each other.

   Neither the first lily nor the last lily can be purple.

   (A) Number Line
   (B) Logic Chain
   (C) Grouping Board
   (D) Hybrid Board

2. A team of six rowers—Highsmith, Jackson, Maurier, Said, Tomkins, and Valadez—is competing in a race. Each rower after the first will be stationed at one of five points along a river. The rower who begins the race will carry a flag that is then handed off to the next rower, in accordance with the following:

   Each rower must compete.

   Maurier must hand the flag to Highsmith.

   Tomkins cannot hand the flag to Said.

   Tomkins cannot hand the flag to Valadez.

   Said must hand the flag to Maurier or Jackson.

   Tomkins or Valadez begins the race.

   (A) Number Line
   (B) Logic Chain
   (C) Grouping Board
   (D) Hybrid Board

3. Tutoring sessions are scheduled for Thursday, Friday, and Saturday. There will be three tutoring sessions each day, in the morning, afternoon, and evening. Each session will be scheduled for one hour or two hours, according to the following rules:

   Two-hour sessions cannot be scheduled consecutively on the same day.

   There must be at least one two-hour session scheduled each day.

   A one-hour session cannot be scheduled in the morning on consecutive days.

   (A) Number Line
   (B) Logic Chain
   (C) Grouping Board
   (D) Hybrid Board

4. Seven campers—Fiona, Lyle, Mila, Praveen, Roger, Viola, and Zenzi—are split into two groups. One group will camp on the east side of the lake, while the other will camp on the west side of the lake. There can be no more than three campers on the east side of the lake, one of whom must be responsible for communicating with the base camp. The campers are divided according to the following conditions:

Either Viola or Zenzi must camp on the east side of the lake, but not both.

If Zenzi camps on the east side, Roger does not.

If Fiona camps on the west side, Praveen also camps on the west side.

If Mila camps on the east side, Viola also camps on the east side.

If Mila camps on the west side, Fiona camps on the east side.

(A) Number Line
(B) Logic Chain
(C) Grouping Board
(D) Hybrid Board

5. Six dolls—H, K, N, O, Q, and Y—are available for a display shelf. The shelf can fit exactly three dolls, each of which must wear a green hat, a red hat, or a silver hat. The dolls will be placed on the shelf according to the following conditions:

If H is included on the shelf, Q is not.

If O is included on the shelf, it must wear a green hat.

If Y is included on the shelf, it must wear a red hat.

Either N or K must be included on the shelf.

If H is included on the shelf, it cannot wear a red hat.

If a silver hat is used, the other two hats must be red.

(A) Number Line
(B) Logic Chain
(C) Grouping Board
(D) Hybrid Board

6. Seven tourists—Grey, Jindal, Kingston, Oh, Petrovsky, Schumer, and Vidal—will each visit exactly one museum exhibit on one of three days. The available exhibits are antique furniture, mummies, or weapons. One exhibit is visited each day and no more than one exhibit may be visited per day. No more than four tourists may visit each exhibit. The visits must adhere to the following conditions:

Grey must visit the museum before Petrovsky.

Vidal cannot visit the mummies exhibit.

Petrovsky and Schumer must visit on the same day.

No more than two tourists may visit the weapons exhibit.

Kingston and Jindal must visit on the same day.

Mummies must be the last exhibit visited.

(A) Number Line
(B) Logic Chain
(C) Grouping Board
(D) Hybrid Board

7. A reading will consist of four short stories and three poems, which must be read in accordance with the following specifications:

No more than two poems can be read consecutively.

The first reading must be a short story.

(A) Number Line
(B) Logic Chain
(C) Grouping Board
(D) Hybrid Board

8. Exactly five cookie varieties—fortune, macaroon, oatmeal raisin, peanut butter, and snickerdoodle—are placed on a placemat around a circular table. Each placemat is numbered 1 through 5, with the 1 at the top of the table and the rest of the placements numbered clockwise around it. Each placemat contains exactly one variety of cookie and conforms to the following rules:

The fortune cookies are next to the oatmeal raisin cookies.

Either the peanut butter cookies or the snickerdoodles are number 1.

The oatmeal raisin cookies cannot be next to the snickerdoodles.

The macaroons cannot be next to the peanut butter cookies.

(A) Number Line
(B) Logic Chain
(C) Grouping Board
(D) Hybrid Board

9. Four contestants on a baking show—Ilana, Julio, Molly, and Oded—will be assigned at least one item to bake from a selection of loaves, pies, rolls, and tarts. Ilana can bake sugar-free and gluten-free, Julio can bake vegan, Molly can bake gluten-free, and Oded can bake sugar-free and vegan. Each contestant will be assigned baking items in accordance with the following conditions:

Molly cannot bake a tart.

Julio must bake a pie.

Molly and Oded cannot bake the same kind of item.

There must be exactly two gluten-free items.

There must be exactly one vegan item.

At least one pie must be sugar-free.

(A) Number Line
(B) Logic Chain
(C) Grouping Board
(D) Hybrid Board

10. Seven books will be stacked one on top of the other next to a bookcase. Each book has a different colored spine and is either lilac, red, silver, or turquoise. The books must be stacked according to the following rules.

No two colors may be stacked consecutively.

At least one book has a spine that corresponds to each of the colors.

No more than two books have a red spine.

A lilac book must be stacked on top of each silver book.

Any turquoise book must be stacked below any red book.

(A) Number Line
(B) Logic Chain
(C) Grouping Board
(D) Hybrid Board

7

Answers

1.   A. Number Line

The threat in this game is that odd rule about the white lilies popping in after two lilies of another color. We're still putting things in order, though, so use a Number Line to keep track of the various ordering possibilities. Notice that our oddball rule means we can't have three lilies in a row that are not white. This allows us to infer that either the fourth or sixth lily must be white.

2.   A. Number Line

The threat to this game is the flag, but since we only have one race and each rower is handing the flag to the next rower, we can use a Number Line to keep track of the order of transfers. Each handoff or excluded handoff becomes a chunk or anti-chunk, respectively.

3.   C. Grouping Board

The threat to this game is the length of the sessions; it's easy to get thrown off by numbers as elements, but this is really just a 3D Grouping game.

4.   B. Logic Chain

The threats here are the named groups and communicator, but don't let them throw you off. This is just an In/Out Grouping game with a special position. It might be hard to recognize it as such because the groups are named, but not all In/Out games are really about being in vs. out. Any game with two groups is a contender, so always check the rule set: if it's all conditionals, the Logic Chain is your best bet.

5.   D. Hybrid Board

This threatening game is a combination of 3D and In/Out. Since there aren't many In/Out rules to track, and since we can't keep track of the 3D characteristics with the Logic Chain, it's best to use a 3D Game Board with an Out group.

6.   D. Hybrid Board

The threat to this game is the undefined group order. This is a trend in Hybrid games that you should be prepared for. Always use the ordered component, in this case the days, as the base. Beneath the base, make a row for the group titles. Above the base, make the rows for the elements. Since there are typically only three groups, you should consider framing around group order, particularly if their order is constrained and if there are rules relating the elements to the groups.

7.   A. Number Line

Where are the rules?! A limited number of constraints can feel like a major threat. But look for what's familiar: we're putting things in order, so the Number Line should be your go-to diagram. In a game like this where you struggle to grasp the nature of the game, it's not a bad idea to try to scratch out a couple of hypotheticals right out of the gate. This will often reveal something essential about how the game works, and, at the very least, it'll give you some good previous work.

8.   A. Number Line

Circle games can feel threatening because, let's face it, who among us can really draw a circle? Luckily, most can be completed using a simple Number Line. Just indicate clearly that the first slot is next to the last slot, and you should be good to go. That said, in some circle games, there are constraints about elements being across from one another. In that case, a Number Line won't do, but don't worry—you can still make it out without drawing a circle. Just draw an asterisk with the number of points equal to the number of slots. That will clearly demarcate which positions are across from one another, and it will make for a nice evenly-spaced, easy to redraw hypothetical.

9.   C. Grouping Board

The threat in this game is the dietary characteristic. While we often use a 3D Board with a characteristic row in a game like this, it would be hard to do that here because each element within a group's column would need its own characteristic slot. We find subscripts helpful for games like this—set up the game on a standard Grouping Board, and beneath the groups, list out the possible subscripts for elements within that group. Just leave room in each slot for a characteristic subscript that can be added either with an element or independent of an element as a placeholder and fill in what you know!

10.   A. Number Line

A stack of something is a lot more threatening than a row of something, but this is still a Basic Ordering game; it's just a vertical one! Use a vertical Number Line whenever you have a game that's asking you to put things in order from top to bottom.

7

CHAPTER 8

Reading Comprehension, The 4-Step Process

In This Chapter, We Will Cover:

- Step 1 – Read the Passage

- Step 2 – Pause and Rehash

- Step 3 – ID the Question/Strategy

- Step 4 – Analyze the Answers

Reading Comprehension, the 4-Step Process

Show us a section of the LSAT and we'll show you a 4-Step Process for tackling it! In RC, that process (necessarily!) starts with reading the passage. Step 2 is your opportunity to collect and organize your thoughts before moving into the questions. Step 3 is where you plan your attack, and Step 4 is where you bring it all home and collect your reward.

In this section, you will learn to:

Read the Passage

- Recognize the function of small-but-important words and phrases
- Read for the right things
- Paraphrase effectively
- Make sound predictions for the direction a passage is likely to take

Pause and Rehash

- Categorize passages based on structure
- Use the Passage Map

ID the Question/Strategy

- Determine when to go back to the passage and when to answer from memory
- Strategize for Inference, Strengthen, Weaken and Application Questions

Analyze the Answers

- Predict traps
- Spot red flags

8

Step 1–Read the Passage

Drill 147: Function Junction, Round 2

Instructions: Little words can make a big impact in RC. A single word or phrase can speak volumes about the direction a sentence, paragraph, or passage is likely to take. Can you pick up what the passage is putting down? Find out with another round of practice!

In each of the following selections, a portion has been highlighted. In the space provided, write a brief description of the function of the highlighted text, and/or what it conveys about the direction the selection is likely to take.

1. Despite unseasonably cold weather on the Fourth of July, the beach was crowded with bathers and picnickers.

   _____

2. It was inevitable that the workers would eventually strike, for there was no willingness to compromise on either side of the dispute.

   _____

3. The Strategic Defense Initiative was doomed to failure because the technical challenges were too great, notwithstanding the immense budgets devoted to the effort.

   _____

4. As long as the economy continues to be perceived as strong, stocks in high-tech industries will experience steady growth in the years ahead.

   _____

5. California has a lower per-capita consumption of energy than any other state in the union with the exception of Vermont, a small rural state with strong ecological sentiment.

   _____

6. Investment in bonds is statistically riskier than investment in stocks; yet, the average investor chooses bonds over stocks when looking for a safe investment for retirement.

   _____

7. The pundit generally has a strong opinion about everything, so it is no surprise that he has a strong opinion about tort reform.

   _____

8. There are four languages officially recognized in Singapore, but the predominant language is Mandarin.

   _____

9. Surveillance cameras not only deter crime but also provide evidence to aid law enforcement when a crime occurs.

   _____

10. The director customarily delegates manpower decisions to the individual department managers.

    _____

11. Regrettably, her decision to follow the broker's advice led to an eventual foreclosure on the property.

    _____

12. The sign language interpreter arrived just as the main speaker was starting his presentation.

    _____

13. This author proposes that Mozart's sudden death was caused by a streptococcal infection, which was epidemic in Vienna at the time.

    _____

14. The trial lasted for two months, but the defendant was ultimately exonerated by the jury.

_____

15. The wax museum had realistic wax replicas of a wide variety of famous figures, including politicians, movie stars, and athletes.

_____

16. The science behind so-called matter transporters used in popular science fiction is unsound because it contains numerous logical contradictions.

_____

17. I enjoy using my vacation time to travel, whereas my husband prefers to stay home and work on house and garden projects.

_____

18. Computer literacy has become an increasingly important part of most high school curricula since the Apple II was introduced into classrooms in the 1970s.

_____

19. The district attorney got the key witness's vital testimony on the record to establish the foundation of the prosecution's case.

_____

20. Manned expeditions to Mars will be possible only once the problem of radiation exposure in space has been solved.

_____

21. In theory, the software should prevent the system from billing a customer twice for the same purchase.

_____

22. The accident rate on the German Autobahn is lower than that on U.S. interstate highways even though there is no speed limit on the Autobahn.

_____

23. Tropical fruits can be characterized by traits that differ from those of temperate fruits, such as the vulnerability of mangoes to low temperatures in which apples or pears are able to thrive.

_____

24. Since rice is an important food for most of the world's people, genetic modification to create more nutritious varieties could help to solve many problems caused by malnutrition.

_____

25. Unmanned probes have gathered sufficient evidence to make doubtful any possibility of life on the other planets and satellites in our solar system.

_____

26. To solve this problem, the board must first recall the product, and then it can address the question of what happened and how it can be prevented in the future.

_____

27. The student's excuse for not turning in the assignment was weak and unconvincing, so it's clear that he will not get a passing grade for the course.

_____

28. With increased concern about global warming, environmentalists have paradoxically become advocates of the nuclear power plants they opposed just a few decades ago.

_____

29. In light of discoveries in neuroplasticity, psychologists are challenging the belief that an individual's intelligence is genetically predetermined.

_____

30. After all, great wealth is not a guarantee of peace of mind.

_____

Answers follow on the next page.

Answers

Note: Your answers may be slightly different than ours, but they should convey similar ideas.

1. Introduce a fact from which to pivot to a contrasting/surprising fact

2. Introduce evidence

3. Indicate that a contrasting fact has no impact on the conclusion

4. Present a condition under which the prediction will be true

5. Introduce an exception to the stated rule

6. Introduce a pivot to a contrasting/surprising fact

7. Indicate a rule that holds true more than half of the time

8. Indicate that a particular thing is the most significant

9. Indicate a pair of consequences

10. Indicate the usual response to a particular situation

11. Indicate the author's negative attitude toward the event described

12. Indicate the timing of a sequence of events

13. Introduce an opinion

14. Present a final outcome

15. Introduce examples

16. Indicate the author's disagreement

17. Introduce a contrast

18. Indicate the timing of a sequence of events

Note: This is unusual! "Since" typically introduces a premise, but occasionally it will express the order in which events occurred.

19. Indicate necessity

20. Indicate necessity

21. Qualify the nature of an assertion

22. Introduce a pivot to a contrasting/surprising fact

23. Introduce a supporting example

24. Introduce evidence

25. Indicate the author's negative attitude

26. Indicate the timing of a sequence of events

Note: "Then" is most often an indicator of the necessary condition of a conditional statement. Sometimes, however, it just expresses the order in which events occurred.

27. Introduce a conclusion that follows from previously stated evidence

28. Introduce a pivot to a contrasting/surprising fact

29. Introduce a refutation

30. Introduce support for a previously stated conclusion

Drill 148: What's Important? Round 2

Instructions: Here's another round of practice separating the wheat from the chaff! Mark up each of the following paragraphs as you would a Reading Comprehension passage.

1. For many years, biological scientists have sought to decipher cellular function by quantifying the degrees of protein and mRNA expression within populations of their cells of interest. Classically, these measurements required combining many cells into a single sample and rupturing their membranes, thus exposing pooled quantities of the target molecule for detection. One limitation of this technique is the reliance on average measurements: it is impossible to distinguish a uniform population of cells expressing intermediate quantities of a molecule from a population composed of separate low and high expressers. The distinction has proven to be important, particularly in the context of drug-targeting of cancer cells; prescribing a dose to hit the "average" cell may completely miss the more aggressive "one percent."

2. "Falsifiability" is the term coined by Karl Popper for the idea that a hypothesis or theory addresses the observable world only insofar as it can be found false as the result of some observation or physical experiment. For instance, the proposition "all cats have fur" can easily be proven false with the observation of a single hairless cat. The proposition "the world will end in the year 3035" is impractical to falsify, but still passes the test of falsifiability in that there exists the logical possibility that 3035 will come and go without the world ending. Popper claimed that a falsifiable theory is the only kind that can truly be scientific, or at least useful to the scientific community.

3.   Quantum mechanics is a relatively new field of physics that was developed in the early 1900s. Although we classically think of a particle as a fixed object, quantum mechanics describes particles as waves, using properties such as position and energy. The quantum mechanical wave describes the probability that the particle's properties take on certain values. Take, for example, the analogy of rolling a six-sided die. For each roll, there is a one-in-six chance that any single number will result. After rolling, however, only one single number will be observed. If the die is rolled enough times, one can deduce that the die has six sides and that each side is equally likely. However, one can never be completely sure because rolling dice is probabilistic in nature. Quantum mechanics states that the same is true of the position (and other properties) of a particle. A particle trapped in a closed box has some finite probability of being at any location within the box. Open the box once and you'll find the particle at only one location. Open the box enough times and you'll see all the particle locations and the frequency at which they are achieved. From this, one can deduce the original properties of the quantum mechanical wave, just as one could deduce the properties of the die.

4.   However, in spite of the well-documented dangers posed by antibiotic-resistant bacteria, many scientists argue that the human race has more to fear from viruses. Whereas bacteria reproduce asexually through binary fission, viruses lack the necessary structures for reproduction and so are known as "intracellular obligate parasites." Virus particles called virions must marshal the host cell's ribosomes, enzymes, and other cellular machinery in order to propagate. Once various viral components have been built, they bind together randomly in the cellular cytoplasm. The newly finished copies of the virus break through the cellular membrane, destroying the cell in the process. Because of this, viral infections cannot be treated *ex post facto* in the same way that bacterial infections can, since antivirals designed to kill the virus could do critical damage to the host cell itself. In fact, viruses can infect bacteria (themselves complete cells), but not the other way around. For many viruses, such as those responsible for the common cold sore, remission rather than cure is the goal of currently available treatments.

Answers follow on the next page.

Answers

Note: Remember, how we notate is subjective, but what we notate shouldn't be. We've included here the important material that you should have noted, but we leave it up to you to come up with a notation system. We find that bracketing is superior to underlining for multiple lines of text, and that labeling anything you bracket or underline with shorthand is a good way to help you relocate relevant information to answer questions later.

1. Too much science. Don't try to figure it out. Tag the measurements/experiments with a word that will let you find it if asked (something like "rupture and measure"). Also, a problem is noted. You don't have to fully understand it, but note that it's something about the average being a problem.

2. Note Popper's theory. It's a bit complicated, but tag the examples and use them to help you understand it. Also, note that the author doesn't weigh in, instead always attributing attitude to Popper.

3. More complicated science. Try to reduce it to the most important concept, using the example/metaphor (which you should have tagged) to help you. We'd go with "quantum mechanics = probability."

4. Note the comparison between viruses and bacteria at the beginning and end of the paragraphs. There's too much science to understand in the middle—tag it with a note to let you know it's describing how viruses work so you can come back here to find the answer to any Identification questions it asks.

Drill 149: Sum It Up, Round 2

Instructions: Most students try to retain too much information while working through an RC passage, or they take notes that are almost as long as the paragraph they're summarizing! For each of the following paragraphs, sum it up as succinctly as possible. Try to capture the paragraph in fewer than ten words.

1. Due to a dearth of angel investors and venture capitalists, many new entrepreneurs are investing their own capital. Some economists argue that, while this requires a significant initial outlay and may carry heavy risks, the rewards can be substantial. However, when such new businesses fail, the consequences may stifle further entrepreneurial risk-taking.

2. Recent interest in dark, psychological themes in entertainment has led to a resurgence in critical discussion of gothic literature. Though gothic literature is often associated with fair maidens in distress and crumbling castles, it has in fact expanded far beyond its early roots. Critics have the option of examining a range of topics, including female gothic, African-American gothic, and queer gothic.

3. Somewhat paradoxically, the prominent virologist Nathan Wolfe considers human immunodeficiency virus (HIV), which has resulted in the deaths of more than thirty million people and infected twice that number, "the biggest near-miss of our lifetime." Despite being the most lethal pandemic in history, HIV could have been far more damaging to the human population. Wolfe notes that it is only through happenstance that this virus cannot be transmitted through respiratory droplets, thereby limiting its rate of transmission.

4. Picasso's *Large Nude in a Red Armchair* marks the extreme of the artist's at times combative relationship with Matisse. The painting is a clear parody of Matisse's earlier *Odalisque with a Tambourine*. Both paintings feature vivid color contrasts, with green wallpaper, vivid reds, glaring yellows, and rich browns. But Picasso's painting, finished in 1929, mocks the achievements of Matisse's earlier work. The sensuous, rich mood of Matisse's painting has been transformed in Picasso's work into something harsh and grotesque.

5. It is clear that the Parthenon frieze is meant to be thought of as a continuous whole. This is particularly interesting because it is unprecedented in Greek art. Continuous friezes on the faces of Greek temples generally depict single subjects, and if continued over all four sides of a building, the four stretches of the frieze are usually thematically separate.

6. Scottish economist Adam Smith's *The Wealth of Nations* heralded the market-based economic system that has increasingly become the norm since the book's publication in 1776. That year predates wide usage of the term capitalism, now commonly associated with Smith, and which Smith refers to as a "system of natural liberty." Smith presented what have become the fundamentals of capitalist economics: supply and demand, the importance of specialization, and the division of labor.

7. The term "free rider" originates from the example of riding public transportation without paying the fare. More broadly, a free rider is anyone who uses or enjoys the benefits of something without paying or takes more than his or her proper share of a publicly shared good that is limited in supply. Free riders can cause others to curtail their own contributions and/or can result in excessive depletion of a common resource, leading to the "free rider problem."

8. While specific rules vary by jurisdiction, all states have some form of a continuing legal education requirement for members of the bar. For example, in New York, requirements vary depending on whether an attorney is experienced or newly admitted to practice and must be completed every two years. The main purpose of continuing legal education requirements is to ensure that attorneys who are licensed to practice are apprised of new legal developments.

9. The War of the Spanish Succession began as a quarrel over whether an Austrian Habsburg or French Bourbon would succeed the childless Charles II of Spain. The conflict eventually embroiled most of Europe and secured an important place in the history of the region. For centuries afterward, school children learned of the Duke of Marlborough's victory at Blenheim and the military brilliance of Prinz Eugen of Savoy, as well as the exploits of Louis XIV of France.

10. Though an echo is a fairly simple acoustic phenomenon—a reflection of sound waves off some hard surface—it occurs only under very specific circumstances. The reflecting object must be more than 11.3 meters away from the sound source or the echo will return too soon to be distinguishable from the original sound. A reflecting object more than about 170 meters, on the other hand, will rarely produce an audible echo, since sound dissipates with distance.

11. According to the modern definition of science, the ancient Greeks were not scientists but philosophers. For example, their investigations were performed in what is now considered an unscientific manner, as is illustrated by Aristotle and his conclusions about the properties of water. Before studying water, Aristotle discovered that matter existed in three main categories: solid, liquid, and gas. He concluded that a solid was the least expandable of the three and verified this by observing that a solid always sank in a liquid of the same type. When Aristotle encountered ice, he postulated that it was an exception to these categories and that the shape of solid water caused it to stay afloat. This, of course, is incorrect.

12. Copernicus's model of the solar system was heliocentric, positing that all of the planets revolved around the sun. Brahe's theory stated that all of the planets revolved around the sun, except the earth, which was immobile, and that the sun actually revolved around the earth. Even if both accurately predicted future movements of the planets, it is easy to see how Copernicus's theory has less of an "ad hoc" quality—and, of course, provides a superior explanation of the mechanisms of the solar system.

8

13. A centuries-old saying that a duck's quack does not echo was confirmed by scientists in the Acoustics Department of the University of Salford. They recorded a duck first in an anechoic chamber filled with sound-absorbing fiberglass wedges, then in an echo chamber with the acoustical properties of a small cathedral.

14. The main reason Boal developed theater workshop styles was to grant audiences agency in order to allow them to create ways to free themselves from oppression. He found that theater audiences were locked into a passive role, similar to the ways in which he saw the oppressed coerced into a subservient role in relation to their oppressors. So, he created the "spect-actor," who simultaneously witnesses and creates theater.

15. For years, medical experts took for granted the idea that blind people can hear better than sighted people. However, functional brain imaging has now allowed researchers to observe the brains of blind people who possess what some have termed "cerebral superpowers," including the ability to understand speech at up to 25 syllables per second. They found that a brain region called V1, situated at the back of the skull and which normally only responds to light, can also process auditory information in the brains of blind people.

16. Invisible theater and guerrilla theater are two forms of street theater with similar origins but very different approaches. Both forms take place exclusively in public places, but invisible theater conceals its performative nature whereas guerrilla theater flaunts it. While invisible theater creates a performance space unbeknownst to its audience, guerrilla theater actively seeks the attention of an audience by explicitly imposing a performance space onto a public place.

17. The role of agency regulations is especially significant in administrative law. At the federal level, for example, Congress may enact a law that sets forth more general statutory guidelines, which are then supplemented by regulations promulgated by the appropriate agency. This approach is common with environmental laws, the specific details of which often require specialized knowledge from scientists, enforcement experts, and policy makers at the Environmental Protection Agency.

18. Consider the case of Phineas Gage, a rail worker who, in 1848, suffered a massive injury to the frontal lobe of his brain. While Gage was ultimately able to function fairly normally, his personality was markedly changed; he became boorish and irresponsible. Gage's case was well documented, allowing modern reconstructions to show that his injury affected areas of the brain that we now know to be related to moral sensibilities and their expression.

19. Nineteenth-century painter Albert Bierstadt's view of his artistic skill as a vehicle for self-promotion was evident in his choices of style and subject matter. From the debut of his career with the exhibition of *Lake Lucerne* (1856), he developed a fixed style that was most easily recognizable for its size. *Lake Lucerne* was by far the largest painting on display at its exhibition and measured over three meters wide. This, coupled with the artist's ability to represent the optimistic feeling in America during westward expansion, led to Bierstadt's explosive growth in popularity during the 1860s.

20. It may also be possible to restore forest health through the application of rock flour. For example, near Asheville, North Carolina, as part of a greenhouse study, hundreds of red spruce and Fraser fir trees were planted in depleted mountain soils that were remineralized with rock flour to varying degrees. Rock-dusted trees not only grew significantly faster than controls, at rates correlating with the application amount, but also manifested improved resistance to disease, demonstrated by increased survival rates. Preliminary field trials have also indicated that remineralization helps alleviate the deleterious effects of acid rain, which drains key nutrients from forest soils.

21. Electroconvulsive therapy (ECT) is a controversial psychiatric treatment involving the induction of a seizure in a patient via the passage of electricity through the brain. While beneficial effects of electrically induced seizures are evident and predictable in most patients, a unified mechanism of action has not yet been established and remains the subject of numerous investigations. According to most, though not all, published studies, ECT has been shown to be effective against several conditions, such as severe depression, mania, and some acute psychotic states, that are resistant to other treatments, although, like many other medical procedures, ECT has its risks.

22. In 1887, an ingenious experiment performed by Albert Michelson and Edward Morley severely undermined classical physics by failing to confirm the existence of "ether," a ghostly massless medium that was thought to permeate the universe. Although the implications of this experimental failure were not completely evident for many years, it ultimately paved the way for Einstein's special theory of relativity.

23. Around 1960, mathematician Edward Lorenz found unexpected behavior in apparently simple equations representing atmospheric air flows. Whenever he reran his model with the same inputs, different outputs resulted, although the model lacked any random elements. Lorenz realized that tiny rounding errors in his analog computer mushroomed over time, leading to erratic results. His findings marked a seminal moment in the development of chaos theory, which, despite its name, has little to do with randomness.

24. The extent to which legal precedent is studied by students depends on the nature of the legal system. In common-law systems, such as the United States and United Kingdom, individual case judgments and legal opinions form critical legal precedent that is necessary in order to interpret and apply statutes and regulations. In civil-law systems, such as those found in much of continental Europe, legal precedent is much less important, as interpretation of laws depends primarily on application of the legal code.

25. Although supernovae explode frequently, few are visible from Earth to the naked eye. In 1604, in Padua, Italy, a supernova became visible, appearing as a star so bright that it was visible in daylight for more than a year. Galileo, who lectured at the local university, gave several lectures that were widely attended by the public. The lectures not only sought to explain the origin of the "star," but also seriously undermined the views of many philosophers at the time that the heavens were unchangeable.

26. The Tokugawa period (1603–1867) in Japan serves as a laboratory for organizational behavior historians for the same reason that Iceland works for geneticists—isolation removes extraneous variables. The Tokugawa shoguns brought peace to a land of warring feudal lords. To preserve that tranquility, the Tokugawa shogunate forbade contact with the outside world, allowing only a few Dutch trading ships to dock at one restricted port. Domestically, in pursuit of the same goal, the social order was fixed; there were four classes—warriors (samurai), artisans, merchants, and farmers or peasants—and social mobility was prohibited.

27. Cells employ many strategies to avoid genetic mutation. From the high fidelity of DNA-synthesizing enzymes to the pro-death signaling that accompanies mutagenic stimuli, such as UV radiation, cellular mechanisms that stymie genetic changes are ubiquitous throughout the natural world. These mechanisms are critical because widespread genomic changes would wreak physiological havoc; indeed, malfunctions in molecular players that safeguard against mutagenesis, such as the protein p53, have been implicated in diseases such as cancer.

28. Trauma theory has likely influenced a number of seminal literary works. For example, in Toni Morrison's *Beloved*, an early trauma returns years later in the form of a mysterious visitor representing a physical embodiment of the trauma that forces it to be dealt with at long last. This closely parallels a central tenet of trauma theory, which is that the feelings associated with trauma, however long repressed, will eventually return.

8

29. Because of the proximity and likeness of Mars to Earth, scientists have long speculated about the possibility of life on Mars. Roughly three centuries ago, astronomers observed Martian polar ice caps, and later scientists discovered other similarities to Earth, including length of day and axial tilt. But in 1965, photos taken by the Mariner 4 probe revealed a Mars without rivers, oceans, or signs of life. Moreover, in the 1990s, it was discovered that unlike Earth, Mars no longer possessed a substantial global magnetic field, allowing celestial radiation to reach the planet's surface and solar wind to eliminate much of Mars's atmosphere over the course of several billion years.

30. The aspect of the aquatic ape theory that captured the public imagination and undoubtedly boosted its standing was that this hypothesis could explain human hairlessness; as with dolphins, this streamlining could facilitate swimming and diving. Proponents noted that the remaining body hair would match the flow of water, and extreme advocates explained the gender difference in hair by suggesting that females much more rarely ventured out of the shallows and into the putatively more dangerous forests and savannas.

Answers follow on the next page.

Answers

Note: Your summaries will probably be different than ours, but make sure that they convey the same information. Also, our notes are not grammatically correct—they are essentially shorthand, so don't confine yourself to thinking in full sentences!

1. Investing in new business risky.

2. Modern gothic lit quite varied.

3. HIV worse if transmitted more easily.

4. *Large Nude* is Picasso mocking Matisse.

5. Continuous Parthenon frieze unprecedented.

6. Smith's fundamentals of capitalism—S&D, specialization, D of L.

7. Free riders deplete common resources.

8. Continuing legal ed. important.

9. War of Spanish Succession important.

10. Echoes depend on distance.

11. Aristotle ice example → ancient Greeks = philosophers, not scientists.

12. Copernicus's model superior to Brahe's.

13. Duck quack doesn't echo.

14. Boal's "spect-actor" idea frees audiences.

15. Brain scans confirm blind hear better.

16. Guerrilla—audience knows. Invisible—audience doesn't.

17. Admin. law needs agency regulations.

18. Brain injury can change personality.

19. Bierstadt self-promoted with style and subject.

20. Rock flour remineralization restores forests.

21. ECT helpful but risky.

22. Ether failure paved way for relativity theory.

23. Lorenz's findings important to chaos theory.

24. Precedent's importance depends on system.

25. Supernova showed the heavens change.

26. Isolation makes Tokugawa useful for O.B. historians.

27. Cells avoiding genetic mutation is important.

28. Trauma theory influences literature.

29. Life on Mars doubtful.

30. Aquatic ape theory offered hairlessness explanation.

8

Drill 150: Where Are You Going with This? Round 2

Instructions: The first sentence in a paragraph can (still!) tell you a lot, and the better you know this test, the more true that becomes. Remember, this test is standardized, and trends in argument structure should help you make accurate predictions about the direction a paragraph is likely to take. Use this drill to practice that skill by writing out the direction you think a paragraph will take after each of the introductory sentences below.

1. Despite these limitations, Shugart's application of computer modeling has proven eerily prophetic of the long-term effects of global climate change on sustainable forest management.

2. Díaz's refusal to reduce his linguistic identity to one variety of a standard language reinforces the cross-cultural sense of belonging experienced by his protagonists.

3. While the archeologists caution against drawing hasty conclusions, several findings support their initial hypothesis that the Neolithic jars were indeed used to store wine.

4. One notable example of how the geopolitical shift rewards emerging economies is the so-called South-South trade.

5. Most of the laboratory-based tests that assess the impact of sleep deprivation on psychological performance have concentrated on simple cognitive and motor tasks.

6. Despite the proliferation of research on climate change vulnerability, the notion of "vulnerability" has not received much attention.

7. This popular criticism reflects dissatisfaction with state-sponsored strategies for language revitalization.

8. In his paintings, Rousseau not only employed an unconventional combination of traditional genres, such as landscape or portraiture, but also juxtaposed dreamlike tropical imagery with urban scenery evoking tabloid illustrations and postcards.

9. Janet Benshoof concedes that the situation of ad hoc tribunals is often uncertain, yet she strongly believes in the importance of the Iraqi High Tribunal in establishing the rule of law in Iraq.

10. This theory may sound compelling, but, in reality, there are several competing explanations for the profitability of the sharing economy in Europe.

8

11. In the course of the study, M. Koob and W. Szybalski developed a comprehensive set of procedures that reduces the risk of compromising the agarose microbeads.

12. To address this concern, most Nordic countries replaced the government-mandated minimum-wage system with union-negotiated wages set by industry.

13. For centuries, scientists have speculated about the expansion rate of the universe, but their estimations were imprecise.

14. Upon further study, the researchers discovered that oxygen vacancies contribute to a considerable photodegradation rate.

15. Given that any structural inadequacies may incur the high costs of remedial work, it is essential to recognize that the legal responsibility for satisfactory execution of the project rests with the contractor.

16. In opposition to the dominant scholarship that interprets El Greco's mastery as a product of the western European Renaissance, some commentators have sought to tie El Greco's work to Byzantine art and culture.

17. There is much debate about introducing stricter regulations to protect child actors in the film industry.

18. Federal expenditures on the United States' international military presence have reached unsustainable levels vis-à-vis the economy's projected growth rate.

19. In line with existing literature, Molyneux makes a distinction between need-based mobilizations rooted in a traditional understanding of gender roles and more politicized movements that focus primarily on defying systemic power imbalances.

20. In order to adjust the philosophy of criminal law to the changing landscape of social relations, we encourage reflection on the state's authority and legitimacy to punish.

Answers follow on the next page.

Answers

Note: Your answers will differ from ours. That's OK! Consider where you landed and where we landed, and if they differ substantially, ask yourself "Which of these sounds more like the LSAT?" Maybe both do, in which case, great! But if only one does, consider how you might align your thinking with ours the next time.

1. Ways in which the model is prophetic. "These limitations" suggests that the critics had their turn already and it's now time to argue in favor of Shugart's application.

2. If Díaz refuses to reduce his linguistic identity in the way described, it seems likely that he has been critiqued for failing to do so, and that this paragraph will defend him from that criticism.

3. What are the findings, and why do they support the hypothesis?

4. South-South trade in detail and how it exemplifies the shift rewarding emerging economies.

5. This presents the old way of doing things. Chances are, there's been some catalyst, and the passage will pivot to why the old way is insufficient or discuss an emerging new way.

6. Definition, or perhaps multiple definitions, of the key term in quotations and/or why it hasn't received much attention and why that needs to change.

7. The opposition to state-sponsored language revitalization programs.

8. How Rousseau developed this style and/or what influence it had.

9. Present Benshoof's argument. Since she's already conceded a point, chances are good that the opposition to her argument preceded it, and it's her turn now.

10. Objections to the theory in the form of alternative explanations.

11. What are the procedures, why are they in place, and what do they hope to achieve?

12. Was this solution effective? Did it lead to any other problems?

13. If that's what they've done for centuries, what changed and why?

14. Why is this the case, and how did they discover it? What implications does this have?

15. This presents a legal problem and a single mandated solution. Expect the paragraph to argue against other possible solutions and support that this is the only viable one.

16. The paragraph will present a recategorization of the artist's work.

17. What are the two sides of the debate? Chances are, the author won't weigh in just yet, and each side will be explored in more detail in a subsequent paragraph.

18. How do the economics of this problem pan out, and how might we solve this problem?

19. This opening line sets up a compare-and-contrast paragraph.

20. If adjustment is necessary, this sets up an "old-way-vs.-new-way" paragraph. Since it mandates "reflection" on the legitimacy of something long held to be legitimate, expect arguments *against* the legitimacy of purely punitive action.

Drill 151: Vocab Lab #14 – Erudite Set

Instructions: Show your erudition (great education) by sprinkling these fancy LSAT words into your next conversation. Choose the answer closest in meaning.

1. Capricious

   (A) reliable

   (B) erratic

   (C) amusing

2. Catalyst

   (A) agent of destruction

   (B) bringer of improvement

   (C) cause of change

3. Didactic

   (A) instructional

   (B) unproductive

   (C) discriminating

4. Ephemeral

   (A) exquisite

   (B) fleeting

   (C) melancholic

5. Hortatory

   (A) acutely harrowing

   (B) crucially enlightening

   (C) strongly encouraging

6. Inexorable

   (A) fearless

   (B) relentless

   (C) helpless

7. Render

   (A) make, turn, give

   (B) break, tear, sever

   (C) stop, terminate, cease

8. Rhetoric

   (A) ambiguous, unclear questions

   (B) satirical, mocking criticisms

   (C) effective, persuasive language

9. Tantamount

   (A) nearly paradoxical

   (B) essentially the same

   (C) preceding logically

10. Vicissitudes

    (A) twists of fate

    (B) decreases in wealth

    (C) principles of ethics

Answers

1. B

Capricious = erratic; acting on *caprice* (whim; random impulse). You can describe nonhuman things as *capricious* (e.g., the weather) without anthropomorphizing them (pretending they're human) too much.

2. C

Catalyst = cause of change. Chemical *catalysts* accelerate reactions but are not themselves used up in those reactions.

3. A

Didactic = instructional; intended for instructional use. *Didactic* can convey additional connotations of moral (or moralistic) instruction or of unwanted, dry instruction.

4. B

Ephemeral = fleeting; lasting only a short time. For bonus points, use *ephemera* (things that last only a short time).

5. C

Hortatory = strongly encouraging; urging onward. The underlying verb is *exhort* (urge; beseech; goad).

6. B

Inexorable = relentless; unyielding; deaf to pleading. The root, *or-,* means "pray"; something *inexorable* cannot be prayed away.

7. A

Render = make; turn; give. You can *render* a car unusable (make it unusable) by *rendering* the tires to your friend (giving them to her).

8. C

Rhetoric = the art of persuasion; the skill of using language effectively. It can also indicate the use of insincere, bombastic, or extravagant language.

9. B

Tantamount = essentially the same (as); equivalent in significance (to). From *tant amount* = amount as much.

10. A

Vicissitudes = twists of fate; ups and downs; changes in fortune. The root of *vicissitudes* is the Latin root *vicis* = change, which also gives rise to *vice versa* and *vice president* (substitute president).

Drill 152: Vocab Lab #15 – More Confusion

Instructions: Here are more LSAT words that are commonly confused with each other (or with other words) or that have something about them that's just plain confusing. For each word, choose the answer closest in meaning.

1. Averse

   (A) opposed to; feeling dislike for
   (B) injurious toward; harmful to
   (C) silent toward; indifferent to

2. Consensus

   (A) compliance
   (B) disunity
   (C) agreement

3. Criterion

   (A) probable outcome
   (B) compilation of parts
   (C) standard for measurement

4. Disparate

   (A) crestfallen
   (B) distinct
   (C) uniform

5. Eschew

   (A) face
   (B) take
   (C) shun

6. Illusory

   (A) false; deceptive
   (B) plain; palpable
   (C) suggestive; implied

7. Imminent

   (A) outstanding
   (B) reckless
   (C) looming

8. Inflammatory

   (A) pacifying
   (B) incendiary
   (C) incombustible

9. Parameter

   (A) subjective evaluation of merit
   (B) value or setting that characterizes something
   (C) guarantee of a benefit

10. Perpetrate

    (A) maintain (an idea)
    (B) designate (a successor)
    (C) commit (a crime)

11. Prescribe

    (A) prohibit; outlaw (a course of action)
    (B) order; recommend (a course of action)
    (C) regard; consider (a course of action)

12. Proscribe

    (A) forbid
    (B) require
    (C) transmit

13. Ramifications
    - (A) origins
    - (B) results
    - (C) observations

14. Surmise
    - (A) believe without absolute certainty
    - (B) demonstrate with absolute certainty
    - (C) declare with intensity

15. Temperance
    - (A) impatience
    - (B) excess
    - (C) moderation

8

Answers

1. A

Averse = strongly opposed to; having a firm dislike for. It's possible to confuse *averse* with *adverse*, which means "unfavorable; disadvantageous."

2. C

Consensus = agreement; solidarity; unity. A *consensus* decision for a group is one reached by mutual agreement. What is not 100% clear, however, is whether that agreement must be unanimous or just by a majority for the agreement to be termed "*consensus*." In your own group processes, be clear about what you mean by "*consensus*."

3. C

Criterion = standard for measurement; a standard by which a judgment or decision can be reached. The plural form of *criterion* is *criteria*. "This is the *criteria*" is therefore incorrect; rather, say "these are the *criteria*."

4. B

Disparate = distinct; dissimilar; different in quality or kind. *Disparate* is kind of a mash-up of *different* and *separate*, but the words are really "similar but different."

5. C

Eschew = shun; avoid; abstain or keep away from. *Eschew* is pronounced as it looks: ess + chew, with the stress on the *chew*, as if the word were a sneeze. *Eschew* is rare and strange enough that its use can stop a conversation. Try it and see.

6. A

Illusory = false; deceptive; based on a wrong perception or *illusion* (an unreal image). It's possible to mix up *illusory* with *allusion* (a reference) or its adjective *allusive*.

7. C

Imminent = looming; about to take place. *Imminent*, with its initial short *i*, is not the same as *eminent* (prominent; high-ranking), with its initial short *e*.

8. B

Inflammatory = incendiary; awaking violent emotion. An *inflammatory* remark metaphorically sets someone on fire. Note that the *in-* of *inflammatory*, *inflame*, and *inflammable* is not a negative (as in *inedible* = not edible). The word *flammable* was supposedly invented so that people wouldn't think that something labeled *inflammable* was not combustible, when in fact *inflammable* very much means "combustible."

9. B

Parameter = a value or settings that helps to describe a system. Before you run a computer model of, say, an economy, you set the *parameters*, e.g., the current rate of inflation. Your choice of *parameters* determines the range of outputs you'll see. But *parameters* are not *perimeters*; you never set the "*perimeters*" of a model. It's always *parameters*.

10. C

Perpetrate = commit (a crime); execute (a harmful action). Don't confuse *perpetrate* with *perpetuate* (maintain; continue indefinitely or perpetually). The word *perpetrator* (criminal; executor of an evil act) should help remind you which is which. Suspected *perpetrators* are sometimes given a "perp walk" in front of the press as they are marched into a police station or court of law.

11. B

Prescribe = order; recommend (a course of action). For your health, a doctor *prescribes* exercise and a daily dose of medicine for you, and you take the second *prescription* as a written document to the pharmacy. (At least, you used to; now it's all electronic.) It's possible to confuse *prescribe* with its near-antonym *proscribe*, the next word.

12. A

Proscribe = forbid; condemn; denounce. *Proscribe* is a very strange word. Root analysis produces "write before or in front of," which doesn't seem that negative. But *proscribe* really meant "publish" (write before an audience), and what was often published were condemnations, forfeitures of property, and other bad things.

8

13.   B

Ramifications = results; implications; offshoots. The issue with this word is not so much that it's confusing or confused with another word, but rather that its nuanced meaning is being lost. *Ramify* = branch; spread out into smaller branches. So *ramifications* should be thought of as that thicket of branching consequences that spread out from some single moment or event.

14.   A

Surmise = believe or guess on the basis of limited evidence. *Surmise* does not mean "infer, conclude beyond the shadow of a doubt" in the sense of formal logic. However, because *surmising* ought to be done with at least some evidence, and maybe because *surmise* sounds fancy, some people may think *surmise* indicates certainty. It does not.

15.   C

Temperance = moderation. *Temperance* movements typically advocate moderation or even abstinence with respect to alcohol. *Temperance* shares a root with *temper* and *temperament*. But *temper* alone has complicated meanings: after all, when you often lose your *temper*, you are said to have a *temper*. So it's probably best just to learn *temperance* as its own word.

8

Step 2–Pause and Rehash

Drill 153: Know Thy Purpose

Instructions: Making a clear and concise passage map is a skill. Using a clear and concise passage map is a different skill. It can be hard to develop the latter until you've developed the former, so use this drill to get a head start as you develop your other passage mapping skills. Use each of the following passage maps to answer the accompanying questions.

P1: Critics don't take author X seriously because he writes fan fiction

P2: History of fan fiction

P3: Defense of fan fiction

P4: Refutation of critics regarding author X

1. Which of the following best describes the role of paragraph three in the passage as a whole?

    (A) It presents the author's main conclusion.

    (B) It presents background information about the subject of the passage.

    (C) It presents information that will then be used to support the author's main point.

2. The primary purpose of this passage is to

    (A) present a critical debate over a literary genre

    (B) defend an author against criticism

    (C) describe an author's role in the development of a literary genre

P1: Introduction of misconception/author foreshadows that she will disagree

P2: Reasons for misconception

P3: Author explains why those reasons are flawed

P4: Author fleshes out what we should be thinking instead

3. Which of the following best expresses the main point of the passage?

    (A) Scholars are deeply concerned that posthumously releasing Jefferson's early writing will tarnish his reputation as an Enlightenment thinker.

    (B) Although many scholars feel that the release of Jefferson's poetry will distort his historical reputation, there are reasons to be skeptical of this concern.

    (C) Jefferson was the most conflicted of the Founding Fathers, as evidenced by the gap between his public statements and his private writings.

4. Which of the following best expresses the purpose of the second paragraph?

    (A) It undermines a claim made by the author in the previous paragraph.

    (B) It explains the problems with a common way of thinking.

    (C) It elaborates on a position introduced in the previous paragraph.

P1: Scientists couldn't explain the crystals found in tree sap

P2: Broader discussion about how crystals usually form in nature

P3: Description of the North Pole / Equator tree sap experiment

P4: Author tentatively endorses the barometric pressure explanation

5. The author's primary purpose is to

(A) present and evaluate a hypothesis

(B) demonstrate the futility of a certain methodology

(C) summarize recent research findings

6. Which of the following best expresses the main point of the passage?

(A) The hexagonal crystals within tree sap may be influenced by the atmospheric pressure to which maple trees are subjected.

(B) Experiments that only make use of extreme environments are inherently suspicious in terms of their wider applicability.

(C) The formation of crystals in nature is primarily a function of the heat and pressure to which certain objects are exposed.

P1: Calhoun: an 18th-century painter, one of earliest at nonrepresentational art

P2: Calhoun's upbringing and education

P3: Calhoun's initial experimentation with "messy art"/resulting backlash

P4: As others followed his lead, he went even further afield

7. Which of the following best expresses the purpose of the second paragraph?

(A) To qualify a claim in the preceding paragraph about the lack of refinement in Calhoun's art

(B) To outline the formative influences on Calhoun's eventual creative pursuits

(C) To argue that Calhoun's teachers had a bigger effect on him than did his parents

8. Which of the following most clearly summarizes the main point of the passage?

(A) Late in his career, Alfonso Calhoun transformed his style from a messy form of realism to wholly unrecognizable nonrepresentational art.

(B) Alfonso Calhoun was an influential artist who first studied under the tutelage of famed French realist Jacques Dubois.

(C) Although derided by many critics at the time, Alfonso Calhoun gave himself and subsequent artists the permission to depart from strict realism.

P1: "Plausible Domain" is a better legal standard than "Provable Interest"

P2: PD allows for ownership in cases that wouldn't be covered by PI

P3: Overall, better for standard to be too permissive than too restrictive

9. Which of the following best describes the function of the third paragraph?

(A) It delineates the historical implications of adopting a certain standard.

(B) It responds to a potential objection to the situation described in the second paragraph.

(C) It illustrates some exceptions to the recommendation in the first paragraph.

10. The primary purpose of the passage is to

(A) argue against a certain criterion for assessing ownership

(B) provide a summary of how a certain criterion came to prominence

(C) describe the differences between two different criteria for assessing ownership

8

Answers follow on the next page.

Answers

1.   C

It can't be A, because the author's main point is in P4, going against the critics in P1. P3 helps the author to defend author X, so P3 acts as support for P4 (C). Choice B seems to better describe P1 and P2, which offer the background on author X and fan fiction.

2.   B

Since the author's main point is refuting the critics of author X, B is the primary purpose. A is true but too narrow, as debating fan fiction is a tool used to refute the critics of author X. It doesn't seem clear that author X was involved in the development of fan fiction as C suggests.

3.   B

Given that the passage map shows that the author is trying to fix someone else's broken thinking, our main point shouldn't just be stating someone else's thinking (A). B captures the purpose of clarifying a misconception, whereas C seems to not touch at all on the idea of correction.

4.   C

In the first paragraph the author hints at the existence of misconception, but P2 would corroborate that, not undermine it (A). The author doesn't explain why the misconception is wrong until P3, so B is a mismatch. P1 introduced the misconception and P2 gives the reasons for it, so C is accurate.

5.   A

Since the author does offer a tentative endorsement, demonstrating futility is too strong (B) and simply summarizing is too neutral (C). "Evaluate" is a verb that indicates that the author offered an opinion without going too far in either direction (A).

6.   A

We want something that sounds like the author's opinion that barometric pressure may explain the crystals in sap. A expresses that idea. B is too general; it isn't focused on tree sap. C is too narrowly focused on the discussion of crystals in P2.

7.   B

"Qualifying a claim" (A) means to narrow the scope of applicability or to cite an exception, but P2 is not undermining or going against P1. C sounds like it's making an unsupported comparison by pitting the two topics of P2 against each other. B better connects the discussion of Calhoun's past to the rest of the passage.

8.   C

A is focused too much on the final stage in P4, while B is more limited to P1 and P2. C does the best job at wrapping its arms around the whole passage by tying together big ideas from P1, P3, and P4.

9.   B

P3 seems to be where the author solidifies her case for PD. She probably wouldn't be listing out historical examples (A) or backpedaling from her thesis (C). Since the situation in P2 could elicit the objection that PD allows for ownership in too broad a range of cases, P3 can be seen as answering that objection (B).

10. A

Since the author's thesis is a recommendation in favor of PD, the idea of summarizing the background (B) seems too neutral and the idea of describing the differences (C) seems too neutral and too limited to P2. The correct answer (A) has some surprising wording, but the author's endorsement of PD could potentially be restated as her rejection of PI.

8

Drill 154: Structure Your Thinking

Instructions: Every RC passage has a different topic, and sometimes, students can't see the forest for the trees. When you're so focused on the details of the passage, it can be hard to see the broad categories into which passages tend to fall. Use this drill to practice categorizing passages using passage maps that we've created for you. For each, select the answer choice that describes the mapped passage most completely.

1. P1: Background of genetic modification in agriculture

   P2: History of genetic modification in food crops

   P3: Genetic modification in food crops to combat world hunger

   P4: Opposition to genetic modification in food crops

   (A) The author reconciles two sides of a debate.

   (B) A debate is presented.

   (C) A thesis is illustrated with examples.

2. P1: Traditional elementary school curricula

   P2: New demands on people entering the workforce

   P3: Integration of technology into elementary education

   P4: Project-based elementary curricula

   (A) Old approach vs. new approach

   (B) A problem is presented, with solutions.

   (C) A thesis is illustrated with examples.

3. P1: Changing landscape of cannabis prohibition

   P2: How to regulate an existing but previously unregulated industry

   P3: Alcohol regulations after prohibition

   P4: Efficacy of noncompliance enforcement

   (A) A traditional view is refuted.

   (B) A problem is presented, with solutions.

   (C) A debate is presented, and the author takes a side.

4. P1: Criticism of Gadley's novels for being unrealistic

   P2: Background on literary genre magic realism

   P3: Qualities of Gadley's novels

   P4: How Gadley's novels align with magic realism

   (A) The importance of something is explored.

   (B) An artist is defended from criticism.

   (C) A traditional theory is refuted.

5. P1: Background on chimpanzee social structure

   P2: Chimpanzee troop that lost its aggressive males

   P3: Chimpanzee troop that became infertile

   P4: Chimpanzee social structure is not genetically predetermined

   (A) A debate is presented, and the author takes a side.

   (B) A traditional theory is refuted.

   (C) A thesis is illustrated with examples.

6. P1: Background on decline of prairie ecosystem

   P2: ID cause: fire suppression

   P3: Role of fire in functioning ecosystem

   P4: Secondary benefits to wildlife

   (A) A problem is presented, with solutions.

   (B) A debate is presented.

   (C) The importance of something is explored.

8

7.   P1: Long-accepted that rats spread bubonic plague

P2: Recent study on spread of disease

P3: Reasons lice as alternate vector fit transmission pattern

P4: Rats vs. lice; conclude probably lice

(A)   A traditional view is refuted.

(B)   A debate is presented.

(C)   Author reconciles two sides of a debate.

8.   P1: Two conflicting views of Trotsky's role in evolution of Communism

P2: View 1: a tragic figure who might have saved Soviet Union from emergence of Stalin

P3: View 2: an architect of the Communist revolution that led to Stalin's reign of terror

P4: Author: both views largely correct, though exaggerated and oversimplified

(A)   A traditional view is refuted.

(B)   A debate is presented.

(C)   Author reconciles two sides of a debate.

9.   P1: Background on third parties in American presidential elections

P2: Some say: quixotic exercises; distract from primary candidates

P3: Others say: important check on establishment; clearly have affected elections (ex. Perot's impact on Clinton's election)

P4: Author: affected elections (ex. did Nader elect Bush?)

(A)   A traditional view is refuted.

(B)   A debate is presented, and the author takes a side.

(C)   Author reconciles two sides of a debate.

10.   P1: History of eruptions of the Yellowstone volcano

P2: New study using remote sensing; ID source of superheated magma

P3: Next eruption: will be destructive and is "past due"

P4: Hypothesis: drilling into core and circulating water could reduce severity

(A)   A problem is presented, with solutions.

(B)   A debate is presented.

(C)   The importance of something is explored.

8

Answers follow on the next page.

Answers

1. **B. A debate is presented.**

There is a debate, but the author's perspective on the issue isn't evident in this passage map, so there is no evidence of reconciliation of the debate (A) or a thesis to be exemplified (C).

2. **A. Old approach vs. new approach**

"Traditional" anything should immediately bring to mind two possible passage structures: the old way vs. the new way or a traditional view is refuted. This map doesn't present a traditional viewpoint to refute—it just presents a traditional approach. A problem isn't presented because new demands aren't necessarily problematic (B), and no thesis is presented to be exemplified (C).

3. **B. A problem is presented, with solutions.**

This map reflects a legal passage, and legal passages often are structured around legal problems and their potential resolutions. Here the problems are cannabis industry regulation and enforcement, and the potential resolutions are those used for alcohol after prohibition. There is no traditional view presented (A) nor is there a debate (C).

4. **B. An artist is defended from criticism.**

When a passage begins with an artist being criticized, it will almost always proceed by defending the artist from that criticism. In this passage map, as in many LSAT passages, that defense takes the form of a reconceptualization of the artist's work. While a literary genre is central to the passage, its importance is not explored (A), and the critic's view that is refuted is not presented as a traditional theory (C).

5. **C. A thesis is illustrated with examples.**

Science passages are often structured around the exemplification of a theory and this one is no exception. The conclusive entry for the fourth paragraph tells us that this author is taking a position, but there isn't a debate presented (A) or a traditional theory to refute (B).

6. **C. The importance of something is explored.**

This author is describing the critical role of fire in the prairie ecosystem. There is no debate presented (B). This science passage, like the last, presents a problem, but unlike the last passage, this one doesn't propose any solutions (A).

7. **A. A traditional view is refuted.**

If a view is "long-accepted," we can expect that the passage will present a catalyst leading to the overthrow of that belief. A debate is certainly presented (B), but that doesn't go far enough: "presented" implies that the author has not weighed in, and that isn't accurate here. "Reconciles" (C) doesn't work either, because the author takes one side over the other, rather than bridging the gap between the two.

8. **C. Author reconciles two sides of a debate.**

"Two conflicting views" indicates a debate, not a traditionally accepted viewpoint (A). The author attempts a reconciliation in the last paragraph, rather than merely presenting the two sides (B).

9. **B. A debate is presented, and the author takes a side.**

There are two sides of a debate set out in the middle paragraphs and the author falls largely on the side of the "others" in P3. The debate isn't reconciled (C), nor is one view presented as more traditional than the other (A).

10. **A. A problem is presented, with solutions.**

A volcano that is "past due" to erupt is a problem. Circulating water to reduce its severity is a solution. The author isn't simply delineating the importance of the topic (C), and there is no debate presented (B).

Drill 155: Vocab Lab #16 – Science Words

Instructions: Science passages can be among the most intimidating, and unfamiliar language is a big part of that intimidation factor. These LSAT words all have to do with science somehow. Some of them have a specific scientific meaning, as well as a more general (but related) meaning. Others are connected to the scientific method or to idealized scientists. For each word, choose the answer closest in meaning.

1. Dubious
   - (A) indisputable
   - (B) deductible
   - (C) questionable

2. Erosion
   - (A) cultivation
   - (B) wearing down
   - (C) building up

3. Hypothesize
   - (A) put forward a testable assumption
   - (B) submit a statement for analysis
   - (C) draw a definite conclusion

4. Inertia
   - (A) ability to accelerate a process
   - (B) tendency to remain unchanged
   - (C) inclination to disintegrate

5. Judicious
   - (A) arbitrary; offhand
   - (B) sensible; wise
   - (C) constant; unvarying

6. Propagate
   - (A) misrepresent (a position)
   - (B) demonstrate (a phenomenon)
   - (C) spread (an idea)

7. Refute
   - (A) duplicate
   - (B) define
   - (C) disprove

8. Scrutinize
   - (A) examine closely
   - (B) reject absolutely
   - (C) fabricate partially

9. Speculate
   - (A) perform a scan
   - (B) offer a guess
   - (C) reflect a worldview

10. Volatile
    - (A) defined by stability
    - (B) subject to rapid change
    - (C) free from interference

Answers

1. C

Dubious = questionable; suspect; doubtful (from the same root as *doubt*). Calling something *dubious* is not necessarily a value judgment, but calling someone *dubious* is throwing shade on a shady character.

2. B

Erosion = wearing down; the process of wear and tear. The verb is *erode*. In environmental science, the physical *erosion* of things such as topsoil happens because of weather. A more abstract concept of *erosion*, e.g., of goodwill, is frequently encountered in other endeavors.

3. A

Hypothesize = put forward a testable assumption (e.g., a *hypothesis*) for the sake of argument or investigation. The process of *hypothesizing* and then testing *hypotheses* via experiment is the crux of the scientific method.

4. B

Inertia = tendency to remain unchanged. According to Isaac Newton, *inertia* is an object's tendency to remain at rest or to remain in straight-line motion (or to remain rotating). More metaphorically, *inertia* means inactivity, sluggishness, or resistance to change.

5. B

Judicious = sensible; wise; measured; using good judgment. Good scientists are *judicious* about how they design experiments and interpret their results.

6. C

Propagate = spread (an idea), generally widely. In physics, light waves are said to *propagate* through various media or through empty space. The related word *propaganda* literally means "*propagation*," but it has come to mean "manipulative political messages that are *propagated*."

7. C

Refute = disprove; falsify; prove to be false. *Refute* is a very important word in science, in law, and on the LSAT.

8. A

Scrutinize = examine closely (and usually critically); subject something to scrutiny. Good scientists *scrutinize* their experimental setups to reduce the possibility for errors and misinterpretations.

9. B

Speculate = offer a guess, educated or otherwise. Far from the traditional world of science—that is to say, on Wall Street—*speculate* means "gamble, make a risky bet" on some unknown outcome.

10. B

Volatile = subject to rapid change (generally unpredictable); erratic; changeable. *Volatile* can also mean "explosive, ready to blow." In chemistry, *volatile* substances evaporate (turn into vapor) very quickly.

8

Drill 156: Vocab Lab #17 – Negative Nancys

Instructions: The following LSAT words all are negative, by virtue of their prefixes *un-, in-, im-,* or *ir-.* Unmask these words by choosing the answer closest in meaning.

1. Unfettered
   - (A) greedy
   - (B) free
   - (C) shackled

2. Unintelligible
   - (A) unsatisfactory
   - (B) unassembled
   - (C) incomprehensible

3. Impermanence
   - (A) continuity
   - (B) penetration
   - (C) instability

4. Unprecedented
   - (A) never before seen
   - (B) never established
   - (C) never exceeded

5. Unimpeded
   - (A) insignificant
   - (B) unabridged
   - (C) unobstructed

6. Incoherence
   - (A) lack of intensity
   - (B) lack of clarity
   - (C) lack of value

7. Unscrupulous
   - (A) unprincipled
   - (B) unmistakable
   - (C) unflagging

8. Inconspicuous
   - (A) not hidden
   - (B) not noticeable
   - (C) not inaccessible

9. Unsubstantiated
   - (A) unsupported
   - (B) unperturbed
   - (C) unquestioned

10. Intangible
    - (A) unable to be believed thoroughly
    - (B) unable to be proclaimed widely
    - (C) unable to be touched physically

11. Untainted
    - (A) not unblemished
    - (B) not indefinite
    - (C) not contaminated

12. Irreconcilable
    - (A) impossible to resolve or bring together
    - (B) impossible to improve or make better
    - (C) impossible to command or dominate

13. Unjustifiable
    - (A) understandable
    - (B) inexcusable
    - (C) inescapable

14. Intransigence
    - (A) inability to influence another's thinking
    - (B) unwillingness to change one's position
    - (C) lack of capacity to explain an idea

15. Unwarranted
    - (A) uncalled for
    - (B) undeniable
    - (C) unprotected

8

Answers

1. B

Unfettered = free; unshackled; uninhibited; released from restraint. *Fetters* are chains or manacles.

2. C

Unintelligible = incomprehensible; not able to be understood. The word seems like a mash-up of *unintelligent* and *legible*, which isn't all that far off.

3. C

Impermanence = instability; lack of lasting existence (*permanence*). Even the pyramids of Egypt are *impermanent*.

4. A

Unprecedented = never before seen; never having happened before (lacking *precedent*). Either a good thing or a bad thing can be *unprecedented*, but it had better be new and worth shouting about.

5. C

Unimpeded = unobstructed; unhindered; not interfered with. That is, the thing has not been *impeded* or blocked.

6. B

Incoherence = lack of clarity, logic, or organization. The parts do not *cohere* (fit and stick together).

7. A

Unscrupulous = unprincipled; unguided by moral rules (lacking *scruples*). Avoid *unscrupulous* partners, since people may think you are, too.

8. B

Inconspicuous = not noticeable; not clearly visible. Trying to be *inconspicuous* often makes you more *conspicuous*.

9. A

Unsubstantiated = unsupported; not proven to be true by evidence. There is no *substance* behind an *unsubstantiated* claim.

10. C

Intangible = unable to be touched physically. *Tangible* property is physical and touchable. In math, a *tangent* curve is one that just touches something else.

11. C

Untainted = not contaminated; not tarnished (in either a physical or moral sense). The love that the band Soft Cell described in the 1980's was not *untainted*. Fortunately for them, they did not call their song "Not *Untainted* Love."

12. A

Irreconcilable = impossible to resolve or bring together (*reconcile*). *Irreconcilable differences* is one of the saddest phrases in the English language.

13. B

Unjustifiable = inexcusable; not able to be proven as right or reasonable. Calling someone's actions *unjustifiable* is a very serious accusation.

14. B

Intransigence = unwillingness to change one's position; lack of compromise; stubbornness. Unlike *resolve* or *resolution,* which are positive characteristics, *intransigence* is unswervingly negative.

15. A

Unwarranted = uncalled for; unjustified; unnecessary. Many small injustices in our daily lives are *unwarranted*, but it is best to sail above these slights as serenely as possible.

Step 3–ID the Question/Strategy

Drill 157: Question Approach

Instructions: Tackling the questions in Reading Comprehension can sometimes feel like a dice roll. When should you answer from memory, when should you research in the passage, and when should you do some combination of the two? Use this drill to practice making those calls quickly and consistently, so you can take the guesswork out of the decision making on test day.

For each of the following questions, indicate whether you would answer the question from your memory (M), research the question (RQ) before checking the answers, or eliminate some answers first then research the answers that remain (RA).

_____ 1. Which of the following most accurately expresses the main point of the passage?

_____ 2. The passage suggests that a porcupine would be unlikely to breed in which of the following circumstances?

_____ 3. The author mentions the word "wabi-sabi" (line 17) primarily in order to

_____ 4. According to the passage, the Zuni language differs from other Native American languages in that it

_____ 5. The author's attitude toward the digitization of medical records can best be described as

_____ 6. With which of the following statements would the author be most likely to agree?

_____ 7. Which one of the following situations is most analogous to the cycle described in lines 27–29?

_____ 8. According to the passage, the primary difference between squid and cuttlefish is that

_____ 9. The author of passage B would most likely respond to the argument in passage A by

_____ 10. Which one of the following most closely describes the author's position on stem-cell therapy?

_____ 11. Which of the following, if true, would most strengthen the researcher's argument that the first manned mission to Mars will most likely occur in the coming century?

_____ 12. The author's main source of disagreement with Hanover is that

_____ 13. Based on the information in the passage, flamingos most likely stand on one leg because

_____ 14. The author would most likely agree with each of the following statements EXCEPT:

_____ 15. It can be inferred from the passage that the hurricane inflicted significantly more damage than expected because

_____ 16. Based on the passage, which one the following would it be most surprising to find at sea level?

_____ 17. The researchers most likely conducted the study in the second paragraph in order to

_____ 18. The information in the passage most strongly suggests that

_____ 19. According to the passage, which one of the following is true about the New York City subway?

_____ 20. Which of the following, if true, most calls into question the reasoning that the philosopher uses to reject Hume's argument?

_____ 21. The purpose of the reference to San Diego's climate (line 33) is most likely to

_____ 22. With which one of the following would the authors of both passages be most likely to agree?

_____ 23. The author's primary purpose in writing this passage can most accurately be described as

_____ 24. The trial judge's reasoning is most similar to which one of the following cases?

_____ 25. According to the passage, which of the following is unique to the Galápagos Islands?

8

Answers

M 1. Which of the following most accurately expresses the main point of the passage?

Main Point questions should be answered from memory. If you don't remember the main point, there's a problem!

RA 2. The passage suggests that a porcupine would be unlikely to breed in which of the following circumstances?

If a question references a subject that you remember, try to knock out answers before researching contenders. If you don't remember the subject, go straight back to research the question or skip.

RQ 3. The author mentions the word "wabi-sabi" (line 17) primarily in order to

If the LSAT gives you a line reference, use it!

RQ 4. According to the passage, the Zuni language differs from other Native American languages in that it

Similarities and differences almost always have questions asked about them, so noting them in the passage pays off. If you do, you can quickly research questions like these and confidently select an answer on the first pass.

M 5. The author's attitude toward the digitization of medical records can best be described as

If digitization of medical records is the primary subject of the passage, then you should come away from the passage understanding the author's opinion toward it. If, however, digitization is a minor detail, you should do some research, before or after looking at the answers, depending on how much you remember about the subject.

RA 6. With which of the following statements would the author be most likely to agree?

Broad Author Agreement questions don't give you a subject to research in the question, so knock off the most egregious offenders and research the answers that remain.

RQ 7. Which one of the following situations is most analogous to the cycle described in lines 27–29?

Line reference = research the question!

RQ 8. According to the passage, the primary difference between squid and cuttlefish is that

Hopefully you marked this difference, so the research is quick and easy.

M 9. The author of passage B would most likely respond to the argument in passage A by

On comparative passages, you should be reading B and thinking "how does this relate back to A?" Then questions like this can be done from memory.

M 10. Which one of the following most closely describes the author's position on stem-cell therapy?

If stem-cell therapy is the main subject of the passage, this can be done from memory. If not, you may have to research some answers.

RQ 11. Which of the following, if true, would most strengthen the researcher's argument that the first manned mission to Mars will most likely occur in the coming century?

Since this is the researcher's argument, rather than the author's, you may not have carefully construed it when you first read it. Just as you would on an LR Strengthen question, make sure you clearly understand the evidence used to support the researcher's claim before you look to strengthen it.

M 12. The author's main source of disagreement with Hanover is that

If Hanover played a big role in the passage, then you'll want to come away from reading with an understanding of the author's reasoning for this disagreement. If the disagreement with Hanover was only a detail, return to the passage to investigate, either before or after looking at the answers, depending on your memory of the disagreement.

RQ 13. Based on the information in the passage, flamingos most likely stand on one leg because

Flamingos are an easy-to-spot subject reference, so go back and get your bearings before you try to answer.

___RA___ 14. The author would most likely agree with each of the following statements EXCEPT:

You'll want to research the answers first for almost all "Except" questions; since the author agrees with four of the statements, it will be difficult to eliminate all four based on your memory of the passage, and the question itself is too broad to research.

___RA___ 15. It can be inferred from the passage that the hurricane inflicted significantly more damage than expected because

Subject references you remember can usually give you some quick eliminations before you research the contender answers.

___RQ___ 16. Based on the passage, which one the following would it be most surprising to find at sea level?

Investigate what sorts of things are expected or unexpected at sea level, then apply that to your evaluation of the answers.

___RA___ 17. The researchers most likely conducted the study in the second paragraph in order to

The "why" is typically more important than the "what" in RC passages, so hopefully you thought through this during your reading and passage mapping enough that you're confident eliminating some answers before researching the contenders. But, if you don't remember the study that's being asked about, research the question before hitting the answers!

___RA___ 18. The information in the passage most strongly suggests that

No subject in the question to research, so start with eliminations then research the contenders.

___RA___ 19. According to the passage, which one of the following is true about the New York City subway?

As long as you recall the reference, go for some eliminations first. If your recollection is faint or you think you took helpful notes on the subject, head back to the passage first.

___RQ___ 20. Which of the following, if true, most calls into question the reasoning that the philosopher uses to reject Hume's argument?

You have to really understand an argument in order to weaken it, so be sure to research the philosopher's reasoning before you tackle the answers.

___RQ___ 21. The purpose of the reference to San Diego's climate (line 33) is most likely to

When they throw you a bone with a line reference, take it!

___M___ 22. With which one of the following would the authors of both passages be most likely to agree?

On comparative passages, always aim to understand the relationship between the two passages before you dive into the questions. That should cover you for a question like this; but, as always, don't force it—if you need to research a couple of contender answers, do it!

___M___ 23. The author's primary purpose in writing this passage can most accurately be described as

You should aim to answer Primary Purpose and Main Point questions from memory.

___RQ___ 24. The trial judge's reasoning is most similar to which one of the following cases?

You can't be successful on an analogy question without a firm grasp of the thing you are analogizing. In this case, that means going back to research the judge's reasoning in the passage before tackling the answer choices.

___RQ___ 25. According to the passage, which of the following is unique to the Galápagos Islands?

Something that makes a place unique is a difference between that place and other places. Differences are noteworthy, so hopefully you can do quick research in your notes and get right to the correct answer.

Drill 158: Vocab Lab #18 – The Good, the Bad, and the Neutral, Round 1

Instructions: Even when you can't define a word precisely, you sometimes know whether it means something good or bad, and that may be enough for your needs.

As fast as you can, classify each of the following words as good (G), bad (B), or neutral (N). As a bonus, define each word...but notice how much longer that takes!

_____ 1. Altruistic

_____ 2. Coercion

_____ 3. Colossal

_____ 4. Deleterious

_____ 5. Eminence

_____ 6. Exacerbate

_____ 7. Intrinsic

_____ 8. Meticulous

_____ 9. Optimize

_____ 10. Perilously

_____ 11. Pernicious

_____ 12. Pompous

_____ 13. Prudential

_____ 14. Scruple

_____ 15. Usurp

_____ 16. Absolve

_____ 17. Appropriated

_____ 18. Bolster

_____ 19. Debased

_____ 20. Deference

_____ 21. Elucidate

_____ 22. Extrapolate

_____ 23. Ignoble

_____ 24. Imprudent

_____ 25. Infringe

_____ 26. Inherent

_____ 27. Invoke

_____ 28. Laudatory

_____ 29. Multifaceted

_____ 30. Prevailing

Answers follow on the next page.

Answers

G 1. Altruistic = unselfish; only concerned with other people's welfare.

B 2. Coercion = use of force to make someone do something against his or her will.

N 3. Colossal = massive; enormous; immense.

B 4. Deleterious = harmful; unhealthy; damaging.

G 5. Eminence = prestige; prominence; being in a leading position in society.

B 6. Exacerbate = make worse or more severe; inflame; irritate further.

N 7. Intrinsic = essential to something's nature.

G 8. Meticulous = detail oriented; precise; painstaking. Note that *meticulous* stays on the positive side; it edges up to the line but doesn't cross into fussy or perfectionist in a negative sense.

G 9. Optimize = make the best use of; adjust to the best possible case.

B 10. Perilously = dangerously; in a risky manner.

B 11. Pernicious = causing gradual damage or injury.

B 12. Pompous = boastful; self-important.

G 13. Prudential = careful and wise in the management of affairs.

G 14. Scruple = doubt or hesitation due to ethical concerns; or an ethical concern itself.

B 15. Usurp = take illegal control; take over command by force.

G 16. Absolve = set free from obligation or guilt.

B 17. Appropriated = taken for one's own use; typically without permission.

G 18. Bolster = strengthen or support.

B 19. Debased = reduced in worth or quality.

G 20. Deference = respectful submission; yielding to the authority or opinion of another.

N 21. Elucidate = clarify; explain; make more *lucid* (clear).

N 22. Extrapolate = predict an unknown by drawing on a previous method, with the assumption that the older method will apply to this unknown.

B 23. Ignoble = not noble; having mean or low motives; of low quality.

B 24. Imprudent = indiscreet; lacking good judgment or wisdom.

B 25. Infringe = actively violate a law or agreement; encroach upon.

N 26. Inherent = existing as an essential, built-in attribute.

N 27. Invoke = appeal to as an authority; earnestly call for help.

G 28. Laudatory = expressing praise; commendatory.

N 29. Multifaceted = having many sides, angles, or aspects.

N 30. Prevailing = current; having the most appeal; gaining ascendancy.

Step 4–Analyze the Answers

Drill 159: Answer Choice Red Flags

Instructions: Have you ever tried to do a set of RC questions without having read the passage? If you have, this drill should feel familiar. When you look at a set of answer choices, there are certain words that jump out as potentially signaling a wrong answer. Maybe they communicate a degree of opinion that seems suspect, or they make an answer feel too broad or, on the other hand, too specific. Of course, without seeing the passage and the questions themselves, you can't know for sure whether these red flags are fatal flaws—plenty of correct answers will contain these elements. What you can know is that these are words worth investigating before you select the answer because they are the words that can make or break your choice.

Each of the following items represents a potential answer choice for an RC question. Highlight any words you think could make or break the answer.

1. Of all Nahiri's innovations in pedagogy, her work in classroom layout had the most lasting impact on modern educational reform.

2. Although Vokel produced a wide array of science fiction blockbusters, he is best known for his smaller independent films.

3. Consuming a diverse array of green vegetables is the most important factor in establishing healthy gut flora.

4. A lack of competition among telecommunication providers is the primary reason that prices for service remain high despite a decline in available options.

5. If the unexpected sectarian violence had not erupted at the end of the last decade, Borowski's economic model for growth in the region would have been accurate.

6. The main competition facing early railways in the Americas was a preexisting system of canals.

7. The majority of buildings built before the advent of transparent aluminum eventually suffered from catastrophic structural failure.

8. Without a dramatic increase in support from the highest levels of government, efforts to reduce greenhouse gas emissions will fail.

9. The inability to burrow underground or find safety in nearby aquatic environments is the primary reason why so many dinosaurs were exterminated in the Cretaceous-Tertiary extinction event.

10. Decentralized cryptocurrencies were the first currencies to operate independently of a centralized banking system.

11. There are fewer than 30 snow leopards living in any single country in the world.

12. The morality of a company's compensation packages for its wealthiest executives should not play any role in determining the manner in which that company is regulated by government agencies.

13. By requiring employees to take implicit bias training, university officials have eliminated the pernicious influence of bigotry from the classroom.

14. The sophisticated use of rocks and sticks by birds to obtain food completely undermines the claim made by some biologists that mammals are unique in their ability to utilize tools to solve complex problems.

15. The policies implemented by the city failed to redress any of the problems raised by the local school board.

16. The newly adopted standards assure that jury tampering will never happen again.

17. There is no situation that warrants the suspension of the right of habeas corpus.

18. Hotels pay little attention to the complaints their customers post online.

19. If the primordial atmosphere had contained free oxygen, and thus an ozone layer, early life could not have formed.

20. Most of Gorofsky's final paintings fail to adhere to the methodologies that made Gorofsky a pioneer of neo-classicism.

21. Beets have not always been one of the top two agricultural sources of sugar.

22. Most contemporary scientists concur that current foods derived from cisgenetically modified organisms are no more likely to cause adverse health effects than are foods derived from unmodified organisms.

23. A university that employs a professor who is accused of academic fraud will probably suffer significant damage to its overall reputation, regardless of the basis for the accusations.

24. A reader cannot evaluate the literary merit of a novel unless he is completely fluent in the language in which it was written.

25. The long-term success of a professional football franchise depends at least in part on the business acumen of executives who contribute little or nothing to the team's on-field performance.

26. The first method bore hardly any resemblance to the second method, but the third method was a stylistic refinement of the second.

27. The challenge of observing the giant or colossal squid in the wild makes it difficult for zoologists to describe its habits accurately.

28. Security for the most prominent celebrities is considerably more sophisticated than it was in the past.

29. To demonstrate that all amphibians must regularly wet their skins in order to remain healthy

30. The recent constitutional crisis is very likely to lead to a permanent shift of power away from the judicial branch of the government.

31. The primary cause of the frequent electrical outages in the community is the poor design of its power infrastructure.

32. Although Lugosi is widely remembered for his portrayal of Dracula, in his own time his fame was overshadowed by that of his friend and colleague Boris Karloff, who enjoyed greater financial and critical success.

33. Most of the main lineages of thoroughbred racing horses in the present day can be traced to the Arabian breeds developed in the mid-eighteenth century.

34. It is used as partial justification for the judge's decision to hold the defendant, Luddite Technologies, responsible for the breach of its customers' privacy.

35. No effective treatment has been developed to reverse the symptoms of any motor neuron disease, although several areas of research are considered promising.

36. Most of the truly exciting bands of the past and present synthesize musical elements in a way that seems novel to contemporary audiences.

37. Before the advent of automated calling, citizens were more likely to engage with telemarketers than they are today, even if they were uninterested in the product or service on offer.

38. They argue that the success of a film studio is now inextricably tied to its production of long-term franchises that develop a committed following over the span of a decade or more.

39. Modern consumer electronics are designed to be less expensive and less durable, potentially contributing to our nation's growing burden of toxic waste.

40. Although a hole in one is a sign of a certain degree of golfing ability, a top professional is not necessarily more likely to achieve one on any given round than is a talented amateur.

8

Answers

Note: We've presented in bold the text we feel could make or break an answer.

1. Of all Nahiri's **innovations** in pedagogy, her work in classroom layout had the **most lasting impact** on modern educational reform.

2. Although Vokel produced a wide array of science fiction blockbusters, he is **best known** for his smaller independent films.

3. Consuming a diverse array of green vegetables is **the most important factor** in establishing healthy gut flora.

4. A lack of competition among telecommunication providers is **the primary reason** that prices for service remain high despite a decline in available options.

5. If the unexpected sectarian violence had not erupted at the end of the last decade, Borowski's economic model for growth in the region **would have been** accurate.

6. The **main competition** facing early railways in the Americas was a preexisting system of canals.

7. The **majority** of buildings built before the advent of transparent aluminum eventually suffered from **catastrophic** structural failure.

8. **Without** a dramatic increase in support from the highest levels of government, efforts to reduce greenhouse gas emissions **will fail.**

9. The inability to burrow underground or find safety in nearby aquatic environments is the **primary reason** why **so many** dinosaurs were exterminated in the Cretaceous-Tertiary extinction event.

10. Decentralized cryptocurrencies were the **first** currencies to operate independently of a centralized banking system.

11. There are **fewer than** 30 snow leopards living in **any single** country in the world.

12. The morality of a company's compensation packages for its wealthiest executives **should not play any role** in determining the manner in which that company is regulated by government agencies.

13. By requiring employees to take implicit bias training, university officials **have eliminated** the **pernicious** influence of **bigotry** from the classroom.

14. The sophisticated use of rocks and sticks by birds to obtain food **completely undermines** the claim made by some biologists that mammals are unique in their ability to utilize tools to solve complex problems.

15. The policies implemented by the city **failed to redress any** of the problems raised by the local school board.

16. The newly adopted standards **assure** that jury tampering **will never** happen again.

17. There is **no situation** that warrants the **suspension** of the right of habeas corpus.

18. Hotels pay **little attention** to the complaints their customers post online.

19. **If** the primordial atmosphere had contained free oxygen, and thus an ozone layer, early life **could not have** formed.

20. **Most** of Gorofsky's final paintings **fail** to adhere to the methodologies that made Gorofsky a **pioneer** of neo-classicism.

21. Beets have **not always** been one of the **top two** agricultural sources of sugar.

22. **Most** contemporary scientists concur that **current** foods derived from cisgenetically modified organisms are **no more likely** to cause adverse health effects than are foods derived from unmodified organisms.

23. A university that employs a professor who is accused of academic fraud will **probably** suffer **significant** damage to its **overall reputation**, **regardless** of the basis for the accusations.

24. A reader **cannot** evaluate the **literary** merit of a novel unless he is **completely fluent** in the language in which it was written.

25. The **long-term** success of a professional football franchise **depends at least in part** on the business acumen of executives who contribute **little or nothing** to the team's **on-field** performance.

26. The first method bore **hardly any** resemblance to the second method, but the third method was a **stylistic refinement** of the second.

27. The challenge of observing the giant or colossal squid **in the wild** makes it **difficult** for zoologists to describe its habits **accurately**.

28. Security for the **most prominent** celebrities is **considerably more** sophisticated **than it was in the past.**

29. To demonstrate that **all** amphibians **must regularly** wet their skins **in order to remain** healthy

30. The **recent** constitutional crisis is **very likely** to lead to a **permanent** shift of power **away** from the judicial branch of the government.

31. The **primary** cause of the **frequent** electrical outages in the community is the **poor** design of its power infrastructure.

32. Although Lugosi is **widely remembered** for his portrayal of Dracula, **in his own time** his fame was **overshadowed** by that of his friend and colleague Boris Karloff, who enjoyed **greater** financial and critical success.

33. **Most** of the **main** lineages of thoroughbred racing horses **in the present day** can be traced to the Arabian breeds developed in the mid-eighteenth century.

34. It is used as **partial** justification for the judge's decision to hold the defendant, Luddite Technologies, **responsible** for the breach of its customers' privacy.

35. **No** effective treatment has been developed to **reverse** the symptoms of **any** motor neuron disease, although **several** areas of research are **considered promising**.

36. **Most** of the **truly exciting** bands of the **past and present** synthesize musical elements in a way that **seems** novel to **contemporary** audiences.

37. Before the advent of automated calling, citizens were **more likely** to engage with telemarketers **than they are today**, even if they were uninterested in the product or service on offer.

38. They argue that the success of a film studio is now **inextricably** tied to its production of **long-term** franchises that develop a committed following **over the span of a decade or more.**

39. **Modern** consumer electronics are designed to be **less** expensive and **less** durable, **potentially** contributing to **our nation's growing** burden of toxic waste.

40. Although a hole in one is a sign of **a certain degree** of golfing ability, a top professional is **not necessarily more likely** to achieve one **on any given round** than is a talented amateur.

Drill 160: I Can Answer That!

Instructions: Most students give too much "wiggle room" to Inference question answers, especially in Most Strongly Supported Logical Reasoning questions, and Reading Comp as a whole. While these questions do ask what is *most* supported by the stimulus/passage, the correct answers rarely require anything other than the smallest leap from the information provided. For each of the following items, write Y if the statement can be inferred from the preceding statements, and N if it can't. There might be more than one inferable statement per set; there may be none. Bonus points if you highlight the word/phrase that makes an item something that *can't* be inferred.

Most people think that skydivers are all adrenaline-addicted daredevils with no sense of fear. Surprisingly, though, many experienced skydivers admit that they are afraid of heights.

_____ 1. Most people have never made a skydive or spoken with an experienced skydiver.

_____ 2. Some people have a perception of skydivers that is not wholly correct.

_____ 3. Many experienced skydivers are not adrenaline-addicted daredevils.

_____ 4. If asked, most people would say that skydivers are daredevils.

_____ 5. Not all skydivers match the preconceptions that many have of them.

Some people who bake cupcakes also like to bake bread. But everyone who bakes cupcakes must know how to use some sort of oven or stove.

_____ 6. Some people who like to bake bread know how to bake cupcakes.

_____ 7. Some people who like to bake bread know how to use some sort of oven or stove.

_____ 8. Most people who know how to use an oven can bake cupcakes.

_____ 9. Some people who know how to bake cupcakes do not like to bake bread.

_____ 10. Everyone who likes to bake bread knows how to bake cupcakes.

While *Don Giovanni* is widely considered Mozart's greatest achievement, eighteenth-century audiences in Vienna were ambivalent at best. The opera mixed traditions of moralism with those of comedy—a practice heretofore unknown among the composer's works—resulting in a production that was not well-liked by conservative Viennese audiences. Meanwhile, however, *Don Giovanni* was performed to much acclaim throughout Europe.

_____ 11. Widely hailed works of art are always well-received.

_____ 12. Mozart's works were more popular in Europe as a whole than in Austria.

_____ 13. *Don Giovanni* was the first opera to mix traditions of moralism with comedy.

_____ 14. *Don Giovanni* faced much criticism in Vienna when first released.

_____ 15. Before *Don Giovanni*, Mozart had not mixed moralism and comedy in any of his known works.

Some critics argue that history textbooks in the United States are far too fact-based and relay the impression that history is composed of "Quick Facts" and diagrams, rather than dynamic events to be critically analyzed. These critics, many of whom are concerned about the general state of public education in the United States, often cite the work of Sandra Wong to support their claims. In her article "Evaluating the Content of Textbooks: Public Interests and Professional Authority," Wong discusses how textbook committees are rarely concerned with the actual substance of the writing in the textbooks they evaluate and are far more interested in things like "charts, illustrations, and introductory outlines."

_____ 16. History textbooks in the US are in dire need of reform.

_____ 17. The problems with US educational materials stem from the general state of the nation's public education system.

_____ 18. At least some of the problems that have been identified with US educational materials relate to systemic issues.

_____ 19. Some critics would agree that current history textbooks ignore important viewpoints when discussing historic events.

_____ 20. Sandra Wong feels that charts, illustrations, and introductory outlines are a necessary, but not sufficient, part of any complete history textbook.

A single short story can suggest a desired response from the reader. It is a difficult task, however, to create a world within a single short story and then create entirely new worlds in other stories while maintaining a consistent flow of ideas. Many authors prefer to use the same setting or character(s) in each story. For example, in Isabel Allende's _Diez Cuentos de Eva Luna_, Allende uses the small town of Agua Santa as the setting for the entire collection.

However, not all authors use this approach to achieve consistency. In _Woman Hollering Creek_, a collection of short stories by Sandra Cisneros, the characters and setting change in each story. While the characters are largely Mexican-American immigrant women, each character also displays a distinct style and literary voice. Much of the burden of connecting the stories is placed on the reader, as aspects of the texts such as mood, circumstance, time, tone, and imagery combine to create the larger world in which the stories take place.

_____ 21. Cisneros succeeds in creating a consistent world within her short story collections.

_____ 22. _Diez Cuentos de Eva Luna_ places the burden of connecting its stories on the reader.

_____ 23. The characters in Allende's stories display distinct styles and literary voices.

_____ 24. Allende is more successful at connecting her short stories in _Diez Cuentos de Eva Luna_ than Cisneros is in _Woman Hollering Creek_.

_____ 25. More short story authors achieve consistency through setting or character than through mood or tone.

8

For many years, most physicists supported one of two cosmological theories: the steady-state universe, or the Big Bang. The theory of the steady-state universe states that the universe has always existed exactly as we observe it at present, whereas the Big Bang theory postulates that the universe was conceived from a singularity in space-time that has expanded into the current universe.

In 1929, Edwin Hubble famously discovered what is now known as Hubble's Law. Hubble's experiment is now a famous benchmark in modern physics. Hubble, using the Mount Wilson Observatory, observed a class of stars known as Cepheid variables, luminous stars that blink and flicker with a rate that depends on their distance from the observer. Using this relation, and over years of observation, Hubble calculated the distance to many of these variable stars. Milton Humason, a fellow astronomer, helped Hubble to calculate the stars' relative velocities to Earth. When Hubble combined the two data sets, he found an interesting relationship: all the stars appeared to be moving away from us. In fact, the speed at which they were moving increased with an increasing distance from Earth.

Hubble realized, from this small set of data, that the earth was a part of the expanding universe. As the universe expands outward in all directions, any observer from a fixed vantage point can look out and see it moving away from them. The farther away any two points are, the more the expansion affects them and the faster they appear to be moving away from each other. Hubble's result was the first experimental proof that we do not live in a steady-state universe, but rather a dynamic and expanding one.

_____ 26. Hubble was not the first to run experiments testing the steady-state universe theory.

_____ 27. Under the steady-state universe theory, stars could be moving away from Earth.

_____ 28. Some evidence against the steady-state universe theory existed before 1929.

_____ 29. Physicists have tested cosmological theories other than the steady-state universe theory.

_____ 30. Most physicists now support the Big Bang theory.

Answers

Note: If specific words would have led us to eliminate an answer in an Inference question (instead of the answer as a whole), we've struck them out. We've also left a note for some particularly tricky ones.

___N___ 1. ~~Most~~ people have never made a skydive or spoken with an experienced skydiver.

___Y___ 2. **Some people have a perception of skydivers that is not wholly correct.**

___N___ 3. Many experienced skydivers are not adrenaline-addicted daredevils.

They may be that in spite of *their fear of heights.*

___N___ 4. If asked, most people would ~~say~~ that skydivers are daredevils.

Just because someone believes something doesn't mean they'd say it if asked.

___Y___ 5. **Not all skydivers match the preconceptions that many have of them.**

___Y___ 6. **Some people who like to bake bread know how to bake cupcakes.**

___N___ 7. Some people who like to bake bread know how to use some sort of oven or stove.

___N___ 8. Most people who know how to use an oven can bake cupcakes.

___N___ 9. Some people who know how to bake cupcakes ~~do not like to bake bread~~.

___N___ 10. ~~Everyone~~ who likes to bake bread knows how to bake cupcakes.

___N___ 11. Widely hailed works of art are ~~always~~ well-received.

___N___ 12. Mozart's works were more popular in Europe as a whole than in ~~Austria~~.

___N___ 13. *Don Giovanni* was the ~~first opera~~ to mix traditions of moralism with comedy.

___N___ 14. *Don Giovanni* faced ~~much criticism~~ in Vienna when first released.

___Y___ 15. **Before *Don Giovanni*, Mozart had not mixed moralism and comedy in any of his known works.**

___N___ 16. History textbooks in the US ~~are~~ in dire need of reform.

___N___ 17. The problems with US educational materials stem from the general state of the nation's public education system.

The critics might agree with this, but it's not established as a fact/the author's viewpoint.

___N___ 18. At least some of the problems that have been identified with US educational materials relate to systemic issues.

Ditto.

___N___ 19. Some critics would agree that current history textbooks ignore important ~~viewpoints~~ when discussing historic events.

___N___ 20. Sandra Wong feels that charts, illustrations, and introductory outlines are a ~~necessary~~, but not sufficient, part of any complete history textbook.

___Y___ 21. **Cisneros succeeds in creating a consistent world within her short story collections.**

___N___ 22. ~~*Diez Cuentos de Eva Luna*~~ places the burden of connecting its stories on the reader.

___N___ 23. The characters in ~~Allende's~~ stories display distinct styles and literary voices.

___N___ 24. Allende is ~~more successful~~ at connecting her short stories in *Diez Cuentos de Eva Luna* than Cisneros is in *Woman Hollering Creek*.

___N___ 25. ~~More~~ short story authors achieve consistency through setting or character than through mood or tone.

___N___ 26. Hubble was not the first to run experiments testing the steady-state universe theory.

___Y___ 27. **Under the steady-state universe theory, stars could be moving away from Earth.**

___N___ 28. Some evidence against the steady-state universe theory existed before 1929.

___N___ 29. Physicists have tested cosmological ~~theories other than~~ the steady-state universe theory.

___N___ 30. ~~Most~~ physicists now support the Big Bang theory.

Drill 161: What's with the Attitude?

Instructions: Questions in RC will frequently ask you to sum up the author's attitude in two words. Even when the answer format is different, prephrasing your own two-word summary can be helpful in allowing you to make some quick eliminations. For each of the following items, select the correct two-word phrase that sums up the author's attitude. In general, they'll consist of an adjective (denoting the strength of the attitude) and a noun (denoting the type of attitude).

1. But what is most striking about the painting is the way Matisse has begun to allow his colors and his forms to play freely, even while they are coordinated. Although this technique is not given the kind of free rein Picasso allows in his Cubist period or in works such as *Minotaur*, it is still a stunning development for Matisse.

    (A) Well-reasoned criticism
    (B) Cautious optimism
    (C) Mixed praise
    (D) Exuberant praise
    (E) Disappointed recognition

2. In arguing against Game Theory's application to tic-tac-toe, critics bring up cogent points. Differentiating a game with few set strategies, including one that always works, from normal Game Theory situations with branching strategies points out a meaningful distinction. However, adherents of Game Theory have addressed many of these points, though not always to the satisfaction of the critics.

    (A) Hasty dismissal
    (B) Balanced analysis
    (C) Moderate criticism
    (D) Unreasoned agreement
    (E) Reasoned agreement

3. The welcome resurgence of board games as a popular pastime was largely started in Germany. There, designers used advanced degrees in mathematics to create game systems much more complex than the games from the last century. As the industry grew in Europe, American companies began to design similarly intricate games while growing their games in a more narrative direction. Now, most designers competently incorporate both mathematically derived systems and narrative elements in their games.

    (A) Neutral background
    (B) Critical analysis
    (C) Tempered praise
    (D) Overall positivity
    (E) Slight disappointment

4. Fad diets are frequently criticized for their often extreme proscriptions against certain types of foods that have become a staple in many diets. Their adherents, on the other hand, correctly point out that avoiding many of these foods, especially those with added sugars, is inarguably an improvement to the average diet. While that is true, completely removing many of these foods is a task that many find impossible, and cheating on the diet once can lead the entire thing to fall apart. So while these diets may be healthy, they rarely lead to healthy diets.

    (A) Neutral presentation
    (B) One-sided analysis
    (C) Balanced pessimism
    (D) Total dismissal
    (E) Optimistic recommendation

8

5. The lemur, endemic to Madagascar, derives its name from the Latin word for *ghosts*. It was deemed a fitting name because of the animal's nocturnal cycle, slow movements, and eyes that glow in the dark. Over the years, this name has been applied to any number of different animals that share those characteristics, highlighting how a name selected for its descriptive powers can sometimes end up leading to confusion.

   (A) Scholarly neutrality
   (B) Scholarly interest
   (C) Scholarly illustration
   (D) Slight confusion
   (E) Extreme confusion

6. Carbon dating has been used by scientists for decades to determine the approximate age of various archaeological items. However, there's a limit to its effectiveness: in items older than 40,000 years, current technology can no longer distinguish between the levels of the carbon-14 isotope necessary to determine the age. This limit is moving further back in time, however, as technology becomes more accurate, and carbon dating has been shown within that limit to be accurate enough for almost all research purposes.

   (A) Complete dismissal
   (B) Reasoned dismissal
   (C) Qualified dismissal
   (D) Qualified support
   (E) Unqualified support

7. A widely held belief is that duck quacks don't echo. Scientists analyzing duck quacks have found that, acoustically, a duck quacking in an echo-free chamber is different from one in an echo chamber. A number of explanations have been posited for the persistence of the belief, from ducks flying in flocks to most ducks living in areas where an echo wouldn't be generated. However, the most likely reason is that a duck quack itself fades in and then out, making it hard to distinguish from an echo.

   (A) Scholarly neutrality
   (B) Hesitant uncertainty
   (C) Qualified agreement
   (D) Relative certainty
   (E) Absolute certainty

8. Explanationism is the idea that prediction is, in itself, insufficient to confirm a theory. To adequately confirm a theory, according to an explanationist, is to see how well it describes events and phenomena that have already been observed. Stephen Brush, a staunch explanationist, would say that a correct prediction does not necessarily confirm the truth of a theory; it could be the case that a theory predicts something and yet does not provide the best explanation of it.

   (A) Neutral analysis
   (B) Neutral exposition
   (C) Qualified agreement
   (D) Qualified disagreement
   (E) Sympathetic exploration

8

9. Spongers typically live solitary lives, but over 22 years of observation, a pattern emerged. The 28 female spongers formed cliques with other female spongers that were not necessarily genetically related to them. This behavior differs from other animal behavior where circumstances, such as genetics or food sources, dictate the formation of groups. The fact that these spongers chose to associate based upon similar, socially learned behaviors makes their cliques a cultural first among animals.

   (A) Scholarly neutrality
   (B) Disinterested analysis
   (C) Convinced of discovery
   (D) Skeptical agreement
   (E) Skeptical neutrality

10. The counterintuitive properties of quantum mechanics, that the attributes of a particle cannot be known in advance of measurement, initially provoked many strong philosophical debates and interpretations regarding the field. In fact, Einstein was deeply troubled by the idea of nature being probabilistic and commented famously that "God does not play dice with the universe." Over the last 70 years, however, irrefutable evidence has abounded that verifies the truth of the theory of quantum mechanics.

    (A) Qualified agreement
    (B) Unqualified agreement
    (C) Scholarly neutrality
    (D) Confused acceptance
    (E) Skeptical questioning

Answers

1. D

By using words such as "striking" and "stunning," the author is praising the work without reservation.

2. B

The author presents both sides as having merit without taking sides.

3. D

Using words such as "welcome" and "competently" shows a positive disposition, and there's no hesitation that would make it tempered.

4. C

The author analyzes both sides but concludes that these diets rarely work.

5. C

Reaching a broader conclusion about how this illustrates a trend moves this from neutrality or interest into illustration.

6. D

Stating there's a "limit" to the technology, as well as stating that it's "accurate enough" for "almost all" purposes, makes this qualified support.

7. D

Since the author states that this is the "most likely reason," the certainty is relative. C is a tempting answer choice, but there's no attribution of who put forth the "fade out" theory, so there's no one for the author to agree with.

8. B

There's no attitude demonstrated in this paragraph, so the correct answer choice has to be A or B. Since the author discusses what the idea is and doesn't analyze the positives and negatives of it, B is the correct choice over A.

9. C

Since the author describes the cause of the group formation to be a "fact," we can support an answer that states she's convinced. Stating that it's a "first" supports discovery.

10. B

"Unqualified agreement" is supported by the "irrefutable evidence" that has "abounded," "verifying" the "truth" of the theory.

Drill 162: It's a Trap! RC Edition

Instructions: The best way to avoid stepping in a pothole is to look for potholes as you walk. The best way to avoid getting caught by a trap answer choice is to look for trap answer choices as you read. Practice recognizing the common RC traps with this drill. For each of the following paragraphs, three questions will be asked, each with two answers. Select the answer that is not a trap answer, and consider what makes the incorrect answer a trap.

Paragraph 1

In the 1960s, Northwestern University sociologist John McKnight coined the term redlining, the practice of denying or severely limiting service to customers in particular geographic areas, often determined by the racial composition of the neighborhood. The term came from the practice of banks outlining certain areas in red on a map; within the red outline, banks refused to invest. With no access to mortgages, residents within the red line suffered low property values and landlord abandonment; buildings abandoned by landlords were then more likely to become centers of drug dealing and other crime, thus further lowering property values.

1. The passage suggests that the banks mentioned in the first paragraph were most likely motivated by which of the following?

   (A) The desire to avoid changing the racial composition of a neighborhood.

   (B) The desire to avoid lending to borrowers of certain racial backgrounds.

2. The first paragraph functions primarily to

   (A) define the concept of redlining.

   (B) argue against the practice of redlining.

3. The passage suggests that which of the following is an outgrowth of the practice of redlining?

   (A) Decreased property value within the red line.

   (B) Racially homogeneous neighborhoods within the red line.

Paragraph 2

Rather than address redlining through enforcement of civil rights laws, the federal government in the 1970s tried to address the problem of poverty within redlined neighborhoods through massive investment in publicly financed affordable housing projects. But instead of interspersing affordable housing into different neighborhoods with a variety of socioeconomic demographics where banks were willing to invest, high-rise public housing complexes were constructed in the redlined neighborhoods. The predictable result was a severe intensification of the concentration of poverty in redlined neighborhoods, which compounded the problems banks used to justify the practice in the first place, including high rates of criminal activity.

4. Which of the following interventions would the author most likely believe to have been preferable to the government's actions in the 1970s?

   (A) Addressing the high rates of criminal activity in redlined neighborhoods.

   (B) Constructing affordable housing in neighborhoods not subjected to redlining.

5. With which of the following would the author of the passage be most likely to agree?

   (A) Federal officials never considered whether to address redlining through the enforcement of civil rights laws.

   (B) Federal officials might have known that large-scale affordable housing projects in redlined neighborhoods would be detrimental to those neighborhoods.

6. The function of the second paragraph is to

   (A) propose solutions that the federal government should undertake to address the problems in redlined neighborhoods.

   (B) describe missed opportunities to address the problems in redlined neighborhoods.

Paragraph 3

Creating a map requires projecting a round surface onto a flat surface, either directly to a plane or onto a cylinder or cone that can be cut and flattened. Any projection unavoidably will create at least one of four types of distortion: (1) feature shape, (2) feature area, (3) distances between points, and (4) direction between points. Different map projections will seek to maintain accuracy for one or more of these properties, but it is impossible to do so for all four. The Lambert conformal conic projection is popular because it accurately portrays shape and directional relationships in the mid-latitudes.

7. The author mentions the Lambert conformal conic projection

   A. because it is popular and accurately portrays shape and directional relation-ships in the mid-latitudes.

   B. in order to illustrate the trade-offs in minimizing different forms of distortion inherent in mapmaking.

8. What can be inferred about a Lambert conformal conic projection of an area in the mid-latitudes?

   A. If it accurately portrays feature area, there will be at least some distortion in distances between points.

   B. It will likely be superior in minimizing more forms of distortion than another type of projection for that same area.

9. According to the passage, a cylinder or cone is suitable for producing a map because

   A. it is preferable for reducing distortion compared to other geometric shapes.

   B. such geometric forms can be cut and laid flat.

Paragraph 4

A new challenge in maintaining accuracy has arisen for mapmakers with the transition to computer generated maps. Geographic Information System (GIS) technology has revolutionized mapmaking and resulted in an explosion of applications, from the GPS guidance system in your car to helping biologists track whale migrations around the world. Vast quantities of geographic data are constantly being accumulated and built into maps. Government agencies and academic departments routinely make their data freely available for all to download from Internet sites. But all the data is formatted for a particular projection. Therefore, it is vital that data formatted for a map with a particular projection undergo a process known as transformation before being imported into a map with a different projection.

10. What is the primary purpose of paragraph two?

    A. To emphasize the way GIS technology has revolutionized mapmaking.

    B. To explain another potential source of distortion in maps related to the projection process.

11. Why does the author mention whale migrations?

    A. To illustrate a potential ramification of the failure of mapmakers to subject data to transformation before incorporating them into maps used for tracking whales.

    B. To provide an example of the diverse range of applications for GIS technology.

12. What is the author's attitude toward the practice of government agencies and academic departments making their GIS data freely available?

    A. Cautionary

    B. Enthusiastic

Answers and explanations follow on the next page.

Answers

Paragraph 1

1. B. The desire to avoid lending to borrowers of certain racial backgrounds.

Watch out for the language match trap in choice A: "often determined by the racial composition of a neighborhood" doesn't imply that redlining was designed to maintain the racial composition of a neighborhood.

2. A. define the concept of redlining.

When a passage talks about something deplorable, be careful not to project your own abhorrence onto the author. In this paragraph, the author hasn't yet weighed in.

3. A. Decreased property value within the red line.

Be careful not to bring your knowledge of a subject to the party. In real life, redlining had the impact of racially segregating neighborhoods, but the passage hasn't mentioned that yet.

Paragraph 2

4. B. Constructing affordable housing in neighborhoods not subjected to redlining.

Don't fall into the "last thing you just read" trap. The last sentence of this paragraph talks about criminal activity, but it is never presented as an alternative intervention.

5. B. Federal officials might have known that large-scale affordable housing projects in redlined neighborhoods would be detrimental to those neighborhoods.

Authors can make subtle statements of opinion by editorializing on the facts. When this author calls the detriment to the neighborhoods "predictable," he suggests that those in the know might have predicted it would happen. The word "never" in choice A is a red flag that we are looking at a Strength Trap!

6. B. describe missed opportunities to address the problems in redlined neighborhoods.

As much as we might want solutions to the problem being presented, that's not what this paragraph is actually doing. Don't get caught wishing, and recognize this subtle trap!

Paragraph 3

7. B. in order to illustrate the trade-offs in minimizing different forms of distortion inherent in mapmaking.

Choice A is a "last thing you read" trap: it recites the basic facts that the passage just mentioned but without addressing the author's purpose in mentioning it. The purpose of a detail is typically found by looking upward in the passage for the context in which the detail was mentioned.

8. A. If it accurately portrays feature area, there will be at least some distortion in distances between points.

Choice A is a logical deduction from the facts in the passage: the Lambert is accurate on two counts, and no projection can be accurate on all four. That means if the Lambert is accurate on one more of the remaining two, it cannot be totally accurate on the fourth. Choice B presents us with a detail creep—the passage talks about popularity and quality but not superiority. It is also stronger than choice A, which should give us pause on an Inference question.

9. B. such geometric forms can be cut and laid flat.

This question is answered at the beginning of the paragraph before the author gets into any discussion of minimizing distortion. There's also no mention of other geometric shapes. So while choice A relates to the big idea of the paragraph, that's actually a trap. It is important to recognize the rare question that just wants you to look at a basic background detail in the beginning of the passage that is mentioned before the author gets into the meat of it.

8

Paragraph 4

10. B. To explain another potential source of distortion in maps related to the projection process.

The information in choice A cites sounds dramatic, but its role is actually just to provide background for the claims that follow. The first sentence signals the continuity between paragraph one and paragraph two and identifies the topic of paragraph two as a "new challenge in maintaining accuracy" in maps, following from the discussion of types of distortion in paragraph one.

11. B. To provide an example of the diverse range of applications for GIS technology.

When passages use examples, take note that most of the time, the example will be the subject of a question. Don't get caught in the "don't have time to research" trap and pick an answer without confirming it. If you've notated well, the information shouldn't be hard to find. A simple "EX" in the margin beside each example will get you there.

12. A. Cautionary

Don't mistake words like "revolutionized" and "explosion" to indicate the author's unbridled enthusiasm. The practice of making data freely available is mentioned in conjunction with the concern that data from different sources can lead to inaccuracies in the absence of transformation.

Drill 163: Counterexample Sample, Round 2

Instructions: Strengthen and Weaken questions are among the toughest on the RC section. Often, you'll be asked to support or undermine a causal claim. That's where counterexamples come in. Correct answers for Weaken questions tend to raise counterexamples, while correct answers for Strengthen questions tend to rule them out. Use this drill to practice coming up with counterexamples, and write them in the space provided. Remember, counterexamples to causal claims can take the form of the cause without the effect or the effect without the cause, but one of them is typically more potent than the other because of the type of causal claim they are refuting. Try to come up with the most potent counterexample possible!

1. Studying too much causes high levels of stress.

2. Lowering the speed limit results in a lower accident rate.

3. Ice ages are caused by decreased solar energy.

4. Eating fast food causes high blood pressure.

5. Overconsumption of chocolate is the cause of acne.

6. Rain is the cause of umbrella use.

7. Aphids will lead to the failure of any vegetable crop they infest.

8. Bad posture is responsible for Carl's back pain.

9. Shampooing every day leads to hair loss.

10. Bill's increased levels of adrenaline stem from prolonged exposure to violent imagery.

8

Answers and explanations follow on the next page.

Answers

Your answers may differ from ours, but make sure that they serve the same function, even if they differ a bit in the specifics.

1. Studying too much causes high levels of stress.

Mark studied for too many hours on Monday but was as relaxed as he's ever been throughout the day. *(If Mark had a high stress day on Monday but hadn't studied, would that be as good? Nope. If one thing is said to cause an effect without implying that it is the only cause of that effect, a counterexample should show the cause without the effect, not the effect without the cause.)*

2. Lowering the speed limit results in a lower accident rate.

Springfield lowered its speed limit but saw an increase in its accident rate. *(Would a town that lowered its accident rate without lowering speed limits be as good? Nope, for the same reason cited for Q.1.)*

3. Ice ages are caused by decreased solar energy.

An ice age occurred in the fifth century BCE, when Earth's received solar energy was especially high. *(Would a period of decreased solar energy that didn't cause an ice age be as good? Nope. Unlike the two above, this claim is that an effect always has a particular cause. In these cases, a counterexample should show the effect without the cause.)*

4. Eating fast food causes high blood pressure.

Suzie only eats at her local fast food restaurant, Burgermeister Burgers, yet her blood pressure is at a perfectly healthy level. *(What if Suzie had high blood pressure but didn't eat fast food? Not as good, because we're not told that fast food is the only cause of high blood pressure.)*

5. Overconsumption of chocolate is the cause of acne.

Augustus has acne but never consumes chocolate. *(What if Augustus eats more chocolate than recommended and has perfect skin? Nope. We're told acne has one cause, so a counterexample needs to show the effect without the cause. We're not told that chocolate always causes acne, so showing the cause without the effect isn't a counterexample.)*

6. Rain is the cause of umbrella use.

Michelle is using an umbrella, yet it is not raining. *(What if it is raining, yet Michelle is not using an umbrella? Nope. Rain is the sole cause, which means we need a counterexample to show the effect without the cause, not the cause without the effect.)*

7. Aphids will lead to the failure of any vegetable crop they infest.

My neighbor's vegetable garden was infested by aphids, but she used some insecticide to get rid of the aphids, and her crop was a success. *(Would non-aphid related crop failure be as good? Nope. When we're told a cause will always have an effect, the counterexample should show the cause without the effect.)*

8. Bad posture is responsible for Carl's back pain.

Carl maintains excellent posture, yet his back pain continues OR Carl's bad posture continues, but his back pain is no more. *(Why both? When we're told that one isolated thing is the cause of another isolated thing but that relationship is not projected beyond that incident, either the cause without the effect or the effect without the cause is a good counterexample.)*

9. Shampooing every day leads to hair loss.

Katarina has shampooed her hair every day for the past eight years and has experienced no hair loss. *(What about hair loss without daily shampooing? Nope. We need the cause without the effect.)*

10. Bill's increased levels of adrenaline stem from prolonged exposure to violent imagery.

Bill had increased levels of adrenaline before he was exposed to violent imagery OR Bill was exposed to violent imagery for a prolonged time and did not suffer increased levels of adrenaline. *(Because this is about an isolated cause of an isolated effect, the counterexample can show the effect without the cause or the cause without the effect.)*

Drill 164: Application

Instructions: Application questions in RC are like Principle Example questions in LR—they give you information, then ask you to find the answer that exemplifies it. The only real difference is the language: instead of calling the correct answer choice an example, it might be called a case to which the principle applies.

For each of the following principles (or styles) that you might come across in an RC passage, determine for each of the following items whether the principle applies to the situation (A), is contradicted by it (C), or doesn't align with it/there's not enough information to tell (N).

The Corinthian architectural style is characterized by a focus on proportion and floral decorations.

_____ 1. A column that conforms to strict mathematical ratios, styled with rose adornments.

_____ 2. A roof supported by columns of varying heights and widths, with abstract adornments.

_____ 3. A sculpture of a potted plant designed by a mathematician.

When designing an experiment, psychologists try to minimize the impact of their involvement by making sure no one with knowledge of the experiment's goals interacts with the subject.

_____ 4. An experiment in which the people interviewing the subjects are all students in psychology classes.

_____ 5. An experiment in which questions are read to the subjects by a computer program.

_____ 6. An experiment in which lab assistants who have helped design the study ask a series of questions, only some of which are related to the goals of the experiment.

In general, increasing the harshness or certainty of punishment decreases the incidence of crime.

_____ 7. Springfield's mayor increased the prison sentences for most crimes committed in its jurisdiction. However, because it didn't announce these changes, Springfield didn't see a decline in the crime rate.

_____ 8. Derringer City saw a decrease in crime after spending money on increasing social services.

_____ 9. San Migorge saw its crime rate plummet after increasing prison sentences for all crimes and investing in an increased police presence.

Economists claim that price and demand are inversely proportional.

_____ 10. Microtendo increased sales of its systems by decreasing their sale price.

_____ 11. Even though demand decreased, BananaSoft made more money overall by increasing the price of its computers.

_____ 12. Because people associate quality with price, any college that has increased the price of tuition has seen an increase in applicants.

Paradoxically, as one becomes more accepting of failure, failure becomes less likely.

_____ 13. Tova Works is recognized as one of the most successful businesspeople. She credits a lot of her success to some early stumbles, which taught her that she could recover and learn.

_____ 14. Despite a crippling fear of failure, Will Doors succeeded through a string of major successful product launches.

_____ 15. Because he knew that fear was the killer of ideas, Paul Treides learned how to mitigate his fear of failure. He immediately saw the success rate of his business pitches increase.

The New Radicalist style is characterized by a mixture of mediums and art that stimulates multiple senses.

_____ 16. Fuzzy Brimhat regularly incorporated materials such as sandpaper, felt, and silk into his artwork.

_____ 17. Polly Jaxer's art is characterized by bright colors that most describe as loud.

_____ 18. Dolly Salva requires any gallery that shows her artwork to play specific musical pieces during its open hours.

The World Statistical Organization has found that the act of measuring something generally drives people to take actions that will move that metric in a desirable direction.

_____ 19. After an analysis showed that its citizens' life expectancy rose each year over the past decade, Brockway politicians proposed a series of bills meant to continue that trend.

_____ 20. After starting a Web site that publicly stated the volunteer rates for their city, Ogdenville saw an increase in the number of its citizens who volunteered on a regular basis.

_____ 21. After publicly committing to monitoring stock market fluctuations, North Haverbrook didn't see an increase in the overall value of stocks, but the decrease in it was less than it otherwise would have been.

When encountering each other for the first time, people of cultures with different languages will begin to learn each other's language through words that are related to the trading of goods and services.

_____ 22. The island nation of Clausatralia was founded by people from New Cleveland. After losing contact and developing their own language, Claustralians still use New Cleveland words for their monetary system and bartering.

_____ 23. Many of the first European traders to Asia only knew local-language words for numbers and phrases such as "this is worth" and "I'll give you."

_____ 24. Early written accounts of trading between Spartha and Corgos include detailed narratives of their different religions and pictographs depicting commodity equivalencies.

Learning about a new culture is best done through authentic immersion.

_____ 25. Marco learned a lot about Italian culture by enrolling in an intermediate class where students were not allowed to speak any language except Italian.

_____ 26. Maria learned more about Russian culture during her three months in Moscow than she did during her entire undergraduate education in Russian studies at USA University.

_____ 27. Sonya's time in Spain solidified everything she learned in her undergraduate Spanish classes.

The Salzberg method of therapy involves the re-creation of the best memories of one's childhood.

_____ 28. During tough periods, Dr. Pepperton encourages his patients to travel to locations that they've referenced in the course of speaking to him about their happy childhood memories.

_____ 29. Dr. Frankeny is skeptical of all so-called therapy "methods," but she uses her hypnotherapy sessions to have her patients recall their best childhood memories.

_____ 30. Nicole has had her most meaningful therapy sessions while confronting painful memories from her past.

8

Answers

Note: For answers that are contradicted, the offending portion of the answer choice has been crossed out.

The Corinthian architectural style is characterized by a focus on proportion and floral decorations.

_A_ 1. A column that conforms to strict mathematical ratios, styled with rose adornments.

_C_ 2. A roof supported by columns of ~~varying heights~~ and ~~widths~~, with ~~abstract~~ adornments.

_N_ 3. A sculpture of a potted plant designed by a mathematician.

(The mathematician may have not conformed to strict proportions.)

When designing an experiment, psychologists try to minimize the impact of their involvement by making sure no one with knowledge of the experiment's goals interacts with the subject.

_N_ 4. An experiment in which the people interviewing the subjects are all students in psychology classes.

_A_ 5. An experiment in which questions are read to the subjects by a computer program.

_C_ 6. An experiment in which ~~lab assistants who have helped design the study~~ ask a series of questions, only some of which are related to the goals of the experiment.

In general, increasing the harshness or certainty of punishment decreases the incidence of crime.

_C_ 7. Springfield's mayor increased the prison sentences for most crimes committed in its jurisdiction. However, because it didn't announce these changes, Springfield ~~didn't see a decline~~ in the crime rate.

_N_ 8. Derringer City saw a decrease in crime after spending money on increasing social services.

_A_ 9. San Migorge saw its crime rate plummet after increasing prison sentences for all crimes and investing in an increased police presence.

Economists claim that price and demand are inversely proportional.

_A_ 10. Microtendo increased sales of its systems by decreasing their sale price.

_A_ 11. Even though demand decreased, BananaSoft made more money overall by increasing the price of its computers.

_C_ 12. Because people associate quality with price, any college that has ~~increased~~ the price of tuition has seen an ~~increase~~ in applicants.

Paradoxically, as one becomes more accepting of failure, failure becomes less likely.

_A_ 13. Tova Works is recognized as one of the most successful businesspeople. She credits a lot of her success to some early stumbles, which taught her that she could recover and learn.

_N_ 14. Despite a crippling fear of failure, Will Doors succeeded through a string of major successful product launches.

(Success in spite of fear doesn't prove that failure wasn't less likely.)

_A_ 15. Because he knew that fear was the killer of ideas, Paul Treides learned how to mitigate his fear of failure. He immediately saw the success rate of his business pitches increase.

The New Radicalist style is characterized by a mixture of mediums and art that stimulates multiple senses.

_A_ 16. Fuzzy Brimhat regularly incorporated materials such as sandpaper, felt, and silk into his artwork.

_N_ 17. Polly Jaxer's art is characterized by bright colors that most describe as loud.

_A_ 18. Dolly Salva requires any gallery that shows her artwork to play specific musical pieces during its open hours.

8

The World Statistical Organization has found that the act of measuring something generally drives people to take actions that will move that metric in a desirable direction.

___A___ 19. After an analysis showed that its citizens' life expectancy rose each year over the past decade, Brockway politicians proposed a series of bills meant to continue that trend.

___A___ 20. After starting a Web site that publicly stated the volunteer rates for their city, Ogdenville saw an increase in the number of its citizens who volunteered on a regular basis.

___A___ 21. After publicly committing to monitoring stock market fluctuations, North Haverbrook didn't see an increase in the overall value of stocks, but the decrease in it was less than it otherwise would have been.

When encountering each other for the first time, people of cultures with different languages will begin to learn each other's language through words that are related to the trading of goods and services.

___N___ 22. The island nation of Clausatralia was founded by people from New Cleveland. After losing contact and developing their own language, Claustralians still use New Cleveland words for their monetary system and bartering.

___A___ 23. Many of the first European traders to Asia only knew local-language words for numbers and phrases such as "this is worth" and "I'll give you."

___C___ 24. Early written accounts of trading between Spartha and Corgos include detailed narratives of their different religions and ~~pictographs~~ depicting commodity equivalencies.

Learning about a new culture is best done through authentic immersion.

___N___ 25. Marco learned a lot about Italian culture by enrolling in an intermediate class where students were not allowed to speak any language except Italian.

___A___ 26. Maria learned more about Russian culture during her three months in Moscow than she did during her entire undergraduate education in Russian studies at USA University.

___N___ 27. Sonya's time in Spain solidified everything she learned in her undergraduate Spanish classes.

The Salzberg method of therapy involves the re-creation of the best memories of one's childhood.

___A___ 28. During tough periods, Dr. Pepperton encourages his patients to travel to locations that they've referenced in the course of speaking to him about their happy childhood memories.

___A___ 29. Dr. Frankeny is skeptical of all so-called therapy "methods," but she uses her hypnotherapy sessions to have her patients recall their best childhood memories.

___C___ 30. Nicole has had her most meaningful therapy sessions while ~~confronting painful memories~~ from her past.

Drill 165: Vocab Lab #19 – History Mystery

Instructions: These LSAT words are all connected with history somehow. Match the words to their closest definitions.

1. Antiquity
2. Constituent
3. Cultivation
4. Deterrent
5. Dissident
6. Doctrine
7. Domestication
8. Evanescent
9. Exponential
10. Ideology
11. Inscribe
12. Perpetual
13. Prevalent
14. Secular
15. Subsist

a. adaptation for human use
b. survive; exist
c. everlasting; never changing
d. core principle taught by a group
e. opposing the established view
f. disincentive; inhibitor
g. widespread; predominant
h. development (e.g., of land for crops, or of the mind with education)
i. engrave; write permanently
j. ancient times
k. nonreligious; temporal
l. fading quickly; soon disappearing
m. component; part
n. system of ideas
o. gaining (or losing) a certain percent in every time period

Answers

1. j

Antiquity = ancient times, often specifically the period of time before the Middle Ages. *Antiquity* can also mean "great age, ancientness."

2. m

Constituent = component; part. In a democracy, government officials are supposed to represent and be accountable to their *constituents*, i.e., voters who delegate authority to those officials.

3. h

Cultivation = development (e.g., of land for crops, or of the mind with education).

4. f

Deterrent = disincentive; inhibitor. Theoretically, a nation's nuclear weapons are thought to act as a *deterrent* to other nations that might threaten war.

5. e

Dissident = opposing the established view. As a noun, *dissident* typically means a person who opposes the political establishment within a territory.

6. d

Doctrine = core principle taught by a group. *Doctrines* may or may not be religious.

7. a

Domestication = adaptation for human use. Many plants and animals that were once wild were *domesticated*, or tamed, before the dawn of written history.

8. l

Evanescent = fading quickly; soon disappearing. The word shares an ancient root with *vanish, vacuum, vanity,* and *void.*

9. o

Exponential = gaining (or losing) a certain percent in every time period. *Exponential* growth is ever more rapid, because the percent increases keep getting bigger in real terms. Nothing can undergo *exponential* growth indefinitely.

10. n

Ideology = system of ideas; especially one by which a group or society is organized.

11. i

Inscribe = engrave; write permanently. *Inscriptions* may last longer than the things they describe.

12. c

Perpetual = everlasting; never changing. The search for *perpetual* motion machines (which defy physical laws) is a curious thread within the history of ideas.

13. g

Prevalent = widespread; predominant. Smartphones have become *prevalent* more quickly than most other technological advances in the past.

14. k

Secular = nonreligious; temporal; living in or belonging to the world (as opposed to a religious realm). From the Latin *saeculum*, meaning "age, generation."

15. b

Subsist = survive; exist. In some contexts, *subsistence* living means living hand-to-mouth, as many people have done (and still do) throughout history. In other contexts, it can refer to living in a lightweight, sustainable way, with minimal impact on natural resources.

Drill 166: Vocab Lab #20 – The Good, the Bad, and the Neutral, Round 2

Instructions: Again, even when you can't define a word precisely, you sometimes know whether it means something good or bad—and that may be enough for your needs.

You've done this before; now do it again. As fast as you can, classify each of the following words as good (G), bad (B), or neutral (N). As a bonus, define each word...but notice how much longer that takes!

_____	1. Attrition		_____	19. Rapport
_____	2. Dichotomous		_____	20. Strident
_____	3. Enumeration		_____	21. Accede
_____	4. Laudable		_____	22. Acquit
_____	5. Onerous		_____	23. Alleviate
_____	6. Palpable		_____	24. Barren
_____	7. Perturbing		_____	25. Conflate
_____	8. Prowess		_____	26. Differential
_____	9. Purported		_____	27. Dire
_____	10. Stoicism		_____	28. Divest
_____	11. Adept		_____	29. Espouse
_____	12. Amass		_____	30. Formidable
_____	13. Conjecture		_____	31. Idiomatic
_____	14. De facto		_____	32. Inclement
_____	15. Diligence		_____	33. Infallible
_____	16. Illuminating		_____	34. Reprisal
_____	17. Impropriety		_____	35. Vigorous
_____	18. Noxious			

Answers

__B__ 1. Attrition = a reduction or decrease in numbers; size or strength.

__N__ 2. Dichotomous = divided into two parts; involving contrast between two things.

__N__ 3. Enumeration = the act of reciting a number of things one by one.

__G__ 4. Laudable = praiseworthy; commendable.

__B__ 5. Onerous = burdensome; oppressive; hard to endure.

__N__ 6. Palpable = able to be felt or perceived; noticeable.

__B__ 7. Perturbing = worrying; upsetting; unsettling; anxiety-causing.

__G__ 8. Prowess = skill; ability; expertise.

__N__ 9. Purported = appearing or claiming to be the case; alleged. Don't fall into the trap of thinking that *purported* (or *alleged*, for that matter) is necessarily negative.

__N__ 10. Stoicism = a lack of emotion toward pleasure or pain. In some circumstances, calling someone *stoic* can be a good thing. But the *stoic* himself would theoretically call that description purely descriptive, not judgmental.

__G__ 11. Adept = skillful; expert (as an adjective); someone who is *adept* at something (as a noun).

__N__ 12. Amass = gather and store; collect.

__N__ 13. Conjecture = educated guess; speculation; opinion formed with incomplete information.

__N__ 14. De facto = in fact; actually.

__G__ 15. Diligence = care and earnest effort put into what you're doing.

__G__ 16. Illuminating = enlightening; informative; offering insight or clarity.

__B__ 17. Impropriety = improper behavior or character; dishonesty; inappropriateness; socially unacceptable standards.

__B__ 18. Noxious = harmful to health; corruptive.

__G__ 19. Rapport = close; amicable relationship in which the involved parties have good communication and a mutual understanding of each other.

__B__ 20. Strident = harsh in sound; loud; grating.

__G__ 21. Accede = agree; give consent; assume power (usually as "*accede* to").

__G__ 22. Acquit = fully discharge from crime.

__G__ 23. Alleviate = lessen; make easier to endure.

__B__ 24. Barren = unable to produce; infertile.

__N__ 25. Conflate = fuse; bring together; combine.

__N__ 26. Differential = showing a distinction; varying depending on certain factors.

__B__ 27. Dire = causing suffering or fear; ominous; urgent or desperate, as in "a *dire* emergency requiring immediate response."

__B__ 28. Divest = strip of power, rights, or belongings. You don't want to be *divested* of stuff.

__G__ 29. Espouse = support; adopt; embrace.

__G__ 30. Formidable = impressively powerful or capable; rousing fear or respect.

__N__ 31. Idiomatic = pertaining to forms of expression that are particular and natural to a people or group.

__B__ 32. Inclement = severe; bitter; cold; wet (as in *inclement weather*). The most common positive form is *clemency*, which you will undoubtedly win for your clients.

__G__ 33. Infallible = incapable of failure or error. Drawn from the negative prefix *in-*, the suffix *-ible*, meaning able, and the root word *fal*, meaning to fail or deceive.

__B__ 34. Reprisal = retaliation; revenge; counterattack. A *reprise* is just a repeated occurrence or a call back to something, but *reprisal* is a very specific, and bad, second round.

__G__ 35. Vigorous = strong; healthy; robust; full of *vigor* (energy).

CHAPTER 9

Don't Stop 'Til You Get Enough

In This Chapter, We Will Cover:

- More Conditional Diagramming!

- More Rule Representation!

- More Prephrases!

Don't Stop 'Til You Get Enough

Some of these drills are so nice, we had to give them to you twice. Some are so nice, we had to give them to you thrice. Some are so nice that...you get the drift. This section of the book is dedicated to drilling foundational skills such as argument breakdown, conditional diagramming, and rule representation for those of you who just can't get enough!

In this section, you will learn to:

Master Conditional Diagramming

- Diagram and chain statements of all difficulty levels

Represent Rules Backward and Forward

- Notate and reverse engineer rules of all sorts

Master the Prephrase

- Effectively prephrase tricky Causal, Conditional, and Quantified questions
- Rattle off Famous Flaws like it's nobody's business

9

Drill 167: Diagramming 101, Round 4

Instructions: Diagram and contrapose each of the following conditional statements in the space provided.

1. All interstate highways require annual maintenance.

2. If it rains more than two inches this month, the city will suspend the current water restrictions.

3. Neusa always eats either oatmeal or eggs for breakfast.

4. Only cats meow.

5. The dresser is black if the chair is also black.

6. No students will travel to the leadership conference without a chaperone.

7. All the homes in the neighborhood had either a tree or fountain in the yard.

8. Every crime scene investigator carried a badge and a flashlight.

9. If the knitter selects the purple yarn, then she will make a hat or a cowl.

10. No hockey player can play without a hockey stick.

11. Whenever it rains more than an inch in a day, Hill Street floods.

12. All the singers at the competition were amateurs.

13. Whomever we choose for the male lead can both sing and dance.

14. The director only wants to see actors who can speak both English and Spanish.

9

15. If a student receives financial aid, she can qualify for a discount at the bookstore.

16. All the deli sandwiches include cheese.

17. None of the beverages at the vegan cafe contain caffeine.

18. Trisha will not attend the conference unless her employer pays for her travel expenses and registration fee.

19. Without a new car, Joshua will not be able to drive to work.

20. Alicia will attend the dance class only if Fatima also attends it.

21. The yoga festival will include both restorative and kids' yoga classes if it has any hot yoga classes.

22. Whenever Yvonne knits, she also watches TV.

23. Lester will plant tomatoes and cilantro only if he also plants basil.

24. None of the musicians at the conservatory played the xylophone.

25. The cat hisses only when he gets a shot.

26. Imogene will apply to the pizza place or the movie theater if she is not hired at the bookstore.

27. All the actors at the wrap party had worked on the movie.

28. Every table was sold with at least two chairs.

29. Penelope will go to the park whenever she has the day off.

30. Carlton will not travel to Europe without a passport.

9

31. Without a local yarn store, Greta will have to buy her yarn online.

32. If Jacob plays a video game, he will not do his homework.

33. If Tristan wins the race, then he had both endurance and speed.

34. Sam will not go to the beach if it is rainy or windy.

35. All dogs like to play fetch.

36. Whenever it is sunny and warm, Britney likes to walk along the beach.

37. Only fresh herbs are included in our lunch special.

38. The dogs bark only when strangers enter the apartment.

39. No customer paid without a credit card today.

40. Every blue skirt in the store has a zipper.

Answers

1. All interstate highways require annual maintenance.

    IH → AM ; ~AM → ~IH

2. If it rains more than two inches this month, the city will suspend the current water restrictions.

    >2″ → ~WR ; WR → ≤2″

3. Neusa always eats either oatmeal or eggs for breakfast.

    NB → O or E ; ~O and ~E → ~NB

    If the entire question is about Neusa's breakfast, you could diagram it as an either/or conditional: ~O → E ; ~E → O

4. Only cats meow.

    M → C ; ~C → ~M

5. The dresser is black if the chair is also black.

    CB → DB ; ~DB → ~CB

6. No students will travel to the leadership conference without a chaperone.

    STLC → C ; ~C → ~STLC

7. All the homes in the neighborhood had either a tree or fountain in the yard.

    NH → T or F ; ~T and ~F → ~NH

    If the entire question is about neighborhood homes, you could diagram it as an either/or conditional: ~T → F ; ~F → T

8. Every crime scene investigator carried a badge and a flashlight.

    CSI → B and F ; ~B or ~F → ~CSI

9. If the knitter selects the purple yarn, then she will make a hat or a cowl.

    P → H or C ; ~H and ~C → ~P

10. No hockey player can play without a hockey stick.

    HP → S ; ~S → ~HP

11. Whenever it rains more than an inch in a day, Hill Street floods.

    >1″ → HSF ; ~HSF → ≤1″

12. All the singers at the competition were amateurs.

    C → A ; ~A → ~C

13. Whomever we choose for the male lead can both sing and dance.

    ML → S and D ; ~S or ~D → ~ML

14. The director only wants to see actors who can speak both English and Spanish.

    DWS → E and S ; ~E or ~S → ~DWS

15. If a student receives financial aid, she can qualify for a discount at the bookstore.

    FA → D ; ~D → ~FA

16. All the deli sandwiches include cheese.

    DS → C ; ~C → ~DS

17. None of the beverages at the vegan cafe contain caffeine.

    BVC→ ~C ; C → ~BVC

18. Trisha will not attend the conference unless her employer pays for her travel expenses and registration fee.

    TC → TE and RF ; ~TE or ~RF → ~TC

19. Without a new car, Joshua will not be able to drive to work.

    ~NC → ~DW ; DW → NC

20. Alicia will attend the dance class only if Fatima also attends it.

    A → F ; ~F → ~A

21. The yoga festival will include both restorative and kids' yoga classes if it has any hot yoga classes.

    HY → RY and KY ; ~RY or ~KY → ~HY

22. Whenever Yvonne knits, she also watches TV.

    K → TV ; ~TV → ~K

23. Lester will plant tomatoes and cilantro only if he also plants basil.

    T and C → B ; ~B → ~T or ~C

24. None of the musicians at the conservatory played the xylophone.

    MC → ~X ; X → ~MC

25. The cat hisses only when he gets a shot.

    H → S ; ~S → ~H

26. Imogene will apply to the pizza place or the theater if she is not hired at the bookstore.

    ~HB → AP or AT ; ~AP and ~AT → HB

9

27. All the actors at the wrap party had worked on the movie.

    WP → M ; ~M → ~WP

28. Every table was sold with at least two chairs.

    TS → ≥2 C ; <2 C → ~TS

29. Penelope will go to the park whenever she has the day off.

    DO → PP ; ~PP → ~DO

30. Carlton will not travel to Europe without a passport.

    E → P ; ~P → ~E

31. Without a local yarn store, Greta will have to buy her yarn online.

    ~LS → BO ; ~BO → L

32. If Jacob plays a video game, he will not do his homework.

    VG → ~HW ; HW → ~VG

33. If Tristan wins the race, then he had both endurance and speed.

    TW → E and S ; ~E or ~S → ~TW

34. Sam will not go to the beach if it is rainy or windy.

    R or W → ~B ; B → ~R and ~W

35. All dogs like to play fetch.

    D → PF ; ~PF → ~D

36. Whenever it is sunny and warm, Britney likes to walk along the beach.

    S and W → LWB ; ~LWB → ~S or ~W

37. Only fresh herbs are included in our lunch special.

    LS → FH ; ~FH → ~LS

38. The dogs bark only when strangers enter the apartment.

    DB → S ; ~S → ~DB

39. No customer paid without a credit card today.

    P → CC ; ~CC → ~P

40. Every blue skirt in the store has a zipper.

    BS → Z ; ~Z → ~BS

9

Drill 168: What's Your Function? Round 4

Instructions: Breaking down arguments into their core components is still step one for almost any Logical Reasoning question, so here is another round of practice!

Each of the following sets of items is an argument, broken up into pieces. Some sentences are also broken up, because single sentences often have multiple clauses that each have a different function. For each item, note whether it's Background info (BG), an Opposing Point (OP), Counter Evidence that would support an opposing point (even if that point has not been explicitly articulated) (CE), a Premise of the argument (P), an Intermediate Conclusion of the argument (IC), or the argument's Main Conclusion (MC). Note that you will generally need to read the whole argument before making your determination, and that it's generally easiest to start by trying to identify the main conclusion and figure the rest out from there.

Argument 1

_____ 1. I need to choose a material from which to construct my home's new deck;

_____ 2. the two options are natural wood planks and polycarbonate planks.

_____ 3. Natural wood is less expensive than polycarbonate,

_____ 4. but it is also more susceptible to weather damage.

_____ 5. Thus, as time passes, a wooden deck will require costly maintenance in order to keep it in acceptable condition.

_____ 6. Polycarbonate is the better choice for a building material.

_____ 7. since it does not need to be maintained in this way.

Argument 2

_____ 8. A number of psychological experiments have confirmed that adults generally exhibit belief perseverance: the reluctance to deviate from a previously-held view despite strong empirical evidence of its falsehood.

_____ 9. It may be the case that the adult mind is inclined to maintain continuity in its beliefs and that conflicting ideas must overcome this "inertia."

_____ 10. However, anyone familiar with children can attest that they are much more likely than adults to change their beliefs quickly, even when not given a strong reason to do so.

_____ 11. Therefore, we can conclude that children's minds are more flexible than adults' minds and can absorb new paradigms more readily.

_____ 12. Any metal used in electric wiring needs to be very conductive.

_____ 13. As a result, the overwhelming majority of electrical wiring is made from copper, which has high conductivity.

_____ 14. Recent articles in engineering trade journals have argued that copper is on the verge of being replaced as the primary metal in wiring.

_____ 15. But in order to rival the role of copper in this industry, an alternative metal would need to be both significantly less expensive and significantly more conductive than copper.

_____ 16. So, no alternative to copper wiring is likely to arise in the near future.

_____ 17. since all metals more conductive than copper, such as silver and gold, are significantly more expensive than copper at the present time.

Argument 3

_____ 18. I am an author of children's literature and have recently decided it will benefit me more to write picture books than to write children's novels.

_____ 19. While I enjoy writing novels,

_____ 20. they are much less profitable.

_____ 21. I estimate that it takes me twice as long to create a book without pictures as it does to complete a picture book,

_____ 22. but I typically receive the same advance for each kind of book.

_____ 23. Additionally, I receive roughly the same amount of money in royalties for each kind of book over a prolonged period of time.

_____ 24. In order to serve at a Petersen High School dance, a prospective chaperone must either be a full-time employee of the school or be at least thirty years of age and the legal guardian of a Petersen student.

_____ 25. Consequently, Imogen is not eligible to chaperone the upcoming Snow Dance

_____ 26. because she is twenty-eight years old and only employed part-time at Petersen.

Argument 4

_____ 27. A photography studio has sufficient space to take a family portrait of four adults and five children.

_____ 28. However, while the Vannoy family consists of four adults and five children,

_____ 29. they cannot all appear in a single photograph taken at the studio.

_____ 30. For safety reasons, there must also be more adults than children in any picture.

Argument 5

_____ 31. Traditionally, dinosaurs were classified into two groups based on the structure of their hip bones.

_____ 32. The ornithischian hip bones resemble those of a modern bird,

_____ 33. while the saurischian hip bones resembles those of a modern lizard.

_____ 34. The recently-discovered Species X must belong to neither of these traditional groups,

_____ 35. because its hip bones have some features in common with the hips of both modern birds and modern lizards.

_____ 36. The Orkham River will certainly overflow its banks this summer.

_____ 37. Farmers have observed that the runoff from snow melting on the nearby mountains has made their fields too soggy for spring planting.

_____ 38. Every time that this has occurred over the previous century, the river has overflowed.

Argument 6

_____ 39. We need to decide upon a location for tonight's dinner gathering.

_____ 40. It would be natural to choose the restaurant whose menu matches what the majority of the group wants to eat,

_____ 41. but recent discussion has made it clear that each of us is in the mood for a different style of cuisine than everyone else.

_____ 42. Since no choice can satisfy most of the group on this basis,

_____ 43. we should choose to dine at La Paz,

_____ 44. which distinguishes itself from the others with its superior ambiance and service.

Argument 7

_____ 45. An outdoor café is encircled by blue maple trees, a species that loses its leaves very early in the autumn.

_____ 46. The leaves on these trees shield the café from direct exposure to the rays of the setting sun;

_____ 47. consequently, they must prevent the café's clientele from unpleasant glare.

_____ 48. Since the outdoor café is typically busiest immediately before sunset,

_____ 49. it must become a much less popular destination in early autumn.

Answers

Argument 1

BG 1. I need to choose a material from which to construct my home's new deck;

P 2. the two options are natural wood planks and polycarbonate planks.

CE 3. Natural wood is less expensive than polycarbonate,

P 4. but it is also more susceptible to weather damage.

IC 5. Thus, as time passes, a wooden deck will require costly maintenance in order to keep it in acceptable condition.

MC 6. Polycarbonate is the better choice for a building material.

P 7. since it does not need to be maintained in this way.

Argument 2

P 8. A number of psychological experiments have confirmed that adults generally exhibit belief perseverance: the reluctance to deviate from a previously-held view despite strong empirical evidence of its falsehood.

P 9. It may be the case that the adult mind is inclined to maintain continuity in its beliefs and that conflicting ideas must overcome this "inertia."

P 10. However, anyone familiar with children can attest that they are much more likely than adults to change their beliefs quickly, even when not given a strong reason to do so.

MC 11. Therefore, we can conclude that children's minds are more flexible than adults' minds and can absorb new paradigms more readily.

P 12. Any metal used in electric wiring needs to be very conductive.

P 13. As a result, the overwhelming majority of electrical wiring is made from copper, which has high conductivity.

OP 14. Recent articles in engineering trade journals have argued that copper is on the verge of being replaced as the primary metal in wiring.

P 15. But in order to rival the role of copper in this industry, an alternative metal would need to be both significantly less expensive and significantly more conductive than copper.

MC 16. So, no alternative to copper wiring is likely to arise in the near future.

P 17. since all metals more conductive than copper, such as silver and gold, are significantly more expensive than copper at the present time.

Argument 3

MC 18. I am an author of children's literature and have recently decided it will benefit me more to write picture books than to write children's novels.

CE 19. While I enjoy writing novels,

IC 20. they are much less profitable.

P 21. I estimate that it takes me twice as long to create a book without pictures as it does to complete a picture book,

P 22. but I typically receive the same advance for each kind of book.

___P___ 23. Additionally, I receive roughly the same amount of money in royalties for each kind of book over a prolonged period of time.

___P___ 24. In order to serve at a Petersen High School dance, a prospective chaperone must either be a full-time employee of the school or be at least thirty years of age and the legal guardian of a Petersen student.

___MC___ 25. Consequently, Imogen is not eligible to chaperone the upcoming Snow Dance

___P___ 26. because she is twenty-eight years old and only employed part-time at Petersen.

Argument 4

___CE___ 27. A photography studio has sufficient space to take a family portrait of four adults and five children.

___P___ 28. However, while the Vannoy family consists of four adults and five children,

___MC___ 29. they cannot all appear in a single photograph taken at the studio.

___P___ 30. For safety reasons, there must also be more adults than children in any picture.

Argument 5

___BG___ 31. Traditionally, dinosaurs were classified into two groups based on the structure of their hip bones.

___P___ 32. The ornithischian hip bones resemble those of a modern bird,

___P___ 33. while the saurischian hip bones resembles those of a modern lizard.

___MC___ 34. The recently-discovered Species X must belong to neither of these traditional groups,

___P___ 35. because its hip bones have some features in common with the hips of both modern birds and modern lizards.

___MC___ 36. The Orkham River will certainly overflow its banks this summer.

___P___ 37. Farmers have observed that the runoff from snow melting on the nearby mountains has made their fields too soggy for spring planting.

___P___ 38. Every time that this has occurred over the previous century, the river has overflowed.

Argument 6

___BG___ 39. We need to decide upon a location for tonight's dinner gathering.

___OP___ 40. It would be natural to choose the restaurant whose menu matches what the majority of the group wants to eat,

___P___ 41. but recent discussion has made it clear that each of us is in the mood for a different style of cuisine than everyone else.

___P___ 42. Since no choice can satisfy most of the group on this basis,

___MC___ 43. we should choose to dine at La Paz,

___P___ 44. which distinguishes itself from the others with its superior ambiance and service.

Argument 7

___P___ 45. An outdoor café is encircled by blue maple trees, a species that loses its leaves very early in the autumn.

___P___ 46. The leaves on these trees shield the café from direct exposure to the rays of the setting sun;

___IC___ 47. consequently, they must prevent the café's clientele from unpleasant glare.

___P___ 48. Since the outdoor café is typically busiest immediately before sunset,

___MC___ 49. it must become a much less popular destination in early autumn.

Drill 169: Rules Represent, Round 4

Instructions: We've said it before (but since this is the last round of this drill, this time we *won't* say it again): you can't master the games section without mastering the rules, so diagram each Logic Games rule in the space provided! There are rules in this drill from all different game types and twists, so be prepared to think about what kind of game a given rule is likely to appear in as you figure out the ideal diagram. You also might need to sketch out a mini game diagram, such as a Number Line or Grouping Board, in which to place some rules.

1. If the kangaroo is showcased, so is the marmot.

2. If Gregory takes one of the cars, then Harriet will not take any of the planes.

3. Velma and Dmitry are selected together or not at all.

4. The musician wears a black suit.

5. Ms. Dumont teaches geography on two days of the week.

6. The novels by Hurston and Morrison are next to each other on the shelf.

7. If Carlos is unavailable, then neither Deidre nor Ephraim will be available.

8. Salt is added if, and only if, paprika is added.

9. There are exactly two lanes between Davis's lane and Jeffrey's lane.

10. Every office on the third floor has been redecorated.

11. The juggler always wears purple and always performs with the clown.

12. The actor performing the *Hamlet* soliloquy performs before the actor performing the *Julius Caesar* soliloquy but after the actor performing the *Othello* soliloquy.

13. Cornelia sits three seats to the right of Graham.

14. Tariq must teach on the day after Methuselah teaches.

15. No more than three roses are chosen for the bouquet.

16. The terrier places at least two ranks above the collie.

17. The jazz song is played after either the rock song or the hip hop song, but not both. (no ties)

18. Patterson and Ohi both exit on the third floor.

19. Either Leonard or Carolyn, but not both, vote after Johanna. (no ties)

20. Grenier is hired after both Knight and Manning are hired.

21. A watercolor painting is never hung next to a painting done in acrylics.

22. The diamonds cannot be kept in the same safe as the rubies.

23. The red painting will be chosen if, and only if, the pink painting is not chosen.

24. Frances will sing either before George or after Javier, but not both and no two will sing at the same time.

25. No doctors are allowed in the green room.

26. If asparagus is included in the menu, then either broccoli or cauliflower is not.

27. Only marsupials are featured in Exhibit Room A.

28. There are at least two workshops following the pottery workshop and before the sketching workshop.

9

29. If the present is wrapped in green paper, it will be chosen first.

30. Brigitte works two floors above Maureen.

31. If red wine is served, then neither fish nor curry is served.

32. Alain is hired three days after Duncan is hired.

33. Monica will visit Singapore only if Paul does not visit Thailand.

34. Norton meets with either James or Hisham first.

35. At least two of the drawers contain sweaters.

36. Jenna does not play the piece by Gershwin.

37. If the greyhound wins a ribbon, then the bulldog wins first place.

38. Burkowicz enters the room at some time after Dumont.

39. *Flashmob* is playing in the third theater.

40. Vaughan Street is next to Kennedy Street.

Answers

Note: Some of these include partial diagrams. If yours are a bit more fleshed out, that's fine. There are also times when more than one way to represent a rule would be correct. We've sometimes included different representations for these rules but just as often included only diagrams of our preferred representation.

1. If the kangaroo is showcased, so is the marmot.

$$K \rightarrow M$$
$$\cancel{M} \rightarrow \cancel{K}$$

2. If Gregory takes one of the cars car, then Harriet will not take any of the planes.

$$G_c \rightarrow \cancel{H}_p$$
$$H_p \rightarrow \cancel{G}_c$$

3. Velma and Dmitry are selected together or not at all.

$$V \leftrightarrow D$$
$$\cancel{V} \leftrightarrow \cancel{D}$$

4. The musician wears a black suit.

$$\frac{B}{M}$$

5. Ms. Dumont teaches geography on two days of the week.

$$\boxed{\begin{matrix} G \\ D \end{matrix}} = 2$$

6. The novels by Hurston and Morrison are next to each other on the shelf.

7. If Carlos is unavailable, then neither Deidre nor Ephraim will be available.

$$\cancel{C} \rightarrow \cancel{D} \text{ or } \cancel{E}$$
$$D \text{ or } E \rightarrow C$$

8. Salt is added if, and only if, paprika is added.

$$S \leftrightarrow P$$
$$\cancel{S} \leftrightarrow \cancel{P}$$

9. There are exactly two lanes between Davis's lane and Jeffrey's lane.

10. Every office on the third floor has been redecorated.

$$3 \underline{\stackrel{r}{} \, \stackrel{r}{} \, \stackrel{r}{}}$$

11. The juggler always wears purple and always performs with the clown.

12. The actor performing the *Hamlet* soliloquy performs before the actor performing the *Julius Caesar* soliloquy but after the actor performing the *Othello* soliloquy.

$$O - H - C$$

13. Cornelia sits three seats to the right of Graham.

$$\boxed{G \, \_\_\_ \, C}$$

14. Tariq must teach on the day after Methuselah teaches.

15. No more than three roses are chosen for the bouquet.

$$R = 3 \text{ max}$$

9

16. The terrier places at least two ranks above the collie.

$$T - \_\_ - C$$

17. The jazz song is played after either the rock song or the hip hop song, but not both. (no ties)

$$R - J - H \text{ or } H - J - R$$

18. Patterson and Ohi both exit on the third floor.

$$3 \ \underline{P} \ \underline{O}$$

19. Either Leonard or Carolyn, but not both, vote after Johanna. (no ties)

$$L - J - C \text{ or } C - J - L$$

20. Grenier is hired after both Knight and Manning are hired.

21. A watercolor painting is never hung next to a painting done in acrylics.

22. The diamonds cannot be kept in the same safe as the rubies.

23. The red painting will be chosen if, and only if, the pink painting is not chosen.

$$R \leftrightarrow \not{P}$$
$$\not{R} \leftrightarrow P$$

24. Frances will sing either before George or after Javier, but not both and no two will sing at the same time.

$$F \overset{G}{\underset{J}{<}} \text{ or } \overset{G}{\underset{J}{>}} F$$

25. No doctors are allowed in the green room.

$$\overline{G}$$
$$\not{D}$$

26. If asparagus is included in the menu, then either broccoli or cauliflower is not.

$$A \rightarrow \not{B} \text{ or } \not{C}$$
$$B + C \rightarrow \not{A}$$

27. Only marsupials are featured in Exhibit Room A.

$$\overline{A}$$
$$non-\not{M}$$

28. There are at least two workshops following the pottery workshop and before the sketching workshop.

$$P - \_\_ - S$$

29. If the present is wrapped in green paper, it will be chosen first.

$$P_G \rightarrow P_1$$
$$\not{P_1} \rightarrow \not{P_G}$$

30. Brigitte works two floors above Maureen.

$$\begin{array}{c} B \\ \sim \\ M \end{array}$$

31. If red wine is served, then neither fish nor curry is served.

$$R \rightarrow \not{F} + \not{C}$$
$$F \text{ or } C \rightarrow \not{R}$$

32. Alain is hired three days after Duncan is hired.

$$| D \_ \_ A |$$

33. Monica will visit Singapore only if Paul does not visit Thailand.

$$M_S \rightarrow \cancel{P}_T$$
$$P_T \rightarrow \cancel{M}_S$$

34. Norton meets with either James or Hisham first.

$$\frac{J/H}{1}$$

35. At least two of the drawers contain sweaters.

$$S = 2+$$

36. Jenna does not play the piece by Gershwin.

$$\cancel{J}_G \text{ or } \frac{G}{\cancel{J}}$$

37. If the greyhound wins a ribbon, then the bulldog wins first place.

$$G \rightarrow B_1$$
$$\cancel{B}_1 \rightarrow \cancel{G}$$

38. Burkowicz enters the room at some time after Dumont.

$$D - B$$

39. *Flashmob* is playing in the third theater.

$$\frac{F}{3}$$

40. Vaughan Street is next to Kennedy Street.

Drill 170: Stem the Tide, Round 4

Instructions: We give you the stem, you tell us the question type! The 18 major question types are as follows: ID the Conclusion, Determine the Function, Procedure, ID the (Dis)agreement, Sufficient Assumption, Necessary Assumption, ID the Flaw, Strengthen, Weaken, Evaluate, Principle Support, Must Be True, Must Be False, Most Strongly Supported, Principle Example, Match the Reasoning, Match the Flaw, Explain a Result.

1. In the conversation, Reed responds to Xiang in which one of the following ways?

_____

2. It would be most important to determine which one of the following in evaluating the argument?

_____

3. The statements above best illustrate which one of the following generalizations?

_____

4. The reasoning in which one of the following is most similar to the reasoning in the argument above?

_____

5. Which one of the following, if true, most helps to account for the unexpected behavior of the coyotes?

_____

6. Which one of the following most accurately expresses the principle underlying the argument?

_____

7. Which one of the following, if true, casts the most doubt on the pundit's claims?

_____

8. The argument depends on assuming which one of the following?

_____

9. Which one of the following conforms most closely to the principle stated above?

_____

10. Which of the following is a point on which Sarah and Luke agree?

_____

11. The physicist's reasoning is flawed because it presumes without giving sufficient justification that

_____

12. Which one of the following propositions does the passage most precisely illustrate?

_____

13. Which one of the following identifies a reasoning error in the argument?

_____

14. Raoul criticizes Martine's argument by

_____

15. Which one of the following, if assumed, most helps to justify the application of the principle?

_____

16. The examples provided above best illustrate which one of the following propositions?

_____

17. Which one of the following can most reasonably be concluded on the basis of the information above?

_____

9

18. The conclusion drawn above follows logically if which one of the following is assumed?

_____

19. Which one of the following most accurately describes the technique Roy uses in responding to Helena's claims?

_____

20. The answer to which one of the following questions would help most in evaluating the argument?

_____

21. The principle stated above, if valid, most helps to justify the reasoning in which one of the following arguments?

_____

22. Which one of the following is an assumption required by the argument?

_____

23. If the statements above are true, each of the following could be true EXCEPT:

_____

24. The journalist's reasoning most closely conforms to which one of the following principles?

_____

25. The reasoning in the argument is questionable because the argument

_____

Answers follow on the next page.

Answers

1. Procedure

2. Evaluate

3. Principle Support

4. Match the Reasoning

5. Explain a Result

6. Principle Support

7. Weaken

8. Necessary Assumption

9. Principle Example

10. ID the Agreement

11. Necessary Assumption

    (*If you listed this as an ID the Flaw stem, you're right too! We've chosen to categorize it as a Necessary Assumption question, however, because the correct answer must be a Necessary Assumption.*)

12. Principle Support

13. ID the Flaw

14. Procedure

15. Strengthen

16. Principle Support

17. Most Strongly Supported

18. Sufficient Assumption

19. Procedure

20. Evaluate

21. Principle Example

22. Necessary Assumption

23. Must Be False

24. Principle Support

25. ID the Flaw

Drill 171: Diagramming 201, Round 3

Instructions: Diagram and contrapose these more complicated conditionals. For an added twist, some of these statements might not even be conditional, in which case you should answer NA.

1. Eric takes the subway and Michael travels on foot, unless we are rehearsing after midnight.

2. Cranium Confection's new headphones will receive a glowing review from critics, but only if either the bass quality is improved or the price point is lowered.

3. Every jellyfish is more than 95% water by weight.

4. In order to receive our weekly newsletter, you'll need to be registered on the site and update your profile information.

5. The alternator belt screeches whenever I put the car into drive or turn sharply.

6. None of the clarinet or bassoon players is both prepared and available to play this weekend.

7. We can leave the shelter, but not until the tornado warning ends or emergency personnel escort us out.

8. All of the alarms Husani set for today's big meeting failed to go off.

9. If neither the principal nor the vice principal sanctions our science experiment, we are guaranteed a failing grade in chemistry.

10. It's impossible to sneeze without both shutting your eyes and holding your breath.

11. Anderson shall build the extension to his home if, but only if, the interest rate on his mortgage lowers.

12. Whenever the judicial and executive branches are opposed to a new law, the legislature will not be able to implement that law effectively.

13. Not only does lemonade sometimes cause tooth erosion, but it can also lower the body's pH.

14. Any of Sona's friends may sign up for either the Saturday or Sunday marathon, except for Carlos.

15. The groundhog seeing its shadow ensures us six more weeks of winter and an increase in cases of seasonal affective disorder.

16. Unless the next few episodes of this show prove to be very popular, this season will be its last.

17. The camping trip is going to be affordable, but only if Francesca and Sarah chip in.

18. Every flower in my aunt's garden is either an annual or a perennial.

19. Gabe needs to grow at least five inches over the summer in order to ride the roller coaster at next year's fair.

20. A strong background in science or mathematics is a prerequisite to leading a successful tech startup.

21. There are many interesting costumes at the party, but none of them is store-bought.

22. Wide swaths of Canada will remain sparsely populated until viable agricultural methods for tundra can be developed.

23. All of Mike's albums that are either R&B or EDM are filed alphabetically and stored in a dehumidified room.

24. Our spring training roster will have to be changed if any of our free agents leave the team during the off-season or retire.

25. A commanding officer can be demoted if, but only if, that officer has unnecessarily risked the lives of his or her unit.

26. Whenever Gregory becomes homesick, he looks up the prices for flights and for buses back home.

9

27. Nightstands from our store that came without an Allen wrench in the packaging are faulty.

28. Only punctures in a tire that are smaller than 2 cm across may be patched.

29. Providing your body with high quality protein and adequate sleep ensures that you will maximize muscle synthesis after workouts.

30. No spectators except for the victim's immediate family will be allowed into the courtroom.

31. Sometimes things are not what they seem.

32. The leak from Ramon's kitchen sink will not be fixed unless the plumber closes the valve in the utility closet and refits the faucet with sealant.

33. Electronics from the U.S. can be used in Japan only if they are plugged into an adapter.

34. Every spice and every sauce listed in the recipe is readily available in most supermarkets.

35. In either comedy or tragedy, a performer needs to find a personal connection to the material in order to be relatable to the audience.

36. An undergraduate degree is a prerequisite for a graduate degree.

37. Of the 27 lipstick varieties on the store's shelves, none are listed as "cruelty free."

38. Charlie will not find love through online dating until Ronald and Dennis help him with his profile.

39. All of this food came from the local farmer's market.

40. A magpie will recognize its own reflection if placed in front of a mirror.

41. It's not safe to leave a pressure cooker unattended without removing it from the heat source and setting it down where it cannot easily be knocked over.

42. The visiting team always loses whenever it has to cross three or more time zones to get to the game.

43. James will sleep comfortably tonight if he remembers to remove the tag from his pajamas.

44. Only those with delusions of grandeur or a strong financial incentive would attempt to summit that mountain.

45. A smooth texture in the custard is ensured by whipping the eggs vigorously.

46. No members of the press except for those from the local newspaper are allowed to film the lottery drawing.

47. I can't remember my dreams unless I am woken up abruptly during the night.

48. Sulfur trioxide is only safe to handle if you are wearing three pairs of gloves and working under a fume hood.

49. Every dog has his day.

50. All of Kristen's taxidermy collection is in good condition except for the octopus.

Answers

1. Eric takes the subway and Michael travels on foot, unless we are rehearsing after midnight.

   ~ES or ~MF → AM ; ~AM → ES and MF

2. Cranium Confection's new headphones will receive a glowing review from critics, but only if either the bass quality is improved or the price point is lowered.

   GR → BQI or LP ; ~BQI and ~LP → ~GR

3. Every jellyfish is more than 95% water by weight.

   J → and 95% W ; ~ and 95% W → ~J

4. In order to receive our weekly newsletter, you'll need to be registered on the site and update your profile information.

   RWN → RPS and UPI ; ~RPS or ~UPI → ~RWN

5. The alternator belt screeches whenever I put the car into drive or turn sharply.

   CD or TS → ABS ; ~ABS → ~CD and ~TS

6. None of the clarinet or bassoon players is both prepared and available to play this weekend.

   C or B → ~P or ~A ; P and A → ~C and ~B

7. We can leave the shelter, but not until the tornado warning ends or emergency personnel escort us out.

   LS → WE or EPE ; ~WE and ~EPE → ~LS

8. All of the alarms Husani set for today's big meeting failed to go off.

   A → ~GO ; GO → ~A

9. If neither the principal nor the vice principal sanctions our science experiment, we are guaranteed a failing grade in chemistry.

   ~P and ~VP → F ; ~F → P or VP

10. It's impossible to sneeze without both shutting your eyes and holding your breath.

    Snz → SE and HB ; ~SE or ~HB → ~Snz

11. Anderson shall build the extension to his home if, but only if, the interest rate on his mortgage lowers.

    BE ↔ IRL ; ~IRL ↔ ~BE

12. Whenever the judicial and executive branches are opposed to a new law, the legislature will not be able to implement that law effectively.

    JO and EO → ~LIE ; LIE → ~JO or ~EO

13. Not only does lemonade sometimes cause tooth erosion, but it can also lower the body's pH.

Not a conditional statement. This is causal, and while some causal statements are conditional (because the cause guarantees the effect), in this one, the cause will only sometimes lead to each of the given effects.

14. Any of Sona's friends may sign up for either the Saturday or Sunday marathon, except for Carlos.

SF and ~C → Sat or Sun ; ~Sat and ~Sun → ~SF or C

15. The groundhog seeing its shadow ensures us six more weeks of winter and an increase in cases of seasonal affective disorder.

GSS → SWW and SAD ; ~SWW or ~SAD → ~GSS

16. Unless the next few episodes of this show prove to be very popular, this season will be its last.

~SL → NEP ; ~NEP → SL

17. The camping trip is going to be affordable, but only if Francesca and Sarah chip in.

CTA → F and S ; ~F or ~S → ~CTA

18. Every flower in my aunt's garden is either an annual or a perennial.

G → A or P ; ~A and ~P → ~G

19. Gabe needs to grow at least five inches over the summer in order to ride the roller coaster at next year's fair.

RNY → G5 and : ~G5 and → ~RNY

20. A strong background in science or mathematics is a prerequisite to leading a successful tech startup.

LSTS → SBS or SBM ; ~SBS and ~SBM → ~LSTS

21. There are many interesting costumes at the party, but none of them is store-bought.

IC → ~SB ; SB → ~IC

22. Wide swaths of Canada will remain sparsely populated until viable agricultural methods for tundra can be developed.

~VAT → SP ; ~SP → VAT

23. All of Mike's albums that are either R&B or EDM are filed alphabetically and stored in a dehumidified room.

R&B or EDM → FA and SD ; ~FA or ~SD → ~R&B and ~EDM

24. Our spring training roster will have to be changed if any of our free agents leave the team during the off-season or retire.

FAL or FAR → RC ; ~RC → ~FAL and ~FAR

25. A commanding officer can be demoted if, but only if, that officer has unnecessarily risked the lives of his or her unit.

D ↔ URL ; ~D ↔ ~URL

9

26. Whenever Gregory becomes homesick, he looks up the prices for flights and for buses back home.

    $H \rightarrow LF$ and LB ; $\sim LF$ or $\sim LB \rightarrow \sim H$

27. Nightstands from our store that came without an Allen wrench in the packaging are faulty.

    $\sim AW \rightarrow F$; $\sim F \rightarrow AW$

28. Only punctures in a tire that are smaller than 2 cm across may be patched.

    $Pat \rightarrow < 2cm$; $\sim < 2cm \rightarrow \sim Pat$

29. Providing your body with high quality protein and adequate sleep ensures that you will maximize muscle synthesis after workouts.

    P and $S \rightarrow MMS$; $\sim MMS \rightarrow \sim P$ or $\sim S$

30. No spectators except for the victim's immediate family will be allowed into the courtroom.

    $SAC \rightarrow VF$; $\sim VF \rightarrow \sim SAC$

31. Sometimes things are not what they seem.

    Not a conditional statement.

32. The leak from Ramon's kitchen sink will not be fixed unless the plumber closes the valve in the utility closet and refits the faucet with sealant.

    $F \rightarrow CV$ and RF ; $\sim CV$ or $\sim RF \rightarrow \sim F$

33. Electronics from the U.S. can be used in Japan only if they are plugged into an adapter.

    $UJ \rightarrow A$: $\sim A \rightarrow \sim UJ$

34. Every spice and every sauce listed in the recipe is readily available in most supermarkets.

    Sp or $Sau \rightarrow AMS$; $\sim AMS \rightarrow \sim Sp$ and $\sim Sau$

    (Note: Because something doesn't need to be both a spice and a sauce to guarantee that it's available in most supermarkets, the conjunction here is "or" rather than "and.")

35. In either comedy or tragedy, a performer needs to find a personal connection to the material in order to be relatable to the audience.

    RC or $RT \rightarrow PC$; $\sim PC \rightarrow \sim RC$ and $\sim RT$

36. An undergraduate degree is a prerequisite for a graduate degree.

    $GD \rightarrow UGD$; $\sim UGD \rightarrow \sim GD$

37. Of the 27 lipstick varieties on the store's shelves, none are listed as "cruelty free."

    $L \rightarrow \sim CF$; $CF \rightarrow \sim L$

38. Charlie will not find love through online dating until Ronald and Dennis help him with his profile.

    $CFL \rightarrow RH$ and DH ; $\sim RH$ or $\sim DH \rightarrow \sim CFL$

39. All of this food came from the local farmer's market.

    F → FM ; ~FM → ~F

40. A magpie will recognize its own reflection if placed in front of a mirror.

    PM → MRR ; ~MRR → ~PM

41. It's not safe to leave a pressure cooker unattended without removing it from the heat source and setting it down where it cannot easily be knocked over.

    S → RH and ~EKO ; ~RH or EKO → ~S

42. The visiting team always loses whenever it has to cross three or more time zones to get to the game.

    C3T → L ; ~L → ~C3T

43. James will sleep comfortably tonight if he remembers to remove the tag from his pajamas.

    RT → SC ; ~SC → ~RT

44. Only those with delusions of grandeur or a strong financial incentive would attempt to summit that mountain.

    AS → DG or SFI ; ~DG and ~SFI → ~AS

45. A smooth texture in the custard is ensured by whipping the eggs vigorously.

    WEV → ST ; ~ST → ~WEV

46. No members of the press except for those from the local newspaper are allowed to film the lottery drawing.

    AF → LN ; ~LN → ~AF

47. I can't remember my dreams unless I am woken up abruptly during the night.

    RD → WA ; ~WA → ~RD

48. Sulfur trioxide is only safe to handle if you are wearing three pairs of gloves and working under a fume hood.

    S → 3G and FH ; ~3G or ~FH → ~S

49. Every dog has his day.

    Dog → Day ; ~Day → ~Dog

50. All of Kristen's taxidermy collection is in good condition except for the octopus.

    ~GC → O ; ~O → GC

Drill 172: Famous Flaws, Round 5

Instructions: For each of the following abbreviated arguments, select which famous flaw is being committed, again! Remember, since there is some overlap among the different flaws, you might prephrase an answer that doesn't appear. That's fine! Figure out which answer is correct and then spend time thinking about why it's correct and how you could have prephrased both answers (assuming, of course, that you were correct with your initial prephrase). For a little added challenge in this final round, we've added an additional answer choice. Enjoy!

1. If Rupert wins the lottery, it is certain that he will finally buy that boat he has been saving up for. But nobody I know will ever win the lottery, so Rupert will not get the boat he has been saving for.

   (A) Circular Reasoning
   (B) Term Shift
   (C) Illegal Negation
   (D) Appeal to Emotion

2. It's been quite some time since Mary has received a raise. However, last Saturday, she volunteered at the community center, and this week, she finally received that raise. Doing good must have resulted in karma rewarding Mary.

   (A) Appeal to Inappropriate Authority
   (B) Ad Hominem
   (C) Appeal to Emotion
   (D) Causation Flaw

3. Economists will tell you that demand for a product and its price will rise in near unison. People must be obsessed with appearing wealthy, purchasing products that are more expensive to demonstrate that wealth.

   (A) Ad Hominem
   (B) Circular Reasoning
   (C) Causation Flaw
   (D) Sampling Flaw

4. While Marisa has always believed in UFOs, her faith in their existence was recently shaken by the revelation that Ellen Tarkanian, a famous UFOlogist, fabricated most of the evidence in her books. Since Tarkanian's books are cited by everyone as the proof that UFOs exist, this revelation must lead us to conclude that there are not, in fact, unidentified flying objects.

   (A) Unproven vs. Untrue
   (B) Circular Reasoning
   (C) Causation Flaw
   (D) Sampling Flaw

5. During the recent world championships, the networks have focused on the inspirational story of Madelaine Aldark. With such an amazing personal history, she's sure to win her events.

   (A) Equivocation
   (B) Opinion vs. Fact
   (C) Appeal to Emotion
   (D) Causation Flaw

6. On regular weekdays, my rush-hour commute to work takes an hour or longer. When I have to work on Saturdays, I take the back roads and usually make it to the office in 45 minutes, despite the lower speed limit. The quicker trip must be due to fewer people driving on back roads compared to the highway.

   (A) Circular Reasoning
   (B) Relative vs. Absolute
   (C) Self-Contradiction
   (D) Comparison Flaw

7. Farland State University recently surveyed recent graduates regarding what changes could be made to improve graduation rates, which have plummeted in the past decade. If the school listens to the feedback, this trend will turn around expeditiously.

(A) Sampling Flaw
(B) Illegal Reversal
(C) Appeal to Emotion
(D) Equivocation

8. Acme Widget Company has had issues with its operations. Staff within each division have failed to coordinate with each other, and division managers haven't coordinated with their counterparts in other divisions. The new CEO has hired strong leaders for each division, and each has gotten her respective division staffs to work well together. Thus, the entire company must be running in sync now.

(A) Percent vs. Amount
(B) Relative vs. Absolute
(C) Part vs. Whole
(D) Possible vs. Certain

9. There are rumors stating that Stu Goodling might be coming out of retirement to play a series of concerts. This is fantastic news for his fans who will be able to see their favorite performer again.

(A) Appeal to Emotion
(B) Possible vs. Certain
(C) Unproven vs. Untrue
(D) False Choice

10. If I work fewer than five days a week, I won't be able to pay my expenses. If I work more than five days a week, I won't be able to study enough to maintain a full course load. Since I must continue to pay all my expenses, I'm going to have to shift to part-time status at college.

(A) Percent vs. Amount
(B) Causation Flaw
(C) False Choice
(D) Equivocation

11. Homeowner: The water level in my pool keeps going down by about two inches per week. I've had multiple plumbing and pool experts check all the water lines, and they are certain that there are no leaks. Thus, the pool liner must have a hole in it, allowing water to leak into the ground.

(A) Appeal to Emotion
(B) Ad Hominem
(C) False Choice
(D) Appeal to Inappropriate Authority

12. Jonquil's financial analyst has provided nothing but successful investment advice. Because of this, Jonquil is planning to ask the analyst to help him with a lawsuit he's involved in.

(A) Opinion vs. Fact
(B) Appeal to Emotion
(C) Appeal to Inappropriate Authority
(D) Sampling Flaw

13. A large group of cat owners were asked what pet they would get next if they couldn't get a second feline. By a wide margin, dogs were at the bottom of the list. This provides strong evidence that dogs are among the least popular pets.

(A) Opinion vs. Fact
(B) Appeal to Emotion
(C) Term Shift
(D) Sampling Flaw

14. Since she knew a new project at work would require a lot of reading, Jana went to her eye doctor to receive a new prescription. Shortly after, her eyes started to become tired. The eye doctor must have made an error with her prescription.

(A) Causation Flaw
(B) Appeal to Inappropriate Authority
(C) Straw Man
(D) Term Shift

15. Donald has swapped his unhealthy snacks for healthier varieties. Therefore, his snacking habit has become healthy.

    (A) Part vs. Whole
    (B) Relative vs. Absolute
    (C) Causation Flaw
    (D) Comparison Flaw

16. Donald has swapped all his unhealthy snacks for healthier varieties. Therefore, his overall diet has become healthier.

    (A) Circular Reasoning
    (B) Relative vs. Absolute
    (C) Part vs. Whole
    (D) False Choice

17. Anybody who is happy will find joy in small victories. Unless one has perspective as to what is really important, one will not find joy in small victories. Allison has a remarkable sense of perspective as to what is actually significant, so she must be happy.

    (A) Term Shift
    (B) Illegal Reversal
    (C) Circular Reasoning
    (D) Straw Man

18. Two of the primary ways that rats can get into a house are through chewing holes in the wall and squeezing through cracks left during construction. Since Abby's house has been checked extensively for cracks and none have been found, it's almost certain that the rats that have been stealing the food in her pantry are entering her house through holes they've chewed in the walls.

    (A) False Choice
    (B) Appeal to Inappropriate Authority
    (C) Illegal Reversal
    (D) Causation Flaw

19. Scientists using Light Detection and Ranging (LIDAR) technology have discovered an ancient Mayan metropolis with about 60,000 residences and a multitude of other structures, including highways. While scientists claim it is in the public interest to research this discovery, the public has largely ignored this news. Therefore, the scientists were wrong to claim that there is public interest in the discovery.

    (A) Equivocation
    (B) False Choice
    (C) Straw Man
    (D) Possible vs. Certain

20. Since scientists now know that the ancient Mayan civilization was far more densely populated than previously thought, it must be the case that it was far more warlike than previously thought.

    (A) Equivocation
    (B) Causation Flaw
    (C) Term Shift
    (D) Sampling Flaw

21. Analyst: Acme Widget Co. needs to get its finances in order if it is to survive. There are myriad ways that it could save money. However, laying off staff is the only option that can, by itself, save enough money to rescue the company. So, Acme Widget must go through a round of staff layoffs.

    (A) Causation Flaw
    (B) Appeal to Emotion
    (C) False Choice
    (D) Unwarranted Prediction

22. Recently, our town added a five-second delay between the time that the crosswalk sign gives pedestrians a green light and the time that the stoplight allows cars to make the turn onto the street these pedestrians are crossing. Since then, the number of accidents involving pedestrians at that intersection has drastically declined. Clearly, the addition of the delay is responsible for this improvement in road safety.

    (A) Causation Flaw
    (B) Appeal to Emotion
    (C) False Choice
    (D) Unwarranted Prediction

23. Politician: Acme Widget Co. is being threatened with shutdown by environmental activists that claim the company is polluting our waterways. But this company has been the lifeblood of our community for generations. My grandfather, and many of yours, too, supported their families by working at the plant. It is therefore in the interest of our entire community to come together to ensure that Acme Widget Co. remains open for generations to come.

    (A) Causation Flaw
    (B) Ad Hominem
    (C) False Choice
    (D) Appeal to Emotion

24. Worker: Acme Widget ownership claims it needs to get its finances in order if the company is to survive, and the only way to do so is by laying off staff. However, they are just resentful that we fought them to get a fair deal in collective bargaining. No layoffs are necessary.

    (A) Causation Flaw
    (B) Ad Hominem
    (C) Unwarranted Prediction
    (D) False Choice

25. Stacy only travels using either NightSKY or QuickJET airlines. For her upcoming trip to Aruba, NightSKY airline has offered her a promotional price much lower than their normal rate. Stacy is therefore likely to pick the NightSKY flight over any offer by QuickJET airline.

    (A) Comparison Flaw
    (B) False Choice
    (C) Self-Contradiction
    (D) Opinion vs. Fact

26. Most smokers are heavy coffee drinkers. So, since Sam drinks a lot of coffee, it is likely that he smokes.

    (A) Term Shift
    (B) Percent vs. Amount
    (C) Relative vs. Absolute
    (D) Illegal Reversal

27. A scientific study on the impact of coffee drinking on heart health indicated that heavy coffee drinkers have an elevated risk of heart attack. If the results of this study are valid, Edouard is at an elevated risk of heart attack since he drinks three cups of coffee a day.

    (A) Unproven vs. Untrue
    (B) Causation Flaw
    (C) Unwarranted Prediction
    (D) False Choice

28. After receiving a recent raise, Soleil analyzed her budget. During this analysis, she noticed that the percent of her paycheck going to rent each month has decreased. While she hasn't heard from her landlord recently, she should remember to send him a thank you note for lowering her rent.

    (A) Ad Hominem
    (B) Appeal to Emotion
    (C) Self-Contradiction
    (D) Percent vs. Amount

9

29. Drinking tea is clearly a great method to decrease the likelihood that one will develop kidney stones. In a recent study of hospital records, those who requested tea with their pre-surgery meal were much less likely to be admitted for kidney stones than those who requested any other beverage.

    (A) Appeal to Emotion
    (B) False Choice
    (C) Causation Flaw
    (D) Sampling Flaw

30. Economist: The vast majority of my fellow economists believe that, under normal economic conditions, tax cuts will produce an increase in national economic output. However, the staggering level of disagreement regarding what constitutes "normal" economic conditions negates relying on such opinions in predicting the effect of tax cuts on economic output. Thus, it is only reasonable to conclude that, under normal economic conditions, tax cuts will result in a decrease in national economic output.

    (A) Unproven vs. Untrue
    (B) False Choice
    (C) Opinion vs. Fact
    (D) Illegal Negation

31. Kirk Vennetorso's previous book, *Charybdis on Dione*, is one of Cheryl's favorite novels. Its strong protagonist and circuitous narrative are her favorite aspects of the novel. Since Vennetorso's new book, *Redbeard*, features a milquetoast protagonist and a straightforward narrative, Cheryl probably won't enjoy it.

    (A) Appeal to Emotion
    (B) Illegal Negation
    (C) Comparison Flaw
    (D) False Choice

32. Mr. Salt Soda asked 1,000 of its Diet Salty drinkers why they choose the diet soda over the non-diet version. Over 700 indicated that they made the decision because of health considerations, and only about 100 chose it for the taste. So, the vast majority of Mr. Salt Soda's customers are not choosing their soda for the taste.

    (A) Part vs. Whole
    (B) Sampling Flaw
    (C) False Choice
    (D) Opinion vs. Fact

33. Only the truly brave will ride the SpineCrusher roller coaster. Wayne must not be as brave as he believes, since he refuses to "Get Crushed," as the ads call riding the coaster.

    (A) Ad Hominem
    (B) Self-Contradiction
    (C) Illegal Negation
    (D) Opinion vs. Fact

34. A few thousand years ago, a once-thriving civilization vanished from the southwestern United States. Some people claim that drought and changing climatic conditions are to blame. Others claim that an epidemic is to blame. However, neither of those alone could have caused such a large civilization to vanish in such a short time frame. So, something else entirely must be at fault.

    (A) False Choice
    (B) Unproven vs. Untrue
    (C) Causation Flaw
    (D) Appeal to Inappropriate Authority

35. Milton is positive that the economy is heading into a recession. But he must be mistaken, for a recession is bad, and thus he's not engaged in positive thinking.

    (A) Self-Contradiction
    (B) Equivocation
    (C) False Choice
    (D) Opinion vs. Fact

9

36. Our area is currently experiencing a false spring, a long stretch of really warm weather in the middle of winter that fools fruit trees into producing flowers that can be damaged if the weather shifts back to wintry conditions. This can result in a greatly diminished fruit crop in the summer. So, this summer will be another bad year for orchards in the area.

    (A) Opinion vs. Fact
    (B) Possible vs. Certain
    (C) Illegal Reversal
    (D) Causation Flaw

37. Music elevates the human spirit. That is why music qualifies as a fine art.

    (A) Opinion vs. Fact
    (B) Appeal to Emotion
    (C) Causation Flaw
    (D) Term Shift

38. Corporate Seed Company Executive: Our company holds patents for seeds that we genetically engineer to be easier to grow, outcompete weeds, and produce greater yields, so it is illegal for farmers to grow these seeds without buying them from us. Yet, we have observed that adjacent to most fields legally growing our seeds are fields full of crops produced from our seeds. It must be that the landowners who own these fields stole our seeds and thus should pay us restitution.

    (A) Causation Flaw
    (B) Illegal Reversal
    (C) False Choice
    (D) Possible vs. Certain

39. Every sentence Maya writes epitomizes what it means to write well—not just in conforming to mundane rules of grammar, but, far more importantly, in the harmony and flow of the tone of each syllable. When her new book is finished, it is guaranteed to be a model of well-crafted prose.

    (A) Relative vs. Absolute
    (B) Sampling Flaw
    (C) Part vs. Whole
    (D) Term Shift

40. Sinclair's mystery novels have achieved critical acclaim. One element of her work that is mentioned in all positive reviews is her mastery of plot. The convoluted, yet logical, conclusions to the mysteries she sets up keep critics guessing while reaching a resolution that is both surprising yet clear. Since she's using similar plotting in her upcoming science fiction novel, it's surely going to be a critical success.

    (A) Illegal Reversal
    (B) Comparison Flaw
    (C) Opinion vs. Fact
    (D) Term Shift

41. The European pied flycatcher must begin its migration from Africa at precisely the right time to arrive in Europe at the peak of caterpillar season; the emergence of caterpillars in turn is triggered by the leafing out of oak trees. Due to climate change, the leafing out of oak trees and peak caterpillar season keeps occurring earlier, but the flycatcher times its departure from Africa based on day length, which varies with the rotation of the earth, not temperatures. So, more and more flycatchers are missing their prime feeding window and starving after their long migration. Thus, the flycatcher will soon start migrating earlier.

    (A) Self-Contradiction
    (B) Opinion vs. Fact
    (C) Illegal Negation
    (D) Causation Flaw

9

42. In a recent court case, the accuracy of a recently developed fingerprint analysis technique was brought into question. While several forensic scientists were brought into court to discuss the technique and its high level of accuracy, the defense called to the stand a lawyer who had a long career in criminal prosecution. This prosecutor discussed all the inaccuracies inherent in fingerprint analysis. Since the prosecutor was involved in many more cases involving fingerprint analysis than all of the scientists combined, his testimony should carry more weight with the jury when they're analyzing the accuracy of the results.

    (A) Part vs. Whole
    (B) Relative vs. Absolute
    (C) Opinion vs. Fact
    (D) Appeal to Inappropriate Authority

43. Good bread cannot be baked without good dough. Since Mary made sure that the dough she created was perfect, she's surely going to end up with good bread.

    (A) Circular Reasoning
    (B) Illegal Negation
    (C) Causation Flaw
    (D) Comparison Flaw

44. Since all living humans who are at least a century old lived through the Great Depression, it must be the case that living through such a financial disaster imparts extended longevity on humans who survive it.

    (A) Illegal Reversal
    (B) Sampling Flaw
    (C) Comparison Flaw
    (D) Causation Flaw

45. During a recent hiking excursion, Sophie kept a log of the species of tree she encountered. The full list had the California redwood, Douglas fir, and Sitka spruce, three of the four largest trees on the planet. Therefore, the forest she hiked through must be massive.

    (A) Part vs. Whole
    (B) Possible vs. Certain
    (C) Unproven vs. Untrue
    (D) Unwarranted Prediction

46. While on a recent hike along a fairly inaccessible riverbank, Hilda and Gertrude saw a large number of animals from a variety of species. While hiking on a well-traveled trail in another forest, they saw only the occasional squirrel. Thus, the forest with the riverbank they hiked along must contain significantly more animals than the one with the well-traveled trail.

    (A) Term Shift
    (B) Equivocation
    (C) Sampling Flaw
    (D) Illegal Negation

47. Karl used to drink three cans of soda per day, each with 65 mg of caffeine. He recently decreased his soda intake to just one can per day in an attempt to lower his caffeine consumption. However, now coffee makes up a larger proportion of his overall beverage consumption, and each cup of coffee contains about twice the amount of caffeine as a single can of soda. Thus, Karl has not succeeded in his goal.

    (A) Unwarranted Prediction
    (B) Percent vs. Amount
    (C) Causation Flaw
    (D) Comparison Flaw

9

48. My opponent claims that tuition for higher education has skyrocketed over the past thirty years, and that the amount of student loan debt owed by the average graduate is resulting in a delayed start to retirement savings and the purchase of homes. But if you give students a free ride, the next generation will never learn the value of money. That's why I oppose her plan to lessen the cost of higher education.

    (A) Straw Man
    (B) Opinion vs. Fact
    (C) False Choice
    (D) Causation Flaw

49. Unless Hans admits to cheating and apologizes, he will be discovered and fail the math class. So, his passing the math class depends on his admitting to, and apologizing for, his cheating.

    (A) Illegal Reversal
    (B) Equivocation
    (C) Circular Reasoning
    (D) Term Shift

50. Many historians have painted a picture of pre-civilization humanity as consisting solely of nomadic communities. However, this is almost surely wrong. Grants given to historians of that era only go to those who are exploring this consensus position, and thus the historians have a reason to argue in favor of the nomadic theory. Additionally, the strongest evidence they cite in favor of the theory—a diet of these early humans consisting mainly of game meat and foraged foods—has recently been called into question. Evidence shows that agriculture started with the planting of food that was traditionally foraged, and game animals were the first to be domesticated.

    (A) Unproven vs. Untrue
    (B) Opinion vs. Fact
    (C) Circular Reasoning
    (D) Self-Contradiction

9

Answers follow on the next page.

5 lb.

Answers

1.	C	14.	A	27.	B	40.	B
2.	D	15.	B	28.	D	41.	A
3.	C	16.	C	29.	C	42.	D
4.	A	17.	B	30.	A	43.	B
5.	C	18.	A	31.	C	44.	D
6.	D	19.	A	32.	B	45.	A
7.	A	20.	C	33.	C	46.	C
8.	C	21.	C	34.	A	47.	B
9.	B	22.	A	35.	B	48.	A
10.	C	23.	D	36.	B	49.	C
11.	C	24.	B	37.	D	50.	A
12.	C	25.	A	38.	C		
13.	D	26.	D	39.	C		

9

Drill 173: Vocab Lab #21 – The Good, the Bad, and the Neutral, Round 3

Instructions: Again, even when you can't define a word precisely, you sometimes know whether it means something good or bad—and that may be enough for your needs.

You've done this before; now do it again. As fast as you can, classify each of the following words as good (G), bad (B), or neutral (N). As a bonus, define each word...but notice how much longer that takes!

_____ 1. Afflict

_____ 2. Confer

_____ 3. Connote

_____ 4. Detriment

_____ 5. Exemplary

_____ 6. Fruitful

_____ 7. Ineffectual

_____ 8. Misconstrue

_____ 9. Persevere

_____ 10. Posit

_____ 11. Reconcile

_____ 12. Staunch

_____ 13. Tenet

_____ 14. Underpinnings

_____ 15. Vexing

_____ 16. Accord

_____ 17. Antecedent

_____ 18. Assent

_____ 19. Concomitant

_____ 20. Contend

_____ 21. Convergence

_____ 22. Dichotomy

_____ 23. Fallacy

_____ 24. Inattentive

_____ 25. Paradoxical

_____ 26. Penchant

_____ 27. Phenomenon

_____ 28. Prominent

_____ 29. Revoke

_____ 30. Salient

Answers

B 1. Afflict = bring pain or suffering upon.

N 2. Confer = consult; compare views; bestow or give. When you graduate from law school in the United States, someone in a fancy academic robe will *confer* the degree of Juris Doctor on you, which is pretty cool.

N 3. Connote = imply the meaning or condition of something.

B 4. Detriment = a cause of harm or loss.

G 5. Exemplary = perfect; ideal; acting as a worthwhile model.

G 6. Fruitful = producing a large amount of fruit; high-yielding; sufficiently productive.

B 7. Ineffectual = unable to deliver desired results.

B 8. Misconstrue = misunderstand; misinterpret.

G 9. Persevere = persist in a course of action even in face of difficulty.

N 10. Posit = presume; suggest; put forward (an idea).

G 11. Reconcile = make compatible; bring together harmoniously; settle.

G 12. Staunch = loyal; devoted; unwavering.

N 13. Tenet = principle or belief held as truth, such as in religion or philosophy.

N 14. Underpinnings = foundation used to support a structure; something that forms the basis of something else.

B 15. Vexing = irritating; annoying; frustrating.

G 16. Accord = grant (such as power or position); agreement; harmony.

N 17. Antecedent = something that precedes or existed before something else.

G 18. Assent = approval; agreement.

N 19. Concomitant = naturally associated; accompanying incidentally.

N 20. Contend = assert in the face of debate.

N 21. Convergence = meeting or coming together.

N 22. Dichotomy = division into two groups that are opposing or mutually exclusive.

B 23. Fallacy = a mistaken idea or flawed reasoning.

B 24. Inattentive = not paying attention; distracted; without concentration.

B 25. Paradoxical = seemingly contradictory.

G 26. Penchant = liking or inclination (usually penchant for).

N 27. Phenomenon = an observable fact or event, especially one that is rare/unusual or whose cause is in question.

G 28. Prominent = important; distinguished; of high rank (when describing a person).

B 29. Revoke = put an end to by taking back; cancel.

N 30. Salient = obvious; standing out; projecting; noticeably relevant or significant. However, something *salient* is not necessarily positive or negative. Contrast *salient* with *prominent*, which does have a positive meaning when applied to a person.

Drill 174: Conditional Fill-in-the-Blank, Round 3

Instructions: You already know that taking the LSAT at the highest level requires that you know your formal logic backward and forward. This drill pulls from the backward side of things (again!) by presenting you with a diagram and *most* of the statement that would generate it, but *without* its conditional indicator word(s). Your task is to look at the diagram and reverse-engineer the statement, filling in the blank(s) with the conditional indicator word(s) that will make the diagram accurate.

1. _____ I become a lawyer, I will be unhappy.

   ~Lawyer→ ~Happy

2. _____ of my neighbors speaks Esperanto.

   Neighbor→ ~Esperanto

3. Kelly will not buy new shoes _____ it is raining.

   Raining → ~New shoes

4. _____ Jack and Jill take the bus will the bus will be late.

   Bus late → Jack AND Jill

5. Andy's eyes hurt _____ it is cold in the office.

   Cold → Eyes hurt

6. Luther will eat either lunch or dinner _____ it's Sunday.

   Sunday → Lunch OR Dinner

7. Amandeep is _____ relaxed when he's at home.

   Home → ~Relaxed

8. I will join the cast of the play _____ Leah does.

   I join → Leah

9. Xouhua is _____ focused and driven when she's teaching.

   Teaching → Focused AND Driven

10. _____ the snake climbs faster or burrows deeper, he will be caught.

    ~Climb faster AND ~Burrow deeper → Caught

11. _____ you play the ukulele, you can be in the show.

    ~Ukulele → In the show

12. The available tickets _____ be overpriced or terrible.

    Available → Overpriced OR Terrible

13. _____ ornithologists have their heads in the clouds.

    Ornithologist → Head in clouds

14. Viet wears his orange hat _____ he's visiting family.

    Visiting family → Orange hat

15. Peggy goes to the market _____ they are having a big sale.

    ~Big sale → Goes to market

16. _____ of the coaches have won gold medals.

    Coach → ~Gold medal

17. Carol _____ be first or last.

    Carol → First OR Last

18. Fredrich will not attend the seminar _____ Baruch does.

    Baruch → ~Fredrich

19. To be in the performance, you _____ wear high-top shoes or knee-high socks.

    Performance → ~High-tops AND ~Knee-highs

20. I will not reach the top of the mountain _____ it doesn't stop snowing.

    ~Stop snowing → ~Reach top

21. _____ carts are permitted on the track.

    Cart → ~Permitted

22. _____ tree was planted correctly.

    Tree → Planted correctly

23. _____ her magic ring, Linda was powerless.

    ~Magic ring → Powerless

24. The pickles were _____ cooked during their preparation.

    Pickle → ~Cooked

25. Dan's ideas are always the best _____ he's desperate.

    Desperate → Best ideas

26. My friend Jake _____ knows what I'm thinking.

    Jake → Knows

27. _____ I eat peanut butter, will I drink a glass of milk.

    Glass of milk → Peanut butter

28. His car _____ be parked in the best spot.

    His car → ~ Best spot

29. Alfredo will _____ clean the bowls.

    Alfredo cleaning → Bowls

30. Bethany is _____ one who will clean the mugs.

    Mugs cleaned → Bethany

31. Donnie is busy _____ the interest rate goes up or the price of oil goes down.

    ~ Interest rate up and ~ Oil price down → Busy

32. I _____ play video games with the volume maxed out.

    Max volume → ~ Video games

33. _____ of the mice lost their ability to hear.

    Mouse → ~ Hear

34. Mickey will fly out for the wedding _____ it's in June and there will be dancing.

    Mickey at wedding → June and Dancing

35. _____ my mom makes my lunch, I will eat a hot dog.

    ~ Mom-made lunch → Hot dog

36. _____ performer on stage has cried at least once tonight.

    Performer on stage → Cried tonight

37. You cannot be a pilot _____ you don't like peanuts.

    ~ Peanuts → ~ Pilot

38. Mark will ace the test _____ he drinks coffee.

    ~ Coffee → Ace the test

39. I will come home for lunch _____ all I have are frozen dumplings in the freezer.

    Home → Frozen dumplings

40. _____ song with a melody and a chorus is a hit.

    Melody and Chorus → Hit

41. Patients _____ know when I am joking with them.

    Patient → Know when I'm joking

42. Sammie _____ has her book when she's in class.

    In class → ~ Book

43. _____ of the contestants on the show won a big prize.

    Contestant → ~ Big prize

44. The _____ meal I eat each day is breakfast.

    Eat → Breakfast

45. You can get a great warranty on printers _____ you buy them online.

    Great warranty → Online

46. Printer warranties are worth it _____ you get the five-year plan.

    ~ Five-year → Worth it

47. I buy a warranty with every printer _____ it is under $20.

    Under $20 → Warranty

48. _____ at the cook-off made a vegan dish.

    At cook-off → ~ Vegan dish

49. Gabe hates _____ of the gifts he received.

    Gift for Gabe → Gabe hates it

50. You will succeed on the LSAT _____ you practice consistently.

    Consistent → LSAT success

Answers

Note: We've included a few options for some of these, but if you have a different answer than ours, it still could be correct. Make sure that if your answer is different, it serves the same function as the answer we've provided.

1. **Unless** I become a lawyer, I will be unhappy.

   ~Lawyer → ~Happy

2. **None** of my neighbors speaks Esperanto.

   Neighbor → ~Esperanto

3. Kelly will not buy new shoes **if** it is raining.

   Raining → ~New shoes

4. **Only if** Jack and Jill take the bus will the bus will be late.

   Bus late → Jack AND Jill

5. Andy's eyes hurt **if/when** it is cold in the office.

   Cold → Eyes hurt

6. Luther will eat either lunch or dinner **if/when** it's Sunday.

   Sunday → Lunch OR Dinner

7. Amandeep is **never** relaxed when he's at home.

   Home → ~Relaxed

8. I will join the cast of the play **only if** Leah does.

   I join → Leah

9. Xouhua is **always** focused and driven when she's teaching.

   Teaching → Focused AND Driven

10. **Unless** the snake climbs faster or burrows deeper, he will be caught.

    ~Climb faster AND ~Burrow deeper → Caught

11. **Unless** you play the ukulele, you can be in the show.

    ~Ukulele → In the show

12. The available tickets **must** be overpriced or terrible.

    Available → Overpriced OR Terrible

13. **All** ornithologists have their heads in the clouds.

    Ornithologist → Head in clouds

14. Viet wears his orange hat **if/when** he's visiting family.

    Visiting family → Orange hat

15. Peggy goes to the market **unless** they are having a big sale.

    ~Big sale → Goes to market

16. **None** of the coaches have won gold medals.

    Coach → ~Gold medal

17. Carol **must** be first or last.

    Carol → First OR Last

18. Fredrich will not attend the seminar **if** Baruch does.

    Baruch → ~Fredrich

19. To be in the performance, you **cannot** wear high-top shoes or knee-high socks.

    Performance → ~High-tops AND ~Knee-highs

20. I will not reach the top of the mountain **if** it doesn't stop snowing.

    ~Stop snowing → ~Reach top

21. **No** carts are permitted on the track.

    Cart → ~Permitted

22. **Every** tree was planted correctly.

    Tree → Planted correctly

23. **Without** her magic ring, Linda was powerless.

    ~Magic ring → Powerless

24. The pickles were **never** cooked during their preparation.

    Pickle → ~Cooked

25. Dan's ideas are always the best **if/when** he's desperate.

    Desperate → Best ideas

26. My friend Jake **always** knows what I'm thinking.

    Jake → Knows

27. **Only if** I eat peanut butter, will I drink a glass of milk.

    Glass of milk → Peanut butter

28. His car **will not/must not/cannot** be parked in the best spot.

    His car → ~ Best spot

29. Alfredo will **only** clean the bowls.

    Alfredo cleaning → Bowls

30. Bethany is **the only** one who will clean the mugs.

    Mugs cleaned → Bethany

31. Donnie is busy **unless** the interest rate goes up or the price of oil goes down.

    ~ Interest rate up and ~ Oil price down → Busy

32. **I cannot/never/do not/etc.** play video games with the volume maxed out.

    Max volume → ~ Video games

33. **All** of the mice lost their ability to hear.

    Mouse → ~ Hear

34. Mickey will fly out for the wedding **only if** it's in June and there will be dancing.

    Mickey at wedding → June and Dancing

35. **Unless** my mom makes my lunch, I will eat a hot dog.

    ~ Mom-made lunch → Hot dog

36. **Every** performer on stage has cried at least once tonight.

    Performer on stage → Cried tonight

37. You cannot be a pilot **if** you don't like peanuts.

    ~ Peanuts → ~ Pilot

38. Mark will ace the test **unless** he drinks coffee.

    ~ Coffee → Ace the test

39. I will come home for lunch **only if** all I have are frozen dumplings in the freezer.

    Home → Frozen dumplings

40. **Any/Every** song with a melody and a chorus is a hit.

    Melody and Chorus → Hit

41. Patients **always** know when I am joking with them.

    Patient → Know when I'm joking

42. Sammie **never** has her book when she's in class.

    In class → ~ Book

43. **None** of the contestants on the show won a big prize.

    Contestant → ~ Big prize

44. The **only** meal I eat each day is breakfast.

    Eat → Breakfast

45. You can get a great warranty on printers **only if** you buy them online.

    Great warranty → Online

46. Printer warranties are worth it **unless** you get the five-year plan.

    ~ Five-year → Worth it

47. I buy a warranty with every printer **if/whenever/every time/each time** it is under $20.

    Under $20 → Warranty

48. **Nobody/No one** at the cook-off made a vegan dish.

    At cook-off → ~ Vegan dish

49. Gabe hates **all/every one/each** of the gifts he received.

    Gift for Gabe → Gabe hates it

50. You will succeed on the LSAT **if** you practice consistently.

    Consistent → LSAT success

9

Drill 175: Famous Flaws, Short Answer Edition, Round 2

Instructions: By now, you should be familiar enough with the famous flaws that you can name them without looking at a list of options. For each of the following abbreviated arguments, record which famous flaw is being committed. Since there is some overlap among flaws there may be instances in which more than one flaw feels appropriate. That's fine! You can list more than one in these cases.

1. Every time Tim goes shopping with Veronica, he spends too much money. When he goes with Marcy, he spends less. So, going shopping with Marcy will guarantee Tim stays within his budget.

   _____

2. The extinction of the dodo was long thought to be caused by overhunting. But the terrain of the land they inhabited makes it highly unlikely that people could have hunted them all the way to extinction. Thus, loss of habitat through timber harvesting must be the real cause of their extinction.

   _____

3. In an effort to improve productivity, Apex, Co. surveyed its employees and found that those who were the most efficient were also those who arrived at work earlier than their scheduled time. Thus, its new policy offering bonuses to individuals for showing up before their scheduled shift will yield an increase in efficiency.

   _____

4. Poli Sci Prof: Anybody who wishes to be successful in a capitalistic society must have some appreciation for the role of wealth in exercising influence in such a society. Thus, only those who master the art of politics can achieve success in a capitalistic society.

   _____

5. Poli Sci Student: Anybody who wishes to be successful in a capitalistic society must have some appreciation for the role of wealth in exercising influence in such a society. Eugene has no desire to be a success in our capitalistic society, so he must not have any conception of the role of wealth in exercising influence in our society.

   _____

6. Terry knows that anyone at his firm who works the required number of billable hours for ten years in a row is guaranteed to make partner. Since his mentor, Shonda, just made partner, she must have met her billable-hour requirements for ten years in a row.

   _____

7. Every winter, Jeffrey turns on the gas furnace that heats his house, and every winter, he catches at least one cold. Particulates released into the air from combustion in the furnace must increase his susceptibility to colds by facilitating the transport of the virus deeper into his lungs.

   _____

8. Far more recreational downhill ski injuries occur at established resorts in the Continental United States than at the fledgling recreational downhill ski resorts recently established in Alaska. This clearly indicates that it is safer to ski at the new Alaskan facilities.

   _____

9. During her recent ski trip, Linda Vann found each ski trail that she skied down to be one-dimensional in the challenges it offered. Clearly the resort she traveled to doesn't offer a variety of challenges for a skier.

   _____

10. In a recent survey, the majority of residents of Caltronia stated that they believed a lack of funding for the education system was the biggest problem in the country. Since this response was by far the most common, the Caltronian government should change its budget priorities to shift more money into the underfunded school system.

   _____

11. Mendelton's Third Theory was based on the belief that a previously discovered document was dated to the late 14th century. Recent carbon-dating tests have revealed that it was actually a fake, created contemporaneously to Mendelton's career. Thus, the Third Theory must be incorrect.

_____

12. Jean's house has recently had a number of leaks in the roof. In order to figure out the problem, she responded to an ad in the paper offering a free inspection by a local slate roofing company that has fixed more roofs than any other local company. During their inspection, they stated that the substandard tar-based roofing material used in the construction of her house was to blame. Jean should therefore replace her current roof with one made of slate.

_____

13. Most of the students in Professor Springsteen's calculus class believe that the final exam will focus almost exclusively on derivation instead of integration. Since Nancy struggles with integration but fully understands derivation, she will probably pass the test.

_____

14. Either oak or maple can be used to construct a stable piece of furniture. However, the price of maple is prohibitively expensive in the creation of large pieces of furniture such as a bed frame, so Wally of Wally's Woodworking will have to make the custom bed frame that was just ordered out of oak.

_____

15. Oak is a stronger wood than maple, so if Wally uses oak in the construction of a new bookshelf, it will be strong enough to support the weight of his client's law books.

_____

16. Jason is a top student who has never failed a class. It's well-known that he has ambitions to attend the prestigious Hale University, and that he eschews extracurricular activities in order to have more time to study. Thus, he will never fail a class.

_____

17. Joe Sadden: The home team, the Platypodes, will win against its competitors because it's going to score more points than the opposing team.

_____

18. Stanlee University requires all students to fulfill a language requirement. Since Stanley needs to fulfill that requirement this semester, and all French classes filled before he was allowed to enroll in any classes, he'll need to enroll in a Russian class.

_____

19. Out of the 100 richest people in the world, 43 are Americans and only 16 are from European countries. So, Americans, on average, must be significantly wealthier than Europeans.

_____

20. In a recent interview, Mae, an astronaut, remarked that there wasn't nearly enough space on the International Space Station. This clearly cannot be true, since space is incomprehensibly vast.

_____

21. Authoritarianism invests all power in a single, strong leader whose word is law. Under this system, the rule of law ceases to exist, and the only important consideration is what the leader decrees. People in this system may exercise limited choice in their personal lives, but they're at the mercy of the leader. This system is clearly inferior to democracy, where each individual has power to effect change in the government.

_____

9

22. In the wake of the devastating oil spill, surveys of people who lost their homes found that the vast majority did not believe that it would be possible for them to rebuild their residences. So, while the environmental effects of the oil spill will be exceptionally negative for the region, another effect of the spill will be its contribution to a population decline in the region.

_____

23. In the wake of the devastating oil spill, surveys of fishermen routinely found that they overwhelmingly believed that restoration of the fisheries was the greatest economic priority. Thus, if decisionmakers fail to prioritize restoration of the fisheries, they will be going against the will of the majority of people in the region.

_____

24. Anybody who wins a local qualifying tournament is automatically granted a position at the world poker championship tournament for a shot at a prize of $4 million. Since Philomena came in third in the local qualifying tournament, she will not be granted a position at the world poker championship.

_____

25. Despite not fulfilling the requirements to receive a promotion and raise this year, Siobhan should be granted an exception because the only reason she wasn't able to fulfill those requirements was that she has a sick father who requires expensive and time-consuming medical care.

_____

Answers follow on the next page.

Answers

1. Relative vs. Absolute
2. False Choice
3. Causation Flaw
4. Term Shift
5. Illegal Negation
6. Illegal Reversal
7. False Choice
8. Percent vs. Amount
9. Part to Whole
10. Opinion vs. Fact
11. Unproven vs. Untrue
12. Appeal to Inappropriate Authority
13. Opinion vs. Fact

14. False Choice
15. Relative vs. Absolute
16. Unwarranted Prediction
17. Circular Reasoning
18. False Choice
19. Sampling Flaw
20. Equivocation
21. Comparison Flaw
22. Opinion vs. Fact
23. Sampling Flaw
24. Illegal Negation
25. Appeal to Emotion

Drill 176: Causal Fill-In, Round 2

Instructions: Strengthen and Weaken questions frequently feature a Correlation vs. Causation flaw. When this happens, there are some common patterns the answer choices fall into. For each of the following causal relationships, fill in a potential answer that follows the given pattern. Note: For some relationships, there may be some patterns that cannot be logically produced or have no logical impact.

The politician called for an investigation into payday lenders. He is clearly desperate to distract the public from the details of his latest scandal.

1. Weaken—ID an Alternative Cause: _____

2. Weaken—Cause without Effect: _____

3. Weaken—Effect without Cause: _____

4. Weaken—Reverse Causality: _____

5. Strengthen—Eliminate an Alternative Cause: _____

6. Strengthen—Same Cause, Same Effect: _____

7. Strengthen—No Cause, No Effect: _____

Local media personality O. MacDonald believes that the cause of the recent "chicken fever" epidemic is the newly-discovered Bahkbahk virus.

8. Weaken—ID an Alternative Cause: _____

9. Weaken—Cause without Effect: _____

10. Weaken—Effect without Cause: _____

11. Weaken—Reverse Causality: _____

12. Strengthen—Eliminate an Alternative Cause: _____

13. Strengthen—Same Cause, Same Effect: _____

14. Strengthen—No Cause, No Effect: _____

In a recent study, people who practiced meditation for three months reported lower blood pressure. Thus, those who want to lower their blood pressure should take up meditation.

15. Weaken—ID an Alternative Cause: _____

16. Weaken—Cause without Effect: _____

17. Weaken—Effect without Cause: _____

18. Weaken—Reverse Causality: _____

19. Strengthen—Eliminate an Alternative Cause: _____

20. Strengthen—Same Cause, Same Effect: _____

21. Strengthen—No Cause, No Effect: _____

The stores in the village that are most profitable are all open on Sunday. Therefore, the camera store in the village, which is never open on Sundays and struggles to stay in business, should start opening up on Sundays.

22. Weaken—ID an Alternative Cause: _____

23. Weaken—Cause without Effect: _____

24. Weaken—Effect without Cause: _____

25. Weaken—Reverse Causality: _____

26. Strengthen—Eliminate an Alternative Cause: _____

27. Strengthen—Same Cause, Same Effect: _____

28. Strengthen—No Cause, No Effect: _____

It must have been because of its convoluted plot that the director's latest film performed poorly at the box office.

29. Weaken—ID an Alternative Cause: _____

30. Weaken—Cause without Effect: _____

31. Weaken—Effect without Cause: _____

32. Weaken—Reverse Causality: _____

33. Strengthen—Eliminate an Alternative Cause: _____

34. Strengthen—Same Cause, Same Effect: _____

35. Strengthen—No Cause, No Effect: _____

Wasps must be attracted to human sweat, as almost all wasp attacks occur to people who are sweating.

36. Weaken—ID an Alternative Cause: _____

37. Weaken—Cause without Effect: _____

38. Weaken—Effect without Cause: _____

39. Weaken—Reverse Causality: _____

40. Strengthen—Eliminate an Alternative Cause: _____

9

41. Strengthen—Same Cause, Same Effect: _____

42. Strengthen—No Cause, No Effect: _____

Leigh, after suffering a thigh injury in her third match of a tennis tournament, withdrew from the tennis tournament before her fourth match. We can thus blame the injury for her withdrawal.

43. Weaken—ID an Alternative Cause: _____

44. Weaken—Cause without Effect: _____

45. Weaken—Effect without Cause: _____

46. Weaken—Reverse Causality: _____

47. Strengthen—Eliminate an Alternative Cause: _____

48. Strengthen—Same Cause, Same Effect: _____

49. Strengthen—No Cause, No Effect: _____

The American composer's latest symphony employing African polyrhythms must have been inspired by his six-week trip to Egypt last year.

50. Weaken—ID an Alternative Cause: _____

51. Weaken—Cause without Effect: _____

52. Weaken—Effect without Cause: _____

53. Weaken—Reverse Causality: _____

54. Strengthen—Eliminate an Alternative Cause: _____

55. Strengthen—Same Cause, Same Effect: _____

56. Strengthen—No Cause, No Effect: _____

The owner of the building painted over a wall of art. He must have mistaken the mural for graffiti.

57. Weaken—ID an Alternative Cause: _____

58. Weaken—Cause without Effect: _____

59. Weaken—Effect without Cause: _____

60. Weaken—Reverse Causality: _____

61. Strengthen—Eliminate an Alternative Cause: _____

9

62. Strengthen—Same Cause, Same Effect: _____

63. Strengthen—No Cause, No Effect: _____

Omar, who plans to major in chemistry, chose to attend Northern State College (NSC). They must have a stellar chemistry department.

64. Weaken—ID an Alternative Cause: _____

65. Weaken—Cause without Effect: _____

66. Weaken—Effect without Cause: _____

67. Weaken—Reverse Causality: _____

68. Strengthen—Eliminate an Alternative Cause: _____

69. Strengthen—Same Cause, Same Effect: _____

70. Strengthen—No Cause, No Effect: _____

Answers

Note: Your answers may differ, especially when identifying alternative causes. That's OK! Just make sure that your answers serve the same function as ours.

The politician called for an investigation into payday lenders. He is clearly desperate to distract the public from the details of his latest scandal.

1. Weaken—ID an Alternative Cause: <u>The politician made investigating payday lenders a significant point in his most recent campaign.</u>

2. Weaken—Cause without Effect: <u>After a previous scandal, the politician did not call for investigating anyone else.</u> *(This isn't as strong a weakener as the others. In general, Cause without Effect works best for arguments in which the claim is that one thing always leads to another. This argument claims only that one thing led to another in a particular instance.)*

3. Weaken—Effect without Cause: <u>The politician has regularly called for investigations into various organizations, even several years before any scandal was exposed.</u>

4. Weaken—Reverse Causality: <u>Payday lenders, hearing about the politician's upcoming call, engineered the scandal.</u>

5. Strengthen—Eliminate an Alternative Cause: <u>The politician has never made any public comments regarding payday lenders.</u>

6. Strengthen—Same Cause, Same Effect: <u>Many other politicians, embroiled in scandals, try to divert attention by calling for investigating unpopular figures.</u>

7. Strengthen—No Cause, No Effect: <u>During periods in which there were no scandals, the politician has never called for public investigations of any type.</u>

Local media personality O. MacDonald believes that the cause of the recent "chicken fever" epidemic is the newly-discovered Bahkbahk virus.

8. Weaken—ID an Alternative Cause: <u>"Chicken fever" is treatable with antibiotics, which suggests that it is bacterial, rather than viral.</u>

9. Weaken—Cause without Effect: <u>People infected with the Bahkbahk virus do not consistently show symptoms of "chicken fever."</u> *(This isn't as strong a weakener as the others. Again, Cause without Effect works best for arguments in which the claim is that one thing always leads to another. This argument claims that an effect has a single cause, but not that the cause will always lead to the effect.)*

10. Weaken—Effect without Cause: <u>Many people exhibit all the symptoms of "chicken fever" without showing any evidence of the Bahkbahk virus.</u>

11. Weaken—Reverse Causality: <u>The Bahkbahk virus is actually a particle formed as a result of the "chicken fever."</u>

12. Strengthen—Eliminate an Alternative Cause: <u>Most patients with "chicken fever" show no evidence of bacterial infection.</u>

13. Strengthen—Same Cause, Same Effect: <u>Every "chicken fever" patient whose blood has been tested has shown evidence of the Bahkbahk virus.</u>

14. Strengthen—No Cause, No Effect: <u>"Chicken fever" has not been observed in anyone who has tested negative for the Bahkbahk virus.</u>

9

In a recent study, people who practiced meditation for three months reported lower blood pressure. Thus, those who want to lower their blood pressure should take up meditation.

15. Weaken—ID an Alternative Cause: <u>Everyone in the study conformed to the meditation instructor's dietary recommendations, which are known to lower blood pressure.</u>

16. Weaken—Cause without Effect: <u>The vast majority of people who practice meditation never notice a decrease in blood pressure.</u>

17. Weaken—Effect without Cause: <u>A recent study of those with low blood pressure found that less than 1 percent meditate.</u> *(This isn't a strong weakener. Effect without Cause doesn't really weaken an argument that says that a cause can have a particular effect. Saying A causes B does not imply that only A causes B. So, even if some people can lower blood pressure without meditation, that doesn't change the argument that meditation can also produce the same effect.)*

18. Weaken—Reverse Causality: <u>Meditation is usually practiced by individuals whose blood pressure is naturally low.</u>

19. Strengthen—Eliminate an Alternative Cause: <u>Participants in the study were required to abstain from using blood pressure medications of any kind.</u>

20. Strengthen—Same Cause, Same Effect: <u>Previous studies have shown that the breathing techniques used in meditation are sufficient to lower blood pressure.</u>

21. Strengthen—No Cause, No Effect: <u>Participants who stopped meditating showed a return to their original blood pressures.</u>

The stores in the village that are most profitable are all open on Sunday. Therefore, the camera store in the village, which is never open on Sundays and struggles to stay in business, should start opening up on Sundays.

22. Weaken—ID an Alternative Cause: <u>The most profitable stores in the village offer high demand products that are not carried by the camera store.</u>

23. Weaken—Cause without Effect: <u>Many of the village stores that fail to make a profit are also open on Sundays.</u>

24. Weaken—Effect without Cause: <u>The computer store in the village recently began running a special to increase business that has been effective, even though the store remains closed on Sundays.</u> *(This is a less effective weakener than the others. The causal claim is that being open on Sundays will cause the camera store to become more profitable, not that it is the only way for the camera store to become more profitable. Thus, showing another way to become more profitable doesn't effectively weaken the claim.)*

25. Weaken—Reverse Causality: <u>The most profitable stores started opening on Sundays in order to accommodate the high volume of customers they had been receiving.</u>

26. Strengthen—Eliminate an Alternative Cause: <u>The most profitable stores are spread out throughout the village and not just located near the primary parking lot.</u>

27. Strengthen—Same Cause, Same Effect: <u>Two electronics shops in the village recently became profitable after extending their hours to include hours on Sunday.</u>

28. Strengthen—No Cause, No Effect: <u>Many of the village stores that are currently struggling to stay in business are closed on Sundays.</u>

It must have been because of its convoluted plot that the director's latest film performed poorly at the box office.

29. Weaken—ID an Alternative Cause: <u>The film had no "big-name" actors to attract audiences.</u>

30. Weaken—Cause without Effect: <u>The film with the best performance at the box office this year has an equally convoluted plot.</u>

31. Weaken—Effect without Cause: <u>Many films whose plots are easy to understand fare poorly at the box office.</u>

32. Weaken—Reverse Causality: <u>The poor box office performance of the original version of the film led to a drastic revision to shorten the run time, which cut out clarifying aspects of the plot.</u>

33. Strengthen—Eliminate an Alternative Cause: <u>The film starred a pair of actors whose films normally perform well at the box office.</u>

34. Strengthen—Same Cause, Same Effect: <u>Most films whose plots are criticized as convoluted perform poorly at the box office.</u>

35. Strengthen—No Cause, No Effect: <u>Most films that perform well at the box office have plots that are easy to understand.</u>

Wasps must be attracted to human sweat, as almost all wasp attacks occur to people who are sweating.

36. Weaken—ID an Alternative Cause: <u>Wasps are attracted to the brightly colored clothes people wear in particularly warm weather.</u>

37. Weaken—Cause without Effect: <u>When exposed to a source of the molecules in human sweat in a laboratory, wasps do not fly toward those molecules.</u>

38. Weaken—Effect without Cause: <u>Some humans attacked by wasps are not currently sweating.</u> *(Not an effective weakener! It's already given that "almost all" attacks occur with the implied cause (sweat). Even if there were some exceptions, the argument already concedes them.)*

39. Weaken—Reverse Causality: <u>The presence of wasps tends to make people nervous, and nervousness makes people perspire.</u>

40. Strengthen—Eliminate an Alternative Cause: <u>Most wasp attacks occur far enough from wasp nests that people would not be perceived as a threat to the nest.</u>

41. Strengthen—Same Cause, Same Effect: <u>Wasps are drawn to mannequins sprayed with human sweat.</u>

42. Strengthen—No Cause, No Effect: <u>Humans who do not possess certain molecules in their sweat are not attacked by wasps.</u>

Leigh, after suffering a thigh injury in her third match of a tennis tournament, withdrew from the tennis tournament before her fourth match. We can thus blame the injury for her withdrawal.

43. Weaken—ID an Alternative Cause: <u>Leigh was ill when she withdrew.</u>

44. Weaken—Cause without Effect: <u>Leigh has suffered thigh injuries in the middle of tournaments in the past, but continued playing after those injuries.</u>

45. Weaken—Effect without Cause: <u>Not applicable. In this scenario, even if Leigh had withdrawn from other events for other reasons, the thigh injury is still likely to be a causal factor in this separate, unique situation.</u>

46. Weaken—Reverse Causality: <u>Not applicable. Due to the chronology of the events (she injured her thigh, and *then* she withdrew from the tournament), it is illogical to suggest that her withdrawal was somehow responsible for her injured thigh. In fact, that just doesn't make any sense at all.</u>

47. Strengthen—Eliminate an Alternative Cause: <u>A medical doctor showed that the only ailment Leigh had at the time of her withdrawal was the thigh injury.</u>

48. Strengthen—Same Cause, Same Effect: <u>In the past, when Leigh has suffered an injury during a tennis tournament, she has always withdrawn.</u>

49. Strengthen—No Cause, No Effect: <u>Leigh has never withdrawn from a tournament in the absence of an injury.</u>

The American composer's latest symphony employing African polyrhythms must have been inspired by his six-week trip to Egypt last year.

50. Weaken—ID an Alternative Cause: <u>The composer had been working under the tutelage of an Ethiopian composer at the time he composed his latest symphony.</u>

51. Weaken—Cause without Effect: <u>The composer has studied music in Egypt every year for the last twenty years, and his latest symphony is the first to use African polyrhythms.</u>

52. Weaken—Effect without Cause: <u>The composer has written numerous symphonies throughout the past decade that employ African polyrhythms.</u>

53. Weaken—Reverse Causality: <u>The composer's love of African polyrhythms inspired his trip to Egypt.</u>

54. Strengthen—Eliminate an Alternative Cause: <u>The composer was not exposed to African polyrhythms before his trip to Egypt.</u>

55. Strengthen—Same Cause, Same Effect: <u>After every lengthy international trip the composer has taken, he has written a major musical work incorporating musical styles to which he was exposed.</u>

56. Strengthen—No Cause, No Effect: <u>The composer never starts composing without a specific inspiration.</u>

The owner of the building painted over a wall of art. He must have mistaken the mural for graffiti.

57. Weaken—ID an Alternative Cause: <u>The owner scheduled the painting of the wall months before the mural was painted.</u>

58. Weaken—Cause without Effect: <u>The owner has not painted over the graffiti on the wall of another building he owns.</u>

59. Weaken—Effect without Cause: <u>The other walls of the building, none of which displayed artwork, were all painted as well.</u>

60. Weaken—Reverse Causality: <u>Not applicable. The sequence of events makes it illogical to suggest that painting over the art caused the owner to mistake that art for graffiti.</u>

61. Strengthen—Eliminate an Alternative Cause: <u>No local laws required the wall to be repainted.</u>

62. Strengthen—Same Cause, Same Effect: <u>The owner of that building is known for painting over other murals that he suspected to be graffiti.</u>

63. Strengthen—No Cause, No Effect: <u>The owner of that building has never painted over a wall that does not have any writing or artwork on it.</u>

Omar, who plans to major in chemistry, chose to attend Northern State College (NSC). They must have a stellar chemistry department.

64. Weaken—ID an Alternative Cause: <u>Omar chose NSC because it is the cheapest school to which he was accepted.</u>

65. Weaken—Cause without Effect: <u>Omar was also accepted to Greenwood University, which has the highest-ranked chemistry department in Northern State, but chose not to attend.</u>

66. Weaken—Effect without Cause: <u>Most students do not choose to attend a college based on the quality of the department they plan to join, but rather on the merits of the college as a whole.</u>

67. Weaken—Reverse Causality:<u> Not applicable. In this case, it is illogical to suggest that Omar's decision to attend NSC is responsible for NSC having a stellar chemistry department . . . unless Omar is really that influential and demanded that NSC go out and hire the best chemistry professors in the country.</u>

68. Strengthen—Eliminate an Alternative Cause: <u>NSC was not the only school to which Omar was accepted.</u>

69. Strengthen—Same Cause, Same Effect: <u>The schools in the country that attract the greatest number of chemistry majors are those that are recognized for having the best chemistry departments.</u>

70. Strengthen—No Cause, No Effect: <u>Prospective chemistry students never enroll in schools with less-than-stellar chemistry departments.</u>

Drill 177: Chain Chain Chain, Round 2

Instructions: Combining several conditional statements is still a skill that will be tested throughout the exam: primarily on Inference questions in Logical Reasoning. Here, a series of conditional statements will be given. Just like last time, use the space provided to write them in formal notation, chain them together, and take the contrapositive of the chain.

1. Palmer refuses to play tennis without Kassie's company, and Kassie plays tennis only when Nelle accompanies her. Nelle never plays tennis on overcast days.

2. To enter DynerCorp's office building, one must present a DynerCorp identification badge. The only way to obtain one of these badges is to be a DynerCorp employee. None of Dynercorp's employees have ever worked for Shanecorp, one of Dynercorp's main competitors.

3. Each member of Zelma's book club attended Orrin's dinner party. None of the guests at the dinner party attended Shadwell's brunch last week.

4. The only truly egalitarian form of government is direct democracy, and direct democracy requires active participation from a significant majority of citizens, which is impossible without a national culture of civic responsibility.

5. No bacteria are eukaryotes, and all organisms that are not eukaryotes are prokaryotes. Every prokaryote is a single-celled organism.

6. Tanisha, who is making a quilt, has a variety of colored fabrics available to her. She will use red fabric only if she also uses yellow fabric. If she does not use red fabric, then she will use green fabric, and she will not use yellow fabric unless she also uses orange fabric.

7. The groundskeeping staff at Longmire Castle will plant one or more varieties of fruit tree in the main courtyard. The staff will plant peaches unless they plant apples, and if the staff plants apples, it will not plant pears. The staff will never allow the courtyard to be planted with neither pears nor plums.

8. Lamar will never go to the movies without Sterne. Any movie that Sterne attends, Ray will attend as well. Priestly will only go to the movies if Ray does not.

9

9. A jeweler is planning a new ring design that will include a variety of gemstones. If the design includes sapphires, it will not include rubies. The jeweler will only include emeralds in designs that also include sapphires, and the jeweler includes garnets in all of her designs unless those designs include emeralds.

10. Malia will not run in next week's marathon unless Aubrey runs. Aubrey will never run in a marathon in which Clifford does not run. Nolan runs in every marathon in which Clifford runs.

11. No human can thrive without a diet rich in nutrients, and a diet rich in nutrients requires both complex carbohydrates and vitamins.

12. Megan always buys her cars at Sal's Used Cars. Sal's only carries four-door sedans, and federal law requires all four-door sedans to be equipped with airbags and antilock brakes.

13. At Orstead College, completing either Sociology 1 or Anthropology 1 makes one eligible for Anthropology 2. Anyone eligible for Anthropology 2 is also eligible for Sociology 2.

14. None of the speakers at the Housing Summit has ever experienced homelessness. To truly understand the needs of people experiencing homelessness, one must have experienced homelessness oneself. Every member of the Youngtown Homeless Advocacy Project truly understands the needs of people experiencing homelessness.

15. No circles are squares, but all squares are rectangles, and the only geometric shapes in Larisa's collage are squares.

16. Only if Abigail works on Saturday will Channie work on Saturday, and Channie will work on Saturday if Bristol does. Bristol works on any Saturday on which Hali does not work.

17. Avery takes the train to Pueblo on each Tuesday. Whenever Avery takes the train to Pueblo, he writes in his journal during the ride. The only pen Avery uses to write in his journal is the Stylus 7A.

18. Unless they vacation in Spruce Junction, the Jabalas will vacation in Paradise Springs. The family will not vacation in Paradise Springs if they decide not to rent a car during their vacation.

9

19. Every doctor at the Lawson Clinic is qualified to diagnose and treat viral infections. The only people qualified to diagnose and treat viral infections are people who continuously study the behavior of infectious disease. Among people who continuously study the behavior of infectious disease, there is no one who is uninterested in microbiology.

20. All plant cells contain vacuoles. Every vacuole is an organelle, and organelles can only be found within living organisms.

21. None of the members of the Harmony Club are members of the Improv Club. Each member of the City Singers is a member of the Harmony Club. Everyone in Sharon's band and everyone in Jaden's band is a member of the City Singers.

22. Siti takes the subway whenever she doesn't take the bus, and she will not take the bus if she is running late or overslept. The subway in the city where Siti lives requires either a single-fare ticket or a monthly pass.

23. No farmers like long winters, and the only people who are citizens of Bart County are farmers. People who do not like long winters invariably appreciate summer.

24. The only candidates who can secure large amounts of campaign funding easily are incumbents. It is difficult to win any election without first being able to easily secure large amounts of campaign funding.

25. All offshore oil drilling is harmful to oceanic animal life. Marianna does not approve of any activity that is harmful to oceanic animal life, and the Committee for Environmental Action will not endorse any action of which Marianna disapproves.

26. Each of the toys currently in Meilin's toy chest is either blue or white. HapCo Toy Company does not manufacture any toys that are blue, nor does it manufacture any toys that are white. All of Meilin's toys are currently in her toy chest.

27. Edward will not be able to renovate his kitchen without replacing his stove. The only renovators local to Edward's community who are qualified to replace stoves are Sanchez and Romero, and Edward will only allow qualified, local renovators to replace his stove.

28. Peter will be promoted only if Carlita is hired to fill his current position, but it will be impossible to hire Carlita without first promoting Anthony. The position to which Anthony could be promoted is the only position for which Xiang could possibly be hired.

9

29. Unless it is Friday, Irena calls her sister at noon. Irena always walks outside on Fridays, and she never visits Greenway Park on days when she walks outside.

30. All cruel people are arrogant, and no one can develop arrogance without first feeling contempt for others, which is incompatible with authentic compassion.

31. None of the restaurants in Uptown Plaza serve trout. The only restaurants at which Gardner will dine are in Uptown Plaza, and Aydin will not dine at any restaurant that doesn't serve trout.

32. Mayburn will inspect the factory only if Wynne does not. Unless Wynne inspects the factory, Thompson will inspect the office. And Gregor must inspect the warehouse if Thompson inspects the office.

33. Vance will attend each workshop on management. Wallace will attend no workshop that Vance attends, and whenever Wallace does not attend a workshop, Basir attends it.

34. None of the guests at the Riverside Inn are members of the wedding party. Each member of the Ivanov family is staying at the Riverside Inn, and all of the caterers are members of the Ivanov family.

35. The only boats at Ocean View Marina are sloops and schooners. For a boat to be called a sloop or a schooner, it must have at least two sails.

36. A group of biologists plans to survey a forest to determine what bird species live there. The biologists know that if chickadees live in the forest, then either bullfinches or flycatchers live there as well. They also know that either kinglets or chickadees live in the forest, and that no forest contains both tanagers and kinglets.

37. Each piece of furniture at Graham's Department Store is on sale, and sale items are always discounted by at least 20%.

38. None of the bills owed by the Kind Hand Corporation are eligible for deferment. All bills currently owed to the Burtland Construction Company are owed by the Kind Hand Corporation.

9

39. If a poem is neither beautiful nor wise, then it is not a great poem. Poems that are either beautiful or wise invariably appeal to a majority of readers. Every poem written by Schulman is a great poem.

40. Without owning a car, it is time-consuming for residents of Country R to commute to and from work. Owning a car in Country R requires registering that car with the Department of Automotives. To register a car with the Department of Automotives, one must come in person to its central offices.

41. Whenever Shari visits her father, who lives in Port Town, he either cooks her dinner or treats her to dinner at a restaurant. The only reason Shari ever travels to Port Town is to visit her father, although she always travels to Port Town on Wednesdays.

42. For a city to be a safe place in which to live, it must have a competent municipal agency devoted to food safety. For a food safety agency to be competent, it must be both well-funded and staffed with food safety experts. Every city in Country Y is a safe place in which to live.

43. Kalani is assigned to the Red Team only if Farid is assigned to the Blue Team. Samuel is assigned to the Blue Team whenever Farid is. Robert and Samuel cannot both be assigned to the Blue Team.

44. Any class that prepares students for success later in life is worth taking, and classes that incorporate writing instruction invariably prepare students for success later in life. Every class, except for some classes in the science department, include at least some writing instruction.

45. At Farrenham University, Chemistry 101 and Physics 101 are both requirements for anyone wishing to take Physics 201. Every physics major at Farrenham must complete Physics 201.

46. Bates is the only attorney qualified to take Larson's case. Bates will never take Larson's case unless his firm assigns him to it, and Bates's firm will assign attorneys to cases only if it believes those cases will contribute to the cause of social justice.

47. As long as I save money responsibly, I will be able to afford a home. However, I will never be able to afford a home without taking out a mortgage, which would necessitate both extensive paperwork and negotiations with a banker.

48. On nights when it does not serve asparagus, Trafalgar's Restaurant also does not serve cucumber. The restaurant never serves jicama on nights when it serves eggplant, and whenever it does not serve cucumber, the restaurant serves eggplant.

49. Jurors should always be skeptical of testimony that is not fully reliable. The only testimony given by the prosecution in this case was eyewitness testimony, and no eyewitness testimony is fully reliable.

50. Whenever she processes a complaint, Nsedu always forwards a copy to her manager. None of the complaints filed with our company this week were processed by Elisa. The only person at our company besides Elisa who processes complaints is Nsedu.

51. One cannot be an ornithologist without also being a biologist, and all biologists share an interest in taxonomy. Among the members of the Zoological Society, everyone who is not an entomologist is an ornithologist.

52. All of the parks in the county, except for some in Silver City, are popular among tourists. None of the parks in Silver City are larger than ten acres, and for a park to adequately accommodate horseback riding, it must be larger than ten acres.

53. Of the members of our band, Hasani is the only skilled horn player. Our newest song, "Fancy," requires a skilled horn player to be performed well. Our next concert will be a failure unless we perform "Fancy" well.

54. The only people qualified to pass judgment on Juarez's book are paleontology experts. One can become a paleontology expert only through years of study, and no one can complete years of study without developing patience.

55. The craters in Calistoga Basin are the only craters in the state, and only a meteorite would be capable of creating such craters. Every meteorite was once a meteor, and every meteor has traveled through space.

56. Ravon is deciding what new articles of clothing to buy. She will not buy a blouse if she does not buy a skirt, and she will not buy a skirt if she buys a pair of jeans. She will only buy a leather jacket if she buys a pair of jeans, and she will not buy leather gloves unless she buys a leather jacket.

57. Sullivan is determining what type of fish he will stock his new aquarium with. He will not choose a platy without also choosing a cichlid. If he chooses a cichlid, he will either choose a tetra or not choose any bettas. If he does not choose a platy, he will choose both a minnow and a guppy.

58. The residents of Palmtown all voted in the national election. One cannot vote in the national election unless one is both registered with the Election Bureau and as a citizen of the nation.

9

59. All air-breathing, aquatic mammals must once have lived on land, and any organism that once lived on land must have had some sort of locomotion system for moving across land. Every porpoise and every dolphin is an air-breathing aquatic mammal.

60. Every player who is not on the blue team is on the red team. None of the players on the red team are on the yellow team, and any player not on the yellow team is also not on the green team.

61. The novels of Cumberson are all thematically dark, and thematically dark novels never appeal to Amanda. However, Fadila invariably enjoys any novel that doesn't appeal to Amanda. Fadila does not enjoy any of the novels of Parre.

62. At our clinic, every doctor who did not graduate from Hoyst Medical School graduated from Laverton Medical School. Graduates of Laverton invariably become highly competent doctors. To be considered highly competent, a doctor must be confident performing routine procedures and have a strong knowledge of general medicine.

63. Mays is not selected if Rahul is not selected. Nestor is selected unless Mays is selected. Rahul and Pindar are never both selected.

64. Unless we leave now, we will miss the ten o'clock train, and we will be late to the play unless we make that train. Anyone who is late to the play is required to wait in the lobby until the end of a scene before entering the theater.

65. If Ramirez swims laps, then either Wanda or Tamiko will play tennis, in which case Sidney will go for a jog. Ramirez swims laps whenever both Violet and Willoughby play basketball.

66. None of the artifacts recovered from Dig Site C are in good condition. Professor Willow will only recover an artifact herself if it is in good condition. The artifacts currently on display at the Glenn University Paleontology Museum were all personally recovered by Professor Willow.

67. Any car part made by either Rice Components or Davidson Automotive will satisfy all of Country J's regulations governing the quality of car parts. Country J's regulations are so strict that car parts capable of satisfying them will invariably be both safe and reliable. Sergio's Auto Shop only carries car parts made by either Rice Components or Davidson Automotive.

68. No pets are allowed at the Coastview apartment complex, which is the only apartment complex located on Parkside Avenue. Seamus will only live in an apartment complex if it allows pets.

69. Landscape painting is the only art form that Hualing practices. No matter how objectively a painter attempts to depict reality, all landscape paintings inevitably express the painter's attitude toward nature. Art that expresses the artist's attitude toward nature is necessarily open to interpretation.

70. The household cleaning fluids produced by the Trugleam Corporation all release benzene into the air, and any airborne benzene is a health risk in poorly-ventilated houses. Hamidi only uses Trugleam cleaning fluids to clean his house.

71. The only fish that live in the Junipero river are rainbow trout and brown trout. Gustavo never goes fishing without Isadoro's company, and Isadoro only fishes on the Junipero River. Every rainbow trout and every brown trout is a freshwater fish.

72. To enroll in Painting 200 at the Manx College of Arts, one must first complete either Painting 100 or Pastels 100. No one may enroll in Painting 300 without first completing Painting 200. Each Manx student enrolled in Sculpture 200 is also enrolled in Painting 300.

73. Formal, academic English requires the first and last words of any book title to be capitalized. *The New Journal of the Humanities* requires all its articles to be written in formal, academic English, and it is the only publication in which Francisca has ever been printed.

74. For a legislator to write a bill that will benefit her constituents, she must gather authentic input from those constituents. It is only possible to gather authentic input from constituents by holding frequent town hall meetings that are accessible to all constituents. Only locations near public transit stops are accessible to all constituents.

75. Sofia will not attend the party unless Zoe attends, and Zoe only attends parties that Xuan attends. Sofia will attend any party that Tilda does not attend, and whenever Rosella attends a party, Tilda does not.

9

Answers

Note: Your shorthand may differ from ours, but the concepts should be the same, and everything should be linked up in the same direction.

1. Palmer refuses to play tennis without Kassie's company, and Kassie plays tennis only when Nelle accompanies her. Nelle never plays tennis on overcast days.

   Overcast → ~Nelle → ~Kass → ~Palm
   Palm → Kass → Nelle → ~Overcast

2. To enter DynerCorp's office building, one must present a DynerCorp identification badge. The only way to obtain one of these badges is to be a DynerCorp employee. None of Dynercorp's employees have ever worked for Shanecorp, one of Dynercorp's main competitors.

   Enter Dyn Building → Badge → Dyn Employee → ~Worked for Shane
   Worked for Shane → ~Dyn Employee → ~Badge → ~Enter Dyn Building

3. Each member of Zelma's book club attended Orrin's dinner party. None of the guests at the dinner party attended Shadwell's brunch last week.

   Z Book Club → Orr Din Party → ~Shad brunch
   Shad brunch → ~Orr Din Party → ~Z Book Club

4. The only truly egalitarian form of government is direct democracy, and direct democracy requires active participation from a significant majority of citizens, which is impossible without a national culture of civic responsibility.

   Egal Gov → DD → Maj Act Part → Nat'l Cult Civ Resp
   ~Nat'l Cult Civ Resp → ~Maj Act Part → ~DD → ~Egal Gov

5. No bacteria are eukaryotes, and all organisms that are not eukaryotes are prokaryotes. Every prokaryote is a single-celled organism.

   Bact → ~Euk → Prok → Sing Cell Org
   ~Sing Cell Org → ~Prok → Euk → ~Bact

6. Tanisha, who is making a quilt, has a variety of colored fabrics available to her. She will use red fabric only if she also uses yellow fabric. If she does not use red fabric, then she will use green fabric, and she will not use yellow fabric unless she also uses orange fabric.

   ~G → R → Y → O
   ~O → ~Y → ~R → G

7. The groundskeeping staff at Longmire Castle will plant one or more varieties of fruit tree in the main courtyard. The staff will plant peaches unless they plant apples, and if the staff plants apples, it will not plant pears. The staff will never allow the courtyard to be planted with neither pears nor plums.

   ~Plum → Pear→ ~App → Peach
   ~Peach → App→ ~Pear → Plum

8. Lamar will never go to the movies without Sterne. Any movie that Sterne attends, Ray will attend as well. Priestly will only go to the movies if Ray does not.

   Pr → ~Ray → ~St → ~La
   La → St → Ray → ~Pr

9. A jeweler is planning a new ring design that will include a variety of gemstones. If the design includes sapphires, it will not include rubies. The jeweler will only include emeralds in designs that also include sapphires, and the jeweler includes garnets in all of her designs unless those designs include emeralds.

   ~Gar → Em → Sapp → ~Rub
   Rub → ~Sapp → ~Em → Gar

10. Malia will not run in next week's marathon unless Aubrey runs. Aubrey will never run in a marathon in which Clifford does not run. Nolan runs in every marathon in which Clifford runs.

    ~Nol → ~Cliff → ~Aub → ~Mal
    Mal → Aub → Cliff → Nol

11. No human can thrive without a diet rich in nutrients, and a diet rich in nutrients requires both complex carbohydrates and vitamins.

    ~Compl Carbs OR ~Vits → ~Diet Rich in Nutr → ~Hum Thrive
    Hum Thrive → Diet Rich in Nutr → Compl Carbs AND Vits

12. Megan always buys her cars at Sal's Used Cars. Sal's only carries four-door sedans, and federal law requires all four-door sedans to be equipped with airbags and antilock brakes.

    Meg Buy Car → Sal's → Four-Door Sed → Airb AND Antilock
    ~Antilock OR ~Airb → ~Four-Door Sed → ~Sal's → ~Meg Buy Car

13. At Orstead College, completing either Sociology 1 or Anthropology 1 makes one eligible for Anthropology 2. Anyone eligible for Anthropology 2 is also eligible for Sociology 2.

    Soc 1 OR Anth 1 → Elig for Anth 2 → Elig for Soc 2
    ~Elig for Soc 2 → ~Elig for Anth 2 → ~Soc 1 AND ~Anth 1

14. None of the speakers at the Housing Summit has ever experienced homelessness. To truly understand the needs of people experiencing homelessness, one must have experienced homelessness oneself. Every member of the Youngtown Homeless Advocacy Project truly understands the needs of people experiencing homelessness.

    Speaker at HS → ~Exp Homel → ~True Underst → ~Memb of YHAP
    Memb of YHAP → True Underst → Exp Homel → ~Speaker at HS

15. No circles are squares, but all squares are rectangles, and the only geometric shapes in Larisa's collage are squares.

    Geo Shap in Lar's Coll → Sq → Rect AND ~Cir
    ~Rect OR Cir → ~Sq → ~Geo Shap in Lar's Coll

16. Only if Abigail works on Saturday will Channie work on Saturday, and Channie will work on Saturday if Bristol does. Bristol works on any Saturday on which Hali does not work.

    ~Hal Sat → Brist Sat → Chan Sat → Ab Sat
    ~Ab Sat → ~Chan Sat → ~Brist Sat → Hal Sat

17. Avery takes the train to Pueblo on each Tuesday. Whenever Avery takes the train to Pueblo, he writes in his journal during the ride. The only pen Avery uses to write in his journal is the Stylus 7A.

    Tues → Av Train to Pueb → Writes in Jour → Styl 7A
    ~Styl 7A → ~Writes in Jour → ~Av train to Pueb → ~Tues

18. Unless they vacation in Spruce Junction, the Jabalas will vacation in Paradise Springs. The family will not vacation in Paradise Springs if they decide not to rent a car during their vacation.

    ~Spru Junct → Par Spr → Rent Car
    ~Rent Car → ~Par Spr → Spru Junct

19. Every doctor at the Lawson Clinic is qualified to diagnose and treat viral infections. The only people qualified to diagnose and treat viral infections are people who continuously study the behavior of infectious disease. Among people who continuously study the behavior of infectious disease, there is no one who is uninterested in microbiology.

    Doc at LC → Qual to Diag/Treat Vir Inf → Cont Study Behav Inf Dis → Int in MB
    ~Int in MB → ~Cont Study Behav Inf Dis → ~Qual to Diag/Treat Vir Inf → ~Doc at LC

20. All plant cells contain vacuoles. Every vacuole is an organelle, and organelles can only be found within living organisms.

    Plant Cell → Vacuole → Organelle → Within Liv Org
    ~Within Liv Org → ~Organelle → ~Vacuole → ~Plant Cell

9

21. None of the members of the Harmony Club are members of the Improv Club. Each member of the City Singers is a member of the Harmony Club. Everyone in Sharon's band and everyone in Jaden's band is a member of the City Singers.

Shar Band OR Jad Band → City Sing → Harm Club → ~Improv Club
Improv Club → ~Harm Club → ~City Sing → ~Shar Band AND ~Jad Band

22. Siti takes the subway whenever she doesn't take the bus, and she will not take the bus if she is running late or overslept. The subway in the city where Siti lives requires either a single-fare ticket or a monthly pass.

Run Late OR Overslept → ~Bus → Sub → 1Fare Tick OR Month Pass
~1Fare Tick AND ~Mon Pass → ~Sub → Bus → ~Run Late AND ~Overslept

23. No farmers like long winters, and the only people who are citizens of Bart County are farmers. People who do not like long winters invariably appreciate summer.

Cit Bart Count → Farm → ~Like Long Wint → Apprec Summ
~Apprec Summ → Like Long Wint → ~Farm → ~Cit Bart Count

24. The only candidates who can secure large amounts of campaign funding easily are incumbents. It is difficult to win any election without first being able to easily secure large amounts of campaign funding.

~Diff to Win Elec → Sec Lg Camp Funds Easily → Incumb
~Incumb → ~Sec Lg Camp Funds Easily → Diff to Win Elec

25. All offshore oil drilling is harmful to oceanic animal life. Marianna does not approve of any activity that is harmful to oceanic animal life, and the Committee for Environmental Action will not endorse any action of which Marianna disapproves.

Offsh Oil Drill → Harm to Oc Anim Life → ~Mar Appr → ~CEA Endorse
CEA Endorse → Mar Appr → ~Harm to Oc Anim Life → ~Offsh Oil Drill

26. Each of the toys currently in Meilin's toy chest is either blue or white. HapCo Toy Company does not manufacture any toys that are blue, nor does it manufacture any toys that are white. All of Meilin's toys are currently in her toy chest.

Mei's Toy → In Mei's Chest → Blue OR White → ~HapCo Manuf
HapCo Manuf → ~Blue and ~White → ~In Mei's Chest → ~Mei's Toy

27. Edward will not be able to renovate his kitchen without replacing his stove. The only renovators local to Edward's community who are qualified to replace stoves are Sanchez and Romero, and Edward will only allow qualified, local renovators to replace his stove.

~Sanch AND ~Rom → ~Qual Loc Renov → ~Repl Stove → ~Renov Kitch
Renov Kitch → Repl Stove → Qual Loc Renov → Sanch OR Rom

28. Peter will be promoted only if Carlita is hired to fill his current position, but it will be impossible to hire Carlita without first promoting Anthony. The position to which Anthony could be promoted is the only position for which Xiang could possibly be hired.

PP → CH → AP → ~XH
XH → ~AP → ~CH → ~PP

29. Unless it is Friday, Irena calls her sister at noon. Irena always walks outside on Fridays, and she never visits Greenway Park on days when she walks outside.

Gr Park → ~Walks Outside → ~Fri → Calls Sis at Noon
~Call Sis at Noon → Fri → Walk Outside → ~Gr Park

30. All cruel people are arrogant, and no one can develop arrogance without first feeling contempt for others, which is incompatible with authentic compassion.

Cruel → Arrog → Cont for Oth → ~Auth Comp
Auth Comp → ~Cont for Oth → ~Arrog → ~Cruel

9

31. None of the restaurants in Uptown Plaza serve trout. The only restaurants at which Gardner will dine are in Uptown Plaza, and Aydin will not dine at any restaurant that doesn't serve trout.

    Gard Dine → Up Plaz → ~Trout → ~Ayd Dine
    Ayd Dine → Trout → ~Up Plaz → ~Gard Dine

32. Mayburn will inspect the factory only if Wynne does not. Unless Wynne inspects the factory, Thompson will inspect the office. And Gregor must inspect the warehouse if Thompson inspects the office.

    May Insp Fact → ~Wyn Insp Fact → Thom Insp Off → Greg Insp Ware
    ~Greg Insp Ware → ~Thom Insp Off → Wyn Insp Fact → ~May Insp Fact

33. Vance will attend each workshop on management. Wallace will attend no workshop that Vance attends, and whenever Wallace does not attend a workshop, Basir attends it.

    Wkshp on Mgmt → V → ~W → B
    ~B → W → ~V → ~Wkshp on Mgmt

34. None of the guests at the Riverside Inn are members of the wedding party. Each member of the Ivanov family is staying at the Riverside Inn, and all of the caterers are members of the Ivanov family.

    Cater → I → R Inn → ~Wed
    Wed → ~R Inn → ~I → ~Cater

35. The only boats at Ocean View Marina are sloops and schooners. For a boat to be called a sloop or a schooner, it must have at least two sails.

    OVM → Sloop OR Schoon → 2+ sails
    ~2+ sails → ~Sloop AND ~Schoon → ~OVM

36. A group of biologists plans to survey a forest to determine what bird species live there. The biologists know that if chickadees live in the forest, then either bullfinches or flycatchers live there as well. They also know that either kinglets or chickadees live in the forest, and that no forest contains both tanagers and kinglets.

    Tan → ~King → Chick → Bull OR Fly
    ~Bull AND ~Fly → ~Chick → King → ~Tan

37. Each piece of furniture at Graham's Department Store is on sale, and sale items are always discounted by at least 20%.

    At Graham's → On Sale → 20%+ Disc
    ~20%+ Disc → ~On Sale → ~At Graham's

38. None of the bills owed by the Kind Hand Corporation are eligible for deferment. All bills currently owed to the Burtland Construction Company are owed by the Kind Hand Corporation.

    Owed to BCC → Owed by KHC → ~Elig for Def
    Elig for Def → ~Owed by KHC → ~Owed to BCC

39. If a poem is neither beautiful nor wise, then it is not a great poem. Poems that are either beautiful or wise invariably appeal to a majority of readers. Every poem written by Schulman is a great poem.

    ~Appeal to Maj → ~B AND ~W → ~Great → ~Written by S
    Written by S → Great → B OR W → Appeal to Maj

40. Without owning a car, it is time-consuming for residents of Country R to commute to and from work. Owning a car in Country R requires registering that car with the Department of Automotives. To register a car with the Department of Automotives, one must come in person to its central offices.

    ~Visit to Cent Off → ~Reg → ~Own Car → Time-Cons Commute
    ~Time-Cons Commute → Own Car → Reg → Visit to Cent Off

9

41. Whenever Shari visits her father, who lives in Port Town, he either cooks her dinner or treats her to dinner at a restaurant. The only reason Shari ever travels to Port Town is to visit her father, although she always travels to Port Town on Wednesdays.

    W → S to PT → Visit Fath → Cooks OR Treats

    ~Cooks AND ~Treats → ~Visit Fath → ~S to PT → ~W

42. For a city to be a safe place in which to live, it must have a competent municipal agency devoted to food safety. For a food safety agency to be competent, it must be both well-funded and staffed with food safety experts. Every city in Country Y is a safe place in which to live.

    Y → Safe → CFSA → Well-Fund AND Exp Staff

    ~Well-Fund OR ~Exp Staff → ~CFSA → ~Safe → ~Y

43. Kalani is assigned to the Red Team only if Farid is assigned to the Blue Team. Samuel is assigned to the Blue Team whenever Farid is. Robert and Samuel cannot both be assigned to the Blue Team.

    K Red → F Blue → S Blue → ~R Blue
    R Blue → ~S Blue → ~F Blue → ~K Red

44. Any class that prepares students for success later in life is worth taking, and classes that incorporate writing instruction invariably prepare students for success later in life. Every class, except for some classes in the science department, include at least some writing instruction.

    ~Sci Dept → Writing → Prep for Succ → Worth Taking

    ~Worth Taking → ~Prep for Succ → ~Writing → Sci Dept

45. At Farrenham University, Chemistry 101 and Physics 101 are both requirements for anyone wishing to take Physics 201. Every physics major at Farrenham must complete Physics 201.

    P Maj → P 201 → C 101 AND P 101
    ~C 101 OR ~P 101 → ~P 201 → ~P Maj

46. Bates is the only attorney qualified to take Larson's case. Bates will never take Larson's case unless his firm assigns him to it, and Bates's firm will assign attorneys to cases only if it believes those cases will contribute to the cause of social justice.

    Qualif Atty for L → B → Firm Assign → Soc Just

    ~Soc Just → ~Firm Assign → ~B → ~Qualif Atty for L

47. As long as I save money responsibly, I will be able to afford a home. However, I will never be able to afford a home without taking out a mortgage, which would necessitate both extensive paperwork and negotiations with a banker.

    Save $ → Home → Mortg → Pap AND Bank

    ~Pap OR ~Bank → ~Mortg → ~Home → ~Save $

48. On nights when it does not serve asparagus, Trafalgar's Restaurant also does not serve cucumber. The restaurant never serves jicama on nights when it serves eggplant, and whenever it does not serve cucumber, the restaurant serves eggplant.

    ~A → ~C → E → ~J
    J → ~E → C → A

49. Jurors should always be skeptical of testimony that is not fully reliable. The only testimony given by the prosecution in this case was eyewitness testimony, and no eyewitness testimony is fully reliable.

    Test from Prosec → EW → ~Full Reli → Skept

    ~Skept → Full Reli → ~EW → ~Test from Prosec

50. Whenever she processes a complaint, Nsedu always forwards a copy to her manager. None of the complaints filed with our company this week were processed by Elisa. The only person at our company besides Elisa who processes complaints is Nsedu.

    Filed this week → ~Elisa → Nsedu → Fwd to Mgr

    ~Fwd to Mgr → ~Nsedu → Elisa → ~Filed this week.

9

51. One cannot be an ornithologist without also being a biologist, and all biologists share an interest in taxonomy. Among the members of the Zoological Society, everyone who is not an entomologist is an ornithologist.

~Int in Tax → ~B → ~O → E
~E → O → B → Int in Tax

52. All of the parks in the county, except for some in Silver City, are popular among tourists. None of the parks in Silver City are larger than ten acres, and for a park to adequately accommodate horseback riding, it must be larger than ten acres.

H Accomm → >10 → ~Silv Cit → Pop Tour
~Pop Tour → Silv Cit → ~>10 → ~H Accomm

53. Of the members of our band, Hasani is the only skilled horn player. Our newest song, "Fancy," requires a skilled horn player to be performed well. Our next concert will be a failure unless we perform "Fancy" well.

~Conc Fail → Fancy → Skill Horn → H
~H → ~Skill Horn → ~Fancy → Conc Fail

54. The only people qualified to pass judgment on Juarez's book are paleontology experts. One can become a paleontology expert only through years of study, and no one can complete years of study without developing patience.

Qual → Pal Exp → Years Stud → Dev Pat
~Dev Pat → ~Years Stud → ~Pal Exp → ~Qual

55. The craters in Calistoga Basin are the only craters in the state, and only a meteorite would be capable of creating such craters. Every meteorite was once a meteor, and every meteor has traveled through space.

Crat in State → Crat in Calistoga → Meteorite → Meteor → Trav through Space
~Trav through Space → ~Meteor → ~Meteorite → ~Crat in Calistoga → ~Crat in State

56. Ravon is deciding what new articles of clothing to buy. She will not buy a blouse if she does not buy a skirt, and she will not buy a skirt if she buys a pair of jeans. She will only buy a leather jacket if she buys a pair of jeans, and she will not buy leather gloves unless she buys a leather jacket.

Leath Glov → Leath Jack → Jeans → ~Skirt → ~Blouse
Blouse → Skirt → ~Jeans → ~Leath Jack → ~Leath Glov

57. Sullivan is determining what type of fish he will stock his new aquarium with. He will not choose a platy without also choosing a cichlid. If he chooses a cichlid, he will either choose a tetra or not choose any bettas. If he does not choose a platy, he will choose both a minnow and a guppy.

~T and B → ~C → ~P → M and G
~M or ~G → P → C → T or ~B

58. The residents of Palmtown all voted in the national election. One cannot vote in the national election unless one is both registered with the Election Bureau and as a citizen of the nation.

Res Palm → Vote → Reg and Cit
~Reg or ~Cit → ~Vote → ~Res Palm

59. All air-breathing, aquatic mammals must once have lived on land, and any organism that once lived on land must have had some sort of locomotion system for moving across land. Every porpoise and every dolphin is an air-breathing aquatic mammal.

Porp or Dolph → Air-br Aq Mamm → Once on Land → Move Sys
~Move Sys → ~Once on Land → ~Air-br Aq Mamm → ~Porp and ~Dolph

60. Every player who is not on the blue team is on the red team. None of the players on the red team are on the yellow team, and any player not on the yellow team is also not on the green team.

~B → R → ~Y → ~G
G → Y → ~R → B

9

61. The novels of Cumberson are all thematically dark, and thematically dark novels never appeal to Amanda. However, Fadila invariably enjoys any novel that doesn't appeal to Amanda. Fadila does not enjoy any of the novels of Parre.

C → Dark → ~App to A → F Enj → ~P
P → ~F Enj → App to A → ~Dark → ~C

62. At our clinic, every doctor who did not graduate from Hoyst Medical School graduated from Laverton Medical School. Graduates of Laverton invariably become highly competent doctors. To be considered highly competent, a doctor must be confident performing routine procedures and have a strong knowledge of general medicine.

~H → L → High Comp → Conf AND Strong Know
~Conf OR ~Strong Know → ~High Comp → ~L → H

63. Mays is not selected if Rahul is not selected. Nestor is selected unless Mays is selected. Rahul and Pindar are never both selected.

P → ~R → ~M → N
~N → M → R → ~P

64. Unless we leave now, we will miss the ten o'clock train, and we will be late to the play unless we make that train. Anyone who is late to the play is required to wait in the lobby until the end of a scene before entering the theater.

~Leave Now → Miss Train → Late → Wait for Scene End
~Wait for Scene End → ~Late → ~Miss Train → Leave Now

65. If Ramirez swims laps, then either Wanda or Tamiko will play tennis, in which case Sidney will go for a jog. Ramirez swims laps whenever both Violet and Willoughby play basketball.

V BBall AND W BBall → R Swim → W Ten OR T Ten → S Jog
~S Jog → ~W Ten AND ~T Ten → ~R Swim → ~V Bask OR ~W Bask

66. None of the artifacts recovered from Dig Site C are in good condition. Professor Willow will only recover an artifact herself if it is in good condition. The artifacts currently on display at the Glenn University Paleontology Museum were all personally recovered by Professor Willow.

C → ~Good → ~W → ~On Disp
On Disp → W → Good → ~C

67. Any car part made by either Rice Components or Davidson Automotive will satisfy all of Country J's regulations governing the quality of car parts. Country J's regulations are so strict that car parts capable of satisfying them will invariably be both safe and reliable. Sergio's Auto Shop only carries car parts made by either Rice Components or Davidson Automotive.

Serg → Rice OR David → Satisfy Regs → Safe AND Relia
~Safe OR ~Relia → ~Satisfy Regs → ~Rice AND ~David → ~Serg

68. No pets are allowed at the Coastview apartment complex, which is the only apartment complex located on Parkside Avenue. Seamus will only live in an apartment complex if it allows pets.

S → Pet → ~CApt → ~P Ave Apt
P Ave Apt → CApt → ~Pet → ~S

69. Landscape painting is the only art form that Hualing practices. No matter how objectively a painter attempts to depict reality, all landscape paintings inevitably express the painter's attitude toward nature. Art that expresses the artist's attitude toward nature is necessarily open to interpretation.

H Art → Landsc Paint → Expr Att to Nature → Open to Interp
~Open to Interp → ~Expr Att to Nature → ~Landsc Paint → ~H Art

70. The household cleaning fluids produced by the Trugleam Corporation all release benzene into the air, and any airborne benzene is a health risk in poorly-ventilated houses. Hamidi only uses Trugleam cleaning fluids to clean his house.

    H → TGC → Benz → Health Risk in Poor Vent
    ~Health Risk in Poor Vent → ~Benz into Air → ~Trug Clea Flu → ~H

71. The only fish that live in the Junipero river are rainbow trout and brown trout. Gustavo never goes fishing without Isadoro's company, and Isadoro only fishes on the Junipero River. Every rainbow trout and every brown trout is a freshwater fish.

    G → I → JR → RT OR BT → Freshw Fish
    ~Freshw Fish → ~RT AND ~BT → ~JR → ~I → ~G

72. To enroll in Painting 200 at the Manx College of Arts, one must first complete either Painting 100 or Pastels 100. No one may enroll in Painting 300 without first completing Painting 200. Each Manx student enrolled in Sculpture 200 is also enrolled in Painting 300.

    S200 → P300 → P200 → Paint 100 OR Past 100
    ~Paint 100 AND ~Past 100 → ~P200 → ~P300 → ~S200

73. Formal, academic English requires the first and last words of any book title to be capitalized. *The New Journal of the Humanities* requires all its articles to be written in formal, academic English, and it is the only publication in which Francisca has ever been printed.

    F → NJH → Form Eng → First Word Cap AND Last Word Cap
    ~First Word Cap OR ~Last Word Cap → ~Form Eng → ~NJH → ~F

74. For a legislator to write a bill that will benefit her constituents, she must gather authentic input from those constituents. It is only possible to gather authentic input from constituents by holding frequent town hall meetings that are accessible to all constituents. Only locations near public transit stops are accessible to all constituents.

    Beneficial Bill → Auth Input → Freq/Access Meets → Near Pub Trans
    ~Near Pub Trans → ~Freq/Access Meets → ~Auth input → ~Beneficial Bill

75. Sofia will not attend the party unless Zoe attends, and Zoe only attends parties that Xuan attends. Sofia will attend any party that Tilda does not attend, and whenever Rosella attends a party, Tilda does not.

    ~X → ~Z → ~S → T → ~R
    R → ~T → S → Z → X

Drill 178: Quanti-YAY or Quanti-NAY? Round 2

Instructions: We've told you before that some of the trickiest Inference Family questions test whether or not you can combine quantified statements. Consider the following pairs of quantified statements. Can they be combined? Use the provided space to either write in the inference, or write in that you can't make one.

A reminder of our guidelines: the *only* way to combine a pair of quantified statements that doesn't include an "All" or a "None" statement is to combine two "Most" statements that have the same first condition. When you do so, you can infer a "Some" statement that links the two second conditions.

To combine a "Some" or "Most" statement with an "All" or "None" statement (aka, a conditional statement), the conditional statement's *sufficient* condition *has* to be the shared term.

The inference will be a "Some" statement in *all* cases *except* those that follow one particular format. If you can build a chain that starts with a "Most" statement and links to a conditional statement like so—"Most A's are B's and all B's are C's"—then you can infer that "Most A's are C's."

Use these guidelines when tackling the items below!

1. No boats with motors are eligible to compete in the annual boat race. Most canoes do not have motors.

2. Proposals must have support from a majority of zoning board members to be approved. Most zoning board members do not support the latest proposal.

3. Most inhabitants of Luxembourg can speak German, and most inhabitants of Luxembourg can speak English.

4. All accountants are good with numbers; they're also all good with computers.

5. Many surfers vacation in Hawaii, and everyone who vacations in Hawaii eats seafood.

6. Most of the school's PTA members made cookies for the bake sale, and most of the people who made cookies for the bake sale made cookies with chocolate chips.

7. Lunch is sometimes served at sales meetings, and most sales meetings are held in the main conference room.

8. Most superheroes are born with their powers, but some get them through accidents.

9. Almost all dinosaurs were small, but the majority of those that capture the imagination of children are huge.

10. Most of the castles of the Mad King Ludwig are well designed, and almost all of them are beautiful.

11. Most of the orchestra members know how to play the violin, and many of the orchestra members know how to play the flute.

12. Most long-haul truckers enjoy books on tape, and most have eggs for breakfast.

13. All of the lecturers at the conference are comfortable with public speaking. Some of the lecturers have introverted personalities.

14. Each vacation package that includes a cruise also includes a flight. Most vacation packages include a flight.

15. Some of the films at the festival were shot in black and white, and some of the films had subtitles.

16. The vast majority of voters in Balavia voted in favor of the referendum, while barely more than 50% of them voted for the ballot initiative.

17. Any scientific theory that has been superseded by another theory has been deemed inadequate. Some scientific theories were superseded because they were supported solely by ruling political groups.

18. Pizza was served at most of the kids' birthday parties, and cupcakes were served at most of the kids' birthday parties.

19. Most multivitamins do not contain iron, and some multivitamins with vitamin C do contain iron.

20. Only marine biologists are allowed to interact directly with the aquarium's penguins. Most of the aquarium's staff are marine biologists.

21. Each of the rings with diamonds has a platinum band. Some rings have diamonds and sapphires.

22. Most plans to terraform Mars are based on technology that doesn't yet exist, and many of those plans would take years to complete.

23. Most of the snack bar's ice cream flavors have chocolate. Some of the snack bar's ice cream flavors have nuts.

24. Some of the tested vacuum cleaners failed to pick up most grains of rice from the carpet. Any vacuum that fails to pick up most grains of rice from the carpet does not pass certification.

25. All issues of *Do You?* magazine include a personality quiz, while most issues of that magazine feature an interview with a famous personality.

26. Each issue of the magazine includes a crossword puzzle. Most crossword puzzles have diagrams that are diagonally symmetric.

27. Every box on the truck contains either kitchen products or cleaning supplies. Most of the boxes on the truck do not contain cleaning supplies.

28. Many impersonations involved impersonating celebrities. Some fraud is committed by people doing impersonations.

29. Only beaches on the south side of the island are open to surfers. Many beaches on the north side of the island have excellent waves for surfing.

30. All gym members have access to the shower facilities. Some of the people in the yoga class are not gym members.

31. Most beginner bowling balls have a polyester coverstock, and many beginner bowling balls are designed to grip the lane and hook.

32. All movies by Mike Inlet feature explosions. The famous Shakespearean actor Robert Coates appeared in exactly one movie by Mike Inlet.

9

33. Most of the gifts were wrapped in blue wrapping paper, and most of the gifts had a yellow ribbon.

34. The restaurant serves brunch only on Sundays. On some Sundays, the restaurant closes early to host a wedding reception.

35. A significant number of ancient civilizations were founded on rivers, and the vast majority of ancient civilizations featured a form of currency.

Answers

Note: Remember that "Some" statements are reversible, so if you presented yours in a different order than ours, no big deal!

1. No inference.

2. The latest proposal will not be approved.

3. Some German speakers can speak English.

4. Some people who are good with numbers are also good with computers.

5. Some surfers eat seafood.

6. No inference.

7. No inference.

8. No inference.

9. No inference.

10. Some well-designed castles are beautiful.

11. No inference.

12. Some people who have eggs for breakfast also enjoy books on tape.

13. Some people who are comfortable speaking publicly have introverted personalities.

14. No inference.

15. No inference.

16. Some voters in Balavia voted for both the referendum and the ballot initiative.

17. Some scientific theories supported solely by ruling political parties have been deemed inadequate.

18. Some birthday parties had both pizza and cupcakes.

19. No inference.

20. No inference.

21. Some rings with sapphires have platinum bands.

22. No inference.

23. No inference.

24. Some of the tested vacuums did not pass certification.

25. Some magazine issues with personality quizzes also feature an interview with a famous personality.

26. No inference.

27. Most of the boxes on the trucks contain kitchen products.

28. No inference.

29. Some beaches with excellent surfing are not open to surfers.

30. No inference.

31. No inference.

32. Robert Coates appeared in at least one movie that features explosions.

33. Some of the gifts have blue wrapping paper and a yellow ribbon.

34. No inference.

35. No inference.

9

Drill 179: Reverse Engineer the Rule, Round 2

Instructions: Knowing how to diagram a rule is one thing. Remembering how to interpret a rule that you've diagrammed is another. Practice that second skill (again!) by decoding the rule diagrams you've been given and reverse engineering the text of the rule. Fill in the text version of each rule in the space provided.

1. $G \rightarrow R$ or $\cancel{M}$

2. $M \rightarrow S$ or L

3. $D - S < \begin{smallmatrix} A \\ C \end{smallmatrix}$

4. $C \rightarrow \cancel{S}$
   $C \rightarrow T$

5. $\boxed{\underline{J\,M}}$

6. $P < \begin{smallmatrix} V \\ N \end{smallmatrix}$

7. $\boxed{\begin{smallmatrix} \cancel{P} \\ \cancel{J} \end{smallmatrix}}$

8. $J \leftrightarrow \cancel{P}$
   $P \leftrightarrow \cancel{J}$

9. $A_j \rightarrow T_h$

10. $\boxed{L \,-\,-\,-\,-\,-\, M}$

11. $\boxed{\begin{smallmatrix} M \\ C \end{smallmatrix}}$

12. $H_a \rightarrow \cancel{K}_P$

13. $B \rightarrow \cancel{G}$
    $B \rightarrow \cancel{H}$

14. $\boxed{P\cancel{M}}$ $\boxed{P\cancel{L}}$ $\boxed{L\cancel{M}}$ ↺↺↺

15. $\boxed{\text{QTW}}$

16. $J-P \rightarrow J_3$

17. $Y - \boxed{RN}$

18.

19. $J_3 \rightarrow L_4$

20. $\boxed{\cancel{D}\cancel{R}}$ ↺

Answers and explanations follow on the next page.

Answers

Note: While you may have phrased the rules differently than we have, make sure that they're conveying the same information. Minor changes can make a big difference in LG rules!

1. $G \rightarrow R$ or $\cancel{M}$

   If G is in a group, either R will be in that group, or M will not be in the group.

2. $M \rightarrow S$ or L

   If M is included, S or L will also be included.

3. $D - S \big\langle {}^A_C$

   S will come after D, but before A and C.

4. $C \rightarrow \cancel{S}$
   $C \rightarrow T$

   If C is included, S will not be included and T will be included.

5. $\lfloor J M \rfloor$

   J will occur directly before M.

6. $P \big\langle {}^V_N$

   P will occur at some point before V and N.

7. $\boxed{\genfrac{}{}{0pt}{}{\cancel{P}}{\cancel{T}}}$

   T will not be in the same group as P.

8. $J \longleftrightarrow \cancel{P}$
   $P \longleftrightarrow \cancel{J}$

   Either J will be in or P will be in, but not both.

9. $A_j \rightarrow T_h$

   If A is in group j, then T will be in group h.

10. $\lfloor L \_\_\_\_\_ M \rfloor$

    L and M will be exactly four spaces apart.

11. $\boxed{\genfrac{}{}{0pt}{}{M}{C}}$

    C and M will be in the same group.

12. $H_a \rightarrow \cancel{K}_p$

    If H is matched with a, K will not be matched with p.

13. $B \rightarrow \cancel{G}$
    $B \rightarrow \cancel{H}$

    If B is included, G and H will not be included.

14. $\boxed{\cancel{PM}} \boxed{\cancel{PL}} \boxed{\cancel{LM}}$

    P and M will not be adjacent. P and L will not be adjacent. L and M will not be adjacent.

15. $\boxed{\boxed{Q T W}}$

    Q, T, and W will arrive consecutively, though not necessarily in that order.

16. $J - P \rightarrow J_3$

    If J is before P, J will be third.

17. $Y - \boxed{R N}$

    Y will go before R, which will go directly before N.

18. $\boxed{\genfrac{}{}{0pt}{}{\boxed{G} H}{K}}$

    K will be in the same group as G or H, but not both.

19. $J_3 \rightarrow L_4$

    If J is third, L will be fourth.

20. $\boxed{D R}$

    D and R will not appear next to each other.

9

Drill 180: Diagramming 301, Round 4

Instructions: Diagram and contrapose each of the following complex conditional rules.

1. She will cite the *Ramirez* case if, and only if, she also cites the *Shepherd* case.

2. The brief will not cite *Powell* or *Klein* unless it cites *Troupe*.

3. She cannot select both an amulet and a crest for her character.

4. He will not visit Dallas unless he also visits Chicago or St. Louis.

5. She will not order orange soda unless she also orders grape soda and cola.

6. She will order orange soda if, but only if, she does not order lemon-lime.

7. She won't order both tea and cola.

8. He will visit St. Louis only if he visits Chicago or Nashville.

9. He will visit Vancouver unless he visits Chicago or Toronto.

10. She will either not go hiking or not go rock climbing if she goes to the beach.

11. The character will not have an ax without a shield and a cloak.

12. Jen will be in the group if, but only if, Lexie is in the group.

13. Either chickadees or nuthatches are in the photograph.

14. A blue jay will be in the photograph unless a woodpecker is.

15. Starlings will not be in a photograph unless chickadees or finches are also.

16. Mary and Kate cannot both work on the project.

17. Brian and Hazel will never be in the group together.

18. If Lexie is in the group, neither Jeremy nor Heather will be.

19. Adam will be in any group that Brian and Jen are in.

20. A playlist will not contain an oldie or a pop song unless it also includes an instrumental piece.

21. A playlist containing a rock or metal song will not contain a hip hop song.

22. The country song will be on the playlist if, and only if, the metal song is not included.

23. The playlist contains a metal song unless it contains both an instrumental and a pop song.

24. She will not order both coffee and tea.

25. If she writes about quantum gravity, she will write about information theory but not about neuroscience.

26. She will order water if she has ordered orange and grape soda.

27. She will order tea unless she orders cola.

28. The brief must cite Hale and Maxwell unless it cites Lincoln.

29. She will cite the *Shepherd* case only if she cites Jones and Lincoln.

30. Any bouquet that contains carnations will also contain gladiolas and fern.

9

31. Any bouquet that contains tulips or daffodils will also contain irises.

32. The bouquet must contain gardenia unless it contains fern and ivy.

33. She cannot cite both the Patton and Wilkinson cases.

34. She must cite either the Hale or Kristoff cases in her brief.

35. Someone will wear a tortoise costume if, but only if, someone else wears a hare costume.

36. There will not be both a witch and a zombie costume at the party.

37. There will never be a ghost and a Frankenstein's monster at the Halloween party.

38. The Troupe case will be cited in any brief that cites Hale or Ramirez.

39. He will visit either Los Angeles or San Diego, but not both.

40. If he visits Boston, he will also visit New York and Philadelphia.

41. He will visit Seattle if, and only if, he visits Vancouver.

42. A photograph contains chickadee if, but only if, it doesn't contain a blue jay.

43. The aviary will feature either robins or starlings, but not both.

44. No photograph will contain both robins and woodpeckers.

45. There will be a vampire costume unless there is an angel costume.

46. No one will wear a princess costume unless a Robin Hood costume is also worn.

47. If there is a zombie costume or a vampire costume, there will be a ghost costume.

48. The film festival will show the horror film if, but only if, it shows the comedy.

49. The epic must be shown unless the foreign film is shown.

50. The comedy is shown only if the art film or romance film is shown.

51. Her character cannot have a sword if she has a crest and a dagger.

52. The character will carry a dagger unless she has a sword or an ax.

53. Her character must have a shield whenever she has either an ax or a crest.

54. Either bamboo or papyrus will be used in the art project.

55. Neither glass nor quartz will be used if metal is used.

56. The project with never include both wool and ceramic.

57. She will not take both biology and physics.

58. She will take statistics unless she takes physics and chemistry.

59. She will not study both German and Spanish.

60. There will be no bamboo used unless ceramic is used.

9

Answers

1. She will cite the *Ramirez* case if, and only if, she also cites the *Shepherd* case.

   R ↔ S ; ~S ↔ ~R

2. The brief will not cite *Powell* or *Klein* unless it cites *Troupe*.

   P or K → T ; ~T → ~P and ~K

3. She cannot select both an amulet and a crest for her character.

   A → ~C ; C → ~A

4. He will not visit Dallas unless he also visits Chicago or St. Louis.

   D → C or SL ; ~C and ~SL → ~D

5. She will not order orange soda unless she also orders grape soda and cola.

   O → G and C ; ~G or ~C → ~O

6. She will order orange soda if, but only if, she does not order lemon-lime.

   O ↔ ~L ; L ↔ ~O

7. She won't order both tea and cola.

   T → ~C ; C → ~T

8. He will visit St. Louis only if he visits Chicago or Nashville.

   SL → C or N ; ~C and ~N → ~SL

9. He will visit Vancouver unless he visits Chicago or Toronto.

   ~V → C or T ; ~C and ~T → V

10. She will either not go hiking or not go rock climbing if she goes to the beach.

    B → ~H or ~RC ; H and RC → ~B

11. The character will not have an ax without a shield and a cloak.

    A → S and C ; ~S or ~C → ~A

12. Jen will be in the group if, but only if, Lexie is in the group.

    J ↔ L ; ~L ↔ ~J

13. Either chickadees or nuthatches are in the photograph.

    ~C → N ; ~N → C

14. A blue jay will be in the photograph unless a woodpecker is.

    ~BJ → W ; ~W → BJ

9

15. Starlings will not be in a photograph unless chickadees or finches are also.

    S → C or F ; ~C and ~F → ~S

16. Mary and Kate cannot both work on the project.

    M → ~K ; K → ~M

17. Brian and Hazel will never be in the group together.

    B → ~H ; H → ~B

18. If Lexie is in the group, neither Jeremy nor Heather will be.

    L → ~J and ~H ; J or H → ~L

19. Adam will be in any group that Brian and Jen are in.

    B and J → A ; ~A → ~B or ~J

20. A playlist will not contain an oldie or a pop song unless it also includes an instrumental piece.

    O or P → I ; ~I → ~O and ~P

21. A playlist containing a rock or metal song will not contain a hip hop song.

    R or M → ~HH ; HH → ~R and ~M

22. The country song will be on the playlist if, and only if, the metal song is not included.

    C ↔ ~M ; M ↔ ~C

23. The playlist contains a metal song unless it contains both an instrumental and a pop song.

    ~M → I and P ; ~I or ~P → M

24. She will not order both coffee and tea.

    C → ~T ; T → ~C

25. If she writes about quantum gravity, she will write about information theory but not about neuroscience.

    QG → IT and ~N ; ~IT or N → ~QG

26. She will order water if she has ordered orange and grape soda.

    O and G → W ; ~W → ~O or ~G

27. She will order tea unless she orders cola.

    ~T → C ; ~C → T

28. The brief must cite Hale and Maxwell unless it cites Lincoln.

    ~H or ~M → L ; ~L → H and M

9

29. She will cite the *Shepherd* case only if she cites Jones and Lincoln.

    S → J and L ; ~J or ~L → ~S

30. Any bouquet that contains carnations will also contain gladiolas and fern.

    C → G and F ; ~G or ~F → ~C

31. Any bouquet that contains tulips or daffodils will also contain irises.

    T or D → I ; ~I → ~T and ~D

32. The bouquet must contain gardenia unless it contains fern and ivy.

    ~G → F and I ; ~F or ~I → G

33. She cannot cite both the Patton and Wilkinson cases.

    P → ~W ; W → ~P

34. She must cite either the Hale or Kristoff cases in her brief.

    ~H → K ; ~K → H

35. Someone will wear a tortoise costume if, but only if, someone else wears a hare costume.

    H ↔ T ; ~T ↔ ~H

36. There will not be both a witch and a zombie costume at the party.

    W → ~Z ; Z → ~W

37. There will never be a ghost and a Frankenstein's monster at the Halloween party.

    F → ~G ; G → ~F

38. The Troupe case will be cited in any brief that cites Hale or Ramirez.

    H or R → T ; ~T → ~H and ~R

39. He will visit either Los Angeles or San Diego, but not both.

    L ↔ ~S ; S ↔ ~L

40. If he visits Boston, he will also visit New York and Philadelphia.

    B → N and P ; ~N or ~P → ~B

41. He will visit Seattle if, and only if, he visits Vancouver.

    S ↔ V ; ~V ↔ ~S

42. A photograph contains chickadee if, but only if, it doesn't contain a blue jay.

    C ↔ ~B ; B ↔ ~C

43. The aviary will feature either robins or starlings, but not both.

   R ↔ ~S ; S ↔ ~R

44. No photograph will contain both robins and woodpeckers.

   R → ~W ; W → ~R

45. There will be a vampire costume unless there is an angel costume.

   ~V → A, ~A → V

46. No one will wear a princess costume unless a Robin Hood costume is also worn.

   P → R ; ~R → ~P

47. If there is a zombie costume or a vampire costume, there will be a ghost costume.

   Z or V → G ; ~G → ~Z and ~V

48. The film festival will show the horror film if, but only if, it shows the comedy.

   C ↔ H ; ~H ↔ ~C

49. The epic must be shown unless the foreign film is shown.

   ~E → F ; ~F → E

50. The comedy is shown only if the art film or romance film is shown.

   C → A or R ; ~A and ~R → ~C

51. Her character cannot have a sword if she has a crest and a dagger.

   C and D → ~S ; S →~C or ~D

52. The character will carry a dagger unless she has a sword or an ax.

   ~D → S or A ; ~S and ~A → D

53. Her character must have a shield whenever she has either an ax or a crest.

   A or C → S ; ~S → ~A and ~C

54. Either bamboo or papyrus will be used in the art project.

   ~B → P ; ~P → B

55. Neither glass nor quartz will be used if metal is used.

   M → ~G and ~Q ; G or Q → ~M

56. The project with never include both wool and ceramic.

   W → ~C ; C → ~W

9

57. She will not take both biology and physics.

    $B \rightarrow \sim P$; $P \rightarrow \sim B$

58. She will take statistics unless she takes physics and chemistry.

    $\sim S \rightarrow P$ and C ; $\sim P$ or $\sim C \rightarrow S$

59. She will not study both German and Spanish.

    $G \rightarrow \sim S$; $S \rightarrow \sim G$

60. There will be no bamboo used unless ceramic is used.

    $B \rightarrow C$; $\sim C \rightarrow \sim B$

PART THREE

Getting the Most Out of Your Work

Cheat Sheets

Wouldn't it be great if you could consolidate all the important information that you've learned about a question or game type into a clear, concise, digestible little package? Enter: The Cheat Sheets! Think of them as a combination pop quiz and crash course. First, we'll pull from the pop quiz side of things and give you a blank Cheat Sheet for you to fill in. Then, we'll pull from the crash course side of things by giving you our filled-in version.

Cheat sheets are also a great place to begin targeted practice. Start by quizzing yourself with a blank sheet to see how much you recall about a question or game type, then review our version before tackling your practice set. Learning Science tells us that writing improves recall, so if our version contains information that your version lacks, fill that information in first before moving into your practice.

Logical Reasoning

ID the Conclusion	
Identifying Language of the Question Stem	
Common Issues at Play in the Stimulus	
Approach to the Stimulus and Prediction	
Common Features of Incorrect Answers	
Common Features of Correct Answers	
General Notes	

ID the Conclusion	
Identifying Language of the Question Stem	"...most accurately expresses the conclusion of the argument?"
Common Issues at Play in the Stimulus	Main conclusion in the middle of the argument. Red herring intermediate conclusion, often in the last line and with a common conclusion indicator such as "therefore" in front of it.
Approach to the Stimulus and Prediction	ID the line of text that you believe to be the main conclusion, then look for an answer that paraphrases it. Beware any text introduced by conclusion indicator words and beware the last line of the argument: neither of these is typically the main conclusion in an ID the Conclusion question. If you find two conclusions, try to determine which supports the other. If there's no clear winner, remember that intermediate conclusions tend to have their support in the same or adjoining lines, and that main conclusions tend to oppose the opposing point while intermediate conclusions tend not to.
Common Features of Incorrect Answers	Premise, intermediate conclusion, a reasonable conclusion the arguer could have drawn but didn't.
Common Features of Correct Answers	They paraphrase the main point made in the stimulus.
General Notes	Sometimes the main conclusion is a judgment on an opposing point (e.g., "Some people think fairies exist, but they are wrong."). The correct answer will typically be an explicit contradiction of the opposing point (e.g., "Fairies do not exist.").

Determine the Function	
Identifying Language of the Question Stem	
Common Issues at Play in the Stimulus	
Approach to the Stimulus and Prediction	
Common Features of Incorrect Answers	
Common Features of Correct Answers	
General Notes	

Determine the Function	
Identifying Language of the Question Stem	"[quoted text] serves which of the following functions?" "...most accurately describes the role played in the argument by [quoted text]?"
Common Issues at Play in the Stimulus	The stimulus is generally more straightforward than in ID the Conclusion questions because the test writers are not trying to hide the conclusion.
Approach to the Stimulus and Prediction	Even though the stem has given you a quoted piece of text to look for, read the argument in its entirety, ID its conclusion and its premise(s), then evaluate how the quoted piece of text fits within that puzzle.
Common Features of Incorrect Answers	Some describe the wrong piece of an argument (e.g., it says the quoted text is a premise when it's actually a conclusion). Other, trickier incorrect answer choices describe the right piece of the argument but misquote how the argument uses that piece (e.g., it says the quoted text is a premise offered in support of conclusion X when in fact the quoted text is a premise offered in support of conclusion Y).
Common Features of Correct Answers	Typically, the quoted text is a premise, intermediate conclusion, main conclusion, or an opposing point. Occasionally, the quoted text is counter evidence that could be used to support an opposing point, whether or not that point has been explicitly articulated.
General Notes	Whenever an answer choice refers to a claim the argument supposedly made, ask yourself: "Did the argument really say that?" to catch those tricky wrong answer choices that misquote the argument.

Procedure	
Identifying Language of the Question Stem	
Common Issues at Play in the Stimulus	
Approach to the Stimulus and Prediction	
Common Features of Incorrect Answers	
Common Features of Correct Answers	
General Notes	

Procedure	
Identifying Language of the Question Stem	"...the argument proceeds by..." "...responds to the first speaker by..."
Common Issues at Play in the Stimulus	An argument with a common valid reasoning structure, such as Reduction to the Absurd, Ruling Out Alternatives, Application of a Principle, or Arguing by Analogy. Two named speakers with colons following their names in separate little paragraphs.
Approach to the Stimulus and Prediction	If there is only one speaker, read the argument and assess whether it has a common reasoning structure. If there are two speakers, figure out which part of Speaker 1's argument Speaker 2 is refuting. Does Speaker 2 point out an assumption, raise an object, point out a famous flaw, or none of the above?
Common Features of Incorrect Answers	Describes the wrong common reasoning structure. The difference between applying a principle to draw a conclusion about a specific example and citing an example to support the existence of a principle is tested frequently. So is the difference between an analogy and an example.
Common Features of Correct Answers	Uses abstract language to describe the structure of the argument.
General Notes	When answers are abstract, replace the abstract terms with concrete terms from the stimulus.

Sufficient Assumption	
Identifying Language of the Question Stem	
Common Issues at Play in the Stimulus	
Approach to the Stimulus and Prediction	
Common Features of Incorrect Answers	
Common Features of Correct Answers	
General Notes	

Sufficient Assumption	
Identifying Language of the Question Stem	"...follows logically if..." "...allows the conclusion to be properly drawn..."
Common Issues at Play in the Stimulus	A new concept introduced in the conclusion. Conditional logic.
Approach to the Stimulus and Prediction	If there is a new concept in the conclusion, it must appear in the correct answer. If the stimulus is conditional, diagram it. Chain the pieces together and ID the missing link in the chain.
Common Features of Incorrect Answers	Doesn't address the new concept in the conclusion. Illegal Reversal.
Common Features of Correct Answers	Bridge Assumptions: If (concept from premise), then (new concept in conclusion). The contrapositive of the most easily-predictable missing link.
General Notes	When evaluating an answer choice, ask yourself: "If this is true, does it make my argument 100% airtight?" Gaps in the stimulus are often pretty clear, and correct answer choices can often be predicted. If there's a new concept in the conclusion, rule out any answer choice that doesn't address it. Sometimes correct answers can be more than is necessary to fill the gap. Other times, they will be just right. Big quantifiers and extreme language are OK because they get the job done. Weak language is suspect because it's often not impactful enough to guarantee the conclusion.

Necessary Assumption	
Identifying Language of the Question Stem	
Common Issues at Play in the Stimulus	
Approach to the Stimulus and Prediction	
Common Features of Incorrect Answers	
Common Features of Correct Answers	
General Notes	

Necessary Assumption	
Identifying Language of the Question Stem	"requires," "depends," "prerequisite," "must be assumed" Also, the plain unqualified language of assumption, presumption, and presupposition (e.g., "The argument presupposes which of the following?" or "The argument presumes which of the following?" or "Which of the following is assumed by the argument?").
Common Issues at Play in the Stimulus	Often these are tricky arguments and gaps in reasoning may be hard to spot. Some will have new concepts in the conclusion but many won't.
Approach to the Stimulus and Prediction	If there's a clear conceptual shift from premise to conclusion, note it. The correct answer might bridge that gap, partially or fully. If the conclusion is an explanation, predict that the right answer will rule out alternative explanations.
Common Features of Incorrect Answers	Too extreme. Big quantifiers and strong degree words are red flags. Out of Scope. Things that strengthen the argument but aren't absolutely necessary.
Common Features of Correct Answers	Defender Assumptions: necessary because they rule out an alternative to the conclusion, or an obstacle that would get in the way of the conclusion following from the premises. Bridge Assumptions are also common in Necessary Assumption questions, connecting the concepts in the premise to a new concept in the conclusion.
General Notes	When evaluating an answer choice, ask yourself: "Does this really need to be true in order for my argument to work?" Negation Technique: If you think an answer is a contender, negate it. Then, consider the argument in light of that negation. If the answer is correct, its negation will destroy the argument. Negate an answer by negating the quantifier or the main verb. Common Quantifier Negations: All—Not all None—Some Most—Half or less To negate a conditional statement, demonstrate that its sufficient condition can happen without its necessary condition.

ID the Flaw	
Identifying Language of the Question Stem	
Common Issues at Play in the Stimulus	
Approach to the Stimulus and Prediction	
Common Features of Incorrect Answers	
Common Features of Correct Answers	
General Notes	

ID the Flaw	
Identifying Language of the Question Stem	"…most vulnerable to criticism…" "…the reasoning in the argument is flawed in that…"
Common Issues at Play in the Stimulus	Roughly half will contain a famous flaw. The other half will hinge on an assumption the argument makes or an objection the argument overlooks.
Approach to the Stimulus and Prediction	Know the famous flaws and how to spot them. If you don't see one, predict the correct answer will address an assumption or an objection.
Common Features of Incorrect Answers	Circular Reasoning and Self-Contradiction appear frequently among the incorrect answer choices. Know what those flaws really look like so these become easy eliminations. Answers that accuse the argument of assuming something that it doesn't really hinge on. Answers that accuse the argument of overlooking something that's actually irrelevant.
Common Features of Correct Answers	The argument assumes/presumes/presupposes/fails to establish…a Necessary Assumption. The argument fails to consider/overlooks the possibility that…an objection. Abstract language describing one of the famous flaws.
General Notes	When abstract language is confusing, pull text from the argument to replace the abstract terms. When evaluating an answer that begins with "the argument assumes" or something equivalent, treat it like a Necessary Assumption answer and ask yourself: "Is that really necessary in order for the argument to work?" When evaluating an answer that begins with "the argument fails to consider" or something equivalent, ask yourself: "If this were true, would it mess up my argument?"

Weaken	
Identifying Language of the Question Stem	
Common Issues at Play in the Stimulus	
Approach to the Stimulus and Prediction	
Common Features of Incorrect Answers	
Common Features of Correct Answers	
General Notes	

Weaken	
Identifying Language of the Question Stem	"...weakens..." "...undermines the conclusion..." "...casts most doubt..."
Common Issues at Play in the Stimulus	Causality. Comparisons.
Approach to the Stimulus and Prediction	If the argument is causal, weakeners most often point to an alternate cause, so always ask yourself: "Could it be something else?" If the argument is comparative, ask yourself: "Are these two things really as similar (or different) as the arguer would have me believe?"
Common Features of Incorrect Answers	Out of Scope. Strengthener.
Common Features of Correct Answers	For causal arguments, alternate causes are the most common correct answer choice type. Other common causal weakeners are counterexamples (cause without the effect or effect without the cause), evidence that the proposed cause and effect relationship is backwards, and information that demonstrates that the effect actually preceded the proposed cause. For comparative arguments that conclude two things are similar, correct answers will typically address a relevant difference. For comparative arguments that conclude two things are different, correct answers will typically address a relevant similarity. For all arguments, information that disputes the applicability of the premise, or that raises an objection to the argument can be a correct answer.
General Notes	When evaluating an answer, ask yourself: "If this is true, does it make my conclusion less likely to follow from my premises?" It's OK to introduce new concepts as long as they are relevant (e.g., a potential objection that the argument hasn't explicitly considered). Weak language is suspect because the answer needs to be impactful.

Strengthen	
Identifying Language of the Question Stem	
Common Issues at Play in the Stimulus	
Approach to the Stimulus and Prediction	
Common Features of Incorrect Answers	
Common Features of Correct Answers	
General Notes	

Strengthen	
Identifying Language of the Question Stem	"...most strengthens the argument" "...most supports the argument"
Common Issues at Play in the Stimulus	Causality. Comparisons.
Approach to the Stimulus and Prediction	If there is a Term Shift, predict that the right answer will help bridge the gap between terms. If the argument is causal, predict that the right answer will rule out an alternate cause, establish a control group, or rule out another causal weakener. If the argument is comparative and concludes two things are similar, predict that the right answer will demonstrate a relevant similarity. If it concludes two things are different, predict the right answer will demonstrate a relevant difference.
Common Features of Incorrect Answers	Premise Boosters: They just give more evidence that the premises are true. Out of Scope. Weakeners: Somewhat counterintuitively, many Strengthen questions have an incorrect answer that is a weakener.
Common Features of Correct Answers	Some are like Bridge Assumptions, connecting the premises to the conclusion. Others, particularly in the most challenging Strengthen questions, are more like Defender Assumptions, ruling out potential weakeners.
General Notes	When evaluating an answer, ask yourself: "If this is true, does it make my conclusion more likely to follow from my premises?" It's OK to introduce new concepts as long as they are relevant (e.g., ruling out a potential objection that the argument hasn't explicitly considered). Weak language is suspect because the answer needs to be impactful.

Principle Support	
Identifying Language of the Question Stem	
Common Issues at Play in the Stimulus	
Approach to the Stimulus and Prediction	
Common Features of Incorrect Answers	
Common Features of Correct Answers	
General Notes	

Principle Support	
Identifying Language of the Question Stem	"Which of the following principles most supports the argument above?"
Common Issues at Play in the Stimulus	The argument will typically include a new concept in the conclusion. Often this concept is a recommendation.
Approach to the Stimulus and Prediction	If the conclusion is a recommendation, predict an answer that will establish criteria for the recommendation in the conclusion you already know are met by the premises: "If (thing from the premises), then (recommendation from the conclusion)."
Common Features of Incorrect Answers	If the conclusion is a recommendation, many incorrect answer choices won't address a recommendation at all, or will address a slightly different recommendation. Others will address the correct recommendation but will be the Illegal Reversal of your prephrase: "If (recommendation from conclusion), then (thing from premises)."
Common Features of Correct Answers	A clear match to the prephrase, or the contrapositive of the prephrase.
General Notes	These can be handled much like Sufficient Assumption questions. There will be a new concept in the conclusion and if an answer choice doesn't address that concept, it's wrong. Direction is important! The trickiest Principle Support questions will have an incorrect answer choice that bridges a gap between the right concepts but which does so in the wrong direction.

Must Be True	
Identifying Language of the Question Stem	
Common Issues at Play in the Stimulus	
Approach to the Stimulus and Prediction	
Common Features of Incorrect Answers	
Common Features of Correct Answers	
General Notes	

Must Be True	
Identifying Language of the Question Stem	"...can be logically inferred from the statements above?" "...which of the following must be true as well?" "...can be properly concluded from the statements above?"
Common Issues at Play in the Stimulus	Conditional logic. Stimuli aren't arguments—they're just sets of facts.
Approach to the Stimulus and Prediction	If the stimulus is conditional, diagram it and chain the statements together. Predict an answer that addresses all or part of your chain. If the stimulus is not conditional, it may not lend itself well to prediction. Make sure you understand the facts before moving into the answers.
Common Features of Incorrect Answers	If the stimulus is conditional, incorrect answer choices will be Illegal Reversals or Illegal Negations of all or part of your chain. If the stimulus is not conditional, incorrect answer choices may be almost-but-not-quite provable or totally Out of Scope.
Common Features of Correct Answers	If the stimulus is conditional, correct answers can match the chain exactly, match only part of it, or match the contrapositive of all or part of the chain. For all Must Be True questions, correct answers might seem incomplete. That's OK. As long as they tell a true story, they don't have to tell the whole story.
General Notes	When evaluating an answer, ask yourself: "If everything in the stimulus is true, does this have to be true as well?" If the answer is yes, pick it. Strong language is OK when the stimulus is conditional. When the stimulus is not conditional, strong language is suspect.

Most Strongly Supported	
Identifying Language of the Question Stem	
Common Issues at Play in the Stimulus	
Approach to the Stimulus and Prediction	
Common Features of Incorrect Answers	
Common Features of Correct Answers	
General Notes	

Most Strongly Supported	
Identifying Language of the Question Stem	"Which of the following is most strongly supported by the statements above?"
Common Issues at Play in the Stimulus	Less likely to be conditional than Must Be True stimuli. Almost all are sets of facts rather than arguments.
Approach to the Stimulus and Prediction	Most Strongly Supported stimuli don't typically lend themselves to prediction. Understand the facts, then let the answers drive your process. Find the most provable.
Common Features of Incorrect Answers	Out of Scope. Too strong to be proven. Big quantifiers and strong degree words are suspect.
Common Features of Correct Answers	Correct answers stick close to the text. They are not creative inferences. Some will be almost-but-not-quite provable. Others will be 100% inferable.
General Notes	When evaluating an answer choice, ask yourself: "If everything in the stimulus is true, does this have to be true as well?" If the answer is yes, pick it. If the answer is "almost but not quite," that choice is still a pretty safe bet. Don't be afraid of answers that sound like they're paraphrasing the stimulus. If they're paraphrasing the stimulus, then they're well-supported enough to be correct!

Must Be False	
Identifying Language of the Question Stem	
Common Issues at Play in the Stimulus	
Approach to the Stimulus and Prediction	
Common Features of Incorrect Answers	
Common Features of Correct Answers	
General Notes	

Must Be False	
Identifying Language of the Question Stem	"…is contradicted by the statements above?" "If the statements above are true, each of the following could be true EXCEPT:"
Common Issues at Play in the Stimulus	Conditional logic. Stimuli aren't arguments—they're just sets of facts.
Approach to the Stimulus and Prediction	If the stimulus has any conditional statements, diagram them. If there is more than one conditional statement, chain the statements together. Predict an answer that contradicts all or part of your chain. If the stimulus is not conditional, it may not lend itself well to prediction. Make sure you understand the facts before moving into the answers.
Common Features of Incorrect Answers	If the stimulus is conditional, incorrect answer choices will often be Illegal Reversals or Illegal Negations of all or part of your chain. Remember, while the Illegal Reversal and Illegal Negation of a statement aren't inferable, they aren't necessarily contradicted. Out of Scope.
Common Features of Correct Answers	If the stimulus has a conditional statement, the correct answer will likely show the sufficient condition of the statement without its necessary condition. If the stimulus has a series of conditional statements that can be chained together to draw a valid conditional conclusion, the correct answer will likely show the sufficient condition of the valid conclusion without its necessary condition. If the stimulus is not conditional, the correct answer will contradict one of the given statements or a conclusion that could be validly drawn from the information given.
General Notes	These questions are all about conditional statement negation: Show the sufficient condition without the necessary condition to prove that the conditional relationship doesn't always hold.

Principle Example	
Identifying Language of the Question Stem	
Common Issues at Play in the Stimulus	
Approach to the Stimulus and Prediction	
Common Features of Incorrect Answers	
Common Features of Correct Answers	
General Notes	

Principle Example	
Identifying Language of the Question Stem	"...the principle stated above..." "...conforms most closely to the principle...?"
Common Issues at Play in the Stimulus	The stimulus is one or two conditional principles. While there may appear to be some conceptual overlap, the principles will not chain.
Approach to the Stimulus and Prediction	Diagram and contrapose each principle. Look for an answer choice that fulfills the sufficient condition of one of the diagrams and concludes its necessary condition.
Common Features of Incorrect Answers	Concludes the wrong thing. Only necessary conditions can be concluded. Eliminate any answer that doesn't conclude the necessary condition of one of your diagrams. Establishes the wrong thing. In order to conclude the necessary condition of one of your diagrams, you have to establish that diagram's sufficient condition. Eliminate any answer that doesn't explicitly fulfill the correct sufficient condition.
Common Features of Correct Answers	Follows the contrapositive of one of the given principles. That's why you always need to both diagram and contrapose!
General Notes	Eliminating answers that conclude the wrong thing will often get you down to two or three contenders.

Match the Reasoning	
Identifying Language of the Question Stem	
Common Issues at Play in the Stimulus	
Approach to the Stimulus and Prediction	
Common Features of Incorrect Answers	
Common Features of Correct Answers	
General Notes	

Match the Reasoning	
Identifying Language of the Question Stem	"…is most similar to the argument above?" "…contains reasoning that most closely parallels…"
Common Issues at Play in the Stimulus	Some are valid arguments, others are not. Many will have unique features worth noting because wrong answer choices won't include them. Many can (and should!) be diagrammed.
Approach to the Stimulus and Prediction	If conditional, diagram the argument. If not conditional, describe the argument in abstract language. Note whether the argument is valid, and if it isn't, whether it contains any famous flaws. Notice any unique features that wrong answer choices are likely to botch. Note the degree of the quantifiers, the number of premises, and the type of conclusion.
Common Features of Incorrect Answers	Conclusion Mismatch: Quantifier, Type. Premise Mismatch: Number, Type. Logic Mismatch: Validity, Flaw. Similar language/subject matter but different logic.
Common Features of Correct Answers	Might be out of order but logically the same.
General Notes	Match the Reasoning questions can often be narrowed to two or three choices using just the conclusion, so this is a good place to start. If the question is conditional, diagram the stimulus, but don't automatically start diagramming every answer. Many can be eliminated by spotting Mismatches without going to the trouble of diagramming.

Match the Flaw	
Identifying Language of the Question Stem	
Common Issues at Play in the Stimulus	
Approach to the Stimulus and Prediction	
Common Features of Incorrect Answers	
Common Features of Correct Answers	
General Notes	

Match the Flaw	
Identifying Language of the Question Stem	"…involves flawed reasoning most similar to…" "…parallels the flawed pattern of reasoning…" "…contains an error in reasoning most similar to…"
Common Issues at Play in the Stimulus	Contains a famous flaw.
Approach to the Stimulus and Prediction	Name that flaw! If you can't, revert to your Match the Reasoning techniques and try to find unique elements that are likely to be botched by incorrect answer choices.
Common Features of Incorrect Answers	Wrong flaw. Valid.
Common Features of Correct Answers	If the stem asks for the answer choice most similar in its flawed pattern of reasoning, the correct answer will have the same flaw and no significant Mismatches. If the stem asks only which argument contains the same flaw, other minor Mismatches are allowable.
General Notes	The flaw is paramount. Find it first!

ID the (Dis)agreement	
Identifying Language of the Question Stem	
Common Issues at Play in the Stimulus	
Approach to the Stimulus and Prediction	
Common Features of Incorrect Answers	
Common Features of Correct Answers	
General Notes	

ID the (Dis)agreement	
Identifying Language of the Question Stem	"...the point at issue between..." "...are committed to disagreeing about..." "...a point of agreement between..."
Common Issues at Play in the Stimulus	Two named speakers with colons following their names in separate little paragraphs.
Approach to the Stimulus and Prediction	Speaker 1 says a couple of things. Speaker 2 only responds to one of them. Figure out which thing that is and you've predicted the point of disagreement/agreement.
Common Features of Incorrect Answers	One or both of the speakers will not have articulated a firm opinion on the matter.
Common Features of Correct Answers	For the more common "Disagreement" version of this question type, if you posed the correct answer as a "yes or no" question to both speakers, one would answer "yes" and the other, "no." For the less common "Agreement" version, the correct answer posed as a "yes or no" question would elicit either a "yes" from both speakers or a "no" from both speakers.
General Notes	Opinions have to be explicit. Don't assume anything about what the speakers believe.

Explain a Result	
Identifying Language of the Question Stem	
Common Issues at Play in the Stimulus	
Approach to the Stimulus and Prediction	
Common Features of Incorrect Answers	
Common Features of Correct Answers	
General Notes	

Explain a Result	
Identifying Language of the Question Stem	"…resolves the apparent discrepancy…" "…contributes to the resolution of the paradox…" "…contributes most to the explanation…"
Common Issues at Play in the Stimulus	A set of paradoxical facts that can be tricky to untangle.
Approach to the Stimulus and Prediction	Think: "How come X happened in spite of Y, because I would have expected Z." X is the unexpected result that has to be explained. Y is the reason you would have expected things to go the other way. Z is the other way you would have expected things to go.
Common Features of Incorrect Answers	Support the expected outcome, thereby furthering the paradox. Explain X or Y, but not how they can exist together. Out of scope.
Common Features of Correct Answers	Explains how both X and Y can exist together.
General Notes	Look out for Except questions. In order to be incorrect, an answer choice must help resolve the paradox: the same criterion that would make an answer correct in a Non-Except question. However, the degree to which an answer must contribute to the resolution of the paradox changes from one question to the next. In order to be a correct answer in a Non-Except question, the answer needs to fully explain the result. In order to be a wrong answer choice in an Except question, the answer just needs to contribute to an explanation of the result.

Evaluate	
Identifying Language of the Question Stem	
Common Issues at Play in the Stimulus	
Approach to the Stimulus and Prediction	
Common Features of Incorrect Answers	
Common Features of Correct Answers	
General Notes	

Evaluate	
Identifying Language of the Question Stem	"…would be most helpful to know when assessing the argument…"
Common Issues at Play in the Stimulus	Statistics. Percentages and amounts.
Approach to the Stimulus and Prediction	If the conclusion is an explanation of a statistical relationship, consider alternate possible explanations. If the conclusion is about percentages and the premise is about amount, or vice versa, consider what needs to be true about one in order to draw a conclusion about the other.
Common Features of Incorrect Answers	Premise Booster. Out of Scope.
Common Features of Correct Answers	Pose a question that, if answered one way, would strengthen the argument and, if answered another way, would weaken the argument.
General Notes	These tricky questions can be thought of as Strengthen/Weaken combo questions. The correct answer choice has to be capable of doing both!

Logic Games

Relative Ordering	
Identifying Markers of the Game Type	
Ideal Diagram	
Common Features of the Standard Games	
Twists to Look Out for and How to Address Them	
General Notes	

Relative Ordering	
Identifying Markers of the Game Type	Task is to put things in order.
	None of the rules refer to definite positions on a Number Line.
	All rules are about the placement of elements relative to other elements.
Ideal Diagram	The Tree
Common Features of the Standard Games	Rules presented in an order where the first few don't overlap.
	If a rule doesn't include a variable already in the Tree, skip it and come back to it at the end. Build your Tree as a cohesive whole, not as a series of pieces you then cobble together later.
Twists to Look Out for and How to Address Them	Either/or rules: Either P is before Q and R or both Q and R are before P.
	Conditional rules: If X is before Y, then T is after Z.
	Both of these can provide framing opportunities. For either/or rules, create one Tree for each option. Then, build the rest of the rules into each Tree.
	For conditional rules, as long as there cannot be ties, create one Tree in which the condition is met and another Tree in which the condition is not. Then, build the rest of the rules into each Tree.
General Notes	These tend to be back-end games, with most of the work done question by question.

Basic Ordering	
Identifying Markers of the Game Type	
Ideal Diagram	
Common Features of the Standard Games	
Twists to Look Out for and How to Address Them	
General Notes	

Basic Ordering	
Identifying Markers of the Game Type	Task is putting things in order.
	Some rules refer to placement on the Number Line, others to relative relationships.
	Conditional Rules.
	Chunks!
Ideal Diagram	The Number Line
Common Features of the Standard Games	Chunks often drive these games. They have limited placement options and can provide opportunities for framing.
Twists to Look Out for and How to Address Them	Mismatches between the number of slots and the number of elements.
	Subgroups (e.g., doctors A, B and C are pediatricians whereas doctors X, Y and Z are family practice docs.)
	We treat both of those as separate game types because they're so common.
General Notes	Contrapose any conditional rules to double their usability.
	If there are multiple chunks, consider whether and how they can intersect.

3D Ordering	
Identifying Markers of the Game Type	
Ideal Diagram	
Common Features of the Standard Games	
Twists to Look Out for and How to Address Them	
General Notes	

3D Ordering	
Identifying Markers of the Game Type	More than two sets of elements that must be put in order. One set of elements, each of which has an additional characteristic.
Ideal Diagram	3D Number Line: a Number Line with additional tiers to accommodate the characteristics/extra set of elements.
Common Features of the Standard Games	Something inherently ordered, such as days of the week or ranks, will form the base of the diagram. The main elements, typically people, will go atop the base, and a row about some characteristic the people have will go atop that.
Twists to Look Out for and How to Address Them	Sometimes the Orientation question can't be answered from the main row of elements alone. If you have it down to two and both look right, jot down the additional row for each. You will likely be able to spot the offense in the wrong answer choice in the additional row, which we call the characteristic row.
General Notes	Sometimes the characteristic row will be the driving force behind the game. Always check in about the numerical limitations of the characteristics (e.g., how many lefties vs. how many righties are possible) and how any vertical chunks (a person and their characteristic) factor in to each diagram you draw. Sometimes the elements are split into subcategories based on the characteristic at the outset of the game (e.g., "F, G, and H are men and L, N, and P are women"). Other times, the characteristic is not linked to particular elements at the outset (e.g., "Four of the seven executives are flying business class and the other three are flying coach"). In these cases, you have to figure out how the elements and their characteristics intersect during the game. Because the 3D Number Line is bigger and more complex, rely on previous work to answer subsequent questions as often as possible, thereby limiting the amount of new work you have to do.

Mismatch Twist	
Identifying Markers of the Game Type	
Ideal Diagram	
Common Features of the Standard Games	
Twists to Look Out for and How to Address Them	
General Notes	

Mismatch Twist	
Identifying Markers of the Game Type	The number of slots is different than the number of elements.

Ideal Diagram	Number Line, with the modifications below.
	
	Too many slots:
	  a) Some elements repeat.
	  b) Some slots are left empty.
	
	Too many elements:
	  a) Some slots have more than one element.
	  b) Some elements don't go. *This is the most common, and when it happens, represent the Out group to the right of the Number Line: __ __ __ __ __ | __ __

Common Features of the Standard Games	An Out group that is the driving force of the game. Limited Group Space inferences based on the small Out group force some elements to always be in.
Twists to Look Out for and How to Address Them	If elements have to repeat or double up in slots, use Numerical Distributions! Elements repeat: Distribute to figure out the number of repeaters and how many times they can/must repeat. Elements double up in slots: Distribute to figure out how many slots can/must have multiple elements and how many extra elements they can/must contain.

General Notes	Contrapose all conditionals to maximize your chances of finding the subtle but important Limited Group Space inferences, e.g.,
	
	  M → G __ __ __ | __
	
	Inference: Because ~G → ~M, and there's only one out slot, G can never be out because there's not room for it to bring M out with it. Therefore, G is always in.
	
	An example of Numerical Distributions to figure out the number of repeaters:
	
	    A B C D 1-1-1-3 or 1-1-2-2 (Either one goes three times and everyone else goes once, or two go twice and two go once.)
	
	    — — — — — —
	
	An example of Numerical Distributions to figure out the number of slots with multiple elements:
	
	    A B C D E F G 1-1-1-1-3 or 1-1-1-2-2 (Either one slot has three elements and the rest have one, or two slots have two elements and the rest have one.)
	
	    — — — — —

In/Out	
Identifying Markers of the Game Type	
Ideal Diagram	
Common Features of the Standard Games	
Twists to Look Out for and How to Address Them	
General Notes	

In/Out	
Identifying Markers of the Game Type	Task is to put things into two groups or, more commonly, to select certain elements (the In group) and leave other elements unselected (the Out group).
	All rules are typically conditional, though there may be one exception on occasion.
Ideal Diagram	The Logic Chain + Placeholder Chart (for a quick Logic Chain tutorial, check out our You Tube Channel!)
Common Features of the Standard Games	You may or may not know how many are in vs. how many are out.
	The Logic Chain should be built rule by rule, skipping any that don't include elements already in the chain, and looping back to those rules at the end.
	Diagram the first rule with room on top and beneath so the chain can be built up and down, depending on which elements subsequent rules include.
	Any strays should be built into the top or bottom of the chain so that they are not forgotten.
	The Big Pause should include looking for pairs that can't be in together and pairs that can't be out together. Use the placeholder chart to represent this information (e.g., if A and B can't be in together, put an A/B placeholder in the out column of the Placeholder Chart).
Twists to Look Out for and How to Address Them	Subcategories of elements: Build the chain based on subcategories, rather than rule by rule, with a line of demarcation between each section. Build rules specific to a subgroup beside that subgroup on the chain. Use Numerical Distributions to determine the different numerical breakdowns of elements per subgroup in the In group.
	Special Positions (e.g., one of singers selected will perform a solo): Diagram rules about the position separately from the rest of the chain. Put an asterisk by these rules, and asterisks beside the elements in the chain about which the rules are written.
	Compound conditional rules that don't build into the chain (e.g., rules that have "and" in the sufficient condition or "or" in the necessary condition): Diagram the rules separately from the chain. Put an asterisk by these rules and asterisks beside the elements that are the sufficient condition in the rules or their contrapositives.
	A bunch of rules that don't build into the chain: the Rule Chart. If an In/Out game can't be tackled using the Logic Chain because too many rules won't build in, make a big T chart. On the "In" side, diagram any rules with an element being in as the sufficient condition. On the "Out" side, diagram any rules with an element being out as the sufficient condition. Contrapose each rule in the appropriate field of the chart, and chain rules together where appropriate.
General Notes	The Logic Chain contraposes for you, so you don't need to diagram each rule first, contrapose, and then build it into the chain.
	X marks the spot when you're looking for Placeholder Inferences. Any time the arrows cross from one column to the other making an X, there's a Placeholder Inference. Place the items connected by the crossed arrows as a placeholder into the column the arrows point to.

Basic Grouping	
Identifying Markers of the Game Type	
Ideal Diagram	
Common Features of the Standard Games	
Twists to Look Out for and How to Address Them	
General Notes	

Basic Grouping	
Identifying Markers of the Game Type	Grouping task. More than two groups. Fixed number of members per group.
Ideal Diagram	Grouping Board
Common Features of the Standard Games	Chunks are often frameable, as many Basic Grouping games have only three groups. Put the chunk in each group and see what happens! Anti-Chunk Standoff. Games with a chunk and one or more anti-chunks often have this kind of advanced inference:
	A B C D E F A and D must be grouped together.
	— — — E and F cannot be grouped together.
	— — —
	1 2 3
	Inference: The AD chunk takes up one group, E and F form a cloud over one row of the other two groups, leaving B and C to form a cloud over the other row of the other two groups, meaning B and C effectively form an additional anti-chunk.
Twists to Look Out for and How to Address Them	Interchangeable Groups: If there is nothing distinguishing the groups from one another, you can often frame out which elements go together, even though you can't tell which particular group they go in. Do so by placing definitive elements such as chunks in a group of your choosing and playing the game out from there. Place a cloud around your group labels to designate that they are interchangeable.
	Mismatches: Build an Out group or track repeaters. If you have an Out group, look out for Limited Group Space inferences. If you have repeaters, use Numerical Distributions.
General Notes	Lots of frameable games!

Open Grouping	
Identifying Markers of the Game Type	
Ideal Diagram	
Common Features of the Standard Games	
Twists to Look Out for and How to Address Them	
General Notes	

Open Grouping	
Identifying Markers of the Game Type	Grouping task. Unknown number of elements per group. "At least one of" and "One or more of" language.
Ideal Diagram	Open Grouping Board
Common Features of the Standard Games	Two standard flavors: A few elements that repeat many times. Group size is limited by the small number of elements. Draw a slot for every element in every group. Many elements that do not repeat. Use Numerical Distributions to figure out the maximum group size so you don't end up with an unwieldy number of slots per group. Rule combinations that establish that all elements must be used between two groups, e.g.: X Y Z Each group has at least one member. — — — Group 1 has more members than group 2. — — — Groups 1 and 2 have no members in common. — — — 1 2 3 Inference: Group 1 has two of the elements and Group 2 has the third.
Twists to Look Out for and How to Address Them	Subcategories of elements: Build in subscripts to represent subcategories in the Grouping Board. Or, build each group in multiple columns, one for each subcategory.
General Notes	These games are driven by numbers! Rules about which groups can and cannot share elements lead to numerical inferences for all groups mentioned in the rule. Don't stop inferring until you've considered both groups mentioned. Sometimes the element set that should form the base of the diagram will be clear from the real-world scenario (e.g., students grouped into teams). Other times, it won't be. When it isn't, the set of elements that would lead to the most inferences about group size should be the base. If there is only one set of elements introduced by the phrase "at least one of" or "one or more of," it will typically be the elements that should be mobile, not the set that should be the base.

3D Grouping	
Identifying Markers of the Game Type	
Ideal Diagram	
Common Features of the Standard Games	
Twists to Look Out for and How to Address Them	
General Notes	

3D Grouping	
Identifying Markers of the Game Type	Grouping task.
	More than two groups.
	Either the elements are divided into subgroups or the groups are divided because they have Special Positions (e.g., one is the manager and the other two, employees), or both.
Ideal Diagram	3D Grouping Board: a standard Grouping Board with additional rows for characteristics, subcategories, or Special Positions.
Common Features of the Standard Games	Numbers of member per group are fixed.
Twists to Look Out for and How to Address Them	Mismatches: Build an Out group or track repeaters. Distribute to make inferences about repeaters, and look for Limited Group Space inferences when you have an Out group.
	Interchangeable groups: Place the definite things, such as chunks, in the group of your choosing and play out the rest of the game. Put a cloud around your group labels to indicate their interchangeability.
General Notes	If elements are divided into subgroups, you can represent one in uppercase and one in lowercase.
	Always write out a roster for each row of the Grouping Board so you remember which sets of elements should be placed in which rows.

Hybrids	
Identifying Markers of the Game Type	
Ideal Diagram	
Common Features of the Standard Games	
Twists to Look Out for and How to Address Them	
General Notes	

Hybrids	
Identifying Markers of the Game Type	Ordering task + Grouping task.
Ideal Diagram	Depends on the game. Grouping Boards can easily be adapted to accommodate ordered groups such as days of the week, and even order within groups, such as time of day.
Common Features of the Standard Games	Groups are ordered from the outset (e.g., Week 1, Week 2, and Week 3) and the only task is to place the elements within those ordered groups. Some people consider Mismatch with an Out group to be a hybridization of the standard game type with In/Out.
Twists to Look Out for and How to Address Them	Groups are not ordered from the outset (e.g., Professor Andreas's research team, Processor Bernard's research team, and Professor Carmichael's research team) and have to be placed in order and filled as you go. For games like this, find the inherently ordered component and make that your base. Build a row of slots beneath the base for the group labels (A, B, and C, in the scenario above), and rows of slots on top of the base for the elements that will be placed into the groups.
General Notes	Hybrid games are all about adaptability. You should recognize the pieces even if you don't at first recognize the whole puzzle. Visualization is important to get to the most appropriate diagram. If you see curveball elements, try to liken them to something familiar and diagram accordingly. Diagram what you know first and build in the curveballs after.

Recycling Bins

One of the most helpful things you can do during your LSAT preparation is recycle questions. Why? Because this test is standardized. Questions, games, and passages are all unique in subject matter, but they follow standard patterns with which every test taker should be intimately familiar by test day. Enter: The Recycling Bins!

Whenever you complete a question, game, or passage that exhibits a standard feature of the LSAT, throw it in the Bin! This could be a standard RC passage structure, a high-level inference common to a particular type of logic game, or a typical trap answer for a certain LR question type, to name a few. Any feature is fair game! Once your Bins are stocked with questions, you can use them in a variety of ways.

When you're doing targeted practice on particular game, passage, or question types, pull relevant items from the Recycling Bin to cement the standard features of that game, passage, or question type in your memory before doing practice sets of new work.

When you're reviewing challenging questions from a PrepTest, section, or practice set, consider whether the question exhibited any standard features. If it did, pull material with similar features from the Recycling Bin to practice addressing those features so future questions that exhibit them won't be as challenging.

When you want to build the intellectual equivalent of muscle memory by practicing the same thing over and over until it becomes rote, pull practice items from the Recycling Bin to ensure that you're practicing with material that reflects common patterns on the test.

OK, enough talk. Here are your Bins! Consider making extra copies while they're blank so you have extra space if you need it.

Logic Games Recycling Bin					
Book/Test	Page or Section	Game #	Game Type	Game Feature	Re-do Dates

Logic Games Recycling Bin					
Book/Test	Page or Section	Game #	Game Type	Game Feature	Re-do Dates

Reading Comprehension Recycling Bin					
Book/Test	Page or Section	Passage #	Passage Subject	Passage Feature	Re-do Dates

Reading Comprehension Recycling Bin					
Book/Test	Page or Section	Passage #	Passage Subject	Passage Feature	Re-do Dates

Logical Reasoning Recycling Bin					
Book/Test	Page or Section	Question #	Question Type	Question Feature	Re-do Dates

Logical Reasoning Recycling Bin					
Book/Test	Page or Section	Question #	Question Type	Question Feature	Re-do Dates

APPENDIX C
Planning and Review

The first step toward getting the most out of your work is effective planning. This entails scheduling your weekly practice and setting intentions for that practice. Learning science tells us that practicing with specific intentions makes you more likely to achieve your goals. Use these documents to get moving in the right direction!

Week 1: Planning and Review

Weekly Prep Plan			
Section	Learning Goals	Activity	Time/Date
LR			
LG			
RC			

PrepTest Plan			
Date	Which PT or sections?	Intentions—What do you want to focus on during this test?	Timing Goals
Overall Score		Section Accuracy	What are you going to work on before the next test?

Navigator Analysis: PrepTest 1

The next step toward getting the most out of your work is effective analysis. After taking a PrepTest, enter it into our online LSAT Navigator to analyze the results. If you haven't used our LSAT Navigator yet, you can access it by registering your book. Instructions for how to do so can be found on page vi, right after the Letter to Students. For each field, record both the number of questions you answered correctly (the first blank) and the total number of questions in that category (the second blank). If, for example, there were 6 Necessary Assumption questions on the test and you answered 4 correctly, you'd enter *4 out of 6*. For Logical Reasoning, the indented entry in each block asks you to add up the entries above it. For Logic Games and Reading Comprehension, questions can (and probably will) count for more than one category. Once you've entered all these numbers, use the chart at the bottom of the next page to analyze your results. Pat yourself on the back for your strengths, and devise a plan for tackling your weaknesses!

Logical Reasoning

- ID the Conclusion: _____ out of _____
- Determine the Function: _____ out of _____
- Procedure: _____ out of _____
  - Describe Family: _____ out of _____

- Necessary Assumption: _____ out of _____
- Sufficient Assumption: _____ out of _____
- ID the Flaw: _____ out of _____
- Strengthen: _____ out of _____
- Weaken: _____ out of _____
- Evaluate: _____ out of _____
  - Assumption Family: _____ out of _____

- Inference: _____ out of _____
- ID the Dis/Agreement: _____ out of _____
- Explain a Result: _____ out of _____
  - Inference Family: _____ out of _____

- Match the Reasoning: _____ out of _____
- Match the Flaw: _____ out of _____
  - Matching Family: _____ out of _____

Reading Comprehension

(Questions and passages can fall into more than one category)

- Natural Sciences: _____ out of _____
- Law: _____ out of _____
- Humanities: _____ out of _____
- Social Sciences: _____ out of _____

- Comparative Passage: _____ out of _____
- Standard Passages: _____ out of _____

- Identification Questions: _____ out of _____
- Inference Questions: _____ out of _____
- Synthesis Questions: _____ out of _____

Logic Games

(Questions and games can fall into more than one category)

- Ordering Games: _____ out of _____
- Grouping Games: _____ out of _____
- Hybrid Games: _____ out of _____
- Other Games: _____ out of _____

- Games with No Twists: _____ out of _____
- Games with Twists: _____ out of _____

- Orientation Questions: _____ out of _____
- Conditional Questions: _____ out of _____
- Unconditional Questions: _____ out of _____
- Tricky/Rare Questions: _____ out of _____

- Could Be True: _____ out of _____
- Must Be True: _____ out of _____
- Could Be False: _____ out of _____
- Must Be False: _____ out of _____

- EXCEPT Questions: _____ out of _____
- Standard Questions: _____ out of _____

Section	Strengths	Areas to Focus On
LR		
RC		
LG		

How to Review Your Work

Once you've completed a PrepTest, you should simply check your answers and figure out why the correct answer is correct, right? Wrong! This common approach to reviewing work is not the way to drive your score upward. Let's look at a more effective method.

There are some basic principles to keep in mind:

1. Simply reading an explanation does not translate into learning something. You have to apply it.

    Whenever the beginning of an explanation helps ideas start to click, stop reading! It's time to shift back to the question, apply what just clicked, and see if you can figure out the rest on your own. Then go back to the explanation when you get stuck again or to further refine whatever dollop of brilliance you just developed on your own.

2. Replaying questions, games, and passages is one of the most effective ways to deepen your understanding.

    This is another way to ensure you're applying what you've learned. Use your Strategy Log and Guided Review sheets to note questions you got wrong, struggled with, or simply took too long to answer. Note your errors and what you'd like to do differently next time. Revisit those questions at regular intervals, between 2 and 10 days after the first attempt, until they become automatic.

The Review Process

1. Complete your question set or practice test under timed conditions, *marking questions you're unsure about or spend too much time on as you go.*

2. *Before you check the answers,* take a second look at all of the problems that you marked in Step 1. Decide to either stick with your current answer or switch to another answer. If you do the latter, you should still track your initial answer.

3. Now, check the answer key. As you do this, mark which problems you answered incorrectly—but *don't indicate the correct answer for that question.*

4. Go back to any question you answered incorrectly and try to find the correct answer.

5. Check to see what the correct answer is for any questions that you just completed a second pass on. Try to explain each of these questions, even if you answered correctly the second time. Focus on why the right answer is right and why the tempting wrong answers are wrong.

6. For any question that you answered incorrectly or marked during any of the above steps, read our explanation on the forums. The goal is to reinforce your thought process for the ones you got right, and correct it for the ones you got wrong. Remember, as you read our explanations, whenever you finish reading a part that explains something you didn't understand already about the question (or passage or game) stop reading and go back and try applying that to the question. The goal is not to passively receive the explanation but to use it to train your brain.

7. Fill out your Strategy Log/Guided Review Sheet for each question you spent too much time on, weren't 90+% certain of, or answered incorrectly.

8. Redo the questions in your Strategy Log/Guided Review Sheet at regular intervals until they become automatic. Give yourself time between these intervals to forget the question specifics, because the act of retrieving the correct approach will strengthen your hold on it.

Let's look at an example to see how this might work:

Suppose you complete a set of 10 Logical Reasoning questions, giving yourself 1:20 per question. You found questions 5 and 6 particularly difficult, so you put a star next to each of them.

After completing the timed set, you go back and take another look to decide to either keep your answer, or change to another one. Then, you grab the answer key and check your answers. You see that you've answered questions 5, 6, and 8 incorrectly. You put marks next to those three questions *without recording the correct answers.*

You head back to 5, 6, and 8 to see if you can figure them out (no time limit). Once that is done, you check the answer key and see that you answered 5 and 8 correctly, but you still picked the wrong answer for 6.

After taking another look at 6 with the correct answer in hand and coming up with an explanation for why it's correct (or struggling with it awhile and deciding that you need some help), you log into the forums and check the explanations for 5, 6, and 8.

Look on the next pages for some specific questions to ask yourself for reviewing each section type, followed by some recommendations on how to review questions if you don't have much time.

Considerations for Review

Logical Reasoning

Question Stem & Stimulus:

1. Did I begin by identifying the question type and recalling my strategy for it?

2. Was my understanding of the stimulus complete and correct? For example, if this was an Assumption Family question, did I identify the argument core accurately?

3. What are the important ideas or keywords in the stimulus? Did I miss any during my initial read?

4. Before I moved on to the answer choices, did I pause to consider what the correct answer choice might look like?

Answer Choices:

1. On my first pass through the answer choices, did I focus on quickly eliminating incorrect answers? Did I make the decision to defer quickly on answers I was unsure about?

2. If I was left with two or three appealing answer choices, how did I choose between them?

3. What parts of wrong answers tempted me?

4. Did I miss any red flags in the incorrect answer choices?

5. What false red flags did I identify in the correct answer?

Timing and Process:

1. Did I allocate my time properly?

2. How does this question relate to other material I've studied? How can I use my experience on this question to avoid making similar mistakes on future questions?

Strategy Log: Week 1 (Logical Reasoning Review)

Date	#/Source	Right? Wrong? Long? Tough?	Review Notes (Next time I see _____, I will _____)	Retry Notes	Done?
					❑
					❑
					❑
					❑
					❑
					❑
					❑

Date	#/Source	Right? Wrong? Long? Tough?	Review Notes (Next time I see _____, I will _____)	Retry Notes	Done?
					❑
					❑
					❑
					❑
					❑
					❑
					❑

Guided Review: Reading Comprehension

Reviewing Reading Comp can be especially tough! Here's a guided review sheet you can use to look for ways to improve. We're including four sheets for week 1 so you can review all the passages on your most recent PrepTest. (That said, if you nailed three out of four passages, save the extra sheets for other tough passages you encounter, or tough passages from your past that you revisit. And if you anticipate needing more than four sheets this week because you're focusing a lot on RC, make some copies of these while they're still blank.)

The first step in RC review is to check the Main Point/Primary Purpose question(s). If you struggled with these questions, generate a new Scale that better reflects the correct answers. Then, check your Passage Map and notations against any Passage Organization question and adjust them as needed.

Next, reread the passage and edit your notations. See something you should have noted? Do so now (it can be helpful to use a different color). Highlight notes that helped you with a question. Also, note if the passage exhibits a common structure:

- The Old vs. The New
- a Traditional View Is Refuted
- a Debate Is Presented
- a Debate Is Presented, and the Author Takes a Side
- the Author Reconciles Two Sides of a Debate

- a Thesis Is Illustrated With an Example(s)
- an Artist Is Critiqued or Defended From Criticism
- the Importance of Something Is Explored
- a Problem Is Presented, With Solutions

Finally, review the questions. For each one:

- Determine your optimal strategy (prephrase from a general understanding; head straight back to research an answer; eliminate some answers and then research).
- If you needed to go back, were your Passage Map and notations good enough to let you quickly find the answer?
- Write a line citation supporting the correct answer.
- Write a line citation for what trapped you into selecting the wrong answer.
- Write out an intention for what you'll do differently next time.

RC Review: PrepTest 1

Passage Work and Understanding	
Passage Type	❑ Does this passage exhibit a common structure? If so, write it down:
Scale	❑ Did your Scale match the correct Main Point/Primary Purpose answers? If not, write a new one here:
Passage Map	❑ Using a different color writing utensil, add notations that would have helped you answer questions. ❑ Highlight notations that helped you in answering any question.

	Questions		
1	☐ Prephrase, ☐ Research, or ☐ Eliminate/Research ☐ Passage Map helped?	☐ Line for correct AC: _____ ☐ Line for incorrect AC: _____	Next time I see _____ I will _____
2	☐ Prephrase, ☐ Research, or ☐ Eliminate/Research ☐ Passage Map helped?	☐ Line for correct AC: _____ ☐ Line for incorrect AC: _____	Next time I see _____ I will _____
3	☐ Prephrase, ☐ Research, or ☐ Eliminate/Research ☐ Passage Map helped?	☐ Line for correct AC: _____ ☐ Line for incorrect AC: _____	Next time I see _____ I will _____
4	☐ Prephrase, ☐ Research, or ☐ Eliminate/Research ☐ Passage Map helped?	☐ Line for correct AC: _____ ☐ Line for incorrect AC: _____	Next time I see _____ I will _____
5	☐ Prephrase, ☐ Research, or ☐ Eliminate/Research ☐ Passage Map helped?	☐ Line for correct AC: _____ ☐ Line for incorrect AC: _____	Next time I see _____ I will _____
(6)	☐ Prephrase, ☐ Research, or ☐ Eliminate/Research ☐ Passage Map helped?	☐ Line for correct AC: _____ ☐ Line for incorrect AC: _____	Next time I see _____ I will _____
(7)	☐ Prephrase, ☐ Research, or ☐ Eliminate/Research ☐ Passage Map helped?	☐ Line for correct AC: _____ ☐ Line for incorrect AC: _____	Next time I see _____ I will _____
(8)	☐ Prephrase, ☐ Research, or ☐ Eliminate/Research ☐ Passage Map helped?	☐ Line for correct AC: _____ ☐ Line for incorrect AC: _____	Next time I see _____ I will _____

Passage Work and Understanding	
Passage Type	☐ Does this passage exhibit a common structure? If so, write it down:
Scale	☐ Did your Scale match the correct Main Point/Primary Purpose answers? If not, write a new one here:
Passage Map	☐ Using a different color writing utensil, add notations that would have helped you answer questions. ☐ Highlight notations that helped you in answering any question.

	Questions		
1	❏ Prephrase, ❏ Research, or ❏ Eliminate/Research ❏ Passage Map helped?	❏ Line for correct AC: _____ ❏ Line for incorrect AC: _____	Next time I see _____ I will _____
2	❏ Prephrase, ❏ Research, or ❏ Eliminate/Research ❏ Passage Map helped?	❏ Line for correct AC: _____ ❏ Line for incorrect AC: _____	Next time I see _____ I will _____
3	❏ Prephrase, ❏ Research, or ❏ Eliminate/Research ❏ Passage Map helped?	❏ Line for correct AC: _____ ❏ Line for incorrect AC: _____	Next time I see _____ I will _____
4	❏ Prephrase, ❏ Research, or ❏ Eliminate/Research ❏ Passage Map helped?	❏ Line for correct AC: _____ ❏ Line for incorrect AC: _____	Next time I see _____ I will _____
5	❏ Prephrase, ❏ Research, or ❏ Eliminate/Research ❏ Passage Map helped?	❏ Line for correct AC: _____ ❏ Line for incorrect AC: _____	Next time I see _____ I will _____
(6)	❏ Prephrase, ❏ Research, or ❏ Eliminate/Research ❏ Passage Map helped?	❏ Line for correct AC: _____ ❏ Line for incorrect AC: _____	Next time I see _____ I will _____
(7)	❏ Prephrase, ❏ Research, or ❏ Eliminate/Research ❏ Passage Map helped?	❏ Line for correct AC: _____ ❏ Line for incorrect AC: _____	Next time I see _____ I will _____
(8)	❏ Prephrase, ❏ Research, or ❏ Eliminate/Research ❏ Passage Map helped?	❏ Line for correct AC: _____ ❏ Line for incorrect AC: _____	Next time I see _____ I will _____

Passage Work and Understanding	
Passage Type	❑ Does this passage exhibit a common structure? If so, write it down:
Scale	❑ Did your Scale match the correct Main Point/Primary Purpose answers? If not, write a new one here:
Passage Map	❑ Using a different color writing utensil, add notations that would have helped you answer questions. ❑ Highlight notations that helped you in answering any question.

Questions			
1	❑ Prephrase, ❑ Research, or ❑ Eliminate/Research ❑ Passage Map helped?	❑ Line for correct AC: _____ ❑ Line for incorrect AC: _____	Next time I see _____ I will _____
2	❑ Prephrase, ❑ Research, or ❑ Eliminate/Research ❑ Passage Map helped?	❑ Line for correct AC: _____ ❑ Line for incorrect AC: _____	Next time I see _____ I will _____
3	❑ Prephrase, ❑ Research, or ❑ Eliminate/Research ❑ Passage Map helped?	❑ Line for correct AC: _____ ❑ Line for incorrect AC: _____	Next time I see _____ I will _____
4	❑ Prephrase, ❑ Research, or ❑ Eliminate/Research ❑ Passage Map helped?	❑ Line for correct AC: _____ ❑ Line for incorrect AC: _____	Next time I see _____ I will _____
5	❑ Prephrase, ❑ Research, or ❑ Eliminate/Research ❑ Passage Map helped?	❑ Line for correct AC: _____ ❑ Line for incorrect AC: _____	Next time I see _____ I will _____
(6)	❑ Prephrase, ❑ Research, or ❑ Eliminate/Research ❑ Passage Map helped?	❑ Line for correct AC: _____ ❑ Line for incorrect AC: _____	Next time I see _____ I will _____
(7)	❑ Prephrase, ❑ Research, or ❑ Eliminate/Research ❑ Passage Map helped?	❑ Line for correct AC: _____ ❑ Line for incorrect AC: _____	Next time I see _____ I will _____
(8)	❑ Prephrase, ❑ Research, or ❑ Eliminate/Research ❑ Passage Map helped?	❑ Line for correct AC: _____ ❑ Line for incorrect AC: _____	Next time I see _____ I will _____

Passage Work and Understanding		
Passage Type	❑	Does this passage exhibit a common structure? If so, write it down:
Scale	❑	Did your Scale match the correct Main Point/Primary Purpose answers? If not, write a new one here:
Passage Map	❑	Using a different color writing utensil, add notations that would have helped you answer questions.
	❑	Highlight notations that helped you in answering any question.

	Questions		
1	☐ Prephrase, ☐ Research, or ☐ Eliminate/Research ☐ Passage Map helped?	☐ Line for correct AC: ——————— ☐ Line for incorrect AC: ———————	Next time I see ——————— I will ———————
2	☐ Prephrase, ☐ Research, or ☐ Eliminate/Research ☐ Passage Map helped?	☐ Line for correct AC: ——————— ☐ Line for incorrect AC: ———————	Next time I see ——————— I will ———————
3	☐ Prephrase, ☐ Research, or ☐ Eliminate/Research ☐ Passage Map helped?	☐ Line for correct AC: ——————— ☐ Line for incorrect AC: ———————	Next time I see ——————— I will ———————
4	☐ Prephrase, ☐ Research, or ☐ Eliminate/Research ☐ Passage Map helped?	☐ Line for correct AC: ——————— ☐ Line for incorrect AC: ———————	Next time I see ——————— I will ———————
5	☐ Prephrase, ☐ Research, or ☐ Eliminate/Research ☐ Passage Map helped?	☐ Line for correct AC: ——————— ☐ Line for incorrect AC: ———————	Next time I see ——————— I will ———————
(6)	☐ Prephrase, ☐ Research, or ☐ Eliminate/Research ☐ Passage Map helped?	☐ Line for correct AC: ——————— ☐ Line for incorrect AC: ———————	Next time I see ——————— I will ———————
(7)	☐ Prephrase, ☐ Research, or ☐ Eliminate/Research ☐ Passage Map helped?	☐ Line for correct AC: ——————— ☐ Line for incorrect AC: ———————	Next time I see ——————— I will ———————
(8)	☐ Prephrase, ☐ Research, or ☐ Eliminate/Research ☐ Passage Map helped?	☐ Line for correct AC: ——————— ☐ Line for incorrect AC: ———————	Next time I see ——————— I will ———————

Guided Review: Logic Games

After finishing a game, check your work to see where you went wrong and find the correct answer to any question you initially answered incorrectly (or, at least, spend some time working through the question again). After that, read through the official explanation, following along by doing the work on your own page. After getting our explanation in your own handwriting, review it to internalize it. Replay the game at regular intervals until you can finish it on time and with perfect form.

The Guided Review sheets that follow will help you identify and correct issues in all stages of your logic games approach. Use one for *every* game that you find challenging. We're including four sheets for week 1 so you can review all the games on your most recent PrepTest. If some were slam dunks, use the extra sheets for other tough games you encounter, or tough games from your past that you revisit. If you anticipate needing more than four sheets this week because you're focusing a lot on LG, make some copies of these while they're still blank!

Once you've filled out four or five of them, look for error patterns in your work:

If you notice a particular game type that you struggle with:

1. Thoroughly fill out the Cheat Sheet for that game type, compare it to ours, edit yours, and then review. Then, start fresh and fill out a blank copy!

If you notice a particular question target that you miss (e.g., *must be true, or could be false*):

1. Recall both the target of the question *and* of the incorrect answers (e.g., *I want an answer that could be true, so I'll eliminate answers that must be false*).

2. Review how to test drive answers and use prior work for that question target.

If you notice that you get tripped up by rare/tricky questions:

1. Review what these questions are asking and the best approaches for them.

2. Consider skipping them to free up time for questions that you're more likely to get correct.

If you notice that timing is an issue:

1. Consider your inferences and Big Pause. Did you rush and miss something? Did you spend too long and find nothing?

2. Recognize when you're staring at the page instead of doing work, and start testing out answers when you are in that mode.

3. Determine if there's a particular game or question type you struggle with, and consider saving them for last.

4. Practice using prior work.

LG Review: PrepTest 1

Picture the Game, Rules, and The Big Pause	
Issues: Did I...	**Fixes: I will...**
Diagram Check	❑ ID basic game type correctly? ❑ Adapt basic diagram to any twists?	
Rules Check	❑ Use clear notation for each rule? ❑ Build as many rules into the setup as possible? ❑ Take contrapositives of conditional rules?	
Inference Check	❑ Make basic inferences (e.g. exclusions from relative ordering)? ❑ Look for rules that share elements and link them when possible? ❑ Look at anti/chunks? ❑ Look at inferences common to the game type/twists?	
Big Pause Check	❑ Identify the least restricted element/strays? ❑ Identify your Most Valuable Relationship? (This could be a rule, inference, or element) ❑ Look for framing opportunities?	
Frames Check	❑ ID any divisions in the rules? ❑ Determine if they had consequences? ❑ Build successful frames? ❑ Build unsuccessful frames?	

Questions			
Orientation Question	**Conditional Questions**	**Unconditional Questions**	**Other Questions**
_____ of _____ correct	_____ of _____ correct	_____ of _____ correct	_____ of _____ correct
Did I... ❑ read rules and eliminate answers?	Did I... ❑ draw a new diagram, follow the inference chain, and ask who's left? ❑ test out answers quickly, if needed?	Did I... ❑ make an inference that helped? ❑ use prior work? ❑ test out answers quickly, if needed?	Did I... ❑ recognize what type of question it is? ❑ use prior work? ❑ test out answers quickly, if needed?

Q#	Type	I Did/Didn't	Fix for Next Time
1	Question type:		
2	Question type:		
3	Question type:		
4	Question type:		
5	Question type:		
(6)	Question type:		
(7)	Question type:		

Picture the Game, Rules, and The Big Pause		
Issues: Did I . . .		**Fixes: I will . . .**
Diagram Check	❑ ID basic game type correctly? ❑ Adapt basic diagram to any twists?	
Rules Check	❑ Use clear notation for each rule? ❑ Build as many rules into the setup as possible? ❑ Take contrapositives of conditional rules?	
Inference Check	❑ Make basic inferences (e.g. exclusions from relative ordering)? ❑ Look for rules that share elements and link them when possible? ❑ Look at anti/chunks? ❑ Look at inferences common to the game type/twists?	
Big Pause Check	❑ Identify the least restricted element/strays? ❑ Identify your Most Valuable Relationship? (This could be a rule, inference, or element) ❑ Look for framing opportunities?	
Frames Check	❑ ID any divisions in the rules? ❑ Determine if they had consequences? ❑ Build successful frames? ❑ Build unsuccessful frames?	

Questions			
Orientation Question	**Conditional Questions**	**Unconditional Questions**	**Other Questions**
_____ of _____ correct	_____ of _____ correct	_____ of _____ correct	_____ of _____ correct
Did I... ❑ read rules and eliminate answers?	Did I... ❑ draw a new diagram, follow the inference chain, and ask who's left? ❑ test out answers quickly, if needed?	Did I... ❑ make an inference that helped? ❑ use prior work? ❑ test out answers quickly, if needed?	Did I... ❑ recognize what type of question it is? ❑ use prior work? ❑ test out answers quickly, if needed?

Q#	Type	I Did/Didn't	Fix for Next Time
1	Question type:		
2	Question type:		
3	Question type:		
4	Question type:		
5	Question type:		
(6)	Question type:		
(7)	Question type:		

Picture the Game, Rules, and The Big Pause	
Issues: Did I . . .	**Fixes: I will . . .**
Diagram Check	❑ ID basic game type correctly? ❑ Adapt basic diagram to any twists?
Rules Check	❑ Use clear notation for each rule? ❑ Build as many rules into the setup as possible? ❑ Take contrapositives of conditional rules?
Inference Check	❑ Make basic inferences (e.g. exclusions from relative ordering)? ❑ Look for rules that share elements and link them when possible? ❑ Look at anti/chunks? ❑ Look at inferences common to the game type/twists?
Big Pause Check	❑ Identify the least restricted element/strays? ❑ Identify your Most Valuable Relationship? (This could be a rule, inference, or element) ❑ Look for framing opportunities?
Frames Check	❑ ID any divisions in the rules? ❑ Determine if they had consequences? ❑ Build successful frames? ❑ Build unsuccessful frames?

Questions			
Orientation Question	**Conditional Questions**	**Unconditional Questions**	**Other Questions**
_____ of _____ correct	_____ of _____ correct	_____ of _____ correct	_____ of _____ correct
Did I... ☐ read rules and eliminate answers?	Did I... ☐ draw a new diagram, follow the inference chain, and ask who's left? ☐ test out answers quickly, if needed?	Did I... ☐ make an inference that helped? ☐ use prior work? ☐ test out answers quickly, if needed?	Did I... ☐ recognize what type of question it is? ☐ use prior work? ☐ test out answers quickly, if needed?

Q#	Type	I Did/Didn't	Fix for Next Time
1	Question type:		
2	Question type:		
3	Question type:		
4	Question type:		
5	Question type:		
(6)	Question type:		
(7)	Question type:		

Picture the Game, Rules, and The Big Pause		
Issues: Did I...		**Fixes: I will...**
Diagram Check	❑ ID basic game type correctly? ❑ Adapt basic diagram to any twists?	
Rules Check	❑ Use clear notation for each rule? ❑ Build as many rules into the setup as possible? ❑ Take contrapositives of conditional rules?	
Inference Check	❑ Make basic inferences (e.g. exclusions from relative ordering)? ❑ Look for rules that share elements and link them when possible? ❑ Look at anti/chunks? ❑ Look at inferences common to the game type/twists?	
Big Pause Check	❑ Identify the least restricted element/strays? ❑ Identify your Most Valuable Relationship? (This could be a rule, inference, or element) ❑ Look for framing opportunities?	
Frames Check	❑ ID any divisions in the rules? ❑ Determine if they had consequences? ❑ Build successful frames? ❑ Build unsuccessful frames?	

Questions			
Orientation Question	**Conditional Questions**	**Unconditional Questions**	**Other Questions**
_____ of _____ correct	_____ of _____ correct	_____ of _____ correct	_____ of _____ correct
Did I... ❑ read rules and eliminate answers?	Did I... ❑ draw a new diagram, follow the inference chain, and ask who's left? ❑ test out answers quickly, if needed?	Did I... ❑ make an inference that helped? ❑ use prior work? ❑ test out answers quickly, if needed?	Did I... ❑ recognize what type of question it is? ❑ use prior work? ❑ test out answers quickly, if needed?

Q#	Type	I Did/Didn't	Fix for Next Time
1	Question type:		
2	Question type:		
3	Question type:		
4	Question type:		
5	Question type:		
(6)	Question type:		
(7)	Question type:		

Week 2: Planning and Review

Weekly Prep Plan

Section	Learning Goals	Activity	Time/Date
LR			
LG			
RC			

PrepTest Plan

Date	Which PT or sections?	Intentions—What do you want to focus on during this test?	Timing Goals

Overall Score	Section Accuracy	What are you going to work on before the next test?

Navigator Analysis: PrepTest 2

Logical Reasoning

- ID the Conclusion: _____ out of _____
- Determine the Function: _____ out of _____
- Procedure: _____ out of _____
  - Describe Family: _____ out of _____

- Necessary Assumption: _____ out of _____
- Sufficient Assumption: _____ out of _____
- ID the Flaw: _____ out of _____
- Strengthen: _____ out of _____
- Weaken: _____ out of _____
- Evaluate: _____ out of _____
  - Assumption Family: _____ out of _____

- Inference: _____ out of _____
- ID the Dis/Agreement: _____ out of _____
- Explain a Result: _____ out of _____
  - Inference Family: _____ out of _____

- Match the Reasoning: _____ out of _____
- Match the Flaw: _____ out of _____
  - Matching Family: _____ out of _____

Reading Comprehension

(Questions and passages can fall into more than one category)

- Natural Sciences: _____ out of _____
- Law: _____ out of _____
- Humanities: _____ out of _____
- Social Sciences: _____ out of _____

- Comparative Passage: _____ out of _____
- Standard Passages: _____ out of _____

- Identification Questions: _____ out of _____
- Inference Questions: _____ out of _____
- Synthesis Questions: _____ out of _____

Logic Games

(Questions and games can fall into more than one category)

- Ordering Games: _____ out of _____
- Grouping Games: _____ out of _____
- Hybrid Games: _____ out of _____
- Other Games: _____ out of _____

- Games with No Twists: _____ out of _____
- Games with Twists: _____ out of _____

- Orientation Questions: _____ out of _____
- Conditional Questions: _____ out of _____
- Unconditional Questions: _____ out of _____
- Tricky/Rare Questions: _____ out of _____

- Could Be True: _____ out of _____
- Must Be True: _____ out of _____
- Could Be False: _____ out of _____
- Must Be False: _____ out of _____

- EXCEPT Questions: _____ out of _____
- Standard Questions: _____ out of _____

Section	Strengths	Areas to Focus On
LR		
RC		
LG		

Strategy Log: Week 2 (Logical Reasoning Review)

Date	#/Source	Right? Wrong? Long? Tough?	Review Notes (Next time I see _____, I will _____)	Retry Notes	Done?
					☐
					☐
					☐
					☐
					☐
					☐
					☐

Date	#/Source	Right? Wrong? Long? Tough?	Review Notes (Next time I see _____, I will _____)	Retry Notes	Done?
					❑
					❑
					❑
					❑
					❑
					❑
					❑

RC Review: PrepTest 2

Passage Work and Understanding	
Passage Type	❑ Does this passage exhibit a common structure? If so, write it down:
Scale	❑ Did your Scale match the correct Main Point/Primary Purpose answers? If not, write a new one here:
Passage Map	❑ Using a different color writing utensil, add notations that would have helped you answer questions. ❑ Highlight notations that helped you in answering any question.

	Questions		
1	❑ Prephrase, ❑ Research, or ❑ Eliminate/Research ❑ Passage Map helped?	❑ Line for correct AC: _____ ❑ Line for incorrect AC: _____	Next time I see _____ I will _____
2	❑ Prephrase, ❑ Research, or ❑ Eliminate/Research ❑ Passage Map helped?	❑ Line for correct AC: _____ ❑ Line for incorrect AC: _____	Next time I see _____ I will _____
3	❑ Prephrase, ❑ Research, or ❑ Eliminate/Research ❑ Passage Map helped?	❑ Line for correct AC: _____ ❑ Line for incorrect AC: _____	Next time I see _____ I will _____
4	❑ Prephrase, ❑ Research, or ❑ Eliminate/Research ❑ Passage Map helped?	❑ Line for correct AC: _____ ❑ Line for incorrect AC: _____	Next time I see _____ I will _____
5	❑ Prephrase, ❑ Research, or ❑ Eliminate/Research ❑ Passage Map helped?	❑ Line for correct AC: _____ ❑ Line for incorrect AC: _____	Next time I see _____ I will _____
(6)	❑ Prephrase, ❑ Research, or ❑ Eliminate/Research ❑ Passage Map helped?	❑ Line for correct AC: _____ ❑ Line for incorrect AC: _____	Next time I see _____ I will _____
(7)	❑ Prephrase, ❑ Research, or ❑ Eliminate/Research ❑ Passage Map helped?	❑ Line for correct AC: _____ ❑ Line for incorrect AC: _____	Next time I see _____ I will _____
(8)	❑ Prephrase, ❑ Research, or ❑ Eliminate/Research ❑ Passage Map helped?	❑ Line for correct AC: _____ ❑ Line for incorrect AC: _____	Next time I see _____ I will _____

Passage Work and Understanding	
Passage Type	❑ Does this passage exhibit a common structure? If so, write it down:
Scale	❑ Did your Scale match the correct Main Point/Primary Purpose answers? If not, write a new one here:
Passage Map	❑ Using a different color writing utensil, add notations that would have helped you answer questions. ❑ Highlight notations that helped you in answering any question.

	Questions		
1	❑ Prephrase, ❑ Research, or ❑ Eliminate/Research ❑ Passage Map helped?	❑ Line for correct AC: _____ ❑ Line for incorrect AC: _____	Next time I see _____ I will _____
2	❑ Prephrase, ❑ Research, or ❑ Eliminate/Research ❑ Passage Map helped?	❑ Line for correct AC: _____ ❑ Line for incorrect AC: _____	Next time I see _____ I will _____
3	❑ Prephrase, ❑ Research, or ❑ Eliminate/Research ❑ Passage Map helped?	❑ Line for correct AC: _____ ❑ Line for incorrect AC: _____	Next time I see _____ I will _____
4	❑ Prephrase, ❑ Research, or ❑ Eliminate/Research ❑ Passage Map helped?	❑ Line for correct AC: _____ ❑ Line for incorrect AC: _____	Next time I see _____ I will _____
5	❑ Prephrase, ❑ Research, or ❑ Eliminate/Research ❑ Passage Map helped?	❑ Line for correct AC: _____ ❑ Line for incorrect AC: _____	Next time I see _____ I will _____
(6)	❑ Prephrase, ❑ Research, or ❑ Eliminate/Research ❑ Passage Map helped?	❑ Line for correct AC: _____ ❑ Line for incorrect AC: _____	Next time I see _____ I will _____
(7)	❑ Prephrase, ❑ Research, or ❑ Eliminate/Research ❑ Passage Map helped?	❑ Line for correct AC: _____ ❑ Line for incorrect AC: _____	Next time I see _____ I will _____
(8)	❑ Prephrase, ❑ Research, or ❑ Eliminate/Research ❑ Passage Map helped?	❑ Line for correct AC: _____ ❑ Line for incorrect AC: _____	Next time I see _____ I will _____

Passage Work and Understanding		
Passage Type	❏	Does this passage exhibit a common structure? If so, write it down:
Scale	❏	Did your Scale match the correct Main Point/Primary Purpose answers? If not, write a new one here:
Passage Map	❏	Using a different color writing utensil, add notations that would have helped you answer questions.
	❏	Highlight notations that helped you in answering any question.

Questions			
1	❑ Prephrase, ❑ Research, or ❑ Eliminate/Research ❑ Passage Map helped?	❑ Line for correct AC: _____ ❑ Line for incorrect AC: _____	Next time I see _____ I will _____
2	❑ Prephrase, ❑ Research, or ❑ Eliminate/Research ❑ Passage Map helped?	❑ Line for correct AC: _____ ❑ Line for incorrect AC: _____	Next time I see _____ I will _____
3	❑ Prephrase, ❑ Research, or ❑ Eliminate/Research ❑ Passage Map helped?	❑ Line for correct AC: _____ ❑ Line for incorrect AC: _____	Next time I see _____ I will _____
4	❑ Prephrase, ❑ Research, or ❑ Eliminate/Research ❑ Passage Map helped?	❑ Line for correct AC: _____ ❑ Line for incorrect AC: _____	Next time I see _____ I will _____
5	❑ Prephrase, ❑ Research, or ❑ Eliminate/Research ❑ Passage Map helped?	❑ Line for correct AC: _____ ❑ Line for incorrect AC: _____	Next time I see _____ I will _____
(6)	❑ Prephrase, ❑ Research, or ❑ Eliminate/Research ❑ Passage Map helped?	❑ Line for correct AC: _____ ❑ Line for incorrect AC: _____	Next time I see _____ I will _____
(7)	❑ Prephrase, ❑ Research, or ❑ Eliminate/Research ❑ Passage Map helped?	❑ Line for correct AC: _____ ❑ Line for incorrect AC: _____	Next time I see _____ I will _____
(8)	❑ Prephrase, ❑ Research, or ❑ Eliminate/Research ❑ Passage Map helped?	❑ Line for correct AC: _____ ❑ Line for incorrect AC: _____	Next time I see _____ I will _____

Passage Work and Understanding		
Passage Type	❏	Does this passage exhibit a common structure? If so, write it down:
Scale	❏	Did your Scale match the correct Main Point/Primary Purpose answers? If not, write a new one here:
Passage Map	❏	Using a different color writing utensil, add notations that would have helped you answer questions.
	❏	Highlight notations that helped you in answering any question.

	Questions		
1	☐ Prephrase, ☐ Research, or ☐ Eliminate/Research ☐ Passage Map helped?	☐ Line for correct AC: _____ ☐ Line for incorrect AC: _____	Next time I see _____ I will _____
2	☐ Prephrase, ☐ Research, or ☐ Eliminate/Research ☐ Passage Map helped?	☐ Line for correct AC: _____ ☐ Line for incorrect AC: _____	Next time I see _____ I will _____
3	☐ Prephrase, ☐ Research, or ☐ Eliminate/Research ☐ Passage Map helped?	☐ Line for correct AC: _____ ☐ Line for incorrect AC: _____	Next time I see _____ I will _____
4	☐ Prephrase, ☐ Research, or ☐ Eliminate/Research ☐ Passage Map helped?	☐ Line for correct AC: _____ ☐ Line for incorrect AC: _____	Next time I see _____ I will _____
5	☐ Prephrase, ☐ Research, or ☐ Eliminate/Research ☐ Passage Map helped?	☐ Line for correct AC: _____ ☐ Line for incorrect AC: _____	Next time I see _____ I will _____
(6)	☐ Prephrase, ☐ Research, or ☐ Eliminate/Research ☐ Passage Map helped?	☐ Line for correct AC: _____ ☐ Line for incorrect AC: _____	Next time I see _____ I will _____
(7)	☐ Prephrase, ☐ Research, or ☐ Eliminate/Research ☐ Passage Map helped?	☐ Line for correct AC: _____ ☐ Line for incorrect AC: _____	Next time I see _____ I will _____
(8)	☐ Prephrase, ☐ Research, or ☐ Eliminate/Research ☐ Passage Map helped?	☐ Line for correct AC: _____ ☐ Line for incorrect AC: _____	Next time I see _____ I will _____

LG Review: PrepTest 2

Picture the Game, Rules, and The Big Pause	
Issues: Did I . . .	**Fixes: I will . . .**
Diagram Check ❑ ID basic game type correctly? ❑ Adapt basic diagram to any twists?	
Rules Check ❑ Use clear notation for each rule? ❑ Build as many rules into the setup as possible? ❑ Take contrapositives of conditional rules?	
Inference Check ❑ Make basic inferences (e.g. exclusions from relative ordering)? ❑ Look for rules that share elements and link them when possible? ❑ Look at anti/chunks? ❑ Look at inferences common to the game type/twists?	
Big Pause Check ❑ Identify the least restricted element/strays? ❑ Identify your Most Valuable Relationship? (This could be a rule, inference, or element) ❑ Look for framing opportunities?	
Frames Check ❑ ID any divisions in the rules? ❑ Determine if they had consequences? ❑ Build successful frames? ❑ Build unsuccessful frames?	

Questions			
Orientation Question	**Conditional Questions**	**Unconditional Questions**	**Other Questions**
_____ of _____ correct	_____ of _____ correct	_____ of _____ correct	_____ of _____ correct
Did I... ❑ read rules and eliminate answers?	Did I... ❑ draw a new diagram, follow the inference chain, and ask who's left? ❑ test out answers quickly, if needed?	Did I... ❑ make an inference that helped? ❑ use prior work? ❑ test out answers quickly, if needed?	Did I... ❑ recognize what type of question it is? ❑ use prior work? ❑ test out answers quickly, if needed?

Q#	Type	I Did/Didn't	Fix for Next Time
1	Question type:		
2	Question type:		
3	Question type:		
4	Question type:		
5	Question type:		
(6)	Question type:		
(7)	Question type:		

Picture the Game, Rules, and The Big Pause		
	Issues: Did I ...	**Fixes: I will ...**
Diagram Check	❏ ID basic game type correctly? ❏ Adapt basic diagram to any twists?	
Rules Check	❏ Use clear notation for each rule? ❏ Build as many rules into the setup as possible? ❏ Take contrapositives of conditional rules?	
Inference Check	❏ Make basic inferences (e.g. exclusions from relative ordering)? ❏ Look for rules that share elements and link them when possible? ❏ Look at anti/chunks? ❏ Look at inferences common to the game type/twists?	
Big Pause Check	❏ Identify the least restricted element/strays? ❏ Identify your Most Valuable Relationship? (This could be a rule, inference, or element) ❏ Look for framing opportunities?	
Frames Check	❏ ID any divisions in the rules? ❏ Determine if they had consequences? ❏ Build successful frames? ❏ Build unsuccessful frames?	

Questions			
Orientation Question	**Conditional Questions**	**Unconditional Questions**	**Other Questions**
_____ of _____ correct	_____ of _____ correct	_____ of _____ correct	_____ of _____ correct
Did I... ❑ read rules and eliminate answers?	Did I... ❑ draw a new diagram, follow the inference chain, and ask who's left? ❑ test out answers quickly, if needed?	Did I... ❑ make an inference that helped? ❑ use prior work? ❑ test out answers quickly, if needed?	Did I... ❑ recognize what type of question it is? ❑ use prior work? ❑ test out answers quickly, if needed?

Q#	Type	I Did/Didn't	Fix for Next Time
1	Question type:		
2	Question type:		
3	Question type:		
4	Question type:		
5	Question type:		
(6)	Question type:		
(7)	Question type:		

Picture the Game, Rules, and The Big Pause	
Issues: Did I...	**Fixes: I will...**
Diagram Check	❑ ID basic game type correctly? ❑ Adapt basic diagram to any twists?	
Rules Check	❑ Use clear notation for each rule? ❑ Build as many rules into the setup as possible? ❑ Take contrapositives of conditional rules?	
Inference Check	❑ Make basic inferences (e.g. exclusions from relative ordering)? ❑ Look for rules that share elements and link them when possible? ❑ Look at anti/chunks? ❑ Look at inferences common to the game type/twists?	
Big Pause Check	❑ Identify the least restricted element/strays? ❑ Identify your Most Valuable Relationship? (This could be a rule, inference, or element) ❑ Look for framing opportunities?	
Frames Check	❑ ID any divisions in the rules? ❑ Determine if they had consequences? ❑ Build successful frames? ❑ Build unsuccessful frames?	

Questions			
Orientation Question	**Conditional Questions**	**Unconditional Questions**	**Other Questions**
_____ of _____ correct	_____ of _____ correct	_____ of _____ correct	_____ of _____ correct
Did I... ❑ read rules and eliminate answers?	Did I... ❑ draw a new diagram, follow the inference chain, and ask who's left? ❑ test out answers quickly, if needed?	Did I... ❑ make an inference that helped? ❑ use prior work? ❑ test out answers quickly, if needed?	Did I... ❑ recognize what type of question it is? ❑ use prior work? ❑ test out answers quickly, if needed?

Q#	Type	I Did/Didn't	Fix for Next Time
1	Question type:		
2	Question type:		
3	Question type:		
4	Question type:		
5	Question type:		
(6)	Question type:		
(7)	Question type:		

Picture the Game, Rules, and The Big Pause		
	Issues: Did I...	**Fixes: I will...**
Diagram Check	❑ ID basic game type correctly? ❑ Adapt basic diagram to any twists?	
Rules Check	❑ Use clear notation for each rule? ❑ Build as many rules into the setup as possible? ❑ Take contrapositives of conditional rules?	
Inference Check	❑ Make basic inferences (e.g. exclusions from relative ordering)? ❑ Look for rules that share elements and link them when possible? ❑ Look at anti/chunks? ❑ Look at inferences common to the game type/twists?	
Big Pause Check	❑ Identify the least restricted element/strays? ❑ Identify your Most Valuable Relationship? (This could be a rule, inference, or element) ❑ Look for framing opportunities?	
Frames Check	❑ ID any divisions in the rules? ❑ Determine if they had consequences? ❑ Build successful frames? ❑ Build unsuccessful frames?	

Questions			
Orientation Question	**Conditional Questions**	**Unconditional Questions**	**Other Questions**
_____ of _____ correct	_____ of _____ correct	_____ of _____ correct	_____ of _____ correct
Did I... ❑ read rules and eliminate answers?	Did I... ❑ draw a new diagram, follow the inference chain, and ask who's left? ❑ test out answers quickly, if needed?	Did I... ❑ make an inference that helped? ❑ use prior work? ❑ test out answers quickly, if needed?	Did I... ❑ recognize what type of question it is? ❑ use prior work? ❑ test out answers quickly, if needed?

Q#	Type	I Did/Didn't	Fix for Next Time
1	Question type:		
2	Question type:		
3	Question type:		
4	Question type:		
5	Question type:		
(6)	Question type:		
(7)	Question type:		

Secret Bonus Section

Yowza! You made it through 5 pounds of LSAT drills! Are you ready to claim your prize? Congratulations, it's...more drills! Consider these the bonus tracks of our LSAT album.

Drill A1: It's a Trap! Fill In the Traps Edition

Instructions: People who look both ways before crossing the street tend not to get hit by a bus, and people who look for trap answers tend not to fall for them. But do you know what trap answers you should be looking for on each of the LR question types? Use this drill to find out! For each of the question types listed below, fill in the traps that you plan to avoid on test day.

1.   Sufficient Assumption:

2.   Necessary Assumption:

3.   Flaw:

4.   Weaken:

5.   Strengthen:

6.   Must Be True:

7.   Most Strongly Supported:

8.   Must Be False:

9.   Principle Example:

10.   Match the Reasoning:

11.   Match the Flaw:

12.   Principle Support:

13.   ID the (Dis)agreement:

14.   Explain a Result:

15. Procedure:

16. ID the Conclusion:

17. Determine the Function:

18. Evaluate:

Answers

Note: Your answers may differ from ours, but make sure they cover the same concepts. If you struggled with this, it's time to make some flashcards!

1.   Sufficient Assumption:

     Illegal reversal/negation. Too weak. Doesn't address the new term in the conclusion.

2.   Necessary Assumption:

     Too strong/extreme language. Sufficient but not necessary.

3.   Flaw:

     Different flaw. Refers to something that didn't happen. Answer choice describes Circular Reasoning (usually incorrect). Answer choice describes Self-Contradiction (usually incorrect).

4.   Weaken:

     Too weak/weak language. Attacks the premise. Strengthens/opposite.

5.   Strengthen:

     Too weak/weak language. Premise booster. Weakens/opposite.

6.   Must Be True:

     Illegal reversal/negation. Term Shift. Extreme language.

7.   Most Strongly Supported:

     Too strong/extreme language. Term Shift.

8.   Must Be False:

     Illegal reversal/negation. Unsupported but not contradicted.

9.   Principle Example:

     Illegal reversal/negation. Language/topic match.

10. Match the Reasoning:

     Illegal reversal/negation. Language/topic match.

11. Match the Flaw:

     Different flaw. Language/topic match. Valid argument.

12. Principle Support:

     Illegal reversal/negation. Too weak/weak language. Doesn't address new term in conclusion.

13. ID the (Dis)agreement:

     Half-scope/only one side discusses. Term Shift.

14. Explain the Result:

     Supports expected. Aligns with unexpected but doesn't explain why.

15. Procedure:

     Refers to something that didn't happen. Different procedure.

16. ID the Conclusion:

     The last sentence. Intermediate conclusion. Premise. Opposing argument. Distorts the conclusion. Similar language but different meaning.

17. Determine the Function:

     Different function. Refers to something that didn't happen. Distorts the relationship to the main conclusion.

18. Evaluate:

     Premise booster. Only addresses one side (strengthen or weaken).

Drill A2: Comparative Narrative

Instruction: Comparison Flaws are common in Strengthen, Weaken, and Evaluate questions. The answer choices for these fall into fairly common patterns concerning similarities and differences. For each of the following arguments based on a Comparison Flaw, prephrase a potentially correct answer.

Mayor: Five years ago, we solved a similar fiscal crisis by enacting a plan that called for increased income taxes coupled with spending cuts. Therefore, we should approve this current bill, which does much of the same.

1. Strengthen:

2. Weaken:

3. Evaluate (answer in the form of a question):

Two plans have been proposed to tackle Caledonia's infrastructure problem. Senator McDonald's plan costs less and focuses on areas that are developing economically. Senator O'Doyle's plan focuses on all infrastructure that needs updating to prevent harm to the economy, and will result in larger long-term growth. Therefore, Senator O'Doyle's plan is the better of the two.

4. Strengthen:

5. Weaken:

6. Evaluate (answer in the form of a question):

Davos O. Kylie's previous medical drama, *Cutting Wit*, featured dramatic relationships and easy-to-follow mysteries each week. His new medical drama, *Over the Knife*, features similar relationships and plotlines. Since his previous show was an award-winning hit among critics, this new show will be, as well.

7. Strengthen:

8. Weaken:

9. Evaluate (answer in the form of a question):

Last year's "Top 100 Video Games of All Time" issue of *Game Informant* focused on games that received critical praise while ignoring many that sold well and were popular among the overall gamer community. Because of this, the issue was widely panned by that community, and sales of the issue were exceptionally low. This year, *Game Informant* based its list solely on sales numbers and a reader poll, so it's sure to sell well and be received better by the gaming community.

10. Strengthen:

11. Weaken:

12. Evaluate (answer in the form of a question):

During this season of *The Fantastic Irish Cooking Show (FICS)*, the two finalists have very different strengths and weaknesses. George is a fantastic plater, with each of his dishes looking like a work of art. Helen, on the other hand, has been frequently criticized for the way her meals appeared on the plate, but consistently received higher marks than George for flavor. Since taste is an important consideration on *FICS*, Helen is certain to take home the prize.

13. Strengthen:

14. Weaken:

15. Evaluate (answer in the form of a question):

Answers

Note: Your answers may be different from ours, but make sure they accomplish the same function! Notes are left in parentheses to more generally describe those functions, when needed.

Mayor: Five years ago, we solved a similar fiscal crisis by enacting a plan that called for increased income taxes coupled with spending cuts. Therefore, we should approve this current bill, which does much of the same.

1. Strengthen:

    The current bill raises taxes for groups of people similar to those whose taxes were raised by the previous bill.

    (Or any other relevant similarity between the bills.)

2. Weaken:

    While income levels were at a historic high during the last fiscal crisis, most people's incomes have decreased since then.

    (Or any other relevant difference between the previous crisis or previous bill and the current one.)

3. Evaluate (answer in the form of a question):

    Are the spending cuts to similar programs and at a similar level to those enacted during the last fiscal crisis?

    (Or any question that asks about relevant similarities/ differences between the bills.)

    Two plans have been proposed to tackle Caledonia's infrastructure problem. Senator McDonald's plan costs less and focuses on areas that are developing economically. Senator O'Doyle's plan focuses on all infrastructure that needs updating to prevent harm to the economy, and will result in larger long-term growth. Therefore, Senator O'Doyle's plan is the better of the two.

4. Strengthen:

    Long-term growth is more important than overall cost when comparing two infrastructure plans.

5. Weaken:

    Cost is a more important consideration than long-term growth when deciding between infrastructure plans.

6. Evaluate (answer in the form of a question):

    When deciding between infrastructure plans, should cost or long-term growth be a more important consideration?

    Davos O. Kylie's previous medical drama, *Cutting Wit*, featured dramatic relationships and easy-to-follow mysteries each week. His new medical drama, *Over the Knife*, features similar relationships and plotlines. Since his previous show was an award-winning hit among critics, this new show will be, as well.

7. Strengthen:

    Many of the writers and actors from *Cutting Wit* who were specifically praised by critics are working on the new show.

    (Or any other relevant similarity.)

8. Weaken:

    Critics almost always praise only innovative shows, and not ones that remind them of other shows.

    (Or any other relevant difference.)

9. Evaluate (answer in the form of a question):

    Are other features of *Cutting Wit* that were praised by critics likely to be featured in this show as well?

Last year's "Top 100 Video Games of All Time" issue of *Game Informant* focused on games that received critical praise while ignoring many that sold well and were popular among the overall gamer community. Because of this, the issue was widely panned by that community, and sales of the issue were exceptionally low. This year, *Game Informant* based its list solely on sales numbers and a reader poll, so it's sure to sell well and be received better by the gaming community.

10. Strengthen:

    This year's "Top 100" issue will also feature a screenshot of each game's final battle, a feature widely requested by readers but ignored in last year's issue.

    (Or any other relevant difference.)

11. Weaken:

    The group that responded to the poll was largely made up of the group of critics whose views determined last year's list.

    (Or any other relevant similarity.)

12. Evaluate (answer in the form of a question):

    Has *GameInformant* made any other changes to the format of the "Top 100" issue that are likely to appeal to readers?

During this season of *The Fantastic Irish Cooking Show*, the two finalists have very different strengths and weaknesses. George is a fantastic plater, with each of his dishes looking like a work of art. Helen, on the other hand, has been frequently criticized for the way her meals appeared on the plate but consistently received higher marks than George for flavor. Since taste is an important consideration on any cooking show, Helen is certain to take home the prize.

13. Strengthen:

    Helen's meals are generally more difficult to prepare than George's, a consideration that the judges also view as important.

14. Weaken:

    While taste is an important consideration, more weight is given by the judges to the aesthetic appeal of a dish.

15. Evaluate (answer in the form of a question):

    Do the judges consider any criteria to be as important, or more important, than taste?

Drill A3: Talking to Yourself, Advanced Edition

Instructions: The speed at which you can attack the answer choices is primarily determined by your ability to stay on task and not do extraneous work. That means asking yourself the right questions as you evaluate each answer choice. Build that skill with this drill!

For each of the following question types, fill in the questions you would ask yourself as you attack each answer.

1. Necessary Assumption:

2. ID the (Dis)agreement:

3. Sufficient Assumption:

4. Flaw:

5. Strengthen:

6. Weaken:

7. Explain a Result:

8. Match the Flaw:

9. Procedure:

10. Principle Support:

11. Match the Reasoning:

12. Must Be True:

13. ID the Conclusion:

14. Principle Example:

15. Determine the Function:

16. Most Strongly Supported:

 1093

Answers

Note: Your answers may differ from ours and that's OK! The language you used can be different, but the concepts should be the same.

1. Necessary Assumption:

    If this answer isn't true (i.e., if I negate it), does it make the argument fall apart?

    Does this rule out a potential objection to the argument?

2. ID the (Dis)agreement:

    If I posed this as a question to both speakers, would one say "yes" and the other "no"?

3. Sufficient Assumption:

    Does the answer, combined with the given premises, absolutely guarantee that the conclusion will be true?

    If there's a new concept in the argument's conclusion, does this answer address it?

4. Flaw:

    Does each piece of abstract language in the answer logically point to a piece in the initial argument?

    Does this describe a necessary assumption the argument makes, or a weakener the argument has failed to consider?

5. Strengthen:

    Does this bridge the gap between the premise and conclusion?

    Does this rule out a potential objection to the argument?

6. Weaken:

    Does this raise a potential objection to the argument?

    Does this attack an assumption the argument makes?

7. Explain a Result:

    Does this help explain how all of the facts in the stimulus could occur at the same time?

8. Match the Flaw:

    What's the flaw in the initial argument, and does this contain the exact same flaw?

9. Procedure:

    If I replace the abstract words in this answer with details from the argument, does it accurately describe the argument?

10. Principle Support:

    Does this answer bridge a gap between the premise and conclusion of the argument?

    If there's a new concept in the argument's conclusion, does this answer address it?

11. Match the Reasoning:

    Does this answer have every major feature of the stimulus argument, and nothing extraneous?

    If the argument is conditional, would it have the same diagram as the argument I'm trying to match?

12. Must Be True:

    Would there be any way to attack this answer if it was the conclusion of an argument that had the stimulus as its premises?

13. ID the Conclusion:

    Is this a paraphrase of the claim that I identified as being the argument's main conclusion?

14. Principle Example:

    Does this scenario fulfill the sufficient condition of the principle and draw a conclusion based on the principle's necessary condition?

15. Determine the Function:

    Does this answer choice accurately describe the relationship between the statement in question and other parts of the argument?

16. Most Strongly Supported:

    Is this answer narrow enough to be supported by the given information?